The Papacy
An Encyclopedia

Published with the assistance of the Centre national du livre in France
and the Goodbooks Foundation

The Papacy
An Encyclopedia

VOLUME 2

Gaius–Proxies

Philippe Levillain, *Université de Paris X*
GENERAL EDITOR

Routledge
New York   London

Published in 2002 by
Routledge
29 West 35th Street
New York, NY 10001

Published in Great Britain by
Routledge
11 New Fetter Lane
London EC4P 4EE

Originally published as *Dictionnaire historique de la papauté*,
© Librairie Arthème Fayard, 1994

Copyright © 2002 by Routledge
Routledge is an imprint of Taylor & Francis Books, Inc.

10   9   8   7   6   5   4   3   2   1

Library of Congress Cataloging-in-Publication Data

Dictionnaire historique de la papauté. English
      The papacy: an encyclopedia / Philippe Levillain, general editor; John W. O'Malley, English language edition editor.
    p. cm.
    Includes bibliographical references and index.
    ISBN 0-415-92228-3 (set)
    ISBN 0-415-92229-1 (volume 1)
    ISBN 0-415-92230-5 (volume 2)
    ISBN 0-415-93752-3 (volume 3)
    1. Papacy—Dictionaries. I. Levillain, Philippe, 1940– II. O'Malley, John W. III Title.

BX955.2 .D53 2002
282'.092'2—dc21
[B]

2001041859

Printed on acid-free, 250-year-life paper
Manufactured in the United States of America

Contents

Entries A to Z

ENTRIES

ENTRIES

GAIUS. See **Caius.**

GALLICANISM. The term "Gallicanism" was coined in the 19th century to encompass the various currents of resistance to the absolutization of papal PRIMACY, and to their ideological referents, which appeared, primarily in France, from the Middle Ages up until VATICAN I. Although they never constituted a coherent doctrine, these currents were based on two essential components: autonomy of the political domain with regard to religion (the separation of powers), and constitutional limitation of the pope's authority. The *Déclaration des Quatre Articles*, adopted by the assembly of clergy in 1682, represented its official position.

Perhaps more significant than the classical distinction between Gallicanism's categorical manifestations—that is, between the political (i.e., royal or parliamentary) and the ecclesiastic (i.e., episcopal or Richerist)—might be its two forms of opposition to the Roman, or ultramontane, ecclesiological model, one of which is archaic (participatory Gallicanism), and the other modern (authoritarian Gallicanism). The first of these is based on a corporative vision of the Church and the nation, and the second on a hierarchical, structured idea. Although, as a whole, they appeal to a common substrate drawn from the example of the Church in its first centuries, and from a certain conciliar tradition, they are two clearly different interpretations that have not elicited the same reactions on the part of the papacy's defenders, and that have followed different evolutionary paths.

Early References. Although more is known about the period after the 16th century, the history of the first centuries of Christianity actually constitutes a privileged reference for any interpretation of the papacy's role and the relations between local churches and the APOSTOLIC SEE. The many examples of concerted actions on the part of the bishops, and of important canonical decisons, furnish proof of a practice that Gallican authors were able to take advantage of. The history of the Middle Ages shows different reactions, dialectically opposed to the practical and theoretical growth of papal authority and aimed at limiting this authority if not at stopping it short. These include the struggle between Papacy and Empire, the accent placed on episcopal authority in the ecclesiastical domain (e.g., Agobard of Lyon, or Hincmar of Reims, in the 9th century), and battles against the privileges of the mendicant orders in the 13th century. Without being limited to France, or even being Gallican, properly speaking, these precedents constitute the arsenal from which later theoreticians would draw when they needed to respond to conflict situations.

The Birth of Gallicanism. The birth of the attitude of national resistance to the papacy's claims, no longer on the level of deeds only, but also on that of general principles, can rightly be seen in the disagreement between BONIFACE VIII and the king of France, Philip the Fair (1285–1314). Assisted by legalists and supported by the clergy (assembly of June 1303), the king called for a council and prepared a response to the BULL UNAM SANCTAM (1302), using a concept from Roman law that makes an absolute distinction between the temporal domain and the spiritual (*Dialogue du clerc et du chevalier, Rex pacificus*). For their part, the Parisian theologians undertook to formulate a statement of doctrine following these perspectives very closely (John of Paris, *Tractatus de potestate regia et papali*, 1302).

Church Reform. Although extreme, this reaction was not isolated; it was part of a more general movement of dissatisfaction and aspiration toward Church reform "in the head and in the members," already present in the general councils of Lyon (1245 and 1274). In 1307, Guillaume Durand the Younger, bishop of Mende, was formalizing these complaints for the Council of Vienne (1311–2) in his *Tractatus de modo generalis concilii celebrandi* (published in 1545). The GREAT SCHISM of the West (1378–1417) was to give new acuity to this point of view by more directly defining the relationship between the pope and the council, and by proclaiming the superiority of the assembly representing the Church militant (Council of Constance, 1414–7). In the progressive development of this decision, French authors (e.g., J. Geron, P. d'Ailly) played a singular role not only in the development of an ecclesiology that was mystical at the same time as it was corporate, but also in the argument with defenders of papal power, founded on early Church law, vestiges of which had been retained in France more than in other places. The king presented himself as the guarantor of these *Libertés Gallicanes* (P. Le Roy, abbot of Mont Saint-Michel, at the Council of Paris, 1398). However, used especially as a means of pressure, the *Libertés* were still an abstract reference for both clergy and royalty, while jurists and parliamentarians used them to accentuate their role as controllers.

Pragmatic Sanction. At the time of the conflict between Pope EUGENE IV and the Council of Basel, the assembly of Bourges (1438) instigated a reception, that is, a registration of the council's decrees, that represented a happy medium between extremes in the council and papal claims. The Pragmatic Sanction of Bourges, which was never fully applied (whence its characterization as an idealized reference) accepted the broad facts of reformational conciliarism, but did so while allowing a more direct intervention by the papacy, primarily in the conferring of benefices. Rome managed to get the text neutralized, although not completely abrogated, by negotiating CONCORDATS with the French monarchy (Amboise, 1472, and especially Bologna, 1516).

Concordat of Bologna. The latter treaty between Francis I and LEO X was less a break than it was a realistic evolution. It codified some of the Pragmatic Sanction's demands regarding Roman interference (trivial names, courts of appeals), while transferring to the monarchy nominations for major benefices that were nevertheless still subject to papal approval. This transfer gave the "Very Christian King" enormous power over the Gallican Church. It was the object of resistance on the part of the Parlement and the University: resistance that showed the normative and already utopian character of the Pragmatic Sanction, and especially the attachment to an "ecclesiology of participation," of which the works of P. Almain (1513) and J. Mair (1516) represented a new evolution in the face of renewed affirmations of the defenders of papal power (Cajetan).

Evolution. Even though the French monarchy's rapprochement with the Holy See, represented by the con-

cordat of 1516, reaffirmed the monarchy in its Catholic interests, it favored a nationalist and regalist interpretation of these interests at the same time. It is clear in this regard that one of the principal components of Gallican behavior vis-à-vis the Council of TRENT remained the desire to restore the religious unity of the kingdom, and consequently to facilitate the growth of a strong state. Preparation of the volumes of *Libertés de l'Église gallicane*, which were aimed at "proving," or establishing the precedents of, this independence, was attributed to this double goal (P. Pithou, 1594, completed by P. Dupuy, 1639). This political Gallicanism was far from being homogenous, however, since it grafted a modern idea of the state onto a medieval substrate, and developed in two different directions. One of these put the accent on the principle of authority (royal Gallicanism) and the other placed it on the role of representative bodies (parliamentary Gallicanism). Almost symmetrically, in the theological order, these same theories gave birth to Richerism, a Gersonian conciliarism set into the new political order (abusively reduced to a kind of presbyterianism), and later to the authoritarian episcopal Gallicanism of the high clergy.

These developments are better understood by taking into account the dialectic movement at their base, particularly the force of ULTRAMONTANISM and its progress, tied to the renewal movement that emerged from the Council of Trent. By favoring a resurgence of papal autonomy, widely promoted by the religious orders (especially the Jesuits) the movement for renewal inevitably provoked a reaction that was both practical and theoretical. Since it was a question of theology, it is not surprising that the University of Paris had been the privileged place for these confrontations. In these internal disputes, the papacy did not seem to be directly engaged, although through the assistance of nuncios and the *parti dévot*, it exercised an undeniable influence (e.g., condemnation of E. Richer by the provincial synods of Sens and Aix, approved by PAUL V in 1612). In the États Généraux of 1614–5, it was the clergy representatives who rejected the article proposed by the third estate on the independence of royal power. It was likewise the activity of the nuncio Spada that protected the writings of the Jesuit Santatrelli (1626) on the subject from being condemned by the theological faculty of Paris.

Jansenism. It was JANSENISM that would instill new vigor into the conflict between the Gallicans and the Romans. By asking INNOCENT X for his judgment on the *Five Propositions* attributed to C. Jansenius, without previously pronouncing their own, the French bishops abdicated their authority to a certain extent. The very reticences that welcomed the constitution *Cum Occasione* (1635) could only encourage greater attention to papal authority, which was committed, primarily, to the undefined concept of INFALLIBILITY. There was a quick reaction that would give an almost definite form to the various currents of Gallicanism. First, the episcopacy, under the leadership of P. de Marca (1594–1662), sought a readjustment of forces by putting the accent on the *reception* of papal decisions, meaning the need for the bishops in question to accept them (clergy assembly, 1655), and then the monarchy pressured the faculty of theology at the University of Paris to obtain official recognition of the "separation of powers" and a negation of infallibility (*Six Articles* of 1663).

Gallican Articles. The *Four Articles* adopted by the clergy assembly of 1682 were to codify these ideas, and they constitute an essential reference in legal and theological development in France. They dealt successively with the separation of powers, the superiority of the council over the pope, the limitation of papal primacy, and the need for the Church's consent for a judgment by the pope to be irrevocable.

There were political concerns behind the articles of 1663 and 1682, including the conflicts with ALEXANDER VII, in 1663, and with INNOCENT XI, in 1682. These entailed moves to put pressure on these popes in specific circumstances; but there was also a comeback for Gallicanism among politicians and progress in the development of Gallicanism among bishops. Roman reactions, remarkable for their prudence and moderation, showed that there was a real attempt to avoid a SCHISM, and to ensure the future. They nevertheless exhibited a certain weakness: rather than directly condemning the affirmations of the *Four Articles*, they stood by canonical measures aimed at signaling papal disapproval and at influencing the search for a compromise (e.g., the BRIEF *Paternae Charitati*, 1682, and especially the refusal to grant investiture to the bishops named from among clerics who had taken part in the assembly). Dogmatically, it was enough to encourage the refutations of the *Four Articles* and to place the most extreme of their commentaries on the INDEX. The conflict reached its apogee in the matter of ambassadorial franchises, where Louis XIV did not hesitate to have a request prepared for the next general council (1688). This was a serious precedent. The constitution *Inter Multiplices*, published by ALEXANDER VIII in 1691, dealt more with the process for promulgating the *Articles* than it did with their content: it limited itself to condemning and nullifying them. Finally, the desired arrangement was negotiated under INNOCENT XII. The bishops named had to recognize the nonnormative side of the declaration of 1682, and Louis XIV had to promise that the *Four Articles* would not be taught.

The Crisis of the "Unigenitus." Even though the king continued his rapprochement with the papacy out of a desire to wipe out Jansenism, he did not keep his promise about teaching the *Articles*. The consequences of this are seen in the way the brief *Cum Alias*, which condemned

Fénelon's *Maxims of the Saints* (clergy assembly, 1700), was received, and especially in the way the bulls *Vineam Domini* (assembly of 1705) and *Unigenitus* (assembly of 1714) were registered, as the bishops had no hesitation about scrutinizing papal decisions before approving them. The anti-Gallican scope of the latter document is undeniable in its principle affirming the irrefragable judgment of the Holy See, as well as in its contents condemning Gallican ideas (propositions 90 and 91). In asking CLEMENT XI to explain himself, and later in calling for a general council (1717), the opposing parties opened themselves up to a direct conflict with the papacy. The conflict was only barely avoided in the early days of the Regency of the duke of Orléans (a refusal to send bulls to the bishops named, 1716–8), although it did grow worse and continued in a number of different forms during the entire century.

Gallico-Jansenism. Resistance to the constitution *Unigenitus*, which so marked the 18th century, considerably influenced the evolution of the main Gallican movements and, thus, the way they were perceived in Rome. This resistance developed on a more general basis, with the more or less explicit rejection of the role the Tridentine papacy assigned itself, in favor of a return to a Christianity that was renewed by conforming to the earliest sources (ENLIGHTENMENT Catholicism). Directly opposed to *Unigenitus*, the Gallicanism of participation, a modern reinterpretation of reformational CONCILIARISM, found new breath among members of Parlement and second-order clergy, often in direct contrast to the authoritarian Gallicanism of the monarchy and the episcopacy. Throughout Catholic Europe there were national variations of these different attitudes, with varying forms of Jansenism on the one hand, and JOSEPHISM and Febronianism on the other. Even though components varied from country to country, they did have a common body of references that showed their more or less real affiliation with the truly Gallican tradition, and they all demonstrated a common objective—opposition to ultramontanism—which they showed by their animosity toward the Society of Jesus, causing its suppression in 1773. The decrees of the synod of Pistoia (1786) were a good example of this Gallico-Jansenist amalgam, and the bull *Auctorem Fidei* (1794), which condemned them, was the best manifestation of the papacy's desire to reject them completely. This is all the more noteworthy since political conditions were hardly favorable to it. On the other hand, adoption of the clergy's Civil Constitution (1790) was a better illustration of the dangers inherent in these perspectives and the need to condemn them as a whole. The history of the document, which was aimed at overseeing reorganization of the constitutional Church, furnished the proof of the harmfulness of the tradition to which it meant to refer. The line of reasoning used by Pius VI (brief *Quod Aliquantum*, 1791) would be used again, and expanded upon, by the neo-ultramontane movement in the 19th century.

Gallicanism in the 19th Century. Negotiating with Pius VII for a new concordat (1801) to reestablish religious peace, Napoleon I was hoping to reconstruct an authoritarian Gallicanism in the service of his power. This restoration was ineluctably weakened, however, by the recognized authority of the Holy See to renew the episcopacy in general. In the new society that came out of the FRENCH REVOLUTION, Gallican principles looked more like servitude to the state in its different constitutional forms than a hope for reform or even a foil favoring a new brand of ultramontanism. If they did show up one last time in an ecclesiastical environment, it was as a reaction to the idea's excesses, and once again in the search for an ecclesiastical position faithful to the old tradition of the Church as much as it was to the necessities of the times (Msgr. Maret, 1805–84). The preparation for, and celebration of, Vatican I (1869–1870) marked the absolute defeat of the different currents of Gallicanism, since not only was the infallibility of the pope defined, but his primacy of jurisdiction was stated in such way that nothing was left in doubt.

Jacques Grès-Gayer

Bibliography

Blet, P. *Le Clergé de France et la Monarchie. Étude sur les assemblées générales du clergé de 1615 à 1666*, Rome, 1959; *Le Clergé de France, Louis XIV et le Saint-Siège de 1695 à 1715*, Rome, 1989.

Costigan, R. F. "Bossuet and the Consensus of the Church," *Theological Studies* 56 (1995), 625–72.

Costigan, R. F. "The Consensus of the Church: Differing Classic Views," *Theological Studies* 51 (1990), 25–48.

Lagarde, De G. *La Naissance de l'esprit laïque à la fin du Moyen Age*, Louvain-Paris, 1963.

Duchon, R. "De Bossuet à Febronius," *Revue d'histoire ecclésiastique*, 65 (1970), 375–422.

Ford, J. T., et al. "Review Symposium 'Triumph in Defeat: Infallibility, Vatican I, and the French Minority Bishops,' by M. O'Gara, 1988," *Horizons* 16 (1989), 353–66.

Gacquère, F. *Pierre de Marca (1594–1662), sa vie, ses oeuvres, son gallicansime.* Paris, 1932.

Gérin, C. *Recherches historiques sur l'asemblée du clergé de France de 1682*, 2nd ed., Paris, 1870.

Gough, J. *Paris and Rome. The Gallican Church and the Ultramontane Campaign, 1848–1853*, Oxford, 1986.

Gres-Gayer, J. "Le Gallicanisme de L. Ellies Du Pin," *Lias*, 18 (1991), 37–82.

Gres-Geyer, J. "The Unigenitus of Clement XI: A Fresh Look at the Issues," *Theological Studies* 49 (1988), 259–82.

Lecler, J. *"Qu'est-ce que les Libertés de* l'Église gallicane?," *Recherches de Science religieuse, 23* (1933), 385–410, 542–68 and 24 (1934), 47–87.

Loyson, J. T. *L'Assemblée du clergé de France de 1682*, Paris, 1870.

Martimort, A. G. *Le Gallicanisme de Bossuet*, Paris, 1953.

Martin, V. *Le Gallicanisme et la réforme catholique*, Paris, 1919; *Le Gallicanisme politique et le clergé de France*, Paris, 1929; *Les Origines du gallicanisme*, Paris, 1939.

Mortimort, A. G. *Les Assemblées du clergé et Louis XIV de 1670 à 1693*, Rome, 1972; *Le Gallicanisme*, Paris, 1973.

Orcibal, J. *Louis XIV contre Innocent XI, les appels au futur concile de 1688 et l'opinion française*, Paris, 1949.

O'Gara, M. *Triumph in Defeat: Infallibility, Vatican I, and the French Minority Bishops*, Washington, D.C., 1988.

Pascoe, L. B. *Jean Gerson's Principles of Church Reform*, Leyde, 1973.

Puyol, E. *Edmond Richer, étude historique et critique sur la rénovation du gallicanisme au commencement du XVIIe siècle*, Paris, 1876.

Schatz, K. *Papal Primacy: From Its Origins to the Present*, Collegeville, Minn., 1996.

Sieben, H. J. *Die Katholische Konzilidee von der Reformation bis zur Aufklärung*, Paderborn, 1988.

Sonnino, P. *Louis XIV's View of the papacy*, Berkeley, 1966.

GAMES, ROMAN EMPIRE. Roman games and spectacles underwent extreme modifications during the centuries of the Republic and the ROMAN EMPIRE, both in terms of their quality and their number: the calendar of A.D. 354 shows 177 days of games that year, an enormous increase since the early days of the Empire. By that time, classic tragedy had almost disappeared from theaters, where the spectacles normally presented were pantomimes or vulgar and obscene *mimi*. Hunts and gladiatorial combats, as well as the executions of condemned prisoners by wild beasts, had developed due to the presence of a large number of exotic animals. Chariot races in the circuses, whose numbers had grown over the centuries, were followed by the spectators with a passion much like the enthusiasm of sports fans today, and the competitions often incited riots and chaos. The athletic games, finally, became a sort of *Vanity Fair* whose protagonists were, in the last days, muscular men who often gave violent performances.

A tradition of thought hostile to the games already existed in the pagan world, and intellectuals like Seneca, (as well as Emperor Marcus Aurelius) considered the spectacles to be vulgar and, in the case of the gladiators and capital punishment, cruel, and gratuitous violence.

As for the Christians, it must be noted that they considered the spectacles and games as manifestations of idolatry. The origins of the games were often religious in nature, and they were accompanied by sacrifices, leading to the prohibition of the Christian faithful from attending or participating. Under Christian emperors, the circus and stadium continued to be dedicated to the gods, whereas the gladiatorial combats were, especially in Rome, only spectacles. In addition, for the Christians there were too many memories of martyrs killed in the arena.

The judgment of the Church Fathers was severe but was constantly repeated and standardized: from Tertullian to Augustine, the circus was defined as *furens*, the games of the amphitheater as cruel atrocities, the theatrical spectacles as impious and obscene, and the exercises and battles in the stadium as the height of vanity. Nevertheless, especially when dealing with the stories of martyrs, comparisons were often made between Christian martyrs and the athletes or gladiators, and the terminology of the games was used to describe their exploits.

What frightened the Church Fathers was the passion with which the spectators followed the games. Novatian (*Spect* I, 4) said that it was difficult to root out because it had a tendency to grow back. The pages of the *Confessions* of St. Augustine (6, 8, 13) describing the approach of Alypius to the combats of the gladiators as almost a disease are an important testimonial to this.

The ecclesiastical hierarchy was therefore opposed to the games due to their idolatrous and bloody nature, as well as the cruelty they inspired in the spectators. The *constitutiones apostolicae* from the second half of the 4th century forbade the faithful to take part in "assemblies" of pagans, spectacles, banquets, or processions (II, 62). Baptism was refused for mimes, circus charioteers, gladiators, runners, and flute, cithara or lyre players from the pantomimes (VIII, 32, 9). Canon LXII of the Council of Elvira, held between 295 and 314, had established the conditions under which *auriges* and mimes could be allowed to take communion, and canons IV and V from the Council of Arles in 314 had excluded the charioteers and active *theatrici* from communion.

The Christian emperors were more or less tolerant toward the games, though Constantine abolished gladitorial combats in 325 with the edict of Beriti (*Cth*, XV, 12, 1) that outlawed gladiators. Nevertheless, one law text (*CIL*, XI, 5265) refers to the combats of gladiators that accompanied the imperial celebrations in Umbria and Tuscany in 333 and 337. The complete disappearance of the games seems to have occurred during the first decades of the 5th century.

Cinzia Vismara

Bibliography

Ville, G. "Les jeux des gladiateurs dans l'empire chrétien," *MEFR*, 71, (1960), 273–335.

Ville, G. "Religion et politique: comment ont pris fin les combats des gladiateurs?" *Annales, (ESC)*, 1979, 651–71.

Weismann, W. *Kirche und Schauspiele. Die Schauspiele in Urteil der lateinischen Kirchenväter unter besonderer Berücksichtigung von Augustin,* Classiciacum XXVII, Würzburg, 1972.

GARB, ECCLESIASTICAL, WITHIN THE VATICAN. The Vatican may be the only place in the world where clothing is not left to anyone's personal taste or affected by fashion. It depends instead on one's position in the hierarchy of the Church, and by the occasion.

It is sometimes difficult to discern the historical origins of vestments, which in many cases have a meaning and make it possible to identify a person's rank in the Church. It may be said that—today, as in the past—the use of vestments at the Vatican obeys the rule of the uniform, both for the clergy and for the pontifical guards.

The variety of garb is striking, but can be explained by a few very simple rules. For ecclesiastics, the cassock is a sign that they are members of the clergy (together with the tonsure, in former times). Black is for everyday use, while colors are used for ceremonial occasions, with specific colors determined by the individual's rank: purple for prelates and bishops, and red for cardinals. This applies for the whole Latin clergy, worldwide. However, it is less and less observed outside the Vatican, since today the clerical suit is a general-purpose uniform and membership in the clergy is sometimes only made obvious at liturgical ceremonies.

This is why the respect for custom, which is actually not systematic at the Vatican, lends a certain exoticism to people's colorful attire, giving the onlooker the impression of being in the midst of a foreign tribe and, for some ecclesiastics, enhancing the feeling of unease that the obligation of certain observances can arouse in Rome.

The cassock's variety of colors has long been extremely subtle. In the past, the episcopal purple was to be a crude blue-mauve, which constituted the lower scale of the scarlet used by cardinals, which was pinkish red and quite different from the bright red used today. The pope is the only one who never wears the black cassock. For prelates, bishops, and cardinals it is everyday attire. In ceremonies and at certain official functions, specific articles of clothing serve as distinctive signs of rank: for prelates, a manteletta (a short knee- length tunic, sleeveless and fastened at the neck); for bishops, a purple rochet (a kind of surplice) and cape; for cardinals, a red rochet and cape. The calotte, or skullcap (either purple or red), the pectoral cross, and the ring are part of the episcopal insignia that bishops and cardinals wear less and less frequently in everyday life, even if they have the option of combining them with the black cassock edged with colored piping and matching sash.

The cardinal's pectoral cross is generally the one the cardinals wore when they were bishops. Since VATICAN

II, simplicity has been the rule, symbolizing the equality in the episcopal office that PAUL VI wanted to convey to the Council Fathers when, in 1965, he gave each one an identical episcopal ring. This was in the form of a cylinder of gold, engraved with a cross between the alpha and omega. Nowadays, to distinguish a bishop or cardinal from among the other clergy, one need only ascertain if he is wearing, if not a colored calotte, then at least a pectoral cross or ring. These latter items can be worn with a clerical suit.

The pope's wardrobe has also been considerably simplified. In liturgical ceremonies, he wears the episcopal accoutrements but keeps the white skullcap. For portraits he wears a rochet over the white cassock, and a red silk cape with an embroidered star. Up until the reign of JOHN XXIII, the pope wore slippers embroidered with a cross. Since then, popes have worn a type of of moccasin or mule, varying in color over the years from fawn to dark brown. It is not unusual, in modern times, however, to see the pope wearing black footwear during ceremonies, just as he has been known on other occasions to leave off the cassock in favor of a skiing or mountaineering outfit. In the open, over his cassock, the sovereign pontiff wears a red cloak laced at the neck, and on his head, over the calotte, a melusine or long-haired felt hat of purple embroidered with gold.

Philippe Levillain

Camauro. The camauro is a headdress worn only by the pope. It resembles a wide skullcap that covers the head, including the ears. The winter version is made of red velvet edged with ermine, while the summer version is made of red satin, without an edging. The sovereign pontiff used to wear it with the mozzetta, a short cape and hood, which was made of the same material as the camauro. In practice, of course, the camauro was only very rarely worn in the hot Roman summers. During the week beginning with Holy Saturday the pope exchanged the camauro and mozzetta of red velvet for ones of white damask trimmed with ermine.

The camauro (which also has several Latin names, including *camelacium, camelaugum, camelaucis,* and *camelausium*) is of monastic origin. In early times the monks wore a head-covering made of camel hair (*camelus*) to keep out the cold. The word is also said to derive from a Greek farmer's headdress known as a *camerion*, which consisted of four triangular pieces of cloth cut in the shape of a cross. Eastern monks wore a camauro with a small cross on the front when raised to the episcopate. Quite popular with the popes of Avignon (where the climate was colder than in Rome), also suggested the "Clementine" headdress of the popes of the 16th and 17th centuries (CLEMENT X wore both headdresses together).

The camauro may also be of imperial origin, since in Byzantium the basileus (king) wore such a head covering in red. To judge from a 9th-century mosaic showing Gregory IV similarly coiffed, the popes were not long in adopting the style. In his edition of the *Liber pontificalis,* Msgr. Duchesne judges it to be the ancestor of the TIARA. The doges of Venice wore something similar, and in the 13th and 14th centuries the archbishops of Benevento also took to wearing it, along with other pontifical insignia (including the tiara), until PAUL II expressly forbade them in 1464.

The shape of the camauro varied at the whim of the pontiffs. In the 17th century, ALEXANDER VII cut out the ear flap, while INNOCENT XI wore it high on the skull, allowing the unfilled space to take very free shapes. In the 18th century, Clement X shortened it to a square cap, stretched over the head like an ecclesiastic's biretta or a toque. For a long time, the popes wore their white calotte beneath the red camauro, removing the latter for sacred functions since it was never a liturgical ornament. PIUS VI gave up the camauro, as did all his successors. PIUS IX and LEO XIII used it only rarely, although in their tombs it was included with their remains. BENEDICT XV adopted it, and PIUS XII wore it on his deathbed. To general surprise, John XXIII used it when barely elected—even, on several occasions, having himself photographed wearing the camauro.

Joël-Benoît d'Onorio

Bibliography

Battandier, A. "Le camauro," *Annuaire pontifical catholique,* 1901.

The Pontifical Gloves. The wearing of liturgical gloves—abolished in the Roman rite after Vatican II—was originally the exclusive privilege of the sovereign pontiff, but was later granted to the bishops and monastic abbots. For example, in the 11th century, LEO IX conferred them (with the dalmatic and liturgical sandals) to Ricaire, the Benedictine abbot of Monte Cassino. Not long after, VICTOR II made the same gesture toward Cardinal-Bishop Umberto, as did CLEMENT IV for the provost of Magdeburg.

Though originally smooth, the papal gloves gradually came to be decorated with embroidery and precious stones, and they matched the colors of the liturgical calendar. Thus they were white, red, purple, or green, although never black because ritual prohibited the wearing of gloves for funeral Masses and the Good Friday service. In practice, the pope wore only white or red gloves, for in past times he only celebrated pontifically twice a year—for Easter and the feast of Sts. Peter and Paul. From the second millennium, the popes's mortal remains were traditionally clothed with red gloves (although those of BONIFACE VIII were of white silk). The last time this was done was at the obsequies of John XXIII in 1963.

The gloves were prescribed only for the eucharistic sacrifice, from the beginning of the Mass up to the offertory, when the pope removed them for the washing of his hands. He only took them up again for the final benediction.

The wearing of liturgical gloves signified chastity of the hands and the purity of the sacrificing pope, clothed to present himself before God and offer Him the oblations. The gloves had to be seamless (in the image of Christ's tunic), symbolizing the oneness of the Church and the integrity of the faith.

Joël-Benoît d'Onorio

Bibliography

Barbier de Montault, *Les Gants pontificaux*, Tours, 1877.
Battandier, A. *Annuaire pontifical catholique*, 1914.

Mule. This is French term designating the shoe that is part of the vestments of the sovereign pontiff. The mule would not have any particular importance were it not linked to the custom, abolished by Paul VI, of the kissing of the pope's feet. In contrast to the Greek Church, which never allowed the use of the symbol of the cross on its dignitaries' shoes, the Roman Church gradually introduced it on those of its head. Monuments decorated with figures show that in the Middle Ages the pope and dignitaries of the Curia wore black shoes, the upper part of which was decorated with a white ornament of varying form. The color red, still used today, was prescribed by the 13th century in the ceremonial of GREGORY X.

It was not until the beginning of the 15th century that the cross appeared as the shoe's principal adornment (this can be seen on Innocent VII's funerary monument in the Vatican Grottoes). Its use was reserved exclusively to the pope (FELIX V as an antipope, had to give it up at the time of his reconciliation with NICHOLAS V), and only if he wore shoes decorated in this way could the pope allow his foot to be kissed.

The ceremoniarius did not fail to mention this particularity. In 1514, Paris de Grassis noted in his diary: "The pope [LEO X] has left Rome without the stole, but, what is worse, without the rochet, and the very worst is that he is wearing boots, which is not proper since those who wish to cannot kiss his foot. When the pope noticed this he smiled, as if it mattered to him scarcely a whit."

The shape of the cross evolved gradually. Up until the 18th century it was a sort of galloon or braid, fairly wide, the upright and the horizontal branches taking up the whole length and width of the upper part of the shoe. This was later narrowed into the form of a Greek cross, decorated at the corners with rays and placed in the middle of the vamp. This form lasted until the beginning of the pontificate of Paul VI, who replaced the red satin or velvet shoe embroidered in gold with a leather pump, reddish brown in color. Since the pontificate of John XXIII, the pope's shoes have been made by a specialist who heads the orthopedic laboratory of the Cottolengo hospital in Turin.

Francois-Charles Uginet

Bibliography

Pouyard, J. "Dissertazione sopra l'antichit . . . del bacio de' piedi de' sommi pontefici all'introduzione della croce sulle loro scarpe o sandali e sopra le diversi forme e colori ed ornati di questa parte del vestiario pontificio negli antichi monumenti sacri," Rome, 1807.

GELASIUS I. *(b. Africa or Rome, ?, d. Rome, 21 November 496.) Elected pope on 1 March 492. Buried in St. Peter's. Saint.*

Son of a certain Valerius, Gelasius was probably born in Rome to a family of African origin. This theory reconciles two apparently contradictory pieces of information: that of the *LIBER PONTIFICALIS*, which calls him an African, and his own account, according to which he was "born a Roman."

Nothing is known of his career before his election as pope. In all probability he belonged to the Roman clergy and became a bishop in Rome, although the theory that he was secretary to his predecessors is without solid foundation. This theory was inspired by the desire to show that Gelasius was the author of a coherent doctrine of papal power, and was based on the stylistic similarities of the letters of SIMPLICIUS, FELIX III, and Gelasius. Such resemblances, however, are due more to the influence of the rules of the CHANCERY. Essentially, the role played by Gelasius in the Roman clergy prior to his election is not certain.

What we know of his papacy comes primarily from the *Liber Pontificalis* and from a note by Dionysius Exiguus. Gelasius did compose six treatises of dogma, and the collections have preserved 104 letters or fragments of letters testifying to his politics and his pastoral activities. According to the dates that can be calculated from the *Liber Pontificalis*, Gelasius was ordained the same day that Felix died: Sunday, 1 March 492. When he began his papacy, Odoacer was ruling in Italy. But since 489 Odoacer had been engaged in combat against Theodoric, king of the Ostrogoths, in the northern part of the country, and the latter's definitive victory in 492 inaugurated a long period of political stability and prosperity in Italy. During his papacy, Gelasius maintained a distant but peaceful relationship with the ruling powers (the court was in RAVENNA), better than his relationship with the emperor, which was marked by the permanent conflict over the Acacian SCHISM.

Gelasius's activity revolved around three primary axes: (1) the debate with the East, which was occasion for the pope to expand forcefully, and sometimes innovatively, the Roman teaching on the nature of papal authority; (2) his pastoral work in the West, which was well documented by his correspondence; and (3) his literary works. In 492, the main figures in the schism of 484 disappeared, but the situation did not change. Emperor Anastasius kept the *Henoticon*, the edict of union composed by Zeno and Acacius (patriarch of Constantinople) in 482, hoping to reconcile the Orthodox and the Monophysites. The Henoticon was ambiguous, however, regarding the COUNCIL of Chalcedon.

Gelasius sent the letter to Anastasius by which the bishop of Rome traditionally announced his election to the emperor—a letter which his predecessor, Felix, in the absence of a Western emperor, had sent to the emperor in the East. But he did not write to the archbishop of Constantinople, Euphemius, whom Felix had refused to recognize, since he kept he names of Acacius and Frauitas in the diptychs. However, Euphemius was a conciliatory individual and, at heart, orthodox. He wrote to the pope that he had reinserted the names of Felix and Gelasius into the diptych, and he affirmed his unqualified adherence to the Council of Chalcedon. But he also asked Gelasius to give up his condemnation of the remembrance of Acacius and Frauitas, a condemnation that would cause riots. The intransigence of Gelasius's reply was characteristic of his attitude toward the East: he incisively, one might even say caustically, rejected the patriarch of Constantinople's proposal, maintaining the Roman demands in their entirety, with no expression of gratitude for the concessions his correspondent had already made. The other letters on this subject, composed over the period from 492 to 494, were marked by the same style. Gelasius forbade Faustus—who was a senator and the legate of King Theodoric to Constantinople, and who was impeded in his mission by the impossibility of receiving communion with the bishop of the capital—to establish any kind of communication with the heretics and their followers. The pope had already neglected to entrust Faustus with a letter for the emperor, which annoyed Anastasius. Gelasius replied to Lawrence of Odria, a suffragan bishop from Thessalonia who was asking him for a "remedy for the faith," with a Chalcedonian confession of faith and a justification for rejecting the *Henoticon*. To Succonius, an African bishop who had survived the Vandal persecution and taken refuge in Constantinople, Gelasius addressed a respectful letter, but one in which he reproached him for being in communion with a heretical clergy. It is not surprising, in light of these letters, that relations with the East were completely broken off after 494. The last of the letters we have is one that the pope addressed to the emperor himself, in 497, and in which he contested the emperor's right to make laws in the ecclesiastical domain without following the opinion of the *sacerdotes*. He also affirmed the right of the Church of Rome to intervene in the East's affairs concerning the faith and ecclesiastic discipline. The letter expressed the essential part of Gelasius's teaching regarding authority, a subject to which we shall return.

But Gelasius showed more flexibility in Rome than he did with his interlocutors in Constantinople. In 495, he reconciled Bishop Vitalis, who had survived the unfortunate legation of 484, following which he had been excommunicated. It is true that Rome's intransigence with the East was not supported by unanimity in the West: the bishops of Gaul, Avitus of Vienne, and Rusticus of Lyon, although they were poorly informed, were concerned with the legitimacy of the causes for the split, and there was even a party in Rome that was in favor of reconciliation with the East, mainly for political reasons. This party was especially visible during the later papacies of ANASTASIUS II and SYMMACHUS. In his letter to Athanasius (494), and at the end of one of his treatises on ANATHEMA, Gelasius affirmed the superiority of the power of clerics over that of princes, and the Holy See's competence to pass laws in religious matters for Churches in general. The most famous of his sayings is from his letter to Athanasius: "There are two principles, august emperor, by which this world is ruled: the sacred authority of pontiffs (*auctoritas sacrata pontificum*) and royal power (*regalis potestas*). For the former, the *pondus* of the priests is all the stronger since, on the Judgment Day, they are to be held accountable even for the kings of men." Gelasius's teaching on the relationship between Church and State had a profound influence on the canonists. But Gelasius was content to hold to the course set by his illustrous predecessors, Ambrose of Milan (with Constance II) and LEO I (with the emperor Leo). He reminded Anastasius of the principles that guided his politics, but contested neither his role as guarantor of the faith nor the right to show interest in religious questions. Gelasius's statement about clerics' responsibility before God for the actions of princes is ambiguous, for we do not know whether it refers to responsibility for their private actions or for their politics. In the former case, it is a question of the spiritual responsibility of the priest; in the second, Gelasius is affirming a hierarchy of power. If he is not reserving this authority only for the bishop of Rome in this text, elsewhere in the same letter (and in his treatise on anathema) he affirms the competence of Rome, as Peter's see, for decisions above those of councils and regional churches. Here, again, he is not being innovative, but Gelasius speaks with unusual strength, and the combination of his independence vis-à-vis the emperor and his consciousness of the universality of Roman authority made him a precurser of pontifical primacy, in the medieval sense of the word.

If relations with the empire held Gelasius's attention for a long time, and if they inspired some of his most universally known writings, the essential part of his activity during his four years as pope was of a pastoral nature, and concerned the West. Three canonical collections have preserved a number of letters and fragments of Gelasius's correspondence with the churches of Italy, and an examination of them paints an interesting picture of the workings of the papacy and the state of churches. From this dossier, however, it is difficult to establish the originality of Gelasius's politics, since to a great extent we are unaware of the reasons why the compilers kept the correspondence of this pope rather than that of some other. Was it because it was more abundant or more specific? Or was it a coincidence, just a chance transmission of texts? (The same question was raised more than a half-century later over the correspondence of Pope PELAGIUS I.) Almost all the letters—with an exception regarding an irregularity committed by the bishop of Ravenna—are addressed to churches of SUBURBICARIAN ITALY and Sicily. It is not surprising that none of the letters were addressed to the provinces of the North, since for the pope it was a question of exercising his metropolitan authority, an authority held in the North by the bishops of Milan and Aquileia.

The subjects with which these letters deal are of some significance. Only one deals with a dogmatic issue, and that is the letter against Pelagianism addressed to the bishops of Picenum—a letter that was called for by a concrete problem of ecclesiastical discipline. None of them were concerned with matters of the East, because it went without saying that the bishops under Roman jurisdiction did not have an opinion different from that of the pope. The letters all concerned "daily life" on the Italian peninsula in the 5th century. Their main themes were ecclesiastical discipline, judiciary problems, and the management of the patrimony.

In the area of church discipline, the pope was especially interested in clergy recruitment. He intervened directly for one candidate or another, he approved one election and contested another, and he reminded his readers of rules in effect in this area. The direction of these interventions was always the same, and was based on three principles: (1) control of clergy recruitment, (2) respect for rules handed down by tradition, and (3) demonstration of flexibility in adapting to the severity of the time (*asperitas temporis*), particulary in authorizing derogations of the strict rules edited by Valerian. It seems as though deacons were rarely interested in becoming priests, since the pope authorized clerics of lower ranks to be raised exceptionally fast to the presbyterate. This was thus a different matter from the demographic crisis in the 6th century, which touched all ranks of the clergy, with the exception of bishops. The dearth of priests was perhaps due to the development of the diaconal program. Conflicts of jurisdiction were rare. The pope's politics of interference was systematic, but we find only a few letters in which the pope admonished bishops for having stepped beyond their rights in acting without previous consultation (e.g., convening an assembly or promoting a clerk). In this area, Gelasius seems to have been reaping the benefits of his predecessors' politics and exercise of authority that was well accepted among Italian churches.

Gelasius was also attentive to the rules for consecrating and giving service to churches, such as reopening for worship a building that had been abandoned for a time, authorizing a procession, or organizing a private oratory. In contrast to his predecessors, however, the pope's primary concern was not the worry of seeing a new building face ruin for lack of means, but he did take precautions so that the bishop could control all his houses of worship. In particular, Gelasius authorized the foundation of two churches consecrated to St. Michael the Archangel: one in Potenza, the other in Lavinium, near Monte Gargano. Tradition, as transmitted by the Belgian chronicler Sigebert of Gembloux in the early 12th century, reports that it was during Gelasius' papacy that the archangel appeared on Monte Gargano, which in the 6th century had become a famous sanctuary. But in Carolingian times, Florus, the deacon from Lyon, only mentioned veneration of the archangel in Rome.

A second group of letters concerns judicial matters. Subjects varied from the nebulous affair of the cleric who "troubled a church," to clerics who squandered Church goods, to a famous case of someone who assassinated a bishop, as well as cases of a simoniac bishop, a parricide, and forgery. On occasion the letters affirm general principles, especially in relationships between the Church and temporal power (in the time of Gelasius, this was the Arian king Theodoric). Several fragments of letters recall the right to asylum and its limits; others recall the duty of a bishop to intervene before a king, regardless of the crime of the accused. As with all papal interventions, even those that have been handed down only in the form of a few lines and which can on occasion look like an abstract announcement of a principle, these latter letters form a legal philosophy on very specific cases. It would be interesting to study certain judicial cases to evaluate the distribution of jurisdictional responsibility between royal power and religious power for crimes concerning an infraction against the penal code that existed before the Justinian Code.

All the other letters concern the management of the Church's PATRIMONY. As far as the principles were concerned, Gelasius was not innovative: the essential theme was the prohibition against alienating Church property. With the exception of a few cases of dishonest clerics, problems usually arose regarding wills. Gelasius did not particularly refer to the difference—a somewhat difficult distinction, it appears—between a bishop's own property (which he acquired before becoming pope) and the rest, which was inalienable. But Gelasius broke a number of wills (and not only those of bishops) because their authors had included Church property in them. However, in the area of management of Church property, he did introduce innovations. For the first time, he pronounced the rule that Church revenue should be divided into four equal parts: one part for the bishop, the second for clerics, the third for the poor, and the fourth for the Fabbrica. Gelasius did not present the rule explicitly as an innovation, but neither did he appeal to tradition; and it is likely that he was its author. Another of Gelasius's letters shows that he sent a DEACON named Corninus to Picenum, with the mission of gathering information for the purpose of evaluating as precisely as possible Church possessions there, and of making a written record of his mission's results. This letter gives credit to the tradition as transmitted by John the Deacon, Gregory the Great's biographer, according to which Gelasius had a register of all the revenue the Church's lands made, a document that GREGORY I, in turn, reformed.

Other than these letters, Gelasius was also the author of six treatises, most of which were inspired by specific questions. The *Breviculus Historiae Eutychianistarum*, or *Gesta de Nomine Acacii* (which perhaps predates his papacy), the *Damnatio Petri et Acacii*, and the *Tomus de Anathematis Vinculo* were inspired by the quarrel with the East. It should also be pointed out that the treatise on anathema was the first of its kind in Rome, and that it reserved for the bishop of Rome alone, as the descendant of PETER, the ultimate right to bind and unbind (the power of the keys). The treatise on the two natures was still concerned with the crisis in the East, but this time it touched on theological questions that separated the Monophysites and the Chalcedonians. The treatise was followed by a large patristic anthology justifying the Chalcedonian position.

The two other treatises concerned the West. Gelasius wrote about the Pelagian heresy on two occasions, one of which we know nothing about, and another, between 490 and 493, when he wrote to a bishop, Honorius of Dalmatia, who had reproached the pope for getting involved in his church's affairs by calling him negligent (he had let himself be influenced by the Pelagian heresy). Gelasius replied, justifying his attitude by his pastoral solicitude. In November 493, the pope addressed all the bishops of Picenum to rectify the Pelagian errors that had been spread by a certain Senex. He also sent a "letter against the Lupercalia" to Senator Andromachus, who had shown attachment to the traditional Roman feast, which at the time still had a carnival nature (Gelasius criticized bawdy songs and immoral behavior) and an element of magic (Gelasius made fun of those Christians who thought it necessary to honor demons in order to chase away misfortune, and reminded them that the public celebration of the Lupercalia in 473 had not kept a great epidemic from breaking out just weeks later). This may have been the last time in the history of Christian Rome that a public celebration of a great pagan feast took place, but it would be incorrect to say that Gelasius forbade it: not only did he not have the authority, but he was content to place before Andromachus the contradiction between his profession of Christian faith and his pagan practices.

The LIBER PONTIFICALIS, which adds to the confusion about political events during the time of Gelasius's papacy, fills out the portrait of the pope. It refers to his role as the builder of basilicas outside Rome: one dedicated to Saint Euphemia, in Tivoli; those dedicated to Saints Nicander, Eleutherius, and Andrew on Via Labicana; and one dedicated to St. Mary on Via Laurentina. None of these buildings is clearly identified, but it is noteworthy that, other than Mary, all these saints were Eastern (Euphemia was patron saint of the Council of Chalcedon).

The *Liber Pontificalis* also makes mention of Gelasius's liturgical work, saying that he wrote hymns "in the style of Ambrose," prefaces, and prayers. We know nothing for certain on this subject, since the sacramentary called the Gelasian Sacramentary was actually compiled early in the 7th century.

Among Gelasius's apocryphal works, the Gelasian decree is also noteworthy. This was a composite work, most probably established early in the 6th century. The decree has five parts, including "a notice concerning the *septiform* Spirit and the names of Christ," a list of the canonical works, and a declaration on Roman PRIMACY and the patriarchal sees (Rome, Alexandria, and Antioch). These three parts are believed to be the work of Pope Damasus. The fourth part is an enumeration of the ecumencial councils and the orthodox Fathers, and the last is a list of the apocryphal works rejected by the Church. Study of the latter two parts shows that the text was compiled before 519—that is, before the extinction of the schism of Acacius—in an atmosphere that was quite favorable to Rome, perhaps in northern Italy or in Provence. It was, however, a private work, rather than an official endeavor.

Gelasius accomplished a considerable amount in his four years as pope. The work was, moreover, too complex for Gelasius to be reduced to the caricatured image of a pope whose intransigence might have lastingly compromised reconciliation with the East. Like all the other popes after 476, Gelasius was confronted by a new political situation: Italy was detached from the empire, and relations between the Church and civil powers needed to adapt to this new fact. Gelasius was fairly involved in the situation, although he kept his concerns for pastoral duties as a first priority, which earned him the personal homage of the anonymous chronicler of the *Liber Pontificalis*: "*hic fuit amator pauperum*" (he was a friend of the poor).

Claire Sotinel

Bibliography

LP, 1, 255–7.

Capelle, B. "Desprecatio Gelasii," *RB*, 66, (1934), 135–44.

Coll. Avell., CSEL 35: *ep. 97*, 400–36; 99, 440–3; 100, 453–64; App. 2, 3, 791–800.

"Decretum Gelasianum de libris recipiendis et non recipiendis," *Texte und Untersuchungen*, 38, 4, 1912.

Gelasius I, *Epistulae LII cum fragm. LXIX*, Thiel, 287–510.

Holleman, A. W. J. *Pope Gelasius I and the Lupercalia*, Amsterdam, 1974.

Nautin, P. "Gélase," *DHGE*, 20 (1984), c. 283–94.

Schwartz, E. "Publistische Sammlungen zum acacianischen Schisma," *Abhandlungen der Bayerischen Akademie der Wissenschaften*, 10 (1934): *Tomus de anathematis uinculo*, 7–15; *De duabus naturis in Christo aduersus Eutychem et Nestorium*, 85–106; *De Damnatione Nominum Petri et Acacii*, 106–11.

Ullmann, W. *Gelasius (492–6)*, Stuttgart, 1981 (*Päpste und Papstum*, 18).

Zeigler, A. K. "Pope Gelasius I and his Teaching on the Relation of Church and State," *Catholic Historical Review*, 27 (1942), 412–37.

GELASIUS II. *John of Gaeta (b. Gaeta, 1060, d. Cluny, 28 or 29 January 1191). Elected pope in Rome on 24 January 1118. Buried in Cluny.*

Gelasius II was born in Gaeta to a wealthy family (he was the son of John Coniulo), and as a child he was entrusted to the care of the monks at Monte Cassino. The monastery, directed by Abbot Didier (the future Pope VICTOR III), was at the time at its apogee, and he received a solid education from the erudite monk Alberic. He composed a number of hagiographical works while there.

While still quite young, he was called to Rome. Beginning in 1088, he was in the service of URBAN II. He was ordained deacon on 23 September 1088; and at about the same time, Urban II named him cardinal deacon of Santa Maria in Cosmedin and head of the papal CHANCERY. A faithful supporter of Urban II (1088–99) and PASCHAL II (1099–1118), he carried out his two duties for three turbulent decades (amid the quarrel over INVESTITURES; and the reign of the antipopes CLEMENT III, THEODERIC, ALBERT, and SILVESTER IV). He had the church of his diaconate completely remodeled, and was quite attached to the reform of the papal chancery, but it was not he who introduced the rules of *cursus* into the chancery. In 1111, John of Gaeta shared the captivity of PASCHAL II and, during these years, he was counted among the moderate cardinals who were concerned with balance. At the time of the Lateran SYNOD in 1116, he stood resolutely beside the pope while he was being seriously attacked for his politics of compromise vis-à-vis Emperor Henry V, and was even accused of HERESY by Bruno de Segni.

At the end of Paschal II's papacy, a time of serious troubles, John retired to Monte Cassino. When the pope died at CASTEL SANT'ANGELO on 21 January 1118, he was called back to Rome at Cardinal-Bishop Pietro da Porto's instigation and was elected pope in Santa Maria in Pallara on 24 January, under the name Gelasius II. The election had hardly taken place when a group of armed men led by Cencius Frangipani broke into the church and captured the newly elected pontiff. This act of violence provoked an uprising by the Roman people, led by the urban prefect Peter and some of the Pierleoni, and Leo Frangipani, Cencius's brother, was forced to release the pope. Gelasius II was led to the Lateran but, because of the troubles, the necessary rites of consecration could not be performed. Informed of the recent events in Rome, Emperor Henry rushed from northern Italy and arrived in the city during the night of the first of March. The pope escaped with most of the cardinals and, after enduring a number of adventures and dangerous situations, took refuge in his native city of Gaeta.

Other than his diaconate, Gelasius had received no other ordination. The emperor attempted to get him to return to Rome, and to be consecrated in his presence. Gelasius refused to enter into talks to help arrive at an amiable resolution. He tried to delay them until the fall, and to have them take place in the context of the Lombard synod. This angered the emperor, and pushed by the Frangipani, who were at the head of his Roman supporters, and advised by erudite Bolognese jurists like the famous Irnerius, he took the step of naming an antipope, claiming that the election of Gelasius had not been valid. On 8 March 1118, Archbishop Maurice of Braga was proclaimed and enthroned under the name GREGORY VIII. On 9 March, in Gaeta, Gelasius II was ordained priest, and on 10 March, bishop. On 7 April 1118, in Capua, he pronounced the excommunication of Emperor Henry and his antipope. Gelasius gave Christianity his own view of these events in his letters.

The antipope, supported by the Frangipani, found almost no partisans outside Rome and its surrounding areas. In Germany, in both Cologne and Fritzlar, Cardinal Legate Conon of Preneste, as ordered by Gelasius II, announced the excommunication of the emperor, the antipope, and their supporters. In early July 1118, as soon as Henry V had left Rome, Gelasius returned, although he could not remain in the city governed by his adversaries. On 21 July, during a solemn office in St. Prassede, he was again attacked by the Frangipani. Still dressed in his liturgical vestments, he managed to escape on horseback. He no longer sought the assistance of the Normans of southern Italy, but rather left Italy, where he had little security. He reached France via boat, with stops in Pisa and Genoa, and he reached Marseille at the end of October. King Louis VI dispatched Abbot Suger from Saint-Denis, who was bearing rich gifts, to head him off in Maguelone. Since a meeting with the king had been foreseen in Vézelay, the pope took the road to the north (via Montpellier, Avignon, Orange, and Vienne, where he held a synod in Lyon), but on 18 January, gravely ill, he had to be transported from Mâcon to Cluny, where he died on 28 or 29 January 1119.

His short and unfortunate papacy, far from putting an end to the quarrel over investitures in the empire, reinforced the division. It was reported that, on his death bed, Gelasius proposed Cardinal Legate Conon of Preneste as his successor, and that after he declined, he recommended Archbishop Gui of Vienne. The latter's papacy (as CALISTUS II) allowed peace to be established on the basis of a compromise, and it allowed the papal schism to be put to an end.

Georg Schwaiger

Bibliography

JL, I, 775–80.

LP, II, 311–21, 347; III, 135–7, 157–66.

PL, 163, 473–514.

Blumenthal, U. R. *The Investiture Controversy,* Philadelphia, 1988.

Blumenthal, U. R. "Gelasius II," *LexMA*, 4 (1987–9), 1197–8.

Brackmann, A. "Drei Schreiben zur Geschichte Gelasius II.," *Neues Archiv*, 37 (1912), 615–31.

Clerval, A. "Gélase II," *DTC*, 6-1 (1924), 1180–82 (updated bibliography by R. Aubert in *DHGE*, 20 [1984], 295).

Elze, R. "Die päpstliche Kapelle im 12. und 13. Jahrhundert," *ZRGKA*, 36 (1950), 145–204.

Engels, O. "Papst Gelasius II. (Johannes von Gaeta) als Hagiograph," *QFIAB*, 35 (1955), 1–45; "Die Hagiographischen Texte Papst Gelasius II, in der Überlieferung der Eustachius-, Erasmus- und Hypolistuslegende," *Historisches Jahrbuch*, 76 (1957), 118–33.

Fürst, C. G. "Kennen wir die Wähler Gelasius II.?" *Festschrift Karl Pivec* [= *Innsbrucker Beiträge zur Kulturwissenschaft*, 12 (1966)], 69–80.

Hüls, R. *Kardinäle, Klerus und* Kirchen Roms, 1049–1130, Tübingen, 1977, 231 ff.

Krohn, R. *Der päpstliche Kanzler Johannes von Gaeta (Gelasius II)*, (Diss.) Marburg, 1918.

Lohrmann, D. "Die Jugendwerke des Johannes von Gaeta," *QFIAB*, 47 (1967), 355–455.

Volpini, L. "Documenti nel *Sancta sanctorum* del Laterano. I resti del 'Archivio' di Gelasi II," *Lateranum* (1986), 215–64.

GENDARMES, PONTIFICAL. The Pontifical Gendarmes was an armed corps that was given the name "Papal Carabinieri" when it was created in 1816 by Pius VII for the purpose of assuring justice and police services throughout the Papal State. Its staff was granted numerous privileges, particularly that of belonging to the Household, or PAPAL FAMILY. In 1849, the force, which was one of the important institutions for the maintenance of order, became the Papal Light Infantry regiment. Nevertheless, in 1852, the name was changed to the more expressive name, Pontifical Gendarmes.

After 1870, the *Gendarmeria* was reduced to some twenty men who served as mounted police for the area that the Italian State considered to be the inviolable enclosure of the papal residence. The *Gendarmeria* regained a certain prestige at the time of the creation of the VATICAN CITY STATE in 1929. It was then placed under the command of the governor of the city, and a colonel commander, himself a former commander in the Italian *Carabinieri*, was named to head it.

The *Gendarmeria* was given the responsibility of policing and maintaining the safety of the Vatican City, the villas of Castel Gandolfo, and some papal palaces in Rome (e.g., the Lateran, St. Callistus). Since the 19th century it has played the role of honor guard, after the example of the PALATINE GUARD, during both ordinary and extraordinary papal AUDIENCES, as well as during the religious functions and ceremonies in which the sovereign pontiff participates.

Excluded from the papal chapel by the *motu proprio Pontificalis Domus* (28 March 1968), the gendarmes was disbanded by a letter from Paul VI to the secretary of state (14 September 1970), which abolished all the papal armed forces except the SWISS GUARD. Its members were turned over to the service of unarmed guards (*vigilanti*), which continue to perform the same duties of policing and maintaining order that the *Gendarmeria* had carried out. Their uniforms were modified and, though the guards were not originally armed, this expression of gentleness had to be given up.

François-Charles Uginet

GENTLEMEN OF HIS HOLINESS. The title "Gentlemen of His Holliness" was created by the *motu propio Pontificalis Domus* (28 March 1968) for the purpose of encompassing with a single name certain lay members of the old papal COURT. This helped distinguish the lay chamberlains (called cape and sword chamberlains) from the ecclesiastical chamberlains. Until they were disbanded, the lay chamberlains, who first appeared in the 16th century, were divided into three classes: the Secret Participant Chamberlains (meaning those who took part at the papal table); the secret chamberlains; and the chamberlains of honor. Only those charged with specific duties belonged to the secret participant chamberlains, as they still retained a certain importance in the daily life of the Papal HOUSEHOLD. The secret chamberlains were divided into secret chamberlains *de numero* (of which there were four), who might eventually substitute for the participant chamberlains in court service, and supernumerary secret chamberlains, an honorific category. The chamberlains of honor were honorary chamberlains, who were also divided *de numero* (four) and supernumerary chamberlains, who served in the throne room.

The word "chamberlain" refers to the person attached to the pope's chamber (*camera*), that is, to the narrow circle of individuals who made up his designated entourage. Depending on time and circumstances, this might include members of the papal FAMILY, the court or the antechamber, and the Papal Household. This entourage was composed of different categories of individuals, many of whom had their own responsibilities, but whose presence was required either permanently or occasionally for the honor service in the successive rooms that gave access to the pope's chamber. Thus the secret participant cape and sword Chamberlains were composed exclusively of the furrier major, the equerry major, the general superintendant of the postal service, the exempt of the NOBLE GUARD, the colonel of the SWISS GUARD, and, until 1918, the master of the Holy Hospice. The case of this latter individual is emblematic of the mechanisms that governed the court: wishing specifically to honor this individual because of his important duties, BENEDICT XV removed him from the group of chamberlains in order to give him special distinction and ranked him immediately after the MASTER OF THE SACRED PALACE.

Even though, in principle, all these responsibilities were to cease upon the death of either the pope or the title holder, most of the responsibilities connected with the title of secret participant cape and sword chamberlains had actually become hereditary. For example, the master of the Holy Hospice, since the time of MARTIN V, was a member of the Conti family (and since 1801, of the Ruspoli family, the continuation of the Contis); the marquis of Sacchetti played the role of furrier major since the mid-19th century; since the 18th century, the equerry major was a Serlupi-Crescenzi; and the Massimo princes were superintendents of the postal service since the time of GREGORY XVI. The *motu proprio Pontificalis Domus* did away with the inheritance of these honors.

The role of Gentlemen of His Holiness is limited to antechamber service at the time of receptions for political figures (state visits, awarding of credentials, official visits, etc.). Even though they no longer participate officially in the chapel, their attendance may be required there for important ceremonies, particularly those in which official representatives of governments are present. The old uniforms, which had retained something of 17th-century Spanish style, have been retired, and the gentlemen now don a black frock coat, closed in front (diplomatic costume), and they wear a long golden chain with the KEYS and the TIARA around their necks.

The honorific titles of the papal court, which for a long time were limited to members of the nobility of the PAPAL STATES, developed extraordinarily in the 19th century, when the cause of the Holy See was confused with that of the Catholic world. In Rome, the "black" nobility (that refused to recognize the end of temporal power), reserved its right to the eminent charges and continued to serve. The aristocracy and the high bourgeoisie of Europe had a real passion for courtly titles and antechamber service. There were advantages in this for everyone: members of the Catholic nobility played a role that they had often lost, or had never known, in their own countries, and the papacy extended its influence into a social and financial elite that was not sparing in its generosity. It appears as though the phenomenon of titles was especially rampant under Leo XIII, but the spirit of recruitment is still very much alive today.

François Charles Uginet

GERMANIC ROMAN EMPIRE. See Holy Roman Empire.

GHIBELLINES.
Since the second half of the 13th century, the term "Ghibelline" has referred to the backers, in northern and central Italy, of the Germanic HOLY ROMAN EMPIRE (*pars imperii, imperatoris*). Ghibellines are defined by contrast to their counterparts, the Guelphs, who were partisans of the pope and the Church (*pars Ecclesiae, Romani pontificis*). The two names are of Germanic origin and stem from the two powerful rival families of the nobility who disputed the imperial crown in the 12th century: the family of "Henry of Waiblingen" (Gueibelinga)—that is, the imperial dynasty of the Salians, of whom the Hohenstaufen claimed to be the descendants; and their adversaries, the prestigious dukes "Welfs of Altdorf" (Otto of Freising, *Gesta*, II, 2).

The state of the sources available does not allow a direct tracing of the paths of these two terms in Italy. They might have reached northern and central Italy as early as the second half of the 12th century with the campaigns of Frederick Barbarossa. According to one legendary tradition, they came out of the war cry of the Welfs and the Hohenstaufen. But these names may not have been adopted until the time of the rivalry between Otto IV and Frederick II (1212–18), and they then would have been simultaneously transformed by popular language and inbued with new meaning. The *ghibellini* were those who backed the Hohenstaufen emperors, who wanted the restoration of the rights of the empire in the *Regnum Italiae*. The Guelphs, their adversaries, formed an opposition movement as polymorphous as it was unstructured, consisting of those who, especially in the papal entourage, were attached to the defense of their territorial rights in the States of the Church. They also included the Lombard and Tuscan communes that feared for their independence.

In diplomatic and narrative sources, the names "Guelphs" and "Ghibellines" were not seen until the

1240s, first in Florence, and then in the neighboring cities of Tuscany and, somewhat later, in northery Italy. As the names gradually passed into the Italian vocabulary of politics and propaganda, the memory of their origin, as well as their earliest meaning tended to fade. Playing on doubtful etymology, some 14th century chroniclers (like Villani and Marchionne Di Coppo Stefani) traced them back to two German barons or Tuscan enemies (Bulfo and Ghibellino). Others, like Pietro Azari and, as early as the 13th century, Saba Malaspina, traced them to two maleficent Tuscan demons ("Gibel" and "Gualef"). Starting in the second half of the 13th century, some witnesses to Italian life (e.g., Humbert of the Romans) thought the names "Ghibellines" and "Guelphs" no longer referred to concrete programs, but were simply names of rival parties to which people belonged by sheer tradition or habit. A century later (around 1380), the famous jurist Bartolo da Sassoferato considered the names to be mere labels devoid of any link to sympathies for the empire or the Church.

Only historical events and the social and intellectual milieu in Italy and the papacy in the 13th and 14th centuries allow the nature of the opposition between *parte ghibellina* and *parte guelfa* to be understood, this includes its meaning and the quite limited possibilities of its effects, both in the area of politics and that of propaganda. Since the 11th century, the *Regnum Italiae*'s juridical adherence to the *imperium* led to increasing conflicts between the German emperor, on the one hand, and the papacy—including a large part of the nobility, the episcopacy, and the Italian communes—on the other. A consequence of Frederick I's offensive imperial politics, especially after the Hohenstaufen takeover of the NORMAN kingdom of Sicily, this conflict turned into an open battle for control of all Italy, one which reached its climax under the reign of Frederick II.

The Hohenstaufen emperors defended their rights and interests tenaciously, which caused an unavoidable polarization in political forces. Their growing presence in Italy also contributed to the problem. This polarization grew into an unstable division between two diplomatic camps—two supple and fluctuating systems of alliance—which were moved by an unceasing antagonism that had broken out between the *pars imperii* and its adversaries.

The Hohenstaufen emperors could count on almost certain assistance from a number of communes and noble dynasties in central and northern Italy that hoped to increase their power and authority by siding with them, even though the independence of the Italian entities risked being compromised by an imperial victory. Despite important conflicts of interests, other communes (the Lombard League) and other nobles sought an alliance of opportunity with the popes, hoping to escape the threat of their common enemy. In the final years of Frederick II's reign (1237–50), and under King Manfred

(1258–66), the *pars imperii*, despite some failures, managed to keep the upper hand in a play of force through frequent returns to the front. It was actually able to operate from the kingdom of Sicily, its power base, even though it had areas of support and partisans—who in the long run were not always disinterested—in central Italy (e.g., Pisa, Siena) as well as in the North (e.g., Cremona, Genoa, Ezzelino da Romano, Oberto Pallavicino, Buoso da Dovara). The politics of alliance of Popes URBAN IV and CLEMENT IV provoked a smaller branch of the French royal family, the Angevins, to enter the lists. The struggle for supremacy in Italy thus took on a definitively European dimension; and, up to the beginnings of modern times, the foreign forces that entered the frey played a decisive role.

After the conquest of the kingdom of Sicily by Charles I of Anjou, the defeat and death of Manfred in Benevento (1266), and the extinction of the Hohenstaufen male line of succession (with the death of Conradin in 1268), the *pars imperii* lost its center of power and its primary support in Italy. But the assistance of Alfonso X of Castille, especially after the episode of Sicilian Vespers (1282), along with the help of the house of Aragon (one branch of which, the kings of Sicily, managed to chase the Angevins from the island onto the mainland in 1296, and then definitively in 1302), provided the *pars imperii* with some compensation, even if it was only temporary. Despite the weakening of the Angevins (during the reigns of Charles II [1285–1309] and Robert the Wise [1309–43]), and their continuous guerilla warfare against the Aragonese (James II [1285–96] and Frederick III [1296–1337]) in southern Italy, the Ghibellines most often found themselves in the underdog position, looking for material and diplomatic support from the empire or from Sicily. This situation explains the episodic nature of all their later undertakings, as, for example, during the campaigns in Italy of Henry VII (1310–3) and Louis of Bavaria (1327–30). Even the transfer of the papal residence to Lyon (1304), and then to Avignon (1316–78), which opened new possibilities for the French monarchy to exercise its influence in Italy, were not sufficient to reinforce the Ghibellines.

Because of foreign support, the development of power structures in Italy influenced all the attempts to give the country a new political configuration. It likewise tempered the radical effects of Guelph and Ghibelline bipolarism, such as permanent instability; traditional rivalries between different cities (e.g., Milan and Cremona, Florence and Pisa); constant changes in equilibrium—both between larger and smaller power structures (communes, lordships, fiefs, Church states, etc.) and within each of them. For the most part, it was local and specific interests that won, due to a tendency to form versatile parties and coalitions based on concrete political interests. In the cities, the selfish concerns of individual groups, which were determined by political, social, and economic factors, had led to the formation of clans and to divisions into diverse, but well organized, *societates* and *partes* that acted autonomously (noble enemy factions; *consorterie; societas militum, societas populi*; professional coalitions among artisans and merchants; coalitions based on territory, *viciniae*, and religious brotherhoods, etc.). Even in the eyes of their contemporaries, one of the primary motives behind these long conflicts (in Florence, for example) that opposed the *maledetti parti* was the competition for power, the responsibilities (*la gara d'uffici*), the jealousy, and the haughty pride (*invidia, superbia*) of each of the groups. It was not rare for a temporarily conquered party to be driven out of a city, or to leave it voluntarily (*fuoriscitismo*), and to then pursue the struggle like a *pars extrinseca*—which kept its organization and its rivals in exile—and to make alliances with its enemies (e.g., other cities or other parties).

These local and regional divisions, changing systems of alliances, and different parties with as many different names were already in existence well before the antagonism between Guelphs and Ghibellines, which merely gave a specific form to what was already in existence. Actually, since the second half of the 12th century, *pars imperii* and *pars ecclesiae* were partners, or possible partners of local and regional clans, who could help them conquer their respective adversaries. It was generally the interests of local power that determined the fluctuating composition of coalitions, and not any avowed preference for "Empire" or "Church." In the end, the supremacy of these interests determined, and also reduced, the margin of maneuver for both the emperor and the pope. In effect, both of them were implicated with their own partisans in the complex play of force of the *partes*, who used them as allies. This also prohibited any stable political restructuring of a global nature in Italy (e.g., the emergence of a dominant central power), regardless of what the people's desire might have been in achieving peace and finding a strong sovereign.

The parties thus followed a specific logic in their makeup, with pragmatic rather than ideological motives predominating. Moreover, the question of Ghibellines and Guelphs was in no way in the foreground of historical developments. Nevertheless, historical research traditionally lends important, and sometimes excessive, meaning to the antagonism. In reference to the history of Italy one often hears of the "period of the Guelphs and the Ghibellines." References to "Ghibellinism" and "Guelphism" (and their respective adjectives) have given an exaggerated ideological dimension to the parties, and there has been a tendency to use these ideas—independent of the terminology of the sources—anachronistically, applying them to phenomena of another order. For example, in reference to theoretical discussions to determine whether the pope or the emperor should hold the *imperium mundi*, the "doctrine of the Ghibelline State" has been referred to (in Dante or Marsilius of Padua), as has Frederick II's "State" (Pepe) of German elector princes (Bock). Modern politics has also seen the use of the terms "neo-Ghibellinism" and "neo-Guelphism."

In Florence, the Guelph and Ghibelline parties were born from a split in the local aristocracy. According to later chroniclers, they sprang from the bloody vendetta opposing the Buondelmonti and Amidei families (1216). But, in reality, their origin went back to the years 1177–9, when, at the same time as other lords of northern Italy, the Uberti and their partisans took sides with Frederick Barbarossa. From this time on, up to and including that of the *popolo*, the two noble factions shared power in the city, with changing fortunes. The Ghibellines counted on the aid of Frederick II and his sons, Frederick of Antioch and Manfred, while the Guelphs sought support from the popes (INNOCENT IV, ALEXANDER IV, Urban IV) and their legates.

From Florence, the partition first won over other cities in Tuscany, and then those in northern Italy, which, like central Italy, had also known periods of regional alliances of Ghibellines and Guelphs. The end of the Hohenstaufen and the rise of the Angevins in southern Italy (1265–8) placed the Ghibellines in a position of weakness. From this time on, the parties' names tended more and more to stray from their original meaning, and they gained their own autonomy. The Ghibellines never found their cohesion again, despite a short renaissance during the period of domination by the Aragons in Sicily (1302). They emerged in local lordships, preoccupied above all with strengthening their own power (Guido Tarlati in Arezzo, William II of Montferrat in the Piedmont, Liguria, and Lombardy; Castruccio Castracani in Lucca and Pistoia, Frederick II of Montefeltre in the Church States, the duchy of Spoleto, and the March of Ancona; the Visconti in Milan; the Della Scala in Verona and Mantua; the Este in Ferrara; and Rainaldo [Passerino] Bonaccolsi in Mantua); and in autonomous communes, with their respective parties (Siena, Pisa, Cremona, Genoa). The Ghibellines only managed to work together during brief periods of German royal campaigns in Italy (Henry VII, Louis of Bavaria), although they never managed to coordinate their actions with the Aragonese in Sicily—which would have been their only chance of success. If they nevertheless shared a certain sense of solidarity, they were indebted in large part to political activity for it, and to propaganda undertakings in the Guelph party (e.g., crusades, accusations of heresy).

The Ghibellines did have a few common characteristics, however, even if they did not have a concretely defined "ideology." These included recalling the rights of the empire (even if this was, for them, only a way of legitimizing themselves, as in the case of the imperial vicariate), which propaganda defended with a traditional juridical reasoning; opposition to the Angevins and to France, even more so than to the popes; a lack of cohesion and continuity in action (and, on the other hand, a certain seduction of "idealists," who fought for a lost cause, and of certain [sometimes religious] protest movements), a stronger aristocratic tone; and inferior means of propaganda than those of the Curia and the French court. It would be going too far, however, to see in the "Monarchy" of the Guelph Dante a manifesto of the "Ghibelline doctrine of the State."

Ernest Voltmer

Bibliography

MGH, Const., 4 (Robert of Naples, Henry VII).

MGH, Const., 5 and 6,1 (Louis of Bavaria).

MGS, SS, 18 (*Annales Placentini Gibellini*).

RIS, 3/2, C. 613 (*Vita Urbani IV*).

RIS, 16/4 (Pietro Azari).

RIS, 30 (Marchionne di Coppo Stefani).

Acta Aragonensia, ed. H. Finke, 3 vols., Leipzig-Berlin, 1908–22.

Bertelli, S. *Il potere oligarchico nello statocittà medievale*, Florence, 1978 (*Strumenti*, 88).

Bock, F. *Reichsidee und nationalstaaten vom Untergang des alten Reiches bis zur Kündigung des deutschen-englischen Bündnisses im Jahre* 1341, Munich, 1943.

Bock, F. "Studien zum politischen Inquisitionsprozess, Johanns XXII.," *QFIAB*, 26 (1935–6), 21–142.

Cardini, F. "Ghibellinen," *LexMA*, 4 (1988), 1436–8.

Dasasso-Ferrato, B. *Tractatus de guelfis et ghibelinis*, in *Tractatus de bannitis*, Lyon, 1533, cc. 127aa–bb.

Davidsohn, *Forschungen*, and Herde, *Guelfen: Quellen und Forschungen zur ältesten Geschichte der Stadt Florenz*, ed. O. Hartwig, 2, Halle, 1880, 40; 223–5 (*Annales Florentini*, II; Pseudo-Brunetto Latini).

Davidsohn, R. *Forschungen zur Geschichte von Florenz*, 4 vols, Berlin, 1908, 29-67 (*Die Entstehung der Guelfen- und Gibellinen-Partei*); *Geschichte von Florenz*, 2/1,2 (*Guelfen und Ghibellinen*), Berlin, 1908.

De Sancto Georgio, B. *De origine Guelphorum et Gibellinorum, quibus olim Germania, nunc Italia exardet, libellus eruditus*, Basle, 1519.

Del Re, G. *Cronisti e scrittori napoletani sincroni editi ed inediti*, 2: *Svevi*, Naples, 1868, 201–408 (Saba Malalspina).

Fasoli, G. "Guelfi e Ghibellini di Romagna nel 1280–1281," *Archivio storico italiano*, 94 (1936), 157–80.

Heers, J. *Partiti e vita politica nell'Occidente medievale*, Milan, 1983.

Herde, P. *Dante als Florentiner Politiker*, Wiesbaden, 1976.

Housley, N. *The Italian Crusades. The Papal-Angevin Alliance and the Crusades against Christian Lay Powers 1254–1343*, Oxford, 1982.

Hyde, J. K. "Contemporary Views on Faction and Civil Strife in Thirteenth and Fourteenth Century Italy," *Violence and Civil Disorder in Italian Cities 1200–1500*, ed. L. Martines, Berkeley, Los Angeles, London, 1972, 273–307.

Jordan, E. *Les Origines de la domination angevine en Italie*, 2 vols., Paris, 1909 (Repr. 1960).

Koenig, J. "Guelphs and Ghibellines," *Dictionary of the Middle Ages*, 6 (1985), 6–7.

Larner, J. *Italy in the Age of Dante and Petrarca 1216–1380*, London, 1980.

Malispini, R. *Storia fliorentina*, ed. V. Follini, Florence, 1816, 79–81 (c. 99).

Mansfield, H. C. "Party and Sect in Machiavelli's Florentine Histories," *Machiavelli and the Nature of Political Thought*, ed. M. Fleischer, New York, 1972, 209–55.

MANSI, 24, c. 125 (Humbert de Romans).

Marongiu, A. "Il regime bipartitico nel trattato sui guelfi e i ghibellini," *Bartolo da Sassoferrato. Studi e documenti per il VI centenario*, 2, Milan, 1962, 333–42.

Muratori, L. A. *Antiquitates italicae medii aevi*, 4, Milan, 1741, 606–14.

Nova Alamanniae, ed. E. E. Stengel, 2 vols., Berlin-Hannover, 1921–76.

Optiz, G. "Ghibellinen und Guelfen," *LTK*, 4 (1960), 881–2.

Ottokar, N. *Il commune di Firenze alla fine del Dugento*, Florence, 1926 (2nd. ed. 1962).

Pampaloni, G. "Guelfi e ghibellini," *Enciclopedia dantesca*, 3 (1971), 301–7.

Pepe, G. *Lo Stato ghibellino di Federico II*, Bari, 1938.

Poulet, C. *Guelfs et Gibelins*, 2 vols., Paris, 1922.

Pullan, B. *A History of Early Renaissance Italy*, London, 1973, 23–48.

Raveggi, S., Tarassi, M., Medici, D., Parenti, P. *Ghibellini, Guelfi e Popolo Grasso, I detentori del potere politico a Firenze nella seconda meta del Duecento*, Florence, 1978.

Salvemini, G. *Magnati e poplari in Firenze dal 1280 al 1295*, Florence, 1899.

Sanfilippo, M. "Guelfi e Ghibellini a Firenze: la "pace" del cardinale Latino (1280)," *Nuova rivista storica*, 64 (1980), 1–24.

Stahi, B. *Adel und Volk im Florentiner Dugento*, Cologne-Graz, 1965.

Stenzel, K. *Waiblungen in der deutschen Geschichte. Ein Beitrag zur Geschichte des deutschen Kaiser- und Reichsgedankens im Mittelalter*, Waiblungen, 1936.

Valeri, N. *Guelfi e Ghibellini a Milano alla scomparsa di Giangaleazzo Visconti*, Milan, 1955.

Villani, G. *Cronica*, ed. F. Gherardi Dragomanni, 1, Florence, 1844, 217–20 (V, 38–9).

Vitale, V. "Guelfi e Ghibellini a Genova nel Duecento," *Rivista storica italiana*, 60 (1948), 525–41.

Waley, D. "Guelfs and Ghibellines at San Gimignano, c. 1260–c. 1320. A Political Experiment," *Bulletin of the John Rylands University Library of Manchester*, 72 (1990), 199–212.

Waley, D. *The Italian City-Republics*, London, 1978, 115–26.

GLOVES, PAPAL. See **Vestments, Pope's Liturgical**.

GONFALON, GONFALONIERE. See **Banners**.

GOSPEL OF PETER. This title refers to a mutilated account of the Passion and Resurrection that was composed in Greek and presented as the Apostle's eyewitness account; it occupies pages 2 through 10 of a manuscript discovered in 1886–7 in the Christian necropolis of Akhmîm in upper Egypt. The text is usually identified as the Gospel According to Peter to which Origen (*Commentaries on Matthew*, X, 17) and Eusebius of Caesarea (*Ecclesiastical History*, VI, 12, 2–6) referred. According to the latter, Serapion of Antioch, a contemporary of Emperor Commodius (180–192), composed a work "to refute the lies contained in this Gospel" for the use of the Christian faithful in Rhossos, who "using this so-called Scripture as an excuse, had been led astray by heterodox teachings."

The author, who obviously knew nothing of Jewish Palestine, its institutions, and its society before the year 70 of the Christian era, seems to have been writing in Asia Minor (rather than in Egypt or Syria, as has often been suggested), in the first half of the 2nd century: his text bears some resemblance to the Christian writings of the period and the region, particularly those of Melito of Sardis and Apollinarius of Hierapolis. He draws freely from the canonical Gospels and from the Apocalypse in order to place the Passion and Resurrection in the light of what the Old Testament had announced. His account, deliberately simplified for didactic reasons, proposed a well-thought-out interpretation of the paschal event; its purpose was to present the event as a glorification of the Lord: the raising of the cross was already a raising up to heaven, and the Resurrection anticipated the Ascension. The text reflects popular theology and concepts popular among Docetist groups, and it may at times have lent itself to a gnostic interpretation. But, as M. G. Mara points out, the doctrinal interpretations of the apocryphal text, "if they do not coincide perfectly with the definitions of modern day orthodoxy," do represent a certain quest conductor "within a philosophical system with poorly defined boundaries." In the opinion of L. Vaganay, the author probably fabricated his material: prompted by a simple but deep faith, he meant to explain the facts of the

canonical Gospels in order to edify his readers with his catechesis. If the story comes from Peter's lips, it is not "literary falsification but dramatic fiction," aimed at making the event come back to life "in all its religious and salvific plenitude." The Gospel of Peter is an apocryphal text, but its message "does not lead us away the Gospel of Jesus Christ."

Luce Pietri

Bibliography

Évangile de Pierre, ed. M. G. Mara, Paris, 1973 (*SC*, 201).

Vaganay, L. *L'Évangile* de Pierre, Paris, 1930.

GOSPELS, THE, AND PAPAL AUTHORITY. The question of the scriptural foundation for the power of the bishop of Rome as successor to Peter can be broken down into at least three questions: Is there a primacy of Peter? Does this primacy represent a specific power, or simply a first place? And finally, does the bishop of Rome as Peter's successor inherit this power?

Various gospel texts are called into service for this debate. Peter is the first named apostle in all four books (Mark 3: 16–19; Matt 10: 2–4; Luke 6: 13–16; Acts 1: 13). Each time Jesus takes a smaller group of apostles with him, Peter is part of that group, and is named first. These episodes include the resurrection of Jairus's daughter (Mark 5: 37), the Transfiguration (Mark 9: 2; Matt 17: 1; Luke 9: 28; cf. 9: 32–33), and the Garden of Gethsemane (Mark 14: 33; Matt 26: 37), three events close to the heart of the mystery of the Passion and Resurrection. Finally, on three different occasions Peter is explicitly singled out among the apostles by Jesus. The three texts are well known. In answer to Jesus' question "But who do you say that I am?" Peter proclaims: "You are the Christ, the Son of the Living God." And Jesus replies: "Blessed are you, Simon, son of Jonah, for flesh and blood has not revealed this to you, but my Father who is in heaven. And I also say to you that you are Peter, and upon this rock I will build my Church, and the gates of hell shall not prevail against it. I will give to you the keys to the Kingdom of Heaven: whatever you will bind on earth will be bound in Heaven, and whatever you loose on earth will be loosed in Heaven" (Matt. 16: 15–19).

As soon as Peter denies Jesus, Luke adds a sentence that refers to a specific function of Peter in the Christian community (Luke 22: 31): "Simon, Simon, behold, Satan demanded to have you, that he might sift you like wheat, but I have prayed for you that your faith may not fail; and when you have turned again, strengthen your brethren." The end of the Gospel of John gives another eminent role to Peter (John 21: 15–17). The resurrected Jesus asks Peter: "Simon, son of Jonas, do you love me?" Three times, Peter affirms his love, and Jesus says:

"Feed my lambs," and "Tend my sheep." Chapter 21 of John's gospel is generally thought to have been added by a redactor.

Claire Sotinel

Bibliography

Pietr, C. *Roma christiana*, Rome, 1976.

GOTHS. See **Barbarians**.

GOVERNMENT (CENTRAL GOVERNMENT OF THE CHURCH). See **Curia**.

GRATIAN. See **Decretum of Gratian**.

GREAT SCHISM OF THE WEST (1378–1417). Starting with CLEMENT V's papacy in 1305, the papacy left Italy and gradually began taking up residence in Avignon. There were a number of reasons for the move, but the pope retained his position as the bishop of Rome. An initial attempt by URBAN V to return to the banks of the Tiber between 1367 and 1370 was unsuccessful. His successor, GREGORY XI, renewed the attempt, responding to the pressing requests of a few mystics and to the worries of the papal administrators in charge of the Church States, where agitation was endemic. But even though Gregory XI returned to Rome in 1377, the CARDINALS, and especially the CURIA, followed him only in part. Thus, nothing was definite when Gregory XI, who never fully recovered from a difficult trip, took his final breath on 27 March 1378.

Two Popes for One Pontifical Throne. The presence of the first CONCLAVE in Rome in seventy-five years aroused the city's citizens to try to influence the course of events and steer the proceedings toward the election of, if not a Roman, at least an Italian pope. The installation of the cardinals in the Vatican for the election was done in a somewhat disruptive atmosphere, and the crowd was threatening on more than one occasion. From the detailed inquiries that gave rise to the choice of Bartolomeo Prignano, archbishop of Bari, historians have been able to retrace the events and feelings of the leading figures in significant detail—all, or almost all, were in fear. But in the days that ensued, no one expressed any doubts about the validity of the election. Prignano donned the TIARA and took the name URBAN VI on 18 April 1378.

The new pontiff's activities quickly shocked his entourage. He was quick to criticize, and, though his criticism was the expression of a mind hoping for reforms, it was nonetheless both awkward and brutal. Having little control over his own actions, he himself was too open to criticism to force his will upon others. Those who bore the brunt of his outbursts looked for ways to defend themselves, and they found them in the dramatic circumstances of his election: CANON LAW declared invalid, *ipso facto*, an act committed under the influence of insurmountable fear. By this reasoning, though Urban could storm all he wished, he was not a legitimate pope and thus no one was obliged to obey him.

Backed by such arguments, some cardinals began to sow doubt in the minds of their colleagues. By the beginning of August, twelve of the sixteen electors had left Rome and drawn up a statement proclaiming the invalidity of the previous election and Urban's inability to govern the Church. Then, continuing the thread of the argument, the rebel cardinals prepared for a new election, and, in Fondi, on 20 September, Cardinal Robert of Geneva, whose family was allied with the French royal family, was elected and took the name CLEMENT VII. Meanwhile, Urban VI created for himself a new college of twenty-nine cardinals, creating an open battle between the two pretenders to the papal throne.

The Division of Christianity. Due to the duration and geographical extent of this schism, it has come to be called the "Great Schism," and many conditions came together to turn the conflict into a matter of concern to all of Western Christianity for two generations. Two cities, fought over the favor of harboring the pontifical throne, offering their respective candidates different contexts and customs. Rome was the spiritual center and the capital of the States of the Church, while Avignon found itself in the heart of the fiscal network, as well as the network of benefices, that was behind the papacy's power in the 14th century. By taking up residence in these cities, the two rival popes were, in effect, splitting the reality of their power. Both had but one objective: to be recognized as the only legitimate pope by the greatest number, regardless of how this was achieved. Because of the Hundred Years War, the split into two camps was in a sense already a *fait accompli*, and the recognition of one pontiff or the other by various princes became just one more piece in the political game. LEGATES in charge of collecting alliances were set out to besiege courts and chanceries; clerics spread lampoons, pamphlets, or treatises; and those with an inclination toward belligerance signed up for a crusade against the "intruder," and blood was spilled on battlefields, in the name of both pontiffs.

The broad outlines of the schism's geography are known: England, Scandinavia, Hungary, Poland, and Venezia were solidly behind the Roman pope, while France, Scotland, and the Iberian peninsula (with the exception of Portugal) sided with Avignon. Castille's affiliation with the Clementine party in 1381 had the remarkable singularity of being the consequence of a contradictory debate in Medina del Campo that lasted six months, regarding the results of a painstaking inquiry into the protagonists of the two elections. Wenceslas, "king of the Romans" and a partisan of Urban, brought most of the Eastern sections of the Germanic Empire in his wake, but a number of Western principalities that had some manner of connection with France leaned toward the Avignon pope. In Italy, even in the Papal States, the Roman pontiff's situation was always precarious, and fidelity was not always certain. The almost permanent state of war that prevailed during this period was continually being fed by the defection of some notable individual, party, or city.

In some regions, the history of the affiliation to one camp or the other is difficult to trace. For example, in the kingdom of Naples the two concurrent dynasties each favored a different pope: the Angevins championed the cause of Avignon, while the Durazzo forged bonds with the Roman pontiff, with no qualms about the need to pursue him in his States. Portugal, Brabant, and the Netherlands were also areas of flux, as they were periodically shaken by violent struggles for the possession of episcopal sees. Some candidates for these sees were more bellicose than others, and, not content with copious supplies of excommunications as ammunition, they pursued the schismatic heretics with arms. In general, the schism found fodder in all the quarrels that divided Christianity.

Reactions Within the Christian Community. In most cases, the faithful behaved as loyal subjects of their princes, who chose their camp of affiliation for them. Some preachers reminded them that it was not their role to try to untangle affairs that for the most part were beyond their purview. The religious life of communities was generally not affected by the schism, except in the troubled areas where warring factions were contesting the validity of the sacraments dispensed by the other camp. In some parts of present day Belgium, the secular authorities intervened to maintain neutrality and to allow worship to take place smoothly. In some areas, groups that were torn apart showed tolerance in their daily relations, and movement from one region to another because of persecution was primarily a concern for clerics.

Neutrality, a sometimes difficult undertaking, was not indifference; it was merely a question of passing through the storm in the best possible way. But it is certain that the scandal of the ecclesiastical body's division could only strengthen those who held that the Church did not need a pope for its existence—and it was those with this view who were the truly "indifferent," and who would be facing the INQUISITION. Following the lead of John Wycliff, in England, anticlerical critics became more vocal. Small groups in search of a more authentic spiritual life increased in Germany. These included the Brothers of Common Life, founded by Gerhard Groote, and the heretical sects of the Free Spirit. It was not easy for the guardians of orthodoxy to distinguish between the humble who wanted to regenerate the Church by beginning to improve themselves and the stronger-minded individuals who wanted to do away with the pope altogether. The time of the schism has often been described as a time of religious slackening. Such an opinion today is not as prevalent. Signs of vitality in the ecclesiastical body could be seen in a number of places, and the idea that reform should concern the head of the ailing body as well as the members was the underpinning for a number of behaviors. In the pilgrims of the Jubilee, in those who heard preachers like Vincent Ferrer calling for the conversion of hearts, and in the numbers of processions and requests received for votive masses could be seen a strong need for expiating misdeeds and a strong desire to belong to the communion of saints. Lack of control and heightened sensitivities sometimes gave rise to unbridled mystical outpourings. In a world prey to a disorder that was said to be inspired by the ANTICHRIST, piety was often expressed in emotional flareups, inspired by an anguish caused by the expectation of the imminent end of time.

There was considerable consciousness among university personalities of their responsibility vis-à-vis the Church. From the earliest moments of the crisis, while some gathered under the banner of one party or the other (Giovanni da Legnano, for example, opted for Urban IV's side), others, like Heinrich von Langenstein and Conrad von Gelnhausen, drew up treatises calling for peace. Some advocated holding a council to put an end to the schism, but this solution was considered unrealistic, since neither pope was ready to convene such a council. At least this was the prevailing opinion in Charles VI's entourage, and Parisian university personnel were actively asked to join Clement's party. The spirit of tolerance gave way to an atmosphere of suspicion, and both Urban's followers and those desirous of holding a council left the capital. This rupture was not without consequences for the reputation of the Univerisy of Paris, and it would be another decade before debates freely and publicly resumed.

How to Return to One Pope? This was the underlying question for the duration of the schism. Two rival heads sharing Western Christianity continued to appear as a monstrosity, perhaps even an intolerable scandal. But this analysis initially gave rise to the desire to have the rights of the sole legitimate pope reign triumphant. It was only with the passing of the years that the desire for union, regardless how it might be achieved, began to replace that of wishing to triumph over the adversary. The spiral of violence and division was slowly replaced with a series of patient efforts and initiatives to reestablish unity.

Urban VI's death in 1389, came during a time of intense belligerence. The college of Roman cardinals took less than two weeks to find a successor, Pietro Tomacelli, who took the name BONIFACE IX. Proclamation of the Jubilee ten years before the fact once again turned all eyes to Rome, and for a while it bailed out the Urbanist coffers. Preparations were being made in the French court for a double offensive, one in the kingdom of Naples, led by the young Louis II of Anjou, and one among the Milanese whose duke had just formed an alliance with the king's brother, Louis of Orleans. It was then that Boniface IX made an overture by sending two Carthusian monks to Charles VI, who, suffering from his first attack of dementia, was unable to receive them. The gesture made a great impression, however, and in the intense prayer movement that was then inaugurated supplications for the king's health and peace in the kingdom went hand in hand with those for union in the Church. The arrival of Pedro de Luna, an Aragonese of the high nobility who took the name BENEDICT XIII following the death of Clement in 1394, blessed this reverse tendency among the followers of Avignon. In France, where members of the University of Paris were putting their minds together in search of alternatives to the "politics of agression," there was hope that the election could be delayed. They then took it upon themselves to pave the new pope's way toward union, which he seemed to call for with his vows. An assembly of clergy decided that the "way of withdrawl," meaning the joint resignation of both popes, was the best solution for extinguishing the schism, and they named the king's uncles and brother to present the plan in Avignon. The delegation noted with surprise that Benedict XIII was not a man to be dictated to, and that he intended to follow the "path of harmony" by negotiating with his rival. Each claimed that the other was less interested in union than in his manner of reaching it, and a climate of antagonism arose between the pontiff and the country that had been his strongest support.

But Benedict XIII was not the only one concerned with the transfer, for the solution advocated by the French actually called for the two popes to resign simultaneously. Achieving such a result supposed a tremendous international cooperation that France flattered herself on having achieved. Richard II of England, accepting a union with Isabelle of France, was unequivocally pledging peace between France and England, and Emperor Wenceslas prepared to go meet Charles VI. Ambassadors were dispatched to the universities and to princes to rally them to the cause of withdrawl and ask them to prepare their respective pontiff for resignation. Although they experienced a variety of receptions (Oxford University took advantage of the situation to publish an urgent plea in favor of the Roman pope), they made contacts that, in some cases, were lasting—even a Franco-Anglo-Castillian delegation was formed to visit both pontiffs. Boniface IX, however, was just as adverse to the withdrawl as Benedict XIII.

The Politics of Withdrawing Obedience. Far from appearing discouraged, the promoters of the "way of withdrawl" decided to go one step further. Since the rival popes were unwilling to step down on their own, the plan was to force them into stepping down. It was among the followers of Avignon, and especially in France, that this tactic was most actively implemented, and a number of its partisans were to a certain extent stimulated by the powerful personality of Benedict XIII, in whom they saw an obstacle to be beaten down. Simon de Cramaud, a former chancelor for the duke of Berry who bore the prestigious title of patriarch of ALEXANDRIA, fine tuned the canonical argument, claiming that a pope who refuses to step down for the pupose of undoing a schism falls into HERESY, since he favors division, which is contrary to the teaching of the one, universal Church. There was, therefore, no longer any need to continue submitting to his authority.

The decision to withdraw obedience gradually ripened. It had already been made in 1396 by the duke of Orleans, but was later postponed, as much by conviction as by political opportunism. The "withdrawal" was also deliberated in an extraordinary assembly of the clergy, in 1398. After hearing a contradictory debate in which Benedict XIII was defended, especially by representatives from the south of France, each of the three hundred participants was called to give his opinion, either orally or in writing. On 28 July, the chancellor of France was able to proclaim that 247 voters had stated their agreement, and the king and the Church in France withdrew their obedience from Benedict.

Agents of the king were dispatched to Avignon to announce the decision and lead the cardinals to support the French decision by leaving the papal court. The majority of the Sacred College effectively seized the road of the right bank of the Rhone, but it appears as though Marshal Boucicaut was working alone when he took over the city and beseiged the pope in his palace. Nevertheless, he was never disowned by the king's council, and Benedict remained a prisoner for nearly five years without anyone being able to extract a frank promise of resignation from him in the event that his rival did decide to abdicate. After a phase of combat in which assistance sent from Catalonia was halted outside Arles, the palace guard passed from the cardinals into the hands of the duke of Orleans, whose representatives kept a half-hearted watch. A network of loyal followers of Benedict had organized resistance, however, and in 1403, when the situation began to be more favorable to him, the pontiff managed to escape to Châteaurenard without great difficulty.

Counting on the support of the king of England and the German emperor, France had launched a large diplomatic offensive toward the chanceries in 1398, hoping to entice all Christendom into its politics of withdrawal. But Richard II's subjects preferred to change kings rather than follow him into an alliance with France, and

Wenceslas was unthroned by his electors in favor of a committed follower of Urban, Ruprecht of the Palatinate. The countries aligned with Avignon thus found themselves almost alone in their withdrawal. Little by little, Provence and the Iberian peninsula, thinking that the Avignonnais were mistreating a pontiff upon whose legitimacy they had never cast doubt, returned to supporting him. In France itself, the idea of restoring obedience was supported by the university in Toulouse and spread under the protection of the duke of Orleans. When Benedict XIII regained his freedom, the prince's skill and the feeling of being stuck at an impasse forced accceptance of a return to obedience. The return nevertheless came with one pressing condition: Benedict XIII was to immediately engage in an active politics of union and agree to withdraw if such a move showed itself to be necessary.

The Impossible Rapprochement of the Two Popes. The warning was taken seriously and the Avignon pope's partisans were expecting him to make a demonstration of good will toward union. Benedict XIII thus dispatched an embassy to his rival, proposing a meeting, and it looked as though it would finally be possible to judge "the path of agreement" on the actual evidence. But the time was not propitious: after rejecting all offers, Boniface IX died in 1404. The ambassadors, who were suspects in his death, were imprisoned and then sent away by INNOCENT VII, the successor to the Roman pope.

This failure was greatly compensated for, in the opinion of Benedict XIII, by the increase in the lands under his obedience. The "conversion" of the Genovese and the variety of trials undergone by his competitor persuaded him to go to Italy. He discreetly sought support among French princes; but it was no longer the time for great enterprises—due to a quarrel between the dukes of Orléans and Burgundy over exercising power in the place of the poor insane king. The threat of the PLAGUE, and growing pressure in favor of withdrawal, forced Benedict XIII to turn back to Provence. In Marseille, he received emissaries from his new rival, the Venetian Angelo Correr, crowned under the name GREGORY XII.

From the moment of his accession to the throne, Gregory took the upper hand. Missives proclaiming that he would be willing to withdraw if his rival would likewise were sent to all the chanceries. Benedict XIII let it be known that he would be willing to withdraw, and a neutral location had to be found to allow the two popes to meet. The city of Savona was agreed upon, and a treaty was drawn up to that effect in April 1407. It was with assurance that Benedict received the large delegation a new assembly of French clergy sent him. The delegation also brought with it a BULL, which was kept secret, excommunicating the king of France in the face of a new threat of withdrawal of obedience. However, it was agreed *in extremis* that the bull would not be presented. Some of the

ambassadors continued their mission to Gregory XII, while the others watched over preparations for the meeting.

Benedict XIII was present in Savona on the day set for the meeting (1 November 1407). Gregory XII had been looking for another meeting place for two months, but had not managed to find one. Clearly, he wanted to avoid a face to face meeting, and his delaying tactics, which were observed by a number of witnesses, including the French ambassadors, ambassadors from Venice and Florence, and the cardinals themselves, failed to change the situation. Observations on the comings and goings of emissaries in both camps strongly suggested that the two rivals were working together to postpone the encounter indefinitely.

Upon consultation, the doctors of the University of Bologna were of the opinion that their pope should honor his commitments; and some (Pietro da Ancharano and Francesco Zabarella, among others) published treatises that were in basic agreement. Feeling the rising tide in favor of union, Gregory began to make threats. In May 1408, nine Roman cardinals decided to break with him and went to take refuge in Pisa. At the same time, France had decided to become neutral, and the bull of excommunication, which Benedict had made public, was simply dismissed. Six cardinals from Avignon, instead of fulfilling the mission of negotiation with which Benedict had charged them, also became dissident and joined their Roman colleagues in Pisa. While the two pontiffs were fleeing to a land of exile, the unionist cardinals decided to take the Church's fate into their own hands.

Pisa, the First Council of Union (1409). The letters with which the cardinals in Pisa announced to the entire world that they were convening a council in the city in the spring of 1409 were a veritable manifesto. The events of the past three years allowed them to accuse both of the rival pontiffs and justify their dissidence at the same time. All Christians were called upon to withdraw obedience from their pontiff and to permit the universal Church to be reunited. Gregory and Benedict would be called upon to withdraw from office, and the two colleges, united, would proceed to the election of a single pastor to be recognized by all. The success of the undertaking would thus rely on the ability of the cardinals to rally the faithful behind them, for the assembly would not be able to claim it represented the Church if it did not include a large number of participants.

Conscious of what was at stake, the unionist cardinals worked diligently to alert the maximum number of people. The convocations were copied by the hundreds and ambassadors were charged with presenting them throughout Christendom. The Byzantine emperor himself was contacted, since in the excitement following the announcement of the first rallyings it was hoped that the grace of union would also touch the "Greeks" (Eastern Churches). All these efforts bore fruit and, starting on 25 March, prelates and delegates began flowing into Pisa from France, Italy (especially central Italy), Savoy, the Netherlands, the principalities of Germany, Bohemia, Poland, Portugal, and England. The numerous lists that have been preserved confirm that there were over five hundred participants, a considerable figure by medieval standards.

While representatives of both sides attended, important parties were missing, including the two rival popes, neither of whom accepted the invitation to attend. Wanting to counter the initiative, each of them, on his own, called his faithful to meet in another council. Benedict's council took place first, in Perpignan, where a crowd of three hundred faithful, composed primarily of Aragonese and Castillians, assured the pontiff of their fidelity, but recommended that he deal with the Pisans. Gregory had much less success in Cividale. Despite the support of Ruprecht of the Palatinate and Ladislas Durazzo, his few partisans quickly scattered when Venice let out word of his defection, while he himself took refuge in Rimini.

More sensitive to the success that their imposing and composite assembly represented than to the opposition of those who were absent, on 10 May the Fathers of Pisa declared that they were forming the council of representatives of the Catholic Church. Having unsuccessfully called Gregory and Benedict to appear on a number of occasions, they had them stand trial in absentia. They drew up counts of indictment, and witnesses were called. The two rivals were condemned as heretics and inveterate schismatics, and deposed from office on 5 June. On 26 June, Pietro Philarghi was chosen by the single college of cardinals to succeed them. The Franciscan, who had been promoted to cardinal by Innocent VII, took the name ALEXANDER V and presided over the final sessions. The mission of reforming the Church was left for a later council, which would take place three years later.

Recognized as the legitimate pontiff by all those who came or sent representatives to Pisa, Alexander V reigned for only a few months. His successor, Baldassare Cossa, had supported the council with his own funds, or rather with the funds he had acquired in Bologna, where Gregory XII had sent him as legate. The personality of the new pope (JOHN XXIII) made him easy prey to criticism, but his authority was in no way questioned by those who gathered in the council in Pisa. Between 1409 and 1412, they were even joined by other Germanic principalities, by Scandinavia, and by Hungary, whose king, Sigismund of Luxemburg, owed his election as king of the Romans (upon Ruprecht's death) to this alliance. Gregory and Benedict, however, refused to give in to the Pisan bloc. Benedict's followers still constituted a following worthy of the name, while Gregory's were more scattered. But the resistance of Ladislas Durazzo, by keeping the Pisan popes from moving back to Rome, had symbolic value: unity was not yet a reality.

The Council of Constance and the Return to Unity (1417). As agreed, John XXIII called a new council for 1412, and a truce with Ladislas led people to believe that it might be held in Rome. Opened in 1413 with very little attendance, it was quickly suspended and, since Rome had again fallen under the control of the king of Naples, another city had to be sought for the gathering. Much more, in fact, was found: namely, a zealous protector of the Church, in the person of Sigismund, the king of Germany and Hungary, who looked to past precedents and dreamed of imperial glory. Preceding the bull of convocation by three months, he let it be known through a universal edict that a council would open in Constance. Willingly or not, John XXIII ratifed the choice of city and prepared to go into the imperial lands for the meeting on 1 November 1414. The participants arrived gradually, and for a period of three years there was an incessant coming and going of delegates, making an accurate count difficult. A number of prelates and ambassadors were accompanied by trains of servants and family members, turning Constance into a lively and colorful crossroads. All the pressing questions of the day were debated, and orators paraded through both the conciliar tribune and the other places where the "nations" met.

As attendees were aware of the numerical preponderance of Italians during the earliest sessions, the assembly decided not to have a vote by individuals, but to divide the participants into four groups, by nationality. To be adopted, a proposition had to collect the approval of the four nations: English, French, Germanic, and Italian. During the first six months, Sigismund and John XXIII were locked in a struggle for presiding over the council. The latter was certainly the pope in the eyes of the participants, but the former had the benefit of being the only spokesman acceptable to both Gregory and Benedict. As for the two rival pontiffs, they were at least in agreement on one point: the illegitimacy of the "little council" in Pisa and of Baldassare Cossa. Gregory showed less intransigence vis-à-vis the imperial initiative than did Benedict, and he agreed to name some legates who had permission to negotiate his retirement, on the condition that negotiation was not done with the Pisan pope. That meant putting Sigismund in the position of arbitrator. Imperial propaganda did the rest, putting the three popes on equal footing, and giving John XXIII the responsibility of setting an example for the others by stepping down first.

John XXIII wanted to force fate at this delicate conjuncture of circumstances. On 21 March, he left Constance in disguise and took refuge in Schaffhouse. But the rallying for which he hoped did not take place. On the contrary, the council Fathers made a decision that was to have broad implications: on 6 April, in the presence of Sigismund, they proclaimed the superiority of the council over the pope (decree *Haec Sancta*). John XXIII did not hold out for long. Agreeing to submit, he returned under strong guard and heard the announcement of his deposition on 29 May 1415. Room was left to deal with Gregory's fate. On the following 4 July, with Sigismund presiding dressed in full imperial insignia, a legate read the bull of convocation of the council that Gregory had drawn up, and then his statement of abdication.

Benedict alone resisted, having retreated to his fortified home in Peñiscola. Sigismund worked to fix the problem. Leaving the council, he took it upon himself to leave for Spain. The interview took place in Perpignan, in the presence of a number of observers. Benedict's proposal was that he alone, as the only surviving cardinal created prior to 1378, would name the future pope. The result of his obstinance was that almost all his remaining followers abandoned him. In an accord signed in Narbonne on 13 December 1415, representatives from Aragon, Navarre, and Castille, as well as from the county of Foix, committed to return to Constance. It took over a year for a fifth nation, Spain, to be added to the council, however. The Fathers of Constance tried Benedict again. Called by ambassadors one last time in 1417, the elderly pontiff refused to cooperate, and a decree again pronounced his depostion, on 3 September 1417.

When that date arrived, the council also enacted a merciless repression of heresy—Jan Hus was condemned on 6 July 1415—and it had set up a number of projects for Church reform, none of which had passed unanimously. A hero for the cause of unity, Sigismund had nevertheless ended up alienating a good number of those assembled because of his attempts to control everything. Rather than come to an impossible agreement on institutional matters, it seemed to be more urgent to find a single pastor for the Church. The last guarantee given to the reformers, the decree *Frequens*, obliged the pope to convene the council with regularity. Then an agreement was reached on an exceptional procedure for electing the new pope: thirty electors were added to the group of cardinals (six delegates for each nation). On 11 November 1417, Cardinal Ottone Colonna became pope MARTIN V, and was greeted as such by all Christendom, except for a handful of Benedict's partisans, who were won over in time.

A Historiographical View. The Catholic Church has never made an official pronouncement on either the canonicity of Urban VI's election or the legitimacy of the council of Pisa. The eventual attribution of the infamous label "antipope" to one pontiff or the other has thus been the sole responsibility of authors, who themselves have been influenced in their judgments by their nationality and their own ecclesiastical ideas. The Great Schism, after dividing the Western Church, divided historians, and

it continues to do so. Baluze and the Gallicans opposed the Ultramontanists, while imperial ideology underpins the work of von der Hardt. The present text of the ANNUARIO PONTIFICIO—which places the Urbanist popes in the line of Roman pontiffs and mentions the popes who came from the council of Pisa only in the margin, after the popes from Avignon—only goes back to 1947. Thus the way was paved for the decision to give the number "XXIII" to the next pope to take the name John. By a curious twist of fate, it happened that a single pontiff, Angelo Roncalli, both took Baldassare Cossa's title and revived a type of conciliar tradition.

Hélène Millet

Bibliography

Bliemetzrieder, F. *Literarische Polemik zu Beginn des grossen abendländischen Schisma*, Vienna, 1909.

Bourgeios Du Chastenet, *Nouvelle Histoire du concile de Constance*, Paris, 1718.

Crowder, C. *Unity, Heresy, and Reform, 1378–1460*, London, 1977.

D'Archery, *Spicilegium*, 1 and 6, Paris, 1723.

De Boüard, M. *Les Origines des guerres d'Italie. La France et l'Italie au temps du Grand Schisme d'Occident*, Paris, 1936.

Esch, A. *Bonifaz IX. und der Kirchenstaat*, Tübingen, 1968.

Finke, H. *Acta concilii Constantiensis*, 4 vols. Münster, 1896–1928.

Fliche-Martin, 14.

Genèse et débuts du Grand Schisme d'Occident, Paris, 1980.

Harvey, M. *Solutions to the Schism*, St.Ottilien, 1983.

Kaminsky, H. *Simon de Cramaud and the Great Schism*, New Brunswick, N. J., 1983.

Landi, A. *Il papa deposto (Pisa 1409)*, Turin, 1985.

MacCarron, D. *The Great Schism: Antipopes Who Split the Church*, Dublin, 1982.

Mansi (26 and 27).

Martene and Durand, *Thesaurus novus anecdotorum*, 2, Paris, 1717; *Veterum scriptorum . . . collectio*, 7, Paris, 1724.

Marzich, G. *The Three Popes: An Account of the Great Schism When Rival Popes in Rome, Avignon, and Pisa Vied for the Rule of Christendom*, New York, 1959.

Millet, H., and Poulle, E. *Le Vote de la soustraction d'obédience de 1398*, Paris, 1988.

Perroy, E. *L'Angleterre et le Grand Schisme d'Occident*, Paris, 1933.

Rusconi, R. *L'Attesa della fine. Crisi della società, profezia e Apocalisse in Italia al tempo del Grande Scisma*, Rome, 1979.

Smith, J. H. *The Great Schism, 1378*, New York, 1970.

Suarez, L. *Castilla, el cisma e la crisis conciliar (1378–1440)*, Madrid, 1960.

Swanson, R. N. *Universities, Academics, and the Great Schism*, Cambridge, 1979.

Ullmann, W. *The Origin of the Great Schism*, London, 1948.

Valois, N. *La France et le Grand Schisme d'Occident*, Paris, 1896–1902, 4 vols.

Vincke, J. *Briefe zum Pisaner Konzil*, Bonn, 1942.

Von Der Hardt, *Magnum oecumenicum Constantiense concilium*, Frankfurt-Leipzig, 1697–1700.

GREEKS IN ITALY. At the end of antiquity, the presence of a Greek population in Italy seems to have been reduced to eastern Sicily and, undoubtedly, southern Calabria. During the high Middle Ages, Greek monks took up residence in Italy in areas that were Latin, but politically Byzantine. They were fleeing from Persian and Arab invasions, and later from monothelitism and iconoclasm. Beginning in the 7th century, DIACONAE and a few Greek monasteries were established in Naples. In Rome, where there was a Greek community, thirteen Eastern popes occupied Peter's throne between 642 and 722. In the 7th century, diaconae (which were quickly Latinized) were also established in the city; their heads were an integral part of the Roman clergy (and by the 11th century, this was also true of the College of Cardinals).

Greek monasteries appeared during the same period. They presented an antimonothelite petition to the council of 649; and the popes sent Greek missionaries into the barbarian West. Between the 7th and the 9th centuries there were about a dozen Greek monasteries in Rome but, starting in the second half of the 9th century, recruitment began to dry up. In the 10th century, Greeks from Calabria visited Rome, and Nil de Rossano founded the abbey of Grottaferrata south of the city. It is still in existence today.

In the 8th century the emperor joined Sicily and Calabria to the patriarchate of Constantinople, and Rome left the empire. In the 9th century, the Western LITURGY was made uniform, using the Roman model. The split that took place in 1054, although it did not break the feeling of common affiliation, did occur at the beginning of the Western Church's process of centralization. The Greek rite and discipline, therefore, began to present a problem, and soon almost no Greek churches could be found outside the areas held by the Eastern Empire. Following the Arab occupation of Sicily in the 9th century, the Greek population that remained tended to migrate toward the north, occupying the northeastern section of Calabria and probably the southwest of the Salento, through some monks went farther north. During Byzantine domination (interrupted by the Norman conquest in the third quarter of the 11th century), the churches in these regions were dependent on the patriarchate of Constantinople including those of Sicily, which were Hellenicized in the 7th and 8th centuries but disappeared almost completely during the Arab period; the metropolis of Reggio and its suffragans; the new dioceses of Sila and their metropolis of Santa Severina, upon which Gallipoli in the Salento also depended; and Otranto, which became the metropolis for new dioceses in Eastern Lucania in 968.

In the 9th century, iconoclasm made its appearance in Otranto and Syracuse. With the Norman conquest, however, these regions returned to following Rome. The civil authorities created Latin dioceses in Sicily; and on the continent, between the conquest and the beginning of the 12th century, Latin bishops replaced Greeks in most sees, with the exception of Bova, Gerace, and Oppido. The Greek rite was practiced until 1537 in the Bova cathedral and until the 13th century in Santa Severina. In Rossano, in 1093, a riot kept a Latin bishop from being installed, and the see remained Greek until 1460. In Gallipoli, a Latinization attempt also failed in the early 12th century, and that see was occupied by Greeks until the 1370s. The Greek rite was practiced in Salento until the 17th century.

Thenceforth, the Greek bishops were dependent on the pope, though they never lost all contact with the East: in 1174, the patriarch of Constantinople replied to Bishop Paul of Gallipoli on a liturgical question, and, at about the same time, Theorien the Philosopher was writing to Greek clerics in Oria. In 1235–6, the metropolitan of Corfu wrote to the Greek clergy of Nardo. Further, in the Latinized dioceses, the existence of a married Greek clergy continued to be recognized. Greek monasticism was also encouraged, although oriented in a cenobitic direction. The monastery of St. Nicholas of Casole (where Nicolas Nectaire would be abbot in the 13th century) was founded in 1099, and at the beginning of the 12th century, St. Barthelemy of Simeri founded Santa Maria of Patire and San Salvatore in Messina (which, like the monastery of Carbona, sheltered an archimandrite). For Rome, these monasteries followed the "rule of St. Basil," and formed the "order of St. Basil" beginning in the 14th century.

The Greek presence in Italy was renewed in the 15th century because of the Turkish occupation of the Balkans. A number of Greeks migrated to Venice, and groups of Albanians, first called as mercenaries by the Aragonese, and then fleeing from the TURKS, took up residence in Puglia, Calabria, and Sicily between the years 1440 and 1530. Many kept their language, their customs, and their rite of worship, albeit with the authority of Rome. A congregation *pro reformatione Graecorum in Italia existentium*, which worked between 1573 and 1596, allowed the persistence of the Greek rite, with priests being trained in the Greek College of Rome. This was a question of simple tolerance, however.

Jean-Marie-Martin

Bibliography

La Chiesa greca in Talaia dall'VIII al XVI secolo, dir. M. Maccarrone, G. G. Meersseman, E. Passerin D'entrèves, and P. Sambin, Padua, 1973, 3 vols. (*Italia Sacra*, 20–2).

Menager, L. R. " 'La byzantinisation' religieuse de l'Italie méridionale (IXe-XIIe siècle) et la politique monastique des Normands d'Italie," *Revue d'histoire ecclésiastique*, 53 (1958), 747–4 and 54 (1959), 5–40; reprinted in *Hommes et institutions de l'Italie normande*, London, 1981.

Sansterre, J. M. *Les Moines grecs et orientaux à Rome aux époques byzantine et carolingienne (milieu du VIe siècle-fin du IXe siècle)*, Brussels, 1983.

GREGORY I. *Called Gregory the Great (b. Rome, circa 540, d. Rome, 12 March 604). Elected pope in January 590, consecrated after imperial confirmation on 3 September of the same year. Buried in Saint Peter's in Rome. Saint, confessor, and doctor (venerated after his death, he appears in the Hieronymian martyrology).*

LEO I and Gregory I are the only popes to be honored with the title "great." Gregory was a citizen of the Byzantine Empire and constantly faithful to his sovereign, but his glory was due as much to his role (amplified by posterity) in the establishment of lasting relations between the patriarchate of the West and most of the Germanic kingdoms, as it was to the circulation of his books throughout Latin-speaking Christianity and into Greek-speaking regions. His origins made him one of the most important individuals in all Italy. He may have been a descendant of the old and very powerful senatorial family, the Anicii. One of his ancestors had been a pope (FELIX III). His father Gordian was senator and one of the *regionnarii* of the Church of Rome. His parents and grandparents are illustrative of the control the Roman nobility exercised, regardless the regime, over the fallen but still prestigious city's civil and religious institutions.

Little is known of his youth, but there is no doubt that he lived opulently; he had estates in the provinces and a large house in the city, as was the case for all nobles. He had a solid classical and juridical education, befitting his rank; an education that was indispensible for taking on the prestigious responsibility of prefect of the city. He thus became familiar with administrative practices. Toward 575, he left the world for the religious life, founding six monasteries on Sicilian land and a seventh (dedicated to St. Andrew) in his Roman house in Clivus Scauri, on the slopes of the Caelius. His admiration for Benedict of Nursia, whose main accomplishments he recounted in his *Dialogues*, in no way implied that he adopted the "Benedictine Rule," since each monastery adopted its own. His vocation urged him to remain in St. Andrew as a simple monk, under the orders of an abbot he had not appointed; moreover, all his written work reveals a demanding faith and a deep mysticism. This exceptional individual thus combined intimate knowledge of civil administration with spiritual demands worthy of the greatest of the Church FATHERS. He was, therefore, noticed by Pope PELAGIUS II (or perhaps by his predecessor), who ordained him deacon and made him his delegate to the emperor. Thus he lived in Constantinople for six years (579–85).

The stay in the capital considerably expanded his horizons. Contrary to what he claims in his works, Gregory I learned enough Greek to communicate and to read certain authors, one of whom was Theodoret of Cyr. He also acquired enough prestige in the Hellenic world, and especially in the imperial family, that several of his works were translated from Latin into Greek, quite a rare phenomenon. Above all he was able to see how the central administration of the empire worked, and he formed relationships with a great diversity of people who lived in the city. His correspondence indicates that he counted among his friends high level administrators, Byzantine nobles (like the Apion family, one of the most influential in Egypt), and Orthodox Spaniards exiled by the Arian kings, like Leandro, the future bishop of Seville and the brother of Isidore. Called back to Rome, he returned to his monastery, this time as abbot. Five years later, in 590, the plague took Pelagius II. The clergy and the "people" of Rome—that is, the senatorial nobility, or a group composed only of its leaders—elected Gregory unanimously. He tried to sway the emperor, Maurice, to refuse confirmation (without it no papal election was valid) but his attempt was in vain. Gregory thus became one of the rare pontiffs to come out of a monastery. The secular clergy soon regretted his election.

Gregory's accession to the highest position of religious responsibility in the West took place while the situation was in constant change. Marked by the turbulance following the war between the empire and the Goths, and then the LOMBARDS, he witnessed the gradual collapse of the old structures; this undoubtedly led him, noble that he was, to emphasize the transitory nature of worldly affairs, as traditional values were vanishing. However, his disillusioned considerations on the misfortunes of time, accentuated by the effects of persistent stomach aches, may be misleading. Gregory was not living in a world in decline, but rather in a world of change; this change concerned only the dominant classes and urban populations. The *paesani*, which included the immense majority of Romans and, therefore, the majority of Church members, continued to live according to the fairly inflexible rules of traditional societies.

Although he may have had reasons to be worried as a noble, some promising perspectives were opening up to the man of the Church. The Spanish sovereigns had just given up Arianism after the conversion of King Reccared (587). Those of Gaul endowed their churches richly and protected their clergies. The leaders of the Irish clans were deeply Christian, while the English kings, especially the king of Kent, were under Frankish influence, and were preparing to convert.

Gregory was first bishop of the "diocese" of ROME, in the present sense of the word. Because almost no letters addressed to individuals residing in the city are extant, his correspondence is poor in this regard. Our information depends on references in his other writings and in biographies written long after his death. There is, however, enough to show the persistence of a large and complex administration, as all the decisions resulted in written acts. This is how we know of his nostalgia for monastic life. Gregory had a talent for management, but was little attracted to it. Gregory led the *episcopium*, the ensemble of services that were there to assist him. There were many of these, and they were well equipped. Seven regional deacons and seven subdeacons were responsible for the seven religious regions of Rome. The notaries formed a *schola*. They were responsible for preserving the archives to facilitate solutions for the many problems that arose and for drawing up official documents or letters. A council composed particularly of the archpriest, the archdeacon, and the primicier of notaries, assisted the pontiff and assured continuity of management in his absence or after his death. Moreover, Gregory named the clerics. The third responsibility was that of buildings, which was given over the the *mansionarii*. At the time, when construction of religious buildings was declining considerably (at least in the empire) Gregory's activity was significantly diminished. Finally, a bishop assisted the poor, with the help of the DIACONIA. His primary biographer tells us that he fed 3,000 regularly.

These purely religious functions are not to be confused with the civil responsibilities incumbent upon bishops since the end of the 5th century. Gregory had to manage the ANNONA, which had remained a civic duty, even though the responsibility was gradually passed from the imperial administration to the municipal administration, of which the pope was head. He was also responsible for the payment of accounts and defined himself, quite justly, as "treasurer" of the state. Likewise, he participated with the generals in the city's defense and acted on behalf of them before the emperor; he even signed a treaty with the Lombards in 595, when no higher authority, either exarch or emperor, was capable of acting in time. Like all bishops in the West or the East, the pope, as prelate of Rome, was the individual ultimately responsible for the local administration, at a time when the exact role played by the SENATE is unknown. These activities presuppose the availability of abundant revenue. This revenue came, for the most part, from the PATRIMONY, which was made up of a certain number of entities grouped according to their geographic location: the patrimony of Sicily, the patrimonies of southern Italy, which had remained Byzantine, the patrimony of Africa, that of Sardinia, and lastly, that of Gaul. To a large extent the revenue was public, which explains, in particular, the sending of inspectors by the central administration (e.g., the ex-consul Leontios). Private gifts and donations amounted to little when compared with the appropriations of public revenues. These included, albeit to a very small degree, profits that came from direct management of the lands belonging to the state. It has become progressively more clear that the greatest part of the total sum came from the fiscal revenues appropriated for the civil budget of the city of Rome (hence the annona), and from the four posts of the ecclesiastical budget. Each patrimony had its rector and was composed of accounting units, the *massae*, numbering some four hundred, whose management was leased out to "conductors" (*contuctores*). The *paesani* paid their taxes to these agents of the Roman Church.

Since the bishop of Rome was the metropolitan of all of southern Italy and the islands (Sicily, Sardinia, Corsica, and the Baleares), he naturally had both the right to consecrate the bishops of his area and the right of appeal for all ecclesiastical affairs, as well as the duty to call his bishops together regularly in a regional council. His representatives, particularly the rectors of the patrimonies, prepared the dossiers and played a determining role in nominations. The example of Januarius, bishop of Cagliari, who was too old to avoid the exactions of his deacons and his priests, is illustrative of the fact that the pope was closely watching over his suffragans.

As patriarch of the West, he had authority over both the bishops of the Byzantine West—in the Balkans, Italy, and Africa—and over all those of the Germanic kingdoms, but relations were strictly limited by the political relationship between the empire and the kingdom in question. He thus intervened constantly in the affairs of Africa and Byzantine northern Italy, sending his representatives, discussing matters with the exarchs, judging appeals, but always bending if the court imposed a decision contrary to his convictions, as is seen in his relationship with the bishops who were partisans of the heresy of the Three Chapters in Istria. He wanted to impose sanctions but Emperor Maurice forbade this in order to avoid both betrayal and the region passing into Lombard authority. On the contrary, he did not write directly to bishops living in the Lombard kingdom, as diplomatic relations were broken between Constantinople and Pavia. The earlier conclusion was incorrect in its belief that the Lombards had dismantled almost all the bishoprics in their state. Likewise, he waited until 599, the date of the Visigoth king's reconciliation with the emperor, to congratulate Reccared on his conversion (587), of which he was not aware until 591. Relations were good with the kings of the FRANKS and the pope was able to write to the bishops in the *Regnum Francorum*, but each time he also addressed a letter of recommendation to the sovereign, who was thus kept current. The primate of the Gauls was in no way the pope's representative. Gregory, who wrote freely to his friends like Leandro of Seville, refrained from dealing with questions of ecclesiastical organization without the approval of local sovereigns. Among the Anglo-Saxons, it seems as though missionaries were sent in reply requests, either from the Catholic queen of Frankish origin, or from her husband, king Ethelbert. In fact, Gregory noted in one of his letters to Brunhild that "the people of the Angles, that is, its leaders, wish to become Christians." Whatever the case might have been, the missionaries were not able to preach without the sovereign's authorization, which does not explain the failure in conversion attempts in other kingdoms, but it does explain the lack of attempts, because the kings forbade it. Nevertheless, relations between the papacy and England were always peculiar, since conversion was the work of one of the pope's men—the monk Augustine, his successor as abbot of St. Andrew—who was sent to Ethelbert. Ethelbert converted on 1 June 597. From what has been said, 10,000 subjects imitated his example on Christmas of the same year.

Gregory claimed an honorary primacy for his patriarchy, in opposition to his representative in Constantinople who, with imperial support, wanted to have the title of ecumenical patriarch.

As pastor, he drew practical conclusions from his theological reflections and the concrete circumstances facing him. Gregory the Great did have a theology, even though it was partially implicit in his pastoral works and contained nothing revolutionary. His concern for responding to the questions of his day explains the great diversity in his actions, their apparent lack of cohesion, and their success, because he completely analyzed situations that turned out to be typical in the ensuing years of the Middle Ages. His idea of the bishop's place in social life was developed in *The Book of Pastoral Rule*. He composed the work in 591, in response to the bishop of Ravenna who reproached him for fleeing from the obligations of the episcopacy. In it, he developed the official doctrine in the empire since the time of CONSTANTINE, a doctrine followed by all the Germanic kingdoms: The bishop should combine great charity for individuals, a pedagogical sense through which he expresses himself differently depending on his audience, and a keen sense of the respect that is owed to the position that his charge has given him in the state. The book, based on a deep knowledge of treatises on the same subject, had considerable success in the West and in the East.

The vain discussion of the truthfulness of the *Dialogues* is founded on a misunderstanding. Gregory, or whoever composed the hagiographical accounts with his name, continues a long tradition of catechesis founded on the telling of simple and edifying stories in the most accessible written language, with no apparent literary effects. This is what explains both his success and the book's translation into Greek.

His tone and style are different in the sermons written for monks or a more enlightened public. The *Moralia on Job* allowed Gregory to develop his thoughts on moral, ascetic, and mystical life.

His letters are remarkable for a number of reasons. Analysis of his phrasing and style shows that the administrative missives were the work of technicians to whom the pope dictated the general theme of the response; the technicians composed the letters according to customs of the papal CHANCERY, which was almost intractable in its wording, its turns of phrase, and its clauses. The pontiff was almost never wrong, for the compiler made a choice that manifestly conformed to the papacy's interests when he composed the "register." The 850 letters preserved do not even constitute a representative sample of what Gregory dictated every day. A careful analysis of them helps to elucidate the papal institution's intentions at the time of their completion.

In the area of liturgy, Gregory manifested the same concern for coherence and pedagogy by adding the final touches to the canon of the mass, which would remain practically unchanged for ten centuries. He also managed to play a role in the form of the chant called "Gregorian."

In the eyes of his contemporaries, Gregory appeared to be the model of the western Byzantine patriarch, faithful to the emperor while at the same time being spokesman for populations placed under his religious and administrative authority, in discussion with the Germanic kings only if their relations with the sovereign from Constantinople were good or nonexistent. After his death, he was increasingly presented as the staunch manager of patrimonies that represented the earliest foundations of the Papal States, and as the pastor who gave the bishop the double advantage of being the "servant of God's servants" (thus a venerable individual), the chief administrator of the city (thus a considerable individual), and the "consul of God" with the right to oversee all the Churches of the West. The growing place of the papacy in the Latin world accentuated the interplay of the different roles and the ever-more-important prestige of Gregory the "Great."

Jean Durliat

Bibliography

PL, 75–9.

JW, 1, 143–219; 2, 696–8, 738.

LP, 1, 312.

Batifol, P. *Saint Grégoire le Grand*, Paris, 1928.

Bede, *Historia Ecclesiastica*, I, 25-2, 1.

Bertolini, O. *Roma di fronte a Bisanzio e ai Longobardi*, Bologna, 1941.

Bonfante, G. *Latini e Germani in Italia*, Brescia, 1959, 3rd. ed. 1965.

Bréhier, L., and Aigrain, R. *De la mort de Théodose à l'élection de Grégoire le Grand, les États barbares et la conquête arabe*, Paris, 1947 (Fliche-Martin, 4).

Commentaire sur le cantique des Cantiques, ed. and trans. R. Bélanger, Paris, 1984 (*SC*, 314).

Cavadini, J. C., ed. *Gregory the Great: A Symposium*, Notre Dame, 1995.

Commentaire sur le premier livre des rois, 1, ed. and trans. A. De Vogüé, Paris, 1989 (*SC*, 351).

Dagens, C. *Grégoire le Grand. Culture et expérience chrétienne*, Paris, 1977.

Dagens, C. "Saint Gregory the Great between the East and West: Historical Crises and the Universalism of Faith," *Communio* 18 (1987), 356–64.

Diacre, P. *Vie de Grégoire de Grand, PL*, 75, 41–62; 63–242.

Dialogues, ed. and trans. A. De Vogüé and P. Antin, Paris 1978–80 (*SC*, 251, 260, 265).

Evans, G. R. *The Thought of Gregory the Great*, Cambridge, 1986.

Gillet, R. "Grégoire le Grand," *DS*, 6 (1967) 872–910.

Gillet, R. "Grégoire Ier," *DHGE*, 21 (1986), 1387–1420.

Godding, R. *Bibliografia di Gregorio magno* (1890–1989), Rome, 1990.

Grégoire le Grand, ed. J. Fontaine, R. Gillet, and S. Pellistrandi, Paris, 1986.

Heinzelmann, M. "Gregor I," *LexMA*, 4 (1987–9), 1663–6.

Homélies sur Ézéchiel, ed. and trans. C. Morel, Paris, 1986–90 (*SC*, 327, 360).

Jenal, G. "Gregor der Grosse und die Stadt Rom (590–604)," *Herrschaft und Kirche*, ed. F. Prinz, Stuttgart, 1988, 109–154.

Le Pastoral de saint Grégoire le Grand, trans. J. Boutet, Paris, 1928.

Magnin, E. *L'Église wisigothique au VIIe siècle*, Paris, 1912.

Markus, R. A. *Gregory the Great and His World*, Cambridge, 1997.

Markus, R. A. *Signs and Meanings: World and Text in Ancient Christianity*, Liverpool, 1996.

Meyvarent, P. *Bede and Gregory the Great*, Newcastle upon Tyne, 1976.

Meyvarent, P. *Benedict, Gregory, Bede and Others*, London, 1977.

Meyvaret, P. "Uncovering the Lost Work of Gregory the Great: Fragments of the Early Commentary of Job," *Traditio* 50 (1995), 55–74.

Modesto, J. *Gregor der Grosse: Nachfolger Petri und Universalprimat*, St. Ottilien, 1989 (*Studien zur Theologie und Geschichte*, 1).

Morales sur Job, ed. and trans. R. Gillet and A. De Gaudemaris, Paris, 1975 (*SC, 32 bis*); ed. and trans. A. De Bocagnano, Paris, 1974–75 (*SC*, 212, 221).

Peterson, J. M. "Homo Omnino Latinus: The Theological and Cultural Background of Pope Gregory the Great" *Speculum* 62 (1987), 529–51.

Pitz, E. *Papstreskripte im frühen Mittelalter*, Sigmaringen, 1990 (*Beiträge zur Geschichte und Quellenkunde des Mittelalters*, 14).

Registre des lettres, livres I–II, ed. and trans. P. Minard, Paris, 2 vols., 1991.

Richards, J. *Consul of God: His Place in History and Thought*, London-Boston, 1980.

Straw, C. *Gregory the Great*. Aldershot, UK: Variorum; Brookfield, VT, USA, 1996.

Straw, C. *Gregory the Great: Perfection in Imperfection*, Berkeley, 1988.

The Earliest Life of Gregory the Great, ed. and trans. B. Colgrave, Cambridge, 1986.

Tweed, R. G. "The Psychology of Gregory the Great (AD 540–604)," *International Journal for the Psychology of Religion* 7 (1997), 101–10.

GREGORY II. *(b. Rome, 669, d. 11 February 731). Consecrated pope on 19 May 715. Buried in St. Peter's in Rome. Saint (early worship, in Ado's martyrology).*

Gregory II was the first native Roman pope since BENEDICT II, and he came to the papacy after a long career in the papal administration. As a DEACON, he had accompanied his predecessor CONSTANTINE I to the East and had participated personally in discussions with Emperor Justinian II regarding the Trullan Synod (Constantinople, 692), certain canons of which Rome did not accept. His papacy was characterized by a new and serious conflict with the Byzantine Empire. Crowned emperor in 717 after a period of internal disorder, Leo III reorganized the financial administration of the empire and again demanded the taxes that were weighing on the vast patrimony the Roman Church possessed in Sicily. Gregory was opposed to this measure, and a group of imperial officers residing in Rome organized a plot against him. The plotters were either killed or banished by the Romans, however. An attempt to intervene militarily by the EXARCH OF RAVENNA met with resistance from the army of the duchy of Rome, to which the duke of Spoleto lent his assistance. The Romans had the same interests as the pope, and in an Italy, where tendencies toward autonomy were developing, detachments from the army, thenceforth recruited locally, were no longer blindly obeying the officers of the Byzantine emperor.

At about the same time a second area of conflict arose between the pope and the emperor, one which was more serious because of its theological nature. In 726, Leo III took a stance against the veneration of images, beginning the iconoclastic crisis that would continue until 843. The veneration of images, especially of icons, had greatly developed in the East, where they were believed to have miraculous powers like relics. But there was also a spiritual current that was hostile to this practice, which was seen by some as a resurgence of idolatry. Like all his predecessors, Leo III felt he had the right to take a stand in a matter of dogma, and he adopted the doctrine favored by the populations of Asia Minor. The Balkans defended image worship, however as did Italy, though it had not greatly developed there. Gregory II strongly condemned the emperor's intervention in the theological domain; he asserted that worship by adoration, which is to be for God alone, must be distinguished from the simple veneration addressed to the saints, to their relics, or to images of them. Leo III paid no attention to his opposition, and, in 730, he forbade the veneration of images and deposed the patriarch of Constantinople, Germain, who refused to follow him. Gregory, of course, protested.

When the imperial edict was made known in Italy, the army from Ravenna and Pentapolis, which was recruited locally (as was also the case for the Roman army), revolted and put the exarch Paul to death. Debarking in Naples, his successor Eutychius formed an alliance with the Lombard king Liutprand, agreeing to help him to subjugate the dukes of Spoleto and Benevento, who had theretofore remained independent, in exchange for assistance against the duchy of Rome. The pope's position was delicate. Despite his conflict with Leo III, he had never failed to assert his loyalty to the emperor. He had already intervened on a number of occasions to get the LOMBARDS to abandon cities they had just taken over, including Sutri, in 727. Liutprand went to set up camp north of Rome. After a decisive interview, Gregory II managed to convince the pious Lombard king to make no alliance with the heretic emperor. Liutprand went so far as to step in between Gregory II and Eutychius, who had to give up all hostile actions against the pope.

Gregory II was also interested in the evolution of the countries north of Italy, whose inhabitants—and even princes, including Duke Theodore of Bavaria—were coming in greater and greater numbers on PILGRIMAGES to Rome. He exchanged letters with Eudes, the duke of Acquitaine, and in 718 the Anglo-Saxon monk Boniface arrived in Rome to request the pope's permission to leave on a MISSION to the pagan Germans. This was an unusual procedure for the time, and one that demonstrated the great respect the Anglo-Saxons held for the papacy. On 15 May 719, Gregory II commissioned Boniface to help the "infidels" to know the Bible and ecclesiastical discipline. Boniface, who had the benefit of the effective protection of Charles Martel, preached in Thuringia and Hesse. He was confronted with problems of church discipline, which are addressed in the correspondence he exchanged with the pope.

The pope convened a SYNOD in 721, which specified the list of obstacles family relationships might present for marriage. In 722, he called Boniface to Rome and consecrated him bishop, making him take the oath of fidelity he required of all his suffagans. The pope's hope was to connect Rome directly with regions that theretofore had been located in the Frankish kingdom's sphere of influence. Boniface returned to Germany, but these provinces ended up being attached to Frankish metropolitans.

Gregory II also contributed to the upkeep and embellishment of monuments in Rome. The uncertainty and volatility of the times led him to have the walls of the city restored, and he founded a monastery in his family home, near Santa Agata.

Jean-Charles Picard

Bibliography

JW, 1, 249–57; 2, 700–42.

LP, 1, 396–414.

MGH, Epist., 3, 698–702.

Bertolini, O. *Roma e i Longobardi*, Rome, 1972.

Duchesne, L. *Les Premiers Temps de l'État pontifical*, Paris, 1911.

Grotz, H. "Les deux lettres de Grégoire II à Léon III empereur," *AHP*, 1980, 9–40.

Howe, John. "The Nobility's Reform of the Medieval Church," *American Historical Review* 93 (1988) 317–39.

Kelly, W. *Pope Gregory II on Divorce and Remarriage: A Canonical-Historical Investigation of the Letter Desiderabiles Motion, with Special Reference to the Response and Proposition*, Rome, 1976.

Llewellyn, P. "The Popes and the Constitution in the Eighth Century," *English Historical Review* 101 (1986).

Moncelle, P. "Grégoire II," *DTC*, 6–2 (1924), 1781–5 (updated by R. Aubert, *DHGE*, 21 [1986], 1420–1).

Noble, T. F. X. *The Republic of St. Peter*, Philadelphia, 1984.

Richards, J. *The Popes and the Papacy in the Early Middle Ages*, 476–752, London, 1979.

Schieffer, R. "Gregor II.," *LexMA*, 4 (1987–9), 1666–7.

Schieffer, R. "Gregor II. Ein Versuch über die historische Grösse," *Historisches Jahrbuch*, 97–8 (1979), 87–107.

GREGORY III. *(d. 10 December 741). Elected pope on 11 February, consecrated on 13 March 731. Buried in St. Peter's. Saint (early worship, he appears in Ado's martyrology).*

Nothing is known of the origins of this Syrian priest before the people unanimously chose him to be pope on the very day of GREGORY II's funeral. He was consecrated five weeks later, after obtaining the approval of the EXARCH OF RAVENNA; he was the last pope to request this approval. In all areas, he energetically pursued the politics of his predecessor. In response to the synodal letter from the new patriarch of Constantinople, Germanus, he wrote to the emperor decrying the iconoclasm he had solemnly condemned during a SYNOD on 1 November 731, which brought together the patriarch of Grado, the archbishop of Ravenna, and ninety-three Italian bishops. The messengers charged by the pope with carrying these texts to the emperor ended up in prison, however. Returning to earlier martial methods, Leo III sent a flotilla to Italy. However, a storm scattered his ships, and the emperor was forced to rely on administrative sanctions. He confiscated the pope's properties in Sicily and Calabria, the only regions of Italy where his authority remained in effect. More precisely, he organized, among peasants, the direct deduction of taxes that the Church had been previously collecting, which gave him access, albeit only for a short period of time, to large sums of cash. In any case, the papacy quickly lost all control of these properties. Leo also transferred Sicily and Illyricum (the Balkans) from the pope's jurisdiction to that of the patriarch of Constantinople. This measure further broadened the split that began in the 4th century between the Latin West and the Greek East.

Starting in the 7th century, the Byzantine provinces of central and northern Italy had shown tendencies to autonomy, and they had practically become independent since the launching of the iconoclastic movement, even if there was still an exarch in Ravenna. The pope continued to behave as a loyal subject of the emperor despite the conflict over dogma, which he thought would be short-lived, but he was led to develop his actions in the temporal domain. It was a normal practice in the empire (and likewise in the Frankish kingdom) for the sovereign to delegate certain public functions to bishops; after 726, the pope went further than the emperor, and progressively had all the administration of the duchy of Rome transferred to his authority. For his part, the Lombard king Liutprand, because he was orthodox, considered himself to be the only truly legitimate political power in Italy, and he took control of Ravenna in 737. The exarch took refuge in the islands of Venezia that had officially remained Byzantine (even though the duke of the province was elected by the people). Gregory III wrote to the patriarch of Grado, asking him to intervene with the duke so that he might help the exarch reconquer Ravenna.

In an attempt to counter the LOMBARD king, Gregory committed the error of allying himself with the duke of Spoleto, Trasamund. Liutprand had intended to subjugate the dukes of Spoleto and Benevento (who up to that time had enjoyed considerable autonomy) and was afraid that they might make common cause with the Byzantines. Since the pope refused to turn it over, Liutprand also occupied the northern part of the duchy of Rome. The Romans then formed an alliance with Trasamund to take back Spoleto, but the duke failed to help them recapture the cities occupied by Liutprand, and reprisals by Liutprand were feared.

It was under these dramatic circumstances that, for the

first time, the papacy thought about placing itself under the protection of the FRANKS. Gregory III wrote several letters to Charles Martel, requesting his intervention. But the powerful French prince refused; he was one of Liutprand's allies, and Liutprand had just helped him in Provence to turn back the Spanish Muslims. At any rate, Martel's power was not sufficiently established in Gaul for him to launch an expedition into Italy. The Lombard king's occupation of Rome appeared to be inevitable when Gregory III died.

As his predecessor had, Gregory III encouraged Boniface's actions in Germany. In 732, he sent Boniface the *pallium*. As archbishop, Boniface was able to consecrate suffragan bishops. He traveled to Rome in 738 for a one-year stay. The pope then asked him to reorganize the network of episcopal sees in Germany. Mercilessly pushing aside the abbot-bishops of the Irish tradition, he set up episcopal sees in the most important cities and towns of Bavaria, Hesse, and Thuringia, organizing, the Church in some areas that had theretofore been untouched by Roman colonization and urbanization. Boniface frequently wrote to Rome; providing an opportunity for the pope to specify the Roman doctrine on family obstacles to marriage, which Gregory extended to the seventh generation.

Gregory III also continued work on the restoration of the Roman walls. He saw to the upkeep of a number of the city's churches, endowing them with valuable liturgical vessels and icons; and he also had work done on the Lateran Palace, which again became the papal residence.

Jean-Charles Picard

Bibliography

JW, 1, 257–62; 2, 700, 742.

LP, 1, 415–26.

MGH, Epist., 3, 476–9.

Bertolini, O. *Roma e i Longobardi*, Rome, 1972.

Duchesne L. *Les Premiers Temps de l'État pontifical*, Paris, 1911.

Moncelle, P. "Grégoire III," *DTC*, 62 (1924), 1785–90 (updated by R. Aubert, *DHGE*, 21 [1986], 1421–2).

Noble, T. F. X. *The Republic of St. Peter*, Philadelphia, 1984.

Richards, J. *The Popes and the Papacy in the Early Middle Ages, 476–752*, London, 1979.

Schieffer, R. "Gregor III.," *LexMA*, 4 (1987–9), 1667.

GREGORY IV. (*d. 25 January 844*). *Elected pope late 827.*

The seventeen-year papacy of Gregory IV was the longest of the 9th century (that of LEO III, which lasted twenty-one years, only spanned sixteen years of the century). Before becoming pope, Gregory was a priest in the church of San Marco, which he had restored and decorated with still-extant mosaics immediately after his election. Nothing is known of his education. After VALENTINE's brief tenure on the papal throne, his election was probably an attempt to continue EUGENE II's work of pacification in the Roman political arena, given what had been concluded with Lothair in 824. The *LIBER PONTIFICALIS* emphasizes the fact that Gregory IV was *genere clausus*, which would strengthen the significance of his election.

At any rate, Gregory IV's papacy cannot be reduced to a simple pursuit of the line followed by Eugene II. As was the case for PASCHAL I, the biographer for the *Liber Pontificalis* took considerable pains to select the facts he recorded, and he emphasized the role of Gregory as a rebuilder and benefactor of churches who worked to make Rome more beautiful. Gregory IV's generosity thus had not only spiritual, but also political value, in the sense that the pope was at the origin of all initiatives for Rome. In reality, the biographer's "omissions" in the *Liber Pontificalis* were programmed. Given the need to mention Gregory IV's numerous works in Rome, he could not drag out his account with details of the vicissitudes of his election and consecration. This omission has great historical value especially if one considers at that time the *constitutio* desired by Lothair was rigorously applied under Eugene II's papacy. According to Einhard, Gregory IV's election was not validated until the imperial legate had examined the regularity of the procedures followed.

Likewise, the *Liber Pontificalis* went quickly over what was the only intervention (and an unfortunate one) by the pope in the international arena, in 833. Deep disagreements had sprung up between the emperor, Louis the Pious, and his sons by his first marriage (Lothair, Pepin, and Louis the German). Lothair convinced the pope to intervene, but Gregory's mediation was a failure. Actually, he paid too much attention to Lothair's interests and failed to win over the Frankish bishops as an authority that could truly represent the "entire" Church. When the episode was over, Gregory IV effectively eschewed international affairs, and for the remainder of his life he concerned himself solely with internal affairs.

The most urgent of these was protecting himself against SARACEN incursions launched from the coast of Latium. They had already attacked Civitavecchia in 813 and 827, but the danger in the Tyrrhenian Sea became much more imminent after their progressive conquest of Sicily (starting in 827), and with the internal wars among the LOMBARDS in the South during the 830s and 840s, when they enlisted Saracen mercenaries. Gregory IV, therefore, decided to build a fortified town near the port of Ostia. He followed its construction personally, giving it his own name, *Gregoriopolis*. With two country *domus* already completed between Rome and Ostia, in Ponte Galeria (formerly the location of a *domusculta* belonging to Hadrian I) and Dragona, this was the first real land development accomplished by a pontiff on his own territory, and the example was followed by other popes. LEO IV gave his name to the "city" that he created when he surrounded the Vatican with walls, as well as to the totally new city he founded to move the inhabitants of Civitavecchia into a more secure location. JOHN VIII did likewise when he fortified the town surrounding the basilica St. Paul's Outside the Walls. The founding of *Gregoriopolis* in 842-3 must thus be seen as a continuation of a clear view of papal power that was prevalent in the area around Rome.

Federico Marazzi

Bibliography

JE, 1, 323-7.

LP, 2, 73-85.

MGH, Epist., 5, 228-232.

MGH, SS, 2, 635-6 and 641.

MGH, SS, In usum schol., 6, 173-4; 7, 36.

PL, 106, 841-63.

Brezzi, P. *Roma e l'Impero medievale*, Rome, 1947.

Clerval, A. "Grégoire IV," *DTC*, 6-2 (1925), 1790 [with a bibliographic complement in *DHGE*, 21 (1986), s.v.].

Duchesne, L. *Les Premiers Temps de l'État pontifical*, Paris, 1898.

Llewellyn, P. *Rome in the Dark Ages*, London, 1971.

Mordek, H. "Gregor IV.," *LexMA*, 4 (1987-9), 1667-8.

GREGORY V. *(Bruno of Carinthia, d. 18 February 999). Elected pope in May 996. Buried in St. Peter's in Rome.*

Gregory V's papacy was eclipsed in history by that of the pope who succeeded him, SILVESTER II (999-1003), who has remained much more famous. Nevertheless, Gregory V's relatively short reign is not without interest. At the time it was rare for a "foreigner," meaning a non-Roman and a non-Italian, to ascend the *Cathedra Petri*. There were as many advantages as risks associated with this status. Gregory V, as a close relative of Emperor Otto III, was able to count on the imperial support of his cousin in case of conflict. On the other hand, what is not known is the extent to which the young German ecclesiastic, son of Duke Otto of Carinthia, was able to appreciate appropriately the balance of power in Rome, for he had been called to the Palatine chapel by Otto III soon after his schooling in Magdeburg.

Whatever the case, Bruno's election as Gregory V took place without the participation of Roman political forces, which at the time were dominated by Senator Crescentius II Nomentanus, the main adversary of Gregory V's predecessor, Pope JOHN XV. Gregory V owed his election solely to imperial will. Because of the external political situation, the decision was initially accepted in Rome. Otto III appeared in Italy in 996 at the head of a substantial army, which he led up to the walls of Rome. On 21 May of that year, the new pontiff Gregory V proceeded to the annointing and CORONATION of his imperial cousin, Otto III. A day later, on 22 May, the pardon of the Roman senator Crescentius, condemned of lese majesty for a plot against John XV, was pronounced. Clearly, the emperor and the pope were betting on a politics of entente with the Roman aristocracy. For Otto III and Gregory V, one thing was clear: the pope, who was a foreigner and a neophyte to Roman politics, found himself in need of Crescentii support if he wished to remain in Rome after the departure of imperial troops.

After the coronation ceremonies, a SYNOD convened at ST. PETER's and jointly presided over by the pope and the emperor dealt with the most acute of the problems in the area of church politics. The dispute over the archbishopric of Reims appears to be one of the most urgent and complex of these problems. In the quarrel, Gregory V had taken sides with Arnoul, the archbishop of Reims, who had been deposed in 991 by a French national COUNCIL. Arnoul's adversary and successor, Gerbert d'Aurillac, the former director of the cathedral school of Reims, whose legitimacy had already been contested by John XV, traveled to Rome, where the decision was temporarily sent back to the synod at St. Peter's. But Gregory V remained faithful to the line defended by Pope John XV, who had openly declared decisions made at the 991 synod in Reims null and void, and who wished to entrust the resolution of the problem to a general synod placed under papal authority. Gregory V went so far as to threaten all of France with anathema (25 May 996). What took place thereafter demonstrated Gregory's lack of authority in Rome. As soon as Emperor Otto III left Rome, in the first half of June 996, the pope, now reduced to his own means, was unable to remain more than a few months in the Eternal City. He was chased by a Roman mob led by Senator Crescentius II, whom the emperor and he had formerly pardoned. In October 996, Gregory's many attempts to reconquer Rome by force failed, only confirming the pope's distress. Gregory V was forced to retire to the North, in Spoleto, where he stayed until the end of the year with Duke Conrad, under whom he had sought protection on Otto's recommendation.

It was in Spoleto that Gregory met with Abbot Abbo of Fleury. Abbo, on behalf of the king of France, Robert II the Pious was engaged in a politics of rapprochement with the papal see. Refusing to support the contested archbishop of Reims, as he had done up to that time, Robert II was counting on an exchange of courtesies. He was thus hoping to obtain the pope's recognition of his anticanonical marriage to Berthe of Bourgogne.

Gregory V's situation worsened seriously with the proclamation in Rome, early in February 997, of an antipope, Archbishop John Philagathos of Piacenza, who took the name JOHN XVI. It did, of course, take time for the news to reach Gregory, who was in northern Italy, and the synod of Pavia, convened by Gregory V and also held in early February 997, made no mention of the antipope in its decisions: only the Roman senator Crescentius was excommunicated. On the other hand, the synod of Pavia did make important decisions regarding the dispute over the archbishopric of Reims. All the bishops of France who had taken part in Arnoul's deposition were threatened with suspension, since they had not listened to the pope who was exhorting them to come justify themselves before a synod. Despite pressure from the king of France, and the political difficulties he was facing, Gregory remained faithful to the line he had so fiercely defended. In fact, he threatened to excommunicate Robert II and the French bishops, who had given their approval to Robert's marriage, and the possibility of an appeal was also rejected. Moreover, the synod condemned all practices of simony with the greatest of severity. In general, Gregory V always assumed his responsibilities with the same zeal. In February 997, he again gave the *pallium* to Archbishop Aelfric of Canterbury, and as soon as he became aware of the election of Pope John XVI, he condemned him for usurping the *Cathedra Petri*.

Consequently, Gregory V remained in contact with Abbot Abbo of Fleury, who certainly played a role in Gregory's decision, during the summer of 997, to authorize the archbishop of Reims, Arnoul, to resume the exercise of his duties.

At the end of 997, Emperor Otto III, whom his cousin the pope had been expecting for such a long time, returned to Italy, and the two met in Pavia in December 997. They passed through Ravenna in early February 998, reached Rome toward the middle of February, and the city fell into their hands almost without a battle. The antipope, John XVI, had already taken flight, but he was apprehended, taken prisoner, and cruelly mutilated. At the end of April 998, Senator Crescentius was executed, and probably toward the early part of May, the antipope John Philagathos was officially deposed, following a procedure held in good and due form.

The emperor's presence in Rome allowed Gregory V to extend his activities to the areas immediately surrounding the city. Thus, in early June 998, the two cousins undertook a joint expedition against Cerveteri, which was occupied by Count Benedict II of Sabina, a relative of Crescentius. In late April the *pallium* was given to Gerbert, now archbishop in Ravenna, which allowed the quarrel in Reims to come to a peaceful resolution. Gerbert's elevation to the most important episcopal see in Italy (other than Rome) was the work of Emperor Otto III, who hoped to make his venerated master less bitter at his defeat in Reims. At the same time, he hoped to strengthen the imperial positions in northern Italy. Did this measure suggest the beginnings of harmonious coexistence and collaboration between the two supreme powers, the temporal and the spiritual? Unfortunately, lack of sources make it impossible to reach a firm conclusion. The signs of distance should not be overestimated, however, even though Otto III, on the occasion of his imperial coronation, broke with the custom of confirming the rights and possessions of the *Cathedra Petri*. One thing is certain: Gregory was not as tightly tied to Emperor Otto as his successor, SILVESTER II would be.

Hans-Henning Körtum

Bibliography

Moehs, T. E. *Gregorius V. (996–999)*, Stuttgart, 1972.
Papsturkunden, 896–1046, II, Vienna, 1988, 637–712.
Zimmermann, H. *Papstregesten*, 911–1024, Vienna-Cologne-Graz, 1969, 296–346.

[GREGORY VI]. *Antipope, elected after 17 May 1012, pope until April 1013.*

After the sudden death of Pope SERGIUS IV on 12 May 1012, and the almost concomitant death of the Roman patrician John II Crescentius, on 18 May, the Roman Tusculani faction managed (probably on 17 May, and in full tumult) to have Theophylact, the second son of Count Gregory of Tusculum, elected pope as BENEDICT VIII. The aristocratic Crescentii faction, who had been in power up to that time, had one of their partisans named pope in a later, canonical, election. This pope he took the name Gregory. The battles that arose within the Roman aristocracy kept him from remaining, and he fled to Sabina, where he was supported by the partisans of the Roman aristocratic faction theretofore in power.

During the campaign of the summer of 1012, Benedict VIII and his partisans conquered almost all the Crescentii possessions. Forced by circumstances, and deprived of all military support, Gregory VI left for Germany in order to get the legitimacy of his election confirmed in a judgment by King Henry II. According to H. Zimmermann, "If there had been no juridical foundation, the trip to the German sovereign by a pope elected by the Crescentii, who were hostile to the emperor, would straightaway have been doomed to fail." On Christmas day in 1012, when Gregory appeared in all his vestments in Pöhlde before the king of Germany, Henry II received him with all the signs of honor, but kept Gregory and his men under guard, postponing his official verdict concerning the contested papal election until his trip to Rome. This was only a formal procedure, however, since Henry had established relations with Benedict VIII much earlier. Shortly thereafter, on 21 January 1013, Benedict VIII confirmed for him his favorite foundation, the bishopric of Bamberg, among other things. In the spring of 1013, Benedict VIII sent Bishop Azzo II of Ostia to Germany as a papal LEGATE. In April 1013, in the framework of a diet of German princes meeting in Grone in Westphalia, the bishop defended Benedict VIII's interests even in the presence of Gregory VI, and he proposed talks to the king regarding his trip to Rome and his imperial coronation by the Tusculani pope. Gregory VI's fate was thus sealed, and the remainder of his life is unknown.

Klaus-Jürgen Herrmann

Bibliography

JW, 1, 514.
LP, 268, n. 4.
Herrmann, K. J. *Das Tuskulanerpapsttum*, 1012–46, Stuttgart, 1973, 5, 7, 25–7.
Struve, T. "Gregor (VI.)," *LexMA*, 4 (1987–9), 1668.
Viard, P. "Grégoire (VI)," *DHGE*, 21 (1986), 1423.
Von Merseburg, T. *Chron. VI*, 101 (*MGH; SS; NS*, 9, 1935), 394.
Zimmermann, H. *Papstregesten*, 1075, 1078, 1108; *Papstabsetzungen des Mittelalters*, Vienna-Cologne-Graz, 1969, 115–7.

GREGORY VI. *(John Gratian, d. late 1047). Pope from 1 May 1045 to 24 December 1046, deposed on that date.*

On 10 March 1045, BENEDICT IX, who had been banished, managed to make his way back to Rome with armed forces. Although he was once again master of the Eternal City, Benedict IX was not in a position to win the confidence of the Romans. An arrangement was made, therefore, for the pope to give up his office to the archpriest John Gratian, who took the name Gregory VI. Gregory was not simply named by Benedict as his successor, but was apparently elected in a vote taken in due form, after the official resignation of Benedict. Large sums of money had paved the way for his election for, even though Benedict gave up his rights, his partisans had not given up theirs. Thus Gregory VI entered into negotiations with the Tusculani party—as well as with the Stephani and SILVESTER III, the pope of whom they were partisans. Gregory apparently quickly reached a deal with the Tusculani, who received monetary compensation for their interests that were still at stake. After piecing all the events together, most sources reduced the issue of these talks to the oversimplified conclusion that Benedict IX had sold the papal throne to Gregory VI—or that Gregory had purchased it. This accord put an end to the Tusculani demands, but the SCHISM with Silvester III remained just as it was. It seemed at the time that, in all likelihood, it would take until March 1046, after the talks with him or with the Crescentii who were supporting him, for Silvester to give up his claims.

From the outset, Gregory's papacy gave considerable satisfaction to those interested in reform who were hoping to see the new pope impose their politics outside the narrow framework formed by factions of the Roman nobility. Gregory VI was unanimously recognized, and in May 1045 he set up acts for receivers of benefices in Italy and France. His position vis-à-vis the German crown lacked stability, however. When Henry III appeared in Italy in the autumn of 1046, Gregory VI went to meet the German sovereign in Piacenza, where he was received, although without being confirmed in his functions as pope. On 24 December, Gregory VI, as had also been the case with Benedict IX and Silvester III, was called to appear at the SYNOD of Sutri. The assembly declared Pope Gregory to be guilty of trafficking in charges (SIMONY), and deposed him.

Following the synod, the pope was incarcerated; after the election of the new pope—Suidger of Bamberg, who took the name CLEMENT II—on 25 December 1046, Emperor Henry III realized that a pope residing in Rome after his deposition could easily become the point of focus for a new schism. Following the precedent set by Emperor Otto I, who had banished Pope Benedict V to Hamburg after his deposition in 965, Gregory VI was banished *ad ripas Rheni*, to the city of Cologne.

His former chaplain, Hildebrand (the future Pope Gregory VII), left with him. At the end of 1047, Gregory VI died, still in exile, an illness that has been difficult to define with any specificity.

Klaus-Jürgen Herrmann

Bibliography

JW, 1, 524 ff.

LP, 2, 270.

Aubert, R. "Grégoire VI," *DHGE*, 21 (1986), 1423–4.

Borino, G. B. "L'elezione e la deposizione di Gregorio VI," *ASR* 39 (1916) 141, 22, 295–410.

Freytmans, D. "Grégoire VI était-il simoniaque?," *Revue belge de philologie et d'histoire*, 11 (1932), 130–7.

Herrmann, K. J. *Das Tuskulanerpapsttum 1012–1046*, Stuttgart, 1973.

Poole, R. L. "Benedict IX and Gregory VI," *Studies in Chronology and History*, Oxford, 2nd ed., 1969, 185–222.

Schmale, F. J. "Die 'Absetzung' Gregors VI. in Sutri und die synodale Tradition," *Annuarium historiae conciliorum*, 11 (1979), 55–103.

Struve, T. "Gregor VI.," *LexMA*, 4 (1987–9), 1668–9.

Wolter, H. *Die Synoden im Reichsgebiet und in Reichsitalien von 916 bis 1056*, Paderborn, 1988, 373 ff.

Zimmermann, H. *Papstabsetzungen des Mittelalters*, Graz-Cologne-Vienna, 1968, 122–136.

Zimmermann, H. *Papsturkunden*, 2, 624–30.

GREGORY VII. *Hildebrand (b. Sovana, circa 1020, d. Salerno, 25 May 1085). Elected pope on 22 April 1073. Buried in the cathedral in Salerno.*

Hildebrand was born in Sovana, in Tuscany, to a family of average means; he went to Rome when he was still quite young and was raised in the monastery of Santa Maria all'Aventino, where the customs of Cluny were observed, and where one of his uncles was abbot. It is likely that he made his profession of vows there. Some of his biographers have claimed that he did so in Cluny, but none are taken seriously. He did form close relationships with a few Roman families, one of which descended from converted Jews. He also certainly had a close friendship with John Gratian, the eminent representative of the clergy who became Pope GREGORY VI in 1045, and who was a meritorious individual worthy of the papacy, even though he did ascend to it in an unusual manner. This relationship and the fact he accompanied Gregory VI to Germany when Henry III deposed him were both beneficial. When he returned to Italy after his patron's death, he remained in service to the Holy See. Named CARDINAL subdeacon of the Roman Church, he was later a LEGATE to France under both LEO IX and Victor II in 1054 and 1056. It was at that time that he became fully aware of the urgency of reform.

In 1057, upon the death of Victor II (the last pope of Henry III, who had died the previous year), Stephen IX ascended to Peter's throne. Hildebrand was sent to Empress Agnes, who was reigning in the name of her young son Henry IV, to obtain agreement and confirmation of the new pontiff's designation. His mission accomplished, he spent time in the kingdom and did not return to Rome until the death of STEPHEN IX (March 1058). Stephen IX had asked that his successor not be named until his legate returned, in order to avoid the possibility that a faction of the Roman nobility opposed to reform and cooperation with the emperor might have succeeded in having one of its members elevated to the papal throne. After his return to the city, Hildebrand and Peter Damian, who had been working for religious restoration for years, got Gerard, bishop of Florence, elected, probably with the agreement of the German Court. Gerard became NICHOLAS II, and named Hildebrand archdeacon of the Roman Church. This position gave him considerable financial responsibility, something his future adversaries would point out when he intractably opposed SIMONY. He then became principal advisor to ALEXANDER II (1061–73), with whom he had dealt previously. During this period he became aware of the danger involved in too much collaboration with the empire, a risk seen in the German monarch's intervention in the affairs of the Holy See at an inopportune time, and, without regard for continuing the work of reform. He also noticed the extent to which certain bishops were opposed to reform, which led him to support the Patarenes, an anticlerical sect whose excesses he would later condemn, against the archbishop of Milan.

The day of Alexander II's funeral (22 April 1073), a great tumult arose in the crowd composed of clerics and laypeople, with shouts of "Hildebrand for bishop!" Cardinal Hugues Candide, formerly an active legate in France and Spain, immediately took matters into his own hands and called the cardinals together. They unanimously agreed to the popular acclamation. Despite its unorthodoxy the election was valid because the cardinal bishops, who, according to Nicholas II's recent decree (1059), were supposed to be consulted first, essentially gave their approval and raised no opposition within their college. Their fellow brothers in the cardinalate followed them. Hildebrand chose Gregory VII as his name, probably both in memory of Gregory VI and in admiration for Gregory I. He informed the imperial court of his promotion and received approval. His experience and his work with the clerics in his entourage on the goals and means of the restoration work that needed to be accomplished, soon pushed him to create a doctrine, that of Gregorian REFORM, which was based on around four essential arguments:

1. The most strongly emphasized objective was that of reestablishing the dignity and the independence of the position of bishop. The struggle against lay investiture, that is, refusing the emperor's intervention (or that of other powers) in decisions on those to be named bishop were to be relentlessly and uncompromisingly pursued, even at the cost of open conflict.

2. This episcopal restoration was, however, only one element (although a fundamental element), in a general societal reform that was the supreme goal of giving freedom and power back to the clergy. Clerics were to be freed from all lay supervision, as this was seen as necessary for man to be released from the demon's servitude and for him to accept service to Christ. However, as the Church was solely in charge of such service, as well as that of abrogating the rules that limited ecclesiastical liberty, it had the duty to maintain regulations and impose them on the entire society. This led to giving the clergy considerable authority over almost all human activities.

3. In order to carry on such a struggle, there could be only one head, a single authority which, by its nature, was unimpeachable, and this was the papacy; this entailed a significant modification in ecclesiastical structures and the transformation of the Church into a monarchy sovereignly governed by Peter's successor.

4. The program thus defined was soon recognized not only as the best of all, but especially as the only program that was capable of succeeding. This meant that all others were bad, blameworthy, and to be condemned. This was the greatest originality in Gregorian reform.

This reform finally questioned seignorial power in cases where lords succeeded in keeping the episcopacy under their control; it likewise questioned the right of the emperor or kings in matters where monarchs retain their prerogatives. It sparked up a series of contestations; among these one with the empire, the battle over INVESTITURES.

After convening a SYNOD to reaffirm the condemnation of simony and NICOLAISM, in Rome during Lent 1074, Gregory began to translate these decisions into concrete actions. In nonimperial countries, his first steps included sending legates, some of whom had a permanent mission, which they accomplished by convening regional synods (Hugues, bishop of Die, did so for France, and Amat of Oleron for the Narbonnaise, Gascony, and Spain). These executives, who for the most part were ardent reformers, often ran into difficulties with civil powers whose rights they contested, as well as with bishops they deposed if they felt the bishop unworthy. This resulted in conflicts, some of which were heated. Such was the case in the French regions in the southern part of the Loire during the years 1075 to 1079. Prelates and great lords protested against the intrusions, which upset a system that consolidated aristocratic control over episcopal sees, and worked to the temporal and spiritual advantage of both parties. Farther north, a few prelates also resisted, while king Philip I retained his prerogatives. Such was also the case in the Iberian peninsula and in England, where William the Conqueror ceded nothing he felt he justly held, although he did favor reform done under the aegis of the archbishop of Canterbury, Lanfranc. In general, results were obtained in all these regions by eliminating those of questionable character and putting dignitaries of quality into place; simony was reduced, as was Nicolaism at least in the high clergy. In most cases, results were gained through firm but prudent action carried out in a manner acceptable to the authorities.

In the kingdoms of Germany and Italy, the work, which was also supported by legates (Anselm of Lucca, in Lombardy, and later Altmann of Passau, in Germany), turned into violent conflict. The Italian episcopacy was at stake and the bishop of Rome intended to be in control of it, but the emperor could scarcely conceive of giving up the investiture that allowed him to govern and administer. In refusal of Gregory's project, he undermined both the pontiff's rights and what the pope considered to be the freedom of the Roman Church. The conflict became open in the spring of 1075 when the pope staunchly renewed his prohibition of lay investiture. Henry IV paid little heed and continued to invest prelates. Called back to order, he convened in Worms, twenty-four German and two Italian bishops who were opposed to the Roman program, who deposed the pontiff in January 1076 as being guilty of diverse crimes and an illegal election. Then he addressed a public manifesto to "the false monk Hildebrand," ordering him to give up Peter's throne. The following month Gregory responded in a like manner, assembling a synod of bishops in Rome that excommunicated the king of Germany and forbade his exercise of power, which was tantamount to deposing him. He absolved the king's subjects of their oath to fidelity with a sentence formulated as an invocation to Saints Peter and Paul, but especially to the former, "in the name of [whose] power" the sovereign was sanctioned "so that the nations might know that you are Peter and that upon this rock the son of the Living God has raised up his Church, against which the gates of hell shall never prevail."

Since he was simultaneously excommunicating and suspending prelates who were guilty or hostile to these measures, it soon appeared in Germany as though Henry had acted lightly and unduly troubled the kingdom and the Church. Through active propaganda and the initiatives of groups in favor of reform, it was concluded that the king should be abandoned. The princes, pushed by the dynasties that were rivals of the Salian dynasty, thus decreed that the king reconcile himself with the Holy See within a period of one year; if not, his fate would be decided by a diet which the pope would both attend and arbitrate. Aware of the danger, the king retreated. He went to the CANOSSA castle, in Emilia, where Gregory was staying, because he had a sure ally in the region in the countess of Tuscany; the king sought his forgiveness like a repentent sinner (January 1077). The pope, who as pastor was incapable of refusing reconciliation to a lost sheep who had returned to the fold, imposed an ecclesiastical penance and give him absolution. He then invited him to reconcile himself with the princes. The princes, however, did not receive him as gladly; some of them named a new king (Rudolph of Swabia). Civil war broke out in the Germanic kingdom and Gregory lost the initiative. He attempted to remain neutral, but since Henry was pressuring him for support, or at least to make a choice, and because he was attempting to restore his authority over the German clergy, he excommunicated Henry and deposed him once again (June 1080).

The king reacted strongly. He again announced his adversary's downfall and, pushing further, had an antipope elected, the archbishop of Ravenna (who took the name CLEMENT III); but above all, he defeated Rudolph, who met death on the battlefield. In 1081 he intervened militarily in northern and central Italy, imposing himself everywhere to some extent. In the summer of 1083, he took over the Roman neighborhood around ST. PETER's and blocked the city, occupying it almost in its entirety during the following spring. Thirteen of Gregory's cardinals abandoned him, siding with Clement III; Clement III was solemnly enthroned in the Lateran and he crowned the emperor. Gregory VII, who was locked up in Castel Sant'Angelo, was freed through the efforts of the Norman "prince" Robert Guiscard, a dangerous neighbor established in the southern part of the peninsula, but always ready to lend his aid against the Germans. Unfortunately, the Roman populace turned against Gregory, holding him

responsible for the pillaging of the city by his ally's troops. Disappointed and exhausted, he went off to die in Salerno on 25 May 1085, apparently vanquished in a conflict that would resurface after his death. The conflict ended with a compromise in 1122, the Concordat of WORMS, which basically favored the papacy's views, if judged by the success of its program of reform.

Gregory VII was a man of high culture and principles and, to the point of being intransigent and occasionally awkward, he was courageous and convinced of the justness of his cause. Authoritarian, abrupt, perhaps slightly inclined to dramatize situations, Gregory VII exposed the reasons and justifications for his interventions in the Church and in the world in a coherent doctrine (his DICTATUS PAPAE), in the two sentences against Henry IV and, in more detailed form, in the two letters he addressed in 1076 and 1080 to bishop Hermann of Metz. The Dictatus Papae is a total of twenty-seven pithy and somewhat curt propositions inserted into the "register" drawn up in 1075, perhaps as a framework for a call to the Roman synod of the same year, or as the outline for a canonical collection. When the canonists of his entourage, or those influenced by him, finished refining it, the doctrine constituted what might be called Gregorian theocracy. The first fundamental argument rested on the affirmation of the preeminent and indivisible sovereignty of the pope over the Church: he is its supreme head, its sole supreme judge, and is the only one with the right to define which truths should be believed. In the life of the Church and in administration of the clergy, all proceeds from him. He deposes and silences bishops (who are elected by the canons of the cathedral), he creates the dioceses, he calls councils. In the religious and spiritual sector, all comes from his competence and his responsibility. All this, put into practice by his legates, and later by services that became increasingly centralized, contributed to the radical transformation of Church structures.

The other fundamental argument rested on the conviction that if human actions are different in their concrete execution, some resulting from material (corporal) facts and others from spiritual data, and if, therefore, we can discern two spheres of activity, it is impossible to separate those that come from the body from those coming from the soul, because any act performed for a temporal enterprise has spiritual value. Therefore, all behaviors should be subject to norms that guarantee this value, norms that only the Church (that is, first of all, the pope) defines and whose application it alone (and especially Peter's vicar) controls. This does not mean that the powers presiding over each of these domains are confused. In reality, they are not: there is an emperor and there are kings, there is a pope and there are bishops, all of whom exercise specific competencies like distinctly different administrations, but the substance of the authority that guides them is the same, such that the Roman pontiff has the duty and the right to monitor acts of the civil power, and to punish those who use them in a manner that might be perverse or dangerous for the salvation of souls, with spiritual sanctions (excommunication), if need be, or via political interventions (deposition). Thus the pope alone has final sovereignty over the world. This was the logic that Gregory VII used when he deposed Henry IV, and when he claimed to place the Iberian kingdoms under the supervision of the Holy See as he was encouraging them to reconquer formerly Christian lands occupied by the Muslims; this endeavor was, for him, an essentially religious enterprise.

Finally, in relation to the first objective of the reform (to christianize society and exalt the spiritual by increasing the power of a clergy conscious of its duties), Gregory VII and the Gregorians worked out a political doctrine that contained within it a new ecclesiology that, reworked in the late 12th and early 13th centuries, would provide the clergy with the fundamental principles of their reflections on relations between Church and State.

Marcel Pacaut

Bibliography

JW, 1, 594–649.

PL, 148, 283–645.

Blumenthal, U. *The Investiture Controversy: Church and Monarchy from the Ninth to the Twelfth Century*, Philadelphia, 1988.

Choux, J. "Grégoire VII," *DHGE*, 21 (1986), 1424–33.

Cowdrey, H. E. J. *Epistolae vagantes*, Oxford, 1972.

Cowdrey, M. E. T. *Pope Gregory VII, 1073–1085*, Oxford, 1998.

Cushing, K. *Papacy and Law in the Georgian Revolution: The Cannonistic Work of Anselm of Luca*, Oxford, 1998.

Das Register Gregors VII., MGH Epist. selectae, 1–2, Berlin, 1920–23, repr. 1955–78.

Fliche, A. *La Réforme grégorienne*, Louvain, 3 vols., 1924–37, repr. Geneva, 1978.

Fliche-Martin, VIII.

Fornasari, G. "Del nuovo su Gregorio VII? Riflessioni su un problema storiografico non esaurito," *Studi Medievali*, 24 (1983), 315–35.

Morghen, R. *Gregorio VII*, Turin, 1942, 2nd ed. Rome, 1974.

Morris, C. *The Papal Monarchy: The Western Church from 1050–1250*, Oxford and New York, 1989.

Pacaut, M. *La Théocracie*, Paris, 1989.

Robinson, L. S. "Pope Gregory VII (1073–1085)," *Journal of Ecclesiastical History*, 36 (1985), 439–83.

Santifallex, L. *Quellen und Forschungen zum Urkunden- und Kanzleiwesen Papst Gregors VII.*, 1, *Quellen, Urkunden, Regesten, Facsimilia*, Vatican, 1957 (*Studi e Testi*, 190).

Sturve, T. "Gregor VII.," *LexMA*, 4 (1987–9), 1669–71.

The Correspondence of Pope Gregory VII, trans. Emerton, E., New York, 1932.

Watterich, 1, 293–546, 740–3, 749–50; 2, 712–13, 751.

Wilken, R. "Gregory VIII and the Politics of Spirit," *First Things* 89 (1999), 26–32.

[GREGORY VIII]. *Antipope (8 March 1118–April 1121, d. after August 1137), previously Mauritus (Burdinus), archbishop of Braga.*

Since the antipope Gregory VIII came from a family of landed nobility in the south of France (or perhaps from Burgundy), where the Bourdin family name is widespread, his name is not necessarily derived from the Roman *Burdinus*, meaning "small ass." Most probably a Cluniac monk from the St. Martial monastery in Limoges, he was called to Toledo, undoubtedly by Archbishop Bernard of Toledo who, as abbot of the Clunisian abbey of Auch, had been sent to Spain by Abbot Hugh of Cluny. The Spanish hierarchy that had just been reestablished, with difficulty, after the Reconquista, was in need of help.

Educated in Toledo by Archbishop Bernard, Maurice became an archdeacon and then was named bishop of Coimbra in 1099. Finally, after making a pilgrimage to the Holy Land between 1104 and 1108, he was named archbishop of Braga in 1109. During the summer of 1109, he personally received the *pallium* in Rome from Pope PASCHAL II. Maurice was extremely cultivated, and in addition to having a keen sense for business matters, he also had diplomatic skills. Faithful to the Cluniac spirit, he was undoubtedly moved by its reformist zeal. During conflicts over jurisdiction with his former protector Bernard of Toledo, primate of Spain and LEGATE, Archbishop Maurice was suspended in 1113–14, but he went to Rome, where Paschal arbitrated the litigation in his favor on 3 November 1114. Two years later, he reappeared in person before the pope to complain about the damage done to his rights as metropolitan. Clearly impressed by the archbishop's skill, Paschal charged him with a mission to Emperor Henry V in northern Italy (late 1116 or early 1117). The emperor essentially wanted an amicable resolution to the quarrel over INVESTITURES, based on those obtained by England and France during the same period. The archbishop of a remote diocese outside the conflict, and one invested with the conciliatory spirit of Cluny, might well have appeared to both parties to be the ideal intermediary. In support of his demands, the emperor left for Rome a second time in early 1117. Paschal II avoided the encounter and fled to Benevento, passing through Monte Cassino and Capua.

During the Easter service at St. Peter's (25 March 1117), Archbishop Maurice celebrated the solemn CORONATION of the emperor (he had been anointed and crowned Roman emperor by Paschal II on 13 April 1111) and of his wife, Mathilda of England. Actually, it was the custom for the bishop highest in the hierarchy to perform this ceremony on solemn feast days. Given the existing conflict, the consequence of this act was that the pope, in a SYNOD in Benevento (April 1117), pronounced the DEPOSITION and excommunication of Maurice and entrusted all his competent bishops with the responsibility of finding a new bishop for the see in Braga.

When Paschal II died on 21 January 1118 and the papal chancellor John of Gaeta was elected pope on 24 January 1118 under the name Gelasius II, Emperor Henry V hurried once more from northern Italy to Rome to restart talks. Gelasius fled to his native city of Gaeta, where he was ordained priest and bishop on 9–10 March, but he refused to return. The Bolognese jurists accompanying the emperor, including the famous Irnerius, considered Gelasius II's election to be invalid. A large part of the Roman aristocracy, headed by the Frangipani, also declared itself to be against Gelasius. On 8 March 1118, Henry V had Archbishop Maurice proclaimed pope and enthroned, under the name Gregory VIII. On 7 April, in Capua, Gelasius pronounced the excommunication of both the emperor and his pope. On Pentecost (2 June), the ANTIPOPE solemnly crowned the emperor in ST. PETER's basilica, just as he had done the year before. Fueled by animosity, Gregory VIII's adversaries described him in the most negative terms, but the evidence seems to suggest that the bishop, certainly serious about wanting reforms, saw perils for all Christianity in the radical demands of the intransigent Gregorians, and that as pope he wanted to act in the service of peace.

Shortly after Pentecost, the emperor left Rome to return to Germany. Gregory VIII, under the protection of the Frangipani, remained in Rome but found few partisans outside the city limits and the immediate area. Returning to Rome in July 1118, Gelasius II was unable to stay, and he departed for France, where he died on 29 January 1119, in Cluny. His successor, Callistus II, immediately proved himself eager to resolve the dispute with Henry V over investitures amicably. Given these circumstances, the emperor severed his connections with the antipope, who took refuge in Sutri. In April 1121, a Norman army under the command of Cardinal John of Crema laid seige to the city, which surrendered after eight days of resistance; and the antipope was delivered to Callistus II. On 23 April, Callistus had him paraded through the streets of Rome riding backwards on a camel, exposing him to the crudest mockery. The unfortunate cleric, thereafter called simply Burdinus, was then condemned to spend his remaining days in southern Italy, in territories subject to NORMAN authority, in La Cava, San Germano (near Monte Cassino), and, under Honorius II (1125), in Fumone, near Alatri. As of August 1137, he was still alive, but still a prisoner in La Cava, near Salerno.

Georg Schwaiger

Bibliography

JL, I, 821; II, 715.

LP, II, 315, 347; III, 162 ff., 169.

Aubert, R. "Grégoire VIII," *DHGE*, 21 (1986), 1433–36.

Baluze, E. "Vita Mauritii Burdini archiepiscopi Bracarensis," *Miscellanea historica*, ed. J. D. MANSI, I, Lucca, 1761, 137–48.

David, P. *Études historiques sur la Galice et le Portugal*, Lisbon-Paris, 1947.

Erdmann, C. "Mauritius Burdinus," *QFIAB*, 19 (1927), 205–61.

Palumbo, F. P. *Lo Schisma del 1130*, Rome, 1942.

Schreiner, K. "Gregor VIII. nackt auf einem Esel," in D. Berg and H. W. Goetz, *Ecclesia et Regnum: Festschrift für Franz-Josef Schmale*, Bochum, 1989, 156–202.

Servatius, C. *Paschalis II.*, Stuttgart, 1979, 128–131, 332.

GREGORY VIII. *Alberto de Morra di Benevento (b. ca. 1105–1110, d. Pisa, 17 December 1187). Elected pope in Ferrara, 12 October 1187, crowned 25 October. Buried in Pisa.*

The son of Sartorius de Morra, called Spanacione, he came from an important family from Benevento. His close relations with the convent of the Augustinian canons regular of St. Martin-de-Laon, where he took his vows, date from his ecclesiastical education in France. Subsequently, the canons were increasingly attracted by the *orbis novus* and merged with the Premonstratensians, although they still continued to offer him their order's habit every year for the remainder of his life. The philosophy of St. Augustine played an important role in his thought, and it is thus not surprising that Pope HADRIAN IV, who himself had been abbot of the canons regular of Saint-Ruf-d'Avignon, made him cardinal deacon of Sant'Adriano in late 1156, and cardinal priest of San Lorenzo in Lucina on 14 March 1158. He had previously studied CANON LAW in Bologna, reaching the level of teacher (*magister*). As part his training he composed an annotation of Gratian's *Decrees*. He served as a LEGATE, and as canon law expert not only in Hungary and Dalmatia (1161; 1162–1165; 1167), where it was hoped he would be elected archbishop of Split, but also in the empire. As part of a sizeable delegation, he brought Emperor Frederick Barbarossa an offer of reconciliation on the pope's behalf in 1163. He also enjoyed very cordial relations with England (1171–1173). He was one of the few supporters of the king of England within the CURIA, and as such, he, along with Cardinal Teodino di San Vitale, helped to get sanctions imposed on Henry II after Thomas Becket's murder. He was also legate in Italy (Novara and Parma, 1177; Northern Italy, 1179; and RAVENNA, 1180). As a reward for his diplomatic skill, Pope ALEXANDER III, whom he knew for a long time and who was especially appreciative of him, named him CHANCELLOR of the Roman Church in 1178. In his new capacity, he compiled a *Forma Dicendi*, a collection of official papal ACTS, and also completed a codification of the *cursus*, a compilation of the very stringent rules governing the euphonious arrangements of sentence endings and phrasing in papal acts. In his honor, the cursus was called *stylus gregorianus*. The fact that during his short papacy Gregory VIII failed to name a new chancellor to succeed him—a custom that would be retained until the time of INNOCENT III—was hardly by chance; he was fully aware of the power associated with the position.

He was known for his strict concept of piety. His election, which took place with the explicit approval of the citizens of Ferrara, appeared to be a clear sign of an internal renewal of the Church and the clergy, although it occured only because of the withdrawal of cardinal bishop Henry of Albano (who belonged to the Cistercian order) and to the defection, due to illness, of the cardinal priest Paolo Scolari, the future pope CLEMENT III. His choice of a papal name (a deliberate homage to GREGORY VII) and his personal role in the founding of a congregation of canons regular of St. Augustine in the churches of Sant' Andrea in Platea and Santa Trinità di Palazzolo in Benevento are confirmation of this renewal. He decreed statutes, inspired by the *ordo antiquus*, that were confirmed in 1187 by Pope URBAN III. His relations with the canons of St. Augustine of Kirkham and the efforts he undertook to promote the renewal of St. Victor in Paris (he had exchanged letters with its abbot, Guérin) likewise reveal the extent to which the currents of reform manifested in the formation of congregations of canons regular were dear to him. Moreover, the good relations he enjoyed with the Hohenstaufen court make Gregory appear a man of conciliation, whose experience and diplomatic skill could get the Curia out of the difficult situation in which it found itself after the conflict that pitted Frederick Barbarossa against Urban III. In the matter of the double election to the metropolitan See of Trier, he demonstrated his willingness to compromise; in the case of the imperial coronation of Henry VI, he likewise showed less intransigence than his predecessors. This attitude may be explained primarily by his concern with organizing a new CRUSADE, in the wake of alarming news from the Holy Land. He begged Genoa and Pisa to assemble a fleet, and he had the crusade proclaimed in Germany and France, among other places, by Cardinal Henry of Albano. If given the chance, would Gregory VIII ultimately have succeeded in establishing harmonious relations with the imperial court, given the religious zeal, that led him to destroy without hesitation the tomb of his schismatic predecessor, Victor IV? That question remains a matter of speculation. The pope's premature death, after only fifty-seven days of papacy, precluded any real answer to it.

Ludwig Vones

Bibliography

JL, 528–35.

LP, 2, 451.

PL, 202, 1537–64.

Aubert, R. "Grégoire VIII," *DHGE*, 21 (1986), 1436.

Fliche-Martin, IX, 2 (1953), 196–98.

Fonseca, C. D. "La professione canonicale del cardinale Alberto de Morra," *RSCI*, 16 (1962) 136–37.

Hottzmann, W. "Die Dekretaler Gregors VIII.," *MIÖG*, 58 (1950), 113–23.

Kehr, P. "Papst Gregor VIII. als Ordensbegründer," *Miscellanea Francesco Ehrle*, II, Rome, 1924, 248–76.

Kleemann, G. *Papst Gregor VIII. 57 tägtiges Pontificat (1187)*. Diss., Bonn, 1912.

Nadig, P. *Gregor VIII.*, Basle, 1890.

Roberg, B. "Gregor VIII.," *LexMA*, 4 (1987–88), 1671.

Sastre Santos, E. "Alberto de Morra, cardenal protector de la Orden de Santiago," *Hidalguia* 31 (1983) 369–92.

Watterich, *Vitae* 2, 682–92.

GREGORY IX. *Hugo or Ugolino ei Conti de Segni (b. Anagni, ca. 1170, d. Rome, 22 August 1241). Elected pope 19 March 1227, consecrated 21 March 1227. Buried in St. Peter's in Rome.*

The third in an uninterrupted series of Roman popes, Gregory IX took INNOCENT III for his model. Like his predecessor, Honorius III, he had gone through all the stages of a brilliant career in the CURIA before his election to the papacy. He endowed the Roman Church with a new CANONICAL COLLECTION and was able to provide definitive rules for the two branches of the Franciscan order. His papacy was characterized by neverending conflict with Emperor Frederick II. His relationship with Frederick demanded much of his energy, as well as his considerable political experience and diplomatic skills, in addition to a certain pugnaciousness. Like Innocent III, he had attended the University of Paris, and he was quite elderly when he reached the papacy. He may have been the oldest pope of the 13th century.

Hugo (or Ugolino, as he is called in a number of sources contemporary to him) was a member of the Conti de Segni family, which owned land in the Anagni region, where he was born (ca. 1170) and reared. Matthew of Paris maintains that Gregory IX died "almost a centenarian," although this statement should not be taken literally. His membership in the Conti de Segni family was affirmed by the *Vita Gregorii IX*, the author of which was most probably the pope's CHAMBERLAIN,

John of Ferentino. His attachment to the Roman Papareschi, or Paparone, family is very problematic. How he was related to Innocent III remains uncertain. The *Gesta Innocentii III* fails to mention a relationship. The *Vita Gregorii IX* calls him *tertio gradu consanguinitatis conjunctus*, which means that they had the same great-great-grandfather. Like a number of other young people belonging to important families of Latium who were destined for an ecclesiastic or curial career, Ugolino was sent to Paris. Honorius III himself recognized this fact in the privilege he accorded to the teachers and students of the University of Paris. Ugolino's stay in Bologna is not documented, but a contemporaneous source considered the future pope to be *juris peritus*, which is confirmed by the intense activity as judge that he was involved in as an AUDITOR during Innocent III's papacy. The bonds he formed with important cultural figures of his time—the Cistercian Rainier, Jacques de Vitry, and Michael Scot—are signs that Gregory IX had broad intellectual interests. The frescoes of the crypt in the cathedral of Agnani that show, among others, the figures of Hippocratus and Galen—rare for icons in the West at the time—show the influence of the canons of Anagni in the first decades of the 13th century, thus reflecting both the family tradition and intellectual milieu that formed Ugolino. As soon as he ascended to the papacy, Innocent III had Ugolino enter his CHAPEL, gave him some judicial cases, and then named him CARDINAL of St. Eustache in his first cardinal promotion (1198). Up to the time of Innocent III's death, Ugolino was seen in the pope's entourage, where he was undoubtedly one of the primary counselors. The pope entrusted him with difficult missions, of both a political (negotiations with Marcward of Anweiler) and judicial nature. Bishop of Ostia in 1206, he became one of the most influential individuals in the College of Cardinals.

In the years 1207–9, he undertook a legation in Germany to attempt to convince the two pretenders to the throne (Otto of Brunswick and Philip of Swabia) to accept papal arbitration. In 1216 he was one of two cardinals charged with finding a compromise to resolve the election of Innocent III's successor. The most important legation during his time as cardinal took him to northern Italy on three different occasions: to Pisa, Genoa, Lucca, and Volterra in 1217 to resolve local political conflicts; to Florence, Bologna, and the Lombard cities in 1218 to impose Frederick II's authority; and in 1221 to seek support for the Holy Land from the Lombard cities after the failure of the fifth CRUSADE, in addition to their collaboration in the struggle against HERESIES. In all cases he showed such skillful diplomacy and thorough knowledge of judicial problems that Honorius III was thoroughly pleased with his performance. After the death of Cardinal John of St. Paul, Francis of Assisi chose Ugolino to protect his fledgling community. In 1217, the future Gregory IX was already able to safeguard the interests of the Roman Curia by encouraging the independence of the Friars Minor of the local church. Hugo apparently took part in the composition of the *Regula Bullata*, which, among other things, called for the insitution of a cardinal protector, a responsibility he was the first to undertake. By 1218, he also took responsibility for the community of St. Claire, whose rule (*Quo elongati*) he composed between 1219 and 1227. It is possible that Francis of Assisi met Ugolino in Subiaco in 1222, which would explain the presence of a portrait of the cardinal in the chapel of St. Gregory. Without ever becoming its institutional protector, Ugolino also had an excellent relationship with the newly established order of Preachers, whose founder, Dominic, he had met a number of times: possibly in 1215, at the time of the LATERAN IV COUNCIL, and certainly in 1217, in the winter of 1219–20, and in 1221, during the Lombard legation. Upon the death of Honorius III (1227), a first papal election *per compromissum* selected the cardinal bishop of Porto, Conrad of Urach, who declined. Ugolino, who took the name Gregory IX, seems to have been elected *per inspirationem*. The election took place on 19 March 1227, in Rome. From early in his papacy, relations with the emperor Frederick II became turbulent. The emperor, who had committed to taking up the cross at the time of his imperial CORONATION, at which Ugolino had been present in his capacity as bishop of Ostia, continually found new excuses to postpone his departure. In August 1227 the emperor was ready, but a sudden illness held him back in Brindisi. The pope, who felt pushed to the limits by this latest delay, rejected the emperor's excuses and proceeded to excommunicate him (29 September). In June 1228 the emperor was finally able to leave. He succeeded in obtaining the liberation of Jerusalem with no resistance whatsoever. This unheard-of feat strengthened the pope's suspicions of the emperor even further, and he held to the excommunication.

The pope gathered an army to thwart the ensuing imperial attacks and invade the kingdom of Sicily. Returning to Italy in June 1230, Frederick II had no difficulty defeating the pope's soldiers, but he was careful to respect the borders of the PAPAL STATES of the Church. A reconciliation between the pope and the emperor took place in July 1230, in Ceprano. The emperor made substantial concessions in Sicily and agreed not to touch the papal teritories. The pope suspended the sentence of excommunication. After a few years of cooperation—the emperor helped the pope in 1234 when the pope had to flee Rome; the pope excommunicated Frederick II's son, Enzo, in 1234, because he revolted against his father—relations between the papacy and the empire again turned violent in 1236. The emperor had demanded that the pope excommunicate the Italian cities against which he was doing battle. Gregory IX replied on 23 October 1236, complaining of Frederick's oppression of the churches in his kingdom. On 20 March 1239, Gregory IX renewed his excommunication of the emperor. The conflict became irreversible. He made a public appeal for a general COUNCIL; treating the emperor like a blasphemer and a precursor to the ANTICHRIST. In his 1239 BULL of excommunication, Gregory IX also let it be known that only a council could attempt to resolve the conflict with the emperor, considered the "great cause among great causes." The council was supposed to be held in Rome during Easter 1241. However, the plan failed because of Frederick II's capture of prelates off the island of Giglio on 3 May 1241, an action with considerable repercussions for public opinion throughout the West. The imperial army entered Rome in early April, but there was no siege of the city. Gregory died in August, courageous and unyielding. The idea of a council was to be taken up later and carried out in Lyon by his successor, Innocent IV.

Gregory IX's accomplishments remained very much in line with his activities as cardinal. His commitment to the crusade and to Church expansion toward the East were undoubtedly the strongest features of his papacy. In order to help keep the crusade movement viable (while tempering its military aspects somewhat under the pacifist influence of Francis of Assisi), he turned to the Teutonic Order. Opening new geographical horizons in Church expansion, he encouraged the missionary efforts of the Franciscans and the DOMINICANS from Finland to Romania and urged the Premonstratensians to establish themselves in Latvia. Francis of Assisi was the first saint to be canonized by Gregory IX (1228). In 1231 and 1232, the pope canonized another illustrious member of the Franciscan order, Anthony of Padua. Dominic, the founder of the Preachers, was canonized in 1234. Gregory IX inaugurated and brought to a completion the CANONIZATION process for two illustrious saints from the Germanic world: Hildegard of Bingen and Elizabeth of Thuringia.

Early in his papacy, the College of Cardinals was composed of 18 members. Five cardinals died during the first six months. The creation of 6 cardinals (18 September 1227) brought the number to 19. Three of these were to become pope: Goffredo Castiglioni (CELESTINE IV), Sinibaldo Fieschi (INNOCENT IV), and Rinaldo of Ienne (ALEXANDER IV), the latter after a relatively important curial career. Gregory IX paid particular attention to individuals from Rome (R. Annibaldi and Barthelemy, for example) and close relatives (Rinaldo of Ienne). The creation of non-Italian cardinals like John of Abbeville, Jacques de Vitry, and Robert of Somercotes, is evidence of Gregory's broad spiritual and intellectual interests.

During his papacy the "courts" or *familiae* of cardinals underwent considerable development. The Roman Curia saw its purview increased, especially in judicial matters. A cardinal's passing into the *familia* was henceforth an important springboard for a career in the Curia, for from Gregory IX's papacy on we see an increasing number of the cardinals' *famiglia* becoming bishops. New ties were thus formed between the central hierarchy and the various dioceses of Christianity. With the great attraction of a career in the Curia, the cardinals were able to rely on highly placed collaborators who often came from the great university centers (e.g., Paris and Bologna). The cultural life of the papal court was enriched. Sinibaldo Fieschi received Frederick Visconti, the future archbishop of Milan, as CHAPLAIN; James of Pecorara had in his service, Roger of Torrecuso who was the author of an important *Carmen miserabile super destructione regni Hungariae*, and Tedaldo Visconti, the future GREGORY X. The English cardinal Robert of Somercotes called on Richard of Fournival, the famous bibliophile and poet.

In his concern with making the corpus of canonical materials produced by the popes more accessible to universities and to practitioners of law, Gregory IX entrusted the Dominican Raymond of Peñafort with distilling previous collections into a new organic compilation. Soon referred to as the *Liber Extra*, it was sent to the universities of Bologna and Paris. Raymond of Peñafort had based his work on Bernard of Pavia's model of the *Breviarium Extravagantium*. Following the instructions given to him, he abridged the individual Decretals and dropped the list of facts, saving only those parts that were juridically essential (decisions and argumentations); 1,771 of the 1,971 chapters of the *Liber Extra* were created this way, 191 were derived from the registers of the first six years of Gregory IX's papacy, and only nine came from elsewhere. Gregory IX's bull *Rex Pacificus* noted formally that the *Liber Extra* would henceforth be the only canonical collection to be a legal source. Because of this, the *Liber Extra* marked the Roman Church's juridictional evolution considerably.

In a series of official letters published in April and May 1231, Gregory IX succeeded in guaranteeing the juridical survival of the young *studium* in Paris, which had been upset by the conflicts and disorder that had spurred most of the teachers and students to leave the kingdom's capital and take refuge in neighboring university cities (Angers, Orleans). The bull *Parens Scientiarum*, promulgated on 13 April 1231, was justly considered the Magna Carta of the university. Two teachers from Paris, William of Auxerre and Geoffroy of Poitiers, who stayed in the Lateran Palace in the spring of 1231, seem to have played a major role in its wording. The most important change concerned the chancellor's responsibilities to the bishop of Paris, who was thenceforth obliged to take an oath to grant the licentiate degrees in the arts and medicine faculties only to candidates who were judged worthy by the teachers. For the faculties of law and theology, which were even closer to the *magisterium*, the bull prescribed a more complex procedure that included an inquiry into the morals, knowledge, eloquence, and potential career of the candidates. There, too, the chancellor's rights of intervention were considerably reduced. After 1231, the discretionary power that the chancellor was still enjoying around the turn of the century had practically disappeared. Thanks to the unreserved support of the papacy, which in this case had used its prerogative of granting appeal in the matter of higher education, the Parisian teachers had won their battle for autonomy against the chancellor.

Upon the death of Gregory IX (1241), the College of Cardinals was divided due to the conflict between the papacy and Frederick II. To force the cardinals' hand, senator Matteo Rosso Orsini locked them up in the Roman palace of the Septizonium, a kind of fortress where a number of papal elections, like those of Innocent III (1198) and Gregory IX (1227) had previously taken place.

Agostino Paravicini Bagliani

Bibliography

Armstrong, R. J. "*Mira circa nos*. Gregory IX's view of Saint Francis of Assisi," *Laurentianum*, 25 (1984), 385–414.

Aubert, R. "Grégoire IX," DHGE, 21 (1986), 1437–38.

Bilan, P. *Storia di Gregorio IX e dei suoi tempi*, 3 vols., Modena, 1872–3.

Brem, E. *Papst Gregor IX., bis zum Beginn seines Pontifikats*, Heidelberg, 1911.

Felten, J. *Papst Gregor IX.*, Freiburg, 1886.

Golubovich, H. "Disputatio Latinorum et Graecorum seu Relatio apocrisarum Gregorii IX de gestis. . . ," *Archivum franciscanum historicum*, 12 (1919), 418–70.

Graefe, E. *Die Publizisik im letzten kampf zwischen kaiser Friedrich und Papst Gregor IX.*, Heidelberg, 1909.

Jackson, P. "The Crusade Against the Mongols," *Journal of Ecclesiastical History* 42 (1991), 1–18.

Kuttner, S. "Raymond of Peñafort as Editor: The Decretals and Constitutions of Gregory IX," *Bulletin of Medieval Canon Law*, 12 (1982), 65–80.

Les Registres de Grégoire IX, ed. L. Auvray, 3 vols., Paris, 1896–1908.

Levi, G. "Documenti ad illustrazione del registro del cardinale Ugolino d'Ostia legato apostolico in Toscana e Lombardia," *ASR*, 12 (1889), 241–326.

Maleczek, W. *Papst und Kardinalskolleg von 1191 bis 1216*, Vienna, 1984, 111–13.

Marchetti-Longhi, G. "Ricerche sulla famiglia di Gregorio IX," *Studi Gregoriani*, 2 (1947), 287–333.

Paravicini-Bagliani, A. *Cardinali di Curia e "familiae" cardinalizie dal 1227 al 1254*, 2 vols., Padua, 1972

(*Italia Sacra*, 18–19); "La storiografica pontificia nel secolo XIII," *Römische historische Mitteilungen*, 18 (1976), 45–54.

Poth, 680–939, 2,099–2,110, 2,136–37.

Roberg, B. "Gregor IX," *LexMA*, 4 (1987–9), 1671–2.

Schaller, H. M. "Die Antwort Gregors IX auf Petrus de Vinea I, 1," DA, 11 (1954), 140–65.

Selge, K. V. "Franz von Assisi und die römische Kurie," *Zeitschrift für Theologie und Kirche*, 67 (1970), 129–61.

Sibilia, S. *Gregorio IX (1227–1241)*, Milan, 1961.

Spence, R. "Pope Gregory IX and the Crusade on the Baltic," *Catholic Historical Review*, 69 (1983), 1–19.

Tautu, A. L. *Acta Honorii III et Gregorii IX*, Rome, 1950 (*Pontificia commissio ad redigendum codicem iuris canonici orientalis, Fontes*, III, 3).

Thouzeiller, C. "La légation en Lombardie du cardinal Hugolin, 1221," *RHE*, 45 (1950), 508–42.

GREGORY X. *Tebaldo (or Tedaldo) Visconti (b. Piacenza, 1210, d. Arezzo, 10 January 1276). Elected pope on 1 September 1271, crowned on 27 March 1272. Buried in Arezzo, beatified by Benedict XIV.*

Noble by birth and a relative of Cardinal Jacques Pecorara, the young Tebaldo Visconti was in the service of Cardinal James of Praeneste for several years. In 1245 he participated in preparations for the first COUNCIL of Lyon, and then studied in Paris between 1248 and 1252. Canon of Lyon and then archdeacon of Liège beginning in 1245 (he stayed in the principality from 1245 to 1265), he was in charge of missions both to Henry III of England and Pope ALEXANDER IV. After December 1265, he joined LEGATE Ottobono Fieschi in England. Invited by Louis IX to accompany him on a CRUSADE, he took up the cross and, left Paris for Brindisi at the end of December 1269. When he learned that the king of France had died in Tunisia, he decided to join Edward, the oldest son of the king of England, in Palestine, where he was continuing the crusade alone. Visconti disembarked in Acre in May or June 1271. It was there, on 23 October 1271, that he learned the news of his election to the Holy See; he would not return to VITERBO until 10 February 1272.

Visconti's election on 1 September 1271 ended the longest vacancy the Holy See had undergone, as it began with CLEMENT IV's death on 29 November 1268. The CARDINALS were seriously divided on what stance to take toward Charles of Anjou, who had profited from the interregnum by reestablishing his authority over the kingdom of Two Sicilies, having himself elected Roman senator for life, and subjugating Tuscany. One faction of cardinals sided with the Florentine Ottaviano degli Ubaldini, who wanted to break with the papacy's politics of entente vis-à-vis Charles of Anjou; the other supported the candidacy of one of the Orsinis, who wanted to maintain the pro-French stance of URBAN IV and Clement IV. Six cardinals, three from each group, were finally named to come up with a compromise candidate. The choice of Visconti, who was neither a priest nor a member of the SACRED COLLEGE, may have been influenced by the minister general of the FRANCISCAN order, Bonaventure. Whatever the case, it is noteworthy that Gregory X learned the news of his election in Acre. His primary objective was that of acting in such a manner that the expedition suspended in 1270 become an undertaking of all Christianity, since the Holy Land held an essential place in the pope's personal piety.

From the moment of his arrival in Viterbo, Gregory X concerned himself with the CANONIZATION dossier of Louis IX. After corresponding with the king's confessor, the DOMINICAN Geoffroy de Beaulieu, regarding Louis IX's religious practices, Gregory X entrusted his LEGATE in France, Simon de Brie, Cardinal of Santa Cecilia, to proceed with an official inquiry, the results of which would reach the CURIA on the day of the pope's death.

On 27 March, after being ordained as a priest on 19 March 1272, Visconti entered Rome, where he was consecrated and crowned. His major concerns could be seen from the earliest days of his papacy. On 31 March, he wrote to Edward of England, who was still in Acre, begging him to continue the defense of the Holy Land. The same day, he informed the archbishop of Sens of his intention to call a general council. In so doing, he was attempting to bring the Greeks back into the Latin Church, free the Holy Land, and correct the moral weaknesses of both the clergy and the populace. He reacted as it were against the actions of his predecessors, who were too wrapped up in matters that were strictly Italian while neglecting the government of the Church itself. This is why he prepared the council with attention to both method and details, and called on a diversity of personalities: the Franciscan Gilbert of Tournai, the master general of the Dominicans, Humbert the Roman, the bishop of Olmutz, and Bruno of Holstein-Schauenberg, each of whom submitted a report on Church reform. The Franciscan Jerome of Ascoli worked on the theological doctrines of the Greeks. Thomas Aquinas was called to the council because of his treatise "Against the Errors of the Greeks," but after leaving Naples in January 1274, he died en route on 7 March without reaching Lyon.

Chosen as the meeting place for this council (13 April 1273), the city on the Rhône offered the advantage of neutral territory, far from Angevin pressure; Pierre de Tarentaise's work for pacification of the archbishopric and the pope's having formerly been a canon in Lyon were further guarantees of success. The pope returned to Lyon between 5 and 9 November 1273. Before leaving Orvieto on 5 June, Gregory X proceeded to name five cardinals to vacant sees: Peter Juliani, called Peter of

Spain, the future Pope JOHN XXI, to that of Tusculum; Bonaventure of Bagnoregio, minister general of the Franciscans, to that of Albano; Vicedomini, the pope's nephew and archbishop of Aix-en-Provence, to that of Praeneste; Bertrand of St. Martin, archbishop of Arles and possibly a protégé of Charles of Anjou, to that of Sabina; and Peter of Tarentaise, the future INNOCENT V, to that of Ostia. This was an important series of promotions, one that included famous scholars and leaders of the mendicant orders, who were called upon to play substantial roles in the council.

The pope solemnly opened the second council of Lyon on 7 May, in the primatial cathedral of St. John, with more than a thousand prelates in attendance, among whom were two hundred bishops; James I of Aragon was the only sovereign present. The council lasted until 17 July 1274. Among its important measures should be noted the constitution *Zelus Fidei*, relating to the crusade, the ultimate objective of the pope's actions. Gregory financed it by establishing in each diocese, for a period of six years, a *decima* levied on church property. He also had a collection of the council's constitutions published on 1 November 1274 and sent to the UNIVERSITIES; it was announced by the ENCYCLICAL *Infras Criptas*. In it were questions relevant to the internal workings of the Church: the nomination of bishops, recruitment of clergy for parishes, the allocation of vacant benefices in the Roman court, the role and number of mendicant orders. The constitution *Ubi Periculum* should be mentioned in particular, since it was one of the most lasting of the council's measures. It regulated procedures for CONCLAVES and papal elections in order to avoid a new vacancy, requiring the cardinals to meet, at the very latest, ten days after the pope's death, in the city in which he died and without waiting for latecomers. Locked up in the papal palace with one servant, the cardinals were to be sequestered, with no communication with the outside. While they worked toward a resolution, their food would be progressively reduced: at the end of eight days they would be left with bread, wine, and water.

The other essential question occupying the council was that of the unification of the Latin and Greek Churches. Michael VIII Paleologus, after his reconquest of Constantinople, sought to consolidate his authority against the Holy Roman emperor and his ally Charles of Anjou. After convincing Louis IX of his willingness to assist the crusaders, he found an attentive listener in Gregory X, who seemed to understand his desire for rapprochement with the Roman Church in order to break his isolation. On 24 October 1272, Gregory officially invited him to participate in the council, provided he accept the doctrine of the Creed (thus, the addition of the *Filioque*), which was already presented to him in 1267, and that the Greeks accept Roman PRIMACY. The Greek delegation was received in Lyon on 24 June 1274, as Michael VIII had obtained recognition of both the primacy and the Creed from the Greek bishops. Unification of the two churches was announced on 29 June and officially promulgated on 6 July. From a diplomatic point of view, Michael VIII appears to have succeeded, since he obtained a one-year truce from Charles of Anjou, starting on 1 May 1275. But Michael had to face the division of his church and the whole of Greek society on the question of unification. The pope's death interrupted these demonstrations of trust, which had inclined his Greek adversaries toward conciliation.

Finally, the pope's reception of the Mongol delegation from Abaqa at the council should be noted. The Mongols offered to ally themselves with the Christians against the infidels, following a mission Gregory X had entrusted to the Polo brothers and the Dominican William of Tripoli to the great Kubla Khan. In matters relating to the Empire, after Richard of Cornwall's death on 2 April 1272 and the rejection of Alfonso of Castille, who was too closely connected to the GHIBELLINES, Gregory X threw his support to Rudolf of Habsburg, who was elected on 1 October 1273. He recognized Rudolf officially on 26 September 1274, after getting him to abandon all claims on Italy and to promise that he would respect the papacy's rights. Leaving Lyon in late April 1275 for Beaucaire, where in May he met Alfonso of Castille to get him to give up his claims (which would be done the following September), the pope reached Lausanne, where he consulted with Rudolf (18–20 October) regarding his going to Rome for the imperial CORONATION and the restoration of the Romagnas. After leaving Lausanne, on his way back to Rome, Gregory X died in Arezzo (where he is buried), on 10 January 1276.

Gregory X broke with the Angevine politics of his predecessors. By linking success in the crusade to the resolution of the Greek problem, he made unification of the churches possible at the time of the council. This put off, *ipso facto*, any expedition against Constantinople. Likewise, by favoring restoration of imperial power, even if it was based in Germany, he sought to counterbalance the king of Sicily's influence in northern Italy. It is nevertheless true that his objective in Italy was to keep the Ghibelline party from gaining power, at any cost. He thus renewed Clement IV's sentences against the cities that supported Conradin (Verona, Pavia, Pisa, and Siena), in April 1272; and in July 1273 he imposed a draconian treaty on the Florentine Ghibellines, who were kept in exile and subordinated to Charles of Anjou. He would end up excommunicating the GUELPHS of Florence and maintaining the sanctions brought against Pisa and Siena, but he discreetly supported Charles of Anjou in Lombardy by sending his nephew Vicedomini to settle points of contention in his favor.

Gregory X's papacy may be considered as a period of spiritual recovery, one that was favored by relative stability in Italy's political situation and in the pope's personal authority, which was unanimously respected. It was, in a sense, an apogee of the papacy that occurred late in the 13th century.

Ghislain Brunel

Bibliography

1274, année charnière: mutations et continuités, Lyon-Paris, 30 septembre–5 octobre 1974, Colloques internationaux du CNRS, 558, Paris, 1977.

Aubert, R. "Grégoire X," *DHGE*, 21 (1986), 1438–9.

Barbiche, B. *Les Actes pontificaux originaux des Archives nationales de Paris, II:* 1261–1304, Vatican City, 1978 (nos. 1460–1559).

Clerval, A. "Grégoire X," *DTC*, 6–2 (1924), 1806–7.

Gatto, L. *Il pontificato di Gregorio X*, Rome, 1959.

Guiraud, J., and Cadier, L. *Les Registres de Grégoire X et de Jean XXI*, Paris, 1892–1960 (BEFAR).

Laurent, M. H. "Grégoire X et Marco Polo (1269–71)," *MAH*, 58 (1941–6), 132–44; *Le Bienheureux Innocent V (Pierre de Tarentaise) et son temps*, Vatican, 1947 (*Studi e testi*, 129).

Roberg, B. "Gregor X.," *LexMA*, 4 (1989), 1672–3.

Vernet F., and Grumel, V. "Lyon (IIe concile oecuménique de)," *DTC*, 9–1 (1926), 1374–1410.

Walter, H., and Holstein, H. *Lyon I et Lyon II*, Paris, 1966.

GREGORY XI. (*b. Pierre Roger Rosiers d'Égletons, Limousin, ca. 1330, d. Rome, during the night of 27 to 27 March 1378). Elected 30 December 1370, crowned 5 January 1371. Buried in Santa Maria Nova in Rome.*

In his funeral oration for URBAN V, Cardinal Guy of Bologne wished for "a pontiff to put those things that have been changed for no reason back into their original state, one who might make innovations disappear. . . , who might not make too many presumptions about himself and who would willingly listen to good advice." Despite the favorable opinion of Msgr. Mollat, this portrait corresponds to a certain extent to Gregory XI, if we make an exception for the steadfastness with which he undertook the plan to return to Rome. He was chosen the day after the CONCLAVE of cardinals began. He was ordained the day before his CORONATION; up to that time he had put off becoming a priest. He was the son of William Roger, later count of Beaufort and elder brother of Pope CLEMENT VI. Made cardinal deacon of Santa Maria Nova by his uncle on 29 May 1348, he spent several years in Perugia studying law. He was showered with BENEFICES, holding at least eighteen archdiaconates at the time of his accession to the papacy. His contemporaries praised his piety, modesty, goodness, and prudence, although these bordered on weakness and equivocation, perhaps because of his fragile health. He endowed his large family with sizeable pieces of property, especially in the Comtat Venaissin. He restored the status of the SACRED COLLEGE and created twenty-one CARDINALS in two promotions (among them were at least two family members and a number of old family friends), assuring a preponderance of native Limousins. Returning, albeit more moderately, to the traditional politics of Clement VI, he assured them that they would enjoy a number of benefices, assigning to each of the twelve cardinals named the first year 4,000 florins in revenues, to be divided up among two or three ecclesiastical provinces.

He weakened the reformist policies that Urban V had wanted to apply, even though he did resume the fight against HERESY in Dauphiné, Germany, Spain (with the inquisitor Nicolas Eymerich), and Sicily. He also supported the rebuilding of the hospital of St. John of Jerusalem and the restoration of the Friar Preachers. He maintained, and even emphasized, centralization in matters of benefices through the practice of reservations, and he frequently returned to measures imposed by his predecessors to fight against the avidity of clerics. Judging by the first study (still in progress) of his general correspondence, he appears to have received supplicants with great benevolence, frequently allowing them to hold more than one office at the same time. Church revenues, it is true, had diminished considerably because of both wars and general poverty.

Gregory XI struggled to bring schismatics back to the Catholic faith by sending DOMINICAN MISSIONARIES to Armenia and FRANCISCANS to Bosnia, and by establishing new episcopal sees in northeastern Europe; when faced with the Turkish threat on Greece, he made an appeal to the king of Hungary.

He took an active role in international diplomacy with the assistance of his LEGATES and his NUNCIOS. He sent Cardinal Guy of Boulogne (1372) to Spain, where a conflict pitted the kings of Aragon, Castille, and Portugal against one another. However, Peter the Ceremonious, king of Aragon, did not give up his territorial claims over Castille until 1375, and despite protests from the pope, he retained a rather nonchalant attitude regarding Church liberties. In England there were a number of causes for friction: competition between beneficiaries of apostolic favors and the king's candidates, a dispute over the competence of the pope's tribunal, and resistance to the system of papal taxation: Gregory XI showed himself to be conciliatory, although the problems remained unresolved. Hostilities had again arisen between France and England. More than the negotiations with sovereigns by cardinals Simon of Langham and Jean de Dromans (1371) and by the bishop of Carpentras and the vicount of Turenne in Bruges (1372), it was sheer exhaustion that gave rise to the truces in Moissac (1374) and Bruges (1375). Charles V used these talks as an excuse for keeping Gregory XI in AVIGNON.

Gregory XI's reign saw the end to hostilities between the kingdom of Naples and the Aragonese occupier of the island of Sicily. After the pope's rejection of an initial plan (1372), an accord was ratified in Aversa (1373). Frederick III, recognized as king of Trinacria, accepted the sovereignty of the pope and Queen Joanna. The negotiator, Jean de Réveillon, bishop of Sarlat, and a new nuncio, Bertrand du Masel, worked to gradually lift the prohibition that had hung over the island for nearly a century and to reestablish, albeit not very effectively, the papal tax system.

In the northern part of the peninsula war was not long in resuming because of the extreme measures of Bernabo and Galeazzo Visconti, lords of Milan, who in 1371 were already occupying the marquis of Este's lands and threatening the Church's possessions. Gregory XI attempted to isolate them by forming alliances with the count of Savoy, the marquis of Montferrat and Este, the lords of Carrarra, Galeotto of Malatesta, the queen of Naples, and the king of Hungary. He had mercenaries recruited who accepted as leaders, in addition to Nicolas of Beaufort and Raymond of Turenne (the pope's brother and nephew), captains like John Hawkwood and Enguerrand of Coucy. He granted INDULGENCES to soldiers who fell in the service to the Church. The Visconti, condemned by Gregory XI in September 1372, were declared perjurers and stripped of their rank of chevalier in March 1373. After the defeat of their troops by the papal armies in the Piedmont in 1373 and Lombardy in 1374, truces were drawn up in Bologna (June 1375), restoring relations with Bernabo.

The success of the papacy and the growing strength of the PAPAL STATES worried the Tuscan cities, particularly Florence. During the great famine of 1374, Florence was refused wheat exports from the PATRIMONY by the abbot of Marmoutier, the pope's vicar general, contrary to Gregory XI's advice. Officers of the papal administration were often abhorred for their greediness and abuses, and, once peace was concluded, hoodlums threatened Tuscany. Florence took advantage of the general discontent to call for a fight for freedom; rebellion broke out even in the Papal States, where there was discontent with the administration of the legates. Gregory XI summoned the Florentines to appear before him, and an interdict was proclaimed (1376). Their nationals were banished from Avignon and their goods confiscated. The Breton troops of Sylvester Budes were sent in under the leadership of Cardinal Robert of Geneva, which led to the massacres of Cesena (1377) and Bolsena. The Florentine government of the Otto Santis had to acccept Bernabo Visconti's mediation, and peace negotiations were opened in Sarzana, in which ambassadors of the emperor, the kings of France, Hungary, and Spain, and Queen Joanna participated.

Meanwhile, the papal court had left Avignon for Italy. In February 1374, Gregory XI had in fact announced in the CONSISTORY his intention to return to Rome. His departure, set for the fall of 1374 or early in 1375, was delayed by the length of the Franco-English negotiations and the hostilities in Italy. Catherine of SIENA's letters and her visit to Avignon in June 1376 may have strengthened the pope's resolve, following a period of inaction. Leaving Avignon on 13 September 1376, Gregory XI embarked in Marseille on 2 October and after four months of difficult travel, during which he endured a number of storms, he reached Rome via the Tiber on 17 January 1377.

The situation nonetheless did not improve: money was in short supply and taxes (*decima* and charitable subsidies) were not coming in regularly. Short term measures had to be taken and loans contracted especially with the duke of Anjou. When he died in March 1378, Gregory XI left the Church in a difficult situation.

Anne-Marie Hayez

Bibliography

Alessandrini, A. "Il ritorno dei papi di Avignone e Sta Caterina da Siena," *ASR*, 56–57 (1933–34) 1–132.

Baluze, E. *Vitae paparum Avenionensium*, ed. G. Mollat, I, Paris, 1914, 415–67.

Clerval, A. "Grégoire XI," *DTC*, 6 (1914), 1807–8.

Davies, R. C. "The Anglo-Papal Concordat of Bruges, 1375," *AHP*, 19 (1981) 97–146.

Dupre-Theseider, E. *I papi d'Avignone e la questione romana*, Florence 1939, 157–227.

Dykmans, M. "La bulle de Grégoire XI à la veille du Grand Schisme," *MEFRM*, 89 (1977), 485–95.

Genése et débuts du Grand Schisme d'Occident, Avignon 25–28 September 1978, Paris 1980.

Glenisson, J. "La question des blés dans les provinces italiennes de l'État pontifical en 1374–1375," *Le Moyen Âge*, 1951, 303–26.

Guillemain, B. *La Cour pontificale d'Avignon*, Paris, 1962.

Hayez, A. M. "D'Urbain V à Grégoire XI: un dangereux retour au passé?" *L'écrit dans la société médiévale. Textes en hommage à Lucie Fossier*, Paris, 1991, 151–164.

Hayez, A. M. "Un codicille de Grégoire XI," *Bibl. de l'École des chartes*, 136 (1968), 223–30.

Lettres (intéressant la Belgique), ed. C. Tihon, Rome-Brussels 1958–75 (*Analecta Vaticano-Belgica*, 11, 20, 25, 28.

Lettres secrètes et curiales intéressant les pays autres que la France, ed. G. Mollat, Paris, 1962–65, (BEFAR, 3e série).

Lettres secrètes et curiales relatives à la France, ed. L. Mirot, H. Jassemin, J. Vielliard, G. Mollat, E., and R. LaBande, Paris, 1935–57 (3e série).

Mirot, L. *La Politique pontificale et le retour du Saint-Siège à Rome en 1376*, Paris, 1899.

Mollat, G. "Grégoire XI et sa légende," *RHE*, 49 (1954) 837–77; "Grégoire XI et les frères mineurs," *Archivum franciscanum historicum*, 56 (1963) 463–66; *Les Papes d'Avignon*, 10th ed., Paris, 1964, 130–42 (bibliography); "Grégoire XI et la péninsule Ibérique," *Journal des Savants*, 1964, 255–60.

Ronzy, P. *Le Voyage de Grégoire XI . . . suivi du texte latin et de la traduction française de l'Itinerarum Gregorii XI de Pierre Ameilh*, Florence, 1952 (*Publ. de l'Inst. français de Florence*).

Schimidinger, H. "Die Rückkehr Gregors XI. nach Rom in den Berichten des Cristoforus von Piacenza," *Ecclesia peregrinans. Josef Lenzenweger zum 70. Geburtstag. . .* , Vienna, 1986, 133–41.

Thibault, P. R. *Pope Gregory XI: The Failure of Tradition*, Lanham, Md., 1986; "Pope Gregory XI (1370–1378) and the Crusade," *Canadian Journal of History*, 20 (1985) 313–35.

GREGORY XII. *Angelo Correr (Venice, ca. 1335–45, d. Recanati, 18 October 1417). Elected 30 November 1406, crowned 19 December. Buried in the Recanati cathedral.*

The first Venetian pope, Correr was professor of theology (1377); canon of Coron (1377); bishop of Castello in Venice (1380); patriarch of Constantinople (1390); titulary of Coron (1395); Negropont, and Crete (1407); apostolic COLLECTOR in the provinces of Aquilea, Zara, Split, Dubrovnik, and Bar (21 July 1387); and nuncio in Naples (1399). He spent a number of years in the CURIA, and was named *referendarius assistens* by INNOCENT VII; rector (4 April 1405) and then LEGATE for the March of Ancona; and finally, cardinal priest of San Marco (12 June 1405). Upon the death of Innocent VII there were two opposing factions tendencies in the SACRED COLLEGE. One wanted to defer the election and attempt to end the Great SCHISM by putting BENEDICT XIII's promises of abdication to the test. The other advocated an immediate election, fearing troubles in Rome should there be a long vacancy, and possible intervention by Ladislas of Anjou-Durazzo, king of Naples, who was resolutely opposed to unification efforts and ever ready to encroach upon the PAPAL STATE. The kingdom of Naples was in effect claimed by Louis II of Anjou, cousin to Charles VI of France. Ladislas feared that the prevailing French influence in the new election might produce a pontiff favorable to his rival. It was decided that no more time should be lost; fourteen cardinals entered into conclave on the evening of 18 November 1406. In five days they fine-tuned a joint declaration: each solemnly promised, if he was elected, to give up his papal office if and when his competitor did likewise, provided that the two colleges of cardinals would unite for a common election; strict deadlines were foreseen. The future papal candidate should thus stand out by virtue of his zeal for unification.

After seven fruitless days, Cardinal Caetani proposed Angelo Correr, a pious, astere, and erudite man who had led an irreproachable life and was already well along in years. Elected unanimously, he took the name Gregory XII in honor of the pontiff who had brought the papacy back to Rome. The following day he renewed the commitment made in the CONCLAVE, and repeated it once more during his first public CONSISTORY. At the time the domain of the Roman papacy—which was almost unchanged from the time of Urban VI—included the empire (with local exceptions), England, Hungary, Bohemia, Poland, Scandinavia, and a good part of Italy—especially the republics of Florence and Venice and the kingdom of Naples. Genoa and Liguria had been lost under BONIFACE IX. The Urbanist positions in Flanders had also been weakened, as was likewise the case in Liege. The power of the papacy was at a low point: the HOLY SEE's vassals had gained considerable independence, and the state of its finances was deplorable. The tremendous cost of maintaining mercenaries, along with papal COURT's expenses, continually depleted the treasury. The APOSTOLIC CAMERA, directed by two of the pope's nephews, Antonio Correr (1407) and Gabriele Condulmer (1408), needed to seek funds from all available sources.

Starting on 10 December, Gregory XII and his cardinals addressed appeals to Benedict XIII and the rest of the Christian world, full of enthusiasm and hope that the end of the schism was at hand. Unfortunately, the future would reveal that Gregory XII's moral virtues were darkened by corresponding defects: stubbornness, indecision, dependence on his entourage, and a senile weakening of mental acuity, with a tendency toward vanity and flagrant nepotism. Over the objection of his cardinals, on 26 February 1407 Gregory XII insisted on naming his nephew Antonio Correr (soon to be bishop of Bologna and CAMERLINGO) to head a delegation to Benedict XIII, with Bishop William of Todi and the physician Antonio De Sutrio; the choice seemed ill-timed, and for good reason. The envoys left Rome on 18 or 19 March 1407 and were received in a first solemn audience in Marseille on 3 April. Negotiations were difficult, with each party proposing meeting places in territory occupied by its own supporters. Finally, Antonio Correr surprisingly accepted an Avignon proposal, and the agreement was concluded on 21 April. The two popes were to meet in Savona before the feast of St. Michael (29 September) or, at the very latest, before All Saints Day in 1407 in order to debate the question of bilateral withdrawal.

Numerous and minute stipulations relating to security gave evidence of mutual distrust. It was a diplomatic victory for Benedict XIII: Savona was a city that supported him, in Genoan territory, which at the time was under French domination. The need to arrange for ships for transportation and security was a large responsibility for Gregory XII. In June, Genoan ambassadors offered him their galleys and every possible guarantee; the pope appeared to accept (on the 11th of the month). He was favorable to assurances provided by Savona on the 13th. In July, however, he told a delegation from Avignon that he could not go to Savona and that another location had to be chosen. From that point on, Gregory XII kept coming up with new obstacles and making evasive moves. He refused the Genoan galleys and tried, in vain, to find some in Venice. The decisive role played by France stirred up hostile powers (like the kings of Hungary and Naples, and the republic of Venice) to exert pressure on Gregory XII to dissuade him from fulfilling the agreement. Their influence, combined with that of his entourage and relatives, could not help but act on an elderly man with a wavering will. Caving in to the pleas of the partisans of union, Gregory XII left Rome on 9 August 1407 with the Curia and the Sacred College, via VITERBO (11–31 August), and went to Siena (4 September 1407–22 January 1408), before continuing on to Lucca (28 January).

For his part, Benedict XIII knowing it to be his advantage arrived in Savona on 24 September. Difficult negotiations were undertaken to find another meeting place, and a number of Italian cities were considered. Benedict XIII went as far as Sarzana, while Gregory XII finally agreed to go to Pisa (1 April). Despite this geographical rapprochement, the encounter never did take place. The growing discontent of the cardinals at Gregory XII's hesitations and equivocation was exacerbated by his plan to create new cardinals. On 9 May 1408 he named four, two of whom were his nephews. Meanwhile, in Lucca, the Florentine diplomats were discreetly encouraging secession. On 11 May, several cardinals left Lucca and traveled to Pisa, on Florentine soil. The split with Gregory XII was soon total. The nine dissidents entered into contact with their colleagues from Avignon. The coalition of the two clans ended up leading to a convocation of a general COUNCIL (without the intervention of either pope), to open in Pisa on 25 March 1409. Its primary result, after the deposition of Benedict XIII and Gregory XII, was the election of a new pontiff, ALEXANDER V (26 June) whom France, England, some Italian states (especially Florence and Venice), and even the king of the Romans and a large portion of the empire immediately supported.

Gregory XII, meanwhile, had to leave Lucca (14 July) to go to Siena (19 July–3 November), and then Rimini, with only five cardinals. In September 1408 he strengthened the Sacred College through the promotion of nine cardinals, but his support crumbled away. He tried to curb the Pisan movement and called a council himself, in Cividale del Friuli, which opened on 26 May 1409. Despite the presence of delegates from the king of the Romans and the king of Naples, the council was poorly attended and produced no concrete results. The eighth and last session was held on 5 September. Gregory XII had long been worried about both his own personal safety and that of his property because of the hostile attitude of the patriarch Antonius of Aquliea. In August, he had already considered a secret departure and entrusted members of his family with some of the decorations from the pontifical CHAPEL. He left Cividale, during the night after the final session; after an adventurous flight he managed to reach the coastline, where a ship sent by King Ladislas, to whom he had appealed, awaited him. He traveled by sea to Pescara, and, he arriving in Gaeta via Sulmona and San Germano at the end of November 1409. There, close surveillance by Ladislas reduced him to semicaptivity. This asylum would soon be less than satisfactory to him. The struggle for the throne of Naples continued between Ladislas and Louis II of Anjou, who was supported by the Pisan party.

In the meantime, Alexander V had died and been replaced by the bellicose JOHN XXIII (25 May 1410). Military action came to an end with the defeat of Ladislas in Roccasecca (19 May 1411), but Anjou did not know how to take advantage of this victory. With encouragement from Florentine diplomats, a reconciliation took place between John XXIII and Ladislas. The latter recognized the Pisan pope (12 May and 16 October 1412), abandoning Gregory XII, who thus lost his last important political support on the peninsula. On 30 October he left Gaeta by sea and, after a perilous journey through the Strait of Messina, he reached Cesenatico on 22 December and on 24 December 1412 entered Rimini, where he enjoyed the hospitality of Carlo Malatesta, his only devoted friend. Through the efforts of the king of the Romans, Sigismund of Luxemburg, the plan for a general council finally took shape. It was to take place in Constance in late October 1414, according to a bull by John XXIII on 9 December 1413. Gregory XII was not invited until 30 July, and he agreed to send two delegates (cardinal Johannes Dominici and John Contarini, patriarch of Constantinople), both of whom had merit in the king's eyes.

The council opened on 5 November 1414 and the delegates of the nations gradually arrived. The primary German representatives who were followers of Gregory, led by the palatine Louis, did not make an appearance until 17 January 1415. Action on the part of the king of the Romans and the non-Italian nations finally led to the flight and the DEPOSITION of John XXIII (29 April 1415). Meanwhile in Rimini, Gregory XII decided to give up his papal office—probably under the influence of Malatesta and his German partisans. Decisive bulls were written between 10 and 13 March. He named Malatesta as his procurator and gave full power to his delegates in Constance to authorize and convene the council in his name. Seeing the proximity of the goal he had so long pursued, the assembly made this concession to him. Thus, on 4 July 1415

(the 14th session solemnly presided over by the king of the Romans), Johannes Dominici officially recognized the council while Malatesta read Gregory XII's act of abdication. The two factions proclaimed themselves united. The council conferred the title of cardinal bishop of Porto on Gregory XII, ranking first just after the pope, and named him legate for life to the March of Ancona. On the evening of 19 July Gregory XII, who had left a PLAGUE-stricken Rimini on 4 June to go to Castello Montefiori, learned of the events of 4 July. The following day he convened his final consistory, took off his papal insignia, and donned the cardinal's habit in joyful resignation and perfect dignity. His cardinals and curialists soon took the road to Constance. In January 1416 he began his residence in Recanati, where he died on 18 October 1417, and where his tomb is located.

Micheline Soenen

Bibliography

Erler, G. *Dietrich von Nieheim. Sein leben und seine Schriften*, Leipzig, 1887.

Erler, G. "Florenz, Neapel und das päpstliche Schisma," *Historisches Taschenbuch*, 8 (1889), 179–230.

Esch, E. *Bonifaz IX. und der Kirchenstaat*, Tübingen, 1969. *Bibliothek des Deutschen historischen Instituts in Rom*, 29.

Eubel, K. "Das Itinerar der Päpste zur Zeit des grossen Schismas," *Historisches Jahrbuch*, 16 (1895), 545–64; "Die "Provisiones Praelatorum" durch Gregor XII. nach Mitte Mai 1408," *Römische Quartalschrift*, 10 (1896), 99–131.

Finke, H. "Eine Papstcronik des XV. Jahrhunderts," *Römische Quartalschrift*, 4 (1890), 340–62.

Fliche-Martin, XIV, Paris, 1962.

Frenken, A. "Gregor XII.," *LexMA*, 4 (1989), 1674–5.

Girgensohn, D. "Kardinal Antonio Caetani und Gregor XII in den Jahren 1406–1408," *QFIAB*, 64 (1984), 11–226; "Venezia e il primo Veneziano sulla cattedra di S. Pietro: Gregorio XII (Angelo Correr), 1406–1415," *Centro Tedesco di Studi Veneziani Quaderni* 30 (1985), 3–32; *DHGE*, 21 (1986), 21, 1440–1.

Hollerbach, J. "Die Gregorianische Partei, Sigismund und das Konstanzer Konzil," *Römische Quartalschrift*, 23 (1909), 129–64; 24 (1910), 3–39; 120–40.

Izbicki, T. "Papalist Reaction to the Council of Constance: Juan de Torquemada to the Present," *Church History* 55 (1980), 7–20.

Lettres de Grégoire XII (1406–1415) [concerning Belgium], ed. M. Soenen, Brussels-Rome, 1976 (*Analecta Vaticano-Belgica*, 30, Documents relatifs au Grand Schisme, 9).

Lisini, A. "Papa Gregorio XII e i Senesi," *La Rassegna Nazionale*, 1896, 97–117; 280–321.

Meister, A. "Das Konzil zu Cividale im Jahre 1409," *Historisches Jahrbuch*, 14 (1893), 320–30.

Mercati, A. "La biblioteca privata e gli arredi di cappella de Gregorio XII," *Miscellanea Francesco Ehrle*, V: Biblioteca ed Archivio Vaticano, Bibliotece diverse (Studi e Testi, 41), Rome, 1924, 128–65.

Mercati, A. "Una fonte poco nota per la storia di Gregorio XII," *ASR*, 50 (1927) 231–38.

Petersohn, J. "Papst Gregors XII. Flucht aus Cividale (1409) und die Sicherstellung des päpstlichen Paramentschatzes," *Römische Quartalschrift*, 58 (1963), 51–70.

Piva, E. "Venezia e lo scisma durante il pontificato di Gregorio XII (1406–1409)," *Nuovo Archivio Veneto*, 13 (1897), 135–58.

Raffaelli, F. *Il monumento di papa Gregorio XII ed i suoi donativi alla cattedrale basilica di Recanati*, Fermo, 1877.

Re, E. "Il tesoro" di Gregorio XII e la sua divisione," *Atti e memorie della Reale Deputazione di Storia patria per le Marche*, III, 1, 1916.

Salembier, L. *Le Grand Schisme d'Occident*, Paris, 1900.

Sauerland, H. V. "Cardinal Johann Dominici und sein Verhalten zu den kirchlichen Unionsbetrebungen während des Jahre 1406–1415," *ZKG*, 9 (1888), 242–92; 10 (1889), 345–98.

Sauerland, H. V. "Gregor XII. von seiner Wahl bis zum Vertrage von Marseille (30 Ap. 1407)," *HZ*, 34 (1875), 74–120.

Schlitz, L. "Die Quellen zur Geschichte des Konzils von Cividale 1409," *Römische Quartalschrift*, 8 (1894), 217–59.

Theod. de Nyem de scismate libri tres, ed. G. Erler, Leipzig, 1890.

Tihon, C. "Les expectatives in forma pauperum de Grégoire XII," *BIHBR*, 6 (1926), 7–101.

Valois, N. *La France et le Grand Schisme d'Occident*, III, Paris, 1901; IV, Paris, 1902.

Zanutto, L. *Itinerario del pontefice Gregorio XII da Roma (9 ag. 1407) a Cividale del Friuli (26 mag. 1409). Studio storico*, Udine, 1901.

GREGORY XIII. *Ugo Boncompagni (b. Bologna, 1 January 1502, d. Rome, 10 April 1585). Buried in St. Peter's in Rome.*

Ugo's father, Cristoforo, was a well-to-do merchant who had married Angela Marescalchi. After getting his diploma *in utroque jure*, he taught at the university in his native city from 1531 to 1539. He then went to Rome where he was given his first responsibilities in the Curia. In 1546, he was named drafter of papal briefs for the Council of TRENT.

Despite his undeniable abilities, his broad juridical knowledge, and his reserved character, he was no stranger to the spirit and morals of the Renaissance, nor to the temptations of the world. Evidence of this is seen in the disconcerting incident of the birth in 1548 of a natural son, whom he had by a girl while he was still a simple cleric. He acknowledged that he had acted deliberately, with the intention of having an heir to his possessions.

The incident had no negative consequences on his future ecclesiastical career, especially since, in the following years, he led a disciplined life and began to make himself known for his irreproachable conduct. This explains the favor he enjoyed with the austere PAUL IV who in January 1556 appointed him to the general commission responsible for Church reform. The same year Boncompagni accompanied the CARDINAL NEPHEW Carlo Carafa on his legation to France and to the court of Philip II, who was living in Brussels at the time.

He was named bishop of Viesti on 20 July 1558 and in that position played an active role in the last part of the Council of Trent, from 1561 to 1563. On 12 March 1565, in recognition of services rendered, PIUS IV named him cardinal. A few months later, he sent Boncompagni as a LEGATE, a role in which he had occasion to be recognized and appreciated by Philip II. Upon his return to Madrid after the death of PIUS IV, which took place on 9 December 1565, Pius IV's successor, PIUS V, named him to head the secretariat of BRIEFS. After the death of Pius V, and with the support of Spain, Cardinal Boncompagni was elected pope in a CONCLAVE that lasted less than twenty-four hours. He took the name Gregory XIII.

The pontiff's actions in the political and ecclesiastical arenas were not always crowned with success. His attempts to form an anti-Turkish alliance among the Catholic powers would fail after the republic of Venice, in 1573, and Spain, in 1581, made separate peace treaties with the Ottoman leadership. The pope's efforts to combat Protestantism also met with failures. In France, even though the Huguenot massacre known as the Massacre of St. Bartholomew (24 August 1572) was celebrated by the pope (who had no knowledge of what was happening behind the scenes) as a victory of the Church over heretics, the Calvinists still held their positions. The pope's political maneuvers against Elizabeth I of England would have no better results. All hopes of seeing her overthrown with the help of Irish Catholics had to be abandoned after two successive attempts at invasion in 1578 and 1579 failed. Initial success in Sweden, with the secret conversion of John III Wasa, also ended in failure, since Gregory XIII did not accept the sovereign's requests, especially concerning the marriage of clerics, the invocation of the saints, and communion under both species. So John III returned to Lutheranism.

In other areas, the Holy See's politics did meet with some success. The support given to Philip II in his battle against rebels in the Low Countries saw the reestablishment of Spanish sovereignty over the southern provinces (Peace of Arras, 17 May 1579). Other successes were registered in the empire, in part because of the dispatch of papal legates to the imperial diets of 1576 and 1582. In Poland, papal recognition in the contested election of king Stephen I Bathory appeared to be decisive for the country's definitive return to Catholicism.

It was in the area of religion that Gregory XIII's work was of fundamental importance in the application of the reforms decided by the Council of Trent. From the earliest part of his papacy, the pope worked to get council decrees applied universally. In Italy, starting in 1573, he established a systematic program of apostolic visits in the Church provinces of the northern and central sections of the peninsula. Although he was aware of the diversity in local situations, he undertook similar actions elsewhere through apostolic nuncios like G. F. Bonomi in the Catholic cantons and F. Ninguarda in lower Austria and the Tyrol. Where Catholic positions were threatened by Protestantism, he used more subtle methods: in 1583, to keep the archbishopric of Cologne from falling into Lutheran hands, he accepted the election of Ernest of Bavaria, even though he had already accumulated four other DIOCESES.

In order to apply his program of spiritual regeneration, Gregory XIII used the new religious orders, especially the Jesuits and the Capuchins. He did not fail to take an interest in the other religious orders. He imposed reform measures on orders that needed them, like the Italian Valombrosians and the Trinitarians in Spain and Portugal. In 1580 he confirmed the reform of the Discalced Carmelites that Teresa of Avila had begun; and, in 1575, he approved the foundation of the congregation of the Oratory of St. Philip Neri.

The pope gave great importance to the training of the clergy. He created a number of COLLEGES, especially in Rome, including, for example, in 1579, the English College, or the Greek College of Sant' Anastasio, the Maronite College, and the Armenian College for the training of Catholic clergy in the Eastern rite. Thanks to Gregory XIII, Rome became the veritable center of ecclesiastical studies and the privileged place for the preparation of future priests. He was so generous in allocating buildings and subsidies for the Roman College of the Society of Jesus in particular that he has been considered the second founder of the university, which today is still called the Gregorian UNIVERSITY.

The missionary activity of the religious orders, especially the JESUITS, received a tremendous impetus under Gregory XIII. He supplied considerable financial aid for the founding and upkeep of the seminaries in Arima and Ausukimono, as he did, likewise, for the new college of the Society of Jesus that was being built in Japan. In recognition of the good works of Jesuits on the Japanese islands and in nearby China (where Father Matteo Ricci had arrived in 1583), in addition to the numerous privileges he granted the Society, Gregory XIII reserved evangelization in that part of the world exclusively for the Je-

suits. The pope also lent his support to the Augustinians and the Franciscans in their missionary activities in the Philippines where, in 1579, he created the diocese of Manila. Nevertheless, it was not only in Asia that Gregory XIII favored missionary work, but also in Africa and Latin America (particularly Mexico and Peru), thus earning him the title "the missionary pope."

In addition to his commitment to promoting missionary expansion, Gregory XIII showed particular interest in the problem of reconnecting Rome to the schismatic churches of the East. Thus, in late 1577 and early 1578, the arrival of the principal representative of the Jacobite Syrian Church, the patriarch of Antioch Ignatius Na'-matallah, raised hope in the papal court for a possible reunion with Rome by the Monophysite Churches (especially the Copts and the Abyssinians, in addition to the Syrians). But the pope died before the talks bore fruit. Contacts between Czar Ivan IV ("the Terrible") led to a similar failure. Ivan request to Gregory XIII in 1581 to use his influence to help conclude peace between Moscow and Poland had led the pope to see the possibility of also reuniting the Russian Orthodox Church and Rome. Papal mediation led to an armistice agreement (15 January 1582), although it bore no fruit in the area of religion. If these efforts for ecumenical rapprochement led to no concrete results, they did at least give the Holy See a better understanding of the situation of the churches of Eastern Europe and the Middle East.

The role played by Gregory XIII in strengthening the central government of the Church was particularly significant. The tendency toward centralism, already outlined under Pius IV and Pius V, intensified during his papacy. He developed and consolidated the institution of apostolic nunciature, which served to help apply the reforms of the Council of Trent. Directly or indirectly, he was responsible for the creation of new nunciatures in Lucerne, Graz, southern Germany, and Flanders (although the latter was not officially created until the time of CLEMENT VIII).

Expansion of the authority of the Congregation of Cardinal Bishops, created by Pius V in 1572, should be considered from the same perspective, that of the centralization in Rome of decisions regarding the religious life of local churches. Within the space of a few years, the congregation held discussions on the most important problems related to the religious life of each diocese, especially those in Italy. A similar orientation was evident in measures to strengthen the congregation in Germany, or in the institution of a temporary cardinal congregation entrusted from 1578 to 1581, with the responsibility of dealing with Philip II's representatives to handle jurisdictional differences that had emerged in connection with Spanish possessions in Italy.

Other than political and religious issues, Gregory XIII entrusted to the member of the Oratory, (future cardinal)

Cesare Baronio, the composition of the new *Martyrologium Romanum* (which would not be published until 1586), and in 1582 he had published the *Corpus Juris Canonici*. The same year he reformed the Julian CALENDAR, after consulting with a number of learned individuals and forming a special commission presided over by the illustrious cardinal G. Sirleto. The new calendar, known as the Gregorian calendar, was promulgated on 24 Feburary 1582. Elimination of the days between 4 and 15 October that year eliminated the excess time that had accumulated since the preceding calculation.

Gregory XIII's intervention in Rome were also numerous in the areas of urban renewal and art. Some of these initiatives were taken looking forward to the HOLY YEAR of 1575, which the pope wanted to celebrate with particular solemnity. It was he who was responsible for the planning of Via Merulana and Via Gregoriana, the reconstruction of the Ponte Rotto entrusted to Matteo da Costello, the creation by Giacomo Della Porta of four fountains (among which were those placed on each end of Piazza Navona), and the beginnings of construction of the QUIRINAL PALACE. Beautification projects were begun in various sacred buildings, including the basilicas of ST. PETER (the Gregorian chapel, designed by Della Porta), St. John Lateran, and St. Mary Major, including St. Stefano Rotondo, where N. Circignani (known as il Pomarancio), Matteo da Siena, and others painted a cycle of thirty-four frescoes from the *Martyrologium*. Work was also undertaken in the Vatican, like the frescoes of the Sala Regia painted by Giorgio Vasari and Federico Zuccari, and those on the ceiling of the hall of Constantine and the gallery of geographical maps along the Belvedere Courtyard.

The money invested in public works, added to the general expenses of the papacy, were bound to have increased the Holy See's deficit. To the draining off of finances we should add the endemic banditry, against which measures taken by the pope were, for all intents and purposes, ineffective. Despite these failures and the setbacks experienced because of certain political and ecclesiastical questions, Gregory XIII's papacy remains of fundamental importance for the history of the Catholic restoration during the period following the Council of Trent.

Agostino Borromeo

Bibliography

Blet, P. *Histoire de la représentation diplomatique du Saint-Siège des origines à l'aube du XIXe siècle*, Vatican City, 1982 (*Collectanea Archivi Vaticani*, 9), 277 ff.

Borromeo, A. "Fonti vaticane riguardanti il cardinale Carlo Borromeo, arcivescovo di Milano: orientamenti per una ricerca," *Studia Borromaica*, 4 (1990), 49 g.

Borromeo, A. "San Carlo Borromeo, arcivescovo di Milano, e la Curia romana," *San Carlo e il suo tempo. Atti del convegno internazionale nel IV centenario della morte* (Milan, 21–26 May 1984), 2 vols., Rome 1986, I, 237–301.

Bues, A. *Die habsburgische Kandidatur für den polnischen Thron während des Ersten Interregnums in Polen 157–273*, Vienna 1984, 135 ff.

Cardinal Giulio Antonio Santoro and the Christian East: Santoro's Audiences and Consistorial Acts, published under the aegis of J. Krajcar, Rome, 1966 (*Orientalia Christiana Analecta*, 177), 20–81.

Carocci, G. *Lo Stato della Chiesa nella seconda metà del sec. XVI. Note e commenti*, Milan, 1961, *ad indicem*.

Catalano, G. "Controversie giurisdizionali tra Chiesa e Stato nell'età di Gregorio XIII e di Filippo II," *Atti dell'Accademia di Scienze, lettere ed Arti di Palermo 15*, part II (1954–55), 5–306.

Del Reguardati, F. M. "Il fenomeno del banditismo sotto Gregorio XIII (1572–1585) e Sisto V (1585–1590). Suoi riflessi sulla nobiltà," *Rivista Araldica* 85 (1987), 198–207.

Fernandez Collado, A. *Gregorio XIII y Felipe II en la nunciatura de Felipe Sega (1577–1581). Aspectos politicos, jurisdiccionales y de reforma*, Toledo, 1991.

Jacks, P. "A Sacred Meta for Pilgrims in the Holy Year 1575," *Architectura*, 30 (1989), 137–66.

Jacks, P. "Gregory XIII," *Dictionary of Art*.

Krasenbrinck, J. *Die Congregatio Germanica und die katholische Reform in Deutschland nach der Tridentinum*, Münster, 1972 (*Reformationsgeschichtliche Studien und Texte*, 105).

Levi Della Vida, G. *Documenti intorno alle relazioni delle Chiese orientali con la Santa Sede durante il pontificato di Gregorio XIII*, Vatican City, 1948 (*Studi e Testi*, 143).

Lukacs, L. *"Die nordlichen päpstlichen Seminarien und P. Possevino (1577–1587),"* *Archivium Historicum Societatis Iesu*, 24 (1955), 3394.

Pecchiai, P. "La nascita di Giacomo Boncompagni," *Archivi d'Italia e rassegna internazionale degli archivi*, II, 21 (1954), 9–47.

Pirri, P. "Gli Annali Gregoriani di Gian Pietro Maffei. Premesse storiche per una revisione critica," *Archivium Historicum Societatis Iesu*, 15 (1946), 56–97.

Polcin, S. *Une tentative d'Union au XVIe siècle: La mission religieuse du père Antoine Possevin s.j. en Moscovie (1581–1582)*, Rome, 1957 (Orientalia Christiana Analecta, 150), passim.

Prodi, P. "San Carlo Borromeo e la trattative tra Gregorio XIII e Filippo II sulla giurisdizione ecclesiastica," *Rivista di storia della Chiesa in Italia*, 11 (1957), 195–240.

Schellhass, K. "Wissenschaftliche Forschungen unter Gregor XIII. für die Neuausgabe des Gratianischen

Dekrets," in *Papsttum und Kaisertum, Forschungen zur Politischen Geschichte und Geisteskultur des Mittelalters Paul Kehr zum 65. Geburtstag dargebracht*, published by A. Brackmann, Munich 1926, 674–99.

Schiffmann, R. *Roma Felix. Aspekte der städtebaulichen Gestaltung Roms unter Papst Sixtus V.*, Berne 1985 (*Europäische Hochschulschriften—Reihe XVIII*, 36).

Stasiewski, B. *Reformation und Gegenreformation in Polen. Neue Forschungsergebnisse*, Münster, 1960 (*Katolisches Leben und Kämpfen im Zeitalter der Glaubens Spaltung, 18*), ad indicem.

Voci, A. M. "L'impresa d'Inghilterra nei dispacci del nunzio a Madrid Nicoló Ormanetto (1572–1577)," *Annuario dell'Istituto Storico Italiano per l'età moderna e comtemporanea* XXXV–XXXVI (1983–1984), 337–425.

Von Lojewski, G. *Bayerns Weg nach Köln. Geschichte der bayerischen Bistumspolitik in der zweiten Hälfte des 16. Jahrhunderts*, Bonn, 1962 (*Bonner Historische Forschungen*, 21).

Von Pastor, L. *Storia dei papi dalla fine del Medioevo*, Italian trans., IX, n. ed., Rome 1955.

Wright, A. D. *The Early Modern Papacy, From the Council of Trent to the French Revolution, 1564–1789*, London, 2000.

GREGORY XIV. *Niccolò Sfondrato (Milan (?), 11 February 1535, d. Rome, 15 October 1591). Elected pope 5 December 1590, crowned 8 December 1590. Buried in St. Peter's in Rome.*

Despite his zeal for reform, Gregory XIV's actions were hindered by illness, by his excessively meek personality, and especially by his lack of political experience. Related through his mother to the Visconti, Niccolò Sfondrato watched his father, a Milanese senator who entered the priesthood after becoming a widower and later became a CARDINAL, show him the path to an ecclesiastical career. After law studies in Perugia and Bologna, he embraced the ecclesiastical state and became bishop of Cremona in 1560. The first prelate to arrive in TRENT for the last session of the council, he participated actively in it. He favored the residence requirement for bishops (against Rome's advice but in agreement with Spain), and was also involved in the revision of the INDEX and the project to formulate a decree on marriage. When he returned to Cremona, he instituted the Tridentine decrees (promulgated in 1580 during a diocesan synod): diocesan visitations, creation of a seminary and introduction of Theatines and Barnabites. Pious and austere, he celebrated mass daily, fasted regularly, and devoted himself entirely to his responsibilities, even after Gregory XIII made him a cardinal (12 December 1583). The close relations he formed with Charles Borromeo, his metropolitan, and with Philip Neri, encouraged him on his path of reform. Upon the death of URBAN VII, the second conclave of 1590, which was dominated by Spanish pressure, just as the first had been, gave the vote to Niccolò Sfondrato, a pro-Spanish moderate, after two months.

Gregory XIV surrounded himself with men who favored Tridentine ideas: the Franciscan Panigarola, and especially his nephew Paolo Sfondrato, whom he made cardinal in an unsual promotion (19 December 1590). The pope attacked three evils hanging over the PAPAL STATE: robbery (he deflected robbers away from Rome and toward the kingdom of Naples); epidemics (he organized the companions of Camille de Lellis into a congregation); and the high cost and low availability of food (he worked to import grain, and he rationed bread). When he fell ill, the pope gradually transferred responsibilities to his nephew, authorizing him to use the *Fiat ut petitur* (cf. DATARY, PETITION). This drew opposition from the cardinals, who forced him to diminish these exceptional powers.

The religious struggles in France remained the pope's primary concern. Gregory XIV sent a new nuncio, Marsilio Landriano, to get the Catholics who supported Henry IV, not yet converted, to mend their ways and publish two letters denouncing him and inviting clerics and lay people to come back into the Church. With 300,000 of the 400,000 ecus taken from the treasury of CASTEL SANT'ANGELO, he formed an ARMY under the command of his nephew, Ercole Sfondrato. But the papal army, composed of Swiss citizens, disbanded even before it reached France.

Gregory XIV published a jubilee, confirmed the structure of the Society of Jesus, regulated the right to asylum in churches (BULL *Cum Alias*, 24 May 1591), regulated the procedures concerning information given to bishops (bull *Onus apostolicae servitutis*, 15 May 1591), completed the work of Sixtus V on the organization of Roman CONGREGATIONS, continued the correction of the Bible and the practice of PATRONAGE (the cupola of ST. PETER'S, the QUIRINAL, the Vatican), and supported Palestrina. His cardinal nominations went primarily to clerics who like him were attached to the idea of Catholic reform. Opposed to the cardinals on the matter of the succession of Ferrara, Gregory XIV became bed-redden in late September 1591 and died surrounded by prayers.

Anne-Cécile Tizon-Germe

Bibliography

Castano, D. L. *Gregorio XIV (Niccolo Sfondrato 1535–1591)*, 1957.

Cloulas, I. "L'armée pontificate de Grégoire XIV, Innocent IX et Clément VIII, pendant la seconde campagne en France d'Alexandre Farnèse (1591–1592)," *Bulletin de la commission royale d'histoire*, 126 (1960), 83–102.

Laurain-Portemer, M. "Absolutisme et népotisme, la surintendance de l'État ecclésiastique," *Bibliothèque de l'École des chartes*, 131 (1973), 487–567.

Moroni, G. *Dizionario di erudizione storico-ecclesiastica*, 32 (1845), 304–309.

Von Pastor, L. *Storia dei Papi*, X, Rome, 1928.

GREGORY XV. *(Alessandro Ludovisi (b. Bologna, 9 January 1554 d. Rome, 8 July 1623). Elected pope 9 February 1621, crowned 14 February. Buried in Sant'Ignazio.*

Although it was of short duration, Gregory XV's papacy nevertheless marked an important period of Catholic REFORM, a half century after the completion of the Council of TRENT: rules for CONCLAVES were set, the Congregation for the PROPAGATION of the FAITH was created, and the first saints of modern Christianity were CANONIZED. These milestones alone sufficed to perpetuate the memory of the pope who reigned over the Church at the dawn of the Thirty Years War.

Born in Bologna in 1554 to Count Pompeo Ludovisi and Camilla Bianchini, the future pontiff belonged to a family of the urban elite that since the 14th century had given the Emilian city a large number of counselors, elders, and senators. He went to Rome from 1569 to 1571 to continue his education with Jesuit teachers in the *Collegio Germanico* and in the Roman College (thus making him the first pope to come out of Jesuit schools). But it was to the University of Bologna that he returned to complete his legal studies, which finished with a doctorate *in utroque jure* (1575). His compatriot Ugo Boncompagni's accession to the papacy (1572) under the name GREGORY XIII opened the door to a career in Rome for him. Ordained a priest, he moved to Rome, where he worked his way into a close-knit group of jurists from Bologna who were in the service of the CURIA. He was named the first collateral judge of the Capitoline Curia. His juridical competence and his conciliatory manner quickly won the favor of the pontiff. In May 1588 he was included by Sixtus V in cardinal legate Ippolito Aldobrandini's entourage during the latter's diplomatic mission to Vienna and to Krakow, but his health prevented him from leaving Rome. In 1591, Gregory XIV called him to participate in the Congregation of Affairs in Ferrara.

After becoming pope in 1592, CLEMENT VIII (Aldobrandini) immediately brought him into the prelature as a referendary to the Two Signatures and named him civil lieutenant in the court of the VICARIATE of Rome; he worked for a short time (April 1597 to May 1598) as its pro-vice-director after the resignation of his compatriot, Ludovico Lambertini. Two years later, on 17 April 1600, he was named auditor for Bologna in the ROTA court (his 584 decisions between 1600 and 1612 were published in 1622 by the lawyer Beltrami). His role as a diplomat grew: Clement VIII entrusted him, successively, with

working out with Spain the question of the archbishop of Toledo's succession, and with canonical reconciliation with Henry IV. Clement sent him on a mission to Benevento in the company of Maffeo Barberini, the future URBAN VIII, in order to negotiate with the vice-kingdom's authorities on questions related to the enclave of Benevento. And it was Ludovisi who finally managed to quell the open conflict between the pope and the Farnese family (Ranuccio, duke of Parma and Cardinal Odoardo). PAUL V (Borghese) named him archbishop of Bologna on 12 April 1612 and entrusted him with an important diplomatic mission to Milan and Turin shortly thereafter, to mediate the conflict that had arisen between Charles Emmanuel I of Savoy and Philip III of Spain over the marquisate of Montferrat. At the end of those negotiations, at the age of sixty-two, he was elevated to the Sacred College (19 September 1616) and he became titulary of Santa Maria in Traspontina (3 December 1618). Established in Bologna, where he worked on clerical reform and protected Domenichino, appreciated by the courts of both Spain and France and far from the Roman struggles for influence, he looked like a *papabile* cardinal even before Paul V's death on 23 January 1621.

The conclave that opened on 8 February 1621 lasted only two days, albeit intense ones. Among the fifty-two cardinals participating in it, thirty-two had been created during the fifteen years of Paul V's papacy. Under the leadership of the CARDINAL NEPHEW of the deceased pope, Scipione Borghese Caffarelli, they formed a majority which, though not solidified, was nevertheless favorable to a solution involving compromise and transition. The fourteen cardinals of Clement VIII and the four of Sixtus V, on the other hand, were divided. The SACRED COLLEGE was divided into various factions according to fluctuating boundaries (the Borghese, Aldobrandini, and Montalto parties; the Spanish, French, and Florentine parties; the partisans of the Sforza, d'Este, Medici, and Farnese families; the "spiritual" party grouped around the Jesuit cardinal Robert Bellarmine), and none seemed capable of winning. Coming into the conclave, the Borghese cardinal's candidate was the cardinal from Modena, Pietro Campori, a cardinal named by Paul V, and one of his confidants. But Campori met with strong opposition. The candidacy of Cardinal Bellarmine was considered in turn; he was held in high esteem, but he was too far from partisan thinking to be able to win. It was left to the head of the Borghese party to propose, within the majority group, a candidate acceptable to the Sacred College as a whole: Scipione Borghese hesitated momentarily between the names of the old Neapolitan cardinal Ladislao of Aquino, who was ill (he died on 12 February), and the archbishop of Bologna, Alessandro Ludovisi, who was sixty-seven years old and already in poor health. The latter candidature immediately won general approval. The Borghese cardinal abandoned the Campori candidacy, and the new pope was elected on the evening of 9 February with the exceptional procedure of vote by acclamation. Prince Federico Cesi, a member of his uncle's conclave and an eyewitness, wrote in his account of the proceedings: "At the time we saw such discord and diversity in human opinion turn into a sudden universal harmony, the marvellous work of the Holy Spirit, at first sketched out and then accomplished in perfect order." The new pope, who took the name Gregory XV in memory of his compatriot and first mentor Gregory XIII, was crowned on 14 February in ST. PETER'S in the Vatican, and took possession of ST. JOHN LATERAN basilica on 9 May.

Gregory XV's first concern was to set up the nucleus of a government, surrounding himself with a familial structure in the style of politico-ecclesiastical nepotism that the Borghese pope had brought to its apogee. On 15 Feburary 1621, the day after his coronation, his nephew Ludovico Ludovisi (1595–1633) was created a cardinal at the age of twenty-five and called to fulfill the functions of cardinal nephew and principal minister for the pontiff. The young man, the son of the pope's elder brother Orazio and Lavinia Albergati, was well educated under the tutelage of his uncle. A student of the Jesuits in the Collegio Germanico and a doctor of law from the university of Bologna, he had come into the prelature in 1619, a proponent of the *Buon Governo* and later of the *Consulta*. He was ordained the day after his uncle's accession to the papacy, his energy and intelligence account for some of the decisive spirit that characterized Gregory's papacy. Made archbishop of Bologna on 27 March, made CAMERLENGO of the Church upon the death of Pietro Aldobrandini, Clement VIII's nephew, as well as legate of Avignon, furnished with well-endowed abbeys, within a few years he amassed considerable revenue and a consistent patrimony for his own profit and that of his family. From the Colonna, for example, he acquired the Colonna palace on Piazza dei S. Apostoli, in May 1622, and in September, for 860,000 ecus, he acquired the historical fiefs of Colonna and Galbrano, as well as the duchy of Zagarolo. He built the two Ludovisi villas at Frascati and on the Pincio, which are no longer extant, and hired Il Domenichino, Guercino, and Guido Reni to embellish them. Moreover, he amassed a remarkable classical art collection and financed works on the Jesuit church of Sant'Ignazio.

Orazio Ludovisi, the pope's brother, moved to Rome on 13 March. He was immediately promoted to general in the armies of the Church and received the duchy of Fiano, which had been repurchased from the Sforza for 200,000 ecus. His son Niccolò was made governor of CASTEL SANT'ANGELO and of the Borgo and received the hand of the heiress to the princes of Venafro. His daughter Ippolita married Giovanni Giorgio Aldobrandini, Clement VIII's nephew and prince of Rossano, who was immedi-

ately promoted to prince of Meldola and duke of Sarsina. A new family was created in the Roman aristocracy.

The memory of Gregory XV's short papacy remains more firmly attached to a group of juridical, disciplinary, and institutional measures that place the Bolognese pope in the line of his compatriots GREGORY XIII and BENEDICT XIV. Setting the rules for conclaves was his first objective. The bull *Aeterni Patris* (15 November 1621) and the detailed measures in the bull *Decet Romanum Pontificem* (12 March 1622) resulted in an electoral code that withstood the test of time and remained in effect until Pius X's reforms at the beginning of the 20th century. The conclave's ceremonial, its electoral system (by vote and accession), the formal arrangements for balloting, the choice of pontiff (election by a two-thirds majority, by compromise, or by acclamation), the method of his acceptance, and finally the rule against voting for oneself were subject to precise and rigorous stipulations. The oath that each cardinal pronounces before placing his ballot justly expresses the combination of human freedom and the will of God that should come into play: *testor Christum Dominum, qui me judicaturus est, me eligere quem secundum Deum judico eligi debere* ("As witness I take my Lord Christ, who will be my judge, that I choose him whom I judge should be chosen according to God.")

The creation of the Congregation for the Propagation of the Faith (*de propaganda fide*) was a seminal date in the history of Catholic missions. Instituted on 6 January 1622, presided over by Cardinal Dean Antonio Maria Sauli (whom Ludovico Ludovisi would succeed as prefect on 12 November), it bought together on 14 January thirteen cardinals, twelve prelates, and a secretary, Francesco Ingoli (1578–1649), who was a professor of law from Ravenna and former preceptor for the cardinal nephew, who would be the guiding spirit of the DICASTERY until the time of his death. So "that they might know and deal with each and every one of the affairs that relate to spreading the faith throughout the entire world" and "watch prudently over all the missions for the preaching and teaching of Catholic doctrine," the pope, via the bull *Inscrutabile Divinae Providentiae* (21 June 1622), conferred upon the members of the congregation "full, free, entire responsibility, authority, and power to make, manage, treat, act, and carry out" (*facenti, gerendi, tractandi, agendi et exsequendi*) in matters of evangelization. The pope, presiding over each meeting, also generously endowed the new dicastery financially while stipulating in his constitution *Cum Inter Multiplices* (14 December 1622), the absolute gratuity of all the ACTS, BRIEFS, letters patent, and writings coming out of the congregation. In Rome the Spanish cardinal Juan Battista Vives, a proponent of establishing a college for the training of missionary clergy, and a member of the congregation since its founding, soon gave its location to the new institution, the Ferrattini Palace (Piazza di Spagna), the future palace for the Propagation and for the Collegio Urbana.

Gregory XV's project, which gave lasting institutional form to previous measures by his predecessors PIUS V, Gregory XIII, and SIXTUS V, was dictated by the urgent need to defend and expand the Catholic faith in a Europe, dramatically reduced by the expansion of the Protestant Reformation, the renewal of Orthodoxy, and the formidable Ottoman power, but to which the discovery and colonization of America, the opening of maritime routes to Africa and the Far East, and shifts in the frontiers of the inhabited world offered extraordinary opportunities for expansion and renewal. The constitution *Inscrutabli* firmly asserted "the commandment given by Our Lord to all His apostles to preach the gospel to every creature" under the charges and prerogatives of the Apostolic See: it was "Peter and his successors" who were responsible for "gathering men who had strayed through diverse superstitions from the four corners of the Earth, to—so to speak—'immolate' them, to strip them of their former lives and bring them in so that they might become a part of Him who is the invisible head of the Church, members of Christ in the visible head of the Chruch; and that thus brought into the family of Christ, they might love that which is of Christ, accomplishing his works with the grace of the Holy Spirit, and that they might be transported into eternal pastures and drink from the inexhaustible torrent of heavenly delights." The Congregation for the Propagation of the Faith, which would develop fully under Urban V, thus became one of the first dicasteries of the Curia and its area of interest extended to the nations of northern, central, and eastern Europe, to the Christian churches in the East, and to the New World. Beyond the political boundaries of monarchies in Europe and the rigid rules of church patronage in Spain and Portugal in their counters and colonies, the new institution marked a decisive step in the extension of Roman centrality; domestic missions and foreign missions thus participated in the renewal of Catholic universality at the dawn of the 17th century.

The canonization of the first saints of the 16th century marked the spiritual culmination of Catholic reform: on 12 March 1622, Gregory XV canonized together with Isidorus, the patron saint of Spanish farmers, Teresa of Avila (1515–82), the reformer of the Carmelites; Philip Neri (1515–95), the founder of the Oratory; Ignatius Loyola (1491–1556), the founder of the Society of Jesus; and Francis Xavier (1506–52), one of Ignatius Loyola's earliest companions and a Jesuit missionary to India and Japan. In the bull *Eximii et Singulares* (28 July 1622), he also gave the Dominican order free rein to discuss the question of the Immaculate Conception within its ranks, although he pronounced no dogmatic definition on the question. An avowed protector of both the Society of Jesus, upon which he lavished privileges and exemptions, and the Capuchins, Gregory XV nevertheless reaffirmed his prohibition made to the regular clergy against preaching and confessing without the permission of the local ordinary, and he renewed Pius IV's severe measures against abusive confessors (*Universi Dominici Gregis*, 30 August 1622). He also pronounced a bull (*Omnipotentis Dei*, 20 March 1623) against sorcerers and magicians. By objectifying the "evil spell," amidst the bloody wave of repression against the cult of magic in the countryside in the early 17th century, the bull indiscriminately placed canon law once again in the service of popular Christian fury and the blind strictness of civil and ecclesiastical courts.

Gregory XV's diplomacy was dominated entirely by the new situation created by the initial successes of Catholic Austria in what was to be the Thirty Years War (1618–48). On 8 November 1620, the Palatine Elector Frederick V, head of the Calvinist Evangelical Union, had fallen in the battle of White Mountain; the Palatinate was immediately occupied by Duke Maximilian of Bavaria (who had the precious collection of manuscripts from the Palatine Library of Heidelberg brought to the pontiff), while in Bohemia and Hungary, the Austrian emperor pursued the politics of forced conversion and repression against the Moravian Brothers. Unreservedly pushing an offensive for the political and religious reconquest of Germany, while at the same time working in favor of Philip III's Spain, Louis XIII's France (where Paris was raised to the status of a metropolitan on 20 October 1622), and even James I's England, in terms of reciprocal arrangements, the pope managed to get the emperor to refer the palatinate electorate to the duke of Bavaria (25 February 1623). The German Holy Roman Empire once again gained a majority of Catholic electors: "Your letter", wrote the elderly pontiff (who would die four months later on 8 July) to the duke of Bavaria in the flowery style of curial Latin "filled our hearts with a shower of delights like celestial manna; the daughter of Zion can finally shake the ashes of mourning from her head, and don her festive gowns." The brief and intense papacy of Gregory XV thus ended in diplomatic and political success, however ephemeral, but it was for his juridical and institutional accomplishments that he is remembered in connection with an exceptionally dynamic moment of consolidation and structuring in the heritage of Catholic reform.

Philippe Boutry

Bibliography

Albrecht, D. *Die deutsche Politik Gregors XV. Die Einwirkung der papstlichen Diplomatie auf die Politik der Häuser Habsburg und Wittelsbach, 1621–1623*, Munich, 1956.

Ciasca, P. "Gregorio XV," *Enciclopedia cattolica* VI (1951), 1146–8.

Gabrieli, G. "Il Conclave di Gregorio XV. Relazione del princ. Federico Cesi," *ASR*, 50, 1927, 5–32.

Keunecke, H. O. "Maximilian von Bayern und die Entführung der Bibliotheca Palatina nach Rom," *Archiv für Geschichte des Buchwesens*, XIX, 1978, 1402–1446.

Metzler, J. "Foundation of the Congregation *de Propaganda Fide* by Gregory XV," *Sacrae congregationis de Propaganda Fide Memoria rerum*, Rome-Freiburg-Vienna, 1971–1976, 5 vols., I/1, 79–111; "Francesco Ingoli, der erste Sekretär der Kongregation (1578–1649)," *ibid.*, 197–243.

Moncelle, P. "Grégoire XV," *DTC* VI/2 (1947), 1815–22.

Navas Gutiérrez, A. M. "Mediación del papa Gregorio XV en un proyecto de matrimonio hispano-inglés," *Miscellanea Augusto Segovia*, Granada, 1986, 179–204; "Los nuncios en España durante el pontificado de Gregorio XV," *Archivio teologico granadino*, L, 1987, 354–403.

Repgend, K. *Die römische Kurie und der Westfälische Friede, Idee und Wirklichkeit des Papsttums im 16 und 17 Jahrhundert, I-Papst, Kaiser und Reich, 1621–1644*, Tübingen, 1962–1965, 2 vols.

Stornajolo, C. "Il conclave in ci fù eletto papa Gregorio XV," *Miscellanea Ceriani*, Milan, 1910, 331–50.

Tedeschi, J. "Appunti sulla *Instructio pro formandis processibus in causis strugum, sortilegiorum et maleficorum*," *Annuario dell'Istituto storico italiano per l'età moderna e contemporanea*, XXXVII–XXXVIII, 1985–86, 217–41.

Von Pastor, L. *Geschichte der Päpste seit dem Ausgang des Mittelalters* XIII. 1 - Gregor XV., Friburg-en-Brisgau, 1928, 25–226 (Ital. trans.: *Storia dei Papi dalla fine del medio evo, XIII - Gregorio XV*, Rome, 1931, 25–226.

Wood, C. H. *The Indian Summer of Bolognese Painting: Gregory XV (1621–1623)*, Ann Arbor, 1990.

GREGORY XVI. *Bartolomeo Alberto (in religion: Mauro) Cappellari (b. Belluno, 18 September 1765, d. Rome, 1 June 1846). Elected pope 2 February 1831, crowned 6 February. Buried in St. Peter's in Rome.*

Although the personality and achievements of Gregory XVI certainly cannot be reduced to his condemnation of Lamennais, of LIBERALISM, and of the first CHRISTIAN DEMOCRACY, a fifteen-year papacy characterized by the dramatic exacerbation of the internal conflicts of the Papal State, pursuit of a resolutely conservative politics of entente with the Crowns, and unyielding affirmation of the authority and rights of the Church bears the mark of rigidity and stasis.

The pope of the revolutions of 1830 was born in 1765 in the States of Terra Firma in the republic of Venice and belonged, through his parents, Giovanni Battista and Giulia Pagani Cesa, to a patrician family from the small city of Belluno. The influence of his sister Caterina, who entered the convent of San Gervasio in 1780 and pronounced her vows in October 1782, was by his own admission a determining factor in his monastic vocation. He, in turn—and in opposition to the will of his parents—entered the Camaldolese convent of San Michele de Murano near Venice, taking the monastic habit at the age of eighteen (13 August 1783) and pronouncing his final vows three years later. He was ordained a priest in 1787. The Camaldolese order (from the hermitage of Camaldoli, in the Tuscan Appenines), founded by St. Romuald early in the 11th century, belonged to the Benedictine family: in the 16th century it split into two different traditions, the eremetic tradition (in Tuscany), and the cenobitic tradition in northern Italy and Rome (San Gregorio in Monte Celio). In the second half of the 18th century the order was hit full force by the general crisis of religious life: the dearth of vocations and the suppression of chapters ordered by the HOLY SEE or imposed by civil powers reduced it from 345 members in 1765 to 196 members in 1803, divided into 27 monasteries. The Napoleonic conquest suppressed all of them, except for those in Rome. Their restoration was incomplete: at the time of Gregory XVI's election the congregation had but seventy-six members, dispersed between Venice and Rome.

It was within this rapidly shrinking universe that the future pope received his spiritual and intellectual education. A professor of philosophy and science, he became a reader in theology in 1790; under the influence of erudite teachers like Mandelli and Nachi his anti-Jansenist ecclesiology deepened. In 1793, he already dreamed of composing a treatise against the theses of the Tuscan Jansenist bishop Scipione De Ricci and the reformational COUNCIL of Pistoia (1786). In August 1795, he left Murano for Rome as a companion (*socius*) of his order's procurator general and completed his work in Roman libraries. In 1799, *The Triumph of the Holy See and the Church over the Assaults of Rejected Innovators Confused by Their Own Arguments*, the result of arduous labor, appeared in Rome in a large volume of nearly five hundred pages, thus establishing the reputation of the papacy's new champion. While the armies of the Directory were triumphing in Italy, the pope was imprisoned and his States were abolished, uncommon assurance was needed to show "the Church and the Holy See triumphing over their enemies." *Eppure così è*, "and yet, it is so," the author retorted, using a phrase from St. John Chrysostom as the epigraph of his work: "It is easier to extinguish the sun than to destroy the Church."

The Triumph of the Holy See (which would be widely reedited and translated after 1831) is part of a broader current of uncompromising apologies of the period by the co-authors of the *Giornale ecclesiastico di Roma*

(Cuccagni and Marchetti) systematized by the recent BULL *Auctorem Fidei* (28 August 1794), promulgated by PIUS VI against the acts of the Council of Pistoia. The force and originality of Mauro Cappellari's thought are nonetheless remarkable. Even though the treatise on papal INFALLIBILITY, that constituted the main part of the work did repeat—in a different order and more systematically than the conciliar, regalian, and Jansenist theses—the classical argument of Roman theologians in favor of PRIMACY, the inability to err, and the indefectibility of Peter's See, the preliminary discourse on the immutability of Church government showed more mettle and sensitivity to the politico-religious reality of the end of the 18th century. As revolutions were upsetting Europe and overthrowing temporal governments, the author exalted the Church, which, by its essence, was immutable, infallible, and invincible, similar today to what it had been in its earliest centuries, monarchical in its structure, and supported by divine promises and the evidence of tradition. From this argument he deduced the necessity for the effective exercise of papal authority and the affirmation of its visibility; but he likewise radically rejected intervention by princes in the area of religion. "The work of the reforming apostles of Pistoia is studded throughout with the heretical adulation of the Throne," he railed. "The Synod grovels before the Throne and it is from the Throne that it awaits the force of law and validity for its decisions . . ." It admits, at the same time, both its powerlessness and the supreme authority it gives the Prince." "Blind and hypocritical! [. . .] If the Church does have the supreme authority in matters of religion that our faith obliges us to recognize in it, it must necessarily possess a constitutional independence in all domains that directly concern religion. The latter does not include only dogma and sacraments, but also morals, discipline, and the clergy." This was the message of the 1799 treatise, a staunch affirmation of the pontiff's infallible authority and an uncompromising rejection of any intervention by the sovereign as "outside bishop."

The work opened the road to Rome for Mauro Cappellari. Called to the capital at the age of thirty-five by the newly elected PIUS VII, in 1800 he was made vicar of the abbey, and then abbot of the Camaldolese monastery of San Gregorio in Monte Celio; in 1801 he became a member of the Academy of Catholic Religion. The French occupation in 1808 forced him to leave Rome and retire to Murano, and then to Padua. But the uncompromising restoration of 1814 under the aegis of Cardinal Pacca engaged him definitively in the service of the CURIA. From its very founding, he was named consultant to the new CONGREGATION of Extraordinary Ecclesiastical Affairs (September 1814), a kind of "think tank" for the SECRETARY OF STATE's office, one of whose most active collaborators he became, and later consultant to the Holy OFFICE (March 1816) and examiner of bishops in theology

(March 1818). Just when it seemed as though he would be elevated to the SACRED COLLEGE during Pius VII's last promotion in March 1823, it was his fellow monk and friend Placido Zurla (1769–1834), four years his junior, who won out: common opinion interpreted the selection as a sign of Cardinal Consalvi's animosity toward Cappellari's intransigence.

The election of a pope (Leo XII, Della Genga) from the *zelante* party in September 1823 nevertheless opened the doors of the Sacred College to him, at the age of sixty. Made a reserved cardinal *in petto* on 21 March 1825, he was announced on 13 March 1826 and made a member of the Congregations of the Holy Office, the Propagation of the Faith, the Correction of Books of the Eastern Church, Studies, and Extraordinary Ecclesiastical Affairs. A few months later, on 1 October 1826, LEO XII named him prefect for the Congregation for the Propagation of the Faith. He expended tremendous effort on this task, restoring the Armenian Catholic metropolis in the Ottoman Empire, and he was particularly devoted to populations recently discovered in Africa and Oceania. Parallel to this, in the Congregation for Ecclesiastical Affairs, he was called by Leo XII to enter into negotiations with the king of Holland that led to a signature of the ephemeral CONCORDAT of 18 June 1827 and the establishment of new boundaries in dioceses in Belgium and Holland. He was also named by PIUS VIII to write the brief of 25 March 1830 to the Rhineland bishops regarding mixed marriages. From those days on, Cardinal Cappellari looked *papabile* within the intransigent party and had as many as 22 votes in the conclave of 1829, after the death of Leo XII.

The end of Pius VIII's brief papacy gave rise to a new and difficult CONCLAVE that lasted 50 days (14 December 1830–2 February 1831), while revolution was hanging over the Romagna and even threatening Rome. Once again, the Crown party (*politicanti*) advocating the cardinals Pacca, and then Macchi, and then Pacca again, clashed with the intransigent party (*zelante*), which upheld, successively, the candidacies of cardinals De Gregorio, Giustiniani (a victim of the "EXCLUSION" in Spain on 9 January) and finally Cappellari, who was elected after three weeks of fruitless division and under the threat of an insurrection (a conspiracy led by the children of Louis Bonaparte was discovered and put down in December, and Louis Napoleon, the future Napoleon III, was expelled from Rome on 11 December 1830). The new pope took the name Gregory, which had not been used since 1622, in memory of Gregory XV, the founder of the Congregation for the Propagation of the Faith, but also in memory of Gregory the Great, the patron of the Camaldolese convent in Rome, and of Gregory VII, the medieval champion in the conflict between the papacy and empire.

The internal affairs of the PAPAL STATES (which had some 2,700,000 inhabitants when Gregory XVI became pope) dominated the early years of his papacy. To the north of the pope's possessions, the four legations of Bologna, Ferrara, Ravenna, and Forli were restored, albeit not easily, in the Treaty of Vienna in 1815, through the skill of Cardinal Consalvi. (Such was also the case for the Marches, although to a lesser extent.) Through their degree of economic, social, and cultural development, and because of their reattachment to the Cisalpine Republic for nearly twenty years (1796–1814), and later to the kingdom of Italy, they constituted a world very distant from the mountains of Umbria, rural Latium, and the Rome of the cardinals and prelates of the Curia. A well-to-do, influential bourgeoisie, the intellectual professions, and the new urban classes had little tolerance for the "government of priests" that almost totally excluded them from political power in the framework of a theocratic absolutism that was accepted with increasing difficulty. Secret societies—*carbonari* of numerous persuasions, and the Freemasons—organized and gave structure to a resistance that was sometimes hidden and sometimes visible to the papal government and its cardinal legates. The memory of the trials organized starting in 1825 by Cardinal Rivarola, the latent civil war between liberal families and "sanfedists" that tore at localities almost everywhere, and also the aspirations of younger generations to the formation of an Italian nation contributed to the fragility of the administration of the papal provinces, where news of revolutions in France and Belgium in the summer of 1830 brought encouragement.

Crowned at ST. PETERS on 6 February, Gregory XVI learned of the uprising in Bologna on the same day. On 4 February 1831, at the instigation of the patriots of Modena led by Ciro Menotti, the second city of the Papal States also joined the insurrection. The pro-legate Paracciani Clarelli had to give up power to a "provisional Commission of the city and the province of Bologna" composed of liberal notables; this commission turned into a provisional government on 8 February, proclaiming the fall of the pope's temporal power. From 5 to 9 February, the movement spread quickly to most of the cities in the Legations, the Marches, and Umbria. On 12 February, Colonel Sercognani's volunteers took control of the fortress of San Leo: Spoleto saw an uprising on 13 February, and Perugia on the following day. Ancona capitulated on 17 February. On 24 February insurgent troops marched on Civita Castellana, threatening Rome, where a tumult, organized for CARNIVAL, had been repressed on 12 February. On 4 March, in Bologna, an assembly of notables that had formed on 26 February announced a provisional statute organizing the United Italian Provinces. The Papal States were on the brink of succumbing.

Gregory XVI named Cardinal Bernetti (who had performed the same duties for Leo XII) as his secretary of state on 10 February: He was torn between recourse to Austria, recommended by the elderly Cardinal Albani, former secretary of state for Pius VIII and zealous servant of Metternich, and a solution based on his own forces, recommended by the *zelante* Bernetti. On 12 February, Cardinal Benvenuti, bishop of Osimo, was named LEGATE *a latere* for the province as a whole, and given full powers. But he had barely arrived in Osimo when he was arrested, during the night of 10 February 1831, led to Bologna, and then imprisoned in Ancona. The Austrian solution won and on 6 March, with the pope's approval, Austrian troops occupied Ferrara and Comacchio; on 8 March, Colonel Sercognani was pushed back past Rieti; on 20 March, the Austrians marched on Bologna, which had been evacuated by the provisional government. On 26 March, in Ancona, the insurgents signed an honorable armistice with Cardinal Benvenuti, and General Zucchi's troops ceased fighting; the Austrians entered Ancona on 29 March. However on 5 April, Gregory XVI retracted Benvenuti's concessions (Benvenuti had been replaced on 14 March by Cardinal Oppizzoni, archbishop of Bologna), denounced the terms of the treaty, and imprisoned the leaders of the insurrection. After intervention forces were withdrawn (July 1831), the revolt continued, although it was mercilessly put down in January 1832 by a new Austrian intervention supported by the papal army; in protest, France occupied Ancona on 23 February 1832, allying itself definitively with the reestablishment of order. Bologna and Ancona were not evacuated by Austria and France, respectively, until 1838.

Gregory XVI immediately had to face pressure by the major European powers to significantly reform the administration and government of his states. On 13 April, the ambassadors of Austria, France, Prussia, and Russia, and the chargés d'affaires from Britain and the Piedmont organized a conference in Rome to address a memorandum to the pope (10 May) proposing partial laicization of local administration, the election of municipal representatives, and the naming of provincial councils, all of which Bernetti was careful to evade. However, on his own initiative, he did proceed in the summer of 1831 to outline an administrative, judiciary, and financial reorganization of the Papal States, accepting some of these suggestions. An edict of administrative reform was completed on 5 July 1831, and an edict of judicial reform on 5 October 1831; rules of civil procedure were completed by 31 October, to be followed by rules of criminal procedure on 5 November, and rules governing crimes and punishments on 20 September 1832. The secretary of state's office was divided into interior affairs and exterior affairs on 10 February 1833. On 11 June 1833 a fund was created for paying off the public debt and reform of the Congregation for the Review of Accounts of the state was inaugurated on 21 November 1833: A congregation for sanitation was created on 20 April 1834.

A few public and private initiatives deserve mention: for example, the creation of chambers of commerce in Ancona and Rome (1831), the *Banca Romana* (22 November 1833), and the savings bank in Rome (14 August 1836); also, the establishment of a salt and tobacco agency (1 July 1831), which was leased out to private concessionaires (the banker-prince Alessandro Torlonia and his associates), and a lottery administration (1 October 1836).

With the replacement of Cardinal Bernetti by Cardinal Lambruschini, a Barnabite monk, and former NUNCIO to the court of Charles X, at the head of the Secretariat of State (19 January 1836), the timid attempts for reform almost completely ceased, giving way to an almost absolute immobilization. The balance sheet of accounts for the previous year of the papacy was final and not subject to appeal: in 1846, the Papal States could count on 9.5 million Roman ecus in revenues, against 10.5 million ecus in expenses: an annual deficit of one million ecus, which was added to a total debt of 37 million ecus. Loans from the Rothschild Bank saved the Papal States financially on a number of occasions. The violent challenge to the papacy's temporal power by the pope's own subjects and the apparent inability of the weak and rigid papal government to face the financial, economic, social, and political imperatives inherent in his territorial possessions, which Gregory XVI saw as the inalienable property of the Church and the guarantee of its independence, committed the pope to a path of systematic recourse to the protection of princes, the legacy of a political theology from the Ancien Régime, and heavily compromised the autonomy of his temporal actions and the scope of his pastoral and spiritual ones.

Although Gregory XVI was not the monkish figure so out of touch with his world and his century as the liberals (and after them, the *Risorgimento*'s historiography) accused him of being, and although he had spent twenty years in the offices of the Curia acquiring hands-on practice with ecclesiastical questions and diplomatic routes, his narrow education (he spoke nothing but Italian and never did leave the peninsula), his abstract intellectual orientation, which was more canonical than theological, his daily habits (frugal and solitary), his unyielding convictions (although they were open to some movement when negotiated compromises were sought), made him almost impervious to contempory spiritual renewal in an age of national and political romanticism.

The brief to the bishops of Poland, the condemnation of the theses of *L'Avenir*, and that of Lamennais himself should be viewed in this context. Poland, insurgent against the Russian occupation in 1831, was quickly crushed and then, once again, brutally subjugated. Called upon by the Russian ambassador, Gagarin, Gregory XVI intervened on 9 June 1832 to condemn those "malicious individuals who, in these unfortunate times, have used the excuse of interest in religion to rise up against the power of legitimate sovereigns, and have plunged their home-land into an abyss of pain, breaking all its legal ties of submission" and call the czar's Catholic subjects to obedience and submission to the "magnanimous emperor."

The newspaper *L'Avenir*, founded by Lamennais and his friends (Baron d'Eckstein, Gerbet, Rohrbacher, Charles de Coux, Lacordaire, and Montalembert) in the climate of intellectual excitement following the revolution of July 1830 in France took a position (16 October 1830–15 November 1831) that was in clear contrast to that adopted by Gregory XVI in Italy and Poland. With the motto "God and Liberty," directly opposing the anticlerical orientation of the July Monarchy, the legitimacy of the GALLICAN episcopacy, and the European balance of the Holy Alliance, *L'Avenir* called for the Church's reconciliation with the current political reality for political and social emancipation, from France to Belgium and from Ireland to Poland, for religious freedom, freedom of the press and of teaching, and for separation of Church and State. The three "pilgrims of freedom" (Lamennais, Lacordaire, and Montalembert), who left Paris on 21 November 1831 after suspending publication of *L'Avenir*, must have had a modicum of innocence and a serious misunderstanding of papal Rome's ecclesiastical and political realities in order to ask Gregory XVI, who had up to that time maintained silence, for explicit approval of their ideas.

Arriving in Rome on 30 December, they were not granted a papal audience until 13 March, and even then it was as chilly as it was disappointing. Meanwhile, the Congregation of the Holy Office prepared a dossier for judgment according to the inquisitional norms in effect at the time. From Metternich to the French episcopacy, hostile steps were being taken. Lamennais left Rome on 10 July. It was in Munich that he became aware of Gregory XVI's first encyclical, *Mirari Vos* (15 August 1832), directed implicitly against *L'Avenir*'s theses. From the outset, the pope recalled the "tempest of disasters and unhappiness" that he had needed to face "from the very first moments," and the second revolt that followed forced him "to use the authority that has been conferred upon us from on high." The times were bad: "It is the triumph of unrestrained maliciousness, of shameless knowledge, of unlimited licence . . . the holy doctrine is corrupted and errors of all fashion are being brazenly propagated." Among the latter, the pope condemned in particular the "shameful alliance formed in opposition to ecclesiastical celibacy," the attacks against "the sanctity and the indissociability of the conjugal bond," the "indifferentism" formerly condemned by Lamennais, and "that absurd and erroneous maxim, or rather that delirium, that freedom of conscience must be assured and guaranteed to everyone . . . that deadly freedom that can not be sufficiently feared, the freedom of the press" and, more generally, "certain doctrines that shake the fidelity and submission owed to princes, and which everywhere ignite the fires of revolt." Bishops, the pope implored, should "work and unceasingly strive to preserve the residue of faith within this conspiracy of the impious," and princes should become convinced that "all that is done for the advantage of the Church is done also for their power and their repose." The first antiliberal encyclical of the 19th century, *Mirari Vos*, thus anticipated the general condemnations of Pius IX's SYLLABUS against "modern society," while remaining ecclesiologically and politically a prisoner of the framework of the alliance between thrones and the altar.

The definitive condemnation of Lamennais did not take place until two years later, however. On 10 September, the publishers of *L'Avenir* submitted and disbanded. But from the winter of 1832 to that of 1834, harrassed by his adversaries' measures, called to make his submission to the encyclical all the more explicit, Lamennais deepened the rift to the point of breaking with Catholicism: Christ became the symbol of man suffering and regenerated, the Church, the image of humanity on the march; common sense was identified with universal progress, religion with "the fertile and eternal divine sap of the universe." In secret, he was preparing a new work, *Words of a Believer*, an eloquent prose poem that was both vehement and prophetic, based in its form and its lexical selections on the verses of Scripture, and completely inspired by a liberating eschatology of the human race. It went on sale in Paris on 30 April 1834. With unusual rapidity for the Roman Church, Gregory XVI issued a condemnation on 7 July, in the encyclical *Singulari Nos*, decrying "this detestable production of impiety and audaciousness," "small in volume but huge in perversity," "in which, through an impious abuse of God's word, people are criminally pushed to sever the ties of all public order, to overthrow authority both the one and the other, to excite, nourish, spread, and fortify sedition in empires, troubles, and rebellions." Despite the appeal for a "return to a better frame of mind" with which the encyclical closed, the break had been consummated.

With regard to the Catholic powers, Gregory XVI was characterized by a prudent maintenance of the status quo in relations between Church and State. The captious JOSEPHIST legislation continued to prevail in Metternich's Austria, as did the concordat of 1817 in Bavaria. With its authority, Rome still supported the princes of an Italy fragmented from Naples to Turin. Promulgating the bull *Sollicitudo Ecclesiarum* (7 August 1831) shortly after his coronation as pope, in which, in case of "political vicissitudes," he recommended seeing to the spiritual needs of Catholic peoples by naming new bishops without necessarily granting formal recognition to new governments, Gregory XVI had given himself a way to solve complex questions regarding legitimacy in Europe, and also in America, and to resign himself, not without occasional difficulty, to what was already a *fait accompli*.

This was the solution that was imposed progressively upon Louis-Philippe's France, where once the anticlerical tensions of the early years were dissipated, the Napoleonic concordat continued to govern religious life with no modifications. This was also the case in Belgium where, againt his will, the pope allowed the alliance of Catholic and liberal forces that took place during the young nation's birth, while attempting to give the nuncio of Brussels authority over the bishops. On the other hand, the Church's situation deteriorated in Spain and Portugal, where the liberal governments of Queen Marie-Caroline and General Espartero, who had defeated the Carlists, and of Dom Pedro and Queen Maria de Gloria, on the other, worked to the detriment of fundamental Church reforms (nationalization of clergy property and of monasteries, dissolution of a number of religious orders and of ecclesiastical courts). Gregory XVI's multiple, and vain, protests and papal diplomatic efforts on the part of bishops and the clergy in support of the legitimist pretenders to the throne (in Spain, in Portugal, Don Carlos, Dom Miguel, whom Gregory XVI welcomed to Rome in 1834 great honors) led to a break in diplomatic relations, with Portugal on 29 July 1833, and with Spain on 31 July 1835. Relations were reestablished only with difficulty—with Portugal in 1841, thanks to Capaccini's skill, and not with Isabella's Spain until the time of Pius IX.

Circumspection and caution remained the rule for dealings with non-Catholic nations, even though Gregory XVI did continue to show intransigence. In no case did he encourage, the conjunction of Catholic and liberal movements, in Poland or in Ireland, and he barely reacted to measures to suppress the Uniate Church in the Ukraine. But he did work to establish more open relations with the British crown, and he hosted a long visit to Rome by Czar Nicholas I in December 1845, in hopes of arriving at some kind of arrangement. In Prussia, the question of mixed marriages (for which Rome refused any religious ceremony if the parents did not agree to raise their children in the Catholic faith) stirred up the resounding "Cologne affair": for having strictly applied the papal conditions, Archbishop von Droste-Bischering was arrested and imprisoned by order of Frederick-William III on 20 November 1837; Gregory XVI made a solemn protest in a public CONSISTORY on 10 December, while Görres alerted Catholic opinion in Europe with a pamphlet, *Athanasius*. In 1838, the king of Prussia also had the archbishop of Poznan, von Dunin, imprisoned, which gave rise to additional papal protestations. The affair was resolved via a compromise with the arrival of Frederick-William IV (1840). Out of fear of Polish nationalism and Rhineland regionalism, the two prelates were freed; but Gregory sacrificed Msgr. von Droste by replacing him with a coadjutor. In Switzerland, the pope denounced the fourteen articles of Baden (20 January 1832), in which the cantons intended to unify the religious life of the Confederation. His firm line—the encyclical *Commissum divinitus* (14 May 1835) condemned the Baden measures as "false, rash, erroneous, prejudicial to the Holy See, destructive to the government of the Church and its divine constitution, and subjecting ecclesiastical ministry Church to secular domination"—brought seven Catholic cantons to break away, an event that led to their crushing defeat during the war of Sonderbund.

It was outside Europe that Gregory XVI's politics would know the most tangible and lasting successes. The former prefect of the Propagation, at whose head he had placed Cardinal Fransoni in 1834, displayed considerable concerted activity, establishing a number of new dioceses in the United States, Canada, and throughout the part of Latin America that had been emancipated from Spain and Portugal, and he set up large missionary districts and a dense network of apostolic vicarates in Africa (where a diocese was created in Algeria in 1838), Asia, and newly discovered Oceania. Although religious persecution had a number of victims in Annam, and although Rome had—without difficulty—to fight the principle of Portuguese paternalism in India and the exclusive authority of the archbishop of Goa, evangelization, financed by the work of the Propagation of the Faith and essentially reliant on the French clergy, experienced a period of growth, and a few new positions came into being. One of these was the letter *In Supremo Apostolatus* (3 December 1839), which condemned the slave trade (but not slavery, which was still practiced by the major Catholic powers); a second was the recommendation on 12 November 1845 to form indigenous clergy.

Seeing more dynamic action at the periphery than in the center of Gregory XVI's papal system is not at all paradoxical. In fact, it was as if, handicapped by the Papal State's difficulties in government and the narrowness of the Ancien Régime's political theology, Gregory XVI nevertheless managed to get quite disparate energies to flow toward Rome and, through them, to consolidate his own authority in the area of ecclesiology and dogma. Thus, the Catholic renewal of the 1840s looked to Rome as the center of Catholic unity—with Montalembert, Lacordaire, Guéranger, and Migne in France; in Germanic Europe with Drey and Mölher in Tübingen, Görres and Döllinger in Munich, and Günther in Vienna; with the foundation of the Catholic university of Louvain in Belgium in 1834; with Wiseman and the conversion of Newman in England; in Ireland with O'Connell; and in Italy itself with Perrone and Ventura, Rosmini and Gioberti. Trips *ad limina* by European bishops slowly began again, a movement for liturgical unity around the Roman rite was strengthened, religious orders for both men and women grew under the aegis of the Roman Congregation of Bishops and Regulars, and a new Roman centralization was born. Parallel to this, the work of the Roman magisterium grew via dogmatic condemnations—of Hermes' neo-Kantian theology (encyclical *Dum Acerbissimas*, 26

September 1835) and Bautain's Fideism in 1841, of the archbishop of Utrecht, Van Buul (4 September 1843), and of the Vintras sect (8 November 1843)—as well as expansion of the activities of the Congregation of the Index, the canonization of Alphonsus Liguori (26 May 1839) and the strengthening of Liguorism in the area of moral theology, the expansion in the veneration of St. Philomena (virgin and martyr of the CATACOMBS), and preparation of a definition of the doctrine of the Immaculate Conception of Mary.

When Gregory XVI died in his eighty-fourth year, on 1 June 1846, in disaffected solitude, revolts were again stirring the Papal States: there was an insurrection in Rimini on 23 September 1845; troubles broke out in Ancona in 1846; there was agitation in the Legations and the Marches; new aspirations for reform were appearing throughout the Papal States. The shadow cast by the deterioration of the pope's temporal powers on a papacy in transition between the ecclesiology of the Ancien Régime (to which Gregory XVI still belonged in so many ways) and the threatening and fertile arrival of "new times," darkened the last days of the life, and even the memory, of the Camaldolese pope.

Philippe Boutry

Bibliography

Bastgen, H. *Forschungen und Quellen zur Kirchenpolitik Gregors XVI.*, Paderborn, 1929.

DeMarco, D. *It tramonto dello Stato Pontifico. Il papato di Gregorio XVI*, Turin, 1948.

Federici, D. *Gregorio XVI tra favola e realtà*, Rovigo, 1948.

Helfert, J. A. *Gregor XVI. und Pius IX. Ausgang und Anfang ihrer Regierung. Oktober 1845–November 1846*, Prague, 1895.

La Condamnation de Lamennais, dossier presented by M. J. and L. Le Guillou, Paris, 1982.

Leflon, J. "Le Pontificat de Grégoire XVI," *La Crise révolutionnaire*, 1789–1846, Paris, 1949, 426–516.

Manzini, L. *Il cardinale Luigi Lambruschini*, Vatican, 1960.

Morelli, E. *La Politica estera di Tommaso Bernetti, segretario di Stato de Gregorio XVI*, Rome, 1953.

Schmidlin, J. "Pontificat de Grégoire XVI (1831–1846)," *Histoire des papes de l'époque contemporaine*, French trans., Lyon-Paris, I.2 (1940), 185–427; *Gregorio XVI. Miscellanea commemorativa*, Rome, 1948, 2 vols.

Schwedt, H. H. *Das römische Urteil über Georg Hermes (1775–1831). Ein Beitrag zur Geschichte der Inquisition in 19. Jahrhundert*, Rome-Freiburg, Vienna, 1980.

Sylvain, C. *Histoire du pontificat de Grégoire XVI*, Lille-Paris, 1889.

GUELPHS. A term used in opposition to GHIBELLINE, the name borrowed for a party in Germany and adopted since the middle of the 13th century in northern and central Italy to refer, first to the supporters of the *pars ecclesiae*, and later to the adversaries of the alliance between the papacy and the house of Anjou. Sources do not say when or how the name migrated to Italy. It is possible that the memory of old ties linking the princely line of the Welfs (related to the Estes) to the house of Canossa and the papacy led to relating the name "Guelphs" to the side of the Church and the popes. But it may also have been adopted for propaganda reasons: first reserved for the adversaries of Frederick II in Italy, the "enemies of the Ghibelline," it came to be applied generally to the partisans of the anti-imperial politics of the Roman CURIA in the struggle for supremacy in Italy.

The name Guelphs first appeared in Florentine and Tuscan sources in the 1240s to refer to the group of those who championed the precedence of *libertas ecclesiae* over *honor imperii*, papal primacy over the emperor and all other sovereigns. Concurrent with this political doctrine, which actually went back to the time of GREGORY VII and INNOCENT III, and was taken to the apogee of its development by BONIFACE VIII, the term "Guelph" was working its way into 14th-century texts devoted to theories of the state, and from there into the Italian vocabulary of political philosophy. Following its own political course, it remained in the vocabulary of political propaganda with the terms "neo-Guelphs" and "neo-Guelphism." Beyond its use in theoretical discussions on the problem of the *imperium mundi*, the name Guelphs and the political movement that was defined as Guelphism concerned the partisans of the autonomy of the communes of northern and central Italy; respect for the particularism of local power structures; and a federalism that, when it was not violated, was even ready to recognize the domination of the empire or another power provided it gave it juridical legitimacy and worked to keep peace. It goes without saying that this politial orientation did not always coincide with the territorial interests of the popes (in the Church States) and the ANGEVINS, nor did it favor the development of the idea of national unification. With the installation of the Angevins in the kingdom of Sicily (1265–1268), Guelphs ceased to be a purely negative term reserved for the adversaries of the empire and those who were opposed to its appetite for concrete as well as theoretical power. The term was thereafter applied to the partisans of the alliance of the popes with the house of Anjou and to the supporters of a sharing of power, such as was established in 1268.

It was in this alliance that the real strength of Guelphism resided, up to the 14th century, even in the time of the Avignon exile. Because of its vitality, it lacked cohesion and presented a multiplicity of forms, depending on the circumstances of the times and the concrete interests of power: like the Guelphism of some popes,

and also that of Robert the Wise of Naples, who sought a reconciliation with the German crown, hoping to pacify Italy or, more precisely, to extend Angevin domination over the entire peninsula, the legitimacy of which would rely on the empire; like the radical Guelphism of the Avignon papacy (JOHN XXII), which supported a French candidate for the German throne and would have loved to completely detach the *provincia Italiana* from the empire; or like Tuscan and Lombard Guelphism, whose financial, military, and ideological center was in Florence, a city that fought for the defense of communal liberties and against the Ghibelline tyrants of northern Italy (the Visconti, the della Scala). There was a coincidence in this latter form of Guelphism and Avignon's hopes to end up with pacification of Italy through collaboration with France, but it was opposed to Angevin Guelphism because of its territorial ambitions.

In contrast to the Ghibelline party, the papacy's actions conferred prestige, solidarity, and ideological coherence to the Guelph party. When the papacy mobilized the instruments of its spiritual power (preaching, the INQUISITION, pursuit of heretics, the CRUSADES) in the service of Guelphism, it brought credibility to a movement that, starting in the 1240s, came into contact with the current of popular piety, with its many orders and brotherhoods sworn to defend the faith and protect the cross. The Ghibellines' identification with heresy (*ghibellini patarini*) and the accusation of heresy made against the Ghibelline *Signori* of northern Italy served to justify the crusades, the first of which, led against Manfred, began in 1255. They then followed, without interruption, until the end of the century (1255–60, 1261, 1263–64, 1265, 1268, 1283, 1291, 1296, 1297–98, 1299, 1302), and reached particular virulence at the time of the conflicts between John XXII and Louis of Bavaria (1231–38).

Beyond these political plans and propaganda arguments, in political reality the Guelphs nevertheless always followed—as was also the case for their adversaries—the logic and specific laws of partisan squabbles. In Florence during the first half of the 13th century, the Guelphs gathered together the adversaries of Uberti, who were linked to the Hohenstaufens, rather than the opponents of the empire or the Hohenstaufens; similarly, in all cities, Guelph parties formed according to the alliances and old local enimities. In Tuscany and the Piedmont (which in the 14th century entered into the Angevin sphere of interest), Guelph partisans were seen as being especially faithful to the kingdom of Naples. On the other hand, there was a contradiction between the Guelphism of a number of nobles or *Signori* (like Malaspina and the Malatesta) and their practical hostility to the German sovereign, whose precedence they still recognized as a way of legitimizing their power; it expressed, much more, their declared enimity against noble families and Ghibelline cities. The Ghibelline dynasties, which had a reputation for tyranny (the Visconti and the della Scala, for example), were the only ones to consider, or even to define, the Ghibellinism that legitimized their power, thanks to the imperial vicariate, as an attitude of conscious fidelity to the empire. In Florence, where the Ghibellines were gradually ousted from municipal positions of power, Guelph was, at the end of the 13th century, the equivalent of "good citizen" or "good patriot." In disputes among clans over influence or responsibilities during this period, the Guelphs split (not only in Florence) into "whites" (moderates, one example of which was Dante) and "blacks" (radicals). The magistrates of black Guelphism supervised the orthodoxy of the individual in charge of each duty and, using the instrument of denunciation that the *ammonizioni* had used to exercise control and coercion, forbade suspects from exercising public duties. In the 14th century, being a "Guelph" in Florence meant belonging to the politico-familial network of the urban oligarchy and recognizing the *status quo* of relations between power and property: The word was a synonym for political orthodoxy and fidelity to the authorities of the city.

Ernest Voltmer

Bibliography

Artifoni, E. "La consapevolezza di un nuovo aspetto politico-sociale nella cronistica italiana d'età avignonese: alcuni esempi fiorentini," *ibid.*, 77–100.

Bonaini, F. "Della Parte Guelfa in Firenze," *Giornale storico degli archivi toscani*, 2 (1858), 171–87, 257–89; 3 (1859), 77–99, 167–84.

Bowsky, W. M. "Florence and Henry of Luxemburg, King of the Romans. The Rebirth of Guelfism," *Speculum*, 33 (1958), 177–203.

Caggese, R. "Su l'origine della parte guelfa e le sue relazioni col Comune," *Archivio storico italiano*, ser. 5, 32 (1903), 205–309.

Cardini, F. "Guelfen," *LexMA*, 4 (1989), 1763–5.

Dorini, U. *Notizie storiche sull'università di Parte Guelfa in Firenze*, Florence, 1902.

Gallavresi, G. "La riscossa dei Guelfi in Lombardia dopo il 1260 e la politica di Filippo della Torre," *Archivio storico lombardo*, 33 (1906), 5–67, 391–453.

Herde, P. *Guelfen und Neoguelfen. Zur Geschichte einer nationalen Ideologie vom Mittelalter zum Risorgimento*, Stuttgart, 1986 (*Sitzungsberichte der Wissenschaftlichen Gesellschaft an der Johann-Wolfgang-Goethe-Universität Frankfurt am Main*, 22, 2).

Pacaut, M. "La féodalité et les villes. Féodalisme et guelfisme," *Études en souvenir de R. Fiétier*, Dijon, 1982, 109–17 (*Mémoires de la Société pour l'histoire du droit et des institutions des anciens pays bourguingons, comptois et romands*, 39).

Pacaut, P. "Aux origines de guelfisme: les doctrines de la ligue lombarde (1167–1183)," *Revue historique*, 230 (1963), 73–90.

Tabacco, G. "La tradizione guelfa in Italia durante il pontificato di Benedetto XII," *Studi di storia medievale e moderna in onore di E. Rota*, ed. P. Vaccari and P. F. Palumbo, Rome, 1958, 97–148.

Tabacco, G. "Programmi di politica italiana in età avignonese," *Aspetti culturali della società italiana nel periodo del papato avignonese*, Rimini, 1981, 49–75 (*Convegni del centro di studi sulla spiritualità medievale, Università degli studi di Perugia*, 19).

Trexler, R. C. *Public Life in Renaissance Florence*, New York, 1980.

Witt, R. G. "A Note on Guelfism in Late Medieval Florence," *Nuova rivista storica*, 53 (1969), 134–145.

HABEMUS PAPAM. This is a shortened form of the words with which the election of a sovereign pontiff is announced from the papal loggia (the loggia of Benedictions) at St. Peter's basilica. Announcement of the conclave's results is preceded by white (or at least light-colored) smoke coming from the chimney located on the roof of the SISTINE CHAPEL. It is with the words *habemus papam* that the name of the new pope is made public. The first CARDINAL deacon (protodeacon) is responsible for the announcement. "*Annuntio vobis gaudium magnum. Habemus papam, Eminentissumum ac* [or *et*] *Reverendissum Dominum,* [*Suam Reverendissimam Excellenciam cardinalem*] [or: *dominum*] [. . . the name of the individual chosen] *qui sibi nomen imposuit* [. . . name chosen by the pope-elect]." The wording, the date of the origin of which is unknown, was initially intended to announce to the Roman people the name of the pope chosen from among the members of the SACRED COLLEGE, whose affiliation with a Roman diaconate was no longer anything more than a reminder that the clergy had been the original electoral body. The announcement was simplified beginning with PIUS XI (1922–39), the first pope since the taking of Rome to give a BENEDICTION *Urbi et Orbi* from the papal loggia. When Pius IX was elected (1846), the announcement information about his episcopal and priestly titles in Rome, after his first name but before his last name.

Between the rising of the white smoke and the announcement made by the cardinal protodeacon a certain amount of time elapses, depending on the conclave. If it is daytime, a virtual guessing game takes place via miming or speculation, by informed entourages circulating around the Sistine Chapel (the Majordomo terrace). One knew, for example, that LEO XIII's successor was cardinal Sarto, in 1903 when a member of the CONCLAVE imitated the motions of a tailor (*sarto* is Italian for tailor) making a cassock.

Sometimes the announcement of the individual's first name suffices. Such was the case at the time of the March

1939 conclave when the announcement of "Eugenium" (Pacelli) unleashed a thundering ovation. Conversely, the phrases announced can also leave the crowd assembled in St. Peter's Square in the greatest of confusion. Such was the case in October 1978 when Cardinal Felici, after announcing "Carolum" completed it with "Wojtyla," pronounced with a Polish accent. Some, in their inability to identify the individual, believed that an African pope had been chosen. In post-Tridentine memory, no announcement of a new sovereign pontiff has been received with either indifference or open hostility.

Philippe Levillain

HADRIAN I. *(d. 26 December 795). Elected pope on 1 February, crowned on 9 February 772. Buried at St. Peter's in Rome.*

Elected without opposition, the deacon Hadrian reconciled in his person both the clergy and the Roman aristocracy. He had been raised by his uncle Theodotus, consul and duke, and then chief notary and head of the diaconate of S. Angelo. He had become cleric (subdeacon) under PAUL I and DEACON under STEPHEN III. He was one of the most noteworthy figures since STEPHEN II. He managed to stop the escalation of violence that had marked the preceding pontificates. He sought out those responsible for murdering Sergius, the assistant to the chief notary and his "second," and exiled some of them to Constantinople. This measure makes clear that ties remained between the pope and the emperor. Paul Afiarta was arrested in his turn, and he too would have ended his days in exile if the authorities of RAVENNA, who had been given the responsibility for incarcerating him, had not had him executed.

But the most serious problem faced by the new pope was that of relations with the LOMBARDS, and the complication of that problem presented by another, the succession of Charlemagne's brother, Carloman, who had died in 771. Soon after his coronation, Hadrian had received an embassy from the Lombard king Desiderius who pressed him to renew the alliance concluded during the time of Stephen III; Desiderius promised to return to the pope all the cities claimed since 776. In the meantime, the aristocrats among the FRANKS of Carloman's kingdom, pushing aside the children of the dead king, rallied around Charles. Carloman's widow, Gerberga, turned to Desiderius, who stood up for the young Frankish princes. He wanted the pope to consecrate them kings; but Hadrian had decided to separate himself from the clan favorable to the Lombards, which was Paul Afiarta's clan. Neither the exchanges of embassies nor the havoc wreaked by the king or the dukes was able to modify Hadrian's attitude. He even refused to meet with Desiderius. At the same time, he sent a message to Charlemagne, which reached him in March 773. In order to force the pope's hand, Desiderius undertook the journey to Rome in the company of the Frankish princes. Hadrian assembled his troops, put Rome on the defensive, and sent three bishops to meet the Lombard king to forbid his entry into the papal territory on pain of excommunication: this is the first known example of the use of ANATHEMA for political ends. The Lombard king did not insist. Charles, in the meantime, had sent ambassadors, to Rome and then to Pavia, in order to keep himself informed of the exact situation. Upon their return, he asked Desiderius to cede to the pope all the cities the pope claimed, promising even to pay damages, but his proposal was in vain. He thereupon decided to invade the Lombard kingdom. After having devastated the Lombard army, he put Pavia under siege through to the following spring. Taking advantage of their newly recovered independence, the inhabitants of the duchy of Spoleto came to make their submission to the pope, who invested their new duke. The leading citizens of a number of cities in Italy likewise asked to have their ties to the papal territory restored. In the spring of 774, Charlemagne decided to make his way to Rome for the Easter celebrations. He arrived on Holy Saturday, and was welcomed with the ceremonial reserved for the exarch. A few days later, on 6 April, a great assembly was held in St. PETER'S. Hadrian presented to the Frankish king the written promise that, he maintained, Pepin had made in his own name and in the name of his sons at Quierzy in 754—a document whose authenticity is the subject of controversy. Charles confirmed it with a new act. It was much more than that which Pepin had actually given the pope in 756: to the exarchate, understood in the widest sense, and to the Pentapolis were added the Lombard duchies of Spoleto, Benevento, and Tuscany, as well as the ancient province of Venetia and Istria, which had been divided among the Lombard kingdom, the Byzantine Empire, and Corsica. It was essentially a matter of giving the papal territories an importance analogous to that of the Lombard kingdom. In fact, Charlemagne did not keep his promise. After the fall of Pavia, he had Desiderius imprisoned, and he made the decision to annex the Lombard kingdom. At this point, he undoubtedly thought there was no need to dismember a kingdom that no longer constituted a threat to the papacy, and he ordered that the pope have restored to him only the cities of the Exarchate that Desiderius had promised, but had kept or reappropriated. These cities first were placed under the administration of the archbishop of Ravenna, Leo, who had freed himself from the authority of the pontifical functionaries.

The Frankish king made two more trips to Rome during Hadrian's lifetime. In 781, he brought his sons Pepin and Louis, whom the pope consecrated, respectively, king of Italy and king of Aquitaine. Hadrian I thereupon abandoned his claims to the duchies of Tuscany and Spoleto in exchange for the payment of the tribute these cities formerly had paid to the Treasury of Pavia. In 787, Charlemagne returned with the intention of securing the effective submission of the duke of Benevento. On this occasion, the pope obtained the cession of the south of Tuscany, with VITERBO, Orvieto, and Soana; the borders of papal Latium would remain practically unchanged until 1870. Since 781, Hadrian had been striking COINS with his effigy and dating his acts by the years of his pontificate rather than by those of the emperor; but this sliding toward full sovereignty was thwarted by the control Charlemagne tended to exercise over the papal ADMINISTRATION.

Emperor Constantine V had died in 775. Power soon passed into the hands of Empress Irene, who resolved in 784 to reestablish the veneration of images. She announced to the pope the convening of an ecumenical COUNCIL for the purpose of putting an end to iconoclasm. Hadrian responded in 786 with two letters addressed to the empress and the new patriarch, Tarasius, in which he developed arguments drawn from the Scriptures and the Fathers in favor of the veneration of images. The council of Nicaea II (the seventh general council) opened on 24 September 787 in the presence of the two legates sent by the pope, including the abbot of S. Saba in Rome; the monks of this monastery undoubtedly had a hand in making up the Roman documents in which quotations from the Greek FATHERS OF THE CHURCH are prominent. The pontifical LEGATES played an important role during the debates, which closed with the reestablishment of the veneration of images and of the communion between Rome and Constantinople. Charlemagne learned of the existence of the council only the following year, when Hadrian sent him a poor Latin translation of its acts. The reaction of Charlemagne and his ecclesiastical counselors, who immediately suspected the Greeks of HERESY, was highly unfavorable (*Capitulary against the Synod* of 788–9): they understood the council to have prescribed the adoration of images, whereas adoration should be directed only to God. Charlemagne considered it his duty to protect the people whom God had entrusted to him from the heresy, and to take the initiative in responding. His refutation was aimed directly at the theses attributed to the Greeks: the *Capitulary on Images* (or the *Libri Carolini*), written between 791 and 794, which he subsequently had approved by a council convened in Frankfurt in June 794 in the presence of the legates of the pope, and which was conceived as the West's answer to the council of Nicaea II. The capitulary was sent to the pope, though whether before or after the council is unknown; Hadrian sent a long letter in which he corrected certain errors of interpretation made by the Franks in their reading of the acts of the council. Charlemagne does not seem to have taken it into account. Constantinople was not informed of this controversy. The council of Frankfurt likewise condemned adoptionism. A clerk from the Frankish kingdom who was to spread Roman practices in Spain stirred up a controversy in which Hadrian had already become involved: he had condemned the unfortunate expression "adoptive son" of God used by the metropolitan of Toledo, Elipandus, in reference to Christ. Since the bishop of Urgel, in the Spanish plain, had taken up the controversial formula once again, Charlemagne called forward his case and had him condemned. But on this point there was complete agreement between the Frankish court and the pope, whose line of argument the council had taken up.

Hadrian's name is likewise attached to two reference works of the Carolingian Renaissance that Charlemagne asked him to write: the *Dionysio-Adriana*, a canonical collection, and the *Adrianum*, an (incomplete) copy of the Gregorian sacramentary, sent in 774 and in 785–6. Hadrian also concerned himself with the city of Rome. The damage caused by the siege of Aistulf had not yet been repaired. He had the aqueducts restored and the roofs of the city's churches rebuilt, for which Charlemagne supplied the beams. He also continued the reorganization, undertaken by Zacharias, of the temporal concerns of the papacy by founding six new *domuscultae* (church-run farms providing income for charitable projects). Well situated near a major road, these continuous domains formed a ring around the city of Rome. The production of the *domusculta Capracorum* near Veii was reserved for feeding the poor of Rome, a hundred of whom were given food every day at the Lateran. Again for the sake of offering hospitality to the poor Hadrian founded or renovated the DIACONIAE: three near St. Peter's for the pilgrims, and three others in the Forum, in refurbished ancient monuments. He had the crypt of Sta. Maria in Cosmedin refurbished as well.

Jean-Charles Picard

Bibliography

JW, 1, 289–306; 2, 701.
LP, 1, 486–523.
MGH, Epist., 3, 567–648, 654–5; 5, 3–57.

Ashanin, C. B. "Western Reaction to the Seventh Ecumenial Council," *Patristic and Byzantine Review* 7 no. 1 (1988), 59–66.
Bertolini, O. "Adriano I," *DBI*, 1 (1960), 312–23.
Duchesne, L. *Les Premiers Temps de l'Etat pontifical*, Paris, 1911.
Jugie, M. "Adrien Ier," *DHGE*, 1 (1912), 614–619 (bibliographical updating, *DHGE*, 22 [1988], 1485).
Lanne, E. "Rome and Sacred Images," *One in Christ* 23 (1987), 1–21.
Libri carolini, MGH, Conc., 2, 3.
Nicee II, 787–1987, Paris, 1987 (articles by E. Lanne and J. C. Schmitt).
Noble, T. F. X. *The Republic of St. Peter*, Philadelphia, 1984.

HADRIAN II. (*b. ca. 820, d. Rome, November/December 872). Crowned pope on 14 December 867. Buried at St. Peter's in Rome.*

Hadrian, a relative of Popes STEPHEN IV and SERGIUS II, had been subdeacon in 842 under GREGORY IV and had held important functions in the LATERAN *patriarchum*. He was a simple, affable man of advanced age. After the pontificate of an authoritarian pope, a milder man was required. Arsenius, bishop of Orta and a relative of the secretary Anastasius, intervened to have Emperor Louis II designate Hadrian. Under the influence of Anastasius, who had became librarian at the Lateran, the new pope, without any disavowal of his predecessor, reestablished good relations with Archbishop Hincmar of Reims and attempted to settle the matter of Lothair II's divorce. But the powerful secretary was soon dismissed following a sordid drama. The pope, before becoming DEACON, had in fact been married and had had a daughter. This daughter was abducted by the brother of Anastasius, named Eleutherius. When Hadrian refused to recognize the marriage, Eleutherius killed both his own wife and the the wife of the pope. He was judged and executed by the imperial agents, and on 12 October 868, the pope excommunicated Anastasius, who had been compromised in the affair.

Lothair II, eager to justify himself before the pope, made his way to Monte Cassino to meet with Hadrian. The pope was planning to open a new investigation concerning the king's marriage, but it all came to nothing, since Lothair II died. His uncles, Charles the Bald and Louis the German, hastily divided up Lorraine between themselves, thereby provoking objections on the part of the pope. Hincmar of Reims let the pope know that he ought not to meddle in political matters. Hadrian—or rather Anastasius Bibliothecarius, who had returned to grace—soon entered into conflict with Hincmar regarding his nephew of the same name, the bishop of Laon, who had appealed to Rome against the schemes of King Charles the Bald and the archbishop of

Reims. Using the "False DECRETALS," which gave extensive power to the bishop and to the pope, Hincmar the Younger presented himself as a victim. On 25 March 871, the pope sent some letters, which were poorly received. The council of Donzy deposed Hincmar of Laon, a decision the pope refused to accept. But Hadrian dared not excite the displeasure of Charles the Bald any further, for he was already planning the succession of Emperor Louis II, who was childless. He needed the help of the secular arm in defending his territories against the dangers posed by the Lombard duke and the SARACENS.

After Patriarch Ignatius had been reinstated in Constantinople, a Roman SYNOD, convened on 10 June 869, condemned the acts of the council that had been called by Photius and that had condemned NICHOLAS I. The pope send his LEGATES to the council of Constantinople, considered the eighth ecumenical council in the West, (October 869), which was to judge Photius and his partisans. Anastasius Bibliothecarius brought the acts of this council back to Rome. The only reason for tension was the sudden reversal on the part of Prince Boris of Bulgaria, who, turning his back on the West, asked BYZANTIUM to send him some priests. Hadrian found his compensation in Moravia. Two Greek missionaries, Cyril and Methodius, began evangelizing the Moravians and developed a LITURGY in Slavonic. Pope NICHOLAS I had invited them to Rome and, after his death, it was Hadrian II who received them. Cyril and Methodius were all the more enthusiastically welcomed because they brought with them the relics of St. CLEMENT, one of the first popes, martyred in the Chersonese. Hadrian approved the brothers' mission and the use of the Slavonic liturgy. He ordained Methodius a priest and had some of his disciples ordained priests. The two brothers spent a year in Rome; Cyril died on 14 February 869 and was buried in the church of S. Clemente. Methodius thereupon was consecrated bishop of Pannonia. He had barely returned to Moravia when he was imprisoned by the authorities under German influence. He appealed to Rome during the pontificate of JOHN VIII, the successor of Hadrian II, who had died on an unknown date toward the end of the year 872.

Pierre Riche

Bibliography

JW, 1, 368–75; 2, 703–4, 745.

LP, 2, 173–93.

MGH, Epist. 6, 691–765.

PL, 122, 1259–1320.

Bertolini, O. "Adriano II," DBI, 1 (1960), 323–9.

Fliche-Martin, VI, 367–95, 469–83.

Lapôtre, A. "Adrien II et les Fausses Décrétales," Revue des questions historiques, 1880, 377–431 (repr., Études sur la papauté au IXe siècle, II, Turin, 1978, 1–55).

Noyon, A. "Adrien II," DHGE, 1 (1912), 619–24 (bibliographic updating, DHGE, 22 [1988], 1485).

HADRIAN III. (b. ?, d. San Cesario on the Panaro, August or September 885). Elected pope on 17 May 884. Buried in the abbey of Nonantola, near Modena. Saint (ancient local cult in the diocese of Modena confirmed by the Holy See in 1891; feast on 8 July).

The brevity of his pontificate makes him, like his predecessor MARINUS I, a transitional pope whose reign is distinguished by no significant undertaking. Born into a Roman family, Hadrian III seems to have been an unremarkable figure before his accession, if we can trust the absolute silence of the sources until 884. His first actions were directed above all at establishing his authority among the factions of the Roman aristocracy—or rather at imposing his own power—by getting rid of the elements that restricted his freedom of movement in the Lateran palace: he reestablished relations with the party, of JOHN VIII, against that of Marinus. Accordingly, he had blinded the chief of the militia, George "of the Aventine," one of the principal opponents of John VIII, deposed by him and then reinstate in his functions by Marinus I. Similarly, he afforded the people of Rome the opportunity to mock the spectacle of the punishment inflicted on a noblewoman named Maria, who was dragged naked and whipped through the city.

In the external realm, Hadrian III devoted the sixteen months of his pontificate to the two great problems of the end of the 9th century, relations with BYZANTIUM and with the Western Empire. On the Byzantine front, the time had come for diplomatic appeasement, after the conflicts that had opposed Marinus I to Emperor Basil and Patriarch Photius; Hadrian III sent a letter giving official notice of his election to the throne of St. Peter, but he had died by the time Basil's response reached Italy. With the respect to the Western Empire, the succession to the imperial throne was once again in question. Emperor Charles the Fat had managed to reunify Charlemagne's shattered domain. But, without a legitimate heir, he sought to entrust the empire to his natural son Bernard. That would come about by means of a formal recognition of filiation by the religious authority. Everything indicates that Hadrian III was, a priori, in favor of such a plan; in the summer of 885, he entrusted Rome to John, the bishop of Pavia and imperial missus, and, on the invitation of Charles the Fat, set out on the route to Germany. He died on the journey, and it is unknown whether he came to his end naturally or as the result of violence (some sources imply that he was assassinated by a member of the family of George of the Aventine whom he had driven away upon coming to power). No sooner had he been buried than the religious of Nonantola opened his tomb to retrieve the pontifical vestments and ornaments.

François Bougard

See also FRANKS.

Bibliography

JW, 1, 426–7; 2, 705.
LP, 2, 225.
Bertolini, O. "Adriano III," *DBI*, 1 (1960), 329–30.
Daniele, I. "Adriano III," *EC*, 1 (1948), 344–5.
Fliche-Martin, VI, 440–2, 498.
Viard, P. "Adrien III," *Catholicisme*, 55 (1962), 474.

HADRIAN IV. *Nicholas Breakspear (b. Abbot's Langley, Hertfordshire, ca. 1110–20, d. Anagni, 7 September 1159). Elected pope on 4 December 1154, crowned on 5 December at St. Peter's in Rome. Buried at St. Peter's in Rome.*

Hadrian IV is the only Englishman to have occupied the see of Peter. He undoubtedly selected his name in honor of HADRIAN I, considered a champion of pontifical rights in Italy. Perhaps he did so also in memory of St. Hadrian (d. 709), abbot of Sts. Peter and Paul of Canterbury. Nicholas was the son of an English cleric who became a monk in the Benedictine abbey of St. Albans (near London). There the young Nicholas received his early education. When he was refused entry into the novitiate, he went to France to pursue his studies. His travels led him to Arles and eventually to St. Rufus, near Avignon. He took the habit in this monastery, which was the center of an important congregation of canons regular, and became prior there and eventually abbot, around 1140. Probably chafing under with his strictness, the canons called for the pope to remove him from his office. In 1145, or shortly thereafter, Nicholas presented himself at the papal court, and EUGENE III engaged him to remain with him. Before 1150, he was promoted to CARDINAL bishop of Albano. Pontifical LEGATE in Scandinavia in 1152–3, he set the ecclesiastical organization of that country on a proper footing according to the Roman model. This task was evidently entrusted to him because of his northern roots and his reputation as an able administrator. He arrived in Norway in July 1152; after lengthy travels in the country for the purpose of gathering information, at the beginning of 1153 he promulgated in Nidaros (today Trondheim) an important body of constitutions according the Church of Norway significant freedom and a strong economic base. In the same year, he set up the ecclesiastical province of Norway, with Nidaros as its metropolitan see. In August–September 1153, he convoked a council of the Swedish church in Linköping in order to get a policy of reform under way. He was not immediately successful in establishing a Swedish archdiocese. Seeking an alternate solution, during his visit to Denmark Nicholas promised Archbishop Eskil de Lund the primacy of Sweden. This reorganization did not take into account the old jurisdictional claims over Scandinavia of the archdiocese of Hamburg-Bremen. He returned to Rome in November 1154.

The success of his mission in the north certainly accounts for his being unanimously elected pope immediately after the death of ANASTASIUS IV. Hadrian IV intervened vigorously when violence broke out once again in Rome. Following an attempt on the life of a cardinal during Lent in 1155, he imposed an INTERDICT on the city. The halting of the PILGRIMAGES, with its economic consequences, forced the Romans into submission; they gave in to the pope's demands and expelled Arnold of Brescia, the instigator of the unrest. After Roger II of Sicily died in February 1154, his son William I succeeded him, without obtaining the recognition of the CURIA. He was excommunicated for having invaded the province of Benevento and Campania. Counting heavily on German support against the NORMANS, in January 1155 the pope renewed the treaty of Constance with Frederick Barbarossa. At this juncture, the German sovereign undertook a military campaign in Italy. His meeting with the pope on 8 June 1155 at Sutri ended in disagreement, undoubtedly due to reciprocal withholding.

Hadrian IV granted his pardon to the king after the king agreed to perform the traditional stirrup ceremony, which he had originally refused. There followed a period of collaboration between the pope and the king. Barbarossa had Arnold de Brescia imprisoned, and then executed on the order of the prefect of Rome. On 18 June, Hadrian IV crowned Frederick emperor at St. Peter's. He modified the course of the ceremony, however, so as to lower the position of the emperor. The consecration provoked clashes between the German Troops and the Romans, who had not been forewarned and who attempted to imprison the pope. The pope left the city along with Frederick. Very quickly, the pope and the emperor came into open conflict, since Barbarossa wanted some former imperial privileges restored, such as his claims to the abbey of Farfa. The emperor abandoned his plans to crush the Romans and to wage a campaign against the Normans. He therefore did not fulfill the obligations imposed by the treaty of Constance—perhaps owing to pressure from the German princes—and returned to Germany in September 1155. Hadrian IV undoubtedly was all the more disappointed because an insurrection of the barons had broken out against William in the south, and because the moment seemed ripe for eliminating the Norman peril once and for all. William I's adversaries had the support of Byzantine troops. The rebels managed to persuade the pope to take advantage of the situation. He made his way to San Germano, and then to Benevento for a longer stay, in order to receive the homage of Robert of Capua, who had reconquered his principality, and that of other great lords of the region. William I thereupon made territorial and ecclesiastical concessions and declared himself ready to crush the Romans in order to make peace with the pope. Yet the majority of the cardinals put pressure on him to refuse these offers. The situation changed completely, however, during the spring of 1156, when William succeeded in crushing the lords' rebellion and driving back the Byzantines. His army laid seige to Benevento. Hadrian IV, who had remained in the city with a few cardinals, began negotiations with the Norman sovereign, which ended in a treaty in the spring of 1156. This marked a step backward with regard to the policy followed by the popes in Sicily over the course of the previous decades; the papacy rallied to the alliance concluded in 1059 with the Normans. The treaty of Benevento put an end to a situation that had been unresolved. The pope recognized William I, as well as a large, unified Norman kingdom that included Sicily, Apulia, Capua, and other regions. The terms establishing the feudal obligations of the Normans could be modified by neither of the parties. In the regions of lower Italy, ecclesiastical nominations were to be free—even if they required royal confirmation—and the APPEAL to the Holy See as well as the visits and the dispatch of legates were to be authorized. On the other hand, there would be no appeals from Sicily, and no dispatch of legates without royal authorization; the privilege conceded by URBAN II to Sicily was therefore upheld.

Hadrian IV returned to Rome in November 1156. Thanks to new bases of support, he consolidated his power in the PATRIMONY OF ST. PETER, thereby counterbalancing the autonomy the Romans continued to enjoy. In 1158, he turned to account the freedom to maneuver that he had arranged for himself in order to negotiate an agreement between the Normans and the Byzantines. But the refusal to recognize the PRIMACY of the pope was an obstacle to union with the Eastern Church. Frederick I had never officially renounced the claims made in the treaty of Constance. For him, the treaty of Benevento violated the agreement concluded between the papacy and the empire, for it seemed to cast a slur on his rights in lower Italy. In 1157, the pope sent to the German lands Cardinals Bernard of S. Clemente and Cardinal Roland of S. Marco (the future ALEXANDER III), both of whom had played a decisive role in the Benevento negotiations. They were given responsibility for making ecclesiastical visits, setting forth the papal policy to the imperial court, and lodging a complaint against the arrest in Burgundy, on his way back from Rome, of Archbishop Eskil de Lund, whom Hadrian IV had made primate of Scandinavia at the beginning of the year. The legates were received in audience at Besançon in October 1157. Barbarossa's chancellor translated the word *beneficia*, used in a letter from Adrian, as "fiefs," which amounted to consideration of the empire as a fief of the Holy See. The German princes were furious. The legates were expelled, and appeals of the German clergy to the Curia were forbidden. But in June 1158, the pope declared that the word *beneficium* should be understood as meaning "benefit" and not "fief." Thanks to this concession, a definitive

break between Hadrian IV and the Germans was avoided, at least in appearance. A disagreement in principle nevertheless remained regarding conceptions of the relations between the Church and the empire. When Barbarossa undertook a new Italian campaign in the summer of 1158, the conflict, originally theoretical, became concrete, opening up specific points of contention. Hadrian IV protested against the new organization imposed in upper Italy by Frederick I and against the encroachment on the part of the imperial administration in the States of the Church. He even attempted to forbid the emperor to intervene in the quarrel between Bergamo and Brescia. In April 1159, the pope suddenly proposed renewing the treaty of Constance. Barbarossa rejected this offer, on the pretext that the treaty had been broken by the pope long before, and demanded instead that it be replaced by an arbitrating tribunal, something Hadrian IV stubbornly refused. The pope insisted that the emperor recognize absolute pontifical sovereignty over Rome and the PAPAL STATES in a vast territorial domain, but Barbarossa likewise claimed rights over Rome. There was a rough attempt to establish contacts between the German court and the Roman communal movement. Hadrian made his way to Anagni, near the Norman kingdom. He incited several northern Italian cities to resistance against the Hohenstaufen, and promised to excommunicate Frederick I within forty days. The death of the pope, in September 1159, put an end to the affair.

Hadrian IV showed himself generous with regard to the monastery of St. Rufus, and understanding with regard to English aspirations. He took the abbey of St. Albans under his wing and accorded privileges to the archdiocese of York, the rights of which he extended over the Church of Scotland. The authenticity of the BULL *Laudabiliter*, authorizing the king of England to conquer Ireland, is contested. In matters respecting the cardinals, Hadrian IV's policy differed from that of EUGENE III, for he elevated no monks to the cardinalate. In 1156, he created four cardinals (among them Boso, the celebrated historian of the papacy), and in 1158, six more. Almost all of them supported Alexander III in the papal SCHISM. Boso presents Hadrian IV as affable, patient, eloquent, inclined to pardon, and charitable. More recent historians, however, have emphasized the energy and the decisiveness of this "action pope" (W. Ullmann).

Karl Schnith

Bibliography

JL, 2, 102–45.
LP,2, 388–97.
PL, 188, 1631–40.
Almedingen, E. M. *The English Pope*, London, 1925.
Bemont, C. "La bulle Laudabiliter," *Mélanges Ferdinand Lot*, Paris 1925, 41–53.

Heinemeyer, W. "Beneficium, non feudum sed bonum factum," *Archiv für Diplomatik*, 15 (1969), 155–236.

Johnsen, A. O. *Studier verdorende Kardinal Nikolaus Brekespears legasjion til Norden*, Oslo, 1945.

Lamma, P. "Adriano IV," *DBI*, 1 (1960), 330–5.

Maccarone, M. *Papato e Imperio dalla elezione di Federico I alla morte di Adriano IV*, Rome, 1959.

Maleczek, W. "Rombeherrschung und Romererneuerung durch das Papsttum," *Rom in hohen Mittelalter*, Sigmaringen, 1992, 15–27.

Noyon, A. "Adrien IV," *DHGE*, 1 (1912), 625–7 (bibliographic updating under "Adrien IV," ibid., 22 [1988], 1486–7).

Rassow, P. *Honor Imperii*, Munich, 2e ed., 1961.

Schmale, F. J., "Adrian IV," *LexMA*, 4 (1987–9), 1823.

Southern, R.W. "Pope Adrian IV," *Medieval Humanism and Other Studies*, Oxford, 1970, 234–52.

Ullmann, W. "The Pontificate of Adrian IV," *Cambridge Historical Journal* 11 (1955), 233–52.

Watterich, 2, 323–74.

Zenker, B. *Die Mitglieder des Kardinalkollegiums von 1130 bis 1159*, Würzburg, 1964.

HADRIAN V.

HADRIAN V. *Ottobono Fieschi (b. Genoa, ca. 1205, d. Viterbo, 18 August 1276). Elected pope on 11 July 1276, not crowned. Buried at Viterbo in the church of S. Francesco.*

Born into the Genoese family of the counts of Lavagna, Ottobono Fieschi was thrust into the forefront of the Roman scene by his uncle, Pope INNOCENT IV. A man of the CURIA he spent his life totally in the service of the popes, his predecessors, and of their diplomacy. After having been his uncle's CHAPLAIN, and then archdeacon and chancellor of Reims, canon of Notre-Dame of Paris, and archdeacon of Parma, he was promoted by Innocent IV to CARDINAL deacon with the TITLE of St. Adriano, at the end of 1251. Under ALEXANDER IV, he continued Innocent IV's policy of family favoritism and increased his influence in the Curia. He thus was able to intervene in favor of John of Parma, minister general of the Franciscans, who was driven to resign in 1257 owing to his Joachimite opinions, and to enable him to avoid the imprisonment to which the proceedings begun by St. Bonaventure would have led.

An implacable enemy of the Hohenstaufen, he stood alongside Cardinal John of Toledo to support and bring to a conclusion the election of Richard of Cornwall as perpetual senator of Rome in the spring of 1261. That was the beginning of a period of sustained relations with England, whose interests he supported by refusing any compromise with Manfred during the election of URBAN IV on 29 August 1261. He was therefore naturally one of the privileged interlocutors of Henry III's ambassadors at the Curia at the beginning of the new pontificate. However, in 1262–3, when Urban IV reoriented papal policy toward a Franco-Angevin alliance, Ottobono Fieschi followed suit, in the interest of his party in Genoa: it was he who urged St. Louis to take to his heart the Sicilian enterprise of his brother, Charles of Anjou; he was one of a trio of trustworthy cardinals sent by the pope in July 1264 to raise troops at Perugia, Assisi, and Spoleto and to preach the CRUSADE against Manfred.

Under CLEMENT IV, he showed the extent of his talents as a negotiator as LEGATE in England. On the way to his legation, he stopped in Genoa to negotiate the free passage of the Angevin troops (he was in Genoa in mid-August 1265), and then he took himself to St. Louis in order to discuss the Angevin project (he was in Paris at the end of August). He arrived in England on 29 October 1265 and succeeded in mediating between Henry III and his rebellious barons during the Diet of Kenilworth on 31 October 1266. He also devoted himself to preaching the crusade in the company of the future popes GREGORY X and BONIFACE VIII. His English legation was accomplished successfully and came to an end in 1267. Fieschi returned to Rome in June 1268 and there continued his work on promoting the Angevin policy, alongside the Genoese GUELPHS in exile—after the victorious uprising of the GHIBELLINES in October 1270—as well as at the CONCLAVE of VITERBO, which ended in the election of Gregory X in 1271, and where he was one of the leaders of the French party. He even met with Charles of Anjou, in residence in Rome, in April–May 1272.

Present at the COUNCIL of Lyon in 1274, he accompanied Gregory X to Lausanne to meet with Rudolf of Habsburg in October 1275; but he attempted to limit Germanic activity to the advantage of the Angevins, in whose favor he intervened in Tuscany in February 1276. Subsequently, he persuaded the new pope, INNOCENT V, to lift the INTERDICT imposed by Gregory X against the cities at war with Pisa.

The election of the successor of Innocent V, who died on 22 June 1276, was overseen by Charles of Anjou, who was present in Rome. It is therefore no surprise that one of his strongest allies, whose influence remained strong within the SACRED COLLEGE, be elected in the person of Ottobono Fieschi on 11 July 1276, after a conclave of three weeks held at St. John of Lateran. Hadrian V only had the time to suspend the constitution of Gregory X on the organization of the conclave. He died soon after in Viterbo on 18 August without ever having been crowned.

Ghislain Brunel

Bibliography

Gatto, L. "Adriano V," *DBI*, 1 (1960), 335–7.

Graham, R. "Letters of Cardinal Ottoboni," *EHR*, 15, (1900), 87–120.

Noyon, A. "Adrien V," *DHGE*, 1 (1912), 627, completed by: "Fieschi (Ottobono)," *EHR*, 22 (1988), 1487.

Roberg, B. "Hadrian V," *LexMA*, 4 (1989), 1823–24.

Schöpp, N. *Papst Hadrian V (Kardinal Ottobuono Fieschi)*, Heidelberg, 1916.

HADRIAN VI. *Adriaan Florensz Dedel (b. Utrecht, 2 March 1459, d. Rome, 14 September 1523). Elected pope on 9 January 1522, crowned on 31 August 1522. Buried at St. Peter's in Rome, then at Sta Maria dell'Anima (1523).*

The importance of this pontificate lies in two distinguishing features: Hadrian VI was the last non-Italian pope before JOHN PAUL II and the first pope of the modern era in favor of reform within the Church, even though the movement for reform undertaken by Luther was still far from having succeeded.

Proposed by CARDINAL Giulio de'Medici, the candidacy of the cardinal bishop of Tortosa, sixty-three years old, was accepted, to general surprise, on 9 January 1522. The cardinal was then in Spain, where he learned the news only on 9 February. After a month of reflection, he accepted, not without reservations, and set out to present himself in Rome.

Adriaan Florensz was born in Utrecht on 2 March 1459. The son of a naval carpenter, of modest origins but preserved from actual want, he studied at the Latin school of Utrecht and Zwolle, where he came under the influence of the *devotio moderna*, before being registered in 1476 at the University of Louvain, where he earned his master of arts degree in 1478 and his doctorate in theology in 1490. He taught there and twice held the office of rector and once that of vice chancellor.

Called to the court of Mary of Burgundy, he was chosen by Maximilian to undertake the education of his grandson Charles. In 1515, he was entrusted with a diplomatic mission to Spain, where he met Cardinal Ximénes of Cisneros. In return for his efforts, he was named bishop of Tortosa in 1516 and cardinal in 1517. He dreamt of returning to Utrecht, where he purchased a house in 1517, but continued his political career in Spain and played a role in the government of Castile from 1517 to 1522.

When he arrived in Rome on 29 August 1522, the "German barbarian" was given a cold, if not hostile, reception by both the people of Rome and the personnel of the CURIA. This reserved intellectual, who had an unusual degree of devotion to his calling (he celebrated mass every day), and was frugal and uncommunicative, disconcerted and worried a population used to luxury. The pope's two governing ideas, set forth in his coronation speech on 1 September 1522, were the continuation of the CRUSADE against the TURKS—which implied the reconciliation of the Christian princes—and the reform of the Curia being prepared for by a cardinals' commission created in February 1523. Hadrian relied on his secretary Dirk Hezius and his friend Willem von Enckenvoirt, whom he had named cardinal. Foreigners who were unfamiliar with the ways of the Curia, they too were exposed to general hostility. Besides its brevity, three reasons stand out for the failure of this pontificate. In spite of his ideal of simplicity (which did not exclude a certain love of art) and strictness, which marked a contrast with the practices of his predecessors, Hadrian was unable to put an end to the archaism of the Papal State in fiscal matters and to the makeshift solutions he condemned, but also had recourse to the sale of offices and positions of responsibility. In spite of the mission entrusted to the NUNCIO Chieregati at the diet of Nuremberg (January 1523) and the acknowledgment of faults committed by the papacy, he did not manage to convince Luther and Melanchhon, whereas he made the German prelates uneasy by his strictness. In spite of his desire for neutrality, he was ultimately constrained by the political nature of the papacy to support Charles V, allied with England, against France (3 August 1523). He died barely thirteen months after his coronation.

Gérald Chaix

Bibliography

Berglar, P. "Die kirchliche und politische Bedeutung des Pontifikats Hadrians VI," *Archiv für Kulturgeschichte*, 54 (1972), 97–112.

Bijloos, J. *Adrianus VI. De Nederlandse Paus*, Haarlem, 1980.

Burmann, C. *Hadrianus VI, sive Analecta historica de hadriano sexto. . .*, Utrecht, 1727.

Ducke, K. H. *Handeln zum Heil. Eine Untersuchung zur Morallehre Hadrians VI*, Leipzig, 1976 (Erfurter Theologische Studien 34).

Ephemerides theologicae Lovanienses, 35 (1959), 513–629, devoted to Hadrian VI, especially the article by L. E. Halkin, "Adrien VI et la réforme de l'Église," 534–52.

Hochks, E. *Der letzte deutsche Papst Adrian VI.*, Freiburg im Breīsgau, 1939; Dutch trans. Bruges, 1944.

McNally, R. E. "Pope Adrian VI (1522–1523) and Church Reform," *AHP*, 7 (1969), 253–85.

Munier, W. A. J. "Hadrian VI," *Theologische Realenzyclopädie*, 14 (1985), 309–10.

Paus Adrianus VI 1459–1523, Gedenkboek. Catalogs, Utrecht, 1959.

Posner, J. *Der deutsche Papst. Adrian VI*, Recklinghausen, 1962.

HAT, HOLY. See **Blessed or Holy Hat and Sword**.

HELSINKI CONFERENCE. The Conference on Security and Cooperation in Europe (CSCE) held in Helsinki

(Finland) from 3 July to 1 August 1975 took on particular importance regarding the configuration of international diplomacy by the HOLY SEE, especially with regard to its relations with sovereign states. For the first time since the preparatory sessions for the Congress of Vienna in 1814, the representative body of the VATICAN city state was invited to participate as a "full member" (and as such, with full responsibility) in a conference with a declared goal that was exclusively political. The difficulties of participation by the authorities of the Roman Catholic Church in conferences of this type were, however, not new, and had already made themselves known in the past, despite the more traditional activities of arbitration and mediation in which the Holy See was not only formally engaged, but to which it was juridically bound. Mandated by PIUS VII (1800–23) to defend the restoration of the PAPAL STATES and having expressed his opposition to one of the projects of the Congress of Vienna, cardinal secretary of state Consalvi referred to the "unfavorable impression that, according to the mentality of the time, makes it appear as though a priest wants to sit in the first row while even the emperors do not" (letter of 21 December 1814 to Cardinal Pacca, pro-secretary of state). Such papal participation was not immediately accepted, including among Catholic nations, and the Holy See itself had affirmed (Article 4 of the LATERAN Accords in 1929) that it wanted to "remain outside both the temporal competition between states and international conferences organized for this purpose," other than in the exceptional case where, in a contentious situation, "the adverse parties would unanimously appeal to its mission of peace." A mission of this kind was carried out by Rome at the time of the Vienna conference on international treaty law (1961). From the very beginning of his papacy, PAUL VI had restored the Holy See's place on the international scene by agreeing to make an apostolic visit to the headquarters of the United Nations. In the case of the Conference on Security and Cooperation in Europe, the invitation was sent to Rome by the Warsaw Pact countries in the framework of an international diplomatic situation rigidified by over two decades of "cold war," but on the verge of gradual improvement: on the European scene, several bilateral treaties (most notably the fundamental treaty signed by the two Germanies) as well as the four-party Accord for Berlin had contributed to a moderate thaw in East-West relations.

During consultations (22 November 1972–25 June 1973) preparatory to the conference, the apostolic pronuncio, Msgr. Zabkat, was reminded that the Holy See would maintain a "very specific" position implying absolute neutrality in the matter of political aims (with neither temporal power nor a specific plan, it fulfilled a spiritual mission of a universal nature) and seeking recognition as a uniquely European entity. This declaration was unanimously approved. The states participating in the conference (officially opened by the first meeting of the ministers concerned on 6 July 1973) had placed their proposals in one or more of the three "baskets" (concerning, respectively, the principles for interstate relations, economic cooperation, and humanitarian issues). On the latter, the Holy See submitted a request aimed at ensuring "respect for the fundamental rights of man, among others, that of religious freedom," which would correspond to the "frontiers of the mind," enjoying the same inviolability as any territorial boundary (6 March 1973). In fact, the issue of human rights proved to be one of the major features of the conference, and one on which the Church was heard. The seventh principle of the final act, adopted on 1 August 1975 by the thirty-three European states participating (Albania was the only absentee), as well as by Canada and the United States, proclaimed "the respect and effective exercise" of these—individual as well as collective — essential rights, and recognized their universality, which was seen as a means of quelling specific regional conflicts. An examination of the stipulations that are specific to international public law demonstrates that, in order to take the form of a transcript, the final Helsinki Act was allowed no binding juridical value for its signatories, but only political and moral force. Following this same principle of analysis, the act, published three days later in the OSSERVATORE ROMANO, nevertheless would not be reduced to a simple declaration of intention, and committed the participants to act in accord with their resolve in the areas dealt with by the conference. In a more directly political manner, the measures that came out of the Helsinki meeting gained a supplementary legitimacy from the size and the importance of the nations involved (powers from both blocs). These measures followed a long period of inactivity in normal bilateral and multilateral diplomatic relations among several of these states.

Thus, without containing actual concrete and immediately implementable measures, the Helsinki Conference contributed indisputably to establishing a climate that welcomed and helped to create further openings. Paul VI, in a message addressed to the conference on the day the final act was signed, and then at the time of the next ANGELUS (8 August 1975), expressed his joy at the attention that had been given to the problem of religious freedom, which had been openly scorned in Eastern Europe. The positions taken and advocated by JOHN PAUL II, from the time of his accession to the papacy, regarding the Eastern Bloc countries—beyond strictly religious concerns—were explicitly connected to the "spirit" of Helsinki. On 5 July 1989, the pope could thus affirm, during a speech given in Helsinki's Finlandia Hall, that the document adopted fourteen years earlier should be seen as "one of the most meaningful tools of international dialogue," allowing Europe to "rediscover her roots," especially her Christian roots, while at the same time fighting for values of universal scope. This almost dual position has a parallel in the international status given the Holy See within the framework of international conferences, allowing it to be a party that is not directly interested in the specific motivations of the different states, but is at the same time actively involved in defining and defending their underlying principles.

Philippe Levillain

Bibliography

Carascosa Coso, A. *La Santa Sede y la Conferencia sobre la seguridad y la cooperación en Europa. Helsinki, Ginebra, Helsinki*, Cuenca, 1990.

Casaroli, A. "Le Saint-Siège et la communauté internationale," *La Documentation catholique*, 73 (1975), 309–17.

Casaroli, A. "Helsinki and the New Europe," *Triped* 58 (1990), 49–60.

Schutze, W. "Détente et sécurité en Europe. Situation actuelle et perspectives d'avenir," Études (July 1973), 177–94.

Silvestrini, A. "La participation du Saint-Siège au processus de la CSCE," *Le Saint-Siàge et les relations diplomatiques. Actes du colloque de l'Académie diplomatique internationale*, Paris, 1989.

Wajsman, P. *Recherches sur la sécurité européene*, thesis Paris-II, 1974.

Zorgbibe, C. "La Conférence sur la sécurité et la coopération en Europe," *Revue générale de droit international public*, 2 (1973), 424–43.

HERALDRY. Interest in papal heraldry is a recent phenomenon. It was not until 1930 that a fully illustrated volume, *Papal Heraldry* (D. L. Galbreath), was published. In 1978, Bruno Heim dedicated a few chapters of his *Heraldry in the Catholic Church, Its Origins, Customs, and Laws* to the papal insignia. And in *Heraldry in the Vatican* (1987), Cardinal Jacques Martin outlined the heraldic monuments of the Vatican and ST. PETER's BASILICA since the time of EUGENE IV's papacy. In the mid-1990s the Italian State Archives were in the process of taking a systematic inventory of all the heraldic monuments in Rome, with the exception of those in Vatican City.

Despite the titles of the works mentioned above, speaking of "papal heraldry" seems inadequate in the specific sense of the word as it is understood by Western and northern European heraldists for whom choosing, granting, using, and, representing arms have been, since the 15th century, subject to clearly defined rules that concern most of the countries that create official bodies to apply them. In Italy, heraldry was not codified before the 18th century, and even then this was not the case in all the states. There was no institution to control the adoption and use of coats of arms. In Italy's case, it is thus more precise to speak of heraldic customs than of heraldry.

Since most of the attributes are of a military nature (helmets, crests, crowns, friezes, trophies, etc.), ecclesiastic heraldry is perhaps not the correct term, except for the escutcheon, the military origin of which was progressively abandoned for purely decorative forms. This peculiarity explains why ecclesiastical heraldry began toward the end of the 13th century, while lay heraldry was flourishing and already on the way to codification. An inquiry into ecclesiastical arms in general, and papal arms in particular, can thus take place effectively without the word "heraldry," but rather with a discussion of the customs and habits observed to represent Church insignia, emblems, and symbols. These customs and habits were deeply influenced by traditional heraldry and, for lack of a better word, quotation marks are used in a discussion of papal "heraldry." Thus, a study of papal heraldry does not follow the normal schema of treatises on heraldry. On the other hand, it does deal with the development, the variations, the introduction, and the abandonment of representations of the sovereign pontiffs' insignia or emblems. These were first of all the CROSS, the universal symbol of Christianity, and then the KEYS of ST. PETER, the symbol of the power to administer the treasures of redemption. After these came insignias of lesser importance: the TIARA, the PAVILION (in Italian, *ombrellino*), and the representation *in effigie* of the apostles PETER and PAUL.

The Cross. Beginning in the 4th century, the cross replaced the earliest symbols for Christ (the fish, the chrism). After it became a liturgical object in the early 8th century, the cross ended up being the universal symbol of Christianity. Pilgrims to Jerusalem sewed it on their clothing, as had the crusaders, who chose different colors depending on their region of origin. The CRUSADES themselves marched under the sign of the cross, and the orders of chivalry adopted it. The emperor's banner, especially that of the Holy Roman Emperor, had a red cross on a white background, and most Italian cities that were prominent in the Middle Ages continue to show it on their coats of arms today: red on a white background, or white on a red background. It is correct to assume that from the earliest times the papal banner, the *vexillum sancti Petri*, had a cross. The popes gave this banner to sovereigns as a personal privilege, either as a sign of vassalage or of infeudation. A later MOSAIC in the Lateran shows St. Peter giving the *pallium* to LEO III and the *vexillum* to Charlemagne. In 1044, BENEDICT IX made a gift of a *vexillum* to Emperor Henry III as he left on a crusade against the Hungarian pagans. In 1076 Pope GREGORY VII sent a *vexillum* as a vassalage to the new king of Croatia and Dalmatia, Zvonimir, at the time of his coronation. The *vexillum* certainly contained a cross from that time on, as a result. We know that the first banner of the Venetian Republic contained a cross. In 1204,

INNOCENT III sent a *vexillum* decorated with a cross and keys to Czar Kalojoanes of Bulgaria. The pope had himself escorted by a *vexillum* carried by a *vexillifer*: ALEXANDER II is said to have given, during a consistory, the banner of St. Peter to the Milanese captain Erembaldo, whom he made flag bearer of the Roman and universal Church. In 1204, as noted above, the cross was accompanied by St. Peter's keys. The LIBER CENSUUM speaks of the cross accompanied by two keys; in 1239 the *vexillum* was depicted "with crosses and keys" (*cum crucibus et clavibus*). In 1316 the city of VITERBO won the privilege of being able to add to its coat of arms a lion passant, the *vexillum* with four keys, one in each quarter of the shield. The commune of Serrona seems to have received the same privilege, since it still bears the cross and keys on its seals. The arms of the diocese of Chieti are identical. Starting in the 14th century, the cross and keys were found more frequently on shields. Cardinal Albornoz, a papal LEGATE, also bore them, and not only on his banner, as was seen in Gubbio (1332) and Bologna (1362). Other representations were found in Perugia in 1466 and 1500. But use of the cross and keys ultimately diminished. They were seen on the banners of BENEDICT XIII (Pedro de Luna), PIUS II, and JULIUS II. Starting in the 15th century, keys and the cross began to be identified with the Church. In 1475, Bernard de Rosier spoke of the "arms of the Church, a white cross on a red background, with keys." The armorials of the latter half of the century, like those of Ingeram, St. Gall, and Grünewald, show a shield with a red cross on silver, and the inscription *Ecclesia*. In the 16th century, the cross disappeared both as an emblem of the pope and as an emblem of the Church (perhaps in the aftermath of the REFORMATION), making way for other symbols: the keys of St. Peter and the pavilion.

The German historian Erdmann's thesis, that the popes added the keys to the cross in order to distinguish their *vexillum* from that of the emperor, does not seem to be well supported. It is worth noting in this regard that the emperors of BYZANTIUM added the letter "B" to the cross, on all four of its extremities.

The Keys of Saint Peter. The custom of using St. Peter's keys as a symbol of papal authority goes back to at least the 12th century. In the old Constantinian basilica of St. Peter there was a mosaic representing Innocent III—the pope who presented the *vexillum* with the cross and the keys to the Bulgarian czar—and a feminine figure holding a gonfalon upon which the two keys of St. Peter stood back to back. During the wars against Frederick II in the second quarter of the 13th century, the soldiers of the papal troops distinguished themselves by a *signum* composed of keys, whence their name *clave signati* ("marked by the key"), just as the Crusaders had been *cruce signati* ("marked by the cross"). After the infeudation of Sicily to Charles of Anjou by the pope, the new king, as a sign of

vassalage, had two keys placed back-to-back on his coins. In the 18th century, the saddle (CHINEA) that the king of Naples offered each year to the pope as a sign of vassalage no longer carried keys on each shabrack, but rather the pontiff's personal arms with the tiara over them.

A number of 13th-century monuments show the keys crossed rather than back-to-back, e.g., in Viterbo (1267), Pesaro, Grottaferrata, and Perugia; they appeared on Orvieto's seals, also. But it was only with the first AVIGNON popes, and contact with Western heraldry, that the keys were placed on a shield and took a heraldic form. The first known example was at the abbey of Sassovivo, near Foligno, and is dated 1214. At the same time, under CLEMENT VI, we see the keys associated for the first time with the tiara, and they also appeared on the Church's BANNERS. A miniature of an early 14th-century manuscript in the Marciana library in Venice, called "The Entrance to Spain," shows its colors: silver on gules (red). First silver, the keys later—and this was one of the few rules to be consistently followed—came to be pictured as one golden and the other silver. The keys' wards, which were cut in the shape of a cross, were always turned upward; only one exception to this is known, in Perugia, dated 1473. Keys standing back to back were found on COINS from 1269 to 1342. They were then replaced by crossed keys, which first appeared in 1314. The keys were called *claves Ecclesiae Romanae* and, in 1512, *insignia Ecclesiae Romanae*. Starting in the 15th century they were always crossed, as back-to-back keys had become the insignia of St. Peter's Basilica. Crossed keys could be presented in a variety of forms. They could stand alone or be accompanied by the tiara or the pavilion, the other emblems of the papacy. Contrary to contemporary usage, which referred to the "tiara and keys," or the "pavilion and keys," the present references are to the "keys and tiara" (meaning they were accompanied by or set underneath a tiara) and "keys and pavilion": for it is the keys that are emblematic of papal power; the tiara and the pavilion are only secondary insignias, and thus subordinate. Thus, representations of the keys of St. Peter are grouped in three categories: 1) crossed keys standing alone, keys with the tiara, and keys and pavilion as independent elements; 2) the same elements placed over a shield; and 3) the same elements placed on a shield, either as a chief (i.e., on the upper part of the shield, separated from the rest by a line of partition) or accompanying a charge (a heraldic figure).

Crossed Keys. *As independent elements*: in general use during the 13th century, they gradually became secondary or ornamental representations, appearing sporadically as independent elements. Primarily decorative, they were seen as early as the reigns of BONIFACE VIII and JOHN XXIII, and on CLEMENT VII's tomb, where they alternated with the arms of the counts of Geneva, and later at La Sapienza (university) in Rome. They were occasionally placed on the canopy over the papal throne, as was the case for GREGORY XI, Pius II (in 1501 in Siena's cathedral) and PIUS V (in the Altemps chapel in Santa Maria in Trastevere, in 1562). The keys occasionally appeared as the insignias of an office: for example, on the seals of the AUDITORS in the CURIA between 1319 and 1450, and those of the Comtat Venaissin's government. In 1314, keys alone were placed on coins by Clement VI, and were still there during BENEDICT XII's papacy. They then disappeared, only to make a brief reappearance in the 18th century under BENEDICT XIV and PIUS VI (*bajocchi*). It might also be mentioned that crossed keys often accompanied the arms of those who held titles to legations in the PAPAL STATES (Bologna, Ferrara, Ancona, Perugia, etc.) and those of the other legates, of whom they were the official insignia.

As crests: from the time of Benedict XII and Clement VI, crossed keys alone were also placed as a crest over the shield on a pope's personal arms. The last Avignon popes, Clement VII (Geneva), Benedict XII (Luna), and CLEMENT VIII (Muñoz), always did so. On rare occasions the keys could be found on the left and right sides of the shield rather than above it; such was the case for INNOCENT VI. This is perhaps explained by the fact that the shield also had a chief with two pairs of crossed keys (thus a total of eight keys). On occasion they were accompanied by other crests. Gregory XI placed the tiara over his shield in the center, with keys on either side. Eugene IV placed the keys on the dexter side, the tiara in the center, and the patriarchal cross on the sinister side. There were thus no strict rules. Two rather strange cases bear mentioning: Eugene IV also stamped his shield with a tiara over which there were keys, but with the bits turned downward. More recently the arms of PIUS XI (Ratti) in St. Peter's set the crossed keys under the charges (an eagle and three bezants) that are "cut off" (i.e. they are not set within a shield), while the tiara sits atop all.

Placed within the shield: there are three variations—a) keys as the only figure, b) keys on the shield's chief, and c) keys accompanied by other charges.

a) The keys as the sole figure: this is a true heraldic presentation. The earliest examples available to us date from the beginning of the 14th century, and are contemporaneous with crossed keys on banners. A manuscript of Pope INNOCENT IV's *Apparatus super Decretalibus* preserved in Trent contains a miniature upon which we see, beside the pope, two horsemen, one of whom is holding a shield with keys. It is assumed that the miniature goes back to an original from the middle of the 13th century. Examples became fairly common in the 14th century. One shield of this sort is in the abbey of Sassovivo, dated 1314. Another in Gubbio, dated 1337, one in Orvieto in 1338, one in a

Vatican manuscript from 1359, and one in a stained-glass window in Bourges from the time of Benedict XIII also deserve mention. One magnificent example of crossed keys is found in a later presentation (14th century) on URBAN V's arms, in the cloister of Saint John Lateran. In general, the shield with crossed keys accompanies the personal arms of a pope, like those on a gold medallion of Eugene IV, or those on a seal from the time of INNOCENT VIII. This custom appears to have been common in the East: it is found on a shield in Rhodes, with the arms of the grand masters Villeneuve, Heredia, and Naillac, next to the arms of Innocent VI, surmounted or not by the tiara. The colors are generally silver on gules (red), as seen on one of the bindings with the arms on the Siena (Biccherne) registers of 1460, on a painting by Bonfigli in Perugia in 1488, and in the St. Gall armorial where the keys, tied together by a blue cord, were erroneously described as those of Rome. The latest representations of the keys on a shield in Rome were those on Julius II's coins. At the end of the 16th century, when the use of these arms appears to have been abandoned, Martin Schrott's roll of arms (1581) presented quite an odd composition: the shield, with crossed keys and stamped with the tiara, is supported by the apostles Peter and Paul, and all this is set upon a SWORD and a patriarchal cross, seen as the symbols of the temporal and spiritual power of the sovereign pontiff.

b) Keys placed on the chief of the shield of the personal arms of a pope: this custom goes back to the time of the Avignon popes. Innocent VI sometimes placed one pair of keys on the chief, and sometimes two pairs. This custom was followed by Urban V, Clement VII, ALEXANDER V, Eugene IV, FELIX V, PAUL II, SIXTUS IV, and ALEXANDER VI, as is seen in Titian's painting (1502) where the general of the Church's army, Cardinal Francesco Pesaro, is seen holding a banner with the papal shield. INNOCENT XII used it again in the 17th century.

c) Keys accompanying charges (symbols) on a shield: crossed keys are never found inside the shield of a pope's personal arms, rather only in the arms of third parties. These are augmentations, to be dealt with below.

Crossed Keys Surmounted by a Tiara. *As independent elements:* from the beginning, the form is purely decorative, and since the Renaissance has been seen quite frequently in Rome. One of the most beautiful examples is in the tiara worn on the head of an angel in St. John Lateran, from the time of CLEMENT XII. Starting in the 18th century, keys surmounted by a tiara became (or, more precisely, were considered to be) the insignias of the sovereign pontiff and the papacy. They appeared on Benedict XIV's coins. Since 1814 they have been found on banners, uniforms, seals, and on the orders and medals of the Papal States. Since the time of the LATERAN PACTS (1929), they have been on the Vatican City flag.

Placed over a shield: This form is the most common representation, and the best known, since the keys and the tiara are, with very few exceptions, always placed over the personal arms of a sovereign pontiff. Their first appearance goes back to Clement VI, and the most recent is associated with JOHN PAUL II. In the beginning, the keys and the tiara were separate. Since the time of MARTIN V, the tiara has gradually been lowered; first it was found between the wands of the keys, although it was then moved down and placed in front, with the crossed keys behind it. Then the keys were moved even lower, behind the shield, and their stems expanded beyond the shield on both sides, either at about the half-way point or toward the lower section. Sometimes the bits emerged on both sides of the shield, as during the time of Felix V and Alexander VII. However, there are no rules, and artistic choice and taste have always decided the placement of the keys surmounted by a tiara in relation to the shield. Nor were there norms regarding the proportion of the keys to the tiara. PAUL IV began to place an angel's head between the keys and the tiara, a custom used later by almost all his successors up to URBAN VIII, and later, also, by Clement XII.

Placed within the shield: There are three variations on keys standing alone.

a) The keys and the tiara as single figures: this form is currently the coat of arms of the Holy See and of Vatican City. It, too, goes back to the Avignon papacy, although it was not prominent until the 15th century. It is superfluous to mention even its most famous representations, but one beautiful example should be borne in mind: on one of the panels on the bronze door of St. Peter's, done by Filarete in about 1455, where the keys and the tiara are seen on a shield, while in the same image we see the arms of pope Eugene IV (familial arms with a chief bearing the tiara), and those of the basilica (with the two keys back to back).

b) The keys and the tiara set on the chief: Clement VI placed the keys and the tiara on the chief of his shield, a representation that was still found during the time of Paul II in the Palazzo Venezia in Rome. Since the time of Martin V, the line of demarcation between the field of the shield and the chief has been abandoned: the keys and the tiara have become, according to the rules of Western heraldry, the "charges." Doing away with partitions, a custom that became general in Rome, allowed for more decorative monuments.

c) The keys and the tiara in the company of charges: we will address this issue in our discussion of augmentation, since it is a question (except in the case already discussed in the two preceding paragraphs) of arms of individuals other than popes.

Crossed Keys Topped with a Pavilion (Ombrellino). It is possible to replace the tiara as the element standing above the keys with a pavilion, or *ombrellino*.

As independent elements: keys and a pavilion are rarer than keys and a tiara, and occasionally these elements are even mixed. The earliest example known to us of keys and a pavilion juxtaposed with keys and a tiara is on the fountain called the fountain of Alexander VI, in the CASTEL SANT' ANGELO. On Pius II's pontifical canopy, which was painted by Pinturicchio (ca. 1501) in the library of the Cathedral of Siena, the keys and the pavilion alternate with the arms of Piccolomini, with a tiara above them. Of similar interest is the representation of the keys and of the pavilion on one of Giorgio Vasari's frescoes in the palace of the Chancery in Rome; it shows PAUL III in 1546, ordering that the construction of the basilica of St. Peter's be continued. In the lower part of the fresco, a crouched, naked old man is holding the keys and the pavilion in one hand, and the tiara in the other. For lack of a better interpretation, it is assumed that the figure represents the Holy See. A pavilion with crossed keys underneath it, dated 1560, can be seen in Corciano, near Perugia. This composition was adopted by a number of Church institutions in modern times. The APOSTOLIC CAMERA used it, as did a few papal institutions like the Lateran university, some cities, and institutions in the old Papal States, and especially the cardinal CAMERLENGO during the vacancy of the Apostolic See, as can be seen by all after the death of a pope. Since 1521, COINS minted during a period of vacancy also have keys surmounted by a pavilion; these are sometimes accompanied by a small shield with the personal arms of the cardinal camerlengo.

As a crest: keys and a pavilion placed above a shield are the exclusive privilege of the cardinal camerlengo having a vacancy in the Apostolic See. It has nevertheless happened that the privilege has been granted to a city or to a family: this issue will be addressed below, in the section on augmentations and privileges.

Placed within the shield:

a) Keys and a pavilion as a single figure: this form has been used by the Holy See since at least 1556. It appears in the two shields at the head of the Colonna family's BULL of EXCOMMUNICATION by Paul IV. The different administrations of the Papal States used it on decrees and ordinances (*bandi*) against posting bills. The shield carrying the keys and the pavilion is generally accompanied by the personal coat of arms of the pope and the holder of the office from which the notice has come. The archives contain hundreds of examples. This custom was probably the origin of an engraving by Jodocus Hondius in 1627, showing a shield with the keys and a pavilion, surmounted by the tiara. In the 18th century, this composition was considered to be the more or less official arms of the Church. This is why Napoleon I placed the keys and the pavilion in the first quarter of his arms as king of Italy, and in the arms of the kingdom of Italy. The *Consulta Araldica* confirmed this usage when it created the arms of the university of Macerata.

b) Keys and pavilion on the chief, the pale, or the accompanying charges: this form is found only in the arms of third parties, and shall be addressed below. However, it should be pointed out that there is at least one case (Bernini's bust of Urban VIII in the Louvre) of keys accompanied not by the tiara or a pavilion, but by the patriarchal cross. Before we deal with the two other papal insignias, the tiara and the pavilion, when they are shown without keys, at least a few lines should be devoted to keys standing back to back, as opposed to crossed, as referred to earlier.

Keys Back-to-Back. We know that St. Peter's keys, seen back-to-back as early as the 13th century, became the exclusive emblem of St. Peter's Basilica. We see them (dated 1438) on the panel of Filarete's bronze door, where they are seen at emperor Sigismund's entrance to the basilica in 1433 and on the *Colonna Santa*. Keys back-to-back can be alone or topped with a tiara. The Saint-Gall armorial and Grünewald show them as gules over argent (silver), tied with a blue cord. In his 1555 armorial, Solis incorrectly attributed them to the Holy See. At the time of the reconstruction of St. Peter's (1535–38), Paul III had designs of two keys flanked by a cross placed on the wall dividing the great nave. They are seen in a number of places around St. Peter's, with the bits always turned downward. During holy years, they are imprinted on the bricks of the Porta Santa. St. Peter's Fabbrica, which, along with the chapter of the basilica, uses these emblems, adding the letters RFSP (*Reverenda Fabrica Sancti Petri*).

Tiara. Generally, the tiara is placed above St. Peter's keys; it is occasionally found alone, however.

The tiara as a single element; placed above a shield: Since the time of JOHN XXII's papacy, the tiara has been placed over the personal arms of the pope. This custom was maintained until NICHOLAS V. Succeeding popes placed keys with a tiara over them above their shields. It is rare, although it does occur, for the tiara to be set over a shield containing keys in a crossed position: one good example of this is found in the 1460 registers of Siena (*Biccherne*). This composition was considered to be the papal arms in Mexico (1645). We have already seen that the tiara in this position can end up being flanked by the patriarchal cross and keys: this was often the case during the COUNCIL of Constance, with the arms of popes ALEXANDER V, GREGORY XII, John XXIII, and Benedict XIII.

Placed within the shield: This position is rare for the tiara, and when it does occur the tiara is always on a chief. The arms of Eugene IV on the bronze pontal of the door of St. Peter's Basilica are noteworthy: in it, we see the arms of the Condulmer family with the tiara on the chief. In the Pienza cathedral, a crozier ornamented with the arms of PIUS XII shows the arms of the Piccolomini family (a cross with five crescent moons), with the tiara on the chief.

It is understood that the pope alone has the right to wear as well as display the tiara on his arms. There are, nevertheless, surprising exceptions. The archbishops of Benevento, referring to a privilege of unknown origin, bore a tiara for a long time instead of the episcopal mitre. This privilege was preserved by the patriarchs of Lisbon, who received it from Clement XII. In Mexico, the cathedrals of the capital and Puebla (de "los Angeles" = *Angelopolitana*) placed, above their respective arms—the representation of the Virgin, in both cases—the tiara with the keys, as can be seen in documents from 1648, 1697, and 1738; on this latter date the figure of the Virgin was replaced by a vase with lilies and a constellation of stars. The seal of the order of St. John in Rhodes from the late 15th century, is also noteworthy; it was probably done by the grand master d'Aubigny. In it, the shield of the order is surmounted by the paschal lamb, and above the entire design are the keys and the tiara, probably as a result of some now forgotten privilege.

The Pavilion, or Ombrellino. It appears as though the *ombrellino*, brought to the West by the Sassanids, originally had only a utilitarian function, as protection against inclement weather. The date at which it became an attribute of pontifical dignity is unknown. On the frescoes of the chapel of the Santi Quattro Coronati, in Rome, dated from the middle of the 13th century, it already had the red and gold colors that it would later retain. It appeared in the same forms at the end of the century, in a mosaic in SANTA MARIA MAGGIORE. But it was certainly used earlier, if we grant that in 1177 pope ALEXANDER III gave it to the *doge* of Venice and his successors at the time of their meeting in Venice with emperor Frederick I, who also used a pavilion. The pavilion's utilitarian role has survived through papal concessions to basilicas, allowing one in case of a papal visit. Due to this privilege, the pavilion was included in the arms of basilicas. Nevertheless, St. John Lateran is the only basilica to make use of it with crossed keys. Some families have taken advantage of a similar privilege, especially those in which one of the members had been given the responsibility of being gonfalonier of the Church.

As an independent element: the pavilion made its appearance under Boniface VIII. It is seen, with a tiara above it, on a marble frieze in the Anagni cathedral. It is also seen in a miniature, from a design by Giotto, representing the opening of the holy year 1300, where it alternates with the arms of the Caetini family.

As a crest: we have found no example of an *ombrellino* surmounting the personal arms of a pope. On the other hand, it is possible to find the pavilion surmounting a shield upon which there are crossed keys. It appears in Bologna in 1422 (statutes of the drapers) and 1509 (statutes of the merchants), and in Perugia in 1466 (deliberations of the priors *delle arti*). One example is that of a pavilion placed above a shield surmounted by the keys and the tiara of pope Clement VII de Medici (miniature from a missal in the SISTINE CHAPEL). The pavilion's shape may vary. Some are rather pointed, others are rounded; the one carried before the sovereign pontiff might be topped by a putti or a dove evoking the Holy Spirit.

The Figures of the Apostles Peter and Paul. Even if these are not, strictly speaking, motifs or "heraldic" symbols or emblems, the figures of the two apostles that replace the much more common angels should be mentioned. They have appeared not only as supporters of the shield, but also as busts, since the end of the 8th century (JOHN VIII) and up to the present day, on the leaden bulls of the sovereign pontiffs. As supporters we see them under SIXTUS V and PAUL V; they also appear in Schrott's armorial (1581). Even though they are usually accessories and decorative, they have a semiofficial character when they hold the printed shields on decrees and *bandi*, starting with GREGORY XV's papacy. They also appear on banners. LEO X and Paul III were exceptions, as they had their arms held, respectively, by lions and unicorns. Today, on the diplomas of the SWISS GUARD, the supporters are two soldiers from the guard, one in the uniform of the 16th century, and the other in the "modern" uniform.

The Personal Arms of the Popes. If a sovereign pontiff's supreme power is represented by St. Peter's keys in various forms or contexts, his reign is represented by the use of his personal arms, be these familial, hereditary, or adopted arms. The earliest examples we have on a monument are the arms of Boniface VIII Caetani (1294–1303). But this does not exclude the possibility of earlier use. Such may have been the case for Urban IV, who was born in the diocese of Troyes, in France. On the monument of his nephew, Cardinal Archer, in Saint Praxed, are the roses and lilies of the family coat-of-arms. Since the time of Boniface VIII, all the popes, with only one exception, used their own arms. Only the humanist Nicholas Parentucelli preferred a shield with keys (with or without the tiara, since both forms are found on his tomb). The only personal mark was the addition of the letters P.N.Q., or N.P.P.Q (*Papa Nicolaus Quintus*, or *Nicolaus Papa Pontifex Quintus*). Whether this choice was a mark of humility or the absence of family arms (the pope's father was a doctor) is unknown.

In representations of their arms, the popes observed the rules of heraldry to a greater or lesser extent. They often followed the Roman custom of "disarticulation," that is,

abandoning partition lines, or the separate use of charges and figures for purely decorative purposes. Only two popes modified their arms as cardinals: Pius VI later took out the North Wind blowing on a fleur-de-lis (beginning in 1785, only the plant, without the chubby-cheeked face of the wind, appeared on coins), and Pius XII gave a more "heraldic" look to the sea and waves of the Pacelli arms.

A few popes, like Boniface VIII, Eugene IV, and HADRIAN VI, did not use a crest above their shield. Nevertheless, since the time of John XXII, shields began to be surmounted by the tiara. Starting with CALLISTUS III, the popes began to use only keys with the tiara over them. The rare cases in which only the crossed keys of St. Peter are placed above the shield have already been mentioned. John XXII Dueze and Benedict XII Fournier (*recte* Novelli) probably had only the arms of the bourgeoisie. Most of the popes, up to the end of the 19th century, had family arms: Pius VI, PIUS X, Pius XI, John XXII, PAUL VI, JOHN PAUL I, and John Paul II chose theirs when they became bishops, as is prescribed by canon law (Pius XI took the arms of another family, with the name Ratti). Three popes of the 20th century who had been patriarchs of Venice and, as such, had placed the lion of St. Mark on the chief of their shields, insisted on keeping it in their arms after their election to the papacy. The case of those who placed the keys and the tiara on the chief has already been discussed, or as an adjoining charge, INNOCENT X kept the Anjou chief of his old arms, as Innocent VIII had done before him with the chief of Genoa. Paul V, INNOCENT XI, and ALEXANDER VIII did not abandon the Empire chief granted to their families, as Paul IV, had done, as well as Pius VI (three years into his reign).

The Italian custom of including the arms, of a religious order on one's arms, if one belonged to it, was followed only by the last four popes who had been regulars: the Dominican Benedict XIII (on the chief), the Franciscan CLEMENT XIV (on the chief), the Benedictine PIUS VII (on part of the dexter side), and the Camaldolese GREGORY XVI (on the dexter of one part, or on the chief). The personal arms of the popes were placed on coins up to the 19th century (with the exception of Benedict XIV and Pius VI's *bajocchi* "with keys" mentioned earlier). The college of jurisconsults of Milan, which adopted the personal arms of its founder, PIUS IV, should also be mentioned, as well as a custom followed by a number of popes: that of replacing inscription periods on the reverse side of their bulls with figures taken from their arms. URBAN VI Prignano used eagles' heads, Julius II Della Rovere used acorns, Paul III Farnese had lilies, Julius III del Monte had small mountains, Clement VIII Aldobrandini had mullets, and Alexander VIII Ottoboni had eagles. The personal arms of the pope, surmounted by a tiara, were often engraved on the FISHERMAN'S RING.

Pontifical Emblems in the Arms of a Third Party. Pontifical emblems may be used as an augmentation in the arms of a private party, or in the arms of families, cities, communities, or institutions. Augmentations may also be grouped according to the length of their use: for the duration of one's mandate, for life, or passed on to heirs. Moreover, they must be classified according to the emblems, primarily "keys and tiara," and the pavilion. Special treatment should be reserved for augmentations in the personal arms of a pope, a custom known as arms of patronage (*armi di padronanza*).

Augmentations through the introduction of papal emblems: These augmentations, if they were granted, could be viewed as privileges granted by the sovereign pontiff. But very few certificates granting such a concession exist. In some cases, it can reasonably be supposed that a certain certificate existed and has been lost. In other cases, for example, the pavilion carried by the abbey of Reichenau or the crossed keys on the chief of the Broni (Pavia) collegiate church, the augmentation was a more or less recognized custom. But in still other cases, one cannot fail to notice a "usurpation" by individual fiat, tolerated or ignored thereafter. In the absence of a controlling body, great latitude was allowed.

Crossed keys alone: Keys were the first emblem to be included in arms, as early as the 14th century. In 1318, the arms of Aimery de Lautrec, the governor of Ancona, had crossed keys on the chief. This is a case of arms of office, like those of the auditor Castagnet, who had the keys over his shield. The keys of St. Peter were fairly rare on family arms. Pope Sixtus IV granted duke Borso d'Este the right to place crossed keys on his chief in 1471. This was one of the cases for which we do have a certificate, which is preserved in the Archivio di Stato de Modena. But Duke Ercole I's satisfaction with the keys waned, and in their place (on the chief) he introduced a pale charged with keys topped by a tiara. This may be considered the beginning of a process of contamination, since these figures were found in arms granted in 1474 by the same Sixtus IV to Duke Frederick of Urbino. Another case of usurpation is that of the Soderini family, which was still showing the keys above three stag heads on its arms in 1519. The family claimed that this augmentation was granted by Paul II. About 1525, like the Este family, they placed a tiara above their keys. A similar case, although this one appears to have been legitimized later, was that of the order of the Golden Militia or the Golden Spur, founded in the 15th century. The new knights legitimately introduced crossed keys into their shields, as a supplementary charge. But later they added the tiara, and even the pavilion. At the time, these entities were generally placed on a small shield outside the one that bore the arms of the knight.

Keys and tiara: The well-known case (Montefeltre) of a papal grant dating back to the 15th century has already been discussed. It was not until the 20th century that two more grants of arms with keys and a tiara would be made. In both cases, papal families displayed a tiara instead of the pavilion that was rightfully theirs. Pius XI's family, the Ratti, had keys and a tiara on its chief; the Pacelli family had them in dexter fields, per pale. Both arms were recognized by the Italian *Consulta Araldica*.

Keys and pavilion: The most frequent augmentation was that of keys and a pavilion, which could show up within the shield (on the pale or on the chief, depending on artistic taste), or on the outside as a crest. Strict rules cannot be given, nor is it possible to draw up a list of the families that have had an *ombrellino* in their arms. The following categories might nevertheless be proposed: families where one member had been a pope, gonfaloniers, and families of gonfaloniers. It is difficult to know why some of these families adopted the augmentation and not others.

At the end of the 16th century, use of augmentation with keys and the *ombrellino* was well established among the popes' families. This practice may go back to the time of Paul III Farnese, but it is difficult to know precisely, since the Farnese family had at least two gonfaloniers among their members. The first certain example was that of the Boncampagni, Pope GREGORY XIII's family, which placed keys and a pavilion on the chief of their arms, a practice that would later be followed by the Chigi, the Albani, the Altieri, and the Ottoboni. Other families placed them on a pale, like the Farnese, or at the base of the chief (Braschi-Onesti). The line of partition is often not used, as was the case for the Pamphili arms sculpted by Bernini in San Andrea al Quirinale. Among the Rezzonico, the pavilion is placed above an escutcheon charging one of the quarterings. There were, likewise, families that never practiced augmentation like the Corsinis, the Orsinis, the Lambertinis, and the Contis. Placed within the shield, the keys and the pavilion were on a red background. Only the Boncompagni Ludovisis had a silver field. The Della Rovere, the dukes of Urbino, had a pale with "keys and a pavilion," but this was on their own, not as a papal family.

Gonfaloniers, not to be confused with the captains general (*capitani generali*) who commanded troops, had an honorary duty that went back to the *vexillifer* of the Middle Ages. It is evident that a captain general could be a gonfalonier. At the time of his nomination, the gonfalonier received one or two gonfalons: that of the Church (*vexillum cum armis Ecclesiae*) and that of the pope (*cum armis suis*). Of the two banners presented to the Swiss by Julius II in 1512 (and originally intended for Francesco Gonzaga), that of the Church bore the keys and the pavilion. After the banner was passed to the gonfalonier, he could add papal emblems (e.g., keys and *ombrellino*) to his own arms (*gestare Ecclesiae claves cum vexillis et ornamentis per alios ganfalonieros gestari solitas*, as a text says in 1662). Originally, this privilege lasted as long as his responsibilities, or sometimes it was granted for life, as was the case for the gonfalonier Jacques Annibal de Hohenembs (1565). It is not clear upon what bases, privileges, or decrees some gonfalonier families appropriated keys or the pavilion as rights of inheritance. But just as was the case for the families of the popes, not every one that had provided a gonfalonier to the church added keys or a pavilion into their arms.

In 1642 Urban VIII excommunicated Odoardo Farnese and forbade him the further use of gonfalonier emblems. Innocent XII abolished the ranks of gonfalonier and captain general, which were replaced by the (just as honorary) title of flag-bearer of the Holy Roman Church (*vessilifero di Santa Romana Chiesa*), which Pius IX made transferable by inheritance within the Roman family of the Naro Patrizi. Aside from those for whom the right to have keys or a pavilion derived from the fact that they had a pope or gonfalonier among their numbers, several families used the same privilege without being able to justify it by a papal concession. Among these were the Pio di Carpi, Varano, Malatesta, Riario, Sforza, Bonelli, and Carpegna families, and the Pucci, from Florence. Most were old families of the Papal states, or important feudatories. It is possible that starting in the 16th century, including keys and the pavilion in one's arms served purely and simply to show possesssion of large fiefs in the states, or a particular bond of vassalage. Beyond the frontiers, the Gonzagas of Mantua sometimes added keys and the pavilion to their arms. Some families from Bologna had this privilege completely documented. In fact, the city of Bologna had the right (like Perugia and Ferrara) to use the pavilion (over the keys, or not) above its arms. The privilege spread to all the families of *anziani*, who rarely failed to surmount their shields with the pavilion, and generally placed it above the shield. Other cities in the Papal States used the keys and pavilion. Besides Bolgona, we find Perugia, which placed its gryphon under the keys and pavilion (1560), in addition to both Ferrara and Osimo. Several municipalities displayed papal emblems on their seals or banners, a custom that has been maintained to the present day. Keys alone are found in Frascati and Stimigliano; keys and a tiara are on Riano's shield; the pavilion alone is found in Valmontona; and keys and a pavilion may be seen in Capranica. Crossed keys are the most frequent elements found as accompanying charges: San Severino Marche and Isola del Liri are noteworthy. Four arms of municipalities should also be singled out: those of Serrone, with the cross accompanied by four keys (identical to those granted to Viterbo in 1316); those of Orte, which received the privilege of adding keys and a tiara in its chief, with the letters MFSRE (*Munus Fidelitatis Sanctae Romanae Ecclesiae*); those of Terracina, to which Paul IV allowed the addition of his own arms above the castle; and those of Subiaco, which received an identical privilege from Pius VI in 1789.

Augmentations of Patronage (Padronanza). Unlike the preceding cases of papal concessions, these augmentations involved a personal decision by the owner of the arms, who wished to show gratitude or special loyalty by including a pope's arms in his own. Most are found in the arms of cardinals, although we cannot exclude an occasional consent by a pope. One exception was by Leo X, who granted his chief as a hereditary privilege to some non-cardinal Florentines, like the Buonarrotis; his was a reference to the Medici arms, that is, bezants with fleurs-de-lis accompanied by the letters "L" and "X." In all the other cases the interested parties placed the personal arms of "their" pope on a chief, on a partition, on the first and fourth quarters of a quartered shield, on a pale, or in a small shield on the bottom. Sometimes, if they lent themselves to it, the papal arms, or at least their charges, were added within the shield as new charges.

This type of patronage goes back to the papacy of Sixtus IV: Cardinal John Sclafenatus (1483–97) placed the oak of the Della Rovere on a chief. The frequency of this use varied from pope to pope. Abandoned by Sixtus IV's immediate successors, it was taken up again by Julius II, when four cardinals adopted the oak. Under Paul III, seventeen cardinals incorporated the Farnese fleurs-de-lis into their arms, under Paul IV, and another nineteen used the Carafa fess. According to one Vatican manuscript, of the 281 cardinals named between 1503 and 1572, 75 adopted arms of patronage. The custom endured throughout the 17th century but declined in the following century. There were still a few examples in the 19th century. In modern times Cardinal Stickler, librarian and archivist of the Holy Roman Church, had a quartered coat of arms that included the anchor of Pius X, the tower of John XXIII, and the church of Benedict XV. Without being cardinals, the majordomo prelates since Pius XII and, starting in 1967, the prefects of the Papal HOUSEHOLD also brought back the custom by including, albeit only for the duration of their tenure, the arms of the reigning pontiff on the dexter side of their shield.

Although there have never been rules for the pope (who is, after all, the sovereign pontiff), but only customs, there were nevertheless somewhat specific directives and recommendations throughout the centuries for the arms of these in the ecclesiastical hierarchy: these were limited exclusively to the use of hierarchical emblems (mitres, croziers, hats, *pallium*, etc.), particularly on seals, and to the use of crowns, mantles, swords of justice, and other exterior ornaments. The choice of a coat of arms, which in principle was mandatory for a bishop, was left (often to the great regret of heraldists) to the taste of prelates. There were few who had family arms, and even fewer who had any knowledge in this domain. As a basic document regulating the heraldry of the Catholic hierarchy, Innocent X's constitution of 19 December 1644 is worthy of note, as is Pius X's *motu propio Inter Multiples Cura* (21 February 1905) and Pius XI's apostolic constitution of 15 August 1934. Decisions regulating partial and minor questions were made by Alexander VII, Benedict XIV, Pius VII, Gregory XVI (who definitively set the number of tassels for hats in 1832), Pius IX, and Pius XII (who forbade the use of insignias of temporal jurisdiction on 12 May 1951). As of the publication of this article, the most recent decision was by Paul VI, on 31 March 1969.

Wipertus Rudt De Collenberg

Bibliography

Galbreath, D. L. *Papal Heraldry*, 2nd edition. rev. by G. Briggs, London, 1972 [the best historical treatment].

Heim, B. *Heraldry in the Catholic Church*, London, 1978 [restates and expands upon *Coutumes et droit héraldiques de l'Église*, Paris, 1949].

Martin, J. *Heraldry in the Vatican*, Van Duren, Gerrards Cross, 1987.

McCarthy, M. F. *Heraldica Collegii Cardinalium: A Roll of Arms of the College of Cardinals 1800–2000*, Thylacine Press, 2000.

Noonan, J. C. Jr., *The Church Visible*, Brooklyn, 1996, 187–200.

Rudt De Collenberg, W. "Augmentations dans l'héraldique à Rome," *Brisures, augmentations et changements d'armoiries. Actes du 5e Colloque international d'héraldique, Spolète 12–16 octobre 1987*, Brussels, 1988, 258–70.

HERESIES.

Early. From the Greek *hairesis*, the etymological meaning of the word is "choice." But in Hellenic historiography, it denotes a current of thought associated with the philosophical schools that were endowed with stable institutions, like Plato's Academy, or the Lyceum. In this case it means a disposition, or an attitude of mind, and does not imply the idea of choice. The Greek-speaking Jews adopted it to refer to tendencies in JUDAISM—the Pharisees, the Sadducees, and the Essenes—without any pejorative connotations. This meaning can still be seen in the Acts of the Apostles to refer to the Sadducees and the Pharisees; Paul began to use it to condemn the formation of "parties" within Christian communities. The New Testament writings attest to the existence of dissent, but names for these errors and their modes of presentation were varied, and suggest no unified concept.

It was the work of Justin, one of the primary Greek apologists of the second century (he was martyred in 165), that gave the first evidence of a unifying description, which later served as an instrument for polemics. Justin pejoratively used the analogy with the Greek schools of thought to designate Christian groups he judged to be deviant; he traced the heresies back to their founders to deprive them of any reference to Christ and to clarify their human, and ultimately diabolical, origin. Taken up by Ireneus of Lyon and refined by Clement of Alexandria and Origen, the model Justin invented was to have decisive consequences for the constitution of heresiology. It implied an understanding of the relationship between orthodoxy and heresy that is connected to the way the Church Fathers conceived of the history of the early Church: heresy, a deformation of the original doctrine, was necessarily inferior, relative to orthodoxy. This simple thesis implied an original purity, a Christianity that had been freed from any influence; justificatory, it did not take into account the way heresy and orthodoxy were identified with respect to one another, or the cultural substrates in which Christianity developed. Used in a noncritical manner up to the present day, it was demolished in 1934 by W. Bauer, who attempted to show that heresy, in forms that would not be called heretical until later, was at the origin of doctrinal development in the history of the Christian communities. It seems unquestionable today that Christianity did not originate in orthodoxy, to which heresies were opposed. In its early period, Christianity knew a diversity of forms and expressions, and we should renounce a simplistic and monolithic view of Christian origins; but making the Church of Rome the standard of "orthodoxy" and supposing that heretical groups came first and were in the majority at the time seems both forced and polemical.

H. E. W. Turner attempted to reply to the limits of Bauer's proposal through a theological analysis of the nature of orthodoxy and heresy. He used a method of analysis that distinguished, within the Christian faith, fundamental fixed elements and flexible elements that shaped its expression and could vary. Heresy then would be going beyond healthy tension, flexible elements spilling out over set elements, or a perversion of set elements. Whatever the limits of their analyses, these two works considerably renewed research in the field by bringing to the fore the diversity and the fluidity of the first centuries of Christianity. They gave birth to a less simple, but more plausible view of Christian origins.

The development of religious sciences that were freer of confessional presuppositions and the substantial renewal of documentation through the discovery of the Essene manuscripts of Qumran and the gnostic manuscripts of Nag Hammadi only reinforced the need to consider a diversity of cultural fields in order to approach the stunning alchemies from which doctrinal formulations came, and to correctly consider the earliest doctrinal statements.

They oblige us to specify the historical and theological pertinence of the word "heresy" as it relates to Christianity. In the 19th and the early 20th centuries the works of the *Quellenforschung* on anti-heretical treatises attempted to define further the elaboration of the concept of heresy by the Church Fathers. By isolating themes and common representations—the emergence of a new literary genre—they highlighted the fundamental schemes of heresiology. By studying the idea of heresy in Greek literature in the 2nd and 3rd centuries, the recent works of Alain Le Boulluec follow the elaboration and fluctuations of the heresiological model that took shape in the 2nd century. Anti-heretical manuals, which drew up lists of branches of Christianity deemed to be heretical, were intended to help aid in their recognition and to head off new heresies.

With the radical change in the attitude of the Roman authorities toward Christianity in the 4th century, as Christianity was becoming the official religion, these lists served as instruments of repression for civil authorities; heresy was thenceforth considered a crime.

Modern research on heresy in the earliest centuries of Christianity, through the study of heretical and suspect writings in light of the patristic texts, leads to a new understanding of the polemics and the pertinence of the dangers as they were perceived. Because they touch the very roots of Christianity, they raise essential questions regarding relationships between faith, history, and theological reflection.

Gnosticism. It was in the 2nd century, as it faced the gnostic sects and had to debate them, that Christianity defined itself and refined the idea of heresy. The modern neologism "gnosticism," from "gnostic," which the heresiologists used to refer to the members of various groups, denotes an ensemble of religious groups that had common traits. The saving gnosis that the gnostic received via revelation shows a radical dualism that often leads to a devaluing of the world; it sets the true God, who is unknown and separate from the world, in opposition to unfinished creation, the work of an inferior god, the demiurge, who is sometimes identified with the God of the Bible. For a long time, gnosticism was known only through Christian accounts that refuted it as a deformation of Christian doctrine through the influence of Greek philosophy and Hellenistic religiosity. The discovery of original manuscripts, especially the 1945 discovery of Nag Hammadi, which completely renewed scholarship in the field, led to both a rethinking of how Christianity developed in the Roman world, and to further questioning about how the earliest doctrinal formulations took shape. Confronted by gnostic thought, Christian thinkers reacted by drawing up lists of authoritative books and formulating official dogmas to serve as norms for the interpretation of the Scriptures. The gnostic sects were absorbed in the 3rd and 4th centuries by the Manichean church.

Marcionism. Marcion, a native of Sinope, spread a doctrine among the Christian community that led to his exclusion from it in 144. He founded a new Church that quickly grew. Marcion had no desire to be the founder of a Church, nor an innovator, but he did consider himself to be the preacher of Jesus's original message. He made a distinction between the good and unknown God, the Father of Jesus Christ, and the just and known God of the Old Testament, the creator of the world. The radical contrast between the message of the God of the Jews and the law of love in the Gospels was based on radical Biblical criticism. For Marcion, the texts were falsified by the Judaizers; he relied on the Gospel of Luke and certain of the Pauline letters, but he eliminated all that seemed to suggest influence from the Old Testament. Marcion's exclusive choice of Scriptures had an indirect, but definite influence on the evolution that led to the canon of Scriptures taken into the Church at the end of the 2nd century, by forcing a refinement in the Christian interpretation of the Jewish Bible and thus defining the canon of the New Testament. The success of the Marcionist Church among the faithful who had converted from paganism is explained by the simplicity of his message of the absolute novelty of the Gospel, by the difficulty of identifying with the heritage of the Jewish Bible, and by the strength of his ascetic teachings. Although it was a true rival of orthodox Christianity, Marcionism would end up being absorbed by Manicheism.

Manicheism. This religious movement dates to Mani, its 3rd-century founder. Long considered to be a heresy, to such an extent that in the Middle Ages the accusation of being a Manichean was a synonym for being a heretic, Manicheism was a dualistic religion of salvation. It was long known only through the indirect testimony of its adversaries, but research on the subject now has the advantage of the discovery of Manichean documents. Born in 216, Mani lived in a community of Elchasaitans until he was twenty-four. Elchasaism is described by patristic texts as a Judeo-Christian baptist sect; in the 4th century it absorbed a number of different baptist communities in Jordan. Mani broke with the community's practices because a revelation came to him bearing the message he was to transmit. Following in the line of Paul, Marcion, and Bardesanes, he was to restore the Church of Jesus and complete the work of the Paraclete according to the word of Jesus. For Mani, the failure of Zarathustra, the Buddha, and Jesus was explained by the fact that they did not write down the texts of their revelations themselves. He composed a corpus of canonical texts containing revelations for the Church. Condemned to death by the Mazdan clergy, Mani died in 277. Structured around a radically dualist myth, organized on the model of the Christian Church, and incorporating a number of earlier revelations, the Manichean Church spread rapidly; it absorbed all known gnostic schools of the 2nd century. It is estimated that Manicheism survived in the neo-dualist sects of the Middle Ages, but the lines of filiation tying the Paulicians, the Bogomils, and the Cathars to Manicheism have yet to be proven.

Montanism developed in Asia Minor in the late 2nd or early 3rd century, as a renewal of apocalyptic fervor with its call to an integral asceticism and its expectation of Christ's imminent return. It owes its name to Montanus, a recent convert who, toward 156, was overcome by ecstatic raptures during which he uttered prophetic warnings. Two women, Maximilla and Priscilla, joined him and also prophesied. The ANATHEMA pronounced by "the great Church" and repressive imperial measures beginning in 331 brought about the disappearance of authentic Montanist documents. It is only through patristic writings that it has been possible to reconstruct the movement's essential characteristics. It made no claims to being a new doctrine; rather, it reevaluated certain elements of traditional doctrine within the framework of a prophetic mission. Montanus announced that the end of the world was imminent and that his mission was to lead to salvation that segment of humanity that gathered in Pepuze, the place of the descent of the celestial Jerusalem. This sacred geography was linked to the organization of the Montanist church, which retained much of the traditional structure, but crowned it with prophetic inspiration. From the expectation of an imminent end came a quite rigorous morality and Encratist tendencies. The break of the "great Church" with Montanism marked the weakening of the role of women and their exclusion from teaching and worshipping in the Church. The split forced the Church to develop a more specific stance on the nature prophecy and its place within the Church as a whole. Violently persecuted, the movement survived in the West until the 5th century in Rome, and until the 9th century in the East.

Novatianism, or the Novatian schism, received its name from NOVATIAN, a Roman priest who challenged the election of Pope Cornelius in Rome (251) with the support of three Italian bishops and founded his own church. He is considered the first ANTIPOPE. The reason for the conflict was the question of the *lapsi*, who had converted during the time of the Decian persecutions. Novatian condemned Cornelius for having readmitted the *lapsi* into the Church; for him, it was not possible to reconcile with them. The schism was born of the desire for a Church of the pure. It must be specified that the ideas of schism, separation from ecclesiastical communion, and heresy were not radically distinguishable in the early Church. Heresy implied SCHISM quite rapidly, and schism presupposed heresy. Pope Innocent persecuted the Novatians and took their churches from them. They disappeared rapidly in the West, but it was not until the 8th century that all traces of them were lost in the East.

Donatism was a schism that divided the Church in AFRICA for over three centuries, from the end of Diocletian's persecution to the Arab invasion. Serious divisions appeared in the Church over what attitude to adopt regarding those who consented to *traditio*, that is, to handing over the Holy Books during Diocletian's persecution. The movement's point of departure, was the election in 312, of Cecilian as bishop of Carthage; the validity of his episcopal consecration was contested by a group of opponents who accused one of the bishops involved in the consecration of being guilty of *traditio*. To oppose Cecilian they elected another bishop, whom Donatus, the real organizer of the schismatic Church, soon succeeded. For him, the validity of the sacraments depended on the holiness of ministers. Under the threat of seeing a Church of the pure develop, St. Augustine established that Christ was the true author of the sacraments. In 313, the Donatists appealed to Emperor Constantine, who refused to recognize their claims and promulgated a law (317) against the schismatics, forcing them to hand over their churches. Resistance was such that in 321 the emperor consented to grant them tolerance. Donatism started to look like a social protest movement with the "Circoncellians," an agrarian proletariat that resorted to violence. In 411, the conference in Carthage outlawed the Donatists; they appear to have disappeared only after the Arab invasion.

Arianism. In about 320, Arius, an Alexandrian priest, spread a doctrine of the Trinity that provoked serious debate. A COUNCIL of Egyptian bishops condemned it. This was the beginning of the Arian crisis, the great historical and religious event of the 4th century.

When Arius entered the debate, Christian thinkers had already worked out the directions Christian orthodoxy might take to define a middle way. Modern researchers use the word "Adoptionism" to refer to the tendency to see Christ as a simple human being, "adopted" as the son of God. A rereading of the heresiologists has shown Adoptionism to be a Judaizing heresy connected to Ebionism. It was only in the 2nd century that the position was condemned as a heresy by Bishop Victor in Rome; it persisted, and seems to have been further elaborated by Paul of Samosate.

In contrast, Monarchianism (from *monos* and *archè*: a single principle) insists above all on the unity of God. This idea was called modalism by the moderns, since according to it the Father, the Son, and the Holy Spirit are nothing more than "modalities" of God's action, and have no reality properly speaking. Rejected by orthodoxy under the name of Patripassianism, this tendency was spread first by Noetus of Smyrna, by Praxeas, and then by Sabellius, whence the name Sabellians, given to his disciples, and Sabellianism to the doctrine.

A third complex tendency sought to articulate the three persons in God. But allowing for a rigorous equality between the Father and the Son meant raising the question of God's unity, and this question would give birth to tendencies toward, and accusations of, ditheism (two gods) and tritheism (three gods). On the other hand, it was possible to choose the simple solution of inequality between the Father and the Son. Subordinationism allowed that the Word was God, but it was less than God the Father who, alone, was the Principle. This tendency appeared early in the 2nd century with Hippolytus of Rome, Origen, and the speculations that developed in ALEXANDRIA. Departing from Origen's traditional trinitarian doctrine, Arius radicalized his subordinationist tendency: only the Father was *agen(n)ètos* (uncreated, unengendered); there can be neither equality nor consubstantiality. The Word is the first-born of all creatures, the power of the Father created it from nothingness in order to confer upon it the work of Creation. Arius wanted to safeguard a strict monotheism, but a monotheism much more philosophical than biblical.

As sole master of the Empire, Constantine decided to convene a council to resolve the Arian quarrel that was dividing the Christians of the East: this was the first "ecumenical" council of Nicaea, held from May to July 325. The Nicaean Creed condemned the Arian propositions and defined the Son as "true God born from true God," "begotten, not created, *homoousios*, consubstantial with his Father." But imperial pressure forced an artificial unanimity. If the Westerners and the Alexandrians easily accepted the *homoousios* that placed the unity of Father and Son above everything else, Easterners saw in the use of the word *ousia* a rebirth of Sabellius's temptation. The Arian crisis rebounded and became a veritable holy war where the religious and political stakes were intertwined, tied to imperial decisions and the role of the great apostolic sees. Aetius, and later Eunome, systematized the thesis of radical Arianism, whence the name Anomoeans and Anomoeanism, since they considered the Son totally different (*anomoios*) from the Father. The extreme reaction to this tendency was that of the Homeousians, for whom the Son was absolutely similar to the Father in substance (*homoiousios*). Emperor Constantius attempted to impose a new wording in an effort to reconcile the differing tendencies; the word *ousia* was forbidden and the Son was defined as similar (*homoios*) to the Father in all things and according to the Scriptures. The partisans of this wording were called Homoians.

The work of Basil of Cesarea, who struggled to overcome mutual misunderstandings by looking for wording that could reconcile Nicaean *homoousios* and the trinitarian doctrine of the three hypostases, would end up bearing fruit. Emperor Theodosius, in the edict of Thessalonica (380), imposed Nicaean orthodoxy on all his subjects. The second ecumenical council of Constantinople (381), in again taking up the Nicaean Creed, closed the debate. Thus the traditional doctrine of the Trinity received its final wording.

But the Christological quarrels that had already germinated during the course of these controversies soon broke up dogmatic unity. Arianism was to survive in the East until the end of the 5th century; in the West, the Goth Ulfila transmitted the Christian faith to the Barbarians under the form of radical Arianism, and it lasted as such until the end of the 6th century.

Apollinarism. Apollinaris of Laodicia and his disciples are considered to be the first Monophysites. In contrast to some anti-Arian polemicists who gave excessive importance to the difference between divine and human nature, he affirmed the unity of Christ by saying that Christ had but one nature in the sense of concrete nature. He could not allow in Christ the existence of a human soul since, for him, this function is filled directly by the Word. He was condemned in Rome in 377, in Alexandria in 378, in Antioch in 379, and at the great council of Constantinople in 381. Imperial decrees confirmed the condemnation. In the East, the movement survived clandestinely until the late 5th century.

Nestorianism. Nestorius, an Antiochian monk called by Emperor Theodosius II to the see of Constantinople, refused to consider Mary the mother of God (*theotokos*), as he refused to see in her anything but the mother of Christ. Seeing the attack this meant for the unity of the person of Christ, Cyril of Alexandria reacted by citing the words of Apollinaris's doctrine "a single nature of the Word incarnate," believing they were Athanasius's words. He thus prepared the lines that would connect Monophysitism to Apollinaris's intuitions. Nestorius's doctrine was condemned under quite confusing circumstances by the Council of Ephesus in 431. Exiled to the great oasis of Egypt, Nestorius died in 451. His doctrine survived him because of the reception it got fifty years later in the Persian Church, which was consequently called the Nestorian Church.

Monophysitism, from the Greek *monos* (single) and *physis* (nature), a generic term referring—in discussions relating to the divinity and humanity of Christ—to a complex doctrinal current that rejected the definition imposed at the ecumenical council of Chalcedon in 451.

In around 445, in Constantinople, the monk Eutyches taught a doctrine using Apollinaris's and Cyril's wording, "one single nature in Christ," which led to rejection of the idea that Jesus, who was consubstantial with God, could be consubstantial with man according to human nature. The condemnation of Eutyches by a synod in Constantinople in 448 raised violent reactions. After the banditry in Ephesus in 449, it was only at the council of Chalcedon, in 451, that orthodoxy was definitively tied to the vocabulary of the two natures, by essentially using the wording from the *Tome to Flavian* proposed two years earlier by Pope Leo. It proclaimed that God the Word, the only Son of God, born of the Virgin Mary in respect to his humanity, is in two natures which remain without confusion, without change, and without either division or separation.

Far from resolving the quarrel, the council of Chalcedon opened a long crisis and engendered a quite complex reaction from the Monophysites. Emperor Justinian, concerned about religious unity, wanted to rally the Monophysites and pronounced the condemnation of the Three Chapters at the council of Constantinople in 553. Poorly received in the West, the decisions aggravated the complaints of the Roman Church against Byzantium, without provoking reconciliation with the Monophysites. The churches that resulted more or less directly from the rejection of the council of Chalcedon's wording defining the unity of the person and the duality of natures in Christ are today called Monophysite, or non-Chalcedonian, churches.

Priscillianism. Somewhere between 370 and 375, Priscillian preached an ascetic doctrine that was quite successful in Spain and the south of Gaul. The basic themes of his teaching were somewhat like an Encratism nourished by a negative concept of the world and all that was material. Use of apocryphal writings with Encratist tendencies put the movement under suspicion of heretical dualism. Priscillian, who had become bishop of Avila (380–81), was condemned by Emperor Gratian and exiled. A council of bishops in Bordeaux condemned him again; under torture, he admitted to crimes of witchcraft and magic and was executed in 385 or 386.

Despite the council of Toledo's condemnation in 400, the movement, sanctified by the martyrdom of its founder, remained very much alive. In the 7th century, the memory of Priscillian disappeared, making room for the great pilgrimage to Compostela.

Pelagianism. Pelagius, a monk of British origin, was the founder of an ascetic movement in Rome beginning in 390. As a moralist concerned about spiritual progress, Pelagius emphasized the importance of effort on man's part. He accentuated the power of free will over divine grace. It was Rufinus who introduced theological theses, properly speaking, into Pelagian circles. Caesestius, one of his disciples, stirred up reactions in Carthage. He was condemned by the council of Carthage in 411. Summoned to explain himself before the SYNOD of Diospolis in 415, Pelagius was declared in communion with the universal Church. But the council of Carthage in 418, and later imperial decrees, condemned the Pelagians. Julian, bishop of Eclanum, took over defense of the condemned heresy and debated Augustine. The council of Ephesus (431) officially condemned Pelagianism. The group would persist clandestinely.

Semi-Pelagianism. This term, which came into general use in the 17th century, referred to a theological movement that developed in the 5th century in Gaul around teachers from Provence or Marseille who disagreed with St. Augustine's ideas on the question of grace and salvation. It was condemned at the 2nd council of Orange in 529.

Francine Culdaut

Bibliography

Bauer, W. *Rechtgläubigkeit und Keitzerei im ältesten Christentum, Tübingen*, 1934, 2nd. ed. by J. Strecker, Tübingen, 1964, and English trans. by R. A. Kraft and G. Krodel, *Orthodoxy and Heresy in Earliest Christianity*, Philadelphia, 1971, London, 1972.

Boularand, E. *L'Hérésie d'Arius et a foi de Nicée*, I–II, Paris, 1972–3.

Brox, N. *Häresie*, RLAC, 13 (1986), 247–98.

Hanson, R. P. C. *The Search for the Christian Doctrine of God. The Arian Controversy*, Edinburgh, 1988.

Koester, H. *Häretiker im Urchristentum als theologisches Problem, Zeit und Geschichte. Dankesgabe an R. Bultmann*, Tübingen, ed. J. C. Mohr, 1964, 61–76.

Le Boulluec, A. "Hérésie," *Encyclopedia Universalis*, 9 (1984), 260.

Le Boulluec, A. *La Notion d'hérésie dans la littérature grecque, IIe–IIIe siècles*, 2 vol., Paris, 1985.

Michel, A. "Hérésie-Hérétique," *DTC*, 6 (1925), 2208–56.

Simonetti, M. *La crisi ariana nel IV secolo*, Rome, 1975.

Turner, H. E. W. *The Pattern of Christian Truth. A Study in the Relations between Orthodoxy and Heresy in the Early Church*, London, 1954.

8th to 13th Centuries. Until the 8th century, the papacy was confronted by heresies of an eminently theological nature, coming primarily from the East. The same was true for the other patriarchies, although in the papacy's case there may have been an honorary preeminence since it was Peter's successor. In the Carolingian Empire, the FRANKISH sovereigns, as new Constantines, most often tried to solve, with occasional unfortunate results, Western theological disputes themselves (Clement, Godescalc, John Scotus Eriugena). It was, in fact, with the Gregorian reform that the papacy intervened more directly; this was furthered by its affirmation of an absolute primacy (the DICTATUS PAPAE, section 26, said: *Quod catholicus non habeatur qui non concordat Romanae ecclesiae*). Herein lies both the affirmation of the Holy See, which was treating SIMONY and NICOLAISM as heresies, and a response to quite diverse movements that were no longer uniquely theological, but also moral, and that shared the reformers' aspirations for a "return to the apostolic life." Even though the question of the "popular" or "intellectual" nature of the heretical movements of the first eleven centuries is subject to debate, we do see the coexistence of 1) movements of recrimination against the clergy before the reform, with the power to stir up social protest (e.g., the Milanese "Pataria"), which were more or less channeled into a reform (the word *patarini* would eventually refer to the Italian Cathars); 2) theological heresies; and 3) protest movements against the established Church in the 12th century (in addition to antiecclesiastical criticism, a favorite activity was anti-sacramental protest). Once it had taken root in Italy and Southern France, Catharism, which came less from a deviation in doctrine than from an entirely separate religion (and thus, early on, did not deserve to be called a heresy), carried a strong anti-ecclesiastical connotation, which it shared, on quite different theological bases, with Waldensianism. All the art of the popes during the Gregorian reform, and later of INNOCENT III and some of his successors, would be based on channeling these morally based aspirations in order to disassociate them from their doctrinal terrain: this is how the return of some of the Waldensians and "*umiliati*" can be viewed as the work of the DOMINICANS. At the same time, the papacy adopted new juridical concepts: the third Lateran COUNCIL made decisions that were not limited to one heresy but rather vast condemnations (March 1179), confirmed and made more specific by LUCIUS III (*Ad Abolendam*, 4 November 1184), who organized the episcopal INQUISITION. Juridical evolution was completed when Innocent III (whose master Uguccio had already qualified heresy as a *crimen publicum*) made the connection with Roman law and assimilated heresy into it as a crime of divine lèse-majesté (*Vergentis in senium*, 25 March 1199). The antiheretical legislation specified by GREGORY IX in February 1231 was less a political "deviation" than a final application of the pontifical theocracy that led the same pope to call Emperor Frederick II heretical because his action made it appear as though he did not respect the "power of the keys."

Monothelitism. This is a continuation of Monophysitism, which saw only one will at work in Christ. It was staunchly condemned by HONORIUS I and MARTIN I in opposition to the emperor of Byzantium. A definitive condemnation took place in 680 at the council of Constantinople.

Iconoclasm. More of a schism, but defined as a heresy, iconoclasm, which was particularly vigorous in the East during the 7th century, confused veneration with worship and advocated the violent destruction of holy images in order to avoid idol worship. Fought by GREGORY II, who defined it as a heresy, it was condemned as being contrary to tradition at the second Council of Nicaea (787), co-organized by empress Irene and Pope HADRIAN I. The council's canons, which were poorly translated, were not received by the Carolingian Church, which rejected them at the Frankfurt synod in 794. In Italy, Claudio di Torino briefly gave new life to this heresy, already eradicated in the West, at the end of the 9th century when he ordered the destruction of crosses.

Adoptionism. Originally a doctrine tending to refute Migezeus's heresy, it became heretical itself when it claimed that Christ had two natures (as in Nestorianism), one of these coming to him via his adoption by the Father. It was refined on the Iberian peninsula by Eliprand of Toldeo, and given additional weight by Felix of Rugen. It was condemned by Frankish theologians, and later at the synod of Rome, in 799.

There were a number of obscure pockets of heresy in France in the first half of the 11th century, some of which paves the way for Catharism (which rejected the flesh and preached extreme abstinence). These groups were undoubtedly targeted by LEO IX's condemnation of the "new heretics" at the council of Reims in 1049.

Berenger of Tours revived the 9th-century eucharistic controversy that had been condemned by the provincial clergy. The early efforts of the Gregorian reformers (Humbert of Silva Candida and the legate Hildebrand, the future GREGORY VII) were set against him and pronounced a judgment of heresy in Rome. There, Berenger recanted at the hands of NICHOLAS II, although he returned to his erroneous ways and was condemned by Gregory VII in 1079.

Evangelical heresies of the early 12th century. Moral and spiritual aspirations had much to do with these, as did the sermons of wandering clerics, often marginal (hermits and parish priests) and sometimes enlightened, who exploited an antiheretical thread that on occasion was rigorously anti-sacramental. Among these were Clement, in Soissons in 1114; Tanchelme in the Netherlands, who was killed in 1115 (he presented himself as the son of God and the husband of the Blessed Virgin); Peter de Bruys in Provence, who was burned in 1132 (his followers were called *Petrobrusiani* when they were condemned at the second Lateran council in 1139); Peter's disciple Henri de Lausanne, who preached in Le Mans and Toulouse before being condemned to silence around 1142 (his followers, called Henricians, were condemned by EUGENE III at the council of Reims in 1148); and Eudes (then "Eon") de l'Étoile in Brittany, around 1140. They were opposed by prominent figures from the Church like St. Norbert of Xanten, St. Bernard of Clairvaux, and Peter the Venerable, who enlightened a papacy not yet ready to take the initiative. Occasionally organized communities appeared, such as that at Mont-Guimer in the diocese of Chalons (LUCIUS II was informed of their success in a long letter from the concerned clergy in Liège), and in Italy around Ugo Speroni (the Speronists were condemned in 1179).

Abelard. Fourteen propositions relating essentially to the Trinity and knowledge by faith, were drawn by William of St. Thierry from the works of this theologian and founder of dialectics. They were refuted by St. Bernard of Clairvaux and condemned at the council of Soissons (1121), presided over by a papal legate. Abelard appealed to the pope and continued his teaching. His second condemnation at the council of Sens (1141) was confirmed by Pope INNOCENT II.

Arnold of Brescia. An instigator of violent anti-ecclesiastical and anti-sacramental criticism, Arnold was condemned at the second Lateran council (1139) and then recanted before Eugene III in 1145. He was excommunicated again in 1148, when he participated in the Roman uprising against the pope. He died in 1155, but his partisans (Arnoldists) were still targeted by the pontifical condemnation of 1184.

Cathars (in France, they were also called Albigensians, and in Italy *Albanenses, Concorenses, patarins,* and weavers. They were universally referred to as Manicheans—and scoundrels). The word *Publicani,* based on *Pauliciani,* which comes from Paul of Samosate, bishop of Antioch in the 3rd century, refers to dualists, with whom they were undoubtedly confused. Inheritors of Eastern Manicheism, they saw history as the opposition of the two principles of good and evil and practiced last-minute penitence (*consolamentum,* which allows one to leave the terrestrial world by refusing to eat). They adapted their beliefs to Western ecclesiastical structures: they had "the prefect," but also bishops and councils. Reinterpreting the Scriptures and using them for their own purposes, they prospered on soil where the way had been prepared by the "evangelical" heresies and opposition to Catholic hierarchy. The lack of structure for the faithful and the success of the Cathars' itinerant preaching, contributed to the failure of both the pope's early attempts to forcefully counter Catharism (CALLISTUS II condemned some form of Catharism in 1119) and that of his legate, after the official condemnation of 1179. Soon however, there was a systematization of the struggle against this heresy, which culminated in the CRUSADE launched by Innocent III and then the work of the Inquisitors.

Josephini. An unknown sect, condemned in 1184 with the Cathars, to whom it was perhaps related.

Passagini. A sect condemned in 1184, known only for its presence in Northern Italy and its Judaizing practices.

Waldensians, or "Poor of Lyon." A movement founded on poverty and preaching (a privilege claimed for simple laypeople), drawing its name from a Lyonnais merchant, Pierre Valdo (ca. 1160–70). Part of the movement was reintegrated into the Church under Innocent III, while another part remained independent and combative.

"Umiliati." An essentially urban community inspired by ideas similar to those of the Waldensians, with whom they were confused in the condemnation of 1184, although they were active in Northern Italy. They were reintegrated by Innocent III.

Amaury de Bène. Taught in Paris (d. 1205). His pantheistic deviations were condemned by his brethren (although never by the pope, despite a bull alleged to be by Innocent III). His disciples (called Amauritians), one of whom was Henri of Dinant (leader of the Dinantists), later adopted his erroneous beliefs, before they were condemned at the council of Paris in 1210, and again by the papal legate Robert of Courçon in 1215.

Satanists or Luciferians. These terms were applied with increasing frequency to any kind of heretic, although they referred particularly to a sect along the Rhine that was pursued by the inquisitor Conrad of Marbourt, who obtained a bull from Gregory IX (13 June 1233) in which it is already possible to recognize some of the themes of witch hunting (the identification of a supposed cult worshipping Lucifer).

Averroists. These were Parisian theologians from the university who, in the wake of Siger of Brabant, followed the Arab philosopher Averroes in his interpretation of Aristotle. The interpretation was condemned in 1270 by the bishop of Paris, Étienne Tempier, and then again in 1277 by the same bishop even before the conclusion of the inquiry with which Pope JOHN XXI had entrusted him.

Apostolics. This sect was formed in Parma under the leadership of Gerardo Segarelli (condemned and executed by the inquisition in 1300), and developed under that of his disciple Dolcino of Novara (executed in 1307). Its violent anti-ecclesiastical criticism and call for poverty and mendicancy were especially popular in Northern Italy. The first papal condemnation of it was under HONORIUS IV (1286).

Fraticelli. These were Franciscans who had broken with their order. They preached absolute poverty and claimed the privileges granted to mendicants by NICHOLAS III and CELESTINE V. They were condemned by BONIFACE VIII in 1296, and by JOHN XXII in 1322.

Olivier Guyotjeannin

Bibliography

DTC and *DS, passim.*

Duprè-Theseider, E. *Introduzione alle eresie medievali,* Bologna, 1953.

Gerkhout, C. T. and Russel, J. B. *Medieval Heresies: A Bibliography, 1960–1979,* Toronto, 1981.

Grundmann, H. *Bibliographie zur Ketzergeschichte (1900–1966), Rome,* 1967.

Kolmer, L. "Christus als beleidigte Majestät: Von der Lex 'Quisquis' (397) bis zur Dekretale 'Vergentis' (1199)," *Papsttum, Kirche und Recht im Mittelalter* [Mélanges H. Fuhrmann], Tübingen, 1991, 1–13.

Mitre and Granda, C. *Las Grandes herejías de la Europa cristiana (380–1520),* Madrid, 1983 (*Fundamentos,* 82).

Moore, R. I. *The Origins of European Dissent,* Oxford, 1985.

Patschovsky, "Häresie," *LexMA,* 4 (1987–9), 1933–7.

Vauchez, A. "De la contestation à l'hérésie," *Histoire du christianisme,* 5, Paris, 1993, 459–79 [with bibliography].

Since the 14th Century. The modern period up to the present day has seen widespread use of a canonical arsenal that, by the 13th century, was fine tuned to combat heresy. This arsenal was clarified as early as 1252 by INNOCENT IV (1243–54), who authorized the use of torture, provided it was applied by secular judges and did not endanger the physical integrity of the individual in question. In 1262, however, URBAN IV (1261–4) authorized the inquisitors to use the procedure themselves, thus opening the door to abuses. This state of affairs only exacerbated the conflicts and the opposition manifested against the Catholic Church's attitude, no longer just because it staunchly demanded to have a monopoly on the totality of revealed faith—as well as its interpretation, which was properly the object of hermeneutics—but also because it appropriated for itself the right to administer justice, on the basis of the divine commandment giving it the power to bind and loose all that existed on earth. Such was at least the theological and dogmatic argument most frequently used. The "treatment" that heretical movements experienced depended on the amount of rigidity granted to the deviant's area of application with respect to expressions of orthodoxy.

Beghards and Beguines. Gathered together since the end of the 12th century in community houses (Beguinages), in groups that were partly religious associations and partly lay organizations, the Beghards and Beguines especially welcomed to the flood of beggars that poured out of the countryside in Liège, starting in 1185. Placed under the sole authority of the bishop, their communities had "an atmosphere somewhere between monastic and secular life" (A. Jundt), as they took vows of chastity and obedience, but did not give up society and temporal affairs. Numbering over a thousand in Paris and Cambrai around 1250 (when there were 2,000 in Cologne), the Beghards competed with parish priests for burials and donations. The internal freedom demanded by these communities, which was most noticeably translated into an exaltation of physical pleasure, first troubled Pope CLEMENT V (1305–14), and then the COUNCIL of Vienne (1311–12), the decrees from which, known as *Clementines*, stigmatized the confusion produced by "those who call freedom of thought the freedom to do whatever they wish." Inquisitorial persecution appeared in a number of locations in the Holy EMPIRE between about 1330 and 1350. The "buffoons," who were also called "lollards" in England, took refuge in France where they took advantage of existing unrest among farmers in the countryside, as well as war; their leader was Jeanne Dabenton, who was burned in Paris (1372) by the inquisitor from the Ile-de-France, Jacques de More. GREGORY XI (1370–8) moderated the zeal of the persecution, as he was aware of the orthodoxy that some had previously held. However, in 1394 Boniface IX (1389–1404) annulled all concessions granted by his predecessor in order to completely eliminate the heresy, which nevertheless did not end until about 1460 in Germany.

Dolcino of Novara. Eschatological sentiment in the early Middle Ages found a major expression in the millenary movement, which foresaw the imminence of the end of time, deduced from the catastrophic situation the Church had survived, and from the corruption of contemporary institutions. The Italian Dolcino of Novara was an eminent representative of this movement at the beginning of the 14th century. Placing his political bets on Emperor Frederick II, who was hostile to the papacy, he foresaw Christ's return in the year 1303. After BONIFACE VIII's death that year, and that of BENEDICT XI the following year, Dolcino, who had a following of some four thousand, began a "guerrilla campaign" (R. Vaneigem), taking over Bergamo and then MILAN, and escaping the INQUISITION three times. In 1305 Dolcino retired to a fortified camp on a summit of the Alps, where he enjoyed DANTE's Parete Calvo support. However, he ended up surrendering in 1307, and was tortured and burned. Some Dolcinists suffered the same treatment in Toulouse in 1322, in Avignon during JOHN XXII's papacy (1316–34), and even in the early 15th century in Germany.

The Flagellants. The famines of 1250, the PLAGUE of 1259, and the bloody conflict that pitted the GUELPHS against the GHIBELLINES provided the background for the birth of the Flagellant movement. The name came from the fact that they used flagellation as a means of contrition and self-punishment, a practice that was first encouraged by a Church sensitive to the spiritual benefits that supposedly devolved from painful repentence. Between 1260 and 1290, it became widespread and associated with hysteria, taking on dangerous dimensions. Nurtured by the tragedy of the Black Death in 1348–9 and linked to millenarian sensibilities, the flagellant movement spread to Bruges, Ghent, Tournai, and even as far as Germany. In 1349, after being initially encouraged and then condemned by CLEMENT VI (1342–52), it acquired patently anticlerical overtones that included refusal to pay the tithe denunciation of trafficking in INDULGENCES, and rejection of veneration of the saints; it thus formed part of the base of support for Martin Luther and the Protestant SCHISM.

Hussites and Taborites. Starting in 1380, the reformist teaching of John Wycliffe in England found a sizeable echo in the countries of Eastern Europe. The rector of the university of Prague, Jan Hus, denounced the opportunism, especially the financial opportunism, of the papacy in the temporal domain. Excommunicated and then called before the council of Constance (1414), despite his imperial safe-conduct, Hus was condemned and burned at the stake. The resistance of a number of prelates who were attentive to their sources of revenue, led them to place the Church of Bohemia under secular control, thus freeing it from submission to Roman power. An incident provoked by King Wenceslas in July 1418 regarding the government of the Prague commune brought matters to a head and set off a popular uprising, the radical wing of which, established on a hill rebaptized Mt. Tabor, took up the interrelated themes of voluntary poverty, egalitarian millenarianism, and free interpretation of the Scriptures. After a number of armed battles that ended in a series of victories and defeats, the fall of the Taborites was determined by the capture of Mt. Tabor in 1452. Along with other dissident currents, like the Bohemian Pikarti, some members joined the community of Moravian brothers, who were great admirers of pacifism.

Anabaptists. The climate of profound religious disturbance created by a number of mystical movements, gyrovagues, and millenarists in a large part of northeastern Europe lasted throughout the tormented 16th century, when a multiplicity of sensibilities and churches, for the most part rather newly established, helped make taking any position an act repaid with violence, and adopting any philosophy a heretical stance that risked universal condemnation. Anabaptism was a perfect example of this, as it suffered the simultaneous hostility of Catholics, Protestants, and civil authorities. Reserving baptism (via total immersion) exclusively for adults as a sign of election and recognition, the movement based itself on "prophets" or "apostles" who were incarnated with strong personalities and freed their followers (largely artisans and rural dwellers from allegiance to any authority whatsoever. Their systematic demands for equality and (essentially material) justice led to armed uprisings in the region around Spire in 1502, and then in Alsace and Swabia. Thomas Müntzer, who was initially a Lutheran pastor, delivered a series of impassioned sermons in Bohemia and in a number of counties in Germany between 1521 and 1525. Then, in April 1525 he founded a church that was immediately repressed. His decapitation on 17 May 1525, together with his disciple Heinrich Pfeiffer, caused the movement to retreat to cities in Austria and Moravia, where there were still many faithful in the middle of the 16th century, before the complete dispersion that resulted from the Thirty Years War.

Jansenism. In the climate of unchallenged monarchical and pontifical absolutism that was the fruit of the Counter-Reformation, the Jansenist quarrel was based on the transitional wording of the theological *disputatio* regarding the spiritual versus the temporal. Born in Holland in 1585, Cornelius Jansenius, shaped by the thought of Augustine, whom he had long studied (in Utrecht, Paris, and later Louvain), did not dare at first to publicize his conclusions about predestination and grace. Jansenius died a victim of the plague in Ypres after addressing a letter to Pope URBAN VIII (1623–44) in which he claimed he was ready to retract "according to what is told to me by that voice of thunder that comes out of the heavens of the Apostolic See." His *Augustinus,* published in 1640, which, because of its position regarding the determinism, material or spiritual, of the human will, seemed to deprive the ministry of the clergy of any utility. It was put on the INDEX in 1642. Jean Duvergier de Hauranne, abbot of St.-Cyran, made it his mission to spread the doctrine professed by Jansenius and managed to attract the sympathy of the Arnauld family, who were protectors of the monastery of Port-Royal. A counselor to Catherine of Medici, and an eminent jurist educated in Bourges by Cujas, Antoine Arnauld devoted himself to battling the JESUITS, whom he reproached in particular for the blind obedience (seen in the maxim *Perinde ac cadaver*) taught by Ignatius of Loyola, whom he referred to as a "Spanish general." His youngest child, the Grand Arnauld, born in 1612, had as his preceptor St.-Cyran, who at the time was overseeing the fate of Port-Royal. Ordained a priest in 1641, two years later he published the treatise *Frequent Communion*, which earned him the vituperation of the Jesuits (who had him imprisoned) and brought him to the forefront of the Jansenist movement. Continuing his polemic against the Society of Jesus, he furnished Pascal with the subject of his *Lettres écrites à un provincial* (1656–57, placed on the Index on 6 September 1657). He died in Brussels in 1694. A certain degree of popular support for Jansenism, out of admiration for its challenge to Rome, quickly dried up under the threat of repression by Louis XIV. The Port-Royal partisans reached Holland, from whence they continued their struggle, and founded a Jansenist church that survived until the 19th century. Pasquier Quesnel tried to safeguard the Jansenist legacy in France, but he was condemned for his opinions in 1713 in the famous BULL *Unigenitus*, forbidden from further theological speculation and reduced to doing manual labor. Jansenism no longer inspired anything but hysterical and convulsive manifestations like those produced in the cemetery of St.-Médard at the time of the inhumation of the deacon of Paris, which gave rise to the famous inscription: "By order of the king, miracles are forbidden in this place."

Pietists. In the line of heretical ideas proclaiming the lack of efficacy, and perhaps even the harmfulness, of mediation by sacraments and the ministers of the church who dispense them—which like many others recurred, were defended, condemned, and then taken up again later—pietism placed the accent on the preeminence in all circumstances of interior conviction and the law of personal conscience. Begun by the Lutheran pastor Philippe-Jacob Spener (1635–1707), the movement sanctioned a certain degree of sensuality, even though it was focused on the promised second coming of Christ at the Parousia. Given its structure through the thoughts and actions of strong personalities like the German Johann-Georg Gichtel (1638–1710), an erudite individual who had taken a vow of perpetual celibacy, the movement was at first a product of isolated individuals focused on their mystical dialogue with Sophia, a spiritual being sometimes identified with the Virgin. It later expanded into religious societies that, in turn, were influenced by German sensibilities in the age of Enlightenment, or *Aufklärung*, which gave pietism a less esoteric and more carnal direction.

François Jankowiak

Bibliography

DTC, *passim*.

Anagnine, E. *Fra Dolcino e il movimento ereticale all'inizio del Trecento*, Florence, 1964.

Aubert, J. M., Metz, R., Sicard, G., Wackenheim, C., and Winniger, P. *Le Droit et les institutions de lÉglise catholique latine de la fin du XVIIIe siècle à 1978. Église et sociétés* [Histoire du Droit et des Institutions de l'Église en Occident, XVIII], Paris, 1984.

Barber, M. *The Cathars: Dualist Heretics in Languedoc in the High Middle Ages*, New York, 2000.

Bemman, R. *Thomas Müntzer, Mülhausen in Thuringen und der Bauernkrieg*, Leipzig, 1920.

Borgomeo, P. *L'Église de ce temps dans la prédication de saint Augustin*, Paris, 1972.

Chatellion, L. *L'Europe des dévôts*, Paris, 1987.

Clanchy, M. T. *Abelard: A Medieval Life*, Oxford, 1997.

Cohn, N. *Les Fanatiques de l'Apocalypse*, Paris, 1983.

D'alès, A. *Priscillien et l'Espagne chrétienne à la fin du IVe siècle*, Paris,1936.

Dictionnaire des hérésies, des schismes, reed. J. P. Migne, *Encyclopédie théologique*, 11–12, Petit-Montrouge, 1853.

Gaudemet, J. *L'Église dans l'Empire romain, IVe-Ve siècles* [Histoire du droit et des institutions de l'Église en Occident, III], Paris, 2nd. ed. 1989 (updates the 1958 edition).

Geremek, B. *Les Marginaux parisiens aux XIVe et XVe siècles*, Paris, 1976.

Greenshields, M. R., and Robinson, T. A., eds. *Orthodoxy and Heresy in Religious Movements: Dicipline and Dissent*, Lewiston, 1992.

Grundmann, H. *Religious Movements in the Middle Ages: The Historical Links between Heresy, the Mendicant Orders, and the Women's Religious Movement in the Twelfth and Thirteenth Century*, trans. S. Rowan, Notre Dame, 1995.

Lafuma, L. *Controverses pascaliennes*, Paris, 1952.

Lambert, M. *The Cathars*, Oxford, 1998.

Leff, G. A. *Heresy in the Later Middle Ages. The Relation of Heterodoxy to Dissent, 1250–1450*. Manchester-New York, 1967.

Le Roy Ladurie, E. *Montaillou: The Promised Land of Error*, New York, 1979.

Marenbon, J. *The Philosophy of Abelard*, New York, 1997.

McDonnell, E. W. *The Beguines and Beghards in Medieval Culture*, New Brunswick, 1954.

O'Shea, S. *The Perfect Heresy: The Revolutionary Life and Death of the Medieval Cathars*, New York, 2000.

Patschovski, A. "Häresie," *LexMA*, 4 (1987–89), 1933–37.

Petré, E. "*Haeresis, schisma et leurs synonymes latins,*" *Revue des études latines*, 1937, 316–25.

Pluquet, Abbot. *Mémoires pour servir à l'histoire des égarements de l'esprit humain par rapport à la religion chrétienne, ou Dictionnaire des hérésies, des erreurs et des schismes*, 2. vols., Besançon, 1817.

Russel, J. B. *Dissent and Order in the Middle Ages: The Search for Legitimate Authority*, New York, 1992.

Schmitt, J. C. *Mort d'une hérésie: l'Église et les clercs face aux béguines et aux béghards du Rhin supérieur du XIVe au XVe siècles*, Paris-La Haye, 1978.

Tourn, G. *The Waldensians: The First 800 Years (1174–1974)*, New York, 1980.

Tourn, G. *You Are My Witness: The Waldensians Across 800 Years*, Cincinnati, 1989.

Vaneigem, R. *La Résistance au christianisme. Les hérésies des origines au XVIIIe siècle*, Paris, 1993.

Vulliaud, P. "Fin du monde et prophàtes modernes," *Les Cahiers d'Hermès*, 1947.

HILARUS (b. *Sardinia, ?, d. Rome, 29 February 468*). *Elected pope 19 November 461. Buried in San Lorenzo-fuori-le-Mura. Saint.*

Hilarus was a deacon when he distinguished himself as LEGATE for the Church of Rome defending papal interests in the "Latrocinium" of Ephesus in 449. Elected pope in 461, he was a faithful successor to Leo, firm in his defense of orthodoxy, and enterprising in his affirmation of Rome's metropolitan privileges.

According to the *LIBER PONTIFICALIS*, (although the evidence is less than convincing), Hilarus was of Sardinian origin, the son of a certain Crispinus, and became a Roman DEACON in 449. Pope Leo chose him, along with Bishop Julian of Puteoli (the priest at St. Clement Renatus) and the notary Dulcifius, to form the legation representing the Roman See at the COUNCIL convoked by Emperor Theodosius II in Ephesus in 449. The council was charged with examining the appeal by Eutyches, the archimandrite in Constantinople who was condemned a number of times in 448 for Monophysitism by Flavian, bishop of Constantinople. The legation was entrusted with a number of letters from the pope, addressed to Emperor Theodosius and Empress Pulcheria, as well as a long dogmatic letter addressed to Flavian in which the pope articulated the Christologic doctrine admitted in Rome "proclaiming the two natures of Christ in the unity of a single person," and condemning Eutyches's errors. When they arrived in Constantinople on 30 July, without Renatus, who had died in Delos, the legation participated in the first session of the council, which was presided over by Dioscorus, bishop of Alexandria, who was quite favorable to Eutyches. Hilarus, who was seated among the low-ranking attendees, took the floor—speaking Latin, and thus needing a translator for all his speeches—on three different occasions. He reminded the council that it was asked not to deal with questions of dogma, and that some papal documents were to be read. At the end of a stormy session that was marred by a number of irregularities, Eutyches was redeemed and Flavian was deposed. Hilarus protested against Flavian's sentence publicly, after which he refused to speak further, take his seat again, or read the papal texts, which might have been taken as approval by Leo. Hilarus may have been one of the individuals expelled by the guard called in by Dioscorus to quiet the opposition. After this first session, Hilarus stayed in Constantinople with the rest of the legation. On 20 August he was in the *martyrium* of St. John's when Dioscorus sent for the Roman emissaries to inform them that they were ordered to take their seats on the council. On the following day, the legates let it be known that their mandate concerned the trial of Eutyches only, and that they were refusing to take their seats. After the session of 22 August, they were called to subscribe to the council's decisions under threat of being detained by force. Hilarus, who was the first to be called, managed to flee, but was enable to deliver the pope's letters to Emperor Theodosius II and Empress Pulcheria. He reached Rome via a roundabout route and arrived, possibly without his companions, before 13 October 449, and probably carrying Flavian's *libellus appellationis*.

Back in Rome, Hilarus wrote to Pulcheria (13 October 449) to explain why he had not been able to give her Leo's letter. In the same missive, Leo wrote to the emperor, underscoring the vigorous stance of his deacon, the only legate he mentioned. Prosper of Aquitaine, in his chronicles, gave special praise to Hilarus's courage. Because of the particular role he played on this occasion, Hilarus is often identified as the anonymous Roman archdeacon whose intention Theodosius of Cyr sought to get Leo to annul the decisions made at Ephesus before 450. The identification is not certain, since it is not known when Hilarus became an archdeacon. He was fulfilling that function before 457, and he was charged by Leo with examining the differences of opinion concerning the way to determine the date of Easter. Disturbed by the incompatibility of the different Greek and Latin systems, Hilarus sought out a certain Victor, a Gaul from Aquitaine, and asked him to establish a system allowing the harmanization of the Alexandrian and Roman computations. Victor finished his work in 457 and sent it to Hilarus, although it is not known to what extent the calculation—which did not resolve all the difficulties—was put into practice outside Gaul.

When Leo died, Hilarus was elected pope (19 November 461), an expected advancement from his role as archdeacon. According to the *LIBER PONTIFICALIS*, he addressed a DECRETAL to the Eastern Churches confirming the synods of Nicaea, Ephesus, and Chalcedon, his predecessor's *Tome for Flavian*, and the condemnations of Eutyches, Nestorius, and all the HERESIES. The text, which was not customary for the time, is not extant today, and nothing is known of Hilarus's relations with the East.

In the West he is known for his work in three areas: combating heresies, affirming Roman disciplinary authority, and municipal activities.

Hilarus had three oratories constructed around the baptistery of St. John LATERAN. The first was dedicated to St. John the Baptist, with an inscription that can still be seen on the old door: *In Honorem Iohannis baptistae Dei famulus offert Hilarus episcopus* ("Bishop Hilarus, friend of God, offers this in honor of John the Baptist"). Another inscription reports that Hilarus was the builder. The mosaic on the vault, which has been destroyed but is known from a 17th-century reproduction and a 16th-century inscription, showed the mystical lamb in the center, surrounded by peacocks with spread wings and other birds. The four evangelists were in the four corners. According to the description by Pancinio (who saw it in 1550), the oratory of Santa Croce, which is no longer extant, as well as the triple portico that led to it, was decorated with a MOSAIC representing the cross held up by four angels, on a gold background. The walls were also decorated with mosaics, depicting the figures of saints Peter and Paul, John the Evangelist, and John the Baptist, as well as Lawrence, Stephen, James, and Philip. The oratory of St. John the Evangelist still exists; it still shows the dedicatory inscription *liberatori suo beato Iohanni evangelistae Hilarus episcopus famulus Christi*, which recalls Hilarus's vicissitudes at Ephesus, and perhaps, more specfically, the protection he found in the *martyrium* of St. John on 20 August 449, the day Dioscorus's emissaries came to get him. The mosaic shows the mystical lamb surrounded by a crown of rivers, around which are birds, hens, ducks, parakeets, and pigeons.

Hilarus also undertook a number of construction projects around the basilica of San Lorenzo, near the cemetery of Verano (S. Lorenzo fuori le Mura). The *Liber Pontificalis* speaks of a monastery, two baths, a *praetorium*, and two libraries. Interpretation of the passage is a matter for debate: the monastery is not identified, but from about the end of the 6th century there is evidence of monastic institutions in San Lorenzo. Even though it was not named, as was the case for all ancient monasteries, its identification with one of the two area monasteries known later, Santo Stefano and San Cassiano, has been suggested. Were the baths, the *praetorium*, and the two libraries connected to the monastery; are they even parts of the same complex? One interpretation posits that the libraries were annexes of the monastery, while the *praetorium* and the baths were for pilgrims. As Duchesne has proposed, the *praetorium* might also be a papal villa near a basilical complex to which Hilarus attached importance, since he is buried there. The library would, in that case, be the pope's. Location of these structures near St. John Lateran is due to an interpolation from the *Liber Pontificalis* denounced by Duchesne. And one more clever hypotheses should be mentioned: that rather than two libraries, the reference was actually to a Bible containing the two testaments. Although there is a manuscript that mentions a division of the Old and New Testaments made by Pope Hilarus, this reading of the *Liber Pontificalis* seems somewhat forced. Hilarus also constructed another monastery, called *ad Lunam*, whose location in Rome is a complete mystery.

The ecclesiastical organization of the province of Gaul was particularly worrisome to Hilarus. In 462 he installed Leontius, bishop of Arles, as his liaison with the other bishops, but this novel measure does not appear to have been very successful. When Leontius seemed ready to take on the preeminent duty the pope proposed, the other bishops of Gaul did not pay much attention to him. This was evident in two different matters involving ecclesiastical discipline: in 462, with bishop Hermes of Narbonne, and in 463, concerning Manuent of Vienne. In both cases the pope called on the bishop of Arles to give him advice, and on the councils that were convened to resolve the matters.

In 465, a council met at SANTA MARIA MAGGIORE to deal with questions concerning the bishops of Spain, who had appealed to the pope. The metropolitan of Tarragona, Ascanius, lodged a complaint against Siluanus of Calabara, who ignored the rights of his metropolitan. The pope reminded all in question of two fundamental principles: the prohibition against bishops naming their successors, and the authority of metropolitans. Beyond the decrees of the synod, the pope sent a letter to the bishops of Spain, in particular to Ascanius of Tarragona. These documents show both the extent and the limits of Roman authority over the churches of the West.

In Rome itself, Hilarus needed—as did his predecessors and his successors—to be aware of the presence of the Arians, who were protected by the prefect of the praetorium, Ricimer. One church, St. Vitale, was reserved for them. But in 467, when Hilarus learned that there were plans to construct a second church, he vigorously opposed it. His successor, Pope Symmachus, referring to him as a paragon of firmness, reported a few decades later that Hilarus did not hesitate in public, in ST. PETER'S basilica, or in the Vatican, to challenge Emperor Anthemius for tolerating such an insult to the Catholic religion, and he won his case. This trait corresponds well with what we know of Hilarus's character.

He was buried in the crypt of the great basilica of S. Lorenzo fuori le Mura, beside popes Xystus and Zosimus. In the *Martyrologium Hieronymianum*, Hilarus is commemorated on 10 September. The written editions give 28 February as the date, which corresponds to the chronology in the *Liber Pontificalis*.

Claire Sotinel

Bibliography

LP, 1, 242–48.
Amann, E. "Hilaire," *DTC*, 6, 2 (1947), 2385–88.
Hefele-LeClerc, *Histoire des conciles*, II, 900–905.
Hilarius, *Epistulae XVII*, Thiel, I, 126–70; *Fragm. epist. ad Nicephorum*, H. Fuhrmann, "Ein Bruchstück der Collectio Ecclesiae Thessalonicensis," *Traditio*, XIV (1958), 374.

See also CALENDAR.

HIPPOLYTUS. *(b. ca. 170, d. 236?). Buried in the cemetery on Via Tiburtina.*

Hippolytus was one of the most important individuals in the life of the Church in the early 3rd century. Nevertheless, tradition has paid him little attention. A Roman priest who may have been born a Greek in the East, he clearly broke with the legitimate hierarchy. In his earliest actions, he showed vehemence and intransigence. He opposed Pope ZEPHYRINUS and his closest counselor, the future Pope CALLISTUS. With the ELECTION of Callistus in 217, Hippolytus was considered the first antipope in the history of the Church. The truth is perhaps more subtle, and there is no trace of him in literary sources. Hippolytus could not resign himself to recognizing Callistus as bishop of Rome, and he took along with him a number of Roman Christians who rose up in rebellion without really defecting or forming a real schismatic community. It is not certain that Hippolytus was ever a bishop. This "splinter" community survived through the papacies of Callistus, Urban, and Pontian.

The break was based on disciplinary issues. Indeed, Hippolytus was always interested in doctrinal thought; even though he still wrote in Greek, he was the first Western exegete of the Scriptures. He showed great intellectual virtuosity thanks to his great familiarity with Greek thought, and Origen, passing through Rome around 212, was favorably impressed by one of his sermons. He left a great number of writings, a list of which appears on his marble statue discovered in 1551 in the cemetery on Via Tiburtina. The list was made by his followers. Among his works are exegetical writings like the *Commentary on Daniel*, some homilies, and canonical and liturgical works, including a *Paschal Canon* (inscribed on his statue); it began in 222 and was calculated on a cycle of sixteen years. His theological works are the most impressive. In about 200 he began with a treatise on the antichrist. The work of his that is best known and was most important for the history of the Church was the *Refutation of All Heresies*, which is often cited under the name *Philosophoumena*, although this corresponds with only its first four books. In it, he refutes thirty-three heresies that were dependent on pagan philosophies. Book IX addressed his disagreements with Callistus (he wrote it after the pope's death). He accused Callistus and his "school" of creating a new legal context and a new morality by granting remission for all sins, accepting the serious lack of internal discipline among the clergy, and legitimizing practices that heretofore had been rejected by the Church.

His theology was both elaborate and complex. On trinitarian doctrine, he opposed those who went so far as to suppress any distinction between persons (Monarchianism and Patripassianism) in order to safeguard divine unity. In this regard, he placed himself in the line of apologists like Justin and Tertullian; he defined the relationship between the Father and the Son in a subordinationist sense, for which he was accused of "ditheism." His concept of the Church was elevated; he saw it as a community of truth, the repository of Scripture and of the teachings of the apostles that was guaranteed by episcopal succession. In the world, the Church must be the community of saints. The intransigent traditionalism that saw in the Church a "society of saints living in justice" was austere and restrictive, and could only clash with Callistus, who was both more pragmatic and far from absolute rigorism. But Hippolytus's thought was strong and founded on solid erudition, and it had tremendous influence among Christians in Rome and, probably, in the East. Under URBAN I and PONTIAN, Hippolytus ceded nothing. Outside intervention allowed him to be reintegrated into the Church, and to become a confessor and martyr. In 235, shortly after the arrival of Maximin of Thrace, the emperor made the decision to exile Pontian, the legitimate bishop, and Hippolytus; they were sent into the mines of Sardinia. In this unfortunate situation, reconciliation came before their deaths, which occurred close together. Pope FABIAN had the bodies brought back to Rome for interment. Hippolytus was buried on 13 August 236 or 237, in the cemetery on Via Tiburtina, which is now named after him, and where his statue is located.

Jean-Pierre Martin

Bibliography

Amann, E. *DTC*, VI, 2, 2487–2511.
Bardy, G. "L'Énigme d'Hippolyte," *Mélanges de science religieuse*, V, 1, 1948, 63–88.
Bertoniere, G. *The Cult Center of the Martyr Hippolytus on the Via Tiburtina*, Oxford, 1985.
Bradshaw, P. *Essays on Hippolytus*, ed. Cummings, G. J., Nottingham, 1978.
Brent, A. *Hippolytus and the Roman Church in the Third Century: Communities in Tension Before the Emergence of a Monarch-Bishop*, Leiden; New York; Koln, 1995.
Camelot, T. *Catholicisme. Hier, aujourd'hui, demain,* 1962, 754–60.
Capelle, B. "Hippolyte de Rome," *Recherche théologique ancienne et médiévale*, XVII, 1950, 145–74; "À propos d' Hippolyte de Rome," *Mélanges de science religieuse*, XIX, 1952, 193–202.
D'alès, A. *La Théologie de saint Hippolyte*, Paris, 1906; *L'Édit de Caliste. Étude sur les origines de la pénitence chrétienne*, Paris, 1914.
Eusebius, *HE*, VI, 20, 2; 22.
Hanssens, J. M. *La Liturgie d'Hippolyte*, Rome, 1959.
Jerome, *De vir. ill.*, 61.
LeClerc, H. *DACL.*, VI, 2, 2409–83.
MacGuire, L. M. R. P. *NCE*, 1967, VI, 1139–41.
Mansfeld, J. *Heresiography in Context: Hippolytus' Elenchos as a Source for Greek Philosophy*, Leiden; New York, 1992.
Osborne, C. *Rethinking Early Greek Philosophy. Hippolytus of Rome and the Presocratics*, London, 1987.
Quasten, J. *Initiation aux Pères d' l'Élise*, Paris, 1957, 193–246.
Richard, M. *DS*, Paris, 1969, 531–71.
Simonetti, M. *Da Clemente a Dionigi, Riv. di St. e Let. relig.*, XXII, 1986, 439–74.
Zani, A. *La Cristologia di Ippolito*, Brescia, 1984.

HOLY CHILDHOOD, PONTIFICAL SOCIETY OF THE.

Having associated fifteen bishops with the Living Rosary created by Pauline Jaricot, Bishop Charles de Forbin-Janson of Nancy conceived the idea of an organization for the propagation of the faith by children for children, in order to "save childhood by childhood." He hoped to assist the children of China, who were dying almost as soon as they were born. He was encouraged in his plan by Jaricot, founder of the Society for the Propagation of the Faith, who suggested the basic principle: to have the children of Europe donate a penny a month to save the young Chinese. De Forbin-Janson's visits to the Middle East and North America strengthened his missionary zeal.

The beginnings of Holy Childhood (its early name) were difficult owing to the opposition of the Gentlemen of the Society for the Propagation of the Faith, who from 1843 to 1858 hindered the expansion of the new organization and divided the French episcopate into pro and con factions. On 19 April 1844, the Lyon Council of the Propagation of the Faith decided to send a circular letter to the bishops of France warning them of the potential "danger" presented by Holy Childhood to the Society for the Propagation of the Faith. In their meeting of the following 26 April, the archbishop of Chambéry agreed to have this circular letter sent to some Italian bishops. During the years 1843–58, Holy Childhood was an issue at more than fifty council meetings, and was invariably considered to be harmful to the "simplicity" of the Society for the Propagation of the Faith.

Holy Childhood, whose symbolic date of foundation in Paris was as early as 20 June 1843, was finally enabled to take off thanks to the intervention of Fr. Jammes, who is considered its second founder. Jammes took over the organization beginning 11 July 1844, after the death of Bishop de Forbin-Janson.

Many years later and following reconciliation with the Society for the Propagation of the Faith, PIUS IX recommended the Society of the Holy Childhood to all bishops, emphasizing the support it gives to the Propagation (apostolic BRIEF *Quum aetate quolibet*, 18 July 1856).

In fact, meeting in synod in 1880, the bishops of China declared quite clearly: "The Society of the Holy Childhood, an apostolic society *par excellence*, has brought the greatest good in China and is a worthy sister of the Propagation of the Faith." "This Society is a service of individual Churches helping educators gradually to awaken a universal mission consciousness in the young and guide them toward sharing their faith and material possessions with the children of less affluent regions and Churches. Since its beginnings, the Society has contributed to a blossoming of missionary vocations" (Statutes of the Pontifical Mission Societies of 26 June 1980, chap. II, art. II, III, n.17). The subscriptions and offerings of the children of all the countries involved form a joint fund directed to the assistance of organizations and institutions in support of children. Every year the society organizes a World Youth Day.

The Pontifical Society of the Holy Childhood has a presence in more than eighty countries, on five continents.

Dominique Le Tourneau

HOLY OFFICE, CONGREGATION OF THE. This is the official name given, from 1908 to 1965, to the dicastery of the Roman Curia originally known as the *Congregatio Sanctae Inquisitionis Haereticae Pravitatis*, and today as the Congregation for the Doctrine of the Faith. Traditionally, it ranks first among the Roman congregations, not only because of the primordial, fundamental role—that of defending the faith—which plays at the heart of the Church, but also because it was historically the first permanent congregation of cardinals to be established within the framework of the Roman Curia.

The origins of the Congregation of the INQUISITION go back to 1542. On 21 July of that year, PAUL III, in his preoccupation with the widespread diffusion of Reformation doctrines throughout Italy, published the constitution *Licet ab initio*. Here, yielding to the pressure of some of the most inflexible personalities of the Curia—such as Cardinal Gian Pietro Carafa and the cardinal of Burgos, Juan Alvarez of Toledo—the pope set up a special permanent commission composed of six cardinals that was designed to deal with HERESY on an international scale. The

cardinals' jurisdiction covered the whole of Christianity. In particular, they could appoint subdelegate inquisitors and hear appeals against judgments these inquisitors handed down.

The new curial agency got down to work immediately. Its activity in suppressing heresy was at times intense, especially when its most influential member, Cardinal Carafa, became pope under the name PAUL IV (1555–9). Still, it was not definitely set up until later, with the constitution *Immense aeterni Dei* (22 January 1588), by which SIXTUS V reorganized the Roman Curia. This document placed first among the Roman congregations the *Congregatio Sanctae Inquisitionis Haereticae Pravitatis* (commonly known thereafter as the *Congregatio Romanae et Universalis Inquisitionis*, or the *Congregatio Sancti Officii*). Its presidency was reserved for the pontiff himself.

The congregation was given broad powers with which to act in cases of clear heresy, schism, apostasy, magic, spells, divination, and abuse of the sacraments, as well as in all other cases where the crime of heresy was suspected. Its jurisdiction extended throughout the Christian world, and all tribunals of the Inquisition were subject to it, except for those operating in the Spanish kingdoms and domains, whose particular privileges were confirmed by the pope.

Among the responsibilities not cited by the constitution, but which the congregation in fact exercised before 1588 and continued later, was the censoring of printed works. Nothing is known about the way relations with the other dicastery competent in this area, the Congregation of the INDEX, were regulated in practice. It was not until 1753, through the constitution *Sollicita ac provida*—which nevertheless confirms the traditional authority of the Congregation of the Inquisition in questions of censorship—that BENEDICT XIV specified that the Congregation of the Index was to concern itself only with works expressly denounced as dangerous, provided there was no judgment pending at the Congregation of the Inquisition.

The activities of the latter congregation remained essentially unchanged until the beginning of the 20th century. The main modifications to the way it functioned were made by PIUS X, in his constitution *Sapienti consilio* of 29 June 1908. Its name was replaced by one that was already in current use and deemed less odious than the former one—the Congregation of the Holy Office. Nevertheless, the reform did not bring about a radical alteration of the dicastery's powers, which remained extremely far-reaching. Indeed, although on the one hand it lost responsibilities relating to certain areas—such as those of a disciplinary nature, which were transferred to the Congregation of the Council—on the other hand it acquired new ones, such as questions having to do with INDULGENCES. The few changes made to the organization of the congregation over the next half-century go back to the years immediately following Pius X's reform. In 1917, under BENEDICT XV, duties regarding indulgences were transferred to the Sacred Apostolic Penitentiary, while the Congregation of the Holy Office was in turn given the duties of the Congregation of the Index, which had been abolished.

PAUL VI carried out a radical reform of the dicastery barely 60 years later. In so doing, he was responding to critics who had arisen on many sides during the work of VATICAN II to oppose the Holy Office's procedures. On the eve of the close of the council, through the *motu proprio Integrae servandae* of 7 December 1965, the pope changed its name to Congregation of the Doctrine of the Faith. He also altered its procedures by relaxing its strictness, giving the accused the broadest means to defend himself, and abolishing as a practical matter the Index of Prohibited Books, which retained only its moral force.

These were not purely external changes. Even though the congregation's duties were still traditional—including trials for crimes against faith, now conducted according to ordinary procedural norms—the very notion of the role entrusted to it was profoundly changed. The principle behind the reform was the one according to which, in the present day, faith is best defended by promoting doctrine. As a result, the dicastery's tasks now include encouraging research in the theological domain and organizing study seminars.

Eighteen months later, with the constitution *Regimini Ecclesiae universae* of 15 August 1967, Paul VI proceeded to carry out a general reform of the Roman Curia. The reform took its inspiration from the new needs of the post-conciliar Church and the criteria of decentralization, reorganization of structures, internationalization, and participation in decision making of the diocesan bishops, and even, when the subject matter called for it, the laity. Regarding the Congregation for the Doctrine of the Faith, the constitution essentially confirmed the norms contained in the *motu proprio* of 1965. The two most important changes concerned, first, the fact that the pope was no longer head of the congregation, which from then on was presided over by a cardinal prefect, assisted by a secretary, an undersecretary, and a promoter of justice. The second change had to do with the fact that, when the dicastery's duties were defined, there was no longer talk of trials regarding crimes against the faith, but only of trials regarding errors in matters of faith. In order to make the congregation's work easier, a few years later Paul VI conferred on its prefect pro tempore the presidency by right of two pontifical commissions: in 1969, that of the International Theological Commission (instituted 11 April of that year) and, in 1971, that of the existing Biblical Commission.

Paul VI's reform was destined to be short-lived. Yet

cases that found a particular resonance in public opinion, like those of the theologians E. Schillebeeckx, H. Küng, and L. Boff, were dealt with according to the new procedures. The reorganization of the Curia that was begun by JOHN PAUL II with the constitution *Pastor bonus* of 28 June 1988 did not substantially alter the congregation's responsibilities; however, according to the principles that inspired the whole document, stress was laid on its duty of ecclesial service and the pastoral spirit that must characterize its actions. Consequently, while affirming that the congregation's primary task is to defend the truths of the faith as well as moral integrity, if need be by resorting to the sanctions provided by canon law, the constitution insisted on the positive role that the congregation is called on to play, for example by laying down that it must promote "studies aimed at increasing the understanding of faith" (art. 49) and strive to be "an aid to the bishops" in matters relating to their actions in the doctrinal domain (art. 50).

Thus, with all vestiges of the Inquisition now vanished, the Congregation for the Doctrine of the Faith has experienced a radical transformation over the past 30 years. From being an agency aimed at suppression and the chastisement of heresy, it has grown to be the dicastery of the Roman Curia charged with safeguarding and promoting the integrity of the faith.

Agostino Borromeo

Bibliography

Borromeo, A. "San Carlo Borromeo, arcibescovo di Milano e la Curia romana," *San Carlo ed il suo tempo: Atti del convegno internazionale nel IV centenario della morte* (Milano, 21–26 maggio 1984), 2 vols., Rome, 1986, 240, 248–53; "Gaspare Visconti, arcivescovo di Milano, e la Curia romana (1584–1595), "*Studia Borromaica* 1 (1987), 25–6.

Del Re, N. *La Curia romana: Problemi e ricerche per la sua storia nell'età moderna e contemporanea*, Rome, 1971, 68–72.

Delgado, G. *La Curia Romana: El gobierno central de la Iglesia*, Pamplona, 1973, 139–62.

Faure, G. B. *Commentarium in bullam Pauli III "Licet ab initio" datam anno 1542, qua Romanam Inquisitionem constituit . . .*, s.l., 1750.

Ferretto, G. *La riforma del B. Pio X, AA, VV., Romana Curia a Beato Pio X sapienti consilio reformata*, Rome, 1951, 43, 44–6, 57–8.

Firpo, L. "Una relazione inedita sull'Inquisizione romana," *Rinascimento*, s.l., 9 (1958), 87–102.

Fitzsimons, E. J. *Competence of the Sacred Congregations in the Reform of Pope Paul VI*, Rome, 1971, 27–38.

Goodman, P. *The Saint as Censor: Robert Bellarmine Between Inquisition and Index*, Leiden; Boston, 2000.

Henner, C. *Beiträge zur Organisation und Competenz*

der päpstlichen Ketzergerichte, Leipzig, 1890, 370–4.

Macedo, F. *Schema illustre et genuinum Sacrae Congregationis Sancti Offici Romani . . .*, Patavii, 1676.

Manzanares, J. "La reforma de la Curia romana por Pablo VI," *Paul VI et les réformes institutionelles dans l'église: Journée d'études, Fribourg (Suisse) 9 novembre 1985*, Brescia, 1987 (Pubblicazioni dell'Istituto Paolo VI, 6), 51 n. 14, 56, 61.

Silvestrelli, A. "La congregazione della Dottrina della Fede," *AA. VV., La Curia romana nella costituzione apostolica "Pastor bonus,"* Vatican City, 1990 (Studi giuridici, 21), 255–37.

Uginet, F. C. "La constitution Regimini Ecclesiae Universae," *Paul VI et la modernité dans l'église, Actes du colloque organisé par l'École Française de Rome (Rome 2–4 juin 1983)*, Rome, 1984 (*CEFR*, 72), 606–7.

von Pastor, L. *Storia dei papi dalla fine del Medio Evo*, It. trans., 16 vols., new ed., Rome, 1942–55, v–xvi, ad indices.

HOLY PLACES.

Until 1917. In the history of the papacy, what people called "holy places" were mostly sanctuaries erected on the exact spots (according to Christian tradition) of Jesus' birth and burial, that is, the churches of the Nativity in Bethlehem and the Holy Sepulcher in Jerusalem.

From CONSTANTINE TO THE CRUSADES. Before Constantine, no certain example of worship was apparent at the places venerated by the Christians who, like Origen, went to Palestine in the 2d and 3d centuries to look for traces of Jesus. After Constantine's conversion to Christianity, he had two sanctuaries consecrated in 335 and 339 on the sites "rediscovered" by Bishop Macarius. The Eastern clergy held worship services there until the crusades. Upon his entry into the Holy City in 638, Caliph Omar allowed the patriarch of Jerusalem to continue using the Holy Places, and dedicated the esplanade of the Temple for Moslem worship. Jews were able to return to Jerusalem for the first time since Hadrian's interdiction in A. D. 135; they built synagogues there and began the habit of praying at the "Wailing Wall." In 1009, the Fatimid caliph Al-Hakim had the sanctuary of the Holy Sepulcher demolished. Then, needing a Byzantine alliance against the TURKS, he authorized its reconstruction in 1028. In 1048, Emperor Constantine Monomachus finished the restoration of the rotunda built over the tomb of Christ, but left the Constantinian church as a crumbling ruin with five bays (one can get an idea of this from the one in Bethlehem, which fortunately was spared).

The question of the Holy Places. The first direct intervention of the papacy puts into perspective the reconquest of territories occupied by Islam, undertaken around 1070 with the encouragement of Pope ALEXANDER II. The idea of a crusade was begun by Pope URBAN II who, at the COUNCIL of Clermont, urged Christians to unite in order to deliver the Holy Places from the power of the infidels. When they took Jerusalem in 1099, the crusaders set fire to a synagogue where some Jews had been locked up. Any Jewish or Moslem establishment was outlawed in the Holy City. The Byzantine patriarch was replaced by a Latin one, who apportioned the buildings of worship between the Christians, divided since 1054 (Latins, Greeks, Armenians, Copts, Syrians); the mosques erected on the esplanade of the Temple were transformed into churches. The crusaders built—between 1131 and 1149—a Romanesque church encapsulating the rotunda of the Holy Sepulcher, the Calvary, and other buildings on that site.

The "question of the Holy Places" quickly arose from daily frictions, sometimes violent, between the different clergies. After the reconquest in 1187, Saladin did not expel the Christians despite their actions in 1099 and permitted the Jews to live in the Holy City once again. The *modus vivendi* between the separated Christians was confirmed, on condition that no clergy had jurisdiction over the others. The ownership of the Holy Places was taken from them definitively, but the Christians had the right to worship there, on the condition that they make repairs in their respective locales (the keys of the Holy Sepulcher are still held by a Muslim family who open and close the only door of the sanctuary each day). After the 14th century, Latin interests were represented by the province of the Franciscans of the Holy Land, by virtue of a treaty concluded in 1333 between King Robert of Anjou and the sultan of Egypt, an accord ratified by CLEMENT VI in 1342.

The rule of the Capitulations (1517–1917). After their victory over the Mamelukes in 1517, the Turks ruled the Holy Land for four centuries. Official tolerance by Islam remained the general rule. The Franciscans defended Latin interests toe-to-toe, by asking for support from the European powers. The statute regarding the Holy Places was entered into the structure of the Capitulations, of which the most famous, signed in 1535, were between Francis I and Suleiman the Magnificent. Renewed on several occasions, they were definitively ratified under Louis XV in 1740: France received, with pontifical approval, the protection of the Franciscans of the Holy Land. In the 19th century, the "question of the Holy Places" was one of the aspects of the "Eastern question." In 1774, Russia had obtained from the Orthodox clergy the same privileges as France had from the Catholics. On the occasion of a "sacristy quarrel" in the Church of the Nativity, a firman (decree) of Sultan Abdul Mejid specified the rights of each of the Christian communities in 1852. In this way, the status quo was defined, as ratified in 1878 by the Congress of Berlin.

Claude Orrieux

Bibliography

Collin, B., *Les Lieux saints*, 1948.

Delpech, F., *Sur les Juifs. Études d'histoire contemporaine*, 1983.

Mendès, M., *Le Vatican et Israël* (French translation), 1990.

Vincent, L. H., and Abel, F. M., *Jérusalem nouvelle*, 1914–26 (a history of the buildings).

Since 1917. The Holy Christian Places are the sites that have been "bathed in the sweat and blood of the Divine Redeemer" (PIUS XI). Since the Muslim conquest (7th century) until the end of WORLD WAR I, these places were ruled by the regime of a protectorate, known as the Capitulations, for which France had the first international recognition at the Congress of Berlin in 1878.

The role of the Allies. After the collapse of the Ottoman Empire, and the Sykes-Picot accords on the sharing of zones of influence in the East, Palestine went back under English control. The English worked at finding a general and definitive solution for the question of the sacred sites, where, for centuries, Greeks and Latins had openly confronted each other. The arrival, during the preceding century, of Anglicans, Protestants, and other sects who also claimed rights to Palestine, would not make things any easier for the new masters.

On the Catholic side, eyes had never stopped looking toward Jerusalem and its neighbors. In 1887, LEO XIII exhorted Catholics to give generously to the collections being taken throughout the Church "so that the monuments which witness such a great and holy mystery, in the city of Jerusalem and the surrounding areas, might be kept and cared for." Pope BENEDICT XV, observing that events and discussions among the Allies did not favor "the development of civil and religious life" in Palestine, clearly stated his opposition against "such sacred places of the Christian religion being given to non-Christians."

On 2 November 1917, Lord Balfour declared that "His Majesty's Government views with favor the establishment in Palestine of a national home for the Jewish people, . . . it being clearly understood that nothing shall be done which may prejudice the civil and religious rights of existing non-Jewish communities in Palestine." In 1920, the League of Nations gave England the mandate over Palestine with the mission "to clarify the future status of the Sacred Sites, while continuing to preserve the existing rights (status quo)." England did this in all honesty and put a commission in place to oversee and "study and rule on all questions and claims concerning the different religious communities."

The Vatican did not oppose "the decision to give the mandate for Palestine to England," but, conscious of the inalienable rights that Christians possessed, it could not "accept that the commission believed it had the right to reopen discussions on the ownership of sanctuaries that, for centuries now, had peacefully been under Catholic custody." To make the mandate applicable, Cardinal Gasparri suggested, in a memo addressed to the council of the League of Nations, that this commission be made up of consuls of the powers in the Holy Land, members of the League of Nations, "giving those in power who have no consuls in the Holy Land the right to name a person of their choice to be part of the commission."

The British plan. In 1922, England had a plan adopted that would have gone into effect after the treaty of Lausanne (1923). This project, prepared by the "Palestine Royal Commission," foresaw the creation of three distinct territories in Palestine: one territory under British control including the Holy Places, an Arab state, and a Jewish state. The Arabs reacted violently against this plan, which took away part of their lands. It would never be applied, but the national Jewish homeland, promised by Balfour, became a reality. To calm people's minds, Sir Winston Churchill, secretary of state for the colonies, declared: "Palestine will not be a Jewish national homeland, but this home will be founded in Palestine." Conditions in the region not yet being settled, Pope Pius XI, in a speech on the occasion of his first CONSISTORY, 11 December 1922, publicly demanded "that the rights of the Catholic Church and those of all Christians be safeguarded and respected." The end of 1922 marked the total failure of the British plan. In 1926–27, the Arabs created the Arab Committee for Palestine. In 1929 in Zurich, the Jewish Agency was created to encourage the immigration of Jews to Palestine.

Faced with the unleashing of passions and the failure of its plan, England definitively gave up on any solution and, according to the recommendations of the League of Nations, settled for purely and simply maintaining the statu quo. The differences between the Christians, together with the hostilities between the Arabs and the Jews, transformed Palestine into a field of battle, which frustrated England's efforts for a solution. The Holy See, moved by a wish for impartiality, condemned any recourse to "violence from whatever source" and reminded people of the necessity of "respecting the rights of each, particular positions and traditions, especially in the religious domain." It insisted that "justice and peace be displayed in the reality of things" and that the order would guarantee security to all the parties in conflict as well as "physical and moral conditions of a greater state of well-being on the material and cultural level."

A viable Jewish state. The influx of Jewish immigrants to Palestine at the end of WORLD WAR II, along with the end of the British mandate, complicated the problem of the Holy Places even more. In response to the support the Jews gave to the Allies, President Harry's Truman, in 1946, approved the request of the Jewish Agency to create "a viable Jewish state" in Palestine. The Arab League, recently founded, made a counter proposition, asking for the creation of a "unique independent State, where Arabs and Jews would be represented proportionately to their number," with the prohibition of any further Jewish immigration to Palestine. Matters, however, had already been set in motion. The English, themselves victims of terrorism, announced in February 1947 that they would leave Palestine on 14 May 1948, returning their mandate to the United Nations, which it had taken over from the League of Nations. On 29 November 1948, the UN approved the division of Palestine into two States, Arab and Israeli, stipulating that "Jerusalem and its suburbs would be set up as a *Corpus separatum*, under the control of the United Nations." Unfortunately, due to the Arab-Israeli war in 1947 and 1948, this new plan for a solution also died away. Immediately after that, Francis Cardinal Spellman, as president of the Catholic Near East Welfare Association, in a letter addressed to the Commission for Political Affairs and Security of the UN, reminded them in the name of the Holy See that "the territory of Palestine is not only the Holy Land for Jews and Moslems, but also for the Christians of the entire world: Catholics, Orthodox, and Protestants." In the ENCYCLICAL *In multiplicibus* of 24 October 1948, PIUS XII asked that Jerusalem and its surrounding areas "where so many precious memories of the life and death of the Savior are found" be given international status, and for the Holy Places "spread throughout Palestine, as well, free access, the freedom of religion and respect for customs and religious traditions." The following month, French intellectuals, among them the duke de Broglie, Paul Claudel, Henri-Daniel Rops, Jean de Fabrègues, Louis Massignon, François Mauriac, and Emmanuel Mounier, worried about the fate of the Holy Land and conscious of the need for Arabs and Jews to find a solution to their conflict through peaceful means, asked "in the name of tradition which makes France a guardian of the freedom of the Sacred Sites" that the French government prepare "a concrete plan" based upon the encyclical of the pope.

"*Corpus separatum*." On 11 December 1948, the General Assembly of the United Nations set up a commission for reconciliation, in charge of proposing a plan. The one submitted by the new commission, which seemed to abandon the principle of internationalization, was rejected by the General Assembly in 1949. Then the commission went back to the 1947 plan. The administrative commission of the UN, after revising it, approved it on 4 April 1950. For first time the question of the Holy Places was dealt with on a high level and moreover, special status of the places was considered as well. Accordingly, the Holy City and its surroundings would be set up as a *corpus separatum* "under the administration of the three religions involved" in the name of the same UN administrative council. Pius XII, in the encyclical *Redemptoris Nostri* (1949), stated that it was necessary to provide for the administration "of all the Sacred Sites" and

that there must be a suitable juridical status for Jerusalem, whose stability, under existing circumstances, could not be assured and guaranteed "except by a common understanding of the nations. . . ." According to the resolution of the administrative council, the control of the Holy Places would belong to the UN. On this subject, the Israeli government, on 28 May 1950, addressed a memorandum to the president of the administrative council, in which it affirmed that "since the Holy Places of Jerusalem are found in a zone limited to three or four square kilometers in the old part of the city and its surroundings," it was ready "immediately, to collaborate in the creation of an international regime whose jurisdiction would be limited to that area." Thus, although Israel reduced the application, it officially accepted the principle of internationalization. The Jordanian government, which initially had not reacted to the resolution of the UN administrative council, on 5 January 1951, preemptorily appointed as "Custodian of the Sacred Sites" one of the "protectors" of Haram ach-Sharif (the mosques El-Aqsa and Omar). This decree respected the rights of Christians, but forbade Jews access to the Wailing Wall.

After the second Arab-Israeli war in 1956, Pius XII, while expressing his hope that war would be banished from history, asked that "the sacred rights of the Church be completely guaranteed." From then on, the question of the Holy Places was going to be tied more and more tightly to the general problem of Palestine. PAUL VI, upon his return from his historic trip to the Holy Land in January 1964, spoke to the College of Cardinals about "the mysterious relationship that exists between this land and Rome." The secular, spiritual, and religious rapport that united Rome to Jerusalem became more visible and tied still more "tightly to the spiritual destinies of the Catholic Church."

Israeli control. The Six Days' War (1967) modified the situation of the Holy Places once again, putting them under Israeli control. In effect, on 27 June 1967, the Knesset (Israeli parliament) voted unilaterally for a law protecting the Holy Places. Paul VI had said the very night before that "the Holy City of Jerusalem should always remain what it represents: the City of God, a free oasis of peace and prayer, a place of meetings, elevation and concord for all with its own guaranteed international status." Paul VI never ceased requesting for Jerusalem each time he could, "a special internationally guaranteed status" by reason of the "particular character of this City, unique in all the world." Others also called for an international solution. In 1973, the bishops of the United States requested that the U.S. Congress recognize the unique status and religious significance of Jerusalem and that "access to the City, by means of whatever international guarantee" be assured. That same year the Catholic bishops of Palestine, on the 25th anniversary of the U.N. Charter of the Rights of Man, expressed the hope that "sincere dialogue, inspired by the principles of the Charter and of the memory of the men, women and children who, in this part of the world, only strive for happiness and the honor of being responsible for their own fates" be engaged. The following year in 1974 the chief rabbi of Israel, Goren Shlomo, declared that the world should know that Jerusalem is the capital of Israel and the soul of the Jewish people, and that it is "our duty to defend the city at the price of our lives." The Israeli decision caused numerous protests.

In 1979, the permanent observer for the Holy See at the United Nations, once again asked for an international guarantee of special status. This did not stop the Israeli authorities from flatly rejecting their earlier endorsement (1950) of internationalization of the old city when it had been under Jordanian administration, since they now controlled the whole city of Jerusalem. In 1980, it declared "Jerusalem the eternal and undivided capital of Israel." The American bishops, wrote to the Foreign Affairs Committee of the U.S. Senate requesting that the position of the Holy See concerning Jerusalem and the Holy Places be read into the official record of the Senate. It stated that in the case of Jerusalem "an appropriate legal guarantee that does not depend on just one of the parties in the case" be given. President Ronald Reagan announced in 1982 that "Jerusalem must remain undivided, but its final status must be defined by negotiations." JOHN PAUL II, in his apostolic letter *Redemptionis Anno* of (20 April 1984) recalled that "all humanity, and in first place the peoples and nations whose brothers in faith are in Jerusalem, Christians, Jews, and Moslems, have reasons to be interested in it and to do all that lies in their power to preserve the unique and specific, sacred nature of the City." In the eyes of the pope, it was not only the monuments, the Holy Places, that must be preserved "but the whole of historic Jerusalem and the religious communities that live there, with their traditions and their aspirations. Different interests and aspirations will only be truly safeguarded and protected thanks to a "particular Statute" (*peculiare Statutum*), internationally guaranteed in "such a way that no party," as John Paul II said, "could reopen the situation for discussion in the future."

All declarations and claims of the Holy See over the Holy Places of Palestine have been aimed at obtaining a definitive international solution that would guarantee the universal character of Jerusalem as the indivisible heritage of three monotheistic religions and would guarantee the freedom of the practice of religion in all aspects.

Edmond Farhat

See also CULTS, EASTERN; PROPAGANDA FIDE.

Bibliography

Collin, B. *Jérusalem et les Lieux saints*, 1984.

Collin, B. *Le Problème juridique des Lieux saints*, 2 vols., Paris, 1956.

Farhat, E. *Gerusalemme nei Documenti Pontifici*, 1987.

Irani, G. E. *The Papacy and the Middle East (1962–1984)*, 1986.

Pastorelli, P. *La Santa Sede e il problema di Gerusalemme, Storia e Politica*, 1982.

Sayegh, S. *Le "statu quo" des Lieux saints, nature juridique et portée international*, 1971.

HOLY ROMAN EMPIRE. The Holy Roman Empire came about through the union of the former empire of Lothair I (855), or Lotharingia, with the kingdom of the eastern Franks, or Germania, which from 919 was ruled by King Henry of Saxony. Henry dominated Lotharingia and bound the kingdom of Burgundy to the Frankish kingdom with feudal ties. His son, Otto I, conquered the kingdom of Italy (951) and was crowned emperor on 2 February 962 by Pope JOHN XII. In 1033, the Burgundian kingdom entered the empire.

The dominating concept of the empire arose from two traditions. According to the first, it expressed the power of its head and his dominance over peoples and kingdoms, a notion that invoked the memory of the Carolingian Empire. This idea, though deep-seated in people's minds and sometimes expressed ceremonially, was not laid down in law because pitted against it was a second tradition, which arose at the rebirth of the idea of empire (800, coronation of Charlemagne; 962, coronation of Otto I). According to this second tradition, the one destined to become emperor was the one the pope crowned in Rome. Thus, the Roman coronation appeared as the authentication of the empire, whose mission essentially was to be the advocate of the Roman Church.

Set against this mutual obligation of Church and Empire was a reality of which people gradually became aware: it was the three kingdoms, in particular that of Germany, that conferred on the ruler his strength and military power. However, these contradictions were not apparent as long as the two powers, pope and emperor, were considered side-by-side at the heart of the *Ecclesia universalis* as distinct, complementary agencies. This complementarity became fully evident during the reign of Otto III, who around the year 1000 founded kingdoms and churches in Hungary and Poland with the agreement of Pope SYLVESTER II, and later in 1046, when emperor Henry III wielded power over the Apostolic See.

The picture of the Empire that has been sketched here underwent profound changes in the wake of Gregorian reform and the ensuing upheavals. First of all, there was a powerful disruption of monarchical authority in the three kingdoms; royal power became purely nominal in Burgundy, the northern Italian cities became emancipated, and the old social structure was abolished by the German high aristocracy. Even more serious, the reformed papacy seems no longer to have thought of the Empire as an entity, as can be seen from the different rules provided by the CONCORDAT OF WORMS for the investiture of bishops in the three kingdoms.

Added to this political enfeeblement of the empire was a decline in the sacred quality of the emperor, who was relegated to the domain of the laity. The emperor also saw the few prerogatives he held in Rome pared down; for example, he lost all rights in the nomination of the pope, who claimed sovereignty in Rome and the PATRIMONY OF ST. PETER. Furthermore, the papacy tried to influence the choice of the king whom it crowned emperor. Pope GREGORY VII was the first to claim the right of approval of the imperial election and imposed an oath of loyalty on the anti-king Rudolf of Rheinfelden.

It fell to the rulers of the house of Hohenstaufen to redress this situation, in particular Frederick I Barbarossa. The principles behind his actions came from two sources. The first was Roman law, which gave the empire its theoretical basis in descent from the Roman Empire, whose continuity was never in doubt. This was the grounds for the titles *Imperium romanum* (Roman Empire), *imperator Romanorum* (emperor of the Romans) and *rex Romanorum* (king of the Romans) applied to the king elected in Germany, who was an imperial candidate; all three titles were official from the 12th century on. Some of Frederick's collaborators, such as his chancellor, Rainald of Dassel, imbued him with ideas of wide-ranging sovereignty, universalism, and a holy empire depending directly on God. Beyond these principles, the Carolingian tradition was the most important political force, evoking the memory of the Frankish conquest and Charlemagne's protection of the entire Christian people.

The restoring of royal rights in the three kingdoms meant using and attempting to legalize the new forces, while cultivating strong points of support for the sovereign. In Burgundy, this strong point was the present-day Franche-Comté, whose heiress Barbarossa had married; in the south, the emperor tried to balance the powerful lay feudality with bishops, whom he granted regalian rights in return for their homage. In Italy, the application of the laws that Frederick had decreed at the Diet of Roncaglia (1158), which prescribed the return to imperial power of the regalian rights usurped by nobles, bishops, and especially the towns, provoked a lengthy conflict with the communes of the Lombard League. This ended only in 1183 with the peace of Constance, whereby the towns won the right to keep and buy back regalian rights and the recognition of their elected magistrates (known as consuls). In each town, the emperor retained some rights of sovereignty; his chief strong point henceforth was central Italy. Finally, in Germany, Frederick used feudal homage and the fortification of their lands to bind to himself the leading lay barons (dukes, Palatine counts, and margraves), as well as the bishops and royal abbots included in the order of princes of the empire (Reichsfürstenstand). In addition, Frederick and his successors strove to increase the royal domain, which covered the whole of Germany (except for the northern plains and Bavaria), but was too dispersed to play a role comparable to that of the

Île-de-France for the Capetian king.

The restoration of the empire was under way when it was obstructed by the struggle between Frederick and the papacy. This conflict of ideas pitted Frederick against the pontifical doctrine of the empire—the pope's emperor-soldier as defender of the Roman Church. Frederick defended his own idea of a sacred empire, directly dependent on God, accession to which was gained through the election of princes. His declaration, which can be read in a deed of 1157, bears the mark of the diet of Besançon. The legate of Pope HADRIAN IV, Orlando Bandinelli (the future ALEXANDER III), had read to the assembly a letter in which, alluding to the empire, Hadrian declared himself prepared to grant Frederick "even more important benefices" (*majores beneficia*). The term was ambiguous; it might mean "benefits" (as the pope declared a little later), but it might also carry the meaning of "fiefs," and it was in the latter sense that—perhaps intentionally—Chancellor Rainald of Dassel translated it.

The scandal that exploded at the assembly was huge and explains the forceful reaction of the emperor, who asserted that he held the empire from God alone. The tension between the two powers reached its climax following the double papal election (September 1159) of Orlando Bandinelli and Octavian of Monticelli: the former (Alexander III) a brilliant canonist and defender of the independence of the Church, and the latter (who took the name Victor IV) a more moderate champion of entente with the emperor. Under the circumstances, Frederick believed he could use the council meeting in Pavia (1160) to impose his pope, VICTOR IV, on Christendom. But his move failed. Victor's rule only covered Germany and royal Italy. Burgundy hesitated, while the rest of Christianity, headed by France and England, recognized Alexander III. The restoration of peace allowed Frederick to reaffirm his authority in Germany and Italy and to carry out his most spectacular diplomatic coup: the marriage of his son Henry, now elected king of the Romans, to the heiress to the kingdom of Sicily. Henry VI, who succeeded when Frederick died on the way to Jerusalem (1190), managed, not without difficulties, to take possession of the Sicilian kingdom, which was thus united with the empire (1194).

Conscious of the danger of the encirclement of Rome and the Patrimony of St. Peter, INNOCENT III took advantage of the German crisis of the double election of Philip of Swabia and Otto of Brunswick (1197–8) to split Sicily off from the Empire by retaining in Sicily the young King Frederick II, son of Henry VI. He did recognize Otto IV, but when the latter broke his promises, he dispatched Frederick to Germany. Frederick had himself elected king of the Romans, abandoning the kingdom of Sicily to his son Henry (1211). The victory of his ally King Philippe Auguste at Bouvines (1214) was also his own.

The new reign initiated a displacement of the axis of empire in 1220, when Frederick recalled from Sicily his son Henry, who was chosen as king of Germany. Frederick himself was crowned emperor by the highly conciliatory Pope HONORIUS II, who allowed him, at least tacitly, to retain the government of Sicily. This brought about the reconstitution of the union of the two monarchies, with the combination of Sicily and Italy becoming the empire's center of gravity. Germany now occupied a secondary place, governed by both the emperor's sons, Henry VII (1220–34) and later Conrad IV (elected in 1237). In a way, the emperor abandoned the kingdom to the lay princes and ecclesiastics whom his constitutions of 1220 and 1232 proclaimed "masters" of the domain they were in the process of building, while he himself remained the supreme source of law and authority in Germany.

In Italy, Frederick, who refused to recognize the peace of Constance, was in more or less permanent conflict with the Lombard towns, which had banded together in a new league. After his victory over the Milanese at Cortenuova (1237), he set about gradually organizing the Italian kingdom in a unified way, even including in it what might be called, from Innocent III's reign, the "pontifical state." This reform unleashed the hatred of popes GREGORY IX and INNOCENT IV against the emperor. Another explanation for this hostility is the alleged tyranny he wielded over the Sicilian Church, and his repeated appeals to the solidarity of the Christian rulers, whom he invited to join him in defending their independence against the encroachments of the Church. Deposed by Innocent IV at the council of Lyons (1245), Frederick continued to fight all his enemies up to his death (13 December 1250). Meanwhile, ignoring the rights of Conrad IV, Innocent IV had invited the Germans to elect a new king. The landgrave of Thuringia, Hermann Raspe, was elected by a few bishops (1246), and on his death, Count William of Holland (1248–56). After William, a double election brought to the throne two foreigners, each chosen by a different group of electors: Richard of Cornwall, brother of the English king Edward I, and the king of Castille, Alfonso X. Politically, Germany no longer had a king after 1257. This was the Great Interregnum, which lasted until the unanimous election of Count Rudolf of Habsburg (1273).

After the interregnum, the link with the empire continued to unravel. In the Burgundian kingdom, where royal authority had long been undermined by the progress of local powers (the counts of Provence, dauphins of the Viennois, counts of Savoy), the policies of Rudolf and his successors would be to maintain their authority as much as possible in the north and to enfeoff the southern regions under the name of the kingdom of Arles to a foreign prince, the last one being the French king Charles V. In northern and central Italy, the absence of any central power liberated the cities, which became sovereign states. In the south, the count of Provence, Charles of Anjou, seized the kingdom of Sicily with the agreement of popes URBAN IV and CLEMENT IV (1266). He and his Angevin successors were virtually party chiefs of the Church (the GUELPHS), even when, after 1282, they had lost Sicily and were reduced to the peninsular section (known from then on as the kingdom of Naples).

Basically hostile to the empire, the Angevins strove to prevent any imperial restoration; thus, after Frederick II, Henry VII of Luxemburg was the first emperor to visit Italy. He was crowned emperor (1312) but did not succeed in imposing his presence as a peacemaker between the two sides. At least his presence revived the hopes of the GHIBELLINES (the champions of the empire). It was by relying on their support and on all the forces hostile to Pope JOHN XXII that Henry's successor, Ludwig of Bavaria, came to Rome and received the crown at the Capitol, an act that made the Roman people seem to be the crowning authority (1328). This episode had no sequel. It fell to Emperor Charles IV, during his two stays in Italy (1355 and 1368), to restore the link with the empire by selling to the lords and cities some much sought-after privileges—acting as agents and representatives on behalf of the Empire—thus making it possible to maintain imperial sovereignty in the north. Only his son Sigismond, king of Hungary (1431) and Frederick III of Hapsburg (1452), were, like him, crowned in Rome with the imperial diadem. Frederick's son Maximilian was the first to abandon the traditional coronation, assuming the title "emperor elect of the Romans." Toward the end of his reign, the name of the empire became official: Holy Roman Empire of the Germanic Nation—that is, arising from the German nation.

The empire took certain features from the most significant traits of Germany toward the end of the Middle Ages. The first was its spread to the Oder and even beyond, as a result of the incorporation of the Silesian duchies from the 12th century on. Next, was the persistence of the elective character of the monarchy. From 1257, election had become the monopoly of the college of the seven electors: the archbishops of Mainz, Cologne, and Trier, the king of Bohemia, the count Palatine of the Rhine, the duke of Saxony, and the margrave of Brandenburg. Highly conscious of their prerogative, they restrained royalty as much as they could, but they also continued to maintain the right of empire on the royal election. Against the papacy, which from Innocent IV's reign once again claimed a right of approval, and against the claims put forth by John XXII, the electors, meeting in Rhens in 1338, announced, following Ludwig of Bavaria, that the chosen king had no need to be approved by the Holy See and was entitled to exercise forthwith the rights deriving from the emperor.

Eighteen years later, there was no longer any question of papal approval in Charles IV's constitution known as the *Golden Bull* (1356). With Germany becoming a federation of princely territories, the kings strove in their turn to build up a strong territorial power (*Hausmacht*) in the hope of gaining the crown and, through it, supremacy over the princes. Their efforts paid off for the Habsburgs and Luxemburgs. Thus, King Rudolf of Habsburg in 1278 conquered the duchies of Austria, Styria, Carinthia, and Carniola, which were added to the family's ancient possessions in Alsace, Switzerland, and Swabia. The *Hausmacht* of the Luxemburgs resulted from the marriage of Henry VII's son, John the Blind, to the heiress of the kingdom of Bohemia. His son Charles IV enlarged the kingdom, making it the most formally organized state in the Empire. In 1364, Emperor Charles IV and Duke Rudolf IV of Austria mutually guaranteed the succession of their lines. This plan was realized first in 1437–38 for a very brief time, then in 1526 for a longer period. At that time, the Habsburgs, masters of a vast patrimony (Austria, Bohemia, and Hungary), ruled the empire with Charles V. They preserved it until its abolition in 1806.

Robert Folz

Bibliography

Beumann, H. *Kaisergestalten des Mittelalters*, Munich, 1984; *Die Ottonen*, Stuttgart, 1987.

Cuvillier, J. P. *L'Allemagne mëdiëvale*, 2 vols., Paris, 1979–81.

Federico Barbarossa nel dibattito in Italia e Germania, ed. R. Manselli and J. Riedmann, Bologna, 1980 (Annali dell'Istituto storico italo-germanico, 10).

Folz, R. *L'idëe d'Empire en Occident (V^e-XIVe siècles)*, Paris, 1953; *La Naissance du Saint Empire*, Paris, 1967.

Fried, J. *Otto III. und Boleslas Chrobry*, Stuttgart, 1989 (Frankfurter historische Abhandlungen, 30).

Gerlich, A. *Habsburg-Luxemburg-Wittelsbach Kampf um die deutsche Krone*, Wiesbaden, 1960.

Haverkamp, A. *Herrschaftsformen der Frühstaufer in Reichsitalien*, 2 vols., Stuttgart, 1970–1. (Monographien zur Geschichte des Mittelalters, I, 1–2).

Higounet, C. *Les Allemands en Europe centrale et orientale au Moyen Age*, Paris, 1989.

Kantorowicz, E. H. *Frederick the Second, 1194–1250*, London, 1931.

Leyser, K. J. *Medieval Germany and its Neighbours (900–1250)*, London, 1982.

Noel, J. F. *Le Saint Empire*, 2nd ed., Paris, 1986.

Rapp, F. *Les Origines médiévales de l'Allemagne moderne*, Paris, 1989.

Stieber, J. W., *Pope Eugenius IV, the Council of Basel and the Secular and Ecclesiastical Authorities in the Empire: The Conflict Over Supreme Authority and Power in the Church,* Leiden, 1978.

Wolf, A. "Les Deux Lorraines et l'origine des princes électeurs du Saint Empire," *Francia*, 11 (1991), 241–56.

HOLY SEE OR APOSTOLIC SEE. The terms "Holy See" and "Apostolic See" refer not only to the Roman pontiff, but also to the Secretariat of State and the other agencies of the Roman Curia, "unless the nature of the matter or the context" implies that only the pope is concerned (CODE OF CANON LAW of 1983, c. 361). This canon also includes the Council for Public Affairs of the Church, which was abolished with the curial reform laid down in the apostolic constitution *Pastor bonus* (28 June 1988) and later became Section II of the Secretariat of State. The reference to other "institutions" has nothing to do with either the congregations or the tribunals of the CURIA (c. 360), but it leaves the door open for the adaptation of the pontifical agencies to the changing needs of government. Such is the broad sense of the term, which was already present in c. 7 of the 1917 Code, following a definition provided by the Holy Office: "documents" of the Holy See should be taken to cover not only those emanating from the Rome pontiff, but also those made by the congregations of the Roman Curia (reply, 13 January 1892). Strictly speaking, however, the Holy See is the Roman pontiff—that is, his office of pontiff of Rome, the papacy, and his primacy as a divine institution that is permanent, although the titular changes.

The documents of VATICAN II frequently employ the term "Apostolic See" (or "Roman Apostolic See," or "Roman See") and only rarely "Holy See," although the expression "Roman pontiff" occurs very often. The Code of 1983 uses "Apostolic See" in 133 canons, and "Holy See" in 38 canons. In both instances—council and Code—the two names "Sedes Apostolica" and "Sancta Sedes" are in a way interchangeable. They denote pontifical power, in the sense that the dicasteries of the Roman Curia are its representatives and executors, as permanent vicar or special delegation. In the Code, as in the conciliar documents, the expression "Romanus Pontifex" defines the responsibilities that derive from the primate of Peter. The Holy See is distinct from the Church, which is "governed by Peter's successor and the bishops in communion with him" (canon 204 § 2), and from the Vatican City State.

Like the Catholic Church, the Apostolic See has the nature of a moral person by divine law itself (canon 113 § 1), both in the internal domain of its organization and in that of international law. This is explained in canon 3, which states that the Code of Canon Law does not abrogate "the pacts entered upon by the Apostolic See with nations or other political societies," nor does it derogate them.

The Holy See and the Catholic Church constitute two distinct juridical persons. Through its divine nature, the Church is a hierarchical society, the hierarchical ministerium being handed down to the apostles' successors, the bishops, who have in Peter's successor "a perpetual and visible principle and foundation for the unity of faith and communion" (Vatican II, dogmatic constitution *Lumen gentium*, n. 18 and 23). The primacy of the Roman pontiff, a perpetual and fundamental institution, ensures unity between the visible head of the Church and its members. The intent of the canonical system is to recognize the juridical personality of the entity formed by the primatial office of the pope and the Curia, considered as a unified whole. "The Holy See is to the Catholic Church what supreme constitutional authority is to the State" (R. Minnerath, *L'église et les états*, p. 76). The juridical personality of the Holy See is thus made up of other entities, which themselves possess their own juridical personalities, as do the papacy and the various agencies of the Roman Curia. Moreover, the Holy See possesses patrimonial capacity (canons 1255 and 1257).

The Holy See possesses the rights and prerogatives peculiar to the Roman pontiff, as supreme organ of direction and representation both of the Church and of the Vatican City State. From the viewpoint of ecclesiastic public law, it is the supreme leader of the Catholic Church, with the triple power to teach, to sanctify, and to govern as the head of the Church. It also acts as patriarch of the West, primate of Italy, metropolitan of the province of Rome, bishop of Rome, and temporal sovereign of the Vatican City State.

The Holy See is, therefore, a subject of the international order. It is the responsibility of the Secretariat of State to develop diplomatic relations with states and other subjects of international law, and to regulate affairs common to the Church and to civil society, if necessary, by means of concordats or similar conventions; in practice, these tasks fall to the pontifical legates, nuncios, and other diplomatic representatives (apostolic constitution *Pastor bonus*, art. 46). Relations established between a state and the Secretariat of State are understood to be between the state in question and the Holy See. The international personality of the Holy See is a reality that has been recognized since the Lateran accords, signed with Italy on 11 February 1929. In article II, "Italy recognizes the sovereignty of the Holy See in the international field as an inherent attribute of its nature, in conformity with its tradition and with the exigencies of its mission in the world."

This juridical recognition had ceased—unlike the juridical personality of the Holy See—with the capture of Rome on 20 September 1870 and the abolition of the Papal States that resulted from it. But it was maintained in practice from 1870 to 1929, demonstrating thereby that the international position of the Holy See was due exclusively to its nature as a direct organ of the Catholic Church. The reasons for this are as follows.

First, the Holy See exercised the active right of legation. The pontifical legates carried out actions that exceeded the limits of temporal sovereignty, and the nuncios preserved the precedence by right that was granted them by the Congress of Vienna (19 March 1815).

Second, the Holy See continued to exercise the passive right of legation, and several states maintained diplomatic relations with it. Some states renewed these relations (e.g., Costa Rica in 1882, Chile on 20 December 1902, Great Britain on 30 December 1914, Monaco on 30 December 1915, Luxemburg in May 1917, Portugal on 11 July 1918, Venezuela on 9 December 1919, Switzerland on 20 June 1920, Paraguay on 6 August 1920, Haiti on 30 September 1921). Others entered into them at the time of the Law of Guarantees (13 May 1871), which defined unilaterally the condition of the Roman pontiff. Sixteen countries were then represented by ambassadors at the Holy See; these numbered 19 at the death of LEO XIII in 1903, 13 at the death of PIUS X in 1914, 28 on that of BENEDICT XV in 1922, and 27 before the signing of the Lateran Treaty.

Third, the Holy See received many extraordinary missions; for example, under Pius X. Such missions came from the emperor of Korea in 1904; the king of Norway and the shah of Persia in 1906; the emperor of Japan in 1907; the negus of Ethiopia in 1907 and 1908; the president of El Salvador, the tsar of Russia, the queen of the Netherlands, the prince regent of Bavaria, and the king of Saxony in 1908; the sultan of Turkey in 1909; and the emperor of China in 1910.

Fourth, the Holy See concluded concordats and other agreements with states, which can be done only according to the rules and the current practice of international law. This was the case with Peru in 1875; Ecuador in 1881 and 1890; Austro-Hungary in 1881; Russia in 1882 and 1907; Guatemala in 1882; Switzerland in 1884 and 1889; Montenegro in 1886; France on 2 April 1886 (establishment of a faculty of theology at the University of Strasbourg) and exchange of letters 16–17 November 1923; Colombia in 1887, 1892, 1898, and 1902; Monaco, apostolic letters of 15 March 1887; Malta in 1889–90; Great Britain in 1890; Spain in 1904; Belgium in 1906; Serbia in 1914; Latvia on 30 May 1922; Bavaria on 19 March 1924; Poland on 10 February 1925; Lithuania on 27 September 1927; Czechoslovakia, *modus vivendi* of 17 December 1927; Romania on 10 May 1927; and Portugal, convention of 15 April 1928.

Finally, the Holy See frequently acceded to the demands of international arbitration that were presented to it. Principal examples include mediation to attempt to prevent the Franco-Prussian War, 1870; arbitration in the dispute between Germany and Spain over the Caroline Islands, 1885; intervention in the dispute between Great Britain and Portugal over the frontiers of the Congo, 1890; arbitration by the pope in the border dispute between Peru and Ecuador, 1893; mediation by the pope proposed by Great Britain and Venezuela to settle the frontiers of Guyana, 1894; arbitration by the pope between Haiti and Santo Domingo regarding a conflict over frontiers, 1895; an appeal by the pope to the emperor of Ethiopia in favor of Italian prisoners of war, 1896; an attempt by the pope to prevent war between Spain and the United States over Cuba, 1898; arbitration by the pope in the border dispute between Argentina and Chile, 1900–3; agreement between Colombia and Peru to submit all future disputes to papal arbitration, 1905; arbitration by the pope in the border dispute between Colombia and Ecuador, 1906; arbitration by the pope in the dispute between Brazil and Peru over possession of gold-bearing deposits, 1909–10; arbitration proposed by the pope to Argentina, Brazil, and Chile, 1914.

The visits of foreign rulers to the pope when he was the "prisoner in the Vatican" were, in effect, solemn recognitions of his sovereignty: Albert I of Belgium, 18 March 1922; the king and queen of England, 1923; Alfonso XIII and Victoria Eugenia of Spain, 19 November 1912; Ras Tafari Makonnen, heir to the throne and regent of Ethiopia, 21 June 1924; Fouad I, king of Egypt, 9 August 1927; and Amanoullah, king of Afghanistan, 12 January 1928). Also significant is the fact that the word "State" was replaced by "powers" in the regulations of the international peace conference held in The Hague in 1898 in order to allow the Holy See to take its place among the states, despite the nonexistence of the PAPAL STATES and the fact that, after the First World War, some states—such as Estonia and Poland—asked to be recognized by the Holy See. Moreover, the German plan for a League of Nations expressly provided for membership of a representative of the Holy See. Even more telling is the fact that the Holy See took part in negotiations with the Italian state with a view to the conclusion of the Lateran accords. To achieve this, it surely was necessary for the Holy See to already exist as a juridical personality, because an international moral person cannot be at one and the same time the subject and object of the same international convention.

The Lateran accords were aimed at ensuring the Holy See "in a stable way, the condition of fact and of right which guarantees absolute independence in fulfillment of its high mission to the world" (preamble). The Holy See agreed that, with these agreements, "adequate assurance is made for what is necessary for providing for due liberty and independence of the pastoral government of the diocese of Rome and the Catholic Church in Italy and the world" (article XXVI).

At the same time, with the express aim of "assuring the Holy See absolute and visible independence and guaranteeing it an indisputable sovereignty even in the international domain," the Vatican City State was created, over which the Holy See exercised "full property right, with exclusive and absolute power and sovereign jurisdiction" (preamble). Vatican City may be conceived as a state that is both the international guarantee and the international seat of the highest organ of the Catholic Church—that is,

the Holy See. From the viewpoint of the Italian government, the Holy See appears as an autonomous, independent body, entirely removed from the sovereignty of the Italian state and beyond the reach of its laws—as regards not only the political and temporal activity on the part of a head of a foreign state, Vatican City, but also all spiritual and religious activity on the part of the supreme head of the Catholic Church with regard to the whole world.

This international juridical personality of the Holy See does not exist solely with regard to Italy, which ratified it in the Lateran accords, extended by those of Villa Madama (18 February 1984). It also pertains within the international juridical system—not only by virtue of its temporal power, as sovereign of the Vatican City State like any other temporal ruler, but also, above all and independently of that, as the supreme institution of the Catholic Church, endowed with a universal spiritual primacy. Here again, through concordats, political powers deal with the Holy See as a representative body of the Catholic Church. In the Lateran accords, the Holy See explicitly demanded recognition of its sovereignty in the international arena "as an inherent attribute of its nature, in conformity with its tradition and the exigencies of its mission in the world" (article II).

Theories differ on the nature of this personality. Does it proceed solely from the fact of being head of the Church and a religious sovereign; or exclusively from the fact of being head of the state of Vatican City and temporal sovereign; or, again, from both at the same time? Is the title therefore single or double? Is there one juridical personality, or a duality of juridical personalities?

Those who hold the "monist" theory are divided into several factions (a) the one holder of international subjecthood would be the Holy See, as supreme institution of the Church; or (b) the two sovereignties would be fused into a single one, that of the Vatican City State having been absorbed by that of the Holy See; or (c) Vatican City would be the sole subject and would provide the Holy See with the means to become a person in international law. By contrast, the "dualist" theory holds that alongside the Holy See, which was a person of international right by virtue of its universal sovereignty in the domain proper to the Catholic Church, the Lateran accords created another person of international right—the state of Vatican City—that is distinct from the Holy See and placed under its authority, designed to guarantee its independence.

In fact, the Holy See considers itself endowed with a double personality, as the Italian state recognized. It is not certain that other states and the international community do likewise in their relations with the Holy See; however, the fact that, by setting up diplomatic relations with it, the states expressed no objection, seems sufficient to deduce that they were willing to take cognizance of the existing situation and thus to recognize that the Holy See is a double subject of international law. The one subject represents and protects the interests of the Church, and the other those of the Vatican City State. This union of the two personalities has no equivalent in the classic examples of union between states. We should reject those opinions on juridical relations between the Holy See and the Vatican City State that present the latter as a vassal state of the Holy See, its "canonical benefice," and that refer to a "protectorate." Also to be rejected are those who seek an answer in the personal and real unions of states, and in a comparison with the seat of international organizations.

This union is truly unique. It is based on three elements: (a) a complete and perfect sovereignty and a personality, likewise complete and perfect, on the part of the two subjects, which is distinct and autonomous in both its juridical claim and its concrete practice; (b) an extremely close link creating a union that is stable, necessary, and inviolable between one and the other, of such a kind as to keep them indissolubly united in the future; and (c) an intimate, immutable subordination of the entity of the state to the extra-state entity, of such a kind as to make the latter, first and foremost, a simple means by which to obtain the finality of the former (P. A. d'Avack, "Santa Sede," *Enciclopedia*, col. 1848).

The unique limitation to this international juridical personality was intended by the Holy See itself. In regard to the sovereignty that it possesses even in the international domain, it "declares that it wishes to remain and will remain extraneous to the temporal disputes between States and to international congresses held for such objects, unless the contending parties make concordant appeals to its peaceful mission, at the same time reserving the right to exercise its moral and spiritual power" (article XXIV of the Lateran treaty). In consequence, the treaty adds that "Vatican City should always and in all cases be considered as a neutral and inviolable territory."

The fact that the Holy See in 1929 obtained Italy's recognition that it had true sovereignty in the domain of international law as an inherent attribute of its nature also shows that the Holy See occupies a place apart in the international community. As a result, if not de jure then at least de facto, it has a supranational character, more moral and political in effect than juridical.

Since 1929, the international role of the Holy See has grown steadily. Besides the appeals to the pope to resolve conflicts (for example, the arbitration of JOHN PAUL II in 1978–79 between Argentina and Chile concerning the Beagle Channel), a constantly growing number of countries—often newly independent—have established or reestablished relations with the Holy See (40 during the first 14 years of John Paul II's pontificate alone, up to mid-1992). The Holy See has also been present in international institutions (from 1957, after an exchange of

notes with the secretary of the UN) as well as in governmental and nongovernmental international organizations, and has participated in international conferences such as the meeting of the Conference on Security and Cooperation in Europe. Vatican City is itself a member of four international institutions (International Astronomical Union, International Institute of Administrative Sciences, International Technical Committee for the Prevention and Extinction of Fire, World Medical Association).

Dominique Le Tourneau

Bibliography

Anzilotti, D. *L'Église et l'État en Italie du Risorgimento à nos jours*, Paris, 1960.

Balladore-Pallieri, G. *Il diritto internazionale ecclesiastico*, Padua, 1940.

Battifol, P. *Le Siège apostolique*, Paris, 1924.

Beales, A. C. F. *The Catholic Church and International Order*, Harmondsworth, 1941.

Bracci, M. *Italia, Santa Sede e Città del Vaticano*, Padua, 1931.

Cammeo, F. *Ordinamento giuridico dello Stato della Città del Vaticano*, Florence, 1932.

Cardinale, I. *Le Saint-Siège et la diplomatie*, Brussels, 1962.

Ciprotti, Pio. "Le Saint-Siège: Sa fonction, sa figure et sa valeur dans le droit international," *Concilium* 58 (1970).

Collective, *Pie XII et la Cité*, Paris-Aix-Marseille, 1988.

D'Avack, P. A. *Chiesa, Santa Sede e Città del Vaticano nel ius publicum ecclesiasticum*, Florence, 1936; "La Chiesa e lo Stato nella nuova impostazione conciliaire," *La Chiesa dopo il Concilio: Atti del Congresso internazionale di diritto canonico, Roma 14–19 gennaio 1970*, Milan, 1972, I, 349–80.

de La Briére, Y. *L'Organisation internationale du monde contemporain et la papauté souveraine*, Paris, 3 vols., 1924–27–30; "La condition juridique de la Cité du Vatican," *RCADI*, 1930, III, 33, 115–65.

Donati, D. *La Città del Vaticano nella teoria generale dello Stato*, Padua, 1930.

Dupuy, A. *La Diplomatie du Saint-Siège après le concile Vatican II*, Paris, 1980.

Jarrige, R. *La Condition internationale du Saint-Siège avant et après les Accords du Latran*, Paris, 1930.

Jemolo, A. C. "Carattere dello Stato della Città del Vaticano," *Rivista di diritto internazionale*, 8 (1929), 25–50.

Köck, H. F. *Die völkerrechtliche Stellung des Heiligen Stuhls*, Berlin, 1975.

Le Fur, L. *Le Saint-Siège et le Droit des gens*, Paris, 1930.

Le Saint-Siège dans les Relations internationales (ed. J. B. d'Onorio), Paris, 1989.

Organizational Diagram of the Institutions of the Holy See

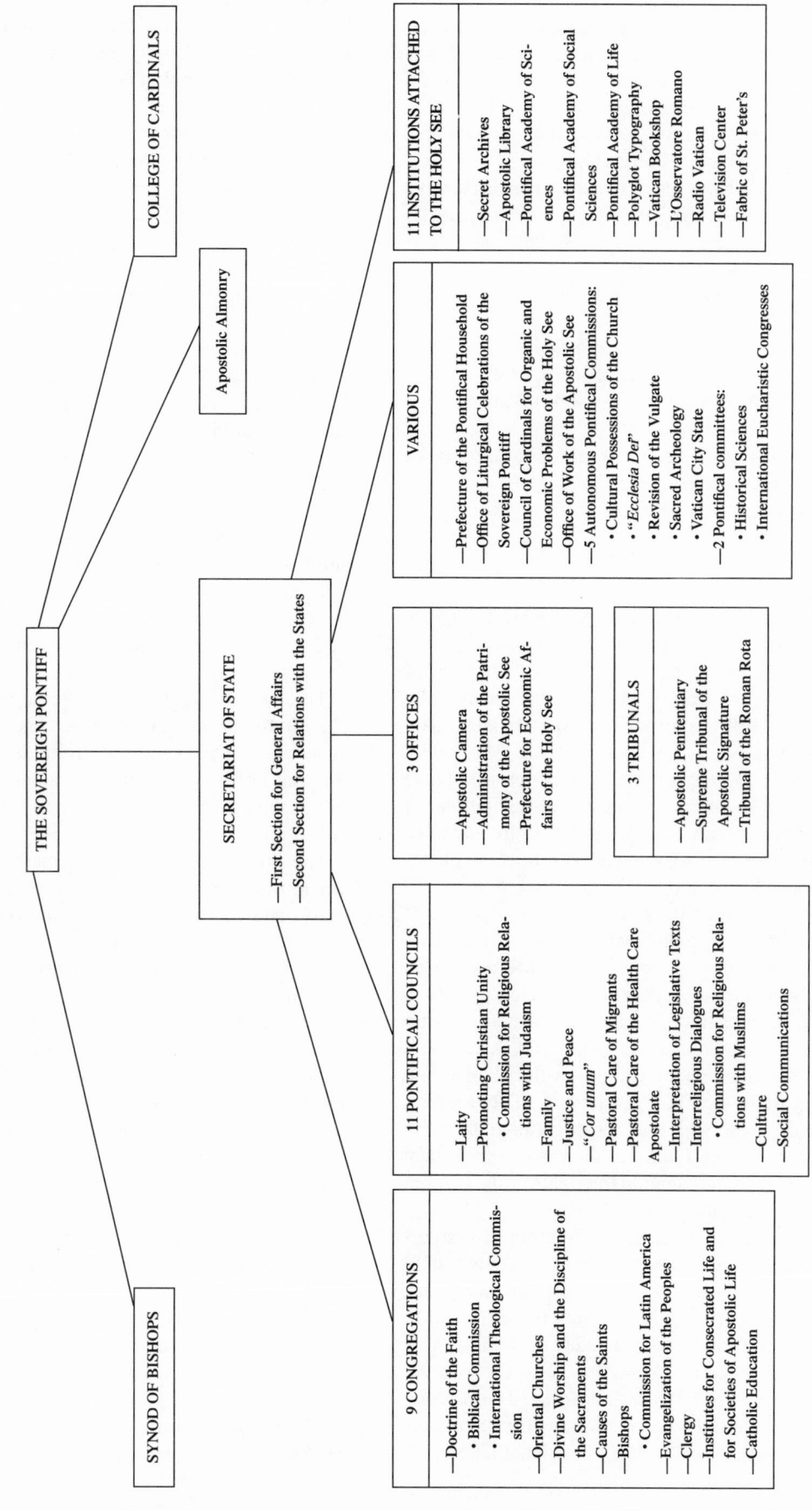

THE SOVEREIGN PONTIFF

- SYNOD OF BISHOPS
- COLLEGE OF CARDINALS
- Apostolic Almonry

SECRETARIAT OF STATE
—First Section for General Affairs
—Second Section for Relations with the States

9 CONGREGATIONS
—Doctrine of the Faith
  • Biblical Commission
  • International Theological Commission
—Oriental Churches
—Divine Worship and the Discipline of the Sacraments
—Causes of the Saints
—Bishops
  • Commission for Latin America
—Evangelization of the Peoples
—Clergy
—Institutes for Consecrated Life and for Societies of Apostolic Life
—Catholic Education

11 PONTIFICAL COUNCILS
—Laity
—Promoting Christian Unity
  • Commission for Religious Relations with Judaism
—Family
—Justice and Peace
—"Cor unum"
—Pastoral Care of Migrants
—Pastoral Care of the Health Care Apostolate
—Interpretation of Legislative Texts
—Interreligious Dialogues
  • Commission for Religious Relations with Muslims
—Culture
—Social Communications

3 OFFICES
—Apostolic Camera
—Administration of the Patrimony of the Apostolic See
—Prefecture for Economic Affairs of the Holy See

3 TRIBUNALS
—Apostolic Penitentiary
—Supreme Tribunal of the Apostolic Signature
—Tribunal of the Roman Rota

VARIOUS
—Prefecture of the Pontifical Household
—Office of Liturgical Celebrations of the Sovereign Pontiff
—Council of Cardinals for Organic and Economic Problems of the Holy See
—Office of Work of the Apostolic See
—5 Autonomous Pontifical Commissions:
  • Cultural Possessions of the Church
  • "Ecclesia Dei"
  • Revision of the Vulgate
  • Sacred Archeology
  • Vatican City State
—2 Pontifical committees:
  • Historical Sciences
  • International Eucharistic Congresses

11 INSTITUTIONS ATTACHED TO THE HOLY SEE
—Secret Archives
—Apostolic Library
—Pontifical Academy of Sciences
—Pontifical Academy of Social Sciences
—Pontifical Academy of Life
—Polyglot Typography
—Vatican Bookshop
—L'Osservatore Romano
—Radio Vatican
—Television Center
—Fabric of St. Peter's

Maccarrone, M. "'Sedes Apostolica' et 'Sedes Apostolicae': De titulo et ratione Apostolicitatis in aetate patristica et in altiore Medio Aevo," *Acta Congressus Internationalis de Theologia Concilii Vaticani II, Romae 26 Sept.–10 Oct. 1966*, Vatican City, 1968, 146–62.

Merle M. and de Montclos, C. *L'Église catholique et les relations internationales*, Paris, 1988.

Minnerath, R. *L'Église et les États concordataires (1846–1981): La Souveraineté spirituelle*, Paris, 1983.

Pernot, M. *Le Saint-Siège, l'Église catholique et la politique internationale*, Paris, 1924.

Puente Egido, J. *Personalidad internacional de la Ciudad del Vaticano*, Madrid, 1965.

Salerno, F. "Sede Apostolica o Santa Sede e Curia Romana," *La curia romana nella Cost. Ap. "Pastor Bonus"* (ed. P. A. Bonnet and C. Gullo), Vatican City, 1990, 45–82.

Schulz, W. *Leggi e disposizioni usuali dello Stato della Città del Vaticano*, Rome, 1981–2.

Wagnon, H. *Concordats et Droit international*, Gembloux, 1935.

HOLY SEPULCHER OF JERUSALEM. (Knightly Order of the). "Continue to respect the land sanctified by the patriarchs, the prophets, by the steps of the Son of God who became the Son of Man, by the apostles, by being always faithful to the spirit of your statutes," said JOHN PAUL II to leaders of this order on 15 May 1986. The pope added: "I congratulate you on the assistance you give the scholastic and ecclesiastical institutions of the diocese of Jerusalelm . . . the schools help guarantee the future presence of the Christian faith in these places and afford considerable aid toward the civil, human and social promotion of these populations."

The order of the Holy Sepulcher has as its primary aim to enhance the practice of the Christian life among its members, in absolute loyalty to the sovereign pontiff in accordance with the Church's teachings. Other aims are to support and aid the charitable, cultural, and social works and institutions of the Church in the Holy Land, particularly those of the Latin patriarchate of Jerusalelm; to encourage the preservation and propagation of the faith in these areas, by urging Catholics the world over to take an interest in them; and to uphold the rights of the Church in the Holy Land (Statutes, 8 July 1977).

From the first centuries of the current era, Christians devoted particular care to the HOLY PLACES, among them the Holy Sepulcher. The churches of the Latin and Syriac rites were the first to ensure its veneration and to tend it. St. Helena constructed a basilica (328) over the Lord's tomb, entrusting its care to cenobites. The Persians set fire to it in 614, and in 638 the Arabs seized Jerusalem. Charlemagne is credited with creating the first capitularies setting up guardians of the Holy Sepulcher (808).

Events in the Holy Land impelled URBAN II to preach the first CRUSADE (council of Clermont, 1095). The knights on whom the Cross was imposed were called Milites Sancti Sepulcri. They liberated Jerusalem under the leadership of Godfrey of Bouillon, who entrusted 50 of them with the honor of serving as the armed guard of the Holy Sepulcher. Some of the knights were members of religious orders, others laymen. His brother and successor, Baudoin I, named the patriarch of Jerusalem head of the order and gave him the power to create, arm, and institute knights. The patriarch, Arnoul of Jerusalem, set up a veritable military and religious order that included canons of the chapter of Jerusalem as well as knights, both being placed under the rule of St. Augustine.

Saladin captured Jerusalem (2 October 1187), which later was retaken and then definitively lost in 1244. The surviving knights, both religious and secular, regrouped at St. John of Acre, which fell in its turn on 18 May 1291. However, in return for a heavy tribute, the sultan in 1333 ceded the Holy Places to Robert of Anjou and his wife, Sancha of Mallorca, rulers of Naples. CLEMENT VI entrusted them to the care of the Friars Minor of St. Francis; their superior, the custodian of the Holy Land, represented the authority of the Holy See. LEO X (brief of 29 October 1518) and later pontiffs confirmed this concession.

The physical defense of the territory of the Holy Places was no longer possible. The order of the Holy Sepulcher, therefore, henceforth devoted itself to the spiritual defense of Christian values in the Holy Land, and to the preservation of its educational and charitable institutions.

The knights settled in their many European houses, the most important being the archpriory of Perugia (Italy) and the priory of Miechow (Poland). In France, the order was introduced by St. Louis in 1254 in the form of a royal archconfraternity. It has existed since 1131 in Spain (where the knights continued to fight the Saracens), and since 1125 in Germany (monastery of Denkendorf). Convents of regular canonesses of the Holy Sepulcher were also founded: Wittstoch (Prussia), Saragossa (Aragon), Charleville—which would become the Ladies of the rue de Bellechasse—near Paris, and others.

INNOCENT VIII incorporated the order of the Holy Sepulcher into that of St. John of Jerusalem (bull *Cum solerti meditatione*, 28 March 1489). But this action met strong resistance, and the bull was not universally applied. Attempts were made to revive the order in 1558 in Flanders and in 1616 in France, but they failed as a result of interventions by the Knights of Malta, who were loath to return the possessions of the order of the Holy Sepulcher.

Nevertheless, Ferdinand of Aragon obtained from ALEXANDER VI the assurance that the pope would revoke the bull of union in part, with the Holy See retaining the post of grand master. Leo X maintained his rights to the Spanish branch, whose monastery of Calatayud was not affected by the extinction of the order (brief of 29 October 1513). Likewise, the monastery of Miechow escaped the turmoil.

After having restored the Latin patriarchate (apostolic letter *Nulla celebrior*, 23 July 1847), PIUS IX reorganized the order (brief *Cum multa*, 24 January 1868). For the first time in four centuries, a patriarch of Jerusalem was named: José Valerga, who received the administration of the order along with its privileges. LEO XIII extended to women the right to belong to the order (brief of 3 August 1888). The new statutes were signed in Jerusalem on 6 April 1892.

PIUS X confirmed the privileges of the order and reserved to himself the title of grand master (apostolic letter *Quam multa*, 3 May 1907). The patriarchate of Jerusalem suffered greatly from the First WORLD WAR. BENEDICT XV gave his blessing to the plan of restoration and approved the foundation of the Work of the Preservation of the Faith, linked to the order of the Holy Sepulcher. Thereafter, the order assumed the title of *Ordo Equestris Sancti Sepulcri Hierosolymitani*, or Knightly Order of the Holy Sepulcher of Jerusalem (Congregation of Ceremonial, decree of 5 August 1931). PIUS XI approved the reformed statutes (19 March 1932), which were then modified by PIUS XII and entrusted by him to a cardinal (apostolic letter *Quam Romani Pontifices*, 14 September 1949).

On 8 December 1962, JOHN XXIII approved the publication of the statutes and entrusted the order with the mission of working to promote the progress of the faith in the Holy Land. PAUL VI sent it this invitation: "Continue to love these holy places, of a predilection ever more intense and more pious . . . continue to promote in it the works of religion, of instruction, of charity which attest to the tenacious and loving presence of the Catholic Church; increase, if possible, your efforts of spiritual and corporal goodwill for these populations. . . ; and make them see that your crusade desires to be of charity, of concord, of peace; of the Gospel of Christ" (allocution to members of the Holy Sepulcher, 30 May 1964). The statutes approved by Paul VI on 8 July 1977 confirmed only that mission.

The order is one of only three chivalric orders officially recognized by the Holy See and some nations. It is under the authority of the cardinal grand master—in 2000, Cardinal Carlo Furno—who directs it in the pontiff's name and resides in Rome. He is aided by the governor general, by the grand magisterium of 16 members from different countries, and by the Consulta, an assembly comprising the grand magisterium and the lieutenants from all countries. The grand prior is, by law, the Latin patriarch of Jerusalem. The order has its seat near the church of St. Onofrio on the Janiculum, in a monastery given by Pius XII.

The order includes 35 chapters, or lieutenancies: 16 in Europe (Germany, England and Wales, Austria, Belgium, Scotland, Spain [Aragon, Catalonia and the Balearics, Castille, Leon], Finland, France, Gibraltar, Hungary, Italy [central, south, west, Sicily], Monaco, the Netherlands, Portugal, Switzerland); 14 in the Americas (Brazil [Rio de Janeiro, São Paolo], Canada [Montreal, Quebec, Toronto], Colombia, Ecuador, United States [south, northwest, west, east, north], Mexico, Puerto Rico); 1 in Oceania (Australia); and 2 in the Far East (Philippines).

The knights and ladies of the Holy Sepulcher (numbering more than 10,000) are divided into three classes: class of knights of the collar and ladies of the collar; class of knights divided into grades, including knight of the grand cross, commander with plaque, commander, knight; and class of ladies divided into the grades of lady of the grand cross, lady of commandery with plaque, lady of commandery, and lady. They are chosen, as is stipulated in the statutes, from among persons who are of deep faith and exemplary moral conduct, and who are particularly deserving with regard to Catholic works in the Holy Land or with regard to the order. They are appointed by the cardinal grand master, with the diploma of nomination bearing the visa and seal of the Secretariat of State. Investiture is carried out, after a prayer vigil, by dubbing according to the ceremony approved by the Congregation of Rites (25 July 1962).

The insignia of the order is the red potent cross, divided into four non-potent crosslets, known as the Jerusalem cross. The statutes explain that "in honor of the passion of Christ, out of respect toward the sovereign pontiff and by obedience toward the vicar of Christ and the bishops, we have adopted 'the holy crosses' in honor of the five wounds of our Lord Jesus Christ in order to distinguish us among the infidels."

The order fulfills its mission by providing material support to the Christian communities in the Holy Land, besides contributing considerably to the functioning of 44 parochial schools in the Latin patriarchate of Jerusalem (approximately 15,000 students, both Christian and Muslim). It meets the needs of the clergy of its 60 parishes and the seminary of Beit Jala (80 seminarians), and it supports numerous benevolent activities, dispensaries, creches, etc. At the suggestion of the Latin patriarch, each lieutenancy may aid in other projects, in agreement with the grand magisterium. From 1980 to 1990, the lieutenancy of France, for instance, helped in the building of a dispensary in Taybeh (a village near Jerusalem), a school (450 students), and a pilgrims' hostel. It supports French coworkers, preferably seminarians, and in the 1990s participated in the construction of an educational complex in Reneh, in Galilee. The order also gives moral support. The knights and ladies visit the Christian communities—the pilgimage to the Holy Land is one of their commitments—and pray with their members. In France, the lieutenancy is in charge of the safekeeping and veneration of the relics of the Passion, exhibited in Notre Dame in Paris.

Dominique Le Tourneau

Bibliography

Allemand, *Précis historique de l'ordre du Saint-Sépulcre de Jérusalem*, Paris, 1815.

Berthod, B., and Bouëssée, J. *L'Ordre du Saint-Sépulcre de Jérusalem et la Terre Sainte*, Lyon, 1990.

Couret, A. *Notice historique sur l'ordre du Saint-Sépulcre de Jérusalem, depuis ses origines jusqu'à nos jours, 1099–1905*, Paris, 1905.

de Bourbon Parme, X. *Les Chevaliers du Saint-Sépulcre*, Paris, 1957.

de Ravestein, M. "L'Ordre du Saint-Sépulcre de Jérusalem," *Revue générale*, 10, 1976.

Giacomini, G. *Storia dei Cavalieri del Santo Sepolcro*, Rome, 1975.

Guigue de Champvans, F. *Ordres de chevalerie du Saint-Siège*, Paris, 1932.

Ortega Costa de Ballestero, J. M. *Breve historial de la Orden de Caballería del Santo Sepulcro de Jerusalén*, Barcelona, 1967; *Homenaje del Capítulo Noble de Aragón, Cataluña y Barcelona a su Orden de Caballería del Santo Sepulcro de Jerusalén*, Barcelona, 1971.

Piavi, L. *Establecimientos y constitución de la Inclita Orden Militar del Santo Sepulcro*, Madrid, 1934.

Posseto, A. *Il Patriarcato Latino di Gerusalemme*, Milan, 1938.

HOLY YEAR.

Middle Ages. When BONIFACE VIII inaugurated the first holy year in 1300, he did not do so on his own initiative but as a response to the request of numerous faithful who were flocking to the city of Rome. These pilgrims had "heard it said from the elders that any Christian who visited the body of the apostles during this centenary year would be delivered from his sins and punishment." The rumor spread like wildfire throughout all of Christendom, which at the time was immersed in a climate of expectation and eschatological tension under the influence of Joachim of Flora's ideas, which the Spiritual Franciscans were spreading. The pope responded favorably to the desire of thousands of pilgrims to visit the city of the apostles. The Florentine chronicler Giovanni Villani mentioned 200,000 people, and Guglielmo Ventura, a contemporary of Villani (not without considerable exaggeration) cited 2 million! More reasonable estimates would be between 10,000 and 30,000 on great holidays.

The bull of 22 February 1300, by which the conditions for obtaining INDULGENCE are precisely defined, accorded the total pardon of sins and punishments to all those who, having duly confessed, visited the Roman basilicas of St. Peter and St. Paul daily for 15 days. The event marked the awakening of the PILGRIMAGE to Rome at the end of the Middle Ages and introduced the practice of the jubilee into the Western Church. The jubilee was an exceptional yearlong period during which divine compassion was overabundant, which is why it is also called a "holy year." No precedent exists for this practice, either in the East or in the West, apart from the providential evidence, invoked by the Romans before the pope, of a 100-year-old man who would have been present for a jubilee in 1200.

The custom of the jubilee year is rooted in Jewish law, in which a jubilee comes about every 50 years, at the end of 7 sabbatical cycles, each of which lasts 7 years. In a jubilee year, slaves were freed and lands returned to their former owners. A few ancient Christian authors used the term *jubilee* to designate an exceptional time of grace and joy, and St. Bernard speaks of it to qualify the indulgence bestowed on the occasion of a CRUSADE. The *vox populi* at the beginning of the 14th century attributed the same spiritual privilege to visiting the apostles' tombs as to the Holy Land. The magisterium, in the person of Boniface VIII, sanctioned this tradition by declaring that for an entire year, from one Christmas to the next, all those who fulfilled the required conditions of devotion could benefit from this exceptional indulgence. In this way, the Church allowed itself to redistribute to the faithful the benefits of the inexhaustible treasure of merits accumulated by Christ and all the saints. This custom is integrated in accordance with the penitential doctrine of the doctors of the Scholastic age. The remission of sins from a jubilary indulgence concerns both the sin and its punishment, which are imputed to the faithful even after death. In the medieval era piety was particularly associated with the salvational solidarity established by the communion of the saints. The ancient gesture of the pilgrimage was thus rekindled with a Roman destination, somewhat rivaled by others at the time.

The jubilee responded so well to both the hopes and expectations of the era that its periodicity was soon reduced. The Roman pilgrims of 1300 believed that there would be 100 years between jubilees. This would, however, deprive entire generations of the benefit of the "great pardon," especially during times of reduced life expectancy. This was no doubt the reason why the pope allowed himself to be persuaded by requests from the faithful to reduce the interval to 50 years. The second jubilee was thus proclaimed in 1350. As in 1300, a very dense crowd arrived in Rome, but Pope CLEMENT VI did not leave his residence in Avignon to honor the city with his presence. Yet, neither PLAGUE nor war discouraged the pilgrims. Some of them, for example the English, even came to Rome despite their sovereign's prohibition.

The succession of holy years was eventually disrupted by the GREAT SCHISM. Each of the two pontiffs wanted to have control over it. Clement VII, the Avignon pope, took the initiative and, in part for financial reasons, advanced the holy year that was supposed to take place to 1390, rather than 1400. BONIFACE IX, as interested as his rival, maintained that the holy year was 1400, but had to deal with the spontaneous reactions of the faithful set out early on the journey because of apocalyptic preaching: In 1399, the Bianchi movement ended with a kind of "march on Rome." (E. Delaruelle).

It is believed that MARTIN V, in 1423, inaugurated a new periodicity of 33 years in memory of Christ's life-time on earth. The jubilee of 1450 marked a renewal of the practice after the disorders of the Great Schism. The incredible influx of pilgrims struck contemporary chroniclers as it had in 1300: "They were arriving like grasshoppers," wrote one of them. Furthermore, it was in this year of grace, on the day of the Pentecost, that the great Franciscan preacher, Bernardin of Sienna, was CANONIZED. Later came the practice of dividing the century into four parts: thus, as of the middle of the 15th century, the jubilees occurred every 25 years.

These vicissitudes already illustrate how anxious the faithful were for jubilary indulgences, not only because these represented the hope of seeing their punishment in purgatory shortened, but also because of their attachment to the throne of St. Peter and his VICAR. The proof of this was in the extension of this privilege to other sanctuaries, beyond of the time of the holy Roman years, according to the formula of the indulgence *ad instar jubilaei*. As of 1390 the popes permitted jubilees in other places of pilgrimage that were particularly celebrated in Christianity or simply protected by influential personalities. Among the most noted, was the Church of Canterbury where, as of 1220, in order to celebrate the 50th anniversary of the "passion" of Thomas Becket, his successor Stephen Langton used the expression "spiritual jubilee." St. James of Compostella claims to benefit from such a favor from the pontificate of CALLISTUS II, but this relies on a bull of dubious authenticity. The documents from the 14th century are more convincing. They accord jubilary indulgence to pilgrims present for the feast of St. James, whenever it falls on a Sunday. The voyage to Puy-en-Velay procures the same benefit for the faithful, but only in years when Good Friday coincides with the holy day of the Annunciation. In 1451 Nicolas of Cusa, the pontifical LEGATE in Germany, conceded indulgences to all those who fulfilled certain devotional conditions and gave alms equal to half the cost of the trip to Rome.

The conditions for obtaining the jubilary indulgence were fixed each time by a special bull and evolved under the pressure of events and the demands of the faithful, who were more and more sensitive to the process of accumulation. If confession remained an indispensable preliminary, the number of BASILICAS to visit grew rapidly. In 1350, three were required after the addition of the LAT-ERAN; in 1373 the number increased to four, including Santa Maria Maggiore. In addition to these visits, the faithful would complete their pious voyage by venerating numerous relics housed in other Roman sanctuaries, which were considered very important in the piety of this period of the Middle Ages. Finally, the obligatory duration of the stay was adjusted to account for the distance traveled by the pilgrim (it was shortened for those traveling long distances). It was then reduced to the minimum time necessary to complete the itinerary, given the limited housing available in the city of Rome.

In fact, the presence of these numerous visitors posed practical problems that were difficult to manage given the episodic nature of the pilgrimages. There were 1,022 hotels in Rome in 1450, according to information from the time, and these were insufficient to house all the pilgrims. Some stayed with friends living in Rome, others went to hospices built for the purpose of housing people from various nations, and the most unlucky slept outdoors, under porticos, on benches, or even in the vineyards outside the city walls. The need for provisions of grain and other food was another concern. Even the circulation of people within the city was a source of worry. The jubilee of 1450 became infamous due to the unfortunate accident on the Sant'Angelo bridge, recounted many times by chroniclers. While a dense crowd crossed the bridge, horses became frightened and reared up, obstructing the passage and causing confusion in which nearly 200 people were killed. These problems, however, did not result from lack of precautions. There were not only castle guards, but also young volunteers responsible for ensuring security and organizing the circulation of crowd with billy clubs in their hands. The pilgrimage to Rome was, therefore, mined with obstacles for the faithful, in addition to the dangers of the trip itself. Once in town, it was necessary to beware of the traps that some Romans set for the naive pilgrims, and pilgrims often left Rome with mixed memories of their experiences, as was true for the poet Pierre Chastellain, wrote who of his joy to depart Rome:

> I believe that the pardon of Rome
> That I am waiting for, will do me good
>
> . . .
>
> He who wants to know what is done in hell
> Should to go to Rome . . .
> Plunder, adultery and usury
> There reign as fixed stars
> Up in heaven, without number or measure.

As these verses suggest, the jubilee years filled the pope's coffers. A significant portion of the sums gathered was used on the spot to cover the expenses for provisions and maintenance of the basilicas. Otherwise, these sums contributed to the growth of papal collections of manuscripts and works of art.

The crowds of pilgrims in Rome during a jubilee gave the city a very colorful, cosmopolitan appearance. In the general anonymity of the crowd were a few conspicuous rich lords or patricians who never moved around without large entourages. Groups from England found themselves with groups from the Iberian peninsula, from beyond the Alps, and from the French and German worlds. It had to be arranged that each pilgrim could make his confession in his own language; Under Martin V's pontificate the first Breton confessor appeared. It is easy to imagine that the observers were struck by this diversity, that made the unity of the Christian world around St. Peter's throne a more concrete reality for all to see. Contemporary historians even wonder if this was not, in fact, one of the successful motivations for this event, given the phenomenon of the "insolent rise of modern States, already partially secularized." The diplomat from Siena, Agostino Dati, described his memory of the 1450 jubilee in the following terms: "My memory of these days is still very vivid, because they showed the triumph and glory of the Christian religion. From the most distant corners of the earth, all the pilgrims came to visit the head of the universal Church and the tomb of the prince of the apostles. Truly it was a year whose memory must be preserved throughout the ages."

Catherine Vincent

Bibliography

Labande, E. R. "O Roma nobilis. . . ," *Villes, bonnes villes, cités et capitales*. Tours, 1989, 141–51.

"Le pèlerinage," *Cahiers de Fanjeaux*, 15.

Rouillard, P. osb, "La vie quotidienne à Rome pendant l'année sainte 1450." *Pèlerins de Rome*, Paris, 199.

Sumpton, J. *Pilgrimage, an Image of Medieval Religion*, London, 1975, 217–56.

Modern Era. The modern Holy Year continued the tradition of the medieval jubilee while reconstructing certain ritual and ceremonial aspects of the liturgical cycle inaugurated in the year 1300, deepening the event's spiritual dimension and above all developing adequate structures to welcome and house the pilgrims who came to Rome from all over Europe.

On 24 December 1499, Pope ALEXANDER VI solemnly inaugurated the rite of opening and closing the holy doors of the four major basilicas of the Holy City, St. Peter's at the Vatican, St. John Lateran, Santa Maria Maggiore, and ST. PAUL-OUTSIDE-THE-WALLS. The ritual was created earlier on, during the course of the 15th century, but it was during the modern era that it acquired its complete liturgical form. From the 19th verse of Psalm 117, recited during the Jewish feast of the Tents (Sukkoth), three verses and their responses were extracted to accompany the three knocks the pontiff gives with a hammer on the *porta aurea* of the ancient basilica of St. Peter: "*Aperite mihi portas justitiae*": (open the doors of justice for me.) "*Ingressus in eas, confitebor Domino*": (when I enter, I will place my confidence in the Lord.) "*Introibo in domum tuam, Domine*": (I will enter your house, my Lord.) "*Adorabo ad templum sanctum tuum in timore tua*": (in your holy temple, I will adore you in fear.) "*Aperite portas quoniam nobiscum Deus*": (open the doors, for God is with us.) *Qui fecit virtutem in Israel*": (Who gave strength to Israel.)

Nonetheless, crisis was not far off. In 1525, when CLEMENT VII presided over the LITURGY of the Holy Year, INDULGENCE was at the heart of the Lutheran criticism of the faith of the Roman Church, which provided salvation through good deeds and the possibility that living people atone for their sins and the sins of those close to them, be they dead or alive, through penance. The papacy and the Roman court were likened to Babylon and denounced vehemently. The practice of indulgence during the jubilee was the butt of sarcasm, and even the practice of the pilgrimage was questioned, on one hand by the Reformation, and on the other by the humanist followers of Erasmus. Two years later, during the night of 6–7 May 1527, Charles V's armies, in part Lutherans, penetrated the Holy City and SACKED it, pillaging its churches and chapels, destroying relics, and raping nuns. In 1550 the ritual of the Holy Year, ordered by PAUL III (deceased on 10 November 1549) and presided over by his successor JULIUS III, did not rediscover either the spirit or the scale of previous jubilees. The council, opened only with difficulty in December 1545 in TRENT, was suspended without a conclusion through September 1549. The reconstruction of St. Peter's basilica was not yet completed, but the early signs of the CATHOLIC REFORM were already manifest. Ignatius of Loyola, and Philip Neri (who contributed that year, with other Roman priests, to establishing the foundations of what would become the archbrotherhood of the Very Holy Trinity welcoming pilgrims and hosting 60,000 to 70,000 faithful with makeshift means) were already present in Rome. Michelangelo, 75 years old at the time, was presiding over the tremendous work on St. Peter's dome and performed his pilgrimage of the four basilicas and seven churches on horseback through special dispensation from the pope.

The Holy Year 1575, presided over by GREGORY XIII, constituted the true beginning of a new cycle in the history of the Christian jubilee: "The jubilee of 1575," notes Paolo Prodi, "marks the beginning of a new period in the history of holy years. It is clearly distinguished from previous jubilees and appears to signal an authentic renaissance, especially regarding the number of pilgrims." The Council of Trent, completed as of December 1563, began to bear fruit for the whole of the Catholic Church. The Catholic reform movement entered its dynamic phase of deepening, consolidating, and expanding ranks. The pilgrimage of the 1575 jubilee was conceived of as an immense enterprise of collective penance centered around the Roman papacy, which had been restored to all its power and splendor. It was a carefully planned event on both spiritual and material levels, and it managed to attract 200,000 faithful to the Holy City. The custom of medieval penance was thus called upon to purify itself in penitence and mortification. Carlo Borromeo, the former secretary of State to PIUS IV, who had become the holy archbishop of Milan and went to Rome in person, insisted,

> You must, my dearly beloved sons, take part in this pilgrimage [*peregrinatione*] leaving aside all forms of curiosity and worldly vanity: for that would be to be a pilgrim for the world, and not for Christ. Banish wild revelling, drunkenness, impurity and all forms of debauched life. Banish lying and calumny, banish the brawling. May holy sobriety, abstinence and Christian modesty accompany your steps; and may all our sensuality be mortified and chastised during this trip.

The pilgrimage to Rome had no meaning except through and in conversion: a significant change in the way of seeing, hearing, and in the entire soul. The archbishop of Milan often quoted by future popes, said, in his admirable pastoral letter of 10 September 1574 to the Milanese diocesans,

> May their eyes be opened, in order to see past errors, the ugliness and danger of sin, the vanity of hopes in this world and the eternal greatness of things of the other life; may their ears be opened to hear in all their brilliance the holy inspiration and voices from heaven may their inner senses be healed and purified, so that they may discern the lies of this world, detest its charms, and so that they may enjoy the gifts of God. . . So that, in a word, they return to their homes free from any servitude to sin, masters of their own passions and in possession of themselves [*possessori e patroni di se medesimi*], in order to be obedient subjects of divine law for henceforth.

The city of Rome, with its relics and churches, remained the focus of this penitential pilgrimage. In paraphrasing St. John Chrysostom's praise of Rome, Carlo Borromeo wrote, "Here is this city where the appearance of the ground, the walls, the altars, the churches and the tombs of the martyrs, where everything offered to the eyes impresses the soul with something sacred, as felt by and impressed upon those who visit these places with the required attitude." The city that welcomed pilgrims, *caput, mater et magistra*, "chef, mother and mistress" of all the churches, according to the words of Pope Gregory XII in his bull of indiction of the jubilee, is called upon to sanctify itself at the same time in order to offer to its visitors neither reason for scandal nor material or spiritual annoyances.

Founded in 1548 with a small group of Roman priests, the archbrotherhood of the Very Holy Trinity of pilgrims and convalescents, which had already assumed an important role during the jubilee of 1550, made a quantitative and qualitative leap in 1575. In that year, it welcomed some 174,367 individuals, according to contemporary statistics, offered them free housing for 3 nights, and provided soup and bread to feed them. The gesture of washing the pilgrims' feet, taken from the Last Supper, performed by the priests and the pope himself during Holy Week, accentuated the collective nature of penance in the modern jubilee.

The holy years in the 17th century marked the height of a massive movement of piety of pilgrims in Rome, called *romei* or *romiers*. The quantitative estimates indicate that there were 180,000 pilgrims in Rome in 1600 and 1625, and a minimum of 160,000 persons housed at the archbrotherhood of the Very Holy Trinity. National pilgrims' hospitals, such as Santa Maria dell'Anima of the Germans, Saint-Julian of the Flemish, Saint-Jacques of the Spanish, Saint Anthony of the Portuguese, Saint-Louis of the French, Saint-Yves of the Bretons, Saint-Nicholas of the Lorrains, and Saint-Claude of the Burgunds, served pilgrims from their respective countries, and both non-Roman archbrotherhoods and Roman brotherhoods welcomed them. The number of visitors for the holy year of 1650 was never surpassed.

The holy year 1675 gathered only 115,000 pilgrims, and the statistic of 100,000 pilgrims for the year 1700 makes the reduction in numbers over the 18th century more palpable. There were 85,000 pilgrims housed in the Very Holy Trinity in 1725, 137,000 in 1750, 100,000 in 1775, and only 94,000 by 1825, the last holy year of the cycle begun in 1575. The gesture of the pilgrimage was, during the 18th century, under the twofold attacks of the Jansenist rigors and the logic of state control by absolute monarchies. The hospitals of the pilgrims' were closed on the routes of Rome during the last quarter of the 18th century, and the pilgrims were hastily identified as poor people, beggars, or vagabonds.

The 19th century had only one jubilee, held in 1825. In 1800, PIUS VII was not elected by the conclave until 14 March and only returned to Rome on 3 July.

The holy year 1825 immediately followed the upheavals caused in the Papal State and throughout Europe by the French Revolution and the Empire. It was ardently desired by Pope LEO XII, despite the political reticence and preventive policing of the Catholic courts of monarchical Europe. It was a successful draw that attracted many more than the "four hundred beggars" of which Stendhal contemptuously speaks in his *Promenades*. It shows, however, an unprecedented narrowing of the geographic area for the pilgrimage to the immediate zone of influence of the city of Rome: central Italy, and in particular, the Abruzzi and the Working Lands (Terre de Labour); the non-Italians represented one percent of the entire group of pilgrims, mainly from Germany and Switzerland. But by maintaining the jubilary tradition with its own authority, the papacy of the Restoration was able to reaffirm, in the face of the world, the sacredness of Rome and its vocation for the universal pilgrimage of the Catholic World, in the penitential tradition of the Tridentine age.

During the first half of 1848, PIUS IX resided at Gaeta, obliged to stay away from the city during the Roman revolution. When he promulgated a jubilee 25 years later (25 December 1874), it could not be held with any solemnity.

Philippe Boutry

Bibliography

Alejandri Barletta, E. "L'arciconfraternita della SS. Trinità dei pellegrini e dei convalescenti e l'anno santo 1575," *Aspetti della Riforma cattolica e del concilio di Trento*, Rome, 1964, 194–205.

Bargellini, P. *L'anno santo nella storia, nella letteratura e nell'arte*, Florence, 1974.

Borzacchini, M. "Un tipo di assistenza ai poveri nell'500: l'arciconfraternita della SS. Trinità dei pellegrini e dei convalescenti," *Storia e politica*, 21 (1982), 363–409.

Boutry, P. "Espace du pèlerinage, espace de la romanité. L'année sainte de la Restauration," in S. Boesch Gajano and L. Sacaraffia, ed., *Luoghi sacri e spazi della santità*, Turin, 1990, 419–44.

Brezzi, P. *Storia degli anni santi*, Milan, 1949.

Cajani, L. "Gli anni santi," F. Fagiolo, J. L. Madonna, *Roma sancta de città delle basiliche*, Milan, 1985, 121–7.

Castelli, G. *Gli anni santi (il grande perdono)*, Bologna, 1949.

Cecchelli, C. "Origini della porta santa," *Capitolium*, 25 (1950), 229–37.

De Blasi, J. *Il Guibileo, Racconto di sei secoli e mezzo (1300–1950)*, Florence, 1951.

Dupront, A. "Année sainte 1975. Tradition et modernité," Paul VI et al modernité dans l'Eglise, Rome, 1984, 339–59.

Fagiolo, M. Madonna, M. L. ed., *L'arte e la storia degli anni santi, Roma, 1300–1975*, Milan, 1984.

Fortini, E. *Storia dell'universale giubileo celebrato nell'anno 1825 dal Sommo Pontefice Leone XII*, Rome, 1900–1.

Garofalo, F. *L'ospedale della SS. Trinità dei pellegrini e dei convalescenti*, Rome, 1950.

Geffroy De Grandmaison, C. A. *La Première Année sainte du XIXe siècle. Le jubilé de 1825*, Paris, 1902.

Gli anni santi, Turin, 1934.

Jung-Inglessis, E. M. *Das Heilige Jahr in der Geschichte, 1300–1975*, Bolzano, *1974*.

Laderchi, G. *S. Filippo Neri l'istitutore e fondatore dell'arciconfraternità della SS. Trinità dei pellegrini e desi convalescenti di Roma*, Rome, 1720.

Lizzani, M. "1850 in forma di giubileo," *Capitolium*, 25 (1950), 29–34.

Martire, E. *Santi e birboni, luci e ombre nella storia dei giubilei*, Milan, 1950.

Moroni, G. "Anno santo," *Dizionario di erudizione storico-ecclesiastica*, 2 (1840), 100–45.

Prinzivalli, V. *Gli anni santi*, Rome, 1899.

Romani, M. *Pellegrini e viaggiatori nell'economia di Roma dal XIV al XVII secolo*, Milan, 1948.

Russo, M. R. "1575: organizzazione e cronaca di un giubileo," *Strenna dei Romanisti*, 36 (1975), 371–85.

Sterpos, D. ed. *I Giubilei, Viaggio e incontro dei pellegrini*, Rome, 1975; *Pèlerins de Rome*, Paris-Rome, 1976.

Strocchi, A. *Compendio degli anni santi*, Faenza, 1826.

Tarugi, G. A. "S. Carlo Borromeo e S. Filippo Neri durante il giubileo del 1575," *Studi Romani*, 23 (1975), 462–72.

Thurston, H. *The Holy Year of Jubilee*, London, 1900.

Wicki, J. "Das neunzehnte heilige Jahr, 1775," *AHP*, 18 (1980), 297–352.

Zaccaria, F. A. *Dell'anno santo. Trattato*, Rome, 1775.

Zawadsky, A. *Jubileo universal del aõ santo. Estudio histórico, 1300–1950*, Cali, 1950.

Contemporary Era. The contemporary version of the holy year increased the extent of the solemn rites performed, and became the occasion for numerous BEATIFICATIONS and CANONIZATIONS. In 1950 PIUS XII added special prayers to the jubilee celebration. At the time, he prayed for the safeguarding of the all holy rights of the Church and for the prompt reestablishment of "tranquillity in the holy sites of Palestine" (bull *Jubilaeum maximum* of 26 May 1949). The apostolic constitution especially proclaimed the universal nature of the jubilary indulgence [*Per annum sacrum* (25 December 1950)], which was extended until 31 December of 1951. The trip to Rome was no longer required. Ordinaries were authorized to designate a cathedral church and three other churches or oratories for the prescribed visits, where services were regularly held in each episcopal town.

PAUL VI, after having reflected on the usefulness of the holy year in the contemporary Church, inscribed the year 1975 as harmonious with the VATICAN II COUNCIL (10th anniversary of the conclusion of the work). He emphasized the jubilee as a time for *métanoïa*, interior conversion of man and, at the same time, maintained the declaration of indulgence. He also instituted a Central Committee for the Holy Year (10 May 1973), presided over by Maximilian de Fürstenberg, who was in charge of organizing the jubilee, and he proposed a prayer for all Christians as a sign of reconciliation.

JOHN PAUL II proclaimed a so-called extraordinary holy year, focusing on the mystery of Redemption, to celebrate the 1950th anniversary of the Passion of Christ in 1983, following the precedent created by PIUS XI in 1933. Two conditions were stipulated to obtain full indulgence: personal sacramental confession and eucharistic communion. Pilgrims in Rome also had to pray in one of the four major basilicas, or in one of the CATACOMBS, or attend one of the pope's general audiences as a time for a solemn catechesis. The arrival of the third Christian millennium was the occasion for unprecedented emphasis on the holy year. In his first encyclical, *Redemptor Hominis* (1979), John Paul II announced that the preparation for the so-called "Great Jubilee" was to be central to his pontificate. In anticipation of the 26th official holy year he outlined a special preparatory program (*Tertio Millenio Adveniente*, 10 November 1994). In general, this program demanded the inner reflection of individual Christians as well as the examination and acknowledgment of all Christian abuses past and present. Furthermore, a special committee was established to instruct Christians in the christological and historic significance of the jubilee. Finally, the three years immediately preceding the jubilee were dedicated to the Trinity: 1997 to the Son, 1998 to the Holy Spirit, and 1999 to the Father. Although interiority, which figured so prominently in 1975, was an integral part of the celebration, John Paul II used the occasion to promulgate a broader, more forward-looking Christian message that underscored the importance of social outreach, responsible economic and political models, and interreligious dialogue, especially among Christians, Moslems, and Jews.

In order to renew Christianity's ancient link with the Middle East, Rome and the Holy Land were made the two preeminent centers of pilgrimage. The multicultural character of the holy year was most evident in the richly embellished ceremony of the Holy Door. On Christmas Eve, John Paul II, in a spirit of innovation, did not use the traditional ceremonial hammer, having determined that it was not of particular symbolic import. Instead, with his hands, he pushed open the door, which stood symbolically wider to accommodate the passing of Christians into the new millennium (Bull of Indiction, *Incarnationis mysterium*, 29 November, 1998). The pope entered the Basilica to the sound of African horns after the Holy Door had been adorned with flowers and perfumes from Asia and Oceania. In another novel gesture, John Paul II became the first pope in the history of the Church to personally open the Holy Doors of all four patriarchical basilicas.

To prepare for jubilee pilgrims, the Italian government expended an unprecedented amount of effort and money on the physical renovation of churches and other monuments of the city, including the cleaning of the facades. In like manner, Bethlehem carried out $200 million worth of renovations. Italian authorities estimated that some 24.5 million people went to Rome in 2000. World Youth Day boasted the largest participation in a single event, attracting more than 2 million young people to the city. The institution of the holy year seems, therefore, quite alive today, the fruit of a pontifical politics that gradually extended its meaning and impact. Given its long history in Christianity, it no doubt constitutes one of the high points

in the life of the Church in terms of its connection to and focus on the person of the pope.

List of Holy Years Beginning in 1300.

1. 1300, Boniface VIII (1294–1303)
2. 1350, Clement VI (1342–52)
3. 1390, Urban VI (d. 15 October 1389)/Boniface IX
4. 1400, Boniface IX (1389–1404)
5. 1425, Martin V (1417–31)
6. 1450, Nicholas V (1447–55)
7. 1475, Paul II (d. 26 July 1471)/Sixtus IV
8. 1500, Alexander VI (1492–1506)
9. 1525, Clement VII (1523–34)
10. 1550, Paul III (d. 10 November 1549)/Jules III
11. 1575, Gregory XIII (1572–85)
12. 1600, Clement VIII (1592–1605)
13. 1625, Urban VIII (1623–44)
14. 1650, Innocent X (1644–55)
15. 1675, Clement X (1670–76)
16. 1700, Innocent XII (d. 27 October 1700)/Clement XI
17. 1725, Benedict XIII (1724–30)
18. 1750, Benedict XIV (1740–58)
19. 1775, Clement XIV (d. 22 September 1774)/Pius VI; 1800, not celebrated—Pius VI
20. 1825, Leo XII (1823–29); 1850, not celebrated—Pius IX
21. 1875, celebrated without the usual solemnities—Pius IX
22. 1900, Leo XIII (1878–1903)
23. 1925, Pius XI (1922–39) 1933, extraordinary holy year (Pius XI)
24. 1950, Pius XII (1939–58)
25. 1975, Paul VI (1963–78)
26. 1983, extraordinary holy year (John Paul II)
27. 2000, John Paul II

Philippe Levillain
Elizabeth W. Russell

Bibliography

Braghin, A. *The Jubilee Guide to Rome*, E. Caruana, et al., eds., C. Merola, trans., Collegeville, Minn., 1998.

Calvesi, M, with Canova, L., ed. *Rejoice!: 700 Years of Art for the Papal Jubilee*, R. Billingsley, trans., New York, 1999.

Elizondo, V. and Sobrino, J., eds. *2000: Reality and Hope*, London and Maryknoll, N.Y., 1999.

"Entering the Jubilee through the Holy Door of St. Peter's," *National Catholic Register* 75 no. 11 (June 1999), pp. 13–19.

Francesco Gioia, H. E., ed. *Pilgrims in Rome: The Official Vatican Guide for the Jubilee Year 2000*, G. Chapman, trans., New York, 1999.

Noe, V. *The Holy Door in St. Peter*, I. Jones, trans., Rome, 1999.

O'Grady D. *Rome Reshaped: Jubilees 1300–2000*, New York, 1999.

Reese, T. J. "A Eucharistic Millennial Jubilee," *Worship*, 69 (November, 1995), 531–7.

Vischer, L. "A Holy Year [2000]," *Mid-Stream*, 26 (October, 1987), 506–22.

HONORIUS I *(Campagna, ?–d. Rome, 12 October 638). Consecrated pope 27 October 625. Buried in Saint Peter's in Rome.*

This son of an honorary consul was probably from a rich family from Campagna. Nothing is known of his life before his accession to the papacy, which in contrast, is rather well known. Besides the note in the LIBER PONTIFICALIS and Honorius's epitaph, we have information from the chroniclers, some of his letters, and even the earliest documents preserved in the LIBER CENSUUM of the Church of Rome. Because he lived in a period of relative calm, the last of the "Gregorian" popes was able, during his long papacy, to consolidate the work of his great predecessor. The breadth of his action stands in contrast to the fate posterity reserved for him.

The obligation to pass on the choice of the Romans to the emperor for confirmation necessitated a delay of five to thirteen months for popes elected between the death of GREGORY I the Great and the accession of Honorius. Moreover, the campaigns undertaken by Heraclius against the Persians kept the emperor away from the capital for a considerable length of time; it was thus decided that the confirmation should be made by the exarch of RAVENNA. Usually confined in northern Italy, the exarch was scarcely able to discuss Rome's choice, as the city was supported by the entire southern part of Italy and the rest of the Western patriarchy. The election of Honorius was thus confirmed in only thirteen days, two days after BONIFACE V's burial.

Relations were good with the LOMBARDS, who were becoming more stable and progressively converting to orthodoxy, especially since civil wars were paralyzing the actions of the kings. Honorius even managed to get the monastery of Bobbio, which was founded by St. Columbanus, to be exempt, meaning that it became dependent only on the papacy. The conjunction of a distancing from the empire and a reconciliation with the Lombards favored the end of the schism of the Three Chapters in northern Italy, which had remained Byzantine; the schismatic Fortunatus, elected in Grado, was unable to keep his power and had to flee to the Lombards, while all the citizens of the empire recognized Honorius elected in his stead.

In Rome, the growing role of the papacy was seen in urban works, which led to a christianization that was more widespread, always with imperial approval. Indeed, Heraclius had the tiles taken off the Pantheon to restore the roof of ST. PETER's basilica. Honorius also built a number of churches, each of which corresponded to an obvious political intention, and he embellished several others, dedicating to them some 2,000 pounds of silver, drawn from the share of Church resources allocated for buildings. In the civil arena, he restored the aqueducts and the mills.

To finance the expenses, the pope managed the public revenues allocated to the budget, both civil and religious. The cartulary drawn up from his register—records of contracts made with public and private individuals—indicates, for example, that he had "rented" a *massa* (fiscal tax base) in Byzantine Tuscany to his representative (*defensor*): the pope gave him management of some of the taxes allocated by the State to the budget of the Church. These rare bits of evidence demonstrate perfect continuity since the time of Gregory the Great who, himself, had applied the methods in use during the time of Gelasius, who, in turn, was continuing a tradition that went back to the establishment of the PATRIMONY OF ST. PETER by Constantine.

Honorius's actions as Western patriarch are also seen in what remains of his correspondence as well as in Bède's *Ecclesiastical History of England*. His authority normally extended from the Balkans to the West. In the regions that had remained Byzantine, it was not contested, as is seen in a number of letters. In the continental States of Lombardy, Gaul, and Spain, he intervened rarely, with the agreement of civil powers, because the kings in question took imperial prerogatives into their own hands. However, in the kingdoms of England, some sovereigns converted and sought in the papacy a counterbalance to Irish penetration. Thus, Honorius sent Birinius to occupy the see of Dorchester in Wessex and gave his support to the foundation of the bishopric of York—where the prelate had the rank of metropolitan—after the conversion of Edwin, king of Northumbria. The see was occupied by the Roman monk Paulin. Nevertheless, he did not diminish the responsibilities of his namesake, the elderly bishop of Canterbury, one of Gregory the Great's last disciples. In the East, in contrast, the Western patriarch intervened clumsily in the theological disputes aroused by the purely political attempts to find a dogmatic wording that could reconcile Orthodox and Monophysites. In 634, Honorius formally approved, in a letter in Latin of which we have a Greek translation, the compromise between orthodoxy and monophysitism that had been devised by Patriarch Sergius of Constantinople: Christ had only one will (monothelism), although he had two natures. But far away from the most active theological centers and too pressed to respond, the pope failed to gauge the importance of the problem. After long tergiversations, the COUNCIL of Constantinople in 680 declared him anathema.

Jean Durliat

Bibliography

JW, 1, 223–26; 2, 698.

LP, 1, 323–27.

PL, 80, 467–94, 601–7.

Bertolini, O. *Roma di fronte a Bisanzio ai Longobardi*, Bologna, 1971, 305–15.

Kreuzer, G. *Die Honoriusfrage im Mittelalter und in der Neuzeit*, Stuttgart, 1975.

Kreuzer, G., "Honorius I.," *LexMA*, 5 (1991), 119–20.

Le Liber censuum de l'Église romaine, ed. P. Fabre and L. Duchesne, 1910, 350–1.

Mansi, XI, 537–63.

Schneider, 21.

Thanner, A. *Papst Honorius I. (625–8)*, Sankt-Ottilien, 1989 (*Studien zur Theologie und Geschichte*, 4).

Zocca, E. "Onorio I e la tradizione occidentale," *Augustianium*, 27 (1987), 571–615.

[HONORIUS II.] *Cadalus of Parma (Verona or Vicenza, 1009–10, -d. Parma, 1071–2). Elected antipope in Basel 28 October 1061, deposed in Mantua 31 May 1064.*

A rich heir to a family of viscounts, he was first a vidame of the church of Verona and vicar for the bishop of the city, and then, starting in 1044, bishop of Parma, probably due to the protection of Emperor Henry III. Remaining faithful to the German court and to his earliest tendencies toward reform in the Church, he was quickly harassed by more radical reformers. After the death of NICHOLAS II, in July 1061, messengers from the Roman NOBILITY, led by Gerardo di Galeria, proposed the rank of dignitary, *Patricius Romanorum*, to Henry IV, who was at the time still under the tutelage of his mother, Agnes. It was in this capacity that the young king nominated Cadalus as antipope against ALEXANDER II. He did so upon the demand and the proposal of some bishops from northern italy, who were also in the court of Basel and had received the approval and the encouragement of the imperial chancellor Wilbert, who was, himself, a native of Parma.

Each for different reasons, the parties favorable to this nomination (the Roman nobility, the bishops of Lombardy, and the German royal court) had rejected Alexander II's election, which was undertaken by Roman reformers who had not consulted the imperial government; the interests of these parties were nevertheless much too divergent for them to be able to support their candidate sufficiently, even to become pope. Despite two armed expeditions against Rome, Cadalus was able to occupy CASTEL SANT' ANGELO for a short period only but could not ascend to St. Peter's throne. After the two enemy popes excommunicated one another, the imperial government, then directed by Archbishop Anno of Cologne, opted, during the synod in Augsburg (October 1062), in favor of Alexander II. Because the schism was not yet out of the way, Anno convoked a synod in Mantua at the urging of the bishop of Ostia, Peter Damian (May 1064). The synod, which convened Italian and German bishops, was then able to pronounce a definitive judgment. With an oath, Alexander II was able to absolve himself of simony. a charge of which he was accused, and finally to ascend to Peter's throne. Cadalus refused to participate in the synod, as he was not allowed to preside over it, and he returned to Parma, again excommunicated. His claim to the papacy was crushed, and people paid little attention to it thereafter. In Parma, he nevertheless retained his duties as bishop, while preserving until the moment of his death a vivid memory of his ill-fated nomination to the papacy, as *Cadalus episcopus et electus apostolicus*.

Tilmann Schmidt

Bibliography

Baix, F. "Cadalus," *DHGE*, 11 (1949), 53–99.

Cavallari, V. "Cadalo e gli Erzoni," *Studi storici Veronesi Liugi Simeoni*, 15 (1965), 59–170.

Herberhold, F. "Die Angriffe des Cadalus von Parma (Gegenpapst Honorius II.) und Rom in den Jahren 1062 und 1063," *Studi Gregoriani*, 2 (1947), 477–503.

Schmidt, T. *Alexander II. (1061–1073) und die römische Reformgruppe seiner Zeit*, 1977 (*Päpste und Papsttum*, 11), 104–33.

Schwaiger, G. "Honorius (II.)," *LexMa*, 5 (1990), 119.

Stoller, M. "Eight Anti-Gregorian Councils," *Annuarium Historiae Conciliorum*, 17 (1985), 254–63.

HONORIUS II. *Lamberto Scannabecchi (d. 13 Feburary 1130). Elected pope and consecrated 21 December 1124.*

Honorius was born Lamberto Scannabechi in Fiagnano, near Imola. He served as archdeacon in Bologna. In 1117, PASCHAL II named him cardinal bishop of Ostia. When GELASIUS II (1118–19) fled to France, Lamberto accompanied him. After Gelasius's death, he became a close adviser to CALLISTUS II. He led the papal legation that concluded the concordat of WORMS with Emperor Henry V in September 1122.

At the end of Callistus II's papacy (1119–24), the main objectives of the Gregorian REFORM seemed to have been attained. The papacy needed only to work to maintain positions secured and to pursue the extension of its universal jurisdiction. In Rome, where rivalries within the NOBILITY persisted, pitting the "imperial" Frangipani against the "Gregorian" Pierleoni, other forces now had to be reckoned with. Diminished outside pressures, such as those exerted by Emperor Henry V (1106–25), made the diversity of opinions among some forty cardinals more obvious. Under URBAN II (1088–99) and Paschal II

(1099–18), most of the clerics admitted into the college of CARDINALS had come from Rome or central or southern Italy. The CURIA had thus strengthened its local, and Roman, influence. The group showed reluctance to meet with the cardinals recently promoted by Callistus II, who was of Burgundian origin, since they were often from France or Burgundy. In the eyes of the old Gregorians, these cardinals from the schools of northern Italy and France, who belonged to a reform circle of canons regular and devoted themselves to the care of souls, looked like "innovators." The latter had at their head Cardinal Aimeric of Burgundy, promoted in 1123 by Callistus II as cardinal deacon of Santa Maria Nova, and then named chancellor, after the LATERAN I COUNCIL (1123). Thereafter, Aimeric (d. 1141) became the decisive authority in matters of papal politics. During both of the following two papal elections, by stirring up trouble and, through suspicious maneuvering, he managed each time to get the candidates of his group, Honorius II (1124) and INNOCENT II (1130), elected, with the support of the Frangipani.

After Callistus II's death (13 December 1124), most of the cardinals thought about electing Cardinal Saxo of Santo Stefano. But three days later (15–16 December), at the request of the cardinal deacon, Jonathas, who was close to the powerful Pierleoni, the cardinals unanimously elected Cardinal Theobald of Sant'Anastasia as CELESTINE II. He had barely donned the red papal mantle (in the church of S. Pancrazio, near the Lateran), when the Frangipani, with Aimeric's approval, stepped in, swords unsheathed, and attacked the newly elected pontiff, proclaiming Cardinal Lamberto of Ostia pope with the name Honorius II. Seriously wounded, Celestine, who had not yet been consecrated, declared his willingness to resign, while his partisans refused to recognize Honorius. Aimeric and Leo Frangipani had to win over the prefect, Urban, and the Pierleoni with large sums of money and many promises before getting rid of resistance. Although Honorius declared his readiness to withdraw, he was elected unanimously and consecrated on 21 December.

Honorius confirmed Aimeric in his duties as chancellor and allowed him to extend his influence even more. The cardinals were almost exclusively non-Roman, which strengthened Aimeric's control. LEGATES were no longer chosen outside the circle. In clear contrast to the popes of the Gregorian period, Honorius favored the new orders of canons regular (Augustinian canons and Premonstratensians, confirmed by the pope in 1126), as well as the Cistercians, who originally had no wish for exemption. Moreover, the pope intervened in the large Benedictine monasteries of Cluny (condemnation of Abbot Pons in 1126) and Monte Cassino (deposition of Abbot Oderisius in 1127).

With the death of Emperor Henry V, in May 1125, the Salian dynasty ended. Among the princes, the ecclesiastical party did not want anything to do with Staufen Duke Frederick II of Swabia, one of Emperor Henry V's nephews. Consequently, under the protection of archbishop Adalbert of Mayence and in the presence of two papal legates, it imposed the election of Duke Lothair of Saxony (30 August 1125). This was the beginning of the conflict between the Staufens and the Welfs (GUELPHS).

Emperor Lothair III (1125–37) sought and obtained from the pope confirmation of his election, something that had never happened before. He made visible efforts to respect the wishes of the Church and the concessions of the concordat of Worms: the king was to give up personally attending episcopal elections; investiture should take place only after consecration; and the oath of faith and homage was to be replaced with a simple oath of fidelity.

For his ecclesiastical politics, Lothair sought the advice of Norbert of Xanten, the founder of the Premonstratensian order and archbishop of Magdeburg. In December 1127, when the Staufen party named Duke Conrad, Frederick of Swabia's younger brother, anti-king, the German bishops sided with Lothair and excommunicated Conrad. On 29 June 1128, Conrad, nevertheless, had himself crowned in Monza by Archbishop Anselm of Milan, where he received the iron crown of the Lombards. The pope then sent Cardinal John of Crema to Pisa, where a synod was convoked to excommunicate Archbishop Anselm. Conrad had returned to Germany without achieving his goals in Italy. In France, Honorius ended the conflict between King Louis VI (1108–37) and the episcopacy. He also improved relations with England, sending papal legates in 1125.

Papal politics were less felicitous when it came to preventing the formation of a southern Norman kingdom. When Duke William of Puglia died in 1127, Roger II of Sicily occupied his land. Negotiations undertaken by Cardinal Aimeric and Cencius Frangipani led to a compromise. With the peace of Benevento (22 August 1128), the pope, in exchange for Roger II's oath of faith and homage, agreed to his control of the territory.

Early in 1130, Honorius fell seriously ill, and Cardinal Aimeric and the Frangipani made their arrangements. The dying pope was taken to San Gregorio monastery, in territory under Frangipani control. An electoral commission composed of the three orders of cardinals was to proceed to a new election after the pope's death and his burial in Sant'Andrea. Five members of the commission belonged to Aimeric's party, and only three were old Gregorians. But when Honorius died (during the night of 13–14 February 1130), Aimeric's preparations could not be carried out. Contrary to all custom, Honorius was shamefuly buried, hurriedly and with no ceremony, in the monastery of San Gregorio; his body was not transported to the Lateran until after Innocent II's election. On 14 February, the schism so painfully staved off in 1124 burst in the open with the double election of INNOCENT II, supported by Aimeric and the Frangipani, and of the old Gregorian, ANACLETUS II, who was the candidate of the Pierleoni family.

Georg Schwaiger

Bibliography

DTC, VII, 132–5.

JL, I, 823–9.

LP, II, 327 ff., 170 ff.

LTK, V, 476.

PL, 166, 1217–1320.

Brezzi, P. *Roma e l'impero medioevale*, 1947.

Deer, J. *Papsttum und Normannen*, Vienna, 1972.

Fink, K. A. *Papsttum und Kirche im abendländischen Mittelalter*, 1981, 36–47.

Fliche-Martin, 9, 42–50.

Grotz, H. "Kriterien auf dem Prüfstand: Bernhard von Clairvaux angesichts zweier kanonisch strittiger Wahlen," in H. Mordek, ed., *Aus Kirche und Reich. Festschrift für Friedrich Kempf*, Sigmaringen, 1983, 237–63.

Haller, J. *Das Papsttum*, I, 1952, 25–35.

Hülz, R. *Kardinäle, Klerus und Kirchen Roms 1049–1130*, 1977, 106 FF., 215.

Jedin, H. ed., *Handbuch der Kirchengeschichte*, III, 2, Friburg-en-Br., 1968, 5–10.

Klewitz, H. W. *Reformpapsttum und Kardinalskolleg*, 1957, 209–59 ("Das Ende des Reformpapsttums").

Malaczek, W. "Das Kardinalskollegium unter Innocenz II., und Anaklet II.," *AHP*, 19 (1981), 27–78.

Maleczek, W. "Honorius II.," *LexMA*, 5 (1991), 120.

March, J. P. *Liber Pontificalis completus ex codice Dertuensi*, 1925, 203–17.

Robinson, I. S. *The Papacy 1037–1198*, Cambridge, 1990.

Schieder, T., ed., *Das Papsttum*, I, Stuttgart, 1985, 176–95.

Schieder, T., ed., *Handbuch der europäischen Geschichte*, II, 1987 (Lit.).

Schmale, F. J. "Das Papsttum im Zeitalter Bernhards von Clairvaux und der frühen Staufer, von Honorius II. bis Cölestin III.," in M. Greschat, ed., *Das Papsttum*, I, Stuttgart, 1985, 176–95.

Schmale, F. M. *Studien zum Schisma des Jahres 1130*, Cologne, 1961.

Seppelt, F. X. *Geschichte der Päpste*, III, 1956, 165–71, 605 f.

Tellenbach, G. "Der Sturz des Abtes Pontius von Cluny und seine geschichtliche Bedeutung," *QFIAB*, 42/43 (1963), 13–55.

HONORIUS III. *Cencius (Savelli?) (Rome, ca. 1160–d. Rome, 18 March 1227). Elected pope 18 July 1216, consecrated 24 July. Buried in St. Mary Major.*

Honorius III succeeded INNOCENT III, "the most powerful pope of the Middle Ages," and he preceded the third Roman pope of the 13th century, GREGORY IX. Honorius III had neither Innocent's high ideals nor Gregory's diplomatic skill. He appears to have pursued the goals of his illustrious predecessor, although in a number of areas his papacy showed signs of a personality that had exceptional administrative skills.

Roman by birth, Cencius probably came from the Savelli family. In his introduction to the *LIBER* CENSUUM, Cencius claims to have been raised by the Roman Church since his childhood, although he makes no reference to his family, which was thus perhaps not a high-ranking one. O. Panvinio (1557) was the first to tie him to the Roman Savelli family. At the time of his papal election (1216), Cencius was already advanced in age: the chroniclers describe him as *senior venerandus* (*MGH SS*, 17, 574) or *jam aevo grandior* (Walter of Coventry, ed. Stubbs, 2, 230–1). He is said, by Bouchard d'Ursberg, to have been in frail health. His advanced age is also visible in his portraits, for example, in the mosaic in ST. PAUL'S OUTSIDE THE WALLS. All this implies that Cencius was born, at the latest, around 1160, thus at the beginning of ALEXANDER III's papacy. He became a canon of St. Mary Major rather early. His entire career took place within the Roman CURIA. He was procurator for Cardinal Hyacinth, the future CELESTINE III. CLEMENT III named him to direct the APOSTOLIC CAMERA, where the earliest evidence of him is on 22 January 1188. Since his first patron's accession to the papacy (1191), his importance within the curial administration only grew; from 1194 to 1198, he directed both the Apostolic Camera and the CHANCERY.

Cencius left important marks of his tenure as head of the Camera. In the Lateran cloister, he had some magnificent bronze doors installed. Most importantly he composed (1192) the *Liber Censuum* of the Roman Church, a volume aimed at gathering all the documents attesting to the papacy's tax rights and rights of vassalage; thanks to the remarkable quality of its internal organization, it quickly acquired an official character. Cencius included in it an important *Ordo romanus de consuetudinibus et observantiis*. An *Ordo romanus ad coronandum imperatorem* and a *Vita Sancti Gregorii* are also attributed to him. He also wrote numerous sermons (Horoy, I, 608–974 and II, 1–395), a new version of which he published after his election to the papacy. On the order of the pope, some manuscripts of his sermons were sent to the Dominicans in Bologna, to Citeaux, and to the chapter in St. Mary Major. Compiling the *Liber Censuum* in all likelihood earned him his nomination as CARDINAL deacon of Santa Lucia in Orthea (his first subscription was dated 4 March 1192). During Celestine III's papacy, Cencius also took an active part in the administration of justice, as an AUDITOR. Innocent III did not renew either of these two duties, and gave him no legation, but did promote him to cardinal priest of Sts. John and Paul in 1200. This demotion, which was considerable when compared with his prestige under the papacies of Clement III and Celestine III, can only be explained by the new pope's hostility toward him. In any case, on the list of subscriptions under Innocent III, Cardinal Cencius is quite often absent.

He was elected pope in Perugia three days after Innocent III's death, on 18 July 1216. On 24 July the cardinal bishop of Ostia consecrated him bishop. The coronation ceremony most probably did not take place in Perugia itself, but rather at ST. PETER's in Rome, on 31 August; and on Sunday, 4 September 1216, the newly elected pope took possession of the Lateran. During his papacy, Honorius III was primarily occupied with pursuing his predecessor's course of action. The CRUSADE, called for by the LATERAN IV COUNCIL in 1215, was one of his major undertakings. Too many obstacles nevertheless kept his efforts from being crowned with success. Among the Christian kings, only the king of Hungary, Andrew II, and the duke of Austria, Leopold VI, committed to go to the East in 1217. The pope placed the crusade under the Cardinal legate Pelagius's care, and the latter's firm and authoritarian conduct caused turmoil. Frederick II had promised to take up the cross in 1215 (Aix-la-Chapelle), and finally declared his readiness to leave in 1219, although he managed to delay the departure a number of times. Frederick II confirmed his intentions in Rome on 22 November 1220, when he received the imperial crown from the hands of Honorius III. On 10 February 1221, Frederick II, in Salerno, finally announced his departure. But the forty galleys that made up the imperial fleet were not sufficient to save Damietta, which had to be evacuated in September 1221. Honorius III composed a severely worded indictment against Frederick II (November 1221). The emperor again put off his departure for the crusade, first until March 1222, and then until July 1225, and finally until August 1227. A conflict with the Italian cities, which broke out after the diet that was held in Cremona at Easter 1226, delayed the emperor's departure one more time. Meanwhile, Frederick II had married Isabella, the heir to the kingdom of Jerusalem.

On 22 December 1216, Honorius III recognized the DOMINICAN order (Order of Preachers). The future pope Gregory IX was named protector of the Order of Minors, whose rule was confirmed by the pope on 29 November 1223. On 30 January 1226, Honorius III recognized the Carmelite order, born from a community of hermits established on Mount Carmel.

With Honorius III, the history of CANONICAL COLLECTIONS entered a new phase. Innocent III had not ordered that a collection of his DECRETALS be constituted. The *Compilatio Quinta*, begun by Tancred in 1225–6, and finished shortly thereafter (February–May 1226), was the first collection of decretals composed at a pope's request. All the decretals it contains, except four, are found in the official registers of the chancery, 570 letters of which were

marked with a cross, certainly made by Tancred at the time of selection. Honorius III addressed the *Compilatio Quinta* to the *studia* of Bologna and Paris on 2 May 1226. On 28 June 1219, the pope forbade the archdeacon of Bologna to admit a student to a *licentia* without preliminary exams. But the name of Honorius III is particularly linked to important decisions regarding the *studium* in the university in Paris. Replying favorably to requests addressed by teachers and students, the pope weakened the position of the bishop's chancellor. Thereafter, a commission of three theologians was empowered to grant the *licentia*, after examining the candidates. When teachers and students decided to take up residence on the left bank, Honorius III blamed the chancellor, who had doubted the legitimacy of such a move. In November 1219, Honorius III published a famous constitution, *Super Speculam*, which forbade the study of civil law and closed the schools of law in Paris. The decision, which at first view was surprising, is explained by the papacy's concern to strengthen the study of theology in Paris, which demanded that a maximum of forces be channeled toward this discipline. In fact, Honorius III allowed students in theology to receive the proceeds from their benefices in their entirety for five years, despite their absence for their studies. In so doing, the pope strengthened canon 11 of the Lateran IV council The idea that the BULL was sought by Philip Augustus to stop the teaching of Roman (i.e., imperial) law in his capital, which would have been a threat to monarchical dignity, is unfounded. In the same bull, Honorius III confirmed the decree from the Council of Tours (1163), forbidding canons regular to study Roman law and medicine. The form used was that of a letter, comparable to modern ENCYCLICALS, addressed to the primary church authorities of the Latin West (patriarchs, metropolitans), as well as to the UNIVERSITIES themselves. Several individuals present at the time in VITERBO, the temporary see of the Roman Curia, were able to influence the composition of *Super Speculam*: Philip the Chancellor, called to the Roman Curia to mediate a conflict between teachers and students; Cardinal Peter of Capua, who had long managed the *studium* in Paris in his capacity as legate; and perhaps even St. Dominic, who is shown to have stayed in Viterbo from November to the middle of December 1219. The general aims of the bull *Super Speculam* coincide with the university interests of the Dominicans, whose Parisian community had just been enriched by a number of prestigious teachers. Promulgated for the *studium* at Paris, *Super Speculam* was already commented on by the canonists of Bologna around 1220. It is part of the *Compilatio Quinta*. Its insertion into the *Liber Extra*, under a form adapted to the needs of the schools, confirmed its nature as a "university charter" par excellence.

From the end of the 12th century on, the papacy had to find enough revenue to maintain a rapidly expanding curial bureaucracy beyond the resources of the Apostolic See itself. Honorius III tried to reserve a prebend in each cathedral church for members of the Curia. In exchange, the pope promised to eliminate the taxes on the bulls produced by the chancery. This proposal, which came from a suggestion by Innocent III, and which Innocent IV renewed in 1244, nevertheless remained a dead issue.

Agostino Paravicini Bagliani

Bibliography

Potth, 468–679, 2059–99, 2135–6.

Boyle, L. "The 'Compilatio quinta' and the Registers of Honorius," *Pastoral Care, Clerical Education and Canon Law, 1200–1400*, London, 1977.

Clausen, J. *Papst Honorius III. (1216–1227)*, 1895.

Horoy, C. A. *Honorii III opera*, 5 vols., 1879–82.

Huillard-Breholles, J. L. A. *Historia diplomatica Friderici Secundi*, 6 vols., 1852–61.

Kuttner, S. "Papst Honorius III. und das Studium des Zivilrechts," *Festschrift M. Wolf*, Tübingen, 1952, 79–101.

Lewry, P. O. "Papal Ideals and the University of Paris, 1170–1303," *The Religious Roles of the Papacy: Ideals and Realities, 1150–1300*, Toronto, 1989, 368.

Maleczek, W. *Papst und Kardinalskolleg vn 1191 bis 1216*, 1984, 111–13.

Mansilla, D. *La documentatio pontificia de Honorio III (1216–1227)*, 1965 (*Monumenta Hispaniae Vaticana, Registros, 2*).

Powell, J. M. "Honorius III's 'Sermo in Dedicatione Ecclesie Lateranensis' and the Historical-Liturgical Traditions of the Lateran," *AHP*, 21 (1983), 195–209.

Pressutti, P. *Regesta Honorii Papae III*, 2 vols., 1888–95.

Regesta imperii, V-2.

Roberg, B. "Honorius III.," *LexMA*, 5 (1991), 120–1.

Rodenberg, C. *Epistolae saeculi XIII e regestis pontificum Romanorum selectae*, I, 1883, 1–260.

Sayers, J. *Papal Government and England during the Pontificate of Honorius III (1216–1227)*, Cambridge, 1984.

Schmidt, T. "Die älteste Überlieferung von Cencius' Ordo Romanus," *QFIAB*, 60 (1980), 511–22.

Tautu, A. L. *Acta Honorii et Gregorii IX*, 1950 (*Pontificia commissio ad redingendum codicem iuris canonici orientalis, Fontes*, III, vol. 3).

HONORIUS IV. *Giacomo Savelli (Rome, ca. 1210–d. Rome, 3 April 1287). Elected pope 2 April 1285, enthroned 20 May, buried in the Vatican.*

Born into the great Roman Savelli family and great-nephew of HONORIUS III, in memory of whom he took the name Honorius IV, Giacomo Savelli, CARDINAL deacon of Santa Maria in Cosmedin, was unanimously elected only four days after the death of Pope MARTIN IV, who had favored French and ANGEVIN interests. The cardinals acted quickly to avoid the pressures that had marked the preceding CONCLAVE. It appeared that a new course would start, and yet the new pope followed the political line of his predecessor, with less excess; it is true that, freed from the tremendously encumbering Charles I of Anjou and natural protector of his heir, who was a prisoner of the king of Aragon, the pope reclaimed a leading role in the affairs of the Italy.

After many years of study at the university of Paris, the future pope was provided with a canonry in Châlons-sur-Marne, and with the rectorate of Berton in the diocese of Norwich. Promoted to cardinal in 1261, he participated in several important negotiations, especially when, in 1276, he was sent with two other cardinals, one of whom was the future NICHOLAS III, to work out an agreement between Rudolf of Habsburg and Charles I of Anjou, from whom he had previously received an oath of obedience to the Roman Church. Even though not much is otherwise known of him, a lot more is known about his family. His father, Luca Savelli, senator of Rome in 1233–4 and 1266, and his wife, Giovanna Aldobrandesca, had another son, Pandulf Savelli, Roman senator at the time of Giacomo's election. The extent of his wealth is also known. When he made his will in 1279, it consisted of a number of houses and towers in Rome, and *castra* and parts of *castra* outside. In fact, the cardinal founded a monastery dedicated to the Virgin Mary and St. Paul on his lands at Albano on 21 October 1282.

Like his predecessors, Honorius IV was given senatorial duties by the Romans and, as vicar, he confirmed the titularies in charge at the time: his brother Pandulf and Annibaldo Annibaldi (sometime in 1285, he named Orso Orsini and Nicolas Conti as titularies). He entered Rome, where he was consecrated, and where he resided most of the time; he was soon installed in the palace that he had built on his patrimonial lands on the Aventine, near Santa Sabina. Also like his predecessors, his short pontificate was dominated by the question of the rivalry between Aragon and the house of Anjou. The failure of the French CRUSADE against the kingdom of Aragon in the summer of 1285 was quickly followed by the death of the two adversaries, Philip III of France (6 October 1285) and Peter III of Aragon (11 November 1285). The crown of Aragon was passed to the latter's eldest son, and that of Sicily to his second born, James (who became king of Aragon in 1291 under the name James II). James, crowned in Palermo on 2 February 1286, was excommunicated by the pope, along with his mother Constance, on 11 April (the sentence was stiffened on 23 May), for refusing to accept the suzerainty of the pope. The eldest son of Charles I of Anjou, Charles prince of Salerno (the future Charles II), had been a prisoner in Aragon since 1284. Through feudal rights, the pope carried out the administration of the continental kingdom, which had come under attack by the Aragonese in Sicily. He showed himself to be quite skillful in maintaining and consolidating Angevin rights: two papal BULLS on 17 September 1285 put the administration of the continental kingdom back in order, one of them by assuring relations between the royalty and local Churches, and the other (*Constitutio super ordinatione regni siciliae*) by giving a veritable code of administrative reform. The latter addressed a number of grievances. Honorius lowered taxes and other charges weighing on communities, limited the minting of new COINS to once per reign, and took a number of measures in penal and feudal matters. The pope also sought to maintain intact the rights of the house of Anjou. On 4 March 1287, he broke the treaty of Barcelona (27 February 1287), by which Charles had given up insular Sicily in exchange for his release. The pope did not lose sight of the possibility of recovering the island through armed force; he thus confirmed levying a three-year decima in Italy, Sardinia, and Corsica, decreed for this purpose by MARTIN IV.

Honorius IV was also active and less fortunate in his dealings with the empire. He had to give up the four-year decima that had been levied to finance the Aragon crusade, in the dioceses near France (Liège, Metz, Toul, Verdun, Basel, Lyon, Vienne, Tarentaise). He also had to annul, because of Rudolf's failure, the coronation of Rudolf of Habsburg in Rome, which was planned on 31 May 1286 for 2 February 1287. Gathered in council and diet in Wurzbrug in March 1287, the empire's electors refused any financial contribution to the *Römerzug* and reaffirmed their imprescriptible right to imperial election; the papal legate only escaped the riot through imperial protection. Virulent anti-Roman hostility erupted in Germany, which also appeared in polemical writings, such as those of Alexander von Roes.

Like his predecessors, Honorius IV painfully tried to pursue the levy of decimas for a new crusade, remaining evasive when he received urgent appeals to lead it from the king of England, Edward I, whose international prestige was at the time great, relative to that of the other Christian nation that had been weakened by wars. In 1286, the pope renewed the condemnation of the heretical sect of the Apostolics, which was born in Parma and was active throughout northern Italy, before a repression for several decades. He also had the decree from the COUNCIL of Lyon I (1274) enforced, disbanding the Friars of the Penitence of Jesus Christ, called *sachets*, and Friars of Our Lady of Val-Vert). And, also in the fashion of his predecessors, he supported and favored the mendicant orders, such as the Dominicans and Franciscans confirming (20 November 1285) the privileges and constitutions of the preachers and minors. He created only one cardinal, his relative Giovanni Boccamazza (cardinal bishop in Tusculano, 22 December 1285). In short, the brief reign of this elderly and ill pope, whose personality remains somewhat unknown, was over before he could leave a clear mark.

Olivier Guyotjeannin

Bibliography

Potth, 1295–1825, 2132–3.

Paravicini Bagliani, A. *I testamenti dei cardinali del Duecento*, 1980 (*Miscellanea della Società romana di storia patria*, 25), 38–39, 197–207.

Pawlicki, B., *Papst Honorius IV.*, Münster, 1896.

Prou, M., *Les Registres d'Honorius IV*, 1886–8.

Roberg, B., "Honorius IV.," *LexMA*, 5 (1991), 121.

HORMISDAS (*Campagna, ?–d. Rome, 6 August 523*). *Elected pope 20 July 514. Buried in St. Peter's in Rome. Saint.*

Hormisdas belonged to a rich family from Campagna. His father, Iustus, was born in Frosinone. He himself had a son, SILVERIUS, who became bishop of Rome in 536–7.

Hormisdas was a deacon at the time of the conflict that pitted Pope SYMMACHUS against his rival Lawrence, beginning in 499. He held a position of confidence and had the responsibility of procuring for the pope, who was called to RAVENNA by King Theodoric, the money needed to finance the trip and help defend his cause. He got the bishop of Milan, Lawrence, to lend Symmachus a large sum of money; his friend Ennodius, a Milanese deacon, both guaranteed the loan to his bishop and provided a number of camels for the trip to Ravenna.

Hormisdas participated in the COUNCIL convened by Pope Symmachus on 6 November 502, to regulate the administration of the Church's property (in 483, the prefect Basilus had forbidden any disposal of Church property). This *scriptura* was annulled because the council considered that no layperson was competent to legislate on the matter, but it did adopt an almost identical measure: prohibition, under penalty of ANATHEMA, of disposing of Church property, unless its upkeep was too costly. The rule was valid for all provincial Churches.

Hormisdas appears to have played an important role in the Roman Church: he was connected to the priest Adeodatus, who held an important position in Rome, and on two different occasions his friend Ennodius predicted he would become pope. When Symmachus died, Hormisdas was elected pope and consecrated on 20 July 514.

Under the reign of Hormisdas, the last upheavals of the Lawrentinian SCHISM subsided and, after more than thirty years, the Eastern Churches returned to the Roman communion. Hormisdas was able to take advantage of specific political circumstances to work on a return to unity, but more than anything he devoted his papacy to affirming the authority of the Roman Church, in the East as well as in the West.

Hormisdas's activity in Rome itself is little known. An ambiguous phrase in the LIBER PONTIFICALIS, which is confirmed by a reference in his epitaph, shows that he brought peace back into the Roman clergy, probably by reestablishing the last of Lawrence's partisans in their duties. The *Liber Pontificalis* also refers to persecution of the Manicheans, whose books are said to have been burned outside ST. PETER's. The incident has not been verified, although it does seem to be in line with both the pope's rigorous orthodoxy and the spirit of the times. Hormisdas had no new buildings contructed in Rome, but he did richly endow the Vatican basilica with liturgical furniture. The *Liber Pontificalis* speaks of a silver crown sent by Clovis; since the king of the FRANKS died in 511, it is not certain that this is exact.

Most of the pope's activity concerned relations with the East. At the time of his accession, Hormisdas had to face a hostile emperor (Anastasius II), and Eastern Churches separated from the Roman communion: even if they were not all Monophysites, they refused the condemnation of the bishops of Constantinople since the time of Acacius, a condition made imperative by Rome since the time of Gelasius.

In 515, the emperor, who was in a position of political weakness, took steps toward reconciliation: he accepted the principle of holding a COUNCIL in Heraclea, called for 1 July 517. The council was to be presided over by the pope, and it would reconcile the Churches. The pope, who was informed of it quite late, replied via a letter (8 July) entrusted to a legation that left Rome on 11 August with a precise duty: the letter was to propose that the Eastern bishops sign a Formula, composed in Rome, by which they publicly accepted the Council of Chalcedon and Pope Leo's letter formally condemning Nestorius, Acacius, Dioscorus, Eutyches, Timothy Aelurus, Peter Mongus, and Peter the Fuller (the bishops of the great patriarchal sees, Constantinople, Alexandria, and Antioch), thus showing their wish to return to communion with the Roman Church, "because in the Apostolic See, the Catholic religion is always spotlessly served," the pope said.

This first legation was not well received by the emperor, and it did not achieve the expected results. But on the way, the LEGATES did enter into negotiations with the bishops of Illyricum, and in February 517, Hormisdas was able to announce that forty bishops of the province had returned to the Roman communion.

In April 517, Hormisdas sent a second legation, still with Ennodius of Pavia, who was this time accompanied by Peregrinus of Misenus. The failure was even more obvious on this occasion: the legates were chased from Constantinople by the emperor, who ordered that all ports be closed to their ship. Despite the order, Ennodius and Peregrinus succeeded in distributing the pontifical letters in the East. The mission as a whole inspired the emperor to pen an angry letter in which he accused the pope of trying to humiliate him.

But on 9 April 518, Anastasius died, apparently by lightning; he was replaced by Justin, the prefect of the praetorium. Justin was a Chalcedonian himself, as was, to an even greater extent, his nephew Justinian, whom he brought into service in the government of the empire. At the same time, popular pressure strove to have the emperor restore communion with Rome. On 15 and 16 July 518, the names of the popes were reinserted into the diptychs, as were those of bishops Euphemius and Macedonius, who had been deposed by Anastasius and sent into exile. In September 518, Emperor Justin, his nephew Justinian, and Patriarch John, wrote to the pope asking for reconciliation.

In January 519, Hormisdas sent a legation with instructions that in fact are not different from those that preceded them, but this time the reception in Constantinople was splendid. The Holy Monday office was concelebrated with the Greek episcopacy, and on Wednesday the Formula of Union was signed. This brilliant success, to which the diplomatic talents of Deacon Dioscorus greatly contributed, was triumphantly announced to the pope. But it was less complete than the enthusiasm of the moment led one to believe: John of Constantinople obtained from the Roman legates the possibility of adding to the pope's text a prologue in which he was careful to affirm the equality of both the old and the new Rome. Moreover, he affirmed his faith in the four ecumenical councils, while up to that time Rome had refused to recognize the Council of Constantinople.

More seriously, even though in Constantinople union around Chalcedonian orthodoxy was indeed realized, such was not the case in the rest of the empire. Hormisdas insistently asked that everywhere the Chalcedonian bishops who had been deposed by the Monophysites be reestablished in their sees. At first, Justin and Justinian put the strength of the empire to the service of this cause. But in Thessalonica, in Antioch, and especially in Alexandria, the failure was patent. As early as 520, the emperor asked the pope to lessen his demands, not to oblige the bishops to strike all their predecessors for over thirty years from the diptychs. Hormisdas conceded nothing, and even encouraged the emperor to use his strength in the service of orthodoxy. This was not the first time since Constantine that the emperor did so, but it was the first time that a bishop of Rome asked that it be done. During the last years of Hormisdas's reign, the situation was less clear; the official victory went to the Chalcedonians, and in the West, it was believed to be complete; but in the East, resistance continued and took root.

While the debates on the condemnation of Acacius were gradually dying down, a new polemic that involved Hormisdas was born. The pope's legates had been called to give their opinions to settle the quarrel between the

Scythian monks, who wanted to introduce into the Creed the words *unus de Trinitae passus est* (one of the Trinity suffered), and Deacon Victor, who considered the words to be Monophysitic. The legates refused to settle the dispute, since their mandate did not give them the necessary authority. The Scythian monks sent a delegation to Rome to present the problem to the pope, and with another question that was raised during the same debates: the African bishop Porsenna had asked him what should be thought of the writings of Faustus of Riez, which had been called Pelagian by the Scythian monks. On 13 August 520, Hormisdas replied to Porsenna: on the Theopaschite question, nothing should be added to the statement of the faith. Regarding Faustus' writings, they were neither canonical nor condemned. The leader of the Scythian monks, Maxentius, strongly criticized the letter, claiming to see in it a forgery unworthy of Hormisdas. But on Theopaschism, Hormisdas reiterated his judgment, which he exclaimed in a letter to the emperor dated 25 March 521, thanks to which the question raised no more trouble for a number of years.

Thus, in these Eastern questions, Hormisdas accomplished a difficult task. Thanks to a confluence of favorable circumstances (the accession of Justin and Justinian), he achieved reconciliation with the East without making the slightest concession either to Monophysitism or, apparently, to the religious ambitions of the imperial city; yet, Monophysitism was not eradicated. Moreover, the lack of understanding between the East and the West in matters of both theological thought and ecclesiology grew. In reconciling with the emperor, Hormisdas further alienated the deeply Monophysite populations from the empire and from Rome.

At the same time, he also made the situation in Gothic Italy more fragile. With the emperor's return to orthodoxy, the Italian aristocracy's attachment to the kingdom, which was governed, after all, by an Arian, showed signs of weakening. More precisely, the party in favor of Constantinople came out strengthened—in conviction, but even more so in numbers. It was Hormisdas's successors, however, beginning with JOHN II, who would suffer the consequences of these changes. During his life, Hormisdas focused in the West— in addition, of course, to exercising his ministry in Italy—with expanding Roman authority in Spain and Gaul. Like other popes of the 6th century, he sought to consolidate the institution of the vicariate: on 2 April 517, he granted unlimited powers to John of Illicitum (or Tarragona), and gave *constitua generalia* for Spain; in 521, he gave the bishop of Seville authority over Baetica and Lusitania. In Gaul, he addressed at least eight letters to Caesarius of Arles and Avit of Vienne.

This sharp consciousness of Roman orthodoxy, accompanied by great political firmness, and this systematic will to affirm Roman authority place Hormisdas in the direct line of the great popes of the 5th century, LEO and GELASIUS. But his papacy was the high point of Roman authority at the end of antiquity: the destruction of the Gothic kingdom soon put the papacy under the very direct control of the emperor, and until the time of GREGORY I the Great, any affirmation of Roman authority vis-à-vis Constantinople would be an act of often ineffectual resistance.

Claire Sotinel

Bibliography

LP, I, 269–74.

Amann E. "Hormisdas," *DTC*, 7, 1, (1927) 761–76.

Fides Hormisdaw papae, Haacke, W. "Die Glaubensformel des Papstes Hormisdas," *Analecta Gregoriana*, 20, 1939, 10–14.

Haacke R. "Hormisdas," *LTK*, 5 (1960), 483.

Hormisdas, *Epsitulae CL*, Thiel, 1, 741–990.

HOUSEHOLD, PAPAL. Since the *motu proprio* of PAUL VI *Pontificalis Domus* in 1968, the pontifical household has been administered by a prefecture of the Roman CURIA under the direction of a bishop with the title of prefect of the papal household (previously known as the prefect of the apostolic PALACE).

History of the Papal Household. Centuries ago the *vice-dominus* presided over the Lateran Palace, and therefore over the papal household. Under ALEXANDER V in 1410, the position became known as master of the Pontifical Household (*Magister domus pontificiae* or *Praefectus aulae*). Then MARTIN V created the position of Prefect of the Holy Palace. URBAN VIII made the prefect a majordomo (*Major domus*) in 1626, with jurisdiction over all ecclesiastical and lay personnel of the palace, and CLEMENT XII added to this position by making him perpetual governor of the CONCLAVE, a way of keeping his position even during pontifical interregnums (apostolic constitution, *Apostolatus officium*, 1732). Over the course of time, the duties of the majordomo of the pope and of prefect of the Apostolic Palaces were sometimes united (PIUS VII, LEO XIII), sometimes separate (PIUS IX), and even eliminated and replaced by the master of the Camera (PIUS XI, 1926).

Fourth of the four high prelates *di fiochetti* (from the name of the feathers decorating the harnesses of their horses), including the vice chamberlain of the Church (who was also, for a time, governor of Rome), the AUDITOR, and the treasurer of the APOSTOLIC CAMERA, the majordomo was the SUPERINTENDENT of the palace and could, for this reason, enjoy certain privileges that were highly prized at the time, such as the addition of ten acorns (instead of six) of a shade of pink to his coat of arms, the inclusion of the arms of the reigning pontiff with half of his own (which is still the case today for the prefect of the papal household), the wearing of a purple *mantelletta* (a small three-quarter length coat without sleeves) even during pontifical funerals, precedence over patriarchs and bishops while attached to the pope's person, seating to the immediate right of the throne, and so forth. Confidential servant of the supreme pontiff, he was also guardian of a series of keys from the ambulatory of ALEXANDER VI (a gallery linking the Vatican to the CASTEL SANT'ANGELO), for the iron cabinet containing the chain of St. Peter in the church of St. Peter's-in-Chains, and of the ciborium enclosing the skulls of Sts. Peter and Paul at the Basilica of St. John Lateran. It was also his duty to seal the casket of the pope whose face he had been the last to see before covering it with the burial veil of white silk. It was not until the end of the 18th century that the majordomo of the pope was almost automatically raised to cardinalate.

The master of the Camera had the duties of a high chamberlain. He was found under the name of *magister aulae palatii* beginning in the early 15th century, and it was through him that visitors might gain access to the pope. He also organized the personnel serving the COURT and set up the weekly schedule of AUDIENCES, both public and private. Guardian of the pontifical seal (the Fisherman's Ring), he stood at the pope's left, and was his servant until his burial (or entombment), only after which could he change his purple clothing for the black mourning cassock.

The papal court of years past, called the papal FAMILY, comprised several categories of people. Palatine Prelates, whose name indicates that they lived in the apostolic palace, included the four Palatine cardinals (chancellor dater, secretary of memorials, secretary of briefs, and secretary of state) as well as the majordomo; the master of the camera; the prefect of the Apostolic Palaces of the Vatican, the Lateran, and Castel Gandolfo; the auditor of the pope (canonical adviser); and the master of the Sacred Palace (a DOMINICAN theologian of the pope). The household also included the secret CHAMBERLAINS of the first class (secret chaplain, prefect of the pontifical chapel, substitute for the secretary of state and secretary of the diplomatic corps, vice chancellor, secretary of the briefs to princes and secretary of Latin letters) and of the second class (*coppiere*, or, in Latin, *pincerna*, which means head cup-bearer or butler of the pontifical table, secretary of the embassies, bearer of papal greetings to sovereigns passing through the city, wardrobe master in charge of the pontifical vestiary, sacristan functioning as the curate of the apostolic palaces, and prefect of pontifical ceremonies). Prelates of the Apostolic Camera—cardinal camerlengo of the Holy Roman Church, vice camerlengo, general auditor, general treasurer and clerics of the Camera—were also part of the family. Domestic Prelates, called *prelati di mantelletta*, belonged to different prelatic colleges: assistant prelates to the throne (patri-

archs, archbishops, and bishops who had received this distinction), apostolic protonotaries (numerary participants called *de numero participantium*, supernumeraries, *ad instar participantium*, titularies or as honors *extra Urbem*), auditors of the ROTA, voting prelates of the Apostolic Signature of Justice, secretary prelates of the larger enclosure (editors of BULLS working in a room of the chancellery called the *parco maggiore*); and the domestic prelates outside the college, so-called because their assignments were outside the diocese of Rome.

Secret Chamberlains (private), were of three kinds: (1) the ecclesiastical chamberlains who formed the prelature called *de mantellone* (from the name of their long purple open coat lined with silk, fastened at the neck and with two long bands of fabric floating from the shoulders like wings, probably vestiges of the wide sleeves of long ago, progressively less used because they got in the way of their work); and the pontifical ceremonialists and the secret supernumerary chamberlains—from two under Urban VIII, the latter became almost sixty under GREGORY XVI and almost 500 under Leo XIII; (2) the lay chamberlains, called secret chamberlains with cape and sword (*cubicularii intimi ab ense et lacerna*), dressed in a black Henri II costume trimmed in white lace with a beret of black velvet adorned with an ostrich feather of the same color and, around the neck, a ruff containing a triple gold chain with the papal emblem. The participant chamberlains included the master of the Apostolic Hospice (in charge of welcoming the sovereigns at the bottom of the staircase of honor, he also watched over the Sistine Chapel during the pope's masses; and stood in the middle of the entry to the presbyterium between the two marble barriers that separate the chapel into two unequal parts); the major quartermaster of the Apostolic Palaces (responsible for the furnishings and the gardens), the head groom or master of the cavalry of the pope (head of the Palatine stables, called *praefectus stabuli*); the general superintendent of the post (*praepositus cursus publici* and then *preafectus tabellariorum*, (organizer of the pontifical messengers and the travels of the pope) who opened and closed the door of the papal carriage); the bearers of the Golden Rose (a faceted jewel of distinction offered by the pope, the fourth Sunday of Lent, to sovereigns, to their wives, and to sanctuaries of deserving cities); the lay secretary of embassy; and the officer of the noble guards of service and the colonels of the Swiss Guard and of the Palatine Guard. The other chamberlains, numeraries and supernumeraries were the coordinators of papal audiences.

Barely six under CLEMENT XIV in 1770, these lay chamberlains reached a record 290 at the end of the 19th century under Leo XIII; (3) the chamberlains of honor were divided into three categories: the ecclesiastical chamberlains of honor in purple dress (*in habito paonazzo*) for positions in the pontifical antechamber, dressed, for papal liturgies, in a scarlet cape with a hood of white ermine in winter or of red silk in summer; the ecclesiastical chamberlains of honor *extra Urbem* with purely honorary functions because they are outside of Rome where they wear their prelate's dress reserved for their respective dioceses; and the lay chamberlains of honor with cape and sword, mainly but occasionally in service in the audience room. At the end of the 19th century, they numbered 290, 203, and 116, respectively.

The Secret Chaplains assigned for sacred duties to the pontiff included the train-bearer of the pope and the cross-bearer, secret chaplains of honor, secret chaplains *extra Urbem*, and secret clerics (for the private chapel), common chaplains (participants or supernumeraries, forming a college for ordinary ceremonies). Among the secret chaplains were also the preacher Apostolic (a Capuchin since BENEDICT XIV), assigned to give the sermons of Advent and Lent for the papal court, and the confessor of the papal family (a Servite of Mary since CLEMENT XIII).

The Familiars of the Pope included the pope's doctor, valet, secret groom, civil servants of the antechamber (named for life and called *bussolanti*, because they stood guard in the archway (*bussola*) of the doors of the pontifical antechamber); there were also twelve sediari, bearers of the *Sedia gestatoria* on which the pope sat for processions.

The staff and the higher officers of the military corps, the NOBLE GUARD, was created by Pius VII in 1801 (in place of the former cavalry of the guard and lighthorsemen dissolved by the French in 1798) to assure the safety and escort of the pope (its members came principally from the pontifical nobility having titles for more than one hundred years). The SWISS GUARD or *cohors helvetica* was instituted in the 14th century. In 1506, JULIUS II formed them into a group of one hundred men. The PALATINE GUARD of honor (two battalions of 500 men), was founded by Pius IX in 1850 to replace the city militia; that same year the pontifical police were created to take over from the pontifical constables of Pius VII.

The Papal Chapel. The papal chapel, which made up the liturgical cortege of the pope during his most solemn and sacred duties, was also part of the papal family. It included the Sacred College of the Cardinals; the college of patriarchs, archbishops, and bishops assisting the pontifical throne, a dignity conferred by letter of the pope and consisting either in holding the missal or carrying a candle (in the latter case, the bearer was called an assistant bishop *a candela*); the vice camerlengo of the Holy Roman Church. Added to this were the lay princes assisting the throne, a very ancient duty that Julius II reserved for the heads of two patrician families of Rome who rode horses beside the papal carriage, the Colonna and the Orsini (the latter would be replaced, in the 20th century, by the Torlonia). The prince of service, in a long black

outfit, stood during the entire liturgy at the right of the throne, beside the cardinal-deacon, holding the pope's train, receiving the incense and kiss of peace before the high prelates *di fiochetti* and, after the offertory, washed the hands of the pope who gives him communion at Christmas and at Easter; the auditor general and the treasurer general of the Apostolic Camera; the majordomo of the pope; the minister of the interior (until 1870); the assessor prelates and secretaries of the Roman CONGREGATIONS and apostolic tribunals; and the dean of the Roman ROTA, who had the privilege of presenting the pope his miter (formerly, the tiara) when there was a pontifical office.

Also part of the papal chapel were the substitute for the secretary of state; the archbishops and bishops not assisting the throne; the apostolic protonotaries; the prelate commander of the Santo-Spirito (a large hospital for the poor, near the Vatican); the regent of the Apostolic CHANCERY (guardian of the seal for papal bulls); the abbot of Monte Cassino and the other abbots *nullius*; the general abbots of the canons regular and monastic orders; the abbot of Saint Jerome *de Urbe* and the general superiors of the mendicant orders; the magistrate of Rome (until 1870); the master of the Apostolic Hospice; the prelate auditors of the Roman Rota; the master of the Sacred Palace; the theologian commissary of the Holy Office; the clerks of the Apostolic Camera; the voting prelates of the Apostolic Signatura; the pontifical master of ceremonies; the secret participating chamberlains, supernumeraries, and those of honor in purple dress.

The college of the advocates of the Sacred Consistory (descendants of the seven defenders of the Church begun by GREGORY I in 568, changed to twelve under SIXTUS IV in 1471) were also part of the chapel as were the secret chaplains and the secret chaplains of honor; the secret clergy of His Holiness; the procurator-generals of the mendicant orders; the preacher Apostolic; the confessor of the pontifical family; the college of the procurers of the Sacred Apostolic Palaces, it the sacristan of His Holiness; the holy canon ministers of the three patriarchal basilicas of St. John Lateran (assistant-priests), of the Vatican (deacon), and of St. Mary Major (pontifical subdeacon); the musician; the candle-bearer acolytes; the clergy of the pontifical chapel; the master-porter of the Red Staff (*a Virga rubea*), guardian of the keys of the room where the pope puts on his liturgical vestments; the guardian of the tiaras; the mace-bearers (pontifical beadles); and the apostolic ushers (*cursores apostolici*), bearers of invitations to pontifical celebrations.

Since Vatican II Council. This litany of titles remained unchanged for a long time, even if, over time, certain positions were not filled (notably after the loss of the Papal States and the fall of Rome, which were fatal to the minister of the interior and the magistrate of Rome), or did not correspond with anything real (cup-bearer, head groom, superintendent-general of the post, and so forth—the latter became purely honorific when, in 1870, with the loss of the Papal States the pope stopped giving banquets and stopped traveling). This heavy organization and this large number, however, changed greatly after the VATICAN II COUNCIL. In 1968, PAUL VI signed the *motu proprio Pontificalis Domus* by which the following were abolished (in the pontifical family as well as in the pontifical chapel): Palatine cardinals, Palatine prelates, prelates *di fiochetti*, princes assisting the throne, His Holiness's majordomo, the minister of the interior, commander of the Holy Spirit, Roman magistrate, master of the Apostolic Hospice, *forriere maggiore* of the Holy Palaces, the *cavallerizzo maggiore*, the superintendent general of the posts, bearers of the Golden Rose, secretaries of the embassies, the officer of the Noble Guard, chamberlains of honor in purple dress and *extra Urbem*, chaplains and secret clerks, the confessor of the pontifical family, the secret taster, the candle-bearer acolytes, the head-bearer of the Red Staff, guardian of the tiaras, mace-bearers, and apostolic ushers. The secretaries of Letters to the Princes and of Latin Letters were abolished in 1973 (*motu proprio, Quo aptius* integrating the Apostolic Chancery with the Secretariat of State). The Noble Guard (which became "of honor" in 1968) and the Palatine Guard were disbanded by Paul VI on 15 September 1970. JOHN PAUL II terminated the *sediari* and the use of the *sedia gestatoria*.

In 1968 some positions were given new names: the Master of the Sacred Palace, a position always filled by a Dominican, became simply the Theologian of the Pontifical Household; the secret chaplain of the sacristy took the name of Chaplain of His Holiness and Vicar-General of His Holiness for the Vatican City; the domestic prelates and the secret supernumerary chamberlains received the title of prelates of honor to His Holiness and of chaplains of His Holiness (honorary titles given to ecclesiastics with that of numerary or supernumerary apostolic protonotaries); also, the lay chamberlains of the cape and sword, secret or honorary, changed their gleaming uniforms for a black habit and their title for that of "gentlemen of His Holiness," as did the *bussolanti* for the name of attachés of the antechamber. Since then, the pontifical household has been divided into two categories: the ecclesiastical pontifical household and the lay pontifical household.

The ecclesiastical pontifical household includes the archbishop Substitute for the Secretary of State; the archbishop secretary for foreign relations; the archbishop Almoner of His Holiness; the vicar-general of His Holiness for the Vatican City (a position given in 1991 to the cardinal archpriest of the Vatican Basilica); the archbishop president of the Ecclesiastical Pontifical Academy (school for Vatican diplomats); the theologian of the Pontifical Household; the numerary and supernumerary apostolic protonotaries; the pontifical "ceremonialists"; the prelates of honor and chaplains of His Holiness; and the preacher Apostolic of the pontifical household.

The lay pontifical household includes the princes assistant to the throne (whose functions—quite rare—are limited to solemn civil ceremonies); the special delegate of the Vatican State; the counselor-general of the Vatican State (a position that has remained unfilled for decades); the commander of the Swiss Guard; the consultants of the Vatican State; the president of the Pontifical Academy of Sciences; His Holiness's GENTLEMEN (for the protocols of greeting civic leaders); the procurators of the Sacred Apostolic Palaces (called "advocates for the Holy See" according to the *motu proprio, Iusti iudicis* of 1988); the attachés of the antechamber and the pope's familiars.

These persons no longer follow the liturgical papal procession but occupy a reserved place at ceremonies. For those occasions, the Pontifical Chapel is actually set up in this manner: all the members of the ecclesiastical pontifical household named above; the college of cardinals; the patriarchs, archbishops, and Latin and Eastern bishops attending the throne; the vice camerlengo of the Holy Roman Church; the archbishops presiding over pontifical councils, the archbishop secretaries of Roman congregations; the archbishop secretary-general of the SYNOD OF BISHOPS; the regent of the apostolic penitentiary; the archbishop secretary of the Supreme Tribunal of the Apostolic Signatura; the dean of the Roman Rota; the higher prelates (secretaries or vice presidents) of pontifical councils and pontifical COMMISSIONS; the abbot of Monte Cassino and the abbots-general of the canon regulars and of the monastic orders; the superior-generals (or, in their absence, the procurator-generals) of the mendicant orders; the prelate judges of the Roman Rota; the voters of the Apostolic Signatura; the canons of the three Roman patriarchal basilicas; the consistorial advocates (now also called "advocates of the Holy See"); the curates of Rome, and the clerics of the pontifical chapel.

It should be noted that, in order to decrease the length of the pontifical processions, the 1968 reform provided that the above-named groups be represented by only two of their members, except for the curates of Rome, who could escort their bishop in larger numbers. Since the papacy of John Paul II, however, the papal liturgical procession only includes the celebrants and master of ceremonies; all the others—when they are present—take their place at the beginning of the celebration.

Moreover, with the reforms, the lay positions ceased to be hereditary since all the ecclesiastical or lay positions of the papal household are assigned by the pope for only five years (though they are renewable). The Prefect of the Pontifical Household, who has the duties of both the majordomo and the Master of the Camera oversees these activities. His prefecture also includes the ancient heraldic commission of the pontifical court, which, fallen into disuse, is only continued in its archives. The prefect handles all nonliturgical protocol for the pope, whom he assists in all his activities within the palace as well as in his movements in Rome and throughout Italy, in concert with the Secretariat of State. He organizes official audiences, both public and private.

Joël-Benoît d'Onorio

Bibliography

Del Rè, N. *La Curia romana—Lineamenti storicogiuridici*, 1970.

D'Onorio, J. B. *Le Pape et le gouvernement de l'Église*, 1992.

Grimaldi, F. *Les Congrégations romaines*, 1890.

Noirot, M. "Famille pontificale," *Catholicisme*, IV; and "Notes sur la prélature," *L'Ami du Clergé*, 29 January, 1948.

Thierry, J. J. *Le Vatican secret*, 1962, and *La Vie quotidienne au Vatican au temps de Léon XIII à la fin du XIXe siècle*, 1963.

Torquebiau, P. "Cour pontificale," *DDC*, IV, 1944, 726–9.

HUMANISM. See **Renaissance Humanism and the Papacy.**

HUMOR. This English word is a doublet for the one referring, according to the *Littré*, to the "liquid substance found in an organized body, the correct balance of which is said to constitute health." The word quickly spread through European culture in the 19th century. In contrast to irony, it expresses detachment via a smile and has a national or ethnic identity that is shaped by a cultural and linguistic code; the forms it takes are often untranslatable from one language or situation to another. Properly speaking, there is no pontifical humor, and the Italian language has a hierarchy of words to designate either sallies (*battute*) or the disposition to sarcastic wit (*fare lo spiritoso*), or humor (*umorismo*). Neither the papal COURT nor the VATICAN CITY STATE has fostered a general disposition to humor as a characteristic form of detachment in the face of situations or circumstances. Humor is situational, and it always occurs within limits that, for the most part, are related to plays on words.

Medieval accounts of papal humor, if the expression is even appropriate for the time, are rare. Biographical sources, like the LIBER PONTIFICALIS, have long been too official and public to show traces of humor; even if the CHANCERY does commonly engage in plays on words, in the etymological sense, this is less out of humor than application (usually refined) of the rules of rhetoric: for example, when a letter by EUGENE III in 1151 opposed the practice of fief incomes allocated in episcopal finances to the profit of lay vassals (*beneficia denariorum quae potius maleficia dicenda sunt*: "benefits [benefices] in silver, that it would be better to call malefits," JW 9454).

It is only in later freer sources of writing—outside chroniclers, letters from visitors to the CURIA or members of it, ambassadorial reports—that traces of humor could be found during some papacies. A systematic study has never been done; the few noted accounts refer more to irony than to what is commonly accepted as humor. They reflect erudite witticisms, expressed in situations of superiority where the pope has intervened before a supportive audience of his cardinals or close associates, and sometimes sharply, made fun of the awkwardness of a supplicant, especially if the latter had not displayed Italian astuteness or the grammatical knowledge of the pope.

It is probably not by chance that there is abundant information from INNOCENT III's time, since he was a young, knowledgable, and authoritarian pope, during a period when documentation changed its form. In 1206, Innocent III did not hesitate to admonish an English cleric, Robert, who was trying to give him a lesson in CANON LAW, saying that the unfortunate cleric drank a little too much English beer while listening to the lectures of his teachers: the episode was narrated by a monk of the abbey of Evesham, which supported Robert in the case brought against him by the bishop of Worcester. Robert had declared: *"Pater sancte, nos didicimus in scholis et haec est opinio magistrorum nostrorum quod non currit praescriptio contra jura episcopalia." Et dominus papa: "Certe, tu et magistri tui multum bibistis de cerevisia anglicana quando haec didicisti," Et quum magister Robertus adhuc idem affirmaret, iterum idem audivit responsum (Chronicon abbatiae de Evesham*, ed. W. D. Macray, London, 1863, 189).

Innocent III replied, off the cuff, in verse and in bad Latin, to a rhymster from Recanati who had asked him a favor. To the veiled request: *Salutat te Scatutius/ et habet te pro dominus* ("Scatuccio greets you; you are his master"), the pope replied: *Si veneris Romam/habebis multam bonam* ("if you come to Rome it will do you great good"). The play here is a "double action" reply, since the pope retorted to the barbarism (*dominus* for *domino*) with another barbarism (*multam bonam* instead of *multum bonum*), and infers that the apprentice poet would do well to leave his province and go to any metropolis (Salimbene, *Cronica*, ed. G. Scalia, v. I, Bari, 1966, 44).

The same literate game is seen in 1256 when, tired of seeing the canons of the cathedral and the monks of Saint-Eloi de Noyon arguing, ALEXANDER IV declared that they were arguing over "goat wool" (the expression, taken from Horace's *Epistles*, I, 18, 15, is, moreover, proverbial in contemporary Italian: Bibl. Nat. Lat. 13777, fol. 68).

The same traits—witticisms, plays on words, rhetorical amusements of the highly literate—appear to characterize what passes for humor among the members of the Curia. In the papacy of Innocent III, there is a good illustration of this in a letter sent by a cleric from the chancery to a friend, the newly elected archbishop of Capua, for whom he had interceded with the pope, undoubtedly to keep him from needing to travel to receive the *pallium*. In it, in a quite refined style, with a combination of scriptural and ancient references, as well as allusions to medical science, he painted a less-than-appealing picture of the Curia's summer sojourn at Subiaco, at the height of the summer (1210). In the letter, Innocent III is called "our father Abraham," although on three occasions he is also mentioned by the nickname that he must have acquired in the Curia, "Salomon [sic] III" (K. Hampe, "Eine Schilderung der Sommeraufenthaltes der römischen Kurie unter Innocenz III. in Subiaco, 1202," *Historische Zeitschrift*, 8, 1905, 509–35).

The familiarity with which the popes did or did not behave within the papal court or vis-à-vis their close entourage determined the witticisms that biographers have delighted in pointing out since the time of Pius IX. A few of the latter's words are famous. When a Jesuit named Alet was presented to the pope, Pius IX observed: "You have the same name as my colonel." The priest replied: "Yes, Holy Father, but with one 'l' only" to which the pope riposted; "Oh, that's right; my colonel has two 'Ls' (wings), but even with two he'd have a hard time flying!" (the play on words being with *ala*, wing). On hearing the news of Frederick Ozanam's wedding, given plaintively to the pope by Father Lacordaire, "My friend Ozanam got trapped into marriage," Pius IX replied, "Are you suggesting that our Savior instituted six sacraments and one trap?" Pius IX is said to have composed a charade when Rome was taken on 20 September 1870, while the cannons were roaring. The image is reported by his biographers, by historians, and by essayists concerned with capturing the Roman spirit. It was this Roman spirit, however, that expressed itself against the popes in the old lampoons inspired by the people of Rome in the torso set on one of the sides of the present Braschi palace. Pius VI, born Giovanni Braschi, paid for it with a lampoon repeated throughout his imprisonment: *"Per conservar la fedel un Pio perde la sede"* (To save the faith Pius is losing the See").

The solemnity with which Pius XI performed his duties did not keep him from occasionally coming up with a good pun, as in the little-known incident when, after receiving a bishop named Msgr. Gatti in an audience, Pius XI remarked *"Non e consueto, che i gatti vengano a baciare i piedi dei ratti"* ("It's not every day that cats (*gatti*) come to kiss the feet of rats"). Ratti was the pontiff's

family name. In contrast, John XXIII's humor was known almost worldwide. At a diplomatic reception to which then Msgr. Roncalli, nuncio in Paris, had been invited, he entered into a friendly discussion with the chief rabbi of Paris, such that when they were asked to move into the dining room, they both, self-effacingly, wanted the other to go first. Gently pushing the rabbi ahead, Msgr. Roncalli said: "Please, first of all, the Old Testament, then the New . . ." On the day of his election, 28 October 1958, as he prepared to appear before the crowds for the *urbi et orbi* benediction, he had trouble raising his arms, cramped in his new papal cassock. Stepping inside, he commented to his assistants: "Do you see, those are the chains of the papacy!" When he later told his friends about the incident, he said, "I felt like a package, all wrapped up, tied, and ready for delivery." On another occasion, a curious visitor who had gotten lost among the rooms and hallways of the papal palace suddenly noticed that one of the mirrors on the wall was moving. John XXIII emerged; seeing the visitor's confusion, he gently approached him, put a finger to his lips, and said: "Shh! I'm lost, too." These *fioretti* made John XXIII quite popular. During the Vatican II council, the two open cafeterias in the conference hall were nicknamed "bar-abba" (*abba*, father, but a play on the name Barabbas). And humorists claim that reversible signs were proposed for hanging outside the toilets; one side was to say *"Libero con sede vacante"* (Free, with an empty see/seat), and the other *"Feliciter regnans in trono!"* (Happy, reigning on the throne!). Paul VI's austerity gave rise to few publicized humorous incidents. On the other hand, Cardinal Guyot after the conclave that elected John Paul I on 26 August 1978 recalled:

> After the *urbi et orbi* benediction, the cardinals spontaneously grouped around John Paul I to surround him. It was then that he remarked, referring to something Saint Bernard had said to Eugene III: "Well! Look what you've done to me! May God forgive you!" And the fact is that the pope in the white cassock went back to the same place at the table that he had occupied the preceding day. This was to the great joy of the cardinals and the servers! And then there is one more anecdote. At the end of the meal, my neighbor, a Spanish cardinal, had a great desire to smoke, which had been forbidden during the conclave. He could not resist any longer, and approached the Holy Father asking for permission to light his cigarette. The new pontiff graciously consented, adding: "Provided the smoke is white, *fumata bianca!*"

The Latin rhetoric that was still used by Msgr. Felici, secretary of the council during Vatican II, has been replaced by quite specific jokes that are the legacy of the Roman tradition or the translation into Latin of a secret irony, which no longer belongs exactly to the domain of humor.

Phillipe Levillain

Bibliography

Andreotti G. "La sciarada di papa Mastai," *Il nostro tempo*, 11.X.1992.

Guyot, *La Documentation catholique*, 75 (1978), 812.

Martin J. "L'humour de Pie IX," *Rivista Pio IX* (1981), 203–9.

Prieto M. *Fioretti de Jean XXIII*, French trans., Paris, 1993.

HYGINUS. *(136–40).*

The episcopacy of the eighth successor to ST. PETER in Rome, as given by all sources, lasted four years (the LIBER PONTIFICALIS speaks of four years, three months, and three days); but his chronology is less than certain. For Eusebius of Caesarea, Hyginus is said to have begun his papacy during the first year of the reign of Antonius Pius (138/139). But, with a duration of four years, Hyginus cannot easily be placed on the list of bishops of Rome. Succeeding Telesphorus, it is necessary to put him between 136 and 140, which seems logical, although it cannot be proven. The *Liber Pontificalis* claims he was a native of Athens, and, which is more significant, that he was a professional philosopher. Yet it was during his papacy that the gnostics Valentinus and Cerdon came to Rome. Hyginus had perhaps to face the first agitation created by the gnostics in Rome (as Irenaeus and Eusebius emphasize). The DECRETALS that are all attributed to him are all apocryphal. He is celebrated as a martyr on 11 January, but none of our sources gives evidence of this end to his life, and excavations undertaken have not allowed confirmation of the *Liber Pontificalis*'s affirmations that his sepulture is in the Vatican, near St. Peter's.

Jean-Pierre Martin

Bibliography

Amann, E. DTC, Paris, 1930, VII, 1, col. 356–7.

Camelot, T. *Catholicisme. Hier, aujourd'hui, demain*, Paris, 1962, V, 1123–4.

Eusebius, *HE*, IV, 10; 11, 1; 11, 6. V, 6, 4; 14.

Irenaeus, *Against Heresies*, III, 3; 4, 2.

Weltin, E. G. *NCE*, 1967, VII, 282.

HYMN, PAPAL. The Holy See got an official hymn in August 1857, when PIUS IX adopted the march without words titled *Musica Festiva*, by the Austrian composer Hallmayr. The hymn was composed in the Viennese style of the time, which led the critics to call it a *saltarello*. Later, in October 1949, as the HOLY YEAR 1950 was approaching, PIUS XII opted for Charles Gounod's *Marche Pontificale*, which was composed for Pius IX's priestly jubilee and first performed in 1869 with seven military bands, the very solemn music was put to words by Msgr. Salvatore Allegra with a transcription, which lasts two minutes and fifty seconds for a choir and orchestra, by Msgr. Alberico Vitalini. A new Latin version was composed in 1991 by Msgr. Raffaello Lavagna, and played first privately on 15 June 1991 on the occasion of JOHN PAUL II's visit to the radiophonic center of Santa Maria di Galeria for the sixtieth anniversary of VATICAN RADIO.

The official public performance took place in October 1993, in the Aula Paolo VI, for the fifteenth anniversary of John Paul II's election.

The official Latin version goes as follows:

O Roma felix! O Roma nobilis!
sedes es Petri, qui Romae effudit sanguinem
Petri cui claves datae sunt regni caelorum.
Pontifex, Tu successor Petri,
Pontifex, Tu magister es tuos confirmans fratres,
Pontifex, Tu qui servus servorum Dei
hominumque piscator, pastor es gregis,
ligans caelum et terram.
Pontifex, Tu Christi es vicarius super terram,
rupes inter fluctus, Tu es pharus in tenebris.
Tu pacis es vindex, Tu es unitatis custos,
Vigil libertatis defensor, in Te potestas.
Tu, Pontifex, firma es petra,
et super petram hanc aedificata est Ecclesia Dei.
O Roma felix! O Roma nobilis!

The English translation is:

O happy Rome! O noble Rome!
You are the See of Peter, who shed his blood in Rome,
and to whom were given the keys of the Kingdom of Heaven.
Pontiff, you, Peter's successor,
Pontiff, you the teacher, who encourage your brothers,
Pontiff, you, the servant of the servants of God,
Fisher of men, are pastor of the flock,
binding heaven and earth.
Pontiff, you are the vicar of Christ on Earth,
Rock among the waves, beacon in the darkness,
Illuminator of peace, guardian of unity,
vigilant defender of liberty; in you is power.
You, pontiff, are the firm rock,
and upon this rock is built the Church of God,
O happy Rome! O noble Rome!

The papal hymn is performed on solemn occasions, such as the pope's receptions in foreign countries and his departures from them; the arrival, in the St. Damasus courtyard in the Apostolic PALACE, of heads of state or of governments on official visits to the Vatican; visits by new ambassadors coming to present their credentials; the appearance of a pope in the central *loggia* of St. Peter's basilica for the *urbi et orbi* blessing on Christmas Day and or Easter Sunday.

The papal hymn is not to be confused with the march called "Silver Trumpets," composed in 1846 by Marquis Giovanni Longhi to greet the solemn entrance of the pope in St. Peter's basilica. This march, suppressed by Paul VI, made its reappearance with John Paul II at the closing of the exceptional holy year of 1983 for the 1950th anniversary of the Redemption.

Joël-Benoît d'Onorio

Bibliography

Battandier, A. "Les airs pontificaux," *Annuaire pontifical catholique*, 1905.
Noirot, M. "Hymne pontifical," *Catholicisme* V.

IMAGE OF ROME IN LITERATURE.

Middle Ages. Virgil was bold enough to predict a never-ending empire for Rome, and an aura of eternity continues to hang over the fallen city. For the medieval mentality, Rome was simultaneously past, present, and future: the moral and cultural primacy of ancient times, guarding its value beyond the loss of political dominion; the presence of the holy apostles buried there, making it the center of Christianity; faith in a mission that remains to be accomplished before the end of time, and the place where some cradle their dreams of spiritual or political universality. Rome is always upright, since it is identified with the fourth empire of Daniel's prophecy, the empire that is to last until the end of time. *Roma caput mundi regit orbis frena rotundi*, "Head of the world, Rome holds the reins of a round globe": since 1030, these medieval verses on the imperial crown represent the endurance of Roman power. "Leader of the world," "honor of nations"—the medievals easily used these fervent phrases of the poets of antiquity. Rome was always grandeur in their eyes; it was the City that had conquered the world, the quintessence of urban civilization. Claudian was widely read. He emphasized the civilizing and unifying work of Rome (*De consulatu Stiliconis*, 150 f.), and Rutilius Numatianus proclaimed a deep attachment to the city that had assimilated and unified everyone it had conquered (*De reditu suo*, 72 f.). The sense of a common heritage was what remained. The quite Christian Prudentius maintained that there was as much difference between Rome and the BARBARIANS as there was between a human being and a wild animal. Rome remained the point of absolute comparison in praising cities: A city that was bettered by no city other than Rome had no rival. The poets who surrounded Charlemagne when he built Aix often referred to it, and when the pirate Hastings took possession of Rouen (according to Dudon de Saint-Quentin), he thought he had taken Rome, since he had never seen such a city. Eternally triumphant in poetry, Rome has always been sung as "the summit, the glory, the jewel, the honor of the world" (Alexander Neckam), in verses of a classical construction with resurgences in enthusiasm in Italy and Germany during times of revival of the imperial idea (under Otto III, for example, or on the occasions of imperial coronations). Rome's great men and her thinkers have been celebrated as the honor of humanity, not only in schools (Alexander Neckam), but also in monasteries (Amadeo of Monte-Cassino, 11th century).

The reader of the Apocalypse may be left with a certain uneasiness, as it tends to identify Rome with the prostitute of Babylon; such may also be the case for the reader of Augustine's *City of God*, since the Romulan city is likened to fratricidal Cain; and likewise for other works composed during times of PERSECUTION. But Eusebius of Caesarea's theory of a providential plan, which makes of Roman unity the predestined condition for Christianization, allows a reconciliation of admiration and defiance. Quite early, the apostles PETER and PAUL redeemed the city that their deaths made holy. If the historical and political superiority of Rome greatly contributed to the establishment of its ecclesiastical primacy, it was the apostles who justified this preeminence, and it was they who made it deserving of the empire. Thus, among the early Christian hymns, those devoted to Peter and Paul, starting with St. Ambrose of Milan, sang of a Rome consecrated by the blood of martyrs. Paulinus of Nola and Prosper of Aquitaine celebrate this transformation: "first among lands, previously only for its empire and its victories, now also for the tombs of the apostles" (Paulinus, *Carmina*, 13, 29–30); "it holds, through religious respect, that which it does not possess by arms" (Prosper, *Carmen de ingratis*).

The theory of this reversal of values is explained at length by Prudentius in his *Against Symmachus*. It unfolds in hymns from the Carolingian period: Paulin of Aquilea underscores the paradox that Rome's felicity comes from a blood which she, herself, shed (*Felix per omnes*). In the 10th century a famous pilgrimage song, *O Roma Nobilis*, perfectly typified the devotional movement that drew pilgrims simultaneously to the city and the saints. One stanza for Rome, "noble and mistress of the world," queen of cities; but its colors were no longer those of her eagles: "red with the crimson blood of your many martyrs, white with the albs and the lilies of your virgins . . ." There is one stanza for Peter, one for Paul, in which one can clearly see how they divvy up the functions that contributed to Rome's power: Peter was power, Paul was knowledge. But also spiritual power and knowledge. But there was no doubt about material decadence. Although it received little emphasis in hymns, it was nevertheless visible in certain malicious attacks (*Versus Romae*, 10th century): "Morals and walls, decrepit Rome, you are crumbling!" The eternal city was in ruins, its eternal empire reclaimed by the Barbarians.

It was Hildebert of Lavardin who gave the most subtle literary form to the melancholy of the ruins that tended to strike the visitor, especially after its SACKING by the Normans. He was also the only one to continue what had been an argument of the pagan apologists of the 4th century: prosperity abandoned Rome when she became Christian. In two magnificently crafted poems, Hildebert first exalts Rome's grandeur, where even in ruins her artistic displays still draw stunned admiration. Rome herself responds and affirms, content with her fate: like that of Christ, her kingdom is not of this world. Thus pagan Rome, mistress of the earth, is contrasted with Christian Rome, in possession of the heavens. With all the counterpoint techniques of ancient rhetoric, Hildebert makes a distinction between false grandeur and true grandeur. But before Petrarch, rarely was false grandeur, that which was only human, treated with so much understanding, admiration, and perhaps even voluntary nostalgia, as by this bishop who, in fact, unhesitatingly placed the emphasis on the spiritual. His sadness at the sight of Roman ruins is less frequent than his simple admiration, which is ultimately darkened by considerations of wealth and the decay of empires. For Flodoard, the 10th century canon of Reims, a trip to Rome was the impetus for composing long poems on the triumphs of Christ and the martyrs. The monuments of Christian Rome and the martyrs' tombs were for him the essential reason for the trip, even though the ancient monuments in the descriptions of the city that had been multiplying since the time of the INVESTITURE CONTROVERSY, were among the "marvels" to be seen along the way to one BASILICA or another and onto which the imagination in search of explanations grafted a growing body of legends.

Less space should be devoted to these legends, most often linked to real places and to the memory of the ancient city, than to the function reserved (in a certain number of hagiographical, epic, or narrative texts) to the city

as a symbolic place. The attractive force of Rome, as she gathers legends around her, also causes a number of narrative traditions to gravitate to her, traditions that originally had nothing to do with the city. The *Romance of the Seven Sages*, a collection of originally Eastern stories, was thus transformed into the *History of the Seven Sages of Rome*, and set in an indistinct background of antiquity with Virgil as its protagonist and Diocletian as the sovereign in most versions. The *Gesta Romanorum* similarly had nothing to do with Rome, other than the names of a few emperors (in the background) whose role is to provide a framework to the narrative. As long as they were written in Latin, there was a preference for references to antiquity, but works in the languages of the people gave Rome another function, in a more contemporary, if not more realistic universe; in them, Rome was the city of the popes. It already was, in one of the most beloved of the lives of the saints, that of saint Alexis, the first Latin version of which came out of a Greek monastery on the Aventine and the milieux related to Otto III, toward the end of the 10th century; it turned the Syrian saint into a Roman who was born, died, and was buried in Rome, and the account of his life in hands stiffened by death can be taken and revealed only by the pope. The French versions introduced into the vernacular literature a bipolarization between Rome and the hero's native country; in *Alexis*, his real country was the desert in the East where long years of asceticism gave him the spiritual strength to return and live as an unknown beggar under the stairway of his Roman house. In the *chansons de geste* and later novels, Rome is more a symbolic place devoid of any concrete description, where the hero finds a necessary reconciliation or a place in the universal order. Rome is the center, either of pardon or of the empire. The pope has the power to bind and to loose, and his intervention is the most necessary in serious cases: incest and bigamy.

The extreme case is the story told in the *Life of Saint Gregory*. Scarred by double incest, Gregory, who was redeemed by going "into the desert," where he remained for years tied to a little wind-whipped island, is miraculously named pope. It is to Rome that his mother, who is also his wife, comes to ask his advice and beg his pardon; to Rome: The pope's see and the center of the institutional Church, the place of normal and harmonious relationships; and it is in Rome that the sad story comes to a satisfactory conclusion. But Rome is not reached as one would wish: A captainless ship takes the hero over a dangerous sea to his destiny. The ship is beached near Rome, but only after Gregory has atoned through a redeeming challenge, and proof is shown to the eyes of men of a spiritual pardon that was obtained not in Rome, but in his earlier solitude. It is only then that the mother appears to receive the official manifestation of pardon, the manifestation of a return to the norm and order. The pardon obtained in Rome is also seen in Philippe de Beaumanoir's *Manekine*, with a theme of incest and after similar wanderings over the sea, as well as in *Belle Hélène de Constantinople*. It likewise appears in *Ile et Galeron*, in *Beuve de Hametone*, and in *Florent et Octavien*, with the theme of a husband with two wives. The center of the world, Rome is thus the positive pole for travels necessitated by a theme of transgression and return to order. It was also a refuge for the hero in *Amis et Amiles*. The need to go to Rome in order to obtain pardon for a particularly serious transgression is frequent, for example, in Germany, in *Tannhäuser*, where the hero is supposed to seek pardon from URBAN IV, in 1260, for his sojourn in the Grotto of Venus. In other texts, while never ceasing to be the city of the pope who holds the power of pardon, Rome is also seen as the center of the empire, the *sine qua non* for the recognition of sovereignty. When this theme is tied to that of marriage, there is no doubt that the concept of a link between woman and land and the origins of power mingles with the reflection of imperial ideology in real life, which, when applied to the myth of the founding of the Roman Empire of the French Eneas brings out much more clearly than does the Aeneid. We see this, for example, in the *chanson de geste* called *The Coronation of Louis* (where the hero is, in fact, split into two, the weak heir Louis and William of Orange), and in the romance *Ile et Galeron*, whose common structure, beyond a few obvious differences, of duplication of an episode where the quest for the empire takes place in Rome has been shown. Apparently, the heroes are somewhat torn between their own country, where they are certain of their power and get married, and Rome, where they receive a universal power, accompanied by another marriage, in exchange for their protection. In fact, even if they appear to run from one universe to another, their personalities mature in Rome: It is in Rome that they go from the local level and from an esprit de corps and lineage to a universal dominion. The pope is there to forgive the flaws inherent in their state as lay people and warriors (including eventual bigamy) in the upheaval of taking power, in exchange for their protection. This was the way the narrative texts portrayed the alliance between the LAITY and the Church, between the pope and the emperor. Armed with the spiritual power that grants absolution and legitimacy, the pope was still not in a position of preeminence. The pardon he showed had already been given, since miracles allowed the penitents to reach him; contact with God took place elsewhere, in solitude. His moral authority made order and the law evident, but it was not he who was admired. Gregory the penitent chained to his rock had more aura than Gregory the pope. The saint (Alexis) was holier than the pope in his ascetic fervor, and the warrior (William of Orange) was braver than he and more confident in the face of Christ's enemies. The pope was shown as easygoing or worried: necessary as an institution, but never exciting.

In the narrations that involved the imperial theme, Rome looked weak and often threatened. The city where the empire of the world was located needed to be protected. Medieval fiction often presented Rome as under siege, with the memory of Attila still in the air, or the Lombard threat that justified a call to the FRANKS, or the threat of the 9th century Saracen raids, or even the Norman pillaging in the 11th century. Some historians multiplied these sieges, such as Jean d'Outremeuse, in whose work Rome was taken over by the Sicambres 410 years after the fall of Babylonia, by the Hungarians and the Danes in 457, by the Franks in 567, and threatened by King Arthur, who is even said to have been recognized as her suzerain (since Geoffrey of Monmouth, Arthur's glory had made contact with Rome obligatory, the ineluctable conquest being avoided by the Romans only through the treason that destroyed the Breton kingdom, as it was on its way to becoming an empire). In the *chansons de geste*, Rome's enemies were universally the SARACENS, and to a certain extent their threat played the dramatizing role held, in today's science-fiction novels, by the forces of evil ready to invade our planet: civilization was in danger. In the Middle Ages, it was Rome that represented civilization, and it was there that the savior won the empire, as had Charlemagne for having crushed the Lombards. The pope, despite the power of the keys, was powerless before the forces of war. It was a weakness analogous to that of the apostles, one that shocked no one: It was normal for him to ask for help, and a hero would rise up to defend him. The grandeur of medieval Rome was spiritual, not material.

Anti-Roman Satire. Nevertheless, it did happen that Roman powerlessness was presented negatively, and in pieces where sometimes acerbic political thought took a literary form. Such were the *Versus Romae* of the end of the 9th century, written by a Neapolitan subject of the *basileus*, who decried Rome in favor of Constantinople, the new Rome, and made fun of her decline. Rome's empire had disappeared, but her pride remained, as did her interest in lucre: Rome paid tribute to the Saracens and sold false relics. She martyred the saints, and now she was selling their bones, or other bones. Without Peter and Paul, she would no longer be anything. Much later, at a time when the papacy was actually more powerful, Giraud de Bari noted maliciously that Rome set rules for the world but was incapable of overcoming her own close neighbors and vassals. Nevertheless, as a general rule, in the abundant satirical literature that attacked Rome and the CURIA, it was not Rome's weakness that was the cause, but rather her failures to live up to the ideals she represented in the eyes of Christians. With rage and disappointment, people cried: "Rome, you have perished!" It was not because she no longer dominated the world, but because she was failing in the spiritual mission that wanted her to be apostolically pure and poor. To this negative current were undoubtedly added memories of the mistrust of the apologists toward Rome's powerful, corrupt, and persecuting empire, which was likened to Babylon in the Apocalypse, and attacks of ancient satirists who were ill at ease in a hard and artificial civilization: "What would I do in Rome? I don't know how to lie," was repeated at every possible opportunity, in imitation of Juvenal. But the great wave of anti-Roman satire was in response to the development of the papal tax system, in a context where Rome was no longer exactly a place, but a term used metonymously for papal authority, regardless where the bishop's chair resided. The voice of the satirists was scarcely heard in the 10th and early 11th centuries, when the papacy certainly deserved criticism, but rather after the GREGORIAN REFORM. Here it took up the themes and accents of the pope's propagandists connected with the struggle against venality, St. Peter Damian and Humbert de Silva Candida. It was an irony of fate that their satire against venality was applied to Roman venality for two centuries after the Investiture controversy; this included moralists like Saint Bernard, because the creation by the papacy of a cash tax base, especially "services" at the time of nominations, was seen only as SIMONY by minds attached to the complete gratuity of divine and spiritual gifts within a framework of a feudal, and not mercantile, society.

Anti-Roman satire was only one aspect (approximately one-third in volume) of a wider protest against any payment in cash for anything other than material goods, a condemnation that included the kings and the administration, judges and courts of justice, and lawyers. It was rarer in countries where systems of cash exchanges and financial innovations had developed earlier (e.g., in Italy), but it was abundant in France, Germany, and England. Beginning in the 12th century, mention of Rome almost automatically unleashed a moral tirade on avarice and venality; inversely, condemning simony led conversation to Rome, which was seen as the headquarters for transgressions against moral purity. The *Tractatus Garsiae* was one of the oldest "tracts" of this type: it was written against URBAN II in 1099, with only the slightest correlation to the pope's real personality. Two powerful new saints appear in it, Albinus and Rufinus (Saint Silver and Saint Gold), who are called to instill some lasting enthusiasm in both pope and prelates. Another text in prose, of which there were a number of versions in the 12th and 13th centuries, was the *Gospel of Saint Mark Silver*, a parody in the style of the gospels about the manner in which a poor man, who can't get through the door, and a guilty rich man are received by the pope. Ill from still not having received anything, the pope was healed by a potion made from gold, and enunciated a new version of the Beatitudes: Blessed are those who possess, for the Roman Curia shall be theirs. Woe to him who has nothing, for it would be better that a stone be tied around his

neck. Masters of ludic verbal techniques, the poets fine-tuned some formidable etymologies and plagiarisms: "Rome nibbles on hands" (*Roma rodit manust*); "what she cannot nibble, she abhors"; "The Roman Curia/Has no need of lambs without wool"; "In Rome it's not a question of three persons in God, but of four coins" (*non est trinus sed quattrinus*); "pope: the poor's peril" (*papa pavor pauperum*); Rome became an acronym for a Biblical maxim that barely needed retouching: *Radix Omnium Malorum Avaritia*, "Root Of all Maleficence: Avarice." The old mottoes were reworked: Rome spelled backwards (*Roma-amor*) is love: of riches, that is. Rome, head of the World? Yes, if "head" (*caput*) comes from the verb "to take" (*capio*). Moreover, Rome was as much a stomach as a head, since she devoured everything. Or else the head is on the tail. The only *libri* that were appreciated in Rome were *libri* (= pounds) of silver, not *libri* (= books) to read. These are representative of the host of accusations where the refrain included the names of the worst traitors greedy for money in the Bible: Giezi, Simon Magus, and Judas.

The masters of anti-Roman satire in the late 12th century—even more than a monk from Cluny, Bernard *Morlaanensis*, who was both heavy handed and prolific ("I certainly have the right to say, I certainly have the right to write: Rome, you exist no longer; your walls have crumbled, your morals have collapsed, and you are of the past. Famous city, you are falling, at present as low as once you were high . . .")—were the school master Gautier de Châtillon and the chancellor of Notre Dame in Paris, Philippe de Grève. The former was versatile, ready to change his tune if a prebend were in the offing, but armed with a technique that made already-outdated arguments and themes acquire unparalleled virulence. De Grève was more humane, outraged by the violence against the defenseless, whose indignation made the contrast between the thunder of triumphant injustice and the silence of forgotten justice resound. Their works, among many others, were seen in poetic collections like the *Carmina Burana*, as well as in others less famous, but in them they vented the rancor of intellectuals in a money-oriented world they failed to understand, and which repulsed them. Works in vernacular languages, written for the laity, were generally more reserved: they spared the pope and attacked his satellites. The result of this was that, generically, "the Romans," including LEGATES, had lots of bad press, even when they resided in Avignon: they represented, for the Recluse of Molliens in the *Roman de Carité*, the "media coverage" of authority, a new system that could only be bad, and Rome was a labyrinth of closed doors that opened only for money, where charity played no role, a place every bit as allegorical and floating as the weak and holy city of fiction. What the medieval imagination rejected for the Holy City was a new worldly domination.

Admiration for antiquity and Rome's Christian past, a dream of grandeur free of violence and avarice, disappointment and rejection before a reality where avarice is at least present: it is striking to see all these themes dealt with side by side, and without transition, in the *De laudibus divinae sapientiae* by Alexander Neckam who, after mentioning the great men of antiquity, admiringly walks the reader of his *mirabilia* through sanctuaries before breaking, with a spiteful adieu to Rome, with her pomp and her lies.

Pascale Bourgain

Bibliography

Batany, J. "Home and Rome, a device in epic and romance," *Yale French Studies*, 51 (1975), 42–60; "Rome dans un schéma narratif bipolaire au Moyen Âge," *Influence de la Grèce et de Rome sur l'Occident moderne*, Paris, 1977, 43–54.

Batany, J. "Les hommes de Rome: géographie et jeux de langage chez deux moralistes français vers 1200," *Jérusalem, Rome, Constantinople,* op. cit., 83–92 (on Hélinand and the recluse Molliens).

Benziger, J. *Invectiva in Romam. Romkritik im Mittelalter von 9. bis zum 12. Jahrhundert*, Lübeck, 1968 (*Historische Studien*, 404).

Bordier, J. "Rome contre Jérusalem: la légende de la Vengeance Jhesuchrist," ibid., 93–124.

de Marco, M. "In margine all'inno *O Roma nobilis*," *Miscellanea Augusto Campana*, Padua, 1981, 231–55.

Graf, A. *Roma nella memoria nell'imaginazioni del Medioevo*, Turin, 1882, 2 vols.

Guerreau, A. "Grégoire ou le double inceste. Le rôle de la papautè comme enjeu (XIIe–XIXe s.)," *Réception et identification du conte depuis le Moyen Âge*, Toulouse, 1987, 21–38; "Inceste et sainteté. La vie de saint Grégoire en français," *AESC* (1988), 1291–319.

Kytzler, B. *Roma aeterna. Lateinische und Griechische Romdichtung von der Antike bis in die Gegenwart*, Zurich-Munich, 1972 (gives important texts in Latin, with bibliographical references and a German translation).

Maddalo, S. *In figura Romae: immagini di Roma nel libro medievale*, Rome, 190 (*Studi di arte medievale*, 2).

Michel, A. "Rome chez Hildebert de Lavardin," *Jérusalem, Rome, Constantinople, l'image et le mythe de la ville*, Paris, 1986, 197–203.

Rom im hohen Mittelalter (Mélanges R. Elze), Sigmaringen, 1992, *passim.*

Schneider, F. *Rom und Romgedanke im Mittelalter*, Munich, 1925, repr. Darmstadt, 1955.

Tellenbach, G. "Die Stadt Rom in der Sicht ausländischer Zeitgenossen (800–1200)," *Saeculum*, 24 (1973), 1–40.

Traube, L. *O Roma nobilis. Philologische Untersuchungen aus dem Mittelalter*, Munich, 1925, repr. Darmstadt, 1955.

Uitti, K. *Story, Myth and Celebration in Old French Narrative Poetry, 1050–1200*, Princeton, 1973.

Yunck, J. *The Lineage of Lady Meed*, Notre Dame (Ill.), 1963.

Modern and Contemporary Eras. In modern literature, Rome plays an important, and ambiguous, role in both the creation and in the deconstruction of images, representations, and myths concerning the papacy from the 16th to the 20th century. The vision of Rome is expressed in a variety of ways in a variety of genres: in poetry, be it *romanseca* in Belli's sonnets, the works of Trilussa, of Pacarella, or foreign in Du Bellay's *Les Antiquités de Rome* and *Les Regrets*, or Goethe's *Roman Elegies*. Likewise, in the novel from Mme. de Staël's *Corinne* and Charles Didier's *Rome souterraine* to Moravia's *Nouvelles Romaines*, Goncourt's *Madame Gervaisais*, Zola's *Rome*, and Fogazzaro's *Il Santo*, papal Rome is part of the story. Similarly, the travel accounts and memoirs, including those of Montaigne, Chateaubriand, Dickens, and Taine, describe the myriad facets of the Eternal City. The image of Rome is also a function of divergent points of view—Roman, Italian, French, German, English, Russian—that weave around it a narrative that opens up a variety of complementary or contradictory perspectives. The way the papacy is presented through them is the result of opposing ideologies, from D'Aubigné's or Garibaldi's Babylonia, to Louis Veuillot's or Palazzeschi's Holy City. Each time, the myth expands or shrinks, is exalted or reduced to nothing. For five centuries, the literature of modern Rome has thus been the deformed mirror in which this unique, changing city in perpetual renaissance is seen.

For the protagonist of a novel, arriving in Rome means, first of all, seeing the dome of ST. PETER'S, which immediately takes on special meaning: it "fills" the narrator of Butor's *La Modification* "with joy"; it "tells" la Ciociara that "she can finally return home confidently, after so many tragedies and upheavals, and that her former existence will continue its course"; it stirs up enthusiasm and a "wave of feelings" that Gogol's *principino* "had been powerless to express," just as it rouses disappointment, as in the beginning of Mme. de Staël's *Corinne* when count d'Erfeuil laconically compares it to the "Dome of Les Invalides." But it is always the point of reference, and, for Cardinal Petralia (in Didier's *Rome souterraine*), who had come to Rome with ambitions of becoming pope, the cross on its top was "the beacon of the world."

The dome's appearances accentuate the progression of Zola's *Rome*: a first "sudden vision . . . paralyzes" Pierre Froment, who is troubled by the pure, almost immaterial beauty of this dome "of such light sky blue" that "it blends into the infinite azure," while its last vision speaks of imminent collapse. Each of the panoramic visions of the city indicates the power relationship before the young man's eyes of the three poles of Rome: St. Peter's, the QUIRINAL, and the COLOSSEUM.

Everyone creates his or her own image of this city where one time is superimposed over another, where everyone feels like he or she is in "the capital, not of Italy, but of a very old and quite special world" (Curvers, *Tempo di Roma*), and where everything seems to try to establish itself forever upon the ruins of one thing or another (Dickens, *Little Dorrit*). This grandiose bric-a-brac characteristic both "amuses" Father Mionnet and "makes him dream" during the course of his *Mission in Rome* (Jules Romains, *Les Hommes de bonne volonté*). For him, Rome is "a quite vast and ancient 'Container' split in places . . . of varying ages and conditions." From the top of the San Pietro terrace in Montorio, Zola's Pierre Froment "gave himself up entirely to Rome, to the living colossus lying there before him, to this earth made from the dust of generations [and whose] glory each century had renewed from the sap of an immortal youthfulness flowing through it." At the Capitol, de Staël's Corinne sings of Rome as the memory of the world, receptacle "of all the marvels that, from the depths of Egypt and Greece, from the far reaches of the centuries, from Romulus to Leo X, have gathered here as if grandeur attracted grandeur, and that a single place had to enclose everything man has been able to shield from time."

From the moment of their arrival, visitors rush toward the two traditional poles of Rome: the Vatican and the great monuments of ancient Rome. "Where would your Excellencies like to be taken?" Franz and Albert are asked in Dumas's *The Count of Monte Cristo*. "Well, first to Saint Peter's and then to the Coliseum," was Albert's immediate reply. With equal energy Corinne announced to Oswald: "Then it is this morning that I will show you the Pantheon and Saint Peter's." In every age, "modern Rome" has difficulty finding a place in literature, architecture, or politics. For Montaigne, it is of unparalleled ugliness, "bastard Rome," with the ruins, violated by time and invasions, reminding him of the nests that sparrows and crows in France had made "in the archways and walls of the churches that the Huguenots had just destroyed" (*Voyage en Italie*).

Three centuries later, for Louis Veuillot, it was the Christian city whose buildings and splendors would be sullied by the Piedmontese's "brutal corruption: they would fill it with barracks, whorehouses, and theaters; they would set up a throne surrounded by spies and soldiers . . . . [But] the modern creations will either fall or become purified" (*Le Parfum de Rome*). More phlegmatic, Mionnet "postpones his judgment." The new city "looks like a disconcerted provincial intruder 'resting on one buttock' and getting ready to leave." Of course, its development has contributed to a "bizarre" placement of "the City of the pope," or at least to highlighting and accentuating its "lack of need of its position," but the city "was not displeasing to him." Moreover, Rome was not "without link or transition with the Rome of earlier centuries. And there were areas from which it seemed to evolve naturally enough."

The idea of continuity—historical and political—dominated Zola's view of Rome, while for Stendhal, as for Charles Didier, papal power was forever incompatible with any form of lay government. In *Rome souterraine*, the attempt to unify Italy through the mediation of a pope devoted to the cause of the *carbonari* failed while Austria was exercising its veto against Cardinal Petralia for pope. However, even before allowing himself to be convinced, Anselm had reminded the cardinal of the story of Alphonse Petrucci "who got LEO X elected to the cry of 'Long live the young!' and whom Leo X had strangled in the CASTEL SANT'ANGELO." For Stendhal, "if religion does not take on a new form, we are going to witness a fight to the death between papism or belief, and representative government founded on examination and defiance" (*Promenades dans Rome*).

The Vatican and the civil government coexisted, each attempting to annex the other. Zola in *Mes Voyages* commented that the pope hoped to regain control of Rome and its finances. On the other hand, he conceded that it was "in the general interest for [the pope] to remain," but only as "BISHOP OF ROME," since Italy, "through him, governed the consciences of the whole world." Nevertheless, "if peace continues, if there are no great European upheavals, the status quo might endure indefinitely; and relations between the Vatican and the Quirinal will get better and better. "Evolution was fatal," the diplomat Narcisse Habert explained to Pierre Froment in *Rome*. "The pope alone will always say no, will always remain unchangeable. But around him, everything goes on and changes . . . . From now on, when a prince has two sons, one stays in the Vatican, and the other goes to the Quirinal."

Beyond political compromise, there exists for Zola a mythic continuity between the different moments of Rome, a continuity that comes from "atavism." The pope and the king reigning one against the other have in their veins the same "blood of Augustus"—emperor and pontiff—which "once again, rose into the cranium of the newcomers, throwing them into the dementia of turning the third Rome into the new queen of the Earth," which "would surpass the two others, the imperial and the papal, by the magnificence of her roads, and the overflowing crowds of her people." And, in the face of construction of new neighborhoods, "Pierre was once again struck by the truth that whoever possesses Rome is devoured by the folly of marble, by the vainglorious need to build and leave future peoples . . . monuments of glory." He laments the "useless and too spacious houses," and the discouraging vacuity where the political indifference of the Pierina's brother finds an echo—for it "was clearly apparent" from his attitude "that if the father was for the pope and the uncle for the republic, he, the son, was certainly for nothing"—that the "third Rome" would leave neither basilica nor Colosseum.

The literary image of Rome takes shape more willingly and more frequently around St. Peter's and the most beautiful churches, on the one hand, and around the Colosseum and the Palatine on the other, depending on the ideological or aesthetic preferences of the visitor. The day after his arrival in Rome, Dickens went to St. Peter's. It was magnificent, of course: "nothing could render . . . the beauty of the place . . . with its elegant colonnade and its bubbling fountains." "The first sight" of the basilica's interior, and especially of the dome, caused an "unforgettable sensation." Even though he had the highest possible idea of the building's beauty, he "did not feel great emotion." Almost fleeing St. Peter's, which he would not have "visited" for anything in the world, he ordered the driver to take him to the Colosseum. This time emotion was there to greet him. "Never in his life, perhaps, will [the visitor] be as moved and overwhelmed by a view that is directly connected to neither his affections nor his pains . . . . It is the most impressive spectacle, the most majestic, the most solemn, grandiose, and imposing that can be imagined." In his entire stay, he "would never succeed in spending a day without returning to it." For Goethe, "when one looks at this monument, the rest all seems small again." On the other hand, Andrea Sperelli, the hero of D'Annunzio's *Pleasure*, feels real passion for the villas, the fountains, the churches of "the popes' Rome." He would have given the entire Colosseum for the Medici villa, the Forum for Piazza di Spagna, Titus's arch for the Fontana delle Tartarughe.

Some prefer, others compare. "The church of Saint Peter," de Staël's Corinne tells Oswald in front of the PANTHEON, "will have a totally different effect on you; you will first believe it to be less vast than it is in reality. The illusion so favorable in the Pantheon comes . . . from there being more space between the columns . . .; but even more so it comes from the fact that there are almost no detail decorations, while Saint Peter's is overloaded with them. (*Corinne ou l'Italie*, 1807). An aesthetic comparison is often followed by an ideological comparison or contrast expressed in a more or less nuanced fashion. For Veuillot, "the world before the pope was Nero's empire"; "from the Coliseum to SAINT JOHN LATERAN, from the great theater of carnage to the great church lies the path to the good Lord." Standing before the "serenity" and the light of the Pantheon, on the other hand, Corinne explains to Oswald that "the pagans divinized life, while the Christians divinized death." Stendhal would finally be in agreement with Mme. de Staël's heroine: at the Chigi palace, her "travelling companions were extremely struck by two small works by Bernini representing *Death and Life*. Life was represented by a beautiful child in white marble . . . standing before a skull, likewise in white marble . . . . This reminds one of Catholicism; the Ancients would have been horrified by such a sight." In St. Peter's, one "stiff statue was a Jupiter. Now it is Saint Peter. It improved in personal morality; but its disciples are not quite what Jupiter's were. Antiquity had neither INQUISITION nor Saint Bartholomew's Day, nor puritan sadness."

Corinne, without mentioning the roar of the lions in her description of Roman activities in the early days of Christianity, nevertheless does not lose sight of the harshness of ancient worship: "Greek religion was not at all, like Christianity, consolation in misfortune, richness in misery, the life to come for the dying; it wanted glory, triumph." Where Corinne exposes and discusses, Mme. Gervaisais chooses: "passion for pagan Beauty, that sincere passion for ancient Rome that managed to hide Catholic Rome from her . . . ."

Stendhal was not able to choose. The two Romes had for a long time been an integral part of his imagination and thought: one affirmation responded to the other. "For those of us who have been translating bits of Livy and Florus for years, their memory precedes all experience," and daydreaming in the Colosseum provides "the most vibrant joys." But the existence of St. Peter's and of "so many magnificent churches spread throughout the world" has determined our sensitivity to "the beautiful." Nothing is "comparable" to the Colosseum, as "nothing can be compared" to a sunset over the dome of St. Peter's. The two monuments are equally capable of stirring this "reverie of Rome that seems so sweet and makes us forget all interest in the active life," to such an extent that when one is "immersed in it . . . if someone told him he was king of the earth, he would not deign to get up and go enjoy the throne; he would put it off until later." Sometimes rage follows enthusiasm. "What abode was ancient Rome; if only its evil star had not allowed on its soil the construction of the Rome of the whores! Saint Peter's excepted, there is nothing plainer than modern architecture . . . ." (*Rome, Naples, et Florence*).

One century earlier, the fate of the Pantheon's statues made the marquis de Sade wax sentimental: "But it is here, Mme. Countess, it is here that the heart is broken, that tears flow despite one's will, when one sees this famous temple of all the gods, this admirable Pantheon, the masterpiece of the beautiful century of Augustus that contains the most beautiful statues in the world, today turned into a wretched, naked, stripped down church" by the religious zeal of "that Ostrogoth URBAN VIII" (*Voyage d'Italie*). In St. Peter's, proclaimed "the most beautiful church of the most beautiful religion in the world," Stendhal did not know whether to "worship" or cry. The canopy's decoration was "necessary," but one moans when one remembers that it was made with bronze taken from the Pantheon.

On the whole, however, the popes, "great princes [friends] of the arts"—whom Stendhal contrasted to "narrow-minded priests" in "fear of Luther"—had preserved more of the great monuments than they had detroyed. BENEDICT XIV undoubtedly saved the Colosseum by turning it into a Christian place: "[W]ishing to remove any excuse from the great lords who, for centuries, had stones taken from it as if it were a quarry, [he] had fourteen small oratories built around the arena." Of course, "if the popes had not come back from Avignon, if the Rome of the priests had not been built at the expense of ancient Rome, we would have many more of the Romans' monuments; but if the Christian religion had not made such an intimate alliance with beauty . . . We, the sons of Christians, would be less sensitive to Beauty."

St. Peter's was born from the Pantheon and the Colosseum. For Corinne, the Pantheon was "a temple set upon a church," in accord with the inspiration of Michelangelo, who "said, when he saw the dome of the Pantheon: 'I will place it in the air.'" Then, recounts Stendhal, "when he was working on the church," Michelangelo, "already quite aged, . . . was found, one winter day, after a heavy snowfall, wandering among the ruins of the Colosseum. He had come to raise his soul to the tone necessary to feel the beauties and the defects of his own design for the dome of Saint Peter's." The basilica exists because "NICHOLAS V, JULIUS II, and Leo X were men worthy of being moved by the ruins of the Colosseum and by the dome of Saint Peter's." For Zola, "the sumptuous, worldly popes of the Renaissance" were able to "passionately resuscitate Antiquity," and the Vatican MUSEUMS were to Father Mionnet's gaily cynical eyes the conservatory of the beauty and the freedom of the world: "He pronounced, to himself, somewhat haphazardly and randomly, the names of the popes of that happy time: Julius II, Leo X, . . . and CLEMENT VII . . . and Alexander Borgia, who nevertheless cannot be left out . . . . It was with a very clear conscience that they offered a definitive refuge . . . to the breasts of the Dianas and the Venuses, and to the sexual organs of the Apollos, the Antinouses, and the Hercules, which had miraculously been spared the furor of the early Christians . . . ." "[W]ith a quite natural inclination, without the least thought of being scandalized," they allowed themselves to be carried away by this free circulation of pleasure, beauty, intelligence, of which the artists of the day made themselves the intermediaries. "Michelangelo and Raphael . . . took responsibility for transitions, for blends, for shading, for repeated motifs. It was they who made a cardinal's mistress bear a resemblance to an ancient goddess, or this same mistress look like a saint in Paradise, or a Greek youth look like a young noble guard; or a virgin resemble a boy . . . ."

The successive lives of Rome thus come together in one harmonious, uninterrupted current: Andrea Sperelli speaks to Elena Muti of his "Catholic and pagan heart." Each stage rejected, each stitch missed soon feels like a gap. Cecile, the anticlerical heroine of Butor's La Modification, refuses to go to St. Peter's, "that gigantic architectural failure," that "immense and extremely wealthy testimony to indigence," or to visit the "interminable corridors" of the Vatican museums "where old stolen statues are so stupidly lined up just about everywhere." But in St. Peter in Chains, the lovers stand sheepishly before Michelangelo's Moses: "The statue was there, like a ghost in an attic and, above all, you felt . . . as though you were missing something essential, something available to you but which was forbidden for you to see because of Cecile, . . . haunted by these prophets and sibyls, . . . conscious of the absurdity of your walks . . . since you knew only too well . . . what there was in Rome besides this Moses." Likewise, if one does not "cross over the bridge" between the antique and Christian worlds, frustration is soon to be born. When, one day, their "wanderings" take them "from OBELISK to obelisk," they "well know that to continue this systematic exploration of Roman themes, they would need to go, once, from Saint Paul's church to Saint Paul's church, . . . in an attempt to deepen or to determine . . . the images connected to these names, these doors to quite strange discoveries . . . about the Christian world itself so fallaciously known."

Zola, like his hero, saw St. Peter's only as "a pagan temple, erected to the god of pomp and light." The pope himself appears as an all-powerful Jupiter, raised upon a red velvet stage, with "flabella waving over the sole sovereign pontiff's head, the great feather fans that in times past swung before the idols of Ancient Rome." It was thus in such a way that the pontiff appeared in Charles Didier's Rome souterraine. In "the wonder . . . the fanatical intoxication . . . the cries" that greeted the passing of a procession, Mme. Gervaisais sees "only a savage and brutish idolatry of the East, a little like the rush of India under the idol of Jaggernat. The Madonna del Parto whose feet she would ultimately kiss when her child was ill at first looks like 'the Idol' to her."

St. Theodore also healed sick children, who were carried into the little church dedicated to him at the foot of the Palatine, as they were once carried to the temple of Romulus, on the site of which it was built. Sade wondered, with exasperated malice, if "it was the same superstition," or if "Saint Theodore actually had the same virtues as Romulus." For Charles Didier, as for Zola, "Christianity just grafted itself onto pagan forms and practices," and Julien Gracq noticed in his trip "around the seven hills" that "almost from the beginning, the churches made peace with the ancient temples."

In the majority of novels or literary writings on Rome, the writers contrast the interior, spiritual life of faith with the elaborate Christian monuments and art. For Oswald, "Italian Catholicism, with all its outer demonstrations, dispenses the soul from meditation and recollection." Pierre Froment wondered if Rome "ever was Christian, beyond the very early period of the catacombs." Taine regretted "not being able to admit that the churches of Rome were Christian . . . . If there is anywhere in the world where it is appropriate to feel tenderness, compunction, veneration, or the either grandiose or painful sense of the infinite, of the *beyond*, it is here, and unfortunately, what is felt here is just the opposite. How often, in contrast, have I thought about our gothic churches—Reims, Chartres, Paris, and especially Strasbourg!" (*Voyage en Italie*).

Stendhal congratulated himself on this "infidelity to hell" of abandoning somber cathedrals: "The popes fell in love with ARCHITECTURE, that eternal art that so easily couples with the religion of terror, but thanks to the Roman monuments they did not stick to the gothic style," which Bishop Fornaro considered to be "pure heresy." In any case, for Stendhal, "as long as man has imagination, as long as he needs to be consoled, he will love to speak to God, and depending on his own individual personality, he [will do so] with greater pleasure under the magnificent arches of Saint Peter's in Rome or in the little half-ruined church of his village." The "sublime" Christmas ceremony in St. Peter's in 1827 left Stendhal "almost as much a believer as a Roman," essentially because of the "stunning" effect of the dome.

"The free thinker . . . who loves lyric theater" and domes has no choice, according to Gracq, but to rejoice that "the most bigoted of the popes" who since the time of Leo X have commissioned work on St. Peter's "have not been able to take away the worldly and courtesan-like beauty that so characterize the church." The "empire of sublime beauty," which gave the "theater" of the Colosseum, gave Michelangelo "ideas for a church."

Contrary to Stendhal, several others were disappointed to find nothing more than spectacle. Immediately after his arrival in Rome, Sade hurried to St. Peter's and "found the façade to be more theatrical than imposing." For Zola, the basilica was just about everything but a church. It was a "giant showroom, a place of wasted space, a cyclopean reception palace." The Gesù was likewise an "opera hall." To Chateaubriand, the galleries and stairways in the Vatican looked like "a theater with abandoned seats, opened to solitude" (*Mémoires d'outre-tombe*). This impression was naturally stronger among Protestants. Dickens declared a mass in St. Peter's, even when the pope was present was neither "impressive nor moving, from a religious point of view." And all the less so, since "behind the altar a huge space had been set up with loggias like those in London's Italian opera, but much more sumptuous in their decoration. In the center of this theater space . . . was a platform with the pope's throne set upon it." The colors—the "bright green" of the carpet, the "unbearable reds," the "crimson," and the "golden borders of the drapes and wall hangings"—all served to reinforce this impression of ostentatious bad taste, transforming it all "into one gigantic piece of candy."

Long after the failure of her honeymoon in Rome, the sumptuousness of St. Peter's would come back to haunt poor Dorothea Casaubon. In her moments of sadness and solitude, she would revisit, for the rest of her life, "the immensity of St. Peter's, . . . the enormous bronze canopy," the agitation of the prophets and evangelists in the mosaics, and the "red wall hangings that were displayed for Christmas, spreading out everywhere like some retinal disease." For Goethe, Christmas mass in St. Peter's was a "spectacle," but a "one-of-a-kind and passably venerable spectacle." Like Oswald, he regretted the formalism of Catholic ceremonies, but decided to "be pleased with what is pleasing" and to "enjoy whatever could be enjoyed." Certainly, "nothing had an effect on him . . ., nothing really impressed him, but [he] admired everything, since it must be admitted that they had perfectly used the Christian traditions. In papal ceremonies, especially in the SIXTINE CHAPEL [sic], everything that tends to be unpleasant in Catholic worship is done with remarkable taste and perfect dignity. But this is possible only in this place where, for centuries, all the arts are at the service of religion." Thus, at a mass during Holy Week where, because of Lent, the cardinals were not "dressed in red, but rather in violet," he recalled the Albrecht Dürer paintings that he had seen just days before: "The ensemble was unique, grandiose, and yet simple." The music was "of unimaginable beauty," especially "the beautiful songs of sorrow."

Oswald remained reticent before these ceremonies that always ran the risk of degenerating into "a spectacle where one plays one's role in relation to someone else's . . .; the regularity of the ceremonies of a court, introduced into a temple, hinders the free impulse of the heart, which alone gives man the hope of approaching Divinity." In his opinion, Roman formalism and dogmatism were harmful to religious meditation, and to morals. "It is after Holy Week," Oswald reminds his companion, "that the greatest number of murders are committed in Rome. The people believe themselves to be, for lack of a better term, funded by Lent, and spend the treasures of their penance by murdering. Criminals have been seen who, still dripping from crimes, felt guilty about eating meat on Friday." The sumptuousness of the Roman churches seems to be no more than homage given to a strong and fearful power, but comparable to any temporal power.

For Taine St. Peter's evokes "a magnificent banquet hall, some royal city hall decked out in all its silver, and crystal . . . to receive some monarch and do honor to the city. The medieval cathedral suggested grandiose and sad dreams . . ., the temple of Catholic restoration inspired feelings of submission, admiration, or at least deference, for this personage so powerful and so established in time, especially so endowed with authority and so well furnished that we call the Church." For Zola, the ferociously temporal aspect of papal power was indubitable. Narcisse Habert attempted to respond to Pierre Froment's perplexities in light of the behavior of Roman prelates by explaining to him "that they leave God in the sanctuary, [that] they reign in his name, convinced that Catholicism is the human organization of God's government, the only perfect and eternal one . . . . While we spend further time . . . furiously discussing the existence of God, they do not allow existence to be placed in doubt, since they are [his] appointed ministers." The arrogance that flows from this certainty is one of the logical consequences of that Roman megalomania which transforms everything into a frenzied will for absolute power, inherited from Augustus, the emperor, and pontiff. So never "have the popes . . . had any other passionate desire, any other secular politic, than that of wanting to reconquer civil authority, the totality of domination, the heart burned by atavistic blood, the red and devourous wave of the blood of the ancestor." The repeated acclamations—"*Evviva il papa re!*"—"the war cry that has allowed so many sins to be committed and so much blood to flow," revolt Pierre and cause him to leave the gallery where he was watching the ceremony done on the occasion of the pilgrimage of Peter's pence. Up in the dome, the young priest "is overcome with emotion before this violent, cruel Rome so little like the Rome of his dreams," and "sees himself as an imbecile, with his dream of a pope purely spiritual confronting this old city of glory and domination clinging to its red."

Sometimes, on the other hand, the magnificence does stir religious sentiment. For Palazzeschi, a ceremony in St. Peter's "is a golden vision in which one feels immersed and transported, it is but a light, a chant," sometimes having "the little woman who has come in from the countryside and finds herself in the middle of it all [exclaim]: Lord, thank you, I am in paradise." For Tolla, Edmond About's heroine, "religion, and especially this splendid Catholicism that reigns in Rome, found . . . a soul that was well prepared. The pomp of the ceremonies, the smell of the incense, the gold, the marble, the sacred music, invincibly captivated her . . . . The childlike enthusiasm she feels for certain images gradually transformed into devotion." All the arts come together for Mme. Gervaisais' progressive conversion: "Little by little in the city of the churches, she gave herself over to the love of marble," and got into the habit of remaining "immobile, contemplative . . . in the middle of this veined stone" where she soon saw come to life "in the flames of the candles . . . a pale glimpse of the afterlife." The

sumptuous ceremonies of Palm Sunday and Easter are "a masterpiece of the triumphal religious spectacle of the 16th century." In the chants of Holy Week she painfully yet sweetly found "the bitter felicity of memory . . . in the melancholy enchantment of a distant harmony." In this "upsetting of her sensibilities" she lost "the haughty strength of [her] ideas . . . , a stoic woman's pride of one who was firmly mistress of herself."

Corinne, on the other hand, tried to attenuate Lord Nevil's reticences as he faced the splendors and the size of St. Peter's, by explaining to him that they also helped to remind man of his smallness, and of his greatness as a Christian. In fact, "prayer alone, the accent of misfortune . . . moves one deeply among these vast spaces" and "one feels that man is imposing by the very infirmity of his nature." Before giving in to the "joyfulness" of the opening ceremonies of the HOLY YEAR, Jimmy, the protagonist in *Tempo di Roma*, had, during his long wait, "meditated . . . on the triumph of death" in the "formidable and dark majesty" of St. Peter's, which, "in the darkness, was stripped down like a mosque [. . . warning] us of both its own nothingness and ours . . . . And there, too, was salvation, beauty, peace."

Walter, the Swiss priest in Guido Morselli's novel *Roma senza Papa*, which pushes the Church's evolution in the 1970s to her apparently logical fictional consequences, first congratulates himself on the "wisdom" that caused "the sumptuous and crushing residence of the Vatican" to be abandoned for the quite sober papal abode of Zagarolo, a little burg to the south of Rome, "since today the See barely relies on the earth." There was no sense of exile in this relocation, but rather "a Jerusalem, the celebration and epitome of asceticism" relative to which "the papacy of other centuries, not only a JULIUS II, but also a PIUS VII, is lost in a fairy tale-perspective, somewhat sullied, I might say, by niggardliness." Nevertheless, upon his return to Rome, he felt the absence of the pope not as an "idea," but as a "wretched lacuna . . . : the city was no longer antique, it was old, for the first time." In contrast, in Palazzeschi's *Roma*, there was a warm consensus of the people regarding the pope, whose "presence . . . in Rome is that of an ever-burning, invisible lamp whose rare and brief appearances are made to thank her for her ever-radiating warmth." Only the white, slight, almost immaterial vision of the pope giving his blessing has been able to give "inward peace" to the Materassi sisters, other Palazzeschi heroines lost in Rome in a "forest of colonnades" that took on the appearance of a nightmare.

It is because of PIUS XII, IN *Roma*, or at least because of "his faith" that Rome owned its escape from destruction in 1944: "The miracle was that of having believed in salvation, and he, who had been the first to believe in it, was the first one to be thanked." The joy of the crowd, in the dazzling sunlight of 6 June 1944, hailing "the emaciated white figure up there in the loggia of Saint Peter's surrounded by magnificently dressed prelates" corresponded to the anguish of the icy afternoon of 24 March when the pope, whom "no one had ever seen so alone, so deprived of decoration," had put out a "warning . . . to the armies of both sides . . . that were fighting over the city."

In literature, the pope is never greater than when he is humble. "How beautiful is this ceremony of papal benediction!" exclaimed Chateaubriand. "All the people falling on their knees under an old man's hand: the pope is the only prince who blesses his subjects." Pius VII's triumphal, but scarcely triumphant, return, in *Mémoires d'outre-tombe*, even brings "the Protestants who witness the scene" to "shed warm tears." "The Holy Father saw nothing, heard nothing . . . and in no way wanted to be carried onto the platform, under the dais and palms; he walked like a shipwrecked man fulfilling a vow to Our Lady of Good Help, and entrusted by Christ with a mission to renew the face of the earth." At the end of the opening ceremony for the holy year, Jimmy looked tenderly and emotionally at "the pope, the only one in the procession [who] was smiling naturally, happily . . . managing to show in the weary motions [of the benediction] a special solicitude for each individual." For Jimmy, the ceremony was a sacred symbol without which life in the world, even in the working-class neighborhoods and factories, would have been darker, shaken, devoid of hope, and impoverished . . . .

The worm, however, is in the fruit. "The holy year," declared Jimmy, "began for me with a disappointment." Even though it was not of a religious nature, but rather stimulated by the fact that, in the "overpopulated island" of St. Peter's square, he could not find his fiancée, there was something emblematic about this disappointment. For reasons that might be diametrically opposed to Prevert's anticlerical outbursts, for example, "Things need to be called by their names/What is, after all, a pope/But a frightful old man" ("Crosier in the air," *Paroles*). Ceremonies in the Vatican and papal appearances often leave a bitter aftertaste. After attending Tenebrae in the Sistine Chapel on Wednesday of Holy Week in 1829, Chateaubriand was prey to "a double sadness." Naturally, "the Catholic heir on the seven hills was there with her memories; but instead of these powerful pontiffs, of these cardinals arguing over the precedence of the monarch, a poor old paralytic pope, with no family and no support, some less than dazzling princes of the Church, were announcing the end of a power that civilized the modern world . . . Christian Rome, in commemorating the agony of Christ, looked like it was celebrating its own."

For Gioacchino Belli, the cardinals during the Lenten services looked like *tanti cadaveri di morti* ("Le Cappelle papale," *Sonetti*). The idea of death hung doubly over the coronation ceremony in Charles Didier's novel. "The

souls of believers never observe without tenderness this sublime, touching spectacle" of the pope kneeling before the altar of the Blessed Sacrament . . . . "[A]las!, this is no longer anything but a dead ceremony." The absentminded Brancador, suspected of treason by the *carbonari*, simply decided to prove his loyalty by assassinating the pope, "believing this would restore his honor through the eviscerated guts of the august old man."

On 18 August 1817, Stendhal attended one of the most beautiful spectacles that he had ever witnessed in his life. The pope came out of St. Peter's, carried on an immense litter: "[W]e saw him, his face wan, kneeling before the Blessed Sacrament . . . , face pale, inanimate, superb," with such 'absence of motion' that a child said to his mother: 'You didn't tell me the pope was dead.'" Stendhal explained: "The pope's position is one of tradition; but since such would be difficult for an old man who is frequently infirm, draperies are arranged in such a way that His Holiness appears to be on his knees, while in reality he is sitting in an armchair" (*Rome, Naples, et Florence*). In *Rome*, the holy aura surrounding the pontiff disappears more violently. The "royal nobility that was his, was but a whisper, a pure soul in an ivory body, so transparent that you could see his soul within, already, as if delivered from the bonds of the earth."

An audience with the sovereign pontiff likewise gives rise to opposing feelings. Veuillot "was going toward him whom God had named to be the living representative . . . of the living God . . . . I prostrated myself before the Immortal . . . and I called him Father. And he, leaning over to bless me, called me 'Figliolo, my son!' This welcoming of so much weakness by so much powerfulness, the gentleness of this majesty, and the tenderness of his smile told me what the dignity of the Christian is" (*Le Parfum de Rome*). Alexandre Dumas, the day of his audience with GREGORY XVI, "felt . . . also the deepest emotion he had ever felt in his life." Nevertheless, it did not keep him from remarking that "sovereigns are like women, they always feel a certain pleasure seeing the effect they produce." The emotion, however, prevailed, and he left the Vatican, "eyes brimming with tears and heart replete with faith," loaded with rosaries and "little wooden and mother-of-pearl crosses" blessed by the pontiff, and comfirmed in his intention to write his new play, *Caligula*, from a Christian perspective.

In his interviews with the pope, Chateaubriand never lost sight of the role the pontiff is capable of playing in the future destiny of both the Church and the world, as much by his writing and speaking as by his political actions. Two days after his arrival in Rome in 1803, as secretary to Cardinal Fesch, Chateaubriand was introduced to Pius VII. In the room, there was a volume of *Le Genie du Christianisme* "politely open on the table." In 1829, he related a long interview with LEO XII to the count de La Ferronays, then minister of foreign affairs, and drew completely political conclusions from it: "in the present state of things, the king can count entirely on the court of Rome." A few days earlier he had written to Mme. Récamier: "The only thing missing in the adventures of my political life was to be in relation with a sovereign pontiff; this completes my career."

Montaigne's audience, two and a half centuries earlier, was characterized by emptiness, when "on 29 December 1580, M. d'Abein, who was then ambassador . . . was of the opinion that he should kiss the feet of the pope." Gesture prevailed over the spiritual:

One or two steps into the room, in one corner of which the pope was sitting, those who entered, regardless who they were, set one knee on the ground, waiting for the pope's blessing . . . after which they stood up and went to the half-way point in the room . . . most not going directly to him in a straight line but rather cutting across the room, veering off slightly along the wall, to come, after this slight detour, directly before him. Being at this half-way point, they again go down on one knee, and receive the second benediction. (*Journal de voyage*) The portrait of GREGORY XIII bears witness to the same absence of passion: "[B]y his nature, he is awkward of speech. In fact, he is a handsome old man . . . of a gentle nature with little interest in the affairs of the world, a great builder . . . , a great chaplain . . . , and . . . he has a voice and mannerisms about which there is nothing extraordinary, either in one way or in another."

The popes of the 16th century who were portrayed by 19th century novelists clearly had more depth. Those of the *Chroniques italiennes* were terrifying. "John Paul Carrafa, the future PAUL IV, even though he was born into "one of the most noble families in the kingdom of Naples, had ways of behaving that were harsh, violent, rude, and in every way worthy of a guardian of sheep." ALEXANDER VI, "that great man who knew everything and could do everything," made him his CHAMBERLAIN; Julius II named him archbishop of Chieti, and Paul III, cardinal. Finally, on 23 May 1555, "after intrigues and terrible disputes among the cardinals locked up in the CONCLAVE, he was made pope under the name Paul IV . . . , those who elected him to St. Peter's throne soon shuddered at the thought of the harshness, of the ferocious, inexorable piety of the master they had just given themselves" (*La Duchesse de Palliano*).

Pope CLEMENT VIII, who reigned at the time of the trial of the Cenci children and their mother in Rome, was on the other hand "sweet and merciful." Unfortunately, an excess of scruples made him fear that the judge Ulysses Moscoti "might have been won over by the beauty of Beatrice, and gone easy on her in the interrogation. It followed that His Holiness took control of the trial away from him and gave it to another, more severe, judge" (*Les Cenci*).

In the story of Father Faria in *The Count of Monte Cristo*, Dumas portrays Pope Alexander VI, a Borgia, as one expert in mortal dinners who uses ingenious accessories, such as an armoire key "with a small iron point," whose prick was deadly, and a "ring with a lion's head" that in "certain handshakes . . . brought death within twenty-four hours." Alexander's appearance at the end of Rolfe's (alias Baron Corvo's) *Dom Tarquinio* was solar and liberating, on the other hand. At the end of "deep labyrinths" and "numerous antechambers" where "a sepulchral odor" reigned, young Tarquinio and his companion Ippolito discovered behind one last "thick, porphyry-colored curtain . . . the flaming sun of the Presence."

Emile Zola, who had no reservations about making a living pope, Leo XIII, a character in a novel, sketched a less than flattering portrait of him in *Rome*. In one scene, Pierre Froment crosses through, in "the black nothingness of the colossal Vatican, a succession of deserted, sumptuous, dead rooms" in his one last attempt to defend his book to the pope. Pierre well knew, after spending a few months in Rome, that he would not find "the ideal pope" of his book, "the predestined individual responsible for the salvation of peoples." During the "barely three-quarters of an hour" of the interview with the pope, he was met with disappointment after disappointment: first, a weak old man, next a "knowledgeable, conciliatory politician"; finally, a "master, so angry, so formidable."

In Fogazzaro's novel, Leo XIII does not get angry. Benedetto, the "Saint," gives the emotional pontiff a speech on the four "evil spirits"—lying, clergy domination, greed, and rigidity—that have entered into the Church, "there to wage war against the Holy Spirit." The reply of the old man, "steeped in gentleness and charity," was measured—the battle against these evils was beyond his strength—"My son . . . some of these words were also long ago spoken in my heart by the Lord."

Zola's Leo XIII thunders that "pure spiritual royalty, sovereignty through charity and love" are nothing more than "wonderful fancy," the "whim of an ignoramus unaware of the conditions under which the papacy has until now lived." In fact, Leo exclaims, "Who will win respect for us? Who will grant us a stone upon which to rest our heads, if we are ever banished . . . ? Who will assure our independence, when we are at the mercy of all the States?"

"*Roma veduta, fede perduta!*" exclaimed an old lady from Novara in *Tempo di Roma*, when a SWISS GUARD prevented her from entering to see her son, a gardener in the Vatican. In *The Count of Monte Cristo*, even though justice is finally rendered in Rome, it was not at St. Peter's but rather in the CATACOMBS where Danglars was held by bandits devoted to the count. Rome was disappointing and could not help being so, since, as Julien Gracq wrote, "to answer . . . to a name that has become nothing but a fable, like Rome, is a wager that cannot be kept." Even Father Mionnet, one of the only characters to find in the Vatican the justification for his "aristocratic" dreams and "success of power" notices that "everywhere the names were larger than objects." For the narrator of Nievo's *Memoirs of an Italian*, Rome's "traditions, memories, glory, majesty make of the city "not only the capital of Italy, but also the capital of the world." Except the new pope, Pius IX, "did not understand or did not want to understand the meaning of the applause that praised him to the heavens, and was a disappointment to the hopes that his partisans for unity had placed on him." Likewise, in Didier's *Rome souterraine*, the papacy was, for Cardinal Petralia, "the last stage of the human spirit, the purest and most perfect social form . . . ."

For Zola's Pierre Froment, Rome was "a center where the entire world converges and ends, but where nothing grows from the soil itself, struck with sterility from the very beginning." All new ideas crashed against "the hard, impregnable bronze door walling in the Vatican, . . . separating it from the rest of the world, so solidly that nothing had entered in for three centuries." It had become a "country guarded by jealous and treacherous dragons," personified in the novel by a frightful gallery of ecclesiastics: Nani, the loveable manipulator, and the assassin Santobono, who was delegated by Sanguinetti, whose "sole goal was the TIARA" (*Rome*). Pierre despaired; Rome spoiled "his dream of a rejuvenated and triumphant Christianity." It became a "city of disaster where he [left] the last shreds of his faith." The successive visits to Cardinal Sarno and his apparent antithesis, the "seductive" Msgr. Fornaro, who had reported his book to the Congregation of the INDEX, made him imagine with terror "what the victorious . . . Church . . . would do to human thought, with courts to judge, police to execute . . . . Everything would collapse into the infantile and the absurd."

"You would take me for a wretched, irritable satirist," said Stendhal, "if I explained the kind of truths that are taught [in the Roman College]. I believe it took a BULL in order to allow—albeit only hypothetically—the system claiming that the earth revolves around the sun to be taught there." Chateaubriand also noticed, with even greater exasperation, this fossilization of papal power. Nevertheless, there would be "immense things for the Holy See to do today . . . , but these ideas cannot penetrate old skulls in the SACRED COLLEGE; the cardinals who have reached the end of their years pass on an elective royalty that soon expires seated on the double ruins of Rome, the popes seem to be struck only by the power of death."

The idea of frustrated hope comes back like a leitmotif: "so much is it true that in Rome things finish, rather than begin" (Modiano, *Livret de famille*), regardless of the point of view adopted. Montfanon, the old papal zouave in Paul Bourget's *Cosmopolis*, cannot stop weeping over the end of his world: "the screening of the old residence

of Pope Urban VII, Sixtus V's successor," was "almost as tragic as the king's [assassination] in 93 . . . . It was the beginning of the agony of that other very great thing that was the Roman nobility."

Two Protestants, nevertheless, experienced a feeling of regeneration. For Goethe, "outside Rome people have no idea of what kind of education one gets there. One must be . . . reborn, and look at his old ideas, as one looks at one's baby shoes."

From her very first visit to St. Peter's, Mary Garland, the young American in Henry James's *Roderick Hudson* feels her entire past collapse as if "a wall in [her] mind had been knocked down at a stroke. Before [her] lies an immense new world, and it makes the old one, the poor little narrow familiar one [she has] always known seem pitiful." On the other hand, for Louis Veuillot, "there is no place on earth where death is so eloquent . . . , where the living make it speak so easily, where it is more honored, adorned, one might even say celebrated. . . ." The death bed of Dario and Benedetta marked the end of Pierre Froment's dream of "a Rome of youth and salvation . . . . Catholic Rome, princely Rome, was dead." From the carriage that brought him back to the station, he saw only a "flat plain, dotted with rubble . . . with nothing living on it but tangles of snakes and bands of rats." Anselme, in *Rome souterraine*, contemplated "that Rome that was twice the queen of the world . . . , stretched out there before his feet, like a cadaver." In Stendahl's *Promenades dans Rome*, "it was necessary to hurry to see the ceremonies of a religion that was either going to change or become extinct." In his *Rome, Naples, and Florence*, "Everything [in Rome] is decadence, everything is memory, everything is dead."

But Roman death can be sweet. Chateaubriand and Stendhal experience the same temptation. "Rome is wonderful for forgetting everything, despising everything, and dying," one of them wrote the evening of Holy Wednesday in 1829. While on the subject of the convent of St. Onofrio, where le Tasse came to die, the other declared: "It is perhaps one of the most beautiful spots on earth to die. The view of Rome from there, so wide, so beautiful, that city of tombs and memories, must make this last step of detachment from things of the earth less painful."

But far from these peaceful ends, some writers emphasize Roman violence and cruelty. "Regarding the pope's State, I had to learn/To take thirst and hunger with patience: It is a pity how people there are so inhumane/How all is so dear and how they pinch," wrote Du Bellay. Stendhal asks, "Do you wish to be oppressed by everyone here, and destroyed?" (*Be Just and Humane*). Until the 19th century, papal power was more often than not portrayed in literature as violent. Editus, the sacristan of the Isle Sonnante, recommended the greatest silence before the Papagault to Pantagruel and Panurge, for "if he ever hears you blaspheming like that, my good men, you are lost. Do you see a basin there in his cage? Thence will come lightning and thunder, devils and tempests, by which you will be instantaneously buried a hundred feet below the earth" (Rabelais, *Fifth Book*).

For d'Aubigné, the popes, "Roman wolves," "monsters of Italy," belonged without distinction to "the sect of torture." In Antonio Fogazzaro's novel, *Il Santo*, one of the guests at the meeting of reformist Catholics organized by the philosopher Giovanni Selva urged the others to prudence, since "well they know, the great Fisherman of Galilee put fish in his pond, while the Fisher of Rome has them fry." On the same theme, Didier concluded the description of the "frightful carnage" awaiting Marius, condemned to being "*mazzolato*," with the cry: "There, O Jesus! man of sweetness and love, this is how they understand charity in your great vicar's metropolis!" The tone was even more brutal in Garibaldi's novel *Clelia*, written immediately after the battle of Mentana, where the priests, who had become "serpents . . . foxes . . . vultures," were responsible for all evil and capable of all kinds of violence. Dickens in his novel describes an execution, which was in no way a Roman specialty, but the indifference to the execution as evidenced by the lotto players is especially chilling: they "positioned themselves in the most appropriate places to count the drops of blood that trickled down, betting on the number."

The Romans, in Moravia's *Nouvelles Romaines* were willingly superstitious. Stendahl wrote: "Everyone here believes more in predictions than they do in the Gospels . . . ." Writing of the conclave following the death of Pius VII, "It might be said in passing that the Gospels do not seem to be given much credit in Rome . . . . The Roman people are," moreover, "shrewd, mocking, and satirical," totally disillusioned. "They are not sad; sadness requires a shred of hope." The Roman *popolani* for whom Belli's sonnets have become the voice, have a consistent ambiguous attitude regarding papal power. The pope, in *Li Baffutelli* and *El Papa nouvo*, was quite right to have the liberals and everyone opposing the regime imprisoned or hung, but "the opening of the conclave," in the sonnet of the same name, stirred up no hope. Whoever the pope might be: "He will begin by having the objects pawned returned,/Will release the thieves from prison/And then, after three or four weeks/As all the Holy Fathers who have preceded him/He will become, God forgive me, a real dog." A hundred years later Alexis Curvers observed: "The Romans are pensive. They have seen too much."

In the 20th century, besides a few anticlerical outbursts like those of Prevert, papal Rome aroused neither anger nor revolt, but rather a feeling of emptiness, abandon. Paleari composed a revealing apologue for Mattia Pascal: the one about the *acquasantiera* and the *portacenere*, the holy water basin and the ashtray. His daughter, Adriana,

had put a holy water basin in the renter's room, which he inadvertently used as an ashtray. The girl took it to wash in, and broke it. Paleari picked up what was left of it and thereafter used it for the same purpose as had Mattia Pascal. "Well," he explained, "Rome's fate is the same. In their own way, the popes made it into a holy water font, and we Italians have used it as an ashtray. We have come from all over to tap the ashes off our cigar, which is the symbol of the frivolity of our wretched lives and the bitter, poisonous pleasure that it gives us." Something has been missing ever since. In the course of another nocturnal walk in St. Peter's square, Mattia Pascal had, without the revolt, the same impression of unfathomable solitude as Pierre Froment after his interview with Leo XIII. In both cases, only the water from the fountains "seemed to be alive," "providing a small voice, a murmur." For not having believed in the reality of the meeting in St. Peter's square that Marcella had promised him for seven o'clock one winter's evening, "Bassetto," the "little" protagonist in a Moravia story, ruined his life. He left the "desert of paving stones" too soon, hopeless, crushed: "Never had I felt as small as that evening, fleeing like a rat in that immensity, under the obelisque with the disappearing peak, up there in the darkness."

Rome was also the city of breakups. Dorothea Casaubon discovered there the extent of her solitude, while in the Vatican library her husband was lost in the research necessary to his great work, *The Key to All Mythologies*, which would ultimately provide the key to nothing. While Cécile was working, the narrator in Butor's *La Modification* intended a visit to the Vatican which, because of the imminent change in life in which he still believed, was charged with special meaning: "So this [visit] will be the first of all those that you will make out of necessity a while from now, without her, after she rejoins you in Paris . . . ; this visit . . . will be like the premonitory ceremony of her absence." Cécile, at any rate, refused to go to the Vatican, "which she abhorred" for being the symbol of Christianity, this "insinuating poison" which, she declared to her lover, "deprived me of so many things and now is depriving me of you." Marie, the friend of Schnier (the "comical artist" in Böll's *The Grimace*), had likewise refused, but for opposite reasons: "visiting Rome with [him who] would [nevertheless] have gladly gone to see the pope with her." But, according to her, "there was something perverse" for an agnostic . . . "wanting to acclaim Saint Peter." The religious difference became unbearable for the young woman, who marries a "member of the national federation of Catholic action," and left for Rome on her honeymoon. Schnier, in despair, thought about going to sing, and then begging, on the stairway of the Bonn train station, while he waited for trains to arrive from Italy, from Rome, and "if Marie managed to pass by [him] without embracing [him], there was always suicide . . . ."

The absence of the pope and papal power can be ardently wished for, as it is for political reasons in the book by Aldo Alberti, *La Lega delle Dame per il trasferimento del papato nelle Americhe*, published in 1986 but set in the years of stuggle for Italian unity. Perina Toso, from Venice, hopes Pius IX "might go do his noble business elsewhere and let us take care of" what he called our "shameful unity." The pope hardly appears in F. Rolfe's *Hadrian VII*, Guido Morselli's *Roma senza Papa*, and Morris S. West's *The Clowns of God*, In Thomas Mann's *The Holy Sinner*, Grigors, who after a long penance for having unknowingly committed Oedipus's sin with his mother, becomes the best sovereign pontiff that can be imagined: "His tolerance and piety rivaled the unshakable firmness he evinced on occasion. His boldness in inciting Divinity to clemency . . . , was a sensation throughout Christianity."

It was precisely on the absence of the pope, supposedly kidnapped and imprisoned by Freemasons in the underground passages of CASTEL SANT'ANGELO, that André Gide's *Les Caves du Vatican* was constructed. Here, Rome and the Vatican became a place of illusion, of doubt and confusion for the victims of the hoax. "Life was becoming decidedly too complicated" for poor Amédée Fleurissoire. "Whom could be trusted, if not the pope? And as soon as the cornerstone gave way . . . nothing more could be considered true." There was nothing astounding in the pope ignoring supplications, since "he is not the real one . . . . The real pope has been confiscated," Amédée explains to his brother-in-law, Julius. Too late, everything had become "suspect."

All these authors who, in one way or another, evoke the pope, the Vatican, or religious life—or their absence—are strangely, foreigners in Rome. There are contemporary Italian novels, such as Esla Morante's *La Storia* and Moravia's *Nouvelles Romaines*, that deal with the absence of the pope in a more radical fashion. In *La Storia*, the "pope, with his glasses," appears in Ida's dreams, just as do other celebrities of the times: "Hitler with his little mustache, . . . and the emperor of Ethiopia with his umbrella," all wrapped up in a kind of whirlwind where the young woman's missing parents are likewise caught. But her son, little Giuseppe, grows up with no religious reference—"neither baptized nor circumcised, and no parish interested in redeeming him"— in the benevolent indifference of the neighborhood that asks nothing about his origins. On the other hand, the arrival of a monk causes stupor among the refugees of Pietralata: "The women, among others, supposed the monk was a false monk, an anarchist in disguise, perhaps, or maybe even some generalissimo from the high spheres." The unfortunate Carlo Vivaldi, who was being sought by the *frate*, likewise became "in their eyes . . . a bizarre and ambiguous adventurer: perhaps linked to a foreign power: or the Vatican?" Someone "even hypothe-

sizes that he is a noble from His Majesty's retinue . . . keeping his identity unknown."

For Moravia, the *Nouvelles Romaines* were "a transcription of Belli's work in the present," which Palazzeschi, in *Rome*, likewise considered to be "the true guide to Rome." The little space given to the Church and the Vatican in the *Nouvelles* is a measure of the change in Roman life, at least in the picture given by Moravia. In it, they appear seldom, and always negatively, in the background, by default. Alfredo, the son of a hawker of pious objects on Piazza Minerva, was unquestionably missing something. Everyone around him was trying to get him to "not question" the reasons his wife left him: "These things happen." Two "disadvantaged" couples, respectively, seek the solution to their unhappiness in a church, and neither finds it. One couple, convinced that the treasures found in churches are there "to do good" for those who need it, such as themselves, locked themselves up in a church to steal a lapis lazuli necklace. The matter ended up in the commissioner's office. The other couple tried to leave their seventh child in a church frequented by rich people so that adoption could save him from the hovel of Tormarancio. They leave the church on Via dei Condotti, and then the one on the Corso, without leaving the baby; then they are chased away by the sacristan of the third one, on Piazza Venezia, because the mother was nursing the baby. St. Peter's, suggested by the father, was immediately rejected: "No, that's a real parade ground . . . they wouldn't even see him." Finally, exhausted, they leave the baby in a comfortable automobile.

In Pasolini's *Ragazzi di vita*, the protagonist lives and dies far from St. Peter's. Likewise, in the 1950s, Paolo, the little hoodlum in Tennessee Williams's *Roman Spring of Mrs. Stone*, where Rome was the place of emptiness and drifting par excellence, replaced the priest with the hairdresser. "Paolo, who was a lukewarm Catholic, did not go to confession but went to Renato for a similar purpose: to give a meaning and a kind of backbone to his butterfly existence."

By the end of the 20th century, papal Rome was really no longer a literary issue: Stendhal's malice, Hugo's fury, Garibaldi's insults, Belli's satires, and the chronicles of Trilussa and Pascarella were cruelly missed. Jimmy, "weary . . . of [Rome's] secrets not penetrated," and "beaten . . . by his own inconsistency," concluded at the end of *Tempo di Roma*: "This is how all things in the world end, they tire of existing because we tire of them . . . ."

Marie-Paule Boutry

Bibliography

About, E. *Tolla*, Paris, 1855.

Albérès, M. *Stendhal et le sentiment religieux*, Paris, 1956.

Alberti, A. *La Lega delle Dame per il trasferimento del Papato nelle Americhe*, Palerma, 1986.

Belli, G. *Sonetti*, Milan, 1952 (composed between 1830 and 1847).

Böll, H. *Ansichten eines Clowns (La Grimace)*, Cologne, 1963.

Boulier, J. "Les Trois Villes," *Europe*, 46, 1968.

Bourget, P. *Cosmopolis*, Paris, 1892.

Bulwer-Lytton, E. *Les Derniers Jours de Pompéi*, London, 1834.

Butor, M. *La Modification*, Paris, 1957.

Corneille, P. *Polyeucte*, Paris, 1643.

Crouzet, M. *Stendhal et l'italianité*, Paris, 1982.

Curvers, A. *Tempo di Roma*, Paris, 1957.

Danadoni, E. *Antonio Fogazzaro*, Bari, 1939.

D'Andlau, B. *Chateaubriand et les "Martyrs," naissance d'une épopée*, Paris, 1952.

D'Annunzio, G. *Il Piacere*, Milan, 1889.

D'Aubigné, A. *Les Tragiques*, Paris, 1616.

De Chateaubriand, F. R. *Le Génie du christianisme*, Paris, 1802; *Les Martyrs*, Paris, 1809; *Mémoires d'outre-tombe*, Paris, 1848.

De Goncourt, E. and J. *Madame Gervaisais*, Paris, 1869.

De Montaigne, M. *Journal de voyage*, Paris, 1774 (written 1580–2).

De Sade, D. A. F. *Juliette*, Paris, 1797; *Voyage en Italie*, Paris, 1967 (written 1775).

De Staël, Mme. *Corinne ou l'Italie*, Paris, 1807.

De Villefosse, L. "Rome," *Europe*, 83–4, 1952.

Dickens, C. *Little Dorrit*, London, 1857; *Pictures of Italy*, London, 1846.

Dickinson, G. *Du Bellay in Rome*, 1960.

Didier, C. *Rome souterraine*, Brussels, 1837.

Du Bellay, J. *Les Regrets*, Paris, 1558.

Dumas, A. *Acté*, Paris, 1839; *Ascanio*, Paris, 1843; *Le Comte de Monte-Cristo*, Paris, 1844–5; *Le Corricolo*, Paris, 1843.

Eliot, G. *Middlemarch*, London, 1872.

Febvre, L. *Le Problème de l'incroyance au XVIe siècle: La religion de Rabelais*, Paris, 1942.

Fogazzaro, A. *Il Santo*, Milan, 1905.

Fumaroli, M. preface to *Madame Gervaisais*, Paris, 1982.

Garibaldi, G. *Clelia*, 1870.

Gide, A. *Les Caves du Vatican*, Paris, 1914.

Gogol, N. "Rome," *Nouvelles*, Paris, 1938.

Gracq, J. *Autour des sept collines*, Paris, 1988.

Hugo, V. *Les Châtiments*, Brussels, 1853.

James, H. *Roderick Hudson*, Boston, 1875.

Lazagna, P. and C. *Pasolini di fronte al problema religioso*, Bologna, 1970.

Lecercle, J. L. "De l'art impassible à la littérature militante; *Les Trois Villes* d'É. Zola," *La Pensée*, 46, 1953.

Mann, T. *The Holy Sinner*, Paris, 1952.

Marchese, A. "Il fu Mattia Pascal, anatomia di un romanzo," *L'analisi letteraria*, Turino, 1976.

Marchi, G. "La Roma di Pirandello," *Studi romani*, 25, 1977.

Michea, R. *Le "Voyage en Italie" de Goethe*, Paris, 1945.

Modiano, P. *Livret de famille*, Paris, 1976.

Montheilhet, H. *Néropolis*, Paris, 1984.

Morante, E. *La Storia*, Turin, 1974.

Moravia, A. *La Ciociara*, Milan, 1957; *Nuovi Racconti romani*, Milan, 1959; *Racconti romani*, Milan, 1954.

Morselli, G. *Roma senza Papa*, Milan, 1974.

Moureau, F., and Bernoulli, R. *Autour du "Journal de voyage," de Montaigne (1580–1980)*, Geneva and Paris, 1982.

Muscetta, C. *Cultura e poesia di G. G. Belli*, Milan, 1961.

Nieto, I. *Confessioni di un Italiano*, Florence, 1867.

Ouvrard, P. *Zola et le prêtre*, Paris, 1986.

Palazzeschi, A. *Roma*, Milan, 1953; *Le sorelle Materassi*, Milan, 1934.

Pascarella, C. *Prose*, Turin, 1920.

Pasolini, P. P. *Ragazzi di vita*, Milan, 1955 and *Una vita violenta*, Milan, 1959.

Pirandello, L. *Il fu Mattia Pascal*, Rome, 1904.

Prévert, J. *Paroles*, Paris, 1945.

Rabelais, F. *Le Cinquième Livre*, Paris, 1564.

Richard, J. P. *Paysage de Chateaubriand*, Paris, 1967.

Rolfe, F. (Baron Corvo), *Hadrien VII*, London, 1904; *Don Tarquinio*, London 1905.

Romains, J. "Mission à Rome," *Les Hommes de bonne volonté*, Paris, 1936.

Siciliano, E. "Moravia e Roma," *Studi romani*, 39, 1991.

Sienkiewicz, H. *Quo Vadis?*, Warsaw, 1896.

Stendhal, *Chroniques italiennes*, Paris, 1839; *Promenades dans Rome*, Paris, 1829; *Rome, Naples et Florence*, Paris, 1817.

Taine, H. *Voyage en Italie*, Paris, 1866.

Ternois, R. "La genèse du premier chapitre de *Rome*," *Mélanges Mario Roques*, III, Paris, 1952.

Trilussa (C. A. Salustri), *Favole*, Rome, 1920.

van Rossum, F. *Critique du roman: Essai sur "La Modification*," Paris, 1970.

Veuillot, L. *Le Parfum de Rome*, Paris, 1862.

Von Goethe, J. W. *Die römische Elegien*, 1793. (1788–9); *Italienische Reise (Travels in Italy)*, 1817.

West, M. L. *The Clowns of God*, 1980; *Lazarus*, 1990.

Wiesman, N. *Fabiola*, 1854.

Williams, T. *The Roman Spring of Mrs. Stone*, 1950.

Zola, E. *Mes Voyages*, Paris, 1958; and *Rome*, Paris, 1896.

Zola et son temps: Lourdes, Rome, Paris, Dijon, 1961.

IMPRIMATUR. The term imprimatur refers to the authorization given by the ordinary of a place to publish (*licentia edendi*) not only books but also "any writing destined for publication," as specified in canon 824, section 2, of the CODE OF CANON LAW of 1983. This authorization is based on the right and the duty of the ministers of the Church to ensure that no attack be made on the faith or morals of the faithful by any means of social communication and to require that the writings of the faithful concerning faith or morals be submitted to their judgment.

Quite obviously, censorship of writings prior to publication was exercised only after the invention of the printing press, following abuses that had been committed. It is in Germany that the first measures to protect the faith were taken, in Cologne (1475) and in Mainz (1486). The papal legate for the jurisdiction of Venice banned (1491) all printing of books by the faithful concerning faith or ecclesiastical matters without the authorization of the bishop. Then ALEXANDER VI (constitution *Inter multiplices*, 1 June 1501) banned the printing of all writing—without the bishop's prior, and non-compensated, authorization to publishers in the ecclesiastical provinces of Cologne, Magdeburg, Mainz, and Trier—under threat of excommunication *latae sententiae*.

This prohibition became general at the LATERAN V COUNCIL (LEO X, constitution *Inter sollicitudines*, 4 May 1515): no work could be published without obtaining two specific permissions: in Rome, that of the vicar of the Roman pontiff and that of the Master of the Sacred Palace; in the diocese, that of the bishop and that of the inquisitor. The Council of TRENT intended to draw up rules for the INDEX. Due to lack of time, it was unable to complete its task. The project was subsequently presented to PIUS IV, who approved it. One of its measures had come from the Lateran V council, although it was strengthened, since sending a manuscript elsewhere to be printed was only to be done with the authorization of one's ordinary. Books by regulars were supposed to be examined by individuals belonging to other religious orders.

BENEDICT XIV prescribed a method for examining and forbiddng books (constitution *Sollicita ac provida*, 9 July 1753). Censorship took place in regard to all books, including those on secular subjects. This is understandable in the context of the time, where it was not rare for authors to deal with the most diverse subjects. PIUS IX reduced the rigorousness of the procedure in the PAPAL STATES (letter to bishops, 2 June 1848) and decided that censorship applied exclusively to books dealing with the following issues: Holy Scriptures, theology, Church history, canon law, natural theology, and ethics, as well as the other religious and moral disciplines. As a general rule, it also applied to all writings dealing primarily with faith or morals. This list of categories would remain almost unchanged in the Code of Canon Law of 1917 (c. 1385, sec. 1, 1).

LEO XIII abolished provisions that had become inapplicable, while retaining others (constitution *Officiorum ac Munerum*, 25 January 1897) that later became part of the Code of 1917. Under the heading "De praevia censure librorum eorumque prohibitione," canons 1384–1405 were divided into two chapters applying to censorship prior to publication and the prohibition of books. PIUS X was the first to use the terms *imprimatur* and *nihil obstat* (i.e., "it may be printed" and "no opposition to publication," respectively) in a legal text; this was in the ENCYCLICAL *Pascendi* (8 September 1907), and later in the *motu propio Sacrorum Antistitum* (1 September 1910), although this terminology was not used in the Code of Canon Law.

Pius X deplored that the *imprimatur* was sometimes given lightly. "Do not be too credulous," he wrote to bishops, "because the author has been able to get an *imprimatur* elsewhere: that *imprimatur* may be apocryphal, or it may have been given without careful examination, or with an excess of benevolence or confidence in the author" (*Sacrorum Antistitum*). In fact, the Holy See has felt obliged to forbid or to withdraw from the market some works already published with the *imprimatur* of the ordinary of the place of publication. This is why ordinaries have been invited to show the greatest of vigilance and to rely on "truly competent" censors (Congregation of the Holy Office, 21 March 1941, 17 April 1942).

The Congregation for the Doctrine of the Faith, which took the place of the Congregation of the HOLY OFFICE (*motu proprio Integrae Servandae*, 7 December 1965), announced that the Index of forbidden books had ceased to exist and was no longer part of ecclesiastical law (notification, 14 June 1966 and decree 15 November 1966). The Congregation for the Doctrine of the Faith published a new regulation for examining teachings (*Nova Agendi Ratio in Doctrinarum Examine*, 15 January 1971). And a further regulation was announced by JOHN PAUL II (Apostolic constitution *Pastor Bonus*, 28 June 1988).

The entire matter of censorship of books prior to publication was reorganized (Congregation for the Doctrine of the Faith, decree *Ecclesiae Pastores*, 19 March 1975) in the late 20th century. These norms were incorporated almost in their entirety into canons 822–32 of the Code of Canon Law of 1983, under the title "Means of Social Communication, Particularly Books." The differences from the Code of 1917 are significant. No longer is a list of books submitted for precensorship; however, all books dealing with faith or morals are reviewed, according to the discretion of the ecclesiastical authority. The specific law should thus determine which books need precensorship (c. 823, sec. 2). Nevertheless, the Church does reserve the right and the duty to oversee the purity of faith and morals. This is one of the areas belonging to the Congregation for the Doctrine of the Faith, as has been continually pointed out (Paul VI, *motu proprio Integrae Servandae*; apostolic constitution *Regimini Eccle-*

siae Universae, 15 August 1966; John Paul II, apostolic constitution *Pastor Bonus*). The local bishop, who has the duty of preaching the Gospel to the entire world (apostolic constitution *Lumen Gentium*, no. 23), has "the duty and the right to examine, even to reprove and to condemn, books and magazines harmful to faith or morals" (directive *Ecclesiae Imago* on the pastoral ministry of bishops, c. 823, sec. 2). The competent authority is the ordinary of the place of publication; a bishop emeritus can thus not give an *imprimatur*.

The Code of Canon Law of 1983 introduced the new option of prior approval, which is required for the following categories of works: (a) books of Scripture and their translations into vernacular languages (c. 825), including the ecumenical translations accompanied by suitable explanations (and taking into account the "directives relative to interconfessional cooperation in the translation of the Bible must be approved by the Holy See or the particular conference of bishops, the office of the secretary for the Unity of Christians, and the executive committee of the Universal Bible Alliance, 1 June 1968); (b) catechisms of Christian doctrine must be approved by the local ordinary (c. 827, sec. 1), and catechisms prepared by a conference of bishops for their territories by the Holy See (c. 775 sec. 2); (c) basic texts used in instruction relative to the Scriptures, theology, canon law, Church history, or religious or moral disciplines require approval by the appropriate ecclesiastical authority (c. 827, sec. 2); (d) the translations of liturgical books prepared by conferences of bishops and of the ordinary of the place for reeditions require approval by the Holy See (c. 826, sec. 1 and 2); (e) prayer books (c. 826, sec. 3), books dealing with religious or moral questions, or books displayed, sold, or given away in churches or oratories (c. 827, sec. 4) require approval by the local ordinary; (f) reeditions of collections of its decrees or acts (c. 828). The *imprimatur* is recommended for other books that focus on the same subjects. The question of knowing if the ordinary of the place can demand that a book be submitted to him before publication is much debated (Congregation for the Doctrine of the Faith, response, 25 June 1980).

Nihil obstat and *imprimatur* are meant to guarantee that writing can be published without harm to faith or morals. The *approbatio* goes further. Indeed, making sure that a catechism, for example, does not contain errors is not sufficient. It still must not contain serious gaps or deficiencies. Each of the categories of books listed above has its requirements. And the approval of the ordinary of the place may be insufficient in certain cases, thus necessitating that of the Holy See. Approval or permission to publish is valid for the original writing but not for new editions or translations (c. 829). It is required for any writing destined for publication. The determining factor is thus the *public* nature of the work. The legal arrange-

ment is therefore not limited to printed texts; it takes into account modern methods of reproduction. Since these norms restrain the free exercise of individual rights, they are interpreted strictly (c. 18). Consequently, precensorship does not apply to other ways of circulating ideas, such as sound recordings or visual reproductions (c. 824). The code is meant specifically for radio or television broadcasts (c. 772, sec. 2 and 831, sec. 2) and refers decisions regarding the norms in question back to the conference of bishops. Members of religious institutes must obtain permission from their superior in order to publish writings on religious or moral questions (c. 832).

When the *imprimatur* and the *nihil obstat* are accorded, mention is to be made in the work, not in a general way as could be done previously by resorting to a phrase like "with ecclesiastical approval," but in a specific way, indicating the name of the individual granting it, and the day and the place of the concession (Pontifical Council for the Interpretation of Legislative Texts, response, 20 June 1987).

The faithful are not to write for branches of the press that openly attack the Catholic religion and good moral standards, except for a just and reasonable cause. Clerics and members of religious institutions will have to obtain the permission of the ordinary of the place, permission that concerns not the content of their intervention but the presence of such a signature in this type of periodical (c. 831). Canon 1369 suggested a "just punishment" for those who, in their writings distributed to the public, or in other means of social communication, blaspheme or do serious harm to good moral standards, utter insults, or encourage hatred or contempt for the religion or the Church.

In the late 20th century, a certain number of sanctions have been imposed. For example, the Holy See forbade the teaching of Charles Curran (1986) because of his stand in matters of sexual morals; of Hans Küng (1979) because of his theories on papal infallibility; of Eugen Drewermann (1991), in the dogmatic domain; of Jacques Polier, in France (1979), for his conception of the Resurrection; and of Louis Bermejo, in India (1988), concerning the identity of the Church. Moreover, certain works or theses have received warnings, without sanctions: Leonardo Boff, in Brazil (1972), Antoine Delzant, in France (1982), and Edward Schillbeeckx, in the Netherlands (1986).

Dominique Le Tourneau

Bibliography

Baura, E. "Il permessa per la pubblicazione di scritti," *Ius Ecclesiae*, 1 (1989), 249–56.

Beste, U., and Noirot, M. "Censura praevia librorum," in P. Palazzini, *Dictionarium morale et cononicum*, 1 (1962), 648–51.

Bonnet, M., "L'imprimatur est-il encore nécessaire?" *Les Cahiers du droit ecclésial*, 2 (1985), 169–86.

Bride, A., "Imprimatur," *Catholicisme*, 5 (1962), 1370–72.

De Echeverría, L., "Regimen de las ediciones de material catequético," *Revista Española de Derecho Canónico*, 40 (1984), 41–62.

Des Valle, J. M. G., commentary to the canons 822–32, in Université de Navarre-Université Saint-Paul, *Code de droit canonique, édition bilingue et annotée sous la direction de E. Caparros, M. Thériault, J. Thorn*, 1990, 481–9.

Fuentes, J. A., "Respuestas de la CP para la interpretación auténtica del CIC de fecha 20.VI.1987," *Ius canonicum*, 28 (1988), 623–34.

García Escudero, J. M., "Censura y libertad," *Arbor* (1952), 177–97.

Gardiner, H. C., and Fortman, E. J. "Censorhip," *NCE* 3 (1967), 391–4.

Grazioli, A., "Censura e licenza nelle pubblicazioni dei sacerdoti," *Palestra del clero*, 8 (1929), 22–3; 10 (1931), 400–3.

Jacquemet, G., "Édition," *Catholicisme*, 3 (1952), 1372–4.

Jombart, É. "Censure des livres," *DDC*, III, 1942, 157–69.

Marsot, G., "Censure," *Catholicisme*, 2 (1949), 797–9.

Morán, S. A., "De la previa censura de los libros de su prohibición," *Revista Española de Derecho Canónico*, 13 (1956), 67–102.

Urrutia, F. J., "De limitibus libertatis scribendi iuxta legem canonicam," *Periodica de re morali, canonica, liturgica*, 65 (1976), 531–45.

Wiest, C., *The Precensorship of Books*, Washington, D.C., 1953.

INCARDINATION. The institution of incardination, which began early in the Church, refers to the ministerial service that a cleric gives to the local Church. The word comes from *cardo*, "hinge," and calls to mind the idea of a connection point around which the incardinated cleric moves, as the door on its hinges. From the very beginning, *incardinare* signified the joining of a cleric to a church, or *titulus*. Clerics so joined were called *cardinales*, or even *intitulati*, or *titulati*, as opposed to those who were not joined and who were described as *vagi*, *acephali*, or *absoluti*. It was absolutely necessary that there not be "gyrovague" or "errant or lost" clerics, according to the statement of a Roman COUNCIL of 826 (Gratian's DECRETUM, dist. LXXII, c. 1). Church discipline in this matter has passed through different phases. Incardination goes back to earlier centuries, for from that period clerics were only ordained for the service of a particular Church, namely those who were necessary or useful for a particular church building in the diocese to which they were automatically incardinated. A vestige of this discipline is maintained in assigning titles or diaconates to cardinals (c. 350 from the CODE OF CANON LAW of 1983).

The first councils insisted on the necessity of an almost indissoluble bond between the cleric and the Church for which he was ordained (the bishop who sought to be transferred to another diocese was even described as adulterous at the COUNCIL of Alexandria in 339). It was thus the rigorous interdiction of any change to another Church, which often took place for less than worthy motives. The Council of Arles, in 314, demanded that a cleric who changed dioceses without sufficient reason be deposed (c. 2 and 21; also the *Canones Apostolorum*, c. 14).

In 325, the Council of Nicaea determined that "it is not permitted for a bishop or other cleric to move from one city to another . . . . If any cleric attempts to escape from this prohibition, his move to another church must be considered invalid and the cleric must be returned to the church for which he was ordained bishop, priest or deacon" (c. 15, included in Gratian's DECRETUM, caus. VII, q. I, c. 19). The interdiction was renewed at the Council of Antioch, in 341 (c. 21), at the Council of Sardica, in 347 (c. 1), at Council III of Carthage, in 397 (c. 38), and so on. It was not, however, always enforced, such that St. Gregory of Nazianzus considered it to have been abrogated by custom. Council III of Carthage itself had studied the possibility of authorizing movement to another diocese, to encourage a better distribution of the clergy among the African Churches. Indeed, the interdiction was mainly disciplinary. The Council of Chalcedon, in 451, renewed the same prohibition (c. 20). It is thus the prohibition of ordinations called "absolute" or "without title," the church being the ordination title or *titulus*. A number of national and provincial councils reiterated the same norm: Carthage (348, c. 5, and 397, c. 21) and Milev (402), in Africa; Toledo I (400, c. 12), Toledo II (527, c. 2), and Seville II (619, c. 3), in Spain; Tours (460, c. 11), Orleans (549, c. 5), and Epaone (517, c. 5) in Gaul. In the 8th and 9th centuries, a change of church with the agreement of the bishop began to be considered lawful.

In effect from the 12th century, *ordinationes absolutae* or absolute ordinations were accepted, first in practice, then in legal texts, following the disappearance of common accumulations of goods for the sustenance of the clergy, and their replacement with individual shares, which became BENEFICES (a system that the Vatican II Council abolished). One additional factor was the growing influence of universities, to which clerics flocked in large numbers, with the encouragement of popes like ALEXANDER II, who authorized the taking of the benefices of nonresidents, unless the nonresident in question was a cleric pursuing studies (decretal *ad Episc. Eboracensem*, c. *Fraternitati*, 5 X, *de cleric. non resi-*

dent., III, 4). In 1179, Lateran III Council forbade (c. 5) the practice of absolute ordinations while allowing them in a case where the patrimonial goods were insufficient for the support of the cleric, thus opening the way to a new title of ordination called *titulus patrimonii* or title of patrimony (C. *Episcopus*, 4, X, *de praebendis*, III, 3: *qui posset sibi necessaria comparare ex bonis patrimonialibus* is not strictly related to incardination), which INNOCENT III instituted in 1208 (DECRETAL, X, 5, 23). The cleric thus acquired unlimited freedom to change dioceses, even without the consent of his bishop. Another practice developed during the same period: the institution of a *titulus beneficii* or granting by a bishop of a benefice to a cleric in his diocese, a title that consisted of no obligation to reside within the boundaries of the diocese. By increasing ordinations without incardination, these two "titles" greatly facilitated the movement of clerics from one diocese to another to obtain a benefice, with less-than-happy consequences for the discipline of the clerics.

The Council of TRENT reacted to this situation with a moderate stance. It decreed the ordinary rule to be ordination after the bishop has provided the ordained individual with a benefice: the *titulus patrimonii* could be allowed in a case "of necessity or usefulness to the Churches" (session XXI, cap. 2, *De Reformatione*). At the same time, it decreed that "in the future no one may be ordained who is not attached [*adscribatur*] to the Church for the service of which he was accepted, so that there is no longer a cleric of variable or uncertain residence" (session XXIII, cap. 16, *De Reformatione*). The application of this measure, as well as others, of the Council of Trent was slow and uneven. This was all the more true, since incardination without concession of a benefice or a definite office only obligated the cleric to perform a limited number of sacred duties. These functions, moreover, were limited to a *locus* or particular territory (cathedral, parish, etc.), since the incardination was made in relation to this *locus* and not in relation to the diocese. These circumstances led to mitigating the discipline drawn up at Trent. INNOCENT XIII (constitution *Apostolici Ministerii*, 13 March 1723, for Spain), and Benedict XIII (constitution *In Supremo*, 23 September 1724), among others, moved in this direction. The Council of Trent's decree was applied especially in conferring minor orders and tonsure. But the spread of seminaries made the *adscriptio* required by the council unnecessary, since it was not possible to carry out the duties it entailed. This was what BENEDICT XIV noted (*De Synodo Dioecesana*, I, lib. XI, c. 2, nos. 8 and 13).

Until the end of the 18th century, a cleric not endowed with a residential benefice or having reasonable grounds to move to another Church could not be retained in his original diocese.

Changes in the 19th century led to an appreciable reduction in the number of ecclesiastical benefices. More-over, it became increasingly impossible to ensure a stable and sufficient *titulus patrimonii*. In view of this situation, Roman congregations and bishops sought solutions. There then appeared, arising out of the law, the *titulus missionis* for the MISSION territories under the Congregation for the PROPAGATION OF THE FAITH; the *titulus servitii dioecesani*, notably in France and Belgium; and the *titulus mensae*, the *titulus administrationis*.

Roman jurisprudence inspired by these new titles, which all strengthened the bond of a cleric to his diocese, affirmed that the bishop could keep a cleric in his diocesan clergy, even against his will. A jurisprudential practice was thus becoming established. The Congregation of the Council ratified it: "Ordinaries have the certain right, if necessitated by the demands of their churches, to forbid priests—even if they were ordained to the title of the patrimony—to leave the diocese without their consent, even if these priests have obtained a residential benefice elsewhere, such as in Rome. However, they must assure them the means to live properly in their diocese" (decree, 22 December 1894).

In addition to the Council of Trent's decrees, the discipline of incardination was made more specific by INNOCENT XII (constitution *Speculatores*, 4 November 1694) and by two decrees (Congregation of the council, *A Primis*, 20 July 1898; and 24 November 1906). The term incardination is of recent usage in ecclesiastical legislation, since it appeared for the first time in a decree of the Congregation for the council (20 July 1898). It was "canonized" by the CODE OF CANON LAW of 1917 (c. 111–17).

In the 1917 legislation, the typical method of incardination was receipt of the tonsure, by which a cleric was attached (*adscriptus*) to a diocese, or to a PRELATURE *nullius*, for whose service he was promoted (c. 111, sec. 2). For members of religious orders, this occurred by perpetual profession, which attached the cleric definitively and in an absolute way to his institute. The extraordinary method was the moving of a cleric already attached to a diocese via the receipt of tonsure to another diocese, in return for letters of perpetual and absolute incardination from the receiving diocese; this happened once the letters of excardination (or *exeat*), which were also perpetual and absolute, were received from the diocese *a quo* (c. 112). This discipline was imposed by the Congregation for the Council (decree *A Primis*, 29 July 1898). Oral or presumed incardination was invalid (Congregation of the council, decree, 15 September 1906). Incardination could also be implicit, by conferring a residential benefice (c. 114), by taking religious vows (c. 585), or by the return into his diocese of a member of a religious order secularized *in sacris*, released from his perpetual vows (c. 641, sec. 1). Incardination could only take place if it was needed by, or useful to, the diocese; after issue of evidence from the preceding ordinary about the qualities of the cleric; and after the interested party had declared under oath that he intended to devote himself throughout his whole life to the service of his new diocese (c. 117).

Excardination is the act by which a cleric leaves his diocese in order to be attached to another, or to a religious institute for simple profession or solemn profession (c. 115 and 585). But as there can be no *cleus vagus*, any excardination must necessarily by accompanied by an incardination. Explicit excardination is realized by letters of excardination; it must be definitive and absolute, that is to say, not dependent upon conditions. Implicit excardination takes place *ipso iure* when a cleric receives a residential benefice in a foreign diocese, with the express authorization of his ordinary; when a cleric receives a residential benefice in a foreign diocese and can count on letters from his ordinary authorizing him to remain *in perpetuum* outside his diocese; or when a secularized cleric expresses a perpetual profession in a religious institute. But excardination can only take place for a just reason and it cannot be imposed on a cleric against his will. It only takes effect when incardination in another diocese has taken place, about which the ordinary must notify the ordinary of origin at the earliest possible time (c. 116).

Incardination thus outlined in the Code of 1917 had a purely disciplinary content. It lost the service content that it previously had: the only service duty that incardination contained for a cleric was a duty of obedience (c. 218). Incardination was therefore not sufficient to specify the service duty of the cleric; the ordination title must be added to it. In addition, what was called for in this conception of incardination was the control that the ordinary exercised over a cleric and, to an excessive degree, over his private life, whereas the pastoral service rendered by the cleric was relegated to lesser importance. Moreover, it was shocking that the content of the duty of ministerial service could vary relative to the importance of the available patrimony to support the cleric. One would even have to allow that pastoral ministry was something extraordinary for the cleric.

The life of the Church and the changes that had occurred in civil society again contributed to an evolution of the institution of incardination and excardination. First of all, the Church concerned herself with a better distribution of the clergy (Consistorial congregation, *Litterae Circulares ad Excmos ac Revmos Italiae Ordinarios*, 24 October 1951; PIUS XII, encyclical *Fidei Donum*, 21 April 1957). The Holy See, also, took into account the needs of groups of faithful requiring a specialized ministry. This primarily concerns priests who go to live in other countries, priests from Europe and from the Mediterranean coast who travel to America or the Philippines (Consistorial congregation, decree *Magni Semper Negotii*, 30 December 1918); priests from Latin America and the Philippines who wish to move to North America

(decree *Ad Fovendam*, 13 February 1960); priests wanting to teach in official centers (Congregation of the council, decree *Cum Plures*, 22 February 1927); priests from Europe emigrating to Australia and New Zealand (Congregation of PROPAGANDA FIDE, decree *Ad Tuendam*, 21 October 1948); spiritual care of the Greek and Ruthenian ordinariates in the United States (Congregation for the Eastern Churches, decree *Cum Data*, 1 March 1929); Eastern priests emigrating to America and Australia to practice their ministry with the faithful of their rite (decree *Qua Sollerti*, 23 December 1929); and clerics of the Eastern rite located outside their patriarchate or region (instruction *Quo Facilior*, 26 September 1932).

A second concern involved emigrants, sailors, and refugees. This entailed the nomination of a prelate for the refugees in Italy (Consistorial congregation, *Notificazione circa la costituzione di un Prelato per l'emigrazione italiana*, 22 October 1920); the creation of a body to facilitate emigration (Pius XII, apostolic constitution *Exsul Familia*, 1 August 1952); and the organization of the Work of the Apostolate of the Sea (Consistorial congregation, *Leges Operis Apostolatus Maris, auctoritate Pii Div. Prov. Pp XII conditai*, 21 November 1957). A third concern was for vicariates for spiritual assistance to the armed forces (Consistorial congregation, instruction *Sollemne Semper*, 26 April 1951). A final concern was the prelature of the Mission of France, whose purpose was to furnish missionary clergy to the French dioceses with the fewest priests (Pius XII, APOSTOLIC CONSTITUTION *Omnium Ecclesiarium*, 15 August 1954).

In all the works and hierarchical structures just listed, it is noted that the concept of incardination from the code of 1917 is insufficient. Thus, a new legal term came into being, the *addictio*, or "aggregation," that is, a service relationship by which the cleric is legally obliged to devote himself completely to the pastoral ministry. The revision of incardination thus had a threefold goal: to assure a better geographical distribution of the clergy; to develop specialized apostolates that might be integrated into particular pastoral structures, distinct from territorial structures; and to permit consecrated ministers to change dioceses for serious personal reasons.

The Vatican II Council (1962–1965) marked a turning point in retaining the first two objectives stated above. Actually, it restored the early meaning of incardination, at once pastoral and pertaining to ministerial service, without altering its disciplinary objectives, thus providing more efficiently for the needs of particular Churches thanks to a better distribution of the clergy. The decree *Christus Dominus*, number 6, stipulated that, to the extent possible, bishops should take "care to send some of their priests into those missions or dioceses [it is a question of missions and countries needing clergy] in order to exercise the sacred ministry in a lasting or a transitory way." The decree *Presbyterorum Ordinis*, number 10, after inviting priests from countries rich in vocations "to be ready to leave willingly, with the permission of their ordinary or at his call, to exercise their ministry in countries, missions, or activities that suffer from a shortage of priests," decided that "the rules of incardination and excardination should be revised: while maintaining this very ancient institution, one must adapt it to the present pastoral needs," that is, to the above-mentioned objectives.

The decrees *Christus Dominus* and *Presbyterorum Ordinis* outlined a new concept of incardination that, much like agregation, demanded complete availability. Diocesan priests were called collaborators with the episcopal order, since, "incardinated or attached to a particular Church, they dedicated themselves entirely to its service, to care for a same portion of the flock" (decree *Christus Dominus*, no. 28). Incardination is thus an act of incorporation into the community or *presbyterium*. Its primary content is a bond of service between a cleric and the hierarchical structure of the Church, be it territorial or personal. It is no longer a simple bond of subordination to the bishop, but of incorporation to a particular Church in order to serve it, and through it, also to serve the universal Church. The service indeed comes first, with the disciplinary aspect as a consequence. Incardination is thus characterized by plenary service, stability, and a community aspect. It can also be deduced from council texts that agregation is a service relationship between a diocesan cleric and a pastoral structure whose content is plenary ministerial service. The bond of incardination is not only stable, but even relative, for any diocesan priest possesses the subjective public right to be granted excardination or agregation by his ordinary for reasons of ministerial service, except serious causes that future legislation must determine. This is a consequence of the universal mission of service communicated by ordination, which is perfectly compatible with incardination. If there is a return to the discipline of the early Church by making incardination an eminently pastoral institution that gives concrete expression to ministerial service, then there is also a break, since the sacred order is no longer considered to grant a concrete and particular mission.

This concrete manifestation first takes place by incardination, by virtue of which the cleric is destined to exercise his ministry within the setting of a particular Church or another particular hierarchical structure; and then, by the granting of an office or assigning duties determined through the intervention of the *missio canonica*. Incardination, or incorporation as a sacred minister to a particular Church or an equivalent entity, is, at the outset, a legal relationship that joins the cleric to the bishop on the one hand, and on the other, to the *presbyterium* and other believers. Because of this, the ordained minister gains rights

and duties toward them; likewise, believers have the right to receive spiritual assets in abundance (dogmatic constitution *Lumen Gentium*, no. 37; Code of 1983, c. 213). The duty of obedience of clerics to their bishop is restricted to their ministry, not to their private lives, which come under their sphere of personal autonomy.

According to Vatican II Council, the particular Church is a "portion of the people of God" (decree *Christus Dominus*, no. 11). The bishop is not the pastor of a territory, but of the community of believers that has been entrusted to him. The territory is no more than an element that serves to define that community of believers. Personal dioceses and personal prelatures (decree *Presbyterorum Ordinis*, no. 10) are equivalent to territorial structures. PAUL VI applied these decrees (*motu proprio Ecclesiae Sanctae*, I, no. 3, 6 August 1966). The Congregation of the Clergy decreed norms regarding how to carry out movements or transfers of priests to other dioceses, by agreements passed between the bishops *a quo* and *ad quem*, written with the participation of the priest, who must accept them and sign them in order for them to have the strength of a norm (*Normae Directivae de Aptiore Cleri Distributione*, 25 March 1980). The Code of 1983 took up these dispositions again under the title *De Clericorum Adscriptione seu Incardinatione* (c. 265–72), taking into account other changes brought about by the council. First it set forth a general principle: "Any cleric must be incardinated either in a particular Church or personal prelacy, or in an institute of consecrated life or a society having that quality," and this in order to avoid absolutely that there be any "acephalous or unattached clerics" (c. 265). This norm expanded the possibilities of incardination, in order to take into account, on the one hand, the flexibility introduced by the council into the organization of the Church by abandoning territoriality as the exclusive criterion for the limits of hierarchical structures and appeal to the personal criterion. On the other hand, incardination was then henceforth possible not only within the structure of the hierarchical organization of the Church, of particular Churches (c. 368 and 372), and personal prelatures (c. 294–7), but also within associations, institutes of consecrated life, and certain societies for apostolic life.

Since tonsure and minor orders were abolished (Paul VI, apostolic letter *Ministeria Quaedam*, 15 August 1972), an individual henceforth enters the priesthood by reception of the diaconate "and is incardinated in the particular Church or in the personal prelacy for the service of which he is ordained" (c. 266, sec. 1). The member of a religious institute who has professed perpetual vows is incardinated as a cleric in this society by the diaconate, unless otherwise precluded by a constitution. The member of a secular institute is incardinated by the diaconate in the particular Church to the service of which he is ordained, unless there is an indult from the

Apostolic See authorizing incardination to the institute (c. 266, sec. 2 and 3).

Incardination cannot be thought of as solely a legal bond. It supposes "a series of pastoral attitudes and spiritual choices" that help shape what a vocation to the priesthood looks like (JOHN PAUL II, apostolic exhortation *Pastores Daba Vobis*, 25 March 1992, no. 31). Indeed, in the hierarchical structures, the ministerial priesthood is manifested in direct service to the believers as such, within the framework of the unique mission of the Church that demands the cooperation of the ministerial priesthood and the common priesthood of all believers (dogmatic constitution *Lumen Gentium*, no. 10). In other kinds of associations, priestly ordination, and the incardination to which it leads, under the circumstances, does not produce such an interrelation within the association, but it does better ensure unity of government in the institution and apostolic activities, when its charisma and its structure call for it.

Incardination in another particular Church cannot take place without a letter of excardination from the bishop *a quo* and a letter of incardination from the bishop *ad quem*, the excardination only taking effect after the stated incardination has been obtained (c. 267). The code foresees an automatic incardination, or *ipso iure*, for the cleric who has moved legitimately from his particular Church to another; he is incardinated with full rights in the second after five years have passed, under the conditions stipulated in c. 268, sec. 1, which reasserts the terms of the *motu proprio Ecclesiae Sanctae*, I, no. 3 sec. 5, and takes the precedent in the matter into account (Supreme Tribunal of the Apostolic Signatura, sentence, 20 June 1977). An actual residence in the diocese is not required, it can be merely formal: the consent of the bishop *a quo* and that of the bishop *ad quem* are required. The effective exercise of the ministry as such is not required since the cleric is able to devote himself to social works, works of education, of charity; or he may be ill, disabled, or too old (Supreme Tribunal of the Apostolic Signatura, sentence in the cause *Miamien Incardinationis*, 27 June 1978).

Perpetual or definitive admission into an institute of consecrated life or into a society of apostolic life leads to automatic excardination from the particular Church of the cleric incardinated in this institute or society (c. 268, sec. 2). The cleric who is a member of a religious institute, who has obtained an exit indult after finding a bishop willing to receive him on probation, is rightfully incardinated into the diocese after a five-year period, except if the bishop has refused him (c. 693), an arrangement that also applies to members of secular institutes (c. 727, sec. 2). The Code of 1983 gives the priest who considers himself wronged by his bishop's refusal to grant excardination the right to appeal this decision (c. 270). This canon leads to the third motive, which demanded a revision of incardination with the coming of Vatican II Council. On the other hand, the convention that the bishops *a quo* and *ad quem* must sign when a priest is put at the disposal of another Church, and which must stipulate the rights and duties of the cleric (c. 271 sec. 1), must be accepted and signed by the interested party (Congregation for the Clergy, instruction *Poatquan Apostoli*, 25 March 1980).

Confirming the previous discipline, the Code reiterates that the diocesan administrator is not qualified to accord incardination or excardination, nor to authorize passage to another particular Church, except after more than one year of vacancy from the see and with the consent of the college of consultants (c. 272).

Dominique Le Tourneau

Bibliography

Bañares, J. I. "Algunas consideraciones a propósito de la incardinación," *Scripta theologica*, 23 (1991), 247–54.

Bernárdez, A. "Incardinación," *Nueva Enciclopedia Juridica*, 12 (1965), 126–9.

Bertone, T. "L'ascrizione dei chierici o incardinazione," *La normativa del Nuovo Codice*, Brescia, 1983, 77–8.

Bondini, L. "De incardinatione et excardinatione clericorum," *Ius pontificium*, 9 (1929), 205–13.

Bride, A. "Excardination," *Catholicisme*, 4 (1956), 864–67; and "Incardination," ibid., 5 (1962), 1408–11.

Colagiovanni, E. "De incardinazione ex jure, vi M.P. *Ecclesiae Sanctae*," *Monitor ecclesiasticus*, (1979), 22 ff.; "Incardinazione ed escardinazione nel nuovo Codice di Diritto Canonico," ibid., (1984), 49–57.

Denis, J. "Les limites de l'obligation incombant à l'évêque de subvenir à l'entretien du prêtre ordonné 'au titre du service du diocèse,'" *Acta Congressus Internationalis Iuris Canonici*, Rome, 1953, 104–15.

Di San Mauro, Z. "Incardinazione," *EC*, 6 (1951), 1743–75.

Herranz, J. "El nuevo concepto de incardinación," *Palabra*, 1966, 26–28.

Hervada, J. "La incardinación en perspectiva conciliar," *Ius canonicum*, 7 (1967), 479–517.

Labandeira, E. "La incardinación *ipso iure* en otra diócesis y su amparo por la Secció 2° de la Signatura Apostólica," *Ius canonicum*, 21 (1981), 393–417.

Maffeo, L. "Incardinazione dei chierici," *Novissimo Digesto Italiano*, 8 (1962), 497–8.

McBride, J. "Incardination and Excardination of Seculars," *Canon Law Studies*, 145, Washington, D. C., 1941.

McBride, J. T. *Incardination and Excardination of Seculars: An Historical Synopsis and Commentary*, Washington, D. C., 1941.

Naz, R. "Incardination," *DDC*, 57 (1953), 1293–96; "Titre d'ordination," ibid., 7 (1965), 1278–88.

Palazzini, P. "L'Instituto della incardinazione secondo lo spirito del Vaticano II," *The World is My Parish*, Malta, 1971, 37–51.

Piontek, C. "De acephali in iure canonico," *ibid.*, 13 (1933), 25–41.

Ribas, J. M. *Incardinación y distribución del clero*, Pamplona, 1971; "Incardinación," *Gran Enciclopedia Rialp*, Madrid, 12 (1973), 524–5.

Schmidt, J. "Status of Incardination of the Establishment of a New Diocese," *The Jurist*, 21 (1961), 296–310.

Schmitz, H. "Die Inkardination im Hinblick auf die konsoziativen Strukturen," *Das konsoziative Element in der Kirche* (under the direction of W. Aymans, K. T. Geringer and H. Schmitz), St. Ottilien, 1990, 701–20.

INDEX. The *Index librorum prohibitorum* was a list, in existence from 1559 to 1966, of works prohibited because of their harmfulness to faith and morals.

The Fragment of Muratori (ca. 196) indicated books of heretical origin "that cannot be received in the Church." The first historically certain condemnation was Arius's *Thalia*, at the Council of Nicaea (325). Pope ANASTASIUS condemned the writings of Origen as more harmful to the ignorant than useful to the learned (400). St. LEO I the Great condemned the writings of the Manicheans in Rome and ordered the Spanish bishops to act similarly toward the writings of the Priscillians. From the first centuries, the question of attitude toward classic pagan books was raised; GELASIUS I rejected some of them (*Decretum Gelasianum*, in 496). Gratian continued this decree (DECRETUM, dist. XV, c. 3). INNOCENT III condemned the writing of Joachim of Fiore against Peter Lombard (LATERAN IV COUNCIL, 11–30 November 1215), a decree that passed into the *Compilatio IV^a* (l. I, t. I, c. 2) then into the DECRETALS of GREGORY IX.

With the spread of the printing press the danger of perversion of the faith and morals grew, all the more so as Protestantism was not long in making its appearance. The Church intervened more often: ALEXANDER VI (constitution *Inter Multiplices,* 1 June 1501), and LEO X (constitution *Sollicitudines,* 4 May 1515) ruled that nothing could be printed without the authorization of the bishop of the place or of his general vicar. The appearance of Protestantism led to the institution of the IMPRIMATUR. The first Indices came into being under pressure from monarchs (Henry VIII of England; Charles V in the Netherlands in 1529, an Index that the University of Louvain revised and completed in 1540 and in 1546; the Republic of Venice in 1543), from theological faculties (the Sorbonne in 1551), or from other bodies (in Florence, Milan, etc.). Leo X and CLEMENT VII especially forbade the writings of Luther. Lists of harmful books gradually appeared in dioceses or provinces. PAUL III entrusted the care of forbidding books marred by heresy to the holy Roman and Universal Inquisition.

Index of Paul IV. In 1557, PAUL IV ordered the composition of a catalog of forbidden books, which was published for the first time in 1559. For each letter of the alphabet there appeared three groups of works: condemned authors or those whose writings were forbidden in advance (*in odium auctoris*); books forbidden because of the danger that their contents presented to faith and morals; anonymous writings or those whose author was concealed by a pseudonym. One clause condemned outright all anonymous writings that had appeared since 1519. An appendix cited the prohibited editions of the Holy Scriptures and gave a list of sixty-two printing houses whose production was suspected of heresy. Beginning in 1561 its strictness made the publication of a *Moderatio Indicis Librorum Prohibitis* necessary.

The Tridentine Index. Accomodating a request from the Council of Trent, PIUS IV had the Index revised and brought up to date (constitution *Dominici gregis custodiae*, 24 March 1564). The second part continued Paul IV's catalog, minus the special clause and the appendix. The first part included ten rules—*Decem regulae generales concilii Tridentini jussu editae*—on the censorship, correction, and sale of forbidden books, the penal sanctions in case of infraction, the condemnation *ipso facto* of certain categories of works, and the way to hear the condemnations brought against heretics. These rules would be the basis of legislation on the subject up to the 19th century. In 1571, PIUS V instituted the CONGREGATION of the Index.

The ten rules underwent a few modifications: GREGORY XIII specified the procedure of interdiction of books (constitution *Ut pestiferarum*, 1572); SIXTUS V completed rule IX (BULL *Coeli et Terrae*, 9 January 1586; bull *Immensa*, 1588); CLEMENT VIII did likewise for rules IV and IX (constitution *Catholicae*, 17 October 1595). The method of condemnation *opera omnia* appeared in 1603, closing at the same time the first class of the Index. ALEXANDER VII eliminated the division by classes (brief *Speculatores*, 5 March 1664).

Leonine Index. LEO XIII adapted the legislation to his time (constitution *Officiorum ac Munerum*, 25 January 1897) and prepared the way for the CODE OF CANON LAW of 1917. The Index appeared in 1900 with a new presentation and rules of interpretation. The works condemned before 1600 disappeared (800 in total). There remained about 4,000, 88 of which were *opera omnia*. The Code of 1917, with a more preventative than penal character, treated the topic in c. 1384–1405. In 1948, there were a total of 109 condemnations under the general clause *opera omnia* and 4,191 condemnations of works.

The Congregation for the Doctrine of the Faith, which replaced the Congregation of the HOLY OFFICE (*motu proprio Integrae Servandae*, 7 December 1965), declared by simple notification (24 June 1966) that the Index of Forbidden Books ceased to be an ecclesiastical law. The reading of a forbidden book no longer led to excommunication. The role of the "commissioner of the Holy Office" for instruction in trials, reserved for DOMINICANS since Paul III, was eliminated by Paul VI (letter to the master general of the Dominicans, 26 March 1966). A few months later the congregation abrogated the Index as well as the corresponding eccesiastical censure (decree, 15 November 1966). The Holy See, however, reserved the right to indicate works that were contrary to faith and morals, and the bishops had a serious duty in this matter with regard to their faithful. The faithful had a serious obligation to refrain from reading or keeping in their possession works that the competent ecclesiastical authority or their well-developed conscience had shown to be contrary to faith or morals.

Catalogs of Prohibited Books. Editions of the Index include: 1559, 1590, 1593, 1596, 1632, 1665, 1681, 1704, 1711, 1716, 1744, 1758, 1786, 1787, 1819, 1835, 1841, 1877, 1881, 1900, 1901, 1907, 1911, 1917, 1922, 1924, 1929, 1930 (in Italian and French), 1938, 1940, 1946, 1948 (last edition published). Unofficial editions include: 1580 (Parma), 1610 (Lyon), 1766 (Venice), 1783 (Parma), 1852 (Montreal), and 1899 (Turin).

Dominique Le Tourneau

Bibliography

Arndt, A. *De disciplina Ecclesiae circa libros usque ad concilium Tridentinum*, 1892; *De libris prohibitis commentarii*, Ratisbonne, 1885.

Boudinhon, A. *La Nouvelle Législation de l'Index*, 1925.

Browne, M. I. "Are non-catholic encyclopedias prohibited 'ipso iure'?," *The Irish Ecclesiastical Record*, 43 (1934), 80–3.

Brys, J. "De lectione pravorum diariorum," *Coll. Brugen.*, 28 (1928), 125–9.

Bujanda, J. M. "El primer índice de libros prohibido," *Scripta theologica*, 16 (1984), 443–50, and *Index des livres interdits, 2: Index de l'université de Louvain 1548, 1550, 1558; 3: index de Venise 1549, Venise et Milan 1554*, Quebec, 1986–87.

Burke, R. *What is the Index?*, Milwaukee, 1952.

Buttignoni, G. "Sulla proibizione dei libri," *Palestra del clero*, 10 (1931), 257–9.

Casati, G. *L'Indice dei libri proibiti. Saggi e commenti*, Milan, 1937.

Choupin, L. *Étude sur la valeur des décisions doctrinales du Saint-Siège*, 1907.

Davidson, N. S. "Rome and the Venetian inquisition in the sixteenth century," *Journal of Ecclesiastical History*, 39 (1988), 16–36.

De Iorio, A. "Indice dei libri proibiti," *EC*, 6 (1951), 1825–9.

Forget, J. "Index," *Dictionnaire apologétique de la foi catholique* (under the dir. of A. D'Ales), II, 4th ed., 1911, 702–16.

Fragnito, G. *La Bibbia al rogo: la censura ecclesiatica e i volgarizzamenti della Scrittura, 1471–1605*, Bologna, 1997.

Gennari, C. *Della nuova disciplina sulla proibizione e sulla censura dei libri*, 1903.

Gennaro, A. "Sulla proibizione dei libri," *Perfice munus*, 7 (1932), 743–4.

Goyeneche, S. "Potestne superior localis prohibere librum aut periodicum suis subditis?," *Commentarium pro religiosis*, 9 (1928), 427, and "An requiratur facultas S.C. Indicis ad retinendos libros prohibitos in armario clauso custodiendo," ibid., 13 (1932), 198–9.

Grendler, P. F. *The Roman Inquisition and the Venetian Press, 1540–1605*, Princeton, N.J., 1977.

Hilgers, J. *Der Index der verboten Bücher*, Freiburg im Breisgau, 1904.

Johnson, H. J. T. "The Roman Index of Prohibited Books," *Downside Review*, 73 (1955), 160–73.

Lecler, M. "Facoltà de leggere libri proibiti," *Perfice munus*, 3 (1928), 865–6.

Lefebvre, Ch. "Index," *Catholicisme*, 5 (1962), 1494–1502.

Moreno, P. A. "El Código y la prohibición de libros," *La ciudad de Dios*, 124 (1921), 382–6.

Mostaza, "De nuperrima editione Indicis," *Periodica de re morali, canonica, liturgica*, 18 (1929), 173–4.

Pennachi, J. *In Const. apost. "Officiorum ac munerum" commentatio*, Rome, 1898.

Periès, G. *L'Index*, Paris, 1898.

Petit, L. *L'Index, son histoire, ses lois, sa force obligatoire*, 1886.

Reusch, H. *Der Index der verbotenen Bücher*, Bonn, 1883–5; *Die Indices librorum prohibitorum des sechzehnten Jahrhunderts*, 1886.

Seidel Menchi, S. *Erasmo in Italia*, Turin, 1987.

Simenon, G. "Lex naturalis servanda in lectione librorum prohibitorum," *Revue ecclésiastique de Liège*, 28 (1937), 257 *sq*.

Thouvenin, A. "Index," *DTC*, 7 (1923), 1570–80.

Vermeersch, A. *De prohibitione et censura librorum*, Rome, 4th ed., 1906.

Wagnon, H. "Le nouvel Index des livres prohibés," *Revue diocésaine de Tournai*, 3 (1948), 3–23.

Wagnon H., and Naz, R. "Index," *DDC*, 3 (1953), 1318–30.

Woywod, S. "Prohibition of books," *The Homiletic and Pastoral Review*, 28 (1928), 1086–95.

INDEX, CONGREGATION OF THE. This Roman congregation, which no longer exists, had as a forerunner a special commission instituted in February 1562, at the time of the 18th session of the COUNCIL of Trent. A council of eighteen priests, it was charged with revising the Index established by PAUL IV in 1559 (whose excessive severity had sparked deep disagreements within the assembly) and with drawing up a new catalog of forbidden books. This catalog was to be published under PIUS IV, in 1564, and would be known as the Index of Trent.

The need to expurgate books of which only certain parts were forbidden by the Index of Trent and the urgency of maintaining continual vigilance toward certain publications brought PIUS V to create, some years later, a specific congregation of cardinals, called the Congregation of the Index. It held its first session on 27 March 1571. Confirmed by GREGORY XIII in 1572, the congregation was organized definitively at the time of the reform of the Roman CURIA brought about by SIXTUS V with the constitution *Immensa aeterni Dei* (22 January 1588). The papal document specified the responsibilities of the congregation. Its essential role was to examine, and possibly to condemn or to correct, books judged contrary to Catholic doctrine or to morality. It also established expurgatory indices that designated which parts of books not completely forbidden were to be corrected or eliminated. In order to accomplish its task, the congregation could use the works of theologians, canonists, and other experts, and appeal to the collaboration of the most reputable universities. In addition, it had the power to grant permission to possess and read forbidden books.

The activity of the congregation received an important impetus under Sixtus V. Beginning in 1590, a new index was printed, but it was never promulgated. Its radical rewriting was published in 1596, under CLEMENT VIII. That was followed by several other indices (among which were those of ALEXANDER VII, in 1664, and BENEDICT XIV, in 1758) up to the last one, in 1948, published by PIUS XII, when the Congregation of the Index ceased to exist as an independent DICASTERY. On the other hand, no full expurgatory index was ever printed, although its drafting was one of the congregation's institutional tasks. It was only in 1607 that the first volume of the expurgatory index appeared. It was prepared by the master of the Sacred PALACE, G. Guanzelle da Brisighella, but was never finished.

With time, the initial severity with which the congregation undertook the prohibition of books abated. The constitution *Sollicita ac provida*, promulgated on 9 July 1753 by BENEDICT XIV, was particularly significant from this point of view. This pope, a man of great culture and of open mind, introduced a norm that was radically innovative relative to the moral philosophy to which the dicastery previously ascribed. In the first place, he established the principle that the congregation was only to be concerned with books expressly denounced as dangerous, unless the judgment in question had been rendered by the Congregation of the Inquisition, since it, too, was competent in matters of censorship. In order to avoid excessively hasty censorship, he established, in addition, that any suspect work be examined personally by the secretary of the dicastery (traditionally a Dominican) and by at least two other experts. A carefully detailed report was to be presented, first to the consultants, then to the cardinal members of the congregation. Finally, special consideration was to be given to Catholic authors censored for the first time. The congregation was to offer them ways to explain and defend themselves, and it was to suspend possible condemnation if the author claimed to be ready to correct the errors that were pointed out to him.

These rules remained in effect even after 25 January 1897, when LEO XIII, acknowledging the critical comments of numerous bishops during the VATICAN I council, undertook the revision of the legislation that regulated the congregation's activities. This revision continued to exist even after the reform of the Roman Curia begun by PIUS X, in 1908, but only for a short time. On 25 March 1917, BENEDICT XV, in the *motu proprio Alloquentes*, finally eliminated the dicastery. Its responsibilities went to a special section of the Congregation of the Holy Office, which continued to draw up the index of forbidden books until it, too, was abolished in 1966 by PAUL VI.

Agostino Borromeo

Bibliography

Arndt, A. *De libris prohibitis commentarii*, Ratisbonne, 1895, 105–8, 195–208.

Catalini, G. *De secretario Sacrae Congregationis Indicis libri duo*, 1751.

Del Re, N. *La Curia romana. Lineamenti storicogiuridici*, 3d ed., 1970 (*Sussidi eruditi*, 23), 325–9.

Dykmans, M. "Les bibliothèques des religieux d'Italie en l'an 1600," *AHP*, 24 (1986), 385–404.

Frajese, V. "La revoca dell'*Index* sistino e la Curia romana (1588–1596)," *Nouvelles de la République des Lettres*, 1 (1986), 21, 25, 33–4.

Larraona, A., and Goyeneche, S. "De SS. Congregationum, tribunalium et officiorum constitutione et interna ordinatione post. Const. 'Sapienti Consilio,'" *Romana Curia a beato Pio X sapienti consilio reformata*, 1951, 105–7.

Pasztor, L. *La Curia romana. Problemi e ricerche per la sua storia nell'età moderna e contemporanea*, 1971, 86–8.

Reale Simioli, C. "Arnaldo Cebà e la congregazione dell'Indice," *Campania Sacra*, 11–12 (1981–2), 96–212.

Rotondò, A. "Nuovi documenti per la storia dell'*Indice dei libri prohibiti* (1572–1638)," *Rinascimento*, 2d ser., 3 (1963), 145–211.

Simoncelli, P. "Documenti interni alla congregazione dell'Indice, 1571–90. Logica e ideologia dell'intervento censorio," *Annuario dell'Istituto Italiano per l'età moderna e contemporanea*, 35–6 (1983–4), 189–215.

Simor, J. "De S. Congregatio Indicis," *Archiv für katholisches Kirchenrecht*, 21 (1869), 46–73.

Tans, J. A. G., and Schmitz Du Moulin, H. *Pasquier Quesnel devant la Congrégation de l'Index. Correspondance avec Francesco Barberini et mémoires sur la mise à l'index de son édition des oeuvres de saint Léon*, The Hague, 1974.

Taurisano, I. *Hierarchica ordinis Praedicatorum*, 1916, 113–21.

Tedeschi, J. "Florentine Documents for an History of the Index of Prohibited Books," *Renaissance Studies in Honour of Hans Baron*, Florence, 1971, 579–605.

Villien, A. "Le Saint-Office et la suppression de la Congrégation de l'Index," *Le Canoniste contemporain*, 40 (1917), 98–111.

INDICTION. See Bull.

INDULGENCES. The indulgence was originally a total or partial remission of temporal punishment incurred for a sin. Borrowed by the Church from the judicial arsenal of the Roman Empire, and mainly used beginning in the 3d century to quickly reconcile Christians who had apostatized during persecution, an "indulgence" was defined in the first DECRETALS (notably in 1172 in a decretal of ALEXANDER III), as the remission of temporal punishments incurred because of sin and coming under ecclesiastic jurisdicition. Never would it apply to spiritual punishments, which come under the sacrament of penance. The principle is that absolution comes from God, and indulgence from the mercy of the Church. The former concerns being admitted into the glory of God, which depends on God's judgment; the latter concerns being reconciled to the heart of the Church, which can be assured.

Since the pope and bishops grant indulgences on the single argument of an act of piety done to this end—be it prayer or mortification—while also requiring subsequent sacramental absolution, the indulgence is therefore not a product of how the act relates to the sin but rather a consequence of the communion of saints, which puts at the Church's disposition a mass of "merits" that is unaffected by nature, since it is normally obtained by the just for the benefit of sinners. Specific references are made as early as the 3d century to the merits acquired by the martyrs, merits that the Church could use for the benefit of Christianity as a whole.

The personal link between the sin and its remission remained nonetheless a very sensitive point up to the 11th century. The pope or the bishop judged the conditions under which the pardon would be granted and was therefore the judge of the shortening or lightening of the trials inflicted on the sinner. It was in fact a question of considering a penance accomplished in advance. The sinner was reintegrated into the community before having completed the length of time spent sleeping on a hard surface, or before finishing the fast or pilgrimage prescribed.

Another factor was introduced through the mentality of barbaric peoples, who put a price on all temporal errors and designed their laws as scales of compensation. This led the Western Church to the writing of penitential books that published the tarif of penance, with which the practice of the indulgence was aligned. Borrowed from Ireland and from insular Britain, the practice spread to the continent in the 6th century. Everything was then translated into days and years of a physical penance based on asceticism. In the 11th century examples of penances so rated were still known.

This rigor was tempered, beginning in the 8th century, by recourse to indulgences, which also had their rate. A certain act of devotion or charity thus justified the commutation of a certain penance, the two being arithmetically defined. The number of physical penances imposed and not accomplished in particular made the use of indulgences necessary as a complement to absolution when an individual was on the verge of death. It was less a question of tempering the severity of penances than of reducing a length often incompatible with life in that century. Thus, originally, an indulgence was not earned only with a few prayers but with acts of mortification, which made the reduction of the penance appear to have reasonable dimensions. The canonic *redemptio* was then the equivalent of the penal *vergeld*.

Beginning in the 9th century, the Church reacted against the spiritual risks tied to the practice of the *redemptio*. SIMONY crept into indulgences, through the work of charity, just as it crept into administration of the sacraments, and the tarifs formerly found in penitential books could be automatically translated for sins: it was known that a certain sin cost a certain amount. The clergy, for its part, was tempted to set the rate of redemption in its best interest. The COUNCILS of the 10th and 11th centuries worked to limit priests' ability to set rates, as an automatic rate appeared to be a better guarantee against simoniacal deviations in the system. It was in the 11th century that general redemption, which escaped bargaining, increased. The principle was finally established, definitively, whereby an indulgence could only follow sacramental absolution.

Early in the Gregorian REFORM, the general indulgence took its place among the affirmations of papal authority. The pope would award a general, but not a plenary, indulgence on the occasion of certain feast days, or when churches were consecrated. The pope was, after all, eager both to encourage the faithful to work together in the great construction movement and to manifest the universality of his temporal power, since it was a question of this power. In the mid-11th century, the plenary indulgence made its appearance, as redemption for a heavy penance at the cost of engaging in a battle for the faith. The first plenary indulgences facilitated the reconquest of Spain over Islam. In 1095, Urban II did nothing more than apply an already proven practice to the CRUSADE in the East. Since it was plenary, the indulgence no longer corresponded to a particular sin and escaped any tarification. It was no longer a compensation. It became the complement of absolution. It then had all the elements that it would retain up to the present time.

A rapid reduction of requirements was then noticed. Relatively minor works of piety or charity led to large indulgences. ALEXANDER III, in particular, allowed plenary indulgences for simple pilgrimages, to Jerusalem, or even to Rome, or even for the observation of a sworn peace, which was paradoxical since this indulgence sanctioned the absence of a sin by the remission of punishments incurred for others. More limited indulgences rewarded, at the discretion of bishops, gifts for the construction of churches or the completion of local pilgrimages or even a simple stop along the way of a longer pilgrimage. Guidebooks for travelers and pilgrims contained the rich catalog of indulgences offered to visitors of sanctuaries situated along the way.

The meaning of the indulgence evolved with the increasing number of crusades. By emphasizing the salvation promised to crusaders who died during the expedition, the Church was implicitly recognizing that indulgences had a spiritual effect in the hereafter; this was contrary to the former doctrine, according to which the effects of the remission only came as a complement to absolution and without prejudice to the individual at the Last Judgment. The new conception was taught in the 13th century in Paris by St. Albert the Great. Others, such as Bonaventure, understood the indulgence as a transferable spiritual good: one could earn it to benefit the souls in purgatory.

From this time, however, the Church hesitated. Some worried about plenary indulgences that were too easily earned, which might discourage Christians from leaving on a crusade. Others, notably theologians, were reticent before an automatic remission, which seemed legitimate when it was dearly earned by a difficult test such as the pilgrimage to the Holy Land or a crusade but seemed excessive when it rewarded a simple act of devotion. On the other hand, the Church was not opposed to encouraging by indulgences the most diverse charitable works. The indulgence was also a good way to lead the faithful to the personal practice of spiritual devotion. Generally, by insisting on the distinction between absolution and indulgence—and with no illusion about the impact of temporal punishment linked to sin—the Church saw in the indulgence a gesture of mercy toward the repentant sinner. It was one of the applications of the communion of saints,

in other words, the pooling of merits acquired by the Church for the benefit of all.

A reaction was then seen to take shape at LATERAN IV COUNCIL in 1215, when the Church was specifying the obligation of a Christian to make a personal and verbal confession each year. Simply attending a religious ceremony was no more than the occasion of a low-level indulgence: one year for the dedication of a church, forty days for the anniversary of this dedication. Papal letters henceforth specified the significance of the indulgence that the preachers, charged with gathering funds for the enterprises of the Church, could grant. From this time on, people showed a certain suspicion toward these collectors who handled the indulgence without proper judgment, but the abuse did not stop, and councils continued to act severely.

Around this time the idea of a jubilee appeared, with an indulgence accorded once every hundred years to pilgrims in Rome. BONIFACE VIII took up this idea and proclaimed a jubilee for the year 1300. CLEMENT VI, in 1343, diminished the interval by half. The GREAT SCHISM, by reducing the Roman papacy to meager resources, certainly favored this practice, which had a jubilee invented from then on each time the papal treasury was empty. Reduced to expedients by a catastrophic administrative and financial situation, the Roman pope of the Great Schism, URBAN VI, moved the jubilee forward by ten years, to 1390. The faithful who were materially incapable of reaching Rome were even awarded a jubilee indulgence for completing the same kind of pilgrimage in their region. Although it was an exceptional pilgrimage in 1300, by the beginning of the 15th century the jubilee was no more than a pretext for collection. The condition was the same everywhere: an offering to the Holy See. It could be seen quite obviously in the 15th century, with the increase in local jubilees that no longer had anything to do with the prayer on the tomb of the Apostle.

A reaction occurred after the Council of Constance, where reformers denounced certain scandals. MARTIN V decided to limit recourse to the indulgence, but successors came back to it, pushed by financial necessity. General pardons unfortunately became more frequent at the time of the Council of Basel. For lack of ecclesiastical reform, the masters of spirituality emphasized the inner life. Consequently, indulgences had no place in the individual exercises of the *devotio moderna* that renewed the forms of spiritual life of both lay persons and clerics.

At the end of the Middle Ages, the practice of indulgences had no more than distant ties with theory. Commutation became the norm: punishment incurred was atoned for in counted money. Collections became more frequent: it was the "pardoners," in whom the people saw no more than preachers selling "forgiveness." False BULLS freely circulated, in the hands of false pardoners, and suspicion grew. The bishops began to worry, and some went so far as to have the pardoners' letters of commission handed over to them. The clergy, on the whole, was also alarmed at practices that turned the generosity of the faithful toward ends that were sometimes disinterested—false pardoners sometimes had a charitable ideal—but often bordered on fraud; hostility was shown toward what looked fairly suited to emptying the collection plates of the Church. What the faithful gave to the pardoner for an indulgence was no longer given to the parish priest. There was thus an organized reaction from the clergy, quite similar to the hostility shown in the 13th century by the secular magistri and the parish priests toward the preachers from the mendicant orders.

Since an indulgence could be negotiated, communities received special concessions. Beginning in the 13th century, the third orders, and shortly thereafter the confraternities, were begging for and receiving indulgences for the benefit of their members. The Franciscans, in particular, would be accused of recruiting for their third order at this price. The princes of the 14th, and especially the 15th, century also had special indulgences granted for their States, most frequently within the context of political negotiations with the Holy See. Everything that could procure alms was, in the 15th century, sanctioned by an indulgence. Such was also the case for the construction of bridges, hospitals, or city walls.

The conditions for an indulgence naturally declined. Indulgences were available for reciting the Lord's Prayer or for an invocation that lasted but a few seconds. The justification was that intentions, alone, counted; there was no longer any relationship between the level of the fault and that of the penalty and its redemption. The Church had to specify that the indulgence was rendered null if the Christian saw in it any moral facility or the ability to sin without risk. The increase in partial indulgences—plenary indulgences, by definition, could not be accumulated—led the faithful to practice a kind of penitential arithmetic, which quickly got introduced into devotions: indulgences were counted, just as the *Our Fathers* and *Hail Marys* of the ROSARY were counted.

By the end of the 14th century, such practices led to a dispute, favored by the crisis of the Great Schism, that worked its way into the great reformation movements within the Church as well as in the political and financial systems of the secular rulers. Theologians, especially, emphasized the need for sacramental absolution: contrition comes first, regardless how charitable one's actions may be.

The primary attacks came from England with the preacher John Wycliff, an Oxford theologian whose anti-ecclesiastical reformism was condemned in 1382, and with Jan Hus, the priest from Prague who was condemned in 1415 by the council of Constance, as much for having raised Bohemia up against Emperor Sigismund as for the theological content of his preaching. More prudent, others throughout the century simply reported the abuses of those taking up collections and showed a certain skepticism regarding the effects of indulgences on the hereafter. An indulgence granted in 1506 to those who would contribute to the construction of the new ST. PETER'S stirred up vigorous reactions. The indulgence proffered by LEO X in 1515 in order to allow the archbishop of Mainz to pay, at his faithful's expense, his debts to the papal treasury burdened by the construction of St. Peter's, aroused violent protests from several theologians who were unhappy about hearing preachers draw an automatic connection between offerings and the redemption of souls in purgatory. Martin Luther went further and, in the theses he published in Wittenberg on 31 October 1517, called the very principle of indulgences into question.

Luther's reaction brought the practice to more reasonable dimensions for a while. In condemning Luther (5 November 1519), Leo X made a careful distinction between the remission of sin and the remission of temporal punishment and considered the indulgence applied to the souls in purgatory to be like an intercession, not as an automatic right. The practice of indulgences nevertheless continued under the supervision of a congregation of indulgences organized by CLEMENT VIII. In 1669 it was integrated into the CURIA by CLEMENT IX. Its responsibilities would be passed to the HOLY OFFICE in 1908, and then to the Ecclesiastical Tribunal in 1917.

Some popes granted indulgences for the simple recitation of a pious formula. Missals for the use of parishoners that were published shortly after WORLD WAR II still showed the specific value, expressed in years and days, of indulgences attached to the recitation of numerous prayers.

Without returning to early usage, since the VATICAN II COUNCIL, the Church has limited the concession of indulgences. The pope still grants plenary indulgences for jubilees, which have become more frequent, and also for benedictions Urbi et Orbi for which the radio, and later television, have increased the diffusion. But the relative importance of the concession has singularly regressed in the face of less formal modes of spirituality.

Jean Favier

Bibliography

Frédéricq, P. "Les comptes des indulgences dans les Pays-Bas," *Mémoires couronnés et autres mémoires publiés par l'Académie royale*, Brussels, 1903, series in octavo, 63, fasc. 5.

Hödl, L. "Ablass," *LexMA*, 1 (1980), 43–6.

Jombart, É. "Indulgences," *DDC*, 5 (1950), 1331–52.

Magnin, E. "Indulgences," *DTC*, 7-2 (1930), 1594–1636.

Paulus, N. *Geschichte des Ablasses im Mittelalter vom Ursprung bis zur Mitte des 14. Jahrhunderts*, 2 vols., 1922–3.

Peter, C. J. "The Church's treasures then and now," *Theological Studies*, 47 (1986), 251–72.

INFALLIBILITY. The Church MAGISTERIUM (the acts of dogmatic or moral teaching of members of the hierarchy, meaning the bishops) is said to be *infallible* when it entails the magisterial authority at the highest degree. At such times, error is not possible, since the Holy Spirit effectively assists in the proclamation of the truth. The magisterium is called "simply authentic" when authority is not exercised at the highest degree. In both cases it requires the adherence of intellect and the will of the faithful.

According to the way it is exercised, a distinction may be made between *extraordinary* magisterium, using the solemn form, as in the case of an ecumenical COUNCIL, or the pope speaking EX CATHEDRA, and *ordinary* magisterium, which refers to the current forms of the teachings of the bishops.

The dogma of infallibility applies to (a) the Church as a whole (VATICAN I COUNCIL, dogmatic constitution *Pastor Aeternus*; Congregation for the Doctrine of the Faith, instruction *Mysterium Ecclesiae*, 24 June 1973); (b) the hierarchy, or infallibility *in docendo*; (c) the faithful in unity with their pastors, or infallibility *in credendo*. The term infallibility, applied to the Roman pontiff, only appeared for the first time in a treatise by Guido Terrena regarding a controversy between some Franciscan Spirituals and JOHN XXII (1316–1334). This article will concern itself primarily with the infallibility of the Roman pontiff, the privileged—although not exclusive—subject of this charism, since he is the visible sign and efficacious instrument of the unity of the Catholic faith.

The Scriptural Foundations of Infallibility. Infallibility is often incorrectly referred to in reference to the Roman pontiff alone. As the VATICAN I COUNCIL stated, "the gift of infallibility has been revealed to us as a perpetual prerogative of the Church of Christ . . . . This gift has been conferred so that the Word of God, in both its written form and its transmission, might be protected and preserved in the universal Church in a fashion that is intact and exempt from any trace of innovation or change" (outline of 21 January 1870).

It is thus first of all the Church that is infallible. There are not two infallibilities, that of the Church and that of the pope, but rather a single infallibility of the Church, the head of which is the Roman pontiff. Even if the term is not found in Scripture, its scriptural foundations are nevertheless sufficiently eloquent. First and foremost, Christ, the Son of God, Word of the Father, presents himself as the eternal, plenary, and indefectible Truth ("I am . . . the Truth," Jn 14:6). If the personal infallibility of Jesus as a man is not acknowledged, then neither can that of the Church be acknowledged. Christ promises indefectibility to his Church, which is built on the faith of Peter: "*Tu es Petrus* . . . , thou art Peter, and upon this rock I shall build my Church and the gates of hell shall not prevail against it . . ." (Mt 16:16–19). After his Ascension into heaven, Jesus entrusted his apostles with the mission of proclaiming the Gospel and announced to them the coming of the Holy Spirit, the Spirit of Truth (Jn 14:17) who would teach them the whole truth (Jn 16:13) and would make them his witnesses to the ends of the earth (Acts 1:18). They would in fact spread the Good News under the guidance of the Holy Spirit (Acts 4:8), convinced that their testimony was a testimony of the Holy Spirit (Acts 5:32). We know the answer the apostles gave to resolve the question of the idolothytes: "It is the decision of the Holy Spirit and ours too . . ." (Acts 15: 28).

Peter received the particular mission of strengthening his brethren in the faith (Lk 22:32; Jn 21:15–17). Since Jesus announced that he was with his disciples until the end of time (Mt 28:20), the Church sees in these texts a promise made, also, to all of Peter's successors.

History. Doctrinal infallibility is attested to by St. Irenaeus. Speaking of the Church of Rome, he wrote: "With this Roman Church it is thus necessary that all Churches be in agreement, because of her eminent authority and because, through her, the tradition coming through the apostles has always been preserved" (*Against Heresies*, III, III, 2). A number of different pontifical interventions give evidence of the recognition of the doctrinal authority of the pope from the earliest moments of the life of the Church: CLEMENT I of Rome (Letter to the Corinthians, ca. 100); St. DIONYSIUS intervened in a doctrinal controversy to condemn the Sabellians and the Arians (letter to Dionysius, bishop of Alexandria, ca. 260); St. FELIX I condemned the error of Paul of Samosata regarding the Incarnation (letter to Maximus, bishop of Alexandria, and to his clergy, ca. 269); St. DAMASUS who, after first being consulted, refused his consent to and denied any value in the Council of Rimini (letter to the bishops of Illyria, ca. 370), and who addressed to Paul of Antioch twenty-four anathemas against heretics (*Confessio fidei catholicae*, 380); St. SIRICIUS condemned the error of the Jovinians (letter to the Church of Milan, ca. 388); St. INNOCENT I made statements at the request of the councils of Carthage (416) and Milev (417) on Pelagianism; and St. CELESTINE I condemned the errors of Nestorius at the request of St. Cyril of Alexandria, in 430, to name but a few.

Interventions by Roman pontiffs and the statements by ecclesiastical writers would increase starting in the 5th century: St. LEO the Great (letter to Flavian, bishop of Constantinople, 449); scriptural canon of the books of the Bible attributed to St. GELASIUS (d. 483); formulary of faith imposed upon the bishops of the East by St.

HORMISDAS (d. 523); approval of the decrees of the Council of Orange by BONIFACE II (d. 532); letter by Theodoret, bishop Cyr, to Renatus, archdeacon of Rome (d. 458); the letters by bishops of Gaul to St. Leo in 450 and 451; and the reprobation of the errors of Nestorius at the Council of Orleans (459).

In the 6th and 7th centuries, we find: St. AGATHO (d. 681) on Monothelism (letter *Ad Augustos Imperatores*); St. HADRIAN I (d. 795) on the worship of images (letter to Constantine and Irenaeus, in 785; letter to Tarasius of Constantinople), whose teachings were accepted by the Council of Nicaea II; as well as recognition of the authority of the See of Rome by the bishops of Numidia, of Byzatium and Mauritania, in 649; and St. Maximus the Confessor (d. 666) on the perpetual indefectibility of Peter.

In the 9th and 10th centuries, St. NICHOLAS I (d. 867) on the PRIMACY of the Roman Church (letters to Emperor Michael, in 860 and 865; to Photius, in 862; to the clergy of Constantinople, in 866); Pope HORMISDAS's formulary of faith at the Council of Constantinople IV (869–70); St. Theodore the Studite (d. 828) appealed to the pope on the question of the worship of images (letter CXXIX); Paschasius Radbertus (d. 860) commented on *Tu es Petrus (Expositio in Matth.*, 1, VIII, c. XVI), just as had Atto of Vercelli (d. 961) and St. Odo of Cluny (d. 942).

In the 11th and 12th centuries, we find: St. LEO IX (d. 1054) reiterated that Peter would never be able to fail (letters to Michael Cerularius, in 1053; to Peter of Antioch, in 1054); as did St. Peter Damian (d. 1072) and St. Anselm of Lucca (d. 1086); INNOCENT II (d. 1143) refuted the errors of Abelard (response to the prelates of the Council of Sens, in 1140); ALEXANDER III (d. 1181) repeated that all those who were in Christ's fold were subject to the magisterium of Peter, as did Yves of Chartres (d. 1171) in his canonical collection; and St. Bernard (d. 1153) denounced Abelard's error (*Epist.* CXC, or *Tractatus ad Innocentium* II).

In the 13th century, Lateran IV Council in 1215 declared the Church of Rome *cunctorum fidelium mater et magistra*. At the Council of Lyon (6 July 1274) Michael VIII Palaeologus submitted the Eastern Church to Rome. Before his accession to the papacy, Innocent III (d. 1216), affirmed the impossibility that the Apostolic See could fall into error (treatise *De sacro altaris mysterio*). St. Thomas Aquinas specified that everything belonging to the domain of faith is the object of infallibility (*Contra errorem graecorum*, c. XXXII; *Quodlibet.*, IX, q. VII, a. 16; *Summa Theologiae*, II–II, q. I, a. 10).

In the 14th century, papal statements increased. BENEDICT XII (constitution *Benedictus Deus*, 29 January 1336) defined the doctrine of the beatific vision, a teaching that was to be subscribed to by all. JOHN XXII (constitution *Licet iuxta doctrinam*, 23 October 1327) condemned the errors and heresies of Marsilius of Padua and John of Jandun.

From the early 15th to the beginning of the 16th century the Gallican theses developed. After JOHN XXIII's deposition in 1417, Pierre d'Ailly (d. 1420), chancellor of the UNIVERSITY of Paris, maintained that "the general council can in many cases judge and condemn the pope, and in many cases a pope can be called to the council, this being in cases where the Church is in danger of destruction" (*Tractatus de Ecclesiae, Consilii generalis, Romani Pontificis et Cardinalium auctoritate*). John Gerson (d. 1429), who succeeded him, affirmed that "in cases of faith, there is no infallible judge upon the earth, or none who can stray from the faith, unless this be the universal Church or a general council which sufficiently represents her" (*Tractatus quomodo et an liceat in causis fidei a Summo Pontifice appellare, seu ejus judicium declinare*). Nicolaus de Tudeschis, called Panormitanus (d. 1445), did not hestitate to prefer the judgment of a private individual to that of the pope, "if he was driven by better arguments and authorities from the New and Old Testaments than the pope" (*Commentaria in Decretal.*, 1. I, tit. VI, no. 3); Denis the Carthusian (d. 1471) proposed the principle that a general council cannot err in matters of faith and morals, since it is assisted by the Holy Spirit (*De auctoritate summi pontificis et generalis concilii*, 1, I, a. 29). Angelo de Clavasio (d. 1495) maintained similar theories (*Summa angelica*, art. *Papa*, q. IX, Venice, 1525).

Among the reactions in defense of the infallibility of the Roman pontiff, the following should be mentioned: Thomas Netter (d. 1445) battled Wycliff, the precursor of the Protestants, relying on the accounts of the Fathers (*Doctrinale antiquitatum fidei Ecclesiae catholicae*); and, as a title to a chapter of the first *Treatise on the Church*, John of Turrecremata (Juan de Torquemada, d. 1468), stated that "the judgment of the Apostolic See cannot err in matters of faith and those that are necessary for salvation" (*Summa de Ecclesia*, 1, II, c. CIX). The interventions of the magisterium also bear mention: MARTIN V, in the BULL *Inter cunctas* (22 February 1418) questioned John Wycliff and Jan Hus. The council of Florence (*Decretum pro Graecis*, 6 July 1439) affirmed the plenitude of the authority of the pope, and the council of Basel condemned conciliarist theories (Pius II, bull *Exsecrabilis*, 18 January 1460). SIXTUS IV, in the bull *Licet ea quae nostro mandato* (9 August 1479) condemned the errors of Peter of Osma.

There were important developments in the doctrine of infallibility in the early 16th century, up to the time of its formal proclamation by the VATICAN I COUNCIL. Robert Bellarmine (d. 1621), using Luke (22:32) as his point of departure, demonstrated that the pope has the gift of indefectibility to strengthen his brethren in the faith (*De romano pontifice*, 1, IV, c. III). With increasing frequency this was seen as a truth of Catholic faith (cf., Suarez, *De fide*, tr. I, disp. V, sec. VIII, n. 4). The

Catholic universities almost all upheld this thesis. John Fisher, chancellor of the University of Cambridge, affirmed in his refutation of Luther that in matters of controversy recourse should be taken to the See of Peter (*Assertionis lutheranae confutatio*, Paris, 1545, *3a veritas*). Ruard Tapper (d. 1559), chancellor of the University of Louvain, urged that unquestioning faith be put in all that has been defined in matters of faith and morals "by the throne of Peter, or by the legitimately assembled general councils" (*Explicationis articulorum venerandae facultatis theologiae Lovaniensis*).

Cardinal Stanislas Hosius (d. 1579) of Poland wrote the *Confessio catholicae fidei* in 1562, Thomas Stapleton (d. 1598) of the University of Douai wrote *Stapletoni Opera*, and Melchior Cano (d. 1560) wrote the *Theologiae cursus completus* all in defense of papal infallibility. Bañez, at the University of Salamanca, took a similar position. For Bañez, "if the question were submitted to a legitimate council, the doctrine of papal infallibility would be defined as being the true faith, and contrary opinion would be struck with anathema" (*Scholastica commentaria in II-II S. Thomae*).

The theories of Tudeschis and Clavasio were echoed in Sylvester of Prierio (d. 1523), Thomas Illyricus (d. 1528), and Alphonso de Castro (d. 1558). The anti-infallibility movement had a sudden resurgence in France with Edmond Richer's *Libellus* (*De ecclesiastica et politica potestate*, 1611). For him, "all controversies are referred to the general council, as the final and infallible tribunal containing all plenitude and power." Richer's theses prepared the way for JANSENISM. Cajetan (d. 1534) refuted the necessary dependence of the pontifical magisterium relative to the council or to the approval of the universal Church. He maintained that the pope's authority is above that of both the general council and the universal Church. Moreover, he tied infallibility to the personal magisterium of the pope, and not to the chair in Rome. Cano, Bellarmine, Suarez, Bañez, and others held similar opinions. Twenty-five bishops from France asked INNOCENT X to condemn the errors of Jansenius (1651), and then thanked him for doing so, recognizing the obligatory nature of the pope's doctrinal decisions. GALLICANISM again became manifest during the conflict that opposed Louis XIV to the Holy See, first in the declaration by the faculty of theology at the Sorbonne in 1663, where it was said that "it is not the faculty's doctrine that the pope is above the general council. It is not the doctrine or the dogma of the faculty that the pope is infallible when there is no intervening consent from the Church" (art. 5 and 6). The clergy assembly of 1682 declared: "Although the sovereign pontiff has the main role in questions of faith, and his decrees concern all the Churches and every one of them in particular, his judgment is however not irreformable, unless the consent of the Church is added" (art. 4). These articles were declared null and void by

ALEXANDER VIII (constitution *Inter multiplices*, 4 August 1690). Gallicanism would subside with time, while there would be no dearth of defenders of papal infallibility.

Vatican I Council. This council proclaimed the complete independence of the pope in regard to councils and the consent of the universal Church, in applying infallibility to matters of faith and morals. It defined as "revealed dogma" that "when [the pope] speaks *ex cathedra*, that is, when fulfilling his duty as pastor and teacher of all Christians, by virtue of his supreme apostolic authority, the Roman pontiff defines a doctrine pertaining to faith and morals which must be held by the universal Church; he enjoys, through the divine assistance that was promised to him by saint Peter, that infallibility with which the divine Redeemer wished His Church to be endowed when she defined doctrine regarding faith and morals" (dogmatic constitution *Pastor Aeternus*). Thus not only is any error excluded, but also the possibility of error.

In order to act with infallibility, the Roman pontiff must speak as pastor of the universal Church in matters of faith or morals and speak to the universal Church in terms that clearly show his intention to formulate a truth in a manner that is both definitive and irrevocable. It was these conditions, and not the form of the document (e.g., encyclical letter, apostolic constitution, etc.) that determined whether an intervention was *ex cathedra*.

On 6 December 1864, PIUS IX confided his intention to convene a council to some cardinals. The bull of convocation (*Aeterni Patris*, 29 June 1868) convoked it for 8 December 1869. It was to be the first Vatican council. The question of infallibility, which was not on the council's agenda, did not get a unanimous vote. In France, the Gallican Declaration of 1682 directly opposed it. However, Joseph de Maistre, with his *Du pape*, and Hughes de Lamennais, with his writings, made the cause progress. The opposition was greater in Germanic countries. Nevertheless, an article that appeared on 6 February 1869 in *La Civiltà cattolica* announced that the council would proclaim papal infallibility by acclamation. A polemic was immediately unleashed in the press. Louis Veuillot made much noise in favor of infallibility. In a pamphlet (11 November 1869), Archbishop Dupanloup of Orleans expressed his fear that the papacy would evolve into a kind of authoritarian monarchy. The opposition of certain German university circles was led by Ignaz Döllinger, a professor in Munich.

At the council, the majority, partisans of infallibility, included the bishops of the countries that were traditionally Catholic, or those having to face Protestantism. Among other things, this majority saw a way to eliminate the remains of Gallicanism and Febronianism, as well as to oppose subjective relativism, which was then so prevalent in society. The minority, on the other hand, included forty-seven German and Austro-Hungarian bishops, some forty French bishops, and twenty-seven Americans. Their concerns primarily entailed seeing a trench dug between the Church and society, or a reappraisal of the divine right of the episcopacy. The opposition was not so much to the principle itself (except Maret, *Du concile général et de la paix religieuse*) as to its opportuneness. Between these two groups there was a third sector of sixteen conciliar Fathers (including Cardinal de Bonnechose, archbishop of Rouen and Archbishop de Lavigerie, of Algiers), who were favorable to infallibility, but within very specific limits, and with wording that would be acceptable to all the conciliar Fathers.

Petitions, or *postulata*, were addressed to the pope on 28 and 29 January 1870. The majority, more than four hundred council Fathers, demanded that infallibility be placed on the agenda of the council. On 1 March 1870, Pius IX gave his approval to proceed to a definition of infallibility. The delegation for the faith composed a text, starting with chapter 11 of the schema on the Church, centered on primacy, to which it added a complement inspired in large part by propositions authored by Deschamps and Cardinal Henry Edward Manning. The schema on the prerogatives of the Roman pontiff was discussed from 13 May to 16 July 1870. Two days later, this text was approved during the last public session of the council, by 533 *placet* and 2 *non placet* (although a good sixty bishops, including the Melkite, Chaldean, and Syrian patriarchs, as well as a few other Eastern bishops who were disappointed with the "Latinizing" of Eastern Christians, had preferred to leave Rome before the vote in order to avoid casting negative ballots). Thus the dogmatic constitution *Pastor Aeternus* came into being. Its prologue recalls the institution of the Church by Christ and the place that papal primacy plays in it. Contrary to some Febronians and Gallicans, the first chapter taught that primacy of jurisdiction was conferred to Peter by Jesus Christ directly and immediately, and not by the intermediary of the Church. Chapter two showed that, through the will of Christ, primacy must last until the end of time. The following chapter defined the nature of primacy, the government of dioceses by bishops acting as true pastors, and the impossibility of an ecumenical council being able to reform a papal sentence. Finally, chapter four defined that the supreme power of the magisterium is included in the primacy of the pope upon certain conditions (the outline adopted had been composed by Franzelin and Kleutgen). The clear result was that papal infallibility is a way for the vicar of Christ to act in carrying out the mission incumbent upon him to oversee the spiritual interests of the faithful; it has nothing to do with temporal affairs. It happened that this affirmation coincided at that time with the loss of the popes' temporal powers, following the occupation and reattachment of Rome to the Italian crown.

The reception of the dogma of the pope's infallibility took place without difficulty; those bishops who were opposed to its formal proclamation by the council accepted it, nonetheless. Adherence by the faithful was immediate and enthusiastic. The only important resistance was from Döllinger and a group of professors, one of whom was Schulte, a professor of canon law at the university of Prague. It was their opinion that the decisions of Vatican I "had created another Church." In August 1870, they gathered in Nuremberg to organize the opposition to the constitutions of the council. A congress that took place in September 1871, in Munich, ratified the schism of the "*old Catholics*." This community was composed of a small group of theologians and canonists, and a few families from the high and middle bourgeoisie of southern Germany, who dreamed of a Church separated from Rome and protected by the State. In Switzerland, where lay opposition was more vigorous, a *Christian-Catholic* Church was formed.

Although the proclamation of the dogma of infallibility was the death knell for Gallicanism, a number of foreign governments showed hostility to the council's decisions. Austria took advantage of the situation to denounce the concordat of 1855 (which its constitution of 1867 had violated). Almost all the German States forbade publication of the council's acts, opening the way to the beginnings of the *Kulturkampf*. The cantons of Basel and Geneva favored the old Catholics excessively.

Vatican II Council. In 1962, Pope John XXIII convoked the VATICAN II COUNCIL. On infallibility, the council ordained that the *people of God* as a whole "cannot be mistaken in faith," the so-called *sensus fidei*, the supernatural sense of faith. "[F]rom bishops to the last of the faithful" (St. Augustine, *De Praed. Sanct.*, 14: 27), it brings "a universal consent to truths concerning faith and morals" (dogmatic constitution *Lumen Gentium*, no. 12). This sense of faith is awakened and sustained by the Holy Spirit and is exercised under the direction of the magisterium of the Church. Manifest examples are furnished by the faith of the Christian people in the Immaculate Conception of Mary and in her ASSUMPTION, truths emphasized by public worship and by consultation of the Church prior to the proclamation of the corresponding dogmas (Pius IX, encyclical *Ubi Primus*, 2 February 1849; PIUS XII, letter *Deiparae Virginis*, 1 May 1946).

This infallibility *in credendo* is closely tied to the communion that the faithful must keep. Speaking of the depository of the word of God, the council specified that in "cleaving to it, the holy people in its entirety, united to its pastors, remains assiduously faithful to the teaching of the apostles and to the communion of brethren, to the breaking of bread and to prayer . . . so that, in the upholding, practice, and confession of the faith transmitted, there is, between pastors and followers, a singular unity of spirit" (dogmatic constitution *Dei Verbum*, no. 10).

The council also spoke about "the *infallibility of the episcopal college*," that is, the extraordinary magisterium and ordinary magisterium. When the episcopal college agrees to teach authentically a doctrine concerning faith or morals, it is Christ's teaching that they are expressing infallibly, even when "they are dispersed throughout the world," while they "maintain the bond of communion among themselves and with the successor of Peter" (dogmatic constitution *Lumen Gentium*, no. 25). This infallibility of the episcopal college may be applied to the ordinary magisterium as well as to the extraordinary magisterium, that is, the magisterium of the bishops gathered in an ecumenical council, where "they act, for the ensemble of the Church, in matters of faith and morals, as doctors and judges to whose definitions one must adhere in obedience to the faith" (dogmatic constitution *Lumen Gentium*, no. 25).

Three conditions must be fulfilled. First, there must be hierarchical communion, that is, of the bishops among themselves and with the Roman pontiff, since infallibility does not apply to bishops taken as individuals. If this communion and this subordination to the vicar of Christ do not exist the exercise of the magisterium is illegitimate or simply nonexistent and in no way obligates the faithful. Second, the teaching must be concerned with matters of faith or morals. The bishop must limit himself to what is proper and specific to the magisterium, thus excluding any personal opinions. It is evident that if under some condition he did offer an opinion that was counter to the teaching of the Roman pontiff, it is the latter that the believer should necessarily follow, without fear of error or of acting badly. Third, it is necessary for the bishop to teach the doctrine in the name of Christ; it is only to the extent that he appeals to the official magisterium that he can impose his own teachings, and it is only in regard to matters of faith and morals that the faithful are held to give the assent of their will.

The pope, who is the head of the college of bishops, is endowed with this infallibility "by the fact of his charge when, as pastor and supreme doctor of all faithful, and responsible for strengthening his brothers in the faith, he proclaims, with a definitive act, a point of doctrine touching on faith and morals" (ibid.). Infallibility thus applies to the Roman pontiff by reason of his charge from Christ to Peter and his successors, as head of the Roman Church.

These definitions "are irreformable *ex sese*, by themselves, and not by virtue of the consent of the Church" (Vatican I Council, dogmatic constitution *Pastor Aeternus*, chap. 4). Vatican II specified that these definitions "are pronounced with the assistance of the Holy Spirit" and thus have no need of approval by others (dogmatic

constitution *Lumen Gentium*, no. 25). The pope is thus not infallible in an absolute fashion, but only when certain conditions come together. The Church's general legislation codifies this doctrine, first regarding the solemn magisterium of the pope: "The supreme pontiff, by virtue of his charge, enjoys infallibility in the magisterium when, as pastor and supreme doctor of all faithful to whom falls the duty of confirming his brothers in the faith, he proclaims by a decisive act a doctrine on faith or morals that is to be held" (Code of Canon Law, 1983, c. 749, sec. 1, which repeats almost verbatim the dogmatic constitution *Lumen Gentium*, no. 25, sec. 3).

A doctrine is considered to be "infallibly defined only if it is manifestly established" (c. 749, sec. 3). Where there is doubt, the doctrine must not be considered infallible, unless there be proof to the contrary.

The Object of Infallibility. This infallibility "extends as far as the depository of Divine Revelation itself" (ibid.). In other words, infallibility pertains to anything that belongs to the domain of Revelation, either because it pertains directly to what has been revealed or because it is necessary to preserve revelation intact and assure its faithful transmission. Under this second condition we find both natural law and a certain number of fundamental truths of a philosophical, historical, scientific, or other order, including an ensemble of truths that have a logical and necessary relationship to the depository of faith, and are implicitly contained in it. These are considered as a secondary object of infallibility.

If the magisterium of the Church had no power over them, it could neither preserve nor conveniently explain the truths of salvation that make up its first object. These truths virtually revealed—or secondary object—are: truths of a spiritual order, such as the preambles to the faith; certain truths of a historical order, like the legitimacy of a council or its ecumenical nature; the objective meaning of an article; the canonization of saints; the solemn approval of religious orders; the recognition of a rite; and so forth.

The magisterium is infallible in each and every one of its acts, meaning each time the pope, or an ecumenical council with the approval of the Roman pontiff, proposes a doctrine with the intention of defining it as being one of faith. The intention is clearly deduced from the terms used.

Dominique Le Tourneau

Bibliography

Alonso, J. M. "La infalibilidad conciliar en la relación del primado y episcopado," *XXII Semana Española de Teología*, Madrid, 1963, 345–406.
Brinklann, B. "Gibt es unfehlbare Aüsserungen des mag-

isterium ordinarium des Papstes?," *Scholastik*, 28 (1953), 202–21.

Butler, B. C. *The Church and Infallibility*, London and New York, 2d ed., 1954.

Caudron, M. "Magistère ordinaire et infaillibilité pontificale d'après la constitution *Dei Filius*," *Ephemerides Theologicae Lovanienses*, 36 (1960), 393–431.

Chavasse, A. "La véritable conception de l'infaillibilité papale d'après le concile du Vatican," *Église et Unité*, Lille, 1948, 57–91; and "L'ecclésiologie au concile du Vatican: l'infaillibilité de l'Église," *L'Ecclésiologie au XIXe siècle*, Paris, 1960, 233–45.

Collective work, *La infalibilidad de la Iglesia*, Barcelona, 1964.

Congregation for the Doctrine of the Faith, declaration *Mysterium Ecclesiae*, 24 June 1973.

Dejaifve, G. "Ex sese non autem ex consensu Ecclesiae," *Salesianum*, 24 (1962), 283–96.

Dell'Addolorata, F. "Infallibilità," *EC*, 6 (1951), 1920–24.

Dublanchy, E. "Infaillibilité du pape," *DTC*, 7 (1923), 1638–1717.

Duprey, P. "Some reflections of infallibility," *Ecumenical Trends*, 18 (1989), 65–9.

Dupuy, B. D. "Infaillibilité de l'Église," *Catholicisme*, 5 (1962), 1549–72.

Hasler, A. *How the Pope Became Infallible: Pius IX and the Politics of Persuasion*, Garden City, N.Y., 1981.

Instruction on the Ecclesiastical Vocation of the Theologian, 24 May 1990.

Küng, H. *Infallible?: An Unresolved Enquiry*, New York, 1994.

Macarrone, M. "Una questione inedita dell'Olivi sull'infallibilità del Papa," *RSCI*, 3 (1949), 309–43.

Michel, A. F. "De l'infaillibilité de l'Église, *L'Ami du clergé*, 71 (1961), 305–10.

Mitchell, G. "Some Aspects of Infallibility," *Irish Theological Quarterly*, 23 (1956), 380–92.

Nau, P. "Le magistère pontifical ordinaire, lieu théologique," *Revue thomiste*, 56 (1956), 389–421.

O'Gara, M. "Reception as key: Unlocking ARCIC on infallibility," *Toronto Journal of Theology*, 3 (1987), 41–9.

O'Gara, M. *Triumph in Defeat: Infallibility, Vatican I, and the French Minority Bishops*, Washington, D.C., 1988.

Proaño, V. "Infalibilidad," *Gran Enciclopedia Rialp*, 12 (1973), 681–7.

Profession of Faith and Oath of Fidelity, 1 March 1989.

Rodriguez, P. "Infallibilis?" La respuesta de Santo Tomás de Aquino (Estudio de la terminología 'infallibilis-infallibiliter-infallibilitas' en sus tratados 'de fide')," *Scripta theologica*, 7 (1975), 51–123; and "La indefectibilidad de la Iglesia," ibid., 10 (1978), 235–67.

Ruffino, G. "Gli organi dell'infallibilità della Chiesa," *Salesianum*, 16 (1954), 39–76.

Sancho Bielsa, H. *Infalibilidad del Pueblo de Dios*, 1979.

Stirnimann, H. "Magisterio enim ordinario haec docentur," *Freiburger Zeitschrift für Philosophie und Theologie*, 1 (1954), 17–47.

Sullivan, F. A. *Magisterium: Teaching Authority in the Catholic Church*, New York, 1983.

Sullivan, F. "On the Infallibility of the Episcopal College in the Ordinary Exercise of its Teaching Office," *Acta Congressus Internationalis de Theologia Concilii Vaticani II, Romae 26 sept.–10 oct. 1966*, Vatican City, 1968, 189–95.

The Gift of Authority: Authority in the Church III: An Agreed Statement by the Anglican/Roman Catholic International Commission (ARCIC), New York, 1998.

Tierney, B. *Origins of Papal Infallibility, 1150–1350*, Leiden, 1972.

Tierney, B. *Rights, Laws, and Infallibility in Medieval Thought*, Brookfield, Vt., 1997.

Torrel, J. P. "L'infaillibilité pontificale est-elle un privilège 'personel'? Une controverse au premier concile du Vatican," *Revue des sciences philosophiques et religieuses*, 45 (1961), 229–45.

Walf, K. "L'infaillibilité comme la voit le 'Code de droit canonique' (canons 749–50)," *Studia canonica*, 23 (1989), 257–66.

INNOCENT I. *(b. Albe, ?, d. Rome, 12 March 417). Elected pope in 401. Buried in Pontian's cemetery in Rome. Feast day 28 July.*

According to the *LIBER PONTIFICALIS*, Innocent was born in Alba, not far from Rome; his father was also named Innocent. Jerome (*Ep.*, 130, 16) said that he was the "successor and [spiritual?] son" of pope ANASTASIUS (399–401). His papacy was thus during the time when the Germanic barbarians were unleashing their fury on the Western Empire, and especially on Italy. Alaric's Goths laid siege to Rome in 408. Innocent was a member of the Roman delegation sent to RAVENNA to negotiate a peace between Emperor Honorius and the king of the Goths. Since the court refused any concession, Alaric entered Rome, which he pillaged on 24 August 410, in the absence of Innocent, who was still in Ravenna (Orose, *Hist.*, VII, 39, *CSEL*, 5, 545). Despite these difficult circumstances, Innocent managed to make the most of the vicissitudes of a time that was ripe with new political developments, to spread the practice of Roman ecclesiastical customs. Thirty-six of his letters have been preserved (*PL*, 20, 460–638), some of which were incorporated into canonical collections at quite an early date.

For Innocent, the bishop of Rome's pastoral solicitude (*cura*), like that of his predecessor, Peter, extended to all

Churches. He affirmed that Rome faithfully guarded traditions that were directly transmitted to her by the prince of the apostles. He thus seized every opportunity to ask the other Churches to conform to Roman custom, proclaiming with calm assurance: "Such is the law of our Church" (*Ep.*, 17, 8, *PL*, 20, 531). More diplomatic than his successor, ZOSIMUS, he had more success in getting his interventions accepted. The demise of MILAN (which had lost its status as capital of the Empire in 402 because of the authority conferred to the episcopal see by men like Ambrose and Simplicianus), was seen by Innocent as an asset to the extent that the other Churches willingly turned toward Rome to have their differences settled.

Innocent I was scarcely an innovator; he was involved, especially, in working with the prescriptions that came out of the Roman council in 386. His activity was aimed at the adoption of the Roman rules already in use regarding the liturgy and Church discipline. Characteristic of this point of view was his letter to Decentius of Gubbio (*Ep.*, 25, *PL*, 20, 551–61 = Jaffe, 311, dating from 416), whose bishopric was located at the border of Milan's influence, but with quite different liturgical customs: the latter stressed the importance of acting as one did in Rome. Since he imagined that all the Churches of the West owed their origin to Peter or to his successors (*Ep.*, 25, 2, *PL*, 20, 552; cf. *Ep.*, 29, 1 or 30, 2), it appeared evident to him that "what has been transmitted to the Roman Church by Peter, the prince of the apostles, and what has been guarded there until now, should be observed by all" (Ibid.). Thus, only the bishop could confirm or admit penitents to reconciliation, and the organization of fasting or the place of the kiss of peace within the mass, were all to be set according to what was done in Rome.

The same spirit was also present in his letters addressed in 404 and 405 to the Gallic bishops Victrice of Rouen (*Ep.*, 2, *PL*, 20, 469–81 = Jaffe, 286) and Exsuperius of Toulouse (*Ep.*, 6, *PL*, 20, 495–502 = Jaffe, 293). These writings are veritable *libri regularum*, to use a term used by Innocent himself in his letter to Victrice (*Ep.*, 2, 1, *PL*, 20, 470): They define the ensemble of rules that should order ecclesiastical discipline. Innocent was pleased to see his bishops consult the Roman see. He had no intention of imposing new precepts, but rather of insuring the observance of those that had fallen into disuse through the negligence of a few bishops, and which Rome had preserved in all their initial purity (*Ep.*, 2, 2, *PL*, 20, 470).

He felt himself particularly qualified to dictate law, and he contributed to an elaboration of canonical legislation fashioned on the model of the imperial chancery. On those points that were controversial at the time, he drew up scriptural dossiers legitimizing Roman practice. For example, to justify the refusal to admit into the clerical state, widowers who were remarried or who had married

a widow, he generally started with Lv. 21:13; then he continued with the Pauline epistles (Tm. 3:2 and Tt. 1:6), and quotes from Genesis 1:28 and Pr. 19:14. This argument was then repeated at each pontifical intervention (*Ep.*, 2; 3; 13; 14). The dossier forbidding the marriage of bishops, priests, and deacons—and imposing continence upon those who had married before their ordinations—was also drawn up in a form that would remain classic in the Western Church. As far as ecclesiastical quarrels were concerned, although Innocent professed that they came out of provincial councils, in conformity with the councils of Nicaea and Sardica, he explicitly reserved the right for Rome to intervene as a last resort (*Ep.*, 2, 6, *PL*, 20, 473).

The conflicts that followed in the wake of Priscillianism, which continued to tear Spain apart despite the decisions made at the Council of Toledo in 400, provided Innocent with the opportunity to intervene there. In response to a group of bishops calling for his intervention, he firmly stipulated that those who refused the decrees of Toledo would be excommunicated (*Ep.*, 3, *PL*, 20, 486–94 = Jaffe, 292).

Innocent's favorite argument for the superiority of the Roman see relative to the other Churches would have been invalid for the great sees of the East. He nevertheless insinuated, in a letter to the bishop of Antioch (*Ep.*, 24, 1, *PL*, 20, 548), that Rome was superior to Antioch to the extent that the latter only had a visit from the apostle as he was passing through, while it was in Rome that he had decided to spend his life. The Eastern Empire was thenceforth completely separated from, even an enemy of, the Western Empire. The bishop of Rome could not plan on getting obedience there; the best he could do was play on conflicts among sees to back one of them or another by giving, or refusing, his communion. He was involved at the time of rivalry between Theophilus of Alexandria and John Chrysostom, bishop of Constantinople, which led to the latter's exile in 404. Each camp sent messengers to Rome, not for the purpose of seeking papal arbitration, but rather to seek solidarity with this prestigious see. Innocent, who sided with John, could only call for the convocation of a SYNOD to judge the matter, break with Theophilus of Alexandria and those who followed him (John's successor in Constantinople, and the bishops of Antioch and Beroea), and send letters of consolation to John and his friends. The matter took a dozen years to die down, and relations between Rome and the main sees of the East were gradually reestablished.

Illyricum, in the Balkans, was a transition zone between East and West that each half of the Empire tried to monopolize for itself. During Innocent I's time, it was attached administratively to the Eastern Empire, but the pope took advantage of troubles which, on a number of occasions, severed communications with Constantinople and tied it to Rome. In June 412 he made Rufus, the bishop of Thessalonica, his vicar for Illyricum (*Ep.*, 13, *PL*, 20, 515–17 = Jaffe, 300). By virtue of a delegation from the Roman primate, the bishop of Thessalonica was able to make all useful decisions, but if there was a need to refer a decision to a higher authority, it was to be referred to the bishop of Rome, and not the bishop of Constantinople. In fact, the institution was conceived especially for periods of crisis and, in more normal circumstances, Innocent preferred to exercise his authority directly (cf. *Ep.*, 17, *PL*, 20, 526–37, dated 414 = Jaffe, 303).

At the time of the Donatist crisis, the African bishops, while showing the greatest of deference to the Apostolic See, failed to ask its opinion or to obey its counsel. The Roman see was not even contacted regarding the great conference of 411.

The situation was quite different for the controversy regarding Pelagius and Caelestius which, it is true, was of concern only to Africa. Condemned in 411 in CARTHAGE, Pelagius had partisans in the East (he was rehabilitated by the Palestinian council of Diospolis in 415), and even in Rome. When two councils, meeting in Carthage and Milev in 416, renewed the sentences from 411, Aurelius of Carthage and Augustine pressured the pope to support the African decisions with all the authority of the Apostolic See (Augustine, *Ep.*, 175, ed. Goldbacher, 653–63). The Roman response (*Ep.*, 29–31, *PL*, 20, 582–97 = Jaffe, 321–3) was to conform to the African desires and draw its theological analyses largely from their line of reasoning. There was more than one view of what Roman primacy meant, however, depending on the Mediterranean coast of its origin. For the African bishops (Augustine, *Ep.*, 177, 19), their "little stream" and the "abundant fount" in Rome both originated from the teachings of Christ, and thus reinforced each other mutually; for Innocent (*Ep.*, 29, *PL*, 20, 583), the see of Rome was the powerful source from whence flowed the waters of the pure doctrine into all regions of the world.

Nancy Gauthier

Bibliography

PL, 20, 460–638 (Jaffe, 285–347). *Collectio Avellana*, *CSEL*, 35, 92–8.

Amman, E. *DTC*, 7, 2, 1940–50.

Caspar, E. *Geschichte des Papsttums*, Tubingen, 1930, 293–343.

Di Berardino, A. dir., *Initiation aux Peres de l'église* (French trans., Paris, 1987), 741–4.

Duchesne, L. *Le Liber Pontificalis*, 220–4.

Green, M. R. *Pope Innocent I*, Diss. Oxford, 1973.

Pietri, C. *Roma christiana*, Paris-Rome, 1976, *passim*.

Wermelinger, O. *Rom und Pelagius*, Stuttgart, 1975, 116–33.

INNOCENT II. *Gregorio Papareschi (d. Rome, 24 September 1143). Elected pope and consecrated 13/14 February 1130. Buried in Saint John Lateran, transferred to Santa Maria in Trastevere after 1308.*

Upon the death (February 1130) of HONORIUS II, whose election in 1124 had been difficult, the cardinals were deeply divided. Oppositions resulted in part from the debates that took place during negotiations for, and the conclusion of, the CONCORDAT of Worms which, in 1122, put an end to the INVESTITURE CONTROVERSY. Even though all were in agreement on maintaining principles in favor of the free election of bishops by chapters, and just as much so regarding the necessity of pursuing the goals of the Gregorian reform, some thought the concordat should be applied without seeking anything more from the emperor or collaborating with him, but still affirming the complete freedom of the Church, disengaging from imperatives that were too political. Others felt that any imperial intervention should be excluded from the ecclesiastical affairs of the kingdom of Italy and should cooperate with the lifeblood of the peninsula. Rivalries among the great Roman families were grafted onto this division, which did fluctuate; this was especially the case for the Frangipani, who were more aristocratic, and the Pierleoni, who were more popular.

With Honorius II almost at death's door and this news stirring up considerable agitation within the city, cardinal chancellor Aimeric, whose influence was great and who was campaigning in favor of the Frangipani, established a commission of eight cardinals, on the advice of his colleagues, for the purpose of choosing the future pope and then getting the choice approved by the plenary assembly. Of the eight, only three were representatives of the Pierleoni family, which nevertheless held a majority in the SACRED COLLEGE. Honorius died during the night of 13/14 February, and Aimeric gathered the six members of the commission together who were present at the time; only one of the six was from the Pierleoni faction. The prelates elected one of their number, by a vote of six to one; it was the cardinal from Sant'Angelo, Gregorio, who was close to the Frangipani family. They quickly engaged the assistance of other cardinals of their persuasion to confirm the balloting. Gregorio, who was led to the Lateran, was dressed in papal robes and took the name Innocent II. A few hours later, the other cardinals, those in the majority, elected cardinal Pietro Pierleoni, who had strongly reacted to the first vote, and who became pope under the name ANACLETUS II.

From a canonical point of view, both elections were irregular, even though a majority of the cardinal bishops, who, based on NICHOLAS II's decree of 1059, had the responsibility of choosing the pope and then proposing their choice to the other cardinals, were on Innocent's side. The reason for this is that this college of a limited number of members had never been convened, nor had it ever met. The commission Aimeric instituted had no decision-making power, especially because its session was held in the absence of two of its members. Neither of the individuals elected was unworthy. Anacletus was probably quite strongly opposed to collaboration with the emperor, but he was not lacking in dignity. Innocent was a well-to-do man, quite attached to spreading and deepening the Gregorian reform, but also attentive to political problems.

Immediately, however, it became necessary for him to be recognized as the only true pope. Powerless to oppose his rival in Rome—where he had to be consecrated in Santa Maria Nuova rather than in SAINT PETER'S—and barely able to count on the Italian bishops, the majority of whom were being especially prudent, and seeing the southern part of the peninsula slip away through the actions of Roger II of Sicily's Normans (at the time, Roger had taken over all the land as a whole, and preferred the other camp), he was forced to leave the city. He spent some time in Tuscany and then in Liguria; on 11 September he disembarked in France, at Saint-Gilles, in the town of Gard.

Like his adversary, Innocent had established contact during these months with the highest political authorities, evidently by presenting himself as the legitimate pontiff. Emperor Lothair, who had been warned by two successive legations, was in no hurry to change his position, letting it be known that it was up to the clergy, first of all, to determine legitimacy. The king of France, Louis VI, took additional actions. Probably on Suger's suggestion, he called the metropolitans of Sens, Reims, and Bourges together with the bishops of their provinces and some abbots, among whom was Bernard of Clairvaux—St. Bernard. The latter, the only one who had been informed by Aimeric and the Frangipani party, took a strong position in favor of Innocent II. Refusing to consider the canonical dossier, except to underscore the choice of the majority of the cardinal bishops within the commission, Bernard enthusiastically declared that Innocent was the legitimate pope, stating that he was more worthy, holier, and elected by the sounder party (*sanior pars*) of the Holy College; he decried the defects and the faults in his competitor. The bishops present thus followed his lead, as did the king. Innocent came to Cluny where he met Suger, and then he traveled to Clermont, where he convoked a synod, during which time Anacletus was excommunicated (October 1130). From there he went to Saint-Benoît-sur-Loire, where he had a meeting with the Capetian monarch, and finally to Reims. Aquitaine, however, which was brought along by the bishop of Angoulême, Gerard, continued to side with Anacletus, whereas the king of England, Henry I, upon the counsel of the archbishop of Rouen and St. Bernard, chose Innocent's party, as did his clergy. In November, after interventions by the archbishop of Magdeburg, Norbert, who was the founder of the Premonstratensians, Lothair did likewise.

Only a certain number of Italian bishops remained to be convinced, and Roger of Sicily had to be stopped. Accompanied by St. Bernard, who acted in vain to reverse the situation in Aquitaine, Innocent met Lothair in Liege; the latter committed to helping reestablish Innocent in Rome, and Innocent, in turn, promised to solemnly crown Lothair there, since he had not yet received the imperial crown. After a sojourn of a few months in France, Innocent returned to Italy and busied himself forming alliances, although this met no real success and never dealt with resolving the situation in Milan in favor of Anacletus. In the spring of 1133, Lothair intervened militarily, although not very forcefully. In April his army was at the gates of Rome, where Innocent had managed to return, even though Anacletus still held a number of areas of the city. He once again declared his decision to assist the pontiff against all enemies, but as soon as he was crowned in the Lateran (4 June), he left for Germany. Innocent was unable to maintain his presence in the capital of Christianity, set up residence in Pisa, and, in May 1135, presided over a council that renewed the sanctions against the opposing party. He worked with St. Bernard to rally the Milanese and, after a number of difficulties, succeeded. In 1136 and 1137, Lothair led a second expedition and inflicted serious defeat on Roger, although the latter managed to reestablish his position. At the time, however, lassitude overcame most of Anacletus's partisans. When he died in January 1138, less than two months after the emperor, his successor, Victor IV, whom his cardinals insisted on electing, raised no substantial obstacles before submitting. Roger II, who was recognized as king by the antipope and excommunicated, remained. Innocent II undertook to restrain him by force, but defeated and taken prisoner, he was forced into a treaty with Roger II. Innocent II, in turn, had to confer the royal title upon him, as well as the possession of the territory he held (treaty of Mignano, July 1139), thus inaugurating, despite himself and notwithstanding a few avatars in the following years, an alliance that would be to the Holy See's advantage for 40 years. The Romans also remained; they revolted in 1143 and planned to proclaim Rome a free commune a few weeks before the pontiff's death on 24 September.

These events give the impression of a papacy marked primarily by undertakings of a political nature, an impression that is reinforced when one considers other interventions in France (strong criticism of Louis VII on the occasion of his conflict with the count of Champagne) and England (support, albeit rather timid, given to King Stephen against Mathilda during the war of succession that took place after the death of King Henry I in 1135). This idea needs some clarification, however. Although it is true that through his intransigence he probably prolonged the schismatic conflict, and that he showed himself to be somewhat vindictive (to the point of deceiving St. Bernard), Innocent II ranks among those who continued the Gregorian reform. That was the motivating concern in his struggle against Anacletus, and the concern that pushed him, as soon as the secession was over, to convene the second ecumenical council in the Lateran (April 1139) for the purpose of continuing and completing the one held in 1123, and promulgating more solemnly the constitutions formulated at the synods of Clermont (1130), Reims (1131), and Pisa (1135). This latter council was against the investiture of bishops by members of the laity and against SIMONY; for the restitution of churches and tithing; and against tournaments and marriages to blood relatives. It was in the name of the same principles, in a realm that was no longer political, that he opposed Louis VII in order to defend the freedom of episcopal elections and conjugal morality (regarding the divorce of Raoul of Vermandois), and that he favored the new monasticism, particularly the Cistercians. It was not just coincidental that important work in reworking and adapting CANON LAW was accomplished during his papacy; gains made from the reform could be monitored and pontifical authority over the Church was solidly established, as seen especially in Gratian's *Decree*, which was compiled and edited between 1140 and 1142.

Marcel Pacaut

Bibliography

JW, 1, 840–911; 2, 715–16, 756–8.
PL, 179, 21–686.
Fliche-Martin, IX, 1.
Grabois, A. "Le schisme de 1130 et la France," *RHE*, 76 (1981), 593–612.
Maleczek, W. "Innocenz II.," *LexMA*, 5 (1991), 433–4.
Schmale, F. J. *Studien zum Schisma des Jahres 1130*, Cologne-Graz, 1961.
Stroll, M. *Symbols as Power: the Papacy following the Investiture Contest*, Leiden, 1991.
Watterich, 2, 174–275.

[INNOCENT III]. *Lando of Sezze. Antipope elected 29 September 1179, abdicated in January 1180.*

Lando of Sezze, cardinal deacon of Sant'Angelo, born to a family of the low nobility in Roman Campagna, a totally inactive and uninteresting antipope, was elected by some implacable partisans and a few of antipope CALLISTUS III's cardinals. Callistus had been forced to step down in 1178 after Frederick Barbarossa's recognition of ALEXANDER III as the only legitimate pope during conclusion of the preliminary sessions for the peace of Agnani and the treaty of Venice, which ended the papacy versus Empire controversy (July 1177). He resigned after a few months, via payment of an indemnity to his family. He was sent to the monastery in Cava.

Marcel Pacaut

Bibliography

JW, 2, 431.
Foreville, R. *Innocent III et la France*, in press (*Päpste und Papsttum*, 26).
Schwaiger, G. "Innocenz (III)," *LexMA*, 5 (1991), 434.

INNOCENT III. *Lotario "de Conti" from Segni (b. Gavignano, near Segni, 1160 or 1161, d. Perugia, 16 July 1216). Elected pope on 8 January 1198, consecrated on 22 February. Buried in the cathedral San Lorenzo in Perugia; his bones, first mixed with those of Urban IV and Martin IV, were transferred in 1605 to the chapel Santo Stefano, then in 1891 to Rome, to Saint John Lateran.*

Nearly two decades long, and marked by the fourth Lateran council like a pause sign in music, Innocent III's papacy, even more diversified than it was brilliant, was enriched by the conjunction—or perhaps the symbiosis—of the pope's exceptional personality and a period of political stability and intellectual activity.

Through his father, Trasimondo, he was born into the powerful seigneurial lineage of the Conti (*Comites*) from Segni, some 50 kilometers southeast of Rome. His mother, Claricia, belonged to the noble Roman Scotti family. Lotario thus had a triple education. He first studied in Rome, probably at the monastery of Sant'Andrea, under the ferula of Petrus Ismahel (whom he would make bishop of Sturi). Supported by cardinal Paul Scolari (the future CLEMENT III), he perhaps was also educated into the LITURGY in the *schola cantorum* at the Lateran. It was probably at this time that he became canon of Saint Peter's. He then went to Paris, where he followed, especially, the teachings of Pierre of Corbeil (whom he would make bishop of Cambrai, and later archbishop of Sens); three of the more noteworthy of his companions were Stephen Langton and Robert of Courson (both of whom he would name to be cardinals), and Eudes of Sully (bishop of Paris in 1196). At the time, the great debates centered on exegesis of the holy scriptures, the theology of the sacraments, and moral questions. He returned to Italy in 1186 where GREGORY VIII ordained him subdeacon. It appears doubtful, today, that he spent a long time studying CANON LAW in Bologna, another city that was going through a period of intense reflection, a representative figure of which was Uguccio of Pisa (bishop of Ferrara in 1190). From his years of apprenticeship, Innocent III drew a deep knowledge of theology and the Scriptures, perfect mastery of juridical vocabulary and concepts, and an intellectual method based in citations and his commentary, as well as in allegory. His work, and then his action, were guided above all by theological and moral thought; served by law, their importance came less from the originality of his personal reflections than from his ability to organize, codify, and elaborate strong syntheses. After his return to Rome, Lotario appears to have remained on the sidelines under Gregory VIII, although he did benefit from the return *en force* of the Roman cardinals under Clement III. It was probably in December 1189 that Clement made him cardinal deacon of Saints Sergio and Bacco. Fortune ebbed once again under CELESTINE III, who came from the Boboni lineage, adversaries of the Scotti. Under this papacy, Lotario was scarcely noticeable, except as an AUDITOR, although his being distanced from the CURIA should not be overly stressed. The pope died on 8 January 1198, leaving a critical situation. Fearing trouble, some of the cardinals, who had met in the Lateran, thought it wise to take refuge in the Frangipani fortified residence, *Septizonium*; Lotario, with the others, decided to remain in the Lateran until the funeral. Even though he was one of the youngest of the cardinals (he was 37 at the time), his election soon took place. His solid education and his energy were undoubtedly arguments in his favor, but the election, about which little is known, can be interpreted neither in simple terms as the victory of one clan over another, nor as one of the temporal over the spiritual party in the Curia: Celestine III's unfortunate dauphin, John of San Paolo, continued to play an important role during the new papacy. Lotario was ordained a priest on 21 February, and made bishop and enthroned on the following day.

Innocent III was immediately confronted by an open struggle with imperial power. In the context of intense reflection on temporal and spiritual powers, which had existed since the time of the Gregorian reform, he provided a remarkable deepening of theory, worked out in his letters and DECRETALS, which has already been carefully examined by historians. Even though the pope's reflection represented an essential step on a path leading to INNOCENT IV and BONIFACE VIII, the word THEOCRACY is too simplistic to characterize it. The key words in Innocent III's writings were *plenitudo potestatis*: not an absolute power over the world and its affairs, but a *plenitudo ecclesiasticae potestatis*, full pontifical power over all churches and all ecclesiastics, which entailed, among other things, undivided mastery of resignations and transferrals of bishops, and of the faculty to tax ecclesiastical benefices throughout Christianity, through levying the decima. It was an absolute power that was tempered by morality and canons. The pope called himself *vicarius Christi*, no longer simply the "vicar of Peter"; he called the Roman Church the *mater ecclesiarum* and the *mater omnium Christi fidelium*. He had the MOSAICS in the apse of Saint Peter's restored: Christ in his majesty is shown surrounded by Peter and Paul, and, below them, by the Roman Church and the pope. But even using and abusing the comparison to Melchisedech, the pope considered the temporal and the spiritual as two essentially autonomous spheres. In this he was following the jurist Uguccio, who affirmed the independence of both the Empire and the papacy (*quoad institutionem neutrum pendet ab altero*). Innocent III added only a correction: the pope could intervene in the temporal domain for religious reasons (*ratione peccati*). He did not intervene in the emperor's election, but examined the moral quality of the individual he was to consecrate; he did not meddle in the government of kingdoms, but he could excommunicate a sovereign and release his subjects from the oath of fidelity if the sovereign was a threat to ecclesiastical order. For the rest, each of the two jurisdictions, represented by a vicar, was independent, or better said, each was associated "as is the moon to the sun"; through consecration, temporal power received its legitimacy "as the moon receives its light from the sun." Only this theoretical background, the basis for a firmly held political line, allowed an approach to the history of the pope's relations with the princes of his day, relations which are incomprehensible if one is forced to keep track of victories and defeats, remarkable feats, and procrastinations.

The affairs of the Empire were necessarily one of the first and the most constant of Innocent III's concerns: It was symptomatic that the pope devoted several years to these affairs, as well as a special catalog (nicknamed *Thronstreitregister* by German historians), a dossier where he registered all documents he considered to be important. When Henry VI died on 27 September 1197, two competitors faced one another: the Staufen Philip of Swabia, Henry VI's brother, elected in March 1198, and the Guelph Otto, elected in June 1198. The two agreed only on excluding Frederick from the succession, the son of the late king and of Queen Constance, heir to the NORMANS in the kingdom of Sicily. In addition to the fact that he was to decide on which of the elected individuals to crown emperor, the pope was doubly implicated in the quarrel, which interfered in the international arena with the conflict between France and England. As an Italian territorial power he clashed with the Empire on boundaries of the PATRIMONY OF SAINT PETER; upon the request of Constance (who had died in December 1198), he assured Sicily that young Frederick, who had provisionally given up his claims to German royalty, would be cared for. Successively supporting each of the three actual, or potential pretenders, Innocent III constantly needed to improvise. First recognized by the pope, Philip launched (January 1199) Markward of Anweiler's troops against Montecassino. The pope then committed, more and more heavily, in favor of Otto. The kingdom of Sicily was saved by the papal troops, and even more so by the death of Markward, who had reached Palermo (1202). But quickly, in the face of Otto's demands and threats in Central Italy, Innocent III built a relationship with Philip. In 1207 he arranged the marriage of one of Philip's daughters to one of the sons of his brother Richard of Segni. Philip's assassination (21 June 1208) forced him to negotiate with Otto, who was crowned in Rome on 4

October 1209. Otto IV immediately resumed his imperial politics of territorial expansion in Italy. In 1210, war had begun again and the kingdom of Sicily was again invaded. On 18 November, Innocent III released the emperor's faithful from their oath of fidelity. On 31 March 1211, he excommunicated him and formed a liaison with the king of France, Philip Augustus, and with Frederick, who was elected and crowned king of Frankfurt on 5 December 1212, and recognized by the pope, whom he thanked with the golden BULL of Egen (12 July 1213), in which he promised to restore the integrity of the PAPAL STATES. Otto IV's already shaken power could not withstand the defeat of Bouvines (27 July 1214). On 1 July 1216, Frederick II promised that after his imperial coronation his son Henry, who had already been crowned king of Sicily, would be a vassal to the Holy See and independent of his own father. The underlying issues were not solved and the contentiousness that had accumulated poisoned the papacies of Innocent III's successors.

There were conflicts with other European monarchies, all just as traditional, caused by either episcopal elections or difficulties applying canonical rules to matrimonial issues. Innocent III, in fact, granted an essential role to the function of bishop, which was increased by CANON LAW, assuring the bases of what has been called the "episcopal reform" of the 13th century (J. Avril). Informed in both its ideology and its institutions by the papal model, the episcopacy would, in fact, have a great century, but it was strictly controlled. Against the archbishop of Canterbury in 1205, Innocent III wanted to impose Stephen Langton: the conflict opened in 1206. The king of England, John, resisted, and an INTERDICT was put upon the kingdom in March 1208. The king, excommunicated, did not submit until 1213, and became a vassal to the pope like the sovereigns of Aragon and Portugal. His power thenceforth legitimate, King John saw himself supported against the English barons by the pope, who annulled the *Magna Carta* (1225) imposed upon the sovereign. Innocent III intervened with similar force in matrimonial affairs, which placed him in opposition to Peter I of Aragon, Alphonse IX of Leon, and Philip Augustus.

Another traditional trait was that papal diplomacy was to a large extent conditioned either by affairs in the East or by its concern for getting France and England into negotiation. Like almost all the representatives of the medieval papacy, Innocent III wanted to work toward unity with the Churches of the East. Although there was some hope with Armenia and Bulgaria, which had broken away from Constantinople, and likewise with the Serbs and the Albanians who were asking for reattachment to Rome primarily for political reasons, these successes faded when his papacy ended. Without neglecting the MISSIONS, which were active in Prussia and the Balkans (the bishopric of Riga was founded), the pope accorded serious attention to the CRUSADE, where failure was obvious, while in the West the Spanish *Reconquista* brought an important victory at Las Navas de Tolosa (16 July 1212). As early as 31 December 1199, the pope provided financing for an expedition to the Holy Land with a tax of one-fortieth on all the ecclesiastical revenues; he and the cardinals were taxed at a rate of 10 percent. We know that the troops of the 4th crusade, who left Venice in October 1202, were progressively turned back from their objective, first by operations in Illyria, and then against Constantinople itself. Overwhelmed, the pope and his legates always withdrew when criticized by the heads of expeditions. Preferring to compromise, they welcomed the installation in Constantinople, in April 1204, of a (Catholic) "Latin Empire" of the East: they could still hope to temper the actions of barons who were especially eager to carve out principalities for themselves, to thus reconstitute, de facto, the unity of the Christian Churches, and have a new base of departure toward the Holy Land at their disposal. Far from attaining this goal, all that was achieved was an accumulation of rancor among the Eastern branches of Christianity, and in the West the crusade ideal ran out of steam. The pope did not give up, however. On 19 April 1213 he called for a new expedition. Seeking to avoid the Venetian monopoly that had weighed heavily in turning back the crusade in 1202–4, he negotiated the transportation of troops with a number of Italian ports. The levying of a new decima was prescribed, and then confirmed, at the fourth Lateran council. For three years, the clergy was to deposit one-twentieth of its revenues; convening the troops was planned for Sicily for 1 June 1217, but the pope's death provisionally interrupted preparations.

The battle against the Albigensian HERESY would affect both the tendencies and the mixed successes of the papacy. Innocent III continued the work of his predecessors, but with more pragmatism and a better sense of contemporary realities; he codified anti-heretical legislation and inserted his ideas on the cooperation of the two powers into the battle. But here again, he was largely overwhelmed by the designs of the laity, occasionally even by the initiatives of his LEGATES. Even though he fully shared their views on purges of the bishops of the south of France, he was reluctant to accept their total support in the struggle—the interested struggle—of the barons of the north against the lords of the south. On 12 January 1208, the papal legate Pierre de Castelnau was assassinated by a servant of the count of Toulouse; an expedition was decided upon, although the king of France, too occupied by England, did not wish to head it. The army and the new legate, Arnaud Amalric, continued their march unaware of the count of Toulouse's submission to the pope. Several years of war, around the decisive battle of Muret (12 September 1213), assured the crusaders' victory. The hostilities, which continued, increasingly became an affair of the kingdom of France, while the pope, not without prevarications, retained his concern for respecting all the steps of judicial procedure as far as the count of Toulouse was concerned, up to the time of his definitive condemnation at the Lateran council. His scruples gave birth, in Languedoc, to a legend about the condemnation of the count of Toulouse having been exacted from him by force.

Successes were more stunning in the spiritual arena. Innocent III, reinforced by the disappointment of the Cistercians, took the battle into the heretical land itself, that of apostolic poverty and preaching to populations that were poorly supervised by the traditional forms of ecclesiastical life. This explains the papacy's approval (and thus the regulation) of new initiatives, moving sometimes to the limits of deviance, that its predecessors in any case had, or would have, rejected. The cases of approval given to the Franciscans are well known. In 1210, most probably, Francis of Assisi and 11 companions took the first step; after initial hesitations, influenced by the cardinals supporting their enterprise, Innocent III decided in their favor and gave verbal approval to a first draft of a rule. From a simple brotherhood, the Franciscans soon became a congregation subject to the pope. They received authorization to preach everywhere and their organization was made official at the Lateran council. In his anti-Cathar preaching, St. Dominic received, if not an official mission, at least formal authority in 1206; he was at the Lateran council. Definitive confirmation of the institution of the Dominicans would come from HONORIUS III, shortly after Innocent III's death, but Innocent approved a number of other initiatives including Guy de Montpellier's hospitallers and St. John of Matha's Trinitarians. Even more original, the *umiliati* were unified under his aegis: These communities of clerics and laypeople, working with their hands, recruiting primarily among the urban artisan class in Northern Italy, had been tolerated with reserve by Alexander III and declared heretical by Lucius III. They saw their rights to meet and preach recognized in 1201. The pope organized them into three branches: a community of clerics, a community of laypeople leading a monastic life, and what was new, a community of laypeople pursuing their lives in the world. The same politics were followed regarding the branch of the Waldensians, Durand of Huesca's "poor Catholics."

These new and fertile initiatives should not overshadow the pope's desire, which was just as strong, although less fortunate, to promote reform in the traditional orders. In 1203 the pope thus prescribed for Italy, France, and England, the holding of triennial chapters general in all the exempt Benedictine monasteries, within the framework of ecclesiastical provinces or kingdoms. Among the canons regular of St. Augustine he intervened more selectively for the reform of some chapters, one of which was that of Saint Peter's. In 1207 Innocent III even planned to regroup cloistered monastics—merging all the

orders—into a *universale coenobium*, dedicated to San Sisto, in homage of SIXTUS II. After his failure, the convent was taken over by Saint Dominic in 1221.

Quite otherwise was the papacy's success in structuring the different bodies of the Curia: the APOSTOLIC CAMERA, as well as, and especially, the chapel and the CHANCERY. It was not by chance that the first rules preserved from the chancery go back precisely to the time of Innocent III, and that this body saw, on bases that henceforth were quite rigorous, to the compilation and preservation of REGISTERS for recording papal ACTS. Innocent III paid special and personal attention to the exercise of justice: Among his contemporaries he earned the nickname "Solomon III." A close examination of the careers of the cardinals in place when Innocent ascended to the papacy, and of the 32 cardinals he created, shows that, without conflicts, the sovereign pontiff did not give the SACRED COLLEGE the entire role it claimed: the decline, starting in the sixth year of his papacy, is emphasized in papal letters via the traditional phrase *de fratrum nostrorum [=cardinalium] consilio*. The cardinals in leadership positions during the preceding papacy were often relegated to honorific positions, devoid of any great influence, such as Cencio, the cardinal deacon of Santa Lucia promoted in 1200 to the rank of cardinal priest (the future Honorius III). Others were not always able to escape disgrace, like Petrus Capuanus, who had failed to control the deviations of the 4th crusade, over which he presided in the company of Soffredo of Santa Prassede. Even though almost all the cardinals created by Innocent III (30 out of 32) were from the Curia, there were few men of confidence, frequently employed as NUNCIOS, legates, or AUDITORS; this tendency was even more marked at the end of his papacy. Those in this category who were most active were Ugolino, a relative of Innocent III (made cardinal deacon of Saint-Eustace in 1198, promoted to the bishopric of Ostia in 1206, several times a legate, and the future GREGORY IX), the Spaniard Pelagius (made cardinal deacon of Santa Lucia in Septisolio in 1205, and then made priest at Santa Cecilia in 1210, and finally bishop of Albano in 1212, and quite often an auditor), and Guala Bicchieri (created cardinal deacon of Santa Maria in Portico in 1205, priest of San Martino in 1211, and several times a legate in Italy and France). Somewhat in the background were collaborators who were nevertheless influential such as John Colonna of San Paolo (made cardinal deacon of Santa Maria in Cosmedin in 1200), chancellor, legate, and auditor, but to a great extent the pope relied on family members, and especially on chaplains, a position which could be used as a reward for a promotion to the rank of cardinal (of the 12 cardinals created from 1205 on, five had been chaplains and one the canon of Saint Peter's). The pope also promoted intellectuals to the rank of cardinal such as Parisian theologian Robert of Courson, who was made cardinal priest of San Stefano Rotundo in 1216, and legate in France from 1213 to 1215.

In what was progressively structured as a veritable Papal State, the pope "was conscious of having begun a new relationship, a relationship of state, with his lands" (E. Dupré-Theseider). In effect, Innocent III pursued the "politics of recuperation" (the term was invented by historian J. Ficker) of his predecessors, directed toward Mathilda of Canossa's contested inheritance, the duchy of RAVENNA and Tuscany. As soon as he was elected, the pope affirmed his positions in Rome, and received the unconditional submission of Conrad von Urslingen, who governed the duchy of Spoleto for the emperor. The struggle with Markward of Anweiler was more difficult, as he kept a firm grip on the March of Ancona and the duchy of Ravenna until the time of his death in 1202. Otto IV, with the "promise of Neuss" (8 June 1201), recognized the land from Radicofani to Ceprano as belonging to the pope, as well as the Exarchate of Pentapolis, the March of Ancona, the duchy of Spoleto, Mathilde's lands, the county of Bertinoro, and all the lands already confirmed by the emperors (the outskirts of Rome, Campagna, and Maremme to the south, and to the north Sabina and Tuscia around Orvieto, Narni, and Viterbo). The papacy actually extended its influence only to the duchy of Spoleto and some possessions in Tuscany. In the March of Ancona, it delegated its claims by supporting the Estes. Increase in pontifical power over lands and communities counted even more than territorial growth. Feudalization was pushed, building a network of *castra speciala* was continued, seigneurial rights (military service, justice, taxation, etc.) were affirmed, interventions in the lives of communes became more delicate, and organization of administrative personnel continued. At the head of the patrimony there was an increase of *rectores*, cardinals but also laypersons from the Roman nobility. This did not happen without crises: factions among barons, agitation in communes that were not exempt from heretical uprisings, and troubles in Rome itself between 1202 and 1205 (Innocent, who sought to reaffirm papal authority relative to the senator and the prefect of the city, was insulted during a procession on 7 April 1203, and left Rome from May 1203 to March 1204). In short, here again Innocent III codified and systematized: Pursuing, above all, the task of his predecessors, he was "an agent for restoration and continuation more than founder of the Papal State's bases" (P. Toubert).

More than 6,000 letters and acts are still extant from his papacy, the most important of these carrying the personal mark of Innocent III. In the winter of 1209–10, he published the compilation of a number of his decretals, a task taken on by his chaplain, Petrus Collivaccinus. Called *Compilatio tertia*, the compilation was sent officially to the university of Bologna. A relatively limited number of sermons were preserved and quickly gathered by Arnaud de Citeaux. W. Imkamp has demonstrated the learned rhetorical construction of the sermon the pope gave at the opening of the fourth Lateran council on the theme *Desiderio desideravi hoc pascha manducare vobiscum antequam patiar* (Lc 22, 15), but all of Innocent III's doctrinal works date back to his time as cardinal. It is interesting to note that, in them, he shows himself to be primarily a theologian, and a "timid" one (M. Maccarone); he is only incidentally a liturgist, and never a canonist. Toward 1194–95, he composed his most famous work, the *De miseria humanae conditionis*, formerly called *De contemptu mundi*. This piece of writing, which strings together the effects of style and structure, looks very much like schoolwork, in both what it says and the way it says it. Relying on a cento of citations, it has been defined as a "little ascetico-moral treatise describing the baseness of the human condition" (M. Maccarone). Its dark pessimism, which engendered the incidental condemnation of some of its propositions by the Catalan inquisitor Nicolas Eymerich (d. 1390), is explained all the more easily by the fact that it was originally conceived as the first panel of a diptych that was to be followed by another dealing with human dignity. The quality of his language and his scholarly, one might even say pedantic, side, explain his rapid and lasting success: Over 600 of his manuscripts are preserved, although rarely under the pope's name. His works were first edited in 1473, and he was still held in honor in Jesuit colleges in the 17th century. Just as scholarly, the brilliant allegorical variations of *De quadripartita specie nuptiarum*, were not really successful. Just as deeply theological, the *De missarum mysteriis* (formerly called *De sacro altaris mysterio*), a long commentary on the papal mass which, with a eucharistic theology still somewhat floating, had the merit of providing a clear wording of the doctrine of transubstantiation. We are also indebted to Innocent III for a commentary on the penitential psalms, which he revised in 1216. Several treatises would later be incorrectly attributed to him, particularly a liturgical compilation, the *Summa de sacramentis*, called *Totus homo* from its inception.

The theological and moral dimensions of Innocent III's work and actions should also be restored, for these dimensions provided unity. This pope, who was also a monarch; this theoretician, who was also pragmatic; this theologian, who was also a judge, clericalized the Curia, had monks serve him at his table, adopted white wool for his vestments, and imposed the same upon the members of the papal household. He returned to the old papal *topos* of the weight of the world's affairs, not in order to speak about lassitude, as his illustrious predecessors GREGORY I and GREGORY VII had done, but according to his biographer, to apply to himself the maxim *Qui tangit picem inquinabitur ab eo* (Si 13, 1), a biblical version of dirty hands: "He who touches tar will be soiled."

Olivier Guyotjeannin

Bibliography

PL, 217, 309–688; treatises and opuscules, Ibid., 691–1130: outdated edition, not yet replaced except for the *De miseria humanae conditionis*, ed. M. Maccarone, Lugano, 1955 and R. E. Lewis, Athens (Georgia), 1978.

PL, 217, 1–308.

PL, 214–16 (Paris, 1855, reproduction of the Baluze edition of 1682), edition currently being replaced by *Die Register Innocenz III.*, ed. O. Hageneder, H. Haidacher et al., 2 vols. already published [the first two years of the papacy], Graz-Cologne, 1964 and Rome-Vienna, 1979; vols. 3 and 4 in preparation by W. Maleczek.

Potth., 1–467, 2041–56, 2135.

Cheney, C. R. *Innocent III (1198–1216) and England*, Stuttgart, 1976 (*Päpste und Papsttum*, 9).

Egger, C. "Papst Innocenz III. als Theologe" *AHP*, 30 (1992), 51–123.

Frenz, T. *I documenti pontifici nel Medioevo e nell'età moderna*, Vatican City, 1989 (*Littera antiqua*, 6), 103–4.

Gesta, in *PL*, 214, XVII–CCXXVIII (this firsthand source, composed in several stages by a cleric who was near the pope, written on the double model of hagiographical literature and the *Liber pontificalis*, stops in 1208; on its stratification: Y. LeFèvre, *MAH*, 61 [1949], 242–5; new ed. in preparation by W. Maleczek).

Imkamp, W. "Sermo ultimus quem fecit dominus Innocentius papa tercius in Lateranensi concilio generali," *Römische Quartalschrift*, 70 (1975), 149–79; *Das Kirchenbild Innocenz' III. (1198–1216)*, Stuttgart, 1983 (*Päpste und Papsttum*, 22).

Kempf, F. *Papsttum und Kaisertum bei Innocenz III.*, Rome, 1954; "Innocenz III. und der deutsche Thronstreit," *AHP*, 23 (1985), 63–91.

Lackner, C. "Studien zur Verwaltung des Kirchenstaates unter Papst Innocenz III.," *Römische historische Mitteilungen*, 29 (1987), 127–214.

Laufs, M. *Politik und Recht bei Innocenz III., Kaiserprivilegien, Thronstreitregister und Egerer Goldbulle in der Reichs- und Rekuperationspolitik Papst Innocenz' III.*, Cologne-Vienna, 1980 (*Kölner historische Abhandlungen*, 26).

Maccarone, M. "Innocent III," *Dictionnaire de spiritualité et de mystique*, 7-2 (1971), 1767–73; *Studi su Innocenzo III*, Padua, 1972 (*Italia Sacra*, 17); "Innocenzo III e la feudalità: non ratione feudi sed occasione peccati," *Structures féodales et féodalisme dans l'Occident méditerranéen (Xe–XIIIe siècle)*, Rome, 1980 (*CEFR*, 44), 457–514.

Maccarone, M. *Nuovi studi su Innocenzo III*, Rome, in press.

Maleczek, W. *Papst und Kardinalskolleg von 1191 bis 1216*, Vienna, 1984 (*Publikationen des hist. Instituts . . . in Rom*, I, 6); "Innocenz III.," *LexMA*, 5 (1990), 434–7.

Moore, J. C. "Lotario dei Conti de Segni (Pope Innocent III) in the 1180s," *AHP*, 29 (1991), 255–8.

Moore, J. C. "Pope Innocent III, Sardinia, and the Papal State," *Speculum*, 62 (1987), 81–101.

Morris, C. *The Papal Monarchy: The Western Church from 1050–1250*, New York, 1989.

Pacaut, M. *La Théocratie: l'Église et le pouvoir au Moyen Âge*, Paris, 1989 (*Bibliothèque d'histoire du christianisme*, 20), 107–24.

Pennington, K. *Popes and Bishops: The Papal Monarchy in the Twelfth and Thirteenth Centuries*, Philadelphia, 1984.

Pennington, K. "The Legal Education of Innocent III," *Bulletin of Medieval Canon Law*, 4 (1974), 70–7.

Powell, J. M. *Innocent III: Vicar of Christ or Lord of the World?*, Washington, D.C., 1994.

Sayers, J. E. *Innocent III: Leader of Europe, 1198–1216*, New York, 1994.

"Thronstreitregister," *Regestum Innocentii III papae super negotio Romani imperii*, ed. F. Kempf, Rome, 1947 (*MHP*, 12).

Tillmann, H. *Papst Innocenz III.*, Bonn, 1954, English trans., *Pope Innocent III*, Amsterdam, 1980.

INNOCENT IV. *Sinibaldo Fieschi (b. Lavagna-Genoa, ca. 1190, d. Naples, 7 December 1254). Elected pope 25 June 1243, consecrated 28 June 1243. Buried in Naples.*

Genoan Sinibaldo Fieschi was one of the intellectual elite of his time and a jurist of tremendous depth. Accustomed to wide geopolitical spaces, he brought—through his canonical reflections and his political actions—hierocratic ideas to a kind of apogee. According to Innocent IV, *christianitas* should serve the universal claims of the papacy, the jurisdictional power of the pope being the pivot around which the social order of all Christianity revolved. Such extreme positions could not fail, in the long run, to provoke reactions, both among the more spiritually oriented members of religious orders, and among movements whose ideals included poverty.

Sinibaldo Fieschi's family on his father's side was one of the most powerful in eastern Liguria. His father, Ugo, count of Lavagna, was the first to bear the name (*Fliscus*), which related to his imperial responsibility as exactor of fiscal charges. Starting in 1166, he established his residence in Genoa, following agreements with the consuls. Young Sinibaldo, who was born between 1180 and 1190, did his earliest studies in Parma under the tutelage of his uncle Obizzo, bishop of the city since 1195. Perhaps following family tradition, he studied in Bologna, where he is known to have been in 1213. However, there is no documentary evidence to confirm that he taught there. In 1223 the young Fieschi was in contact with the cardinal LEGATE Ugolino, the future GREGORY IX. His first duty in the Curia, as *auditor litterarum contradictarum* (starting on 14 November 1226), was the crown in his excellent education as a jurist. His rise to the Roman CURIA was rapid: on 31 May 1227, shortly after his election to the papacy, Gregory IX called him to the head of the papal chancery and, on 18 September, he made him cardinal of San Lorenzo in Lucina. Rector of the March of Ancona between 1234 and 1239, he continued to reside in the Curia, as is shown by the list of his subscriptions to Pope Gregory IX's privileges.

On 25 June 1243, Sinibaldo was elected pope after a long vacancy, during the course of which he fell seriously ill. Frederick II who, for the occasion, had not freed the two cardinals he had imprisoned in 1241 off the coast of the island of Giglio, hailed the news *gaudio magna*. The election was the fruit of a compromise among the cardinals, prefiguring the capitulations in the early 14th century concerning two objectives: Church reform and peace with the emperor. At first, Frederick II accepted the peace proposals of the newly elected pontiff, who was demanding freedom for the island of Giglio's prisoners and open access to the city of Rome for the pope, but suddenly, and for reasons that are difficult to discern, he withdrew his ambassadors. The pope entered Rome on 20 October 1243. On 28 May of the following year he proceeded to nominate ten new cardinals. There was supposed to be a meeting between the emperor and the pope in Narni on 7 June 1244, but this time it was the pope who decided to flee from the Church States. A Genoan boat took him to his native city, where he fell ill (July–October). In the autumn, he set out across the Alps and arrived in Lyon, the imperial city near the kingdom of France (far from Italian conflicts) with great possibilities for access. Three weeks after his arrival in Lyon, on 27 December 1244, Innocent IV called for a council for the feast of Saint John in the following year. A convocation was also addressed to the emperor. For the first time, the superiors general of the mendicant orders were invited to a general council. The affairs of Rome and the PATRIMONY were left to four cardinals (Reginald of Segni, Stephen Conti, Richard Annibaldi, and Ranuccio Capocci), who remained behind in Italy.

Three months before the council was opened (13 April 1245), the pope renewed the excommunication of Frederick II and his son, King Henry (VII). A late attempt (May 1245) on the part of the patriarch of Antioch, Albert—a friend of the emperor who enjoyed unquestioned prestige within the Roman Curia—to reconcile the pope and the emperor failed because of Innocent IV's misgivings. This was the first time since the great Lateran COUNCILS that the foreground of the council scene was occupied by problems that were essentially political, as opposed to disciplinary or pastoral, such as Church reform or combating HERESY.

The first council of Lyon did not excommunicate the emperor again, probably because, according to Innocent IV, his bull of 13 April 1245 had no need of the council's confirmation. The pope alone was authorized to depose the emperor because the latter's position was created by the pope.

At the height of the polemic against Frederick, someone within the Roman Curia composed the *Eger cui lenia*, "one of the fundamental texts of pontifical theocracy." The author systematically refuted all the arguments advanced by imperial propaganda (Pierre de la Vigne) immediately after the council, and arrived at the claim "that he does not recognize the Son of God, heir to the universe, as Lord and God, he who claims to be exempt from submission to his vicar." The pope, Christ's vicar, possessed "a general legation" from the king of kings, from whom he had received "the fullness of power to bind and unbind not only whomever, but also whatever upon earth, such that no thing or matter was excepted, this power embracing more generally the entire universe." The pamphlet does not appear to have been written by the pope himself (despite the account of Tolome of Lucca), but it nevertheless does not contradict what Sinibaldo Fieschi had affirmed in his *Apparatus* regarding the difference between the two powers. It was aimed especially at establishing that the emperor, through his faults and his excesses, had made himself "unworthy of the Empire, of any honor or any dignity," and that the Lord had deprived him "of the dignity of the Empire and kingdoms."

Lyon I in itself had not eliminated Frederick II, who was at the time still sufficiently strong to have influence in Lyon. On the instigation of Innocent IV's parents, the city of Parma revolted on 16 May 1247, obliging the emperor to interrupt his excursion to the city of the council. On 18 March 1248, the city of Vittoria, built by the emperor to lay siege to Parma, was taken by the besieged. The defeat constituted a decisive turning point in Frederick II's reign. Mediation by the king of France once again failed and the pope renewed his excommunication. On 1 November 1248, William of Holland was proclaimed king at Aix-la-Chapelle.

The pope decided to delay publication of the conciliar canons, in order to make some corrections in them. Moreover, he, himself, wrote the commentary on them in his *Apparatus*. Their distribution took advantage of the well-established existence of the collections of *decretals*. Twenty-three decrees were added to complete Gregory IX's *Liber Extra*. They would appear again (with the exception of the second), with excerpts from the bull of deposition *Ad Apostolicae Dignitatis*, in BONIFACE VIII's *Liber Sextus*.

During his stay in Lyon in 1245, Innocent IV instituted a *studium generale* to follow the travels of the Roman Curia. By this decision, the pope, who was undoubtedly trying to emulate Frederick II, the founder of the *studium* in Naples, accorded privileges of *studia* to a number of private schools of law, both civil and canon, that existed within the Roman Curia. The *Studium Curiae*, or to be more precise, the different (private) schools of (civil and canon) law within and around the Curia, were supposed to articulate the *opinio Curiae* in matters of canonical legislation.

During the council, Innocent IV allowed the cardinals a red hat, probably to strengthen their symbolic connection to the pope (one of whose traditional signs was a red cloak, or *cappa rubea*). The cardinals wore the hat for the first time during Innocent IV's visit to Cluny (November 1245).

Open to the world by virtue of his social and geographical roots, Innocent IV took an interest in increasing his knowledge, primarily concerning the Tartars and the Far East, and he made a number of diplomatic overtures. It was in Lyon, at the court of Innocent IV, that the West was able to collect first-hand information on the Tartars, thanks to a certain "archbishop Peter," a prelate who was probably of Russian origin, and to John of Toledo's chaplain, Roger of Torrecuso, the author of one of the most reliable sources of information on the Tartar invasion of Hungary, the *Carmen miserabile super destructione regni Hungariae*. Roger had been taken prisoner by the Mongols in 1241 and 1242. Moreover, the pope planned two embassies, which he entrusted to Lawrence of Portugal (whom we know only from the pope's missive) and John of Plan Carpin. The latter was sent into the heart of Asia. Departing from Lyon on 16 April 1245, he returned two years later in 1247. Innocent IV entrusted the mendicant orders with other missions. The minister general of the Franciscans, John of Parma, was sent to the court of John III Ducas Vatatzes, the Byzantine emperor of Nicaea, with the mission of convincing him to withdraw his support for Frederick II, and to explore the possibility of opening negotiations for peace and unity. In a wide range of diplomatic and missionary activities, Innocent IV sent one of his primary advisors, the Spanish Franciscan Lope Fernandez of Ayn into the Maghreb. Armed with plenipotentiary powers, he was to attempt to negotiate concessions with the caliph Al-Said for freedom of worship and, for cases of conflict or danger, for allocating a certain number of set locations to facilitate the Christians' gathering and returning to the country of their origin.

In 1215 the fourth Lateran council had officially sanctioned the granting of a plenary INDULGENCE to the crusaders, albeit not without expressing fears about the negative effect that excessive recourse to indulgences might have on penitential practices. Innocent IV, however, granted a plenary indulgence to the widows and prosecutors of the crusaders. In 1249 the pope wanted ten young students to travel to the university of Paris to learn Arabic and other Eastern languages. In the climate of the 13th century, the Curia's manifest interest in Eastern languages, under the impetus of Innocent IV, who, because of his (Genoan) family origins was accustomed to a wide geo-cultural horizon, was shared by the most important heads of the mendicant orders.

Gregory IX and Innocent IV reached the point where they had to intervene in the question of the Talmud, which in the mid-1230s exploded with rare violence among members of the *studium* in Paris. Gregory IX acted on the instigation of a French Jew, Nicolas Donin, who converted to Christianity in 1236. Donin gave him a dossier of 35 accusations against the Talmud in 1238–9. Innocent IV had not taken the initiative, either. He did so at the request of the chancellor and the doctor regents of the university of Paris. According to Innocent IV, the Talmud contained "inextricable and manifest fabrications" regarding the Virgin Mary, as well as errors and inanities that made it blasphemous "toward God and Christ," and was thus worthy of condemnation. The pope then informed cardinal legate Eudes of Châteauroux that after his own examination, the Talmud should be tolerated in the parts that entailed no injury to the Christian faith. The cardinal legate nevertheless overturned the pope's position, declaring that these books "were so full of controversial declarations that they could not be tolerated without harm to the Christian faith," and decided not to return the "intolerable" books to the rabbis, but rather to condemn them officially. Innocent IV took no measure to extend the inquiry beyond Paris, and appealed to no sovereign outside Saint Louis.

Toward the middle of the century, when the famous quarrel between the secular teachers and mendicants (1253–9) broke out, the papacy, after a few hesitations ended up rallying to the cause of the FRANCISCANS and the DOMINICANS. The friars' prestige within the Parisian schools and their theological positions thus got official recognition at the highest level. In April 1253, the secular teachers decided no longer to accept anyone into their body who had not first taken an oath to their statutes. This measure was aimed at eliminating Dominican and Franciscan teachers. On 1 July 1253, Innocent IV, doing a spectacular about-face, ordered the secular teachers to accept the teachers of the mendicant orders. In 1254 however, Innocent IV, in his desire to "govern in a manner with which no curious critic could find fault," declared himself to be in favor of the demands of the secular teachers, of giving financial assistance to William of Saint-Amour, and of imposing restrictions on the mendicants. ALEXANDER IV, who had previously been cardinal protector of the Franciscans, annulled these measures from the very beginning of his papacy. William of Saint-Amour's *De periculis novissimorum temporum* was finally condemned by Alexander IV, based on the report of a commission of cardinals.

Toulouse, the first and only university foundation instigated by the papacy in the Middle Ages, had no success as long as its vocation remained linked to the battle against heresies. Innocent IV tried fruitlessly to relaunch the Toulouse *studium* by granting it the same privileges as Paris (*Parens scientiarum*), on 22 September 1245. Success came only when the *studium* managed to establish itself locally, that is, to free itself from the original stigma of being too closely tied to the battle against heresies.

When he was elected, Sinibaldo was in the process of composing his masterpiece, his Commentary on Gregory IX's *Decretales*, called *Apparatus in quinque libros decretalium*, a difficult work, even for his contemporaries. His papal legislation included three collections of decretals. The first two were probably added to the *Liber extra*, but the pope preferred to send the *studium* in Bologna a definitive and separate list of official decretals, which were called *Novellae*, and were independently distributed. Most of them were subsequently incorporated into the *Liber Sextus* (1298). With the constitution *Ad extirpandam* (1252), Innocent IV judged the use of torture in the INQUISITION's trials of heretics to be legitimate.

Innocent IV made two of his nephews cardinals. One of them (Ottobano) became pope in 1276 (HADRIAN V). For 50 years, the Genovese Fieschis had an uninterrupted presence in the Roman Curia. As such, it was the best represented non-Roman family in the Curia during the 13th century. Innocent IV died in Naples and was buried in the old cathedral of the city (destroyed in 1294). At the beginning of the 14th century, archbishop Humbert of Ormont (1308–20) had the tomb transferred to the new cathedral. The present tomb is almost entirely the work of the 16th century, as is its recumbent effigy.

Agostino Paravicini Bagliani

Bibliography

Potth., 943–1286.

Abate, G. "Lettere secrete d'Innocenzo IV," *Miscellanea Francescana*, 55 (1955), 317–73.

Bernal Palacios, E. "Repertorios del comentario de Innocencio IV a las Decretales de Gregorio IX," *Escritos del vedat-Anvario*, 17 (1987), 143–72.

Böhmer, J. F., Ficker, J., and Winkelmann, E. *Regesta Imperii*, V, 3, Innsbruck, 1892.

Dolcini, C. "Eger cui lenia, 1245 (46): Innocenzo IV, Tolomeo da Lucca, Guglielmo d'Ockham," *RSCI*, 29 (1975), 147 f.

Dufeil, M. M. *Guillaume de Saint-Amour et la polémique universitaire parisienne 1250–1259*, Paris, 1972.

Fried, J. "Auf der Suche nach der Wirklichkeit. Die Mongolen und die europäische Erfahrungswissenschaft," *HZ*, 243 (1986), 287–332.

Haluscynski, T. T., and Woinar, M. M. *Acta Innocentii papae IV (1243–1254)*, Rome, 1961.

Huillard-Bréholles, J. L. A. *Historia diplomatica Friderici secundi*, VI, Paris, 1861.

Le Bras, G. "Innocent IV romaniste. Examen de l'Apparatus," *SG*, 11 (1967), 305–26.

Lefebvre, C. "Sinibalde dei Fieschi," *DDC*, 7 (1965), 1029–62.

Les Registres d'Innocent IV (1243–1254), ed. E. Berger, 4 vols., Paris, 1884–1921.

Melloni, A. *Innocenzo IV. La concezione e l'esperienza della cristianità come regimen unius personae*, Genoa, 1990.

Pacaut, M. "L'authorité pontificale selon Innocent IV," *Le Moyen Âge*, 66 (1960), 85–119.

Pagnotti, F. "Niccolò da Calvi e la sua Vita d'Innocenzo IV con una breve introduzione sulla istoriografia pontificia dei secoli XIII e XIV," *ASR*, 21 (1898), 1–120 (reedition of the *Vita*: A. Melloni, *Innocenzo IV*, [*op. cit. infra*], 259–93).

Paravicini Bagliani, A. *Cardinali di Curia e "familiae" cardinalizie dall 1227 al 1254*, Padua, 1972, 2 vols.

Paravicini Bagliani, A. "La fondazione dello Studium Curiae: una riletture critica," *Luoghi e metodi di insegnamento nell' Italia medioevale (secoli XII–XIV)*, Congedo Editore, 1989, 59–81.

Piergiovanni, V. "Sinibaldo dei Fieschi decretalista. Ricerche sulla vita," *Collectanea Stephan Kuttner*, IV, *Studia Gratiana*, 14 (1967), 126–54.

Pisanu, L. *L'attività politica di Innocenzo IV e i Francescani (1243–1254)*, Rome, 1969.

Quintana Prieto, A. *La documentation pontificia de Innocencio IV (1243–1254)*, Rome, 1987, 2 vols.

Rembaum, J. E. "The Talmud and the Popes: Reflections on the Talmud Trials of the 1240s," *Viator*, 13 (1982), 215 f.

Roberg, B. "Die Tartaren auf dem 2. Konzil von Lyon 1274," *Annuarium historiae conciliarum*, 5 (1973), 251 f.

Roberg, B. "Innocenz IV.," *LexMA*, 5 (1991), 437–8.

Tisserand, E., and Wiet, G. "Une lettre de l'almohade Murtada au pape Innocent IV," *Recueil cardinal Eugène Tisserand*, I, Louvain, 1955, 113–37.

Wolter, L. and Holstein, H. *Lyon I et Lyon II*, Paris, 1966.

INNOCENT V. *Pierre of Tarentaise (b. Tarentaise, Department of the Loire, Arrondissement of Saint-Étienne?, ca. 1224, d. Rome, 22 June 1276). Elected pope 21 January 1276, crowned 22 February 1276. Buried in Saint John Lateran. Beatified in 1898 by Leo XIII.*

During the first part of his life, Pierre of Tarentaise followed the classical path of a young DOMINICAN. He entered the Dominican convent of Lyon in about 1240, and did not leave until 1255, to acquire a degree in theology in Paris. Doctor in 1259, he was one of the five teachers (with Albertus Magnus and Thomas Aquinas) who worked out a new rule of studies for the Dominicans during the chapter general of Valenciennes in 1259. He taught in Paris until July of 1264 when he took over the duties of prior for the province of France. Relieved of his duty in June 1267, he began to teach again until

1269, and then definitively gave up teaching after his re-election in May 1269 as provincial for France. It was during this university period that he composed his commentaries on the Scriptures and his *Questions*.

Named archbishop of Lyon by GREGORY X, he took possession of his see between August and October 1272. As the pope had chosen him with a future COUNCIL in Lyon in mind, Pierre of Tarentaise busied himself reestablishing peace in his city and regulating conflicts of jurisdiction between the archbishopric and the king of France. The situation seemed relatively settled in Gregory X's eyes, such that on 13 April 1273 he announced his choice of Lyon as the meeting place for the council.

Shortly thereafter, between 23 and 28 May 1273, the pope named him cardinal bishop of Ostia, at the same time as Bonaventure. Concecrated bishop before 9 August 1273, Pierre administered his diocese until the time of his replacement by Aymar of Roussillon in April 1274. Free of all obligations, he devoted himself to the council, which opened on 7 May 1274, and actively assisted the pope during it. In late 1274 or early 1275, he left Lyon for the court of Philip the Hardy, where, among other things, he dealt with the question of the marriage of Jeanne of Navarre to the king's second son. He returned to Lyon, but left the city with the pontiff to participate, in May, in the meetings in Beaucaire with Alfonso X of Castille, and in October, in meetings in Lausanne with Rudolf of Habsburg. He preceded Gregory X on the road back to Rome, where he learned of his death and immediately rejoined Arezzo. It was at the conclave of Arezzo that for the first time Gregory X's constitution *Ubi Periculum* was applied. The Franco-Angevin and Roman parties, too opposed, did not manage to gain a majority in their favor, and thus decided to agree on a less committed figure: Pierre of Tarentaise was thus elected on the first round of balloting on 21 January 1276. His election was well received by Charles of Anjou, whom he met in Viterbo between 7 and 15 February. Crowned in Saint Peter's in Rome on 22 February, he established his residence in the Lateran palace.

The first Dominican to ascend to the papal throne, Innocent V broadly outlined his action plan in the BULL *Fondamentum aliud*; in the direct line of Gregory X's politics, freeing the Holy Land was his primary goal and the main focus of all his efforts. Nevertheless, his appeal for a CRUSADE ran up against the rivalries of sovereigns and princes who had promised to take part in it. Innocent V thus had to intervene in the latent conflict opposing Michael VIII Paleologus and Charles of Anjou. He sent an embassy to Constantinople to negotiate a new truce, but the delegation learned of the pope's death in Ancona and returned to Rome without pursuing its mission. The Union of Churches, proclaimed at the council of Lyon, ultimately failed.

The pope took an active part in regulating the many conflicts in Italian internal affairs, always with the cru-sade in mind. His action was a determining factor in the signing of the peace treaty between Genoa and Charles of Anjou (18 June 1276), which led to removal of the proscription over Genoa, as Innocent V was hoping to be able to count on the powerful maritime republic's collaboration in the case of a crusade. Peace was also signed on 13 June between GHIBELLINE Pisa and the cities of the Tuscan GUELPH League. Pisa allowed the pope to choose the city's chief magistrate and the other magistrates, the Guelph army was dissolved, and the censures weighing on the cities of the league were lifted a few days after the death of Innocent V, whose final efforts were turned primarily toward consolidating peace in Tuscany and Liguria.

In Rome itself, Innocent V's papacy marked a break with the attempts of his predecessor to free the Holy See from the grip of the Angevins. In his desire to set up residence in Rome, the pope had to compromise with Charles of Anjou, who had taken advantage of Gregory X's distance to reinforce his power. The same day that Charles of Anjou went to the Lateran to pledge homage to the pope for the kingdom of Sicily, 2 March 1276, Innocent V confirmed him in his duties as senator of Rome and imperial vicar of Tuscany. The pope delayed the coronation of Rudolf of Habsburg in Rome, expecting the restitution of the Romagnas, promised to GREGORY V.

From the point of view of ecclesiastical affairs, Innocent V scarcely had time to leave his mark. Even though it was to him that cardinal Simon of Brie communicated the depositions collected for the canonization of Saint Louis, he was not able to bring the procedure to a close. He likewise relaunched the canonical inquiry concerning Saint Margaret of Hungary. Innocent V died on 22 June 1276 and was buried in the presence of Charles of Anjou, who intervened personally to have his body laid to rest in the Lateran, under the papacy of JOHN XXI.

Ghislain Brunel

Bibliography

Forget, J. "Innocent V," *DTC*, 7–2 (1922), 1996–7.

Laurent, M. H. *Le Bienheureux Innocent V (Pierre de Tarentaise) et son temps*, Vatican City, 1947 (*Studi et testi*, 129).

Roberg, B. "Innocenz V.," *LexMA*, 5 (1991), 438.

INNOCENT VI. *Étienne Aubert (b. Les Monts, commune of Beyssac [Corrèze], 1282 or 1295, d. Avignon, 12 September 1362). Elected pope 18 December 1352 and crowned on 30 December. Buried in the Charter House (Chartreuse) in Villeneuve-lès-Avignon (Gard).*

In contrast to the papacy of his predecessor, CLEMENT VI, that of Innocent VI was marked by a spirit of reform. His lack of diplomatic success was due in part to his hesitations, which imperiled even the results of the politics of reconquest of the Church States, so masterfully undertaken by cardinal Gil Albornoz.

Étienne Aubert was the son of Adhémar, a member of a family that did not belong to the nobility, but which had been assimilated into the petite noblesse around Pompadour and had later taken up residence in the hamlet of Monts in Limousin. Aubert studied civil law at the university of Toulouse, received his diploma as *licencié* in 1321, and his doctorate in 1329 or 1330; he then taught for a short period at the same university. Thereafter, he balanced an administrative career with the royalty and his ecclesiastical career. He was first judge in the court of civil appeals (June 1321), and then ordinary judge and guard of the seneschal seal (July 1321) of Toulouse; he was lieutenant for the seneschal of Toulouse and Albi (1328–9), and later judge magistrate of Toulouse, probably from 1330 to 1334. Called into the service of Philip VI, who gave him the title clerk and counselor, he was one of the commissioners entrusted (1335–6) with settling the serious matter involving Aimery Bérenger, which led to the reorganization of the administration of the municipal magistrates in Toulouse. As clerk of the great chamber of the Parlement in 1336, he received (April and July 1337, and January 1338) three diplomatic missions to the king from BENEDICT XII; they concerned defending the freedom of the church in the kingdom, and the conflict between France and England. At the same time, generous benefices were allocated to him, and they were renewed every three years at least until 1334. He had become subdeacon at least as early as 1324. He enjoyed the support of one of his relatives, Audoin Aubert, whose prebended canonicate of Orense, Spain, he was given. (Audoin Aubert's career was in the service of a family, the Arrabloys, that was quite devoted to the king of France; he died in 1323 as CHAPLAIN and CHAMBERLAIN for cardinal Peter of Arrabloy, former guardian of the royal seals.) To several rich canonicates, Étienne added the archdiaconates of Souvigny, in the church of Clermont, of Cambrai, and of Brabant. It was from a mission for the king in AVIGNON that he brought back his nomination as bishop of Noyon, on 23 January 1338. He remained the king's advisor and continued to serve him as a diplomat, particularly in matters concerning the pope. Although he never fulfilled the duties, the king also named him captain and lieutenant for the reformation of Languedoc in August 1340, shortly before he was transferred to the bishopric of Clermont on 11 October. One record from his *familia* as bishop of Noyon is clear evidence that he had at his disposal a powerful network of relations in the CURIA. He was included in his compatriot Pierre Roger's first set of promotions to cardinal, on 20 September 1342, with the presbyterial title of Santi Giovanni and Paolo. On 29 June 1348 he took the place of John of Gaucelme as great penitentiary, and fulfilled this important duty well until his election. He was finally transferred to the bishopric of Ostia and Velletri on 13 February 1352. The CONCLAVE following the death of Clement VI was a passionate one in which the oligarchical demands of the SACRED COLLEGE came to a peak in the first capitulations in its history. The cardinal of Ostia appears to have been the candidate for compromise: He was elected pope on 18 December 1352 and crowned on 30 December.

Although he did annul (in the name of his *plenitudo potestati*) the capitulations to which he had subscribed only with the greatest of reserve regarding their canonical nature, he did wait until 6 July 1353 to do so, and he put an abrupt end to the cardinals' demands for control over the papacy. Under his reign, the average annual receipts of the APOSTOLIC CAMERA grew to some 65,000 florins, thanks to progress in the papal tax system; but the expenses of Albornoz's campaign in Italy, which alone comprised half of the expenses, emptied the papal treasury and forced the pope to sell some of his objects of value, and even to borrow funds. He continued, as had Clement VI, to favor clerics from France, especially from the southwest, in his recruitments for the Curia and the Sacred College. Innocent held three consistories naming cardinals, an Italian (Francesco degli Atti), an Aragonese (Nicolas Rosell), against 13 Frenchmen (two from the north and eleven from Languedoc, five of which were from the region of Limoges, and three of these were nephews: Audoin Aubert, Étienne [II] Aubert, and Pierre of Monteruc).

His politics of reform was evident in two primary areas. The first of these restricted the daily life of his own house and sought to moderate that of the cardinals (constitution *Ad Honorem*, 1357) and the Curia, and entailed attempts to limit the accumulation of benefices and dispensations of residence. These had been accorded quite liberally by his predecessor at the expense of the care for souls, and forced most of the beggars who had rushed to the Curia to return to their dioceses under the threat of excommunication. On the other hand, he uncompromisingly imposed moral improvement in both recruitment and discipline in a number of convents of Dominican friars, supporting master general Simon of Langres, who had been the object of scathing attacks within his order. He did not deal gently with the Franciscans, either the spirituals or the *fraticelli*, against whom he unleashed the fury of the inquisitors, and sought, awkwardly, to reform the order of the hospitallers of Saint John of Jerusalem. He also founded the charter house of Val de Bénédiction in Villeneuve-lès-Avignon, in his former palace as cardinal (1356–62); the college of Saint-Martial, in Toulouse (1359); and a school of theology in Bologna (1360).

Despite his great concern for ecclesiastical and religious matters, his attention was drawn away by political and diplomatic questions, among the most pressing of which was the situation with the Church States. Without really intending to take the papacy back to Rome, an intention that URBAN V and GREGORY XI would have, he understood that restoring papal authority in his Italian lands was an absolute priority. He was wise to name (June 1353) the Castillian cardinal Gil Albornoz as LEGATE and vicar general in the Church's territories: Albornoz had already proven himself during the Spanish *Reconquista* against the Moors. The methodical submission of the Church lands to papal power between 1353 and 1361 was, moreover, due much more to the skill of Albornoz than to that of the pope, whose support for his legate was not unfailing, as he showed himself to be both indecisive and insensitive to pressures from the devious and ambitious Bernabò Visconti's partisans, who were powerful even within the Sacred College. Innocent VI was unable to appropriately appreciate his legate's methods, which contrasted with the politics of conquest by force of his predecessors, especially Bertrand of Pouget (1321–34). Albornoz greatly benefited, especially in the beginning, from the Holy See's financial support. He practiced a flexible politics of separation from enemy coalitions, each in time, and adapting acts of subordination to papal power to each case individually, depending on the circumstances, via concession of a vicarate or a reduction in communal statutes. This was all crowned by a network of imposing fortresses and holding regional or provincial "parliaments" (it was at the parliament of Fano, in April/May 1357, that the famous "Church Constitutions," or "Egidian Constitutions" were promulgated). Despite his resistances, Albornoz, refusing any alliance with the Visconti, was forced to leave the Italian scene for nearly a year, to the profit of the unscrupulous and ineffective Androuin de La Roche, abbot of Cluny (August 1357–September 1358).

In order to succeed in his Italian politics, the pope needed, if not the support, at least the neutrality of the king of the Romans, Charles IV; similarly, Charles IV was eager to be crowned emperor. Although, after returning Cola di Rienzo to the pope (1354) as a guarantee of his loyalty, he was effectively (and hastily) crowned in Rome on 5 April 1355 by legate Pierre Bertrand of Colombier, the emperor did not prove to be a steadfast ally against Bernabò Visconti. He had nothing more pressing after his return to Italy than to convoke a diet in Nuremberg for November 1355, for the purpose of dealing, among other things, with the election of the king of the Romans. As a result of a compromise between Charles IV and the electors, the "Imperial Code," called "The Golden Bull" in the 15th century (promulgated in two parts: Diet of Nuremberg, 10 January 1356 and Diet of Metz, Christmas 1356, in the presence of cardinal legate Talleyrand of Perigord), to a certain extent put a stop to the conflict between the Church and the Empire. This was to the pope's disadvantage because it reserved

the elective right for seven great electors and instituted a vicarate, in the case of vacancy, to be filled by the Palatine elector and the duke of Saxony; the individual elected thenceforth was invested with the power to administer the Empire after his election, rather than after confirmation. The approval and confirmation claimed by the pope were passed over in silence, and the vicarate, in case of vacancy, no longer belonged, ipso facto, to the pope. Innocent VI did not decry the edict, which theoretically left him more freedom in Italy. He was more evasive regarding the emperor's aims to have the decretals *Romani principes* (1312) and *Pastoralis Cura* (1314) annulled, promulgated by Clement V, affirming the superiority of the Church over the Empire and the elected individual's obligation to swear an oath of fidelity to the pope.

As in the case of Clement VI, the pope was unable to curb developments in the conflict between France and England and in internal troubles in France. Intervention by cardinal Gui de Boulogne, who was acting on behalf of the king of France and not of the pope, only made things worse (Treaty of Guines, 1353; Treaty of Mantes, 1354). The sovereign pontiff, who took pains to hide his predilection for France, nevertheless increased peace initiatives, although these had no lasting results. The consequences of the war were felt even behind the walls of Avignon, where the pope hastily had a new wall built to protect the Great Companies; it was begun in 1355 and completed under URBAN V. He was also unsuccessful in Spain. The unfailing support for Blanche of Bourbon, who was persecuted by her husband, Pedro I of Castille, was only one aspect of the violent conflict that set the king against the papacy. The pope meddled in the serious dynastic quarrel with international stakes, stirred up by a revolt by one party of the nobility against the king (1353–4), creating serious difficulties in receiving revenue from the Apostolic Camera in Spain, especially after the reiterated promulgation of sentences of excommunication against the king. There was a final failure, despite some misleading successes on the part of the cardinal of Boulogne, in his arbitration attempts with Castille, Aragon, and Navarra.

Innocent VI showed a real lack of judgment in questions regarding the East; he had no principled line of conduct, but rather a pragmatic reaction to events: He wanted to continue Clement VI's politics, but without spending the same amounts of money. He concentrated his diplomacy on settling the conflict involving Genoa, Venice, and Aragon, which took precedence over any aid to the Holy Land. His efforts were in vain because the Turkish threat hanging over Constantinople was increasing. He mistakenly guessed that aid to Smyrnia was a more urgent issue than aid to the Eastern Empire, which itself was divided. The little crusade that followed the naming of the Carmelite Pierre Thomas as legate resulted in an advantage for the king of Cyprus. In matters concerning the Orient, the pope recognized the order of brothers of Grand Armenia, which was under the rule of Saint Augustine, and subject to both the constitution of the Dominicans and their master general; he also imposed the same rule upon the Basilians of Italy.

Weakened by illness (gout appears to have kept him from consistently carrying out all the duties of his office), the pope died in Avignon. After his funeral, at Notre Dame des Doms, he was buried (22 September) in the chapel of the Holy Trinity in his charter house in Villeneuve-lès-Avignon, in the mausoleum that he had had constructed in 1361 by Bertrand Nogayrol, the architect for the Apostolic Palace.

Pierre Jugie

Bibliography

Aux origines de l'État moderne. Le fonctionnement administratif de la papauté d'Avignon. Actes de la table ronde de l'École française de Rome (Avignon, 1988), Rome, 1990.

Baluze, É. *Vitae paparum Avenionensium*, ed. G. Mollat, I, Paris, 1914, 309–48 [text for 4 lives] and II, Paris, 1927, 433–89 [notes].

Gilles, H. "Le clergé méridional entre le roi et l'Église," *Les Évêques, les clercs et le roi (1250–1300). Cahiers de Fanjeaux*, 7 (1972), 393–417.

Giunta, F. "Sulla politica orientala di Innocenzo VI," *Miscellanea in onore di Roberto Cessi*, I, Rome, 1958, 305–20.

Guillemain, B. *La Cour pontificale d'Avignon, 1306–1376: étude d'une société*, Paris, 1966.

Innocent VI (1352–62), *Lettres secrètes et curiales*, ed. P. Gasnault, M. H. Laurent, and N. Gotteri, Paris, 1959–76, 3 vols and 1 fasc., in preparation, publ. to the end of the 4th year of papacy, 30 December 1356; until this work is completed, see, for the 9th year (1361), the edition by E. Martene and U. Durand, *Thesaurus novus anecdotorum*, II, Paris, 1717, 843–1027.

Mollat, G. "Innocent VI," *DTC*, 7 (1927), 1997–2001 [sources and bibliography]; *Les Papes d'Avignon (1305–1378)*, 10th ed., Paris, 1964, 104–15 [sources and bibliography].

Seibt, F. *Karl IV. Ein Kaiser in Europa (1346–1378)*, Munich, 1979.

Suarez Fernandez, L., and Reglà Campistol, J. *España cristiana, crisis de la Reconquista, luchas civiles*, Madrid, 1966 (*Historia de España*, dir. R. Menéndez Pidal, XIV), 19–56.

Waley, D. "Lo stato papale del periodo feudale a Martino V," *Comuni e signorie nell'Italia nordorientale e centrale: Lazio, Umbria e Marche, Lucca*, Turin, 1987 (*Storia d'Italia*, dir. G. Galasso, VII, 2), 293–300 and bibliography 317–19.

Williman, D. "Memoranda and sermons of Étienne Aubert (Innocent VI) as bishop (1338–1341)," *Mediaeval Studies*, 37 (1975), 7–41.

Wood, D. *Clement VI. The Pontificate and Ideas of an Avignon Pope*, Cambridge, 1989, 96–121.

INNOCENT VII. *Cosma de' Migliorati (b. Sulmona, 1336, d. Rome, 6 November 1406). Elected pope 17 October 1404, crowned 11 November. Buried in Saint Peter's in Rome.*

He succeeded URBAN VI (1378–89) and BONIFACE IX (1389–1404) in following Rome during the GREAT SCHISM OF THE WEST. His reputation as a man of integrity, as a man who was both conciliatory and ascetic, brought hope. However, his lack of energy and his timidity led to the failure of the few efforts he undertook to end the division within the Church. He had been educated as a jurist (he had a degree in canon law) and had taught in Perugia and Padua. During the schism, he was chancellor of the church of Capua (1379), cleric of the Chamber of the SACRED COLLEGE (1380), prevost of the church in Valva, papal CHAPLAIN, collector in the service of the APOSTOLIC CAMERA in England, archbishop of Ravenna (1387), and then archbishop of Bologna (1389). Boniface IX brought him into his college of cardinals by giving him the title Holy Cross of Jerusalem (1389). He then sent him as a LEGATE to Lombardy and Tuscany, his mission being to reconcile Galeas Visconti on one hand, and the cities of Bologna and Florence on the other (1390).

Innocent VII's papacy was short but eventful. In his very first year the pope faced a popular revolt. Supported by Ladislas, the king of Naples, and stirred by the Colonnas, the Romans rose up against the presence of mercenaries in the ruined city. Innocent took refuge in the Vatican. Feeling that his uncle was in danger, the young Roman senator Louis had the 11 magistrates responsible for negotiating with the pontiff assassinated. The pope owed his safety only to his flight to VITERBO, with his entire CURIA, on 6 August 1405. The populace then invaded the Vatican and sacked the CHANCERY, slashing up hundreds of registers. When calm was restored, the pope was able to return to Rome on 13 March 1406.

Despite the commitment he had made (14 October 1404) during the CONCLAVE—that if elected he would attempt to reestablish unity, even by transfer of his title— Innocent stubbornly refused to meet BENEDICT XIII, his rival in Avignon. After the failure of official negotiations that took place in Rome in 1404–5 between the partisans of the two adversaries, the UNIVERSITY of Paris demanded his abdication and Benedict branded him with ANATHEMA. The pope announced the holding of a council in Rome for his followers. Foreseen for November 1405 but deferred, ostensibly because of troubles in the city, Innocent called the council off in 1406 because of a lack of participants. The pope then received a Castillian embassy, which encouraged him, albeit in vain, to transfer. He died of an apoplectic fit in the fall.

The Great Schism should not overshadow the few successes of his papacy: an attempted reform of the Franciscan order by reducing the duration of provincial responsibilities to six years; exemption of any temporal jurisdiction for the "Anima," a hospice founded in Rome in 1389 for German pilgrims who were ill or overly fatigued from their travels; the BULL *Ad exaltationem*, which reorganized the university of Rome, which added Greek to its curriculum. Sensitive to the new culture of humanism, the pope liked to choose apostolic secretaries for the beauty of their language. In June 1405, Innocent VII had named 11 cardinals, among whom were three future popes: Angelo Correr, his successor in the Roman obedience (GREGORY XII), Pietro Philarghi, the first in the Pisan obedience (ALEXANDER V), and Oddo Colonna, the pope of refound unity (MARTIN V).

Monique Maillard-Luypaert

Bibliography

Bliemetzrieder, F. "Die Konzilsidee unter Innocenz VII. und König Rupprecht," *Studi Mediaevali*, 27 (1906), 355–67.

Bolino, G. "Papa Innocenzo VII di Giuseppe Capograssi," *Bolletino della Deputazione Abruzzese*, 70 (1980), 487–510.

Brand, P. "Innocenzo VII e il delitto di suo nipote Ludovico Migliorati," *Studi e documenti di storia di diritto*, 21 (1900), 179–215.

Finke, H. "Zum Konzilsprojecte Innocenz VII.," *Römische Quartalschrift*, 7 (1893), 483–5.

Gualdo, G. "'Litterae ante coronationem' agli inizi dell'400. Innocenzo VII e Gregorio XII," *Atti del Istituto Veneto di Scienze, Classe di Scienze Morale*, 140 (1981–2), 175–98.

Kneer, A. "Zur Vorgeschichte Papst Innocenz VII.," *Historisches Jahrbuch*, 12 (1891), 347–50.

Lettres d'Innocent VII (1404–1406), M. Maillard-Luypaert ed. (*Analecta Vaticano-Belgica. Documents relatifs aux anciens diocèses de Cambrai, Liège, Thérouanne et Tournai. Documents relatifs au Grand Schisme*, 8), Brussels, 1987.

Mollat, G. "Innocent VII," *DTC*, 7 (1922), 2001–2.

Tellenbach, G. *Repertorium Germanicum. 2. Verzeichnis der in den Registern und Kameralakten Urbans VI., Bonifaz' IX., Innocenz' VII und Gregors XII., vorkommenden Personen, Kirchen und Orte des Deutschen Reiches, seiner Diözesen und Territorien (1378–1415)*, Berlin, 1961.

INNOCENT VIII. *Giovanni Battista Cibo (b. Genoa, 1432, d. Rome, 25 July 1492). Elected pope 29 August 1484, crowned 12 September. Buried in Saint Peter's in Rome.*

Son of Arano Cibo, who was a Roman senator in 1455, and of Teodorina de Mari, a Genovese patrician, Giovanni Battista Cibo was born in Genoa in 1432 and spent his youth in the court of Naples, a city where his father had duties in the administration of justice. Before joining a religious order he had two illegitimate children, Teodorina and Franceschetto. He studied in Padua, and then in Rome, where he was taken in by cardinal Calandrini, NICHOLAS V's half brother. In April 1467, PAUL II granted him the bishopric of Savona, which SIXTUS IV, in 1472, exchanged for that of Molfetta. Thanks to his friendship with the future JULIUS II, he had a rapid rise in the Curia. In 1473 he was named cardinal, titular priest of Santa Balbina, which he would later exchange for Santa Cecilia. When Sixtus IV died in 1484, hostilities between the factions were renewed in Rome and the SACRED COLLEGE itself divided into two groups. The first had cardinal Rodrigo Borgia at its head and was supported by the Orsinis, while the second, led by cardinal Giuliano Della Rovere, was supported by the Colonnas. The conclave finally met on 26 August and cardinal Cibo was elected through the machinations, which may not have been completely exempt from SIMONY, of cardinal Della Rovere. The new pope then took the name Innocent VIII.

An indecisive man of little character and precarious health, Innocent VIII was dominated by the powerful cardinal Della Rovere, who inspired much of his political action. It was Della Rovere who got him to help the Neapolitan barons who had revolted against King Ferdinand. In the eyes of the pope, Ferdinand was guilty of having refused to pay the Holy See his investiture toll on several occasions. The war dragged on, provoking the hostility of the king of Hungary, Mathias Corvino, the king's son-in-law, and the duke of Milan, Gian Galeazzo Sforza. This pushed the pope to ask France for assistance. In September 1486, peace was concluded between the pontiff and the king of Naples, since the latter was in fear of new interventions against the kingdom by the Angevins. Nevertheless, relations between Rome and Naples did not improve, and Ferdinand did not curtail his hostile behavior toward the pope. This is why, at the time of the CONSISTORY of 1489, Innocent VIII excommunicated him and again appealed to the king of France, to whom he officially proposed conquest of the kingdom of Naples. It was not until January 1492, under French pressure, that King Ferdinand showed himself to be more conciliatory, and peace was finally reestablished a few months before the pope's death, which took place during the night of 25 to 26 July.

The entente with Florence marked the second period in Innocent VIII's papacy. Actually, to get out of the isolation that his support of the Neapolitan barons had provoked, and to ease his financial situation, which was burdened by debts, the pontiff went to Lorenzo de' Medici, to whose bank the APOSTOLIC CAMERA was heavily indebted. In order to strengthen this new alliance, he favored the marriage of his son Franceschetto to Lorenzo's daughter, Maddalena. The wedding took place (January 1488) in great pomp in the Vatican palace. It was looked upon disapprovingly by some, in particular Giles of Viterbo. Moreover, the following year, during the only promotion of cardinals of his papacy, Innocent VIII raised Lorenzo's young son, 13-year-old Giovanni, the future LEO X, to the rank of cardinal. Others who were made cardinal at this time were his nephew, Lorenzo Cibo, Antonietto Pallavicino, Andrew of Épinay, Peter of Aubusson, Maffeo De Gerardis, Federicus of San Severino, and Ardicino Della Porta.

Also noteworthy among the other political acts of his papacy was his recognition of Henry VII Tudor as king of England, after the War of the Roses, by right of conquest, heritage, and national choice; and approval of Henry VII's marriage to Elizabeth of York, Edward IV's daughter, a union that would give birth to Henry VIII. Moreover, he gave the title "Catholic King and Queen" to Ferdinand V and Isabella of Castille, following the taking of Granada (2 January 1492) and expelling the Moors from Spain. This news was received enthusiastically in Rome and gave rise to great festivities, both religious and civil.

In the matter of the internal politics of the PAPAL STATES, Innocent VIII attempted to govern with the support of local oligarchies. Thus, for example, the lordship of Imola and Forlì was confirmed for Girolamo Riario who, nevertheless, had his responsibilities as captain general of the Church taken away. The Della Rovere family kept control of the government of the Church, as it had under SIXTUS IV, not only with cardinal Giuliano, but also with the assistance of Giovanni Della Rovere, who was given responsibility as captain general. After a period of strong opposition, even the noble Roman Colonna and Orsini families reached an agreement that reestablished their preeminence in the regions around Rome, to the detriment of papal power. In 1490 Innocent VIII accomplished a timid change in the politics of nonintervention in papal lands, when he allocated as a fiefdom to his son, Franceschetto, the lands that had belonged to the counts of Anguillara. In Rome, on the other hand, he pursued the work of Sixtus IV, seeking to reduce still further the power of the old municipal class and favoring the arrival of foreign merchants and bankers.

Like his predecessors, he attempted to organize a new crusade against the TURKS, but after talks with the Christian princes failed, Innocent VIII ended up reaching an agreement with the sultan, Bajazet II, in 1489. He was the first pontiff to make diplomatic ties with the infidels. Prince Djem, his rival and the sultan's brother, had to be kept in Rome by the pope, to whom Bajazet had given the Holy Lance (a relic of inestimable value, since it was believed to have been the weapon that pierced Jesus' side on the cross) and paid an annual tribute of 40,000 ducats. The treaty was certainly the fruit of the disastrous state of the Holy See's finances and the extravagant and worldly life of the Curia. The Curia had become a veritable princely court in which the cardinals themselves behaved like "great lords." In order to face the Curia's enormous expenses, Sixtus IV had already had to sell some offices. Innocent VIII devoted himself to a politics of creating colleges, most notably to raise the extraordinary sums required by the wars in which he was involved. In May 1486 he created the college of the 52 *plumbatores* of papal BULLS, which brought him 26,000 golden ducats. In 1487 he increased the number of apostolic secretaries to 30; up to that time there had been only six. In 1490 he instituted the 30 agents for the Apostolic Camera's contracts. Simultaneously, he raised the price for a number of offices of the Curia that were already in existence. Even the duty of Vatican librarian became venal.

Innocent VIII's name in the area of religious affairs is primarily linked to the famous bull *Summis Desiderantes Affectibus* (5 December 1484), which legally allowed the Inquisition to intervene in repressing witchcraft. The document also authorized two DOMINICAN inquisitors, Henrich Krämer and Jakob Sprenger, to go to Germany to prepare trials against presumed witches who, once they were found guilty, were to be severely condemned. After returning from this mission, the two inquisitors published the famous book *Malleus Maleficarum* (Cologne, 1486), where principles are set down and illustrated with examples to explain and repress the heresy of witchcraft. Witchcraft certainly had been a widespread belief for a long time, and had been condemned by the Church for just as long, but it is doubtless that this bull unleashed an especially cruel repression. On a number of occasions, Innocent VIII had to concern himself with Spanish Jews, especially with the Jews who had converted to Christianity but who were suspected of continuing in their practice of JUDAISM. The Spanish Inquisition had looked into their behavior with particular sternness, but since the inquisition itself did not appear to have much success in resolving the situation, King Ferdinand took extreme measures. On 31 March 1492, he published an edict forcing all Jews to become Christians or to leave any land under the Spanish crown.

Innocent VIII is also credited with the condemnation of Pico della Mirandola's 900 theses (4 August 1486) on dialectics, morals, physics, mathematics, theology, the Kabbala, and a number of other sciences that were suspected of HERESY. The pontiff refused to discuss the issue publicly and condemned them en masse. An antedated statement of self-defense by Pico did not manage to avoid the pope's negative judgment.

Without being able to make a comparison with Sixtus IV's patronage, most notably because of financial difficulties, it nevertheless remains that in the area of art, Innocent VIII's role was significant. In Rome he restored a number of churches and completely reconstructed the church of Santa Maria in Via Lata. In the Vatican he had a grandiose palace built for the offices of the Curia, although it is no longer extant; and near it, he had the famous Belvedere built, which Julius II later began to connect to the Vatican. Five miles from the city, in the Tiber valley, Innocent VIII had begun to construct a hunting pavilion that was to become the magnficent Villa de la Magliana. Famous artists worked for Innocent VIII: Antonio Pollaiuolo, who also erected his funerary monument at the request of the pope's nephew, Lorenzo Cibo; Pinturicchio, who painted the Belvedere's lunettes; Andrea Mantegna, who was entrusted with both the decoration of the Belvedere's chapel and with frescoes that are no longer extant today because of the construction of the new wing of the Vatican palace under Pius VI. Works by Filippino Lippi, Antonazzo Romano, and Perugino are also noteworthy.

Anna Esposito

Bibliography

Aubenas, R., and Richard, R. *La Chiesa e il Rinascimento (1449–1517)*, II, Italian ed. P. Produ, Turin, 1972, 144–52.

Burckardus, J. *Liber notarum ab anno 483 usque ad annum 1506*, ed. E. Celani, I, Città di Castello, 1909–10 (RIS/2, XXXII, 2), 22–370.

Caravale, M., and Caracciolo, A. *Lo Stato pontificio da Martino V a Pio IX*, Turin, 1978, 118–29.

Dispacci e lettere di Giacomo Gherardi da Volterra nunzio pontificio (1487–1490), ed. E. Curas, Rome, 1909 (*Studi e testi*, 21), 103–9.

Fedele, P. "La pace del 1486 tra Ferdinando d'Aragona ed Innocenzo VIII," *Archivio storico per le provincie napoletane*, 30 (1905), 481–503.

Infessura, S. *Diario della città di Roma*, ed. O. Tommasini, Rome, 1890 (*Fonti per la storia d'Italia*, 5), 170–277.

Pasquier, J. "Innocent VIII," *DTC*, 7-2 (1923), 2002–2005.

Pastor, 5.

Rodocanachi, E. *Histoire de Rome. Une cour princière au Vatican pendant la Renaissance (1471–1503)*, Paris, 1925.

INNOCENT IX. *Giovanni Antonio Facchinetti (b. Bologna, 20 July 1519, d. Rome, 30 December 1591). Elected pope 29 October 1591; crowned 3 November 1591. Buried at St. Peter's in Rome.*

The illness of GREGORY XIV brought about negotiations for his succession beginning in the fall of 1591 and, in the competition, Giovanni Antonio Facchinetti, despite his age, found himself in first place: Two days of CONCLAVE were enough for him to be elected. In his favor, the new pope had the support of Spain and a reputation as a cleric resonating with the Counter Reformation. After studying law in Bologna, Giovanni Antonio Facchinetti entered the service of Cardinal Alexander Farnese, whom he represented during four years of legation at Avignon. PIUS IV made him bishop of Nicastro in Calabria in 1560. The new bishop participated in the COUNCIL OF TRENT, visited his diocese, and founded a seminary there. In 1566 PIUS V sent him as a NUNCIO to Venice; he was therefore one of the instigators of the league against the TURKS, which was victorious at LEPANTO. In 1575 he renounced his diocese due to precarious health, but in 1576, GREGORY XIII made him patriarch of Jerusalem and used him during the INQUISITION. The pope repaid him for this unending activity by making him a cardinal on 12 December 1583.

After his election, Innocent IX began his duties with zeal, inviting the cardinals to assist and counsel him, giving a number of audiences, keeping busy with the provisioning of Rome, and regulating traffic on the Tiber. He renewed the BULL of Pius V on the alienation of ecclesiastical possessions and made an important change in the SECRETARIAT OF STATE, which would have affected the future if his pontificate had been longer. He divided the secretariat into three sections, one for France and Poland, one for Italy and Spain, and the last for Germany. He also restored the Congregation of Germany and revived the policy of hoarding stores in the CASTEL SANT'ANGELO. He reorganized and reduced the expenses of the PAPAL ARMY in France, while pushing it toward immediate action. Especially, he showed an inclination toward spiritual weaponry by making Filippo Sega, who had been in Paris since 1590, a cardinal. During a PILGRIMAGE, the pope caught a chill and died on 30 December 1591, after two months' reign.

Anne-Cécile Germe-Tizon

Bibliography

Cloulas, I. "L'armée pontificale de Grégoire XIV, Innocent IX et Clément VIII, pendant la seconde campagne en France d'Alexandre Farnese (1591–1592)," *Bulletin de la commission royale d'histoire*, 126 (1960), 83–102.

Laurain-Portemer, M. "Absolutisme et népotisme. La surintendance de l'État ecclésiastique," *Bibliothèque de l'École des chartes*, 131 (1973), 487–567.

Moroni, G. *Dizionario di erudizione storico-ecclesiastica*, 36 (1846), 10–12.

Pastor, 22.

INNOCENT X. *Giovanni Battista Pamfili (b. Rome, 6 May 1574, d. Rome, 5 January 1655). Elected pope 15 September 1644; crowned 4 October. Buried at St. Peter's in Rome.*

If the ten years of Innocent X's pontificate retain (to use Ranke's expression) "a bad reputation," they owe it more to familial vicissitudes than to the event that was, nevertheless, the most decisive one of his reign: the conclusion of the peace of Westphalia (1648), in which the monarchical principle *cujus regio ejus religio* (each shall have the religion of his kingdom) triumphed over the Catholic upsurge and missionary expansion that had been the main feature of the papacies of GREGORY XV and URBAN VIII. A transitional pontificate, the reign of Innocent X still deserves attention, for it marks the decline of nepotism and the difficult entry of the Church into the modernity of the age of absolutism.

The second son of Camillo Pamfili and Maria Flaminia Del Bufalo, the future pope came from two powerful families of the Roman nobility; the Pamfili, originally from Gubbio, had lived in Rome since the end of the 15th century. Giovanni Battista was quickly destined for an ecclesiastical career under the wing of his paternal uncle, Cardinal Girolamo (1545–1610), AUDITOR and the dean of the tribunal of the Rota and a disciple of Saint Philip Neri, raised to the SACRED COLLEGE on 9 June 1604 by CLEMENT VIII, who soon made him vicar of Rome. At the end of his university studies at the Sapienza, where he obtained a doctorate *in utroque jure* on 17 September 1597, Pamfili was ordained a priest and began a rapidly rising career in the judiciary offices of the CURIA. Promoted to advocate of the consistory (1601), he succeeded his uncle Girolamo as auditor of the tribunal of the Rota (1604) and became close friends with the auditor of Bologna, Alessandro Ludovisi. The latter, who became pope under the name of Gregory XV, named him NUNCIO to the court of Naples (26 March 1621) where he remained for four years. He then accompanied the young cardinal Francesco Barberini, nephew of Pope Urban VIII, as his datary and counselor during his mission to France and Spain (1625). Pamfili was promoted upon his return to Latin patriarch of Antioch (19 January 1626), and then Urban VIII named him nuncio to the court of Spain (30 May 1626). Made a cardinal *in petto* the following year (30 August 1627), he was raised to the Holy College on 19 November 1629, and upon his return to Rome obtained the prefecture of the congregation of the council. The CONCLAVE that opened at the end of the 22-year pontificate of Urban VIII, who died 29 July 1644, lasted 37 days. The Sacred College, composed almost totally of associates of the dead pope (48 of the 56 cardinals present), was deeply divided between a powerful Austro-Spanish party (which numbered, at its head, within the conclave, cardinals Albornoz, archbishop of Tarento, and von Harrach, archbishop of Prague), hostile to the policy of Urban VIII during the Thirty Years' War, and a French party, led by the cardinal nephew Antonio Barberini and vigorously supported from Paris by the young King Louis XIV, but did not take into account the party of the "old cardinals" of Cardinal Gaspare Mattei, with a Spanish-loving orientation, and that of the "young cardinals" led by the cardinal nephew Francesco Barberini. The man who would take the role of *papabile* at the opening of the conclave (9 August) belonged to the latter group: Cardinal Giulio Sacchetti, the protégé and confidant of the deceased pope, whose age nevertheless was held against him (57 years old) as was his former friendship with Mazarin; immediately he was excluded by Spain. The Spanish party's candidate, the old cardinal Francesco Cennini, an associate of Paul V, was not, however, able to get more than 25 votes. A compromise was reached between the two Barberini cardinals and the Spanish party, bringing forth Pamfili's name. Without waiting for the French ambassador to consult his court (where Mazarin announced his complete opposition to the proposition on 19 September), on 14 September the conclave elected the Roman cardinal who took the name of Innocent X in memory of INNOCENT VIII, who had protected the establishment of the Pamfili family in Rome; he was crowned on 4 October.

The familial and political logic of nepotism forced the new pontiff to choose one of his relatives as cardinal nephew, as his predecessors had. But, "the misfortune of Pope Pamfili" as Ludwig von Pastor notes, not without humor, "was that the only person in his family who would have had the qualities necessary to fill such a position was a woman": his sister-in-law Olimpia Maidalchini, wife of his dead older brother, born in 1594 at Viterbo, intelligent, cultivated, eager and enterprising, who quickly gained an irresistible hold over the pope. The family saga of the Pamfili would considerably influence, to the great delight of the Roman *Pasquino*, the French "canards" and Protestant propaganda, the history and image of the pontificate. In the first part of his pontificate (1644–7), Innocent X placed the Church government in the hands of Olimpia's son, Camillo Pamfili, promoted to cardinal nephew on 14 November, and also general of the Church, LEGATE to Avignon, secretary of the BRIEFS, and prefect of the tribunal of the Signature of Justice. He also brought him together with Cardinal Panciroli, as Secretary of State, who assumed the direction of Church and state business until 1651. In a second stage (1647–9), the defection and disgrace of Camillo Pamfili (who renounced his cardinalate on 21 January 1647 in order to marry the beautiful and extremely rich Olimpia Aldobrandini, great-niece of CLEMENT VIII and the widow of Paolo Borghese on 10 February, against the wishes of the pope and his mother) brought about the promotion of a cardinal nephew of only 17 years, Francesco Maidalchini, Olimpia's nephew, who quickly showed he was incapable of fulfilling his duties. Between 1649 and 1651 Olimpia, in turn, fell into disgrace (fall 1649) and one of her cousins, the mediocre Camillo Astalli, was adopted by the pontiff, raised to the Sacred College (19 September 1650) and given all the prerogatives of a cardinal nephew. This new equilibrium did not last and gave way to a fourth stage (1651–5), which saw, in succession, the return to grace of Camillo Pamfili, his wife, and his young children (8 January 1651); the disgrace and death (3 September 1651) of Cardinal Panciroli; the promotion of the nuncio Fabio Chigi, recalled from Germany and made cardinal (10 February 1652) and secretary of State; the return to grace of Olimpia (11 March 1653); and the ultimate favor of Cardinal Decio Azzolini, who unsuccessfully threatened the position of Fabio Chigi, the next successor to Pope Innocent. The wandering heart of the weak, old pontiff and the intrigues of his entourage could only lead to derision or scandal. Nonetheless, they had a decisive historical significance: The questioning of nepotism as a system of government, and the increase in strength, after the middle of the 17th century, of a new actor within the government of the Curia—the cardinal secretary of State. A double conflict with France and the Barberini party also dominated the chronicle of this pontificate. From Paris, Mazarin, who had not accepted the choice of the conclave, withdrew his support from his ex-ally Antonio Barberini (October 1644) and recalled his ambassador. Innocent X replied by promoting cardinals who were clearly anti-French (6 March 1645), and in June, opening a fiscal inquiry into the squandering of funds by Urban VIII's nephews during the war of Castro against the Farnese (Francesco Maria Farnese was one of the new cardinals). On 28 September, Cardinal Antonio Barberini secretly fled to France by sea. On 15 October, Cardinal Francesco and Prince Taddeo placed the coat of arms of France on their palaces and fled with their families the night of 16 January 1646: Their possessions were confiscated during the CONSISTORY on 3 February 1646, while Antonio Barberini, and then his brothers, were received with the greatest honor at the French court. After the failure of Abbot Henri Arnauld's mission (spring 1646), the Franco-Spanish War extended as far as Orbetello, threatening the lands of Prince Ludovisi, the nephew of Innocent X. The latter had to yield: ambassador de Fontenay entered Rome (24 May 1647), Mazarin's brother was promoted to cardinal (7 October 1647), and Cardinal Francesco Barberini returned to Rome where he got back his possessions and his titles (27 February 1648) five years before the return of his brother Antonio (12 July 1653). But Innocent X also welcomed the cardinal de Retz, archbishop of Paris and Mazarin's adversary during the Fronde (1 December 1654) with great honors.

It was a belated and pathetic revenge, for Europe's equilibrium had changed rapidly during the interval. If Innocent X appeared to take sides with Spain by refusing to recognize the independence Portugal regained in 1640, he acted entirely differently toward Masaniello's revolt in Naples (7 July 1647), which was a severe blow to Spain's order in Italy. After having condemned the insurrection, he tried mediating, in vain, with Spain in order to reduce the military presence in the city. He also disapproved of the bombardment of Naples by Don Juan of Spain's fleet (October 1647). In Germany, the peace of Westphalia (24 October 1648), which marked the end of the cruel Thirty Years' War, sanctioned the new political and religious balance born of the Reformation during the 16th century, confirmed the elimination of a large number of abbeys and bishoprics as well as the secularization of a considerable portion of Church properties, and affirmed the principle that subjects everywhere should adhere to the religion of their princes. In the name of the pope, the nuncio of Cologne, Fabio Chigi, practically excluded from these negotiations, registered a solemn protest against the treaties in the BRIEF *Zelus domus meae* (dated 26 November 1648 and published 20 August 1650). In this document, the Holy See wanted it known that they rejected the partitioning that would put an end to any Catholic attempt to reconquer territories lost during the Reformation. The persecution of Catholics in puritan England, as well as the bloody war of extermination and colonization that took place in Ireland under General Oliver Cromwell (August 1649 through May 1650), show the powerlessness of the Holy See in Protestant countries. The encouragement gained from Venice during the war of Candia against the Turks did not allay the aggravation of tensions over ecclesiastical privileges in the republic. Papal government was not strengthened just within the PAPAL STATES: after the initial reconciliation with the Farnese, a new war over Castro, a feudal possession situated in the heart of the PATRIMONY OF SAINT PETER, followed; the city of Castro was occupied (2 September 1649), and then razed to the ground. And thus, everywhere in Europe, the affirmation of the states led the papacy to undertake, mostly in vain, a battle to affirm the rights of a Church excluded from the new political policies at the dawn of the age of absolutism.

Innocent X's religious policy deserves to be appreciated in light of this ostensible weakening of the Church's diplomatic situation in Europe. Everywhere in the world the pope protected the activities of the CONGREGATION OF PROPAGANDA and especially encouraged the MISSIONS in the Philippines. Nevertheless, he condemned, against the recommendation of the Society of Jesus, the adaptation of Chinese rites (12 September 1645). In Italy, he used his authority to support a vast movement of reform of monastic life from 1649 on, which ended in regrouping or eliminating many smaller groups that held only a few monks and that had become isolated from any religious change. In Rome itself, Pope Pamfili pursued a policy of beautifying the holy city through an active and lavish maecenas.

He gave Cavalier Bernin the job of decorating the columns and mosaic pavement of the great nave of ST. PETER'S BASILICA in the Vatican, and to Alessandro Algardi the construction of the monumental altar of St. Leo the Great. The piazza Navone, where the Pamfili palace was located, was admirably redesigned along the lines of Domitian's circus, which had been there before, enhanced by a new church, Sant'Agnese in Agone, destined for the role of family chapel for the Pamfili, and adorned with the monumental Fountain of the Four Rivers and its obelisk by Bernini. Bernini's rival, Borromini, was assigned the reconstruction of the façade of the basilica of ST. JOHN LATERAN. On the Janiculum, Prince Camillo Pamfili built the magnificent villa that still bears his name, beyond the San Pancrazio gate. The HOLY YEAR of 1650, which attracted some 500,000 pilgrims to Rome (150,000 were housed at the hospice of Most-Holy-Trinity-of-Pilgrims near the Ponte Sisto at the expense of the Holy See) marked the quantitative and spiritual apogee of religious fervor during the baroque age.

The Holy See's position on JANSENISM was the action during this pontificate that had the most long-range influence on theology and religion. Faced with the progress of the theses of Jansen in Flanders and Port-Royal in France, and the success of the treatise *De la fréquente communion* (1643) by Antoine Arnauld, the Holy See, alerted by the nuncio Guido di Bagno and pressured to make a decision by Jean-Jacques Olier and Vincent de Paul, progressively moved toward a doctrinal pronouncement. The Holy Office, then a special congregation of cardinals formed and personally presided over by Innocent X (12 April 1651), examined the suspect texts and the positions of its adversaries for a long time. The condemnation of five proposals drawn from Jansen's *Augustinus* by the bull *Cum occasione impressionis libri* (31 May 1653), though it began more than a century of divisions within the Church, marked a decisive turning point in the search, by Catholic theology, for a balance between divine grace and human freedom. Published in Rome on 9 June, it received the authority of a royal sanction by Philip IV and Louis XIV (thanks to the active support of Cardinal Mazarin), not without encountering resistance in Flanders and in France.

Innocent X died in Rome at the age of 81 on 5 January 1655: The chronicle reports that his sister-in-law Olimpia refused to pay the cost of his entombment, a final small-minded shadow over a difficult pontificate, which still was a significant historic transition between the age of the successesful Catholic reform of the early 17th century and the new era for the Church generated by the triumph of monarchical absolutism of the 17th and 18th centuries.

Philippe Boutry

Bibliography

Albert, M. *Nuntius Fabio Chigi und die Anfänge des Jansenismus, 1639–1651. Ein Römischer Diplomat in theologischen Auseinandersetzungen*, Rome-Fribourg-Vienna, 1988.

Boaga, E. *La soppressione innocenziana dei piccoli conventi in Italia*, Rome, 1971.

Campanelli, M. "L'ordine dei Minimi e la reforma innocenziana del 1649," *Annali della facoltà di lettere e filosofia di Napoli*, 15 (1972–3), 109–43.

Ceyssens, L., and Legrand, A. "La correspondance du nonce de Madrid relative au jansénisme (1645–1654)," *Antologica annua*, 4 (1956), 549–640; *La Correspondance antijanséniste de Fabio Chigi, nonce à Cologne, plus tard pape Alexandre VII*, Brussels-Rome, 1957.

Ceyssens, L., and Legrand A. *La Première Bulle contre Jansénius. Sources relatives à son histoire (1644–1653)*, Brussels-Rome, 1961–2.

Ciampi, I. *Innocenzo X Pamfili e la sua corte*, Imola, 1878.

Coville, H. *Études sur Mazarin et ses démêlés avec le pape Innocent X*, Paris, 1914.

Esposito, L. G. "Soppressione e consegna dei *conventini* domenicani in Calabria," *Visita storica calabrese*, 4 (1983), 175–212.

Feuillas, M. "Innocent X," *Dictionnaire du Grand Siècle*, Paris, 1990, 756–7.

Hammermayer, L. "Grundlage der Entwicklung des päpstlichen Staatssekretariats von Paul V, bis Innocenz X. (1605–1655)," *Römische Quartalschrift*, 5 (1960), 157–202.

Incisa Della Rocchetta, G., and Kybal, V. *La nunziatura di Fabio Chigi (1640–1651)*, Rome, 1943–6.

Innocenzo X Pamphili. Arte e potere a Roma nell'età barocca, A. Zuccari and S. Macioce ed., Rome, 1990.

Luzi, R. "L'inedito Giornale dell'assedio, presa e demolizione di Castro (1649) dopo l'assassinio del vescovo barnabita Mons. Cristoforo Giarda," *Barnabiti Studi*, 2 (1985), 7–55.

Mastroianni, F. F. "L'inchiesta di Innocenzo X sui conventi capuccini italiani (1650). Analisi dei dati," *Studi e ricerche francescane*, 14 (1984), 143–280.

Pastor, 30.

Repgen, K. "Die Proteste Chigis und der päpstliche Protest gegen den Westfällischen Frieden (1648–1650). Vier Kapitel über das Breve *Zelo domus Dei*," *Staat, Kirche, Wissenschaft in einer pluralistischer Gesellschaft, Festschrift zur 65. Geburtstag von Paul Mikat*, Berlin, 1989, 623–47.

Wright, A. D. *The Early Modern Papacy: From the Council of Trent to the French Revolution, 1564–1789*, London, 2000.

INNOCENT XI. *Benedetto Odescalchi (b. Como, 19 May 1611, d. Rome, 12 August 1689). Elected pope on 21 September 1676, crowned at St. Peter's in Rome.*

The Odescalchis were a very ancient noble family that could be traced back to the paladins who had followed Charlemagne into Italy. Bankers, diplomats, bishops, and magistrates, their social and religious role was important in the Como region and in Lombardy during the 15th and 16th centuries, and was widened in the 17th. Private tutors first guided Benedetto Odescalchi in his studies, introducing him to religion. He then attended the best colleges in Como, where his family was very prestigious. With Benedetto, the family moved to Rome, and with Livio (1652–1713), his nephew, who participated in the defense of Vienna against the TURKS, they extended their influence to Hungary and Slavonia. In 1697, Livio was a candidate for the throne of Poland. This family interest in European politics may be seen in Benedetto as well. During his pontificate, he was closely involved in political and social problems of the time, though this was not in keeping with his more reflective personality.

His early studies finished, he was admitted to the JESUIT college of Como, an establishment attended by the young aristocrats of the city. The Odescalchis were honored there in memory of the hospitality they had offered to the first Jesuits who had come to Como to fight against the Calvinist HERESY. They had first lived in a house that the family had put at their disposal (around 1563). His youth was marked by the loss of his father in 1622, and then of his mother during the plague of 1630. One of his uncles, Papirio, took him into his home in Genoa and directed his administrative studies. From 1626 to 1632, he often went to Genoa, Milan, Como, and Mendrisio, and became familiar with the business world and administrative problems. In 1635 he was named governor of the state of Milan. Still, just before his transfer to Rome, Benedetto Odescalchi did not seem to have chosen a real direction for his life. In the Holy City, he took classes in canon and civil law and obtained his diploma in Naples (21 November 1639). It was during this later period of university studies that he began to feel a clear ecclesiastical calling. He was influenced by new Roman friendships with Capuchins and especially several great protectors like cardinals Alfonso de la Cueva, Francesco Barberini, and Giambattista Pamfili (later INNOCENT X). It was in these ecclesiastical surroundings and in the CURIA that he found the definitive orientation for his life. When he labored in the congregations, his administrative experience, together with human and religious qualities, got him noticed. URBAN VIII Barberini favored him and, quickly, he was given extensive duties and weighty responsibilities. In several years he was named participating PROTONOTARY, commissioner general of stamps (a duty linked to the collection of taxes), and governor of Macerata (1644). On 6 March 1645, he was made cardinal-deacon of Sts. Cosmas and Damian. A very straight and narrow career, certainly due to the qualities of the man much more than to influential friendships that he had known to cultivate, and

even less to personal ambition, even if receiving the purple so young (he was only 34 years old) excited jealousies. For whatever reason, his nomination to the cardinalate, granted by Innocent X (1644–55), the successor of Urban VIII, emphasizes the continuity and importance of the favor that his family enjoyed in the highest levels of the Curia. After a short, but still administrative, digression (like the legation to Ferrara during the famine of 1648) and several duties inside the Curia (with the congregations of bishops and regulars, of guidance, and for good government), Cardinal Odescalchi was called to the bishopric of Novara (April 1650) although he was not yet a priest. His ordination took place on 20 November 1650, and he received his episcopal consecration on 30 January 1651. He remained at this see, previously occupied by great bishops like Speciano and Bascapè, until March 1659, when he returned to Rome. During his episcopal ministry, he showed great zeal and was totally engaged in charitable and pastoral duties. The great figure of St. Charles Borromeo was a constant example for him and it could be said that the ideal model of a good bishop proposed by the COUNCIL OF TRENT found a new application in him, though his name is not found among the great bishops of the 17th century in Italy. Cardinal Odescalchi did not have the temperament of an intransigent reformer and did not lead a stunning pastoral initiative. Honors did not attract him, and he preferred to work conscientiously and methodically and live a discreet life consecrated to meditation and piety. At the time of the CONCLAVE after the death of CLEMENT X (1676), Cardinal Odescalchi was in a favorable position. He was one of the best known and loved churchmen, and he had demonstrated his wisdom in the management of temporal affairs. He had also shown a great human sensibility by taking care of populations in the PAPAL STATES, especially during the famines and social crises during the 1640s. The Romans often saw him in the halls of hospitals or in the slums periodically inundated by the Tiber. The members of the SACRED COLLEGE, some of whom were highly intellectual and agile politicians like Cardinals Cibo, Ludovisi, or Barberini, easily came to an agreement, despite French opposition at the beginning, on a man in whom they saw a perfectly harmonious collection of significant experience. His first biographers, from Gaspar to Marracci (who was his confessor) and Lippi, give credit for this to the strictly spiritual and ascetic elements of his personality. In fact, it was these religious qualities that inspired his pontificate. Innocent XI tried to give a clearly religious quality to his pontificate (note the 14 articles of reform that he had all the cardinals sign), without tolerating any attack on the prerogatives and temporal privileges of the Church. Having taken the name of the pontiff who had named him cardinal, he had to confront three particularly thorny politico-religious situations of his time.

On the political level, he tried to eliminate the traditional rivalry between the Bourbons and the Habsburgs. In effect, he was aware that Christian Europe could only be united and live in peace if there was a perfect understanding among its members. On the other hand, the unity that Innocent XI sought was based on religion, more than on the political or military level. In this traditional vision of a Christian Europe, these kingdoms of ancient Catholic tradition were therefore indispensable. He would have liked them to be at the head of a new offensive against all that troubled or threatened the unity of Europe, like the propagation of Protestantism, the diffusion of the lay spirit, and the designs of the Ottoman Empire on the East and the European community itself, but France created the greatest obstacles to the accomplishment of this plan, through the "Very Christian" Louis XIV. In addition to more immediate political objectives such as pushing back his borders to the Rhine at the north and east, Louis XIV showed a marked desire for hegemony in the European theater. The anti-Austrian alliance with Poland, tolerance shown regarding the Ottoman Empire, the sympathy shown toward the king of England, and the weakening rigor with which the French territory combated heresy were different aspects of this policy that the pope distrusted. He saw in Louis' actions a general ambition where the national and hegemonic elements predominated to a worrisome extent, while the traditional danger that the Ottoman Empire posed for the West became more and more threatening with the election of the Grand Vizier Kara Mustafa, against whom only a united response from Europe could secure any concrete results. The difficult peace of Nimègue (1678), which established a momentary truce between the imperial bloc and the crown, only partially satisfied Innocent XI, who would have wished for a more explicit involvement by Louis XIV for the Catholic cause. Upon the announcement of peace, there was no exultation in Rome where a simple Te Deum *in forma paupertatis* at the church of Gesù was held. The plan for an anti-Turk league of Christian states made little progress because of the divisions in the Slavic world and the leaning of Sobieski toward Louis XIV, which increased the insurmountable rivalries between the States. Louis XIV only promised that he would intervene to defend Poland and Venice if the Turks attacked. The pope redoubled his efforts to find a way to hinder the Ottoman troops' advance. Their defeat before the walls of Vienna on 12 September 1683, opposed by a coalition force of Imperial, Polish, and Bavarian troops, was one of the capital events of modern history, but it was also a final sign of divisions that frustrated Innocent XI. Through his anti-Turk league, the pope wished to build a Christian world, not just an instrument capable of guaranteeing peace on the military level, which did not interest him. He would make this known himself by emphasizing the originality of his role and his mission: "We are the leader of Christianity, but we cannot be one for a league or an army."

In France, other difficult problems faced the pope in the jurisdictional realm with the question of regalia, which were prerogatives reserved for the crown on matters of ecclesiastical benefices and nominations for episcopal sees. These rights, acquired during the Middle Ages, had been enlarged little by little and Louis XIV was claiming them for all territories controlled by the French crown, retroactively. Innocent XI, appealed to by certain bishops engaged in the Jansenist controversy, reopened this contentious matter, admonishing the king in three BRIEFS that he addressed to him from 1678 to 1680. Then the affair became more complicated, partially due to the direct intervention of the French clergy who took the king's side (assemblies of 1680 and 1681) and claimed the principle of independence of the sovereign in temporal matters. Their positions hardened, despite the good sense Bossuet recommended. In Rome, discussions between the pope and the French ambassador, Cardinal d'Estrées, were broken off and on 11 April 1687, a brief by Innocent XI rejected and condemned the assertions of the assemblies. The risk of a rupture with disastrous effects convinced Louis XIV to dissolve the assemblies and resume the talks that, for the moment at least, ended in a compromise. Innocent XI refused the consecration of bishops named during the assembly of the clergy in 1680–1, but he took a more tolerant attitude in opposition to the four contested articles on the freedom of the Gallican Church.

A new crisis with the French crown arose regarding the question of quarter, otherwise known as the free zone reserved for ambassadors in Rome. The progressive growth of immunities and exemptions had given way to considerable abuses that particularly hindered the administration of justice. In this case also, the pope had inherited thorny problems from his predecessors, but his temperament led him to meet the most burning issues head on. He did not hesitate to restrain the freedoms given the diplomatic missions in Rome. The protests from Venice, Spain, and France did not make him back down. When Lavardin, the new French ambassador, took up his new post without being aware of the pope's positions, the pope thundered against both him and the French king in the bull *In coena Domini* and put a papal interdict on the national church of Saint-Louis-of-the-French where the ambassador had gone to hear mass on 24 December 1687. Two years later, Cardinal d'Estrées returned to France without ever having been received by the pope.

On the strictly religious level, the pontificate of Innocent XI coincided with the culmination of the controversy over "the prayer of guilt" and the problems related to conscience and its moral judgments. Those were some of the great themes that marked not only the formulation of doctrine, but also the religious and moral sensitivity of the baroque period. The final formulations on the manner in which the soul experiences the divine were written in line with a debate that had passionately engaged theologians, masters of different schools of spirituality and directors of conscience since the early 17th century. Although there were numerous solutions proposed, the insistence that everything be attributed to God and none to the individual had led people to believe that abandoning the soul completely to God was a possible response to the problem. What's more, this corresponded perfectly with the deepest aspirations of a culture searching for a direct experiencing of God. This was given the name QUIETISM in the history of spirituality. Under Innocent XI, the question was asked again, forcibly, regarding practical aspects of prayer, of abandonment to God, of the perfect quietude in Him of all the forces of the soul and the mind. The pontiffs had already intervened to condemn the excesses of these doctrines, which underestimated the role of human nature to the ascetic life and in the dialogue with God, and many statements of position had sanctioned the influence of these doctrines on the spirituality of the time. In the 1670s a Spanish priest was particularly active, whose *Spiritual Guide* was published in 1675, with 12 editions in 10 years, not counting the translations into different languages. Around Molinos, men and women of Roman high society gathered, along with ecclesiastics, nuns, and simple and uncultivated folk. The pope did not hide a certain sympathy for Molinos (there was even talk of a promotion to cardinal) despite the firm opposition of leaders of other spiritual schools like Father Paolo Segneri and masters from the Society of Jesus, but in 1685 the Spanish priest was arrested and accused of having corrupted the principles of Christian asceticism and led his disciples into immoral practices. In this rapid change of opinion on Molinos, it is difficult to understand the role of Innocent XI, and it was opportunism that led him to adopt certain positions. Just as incomprehensible was the granting of a cardinal's hat to the Oratorian Matteo Petrucci (1686), a very great personality in the spiritual realm, but who was also the center of bitter polemics regarding his doctrines, openly accused of Quietism. Whatever may have been, it was the pope's job to officially sanction the incompatibility of Quietist doctrines with Catholic orthodoxy. In the document *Coelestis pastor* on 20 November 1687, he condemned 68 of Molinos' propositions.

The controversy over grace, especially, continued to perturb the Catholic world and Innocent XI's pontificate. The difficult question of the relationships between divine grace and human freedom had interested the greatest minds of the century: from Jansen to Duvergier, from Pascal to Arnauld. Theoretical speculation mingled with politics and polemics among religious orders, and theological traditions, finally descending into devotional practice and religious life. Although the most bitter phase of the conflict that opposed rigorism and moved toward more moderate positions was nevertheless practically over as a result of repeated interventions of the Holy See from 1641 to 1656 against the theses of the *Augustinus* of Jansen, in 1679 Innocent XI condemned 65 laxist propositions, which were not acceptable to a man of perfect orthodoxy like the pope, whose extremely rigorous religiosity brought him closer to his more austere contemporaries.

Innocent died on 12 August 1689 at the QUIRINAL palace. An overall judgment of his pontificate cannot fail to bring out, as a central and characteristic element, his extraordinary engagement in returning the Church to its traditional role of referee and mediator between peoples, at the moment when many cases escaped its reach. It could even be said that his government reflected many tendencies of the Church during the 17th century: a reaffirmation of its spiritual authority, a desire not to stand by powerlessly while modern States took over, and a similar social preoccupation, especially with the great problems of poverty and poor relief. This pope especially tried to give the Church back its religious dimension by eliminating the too-worldly elements that had tarnished its image. The absolute refusal of nepotism was significant, like the sympathy he felt for the currents that demanded a Christianity stripped of easy accommodation and laxness that had been introduced not only into religious practices but also in certain solutions proposed by the moralists of the 17th century. A papacy that, on one hand, was far from the image of the great popes, patrons, and temporals of the baroque age ("With Innocent XI, there was no ambition to leave behind a lasting memory, but only piety," said his contemporaries). On the other hand, it seems to be interwoven with the first indications of modernity, certainly more sensitive to the Pascalian uneasiness than to the casuistic intricacies in which theologians and preachers, trying to interpret the new questions posed by religious conscience, had succeeded in limiting Christianity. The process for the sainthood of Benedetto Odescalchi was opened 11 April 1691, but it was not until 7 October 1958 that PIUS XII beatified him.

Luigi Fiorani

Bibliography

Blet, P. "Innocent XI et l'assemblée du clergé et Louis XIV de 1670 à 1693, Rome, 1972.

Colombo, G. *Notizie biografiche e lettere di papa Innocenzo XI*, Turin, 1878.

Correspondance du nonce en France Angelo Ranuzzi (1683–1689) (= Acta nuntiaturae gallicae, 10–11). ed. by B. Neveu, Rome, 1973.

De Bojani, F. *Innocent XI: sa correspondance avec ses nonces (1676–1684)*, Rome-Paris, 1910–12; "L'affaire du 'Quartier' à la fin du XVIIe siècle. Louis XIV et le Saint-Siège," *Revue d'histoire diplomatique*, 1908, 350–78.

Epistolae ad principes (1676–1689), ed. I. I. Berthier, Rome, 1891–4.

Epistolario innocenzano . . ., ed. P. Giani, Como, 1977.

Gerin, C. *Louis XIV et le Saint-Siège*, Paris, 1894 (see other works by the same author).

Maras, R. J. *Innocent XI, Pope of Christian Unity*, Notre Dame, Ind., 1984.

Michaud, E. *Louis XIV et Innocent XI d'après les correspondances diplomatiques inédites*, Paris, 1882–3.

Neveu, B. "Episcopus et princeps Urbis: Innocent XI réformateur de Rome d'après des documents inédits (1676–1689)," *Römische Kurie, Kirchliche Finanzen, Studien zu Ehren von Hermann Hoberg*, Rome, 1979, 597–633.

Orcibal, J. *Louis XIV contre Innocent XI. Les appels au future concile de 1688 et l'opinion française*, Paris, 1949.

Pastor, XI, 2, 3–384.

Sauer, A. *Rom und Wien im Jahre 1683 . . .*, Vienna, 1883.

Wright, A. D. *The Early Modern Papacy: From the Council of Trent to the French Revolution, 1564–1789*, London, 2000.

INNOCENT XII. *Antonio Pignatelli (b. Spinazzola, Bari, 13 March 1615, d. 27 September 1700). Elected pope 12 July 1691. Buried at St. Peter's in Rome.*

Pignatelli belonged to a family of ancient southern nobility and was born in the paternal castle of Spinazzola, in Apulia. His father, Prince Francesco di Minervino, sent him to Rome for his university studies. He spent time with the JESUITS at the Roman College, which, in the mid-17th century, had greatly revised the teaching of law and created a new chair in canonical law. Antonio Pignatelli got his diploma in law and entered the prelature thanks to his friendly rapport with influential Roman churchmen, particularly URBAN VIII. He became vice-legate of Urbino, inquisitor in Malta, and governor of VITERBO. Then began a fine European diplomatic career in prestigious postings. He was NUNCIO to Florence in 1652, then to Poland in 1660, and to Vienna to the imperial court in 1668. Despite several transitory incidents (such as the episcopate of Lecce and the fact that he was not made cardinal), CLEMENT X named him secretary of the Congregation of Bishops and Regulars in 1673. He finally obtained his cardinal's hat in 1681, with a singularly long delay if one compares it to the rapid rise of other great prelates of the CURIA. INNOCENT XI, who had called him to the SACRED COLLEGE, then gave him the government of the diocese of Naples (20 September 1686). Besides its population (statistics tell of around 400,000 inhabitants), this turbulent capital of the viceroyalty was characterized by a plethora of clergy, an infinity of churches and monasteries, and a group of intellectuals very pugnaciously opposed to the Curia. Historians have recognized Pignatelli for his moderation, a deep religious sensibility, and a great love for the poor.

The conclave lasted five months, from February to June 1691. Interminable discussions, as well as alternating vetoes by the great powers, presaged the difficulties and pressures that the pontificate following that of ALEXANDER VIII would experience. Cardinal Gregorio Barbarigo, bishop of Padua, seemed to have the best chance of winning. He was a saintly man, a pastor of great spiritual depth, yet very human. However, the extreme complexity of the political situation weighed heavily upon the work of the conclave. Because the cardinals of the imperial party opposed Gregorio Barbarigo, and the French, though they saw good qualities in him, would not vote for him, his candidacy was no longer promoted, except by the *zelanti* of the Curia. It was then that a compromise was found with near unanimity of the Sacred College, in the person of Cardinal Pignatelli. He was elected pope on 12 July 1691 at age 76. At the opening of the CONCLAVE he had in progress a synod of his diocese and, in addition to his known juridical and diplomatic skills, he also showed evidence of a pastoral openness, which was certainly one of the determining factors in his election. Despite the brevity of his pontificate, he had to confront very important doctrinal and political problems that had already tested the preceding popes. Innocent XII distinguished himself by the stability of his positions and by a definite autonomy in his choices of government. This differed significantly from the style of his predecessor, Alexander VIII, and was closer to that, more clearly religious, of Innocent XI, under whose protection he had served at the Curia. He was, however, sometimes independently inspired, as in the case of the bull against nepotism *Romanum decet Pontificem* on 22 June 1692, because he wanted it to be a distinctive document of his pontificate, despite resistance from many prelates.

Again, religious questions were linked to political problems in the context of new divergences between the European powers on the subject of the successions to the thrones of Poland and Spain. Although the Holy See had largely rejected the Jansenist theology and ethics in their theoretical forms and practices, these were far from disappearing from Church life at the end of the 17th century. The rigorist theses and attitudes were fed by some very active intellectuals and supported by groups of devotees and spiritual masters, especially in central Europe. At the time of Innocent XII, several small, more combative groups had left France and moved to Belgium and Holland, where they increased their activity, often in conflict with directives from Rome. The University of Louvain was their fortress. In the early days at least, they achieved a certain understanding with Innocent XII, who accepted their literal adhesion to the censures formulated by ALEXANDER VII regarding the five propositions of the *Augustinus* of Jansen. The pontiff asked the Belgian bishops to be moderate. On 25 November 1696, he sent them a letter that expressed his openness of mind. The necessity of accepting the decree of Alexander VII was reaffirmed, but the letter also stated that they were to be content to only accept the formula, without trying to learn the degree of interior assent of the signers, for the Church did not judge such things. The doctrinal opposition between Bossuet and Fénelon, which was reaching its most acute phase in the latter years of the 17th century, was a very painful affair on which Innocent XII was asked to take a position. The problem that was central to the long disagreement that opposed the great bishop and writer concerned, once again, the manner of conceiving the great questions of spiritual life about the contemplation of God, individual asceticism, and prayer. Their positions were quite different on these issues. Bossuet, more sensitive to the positive aspects of human nature and history, accentuated the dimension of striving and internal purification. Fénelon emphasized the necessity for confident abandonment to God, as the method of attaining the highest levels of contemplation. The difference between the two men grew more complicated when Fénelon took a position in favor of Jeanne Guyon, a woman of high society who remained a widow at only age 28 and who had devoted herself to religious life and works of charity. In 1685 at Grenoble, she had published a famous and controversial prayer manual: *Le Moyen court et très facile de faire l'oraison*, which had a large circle of readers, and quickly aroused great misgivings about the manner in which it suggested that difficult problems of spirituality be resolved. All in all, her critics said she took a position unilaterally centered on abandonment to God, to the detriment of interior mortification and personal engagement in Christian virtues. Sacramental practice itself was slighted in the manual; the author had admitted to not having confessed for 15 years. Mme Guyon, though protected by Mme de Maintenon, the morganatic wife of Louis XIV, was interrogated between July 1694 and March 1695 by a commission in which Bossuet was an influential member. Fénelon took her defense, and they arrived at a provisional agreement with a protocol of 34 articles that attempted to reconcile the varying positions. The polemics began once more with the simultaneous publication of *Explications des maximes des saints sur la vie intérieure* by Fénelon and of the *Ordonnance et instruction pastorale sur les états d'oraison* by Bossuet, which rekindled discussions and provoked an intervention by Rome. Reasons of political opportunism were not unrelated to Innocent XII's position against the theses of intense perfection, as through love, exempt even from the desire for one's own salvation, as maintained by Fénelon. They were condemned in 1699. Still, Innocent XII recognized the attachment of the bishop of Cambrai to the Roman see and the speed with which he submitted, whereas Bossuet's behavior seemed rather opportunistic.

One of the greatest consequences of his pontificate was, without a doubt, the improvement of relations with Louis XIV and, more particularly, resolution of the deadlock over the question of the bishops who had participated in Gallican assemblies of 1682 and adhered to anti-Roman theses that had been formulated then. Certainly, the king was going through a very delicate phase with regard to the new alliances that had reunited the monarchies of central Europe. Alexander VIII had already stated his opposition to the Gallican deliberations, on principle, not long before his death, and Innocent XII was not unhappy to return to the question on a strictly practical level, to see if several concessions were possible. The bishops named by the king, who had not taken part in the assemblies, were confirmed by the pope on condition that the king not try to force them to follow the four Gallican articles. Concerning the bishops who had intervened in the assemblies, the pope made their recognition contingent upon a declaration of obedience and a retraction of their accord. These maneuverings were prolonged, but the king yielded to the determination of the pope and informed Innocent XII on 14 September 1693 of the abrogation of the edict of 1682. "Louis XIV did not go to Canossa, but he made his bishops, his docile instruments, take that path," commented Ranke. Most important is that thanks to this accord, the Catholic hierarchy was reestablished in France. Not everything was clear, however, and the decision was often applied in a slapdash fashion, so that the right of regalia remained virtually in effect.

On the political level, the new closeness between France and the Holy See worried the other powers, but Innocent XII pursued his line of noninterference in purely temporal affairs, which allowed him to avoid becoming the prisoner of the coalitions. In the case of the succession to the throne of Poland, he first supported the candidacy of the French Catholic Conti, but recognized the election of the Lutheran Frederick Augustus of Saxe without difficulty. One unquestionable accomplishment of this attitude was that he was able to include in the treaty of Ryswick in 1697 between Louis XIV and the great coalition the clause guaranteeing the maintenance of the Catholic religion in the states that would pass under protestant domination as a result of peace treaties. Despite this, opportunists and political calculations or real about-faces, like those that Frederick Augustus used to affirm his independence from the prerogatives of the Holy See, often caused him difficulties, notably in the election of bishops.

Innocent XII tried to correct certain striking faults of the papal administration such as the venality of certain exactions, the dispersion and inefficacy of the tribunals, and specific abuses such as the enormous costs of the court. Having known poverty personally in Naples, he wanted to confront the problems of indigence and begging that were found in Rome in striking proportions. He was inspired to gather large numbers of the indigent, considered to be a menace to social tranquillity, in large hospices. He consulted theoreticians with much experience such as Baldigiani and the Frenchmen Chaurand and Guévarre, and, finally, he himself launched the "great enclosing" by setting up the Lateran palace to receive the poor who were unable to work. About 5,000 indigents streamed in. False paupers were expelled or otherwise dealt with. With the enlarging of the San Michele institution at Ripa Grande for educating the young, and with other interventions like the allocation of large sums of money for charitable organizations, Innocent XII showed himself to be one of the most open pontiffs of the modern period to problems of society, even if he seemed not to have thought about the causes of the inequalities and long-range implications.

His pontificate, short but productive, was entirely consecrated to reaffirming the prerogatives of the Church confronting the Gallican and jurisdictionalist tendencies, to diminishing long-standing but harmful traditions (like nepotism and selling of posts) in ecclesiastical life, and to bettering the functioning of the Roman Curia, trying to find a middle ground between probabilism and rigorism (accepting the ethic of the Jesuit Tirso Gonzales, an antiprobabilist, and refusing to condemn the *Nodus praedestinationis* by Sfondrati, accused of laxism), and finally, of attempting to control poverty by looking for some form of coercive discipline. Innocent XII was living at the end of the century, in both a chronological and figurative sense. At least on the level of spiritual history, we must recognize that his interventions against Quietism and against the final formulations of "pure love" accelerated the twilight of a devout sensibility that had moved through mystical and spiritual Europe during the second half of the 17th century.

Luigi Fiorani

Bibliography

Aragona Pignatelli, F. *Innocenzo XII e la sua famiglia*, Naples, 1946.

Campello Della Spina, G. B. *Diario del pontificate di Innocenzo XII*, Rome, 1887.

De Forbin, M. "Le cardinal de Forbi-Janson à Rome, le conclave d'Innocent XII," *Revue d'histoire diplomatique*, 38 (1924), 132–213.

De Maio, R. *Società e vita religiosa a Napoli nell'età moderna (1656–1799)*, Naples, 1971, 23–4 and *passim*.

Fantasia, M. *Innocenzo XII*, Molfetta, 1966.

Fatica, M. "La reclusione dei poveri a Roma durante il pontificato di Innocenzo XII," *Ricerche per la storia religiosa di Roma*, 3 (1979), 133–79.

Jovet, C. "Le père Guévarre et les bureaux de charité au XVIIe siècle," *Annales du Midi*, 1, (1889), 305–51.

Pastor, 32.

INNOCENT XIII. *Michelangelo Conti (b. Poli, Rome, 13 May 1655, d. Rome, 7 March 1724). Elected pope on 8 May 1721. Buried at St. Peter's in Rome.*

The illuminations and the triumphal arches with which the Roman people welcomed the election of Cardinal Michelangelo Conti to the pontificate could not hide the importance of the problems left by the unforeseen death of his predecessor, CLEMENT XI.

These problems had been brought about by the irresolution of the pro-imperial groups who could no longer count on the Spaniards. In effect, because the crown of Spain had fallen to a Bourbon, the Spanish were voting as a group with the French cardinals. The search for balance was difficult and took some time. Illustrious *papabili*, like Secretary of State Paolucci, against whom Vienna had used its veto, were sacrificed. Finally, the cardinals thought of Cardinal Conti, who was unanimously elected on 8 May 1721, for he promised to be ready to follow a policy of equilibrium between the two blocs.

Although born at the castle of Poli in the Roman countryside above Palestrina, he was considered a Roman pope. One of his ancestors had been a famous pope, INNOCENT III, whose name he took. He began his studies at Ancona with his uncle the bishop, and then continued at the Roman College of the Jesuits. His first advances in the prelature were as governor of Ascoli, then of Frosinone and VITERBO in 1693. In 1695 he was named to the nunciature to the Swiss Cantons and, in April 1698, to that of Lisbone. Finally, on 7 June 1706, Clement XI named him cardinal. He returned to Rome in 1710 and, after episcopal visits to Osimo and Viterbo, he resigned his non-Roman duties for reasons of health. All in all, his diplomatic career had taken place without upsets, except for the support that he had given Portugal when it entered the alliance, which had displeased the French diplomats.

His pontificate, therefore, began under the aegis of equilibrium. He had shown great dexterity when he named his first collaborators and called men to him who had proved themselves under Clement XI (Paolucci was named vicar general of Rome, Olivieri was confirmed as secretary of Briefs, Corradini was named datary, and Spinola secretary of state). Given the brevity of his pontificate, he was only able to deal definitively with two problems that had been pending for a long time. The first concerned the investiture of the fief of Naples and Sicily for which the emperor had waited a long time; the second, the restitution of Comacchio, the Ferrarese village occupied by the imperial troops in 1708. Taking advantage of his good relationship with Emperor Charles VI and wishing to settle the conflicts between the Catholic powers, he succeeded in putting an end to the affair, pending for over 20 years, of the investiture of the emperor in southern Italy. Still, Innocent XI did not make his decision until after consulting the cardinals and reestablishing the fiscal rights of the Holy See in these territories. The investiture took place in June 1722 and led to the changing of imperial representatives. The very faithful cardinal Althann left Rome to assume the position of viceroy in Naples (where he met with fierce opposition from the group of intellectuals with Giannone and Argento at their head), and was replaced by Cardinal Cienfuegos. The favorable solution of this affair made the pope hope for a similar one for the case of Comacchio, which, for the Holy See, had become a symbol of the inviolate character of the ecclesiastical state. However, the talks begun in June 1721 went extremely slowly and agreement on the formula of restitution was very difficult. Innocent XIII would not see its end; it would be left to his successor BENEDICT XIII (1725). In short, the relationships of Rome with the imperial court remained tense, even though they never attained the stiffness seen during Clement XI's time, and the results were meager. In fact, the Empire reaffirmed its rights over Parma and Piacenza. In Spain, things did not go any better. The CONCORDAT was not signed, despite the reprimands from the Holy See via the NUNCIO Acquaviva, who was reproached for a lack of aggressiveness.

The long quarrel that divided the Holy See from the French bishops on the question of Jansenism and the bull *Unigenitus* took a rather odd turn. Upon his election, seven French bishops who believed rumors that he was sympathetic to the opposition sent him a letter (dated 9 June 1721) containing very harsh criticisms of the contents of the anti-Jansenist bull of Clement XI, in which they saw "religion attacked in its dogma, Christian morality in its foundations and in its spirit." Their protests went as far as to ask for the abrogation of the papal document. A flood of polemics arose; to cut it off, the pope handed the document to the INQUISITION, which condemned it on 8 January 1722, and imposed the pure and simple acceptance of the Clementine constitution.

Innocent XIII was able to do little for the PAPAL STATES. He was content to remind people, in a letter on 17 September 1721, of the dispositions of the preceding popes concerning the interdiction of hoarding grain, the ANNONA, the authorization of partial exportation by the grain producers, and the maintenance of the freedom of commerce in the interior.

His 30 months of government would not allow him to deal with the more urgent problems of the Church, nor to imprint them with his personal stamp. In fact, he toed the line of his predecessors, limiting himself to looking at and clarifying official documents and, when necessary, asking for them to be applied. This was the case for the decree of *Propaganda Fide* on 13 September 1723, addressed to the general of the Society of Jesus to ask the missionaries to conform in a stricter fashion to the papal dispositions opposing the acceptance of Chinese rites.

Luigi Fiorani

Bibliography

Michaud, E. "La fin de Clément XIII," *Revue internationale de théologie*, 5 (1897), 42–60, 304–31.

Pastor, XV, 391–460.

Seppelt, F. *Geschichte der Päpste*, V, 413–15.

Von Mayer, M. *Die Papstwahl Innocens XIII.*, Vienna, 1874.

INQUISITION.

Middle Ages. The Inquisition in the Middle Ages (13th century) was originally a judicial procedure with a gradual, almost haphazard, development. The word itself is a literal transposition of the Latin *inquisitio*, which means "search" (its result, an inquest or inquiry, comes from *inquesta*). A simple process, the Inquisition soon combined with an ensemble of solutions that were more or less innovative, but always performed hastily in order to combat HERESIES; later an emergency Church tribunal was named to work in cooperation with civil authorities, albeit not always by delegation or papal injunction. Even though the papacy played a central role in its spread, the larger context for the birth of the Inquisition must be borne in mind. The many imitations to which it gave rise should not be forgotten: the famous "inquiries" begun by St. Louis in his kingdom thus borrowed much from the model.

Originally, only accusatory procedures were known in CANON LAW: the judge began legal proceedings only after an accusation was made, upon which furnishing proof was incumbent. The practical limits of the system were at first rejected by the progressive appearance of the denunciatory procedure, but the decisive step was taken when several decretals by INNOCENT III (1198–1213) juxtaposed the inquisitory procedure with these two others. This conceptual revolution was profound: "notoriety" (*fama publica*) became a kind of collective accusation, and the judge could open a procedure against a suspect without consultation. He then needed to seek specific accusers (thus allowing an accusatory procedure to be opened), or take it upon himself to furnish the proof: he searched ("inquisition") for the proof by assigning witnesses and collecting their depositions, including those of the defendant. The defendant, if guilty, was left only with a choice between perjury and self-accusation, because his depositions, as well as those of his witnesses, were made under oath. The system was not designed until after the judicial practices and experiences of the 12th century had been assimilated. These included the growing role of witnesses and written documents, which could be analyzed at one's leisure, and the new role of the confession, founded on the Roman adage *Confessi pro judicatis habentur* ("Those who confess condemn themselves"), which invaded other domains as diverse as composing private acts and auricular confession. So many free and spontaneous confessions would soon involve the judge in seeking, indeed even extorting confessions; and, at the same time, another overlap with the law and knowledge of antiquity—torture was reintroduced into the field of justice. It followed almost as logically that once the inquisitory procedure was applied to the search for heresy, the seriousness of the stakes and the theological practice of the judges led to a refinement in investigative techniques: weighing and cross-checking accounts through methods that today are referred to as police tactics, psychological harassment, trick questions, and infiltration by spies.

In the beginning, however, the inquisitory procedure was developed only to deal with matters of ecclesiastical discipline (SIMONY, elections of abbots that were contested, etc.). Later, it was applied to battling heresies that had become all the more threatening because they were upsetting a growing movement for stricter supervision of subjects and believers. In order to do so, the Inquisition as a procedure had to be combined with other elements: a system of penal laws, punishments and a body of judges. These components came together in a way that was as gradual as it was pragmatic. The medieval Inquisition was plural; an emergency measure, it never did become a stable institution, and it remained subject to the pressure of internal as well as political factors that affected the choice and the activity of its main figures.

In terms of the juridical arsenal of repression, the synthesis of the 13th century was as original as it was complex. The legal renaissance of the 12th century, which drew heavily on old Roman law, offered key concepts, specifically those of a "public matter" (*res publica*) and "majesty," against which heresy was seen as an attack. In the early Middle Ages, the heretic had been considered despicable; it was thus necessary to cut him off from the body of the faithful (excommunication), to punish him by measures that were for the most part temporary and medicinal (exile, confiscation of property), and this was done with the assistance of a "secular arm" to which the clergy appealed on more than one occasion. In the 12th century, the heretic became above all a disturbance to order, an enemy of society: it was Innocent III who, in 1199, took a decisive step by likening heresy to the crime of lèse-

majesté, which lay monarchies had also rediscovered (decretal *Vergentis in senium*, sent to the clergy and people of Viterbo). Canonical legislation thus worked out a reconciliation, not only with the penal law of antiquity (especially on the critical issue of definitive confiscation of property, which was appealing to more than one prince), but also with the Germanic tradition (royal and episcopal capitularies from the Carolingian era) that punished sacrilege with severe physical measures (e.g., mutilation, death) and which had already lit a long series of fires throughout the 11th and 12th centuries. During the 12th century, there was even a short liaison with the right to wage war, where the battle against heresy became a "just war at the very time that a theology of the CRUSADES was being shaped (URBAN II wrote: "We do not consider as murderers those who, ardent in the defense of their mother the Catholic Church, put the excommunicated to death"). An important moment in the battle against heresy, in the collaboration between pope and emperor, between bishops and princes, LUCIUS III's decretal *Ad Abolendam* (4 November 1184) dealt only with the accusatory procedure and remained strangely vague on the matter of penalties. When the fourth Lateran council evoked in 1215 the possibility of recourse to a personnel specialized in the battle against heresy, everything showed that it was aiming at traditional repression, within the diocesan framework (episcopal visitations, diocesan synods), with the assistance of not less traditional synodal witnesses (so named because, at the bishop's urging, clerics and laypeople rose up during synods as accusers or informers against heretics). For the final step to be taken, in the years 1220 to 1230, the combination, the systematization, and the stiffening of civil laws and papal interventions were needed. The array of penalties, where burning at the stake had become the common punishment, was shaped by civil authorities in agreement with the papacy (e.g., young emperor Frederick II and the statute of Catania, composed in 1224 against the heretics of Lombardy; and the Roman senator Annibaldo, in 1231), or in a profusion of statutes coming out of provincial councils called by papal LEGATES (for the Languedoc and Toulouse, in 1229, for Beziers in 1233). The papacy did not directly intervene, except to gather the essential facts ("statutes of the Holy See," developed in 1231 by fusing one of Gregory IX's constitutions and some of Annibaldo's statutes), and to urge communes, princes, and bishops to speed up their deliberations and promulgate the legislation. It is revealing that even after 1231 a number of points had to be specified at the local level (for example, for the Languedoc, in four regional councils spanning the years 1243 to 1254) and that the popes themselves did not cease producing new, abundantly glossed decretals, the majority of which would be coordinated only with difficulty in Boniface VII's *Sexte*.

In the first three decades of the 13th century, at the time of this legislative explosion, the human resources that battled heresy were particularly varied. In a city in Lombardy, a bishop sought collaboration with the chief magistrate of the commune to punish heretics in the name of imperial constitutions that had been distributed by the papacy; he was often pressed by a legate, who was soon supported by militias of the faith, whose mind-set was akin to that of the military orders. In southwestern France, the crusade combined its efforts with episcopal repression, which was goaded by the legates. In the Rhineland, the Dominican Conrad Dorso and Jean le Borgne, who in 1227 were adjuncts to a papal commissioner (the director of the cathedral school in Mainz, Conrad of Marburg), formed a kind of itinerant commission of inquiry that stimulated diocesan tribunals; in their proceedings they played the role of the old synodal witnesses, while Gregory IX was negotiating for more active collaboration with the princes of the Empire. Prepared by this period of improvisation, the classical Inquisition found some of the impetus for its birth in a number of papal letters in the period from 1231 to 1233. In 1231, even while his legislation was expanding the role of the Church in the direct punishment of heresy, Gregory IX extended Conrad of Marburg's powers by placing the inquisitory procedure in his hands. Similar missions were entrusted to Dominicans from the Empire in late 1231 (among others, to the priors of Ratisbonne, Friesach, and Strassbourg), and later in Burgundy to three other Dominicans (one of whom, the famous Robert le Bougre, whose nickname was due to his past as a former Cathar), by stipulations in a letter that has been lost (19 April 1233). With no limitations whatsoever, the DOMINICANS intervened in almost the entire kingdom of France in the same years; in 1235, Robert le Bougre became papal inquisitor for the entire kingdom, with the exception of the Languedoc (he would be suspended in 1239, probably less for his implacable severity than for his misunderstandings with the bishops of the kingdom). Even though these "inquisitors" were presented only as helpers of the ordinary, the reticence with which they were received can be understood. Specifically entrusted with seeking out *pravitas heretica* and freed from other duties, they were more mobile and less constricted by local pressures. The papal commission (which took the form of a delegation, against which the jurists were now preparing their weapons) implied that appealing a sentence to Rome was, a priori, impossible (it could be done, but only with difficulty), and that the commission was linked to the person of the pope himself, and thus for the length of his life.

During the 13th century, necessity led to expansion. Under Alexander IV, inquisitors were subject to the jurisdiction of the legates themselves, and a canonist soon compared them to proconsuls. In 1267 their mandate was no longer tied to the individual pope, but became perpetual, barring revocation, which was always possible, and without excluding possible recourse to temporary commissions. It is easy to see how historians have had difficulty charting intrigues that were continually moving, and whose most constant and active centers on French soil were Toulouse, Carcassonne, Avignon, Besançon, Paris, and sometimes Tours and Poitiers. It is also possible to understand the coexistence, even the rivalry, of an episcopal Inquisition, assured by the ordinary, and a "legatine" Inquisition (directly delegated by the pope). The latter term is ambiguous, since it confuses the activity that was (rarely) assumed by legates and, much more often, by special commissions. Out of necessity, these delegates were, for the most part, regulars (hence the unfortunate expression "monastic Inquisition"), and among them particularly were Dominicans. The context for the birth of the order of preachers in Cathar lands, the order's close ties to the Holy See, and its very vocation of combating heresy via the spoken word directly explain the important role it assumed in the Inquisition, but also the evolution of some of its characteristics. In some periods this involved harshness, and throughout, the use of the Inquisitorial procedure itself in the much wider context of reconquering minds through preaching and theological disputation. It even left its mark in keeping and using registers of depositions, something that benefited from the great innovations of the 13th century in the use of books (e.g., reference systems, alphabetical indexing). Widely present in the decades when the Inquisition was most active, the Dominican order also made a mark that other protagonists would inherit. The role of the Franciscans was not negligible, and the monastic Inquisition on the whole went through periods of crisis (in Toulouse, the Dominicans were isolated from 1250 to 1255), to the profit of the episcopate, even before the installation of a more serene collaboration in the 14th century. Bishops were actually associated with the Inquisition more or less willingly; in many cases they were directly responsible for the procedure, and sometimes proved to be just as meticulous in their quest and just as efficient in their aggression (one case in point was Jacques Fournier, a former Cistercian and the future BENEDICT XII, when he was bishop of Pamiers and later Mirepoix). The Inquisition was unable to function without the active support of temporal princes, however. As a result, its spread in time, as well as in space, differed considerably. Aragon was the only Iberian monarchy to support the papal Inquisition directly and Venice was always prudently reticent. The struggle against the English Lollards was a purely royal and episcopal matter, and the papal Inquisition was almost nonexistent in the Scandinavian countries; France, Italy, Germany, and, from there, the Netherlands and the kingdoms of the European East were its preferred lands.

There was nothing in the scope of the Inquisition that did not undergo great variation, as the evolution of the concept of heresy dictated. Even though the Waldensians and the Cathars were naturally singled out, the Inquisition managed to spread to cases of apostasy of converted Jews and Muslims, as well as to those of sorcery. In 1260, Alexander IV drew a line between complicated cases of heresy, which were subject to the Inquisition, and the "simple" cases of diviners and sorcerers, which were dependent on diocesan curias, although this line was moved by JOHN XXII to the benefit of the courts of the Inquisition. Heresy was soon extended to any deviation relative to the Roman "line." The development was obvious under John XXII, who fought Spiritual Franciscans and Beguins with the Inquisition; starting in 1323 it included anyone who proclaimed the complete poverty of Christ. Beginning in the 13th century, the political extension took place within the framework of the pope's struggle against Frederick II; even in the 14th century, with the GREAT SCHISM, the Inquisition's sphere of influence was extended to include the schismatics.

Beginning in the mid 13th century, manuals and other documents abounded, with their production reaching its apogee in the 14th century. This literature, for internal use, was supposed to synthesize a plentiful legislation and to give exact formulas for the mastery of a complex procedure. Its purpose was also to furnish pragmatic advice ranging from advice of a psychological nature to treatises in proper form regarding heretical opinions, their evidence, and how to flush them from behind behaviors and pat expressions (the most famous of this was that of the inquisitor Bernard Gui). The procedure was bracketed between sermons (initial and final), developing at the same time into a ceremonial display showing a deep split: the effects on the laity can be imagined, especially when the secular arm was supervising the process. The parish community gathered and a "period of grace" was prescribed, which allowed the heretics to give themselves up and thus benefit from clemency measures, at the same time that the search for witnesses began. The proceedings ordinarily associated two judges (the norm was set at the council of Vienne), two inquisitors, or one inquisitor and one adjunct (*socius*), the latter of whom might be the bishop, who was more closely incorporated during the 14th century. Imprisonment of the accused and their interrogations continued the proceeding, which ended with the proclamation of the sentence and administration of the punishment, which once again were brought to conclusion by a public meeting and sermon. In this sense, the object was less repression itself than persuading (at any price) the heretic's recantation. The Inquisition first worked as an emergency measure (let us bear in mind the massacre of Conrad of Marburg and his colleagues in 1233; of Peter of Verona, the inquisitor

from Milan, in 1245; and the inquisitors from the Languedoc in Avignonet, in 1242, which was an excuse for the massacre in Montsegur). This explains the harshness of the earliest procedures and the use of exceptional methods, so well refined after the Middle Ages (as a precaution, the accused was often left in ignorance regarding which witnesses had made depositions against him). It should also be noted that the range of punishments, which was quite open, was more than anything a ploy against a hardening of spirit, and that the greatest tenacity was consequently reserved for those who had relapsed, returning to their heresies after an initial recantation. The death penalty was not pronounced as such, but only that an individual was "handed over to the secular arm" (indicating burning at the stake and confiscation of goods) and that the other punishments were, in a way that was much more monastic than civil, punishments of "penance," which were certainly to be feared but greatly foreign to the lay system of justice at the time. These included the defamatory wearing of yellow crosses; expiatory pilgrimages; and enclosure that was, in principle, perpetual (being "walled in," with degrees between the "strict wall," with shackles and bread and water, and the "wide wall," where the prisoner was physically able to walk around in his prison, with the benefit of "permissions"). Despite sad memories of a strictly totalitarian logic, it can be seen that inquisitorial repression was in no way like the more savage and final repression that lay princes or the crusaders carried out, aiming at past faults.

At the same time, the delicate question is raised regarding the working of the instruction and its most inhumane aspects. Sources here are relatively scarce. The non-sedentary nature of the phenomenon, sometimes even the riots or surprise attacks aimed against the archives as much as at the inquisitors themselves, explain why only a few registers are extant today, these being of sentences and, even more so, of depositions of witnesses: irreplacable sources with a richness that goes beyond the history of religion, but which are particularly fragmentary and especially difficult to use (the words of the accused being transcribed by the notary, and penned in rigid phrasing) and badly preserved through the ages (the only detailed texts available are from the late 13th century).

The first point in the proceedings: The inquisitor sought "advice" from the jurists and the ordinary's opinion, even if the latter was not directly associated with the proceedings. Quite often there was a lack of detailed affidavits to help us judge what was hidden behind stereotyped phrases mentioning the "advice taken" for the regularity of sentences. Even if it was unquestionable that "advisors," whose numbers varied but were usually quite high, were finally acquainted with the dossiers prepared by the inquisitor, it was difficult to know if they were allowed to examine them seriously. It is probable that, in critical periods, the local lay jurists and local clerics were afraid of betraying a passive sympathy for heresy. Once the great anti-Cathar repression of the 1230s through the 1260s had passed, a few isolated cases showed that sentences could be reduced.

Problems, as can be imagined, were more delicate when it was a matter of the use of torture. The almost logical outcome of the procedure and the search for a confession, long codified by jurists but discreet in written records, it was part of a much wider procedure where psychological pressure was ubiquitous; thus Bernard Gui's sadly famous *Vexatio dat intellectum*: "[Intellectual] torment gives intelligence [to those who play the idiots]." The jurists did set limits on torture (it should cause neither death nor mutilation), and especially justifications, since the Church had a "distaste for blood." Because its application was often handed over to secular judges or laypeople (whose very practices in this domain became more frequent and still remained brutal), it was all the more easily done in the presence of the inquisitors; in 1256 Alexander IV (for Toulouse) and in 1262 Urban V, in a general way both authorized the two associate inquisitors to excuse one another from the prohibitions set by the Church for the use of torture. The final figures are difficult, if not impossible, to discern. In any case, it seems sure that until the 1260s, sources do not allow explicit traces of torture to be found, but later, particularly in the 14th century, the practice became tragically commonplace. Evidence of this can be seen, from some research, by the paucity of confessions explicitly obtained "without torture" or "outside" (thus after) torture.

A numerical tally for repression is similarly impossible. Reliable statistics are partial and of later date, even if in some cases the lay accounting records (accounts "in process," meaning of confiscations, in France) reinforced evidence from inquisitors' registers. In the diocese of Turin, G. Merlo counted a little over 200 condemnations between 1312 and 1395 (approximately one-fourth of the accused were women), of whom 22 received the death sentence and 41 wore crosses, and there were some 150 sentences that ranged from fines (of which there were five in village communities) to PILGRIMAGES. Activity was of course more intense in the south of France between 1230 and 1330, where it was not a question of pursuing Spiritual Franciscans or pacifying Waldensian communities in the mountains. After Montsegur, a quite partial compilation (probably less than a third) of the inquisitorial registers of Jean de Saint-Pierre and Bernard de Caux leave traces of 5,471 depositions, but a later, and thus less repressive period, would have to come before a breakdown of these punishments could be done. The sentences pronounced in Quercy from Advent, 1241, to the Feast of the Ascension in 1242 (427 pilgrimages to Compostela, 2 to Rome, and 108 to Canterbury, 79 bearing of crosses) ac-

tually concerned only heretics who had spontaneously confessed during the grace period. The most interesting calculations were done by A. Palès-Gobilliard from the archives of Bernard Gui, inquisitor in Toulouse starting in 1307. From 1307 to 1323, Gui pronounced 501 condemnations and 243 remissions of sentences (which, for the most part, ended imprisonment after a minimum of three years in detention). Eighty of the condemnations were made against individuals already deceased, and whose bones were exhumed and burned. The other 421 concerned 401 accused (of which 177 were women) and 20 increases in sanctions. Twenty-nine individuals were sent to be burned at the stake; the "strict wall" was imposed on 13 who were condemned, and the "wide wall" on 231 others (perpetual, in principle, but the majority of them remained imprisoned for 7 to 12 years), defamatory sentences involving the loss of civil rights and pilgrimages were imposed on 107 individuals. Repression was thus no longer an emergency measure, but the activities it included do deserve mention: there were 113 detainees in the Inquisition's prison in Toulouse in the autumn of 1310 and, of a total of 638 individuals charged by Bernard Gui, 10 died during a particularly trying "preventive" detention.

At the end of the Middle Ages, the Inquisition began to decline, less from a shortage of heretics than from competition from new protagonists, beginning with monarchies. On 1 August 1458, while Nicholas V was naming an inquisitor for the entire kingdom of France (with the exception of the East), he expanded his area of reponsibility to cases of blasphemy and divination, totally taking it out of the ordinary's hands (his sentences could be pronounced in the bishop's absence). Nevertheless, in 1478, while the Curia was naming an inquisitor in Bourges, its choice fell upon the duke of Bourbon's confessor. When the priest Jean Lailler, in Paris, was spreading the most radical of Wycliff's theses and those of denigrators of the Curia and of St. Francis (whom he put in hell), the papal inquisitor only managed, in his inaction, to avoid open conflict with the opposition of the university, the bishop, and the parlement. In 1485, the papal inquisitor "for France, Aquitaine, Gascony, and Languedoc" called himself an inquisitor "from the Holy See and parlement." Evidence, in the best and worst senses, of the building of a papal monarchy in the 13th century, the medieval Inquisition thus began to fail with the building of monarchical States in the 15th century. It was another monarchy, in Spain, that would give it its second breath.

Olivier Guyotjeannin

Bibliography

Artini, P. A. "Per una storia dell'inquisizione medievale: l'inquisitio trentina del 1332–1333," *Archivio storico italiano*, 150 (1992), 83–113.

Courtenay, W. J. "Inquiry and Inquisition: Academic Freedom in Medieval Universities," *Church History*, 58 (1989), 168–91.

Davis, G. W. *The Inquisition at Albi, 1299–1300: Text of Register and Analysis*, New York, 1948.

Despy, G. "Les débuts de l'Inquisition dans les anciens Pays-Bas au XIIIe siècle," *Problèmes d'histoire du christianisme*, 9 (1980), 71–104.

Dossat, Y. *Les Crises de l'Inquisition toulousaine au XIIIe siècle (1233–1273)*, Bordeaux, 1959; *Église et hérésie en France au XIIIe siècle*, London, 1982 (reprint of articles).

Douais, C. *Documents pour servir à l'histoire de l'Inquisition dans le Languedoc*, 2 vol., Paris, 1900.

Duvernoy, J. *Le Registre d'inquisition de Jacques Fournier évêque de Pamiers, 1318–1325*, Paris-La Haye, 3 vols., 1978.

Eymerich, N., and Peña, F. *Le Manuel des inquisiteurs*, trans. L. Sala-Molins, Paris-La Haye, 1973.

Gonnet, G. "Bibliographical appendix: recent European historiography on the Medieval Inquisition," in G. Henningsen and J. Tedeschi, *The Inquisition in Early Modern Europe*, Dekalb (Illinois), 1986, 199–223.

Gui, B. *Manuel de l'inquisiteur*, ed. and trans. G. Mollat and G. Drioux, Paris, 2. vols, 1926–7.

Guiraud, J. *Histoire de l'Inquisition au Moyen Âge* [XIII siècle], Paris, 2 vols., 1935–8.

Hamilton, B. *The Medieval Inquisition*, New York, 1981.

Inquisition im Mittelalter, P. Segl. ed. Cologne-Vienna, 1993 (*Bayreuther historische Kolloquien*, 7).

Kieckheffer, R. *Repression in Medieval Germany*, Liverpool, 1979.

Lea, H. C. *Histoire de l'Inquisition au Moyen Âge*, French trans. S. Reinach, Paris, 3 vols., 1900–1; reprint Grenoble, 1990 (ed. London, 1888).

Maisonneuve, H. *Études sur les origines de l'Inquisition*, Paris, 1942 (2nd ed. 1960).

Merlo, G. *Eretici e inquisitori nella società piemontese del Trecento*, Turin, 1977. É. Griffe, *Le Languedoc cathare et l'Inquisition (1229–1329)*, Paris, 1980.

Molinier, C. *L'Inquisition dans le Midi de la France au XIIIe et au XIVe siècle: étude sur les sources de son histoire*, Toulouse, 1880; critical complement by Ch. Douais, "Les sources de l'histoire de l'Inquisition dans le midi de la France aux XIII et XIVe siècles," *Revue des questions historiques*, 30 (1881), 383–459.

Palès-Gobilliard, A. *L'Inquisiteur Geoffroy d'Ablis et les cathares du comté de Foix (1308–1309)*, Paris, 1984.

Palès-Gobilliard, A. "Pénalités inquisitoriales au XIVe siècle," *Crises et réformes dans l'Église (Actes du 115e congrès national des sociétés savantes, Avignon, 1990)*, Paris, 1991, 143–54.

Paolini, L., and Orioli, R. *Acta S. Officii Bononie ab anno 1291 usque ad annum 1310*, Rome, 3. vols., 1982–4.

Paolini, L. *Il "De officio inquisitionis": la procedura inquisitoriale a Bologna e la Ferrara nel Trecento*, Bologna, 1976.

Patchovsky, A. *Die Anfänge einer ständigen Inquisition in Böhmen: ein Prager Inquisitiorien-Handbuch aus der ersten Hälfte des 14. Jahrhunderts*, Berlin-New York, 1975.

Shannon, A. C. *The Medieval Inquisition*, Washington, D. C., 1983.

Van der Vekene, E. *Bibliotheca bibliographica historiae sanctae Inquisitionis*, new. ed. Vaduz, 2 vols., 1982–3.

Vidal, J. M. *Bullaire de l'Inquisition française au XIVe siècle et jusqu'à la fin du Grand Schisme*, Paris, 1913.

Vincke, J. *Zur Vorgeschichte der spanischen Inquisition: Die Inquisition in Aragon, Katalonien, Malorca und Valencia während des 13. und 14. Jahrhunderts*, Münster, 1941.

Modern Era. The Inquisition, as an invested tribunal delegated by the papacy and with special jurisdiction over offenses against the faith, was an institution of medieval origin. The period of its greatest activity, in the second half of the 13th century, coincided with the repression of Catharism. It then experienced a period of decline: some courts disappeared, while others were barely active.

A new chapter in the already secular history of the institution was opened in the second half of the 15th century with the progressive establishment of the tribunals of the Spanish Inquisition. On the Iberian Peninsula, the Inquisition had only been in effect in the kingdoms under the crown of Aragon, where it appears as though, beginning in the first half of the 15th century, its activity was reduced. Early in their reign, the Catholic king and queen, Ferdinand of Aragon and Isabella of Castille, who had been impressed by the worrisome dimensions that the phenomenon of crypto-Judaism was taking on in their possessions, felt a need to reshape the tribunal and established it in Castile.

It frequently happened that Jews who had been baptized (not always completely willingly) went back to the clandestine practice of the religion of their forebears, but the motives that encouraged the sovereigns to ask the Holy See to create new courts of the Inquisition in their kingdoms were not exclusively religious. There were also motives of a political nature, where it seemed evident that there could be no political unity without religious unity. There were also social factors, most notably the pressure brought to bear by a movement of public opinion expressing Christian hostility against an element that had not been assimilated into society.

As a whole, this was a question of creating a body that was clearly different from what preceded it, one upon which the crown was able to exercise a certain amount of control. Ferdinand and Isabella saw their wishes granted with a BULL of SIXTUS IV (promulgated 1 November 1478), which gave the sovereigns the right to name inquisitors and to send them wherever necessary.

The violent repression against the *conversos* that followed the creation of the first courts in 1480, led the pope to modify this early concession. The definitive structure of the institution was set in 1485 by INNOCENT VIII. Sovereigns had the right to name an inquisitor general to head it; the pope would confer the necessary jurisdiction upon him, particularly the ability to name local inquisitors. Consequently, in 1486, the Holy See granted the inquisitor general the power to judge appeals against the sentences of peripheral courts. In time, this power was interpreted to mean that the judgment in appeal given by the inquisitor general concluded the procedure, with no possibility of another appeal to the Holy See. This was the foundation of the autonomy claimed by the institution vis-à-vis Rome. Nevertheless, starting in about 1488, the inquisitor general was joined by a general council known as the *Suprema*, the members of which were named by the king and queen, which would represent the "long arm" (*longa manus*) of the monarchy in the affairs of the Holy Office. During the following period, the only institutional innovation would be the introduction of the Holy Office into the American colonies. Tribunals were created in Mexico City and Lima in 1569, and in Cartagena de Indias in 1609.

In a way, the Portuguese Inquisition's origins were tied to the institution of the Spanish Inquisition. Beginning in 1515, King Manuel had tried in vain to get the Holy See to establish a court similar to the one in the neighboring country. He based his request on the fact that a number of *conversos* pursued by the Spanish Inquisition were fleeing from Castille and seeking refuge in Portugal. A new attempt was made in 1531 by JOHN II, but a first papal concession of 17 December of that same year was revoked less than a year later. CLEMENT VII judged in fact that he had been poorly informed about the real situation of the converted Jews (*cristãos-novos*), many of whom had been forcibly baptized. They sent representatives to Rome, and the pressure they brought to bear in the Curia dragged out the diplomatic talks in which the sovereign had been involved for over 15 years.

In 1536 the foundations of the new institution were set in a bull of PAUL III which was not satisfactory to the king. It was only on 16 July 1547, after numerous incidents and tedious discussions that included Emperor Charles V, that JOHN III obtained the promulgation of a bull creating a tribunal analogous to the one already in existence in Spain. It was in this way that the inquisitor general of Portugal also gained both the power to name peripheral inquisitors and jurisdiction of appeal on the sentences of lower courts. He was assisted in his tasks by a general council (*Conselho Geral do Santo Ofício*), whose members were named by the king. Following the

example of the Spanish institution, the Holy Office of Portugal thus succeeded in assuring a certain autonomy relative to the papacy.

The Roman Inquisition's foundation was later than those on the Iberian peninsula, which came into being primarily to repress crypto-Judaism. The Roman institution was established primarily to confront the danger of Protestantism.

In the early 16th century in Italy, as elsewhere, the medieval Inquisition was undergoing a period of crisis. The weak activities of the tribunal facilitated the propagation of Protestant teachings. Luther's writings circulated in Lombardy as early as 1519. A few years later, Venice became the main center for the spread of Protestant thinking on the peninsula. Nevertheless, the Church did not react until 1542, when Paul III created a special commission of cardinals, which was to become the Congregation for the Inquisition, or of the Holy Office. The foundation was thus laid for the inquisitional machinery which, in time, would be called the Roman Inquisition.

The sphere of influence and the organization of the Congregation, which were later expanded, were established definitively within the framework of the reform of the Roman Curia undertaken by Sixtus V in 1588. The DICASTERY was to direct, promote, and coordinate the activities of all the tribunals of the Inquisition (with the exception of those on the Iberian peninsula). Moreover, it could both proceed directly against those suspected of heresy and recall pending cases and judge appeals against the sentences of peripheral courts. As its archives were until recently inaccessible, little is known about the congregation's activities. Nevertheless, it appears as though the dicastery in fact concerned itself almost exclusively with courts operating on the Italian peninsula and the neighboring islands (with the exception of Sicily and Sardinia, which were under the purview of the Spanish Inquisition), as well as in Avignon, the Comtat Venaissin, and the Spanish Franche-Comté. At the beginning of the modern era, the Inquisition worked in two other geographical regions, France and the Netherlands.

In the early 16th century, the medieval Inquisition was still surviving in France. With the Reform spreading, repression of heresy passed gradually into the hands of royal power, which exercised it through parliaments. It was not until 1557, under Henry II, that an attempt to introduce the Roman Inquisition took place, but the opposition of the Parlement in Paris doomed it to failure. The institution continued to exist in name, but when it was suppressed, during Louis XIV's reign, the last existing court, that of Toulouse, had a titulary in name only, who did not even live there.

The situation was different in the Netherlands, where in the Middle Ages the delegated Inquisition had operated under the DOMINICANS. In this case also, the penetration, first of Lutheran and later of Anabaptist doctrines was to force a radical reformation of the institution. In April 1522, Charles V conferred the responsibility of inquisitor general upon a member of the Council of Brabant, F. van der Hulst. Although he was a layman, van der Hulst saw his charge confirmed by HADRIAN VI on 10 June 1523. The flagrant abuses and serious irregularities committed by the new inquisitor would provoke his dismissal a few months later. Charles V then opted to have a different structure put into place. The sovereign had the right to name inquisitors, whom the Holy See would later confirm, and upon whom it would confer the necessary powers. Consequently, in 1529 and 1531, Charles V took rigorous measures (the sadly famous "placards") stipulating severe punishments for both propagators and disciples of the new teachings. The subsequent spread of Calvinism pushed the emperor to again institute tribunals whose actions, in 1546 and 1550, were to unfold under the control and the support of civil authorities. However, the revolt that broke out against Spain and popular aversion to the tribunal forced the son of Charles V, Philip II, to temporarily suspend its activities. After the pacification of Gand in 1585, he abolished it, leaving the matter of repressing heresy to bishops alone.

In the second half of the 16th century, the three truly active institutions were, therefore, those in Spain, Portugal, and Rome. They were of similar, although not identical, organization. In principle, the sovereign pontiff was at the head of the inquisitional framework. In fact, he exercised his powers directly over only the Roman Inquisition. As has already been seen, the Spanish and Portuguese Inquisitions, while they recognized the supreme authority of the pontiff, had managed, in fact, to gain considerable autonomy. Despite that, the three principal Inquisitions were of analogous structure. A collegial body (the Congregation of the Inquisition, for the Roman Inquisition; the Consejo General, or Suprema, for the Spanish Inquisition; and the Conselho Geral, for the Portuguese Inquisition), had the task of directing, coordinating, and controlling the activities of the peripheral tribunals. Moreover, the three bodies acted as courts of appeal for all appeals against first-degree sentences made by local inquisitors.

Below the three central bodies there was a network of tribunals whose territorial jurisdiction was of a different extent in the Iberian Inquisitions and in that of Rome. In effect, while in the Roman Inquisition, inquisitorial districts generally coincided with diocesan boundaries, in the Spanish and Portuguese Inquisitions the districts were wider, sometimes even considerably so. Thus, the juristiction of the tribunal of Lisbon included not only islands and strongholds in North Africa, but also Angola and all of Brazil.

Similarly, there were differences in the matter of personnel. In the Roman Inquisition, the judges were Dominicans (except in Florence and Venice, whose tribunals were traditionally given to the Franciscans), and they were theologians. The Spanish and Portuguese inquisitors were generally chosen from among the ranks of the secular clergy. These most often had been trained as jurists. Given the differences of size among inquisitorial districts, there were a number of inquisitors, from two to four, at the head of the Iberian tribunals. The Italian tribunals tended to have only one inquisitor, who was assisted by an associate (*socius*). The only exception to this was in the kingdom of Naples, where the Roman Inquisition was represented by a delegate from the Congregation of the Inquisition who resided in Naples. In the rest of the kingdom, the peripheral tribunals were directed by the bishops of the respective dioceses, who intervened in the capacity of ordinary judges in matters of faith.

Below the inquisitors there were personnel, the number of which differed depending on the Inquisition in question: fiscal procurators (who supported the prosecution); secretaries; notaries; miscellaneous employees; advisors; and close associates, meaning laypeople who, in exchange for certain privileges, cooperated free of charge with the activities of the courts, especially in gathering information and arresting the accused. Even though a fair amount is known about the Inquisition's bureaucracy, such is not the case for its finances. The subject has been discussed with more fiction than fact, given that the tribunals had the ability to confiscate the property of those who were condemned. In reality, according to what is known, with the exception of specific periods, the three Inquisitions never did benefit from substantial revenues, and expenses generally surpassed the revenues that came in from sequestrated property and other eventual sources of finance.

The procedures followed by the different Inquisitions were fundamentally identical. This was due to the fact that the inquisitorial process was definitively established in the 13th and 14th centuries. The relative norms had been gathered together in the canonical collections (*DECRETALS*, *Sexte*, *Clementines*) and remained unchanged, except for a few minor adjustments in more modern times due to the characteristics of each national Inquisition.

A trial during the Inquisition began when the inquisitor learned (generally after a denunciation had been made) facts that cast doubt regarding the orthodoxy of an individual. Information was gathered and statements were taken, leading to charges brought against the individual. In cases where the items collected justified it, a decision for preventive incarceration was made. Then the true trial began, in the course of which a formal interrogation of the accused was carried out, and the testimonies made against him or her were made known, albeit without divulging the name of the individuals giving those testimonies. When interrogations revealed serious signs that the accused was lying or was failing to divulge a part of the truth, torture could be utilized after a specific procedure had been carried out, supposedly entailing the participation of the bishop of the diocese where the tribunal acted (the famous interlocutory judgment). In the tribunals of the Inquisition, as in secular tribunals, torture was considered to be the most certain means of reaching the truth. It was the "queen of proof." This is why, if the accused confirmed his preceding declarations of innocence while being tortured, he was acquitted. On the other hand, if he changed his previous deposition, his confession had to be subsequently confirmed in order for it to be considered juridically valid. After enough evidence was collected to make a decision regarding the fate of the accused, the inquisitors pronounced their sentence, in consultation with the advisors and after getting the approval of the diocesan ordinary. The sentence could be an acquittal; a condemnation to minor punishment if there was a suggestion of heresy, which could be light (*suspicio levis*) or grave (*suspicio vehemens*); or burning at the stake, with eventual confiscation of property, if the condemned individual's heterodoxy was fully proved and if he remained obstinate, meaning if he confirmed his heterodox beliefs. Capital punishment was not carried out by the tribunal of the Inquisition, but by civil authorities to whom the individual was turned over after the judgment was handed down (*traditio brachio saeculari*). If the condemned individual was judged in absentia, or if he had already died by the time of the trial, an effigy was burned in his place (a procedure called *relajación en efigie* in the Spanish Inquisition). The sentence was generally carried out in public, during solemn ceremonies (in Portuguese, *auto da fe*, in Spanish, *auto de fe*).

Although these proceedings originated in the Middle Ages, it should be noted that in modern times they were generally administered with less harshness. For example, the right of the accused to have someone defend him or her (or a lawyer designated by the court when the accused did not have the means to hire one) was recognized, as was the right to appeal the sentence, which was excluded in the Middle Ages. Moreover, torture and capital punishment were administered somewhat more sparingly. According to the data we have for the Spanish Inquisition, between the second half of the 16th century and the first half of the 17th, the percentage of those tortured varied, depending on the tribunal, from 7 to 11 percent of the number accused.

Similarly, from 1540 to 1700, of a total of 44,674 cases, only 1.8 percent of the accused were effectively condemned to death, while 1.7 percent of the trials concluded with a burning in effigy. Unfortunately, we do not have general data on the Roman Inquisition to allow comparison with the Spanish Inquisition. The partial data available seem to indicate that the Italian tribunals were quite prudent in decisions regarding the death penalty. Thus, for example, of the 1,000 first accused who were brought before the tribunal of the Inquisition of Aquileia-

Concordia between 1551 and 1647, only 5 (i.e., 0.5 percent) suffered capital punishment. The number of those condemned to death in the Portuguese Inquisition appears to have been higher. Of 13,255 trials that took place from 1540 to 1629, death sentences (in *carne* and in *estatua*; the source available does not make a distinction) represented 5.7 percent. Nevertheless, the fact that the data refer to the early period of the Portuguese tribunal's activity should be borne in mind; it was during this period that repression was the harshest.

Naturally, these figures are not sufficient to conclude that the Inquisition was a soft and equitable judicial court; famous trials, and even entire periods of the history of its tribunals show that such was not always the case. They show only that the most recent research has helped to add nuance to a demoniacal image often based on less-than-reliable historical data, which a certain historiography of the past wanted to give to the Inquisition of the modern era, turning it into an institution founded on arbitrariness and cruelty.

Despite a considerable bibliography, the present state of works does not allow us to outline a historical evolution of the institution as a whole. However, two periods for the three primary Inquisitions can be distinguished. The first, the shorter of the two, went up to the years immediately after the conclusion of the COUNCIL OF TRENT; the second began in the last 20 years of the 16th century and lasted until the progressive disappearance of the tribunals at the end of the 18th century and the beginning of the 19th.

The first period was characterized by particularly intense repressive activity: against the *conversos* and the *alumbrados* (who belonged to a pseudo-mystical sect of a heretical nature) in Spain; against the *cristãos-novos* in Portugal, and against Protestants of all confessions in Italy. It was a period during the course of which unfounded suspicions were brought against high-ranking Church figures such as cardinal Giovanni Morone and the archbishop of Toledo, Bartolomé Carranza.

During the second period, after the Council of Trent, the situation changed for the Spanish and Roman Inquisitions, but not for the Portuguese. Although it was less intense, the latter continued to focus its repressive activity on the minority of *cristãos-novos*, who represented 80 percent of the accused up to the end of the 18th century. Things evolved differently in Spain and Italy. Since the groups of Protestants had been eliminated and the pressure exerted on the converts from Judaism and Islam had lessened in Spain, the inquisitors' attention turned to the mass of "old Christians," within the framework of the general effort accomplished by the Church, after the Council of Trent, to stimulate and regulate the religious life of the clergy and the Christian people. In this context, the Inquisition charged itself with pursuing those offenses that implied, or that might imply, deviations from specific teachings including blasphemy, abuse of the sacraments, bigamy, or magic with invocation of the devil.

A separate sector of the Holy Office's activity originated in Portugal in 1547, in Spain in 1551, and in Italy in 1559. This entailed the publication of special lists of forbidden books (the inquisitorial indexes) and controlling their use through regular customs inspections and periodical visits to libraries. Through its activity in the areas of justice and surveillance of the press (which, in the Roman Inquisition, was coordinated by a special congregation of cardinals created in 1571), the inquisitorial machinery stretched a kind of sanitary cordon around the populations of Catholic countries, thus impeding the arrival of heretics and the introduction of heretical teachings.

Beginning in the first third of the 17th century, however, despite a few resounding trials like those of Galileo and the Portuguese Jesuit Antonio Vieira, the institution entered into a period of decline that would lead to its gradual disappearance. In the Italian states, under the impulse of philosophical ideas, the sovereigns abolished the tribunals. Such was the case in Naples in 1746, in Milan in 1779, in Florence and Palermo in 1782, and in Venice in 1798. The Iberian Inquisitions would survive somewhat longer, but they, too, would ultimately succumb to liberal ideology. The Portuguese Inquisition would finally become extinct in 1821, to be followed by the Spanish in 1834.

Thereafter, the only inquisitorial tribunal to survive was that of the Roman Congregation of the Holy Office. As has already been said, little is known of its activities because its archives have, until recently, been inaccessible. Nevertheless, it is certain that it was primarily involved in solving problems in matters of faith that arose because of mixed marriages (those celebrated between a Catholic and a non-Catholic) and, especially, examination and subsequent condemnation of works or teachings judged to be dangerous relative to orthodoxy or morals. Teachings such as Hermesianism (first half of the 19th century; from the name of the theologian Georg Hermes) or modernism, or, more recently, liberation theology, have been the object of condemnations by the Congregation. Since 1965 the Congregation has undergone a radical reform and has been renamed Congregation of the Doctrine of the Faith.

Agostino Borromeo

Bibliography

Azevedo Mea, E. "A inquisição do Porto," *Revista de História*, 2 (1979), 5–17; *Sentenças da inquisição de Coimbra em metropolitanos de D. Frei Bartolomeu dos Mártires (1567–1582)*, Porto, 1982.

Benassar, B. *L'Inquisition espagnole, XVe–XIXe siècle*, Paris, 1979.

Béthencourt, F. "Declínio e extinção do Santo Ofício," *Revista de História Económica e Social*, 1987, 77–85; *O imaginário da magia. Feiticeiras, saludadores e nibromantes no sec. XVI*, Lisbon, 1987.

Beuningen, P. T. *Wilhelmus Lindanus als inquisiteur en bishop. Bijdrage tot zijn biografie, 1525–1576*, Assen, 1976.

Borges Coelho, A. *Inquisição de Evora*, 2 vols., Lisbon, 1987.

Borromeo, A. "The Inquisition and Inquisitorial Censorship," *Catholicism in Early Modern History. A Guide to Research*, ed. J. O'Malley, Saint Louis, 1988 (*Reformation Guides to Research*, 2), 252–72.

Canosa, R. *Storia dell'inquisizione in Italia dalla metà del Cinquecento alla fine del Settecento*, 5 vols., Rome, 1986–90.

De Azevedo, J. L. *História dos Cristãos Novos portugueses*, II, Lisbon, 1975.

Dedieu, J. P. *L'Administration de la foi. L'Inquisition de Tolède (XVIe–XVIIIe siècle)*, Madrid, 1989 (*Bibliothèque de la Casa de Velázquez*, 7).

Duke, A. C. "Salvation by Coercion: The Controversy Surrounding the 'Inquisition' in the Low Countries on the Eve of Revolt," *Reformation Principle and Practice*, ed. P. N. Brooks, London, 1980, 135–56.

Firpo, M. *Dal sacco di Roma all'Inquisizione: Studi su Juan de Valdes e la Riforma italiana*, Alessandria, 1998.

Firpo, M., and Marcatto, D. *Il processo inquisitoriale del cardinal Giovanni Morone. Edizione critica*, 5 vols., Rome, 1981–9.

Firpo, Massimo, and Dario Marcatto, eds. *I processi inquisitoriali di Pietro Carnesecchi, 1557–1567,* Vatican City, 1998-.

Ginzburg, C. *Il formaggio e I vermi Il cosmo di un mugnaio del '500*, Turin, 1976.

Ginzburg, C. *I benandanti. Stregoneria e culti agrari tra Cinquecento e Seicento*, Turin, 1972.

Herculano, A. *História da origem e estabelecimento da inquisição em Portugal*, 3 vols., ed. V. Nemésio and A. C. Lucas, new. ed. Lisbon, 1975–6 (*Obras completas de Alexandre Herculano*).

Historia de la inquisición en España y América, ed. J. Pérez Villanueva and B. Escandell Bonet, I, Madrid, 1984.

I documenti del processo di Galileo Galilei, ed. S. Pagano, Vatican City, 1984.

Inquisição. Comunicações apresentadas ao 1o Congresso Luso-Brasileiro sobre Inquisição realizado em Lisboa de 17 a 20 de fevereiro de 1987, 3 vols., ed. M. H. Carvalho Dos Santos, Lisbon, 1989–90.

Inquisición española y mentalidad inquisitorial. Ponencias del Simposio Internacional sobre Inquisición, Nueva York, abril de 1983, ed. A. Alcalá, Barcelona, 1984.

Inquisition and Society in Early Modern Europe, ed. S. Haliczer, London, 1987.

Ioly Zorattini, P. C. *Processi dei S. Uffizio di Venezia contro ebrei e giudaizzanti*, 12 vols., Florence, 1980–90.

Kamen, H. *The Spanish Inquisition: A Historical Revision*, New Haven, Conn. 1998.

La inquisición española. Nueva visión, nuevos horizontes, ed. J. Pérez Villanueva, Madrid, 1980.

Lea, H. C. *A History of the Inquisition of Spain*, 4 vols., New York, 1906–7 (Spanish trans. ed. A. Alcalá, Madrid, 1983).

L'inquisizione in Italia nell'età moderna. Archivi, problemi di metodo e nuove ricerche. Atti del seminario internazionale, Trieste 18–20 maggio 1988, Rome, 1991 (*Pubblicazioni degli Archivi di Stato—Saggi* 19).

Maqueda Abreu, C. *El auto de fe*, Madrid, 1992.

Marchetti, V. *Gruppi ereticali senesi del Cinquecento*, Florence, 1975.

Mentzer, R. A. *Heresy Proceedings in Languedoc, 1500–1560*, Philadelphia, 1984.

Montagnes, B. "Un inquisiteur de Toulouse accusé d'hérésie en 1534: le dominicain Arnaud de Badet," *RHEF*, 71 (1985), 233–52.

Monter, W. *Frontiers of Heresy. The Spanish Inquisition from the Basque Lands to Sicily*, Cambridge, 1990.

New, I. "Die spanische Inquisition und die Lutheraner im 16. Jahrhundert," *Archiv fur Reformationsgeschichte*, 90 (1999), 289–319.

Osbat, L. *L'inquisizione a Napoli. Il processo agli ateisti, 1688–1697*, Rome, 1974 (*Politica e storia*, 32).

Perfiles jurídicos de la inquisición española, ed. J. A. Escudero, Madrid, 1989.

Prosperi, A. "L'inquisizione: verso una nuova immagine?" *Critica storica*, 25 (1988), 119–45.

Pullan, B. *The Jews of Europe and the Inquisition of Venice, 1550–1670*, Oxford, 1983.

Romeo, G. *Inquisitori, esoricisti e streghe nell'Italia della Controriforma*, Florence, 1990.

Romeo, G. "Note sull'Inquisizione romana tra il 1557 e il 1561," *Revista di Storia e Letteratura Religiosa*, 36 (2000), 115–41.

Saraiva, A. J. *A inquisição portuguesa*, II, Lisbon, 1956.

Scheerder, J. "De werking van de inquisitie," *Opstand en pacificatie in de lage Landen*, Gand, 1976, 153–65.

Sutherland, N. M. M. "Was There an Inquisition in Reformation France?" *Les Réformes: enracinement socio-culturel. XXVe Colloque international d'études humanistes, Tours, 1er- 13 juillet 1982*, ed. B. Chevalier and R. Sauzet, Paris, 1985, 363–74.

Tanon, L. *Histoire des tribunaux de l'Inquisition en France depuis le haut Moyen Âge jusqu'à la Réforme*, Paris, 1893.

Tedeschi, J. *The Prosecution of Heresy. Collected Studies on the Inquisition in Early Modern Italy*, Binghampton, NY, 1991 (*Medieval and Renaissance Texts and Studies*, 78).

The Inquisition in Early Modern Europe. Studies on Sources and Methods, ed. G. Henningsen, J. Tedeschi, and C. Amiel, Dekalb, Illinois, 1986.

Valvekens, P. E. *De inquisitie in de Nederlanden der zestiende eeuw*, Brussels-Amsterdam, 1949.

Van Der Vekene, E. *Bibliotheca bibliographica historiae sanctae Inquisitionis. Bibliographisches Verzeichnis des gedruckten Schrifttums zur Geschichte und Literatur der Inquisition*, 3 vols., Vaduz, 1983–92.

INSIGNIA, PAPAL. See **Heraldry**.

INSTITUTE FOR THE WORKS OF RELIGION. See **Finances, Papal**.

INTERDICT. Personal interdict is a penal sanction ("censure," along with excommunication and SUSPENSION) administered by the pope or a bishop who deprives one of the faithful, either a cleric or layperson, of spiritual goods (e.g., sacraments, the divine office, ecclesiastical burial) until the time of absolution. Local interdict can be levied upon a church, a parish, a religious community, a diocese, or a country. It was often for political reasons, especially after the GREGORIAN REFORM and up to the end of the 12th century, that the pope used, and even abused, this means against kings or territorial princes for the purpose of forcing the subjects of the recalcitrants in question to submit; examples include the threat of an interdict against the kingdom of France by GREGORY V; the interdict of Reims by PASCHAL II; that of the kingdom of France in 1146; and that of the royal domain in 1200. Beginning in the 13th century, there was little political use of the interdict; it became confined to the domain of religion. The COUNCIL OF TRENT retained the practice, but its application became ineffective outside strictly defined places (such as a parish or a religious community), or even became the object of scandal. In 1839–40, the interdict against Prussian bishops nevertheless had favorable results in a specific political context. It remains on the list of punishments in the codes of 1917 and 1983.

Gérard Giordanengo

Bibliography

Bongert, Y. "L'interdit, arme de l'Église contre le pouvoir temporel," *Église et pouvoir politique. Actes des journées internationales d'histoire du droit d'Angers*, Angers, 1987, 93–116; "Un 'scandale' à Lille au XVIIe siècle: l'interdit de l'église de Saint-Maurice (1662–1663)," *Études d'histoire du droit canonique dédiées à G. Le Bras*. Paris, 1965, 457–88.

Godefroy, L. "Interdit," *DTC*, 7 (1927), 2280–90.

Jombart, É. "Interdit," *DDC*, 5 (1953), 1464–75.

INVESTITURE CONTROVERSY. The Investiture Controversy took place in the later phase of the 11th-century Gregorian reform. The term refers to the conflict that arose between papacy and monarchy with regard to the latter rulers' participation in the appointment of bishops and abbots through traditional investiture. The dispute, particularly severe in the Holy Roman Empire (1075?–1122; Germany, Italy, and Burgundy), also spread to France (1077–1107) and England (1099–1107). It ultimately led to a reorganizing of the ties between the Church (*sacerdotium*) and the monarchy (*regnum*). The Carolingian order, in which Church and monarchy coexisted within a Church guided by Christ, gave way to the subordination of the whole of the laity, including kings and emperors, to the pope, who from then on was the monarchic head of a strictly hierarchical Church.

The Notion of Investiture. The first written reference to a king's handing over of the episcopal crosier to endow an elected bishop with the episcopate dates to around 900. The gesture exemplified the custom, developed over a century, that gave the kings and princes of the German states who were heirs to Rome a leadership role at the heart of the Church.

In the 10th century, under the Ottonians, this new ceremony became obligatory. Toward the middle of the 11th century, a second symbol, the ring, was added to the crosier. According to Peter Damian, the doubtless much older formula *accipe ecclesiam* ("receive the Church") was uttered when the crosier and ring were bestowed. It signaled that the handing over concerned the episcopacy as a whole—that is, both function and possessions. The use of the term *investitura* to mean the transfer of the symbols is not attested until ALEXANDER II's reign (1061–73), but the appearance of the verb *investire*, by itself, is much earlier.

The form the investiture took varied a great deal, but the transfer of the ring and crosier, which had been brought back to the royal court after the death or resignation of the previous bishop, took place following the *immixtio manuum* (the Carolingian *commendatio*) of the future bishop or abbot. From the end of the 11th century, the two actions were embraced by the one term, *hominium* or *homagium*. In the sources, *hominium* was, in turn, often confused with the general idea of investiture. However, a clear distinction should be made between investiture of election and that of consecration, though it should be noted that royal investiture was the determining factor at elections of bishops and abbots. Moreover, the popes did not take exception to royal investiture, and it was the clear expression of royal power. Through investiture, sovereigns were assured of the loyalty of bishops and abbots, who were rich and politically powerful. Furthermore, these clerics were subject to the *servitium regis*, with its seigniorial taxes, obligations of hospitality and escort, and the service that each vassal owed in war and to the court. In Germany, in many cases there were additional obligations to the Landgrafs, among other public duties.

Interdiction of Investiture. The earliest criticism that has come down to us was voiced by Humberto da Silva Candida in 1057–8, but it had no repercussions. A letter written by Pope NICHOLAS II conveyed a conciliar decree of 1059 whereby no cleric or priest should receive a church from a member of the laity, either free or against payment, but that concerned only the lower clergy. Not until the reign of GREGORY VII was the royal investiture of bishops and abbots forbidden, the measure being applied possibly in 1075, in the case of Milan. The following documents support this hypothesis: a reference by the chronicler Arnulf of Milan (now invalidated, thanks to Hilpert's perspicacity); two letters of Gregory VII, dating from 1077 and 1078, in which he speaks of an interdiction of investiture that had previously been decreed; and a very vague letter that Gregory sent in 1075 to Henry IV. The hypothesis is contradicted, however, by the instructions that Gregory sent Henry IV in the summer of 1075 concerning the reinvesting of the holder of the bishopric of Bamberg. Whatever the truth of the matter, in March 1077 Gregory described secular investiture as an outdated, undesirable practice. In May, he gave instructions to his legate Hugh of Die to forbid the laity to take part in the elevation of bishops at a synod. This was proclaimed outright at Autun in the fall and at Poitiers in January 1078. The first general interdiction of investiture to come from Gregory himself of which the text has been preserved was promulgated by the pope at the council of November 1078. It states that no cleric should receive the investiture of a bishopric, abbey, or church from the hand of the emperor or the king or from any member of the laity whatsoever, man or woman. This is the core of the arrangement, which was again reinforced in 1080 at the Lenten synod. Gregory's successors abided by this interdiction, which Pope URBAN II extended to the *hominium* at Clermont in 1095. Under PASCHAL II, this extension was not applied in England. But aside from the brief period (1111–12) when his hands were tied by the privilege granted to Henry V, Paschal II also abided by the strict interdiction of investiture that he had imposed on England and France. For the empire, the regulation came up only with the concordat of Worms in 1122.

Political Consequences of Interdiction. When Gregory VII deposed and excommunicated Henry IV for the first time in February 1076, the decree prohibiting investiture had not been promulgated, yet Henry certainly invested bishops in Milan, Fermo, and Spoleto after his deposition. Since the 10th century, the German kings and emperors had so obviously relied on collaboration with the Church (the "Kirchensystem" of the Ottonians and Salians) that interdiction of investiture shook the foundations of royal power. At the diet of Worms in 1076, the German and Italian episcopacies had more or less remained united behind the king. The interdictions of investitures, the election of the anti-king Rudolf of Swabia (15 March 1077), and Gregory's definitive condemnation of Henry brought about a coalition against the bishops and abbots, formed by nobles hostile to the monarchy together with partisans of the pope. Negotiations and disputes between the parties alternated, and a compromise was not reached until 1109 (*Tractatus de Investitura*). Henry's designation of Archbishop Guibert of Ravenna as antipope (25 June 1080), Guibert's enthronement under the name of CLEMENT III (24 March 1084), and Gregory's recognition of Rudolf (7 March 1080) changed the Investiture Controversy into a conflict of principle on the relations between *regnum* and *sacerdotium*. It was already so recognized by contemporaries, as we know from the voluminous, scurrilous writings that came out at the time (MGH, *Libelli de lite*).

In France, the Investiture Controversy took a far less dogmatic form than in the empire. Philip I (1059–1108) and Louis VI (1098–1137), together with the French nobility, also exploited to the utmost the power and possessions of bishoprics and abbeys in order to strengthen their own positions. But, unlike in Germany and England, from the end of the Carolingian period the monarchy and nobles wielded this influence in equal measure. Out of roughly 77 dioceses, at the time around 25 were "royal" dioceses. True, tensions were high between Rome and Philip I, but they were caused by the question of the application of ecclesiastical reform in the French Church and by Philip's moral shortcomings (matrimonial lawsuits), not by investiture. For Philip, Urban II's excommunication and interdict were merely pastoral sanctions. The interdiction of investiture pronounced in 1077–8 was just one more complication in the exercise of royal sovereignty over the Church, which, in any case, had always been a source of trouble for the Capetians.

When episcopal investitures were disputed, both the pope and the king showed moderation and had second thoughts. Even under Paschal II (in Beauvais and Paris), a way was always found for tacit agreement; in 1098 there was no official renunciation of investiture, doubtless owing to the influence of Yves of Chartres, who, in separating the temporal from the spiritual, believed it possible for the king to grant an ecclesiastical benefit without the crosier and ring. The idea gradually took root, and at a canonical election—without investiture, but with the bishops taking the oath of fidelity—the king was allowed to hand over the episcopal regalia. When they met at Saint-Denis (30 April–3 May 1107), Pope Paschal II and kings Philip and Louis VI seemed to have found a compromise on this basis.

The reign of William I (1066–87), who conquered England with the help of the future Pope Gregory VII, put an end to the growing autonomy of the English Church vis-à-vis Rome. Papal indulgence made it possible to prevent an Investiture Controversy from arising up to the period of Henry I (1100–35) and Anselm of Canterbury. In exile following his disagreement with William II (1087–1100), Anselm heard the interdictions of investiture and *hominium* pronounced in Rome by Pope Urban

II at the council of 1099. He considered them absolute obligations; therefore, on being appointed archbishop of Canterbury, he refused Henry I the *hominium* and act of investiture. The rupture between the two men sent Anselm once more into exile. To forestall a threat of excommunication, most likely on the occasion of a meeting at Laigle (July 1105) and after further talks, Henry I declared before the end of 1105 that he had renounced investiture, but he continued to affirm his rights to the *hominium* of prelates. Paschal II finally (23 March 1106) came up with a dispensation that allowed Anselm to consecrate bishops who had sworn *hominium* to the king without being invested. He personally absolved Anselm of Urban II's interdiction. The compromise was promulgated in August 1107 by Henry I to the court, during an assembly. The king renounced investiture of the person elected at court, handed him the temporal insignia, and in exchange obtained the *hominium* from the ecclesiastic. Yet in practice, royal power was untouched.

Uta Renate Blumenthal

Bibliography

JL, 4405/44–6.

MGH, *Libelli de lite*.

Blumenthal, U. R. *Papal Reform and Canon Law in the Eleventh and Twelfth Centuries*, Brookfield, Vt., 1998.

Blumenthal, U. R. *The Investiture Controversy: Church and Monarchy from the Ninth to the Twelfth Century*, Philadelphia, 1988.

Cowdrey, H. E. J. *Pope Gregory VII, 1073–1085*, Oxford, 1998.

Cushing, K. G. *Papacy and Law in the Gregorian Revolution: the Canonistic Work of Anselm of Lucca*, Oxford, 1998.

Epist. I, 134 = *PL*; 144, 221.

Lynch, J. H. "Hugh I of Cluny's Sponsorship of Henry IV: Its Context and Consequences," *Speculum*, 60 (1985), 800–26.

Morris, C. *The Papal Monarchy: the Western Church from 1050–1250*, Oxford; New York, 1989. See Gregory VII and Innocent III.

Registrum; III, 3i, 7, 10; IV, 13, 22, 33; V, 18; VI, 5b, c. 3, VII, 14a, c. 1–2.

Rimberti, V. ed. G. Waitz, *MGH, SS, ref. germ.*, 1884m 81–100, c. 11.

Robinson, I. S. *The Papacy 1073–1198: Continuity and Innovation*, Cambridge, 1990.

Tierney, B. *The Crisis of Church and State, 1050–1300*, Englewood Cliffs, N.J., 1964.

Wilken, R. L. "Gregory VII and the Politics of the Spirit," *First Things*, no. 89 (January, 1999), 26–32. See Gregory VII.

ISRAEL AND THE HOLY SEE. See **Judaism.**

JANSENISM. This generic term encompasses a multi-faceted movement linked to the Catholic REFORM, whose principal characteristics are a systematic fidelity to Augustinianism, a moral rigorism, and a demanding spirituality with an individualistic tendency.

The *Augustinus* of Cornelius Jansen (1585–1638), bishop of Ypres, published after his death, intended to prepare the ground for the resolution, according to the method prescribed by the HOLY SEE, of the disputes *De auxiliis*, suspended in 1607. In this work of positive theology, Jansen hoped to present a synthesis of the thought of St. Augustine on grace and free will. A work dear to his heart, he did not follow it to its perfect conclusion, for, hoping to publish it with the support of Rome, he undoubtedly would have made the adjustments necessary for toning it down. In undertaking it, the former professor from Louvain was seeking to counteract the growing influence of Molinism. His adversaries had no difficulty underlining the dangers of his effort: was it not risking a renewal of the errors condemned in Baius, a Louvain theologian of the 16th century, and, above all, was it not going against the prohibition issued by PAUL V in 1611, against publishing on these topics? The prohibition, certainly, was little observed. From the perspective of the reforming papacy, the attitude of Jansen and of his French correspondents, who were soon called "Jansenists" as a way of implying their heterodoxy, could actually appear rather bold.

The work has characteristics that allow us to bring together the multiple tendencies of the movement: an intellectual assurance, and an absolutization of truth that fails to take sufficient account of ecclesiastical authority and its heavy-handedness. It is significant in this respect that Jansen, whose inclination was clearly ultramontanist, differed very little from his friend Saint-Cyran, who rather favored an "episcopalist" ecclesiology that would later be called "GALLICAN." This individualism, the roots of which are at once intellectual, spiritual, and sociological,

would remain powerful during the growth of the movement, certainly intensified by the religious and political resistance against which it had to try its strength.

If the *Augustinus* was generally condemned for having contravened the prohibition against writing on these subjects (*In eminenti*, 1643), the spiral of pontifical interventions that followed was more closely tied to the hazards of internal French politics. The judgments clearly demonstrate that, from the Roman perspective, the question of papal authority was becoming more important than theological distinctions—a point the Augustinians failed to perceive sufficiently, but which their anti-Jansenist adversaries knew how to exploit admirably. In presenting a maximalist account of the decisions of the papal MAGISTERIUM, the Molinists forced their opponents to challenge it, and therefore to manifest a negative, disrespectful, and, finally, inadmissible insubordination. The BULL *Cum occasione* (1653) condemned five propositions implicitly linked to the *Augustinus*, mentioned twice in the document, though it said nothing more about their presence in the book. It expressed the desire, on the part of INNOCENT X, to put an end to a theological dispute that neither the Paris faculty of theology nor the assembled clergy of France had been able to resolve. By condemning an abstract heresy, on the insistence of the majority of the French episcopate, Rome was demonstrating its preeminence and its definitive role in the defense of orthodoxy. It must be emphasized that, by giving form to Jansenism, the anti-Jansenists hoped above all to strengthen ULTRAMONTANISM, especially with regard to papal INFALLIBILITY. The case of Cardinal Albizzi (1593–1684), put forward by L. Ceyssens, is a good illustration of this policy, influential in the Roman CURIA, of attaching greater importance to legal correctness than to theological ideas. By explicitly attributing the five condemned propositions to Jansen, an assembly of prelates, presided over by Mazarin, certainly went beyond the contents of the document and the primary intention of Innocent X. It forced the hand of the papacy, which, after that, would find it difficult to draw back. ALEXANDER VII confirmed, on his own, the presence of the propositions in the *Augustinus* (the "fact" of Jansen) and added—with an alarming precision—that these had been condemned in the sense the author meant them (*Ad Sanctam Petri Sedem*, 1656). As Antoine Arnauld had already emphasized in some polemical writings, this was to require blind adherence, contrary to evidence. The clergy of France once again insisted along these lines by imposing a formula of explicit adherence (1657). After some hesitation, Alexander VII ratified the measure by stipulating a form of oath, scarcely more moderate (*Regiminis apostolici*, 1665). It was part of the logic of this intervention that the insubordinate ones were to be censured not only for heterodoxy, but also for temerity, that is, for refusal to obey the ecclesiastical authority. That had already happened at the Sorbonne to Antoine Arnauld, expelled from the Paris faculty of theology, along with a hundred or so doctors who refused to condemn him (1656). Nevertheless, when the reservations expressed by several members among the best of the Gallic episcopate caused them to be accused, the episcopalist sensibility of their colleagues was awakened. To avoid the threat of a schism, CLEMENT IX, at the request of the French court, accepted a compromise that sanctioned, without really making it clear, the position advocated by the recalcitrant Augustinians in support of an outward obedience to the decisions of the Church that left intact the rights of the conscience. The "Peace of the Church" (1669) should therefore have marked the end of a period of tensions in which the political and ideological aspects more and more took precedence over the purely doctrinal content. The error defined by these five propositions being taught by no one, represented more of an abstraction than a particular doctrine. That is what the Augustinians affirmed, more determined than ever to be of service to the Church, especially in the controversy with the Protestants. If in Rome they could count on the sympathy of a curialist group committed to the spirit of the Tridentine reform, enemies of a relaxed morality, and unfavorably disposed to the Jesuits, the Jansenists had powerful enemies there as well. This opposition, which associated itself in the political realm with the a priori views of the monarchy since it saw the Port-Royal circle as made up of slingers and "republicans," can perhaps best be accounted for by the theological approach particular to the Jansenist circles. As B. Neveu and L. Ceyssens have shown with evidence, by referring in an absolute way to St. Augustine, the "doctor of grace," the authors of the party seemed to minimize and above all to limit the authority of the living magisterium. The opposition seems irresolvable, if one compares the formula of Antoine Arnauld, "The definitions of the Council of TRENT and of the popes must be explained through St. Augustine," with that of Cardinal

Albizzi, "*la vera mens* of St. Augustine was explained by the council of Trent." Aware of these viewpoints, the disciples of St. Augustine sought to neutralize them by establishing observers in Rome, responsible for defending their views (S. J. du Cambout de Pontchâteau [1677–80] and L. P. du Vaucel [1680–1703]. In this, they had some success, in the condemnation of laxist propositions (1670) and the refusal to condemn Jansenist propositions denounced to the Holy Office (1679). The particular personality of the Odescalchi pope, and also the influence of the eminent curialists A. Favoriti and his nephew, L. Casoni, can be detected here. The taking of positions on the affair of the REGALIA by bishops and theologians linked to the movement had also favored such a rapprochement. When placed within the greater context of the whole Jansenist quarrel, the behavior of INNOCENT XI also emphasizes the moderation of principle that Rome intended to maintain and above all the desire to position itself above the parties in a dispute. This conduct can be found also in popes less favorably disposed, ALEXANDER VIII, who allowed the censure of rigorist propositions (1690) but condemned the error of philosophical sin (1690), and INNOCENT XII, who urged the bishops of the Netherlands to put an end to persecution of the Jansenists (1694). It was therefore external pressures, principally those of a political nature on the part of Louis XIV but also the less obvious pressures exerted by an anti-Jansenist coalition, that would produce a new series of decisions from the magisterium, the importance of which is also linked to the Gallican principles set forth in the articles of the assembly of the clergy of 1682. These articles, by challenging any intervention on the part of the HOLY OFFICE, or by refusing the recording of simple briefs, forced the publication of dogmatic constitutions more markedly magisterial in character. Moderation, however, characterizes the constitution *Vineam Domini* (1704), censuring the publication of a "case of conscience" favorably resolved by the Paris faculty of the theology. *Vineam* only repeated the previous condemnations concerning the "fact," without taking into account the principles expanded in this "case" principles that later would be censured in *Unigenitus* (1713).

The genesis of this last document, destined to leave an enduring mark on the history of the 17th century, has been amply elucidated by the works of J. A. G. Tans and L. Ceyssens and of P. Blet. The former two emphasize the influence of which CLEMENT XI was the object, especially that of Cardinal C. A. Fabroni (1651–1727), the principal author of the document, and the partisan manner in which the study of the book and the composition of the document were carried out. The latter clearly describes the political pressures exerted by the Bourbon monarchy and the hopes raised in Rome by this weakening of the Gallican principles. The content of the constitution, 101 propositions drawn from the influential

Réflexions morales sur le Nouveau Testament (1687) by Pasquier Quesnel, condemned *in globo*—that is, without a precise description of the theological error in each—forms a whole that clearly sets in place an irreducible opposition between two interpretations of post-Tridentine Catholicism. It deals with the subjects of grace, on which the magisterium takes a position favorable to Molinism, and also of ecclesiology, represented by a "Gallicanism of participation," along the line of the conciliarist renewal attempted by E. Richer at the beginning of the 17th century. There are also topics dear to the Catholic Reform in France, such as the place of Holy Scripture, liturgical participation, and the spiritual life. The Gallico-Jansenist front that opposed the reception of the constitution was very heterogeneous, as is evidently proved by the content of the numerous objections, but the refusal of religious and soon political obedience manifested by it facilitated its being identified as a single party. By asking Clement XI to explain himself, that is, to recognize the limitations of his intervention, the opposition touched on a particularly sensitive point. It seems that if the pontiff had used the language of his successor BENEDICT XIII (*Demissa preces*, 1724), the storm would probably have subsided, but at the price of a visible weakening of papal authority and of the personal infallibility implicit in it. The appeal to a future general council issued at the Sorbonne by four bishops (March 1717) followed by a minority of their colleagues and members of the Gallican clergy, raised the challenge to a higher level. A new constitution, *Pastoralis officii* (1718) condemned it, yet without excommunicating the appellants. The SCHISM of the Church of the United Provinces (1723), facilitated by the intervention of the French anti-constitutionalists, could only comfort Rome in its inflexibility. The equally tough attitude of the government of Louis XV would also shift the principal elements of the Jansenist resistance into the political realm, helping to weaken it by dividing it.

In the theological realm, the Jansenists continued to stress a negative perception of the papal magisterium, linked to the repression, which would end ironically in the suppression of the papal magisterium's most militant ally, the Society of Jesus, (1773). The rift, however was much more profound in religious matters, as manifested in the persistent influence of Jansenist ideas in the Europe of the ENLIGHTMENT, for which the *Unigenitus* became the obvious symbol of a regrettable decadence and of the need for renewal. The filiation is undoubtedly more intellectual than spiritual, in the degree to which this movement—the representatives of which could be found among the erudite within the clergy and the laity—took up the themes of the preceding period, with a perspective close to that of the humanism of the Renaissance. To the authoritarian Christianity of the Ultramontanists and the Molinists they countered once again with the ancient primitive model, a combination of intelligent rigor and

shared responsibility. The success among the elites of this enlightened approach (Catholic *Aufklärung*) in most European countries foreshadowed a lasting weakening of the Tridentine thought thus objected to and the inevitable decline of the PRIMACY of the pope to an honorific primacy. They had sized up the situation in Rome, where these influences were not negligable, and that accounts for the severe reactions of the papal bull *Auctorem fidei* (1794) to the statutes of the diocesan SYNOD of Pistoia (1786) and the desire to put an end once and for all to a particularly threatening drift of things. By a twist of historical fate, the disorder arising out of the FRENCH REVOLUTION and the reestablishment of Catholicism by the CONCORDAT of 1801, which encouraged a revival of the papacy, wiped out this evolution.

Jacques Grès-Gayer

Bibliography

Armogathe, J. F. "Jansénisme," *DS*, 8 (1974), 101–48.

Blet, D. *Le Clerge de France, Louis XIV*, Louvain, 1987.

Callaey, F. "La critique historique et le courant pro-janséniste à Rome au XVIIIe siècle," *Nuove Ricerche storiche sul Giansenismo*, Rome, 1954, 185–94.

Ceyssens, L., and Tans, J. A. *Autour de l'Unigenitus et le Saint-Siège de 1695 à 1715*, Rome, 1989.

Ceyssens, L. *Le Cardinal François Albizzi (1593–1684). Un cas important dans l'histoire du jansénisme*, Rome, 1977.

Ceyssens, L. "Les cinq propositions de Jansénius à Rome," *Jansenistica Minora*, XI.

Ceyssens, L. "L'origine romaine de la bulle *In Eminenti*," *Jansenistica. Études relatives à l'histoire du jansénisme*, Mechlin, 1957, 9–110.

Cognet, L. *Le Jansénisme*, Paris, 1961.

Doyle, W. *Jansenism: Catholic Resistance to Authority from the Reformation to the French Revolution*, New York, 2000.

Gres-Gayer, J. "The *Unigenitus* of Clement XI: A Fresh Look at the Issues," *Theological Studies*, 49 (1988), 259–82.

Neveu, B. "Juge supréme et docteur infaillible: le pontificat romain de la bulle *In Eminenti* (1643) à la bulle *Auctorem fidei* (1794)," *MEFRM*, 93 (1981) 215–75.

Neveu, B. "La correspondance romaine de Louis-Paul du Vaucel (1683–1703), *Actes du colloque sur le jansénisme organisé par l'Academia belgica* (Rome, 1973), Louvain, 1977, 105–85.

Neveu, B. *S. J. du Cambout de Ponschâteau (1634–1690) et ses missions à Rome*, Paris, 1969.

Orcibal, J. *Jansénius d'Yprès (1585–1638)*, Paris, 1989.

Orcibal, J. "Jansénius et Rome," *Actes du colloque sur le jansénisme organisé par l'Academia belgica* (Rome, 1973), Louvain, 1977, 27–45.

Pasztor, L. "La Curia romana e il giansenismo. La preparazione della bolla 'Auctorem fidei,'" *Actes du colloque sur le jansénisme organisé par l'Academia belgica* (Rome, 1973), Louvain, 1977, 89–102.

Plongeron, B. "Recherches sur l'*Aufklärung* catholique en Europe occidentale (1770–1830)," *Revue d'histoire moderne et contemporaine*, 16 (1969), 555–605.

Rosa, M., ed., *Cattolicesimo et lumi nel settecento italiano*, Rome, 1981.

Sedgwick, A. *Janenism in Seventeenth–Century France*, Charlottesville, Va., 1977.

Stella, P. *Studi sul Giansenismo*, Bari, 1972.

Van Kley, D. K. *The Damiens Affair and the Unravelling of the Ancien Régime 1750–1770*, Princeton, 1984.

Van Kely, D. K. *The Jansenists and the Expulsion of the Jesuits from France 1757–1765*, New Haven, Conn.; London, 1975.

Weaver, F. E. *DS*, 13 (1931–52).

JESUITS. The relationship of the Society of Jesus to the papacy is defined in the *Constitutions* of this order by the founding vow of Ignatius Loyola and his first companions: "It is good to remember the intention with which the Company made the vow of obedience, without making excuses, to the Sovereign Vicar of Christ: it is a question of being sent among the faithful or the infidels, wherever he would consider it useful for a greater divine glory and an even greater good for some souls" (*Septima pars*, cap. I, 603).

Thus oneness of direction is maintained despite dispersion. Its object is not daily administration, but the universal mission. Putting oneself at the disposition of the pope is most clearly marked by the fourth vow, the special vow of obedience, which is not pronounced by every member of the order, but only by the professed. They vow solemnly to listen to the words of the pope and not to ask him for money for the MISSIONS. The general must explain the importance of this vow to each new pope. As a consequence, this order has been linked to the papacy since its birth.

The popes provided the Jesuits with favors and protection and have never hesitated to intercede in matters of government, often going as far as suppression. The CARDINALS and the CONGREGATIONS also played their part in this story. Since 1539, the order is no more monolithic than the CURIA. The respect for the one who sends them on missions does not preclude a certain diversity of attitudes, not surprising in a diverse group spread across the world. It is virtually impossible to separate the order and the Curia, because the Jesuits are present in the entourage of the popes, in numbers that vary according to the pontificates, and appear as cardinals, confessors, or experts in congregations. The oblation to the pope and the mission predate the order. For the vow of Montmartre, 15 August 1534, Ignatius and his six companions decided, if they were unable to reach Jerusalem, to put themselves at the

pope's disposal. It was a personal and original vow during a time when religious were highly criticized. The pope's acceptance would be the foundation of the future Society of Jesus. In November 1539, the companions offered themselves to PAUL III who sent them to Italy and an ecclesiastic future. But what form of life should they take, and how would they keep united? The BULL *Regimini militantis Ecclesiae* approved the first sketch on 27 September 1540. The members were permitted to name a superior and to compose *Constitutions*, but their number, after pressure from several curialists, was first limited to 60. Paul III eventually eliminated this constraint. The Society enjoyed the benefits and privileges of pontifical favor and, beginning in 1540, could preach, confess, and absolve. To aid the full members, coadjutors were established, both priests and laymen, who took only three vows, but were members of the order. In 1548, the *Exercises* were approved and recommended by the BRIEF *Pastoralis Officii*.

The three successors of Paul III were not as well disposed toward Ignatius and his order. JULIUS III approved the foundation of the Roman College and gave the Jesuits the German College; MARCELLUS II wanted to use them as "soldiers"; and PAUL IV put an end to liberality, attempting to join the order to his own foundation, the Theatines. At war with Spain, he went as far as to search Ignatius' home. Ignatius, feeling his death approaching, still asked for benediction. This distrust should not overshadow the work accomplished by the company since 1539 in the service of the pope. The pope established objectives for dealing with infidels, and Ignatius sent his men throughout Europe according to requests and opportunities. Not only did the pope recommend them, he protected them from their detractors; he sent Laynez and Salmeron to the COUNCIL OF TRENT as his theologians.

Lasting uncertainties about the *Constitutions* marked the century immediately after the death of Ignatius in 1556. Without questioning the existence of the Society, several popes were hostile about its specifics. The Franciscan SIXTUS V disapproved of blind obedience, the account of conscience, and the different degrees of membership. In 1590 he forced the Society to remove the words "of Jesus" from its name. Other popes forced a series of modifications, almost always undone by their successors. Under Paul IV, beginning in 1557, then under PIUS V, members had to recite the office in choral fashion, as did traditional orders. The nature of their vows was viewed differently by the popes and the lifetime duration of the generalship was the object of controversy. Paul IV limited it to three years with a possibility of reelection, but this was rescinded by CLEMENT VIII. The general congregations were occasions of intervention: some by Paul IV who retracted the necessary pontifical approval, and in 1573 by GREGORY XIII who forbade the election of a Spaniard and then expressed the desire to see Father Mercurian follow Father Francis Borgia. In 1646 INNOCENT X added the requirements of the meeting of a general congregation every nine years. Though this disposition was not reversed until 1746 (by BENEDICT XIV), others concerning changing the general's assistants at each annual meeting and changing each individual superior every three years did not last; ALEXANDER VII suspended then discarded them in 1663.

These interventions are linked to government in general, and to internal dissentions. Paul IV felt that the system instituted by Ignatius was tyrannical. Under Sixtus V, Mariana wanted to make some changes in the *Constitutions*, and the Spanish Inquisition pursued the Jesuits. In the early 17th century, Spanish intrigues, relayed by the NUNCIO of Madrid, again threatened the Society and Father Aquaviva, whose authority they wanted to limit. Clement VIII encouraged a general congregation to examine the situation. In 1645 a former Jesuit, Scotti, hoped to see INNOCENT X reform the *Constitutions* in the same way. The same popes were not always critics. Pius V confirmed the disputed points in the *Constitutions* in 1584. Sixtus V knew how to use the Society to help him defend his prerogatives. Other pontiffs showered the Jesuits with clemency and favors. Paul V approved the measures taken against their detractors and, in 1609, began the process of Ignatius' beatification. Then came decades of good fortune. Francis Xavier was beatified in 1619, and then canonized with Ignatius in 1622–3; it was Francis Borgia's turn in 1624. In 1640, Pope URBAN VIII decreed a jubilee for the hundredth anniversary of the order.

The popes never stopped using the Society. In the Jesuits they found valued experts like Canisius, to help refute the Protestant writers and others to defend their authority before that of kings such as Bellarmine. Beginning with PIUS IV, with the Roman Seminary in 1564, the training of priests was an essential assignment. The conferring of degrees in philosophy and theology was entrusted to them in 1561, and in 1571, the possibility of teaching publicly in university cities. Financial support, privileges, and recommendations to kings accumulated for the schools that soon multiplied, accompanied in the 17th century by the Marian Congregations on the Roman model.

The missions also benefited, Japan was reserved only for Jesuits from 1585 to 1600. In 1609 the secular hierarchy supported Jesuit missionaries everywhere. Even in Rome, Jesuits preached to the popes and their families, as well as to certain cardinals. The first Jesuit to receive the cardinal's hat got it from Clement VIII. The Society was represented in the Curia, where it could count on many others who were very faithful former students. Under GREGORY XV it was protected by Cardinal Ludovisi. The Roman College trained Pope Urban VIII, and his nephew took part in the centennial celebration.

The second century of the company was dominated by two great quarrels, on morality and on rites. The question of probabilism resulted in the Jesuits being accused of laxism: When in doubt about what is permitted, may one follow any probable opinion (that is, which has not been rejected by the Church), or only the one that is the more probable (which is probabiliorism)? The Society was never unanimous on this issue. A doctor from Salamanca, Father Gonzalez, believed in the second solution, and he was elected general in 1687 after three ballots and the intervention of INNOCENT XI. If this pope actually decided to act against probabilism by relying upon a decree of the Holy See from 1680, which had been kept partially secret, he was less categorical about it, and in 1706 asked the Jesuits not to give ammunition to the critics in his entourage. Had not Cardinal Casanata declared that the Church could cut off its right hand if it did not need it any more? However, the popes defended the Society during its disputes with Louis XIV, and canonized Stanislas Kostka, John Francis Régis, and Aloysius Gonzaga.

This protection was not without interventions, especially on behalf of Eastern missions, where, since 1630, conflicts continued with Capuchins and Franciscans who complained about the Jesuits to the pope. Questions of jurisdiction in Indochina were a weighty topic after 1670, especially with the Missions Etrangères in Paris, but also with the PROPAGANDA that tried to limit the privileges of the Society by saddling it with French apostolic vicars. Tensions were high between the Curia and the religious orders at the beginning of the 18th century. The same was the case for Malabar rites after 1706. The LEGATE, supported by the Holy Office, outlawed certain practices. Clement XI, confirming this ban, left some latitude. He decreed an oath of obedience for all missionaries, while establishing a special ministry to work with the pariahs. China, in particular, was the subject of a heated dispute, both pastoral and legal, between the foreign missions and the Holy Office. Clement XI required an oath of obedience from missionaries in 1715. In 1723, under Innocent XIII, when the secretary of the Propaganda accused the Jesuits in China of disobedience, the sending of Jesuit fathers to the Far East was suspended and the Society was threatened: if it did not moderate its behavior, it would lose its novices. During these crises, weathered since 1540, the *Constitutions* were at times partially overridden, but still remained the foundation of the order.

The Society, despite its enemies in the Curia, had more favorable times under Benedict XIV, who ended the dispute about the rites and put an end to the requirement for a general congregation every nine years. Against its adversaries in Rome and the Catholic monarchs, the Society could usually count on the popes' support. It did not diminish when CLEMENT XIII wrote to Louis XV and the bishops of France in 1762 *Sint ut sunt, aut non sint*. After the expulsions of the Jesuits from Portugal, France, and Spain, the Bourbon kings demanded that Clement XIII destroy the Jesuit order. He refused, but died soon afterward. Intrigues doubled at the CONCLAVE and the *papabile* promised to disband the Jesuits in order to get elected. When he became CLEMENT XIV, the Franciscan cardinal Ganganelli was slow to honor his promise, but Spain and France threatened to break with Rome. Spanish ambassador José Moñino was able to bribe some of the pope's confidants. The loss of Austrian support left the latter at the mercy of the Bourbons, and this meant the end for the Society. Clement XIV, without consulting the SACRED COLLEGE, published the brief *Dominus ac Redemptor*, inspired by Moñino, and dated 21 July 1773.

This conclusion was justified by a desire to assure lasting peace for the Church, which the continued existence of the Society made impossible. The pope kept the power to create and provide for missions and forbade any writings about ex-Jesuits, who were to be treated with charity. The Society acquiesced. The brief was not published, however, in Silesia or in White Russia. Where the rulers forbade this publication, the company survived. While a Jesuit refuge in Eastern Europe was taking form, with the discreet assent of the pope, the ex-general Ricci, after a hasty and summary trial, was imprisoned in CASTEL SANT'ANGELO. He died there in 1775 after having stated that he and the Society did not deserve such treatment. Pius VI, elected shortly before this, was not able to free him because of Spanish demands, but later released several of the dead general's companions. He used ex-Jesuit canonists during his conflicts with Joseph II.

After several attempts, the order rallied in Russia. In 1801 Pius VI authorized the Jesuits to return to their former life, to open schools and administer the sacraments, powers extended to the Two-Sicilies for a time in 1804. In 1806 Father Brzozowski became general, but it was not until PIUS VII returned to Rome in 1814 that princes and bishops petitioned for the order to be officially reestablished. The pope commanded Secretary of State Pacca and other cardinals to prepare the guidelines. Thus the document *Sollicitudo omnium ecclesiarum*, of 7 July 1814, reestablished the Society in order to give St. Peter's ship "experienced and careful oarsmen" to keep it from foundering. The paper was promulgated on 7 August at the church of St. Ignatius. The Jesuits had regained their former circumstances, could receive novices, and regained their privileges and houses held under the papacies of Pius VII through Leo XII.

Their relationship with the papacy became more limited at first under the pontificate of PIUS IX. Before the Roman revolution of 1848, the pope rarely supported them against their adversaries and even asked them to leave his States after their expulsion from Naples and from Piedmont. The situation changed again with the pope's return from Gaeta and the election of Father

Beckx in 1853, the influence of the Jesuits dominated the Curia. Among the *Zelanti*, Jesuits advised the pope, sat on the commissions, and were useful assistants in fighting liberal ideas, defending his temporal power, and promoting ultramontanism. The foundation of the monthly *Civiltà Cattolica* in 1866 answered this need. The Roman fathers still played an important role in all the theological controversies and in the Thomist renewal. Although there were only eight among 96 consultants preparing for the First Vatican Council, the Jesuits were influential there, as much on the Commission on Doctrine as they were as counselors to several bishops. The preparatory work, however, occasioned internal debates for the Jesuits with the general. Father Franzelin and Father Schrader had to justify several planned decrees.

The obedience of service to the pontiff also characterized the pontificates from Leo XIII to Pius XII, even if there were different undercurrents in the Society, as there were in the Church, perhaps better called reserves. They appeared during the Ralliement in France. The general insisted on applying Leo XIII's directives on social questions and on syndicalism, but *Études* did not have the same views as *Civiltá Cattolica*. The superiors had to publicize the encyclicals and Father Liberatore had taken part in the explanation of *Rerum novarum*. Some Jesuits were present in different commissions on historical studies and liturgy. They were at the heart of debates on exegetical methods, theology, and CANON LAW, which did not occur without internal disagreements. Leo XIII counted on them to favor neo-Thomism. Their role in teaching in Rome was even greater when the Roman College, reopened in 1824, became the Gregorian University. Several institutes were given to them in Rome, (the Biblical Institute) and elsewhere (St. Joseph's University in Beirut). Missions were still stressed: INDULGENCES, permissions, and new apostolic prefectures were created to handle the requirements of the Far East, without forgetting the nearer tasks such as the Italian work on the Holy Family. Under Pius XI, Father Leiber and Father Bea participated in the composition of *Mit brennender Sorge*, assisting Cardinal Pacelli. When he became Pius XII, he then took them into his entourage as personal secretary and confessor, with Father Heinrich as librarian. Despite certain legends, their role was only that of counsel, with the pope making the final decisions. He depended upon certain Jesuits for questions about exegesis, to prepare theological dossiers, for *Mystici corporis*, or on the dogma of the Assumption. Father Grundlach and other non-Jesuits theologians were also often consulted. Although the theological renewal, especially in France, was sometimes undeniably defied, it prospered due to other members of the Society, such as Father de Lubac and Father Teilhard de Chardin.

Numerous Jesuits participated in the Second Vatican Council, some worked on the preparatory schemes, others later on the commissions, such as Fathers de Lubac, Daniélou or Rahner, and others as counselors to bishops. The post-council period was marked by palpable pontifical anxiety expressed as watchfulness on the part of Paul VI at the end of the 31st congregation in 1966. An incident occurred during the 32nd congregation, which was trying to abolish grades of membership, demonstrating opposition to the pope and Cardinal Villot (Secretary of State) who were known to be hostile to the plan. On 15 February 1974, Paul VI wrote to General Arrupe that no innovation would be allowed. The *Constitutions* were, therefore, never changed.

After protestations by the bishops and the nuncios against some viewpoints taken here and there by Jesuits and some continuing concerns of Paul VI, his short-lived successor JOHN PAUL I prepared a document on the Society. JOHN PAUL II published it on 8 February 1978, asking for teaching and writings to clarify the issues and for a more solid doctrine. The general offered his resignation in vain, then, in 1981, renewed his obedience and that of his Society. His poor health that year was the occasion for an exceptional intervention, when John Paul II, instead of Father O'Keefe, designated by Father Arrupe, named Father Dezza, Paul VI's former confessor, along with Father Pittau as his personal representative to the Society. The Jesuits obeyed and the pope announced this publicly in 1982. He reminded us of the traditional tasks of the Jesuits, adding to them the implementation of the Second Vatican Council, ecumenicism, the promotion of justice without compromising their sacerdotal character, and viewpoints adopted by the 32nd general congregation. These tensions, often born from pastoral differences, should not overshadow the role of numerous Jesuits in the dicasts, synods, and the preparation of encyclicals and the function of the *Civiltà Cattolica* as the semi-official organ of the Holy See, under the control of the Secretary of state.

Olivier Chaline

Bibliography

Alden, D. *The Making of an Enterprise: The Society of Jesus in Portugal, Its Empire, and Bogard, 1540–1750*, Stanford, 1996.

Bangert, W. V. *A History of the Society of Jesus*, St. Louis, 1972; 2nd ed. 1986.

Brucker, J. *La Compagnie de Jésus. Esquisse de son Institut et de son histoire*, Paris, 1919.

Cordara, G. C. *On the Suppression of the Society of Jesus: A Contemporary Account*, Chicago, 1999.

Idigoras, I. T. *Ignace de Loyola pèlerin de l'absolu*, Paris, 1990.

Lacouture, J. *Jésuites*, Paris, 1991–2, 2 vols.

O'Malley, J. W. *The First Jesuits*, Cambridge MA., 1993.

O'Malley, J. W. *The Fourth Vow in its Ignation Context*, Studies in the Spirituality of Jesuits 1511, St. Louis, 1983.

O'Malley, J. W., et al., eds. *The Jesuits: Cultures, Sciences and the Arts, 1540–1773*, Toronto 1999.

Ravier, A. *Ignace de Loyola fonde la Compagnie de Jésus*, Paris, 1974.

Ravier, A. *La Compagnie de Jésus sous le gouvernement d'Ignace de Loyola (1541–1556)*, Paris, 1991.

Synopsis Historiae Societatis Jesu, Louvain, 1950.

Van Kley, D. K. *The Jansenists and the Expulsion of the Jesuits from France*, 1757–65, New Haven, Conn., 1975.

JEWS. See *The Deputy*; **Judaism**; **World War II.**

JOAN. *A woman supposed to have occupied the papal seat in the 9th century, disguised as a man.*

This fiction, whose first known mention comes from around 1255, was taken for truth during the Middle Ages. The gradual refutation of this legend began in the 16th century. The story, whose memory remains alive yet today, was immensely popular; beyond its romantic quality, it questioned a fundamental prohibition of Catholic Culture—the refusal to ordain women. It also asked the troubling question of pretense: what happens when a supreme and divinely sanctioned power lets itself be usurped? Thus, the legend played a powerful role in the controversies that occurred from the 13th century on around the status of the Roman Church and of its MAGISTERIUM.

The story rapidly took established form. In a version from the late 13th century, around the year 850, a woman, born in Mainz of English parents, dressed as a man in order to follow her beloved, who was devoted to his studies and therefore destined to live in an exclusively masculine world. She thrived in that milieu to the point that, after studying in Athens, she was welcomed in Rome, allowed to enter the hierarchy of the CURIA, and finally to be elected pope. Her pontificate lasted more than two years and was interrupted by a scandal: Joan, who had not given up the pleasures of the flesh, found herself pregnant and died in the course of a procession from St. Peter's in the Vatican to St. John Lateran, after giving birth in public. Several versions of the story claim to offer hints, proofs, or even a memoir of the female pope. For example since that time, the sex of the pope is supposedly manually verified during the course of the CORONATION. Pontifical processions supposedly leave the direct route between St. Peter's in the Vatican and the Lateran when they reach the church of S. Clemente in order to avoid the place the birth occurred. A statue and an inscription at this spot are supposed to have commemorated this deplorable incident.

It is difficult to establish the origins of this story, the earliest surviving document of which is in a chronicle of the convent of Metz written around 1255 by the Dominican Jean de Mailly. The speed and the geographical spread of the legend suggest that the rumor of a female pope had been circulating for some time before it was written down. It probably originated in Rome, a city that, in the 12th century, was undergoing serious antipapal disturbances. The supposed rite of verification of virility of the popes may have played a decisive role, although mention of this does not appear until 1295. In the coronation ceremonies of the popes as they were performed in the Lateran palace from the end of the 11th century, the future pope used two chairs whose seats were deeply indented—supposed to be the ancient curule chairs symbolizing the collegiate aspect of the Curia. The strange shape of the seats, the obscurity of the rite and a naïve or malicious interpretation may have changed them into "pierced chairs" whose purpose was to be permit officials to touch the genitals of the future pope.

The brief, tentative mention of the female pope in the chronicle of Jean de Mailly was rapidly reproduced and elaborated in Dominican circles: around 1260, it found its way into a collection of *exempla*, the *Traité des divers matériaux de la prédication* prepared by the preacher Stephen of Bourbon, who came from the same Dominican province as Jean de Mailly. But this use for preaching would not have gone far, considering the dangerous nature of the anecdote; only the preacher Arnold of Liège is known to have used it in his collection, the *Alphabetum narrationum* (around 1307). However, the story, told in the manner of a historic legal case, was placed in a chronicle that would be very widely read: the *Chronique des pontifes romains et des empereurs*, written by the Dominican Martin the Pole, or by his followers, around 1280. From then on, the story of the female pope showed up in innumerable universal chronicles of the Middle Ages. The mention of this episode seemed to carry no subversive intent against the papacy: not only was there no attempt to censor or refute the story, at least not until the 15th century, but it was told in circles close to the pope. Martin the Pole was the CHAPLAIN of several popes, and in 1474, the humanist Platina, officially charged to write a *Lives of the Popes*, included the female pope, Joan. Legal interest in this case and religious control over possible interpretations of the incident perhaps explain its inclusion in this collection. However, Joan quickly became a subversive figure. At the same time as the Dominicans, the Franciscans had incorporated this story into their chronicles, with slightly different versions that emphasized the diabolical aspect of the usurpation. In spiritual Franciscan circles of the early 14th century, notably that of William of Ockham, Joan became the historical proof of a sa-

tanic occupancy of the papal see and foreshadowed the so-called indignity of JOHN XXII, the great breaker of the spirituals.

On a more fundamental level, Joan appeared as a sort of pseudo-pope who had the exterior trappings of legitimacy without the inner reality. She justified the distinction the spirituals made between real and false popes: only the latter condemned the rule of absolute poverty. Paradoxically, this distinction helped build the idea of papal INFALLIBILITY: the dogma pronounced by the "real" popes would remain unassailable. During the time of the GREAT SCHISM, at the end of the 14th century and the early 15th, Joan was enrolled in opposite camps; she proved the legal possibility and the superior necessity of being able to depose a pope, which provided for only in the case of HERESY. Thanks to Joan, the notion of error in the person and the circumstances of the pope's election henceforth played a role in the controversy. From then on, Joan became a more and more undesirable person for the Church; the Hussites and the Lutherans a century later used this story as an example of Roman corruption, a Roman image of the whore of Babylon. This polemic and violent use led, in 1562, to the first scholarly refutation by the Catholic church, done by the Augustine monk Panvinio. A century later, Calvinist scholars agreed that the female pope never existed, but the power of this story was such that it survived for a long time after that in anticlerical polemics and in European literature.

Alain Boureau

Bibliography

Boureau, A. *La Papesse Jeanne*, Paris, 1988.

Boureau, A. *The Myth of Pope Joan*, trans. L. G. Cochrane, Chicago, 2001.

Pardoe, R. A. *The Female Pope: The Mystery of Pope Joan*, New York, 1988.

Stanford, P. *The Legend of Pope Joan: In Search of the Truth*, New York, 1999.

Van der Helder, E. M. *Pope Joan in Legend and Drama: A Case Study in German Medieval Drama*, Armidale, 1987.

[JOHN]. *Antipope (844).*

Little is known about the attempt made by a certain John to proclaim himself ANTIPOPE after the death of GREGORY IV. John was a DEACON in the Roman Church whose election to the pontifical see was attempted when the rumor spread in Rome that the Roman nobility had decided to elect the archpriest SERGIUS. The LIBER PONTIFICALIS confirms that partisans for John were recruited in the countryside and fled after having helped him enter the Lateran by force. But the mention of these "countrymen" is drawn, according to Duchesne, from the story of the usurpation of Antipope URSINUS with respect to DAMASUS I, and therefore it does not mean much. The *principes* of Rome came in and elected SERGIUS II pope; they went with him to the Lateran palace, seized John, and imprisoned him. Then an assembly of bishops organized by the *principes* intervened and deposed John. They asked for his death, but Sergius II magnanimously spared his life and probably had him shut away in a monastery. The most plausible explanation for this episode lies in the absence of the Lateran clergy among Sergius II's supporters, which would mean that this clergy made an attempt to elect a pope who was not linked to any aristocratic Roman family.

Federico Marazzi

Bibliography

JE, 1, 327.
LP, 2, 86, 196.
Brezzi, P. "Giovanni," *EC* 6, 582.
Duchesne, L. *Early History of the Christian Church*, London, 1907.
Schieffer, R. "Johannes (VII)," *LexMA* 5 (1990), 540.

JOHN I. (*b. Tuscany ?, d. Ravenna, 18 May 526) Elected pope on 13 August 523. Buried in St. Peter's in Rome, Saint.*

The brief pontificate of John I is notable for the persecution he suffered from King Theodoric, and for the embassy he led to Constantinople on order of the king; John was the first bishop of Rome to visit the new capital of the empire.

According to the *LIBER PONTIFICALIS*, John was born in Tuscany, and his father was named Constantine. It is possible that he is to be identified with a Deacon John mentioned three times before his election as pope, but the name Johannes is too often common in 6th-century documents (three popes bear this name) for the identification to be certain. In September 506, a deacon with this name signed a statement in which he recognized the authority of Pope SYMMACHUS after having long supported his competitor, LAWRENCE. If this deacon was the future pope, he would have been part of a group close to the senatorial aristocracy and favorable to reconciliation with the Eastern Church. These two traits are not incompatible with John's acts as pope. It was also a Deacon John whom Senator Senarius questioned about baptism, sin, and grace. Senarius, mentioned until 515–6, was an important servant of the king of the Goths, and the person whom he consulted was a learned man, though nothing proves that he was Roman other than the fact that the LITURGY he describes is Roman. It is not impossible that he was the future pope. His response is a treatise on baptism with a distinctly Augustinian flavor. Finally, Boethius dedicated three of his works on religious ques-

tions to a Deacon John: *Utrum Pater et Filius et Spiritus sanctus de divinitale substantialiter praedicentur, Quomodo substantiae in eo, quod sint, bonae sint*, and *Liber contra Eutychem et Nestorium*. This Deacon John, like the first, was close to aristocratic society and interested in the Eastern question.

If these three people are one and the same, and to be identified with John I, his election represented a triumph for the pro-Eastern party that went far beyond the simple ecclesiastical reconciliation achieved by HORMISDAS. But his election would also have been a provocation to Theodoric, who would presumably have had no influence in the choice of the new pontiff. This would explain why Theodoric's successor chose directly to impose his candidates Boniface and Felix.

Whatever the truth may be, the election of John marks—at least chronologically—the beginning of the conflict between the SENATE and the king. John was elected in August 523, after a short vacancy. In the months that followed, a letter from Senator Albinus (consul in 493) was intercepted and interpreted as an act of treason against the Ostrogothic government. Boethius tried to cover up the affair, but Senator Cyprian brought it before the king, who brought Albinus to trial for high treason. E. Stein puts forth the hypothesis that Albinus's letter was one of several announcing to Constantinole the election of Pope John. Boethius was arrested and imprisoned at Pavia. This affair was only the beginning of Theodoric's worries: the king then learned that Emperor Justin had undertaken a major campaign to root out Arianism, confiscating Arian churches and forcing conversions. This news led the king to send an embassy to Constantinople, led by Pope John, to order the emperor to cease persecuting the Arians, under threat of reprisals against the Roman Church. Besides the pope, the embassy included the bishops Ecclesius of Ravenna, Eusebius of Fano, and Sabinus of Campania, senators Theodorus and Importunus, and two other patricians, both named Agapitus.

All the work of John in Rome dates from before this journey, which would cost him his life. He had restored the cemetery basilicas of Achilles and Nereus, Felix and Andreatus, and Priscilla. He benefited from the gifts of Emperor Justin and placed the ornaments offered in the basilicas of St. Peter's, St. Paul's, and St. Mary Major, also repairing the confession of St. Peter. This imperial generosity confirms that John's relationship with the East was good. John consecrated fifteen bishops, a number consonant with the brevity of his pontificate.

In 525, John consulted the canonist Dionysius Exiguus on the computation of the date of EASTER and decided to adopt the Alexandrine calculation for Rome. This additional sign of sympathy toward the East is interesting because the date of Easter had been the subject of raging debate during the Lawrentian SCHISM. This connection is not without interest for the identification of John with his namesake, the Lawretian deacon.

At the end of 525, John was called to Ravenna by the king. According to the account by the Anonymous of Valois, the interview was tense: Theodoric demanded that the pope tell the emperor to annul the Arian conversions to Catholicism; John refused to act against his own conscience, but he promised to relay the rest of Theodoric's message faith fully. The delegates left Ravenna by ship, and, following an uneventful voyage, arrived in Constantinople, where they were sumptuously received: a procession was organized to greet them long before they reached the city, and the emperor himself met the pope and prostrated himself before him. For the holy days of Christmas and Easter, John celebrated mass according to the Roman ritual, and, according to the *Liber pontificalis*, Justin had himself crowned by the pope. All eyewitness reports agree that John won the case on all accounts. On the return voyage to Ravenna, one of the two senators named Agapitus died. John met a hostile reception from Theodoric, perhaps because, before or during the pope's voyage, tension was increasing between the king and the senators (Boethius and Symmachus, his father-in-law, were both executed); perhaps because the news of the welcome given in Constantinople to the bishop of Rome seemed like proof of treason to Theodoric; or perhaps because the aging monarch (he would die three months later) was obsessed by his worries. In any case, Theodoric commanded John to reside in Ravenna, or perhaps even had him imprisoned there. Following ill treatment, the nature of which is not described in the sources, John I died. His epitaph is preserved in two manuscripts. According to the Anonymous of Valois, miracles began to occur immediately after his death. Several decades later, Pope Gregory I attributed several miracles to Pope John during the course of his final voyage, and another posthumous one.

Claire Sotinel

Bibliography

LP, I, 275–8.
Amann, E. "Jean 1er," *DTC*, 8–1 (1924), 593–5.
De Rossi, *Inscr. Christ.*, II, 57.
Goubert, P. "Autour du voyage à Byzance du pape Jean 1er," *Orientalia christiana periodica*, 24, (1958), 359–62.
Iohannes Diac., *Ep. and Senarium, PL*, LIX, 399.

JOHN II. *Mercurius (b. Rome, d. 8 May 535). Elected on 2 January 533. Buried in St. Peter's in Rome.*

Mercurius was of Roman birth and the son of a certain Projectus, according to the LIBER PONTIFICALIS, and was a priest of the title of St. Clement under Pope Hormisdas (514–23). He is mentioned in several inscriptions, including the dedication of an altar in the basilica of St. Clement.

John was elected to succeed Boniface II (d. in October 532) after a vacancy of more than two months which seem to have been filled with intrigues and corruption. Accusations of SIMONY (bribery) led King Athalaric to issue a decree—John II was notified—that reinforced a senate action taken in 530 to repress simoniacal practices (*Variae*, IX-15). Cassiodorus, named prefect of the pretorium of Italy in September 533, also wrote John a letter asking for his prayers.

John II found himself embroiled in the Theopaschite controversy. The doctrine that one member of the Trinity suffered in the flesh, put forth by Scythian monks in order to combat the Nestorians, had been rejected by Pope Hormisdas. It was, however, used by Emperor Justinian, who—without consulting Rome—published an edict defining faith on 15 March 533, directed against the Nestorians. In it he emphasized the unity of the person of Christ (but without using the Chalcedonian term "two natures"). John II was therefore pulled in two opposing directions. First two envoys to Rome from the Acoemetae ("sleepless") monks in Constantinople, Abbot Cyrus and Eulogius, denounced the monophysite formulas used in official documents and protested against the accusation of Nestorianism and the excommunication measures taken against them. On the other hand, the pope received from Justinian a letter dated 6 June 533, delivered by two bishops, Hypatius of Ephesus and Demetrius of Philippus, to which was joined a letter (now lost) from Patriarch Epiphanius of Constantinople. Rich gifts for St. Peter's basilica accompanied these two letters. In his letter, Justinian proclaimed that the Holy See is the leader of all the holy churches and confirmed the need for all churches to join together with Rome; he invited the pope to confirm the imperial Christology by condemning the monks for Nestorianism, by recognizing the orthodoxy of the saying "One of the Trinity suffered in the flesh," and by confessing that Mary was truly the Mother of God. The pope, advised that Patriarch Epiphanius, had already approved this profession of faith, was invited to show his agreement by writing letters to the emperor and to Epiphanus.

John II seemed to have tried to convince the envoys to follow the Christological formulas put forth by Justinian, but he ended up excommunicating them. On 25 March 534, he sent the emperor a letter in which he unreservedly approved the imperial theology, adding that he had received the agreement of the bishops and asking that they show understanding in the case of the excommunicated monks, if the monks agreed to recant (JK, 884). He joined to this letter a dogmatic narrative that he had had approved by the bishops, the SENATE, and the people of Rome.

Not long after this, the pope had to answer a group of senators (including Cassiodorus, then prefect of the pre-

torium) who asked him to account for his positions. John declared to them (JK, 885) that he had responded affirmatively to Justinian on each of three points:
• Could Christ be said to be "One of the Trinity"?
• Did the Christ God suffer in the flesh while remaining impassive in his divinity?
• Should Mary always a virgin, be truly called the Mother of God, Mother of God the Word who became incarnate within her?

The pope justified his approval with many quotations from Scripture and other Christian writings (mostly in Latin). His reply also contains (for the first time in a surviving Roman document) the twelfth ANATHEMA contested by Cyril of Alexandria, confessing that the Word had suffered in the flesh. John also notified his correspondents of the condemnation of the Acoemetae monks as Nestorians and requested that they not communicate further with the monks.

In his relations with the Western Church, John II received a *relatio* from Bishop Caesarius of Arles and some Gallic bishops concerning the improper conduct of their colleague Contumeliosus of Riez, in Provence. In three letters written in April 535, addressed to Caesarius of Arles, the Gallic bishops, and the Church of Riez (JK, 886–888), the pope announced his deposition of Contumeliosus and ordered his banishment to a monastery and the nomination of a temporary visitor for the Church of Riez pending the election of a new bishop. To Caesarius of Arles, he sent along canons intended to enlighten him on the proper course of action.

The African bishops also sent John a letter concerning problems posed by the Arians and by some African clerks who were going to Italy without permission, but this situation was to be resolved by his successor, AGAPITUS I. John's hasty approval of the imperial Christology, which demonstrates that the Roman Church did not have the means to counteract imperial demands by playing into the hands of the Monophysites—certainly at the time more to be feared than the Nestorians—resulted in undermining the decrees of the council of Chalcedon and committing succeeding popes on the doctrinal level.

Christiane Fraisse-Coué

Bibliography

Amann, E. *DTC* 8, 895–7.
Batiffol, L. "L'empereur Justinien et le Siège apostolique," *Cathedra Petri*, Paris, 1938, 267–79.
Epistula, ACO, IV, 2, 206–10.
Epistulae, Coll. Arelatensis, 12–14, 45–8.
Iohannes, *Epistula, Coll. Auel.*, 84, CSEL, 35, 1, 320–8.
Liber pontificalis, I, 285–6.
Magi, L. "La sede romana nella corrispondenza degli imperatori e patriarchi bizantini (6th–7th century)," *Bibliothèque de la RHE*, 57, Rome (1972), 107–18.

JOHN III. (*b. Rome ?, d. Rome, 13 July 574). Elected pope 17 July 561. Buried in St. Peter's in Rome.*

Little is known about the long pontificate of John III, perhaps because it took place during one of the most confused periods in the history of Italy, during the 6th century. We know nothing about John's life before he became pope, except that he was Roman and that his father's name was Anastasius, which perhaps indicates a Greek family origin. At the death of PELAGIUS I, Rome had been under Byzantine control for many years, and according to the procedure imposed by Constantinople, the name of the elected candidate had to be submitted to the emperor for approval. This explains the long vacancy between the death of Pelagius on 3 March and the ordination of John on 17 July. Although the Byzantines held Rome, the suppression of the Gothic kingdom was still accompanied by many military troubles, as mentioned in the *LIBER PONTIFICALIS*. The Franks, whom the Goths had called in for assistance, tried to conquer northern Italy, and the exarch (viceroy) Narses had to fight them, probably before 565. After his victory, he faced the revolt of his general, Sindual, in 566 or 567. Even if these battles did not directly threaten Rome, they put military pressure on it. Nevertheless, in the section on John III in the *Liber pontificalis* is found the famous phrase "All Italy was full of joy," which is echoed in the chronicle of Prosper of Aquitaine: "The patrician Narses . . . returned Italy to the Roman Empire, restored the destroyed cities, and having chased away the Goths, gave back to the peoples of all Italy the joy of their origins."

The fragility of this joy, however, became apparent during the pontificate of John III. The *Liber pontificalis* tells how the Romans complained to the emperor about the extortions of Narses—probably they were simply discovering the heavy hand of the Byzantine government—and how this prompted the exarch's decision to leave Rome for Naples. The pope visited Narses to ask him to return to Rome. This exceptional episode shows how strongly John III was linked to the Byzantine milieu. He persuaded the exarch to return, but the circumstances of this return are confused. A tradition abundantly confirmed, but with many aspects still suspect, has inspired debate for centuries: Narses, to get revenge on the Romans, is said to have called in the Lombards to invade Italy. All we can be sure of is a chronological concurrence: Narses' disgrace, after the death of Justinian, is dated 567; the Lombards entered Italy in the spring of 568; and Narses returned to Rome in 571. A contemporary chronicler says that, when he returned, he looted the Capitol and the PALATINE of the statues that were still there.

The end of John III's life shows that the relations between the Byzantine rulers and the Roman people were in any case bad. Upon his return from Naples, the pope did not re-enter the city but instead moved into the cemetery of

Pretextat, on the Appian Way, several hundred meters from the Lateran and outside the walls. He lived there for a long time and performed many ordinations there. It is not known what powerful forces kept him from residing in Rome.

The few known religious events of John's pontificate are also linked to the political situation. The only letter of this pope that has been preserved is a rescript in which he gives the bishop of RAVENNA, Peter (elected 569), the *pallium*, insignia of archepiscopal dignity, for the first time. In this way the pope blessed the ascension of this city, the Byzantine bridgehead in Italy.

The Lombard invasion changed the situation of all the schismatic churches of northern Italy. Although the bishops of Aquileia, in refuge at Grado, continued to defend the Three Chapters, the bishop, clergy, and aristocracy of MILAN, who had fled as far as Genoa, were asking to return to the Roman communion. In the presence of the future pope Gregory I then the prefect of Rome, Bishop Laurentius presented Pope John with a document signed by the clergy and the Milanese aristocracy, declaring their acceptance of all the councils' decisions and their communion with the see of Rome, and implicitly condemning the Three Chapters. This event, known through the testimony of Gregory himself, involved only the regions of Liguria still under Byzantine control.

In Rome itself, John III organized the suburban cemeteries; progressively neglected, they had become simply sites for the veneration of martyrs, and their care required that special measures be taken. John III gave to the Lateran the task of attending to Sunday masses in the cemeteries. He also finished the rebuilding of the basilica of Pope Julius, begun by his predecessor, and dedicated the new church to St. Philip and St. James (the Santi Apostoli), as recorded in inscriptions preserved until the 15th century. Despite his differences with the Roman people, John III, was buried in St. Peter's.

Claire Sotinel

Bibliography:

LP, 1, 305–7.

Johannes III, *Exemplum praecepti ad Petrum episcopum Ravennatem de usu pallii*, *MGH*, 1, 230.

Leclercq, H. "Jean III," *DACL*, 13–1, (1937), 1222.

JOHN IV. (*b. Dalmatia, ?, d. Rome, 22 October 642). Elected pope 24 December 640. Buried in St. Peter's in Rome.*

The short duration of the pontificate of John IV is not surprising for a period in which the Romans considered this post as the crowning achievement of a long career and the emperor preferred elderly popes who were likely to be more acquiescent, or at least sooner replaced. However, the firmness with which John faced up to imperial politics shows the growing power of the patriarchate in the West.

This Dalmatian, son of the scholasticus (legal advisor) Venantius—who probably worked for the exarch or another high civil official—might appear susceptible to influence. At the head of the Roman church, however, he expressed his hostility towards monothelitism (the theory that in Christ there was only one will, rather than both human and divine wills). As soon as he was elected, he called an Italian SYNOD to condemn the document (*Ecthesis*) of Sergius, which affirmed monothelitism, and to justify the contested formulas of his predecessor, HONORIUS I. Relations with Pyrrhus, successor of Sergius in the see of Constantinople, remained tense. The danger created by Muslim advances worried the imperial court, while the support of the Palestinian and African clergy encouraged the pope. Nevertheless, nothing decisive happened.

The situation was the same in the West. John was elected while he belonged, as archdeacon, to the council of the *servantes locum sanctae sedis apostolicae*, who were in charge of managing the Church in the period between the death of a pope and the election of his successor. As such, he and his colleagues received a delegation of bishops, priests and English abbots who had come to consult with Pope SEVERINUS but arrived after his death—evidence that pontifical authority was becoming recognized in the Britain. The kings of the FRANKS also applied to the pope to obtain the EXEMPTION of a monastery, which was thus taken away from the authority of the ordinary and put directly under the authority, of the pope; this allowed the kings to dispose of it as they wished. A collaboration was shaping up between the foremost political power of the West and its most prestigious moral authority, whose approval was now sought. The pope also wished to impose his authority in Ireland, by forcing the Irish to adopt the Roman way of calculating the date of Easter and other Roman customs.

In Rome, John increased the prestige of the city, enriching it with relics from all over his patriarchate. He sent for the remains of Sts. Venantius, Anastasius, and Maurus in Dalmatia and had a chapel built for them whose mosaics are still partially preserved. These relics contributed to John's prestige because they came from his homeland, and the most important of the saints, Venantius, had the same name as his father. His concern for Dalmatia was also evident in the expense he incurred to ransom Dalmatian prisoners captured by the Slavs and the Avars.

Jean Durliat

Bibliography

JW, 1, 227–8; 2, 698–739.

LP, 1, 330.

PL, 80, 601–650.

Bede, 2, 19.

Bertolini, O. *Roma di frone a Bizanzio e ai Longobardi*, Bologna, 1974

Schwaiger, G. "Johannes IV.," *LexMA* 5 (1990), 538–9.

JOHN V. (*b. Antioch, ?, d. Rome, 2 August 686*). *Elected pope on 23 July 685. Buried in St. Peter's in Rome.*

This pontificate of one year and ten days' duration left few records. John was born in Antioch, but his father, Cyriacus, probably fled that city during the Arab conquest. By 680, John was playing an important role in the Church of Rome. Pope AGATHO made him one of his three emissaries to the imperial court during the third council of Constantinople (680–1). John brought back the acts of the council and the results of negotiations that led to the confirmation of the election of LEO II. The exarch of RAVENNA quickly ratified John's election, and three of his suffragans consecrated him less than one month after the death of his predecessor. He distributed 1,800 sous, or 25 pounds of gold, to the clergy, monasteries, the poor under the care of the episcopal deacons, and the people in charge of the upkeep of the churches. These gifts were customary at the installation of a new pope, explaining in part why old men were usually chosen for this position: gifts came more frequently.

John punished the bishop of Cagliari, who had been promoted to the rank of archbishop, and wanted to name his suffragans independently. He also suspended the bishop of Porto Torres, who had been consecrated without his authorization, but reinstated him after this demonstration of his authority.

Jean Durliat

Bibliography

JW, I, 242–3; 2, 699.

LP, I, 366–7.

Bertolini, O. *Roma di fronte a Bisancio e ai Longobardi*, Bologna, 1971, 395–6.

Schwaiger, G., "Johannes V," *LexMA* 5 (1990–), 539.

JOHN VI. (*b. Greece, ?, d. Rome, 11 January, 705*). *Elected pope 30 October 701. Buried in St. Peter's in Rome.*

During the pontificate of John VI, the pope became defined as the political leader from Rome to the outer edges of an increasingly weak empire, and as head of the Church in England. When the exarch Theophylact returned from Sicily to RAVENNA, the army of "all Italy"—actually that of Ravenna and of the Pentapolis, since it was usual to take this part for the whole—rebelled and went out to confront him. Theophylact was forced to take refuge in Rome, where he had perhaps been planning to punish the supporters of SERGIUS, John's predecessor, in the name of the emperor. John closed the gates of Rome and sent priests who succeeded in ending the revolt. He thus found himself in the position of protecting the exarch, even though the latter was the head of civil and military administration for all Italy. Theophylact was evidently incapable of

contesting the election of the pope, and he even condemned the informers who, had acted on his behalf against Sergius.

Master at home and arbiter of Byzantine affairs in Italy, John still had to face a Lombard attack organized by the duke of Benevento, who was taking advantage of the troubles that were weakening his opponents. Although he was Catholic, he invaded Campania and arrived at the walls of Rome; to him, the pope was only the leader of an enemy territory. No one was able to stop him by force, so John had to negotiate with him, using priests as intermediaries. After a series of gifts, the ransom of prisoners, and the forfeit of three cities on the left bank of the Liri, the duke went home. It was clear that the pope could no longer count on the emperor's assistance or that of the exarch, and that he could no longer fight alone against a Lombard attack.

Though weak in Italy and practically ignored in Spain and Gaul, the papacy was gaining prestige in England, where people were begging him to arbitrate their religious conflicts. Wilfrid, removed from the office of archbishop of York for the third time, arrived in 703 to ask the pope to judge his case on appeal. A long council held in Rome finally found him in the right, and John wrote a long letter to the kings of Northumbria and Mercia. He took the occasion to confirm Beorhtweald as archbishop of Canterbury (693–731) and asked him to set Wilfrid's affair straight with a regional council. If not, the pope himself would do it.

In a reign of less than three and a half years, John also found time to have a church built in honor of St. Andrew and to undertake several other projects.

Jean Durliat

Bibliography

JW, 1, 245–6; 2, 700–41.

LP, 1, 383–4.

PL, 89, 59.

Bertolini, O. *Rome di fronte a Bisanzio e ai Longobardi*, Bologna, 1971, 408–10.

Diacre, P. *HL*, 6, 27.

Guillou, A. *Régionalisme et indépendance dans l'Empire byzantin au VIIe siècle: L'exemple de l'Exarchat et de la Pentapole d'Italie*, Rome, 1969, 211.

Mansi, 169.

Schieffer, R. "Johannes VI.," *LexMA* 5 (1990), 539.

JOHN VII. (*b. Greece, ?, d. Rome, 18 October 707*). *Elected pope 1 March 705. Buried in the chapel he built at St. Peter's in Rome.*

The only pope who was the son of an imperial official, John VII was the last to consider—in a highly anachronistic way—the Roman pontificate as coming under the authority of the Eastern Empire. His mother belonged to the Roman NOBILITY, and his father was responsible for the palace where the representative of the Byzantine exarch in Rome lived. John received a solid intellectual and artistic education and became administrator of the pontifical lands along the Appian Way. After his election, he had a new episcopal palace (*episcopium*) built near the Greek quarter and the PALATINE and undertook a vast program of construction and decoration of Roman churches. Besides a chapel in honor of the Virgin destined for his tomb, he supported important work at Sta Maria Antiqua, where the frescoes reveal strong influence from the art of Constantinople. John's biographer notes with irony that the pope often had himself represented on the walls of buildings. His activity can be seen as important to the diffusion and survival of contemporary Byzantine art, since many works in Constantinople fell victim to iconoclasm.

John's attitude toward the emperor was marked by great deference, which displeased the Roman populace. Justinian II had returned to imperial power in 705, and in 706 he sent the pope a copy of the canons of the Quinisext council—also called the second Trullan council—which had met in 692. Sergius I had refused to endorse these canons. John, fearing the wrath of Justinian, sent back the canons without calling a council to examine them. He obviously overestimated the capacity of the emperor to intervene.

Although strongly preoccupied with his relationship with Constantinople, John did not forget the West. He wrote to all the English clergy and accorded the *pallium* to the bishop of Vienne. But it was with the Lombards that he pursued a relationship most consistently. For the first time, the relations between the two became almost cordial. The duke of Benevento made no move to attack Rome, and King Aribert II returned the patrimony of the Cottian Alps (in fact, of Liguria) conquered by Rothari (625–43). The lands remained in Lombard hands, but the fiscal revenues went to the pope.

Jean Durliat

Bibliography

JW, 1, 246–7.

LP, 1, 385–7.

Breckenridge, J. "Evidence for the Nature of Relations between Pope John VII and the Byzantine Emperor Justinian II," *Byzantinianische Zeitschrift*, 65 (1972), 364–74.

Nordhagen, P.J. *The Frescoes of John VII in S. Maria Antiqua*, Rome, 1968.

Schieffer, R. " Johannes VII.", *LexMA* 5 (1990), 539.

Schneider, 25, 27.

JOHN VIII. *(b. Rome, end of 8th century, d. Rome, 15 December 882). Elected pope at the end of December 872. Buried in St. Peter's in Rome.*

When HADRIAN II died, the Roman clergy chose another old man to replace him: John VIII. He had long worked for the Lateran *patriarchum* with NICHOLAS I. Named archdeacon, he was considered a level-headed man. As his biographer A. Lapôtre wrote, "At the hour of his consecration as pope, during the solemn procession which led him from the Lateran palace to the other side of the Tiber into the basilica of the Prince of the Apostles, more than one among the ambitious or restless men who had been supplemented must have said to themselves, seeing the old archdeacon pass by, that the wait would be neither too long nor too painful." Among the ambitious was Formosus, bishop of Porto, who had failed to become a bishop in the Bulgarian lands and now wanted to possess the pontifical crown.

John VIII, a man with wide business experience, proved to be a good manager. The ample treasure of the Lateran allowed him to enlist men to fight against the SARACENS threatening the West, to pay the sailors of Amalfi and Naples, and to undertake major construction projects in Rome. He had the walls of the Vatican reinforced and enclosed St. Paul's Outside the Walls with a defensive wall, which gave the monastic compound the name Johannopolis. His love of beautiful horses and rich tableware allowed the pope to increase the external prestige of the papacy. From the beginning of his reign, however, he showed a desire to follow his predecessors' example.

The Council of Constantinople, which the Catholic Church calls the eighth ecumenical council, had condemned the former patriarch Photius and reestablished good relations with Rome. In its final session, the Bulgarian prince Boris obtained the consecration of a bishop for his country from the patriarch Ignatius. John VIII, wishing to protect the rights of the Roman church in Bulgaria, sent a legation to Constantinople. When it arrived, it found that Ignatius had just died, and his replacement was none other than Photius, back in favor. John VIII, increasingly threatened by the Arabs and no longer able to expect much help from the West, did not want to quarrel with Emperor Basil the Macedonian. The Roman Church confirmed Photius on the condition that he express his regrets for his past conduct toward Rome. In addition, the pope wanted BYZANTIUM to renounce all claim to controlling the Bulgarian Church. A council was organized by the emperor in November 879 and lasted until March 880. It is difficult to ascertain its results because the letters of John VIII, translated into Greek, have been falsified to enhance Photius's role.

It seems, however, that peace was made, and that even the question of the *Filioque*, brought up during the last two sessions, caused no new difficulties, since the Roman Church had refused to recite the Credo with the new formula since the reign of Leo III, holding to the Nicea-Constantinople definition instead. Finally,

Photius abandoned his claims to the Bulgarian Church. However, Boris refused to exchange his Greek clergy for a Latin clergy, and, between Byzantium and Rome, kept his autonomy. Relations between Photius and John remained good until the end of his pontificate. This must be emphasized because for a long time certain Roman historians posited a "second schism with Photius," a hypothesis successfully countered by Lapôtre in 1895 and later by E. Amann and especially F. Dvornik.

Hadrian II had saved his best welcome for Cyril and Methodius, apostles of the Moravian people; Cyril died in Rome, and Methodius was consecrated archbishop of Pannonia. When John VIII learned that Methodius had been taken prisoner on the urging of the German clergy, he intervened vigorously. Methodius, once he was freed, went back to his evangelization. Some clerics reported to the pope that Methodius's doctrine was not orthodox and that he sang mass "in a barbaric manner"; John VIII therefore called the bishop to Rome and, after discussion, accepted his innovations. He wrote to Duke Svatopluk that he was authorizing Methodius to sing mass in the Slavonic language and to translate the Scriptures because, he said, "He who made three main languages, Hebrew, Greek and Latin, also made all the other languages to sing his praise and glory." Thus for the first and last time before the VATICAN II COUNCIL, a pope accepted a LITURGY that was not in Latin. The opponents of Methodius, with Bishop Wiching as their leader, did not relent. As long as John VIII lived, he protected Methodius, but after the death of the pope and the archbishop, the disciples of Methodius were persecuted, and their enemies succeeded in obtaining an interdiction of the Slavonic mass from Pope Stephen V in 885.

From the beginning of his pontificate, John VIII reminded King Charles of France and King Louis of Germany, that they should respect the warnings of the Roman Church regarding the succession of Lothair II, king of Lotharingia. He required that the new bishops of Cologne and Trevi come to receive the *pallium* in Rome. When Emperor Louis II died childless (875), the pope intervened to choose his successor. He asked Charles the Bald to seek the imperial crown because he had distinguished himself from his rivals, the sons of Louis the German, "by his virtue, his battles on behalf of religion and law, his care to honor clerics and to educate them." Charles quickly superseded the other princes and had himself recognized by the Italian aristocracy; he was crowned by the pope on 25 December 875. Among the gifts he gave John were a Bible, preserved today in St. Paul's Outside the Walls, and the famous throne called St. Peter's, today enshrined in front of the canopy of St. Peter's in the Vatican.

The pope hoped that Charles would use his forces against the Saracens, but the new emperor merely designated the duke of Spoleto, Lambert, to defend the PAPAL STATES. John designated the archbishop of Sens,

Ansegius, as pontifical vicar in Gaul and in Germany, which upset Archbishop Hincmar of Reims. After Charles the Bald left for France, John had to face interior unrest in 876, as well as Saracen attacks. He dismissed Bishop Formosus and some high lay officials (SYNOD of Saint Mary of the Martyrs, 19 April). He went to Capua and Naples to rally the minor princes and organize a defense against the Saracens. He obtained more political authority from the emperor and treated Lambert of Spoleto as a subordinate. But faced with mounting peril, John called for the emperor to return to Italy. His numerous letters, written by Anastasius the Librarian, show his impatience. Charles finally met the pope in Pavia (September 877) but, threatened by Carloman, son of Louis of Bavaria, he had to return to France. He died in the hamlet of Maurienne while John speedily returned to Rome.

Threatened by the Saracens, by the supporters of Formosus, and by Lambert of Spoleto and Adelbert of Tuscany—who were working on their own behalf—John decided to imitate his distant predecessor STEPHEN II. He went to France to beg for help from the new king, Louis the Stammerer. A great council was held at Troyes in August 878. The pope crowned Louis and established good relations with Boson, the king's uncle, by encouraging him to hope for the imperial crown. After the king's death, however, Boson had already secured the throne of Provence, so John suggested that Charles the Fat, son of Louis the German, receive the imperial crown. Charles accepted and was crowned in Rome on 12 February 881. Attacks by the Normans forced him quickly to return home across the Alps. John VIII, left alone at the mercy of Saracen attacks, died soon afterward, perhaps assassinated by some cleric in his entourage.

The tragic end of John VIII should not obscure his greatness or the importance of his papacy. Through his writings and his actions, the pope affirmed that Rome was the royal and sacred city, source of the faith and head of what he called "Christendom," which meant not the Church of clerics, but the church of all Christian people.

Pierre Riche

Bibliography

LP, 2, 221–3.

MGH, Epist. 7, 1–133.

JW, 1, 376–422; 2, 704, 746.

Lapôtre, A. *L'Europe et le Saint-Siège à l'époque carolingienne: Le pape Jean VIII*, Paris, 1895.

Amann, E. "Jean VIII," *DTC*, 8 (1922), 601–13; *L'Époque carolingienne*, Paris, 1947 (Fliche-Martin, 412–45, 489–97).

Lohrmann, D. *Das Register Papst Johannes VIII.*, 872–82, Tübingen, 1968.

Schieffer, R. "Johannes VIII," *LexMA*, 5 (1990), 539–40.

JOHN IX. *(b. Tivoli, ?, d. January 900). Elected pope in January 898. Buried in St. Peter's in Rome.*

Born the son of a certain Ramboald, John was ordained as a presbyter by Pope FORMOSUS. As soon as he had risen to the papal throne, he had to confront Formosus' opponent SERGIUS III, who had in all likelihood been elected pope by another Roman faction shortly before John IX was. His pontificate began in January 898. It is uncertain whether the new pope received the support of Emperor Lambert at the outset. Nevertheless, it was definitely with the emperor's approval that John IX called a synod to meet at Ravenna. This COUNCIL was probably not preceded by a Roman synod, despite the claims of earlier scholars that may still be found in recent works. The decrees of Ravenna, made up of teachings drawn from Formosan polemics, succeeded, in accordance with the politics of Theodore II, in rehabilitating Pope Formosus. With another specific decree, Sergius was deposed, along with several of his supporters, and excommunicated for having profaned Formosus.

Other chapters of the decrees must have supported Lambert of Spoleto and defended his sovereignty, since the imperial coronation of Lambert was recognized and that of Arnoul rejected. Concerning the papal election, the council wished to return to the practice of *constitutio romana* (consecration only in the presence of imperial delegates). These chapters not only showed themselves willing to put an end to the Roman crisis and that of the papacy but also revealed the state of dereliction in which Rome and the papacy lay at the end of the 9th century.

The premature death of Emperor Lambert (15 October 898) prevented all these intended reforms. For the first time since the pontificate of Formosus, the papacy, under John IX, found both within and outside Italy the stirrings of greater autonomy. For this reason, John wrote a letter addressed to Stylianos proposing compromise between the factions of the Ignatians, led by Stylianos and Patriarch Antony I Cauleas (893–901) of Byzantium. He attempted to send a legation to Moravia to restore order and intervened in the SCHISM of Langres. Decrees addressed Italian recipients were mostly related to current events there. Recently, John IX has been given credit for establishing relations with Asturia and Galicia as well as for the convocation of a synod at Viviers, but these acts are not at all certain. It is possible that the hymn sung the Saturday after Easter, in which a Pope John is mentioned, refers to John IX.

Klaus Herbers

Bibliography

JL, I, 442–3; II, 705, *MGH*, II, 123–6.

Duhr, J. "Le concile de Ravenne en 898; la réhabilitation du pape Formose," *Recherche de science religieuse*, 22, (1932), 541–79.

Hartmann, W. *Die Synoden der Karolingenzeit im Frankenreich und in Italien*, Paderborn, 1989.

Mansi, *LP*, 2, 232.

Petrocchi, M. "La personalità di un papa tiburtino: Giovanni IX (898–900)," *Atti e Memorie della Società tiburtina di storia e d'arte*, 39, 1966.

Pokorny, R. "Ein unbekanntes Brieffragment Argrims von Lyon-Langres aus de Jahren 894–895 une zwei umstrittene Bischofsweihen in der Kirchenprovinz Lyon: Mit Textedition und Exkurs," *Francia*, 13 (1985) 602–22.

Schieffer, R. "Johannes IX.", *LexMA*, 5 (1991), 540.

Scholz, S. *Transmigration und Translation. Studien zum Bistumswechsel der Bischöfe von der Spätantike bis zum Hohen Mittelalter*, Cologne, Weimar, and Vienna, 1992 (*Kölner Historische Abhandlungen*, 37), 225–8.

Schröder, I. *Die westfränkischen Synoden von 888 bis 987 und ihre Überlieferung*, Munich, 1980, 373–5.

Villoslada, R. G. "El himmo al papa Juan (IX?) de las Landes Coruomaniae," *Miscellanea Counillas*, 32 (1974), 185–205.

Zimmermann, H. *Papstabsetzungen des Mittelalters*, Graz, Vienna, and Cologne, 1968.

Zimmermann, H. *Papsturkunden*, 13–23.

JOHN X. *(b. Tossignano, d. 929). Elected pope at the beginning of April 914. Deposed in 928.*

This pope had been a deacon in Bologna, where he was expected to succeed to Peter IV as bishop, but in 905, shortly before that was to occur, he was elected archbishop of RAVENNA. Governing Ravenna under the name John XI, he was apparently on good terms with the king of Italy, Berengar I of Frioul (888–924). He worked in vain with the Church in Rome to have Berengar crowned Roman emperor instead of Emperor Louis III of Lower Burgundy (901–28), who was deposed and blinded. The clan of the nobility that then dominated Rome with the exarch Theophylact summoned John from Ravenna to make him pope. His adversaries accused him of having changed dioceses twice—this was an infraction of the canons on changing sees—and alleged that he had been called to Rome owing to an affair he had had with Theodora, the wife of Theophylact, even before he had been sent to Bologna.

John's energetic political activity earned him the enmity of the Roman NOBILITY. When the Roman senatrix Marozia, daughter of Theodora, was in power, he was overthrown and, after a year in captivity at Veroli and then in Rome, he was assassinated in a Roman dungeon around the middle of 929. It is surmised that the pope's fall coincided with his brother Peter's being named marquis of Spoleto under unusual circumstances, so that Marozia and her husband Guido of Tuscany (917–29) feared their sovereignty was threatened. After the retaking of Rome in 927, Peter (who had been expelled from the city) and the pope were accused of having made an alliance with the pagan Magyars.

Some great political events are associated with the pontificate of John X. In 915, a coalition of Italian princes created on the pope's initiative and supported by a Byzantine fleet and Roman troops commanded by the pope himself drove the Saracens out of their stronghold at the mouth of the Garigliano. The next important event was the imperial coronation of Berengar I in Rome in December 915; after Berengar's assassination in 924, John summoned Count Hugh of Arles—half-brother of Guido of Tuscany, reigning in Provence for Emperor Louis III the Blind—and concluded an alliance in Mantua (926) with Hugh, who had become king of Italy. That same year, the pope met in France with Count Herbert II of Vermandois (902–43) to plead the case of Charles III the Simple (893–929), the Carolingian king who had been deposed and imprisoned in 922–3 and had been unable to obtain reinstatement. After arbitrating a SCHISM declared at Liège (920–1), the pope, in two important mandates in favor of Charles III, had categorically recognized the right of the king to choose bishops, a decision that GRATIAN did not include in his Decree. In 916, again to reinforce royal authority, the pope sent a legate, bishop Pierre d'Orte, to Germany to the SYNOD of Hohenaltheim.

From Byzantium, John received several letters from Patriarch Nicholas the Mystic (901–25) and sent legates who helped end the dispute over tetragamy that had arisen as a result of the fourth marriage in 907 of Emperor Leo VI (886–911). At the same time, John worked to obtain peace between Bulgaria and the Byzantine Empire, and then between Bulgaria and Croatia. According to a later tradition, he recognized Simeon of Bulgaria (893–927) as tsar. Moreover, in a papal letter of 925 addressed to Tomislav of Croatia (910–28), the title king of Croatia is used for the first time in the surviving record. In 925, legates of the pope went to the synods of Split in Dalmatia to enforce the rights of the metropolitan of Split against the bishop of the Croats, whose residence was in Nin.

In Rome, as an inscription verifies, the pope pursued the renovation of the Lateran palace, which had crumbled in 897. From his pontificate, twenty authentic pontifical acts are preserved. Some of them are rescripts—for example, those sent in response to a question from Reims around 914 on the mission among the NORMANS, and those from Cologne on various problems related to penance. The other documents are confirmations of rights and property ownership sent to monasteries and cathedrals. The *pallium* was given to the metropolitans of Canterbury, Hamburg, Liège, Reims, Grado, and Narbonne, where John X had to end a schism that had arisen under ANASTASIUS III, his predecessor. In 928, the reformed abbey of Cluny, under the pope's protection since its foundation in 910, obtained its first papal privilege, which put an end to a dispute with its sister abbey, Gigny, over the will of their founding abbot, Berno (d. 927), and

assigned the monastery to the protection of King Raoul of France (923–36). In 917, the abbey of Fulda in Hesse was given EXEMPTION and immunity.

Despite his lack of political success in Rome, John X is considered an important pope. His elevation to the Roman papacy when he was archbishop of Ravenna reawakened certain disputes—and lampoons—on the legitimacy of Formosus (891—96), who was also a bishop when he became pope. But it is from this reign that the preeminence of the pontiff over the episcopacy is dated, so that a change of see no longer conflicts with the *matrimonium mysticum*.

Harald Zimmermann

Bibliography

Schieffer, R. "Johannes XI," *LexMA*, 5, (1990), 540–541.

Scholz, S. *Transmigration und Translation*, 1992, 171, 243 *sq*.

Venni, I "Giovanni X," *ASR*, 59 (1936), 1–137.

Zimmermann, H. *Das dunkle Jahrhundert*, Braz, 1971; "Die ersten Konzilien von Split im Rahmen der Geschichte ihrer Zeit," *Medioevo e Umanesimo*, 49 (1982), 3–20.

Zimmermann, H. *Papstregesten 7–39; Papsturkunden 61–99*; "Der Streit um das Lütticher Bistum bis vom Jahre 920–921," MIÖG, 65 (1957).

JOHN XI. (b. ?, d. beginning of January 936). *Elected pope in early March 931. Probably buried in St. John Lateran.*

It is certain that this pope's mother was the senatrix Marozia, who reigned in Rome at the time of his election; it is not certain, however, that his father was Duke Alberic I of Spoleto, Marozia's first husband, even though the future prince of Rome, Alberic II (932–54), is referred to as the brother of John XI. Contemporary sources, such as the chronicler Liutprand of Cremona, stated that the future pope was the illegitimate son of Marozia by Pope SERGIUS III (904–11), a claim that modern researchers have discounted. At any rate, it must have been his influential mother who enabled John to ascend onto St. Peter's throne while he was probably still young, even though it seems that he had earlier been a cardinal-priest at the church of Santa Maria in Trastevere.

Only five authentic pontifical documents survive from John XI's papacy. This may be due to the fact that he was implicated in the fall of his mother from power—or, rather, in the Roman revolt against her third husband, King Hugo of Italy (926–48)—and was imprisoned at the end of 932 by the new master of Rome, Prince Alberic II. This obviously limited what John could accomplish. Three of these five acts were on behalf of Abbot

Odo of Cluny, for his monasteries of Cluny and Deols. The monastery of Vézelay in the diocese of Autun, which was under papal protection, as well as the cathedral of Autun, are the addressees of the other two texts; undeniably the most important action recorded was the privilege established for Cluny in March 931, which for the first time confirmed the EXEMPTION, immunity, and pontifical protection of the monastery, enabling it to take other abbeys under its wing to reform them. This innovative authorization created the canonical conditions necessary for the development and diffusion of Cluny's reforms. Odo probably asked personally for this privilege while in Rome, after he had been given other monasteries to direct.

Among the other important events of John XI's reign was the concession in 931 of the *pallium* to Archbishop Hilduan of Milan, who had been evicted from Liège, and another in 932 to Archbishop Artaud of Reims, whom King Raoul of France had just invested instead of Hugh of Vermandois, still a minor. Both cases were undertaken to settle ecclesiastical problems. Hugh, king of Italy, intervened for Hilduin; from Reims, a legation was sent to Rome.

In 932, LEGATES from the pope went to Constantinople to participate in the enthronement as patriarch of the minor son of the emperor, Theophylact (933–56) and to show the pope's approval of this act, which raised canonical objections. The principal information about this event exists in a letter addressed to the pope by the Byzantine emperor Romanus I (844–920), in which the desire for an alliance between the family of Marozia and the imperial family is advanced as a political argument.

There is little information about the final years of John XI's papacy. Even the date of its end is approximate, and it is not certain where he is buried.

Harald Zimmermann

Bibliography

Duchesne, L. "Serge III et Jean XI", *MAH*, 33 (1913), 42–64.

Schieffer, R. "Johannes XI," *LexMA*, 5 (1990), 541.

Zimmermann, H. *Papstregesten*, 40–46; *Das dunkle Jahrhundert*, Graz, 1971, 77 sq; *Papsturkunden*, 105–15.

JOHN XII. *Octavian (b. Rome, 937, d. in the Roman countryside, 14 May 964). Elected pope 16 December 955. Deposed 4 December 963. May be buried at St. John Lateran.*

John XII was the son of Alberic II of Spoleto, lord of Rome. At the end of August 954, Alberic, on his deathbed, made the Roman nobility promise to elect his son Octavian as pope after the death of AGAPITUS II (which occurred in December 955). Such an oath was against all canonical norms. It is not known whether Octavian was the required canonical age at the time of his election, or even if he had already received religious training. He changed his name to John XII, the beginning of the medieval practice according to which a pope took a new name.

John XII represented in one person both the temporal power and the spiritual authority over Rome. Morally dissolute, he nevertheless carried on with the measures of religious reform his father had supported, for instance at Farfa and at Subiaco. When he came into conflict with King Berengar II of Italy and his son Adalbert, he asked King Otto I of Germany for help, and crowned him emperor in 962. From then on, imperial dignity was linked to the German crown. Unlike his father, Alberic, John developed a policy of wide-ranging territorial expansion; nevertheless, his offensive against Capua was repelled in 959.

At the same time, King Berengar II was threatening the Papal States. Forced by these circumstances, and probably by a Roman opposition group, in the fall of 960 John had to appeal to Otto for help, as popes Stephen II and Leo III had gone in their time to the king of the FRANKS. The papal legates, however, were not content merely to transmit the pope's message; they also expressed their disapproval of his morals and his administration. In August 961, Otto I set out on a second expedition into Italy; since Berengar had withdrawn into remote strongholds, Otto was able to advance as far as Pavia. On 2 February 962, he made his entry into Rome after having sworn to protect the pope; on the same day at St. Peter's, John crowned him emperor, with his wife Adelaide. After difficult negotiations, during which the DONATION OF CONSTANTINE was probably displayed, Otto on 13 February 962 gave the pope the so-called *Privilegium Ottonianum*. In this, he was following the examples of kings and emperors who had preceded him, particularly the "Donation of Pepin." The *Ottonianum*, of which a copy is preserved in the Vatican ARCHIVES, confirms the rights of the Papal States while stipulating that the freely elected pope must, before his consecration, take an oath of loyalty in the presence of imperial delegates. The day before, John XII had, among other things, agreed to found the archdiocese of Magdeburg as a missionary center for the Slavic countries, a project that during AGAPITUS II's time had met strong opposition from Archbishop William of Mayence.

The intervention of Otto into Italian affairs limited the political possibilities for John. Therefore, as soon as the emperor had left Rome to fight against Berengar II, the pope made alliances with Adalbert, the son of Berengar, and with BYZANTIUM. This caused Otto to return to Rome, and John had to flee. He was summoned several times to appear; during a SYNOD called by the emperor, John was declared guilty of apostasy and of violating the residency requirement, and he was deposed on 4 December 963. In his place, the chief notary (*protoscriniarus*) Leo, a lay person, was elected; he took the name LEO VIII. Otto had already modified the *Privilegium Ottonianum*: in the future, the consent of the emperor was to be the necessary condition for any papal election.

After the departure of Otto from Rome, however, John was able to retake the city. In February 964, a council, over which he presided at ST. PETER's declared the imperial synod unlawful and deposed and excommunicated Leo VIII. In Rome, John was unforgiving with the supporters of Otto and Leo. However, obviously fearing a new imperial punishment, John did not delay in making friendly overtures to the emperor. But struck down by apoplexy on 7 May 964—allegedly in the act of committing adultery—he died on 14 May 964.

Rolf Grosse

Bibliography

LP, 2, 246–249.

Chraska, W. Johannes XII. *Eine Studie zu einem problematischen Pontifikat*, Aalen, 1973.

Hehl, E. D. "Der wohlberatene Papst. Die römische Synode Johannes XII. vom Februar 964," *Ex ipsis rerum documentis. Beiträge zur Mediävalistik: Festschrift für H. Zimmermann zum 65. Geburtstag*, ed. K. Herbers, H. H. Kortum, C. Servatius, Sigmaringen, 1991, 257–75.

Schieffer, R. "Johannes XII," *LexMA*, 5, (1991), 541 sqq.

Ullman, W. "The Origin of *Ottonianum*," *Cambridge Historical Journal* 11 (1953–5), 114–28.

Wolter, H. *Die Synoden im Reichsgebiet und in Reichsitalien von 916 bis 1056*, Paderborn, Munich, Vienna, and Zurich, 1988, 69 ff.

Zimmermann, H. *Papstregesten*, 98–139; *Papsturkunden*, 1, 249–93; "Partieungen und Papstwahlen in Rom zur Zeit Kaiser Ottos des Großen; *Römische historische Mitteilungen*, 8–9 (1964–6), 29 (reprinted as *Otto der Große*, Darmstadt, 1967, 325); *Papstabsetzungen des Mittelalters*, Graz, Vienna, and Cologne, 1968, 77–92, 235 ff., 252–72. *Das dunkle Jahrhundert*, Graz, and Cologne- Vienna, 1971.

John XIII. (*b. Rome,?, d. Rome, 6 September 972). Elected pope and installed 1 October 965. Buried at St. Paul's Outside the Walls.*

John XIII, son of a certain Bishop John, was bishop of Narni when he was elected as the successor to Leo VIII (d. March 965), after a vacancy of six months. Barely ten weeks later, he was overthrown by a revolt in Rome and banished, but he was able to escape and to retake the city. The remainder of his pontificate passed without incident, in accord with Emperor Otto the Great, though the pope was able to preserve his autonomy from the emperor.

After the death of Leo VIII, Otto the Great, undoubtedly at the request of a Roman legation, had sent the bishops Otger of Spire and Liutprand of Cremona to Rome for the election of the new pope. Apparently after difficult negotiations, Bishop John of Narni was elected and took the name John XIII in the presence of the imperial delegates. He was closely linked with the ruling Roman families, and his election must be viewed as a compromise between the Roman and imperial viewpoints. Though not a Crescentii, he favored their advancement. After receiving his training at the LATERAN palace, he had risen in Rome through all levels of the ecclesiastical hierarchy. Beginning in 961, he is mentioned as bishop of Narni; from 961 to 962 he simultaneously held the position of Roman librarian. He played an equivocal role during the conflict between Otto the Great and JOHN XII.

Just ten weeks after John XIII's election as pope, a riot broke out in Rome, led by the urban prefect Peter, Count Rofried of Campania, the *vestararius* Stephen, and some army commanders; this revolt was probably provoked by a faction hostile to the ruling Roman families and eager for greater power, a class to which Leo VIII also owed his rise. John was first imprisoned in CASTEL SANT' ANGELO, then banished in the Roman countryside. However, he escaped, gathered some troops, and sent a request for assistance to Otto the Great in Saxony. The emperor had only to show himself in Italy, and the Romans brought the pope back to Rome in November 966. After Otto made his entry into the city, the rioters were severely punished.

The rest of John's papacy was uneventful; he had a perfect understanding with the emperor, who remained in Italy from 966 to 972. Otto the Great and John XIII together presided over the synods of Rome and of Ravenna in 967. It was especially at Ravenna, where there was a very well attended assembly that important questions were discussed: the foundation of the archdiocese of Magdeburg and the restitution of the EXARCHATE of RAVENNA to the pope. In 962, John XII had already given his consent for Magdeburg to become a metropolitan see; on 20 April 967, John XIII prepared a document that made Magdeburg an archbishopric and gave it dominion over the dioceses of Brandenburg and Havelburg. In addition, the archbishop and his successors were allowed to ordain other bishops, principally at Merseburg, Zeitz, and Meissen. The foundation of the new metropolitan see would not become effective until 18 October 968, when John XIII named Abbot Adalbert of Wissemburg as the first archbishop of Magdeburg and gave him the *pallium*. At the same synod of Ravenna, Otto the Great restored the Exarchate of Ravenna to the pope, which he had already done in 962 in the *Privilegium Ottonianum*, though without completely renouncing his supremacy over it. From Ravenna, John XIII and Otto the Great invited Otto II, who was in Germany under the protection of Willigis of Mainz, to come to Rome; there, on Christmas Day 967 in ST. PETER's, he was crowned co-emperor by the pope, according to Carolingian custom. On 26 May 969, a Roman synod presided over by the pope made Benevento a metropolitan see; John XIII had already given the same rank to Capua in 966. This ecclesiastical reorganization of southern Italy created some tension in relations with the Byzantine Empire. In 971, the pope failed in an attempt to create a new archdiocese in Vich, Catalonia. A little before his death, the pope was participating in the conclusion of the a peace treaty and the recognition of the imperial dignity of Otto I by John, the Roman emperor of the East; on 14 April 972 in St. Peter's, John XIII united Otto II and the Byzantine princess Theophano in marriage and crowned her empress.

Rolf Grosse

Bibliography

LP, 2, 252–4.

Schieffer, R. "Johannes XIII," *LexMA*, 5, (1991), 542.

Wolter, H. *Die Synoden im Reichsgebiet und in Reichsitalien von 916 bis 1056*, Paderborn, Munich, Vienna, and Zurich, 1988, 88 ff.

Zimmermann, H. *Papstregesten*, 152–203; *Papsturkunden*, I, 333–433; "Parteiungen und Papstwahlen in Rom zur Zeit Kaiser Ottos des Großen," *Römische historische Mitteilungen*, 8–9 (1964–6), 66–81, 87 (reprinted as *Otto der Große*, Darmstadt, 1967, 381–403, 414); *Das dunkle Jahrhundert*, Graz, Cologne, and Vienna, 1971, 153 ff.

JOHN XIV. *Peter (d. 20 August 984). Elected pope in September 983. Buried at St. Peter's in Rome.*

John XIV owed his ascent to St. Peter's throne to imperial nomination alone: no contemporary source suggests that Emperor Otto II even tried to have his choice ("election" in the etymological sense) ratified by the clergy and the Roman people. After the death of Benedict VII (July 983), Otto II first chose the prestigious abbot of Cluny, Maiolus, but he refused the pontificate. The emperor then chose Peter, bishop of Pavia since 971, and his arch-chancellor for the kingdom of Italy since the end of 980. Faithful to Otto II, with judiciary powers such as *missus sacri palatii* (legate of the sacred palace, 981–3), Peter seems to have accompanied his sovereign on his expedition to southern Italy. Once he was "elected" pope, Peter took the name John rather than keep the name of the Prince of the Apostles.

The new pope was too attached to the emperor not to suffer after the death of the latter (7 December 983). The antipope BONIFACE VII, probably supported by a large part of the forces prevailing in the city of Rome, was able to seize power again and capture John XIV in April 984. John was imprisoned in CASTEL SANT'ANGELO and soon died there of starvation. Because of the brevity and weakness of his reign, very few documents bear his name.

Hans-Henning Körtum

Bibliography

LP, 2, 259.

Pauler, R. *Das* Regnum Italiae *in ottonischer Zeit*, Tübingen, 1982, 118–20.

Schieffer, R. "Johannes XIV.," *LexMA*, 5 (1990), 542.

Zimmermann, H. *Das dunkle Jahrhundert*, Graz, Cologne, and Vienna, 1971.

Zimmermann, H. *Papstregesten*, 250–5; *Papsturkunden*, I, 549–53.

JOHN XV. *(d. March 996). Elected pope in August 985.*

Unlike his predecessor, John XIV, who was installed by imperial will alone, Pope John XV owed his election in large part to the Roman aristocracy and to the party of John Crescentius, who had supported the antipope BONIFACE VIII until his death. John XV was the son of a priest, originally from the fourth region of Rome (Gallina Alba), and a former cardinal-priest of San Vitale. He at first looked indebted to the Crescentii, nobles of the city and true masters of a papal state in development (John, and then Crescentius II Nomentanus). The empress mother Theophano, wishing to preserve the rights of her young son Otto III in Germany, could only endorse this state of affairs during the course of a stay in Rome (990).

Nonetheless, the pope tried to disengage himself from the Crescenti's patronage. Driven out of Rome for a brief period (March 991), he looked for a counterbalance in active foreign politics. Ties with the German regents Theophano and later Adelaide, and with Otto III, were an essential element of his policy. This was undoubtedly why he canonized Bishop Ulrich of Augsburg, a model Ottonian prelate (993).

The pope was able to impose his mediation in a conflict between the king of England, Ethelred II, and the duke of Normandy, Richard I (March 991), and also to take positions, as intransigent as they were ineffective, in the affair of Reims. In June 991, at the council of St. Basil of Verzy, the king of France, Hugh Capet, had urged the dismissal of Archbishop Arnoul of Reims and his replacement by Gerbert d'Aurillac, the future Pope Sylvester II. John XV refused to confirm the dismissal of Arnoul, and in 992, through his legate Leo, he called the French bishops to the synod of Aix-la-Chapelle, and then summoned the kings of France, Hugh and Robert, to Rome. The pope did not give in when faced by resistance from the episcopate and the royalty of France. Reinforced in his determination by a visit from Abbon, the abbot of Fleury (St.-Benoit-sur-Loire), during summer 994, he sent his legate Leo back to Otto III with the same goal: to summon the archbishops before a new synod, this time in Mouzon (June 995). They were once again notably absent, but Gerbert was dismissed.

John XV was no less active in eastern Europe. At the end of the year 988, he sent a delegation to Russia, where Prince Vladimir of Kiev had just converted upon sealing an alliance with the BYZANTINE Empire. It was probably in 992 that Mieszko of Poland gave his kingdom to the see of St. Peter in order to keep his distance from Germany. The pope also gave active support to the missionary activities of Adalbert of Prague in Bohemia.

The growing tension between the aristocracy and the Roman clergy may not have been the only reason for the increasing criticism of the authoritarianism of the pope. Abbon of Fleury himself testified that corruption then reigned in the CURIA. In March 995, John XV again had to leave Rome to take refuge in Sutri. An order from Otto III, now an adult, induced Crescentius to allow the pope to return to the LATERAN, but John was carried off by an illness before he was able to meet Otto, who had begun to march on Rome in February 996.

Hans-Henning Körtum

Bibliography

LP 2, 260.

Schieffer, R. "Johannes XV.," *LexMA*, 5 (1990–), 542.

Zimmermann, H. *Das dunkle Jahrhundert*, Graz, Cologne, and Vienna, 1971.

Zimmermann, H. *Papstregesten*, 256–96; *Papsturkunden*, I, 555–635.

[JOHN XVI]. *John Philagathos (d. 26 August 1001). Antipope from February 997 until May 998.*

John Philagathos was a Greek from Calabria, originally from Rossano. Nothing about his early career foretold that he would become antipope against GREGORY V. He owed his early promotions to the Ottonians, especially the wife of Otto II, the Byzantine Theophano. From February 980 to September 982 and again from April 991 to May/June 992, he was listed as the imperial chancellor for Italy. In 982, with the title of *archimandrita*, he received the rich abbey of Nonantola, near Modena, from Otto II. From 3 January 989, he was registered as the bishop of Piacenza, probably independent from the metropolitan see of RAVENNA. According to a later and very hostile mention in the *Honorantiae civitatis Papiae*, he was also in charge of imperial financial administration in Italy (*magistratus camere regis*). In 995–6, he was sent on a mission to Byzantium with Bishop Bernward of Wurzburg, to ask for a Greek princess as a bride for Otto III.

The German pope GREGORY V, installed by Otto III (May 996), not knowing either how to win over the Roman aristocracy led by Crescentius II Nomentanus or how to maintain good relations with the emperor, was soon expelled by the Romans when Otto III had to return to Germany. In February 997, when the pope was in northern Italy, Crescentius and his party proclaimed the throne of St. Peter to be vacant and elected as pope John Philagathos, who was in Rome; the election took place with the assent of Leo, an envoy from the Byzantine court. The scarcity of sources (no acts of John XVI were kept) makes it difficult to evaluate this event. It seems that Crescentius thought he could get Otto III on his side by naming John, and that the Byzantine court would be happy to see a Greek ruler in a Rome detached from the rest of Italy; the motivations of John, besides ambition, are unclear.

John was barely recognized except in Rome and its suburbs, and Otto III soon renewed his support for Gregory V, took away John's offices in northern Italy, and had him excommunicated. His fate was linked thenceforth with the possibility of a demonstration of imperial force in Rome. As soon as the arrival of Otto III and his troops was announced in December 997, John fled to Calabria. Rome was taken in February 998, and Gregory V was reinstalled. Captured, blinded, and mutilated, John was brought back to Rome and dragged through the streets, mounted backward on an ass. Solemnly judged and deposed in May 998, he was shut up in a Roman monastery, where he died several years later.

Hans-Henning Körtum

Bibliography

LP, 2, 261 ff.

Nitschke, A. "Der Miβhandelte Papst," *Staat und Gesellschaft im Mittelalter und früher Neuzeit: Gedenkschrift Joachim Leuschner*, Göttinger (1983), 40–53.

Pauler, R. *Das Regnum* Italiae *in ottonischer Zeit*, Tübingen, 1982, 83–8.

Zimmermann, H. "Johannes XVI.," *LexMA*, 5 (1990–), 542–3.

Zimmermann, H. *Papstregesten*, 313–35; *Papsturkunden*, I, 549–553.

JOHN XVII. *John Sicco (b. Rome, ?, d. 6 November 1003). Elected pope 16 May 1003. Believed to be interred in St. John Lateran.*

After the death of Silvester II on 12 May 1003, at the instigation of the Roman noble John II Crescentius, John Sicco was elected pope, taking the name John XVII. John Sicco came from the part of Rome called Biberatica; we know practically nothing about his family, except that his father was also named John. An epitaph dated

1040 names as members of his family Bishop John of Palestrina and the *secondicier* Andrew. It is believed that his family was close to the reigning Crescentii family, especially to the son Crescentius Nomentanus, overthrown and executed in 998, and to John II Crescentius, who had been in power in Rome since the death of Emperor Otto III.

Because of the brevity of John XVII's pontificate, only a few things are known about his activities. The privilege established for the monastery of San Giovanni di Marzona (diocese of tlhe Città di Castello) should be attributed not to this pope but to JOHN VIII, and it is doubtful that John XVII worked, as some have maintained, in favor of the collegiate church of Orvieto. It can only be confirmed that he supported the mission to the Polish people and the Christianization of the Slavs. Perhaps at the beginning of the year 1003, John XVII renewed the privilege of the mission to the Slavs during a meeting in Rome with the envoy of the missionary in Poland, Anthony, disciple of Bruno of Querfurt. This privilege had been given the previous spring by John's predecessor, Sylvester II. It has been speculated that the Polish ruler Boleslaw Chrobry used the envoy to persuade the pope to give him the royal crown, but the only source mentioning this possibility nullifies this hypothesis.

John XVII died on 6 November 1003. There are no reports about the precise circumstances of his death; one source mentions that the pope may have been poisoned, but this is not very credible.

Klaus-Jürgen Herrmann

Bibliography

JW 1, 501.
LP 2, 265.
Amann, E. "Jean XVII," *DTC*, 8-1 (1947), 629.
Gerstenberg, O. "Studien zur Geschichte des römischen Adels im Ausgang des 10. Jahrhunderts," *Hist. Vierteljahrschrift*, 31 (1937), 23.
Kölmel, W. *Rom und der Kirchenstaat im 10, und 11. Jahrhundert bis in die Anfänge der Reform*, Berlin, 1935, 43 f.
Poupardin, R. "Note sur la chronologie du pontificat de Jean XVII," *MAH* 21 (1901), 387–90.
Schieffer, R. "Johannes XVII.," *LexMA*, 5 (1990), 543.
Zimmermann, H. *Papstabsetzungen des Mittelalters*, Vienna, Cologne, and Graz, 1968, 114.
Zimmermann, H. *Papstregesten*, 975–9.

JOHN XVIII. *John Fasanus. (d. end of June 1009). Elected pope 25 December 1003. Buried at St. Paul's Outside the Walls.*

After the sudden death of his predecessor, JOHN XVII—probably owing to the support of John II Crescentius, a Roman noble—John Fasanus, a member of the Crescentii faction or even of the family, cardinal-priest of St. Peter's, was consecrated pope, taking the name John XVIII. Son of a priest, Ursus, and his wife, Stephanie, John was originally from Rome's Porta Metronia quarter.

During his entire pontificate, John XVIII tried stubbornly—but finally without success, as a result of the resistance put up by the nobility—to establish closer contacts with the German king Henry II. Shortly after his consecration, he sent Leo, bishop and Roman librarian, to the king's court to begin negotiations concerning, among other things, the reestablishment of the bishopric at Merseburg, which had been suppressed by Benedict VII in 981. In March 1004, the pope received the king's delegation in Rome and confirmed the reestablishment of the see of Merseburg. In June 1007, envoys of the king again stayed in Rome and informed the pope of the foundation and endowment of the new bishopric of Bamberg by the king. After a synod at St. Peter's, the pope took the see under his personal protection. After that, the John was careful to maintain good relations with the court and episcopate of Germany: at the beginning of the year 1008, to please the king, he ordained one of Henry II's supporters as the new bishop of Asti after his predecessor in this post—apparently a partisan of Arduin, king of Italy—had been removed by Henry. Then, in October 1008, he gave the *pallium* to Archbishop Megingaud of Trevi.

The pope displayed particular energy in French ecclesiastical affairs, and several privileges in particular show his determination to reinforce monastic institutions. The monastery of Saint-Maur-des-Fossés (diocese of Paris) obtained the right to elect freely its own abbot, as did that of Saint-Victor of Marseille, which also received EXEMPTION. The monastery of Villeneuve-lés-Avignon was placed under papal protection. In addition, confirmations of property were sent for the monastery of Saint-Florent-lés-Saumur, for Psalmodi, a reestablished monastery (diocese of Nimes), for the cathedral of Angers, for Arles, and for the church in Toulouse. The reforming abbey of Fleury provoked the most forceful action of John XVIII. At the end of the year 1007, the pope learned from his legate in France, Peter of Piperno, that, in a synod held at Orleans at the end of autumn, some of the French episcopate, including Archbishop Lietry of Sens and Bishop Foulque of Orleans, were contesting the power of the pope and had even tried publicly to abolish a pontifical privilege established for the abbey of Fleury, by John's predecessor Gregory V. In a mandate addressed to King Robert II of France in scorching terms, John XVIII threatened to declare his kingdom ANATHEMA if the French did not respect the acts of the pope. He summoned Archibishop Lietry, Bishop Foulque, and Abbot Gauzlin to Rome to him for the next celebration of Easter in 1008. Probably, in the context of the same trip, the papal legate gave the king of France another papal mandate to stop all violent attacks against the Jews in France.

At the end of May 1004, John XVIII showed Rome the attention he was paying to missionary work. At the request of Anthony, a missionary to the Slavs who was in Rome, he canonized the brothers Benedict, John, Isaac, Matthias, and Christian, who had all been assassinated in November 1003 while preaching in Poland with the support of John XVIII's predecessor. During his entire papacy, he had an ambivalent relationship with John II Crescentius. The intensive contacts with the court of the king of Germany and their implications for internal Roman politics forcefully provoked the overthrow or deposition of John XVIII, who died as a monk in the Roman monastery of ST. PAUL'S OUTSIDE THE WALLS at the end of July 1009.

Klaus-Jürgen Herrmann

Bibliography

JW 1, 501–3.

LP, 2, 266.

Amann, E. "Jean XVIII," *DTC* (1947), 629–30.

Colini, A. M. "L'epitaffio del fratello di Giovanni XVIII," *ASR*, 99 (1976), 333–5.

Schieffer, R. "Johannes XVIII.," *LexMA*, 5 (1990), 543.

Wolter, H. *Die Synoden in Reichsgebiet von 916 vis 1056*, Paderborn, 1988, 235 f.

Wimmermann, H. *Papstabsetzungen des Mittelalters*, Cologne, Vienna and Graz, 1968, 114.

Zimmermann, H. *Papstregesten*, 980–1035; *Papsturkunden*, 24, 408–42.

JOHN XIX. *Roman of Tusculum (d. 20 October 1032). Elected pope on or before 19 April 1024.*

When BENEDICT VIII died on 9 April 1024, the Tusculani faction encountered no resistance to having his brother Roman elected under the name John XIX. The new pope, third son of Gregory of Tusculum and his wife Mary, was still a layman when elected; during the pontificate of his brother Benedict, he had had judicial powers, as a senator, in the PAPAL STATE. John XIX tried to bring peace to the papacy's relations with the Roman clan of the Crescentii, leaving them in leadership posts in the Papal State and even offering offices to them. His older brother Alberic III—who until then had held, as consul and dues, the judicial powers of the urban prefect—took a post at the papal COURT.

In the wake of the German policies of his brother Benedict, John XIX also tried to seek a cooperative relationship with the new king of Germany, Conrad II (1024–39), but Conrad considered the pope only as a puppet to do his bidding. Having been crowned emperor with all due solemnities on 26 March 1027, Conrad

forced the pope, at a SYNOD held at the LATERAN on 6 April 1027, to rescind a decision made before December 1024, that had given autonomy to the patriarchate of Grado; John was now required not to give the patriarchate to anyone except Poppo of Aquileia, a supporter of Conrad, and to put Grado under his control. For this obliging gesture, Conrad granted not a single privilege to the Roman church. The emperor dragged the pope deeper into his own schemes when John XIX consented to the transfer of the see of Zeitz to Naumburg, and even suffered silently an affront done to him by Bishop Warmann of Constance, who, with Conrad's support, publicly burned a privilege that he did not like, which the pope was sending to Abbot Bernon of Reichenau. The "German trauma" of John XIX also marked his relationships with most of the German archbishops: in January 1032, Archbishop Bardo of Mainz easily regained the *pallium* that BENEDICT VIII had taken away from his predecessor; relationships with archbishops Pilgrim of Cologne and Poppe of Trevi, were infrequent, with no evidence of closer ties.

While John XIX demonstrated great cooperativeness with German interests, he also showed himself to be open to reforming ambitions, especially in France. The relationship of the pope with Abbot Odilo of Cluny, in particular, led not only to the formulation of the rights of abbeys associated with Cluny, but also that of the rights of the Holy See: Bishop Gauzlin of Mâcon and a faction incited by other bishops attacked the fullest privilege of EXEMPTION established by John XIX in 1024 for the monastery of Cluny. During a synod that met at Anzio, they went so far as to question the right of the pope to decide such matters. John XIX reacted strongly to these attacks: on 28 March 1027, in the presence of Conrad II, he renewed all the privileges his predecessors had given this reforming monastery and also renewed its plenary exemption. In a private letter addressed to King Robert II of France (988–1031), the pope expressed his unhappiness with the opposition led by the bishops and recommended the monastery to him for special protection, while threatening Bishop Gauzlin with excommunication. Other than this, John XIX's lack of interest in questions that concerned only the French episcopate was striking: he dealt with them only in the context of monastic affairs. The claim that John XIX recognized the apostolicity of St. Martial in favor of the monastery of Saint-Martial in Limoges has recently been questioned.

Another famous reforming abbot, William of Saint-Bénigne of Dijon, met with the pope and asked him to give his protection to the monastery at Frutuaria, which William had founded; the second Tusculani pope also energetically supported Tuscan reform. On the other hand, one cannot say that John had a clearly defined plan for reform of existing MONASTICISM.

In southern Italy, John XIX did not continue the confrontational policy with Byzantium of Benedict VIII, but tried rather to achieve, through negotiations, an amicable agreement. According to the records of Raoul Glaber, in 1024 Byzantium had suggested to the pope that they separate their respective spheres of interest and recognize the Roman Church of the East as supreme in its domain. It seems that only a storm of protest was able to restrain John XIX from approving this plan. The important thing is that the pope was able to achieve a balance of power with Byzantium regarding the ecclesiastical administration of southern Italy; having given up direct supervision of the Catepanate, the pope seems to have received the promise that he could develop a zone of obedience where the local Greek administration—as well as the stubbornness of Benedict VIII—had previously made that impossibile. This resulted in the most lasting effect of John XIX's actions as pope: his diplomacy greatly increased the influence of the Roman Church in the southern parts of Italy.

At the imperial coronation of Conrad II in March 1027, the pope met Canute, king of England (1016–1035) and of Denmark (beginning in 1018); on this occasion, John XIX renounced the payment of money linked to the receipt of the *pallium* and also suspended the fees which were burdening the English *schola* of Rome. In gratitude, Canute granted the pope a regular payment known as Peter's pence.

Klaus-Jürgen Herrmann

Bibliography

JW, 1, 514–19; 2, 709–48.

LP, 2, 269.

Cowdrey, H. E. J. *The Cluniacs and the Gregorian Reform*, Oxford, 1970.

Herrmann, K. J. *Das Tuskulanerpapsttum* 1012–46, Stuttgart, 1973.

Lemarignier, J. F. *L'Exemption monastique et les origines de la réform grégorienne*, Dijon, 1950, 288–334, esp. 327.

Michel, A. "Die Weltreichs- und Kirchenteilung bei Rudolf Glaber," *Historisches Jahrbuch*, 70 (1951), 53–64.

Santifaller, L. "Chronologisches Verzeichnis der Urkunden Papst Johannes XIX.," *Römische Historische Mitteilungen*, 1 (1958), 35–73.

Schieffer, R. "Johannes XIX.," *LexMA*, 5 (1990), 543.

Wolter, H. *Die Synoden im Reichsgebiet und in Reichsitalien von 916–1056*, Paderborn, 1988, 325 f.

Zimmermann, H. *Papsturkunden*, 2, 550–97.

JOHN XX. Through an ONOMASTIC (enumeration) mistake, the name John XX was never taken by any pope. This may be explained by a confusion of the papal lists at the naming of John XXI, elected in 1276; there had been at least eleven popes and an antipope named John elected between 872 and 1024, often for very short terms (John VIII–John XIX), and among them were five elected between 983 and 1003 (John XIV–John XVIII).

Olivier Guyotjeannin

JOHN XXI. *Pedro Julião, surname Hispanus, or Hispanus Portugalensis (b. Lisbon, 1210–1215, d. Viterbo, 20 May 1277). Elected pope 8 September 1276. Crowned 15 September 1276. Buried at the cathedral of Viterbo.*

Petrus Hispanus, son of a doctor Julião (not to be confused with the Bolognese decretalist of the same name from the end of the 12th–early 13th century) is called *clericus universalis* by Ptolemy of Luxor and *magnus sophysta, logicus, disputator atque theologus* by Salimbene of Adam. In him, one of the principal scholastic philosophers of the 13th century ascended St. Peter's throne; his scientific activity also extends into the domains of medicine, mathematics, and theology. After having received his initial education at the cathedral schools in Lisbon and León, he studied philosophy and medicine in Paris, where he had Albert the Great, Lambert of Auxerre, and probably also William of Sherwood as teachers. Named *de Montibus*, he obtained the rank of *magister*, and undertook his first teaching in the faculty of arts. After possibly studying at Montpellier and at Salerno, he returned to finish his studies at the University of Siena, where he gave classes in medicine beginning in 1245. His path then led him to the court of Emperor Frederick II, where he studied physics with the emperor's doctor, Theodore, and finally to the papal CURIA. Doctor to a series of cardinals—among them Ottobone Fieschi (the future HADRIAN V), and the personal physician of GREGORY X, he quickly established himself there, thus accelerating his ecclesiastical career considerably. He is listed as the dean of the church in Lisbon, then as archdeacon of Braga and the archdeaconry of Vermuy, and as prior in the church of Santa Maria de Guimarães. In 1272, he was elected archbishop of Braga, but this appointment never received the necessary papal confirmation. On 3 June 1273, Gregory X named him cardinal bishop of Tusculum, which permitted him to assume a position on the Curia and to be chosen as the new pope by the CONCLAVE of 1276, owing to the support of Cardinal Giovanni Gaetano Orsini, the future NICHOLAS III.

During his very brief pontificate, John XXI soon after his election rescinded the constitution *Ubi periculum* by which Gregory X had set rules for holding a conclave. He attempted to interfere in the dispute between France and Spain over Navarre, and he tried, based on his experience acquired at the second COUNCIL of Lyon, to further a reunion with the Greek Church. His main accomplishment, however, was the mission given to Stephen Tempier to undertake a thorough investigation of errors whose origin was supposedly the teachings of the University of Paris, and to report his findings. Animated by religious zeal and influenced by conservative circles, Tempier brought together a commission of theologians without having previously informed the Holy See. Beginning on 7 March 1277, they condemned 219 theses, some going as far back as the philosophers Aristotle, Avicenna, Averroes, and Boethius; others were supposed to be about immoral writings, or to concern magic and sorcery. As a result, the investigation attained an importance far greater than the pope had originally intended. Siger of Brabant had already left Paris, but the censorship—which initially attacked, the radical Aristotelianism of the faculty of arts of Paris—immediately touched not only conservative theologians such as Giles of Rome, but also the philosophy of St. Thomas Aquinas, so that Albert the Great felt compelled to make a trip from Cologne to Paris to defend his former student. John XXI himself felt obliged, at the end of April, to ask Stephen Tempier to extend his investigation to the faculty of theology. Only the pope's sudden death, caused by the collapse of the ceiling of his study at VITERBO, brought some'calm, owing to the vacancy of the apostolic see and the weakening of possible actions by the Curia.

The principal philosophical treatise authored by John XXI is found in *Summulae logicales*, which would become the main text on logic for the Middle Ages, as well as a first attempt at systematizing classical logic; it earned him the title of *Summulistarum princeps*. He was also a distinguished commentator on the treatises of Aristotle, especially *De animalibus* and *De anima* (whose authenticity has been questioned), which he read in the Augustinian tradition; he revised their interpretation based on his knowledge of the Arab commentators Averroes, Avicenna, Al-Gazali, and Avencebrol. Though he is not numbered among the foremost scholastics, his notion of "concept" (*terminus*) prepared the way for the future nominalism. He represents the *summus medicorum monarcha* of the Middle Ages, but his plan to integrate medicine into a scholastic survey between logic and natural philosophy remained unfinished. His most popular work, and the one that survives in the most manuscripts, is the *Thesaurus pauperum*, a compilation of medical recipes that some manuscripts call the *Summa experimentorum medicinalis*. His attitude toward medicine is dominated by his concept of *Christus medicus*, Christ as the supreme doctor, since all cures come from God as "father of the poor" (*pater pauperum*) and from Creation.

Ludwig Vones

Bibliography

LP, 2, 457–58.

Poth., 21150–249.

Brasao, E. "Oünico papa português: João XXI," *Anais da Academia Portuguesa da História*, II, s. 26 (1980), 381–404.

Da Cruz Pontes, J. M. "À propos d'un centenaire: Une nouvelle monographie sur Petrus Hispanus Portugalensis, le pape Jean XXI (m. 1277), est-elle nécessaire?" *Recherches de théologie ancienne et médiévale*, 44 (1977), 220–30.

De Rijk, L. M. "On the Life of Peter of Spain, the author of the Tractatus, called afterwards Summulae logicales," *Vivarium*, 8 (1970), 123–54.

Exposiño sobre os libros de Beato Dionisio Areopagita, ed. Alonso Alonso, Lisbon, 1957.

Grabmann, M. "Handschriftliche Forschungen und Funde zu de philosophischen Schriften des Petrus Hispanus, des späteren Papstes Johannes XXI. (gestorben 1277)," Munich, 1933 (*Sitzungsberichte der Bayerischen Akademie der Wissenschaften, Phil.-Hist. Abteilung*, 9).

Le Registre de Jean XXI (1276–1277), ed. L. Cadier, Paris, 1898.

Lohr, C. H. *Commentateurs d'Aristote au Moyen Âge latin: Bibliographie de la littérature secondaire récente*, Fribourg-Paris, 1988 (Vestigia, 2), 200–3.

Moreira De Sa, A. "Pedro Hispano, Prior da Igreja de Santa Maria de Guimarães e Arcebispo da Sé de Braga," *Biblos*, 30 (1954), 1–24.

Obras filisóficas, ed. M. Alonso Alonse, 3 vols., 2nd ed., Barcelona, 1961.

Roberg, B. "Johannes XXI.," *LexMA*, 5 (1990), 544.

Schipperges, H. "Grundzüge einer Scholastischen Anthropologie bei Petrus Hispanus," *Portugiesische Forschungen der Görresgesellschaft*, 7 (1967), 1–51.

Stapper, R. *Papst Johannes XXI, Eine Monographie*, Münster, 1898.

Summulae logicales, ed. O. N. De Rijk, 1972.

Tractatus syncategorematum and Selected Anonymous Treatises by Peter of Spain, ed. and trans. by J. P. Mullally and R. Houde, Milwaukee, 1964.

Wach, M. F. "The Measure of Pleasure: Peter of Spain on Men, Women, and Lovesickness," *Viator*, 17 (1986), 173–96.

JOHN XXII. *Jacques Duèse (b. Cahors, 1244?, d. Avignon, 4 December 1334). Elected pope August 7, 1316. Crowned on 5 September 1316. Buried at the cathedral of Notre-Dame-des-Doms in Avignon.*

Jacques Duèse was born in Cahors, in a well-to-do middle class family. Destined for the clergy, he studied law, receiving a doctorate *utriusque iuris*, which took him from Cahors to Montpellier and Orleans. He also enrolled in the faculty of theology at Paris but did not graduate. He then taught, probably in Toulouse, while accumulating benefices: archpriest of Cahors, canon of Saint-Front de Périgueux, archpriest of Sarlat, dean of Puy. He obtained the favor of the king of Naples, Charles II of Anjou, whose cleric and intimate he was before

1298, and must have been part of the entourage of St. Louis of Anjou—whom he would later canonize—during the several months that the young archbishop of Toulouse spent in his diocese (1297). Elected bishop of Fréjus in 1300, he was called by Charles II to be chancellor of the kingdom of Sicily in 1308 and continued to fulfill this appointment after the death of Charles and the accession of his son, Robert (5 May 1309). Clement V then transferred him to the see of Avignon, the city where the pope then lived (18 March 1310). The pontiff used him for missions relating to the trial of BONIFACE VIII, and then to the COUNCIL of Vienne, where this jurist played an essential role behind the scenes. Created cardinal with the TITLE of Saint-Vital in December 1312, he was promoted bishop of Porto in April 1313.

CLEMENT V died on 20 April 1314 at Roquemaure, and the CONCLAVE should have taken place in the manner prescribed by the late pontiff (constitution *Ne Romani*, 1312) and by GREGORY X (*Ubi periculum*, 1274): the cardinals were to meet in the diocese where the CURIA resided (more precisely, where the letters and apostolic causes where heard). If the cardinals disagreed and left the conclave, individually or together, the public powers (magistrates of the city, according to the constitution of Gregory X, or even the princes, according to the interpretation of John Andrew) had the right to require them to go back to their deliberations.

The cardinals, 23 in number (the 24th, Luca Fieschi, was then in Italy), met toward the first of May in the episcopal palace of Carpentras, where the Curia met. Three factions immediately formed: a Gascon faction that gathered ten cardinals around Arnaud de Pellegrue, all of whom had been created by Clement V and supported by his nephews, the viscount of Lomagne, Bertrand de Got, and Raimond Guilhem de Budos; an Italian faction strongly opposed to the former, but whose seven members, distrusted one another; and a French faction which included, in a group with little unity, three southerners from Languedoc, a Quercy native (Jacques Huèse), and two Normans. The first candidacy, that of an eminent jurist, the Languedocian William of Mandagout, presented by the Italians, failed because of the opposition of the Gascons and the personal ambition of another Languedocian, Berenger Fredol L'Ancien. The conclave quickly found itself at an impasse, each member stubbornly refusing to compromise.

Serious trouble then broke out in the town between the servants of the Italian cardinals and those of the Gascons; bands of mercenary soldiers paid by the nephews of the dead cardinal soon aggravated the violence. The conclave found itself besieged, and the Italian cardinals, directly under fire, were saved only by their flight from the episcopal palace (24 July 1314). The entire SACRED COLLEGE scattered "like terrified partridges" (as noted by Guillaume de Naugis) to Avignon, Orange, or Valence.

The Church was in danger of SCHISM, since the Gascon faction was ready to hold an election without the other cardinals. To force the conclave to return required admonitions from the Christian princes, especially Philip the Fair. He gathered groups of jurists and maintained a firm attitude toward the cardinals, but he died during these proceedings (24 November 1314). His son, Louis X, continued his father's policies, sending a mission that succeeded in driving away Clement V's nephews and working to convince the cardinals to meet again in Lyon. In spring 1316, the brother of the king, the count of Poitiers, sent in turn, succeeded in doing so. The situation fell apart again, however, when the king died suddenly. The count of Poitiers, whose own interests were calling him back to Paris, decided to force the issue: he locked the cardinals in the Dominican convent of Lyon and departed, leaving the count of Forez to maintain order and guard the conclave (28 June 1316).

A first candidate, Arnaud Fournier, a moderate Gascon, was turned down by the count of Forez, who had received precise instructions. The nominations of Arnaud de Pellegrue (Gascon) and Guillaume de Mandagout were maintained, while that of Berenger Fredol had several supporters. Again, as at Carpentras, there was an impasse. Then a compromise candidate, Jacques Duèse, was proposed and elected on 7 August 1316, after a vacancy of more than 27 months. The compromise had been developed by some of the Italians, worried about the machinations of the Colonnas and by the Gascons; the new candidate had the support of the count of Poitiers and of King Robert of Naples. The election was unanimous: the last dissenting members, making the best of a bad thing, rallied in favor of the candidate who appeared likely to be a transitional pope, considering his age (72, or perhaps a bit less). Jacques Duèse took the name John XXII and, by 9 August, announced the reopening of the hearing of contested cases for 1 October at AVIGNON. The papacy was settling rather permanently on the banks of the Rhone River.

Experienced in civil and ecclesiastical matters, the new pontiff was a man of lively intelligence, very active despite his age. His vehement, quick-tempered personality sometimes led him to be unjust, but people praised his pure morals, his simple lifestyle, and his sincere piety. He fought against SIMONY, but succumbed to the temptation of NEPOTISM. His many nephews and their allies took important places in the pontifical court. It is true that he needed trustworthy men in his entourage, because his election had not pleased everyone, and, in the beginning of his papacy, he had to thwart several plots against him. The most famous was instigated by the bishop of Cahors, Hugh Geraud, who was condemned, and burned at the stake for having tried to use the weapons of poison and magic against the pope (September 1317).

The accomplishments of John XXII concerning the inner government of the church took place on several levels. In legislative matters, he promulgated the DECRETALS of his predecessor, Clement V (the *Clementines*), most of which had been taken at the council of Vienne. He himself wrote a certain number of texts that were later gathered, into two collections, the *Extravagantes communes* and *Extravagantes Johannis XXII*, to become part of the *Corpus iuris canonici*.

The pope busied himself in trimming dioceses that had grown too large to be conveniently managed by their bishops. Thus, in 1317–1318, he split up the huge diocese of Toulouse, from which Boniface VIII had already removed the diocese of Pamiers, creating the new diocesan divisions of Lavaur, Lombez, Mirepoix, Montauban, Rieux, and Saint-Papoul, for which Toulouse was metropolis. In the same way, Alet and Saint-Pons of Thomières were detached from Narbonne, Vabres from Rodez, Castres from Albi, Condom from Agen, Sarlat from Périgueux, Luçon and Maillezais from Poitiers, Tulle from Limoges, and Saint-Flour from Clermont.

In other ways, John XXII continued and emphasized the centralist policy of his predecessors, aiming to control—especially as a fiscal goal—the nominations to ecclesiastical benefices. In the beginning of his pontificate, the BULL *Ex debito* (15 September 1316) unified and prolonged the existing legislation on this matter. From then on, all major or minor benefices, that had become vacant—by death *apud Sedem Apostolicam* (an expression already extended to an area comprising anything within two days' walking distance of the pope's residence), by deposition or forfeiture, by renunciation into the hands of the pope, by transfer to another benefice enacted by the pope, by rejection of postulancy or of election, or by the acceptance of other benefices conferred by the pope in the form of a provision or of expectative—were reserved exclusively for pontifical conferral. The number of benefices thus put at the disposition of the pope was greatly increased when, by the bull *Exsecrabilis* (19 November 1317), the accumulation of more than one benefice *cum cura animarum* and a benefice *sine cura* was basically forbidden: the clerics then had to resign from benefices exceeding that number, which then went to papal advowson. In addition, all the advowsons and the accumulations of benefices were the occasion for lucrative taxes: unfilled common and small services, ANNATES, and so forth. Thus, the papal treasury experienced healthy growth under John XXII's pontificate and rigorous administration.

As soon as he took St. Peter's throne, John XXII found himself faced with the longstanding problem in the Franciscan order posed by the coexistence of a majority (the "community") satisfied with an ideal of poverty mitigated by the legal fiction of ownership exercised by the Holy See on property put at the disposition of the brothers, and by recognition of a *usus facti* (as separate from a *usus iuris*) authorized on worldly goods, and of the "spirituals," led by Angelo Clareno and Ubertino of Casale, who claimed they must live like St. Francis himself, in complete destitution. Appeased at the end of Clement V's pontificate by measures that reassured the spirituals but maintained the unity of the order, the conflict was reborn during the long simultaneous vacancy of the Holy See and of the office of minister general of the Friars Minor, to which Michael of Cesena, a member of the community very hostile to the centralizing tendencies of on the spirituals, was finally elected 29 May 1316. At Michael's request, the pope called the spirituals to Avignon. They unwisely chose Bernard Delicieux to defend them; Bernard was well known at the papal court for the revolts he had provoked against the INQUISTION. John XXII reacted strongly: Bernard and his companions were put in prison, Angelo Clareno and Ubertino de Casale were dismissed from the Franciscan order (the former joined the Celestines, and the latter, given an office in the Benedictine monastery of Gembloux, nevertheless stayed at the Curia in the *familia* of Cardinal Napoleon Orsini) and stubborn resisters were burned at the stake. The bull *Sancta Romana* (30 December 1317) condemned the spirituals and those who held similar views (called *fraticelli*—the first appearance of the word—beguines, *bizoques*, etc.). The bull *Quorumdam exigit* (7 October 1317) laid out a hierarchy of the three religious virtues, placing obedience at the top, before chastity, and poverty.

The conflict surfaced again in 1321, but this time the areas of the split were different. The occasion was a preacher from Narbonne who claimed, among other things, that Christ and his apostles had not owned any property, either privately or as a group. Pursued by the inquisitor, he was assisted by the lector of the convent of Narbonne, and the case was sent to the court at Avignon. A great theoretical debate took place on the poverty of Christ; the stakes were the state of ecclesiastical property in relation to Christian perfection. Unanimously, the Franciscans consulted by the pope or gathered at the general chapter meeting in Perogia (June 1322) insisted on the absolute poverty of Christ, whereas all the other pontifical advisers, theologians, or prelates were inclined to consider heretical the proposal that Jesus and his apostles had no possessions. After consultation and reflection, the pope cut short the doctrinal debate and listed the legal consequences. On the theoretical level, they were addressed in the document *Cum inter nonnullos* of 12 November 1323, declaring the proposal to be heresy; as a canonical matter, by 8 December 1322, the decretal *Ad conditorem canonum* restored to the Franciscan brotherhood the properties that the Holy See had held in its name until this time. This drastic change in the concept of poverty that was the foundation of Franciscan life was badly received by the brothers, and groups of rebellious *fraticelli* developed in various locations, notably in Italy. Even more serious, the minister general Michael of Cesena, the former critic of the spirituals, was now preaching resistance; called to Avignon, he fled away in May 1328, accompanied by the former bursar of the order, Bonagrazia of Bergamo, and the theologian William of Ockham, to seek shelter at the court of Louis of Bavaria and rejoin the antipope NICHOLAS V. The majority of the order, nevertheless, remained faithful to John XXII, but it took some time for the last of the little clusters of *fraticelli* to disappear.

The Franciscan problem was compounded by the Italo-Germanic problem. When Emperor Henry VII died (1313), the electors of the HOLY ROMAN EMPIRE were divided, and a double election took place; the duke of Bavaria, Louis, had himself crowned at Aix-la-Chapelle (Aachen), while Duke Frederick of Austria was enthroned in Bonn. The war between these two competitors ended in favor of Louis of Bavaria, winner of the battle of Mühldorf (28 September 1322), in the course of which Frederick was taken prisoner.

John XXII took advantage of the conflict to affirm the supremacy of the papacy over the empire. In 1317, he declared the empire vacant and gave the vicariate of Italy to the king of Naples, Robert of Anjou. After Mühldorf, Louis of Bavaria sent a vicar to Italy to help the Gnibelline leaders Matteo Visconti and Cangrande della Scala; the pope then affirmed his right to decide the validity of the imperial election. Louis replied by giving his protection to the *fraticelli*. Excommunicated by the pope on 23 March 1324, Louis issued the appeal of Sachsenhausen (22 May), in which he accused John XXII of HERESY. His rebellion received a great deal of support from a work that appeared at that time, the *Defensor pacis*, written by two former teachers at the University of Paris, John of Jandun and Marsilio of Padua. The authors argued the sovereignty of the empire over the papacy, a human institution that had taken shape only as a the result of multiple usurpations; in the Church, the supreme authority lay in the council, bringing together delegates of all Christians, clerics and laymen, called by the "faithful human legislator who has no one above him"—that is, the emperor. The pope had no power except that given him by the council and the emperor, and he could be judged and deposed by them. Reinforced by these theories, which naturally were condemned by the pope, Louis of Bavaria entered Italy, took the crown of king of Italy at Milan (11 May 1327), and then went to Rome, where he had himself elected emperor by an assembly of the people and was crowned at St. Peter's (17 January 1328) by bishops rebelling against the pope. The pope had already reacted by declaring Louis dispossessed of his lands, and a heretic; the emperor called an assembly of laymen and clerics (14–18 April 1328) that deposed John

XXII and elected a new pope, Pietro Rainallucci of Corvara, a Franciscan, who took the name of NICHOLAS V. But Louis of Bavaria could not hold Rome; he returned to the north, abandoning Nicholas V at Pisa.

Although the antipope renounced his adventure and yielded to John XXII (1330), the latter pursued a diplomatic offensive with the goal of isolating the emperor to force him to abdicate. This project almost succeeded but was ruined by an about-face by Robert of Anjou, who was being advised by Cardinal Napoleon Orsini and who was worried about the transfer of the kingdom of Arles to the Kingdom of France, as provided in the diplomatic scheme of the pope (1334).

The final years of John XXII's pontificate were marked by the theological controversy on the beatific vision. On 1 November 1331, in the cathedral of Avignon, John XXII gave a sermon in which he stated that the souls of the righteous, before the resurrection of their bodies, did not have the benefit of the direct vision of God. Placed "under the altar" (Rev. 6: 9), they were consoled and protected by the humanity of Christ, but not until after the Last Judgment, when they were reunited with their resurrected bodies, were the souls, now "on the altar," able to gaze with beatitude on the divine essence (beatific vision).

The pope returned to this topic on several occasions in his sermons in the following weeks. Although this thesis found a few supporters, including the minister general of the Friars Minor, Guiral Ot, it disturbed most theologians, especially Dominicans such as John of Naples, Durand of Saint-Pourçain, Thomas Waleys, and Cardinal Jacques Fournier (the future BENEDICT XII, who would put an end to this controversy with his *Benedictus Deus* of 29 January 1336). Despite the strong opposition he encountered, the pope stubbornly stood his ground and gathered a group of *auctoritates*, (patristic texts in his favor, drawn primarily from St. Augustine and St. Bernard). The controversy grew from 1333 to 1334 as the pope tried to convince the rulers and the universities. Yet at no time did he attempt to use his authority as pope to impose his opinion, which remained that of a private theologian. When he had Thomas Waleys brought before the Inquisition—a man who, in Avignon itself, had defended the opposing view zealously and had even dared to insinuate that theologians who agreed with the pope did so only in the hope of receiving large prebends (payments)—it was to require him to answer for statements about the resurrection and judgment, but not to discuss the beatific vision.

The stubbornness of the pontiff did not stand up to his final illness. Conscious of having professed a thesis that went against general traditional beliefs, John XXII retracted it on his deathbed. On 3 December 1334, in the presence of the cardinals, he confessed "that souls separated from bodies and fully justified . . . see God and the divine essence face to face and clearly, as much as the state and condition of the separated soul can bear." The last statement was an important restriction: the theological question remained open on the difference between the state of a separated soul and that of a soul reunited with its body. The next morning, the nonagenarian pope passed away. He was buried at Avignon, in his former cathedral of Notre-Dame-des-Doms.

Louis Duval-Arnould

Bibliography

Albe, E. *Autour de Jean XXII: Les familles du Quercy,* Rome, 1902–1904, 2 vols. (taken from *Annales de Saint-Louis-des-Français*, 6–8, [1901–1904]).

Baluze, E. *Vitae paparum Avenionensium*, ed. G. Mollat, Paris, 1916–1928, I, 107–94; II, 175–98; III, 244–478.

Caillet, L. *La Papauté d'Avignon et l'Église de France: La politique bénéficiale du pape Jean XXII (1316–1334)*, Paris, 1975 (*Publications de l'université de Rouen*).

Coulon A., and Clémencet, S. *Jean XXII: Lettres secrètes et curiales relatives à la France*, 10 fasc., Paris 1900–1973.

Duval-Arnould, L. "Élaboration d'un document pontifical: Les travaux préparatoires à la constitution apostolique *Cum inter nonnullos* (12 novembre 1323)," *Aux origines de l'État moderne: Le fonctionnement administratif de la papauté d'Avignon*, Rome, 1990 (CEFR, 138), 385–409.

Dykmann, M. *Les Sermons de Jean XXII sur la vision béatifique,* Rome, 1973 (*Miscellanea historiae pontificiae*, 34).

Guillemain, B. *La Cour pontificale d'Avignon (1309–1376), étude d'une société*, Paris, 1966 (*BEFAR*, 201).

Heft, J. L. *John XXII and Papal Teaching Authority,* Lewiston, NY, 1986.

Heft, J. L. "Nicholas III and John XXII: Popes in Contradiction," *Archivum Historiae Pontificiae* 21, 1983, 245–7.

Meadelsohn, W. R. *Pope John XXII and the Heresy of Magic*, 1990.

Mollat, G. *Jean XXII, Lettres communes,* Paris, 1904–1946, 16 vol.

Mollat, G. *The Popes at Avignon*, trans. Love, New York, 1963.

Tabacco, G. *La Casa di Francia nell'azione politica di papa Giovanni XXII*, Rome, 1953 (*Istituto storico italiano per il medio evo, Studi storici*, 1–4).

Tierney, B. *Origins of Papal Infalibility 1150–1350*, Leiden, 1972.

Turley, T. "John XXII and the Franciscans: A Reappraisal," *Popes, Teachers, and Canon Law in the Middle Ages*, ed. Sweeney, J. R., and Chodorow, S., Ithaca, N.Y. and London, 1989, 74–88.

Valois, N. "Jacques Duèse, pape sous le nom de Jean XXII," *Histoire littéraire de la France*, XXXIV, Paris, 1914, 391–630.

Weakland, J. E. "John XXII before his Pontificate, 1244–1316: Jacques Duèse and his Family," *AHP*, 10 (1972), 161–185

[JOHN XXIII]. *Baldassarre Cossa (b. Procida, ca. 1360, d. Florence, 27 December 1419). Elected pope in the Pisan obedience, on 17 May 1410. Crowned on 15 May 1410. Deposed by the council of Constance on 29 May 1415. Buried in the baptistry in Florence.*

Baldassare Cossa, son of Giovanni, lord of the isle of Procida near Naples, was born into a family that drew more resources from the sea than from the land. Despite their reputation as pirates, the Cossa married in high society. Baldassarre's mother and his brother Marino's wife were Barriles, and his other two brothers found wives in the Brancacci and Caraccioli families. By temperament, Baldassarre Cossa was not suited to be a cleric. His weaknesses were emphasized by his adversaries, more of whom left behind records than did his supporters: one must use their witness with caution. They said, wrongly, that he had two natural children, but his liaison with his sister-in-law, on the other hand, was genuine. Because he was more suited to business than to the life of the spirit, his rise in the clerical ranks seemed suspicious. His father's money was probably responsible for his promotion to the rank of doctor of canon law that the University of Bologna granted him a little before 1389. He owed his career to the Neapolitan popes who took over the Roman see during the GREAT SCHISM. Already a canon of Bologna in 1386, he was admitted as a simple "regular" to the entourage of BONIFACE IX, and then became CHAMBERLAIN in 1392. In 1396, the post of archdeacon of Bologna opened greater possibilities. With this title, he had the right to oversee the affairs of the university; even more, he could hope to follow in the footsteps of his predecessors, all promoted to cardinal. Boniface IX gave him the purple, with the TITLE of San Eustachio, in 1402.

In the months that followed, the pope made Baldassare Cossa his LEGATE to Bologna, with the mission of recovering the city, then under Visconti domination. The cardinal took control of an army and in September 1403, became master of the city. INNOCENT VII and then GREGORY XII confirmed his legation. In 1409, the humanist and curialist Antonio Loschi described Cossa's government in glowing terms, but the Council of Constance accused him of behaving as a tyrant. Modern historians note that his personal account with the Medicis of Florence grew at a regular pace, unlike the apostolic treasury.

Having quickly joined his unionist colleagues who broke with Gregory XII in May of 1408, Cardinal Cossa joined his voice to theirs to call all Christians to unite in a COUNCIL at Pisa. The choice of this city, then dominated by Florence, had been delicate, and his intervention with the city's leaders eased the undertaking. To go to Pisa, he went to his bank and withdrew almost all his money; probably he contributed heavily to the financing of the assembly. After having deposed the two rival popes, the Pisan cardinals chose the cardinal of Milan over Cossa to preside over the destinies of the Pisan alliance.

The new pope, ALEXANDER V, was followed by everyone who had participated in the Pisan Council, but he could not go to Rome, which was controlled by Ladislas of Durazzo, who had sided with Gregory XII. To oppose Ladislas, the Pisans had chosen to support the pretensions of Louis II of Anjou to the throne of Naples. Cardinal Cossa again became a leader in battle; despite his family ties on Ladislas's side, he immersed himself totally in the war and was first to enter Rome, in October 1409. Then the energetic legate went back to his home in Bologna, where Alexander V joined him. The pontiff died there—a natural death, no matter what rumor imputed to Cardinal Cossa.

On 17 May 1410, after three days of CONCLAVE, Baldassarre Cossa was elected. He was ordained a priest before being crowned. He suspended the BULLS of Alexander V in favor of the mendicants, but he continued his policy of benefices, and he tried to raise a TITHE to pay for the Italian war. Meanwhile, Ladislas of Durazzo had retaken Rome, and Louis II of Anjou was in great need of support. The pontiff assumed direction of military operations and, after his entry into Rome on 12 April 1411, a victory at Roccasecca seemed to consolidate his position. The prince of Anjou, however, went back to France with no intention to return.

In order to remain in Rome, John XXIII chose to make peace with Ladislas (June 1412). The time had come to keep the promise made in Pisa to call a council again for the reform of the Church. Recent promotions of cardinals seemed a good omen, for men like Pierre d'Ailly and Francesco Zabarella, known for their openmindedness, had been chosen. But the Council of Rome drew few participants; in March 1413, the pope decided to end it, without making any other commitment. In June Ladislas entered Rome again, sacking it and driving the pope north. In his retreat, the pope found himself confronted with pressing demands from Sigismund, king of Hungary, who had just been elected king of the Romans thanks to his clever religious politics. Confronted by the partisans of Gregory XII, this candidate for the imperial throne promised to guarantee the unity of the Church rather than to uphold the Pisan legitimacy, and he proposed to recall the council to deal with all schismatics.

This brought him the sympathy of the reformers. John XXIII was in no position to negotiate; he resigned himself to accepting imperial hospitality and, even before he had released a bull of convocation, Sigismund issued an edict announcing the opening of the next council at Constance on 1 November 1414.

John XXIII arrived promptly for the meeting. By the first session he realized that even the most unionist prelates were ready to sacrifice him to achieve their own goals. In view of the experience of Gregory XII and BENEDICT XIII, he was urged to set an example and resign rather than be deposed. The partisans of this idea urged him, with the support of Sigismund, and the atmosphere grew tense. To avoid the trap closing around him, John XXIII left Constance in disguise during the night of 20–21 March 1415 and fled to Schaffousen to stay with the duke of Austria. Some cardinals tried to intervene between the two camps, but with Sigismund threatening him, John chose to take flight and tried to cross the Rhine. This succeeded in discrediting him in the eyes of the council: having proclaimed the supremacy of the council over the pope, they sent out a summons for John to appear before them, which caught up with the fugitive at Freiburg. Sigismund induced the duke of Austria to turn the city over to him, and he captured the pope.

At that, Baldassare Cossa ceased all resistance. The council fathers held his trial and issued accusations of ambition, SIMONY, bad conduct, and tyranny. He was deposed on 29 May. Imprisoned in the castle of Radolfzell on Lake Constance, he received his sentence humbly. His imprisonment did not end until June 1419. He soon made an act of submission before MARTIN V, who gave him the title of cardinal of Frascati. Six months later, he died. He was buried in the baptistry of Florence, where his tomb is ornamented with the work of Donatello and Michelozzo.

Hélène Millet

Bibliography

Blumenthal, H. "Johan XXIII, seine Wahl und seine Persönlichkeit, *ZKG*, 21 (1901), 488–516.

De Niem, T. "De vita . . . Johannis XXIII," ed. H. Von Der Hardt, *Magnum oecumenicum Constantiense concilium*, vol. 2, Frankfurt and Leipzig, 1697, 335–460.

Esch, A. "Das Papstum unter der Herrschaft des Neapolitaner," *Festschrift für H. Heimpel*, 2, Göttingen, 1972, 713–800.

Favier, J. *Les Finances pontificales à l'époque du Grand Schisme d'Occident 1378–1409*, Paris, 1966, 680–3. (BEFAR, 211).

Girgensohn, D. "Antonio Loschi und Baldassarre Cossa vor dem Pisaner Konzil von 1409," *Italia medioevale e umanistica*, 30 (1987), 1–93.

JOHN XXIII. *Angelo Giuseppe Roncalli (b. Sotto il Monte, 25 November 1881, d. Rome, 3 June, 1963). Elected pope 28 October 1958. Crowned 4 November. Buried in St. Peter's in Rome.*

If no pope was elected very young, it was also rare to be elected to the pontificate at such an advanced age as Cardinal Roncalli. He was almost 77 years old. This seems to support the thesis that the members of the CONCLAVE, after eleven ballots, made a prudent choice in order to assure the Church a pontificate of transition.

The life of Cardinal Roncalli up to that point seemed to guarantee this. Born at Sotto il Monte (near Bergamo) in a large, poor family (ten children), Angelo Roncalli stayed faithful to his origins, as seen in his ideal of priesthood: "I became a priest . . . only to do good in as many ways as possible for the poor" (*Lettere ai familiari*, I, 9). A seminarian at age 12, he followed a traditional ecclesiastical itinerary—marked however, in October 1902 by his meeting an exceptional spiritual director, the Redemptorist Francesco Pittochi. It was the latter who led him to adopt a motto as simple as it was radical: "God is all, I am nothing" (*Journal of a Soul*, 16 December 1902). After studies in theology in Rome, where his friends included future representatives of Italian modernism, he was ordained as a priest in 1904. He was soon named secretary to the new bishop of Bergamo, G. Radini-Tedeschi, with whom he stayed until the latter's death in 1914. During the years spent in daily contact with this prelate, the young priest broadened his horizons and acquired his great pastoral sensitivity. It was also during this period that he made contact with liturgical and ecumenical movements little known then in Italy and tackled the growing problems of social justice in his region with a spirit of open dialogue.

After the death of Monsignor Radini, Fr. Roncalli was a soldier from May 1915 until September 1918, first in the health service and then as a military chaplain. At the end of the war, he founded a student house and was spiritual director of the seminary for two years. In early 1921 he began his Roman career. Called to the Congregation for the PROPAGATION OF THE FAITH, he was in charge of raising the funds necessary for the MISSIONS. He held this post until 1925, thus beginning directly to serve the HOLY SEE, which for many years kept him away from the pastoral duties he desired deeply. From 1925 to 1934, PIUS XI, who had named him bishop, sent him to Orthodox Bulgaria, first as an apostolic visitor and then as an apostolic delegate. During the next ten years (1935–1944), he was the apostolic delegate in Istanbul for Greece and Turkey. These were long, lonely years spent in lands that were hardly welcoming to a Catholic prelate; there were tensions with Rome over different views of the proper attitude toward Christians of other creeds, and over ties between the Vatican and the Fascist Italian government. But they were years when contact with the Orthodox churches gave him a growing sense of unity of the Church; he also experienced a Muslim universe undergoing a radical secularization, and was becoming aware of the limits of the Eurocentrism of ecclesiastical circles. In 1938–1939, war broke out. Roncalli found himself in a priviledged but uncomfortable position. His behavior remained inspired by pastoral demands which took the shape of saving Nazi victims in occupied Greece, and in particular, Jews who were trying to escape deportation.

As papal NUNCIO to Paris beginning 1 January 1945, Bishop Roncalli took over from Bishop Valerio Valeri, whose removal General de Gaulle had requested because of his compromises with the collaborationist Vichy government. Roncalli had to manage, with an amiability that was sometimes taken for naïveté, the difficult transition from a diffuse collaborationist attitude, widespread among the French episcopate, to loyal relations with the new government. Paris complemented his previous experiences: relationships with Marxists were tense; a dying colonialism was unleashing war in Algeria; and the dechristianization taking place in one of the most ancient of Christian nations was forcing a radical pastoral renewal. The ten years spent in France therefore enriched Roncalli's personality by helping him become aware, in an intense way, of some of the most significant upheavals in contemporary Catholicism. In 1953, named patriarch of Venice, he ended his long diplomatic career and began his pastoral ministry. At age 72, he saw Venice as a long-desired haven: "It is interesting that Providence brought me back where my priestly vocation began, that is, to pastoral service . . . At present, I am placed in front of the true interests of the souls of the Church . . . It fulfills me, and I thank the Lord" (*Journal of a Soul*, 1953). However, he remained only about five years in Venice, during the end of the pontificate of Pius XII, which was marked by the cold war and an immobility in ecclesiastical structures. Still, it was a precious experience, that the future pope would remember vividly because of his direct contact with the demands and problems of Christian life.

The conclave that opened on 25 October 1958, after the death of Pius XII, took place in a difficult climate. Within the Church, the preceding very lengthy pontificate had established an increasingly personal and centralized way of government, which had created tensions and a certain amount of resistance to change during the last few years. The Catholic movements for renewal (biblical, liturgical, and ecumenical), active at the fringes of the Church, were considered with suspicion, and feelings of unrest were suppressed rather than confronted. The cold war dominated the political scene, while the process of decolonization in Asia and in Africa created serious questions for the future. Over all hung the terrible possibility of nuclear war.

Nevertheless, the conclave was short, lasting only three days. The natural candidate for the succession was the archbishop of Milan, Giovanni Battista Montini. But Pius XII had never made him a cardinal, even though the see of Milan was traditionally held by a cardinal. Choosing him would have made the election a rupture with the tradition that a pope was chosen from among the cardinals. The majority of the electors then sought a candidate who would bring a brief period of détente, a moment of reflection and pause. They wished to avoid continuity with Pius XII, yet also to avoid taking a totally different direction. Cardinal Roncalli appeared to solve this problem. He was a very different prelate and, on certain issues, opposed to Pius XII. A peasant from the north of Italy would be taking over from a Roman noble; a bishop who had felt fully at ease only in his Venetian bishopric and who, once he had undertaken diplomatic functions, had always tried to keep some pastoral activities, would succeed a diplomat without pastoral experience; a man who appeared naturally accommodating would follow a strong and authoritarian personality. On the other hand, Cardinal Roncalli's obedience to the Holy See and his natural sense of moderation had always kept him from exceeding the responsibilities he was assigned, which had added to his image as a gentle prelate, reassuring to all. Finally, his advanced age guaranteed a short pontificate. During the NOVENDIALS he had probably noticed a growing sympathy toward himself, and he was not completely surprised when a majority of the cardinals supported his nomination (the other candidate was Cardinal Agagianian, of Armenian origin).

From the beginning, the new pope gave the impression of having a very precise concept of the pontificate and of not resigning himself to a simple role of transition, but rather of wanting fully to exercise his duties as pope, as he saw them. First, he chose an unexpected name, John. This had not been used since 1415, when a certain JOHN XXIII, now considered an ANTIPOPE, had been deposed. By this choice, as a good historian, John XXIII showed an objective and serene detachment from past events, even if they were disastrous. In his CORONATION speech (4 November 1958), he stated that one should not look to the pope as a head of state, a diplomat or, even less, a scholar or an organizer of collective life. To introduce himself, he used an image that was dear to him: the one in which the son of Jacob says to his brothers, "I am Joseph, your brother," showing thus his desire to share in the human condition. This did not stop John, however, from feeling deeply his role as a father and pastor. Given the solemnity of the moment, public opinion saw in these words the dawning of a new conception of the papacy.

The first innovations took place in two directions. First, the pope normalized the life of the Roman CURIA by nominating as secretary of state, a position vacant since 1944, a Domenico Tardini, his former superior and

critic. He also reestablished work audiences for the officials of different sectors of the Roman Curia, thus facilitating simple and habitual relations between the pope and his co-workers. Quickly, he named several new cardinals, who renewed and rejuvenated the SACRED COLLEGE. Next, he reaffirmed his role as bishop of Rome by solemnly taking possession of the BASILICA of the LATERAN, the cathedral church of Rome, and then by beginning a pastoral ministry, visiting places of suffering in the city (prisons and hospitals) and Roman parishes. It should be emphasized that, for centuries before this, the popes had completely ignored the fact that they were also bishops in the Church of God, even though with a primordial role. This implied a real consideration of bishops and a reevaluation of their role and that of the local churches, which were to become major participants once again in ecclesiastic life and not just the recipients of Roman decisions. John XXIII was always sensitive to everything in the Church that was an expression of communion and brotherhood, vitality, and youth. From this viewpoint, he pressed each church, ancient or new, to bring its special contributions or charisms into the universal Church.

The Italian church was the first to feel these new orientations. Having always been protected and guided by the Roman see, it was now forced to act autonomously, which did not instill a welcoming climate of understanding with the new pontiff. Basically, the positions of the Italian episcopate, very often conservative, became the result of free choice. Moreover, the pope pulled the Church and the papacy out of Italian politics, especially regarding the existing parallelism that had led to a fundamental identity between the Catholics and the Christian Democratic party. Two deep convictions guided the pope in these actions. First, history was a process of continual transformation that, in order to be understood, required a real openness and not an unchangeable *a priori* judgment. Second, there was a clear distinction between the political milieu and that of the faith. This is why he considered it a real temptation for bishops to "declare themselves for one fraction, or faction, over another" (13 August 1961).

From the beginning of his pontificate, John XXIII noticed the timid signs of thawing coming from the East, and he abandoned the rigid choice of the Church that had made the West, especially the United States, the defender or even incarnation of Christian civilization. To open dialogue with everyone, John XXIII wanted a Church "endeavoring to serve man as such, and not just the Catholics" (25 June 1962), and whose goal was to place the Gospel "above all opinions and parties that agitate and upset society" (13 August 1961). It was not a question of changing sides or blessing what had been previously condemned, but rather of refusing to take sides and of seeking any encounter with a sincere will for peace that would appear credible to all people. In the second half of October 1962, the Cuban crisis between the United States and the Soviet Union gave the pope a chance, in his message on 25 October, to speak to all heads of state without distinction. He thus helped to avert an imminent war, and he definitively confirmed the beginning of an era of openness for the Church of Rome. This was the dawn of OSTPOLITIK. The presence of two representatives of the patriarch of Moscow among the observers from other Christian churches during the sessions of VATICAN II, the exchange of messages between Soviet premier Nikita Khrushchev and the pope on Christmas 1962, and, for the first time, the publication in *Pravda* of portions of the pope's Christmas speech were also signs of détente. This finally manifested itself as concrete action in early February 1963, with the release of 70-year-old Bishop Slipyj of Ukraine, whose long imprisonment represented one of the main points of friction between the Vatican and Moscow. But the most remarkable event was the visit of Khrushchev's daughter and son-in-law to John XXIII on 5 March 1963. This was a moment of great tension between the pope and the Curia, who—especially Cardinal Ottaviani, then secretary of the Holy Office—opposed this meeting with all the means at its disposal. This opposition was finally expressed through a vehement campaign of criticism, with absolute silence of the *CIVILTÀ CATTOLICA* on this subject, and by the refusal of the SECRETARIAT OF STATE to publish—as the pope expressly desired, in response to all the accusations that were being brought—the notes on the audience written by the only witness, the interpreter F. Koulich. The events of these final years showed the effectiveness of this embryonic *ostpolitik*. The keenness of his perception of the signs of the times and historical changes remains one of the most surprising aspects of John XXIII's personality.

Because of his diverse experience, John XXIII had a very vivid perception not only of the evils of his time, but also of the ferment of renewal active in the church. This is why he decided that the scope, seriousness, and novelty of the problems could not be handled by just one man, but instead required the attention of all the bishops of all the churches worldwide, and, through them, of all the faithful. Less than three months after his election, on 25 January 1959, the pope announced the convocation of a new general COUNCIL, an initiative that he always claimed was his own personal idea and responsibility. Simultaneously, he opened a diocesan SYNOD for Rome and began the revision of the canonical code published in 1917.

The announcement of a new council almost a century after VATICAN I raised a storm of emotion and great hopes for renewal, but also opposition and resistance. First, John XXIII had to confront the widespread opinion that, after the proclamation of papal INFALLIBILITY at the council of 1870, there was no reason to hold such assemblies.

Moreover, many feared that the council would bring out problems and difficulties that it was preferable to ignore or to resolve in an authoritarian fashion. This pontificate was in a sense dominated by the preparation and opening of the council, which John XXIII called the "Second Vatican Council" to show that it was a "new" council and not a codicil to the preceding one. The pope intended not simply to hold an assembly similar to a modern parliament, but rather to apply an ancient form of exercise of the Church's authority. When he perceived a need in the Church for innovation, he responded by going back to the most ancient tradition, thus linking the present with the past.

Preparations for the council were entrusted to the secretary of state, Cardinal Domenico Tardini, on the express condition that he call bishops and theologians from all over the world and from all orientations. More than 2,000 bishops sent propositions and advice. To facilitate relations with non-Christian churches, John XXIII created, in the spring of 1960, the Secretariat for Christian Unity, directed by a Jesuit, Cardinal Agostino Bea; it was to play a decisive role in promoting the ecumenical spirit. The first positive result was the active presence of about a hundred observers from non-Christian churches at the meetings of the conciliar assembly. On 11 September 1962, the night before the opening of the ecumenical meeting, John XXIII taped a radio message of great theological and historical significance. In it, the public above all heard that, in developing countries, the Church should be "a Church for all, particularly the poor." This statement had far-reaching echoes, principally in the Latin American churches.

The most important act of John XXIII's pontificate, one that was the most absorbing for the Catholic Church at the time, was the speech he gave at the opening of Vatican II Council. Historic research confirms that it was personally written by the pope, as shown in the manuscript of the text. It did not set a program for the council, which should be–according to the pontiff—up to the assembly to establish; rather he defined Christian behavior for the contemporary era, Christian behavior that should be governed by the needs of the *aggiornamento*, by the choice of an attitude of mercy and not of condemnation, and by the rejection of "prophets of doom . . . who see our time as only corruption and ruin," from whom the pope announced he was officially dissociating himself. Moreover, the pontiff rejected a pessimistic spiritual behavior that had taken shape in vast areas of Catholicism since the FRENCH REVOLUTION and that stopped people from seeing "the new order of human relationships" toward which the world seemed to him to be headed.

John XXIII treated the council fathers with the greatest discretion, but he followed the council's activities on an hourly basis. He intervened directly only twice, in order to guarantee the freedom of the fathers and respect for the will of the majority. The first time was in mid-October 1962, when he agreed to put off election of members of the conciliary COMMISSIONS so that the fathers could exchange opinions and so the elections could be held using lists prepared by the episcopates themselves and not from the alphabetical list of the 2,000 participants in the council, which would have led to domination by the Curia's candidates. The second intervention took place after the vote of 21 November. In that vote, a majority—but not the two-thirds required by the formal rules—voted against going ahead with a discussion of a very delicate preparatory plan concerning the relationship between the Scriptures and tradition. The pope intervened because he felt that the majority view expressed was sufficient to represent truly the will of the council; and, understanding the difficulties that existed, he decided that the text should be reviewed by a mixed commission including both the members of the Commission on Doctrine and the members of the Secretariat for Unity. By acting in this way, he proved wrong those who believed that the council was only a simple formal act of solemn approval for texts drawn up by the preparatory committees dominated by the Roman Curia. He chose the longest route for the council, but the most productive. At the end of the first session (8 December 1962) one preoccupation was dominant: the future of the council. In September the pope's physicians had diagnosed an irreversible, fast-acting cancer, and the his activities had been cut back. People wondered if it would be possible to continue in further sessions. To achieve this goal, the pope had created a commission of coordination and formulated norms for the intersession period, even setting the date for reconvening. A letter on the feast of the Epiphany 1963 to all the bishops of the world was John XXIII's last direct intervention regarding Vatican II Council. Feeling that death was near, he entrusted to the bishops the smooth running of the council he had conceived and launched, which would remain the great work of his pontificate.

On 11 April 1963, John XXIII still had enough strength to put out the last, and also the most important, of his eight ENCYCLICALS: *Pacem in terris*, addressed not just to Catholics but to all people of good will. (The encyclical *Mater et Magistra* (5 May 1961) also was of particular importance because it approved the use of the inductive method in elaborating the social doctrine of the Church.) In *Pacem in terris*, two fundamental principles were proclaimed. First, it was impossible to think that "in the atomic age war may be used as an instrument of justice," and, consequently, that there was such a thing as a just war. This was the conclusion of a theological debate that had lasted for centuries and which until now had always admitted that a just war was possible. The condemnation of any type of warfare obviously asked for the si-

multaneous and reciprocal reduction of existing arms and, as a result, the refusal of a peace based "upon a balance of terror." Then, opening the theme of collaboration between peoples—and therefore also of Christians with non-Christians—he admitted that the time was ripe for "reconciliations and meetings of a practical order that yesterday were deemed inconvenient or not productive." According to him, it was a question of distinguishing between error and the person making the error, and of not identifying false philosophical doctrines with historical, political movements generated by them. Indeed, while ideologues stick to unchangeable formulas, movements evolve. This meant the rejection of ideological barriers and the transcending of the resulting culture of the adversary.

On 22 May 1963, the pope greeted and blessed the crowd in the courtyard of St. Peter's for the last time. On 3 June, Pentecost, the entire world followed with emotion the final agony of the octogenarian pope, who shared even his final hours fraternally with all. He had truly been a pope of transition, in the stronger sense of the word, for he had ended the Constantinian era of the Church and begun a new historical period. His pontificate, which lasted less than five years, led the Catholic church in a profound and complex renovation that saw it abandon its concept of a defended fortress in order to assume a more open and welcoming stance towards humanity on the eve of a new millennium. The task that John XXIII attempted to accomplish could not, in all likelihood, have been accomplished in one pontificate. It seems that he foresaw and prepared for, rather than accomplished, a change of direction. That is what springs forth from the pages of the extraordinary spiritual journal that John XXIII kept from 1895 until his death, which was edited after his death under the title *Journal of a Soul*.

Giuseppe Alberigo

See also JUDAISM; WORLD WAR II.

Bibliography

Aime-Azam, D. *L'Extraordinaire ambassadeur*, Paris, 1967.

Alberigo, G. "Jean XXIII: itinéraire spirituel," *La Vie spirituelle*, 69 (1989), 389–413.

Alberigo, G. "Johannes XXIII," *Theologische Realenzyklopedie*, 17 (1987), 113–18; "Jean XXIII," *Histoire des saints et de la sainteté chrétienne, X: Vers une sainteté universelle*, Paris, 1988, 153–64.

Alberigo, G. "L'inspiration d'un concile oecumenique: Les expériences du cardinal Roncalli," *Le Deuxième Concile du Vatican (1959–1965)*, Rome, 1989, 81–99.

Alberigo, A. and G. *Giovanni XXIII profezia nella Fedeltà, Brescia*, 1978.

Alberigo, A. and G. "La miséricorde chez Jean XXIII," *La Vie spirituelle*, 72 (1992), 210–15.

Algisi, L. *Jean XXIII*, Paris, 1961 (*Giovanni XXIII*, Turin, 1981).

Capovilla, L. *Giovanni XXIII: Quindici letture*, Rome, 1970.

Della Salda, F. *Obbedienza e pace: Il vescovo A. G. Roncalli tra Sofia e Roma 1925–1934*, Genoa, 1989.

Fede, tradizione, profezia: Studi su Giovanni XXIII e sul Vaticano II, Brescia, 1984.

Feldman, C. *Pope John XXIII: A Spiritual Biography*, trans. P. Heinegg, New York, 2000.

Gritti, J. *Jean XXIII dans l'opinion publique: Son image à travers la presse et les sondages d'opinion publique*, Paris, 1967.

Hallahan, K. P. "Pacem in Terris," *The New Dictionary of Catholic Social Thought*, ed. J. A. Dujer, Collegeville, 1994, 696–706.

Hebblethwaite, P. *Pope John XXIII, Shepherd of the Modern World*, Garden City, 1984.

Jacquemet, G. "Jean XXIII," *Catholicisme, 6* (1966), 494–48.

Jean XXIII devant l'histoire, ed. by G. Alberigo, Paris, 1989.

John XXIII. *Il cardinale Cesare Baronio*, Rome, 1961; *Mons. Giacomo Maria Radini Tedeschi, vescovo di Bergamo*, Rome, 1961; *Souvenirs d'un nonce*, Cahiers de France (1944–1953), Rome, 1963; *Gli atti della visita apostolica di S. Carlo Borromeo a Bergamo, 5* vols., Florence, 1936–57; *Discorsi, messaggi, colloqui, 6* vols., Rome, 1960–7; *Journal of a Soul*, Garden City, NY, 1980; (*Il giornale dell'anima*, ed. by L. Capovilla, Cinisello B., 1990; a more complete edition ed. A. Melloni, Bologna, 1989); *Lettere ai familiari 1901–1962*, ed. L. Capovilla , 2 vols., Rome, 1968; *Lettere 1958–1963*, ed. L. Capovilla, Rome, 1978.

Manzo, M. *Papa Giovanni vescovo a Roma*, Cinisello B., 1991.

Melloni, A. *La Fine del passato: A.G. Roncalli vicario e delegato apostolico fra Istanbul, Atene e la guerra (1935–1944)*, Genoa, 1993.

Neuvecelle, J. *Jean XXIII: Une vie*, Paris, 1968.

Paxia, G. *The Artist and Moral Responsibility: Teachings of Pius XII and John XXXIII*, San Francisco, 1998.

Trinchese, S. *Roncalli e le missioni: L'Opera della propagazione della fede tra Francia e Vaticano negli anni'20*, Brescia, 1989.

Willam, F. M. *Vom jungen Angelo Roncalli (1903–1963)*, Innsbruck, 1967.

Zizola, G. *L'Utopia di papa Giovanni*, Assisi, 1973.

JOHN PAUL I. *Albino Luciani (b. Canale d'Agordo, 17 October 1912, d. Rome, 28 September 1978). Elected pope on 26 August 1978. Consecrated on 3 September 1978. Buried at St. Peter's in Rome.*

Albino Luciani was the third patriarch of Venice, from a modest, rural background, to be elected pope in a century that saw six northern Italians rise to the see of St. Peter. He was born in Canale d'Agordo in the province of Belluno. His father, a migrant laborer with socialist leanings, worked mostly in France, until he found a job as a glassmaker in Murano. His mother, a fervent Catholic, encouraged the early vocation of the young Albino, a gifted student who attended the minor seminary of Feltre, the major seminary of Belluno, and the Gregorian University in Rome, where he received a doctorate in theology with a thesis on "The origin of the soul in the thought of Rosmini."

Ordained a priest on 7 July 1935, Luciani served as a curate in Canale d'Agordo and taught at the Technical Mining Institute. He was professor of dogmatic theology and vice rector of the seminary at Belluno in 1937. He was interested in many subjects—Scripture, patristics, morals, CANON LAW, art history—which he taught occasionally. From 1947 on, he worked in the administration of his diocese as secretary of the interdiocesan SYNOD of Feltre and Belluno in 1947, prochancellor, provicar, and finally vicar-general of Belluno. As director of the Catechetical Bureau of Belluno, he planned the year's activities and the Eucharistic Congress held there in 1949; he collected the talks from it in a book, *Catechesi in bricciole* ("Catechesis, Bit by Bit"), which went into six editions in Italy and was translated into Spanish.

Fr. Luciani was made bishop of Vittorio Veneto on 15 December 1958, and JOHN XXIII ordained him in St. Peter's on 27 December 1958. Named archbishop patriarch of Venice on 15 December 1969, he took possession of St. Mark's cathedral on 3 February 1970, received Pope PAUL VI there in September 1972, and was made a cardinal on 5 March 1973.

This churchman was a well-educated writer who used simple language to spread the evangelical message to the people and knew how to use anecdotes to great effect. In his *Messenger of Saint Anthony*, he writes letters to famous people of the past: to Jesus, of course, but also to Dickens, Dante, Péguy, Chesterton, and to a few imaginary characters like Figaro or Pinocchio. Very close to his clergy, Cardinal Luciani meditated on identity and asked the servants of Christ to imitate their Master in every way. He showed great concern for the poor, the sick, and children, and was particularly interested in his countrymen who emigrated, whom he visited in France, Germany, Portugal, Burundi, and Brazil. He gave the island of San Giorgio in Alga to the city of Venice so a center for study, research, and experimentation to safeguard the city could be founded there.

Cardinal Luciani, as vice president of the Italian Episcopal Conference from 1972 on, fought against the introduction of divorce into Italian law, dissolved the Catholic youth organizations that accepted this "reverse sacrament," and spoke against the false pluralism that he differentiated from "holy pluralism." In an article in *L'Osservatore romano* on "The Responsibility of Theologians" (23 January 1972), he stated that theologians abuse their freedom if they forget that theology is a holy science. He was very severe with theses on the theology of liberation.

After the death of Paul VI, who had treated the patriarch of Venice with much consideration—inviting him to the synod of 1971 and complaining that he did not come to Rome often enough—the name of Albino Luciani was no better known than any other to the journalists analyzing the electoral chances of various Italian cardinals and predicting that it would be a very long CONCLAVE. However, on 26 August 1978, in the Sistine chapel, the will of the conclave to elect a pastor—a man of position with a feeling for collegiality—led two chief electors, Cardinal Felici, prefect of the tribunal of the Apostolic Signatura, and Cardinal Villot, secretary of state, to suggest the nomination of the patriarch of Venice. In uncomfortable quarters and stifling heat, the suggestion pleased a majority, who showed this by casting their votes on the fourth ballot for a little-known cardinal in order to choose an Italian who was neither Cardinal Siri (archbishop of Genoa, who had reservations about VATICAN II) nor Cardinal Benelli (former substitute secretary of state for Paul VI, archbishop of Florence).

Albino Luciani astonished everyone by choosing a double name for the first time in the history of the Roman pontificate: John Paul, in honor of his two predecessors, to show his willingness to continue their work in the application of Vatican II. Vatican experts and the public quickly interpreted the double name in this way, but it also referred to the basilica of Sts. John and Paul (Zannipolo), pantheon of the doges of Venice. The election of John Paul I, the smiling man whose motto was "*Humilitas,*" was well received: "I was hoping for a pastor and we got a pastor, and a pastor who was part of the Second Vatican Council and has tried to apply its reforms . . . He is a sweet tenacious man who is clear-thinking, with firm speech, and who is easy to approach," commented Cardinal Marty, archbishop of Paris. On 3 September, during the ceremony of enthronement, the giving of the *pallium* replaced that of the TIARA, the triple crown that Paul VI had stopped using. The emotion of the public increased when it learned on 5 September, that a great partisan of ecumenism, the patriarch of Leningrad and Novgorod, Monsignor Nikodim, whose people were suffering many persecutions, had died of a heart attack while speaking with the new pope. Soon, however, those around him noticed that John Paul was not skilled in diplomacy, that he understood the CURIA very little, and that he had just begun to learn English. His already full days were lengthening, and files were piling up on his desk.

During public audiences on Wednesdays, John Paul I gave the impression of being a cultured man, citing not only the Bible but also the Fathers of the Church, the great spiritual writers, and authors from the past two centuries. At the first audience on 6 September he shared his happiness about the Camp David meeting of Presidents Jimmy Carter, Anwar Sadat, and Menachem Begin. The last three Wednesday audiences of his papacy focused on the three theological virtues: faith, hope and charity. On 13 September, he declared that Pope JOHN XXIII had hoped that, with the council, the Church would make a leap forward, "a leap onto the road of certain, unchangeable truths, and not onto the road of truths that would change." He declared, "The *aggiornamento* consists of proposing truths in a manner adapted for these modern times." On 20 September, he clearly warned his peers: "It is untrue to say that political, economical and social liberation coincide with salvation in Jesus Christ; that the Kingdom of God may be identified with the kingdom of man, that *Ubi Lenin, ubi Jerusalem* ('Wherever Lenin is, there is Jerusalem')." This was the first time that a pope officially mentioned Lenin and his cult. This prophetic phrase denounces Marxism-Leninism, then at the peak of its expansion. In a letter to the public on 20 September 1978, John Paul I encouraged the efforts toward peace of the episcopates in Argentina and Chile and urged them to call "governors and governed to mutual understanding" in the affair of the Beagle Canal, which was threatening to start a war between those nations. Besides the traditional ALLOCUTIONS to the diplomatic corps, the SACRED COLLEGE, the press, the mayor of Rome, and the special missions sent to Rome for his installment, John Paul I spoke to the clergy of Rome about clerical discipline, to the bishops of the United States on the sanctity of the Christian family, and to the bishops of the Philippines on evangelization. He preached love for the poor, insisted on the authority of the bishop as the servant of God, deplored liturgical irregularities, and spoke against violence in the name of Christ.

On 29 September, his personal secretary, Fr. John Magee, found the pope dead in his bed. The doctors diagnosed the cause as a heart attack and set the time of death as approximately 11 PM on 28 September. John Paul I had not been in good health. The day before he died, he had declared, to the surprise of his listeners, "The pope now speaking to you has been in the hospital eight times, and has undergone four operations." In his youth he had a serious lung infection; for a time, he had lost the use of his left eye, and had also he had several angina attacks. In Rome, during the stifling heat of summer's end, he found himself burdened with a crushing workload. To his secretary of state, Cardinal Villot, who remarked on his fatigue and his swollen legs, and advised him to take care of himself, the pope had once replied, "If the pope dies, they'll get another." John Paul I had been scheduled to give a speech to the procurators of the JESUITS on 30 September. The text, sent in the form of a letter from JOHN PAUL II to Father Arrupe, general of the Jesuits, recalled the need for doctrinal training, asked that Jesuit teachings and publications avoid being a source of confusion and disorientation, and emphasized that the mission was to announce the Christian message, whose true interpreter is the Church magisterium.

Yves-Marie Hilaire

Bibliography

Acta Apostolicae Sedis, 70 (1978), 677–903.

Catholic Documentation, 24 September 1978 and 15 October 1978.

Cornwell, P. *A Thief in the Night: The Death of Pope John Paul I*, London and New York, 1990.

Giulio, N. *Trenta giorni: Un pontificato*, Gorle, 1984.

Grootaers, L. *De Vatican II à Jean Paul II, le grand tournant de l'Église catholique*, Paris, 1981.

Levillain P., and Uginet, F. C. *Le Vatican ou les frontières de la grâce*, Paris, 1984.

Luciani, A. *Illustrissimi*, Padua, 1976.

Wenger, A. *Le Cardinal Villot* (1905–1979), Paris, 1989.

Yallop, D. *Au nom de Dieu*, Paris, 1984.

Yallop, D. A. *In God's Name*, Toronto, New York, 1984.

JOHN PAUL II. *Karol Wojtyla (b. Wadowice, 18 May 1920). Elected pope 16 October 1978. Installed 22 October 1978.*

Of all the pontificates of the 20th century (nine), John Paul II's is unique for having been placed, from its beginning, under the worldwide public scrutiny of believers and nonbelievers alike. According to the Vaticanist Domenico Del Rio of *La Republica*, he is "A man who reassures a world that wants reassurance."

John Paul II was popular from the first night of his election on Monday, 16 October 1978. An unknown to the public troubled by the extraordinary brevity (34 days) of the pontificate of his predecessor JOHN PAUL I, and a possible papal candidate (*papabile*) little spoken of by Vaticanists, Karol Wojtyla took a doubly significant name chosen by Cardinal Albino Luciani only 5 weeks before. The new pope appeared on the balcony of Benedictions of ST. PETER'S BASILICA giving the impression of strength that no one had thought the Catholic church was capable of in the midst of crisis that was shaking it. At age 58, Polish and multilingual, he brought to the HOLY SEE the stature of a bishop experienced in the debate between the post-council Church and the modern world. At his installation ceremony (22 October), he expressed his thoughts on the responsibility that had been offered to him, and that he had accepted: "Be not Afraid." They were words full of meaning: do not be afraid of a non-Italian pope; do not be afraid of the current difficulties of the Church; do not be afraid of a world torn by war, nuclear threats, and terrorism (which Italy in particular was experiencing, as the assassination of Aldo Moro in May 1978 had shown dramatically).

How was this Polish pope going to govern the Church when he had not master all its machinery, unlike PAUL VI or PIUS XII? How would this non-Italian adapt his experience as a pastor to a Roman catholicism with its own style and praxis in the world's eyes? Strengthened by their Italian origin, his predecessors with little experience with the CURIA (PIUS X, John Paul I) knew how to make connections between their diocesan experience and the supreme command. JOHN PAUL I, who had been quite ill, was rapidly overwhelmed in trying to run a government more complex than he imagined. The vitality of the new pope contrasted with that of his predecessor, whose sudden disappearance gave credibility to the idea that the Holy See needed a man of character, who represented a post-council Church. The VATICAN II COUNCIL had shown the world strong personalities that were not necessarily Italian. The vague longing for the time of a pope "from somewhere else" had replaced the time of the election of popes from within the patrician Italian families and the Roman nobility. A harmony developed between the CONCLAVE, which probably saw in the archbishop of Cracow, a representative of a large Catholic country ruled by communism and closely watched by the Soviet Union, and public opinion, which saw him as a defender of the faith against its greatest enemy (atheistic materialism). The pontificate entrusted to an athlete of God offered the promise of a great spiritual and geopolitical debate. The sacred monsters of the international scene who had led people in the name of ideologies either friendly or rival, were all gone now: Stalin in 1953, Churchill in 1965; de Gaulle in 1970; Mao Tse-Tung in 1976. Their successors now continued their conflicts, using the logic of acquisitions or threats. The religious fact was now registering in people's memories as a sculptural relief worn away by 20th-century society for which the Berlin Wall (1962) was the symbol, in Europe, of two opposing ideas of progress and happiness, where decolonization was leaving adrift whole continents suffering growing pains and lack of harmony. To this empty international scene, John Paul II brought, if not general hope, at least a promise of dialogue with the world, referring to the debate between man and history.

The pontificate of John Paul II was called by the general public to review and clarify the role of the Church in the last quarter of the 20th century. The role of a responsible modernity was assigned to it. It was logical from the beginning that since the pope was considered a man given an authority which, it was felt quickly, he would totally accept without reservation, the pontificate would become the subject of conflicts. One way he differed from his predecessors was that he had received an inheritance: the VATICAN II COUNCIL, whose spirit had marked the second half of the 20th century—*aggiornamento*; debates; pastoral overture—and whose writings were not well known, an invisible cathedral whose inspiration and layout were only in people's memories.

His papal name, announced by posters on the walls of Rome during the *novendials* by *Communione e Liberazione*, a movement defending the strict application of the Vatican II against the partisans of a freer interpretation, became the symbol of an active synthesis of the initiative of JOHN XXIII in 1959 and its gradual realization by PAUL VI in the broadest possible form for an assembly of about 2,500 people. LEO XIII (1878–1903) had inherited issues involving defense of the Church against the modern world (from PIUS IX) and those resulting from an unfinished council (VATICAN I), marked by the painful vote on papal INFALLIBILITY. John Paul II, on the other hand, was left with the aftermath of a council that had aroused nostalgia and caused disturbances in the 1970s, in regard to which the Church and its observers expected clarification. This is why no other pontificate, even in the recent past, had been the object of so many assessments with the media's help: for his 5th anniversary in 1983, his 10th in 1988, and his 15th in 1993. So many expressions of encouragement, of disappointments, of indirect warnings (which, by nature, the HOLY SEE ignores) show the place of importance given to the papacy in the modern world. This was a strange situation, if one considers that in 1870, after the taking of Rome, the Holy See, deprived of its states, was considered an institution about to disappear, and that the popularity of John XXIII was mostly due to an appreciation for bringing together a council that was viewed as a return to conciliarism, or the opening at all levels of a democratic discussion without limits in the Church.

John Paul II needed to make some choices. His election implied this. The situation full of passion, gave those choices, which he made gradually, an aura of mystery that in the first days (and still somewhat today), clouded judgments and replaced them with questions on the *Forma mentis* and the piety of a Polish pope, whose first voyage in Europe was to Poland (2–10 June 1979); on his entourage and his ties with Poland where, from 1979 to 1999, he went seven times; on his daily life, that of an active pope, welcoming, natural, a bit in the style of John XXIII who however, was 77 at the time of his election in 1958, and was hailed as a pope of transition. Definitely the pope's age played a role. It was easy to see that, at age 58, he would, barring an accident, have a long pontificate. The conclave had perhaps weighed this advantage, which may have influenced it all the more in the light of the reform introduced by Paul VI on 21 November 1970 (*motu proprio Ingravescentem aetatem*) that barred cardinals over age 80 from electing the pontiff (but not making

them ineligible for election themselves). The emotion raised by the attempt on his life in front of St. Peter's during a general AUDIENCE on 13 May 1981 gave rise to astonishment that someone would dare to kill John Paul II.

The mystery surrounding him gave rise, in several years, to a return to the holy in carrying out the role of the vicar of Christ, which can explain the extraordinary popularity of John Paul II despite more and more attacks on some of his actions, especially in the area of the prevailing importance of the Christian ethic. The man, Karol Wojtyla, and the pope have become one in the eyes of public opinion for which the papacy now presents itself as defending of human rights as the basis for Christianity in the 21st century.

Karol Wojtyla: The Beginnings of a Vocation (1920–46). Born in 1920 in a small poor parish (Wadowice) located 50 kilometers southwest of Warsaw, Karol Wojtyla was the second son of Emilia Kacrorowska and Karol Wojtyla, a retired officer. He lost his mother in 1929 and his older brother Edward in 1938 during an epidemic of scarlet fever, which he caught at the hospital of Bielsko where he was an intern. His father died in 1941. At age 21, Karol Wojtyla faced a challenge alone: assume his Polish identity and make his way in the world from a country controlled by Nazi Germany since September 1939. In a short time, the Polish Church, which was the soul of a country at the crossroads of Europe, split between neighbors sensitive to its riches and its population, had been pulled apart. In 1938, there were three archbishops, 15 diocesan bishops, an ordinary military bishop, 20 auxiliary bishops, 40 male congregations with 6,000 members, and 50 female congregations of 16,000 sisters. Poland had 11,000 priests. A number of parishes owned farms whose revenues gave the clergy relative affluence as in the Ancien Régime in France, giving the clergy social status. The clergy were trained in state universities that all (except Poznán) had a faculty of theology. A number of them, before or after their studies, were sent to European universities to perfect or begin their training (Rome, Strasbourg, Paris). The wealth and high rank of the average clergyman, in the bosom of a Church with an obvious hierarchy in relationships and titles—the archbishop of Cracow had the title of "Prince" beginning in 1484—were appreciated by the faithful for whom the Caritas organization (among others) practiced charity without distinction. The Nazi invasion materially undermined the Polish Church and meant to end its social and spiritual domination by attacking the clergy. Karol Wojtyla, who had followed a course of studies favored by his social milieu, had enrolled in 1938 in the school of letters in Jagiellonian University in Cracow to specialize in Polish philology. The entry of Nazi troops brought about the closing of the university, the deportation of the professors, and the sending of the students to work camps. Karol Wojtyla found a job as a worker in a stone quarry at first, and later in a factory that made chemicals (Solvay).

It is at the juncture of this passive resistance with a strong sense of what was appropriate and of the perception of the stakes for which Poland was the martyr that his religious vocation was born. This vocation, different from the traditional biographies of the popes, was not there as a continuous path, getting firmer as it went from religious education to entry into holy orders. Karol Wojtyla had a deep liking for literary studies; it was obvious right after his election in 1978 that he had participated actively in the creation of the Rhapsodic Theater, a group of underground anti-Nazi comedians founded at the beginning of the war in Cracow. From this experience came *The Jeweler's Shop*, a drama in verse published in *Znak* [The Sign] in 1960 with a revealing subtitle: Meditation on the Sacrament of Marriage that Sometimes Becomes a Drama. In these years of young adulthood, in a solitude sustained by a natural religious life and the company of enthusiastic fellows eager to save their banned culture, Karol Wojtyla chose the priesthood. One could not go much further in a fighting spirit in the midst of a devastated civilization with an uncertain future: "I worked in the factory, devoting myself, as much as the terror of the Occupation allowed, to my love of literature and the dramatic arts. My vocation took shape in the middle of all that, as an inner truth of absolute and indisputable clarity." Jagiellonian University had reopened clandestinely at the beginning of 1942. In October, Karol Wojtyla, resolute, enrolled in its seminary. Classes were held at night. In October 1944, after a rebellion in Warsaw, Cardinal Sapieha decided to hide the seminarians in the episcopal palace. This cautious concealment lasted until the liberation of Cracow on 17 January 1945. Karol Wojtyla was ordained a priest on All Saints' Day 1946. Cardinal Sapieha immediately sent him to Rome to complete his theological training at the Angelicum, a university run by the DOMINICANS (the Pontifical University of St. Thomas Aquinas). He remained there for two years and wrote a doctoral thesis on "Faith in the Thought of St. John of the Cross" (defended in 1948 at Jagiellonian University). At the end of this Roman education, at the request of the archbishop of Cracow, Father Wojtyla returned to Cracow after staying in France (where he attended the Catholic Institute in Paris, met theologians such as Father Henri de Lubac whom he would make a cardinal in 1989, and was impressed by the experience of the worker-priests developed by the Mission of France), in Belgium where he met, among others, abbé Cardjin, founder of the Young Catholic Workers (JOC, *Jeunesse ouvrière catholique*) in 1925; and in Holland. He was

then named head vicar in Niegowic, a small rural parish in the diocese of Tarkow, then at Saint-Florian, the most important parish of Cracow. The exercise of his ministry went hand-in-hand with his work on a doctorate in philosophy on the German philosopher Max Scheler.

In 1953 he was named professor of moral theology and social ethics in the faculty of theology of Cracow, which was closed in 1954. F. Wojtyla was then named professor of ethics at the Catholic university of Lublin where he founded, in 1956, an institute of moral theology which he would direct until 1978. On 28 September 1958, Pius XII (who died on 9 October) named Wojtyla auxiliary bishop of Cracow in the cathedral of Wawel where, on 1 September 1939, he had heard the first German bombardments. He became, at age 38, the youngest bishop of Poland. Without knowing it, Pius XII had opened to this new bishop the doors of the council that John XXIII would announce on 25 January 1959.

The priestly itinerary of Bishop Wojtyla was that of a strong, gifted person whose talents were perceived and pushed by the archbishop of the diocese where he was incardinated. This type of active vigilance and confidence often leads to the episcopate, an office for which the influence of the bishop or archbishop of the area is generally the determining factor for Rome' decision. The progressive training of Karol Wojtyla (six years of perfectly planned studies) created a vocation in the service of the Church. In this sense, it involved, little by little, a connection between a natural attachment to a divine institution embedded in the vicissitudes of history—the bishop and his clergy, *defensores civitatis*—and a reflection on faith in the modern world. Faith in search of understanding (*Fides quaerens intellectum*): For Karol Wotjyla, this properly Thomist approach came from a scholastic appreciation of dogma. "An intellectual turmoil took place in me," said John Paul II later to André Frossard, "at the beginning of my studies, with my first contact with a simple manual of metaphysics, or 'philosophy of being.' This intellectual discovery which could be defined, according to Aristotle, as a discovery of 'primary Philosophy' or of the most basic dimension of our knowledge as much pre-scientific as properly scientific, formed a lasting basis in my mind for the intellectual understanding of God." This research of "being" in nature, given to man by God, led Karol Wojtyla to go toward Thomism, which postulated the coincidence between the "transhistoric" context of a being created in the image and resemblance of God and to the transitory historical context that is superimposed upon him, a humanity "written in time with the whole visible world" which "manifests at the same time that which resists time, destruction and death. . . . Every man, then, is born into this world to witness the truth according to his particular vocation." *Defensores civitatis. Defensores veritatis.* John

Paul II would write *"Veritatis splendor,"* in 1993. This explains the pope's systematic attempt to present a Christian ethics beginning in 1979 in line with his principal work, *Love and Responsibility*, published in 1960 (and translated into several languages in 1968).

Wojtyla's pastoral work from 1948 to 1958 took place in a climate typical of the state of watchful exploration of a Church rooted in society in the years following WORLD WAR II. The Communist leaders looked for a rapprochement that realism demanded of them, to which the archbishop primate of Warsaw, Cardinal Wyszynski, acquiesced on 14 April 1950. The government would protect the existence of religious orders, the Catholic university of Lublin, the theological faculties of Cracow and Warsaw, and catechism in the schools. The efforts to influence the hierarchy of the Church through the election of capitular vicars (compliant men) in the territories taken back from Germany were unsuccessful, but on 9 November 1953, a decree imposed strict state control over all nominations to ecclesiastical positions. The Church refused this arrangement outright, which would lead progressively to control. On 24 September, Cardinal Wyszynski was condemned to solitary confinement for three years. Monsignor Klepecz of Lodz replaced him as president of the episcopate and advised the clergy to be cautious. The most active journals coming from lay Catholic sources, such as *Tygodnik Powszechny* [The Universal Weekly] were banned. The weekly linked to this journal, *Znak*, to which Karol Wojtyla contributed, went underground. This test of the Polish Church failed because the Church's resistance, in those years, was led by a people who, after all the complex reapportioning of territory in 1946–47 (in favor of Germany and the Soviet Union and then, inversely, in favor of Poland and other countries), believed in a Poland that had become "one of the most monolithic States of Europe as far as the ethnic and religious profile was concerned" (J. Kloczowski), with 95 percent of Poles baptized as Roman Catholics. In response to the negative remarks made by the Communist government against Church structures, the hierarchy could count on a popular piety demonstrably stronger than any allegiance to apparent democracy. In this way, Cardinal Wyszynski was able, with a pastoral letter, to call on the Polish people in August 1957. In it he reminded them that Poland "was linked by the Roman Church to the Western Church" and instituted a novena in preparation for the millennium of Polish Christendom. Polish piety and fervor were supported by intense pastoral activity of the clergy whose intellectual training and spirituality were exemplified in Wojtyla. During these years the ethics professor organized seminars in the countryside, by lakes or rivers or on mountain paths, for the seminary students of Lublin, while contributing regularly, as much as he could, to *Tygodnik Powszechny* or to *Znak* (which he continued until 1978) and recording his emotions in poems published under the name of Andreas Jaw-

ien (*Jawien*: Polish for "he who reveals the truth"). Photos of Karol Wojtyla on bike trips, in canoes, would spread worldwide after his election, uncommon expressions of the vitality of this successor of St. Peter.

The Bishop, the Archbishop: The Apostolic Destiny (1958–78). Named auxiliary bishop of Cracow, Wojtyla chose as his motto *"Totus tuus"* ("Entirely yours"). His function, at the side of Archbishop Eugenius Baziak, did not stop him from continuing to organize outdoor seminars. His teaching at the university of Lublin became less regular. In 1962, when the archbishop of Cracow died, he was appointed interim administrator of the diocese of Cracow. There were three candidates for the seat of cardinal archbishop of Cracow: Bishop Wojtyla and two prelates from aristocratic backgrounds. The Polish government expressed a clear preference for the auxiliary bishop of Cracow, who was 42 years old. The Holy See, which was not linked to Poland by any type of concordat stalled for time. Finally, Paul VI named Bishop Wojtyla archbishop of Cracow on 13 January 1964. He was consecrated on 13 June. The Vatican II Council was going into its third session.

Named bishop at the very end of the pontificate of Pius XII and promoted to the see of Cracow at the beginning of Paul VI's pontificate, Karol Wojtyla owed his rapid rise (he was made cardinal in 1967) to the combination of his personality, typical of the Polish Church in reconstruction, and the Holy See's new appreciation of the Polish Church, beginning when the Vatican II Council changed the Holy See's views on the churches of silence, meaning those of the Eastern-bloc countries. In the mind of John XXIII, the 21st Ecumenical Council should gather the bishops of the entire world together, and the pope applied Canon 331 of the Code of CANON LAW of 1917 in the broadest way possible, concerning the categories of who should be invited to attend the council. The participation of church hierarchy of the Eastern-bloc countries was solicited, but this depended on the good will of the states. Those in which the governments had succeeded in controlling Catholicism using methods of harsh repression or a successful call for collaboration (Hungary, Czechoslovakia, and Yugoslavia) were very wary of the council. Those in which Catholics were a minority (Albania, Bulgaria, and Romania) created obstacles.

Wojtyla, consulted during the preparatory phase of the council, had already made his mark as a key figure in the Polish episcopate when the question of nomination to the residential see of Cracow arose. It made the diocese think about the question of the relationship between the Church and the world proposed at the council in the plans of 1962 (the future document *Gaudium et spes* of 1965). He had intervened as an experienced pastor on questions of religious intolerance, unbelief, and religious freedom. All of Wojtyla's proposals included both a geopolitical and an ecclesiastical analysis of the situation of contemporary man in a society far from God, the principle of being. He called upon the strength of conviction without considering that condemnation might be a useful response. That is why he did not sign the request of the council fathers who, in 1965, wanted an explicit condemnation of atheism, the source of communism. On the contrary, he wanted the Church to show the world its supernatural calling. This is why, in 1965, he aligned himself with the minority of the council who opposed a description of the Church (document *Lumen gentium*) based upon the "People of God" rather than on the hierarchy as representative of its divine institution. Wojtyla's positions at the Vatican II have not been studied well, but show that the spirit of his pontificate, through his administration of the Church, already existed between 1962 and 1965: a Church that was strong with respect to a society that God was not abandoning to man, but which man was destroying by opposing the principle of truth that God had entrusted to him.

The relative freedom enjoyed by the Church in Poland after Gomulka came to power in 1956 was threatened right after the council with the entry of Russian tanks backed by part of the forces from the Warsaw Pact into Prague in August 1968. The Polish government, which was watching the strengthening of Moscow, took the initiative. The young Cardinal Wojtyla refused, under these conditions, to participate in the SYNOD of 1967 for which the Polish authorities had not been willing to approve a passport for Cardinal Wyszynski, who, it was known, wanted a firm condemnation of communism. However, Cardinal Wojtyla was present at all the synods after that, every two or three years. He defended the principle of COLLEGIALITY in 1969. In 1971 he was elected (on the second ballot) to the third position of the *Concilium* of the General Secretariat and intervened on the question of the celibacy of priests, strongly asserting the "naturalness of celibacy and the priesthood." About the relationships between individual churches and the Universal Church, he said: "Communion exists when individual churches communicate to the others the bonds which are particular to them within the unity of the Universal Church, at the foundation of which the Lord placed Peter." In 1974 the archbishop of Cracow spoke on liberation theology to remind people that MARXISM left the Church only one freedom: that of not existing. At these synods, Cardinal Wojtyla spent more time with the French-speaking circle (presided over by Cardinal Suenens, the primate of Belgium) than with the Italian-speaking circle. In 1976 he was chosen by Paul VI to preach the Lenten retreat the Vatican. After his elevation to cardinal, the archbishop of Cracow had also been named member of several Roman CONGREGATIONS: for the clergy, for the divine worship, and for Catholic education (1978). Finally, since the Vatican II Council had brought together Church fathers who,

until then, barely knew each other, he traveled extensively in North America (to the Eucharistic Congress in Philadelphia in August 1976, during which the Harvard student newspaper published his photo on the front page with the headline "Cardinal Wojtyla, Probable Successor to Paul VI"), to Africa, to Southeast Asia, and to Australia. He was not the only cardinal to lead a similar post-council life.

The Conclave of October 1978 (14–16 October). The death of Paul VI, which the pope approaching age 80 waited for with confident serenity, offered choices to the conclave as never before in the history of the papacy. The tradition of an Italian pope was compelling and two of them had been instrumental in creating the council. It was claimed that Cardinal Alfrink (archbishop of Utrecht, age 78), one of the great leaders of Vatican II had stated: "The worst of the Italian popes will always be better than the best foreign pope," but the heritage of Paul VI was weighty and in question. The pontifical authority was shaken, and the Church was focused (by the very will of the pope) on the office of the sovereign pontiff. The analysis of the consequences of Vatican II was dividing the Italian church. Was it a useless and harmful council? The archbishop of Genoa, Cardinal Siri, defended this thesis methodically and relentlessly, or was it a council whose work constituted a basic reference to be put into practice with firm resolve? This was the opinion of a majority of the cardinals, ready to trust Italian savior-faire. Paul VI had implicitly designated a successor in Cardinal Benelli (archbishop of Florence, age 57), former SUBSTITUTE, created cardinal at the CONSISTORY of 1977. A compromise was found in August 1978 with the name of Cardinal Albino Luciani, patriarch of Venice, age 66, and caring pastor. Had not Venice given the world PIUS X in 1903 and especially John XXIII in 1958?

The death of John Paul I who had led the "pontificate of the smile" changed the stakes for two reasons: the proof was there, even in 33 days, that the best of the Italian cardinals was not necessarily the best pope; the members of the conclave knew each other and there was an agreement by the opposing Siri-Benelli factions that a new Italian cardinal, whether he was in the Curia or not, no longer seemed a logical solution.

In conversations among the cardinals during the novendials in August 1978 and at the beginning of the conclave Cardinal König (archbishop of Vienna, age 73) supposedly put forth Wojtyla's name, but was convinced by Cardinal Wyszynski not to pursue it further in light of what was believed to be a slim chance of confirmation. It is difficult to believe that the primate of Poland would have opposed the election of a man who, during the turmoil in the Polish Church, had been perfectly loyal, regardless of their differing views on the Church's role in Poland. Witnesses observed the two cardinals in prayer, alone, in front of the *Pietà* in the basilica of St. Peter's on Friday, 13 October, the night before the end of the conclave; their emotional embrace in St. Peter's Square during the giving of the *pallium* on 22 October attests to the contrary. It was an easy matter for Cardinal König to repeat his preference for a non-Italian pope. Participants murmured that John Paul I had voted in August 1978 in favor of Cardinal Lorscheider (archbishop of Fortaleza, age 54), an influential person at the Vatican II. It seems that a group also gathered around Cardinal König, including Cardinals Suenens, Marty (archbishop of Paris), Gouyon (archbishop of Rennes), Pappalardo (archbishop of Palermo), Colombo (archbishop of Milan), Arns (archbishop of São Paulo), Lorscheider, Thiandoum (archbishop of Dakar), if not to favor Cardinal König's preference, at least to discuss a non-Italian choice to favor, beginning thus a move against a Curialist likely to block the work of Vatican II.

The election of Cardinal Wojtyla was accomplished after seven or eight rounds of balloting (two each half-day, beginning on Sunday, 15 October). It seems that votes at first were divided between Siri and Benelli, the archbishop of Genoa slightly ahead of the archbishop of Florence (there were 29 Italian cardinals); other votes were scattered, some going to Cardinal Wojtyla even during the first round. A huge crowd, on the evening of 15 October, was waiting for white smoke and got progressively more disappointed when black smoke issued forth several times. The conclave had hoped for a speedy election that would show a harmony that the public almost demanded. It was probably during lunch on Monday, 16 October, that things turned around, due to the intervention of Cardinal König who succeeded in convincing the very anti-Communist North American cardinals (Cardinal Krol, conservative archbishop of Philadelphia, of Polish background), and those of the Canadian and German episcopates (following the reconciliation of the German and Polish Churches). There are questions as to whether the archbishop of Cracow was elected by 99 votes out of 109 or by 103 out of 109, and whether he refused the first time, requiring a second ballot to win him over. At almost 8 PM, Cardinal Pericle Felici, whose duty it was as the last cardinal deacon, announced to the crowd gathered in St. Peter's Square, smaller than the one the previous evening, and more partisan: "*Habemus papam . . .*" and, pronouncing in the Polish manner—"*Woeeteelah*"—the name of the new pope. There was confusion for a short time, some thinking it was an African pope, but this was soon clarified upon the pope's appearance.

The Heritage and the Imprint (1978–2001). John XXIII and John Paul I had been no better known to the public than John Paul II. Paul VI was better known, because his speech at the opening of the Vatican II Council had been published and his election had been predicted as probable. Karol Wojtyla's past was hurriedly examined with a

magnifying glass by the media. It proposed a little-disputed image of the new pope which, after the gradual and voluntary effacement of Paul VI, contributed to establishing him as a distinct and strong personality. Within several days, a picture of the new pope was made clear by the press. The public was curious; a curiosity not unlike that of those in the 19th century toward foreign-born rulers sent to them by the European powers at the whim of secret treaties. A picture unfolded of a man who had been archbishop of a nation martyred in history, ruled as a Communist state under Russian control; an athlete, actor, poet, a writer with more than 300 published works; a blond, handsome former blue-collar worker; a multilingual man seemingly with no secrets. The public had forgotten that Pius XI had been an athlete, a writer, and an avid reader, as were Pius XII and Paul VI, but these were Italians, and Italy produced popes like the "grande écoles" produced elites.

The election of a Polish pope probably pleased Italian lay society the most. The crisis of Christian democracy, ongoing since the end of the 1960s, raised the question of hegemony exercised since 1947 in varying degrees by a Christian party and of its ties (though these were loose since the early 1970s) with the Holy See, and made them somewhat open to the change. The emotional atmosphere created by the kidnapping (March 1978) and assassination of Aldo Moro, to whose kidnappers Pope Paul VI had proposed the trade of Moro's life for his own (April 1978) had reintroduced religion into a political arena that was trying to eradicate its Christian roots, planted after World War II, by rejecting both Italian communism and a creeping perpetuation of fascism. A non-Italian pope might allow this. In his installation homily of 22 October, John Paul II, however, placed himself right in the direct line of the history of the Roman papacy: "On St. Peter's throne, today, sits a pope who is not Roman. A bishop who is a son of Poland. But from this instant, he becomes Roman also. Yes, Roman. . . ." Elsewhere people wanted to hear words that were more conciliar than institutional, and John Paul II was quick to pronounce them on 17 October at a mass celebrated in the SISTINE CHAPEL before an open conclave:

> First of all, we must insist on the lasting importance of the ecumenical Second Vatican Council, and this means, for us, the formal commitment to carry out its decisions [. . .] But just as the council does not exist only in documents, it does not end with its implementation in the immediate post-Council years. We therefore consider it a primary obligation to promote the application of liturgical norms which come from ecclesiastical authority and exclude the arbitrary and uncontrolled innovations as well as the stubborn rejection of what has been legitimately planned and introduced into the sacred rites.

This preplanned speech was obscured by the famous appeal at the end of the homily on 22 October: "My brothers and sisters, don't be afraid to welcome Christ and accept his power [. . .] Be not afraid! Open, throw wide all doors to Christ [. . .] Be not afraid! Christ knows what is in the hearts of men! And he alone knows!" This was a sample of the pontifical policy, so much discussed and followed, because the mystery of his election seemed to bring with it attitudes no less mysterious, ready to synthetize multiple demands and expectations, if not contradictory ones.

At the center was the Church of St. Peter with the pope as its vicar; "One, holy, apostolic." A catholic Church, that is to say, carved into the history of salvation as the fulfilment of the promise made to Israel, before all other monotheistic churches. Ecumenism, to which John Paul II subscribed, must come as the result of an agreement on the primacy of St. Peter's see. The discussions with the Anglicans, which almost succeeded in 1989, touched on the question of the difference between primacy and precedence; the Catholic Church as "One", the 92 voyages made by John Paul II between 1979 and the end of 2000 supported this goal, and he did not hesitate to excommunicate and isolate Monsignor Lefebvre and his followers in schism on 30 June 1988. A Catholic Church as "apostolic": John Paul II, also through his voyages, wished to demonstrate the principle of collegiality. The Catholic Church as "holy": the call to sanctity and the review of the ways of achieving sanctity, is one of the recurring themes of a pontificate that wishes to make known the specific virtues of the blessed ones and the saints, that honored the greatest cult sites with its presence, especially Marian ones. John Paul II has, from the beginning of his pontificate, felt that the continued attention paid to his activities gave him a way to spread a model of pontifical piety reserved until then to the personal (and logical) life of a reigning pope: prayer. This meditative pope, enclosed in an athletic body, whose fervent attitudes show through his gestures, has given the world the impression of solitude in the exercise of his functions as well as an exceptional relationship to the supernatural through public piety. He combined public and personal, incorporating the crowds touched by the comings and goings of a pope who made each stop, each meeting a step on the road of his mission: the resurrection, in the late 20th century, of transcended Christianity in the name of a historic call to the values which it is his responsibility to represent.

John Paul II chose two ways to accomplish this: an even more progressively centralized government and a more and more precise prophetism. Since 1979, he has created 154 cardinals, in eight consistories, renewing—with the help of Paul VI's dispositions—almost all of the SACRED COLLEGE where the Europeans are now in the minority. Beginning in 1979, he established a model for bishops corresponding to his own: pastors, intellectuals,

teachers, including members of the regular clergy. He inspired a general enthusiasm among youth in his annual and symbolic PILGRIMAGES. He received, in private or public audiences, those who acted upon his message. He also demonstrated the complete independence of the Holy See from civil society by receiving both Yasser Arafat (15 September 1982) and Kurt Waldheim (in 1989). This spirit of freedom was given to him by the circumstances of his election and was recognized as soon as he used it. It was John Paul II who, according to the plans drawn up in 1978, completed the new CODE OF CANON LAW (1983) promised by John XXIII in 1958, reflected upon the heritage of Vatican II (during the extraordinary synod of 1985), met the man who had tried to assassinate him (17 December 1983), went to a meeting of Calvinsts in Geneva (12–17 June 1984), and undertook a historic journey to Israel in 2000. The same man was one of the driving forces behind the fall of the Berlin Wall in 1989 through ecumenical activities, calling for faith in mankind against a totalitarian society. The chronology of John Paul II's pontificate can be broken up into short periods. From 1978 to 1985 he assumed the heritage of Vatican II with an authoritarian interpretation of it; from 1985 to 1989 he reaped the fruits of it; from 1989 to the present he has proposed a demanding interpretation of the Church of which his ENCYCLICALS *Veritatis Splendor* and *Fides et Ratio* are the greatest expressions.

The Case for John Paul II. A cause in the Church, consists of the introduction—today—of a person for BEATIFICATION or CANONIZATION. It is the introduction of a file in which the historical portion plays an important part: that of examining the vocation that manifested itself throughout life, that is attested to by testimonies among which miracles performed after death constitute a strong part. Few popes have been beatified or canonized. PIUS X, of the modern popes, is the most recent instance. Paul VI, introduced in 1965, in full council, the causes of PIUS XII and of John XXIII and John Paul II beatified the latter in October 2000. The need for significant models led John Paul II to collective canonizations that astonished the public (117 Catholics martyred in Vietnam from the 18th and 19th centuries on 19 June 1988, and 120 Chinese martyrs in 2000). This collection of saints, including natives, missionaries, clerics, and religious individuals of various nationalities demonstrates the will to remind people of the meaning of faith; an explanation of the vocation, an acceptance of the meaning of the vocation in martyrdom. In all, by the end of 2000, John Paul II had proclaimed 994 Blesseds in 123 beatification ceremonies and 447 saints in canonization ceremonies.

John Paul II has been referred to as "an unclassifiable pope" (René Rémond, *Le Monde*, October 1988), an enigma (Juan Arias, 1986), a "superstar," a traditionalist, and a progressive moderate in Vatican II who became a traditionalist 15 years later. Although he may be any one or all of these things, what is certain is that his pontificate has been the most influential of the 20th century.

Philippe Levillain

Bibliography

Abu-Rabi, I. M. "Pope John Paul II and Islam," *Muslim World* 88 (1998), 279–96.

Alberigo, G. "Jean Paul II: Dix ans de pontificat," *Études*, 368/5 (1988), 669–81.

Amerio, R. *Ista Unum: Étude des variations de l'Église catholique au XXe siècle*, Paris, 1987.

Aparicio Manso, E. "Juan Pablo II, misionero de la juventud," *Burgense, Collectanea Scientifica*, 32/1 (1991), 231–77.

Arias, J. *L'Enigma Wojtyla*, Madrid, 1986.

Bernstein, C. *His Holiness: John Paul II and the Hidden History of Our Time*, New York, 1996.

Bertetto, D. "Maria en el magisterio de Juan Pablo II," *Scripta theologica*, 20 (1988), 129–62.

Brodevani, E. "Giovanni Paolo II e la scienza," *Aggiornamenti Sociali Milano*, 34, 9–10 (1983), 579–97.

Buttiglione, R. "La Pensée de K. Wojtyla sur la relation hommefemme," *Laval théologique et philosophique*, 40/1 (1984), 3–29.

Casanova, A. "Crise de civilisation et libération: Les solutions de Jean Paul II," *La Pensée*, 247 (1985), 86–98.

Chelini, J. *L'Église de Jean Paul II face à l'Europe: Dix années d'action, 1978–1988*, Paris, 1989.

Clarke, W. N. "The Complementarity of Faith and Philosophy in the Search for Truth," *Communio* 26 (1999), 22–39.

De Roeck, J. *Jean Paul II*, Paris, 1978.

Dyduch, J. "La contribution de Mgr Karol Wojtyla à la doctrine du laïc à Vatican II," *Analecta Cracoviensia*, 20 (1988), 151–64.

Echeverria, E. J., and Echeverria, D. R. "John Paul II and America's New Birth of Freedom," *Josphinum Journal of Theology* 6 (1999), 60–74.

Frossard, A. *Le Monde de Jean Paul II*, Paris, 1991.

Frossard, A. *N'ayez pas peur. Dialogues avec Jean Paul II*, Paris, 1982.

Gneuhs, G., ed. *The Legacy of Pope John Paul II: His Contribution to Catholic Thought*, New York, 2000.

Gray, C. B. "Images and morals of John Paul II," *Irish Theological Quarterly*, 53/4 (1987), 303–19.

Grootaers, J. *De Vatican II à Jean Paul II: Le grand tournant de l'Église catholique*, Paris. 1981.

Hebblethwaite, P. *Introducing John Paul II*, London, 1982.

Hebblethwaite, P. *The Year of Three Popes*, London, 1978.

Hervieu-Leger, D. "Jean Paul II: La stratégie de concentration catholique," *L'Année sociologique*, 38 (1988), 213–31.

Huerga, A. "Karol Wojtyla, commentateur de saint Jean de la Croix," *Angelicum*, 56 (1979), 358–66.

Joblin, J. "Jean-Paul II et les socialismes. L'arrière-plan de l'éthique de la décision," *Nouvelle Revue théologique*, 108 (1986), 1 and 2, 47–63 and 239–48.

Johnson, P. *Pope John Paul II*, London, 1982.

Kalinowski, G. *Autour de "Personne et acte" de Karol Wojtyla: Articles et conférences sur une rencontre du thomisme avec la phénoménologie*, Aix-en-Provence, 1987.

Kallarangatt, J. "Fides et Ratio: It's Timeliness and Contribution," *Christian Orient*, 20 (1999), 22–39.

Kydrynski, J. "Les jeunes années de K. Wojtyla," *Perspectives polonaises, Varsovie*, 28 (1985) 15–23.

Landes, R. "From the Peace of God to the Promise Keepers: End of the Millennium Phenomena," *Modern Believing* 40 (1999), 6–17.

Lord, Layford *Pope John Paul II: Authorized Biography*, London, 1982.

Mattheuws, A. "De la Bible à Humanae vitae. Les catéchèses de Jean Paul II," *Nouvelle Revue théologique*, 111 (1989), 228–48.

Montalbo, M. Jr. "Karol Wojtyla's Philosophy of the Acting Person," *Philippiniana Sacra*, 23, 69 (1988), 333–86.

O'Connor, E. "The Roots of Pope John Paul II's Devotion to Mary," *Marian Studies*, 39 (1988), 78–114.

Peyrous, B. "La sainteté dans l'Église depuis Vatican II," *Nouvelle Revue théologique*, 107/3 (1985), 361–75.

Sacco, U. C. *John Paul the II and World Politics: Twenty Years of a Search for a New Approach*, Leuven, Peeters, Hadleigh, 1999.

Serretti, M. "Etica e antropologia folosofica: Considerazioni, su Maritain et Wojtyla," *Sapienza* 38.1 (1985), 15–31.

Silva, G. S. "La idea de la técnica moderna en el Magisterio de la Iglesia desde Pio XII hasta Juan Pablo II (1985)," *Anales de la Facultad de Teologia*, 38/2 (1989), 1–166.

Sudia, A. "El 'modelo polacco' en lo politico latinoamerican," *Theologia Xavieriana*, 37/83 (1987) 219–41.

Sztafrowski, E. "The Roman Curia of John Paul II," *Prawo Kanoniczne*, 33 (1990), 21–81 (in Polish)

Szulc, T. *Pope John Paul II: The Biography*, New York; London, 1995.

Walsh, M. J. *John Paul II*, London, 1994.

Williams, G. H. *The Mind of John Paul II, Origins of His Thought and Actions*, New York, 1981.

Wojtyla, K., translated into English; *Easter Vigil and Other Poems*, New York, 1979; *The Jeweler's Shop: A Meditation on the Sacrament of Matrimony Passing on Occasion into Drama*, New York, 1980; *Faith According to John of the Cross*, San Francisco, 1981.

Wynn, W. *Keepers of the Keys: John XXIII, Paul VI and John Paul II: Three Who Have Changed the Church*, New York, 1988.

JOSEPHISM. This is the name given to the religious policies of the Austrian monarchy during the ten-year rule of Emperor Joseph II (1780–90). The assortment of measures taken were take result of the political vision of an enlightened despot, well versed in Enlightenment philosophy and yet still a good Catholic, and still able to maintain relationships between the Church and the state. Josephism, strongly criticized by conservatives and a portion of the Catholic hierarchy, has been variously appreciated by historians. In our opinion, if you take into account the last years of research, as much Austrian as international, it was more the result of a religious evolution that took place throughout the whole 18th century, even if the emperor, with his usual fiery passion, gave it his own personal stamp, which would deeply mark the future development of Austrian Catholicism. This is why it seems necessary to show the steps which, little by little, transformed Tridentine Catholicism, which had been rather successfully imposed by the Habsburgs before 1740, and show the role that owes as much to JANSENISM as it does to a reforming Catholicism.

The first crack in the system (in the 17th century) was actually opened by the Jansenists, protected by Empress Maria Theresa, who was deeply convinced of the need for evolution within the Church and in the relationships between Church and state. Two criteria defined the Jansenist attitude in 18th-century Austria: first, a sort of moral rigor, as opposed to the perceived laxness of the JESUITS, and second, the serious study of the Bible and the Church Fathers, which intellectually corresponded to the rejection of modern scholarship and Aristotle's philosophy, still all powerful in the theology schools and diocesan seminaries. Instead of Aristotelianism, as interpreted by the Jesuits, which had dominated the intellectual life of the baroque period, they preferred Cartesian philosophy and the history of the Church. However, it is clear that in no case would Austrian Jansenists have accepted the rigorous Augustinianism of Jansen or his doctrine of grace. The base of their religious view rested upon the *Catechism of Montpellier*, the work of Charles Joachim Colbert de Croissy. Following that, the *Nouvelles ecclésiastiques*, published in Utrecht by Count Dupac de Bellegarde, was widely read while the ideas would be taken up again beginning in 1776 by a more accessible newspaper in the German language, the *Wiener Kirchenzeitungen*.

Like their French contemporaries during the Enlightenment, the Jansenists were hostile toward private masses and the small devotions that popular piety engendered. They wanted a stripped-down Church and favored the neoclassic style, which became dominant after 1780. They went as far as to condemn PILGRIMAGES, which, giving rhythm to religious life in rural parishes, sometimes gave way to licentiousness, which their moral rigor condemned. Everything set them against the dominant movements in the clergy as well as in the Christian people of Austria; they advocated a cultural revolution within Austrian Catholicism. Nevertheless, they found support among the conservatives who favored this "reforming Catholicism" and encouraged evolution of the Austrian episcopate, a major step because the religious reforms had been imposed from above onto the frankly reticent faithful.

If Jansenism was tightly linked to a culture of primarily French expression, "reforming Catholicism" was born in Roman surroundings in the 1720s, as a reaction against Jesuit domination. This was the movement of the *sana dottrina*, which advocated, as did Jansenism, a return to the original sources of Christianity: the Holy Scripture and the writings of the Church Fathers. At the Roman *Collegium Germanicum*, where the future bishops of central Europe were trained, it influenced the "reforming bishops" of the monarchy, Counts Thun, Firmian, Waldstein, Schaffgotsch, and Hallweil, and especially the two prelates who occupied the see of the archbishop of Vienna in the second half of the 18th century, Counts Trautson (1751–7) and Migazzi (1757–99). The latter, in particular, played a considerable role in the evolution of Austrian Catholicism, as much by his role as archbishop of Vienna under four successive rulers as by his own evolution: a reformer in the beginning, he became frightened by the consequences of his own boldness and took much more conservative positions beginning in 1765, before joining the reactionary camp of Joseph II. By helping Maria Theresa to break the Jesuit monopoly and by founding a diocesan seminary in Vienna, he helped shape a generation of reforming priests who quickly occupied key positions in the Austrian capital: the chapter of St. Stephen's cathedral, chairs in the theology faculty at the university, the censorship commission.

In 1759, a crisis whose origins are still little understood had ended in a reform highly influential for the future of Austrian Catholicism. Using her power as ruler, Maria Theresa had basically taken control of the censorship commission from the Jesuits, who had dominated it for more than a century. As Klingenstein has shown, this reform coincided with a secularization and liberalization of action, not with a suppression of censure, for in the course of the quarter-century during which Austria opened itself to foreign influences (1765–90), censorship was never abolished. Still, beginning in 1765, it was possible to purchase, in Vienna bookstores, just about any published book (except the smutty works popular in the 18th century). The ruling powers had, therefore, taken control of intellectual life and could turn opinion to their own ends. Joseph II did not hesitate to use this to promote his own political views.

In 1780, at the end of the co-regency (from 1765 to 1780, Joseph II had shared his reign with his mother) and the death of Maria Theresa, the situation changed markedly. If his mother had favored Jansenists to the point of taking Canon Ignace Muller as her confessor (from 1765 to 1780), Joseph II liked them very little despite the similarity of their ideas to those of his own program, because the Jansenists were as hostile as the conservatives toward the sort of State-led Catholicism Joseph II envisaged.

Joseph II's reforms were as severe a shock for the pastors as they were for the faithful. He shocked most Austrian Catholics by changing the relationship between the Church and the state. He gave this task to a commission that was inspired by the ideas of Hontheim (*alias* Febronius), the chancellor of the University of Treviso, according to which the Church's main function was to dispense the sacraments and take care of the moral instruction of its followers. As "Supreme Protector of the Church in Austria," the emperor demanded total submission of the clergy and instituted reforms inspired by Jansenism.

More than 400 convents were closed and their properties, which had come from donations made long ago by the faithful, were transferred to a state foundation, the "funds of religion," whose revenues were used to cover other expenses of the Church. The maintenance of many religious houses that were three-fourths empty was difficult to justify, especially to the viewpoint of the Enlightenment, in which most of the regular clergy were seen as "idle," with nothing to justify their existence. A religious person could only justify his position if he were a pastor or a teacher. This action could be justified on its general principles but was criticized due to its methods.

The execution of these measures was sometimes assigned to "strong characters" who destroyed libraries and sacked convent buildings, shocking the faithful nearby and contributing to the alienation of many Austrian Catholics toward Josephism. "Enlightened" prelates allowed an anticlerical propaganda to spread, which mocked traditional forms of piety and showed a biting irony toward the adversaries of the Josephist Church. However, the "funds of religion" were never used for profane goals and served to complete the work of the Counter Reformation on the pastoral level. Some clerics were used as curates in parishes that had been poorly served until then, and the monies freed up were used to create new bishoprics and new parishes, to better reach the population—a project deferred for more than a century by Catholic aristocrats (often quite pious) reluctant to return possessions that had formerly belonged to the

Church. The results of this policy were spectacular. Five new bishoprics were established under Joseph II (Linz, Sankt-Pölten, Ljubljana, Hradec Kralove, and Ceske Budejovice) and the government created an impressive number of parishes: 263 in lower Austria alone, 180 in Moravia, and more than 1,000 in Hungary. The result was better-instructed believers, better served by a clergy closer to them. This was a positive application of the program of Catholic reforms.

The State also involved itself deeply in parish life: religious confraternities were bullied, when they were not simply dissolved; processions and pilgrimages that were so large a part of traditional devotions were suppressed. Imperial orders directed preaching, liturgy, funerals, and the decoration of churches, so that the King of Prussia, Frederick II, made fun of Joseph II's mania for interfering in the religious life of his subjects, calling him "my brother the sacristan." Civil servants had orders to attend sermons to make sure that priests did not criticize the government or the emperor. Denunciations of recalcitrant priests increased, bringing changes and sanctions. Finally a bureaucratization of pastoral activities and a cold regularization of religious services, administered by "enlightened" churchmen appealed to reason and not to the hearts of the faithful. These criticisms were directed at the new generation of priests trained in the general seminaries.

Joseph II suppressed the diocesan seminaries and convent schools, whose obedience left something to be desired, in order to create State establishments, called general seminaries, which were withdrawn from the authority of bishops, and were administered by teachers accustomed to the new ideas. They were run with military discipline, teaching a hatred for Rome and persuading the seminarians that they were the pillars of the Josephist Church. The emperor would probably have acted more moderately if he had not been so strongly opposed by prelates as intractable as Cardinal Migazzi. The archbishop of Salzburg, Count Colloredo, and the bishops of Hradec Kralove and Ljubljana spontaneously instituted reforms in order to get reputations as "philosopher" prelates. Other sees were progressively filled with candidates accustomed to the new ideas, who had been part of the ecclesiastical commission and who allowed the development of an anticlerical propaganda against the opponents of the Josephist Church.

To show that the era of the Counter-Reformation and the all-powerful Roman Church was at an end, Joseph II promulgated the Edict of Tolerance on 13 October 1781, which gave freedom of religion to Lutherans, Calvinists, and Orthodox, and returned civil rights to Hungarian Protestants. Still, Catholicism remained the "dominant" religion of the State; non-Catholic religious buildings were not allowed to have fronting squares or bell towers, and the state civil records remained in the hands of the

Catholic clergy. These measures were greeted gratefully by the crypto-Protestant communities of Austria and Bohemia, which had continued to read the Bible and sing canticles secretly. In Hungary, where half the population was still not Catholic (in 1790, 25 percent were Calvinist, 5 percent Lutheran, and 20 percent Greek Orthodox), this action caused the Protestant nobility to rally to Joseph II's policies. As for Jews, although they did not receive full civil rights, their treatment was better: they were authorized to perform manual work, found industrial businesses and attend universities, and laws requiring them to dress differently were abolished. If these reforms were well received in the communities of Bohemia and Austria, who wanted a progressive integration, the Jews of Galicia were much less enthusiastic.

In a more general way, most of the religious reforms were badly received and led to a conflict with the Holy See. The clergy, with Cardinal Migazzi at their head, took positions completely hostile to the reforms and the enlightened prelates. The conservative hierarchy criticized the general seminaries so vigorously that their introduction into the Austrian Netherlands in 1787 sparked the first revolt against Joseph II. The people remained strongly attached to the baroque forms of piety, the beautiful ceremonies and richly decorated churches, the cult of saints, the feast days, and especially the processions and pilgrimages. An austere and cerebral piety did not suit them. Besides, the rural population remained faithful to the regular priests persecuted by Joseph II, so that their allegiance was stretched between an emperor who had done so much for their welfare by abolishing the feudal servitudes in 1781 and who, on the other hand, challenged their vision of the world and their concept of religion. The peasants, along with the majority of the clergy, constituted a powerful force of resistance against Josephism and an extraordinary bastion of conservatism.

Another action worried the Holy See. By extending to the entire monarchy the Hungarian practice of *placetum regium*, it was forbidden for bishops to write directly to the Holy See or to its representative in Vienna, the papal NUNCIO. All correspondence had to pass through the imperial chancellery first. On the other hand, the nomination of bishops remained unchanged. In the dioceses belonging to the Holy Roman Empire, bishops continued to be elected by the canons of the cathedral chapter, whereas in Hungary, it was a royal privilege given by Rome to St. Stephen to name the bishops.

Josephist policy provoked a conflict with the CURIA, that Chancellor Kaunitz, as a true philosopher took ironically. PIUS VI, worried about maintaining Church unity, decided to travel to Vienna in 1782. If his welcome by the population was overwhelming, the court only showed a polite respect, and Kaunitz gave the pope a cold shoulder. Conversations accomplished nothing, with each speaker maintaining

his own position. Pius VI did not insist on the abolition of the reforms, but did require upholding the BULL *Unigenitus*, which condemned Jansenism. The pontiff was reassured of the most essential thing: He would maintain his PRIMACY on the questions of doctrine and would let the emperor handle questions of discipline. A trip made by the emperor to Rome in 1783 confirmed these provisions.

Finally, Joseph II continued the educational policies begun under Maria Theresa. The most original aspect of the Enlightenment had been very ambitious school reforms, accomplished before Joseph II's reign, which put Austria on a par with the German states (Prussia and the Rhine electorates). This was the work of Maria Theresa and the prelate Ignace Felbiger (1773 for Austria, 1777 for Hungary); it gave secondary education to the clergy and retained tight control over primary schools. By reforming the schools and colleges, Maria Theresa had prepared for the future and placed the monarchy in a position to bring progress to the empire. In 1783 the Commission on Education and Censorship saw its power given to the Austrian monarchy. From then on, education was a function of the State but in a confessional perspective, as the emperor believed that religion gave the best moral instruction. The teaching profession would be closely watched by inspectors; efficient for primary instruction, this system proved to be mediocre for secondary schooling and disastrous for the universities, which Joseph II saw as schools for training professionals such as government workers or doctors.

Despite Josephist policies, Austrian culture remained deeply influenced by Catholicism, while the Enlightenment represented more of a religious modification for it than a dechristianization; while the elite gravitated toward a more intellectual religion, the masses remained faithful to traditional methods of worship. By the creation of general seminaries and the progressive selection of reforming prelates for strategic positions, the Josephist Church was victorious and gave new direction to a Church profoundly marked by the Counter-Reformation. However, Joseph II's reforms also increased pastoral care and, once the more unpleasant aspects of Josephism were erased (general seminaries in particular), the Austrian monarchy was a bastion of religion during the revolutionary time and once again deserved its name, after 1792, of "Catholic Austria."

Jean Beringer

Bibliography

Fejtö, F. *Joseph II. Un Habsbourg révolutionnaire*, Paris, 1948.

Hersche, P. *Der Spätjansenismus in Oesterreich*, Vienna, 1977.

Klingenstein, G. *Staatsgewalt und Kirchliche Autorität. Zur Studie der Zensor in Oesterreich des Aufklärung*, Graz, 1973.

Kovacs, E. *Katholische Aufklärung und Josephinismus*, Vienna, 1979.

Maass, F. *Der Josephinismus. Quellen zu seiner Geschichte in Oesterreich 1760–1790*, 5 vols., Vienna, 1951–61, *Fontes Rerum Austriacarum*, II, 71–75.

Mitrofanov, P. *Joseph II. Seine politische und kulturelle Tätigkeit*, 2 vols., Vienna-Leipzig, 1910.

Valjavec, F. *Der Josephinismus. Zur geistigen Entwicklung Oesterreichs im 18. und 19. Jahrhundert*, Munich-Vienna, 1944.

Winter, E. *Joseph II. Von de geistigen Quellen und letzten Beweggründen seiner Reformideen. Darstellungen aus dem Kultur und Geistesleben Oesterrichs*, Vienna, 1946.

JUBILLEE. See **Holy Year.**

JUDAISM.
Up to 1870. The standard picture of papal-Jewish relations up to modern times is dominated by two figures, Gregory the Great (GREGORY I) and INNOCENT III. This is a great historiographical paradox. Pope Gregory's letters clearly set a pattern. Over 25 of them have been preserved, and much of what they say has also been inserted into the canons, whether in Gratian's *Decretum* or in GREGORY IX's *Decretals*. Their message is simple: Various laws require that Jews be inferior to Christians and be highly regulated toward this end; at the same time, Christians (and the Church) are held to respect Jewish rights, including the right freely to practice Judaism; nor may Jews forcibly be converted. This policy represents the papal standard of behavior through the 16th century, if not beyond.

However, and this is the paradox, Gregory's legacy was not continuous. Its persistence was really owed to the activity of 10th- and 11th-century canonists, not the innate staying power of the words of Pope Gregory himself. A search of all the legal and theological materials produced in the 350 years between 603, Gregory's death, and a tract composed by Gerhard of Mainz in 938 reveals that Gregory's letters on the Jews were never cited. What remained was the ominous tone and implications of the 9th-century Agobard of Lyons: "Since, he said, they [the Jews] dwell among us, we ought not to be malignant toward them, nor should we threaten their lives, safety, or property." Otherwise, Agobard argued for nearly total Jewish-Christian segregation. Innocent III is blamed for bringing this segregationist policy to a head during the LATERAN IV Council of 1215.

In fact, this council did issue severe laws concerning Jews. It is responsible for the first demand that Jews wear distinguishing clothing. Innocent based his call on the commandment in the Torah that Jews are to wear fringes on their garments (as seen on the modern *tallith*, or prayer shawl) and indicated that what the Torah ordered should still be observed. However, only a few years after the 1215 COUNCIL, the demand was converted into the derisive sign Jews were forced to sew on their clothing; although enforcement was not continuous, there certainly was enforcement. It is because of this order to wear special clothing that Lateran IV has received so bad a name. The wording of the conciliar edict shows it was originally intended to prevent sexual relations between Christians and Jews, whose prohibition was traditional; Hrabanus Maurus, for instance, had forbidden such relations in the early 9th century, although we have little direct evidence on the subject. The infamy of the Jews' unique dress came later.

More important, the real beginning of laws calling for social separation comes from Paul in I Corinthians, 10:16–22, a call incorporated by the early Middle Ages into the Visigothic law *Christianorum ad aras*: Christians were to dissociate themselves from the altars of all non-Christians and so avoid "pollution" of themselves as members of the body of Christ and in the reception of the Eucharist; Paul was explicit. Consequently, and with Paul's admonition frequently recalled, early medieval councils and Church leaders issued canons seeking segregation, prohibiting, for example, Jews and Christians from dining together, as well as forbidding Jews to show themselves in public during Easter week. All social contact was condemned. Agobard of Lyons, in particular, was obsessed about Jews and Christians sharing the same table, lest the Christian thereby be sullied and made "impure"; he had metaphorized any meal into the table of the Eucharist: prohibiting "anyone who has become impure through fraternizing and dining with Jews from breaking bread with any of our priests." This was the notion of I Corinthians 10:16, as well as the Visigothic law *Christianorum ad aras* elaborated. Jews were also not permitted to have Christian servants (or slaves) in their homes; here the fear of sexuality was acute.

To this was added a fear of Judaizing. The origins of this fear were again in Paul, Galatians 4 and 5, arguing that like the son of Hagar, those (Christians) who impugned their faith by practicing circumcision, should be expelled. By the Visigothic period, the Judaizers had become like the Jews themselves, in particular, "backsliding" converts. The Spanish Visigothic rulers, with the probable collaboration of some ecclesiastics, and with the reluctant consent of others, demanded that all Jews be baptized. Most eventually were, unwillingly, and quickly reverted to Judaism. The body of Visigothic law generated to reverse this process also perceived Jews as a *genus*, a virtually racial category, so that the laws specify "baptized Jews." From the 9th-century missives of Agobard of Lyons, it is clear that this experience was traumatic, to the extent that it informed attitudes toward *con-*

versos in the 15th century and afterward. It also affected attitudes toward the many Jews who returned to Judaism after the forced baptisms that took place especially during the CRUSADE of 1096.

In the view of all this, we should not see Lateran IV's attempts at social segregation as innovative. Arguably, one may say they were pursuing an equilibrium between privilege and restriction; separation, distance, but also acceptance of Jews and Judaism, much, therefore, as Gregory the Great had specified. Indeed, in one realm, there was outright mitigation in 1215, that of lending at interest. Jews, unlike Christians, were permitted to take *non immoderatasve usuras*; the right to do this was not papally abrogated, in fact, until 1682. If there was a culmination of anything in 1215, therefore, it was of the search for a Jewish-Christian equilibrium, of the kind expressed in the *proemia* to all papal BULLS concerning Jews. Clauses saying "the Jews are worthy of hatred," were actually preludes to additional clauses saying that "nonetheless Jews should be tolerated (*tolerare*)." Conversely, bulls saying that the Church accepted Jews were most often introductions to excoriation and restriction. The drive toward this equilibrium had been somewhat interrupted by the forced conversions and relapses following 1096. Still, through the 13th century, and in fact through the later 16th, the drive toward a balance prevailed.

The fundamental move toward equilibrium may be seen in the pre-crusade texts of Burchard of Worms and Ivo of Chartes, who, indeed, cite Gregory the Great and also speak of murdering Jews as "destroying God's image." ALEXANDER II, who made the first unambiguous statement on the legal and political place of Jews in European society (about 1063), did not invoke Gregory's words. He said, rather, that Jews were not to be treated as enemies, much as the Muslims in Spain should be. (The pope was clearly under Cluniac influence in this regard, including the ideals of the *Reconquista* and the just war; in the 11th century, the wars between Christians and Muslims were only beginning to acquire the sense of a grand war between the faiths, the same sense that would fuel the imminent crusades). Jews, Alexander continued, were passive, "everywhere ready to be subservient," meaning to accept the dictates of the canons that consigned them to inferiority with respect to Christians. The notion that Jews did not consider, nor were they capable of, harming Christians (*nec sciunt, nec possunt contra Christianos*) was still being repeated by Humbert of Romans, master general of the Dominican order, in preparation for the Council of Lyons in 1274. This view was reflected in the thinking of Thomas Aquinas, who portrayed Jews as the necessary balance on a scholastic scale. They represented the fruits of bad faith, which were exemplified by the Jews' miserable presence in Christian society. The Jewish presence was thus necessary, and Jews were

entitled to justice, but certainly not to judicial equality in modern terms.

It was this thinking and tradition that motivated Innocent III. One sees this in his letters, some offering privilege and protection, others effecting enormous anger. If Jews forced (already illegal) Christian wet nurses of their children to spill their milk into a latrine following reception of the Eucharist, then this insulted Christianity; to Jews the object was no doubt to prevent the transmission of magically potent substances. Innocent, in his terms, was justly angered, but Jews were also entitled to a papal rescript saying that having asked for protection (the form of the text is the traditional *tuitio* charter between a ruler and dependent subjects, however in a formulation that apparently remained valid only for Jews), they were entitled to receive it. No one was to disturb their prayers and no one was forcibly to baptize their children. The decrees of Lateran IV must be viewed in this light.

INNOCENT IV sharpened the definitions of Jewish protection. He stated outright that the Jews were entitled to justice. He decried the blood libel at Valreas, and said they were equally entitled to keep their (rabbinic) literature because it was necessary for Jews to understand their religion. Yet Sinibaldo Fieschi was also a great canonist. When he said these things, he was well aware of a certain ambivalence. For as a canonist, this same pope had written that Jews might be punished directly by the Church should their literature, the same literature he had said they might retain, impugn Christianity or should it pervert the Jews' own beliefs. This last, the charge of being a *Nova Lex*, was that laid at the feet of the Talmud in the early 1240s; on these grounds the Talmud was burned at least twice in Paris in those years. Innocent IV also indirectly approved what amounted to forced preaching to the Jews of Aragon.

It would be easy to attribute these inconsistencies in papal policies to pressures applied by the mendicants, the Dominicans in particular, who led the attack on Jewish literature, and whose Master General Raymond of Peñafort had edited the *Decretals* of Innocent's immediate predecessor, Gregory IX. Yet the real moving factor in defining precise lines of Jewish justice was the concept of *caritas*, a term sometimes alternating with the notion of *misericordia* toward the Jews, meaning that the very justice on which the world rested applied to Jews as well as to the faithful. It even affected Dominicans like Raymond of Peñafort as well as Humbert of Romans. One need note that in editing the decretal of Innocent III, which was to be known as the *Constitutio pro iudaeis*, the bull *Sicut iudaeis non*, which was also to be repeated for emphasis (as a decretal, it was permanently valid law), Peñafort himself removed an opaque but clearly threatening addendum of Innocent III saying that the protections of the text applied only to those Jews who did not plot against or threaten their Christian hosts. The Jewish right to live in Christian lands, even if one sought to convert them, expurgate their books, and keep a tight lid on their behavior, was beyond reproach, so much so that when a late 15th-century Franciscan tried to have Jews expelled on the grounds that they had violated this trust, he rested his case on Roman law, which offered similar guarantees (and, by implication, threats). No one, it seems, would take on the doctrines of *Sicut iudaeis non* outright. Not even BENEDICT XIII violated these doctrines, even in his drastic *Etsi doctoris gentium* of 1415. He did not violate them because he believed the force of law would bring Jews to the baptismal font. Benedict's 16th century successor Paul IV believed the same, and he, too, despite many restrictive edicts, left the doctrines of *Sicut iudaeis non* intact.

The fingerprints, so to speak, of *Sicut iudaeis non* are visible even in matters that verged on disrupting the balance. Thus, Innocent IV said flatly that justice demands the Jews be allowed the literature that preserves their faith. MARTIN IV said in 1281 that the inquisition might not deal arbitrarily with Jews. They were not to be charged simply for *familiaritas* with converts. Only true instigators of apostasy (aiding Jews to return to Judaism) made Jews liable to inquisitional intervention. Finally, the bull allowing Franciscans to preach to Jews, *Vineam sorec* (1278) of NICHOLAS III, has an extraordinary penalty clause. Jews not appearing for sermons would be reported to the pope, who would "consider" a remedy. No such empty penalty clause exists elsewhere, certainly not in bulls concerning Jews.

To upset the norm required real extremes. In the early 14th century, JOHN XXII had to resort to charges of Jewish necromancy to expel the Jews, very briefly it turned out, from Avignon. This charge was repeated in 1569 and 1593 in the PAPAL STATES, where the expulsion was definitive, except from Rome and Ancona. Even *Turbato corde*, the bull (1267) allowing inquisitors directly to prosecute Jews is limited to Jews who provoke apostasy. The law of the Church was, for the popes, indeed the law. It was so much the law that in 1354 the Jews of Barcelona told Pedro IV of Aragon that if the king did not turn to the pope to get a definition of when the inquisition might prosecute Jews, then they would do so themselves. They were most confident in the result, which possibly was the statement of Nicholas Eymerich in his later 14th century manual that the inquisition could try Jews as Jews (with no reference to apostasy) only if they denied God.

Something, however, was undermining this stability. It was not the question of the Talmud in the 1240s, which was a local Parisian affair and was moved by the rebellious secular clergy, as attested by the signatures on the condemnation of 1248. The popes soon realized that the attack on post-Biblical rabbinic law was also a muted attack on their equally post-Biblical law, mounted by those who still wanted to argue the primacy of the *Sacra Pagina*, and they limited condemnation to questions of blasphemy in the Talmudic text; real attacks stopped where the promoters were not royalty. The Spanish Dominican campaigns against the Talmud, too, died down in the late 13th century. The apparent claim of Ramon Martì, that current Judaism was a perversity, heretical unto its (biblical true) self, and a construct of the devil, never took hold; Judaism, of course, could never be a heresy in the sense of being heretical to Christianity for the obvious reason that one cannot be a heretic before one is baptized formally as a believer. So arcane, in any case, was Martì's *Pugio Fidei*, that when Petrus Galatinus plagiarized it wholesale in the early 16th century, it was a long time before the truth came out. Finally, even Franciscan preaching, which took on quasi-apocalyptic dimensions in the 15th century, and which viewed interest, especially interest taken by Jews, as gangrenous, did not deflect papal policy. The popes supported this lending until 1682. Observantine Franciscan support of blood libels was not effective. Sixtus IV, himself a Franciscan Conventual, who had been minister general of the order, was ultimately angered by the ritual murder libel at Trent in 1475.

The real movement toward instability began more subtly, as was implied above, in the wake of the crusades. Jews who had converted, forcibly or not, all slipped back into Judaism. The then anti-pope Wibert (CLEMENT III) protested bitterly. What the official pope, URBAN II thought, is not known. However, various chroniclers were highly exercised by these events, which they saw as the Judaizing so feared and prominent in early medieval legislation. It is no accident that these fears were paralleled by the growth, in the 12th and 13th centuries, of libels of ritual crucifixion, ritual murder, and eventual the host libel. All pointed to Jewish assaults on Christian integrity, on the mystical and real Corpus Christi. The libels, in fact, all unite in the story of Werner of Oberwessel as told in the late 13th century, who is at once named the *corpus mysticum* and the *corpus verum* (the Bollandists perpetuated this precise story in the 17th century). It is against this background that the application to the Jews of Paul's dictum in Galatians about expelling the son of Hagar began to make sense; so said the jurist Oldradus da Ponte in the early 14th century. Real expulsion in punishment for irreparable crimes was permissible. That which some have called grand vacillations in papal policy in the 14th and 15th centuries were really a grappling with the question of whether Jews were no longer entitled to the protection of *caritas* or *misericordia*.

In light of this, SIXTUS IV, was pulled to extremes, condemning the "filth" of Jewish expression, yet also condemning the violence done to justice at Trent in 1475. Seventy-five years later PAUL IV insisted that something radical had to be done. He may have been moved chiliastically, as is clear in a letter he wrote his sister about his times. He may have been moved to react to Protestantism or by the fears of new blood libels in Rome itself, and even more by reforming documents like the *Libellus ad Leonem Decem* of 1513, which urged unprecedented missionary activity among Jews. *Caritas* would stand. The Jews, therefore, would not be expelled, but they would live in a ghetto until the "pious lashes" (*piis verberibus*, in the words of the *Libellus*) of rigid legal application persuaded them that the time to realize the vision of Paul in Romans 11 had arrived. Concurring, PIUS V and CLEMENT VIII also thought it was necessary to expel the Jews from all localities of the Papal State, save Rome, Ancona, and the French papal posessions in and near Avignon. GREGORY XIII forced the Jews (quite illegally, as NICHOLAS III had recognized in 1278) to attend conversionary sermons. This policy became static.

The policy was to be made weightier, however, in the mid-18th century. The threat of incipient modernity moved BENEDICT XIV not only to tighten the already heavy ghetto restrictions, but also to rage at Polish Jews; they were, he said, "corrupting" Polish bishops by borrowing from the latter, who, themselves, took a share of the Jewish profits (1751). Yet, CLEMENT XIV, while still Cardinal Ganganelli, had repeated the 13th century papal condemnations of the blood libel. The old limits had not crumbled completely, but there would be no easing either. Papal policy toward Jews, now focused primarily, but not wholly, on the Jews of the Papal State, remained fixed until 1870. The Roman Ghetto and the Papal State fell simultaneously on 20 September of that year. Only then, in response to the libel at Polna in Bavaria in 1899, did LEO XIII make the total break and refuse to republish the letters of his medieval predecessors denouncing the blood libel. The old and the new, in fact, had merged. For contemporaneously, Monsignor Lorenzelli, the papal nuncio in France, was condemning one Abbé Pichot, a teacher of mathematics and science (in Limoges). Pichot, he said, was "*il sacerdote piu' dreyfusardo e piu' giudiazzante che si conosca*," who was guilty, too, of manifesting a spirit that was both "*umanitario* [he means lay and secular] *e dreyfusardo*." Dreyfus, secularism, Judaizing and ritual murder were all one, together embodying the modernity the Church so feared. In the context of a papacy without a state, a direct product of the emergence of the modern Italian state, an event itself linked intimately to the French abandonment of PIUS IX's regime following Pius's refusal to restore the surreptitiously baptized Edgardo Mortara to his family in 1858, the nearly two-millennia-old anxiety over (alleged) Judaizing had assumed an unprecedented dimension.

Kenneth Stow

Bibliography

Baron, S. W. *A Social and Religious History of the Jews*, 2nd ed. 18 vols., New York, 1983.

Browe, P. *Die Judenmission im Mittelalter und die Paepste*, Rome, 1942.

Caffiero, M. "'Le insidie dè perfidi Giudei,' Antiebraismo e riconquista Cattolica alla fine del settecento," *Rivista Storica Italiana* 105 (1993): 555–81.

Davies, W. D., and Finkelstein, L. *The Cambridge History of Judaism*, 3 vols., Cambridge, 1984.

Davies, W. D. *Christian Engagements with Judaism*, Morrisburg, PA, 1999.

Die Paepstlichen Bullen über die Blutbeschuldingung, Munich, 1900, no author.

Foa, A. "Il gioco del proselitismo: politica delle conversioni e controllo della violenza nella Roma del Cinquecento," in ed. M. Luzzati, M. Olivari, A. Veronese. *Ebrei e Cristiani nell'Italia Medievale e Moderna: Conversioni, Scambi, Contrasti*, Rome, 1988.

Grayzel, S. *The Popes and the Jews in the Thirteenth Century*, vol. 1, Philadelphia, 1933; and vol. 2, ed. K. Stow, New York, 1989.

Kedar, B. Z. "Canon Law and the Burning of the Talmud," *Bulletin of Medieval Canon Law* 9 (1979): 79–82.

Parente, F. "La Chiesa e il Talmud," in ed. C. Vivanti, *Gli ebrei in Italia, Storia d'Italia, Annali 11*, Turin, 1996.

Rodochanachi, E. *Le Saint-Siège et les Juifs, Le Ghetto a Rome*, Paris, 1891.

Rosa, M. "Tra tolleranza e repressione: Roma e gli ebrei nel '700," *Italia Judaica III*, Rome, 1989.

Simonsohn, S. *The Apostolic See and the Jews*, vols. 1–6, and vol. 8, Toronto, 1988–1991.

Stow, K. R. *The '1007 Anonymous' and Papal Sovereignty: Jewish Perceptions of the Papacy and Papal Policy in the High Middle Ages*, Cincinnati, 1984.

Stow, K. R. "The Avigonese Popes, or After the Expulsion," in ed. J. Cohen, *From Witness to Witchcraft: Jews and Judaism in Medieval Christian Thought*, Weisbaden, 1996.

Stow, K. R. "The Burning of the Talmud in 1553, In the Light of Sixteenth Century Catholic Attitudes Toward the Talmud," *Bibliothèque d'Humanisme et Renaissance* 34 (1972): 435–59.

Stow, K. R. *Catholic Thought and Papal Jewry Policy: 1555–1593*, New York, 1977.

Stow, K. R. "Expulsion Italian Style: The Case of Lucio Ferraris," *Jewish History* 3/1 (1988): 51–64.

Stow, K. R. "The Good of the Church, The Good of the State: The Popes and Jewish Money," in ed. D. Wood, *Christianity and Judaism* [= *Studies in Church History* 29] Oxford, 1992.

Stow, K. R. "Papal and Royal Attitudes Toward Jewish Lending," *AJS Review* 6 (1981): 161–84.

Stow, K. R. "Papal Mendicants or Mendicant Popes: Continuity and Change in Papal Policies toward the Jews at the end of the Fifteenth Century," in ed. L.

Simon and S. McMichael, *The Friars and the Jews*, Leiden, 2000.

Stow, K. R. *Taxation Community and State: The Jews and the Fiscal Foundations of the Early Modern Papal State*, Stuttgart, 1982.

Synan, E. *The Popes and the Jews in the Middle Ages*, New York, 1965.

After 1870. When Rome fell into the hands of Italian soldiers in September 1870, the pope lost his temporal power. From then on, he no longer ruled the Jews in the Roman ghetto, which was demolished 15 years later, and his relations with the Jews were forcibly confined to things of the spiritual domain. Nevertheless, the interventions of popes concerning Jewish citizens of many countries had an inevitable political effect.

During the liberal period of his pontificate, before 1850, PIUS IX had taken several measures favorable to the Jews in the PAPAL STATES, but returning to more conservative ideals after the "Springtime of the People," he reinstated the restrictions of his predecessors. In 1858 the Mortara affair, which resulted in a policy of forcible conversion of young children, took place; despite the interventions of Catholic rulers like the emperor of Austria and Napoleon III, Pius IX energetically refused to return children against their parents' will to their families. The Jews had to wait for the end of the pope's temporal power to obtain their emancipation and open their ghetto; they were the last Jews in all of Italy to receive these freedoms, which King Victor Emmanuel established in the country as he united it. Convinced that the century was bringing "modern errors," Pius IX offered his support to Catholic groups opposed by many Jews who owed their freedom to the new ideas of the Enlightenment.

Just before the violent Nazi persecutions began, the papacy began to react favorably toward the Jews, though the pogroms in Russia aroused very little compassion and, from Pius IX to BENEDICT XV, popes persisted in showing hostility toward Jews, sometimes ostentatiously, at other times mitigated by a gesture of good will or a private word. Although he had still not opened the doors of the ghetto of Rome, Pope Pius IX forbade a procession in Brussels that was to commemorate the 500th anniversary of the miracle of the bleeding hosts, after a pretended profanation by the Jews. In 1892, LEO XXIII addressed the Protestants and Jews in his call to the Catholics of France to fight against freemasonry, the enemy of religion; then, three years later, he encouraged a violently anti-Semitic clerical coalition in Austria. During his pontificate, the organ of the JESUITS, la *Civiltà Cattolica*, very close to the HOLY SEE, regularly published the worst anti-Jewish accusations from medieval times, such as ritual murder. It adapted its anti-Semitism to the taste of the end of the century by denouncing the wicked Jewish domination in finances, journalism, and politics acquired during the FRENCH REVOLUTION by abusing the equality and the brotherhood that were proclaimed. However, LEO XIII tried to calm passions during the Dreyfus affair.

His successor PIUS X held certain Jews in esteem but showed a great dislike for Judaism and Jews in general. On several occasions he vigorously opposed the proofs of loyalty to the kingdom of Italy shown by a Jewish community. In January 1904, he held a private interview with Theodor Herzl, the founder of political Zionism. The author of *The Jewish State* spoke of his theory of "extraterritoriality" for the HOLY PLACES, but the pope told him he disapproved of founding a Jewish state in Palestine. He planned missionary actions to convert the Jews who were living in the Holy Land. "The Jews have not acknowledged Our Lord, this is why we cannot recognize the Jewish people" he said, in explanation. During his brief pontificate, Benedict XV (1914–22) listened with a more willing ear to the plans of the Zionist representative N. Sokolov (May 1917), but showed some worry about the holy places when the possibility of an Anglo-Zionist collaboration began. The diplomacy of the Holy See tried, sometimes in tandem with Italian diplomacy, to keep what they had acquired at the end of the Ottoman Empire. PIUS XI was confronted with cohabitation with Italian fascism and its relatively discreet anti-Semitic connotations and the burgeoning anti-Semitism in Nazi Germany. The condemnation of l'Action français in 1926, and especially the explicit decree of the month of March 1928 removed Catholics from virulent anti-Semitism. The Holy See condemned "particularly and without reservation the hatred that currently is called anti-Semitism." However, it decided that same year to dissolve *The Friends of Israel*, suspected of ambiguous love of Jews. The pope continued to be quite unwilling to come forth on the subject of Zionism. The Vatican press closely followed the progression of the Zionist installation, while remarking on the confirmed agnosticism of the more militant members. The *Civiltà Cattolica* continued to be hostile to Judaism.

When the Nazis seized power, the Catholic Church was also threatened with persecution. Pius XI thought to preserve it by accepting the CONCORDAT with Nazi Germany during the summer of 1933. A little before then, in April 1933, Edith Stein, a Jew who converted to Catholicism and entered a convent, wanted the pope to put out an ENCYCLICAL exclusively devoted to the Jewish question. Such a text never saw the light of day but four years later, in March 1937, Pius XI firmly condemned Nazism in *Mit brennender Sorge*, an encyclical written in German for German Catholics. He did not shrink from stating clearly his rejection of Nazism and its racist theories, publishing his opinions through the official organ of the Vatican, *L'Osservatore romano*. He retired to Castel Gandolfo when Hitler visited Rome on 3 May 1938. Several months later, before a group of Belgian pilgrims, he clearly enunciated the official line of Catholicism regarding Judaism in the famous phrase: "Anti-Semitism is inadmissible; spiritually we are all Semites." He was the instigator of the energetic protest of Cardinals Van Roey, the primate of Belgium, and Verdier of Paris after the "Kristallnacht" that ravaged German synagogues. He even interceded through ambassadors to assist the emigration of converted Jews or half-Jews, if not of Jews, to America. He could not do any more, for he died 10 February 1939.

Cardinal Pacelli had an interview with Sokolov in 1917 on the subject of the holy places. Quite knowledgeable about Germany, PIUS XII expressed his aversion for Nazism and the anti-Semitism it propagated. After the promulgation of racial laws in Italy in 1939, the new pope offered his services to university scholars excluded from their profession. During the war, many Italian Catholics saved Jews thanks to the efficient support of the pope who asked monasteries to open their doors to the persecuted; among them, several even took refuge in the Vatican. Father Marie-Benedict, a Capuchin monk who organized the flight of Jewish refugees to Italy, asked Pius XII for help and received passes to enter several embassies. The rescue action, first for baptized Jews and in other individual cases, increased in 1942. When the cardinal of Toulouse, Monsignor Saliège, protested against the massive arrests of Jews in August of that year, *L'Osservatore romano* and RADIO VATICAN, at Pius XII's request, printed and announced the text. The Christmas message of 1942 outlined the horror of racial persecutions. Everywhere in Europe the Holy See supported priests and institutions when they turned to it to act in favor of the Jews. It was with the full support of Pius XII that the nuncio Roncalli in Istanbul aided and rescued racial victims of Nazism. After the war, the Holy Father answered favorably—but his wish was not always followed—the request of the secretary general of the Jewish World Congress that orphans taken in by Catholics might, without delay, be able to return to their religion.

On the other hand, he did not raise his voice against the massive executions, deportations, and extermination camps, though he knew about them. Many Catholics were disappointed when waiting for a public pronouncement from the spiritual leader of their Church and this silence on the part of the pope still sits heavily in the memory of genocide. The warmth of thanks expressed by the Jews of Rome during the liberation gave way little by little to criticism that culminated in the violent denunciation by R. Hochhuth in the play *The Deputy* (1963), which provoked some great controversy.

The "shoah" (catastrophe) and the creation of ISRAEL brought about a change in Christian attitudes toward Jews. Anticipations of the change can be detected in the last part of Pius XII's pontificate, through many official positions taken by bishops of Western Europe, and especially by the approval of "Ten Points of Seelisberg" (Au-

gust 1947) by Vatican insistence. The historian Jules Isaac, the initiator of this charter, obtained an interview with Pius XII in June 1949 and felt he was heard "with good will and understanding sympathy." The correction of a humiliating discrimination for Jews in the prayer for Good Friday was gradually obtained, first by a note from the Congregation of Rites about the meaning of the expression *perfidis judaeis* (August 1948), and then by the reestablishment of the genuflection. The term *perfidis* disappeared under JOHN XXIII and the words of the prayer were totally changed in 1966 under PAUL VI. During the 1950s, the signs of understanding increased in the Vatican media, particularly at Christmas or Unity Week; the philo-Semitic orientation of certain religious orders, the effort to understand Judaism in theology schools, and meetings in ecumenical settings no longer met with distrust of Roman congregations. Pope Pius XII's approval of the use of modern tools in biblical study also opened the door to the study of post-biblical Judaism. Restoring most of the Jewish children hidden in convents to their families also showed respect; not doing this was considered a distressing exception.

These changes, which at first seemed somewhat haphazard, bear the mark of the papal will after John XXIII took St. Peter's throne. Though it is not certain that all the proposals and intentions credited to him by the Jewish public were authentic, without doubt he did display a sympathetic interest in Judaism and his courageous behavior during the war was not by chance. John XXIII quickly corrected several prayers considered disparaging toward the Jews, received several delegations, encouraged or accepted from several theologians some contacts between Jews and Christians. Following his example, many Christian leaders spoke up loudly against the resurgence of anti-Semitism in Europe in 1960. Two of John XXIII's meetings are famous: the one with Jules Isaac on 13 June 1960, and one with the United Jewish Appeal on 17 October 1960. At each of them, he spoke warmly: "You have a right to more than hope" and "I am your brother Joseph." After the announcement of the COUNCIL, the choice of Cardinal Bea to prepare the position on Jews showed the importance and the difficulty of the subject.

The first version prepared for the VATICAN II Council, imperiled by leaks and by the many political obstacles to the project, was reintroduced (December 1962) thanks to the unfailing support John XXIII gave to Cardinal Bea. The position paper was worked and reworked several times and tacked on to different declarations, or set apart, according to the sessions. It ran up against two sorts of opposition: that of conservatives hostile toward Judaism and that of the representatives of Eastern Christianity, worried about possible dangerous political consequences. In 1964 a flood of articles and multiple pressures made the editing difficult, and several strong expressions were tempered in order to get a wider consensus. The vigorous support of John XXIII was continued by PAUL VI. The amended text was approved by preliminary vote on 20 November 1964 and definitively adopted on 15 October 1965: *Nostra aetate* was promulgated 28 October 1965, becoming the basis for Judeo-Christian dialogue in the future, and enriching ecumenical discussions.

For those who had been won over by John XXIII's spontaneity in his relationship with the Jews, the apparent withdrawal of Paul VI during the council debates could have seemed like indifference to this topic. At the beginning of his pontificate, Paul VI on several occasions justified Pius XII's attitude during the war, even taking the initiative to have the important series of documents from the Vatican Archive that pertained to the issues published. A certain personal reticence surfaced in political meetings with Israeli leaders, including during his trip to Israel in 1964. The personal contribution of Paul VI was in another domain, that of inserting bits of dialogue in such a way that they could assist the implementation of conciliar decisions. The many associations, encounters, or ceremonies that mark the reconciliation during the council appear sometimes as brief flashes, whereas the dialogues encouraged by the pope within the Catholic world and on the ecumenical level succeeded in maintaining a regular and friendly dialogue. In 1966 a Vatican commission was created on the relationships between Jews and Catholics; in 1970 the International Catholic-Jewish Liaison Committee and in 1974 the Commission for Relations with Judaism showed a desire for regular progress by taking the necessary time. From the work of these commissions and the important work of theologians came influential texts such as the *Orientations and Suggestions for the Application of Nostra aetate* (3 January 1975, first text of the holy year) and in 1985 with the *Notes for a Correct Presentation on Jews and Judaism*, rich material intended for preachers and catechists. The 1975 text shows the progress made, beginning with the council's principles:

> Spiritual ties and historical relationships link the Church to Judaism, and condemn any form of anti-Semitism as going against the spirit of Christianity [. . .] What is more, these links and relationships impose the necessity for better mutual understanding and a renewed esteem for one another [. . .] May Christians learn by what essential traits Jews define themselves in their religious life [. . .] The relations between Jews and Christians, when they exist, have rarely gone farther than monologues. What we need to establish from now on is a true dialogue.

The pope's speech to the Liaison Committee on 10 January 1975 contains the first positive evaluations of the post-biblical relationship from the mouth of a reigning pontiff. The pontificate of JOHN PAUL II, after the end of January 1978, was marked by the deepening of the earlier dialogue in the practical sense (see the *Notes* mentioned above) and in the theological and religious sense, and finally in the eradication of anti-Semitism as a "sin against God and humanity" (speech in Prague 6 September 1990). More than his predecessor, John Paul II knew how to make declarations during certain catechisms or meditations, and he often met with Jewish groups.

The man who had aided the Jews of Cracow against the Nazis when he was only Father Wojtyla gave great attention from the beginning of his pontificate to commemoration of the genocide of the Jews. He visited Auschwitz-Birkenau on 7 June 1979 and denounced Nazism and its resurgences several times (16 November 1980 in Cologne' speech on the Warsaw ghetto at the audience of 14 April 1983; recognition of Christian errors in Austria 10 September 1983; speech about Mauthausen in 1985; numerous speeches and messages on the *shoah* beginning with the apostolic letter of 17 August 1989). However, these words often met with skepticism from Jews for several reasons: distrust of the pope's Polishness, hope for a greater accounting of the specific fate of the Jews, and actions judged to be contradictory such as the reception of Austrian chancellor Kurt Waldheim at the Vatican (25 June 1987). The main moments of crisis were the canonization of Edith Stein and Father Kolbe, the boycott of the pope's visit by Jewish Americans after his defense of Pius XII, and especially the long crisis over the Carmelite convent at Auschwitz. The collection of money for this project during John Paul II's visit to Belgium in 1985 opened a long controversy that has not yet ended about the "recovery" of the *shoah* by Catholicism. The disagreement of the Catholic protagonists and the Jews' overestimation of papal power over the Carmelite order increased suspicion of a deliberate Vatican strategy and slowed down the Judeo-Christian dialogue.

A second aspect of John Paul II's actions was the attempt to deepen the institutional dialogue that Paul VI felt was very important. In March 1979 the pope asked the participants to continue this method. On 6 March 1982 he expressed his desire for a more definitive advancement, with numerous meetings and tight collaboration. The *Pastoral Directives for Dialogue in the Diocese of Rome* (25 January 1983) prove that this was not simply a pious vow; the *Notes* of 1985 extended this directive to all Catholicism. A remarkable and often misunderstood aspect of this effort to understand is the bringing in of Jewish university staff and students to prestigious Roman training institutions (*Gregoriana, Biblicum*).

The most spectacular gesture of the new closeness was the pope's visit to the synagogue of Rome on 13 April 1986; the whole world understood its symbolism: the meeting as equals of the bishop of Rome and the head rabbi and the warm words: "You are our favorite brothers, and, in a way, you could say our elder brothers." The clarity of the course laid out for the future made this meeting one of great import. The same atmosphere was felt again at the Assisi meeting in October of that same year, but the ensuing dialogues had to deal with a serious crisis for both religious and political reasons at the same time.

In 1987 John Paul II called on the Vatican Commission for Religious Relations with the Jews to inquire into the question of what responsibility, if any, the Church and Christianity bore for the slaughter of millions of Jews in Europe during World War II. Their eagerly awaited findings, in a documented titled "We Remember: A Reflection on the Shoah," released in March 1998, was hailed by the pope as an important part of Church preparations for the upcoming millennial celebration. Although noting that the Holocaust had taken place "in countries of long-standing Christian civilization," the report argued that the Church itself bore no responsibility for it. Rather than flowing from any kind of anti-Jewish sentiment associated with the Church or Christianity, the kind of antipathy to the Jews that culminated in the Holocaust, the report argued, was due to something very historically distinct. This was anti-Semitism, a product of modern nationalist movements, which had arisen in the 19th century, and which was hostile to the teachings of the Catholic Church. Considerable disappointment was registered among Jewish leaders over this statement, which from their point of view failed to recognize the historical role of the Church in promulgating anti-Semitism, and failed to criticize Pius XII's failure to speak out publicly against the genocide of the Jews.

Two years later, in March 2000, as part of the jubilee year observances, John Paul II issued a dramatic apology on behalf of the Church. Calling for a "purification of memory," he expressed sorrow for the sins done to the Jews (along with various other groups) in the past, although he did not specifically attribute any of the responsibility to actions of the institutional Church itself.

From the moment Israel was created, the Holy See's position was expressed in the encyclicals *Auspicia quaedam* (1948), *In multiplicibus curis* (1948), and *Redemptoris nostri* (1949). The essential demand was for "international rule" of Jerusalem. The United Nations voted in favor of this solution on 9 December 1949, but did not enforce it after 1950. There were few signs of a de facto recognition of the State of Israel under Pius XII (one being the reception of Minister Sharett in 1952). John XXIII sent President Ben Zvi an official letter after his election. His encyclical *Pacem in Terris* was beautifully published in Hebrew. If there was a lot of talk about Paul VI's pilgrimage to the Holy Land, its success on an ecumenical level contrasts with the political reticence evident in his very brief stop in Israel (January 1964). The Six Day War opened a new active area for Vatican diplo-

macy, especially in the United Nations. As a result, a vague request for an "appropriate statute" for Jerusalem replaced the demand for internationalization. Worried about Christians leaving Jerusalem, the pope increasingly emphasized the importance of people rather than the Holy Places themselves, as venerable as they might be (for example, in the encyclical *Nobis in animo* 25 March 1974). The same slow evolution of terms showed up regarding the Palestinian problem. Worried by mounting violence, Paul VI spoke several times on behalf of Israeli prisoners, but Vatican interventions on behalf of Monsignor Capucci, imprisoned for arms trafficking, angered Israel; it took a personal message from the pope to President Katzir to get the prelate freed and deported to Rome in November 1977.

Several Israeli heads of government and ministers of foreign affairs were solemnly received at the Vatican: Abba Eban (6 October 1969), Golda Meir 15 January 1973 in a tenser political atmosphere), Moshe Dayan (12 January 1978, with warmth and hope). The Israeli law of 1 April 1978 against missionary activities provoked much criticism from Catholics.

After the Israeli-Egyptian peace treaty, John Paul II continued to insist in finding a solution for the Jerusalem problem that took into account the religious, international, and human viewpoints, in particular in his letter *Redemptoris anno* (1984), that also expressed, the necessity for assuring the security of the Jewish people living in the state of Israel. The nomination of Monsignor Sabbah, a Palestinian, as the Patriarch of Jerusalem in January 1988 was a sign that Arabic-speaking Christians were to be taken into account. Although the pope received the Israeli minister of foreign affairs Yitzalk Shamir (7 January 1982) and Prime Minister Shimon Peres (19 January 1985), he upset the Israelis by receiving Yasser Arafat, the head of the PLO, twice (15 September 1982 during Beirut's occupations by the Israeli army, and 24 December 1988). During the period of strained relations, the Jewish negotiators insisted on the decision, postponed since 1948, for full normal diplomatic relations with the state of Israel. Such recognition finally occurred at the end of 1993, when the Vatican signed an agreement with the Israeli government establishing full diplomatic ties.

In March 2000, as part of the highlights of the pope's jubilee celebrations, John Paul II undertook a six-day trip to Israel, which proved deeply moving to Israelis, who were struck by the pope's sincere sadness for the historic persecution of the Jews and for the horrors of the Holocaust. The pope's visit to the Yad Vashem Holocaust memorial and, especially, his poignant visit to Jerusalem's Western Wall, where he prayed and left a message asking God's forgiveness for what had been done to the Jews in the past, did much to build better relations between the Church and the Jewish community.

The last 30 years of the 20th century saw the developing of common actions and deepening dialogues between Jews and Christians, but not without difficult times. The comparison between pre-council texts that dealt with this and the declaration of John Paul II made 6 December 1990 show the progress in understanding and the rich pastoral and theological implications of this attitude.

Jean-Marie and Dominique Delmaire

Bibliography

SIDIC, Rome, VIII, 3 (1975) and XVIII, 3 (1985) and XIX, 1 (1986).

Carroll, J. *Constantine's Sword*. Boston, 2001.

Delmaire, M. "Une ouverture prudente: Paul VI, le judaïsme et Israël," *Paul VI et la modernité dans l'Église*, Rome, 1984, 821–35

Ferrari, S. "Le Saint-Siège, l'État d'Israël et les Lieux saints de Jérusalem," in J. B. D'Onorio, *Le Saint-Siège dans les relations internationales*, Paris, 1989, 301–21.

Fumagalli, P. F. "L'Église et le peuple juif. Vingtcinq ans après le Concile Vatican II," *SIDIC*, Rome, XXV, 2 (1992), 20–31.

Hoch M. T., and Dupuy, B., eds., *Les Églises devant le judaisme. Documents officiels 1948–1978*, Paris, 1980.

International Catholic-Jewish Liaison Committee, *Fifteen Years of Catholic-Jewish Dialogue 1970–1985. Selected Papers and Documents*, Vatican, 1988.

Irani, G. E. *The Papacy and the Middle East*, Notre Dame, 1986.

Juifs et chrétiens "Pour une entente nouvelle," visite de Jean Paul II à la synagogue de Rome, Paris, 1986.

Lapide, P. E. *Rome et les Juifs*, Paris, 1967.

Laurentin, R. *L'Église et les Juifs à Vatican II*, Tournai, 1976.

Mendes, M. *Le vatican et Israël*, Paris, 1990.

Fundamental Agreement Between the Holy See and the State of Israel. On 30 December 1993, a "fundamental agreement" was signed between the Holy See and the state of Israel:

PREAMBLE:

The Holy See and the state of Israel,

Mindful of the singular character and universal significance of the Holy Land;

Aware of the unique nature of the relationship between the Catholic Church and the Jewish people, and of the historic process of reconciliation and growth in mutual understanding and friendship between Catholics and Jews;

Having decided on July 29, 1992 to establish a bilateral permanent working commission in order to study and define together issues of common interest, and in view of normalizing their relations;

Recognizing that the work of the aforementioned commission has produced sufficient material for a first and fundamental agreement;

Realizing that such agreement will provide a sound and lasting basis for the continued development of their present and future relations and for the furtherance of the commission's task,

Agree upon the following articles:

ARTICLE 1

1. The state of Israel, recalling its Declaration of Independence, affirms its continuing commitment to uphold and observe the human right to freedom of religion and conscience, as set forth in the Universal Declaration of Human Rights and in other international instruments to which it is a party.

2. The Holy See, recalling the Declaration on Religious Freedom of the Second Vatican Council, *Dignitatis humanae*, affirms the Catholic Church's commitment to uphold the human right to freedom of religion and conscience, as set forth in the Universal Declaration of Human Rights and in other international instruments to which it is a party. The Holy See wishes to affirm as well the Catholic Church's respect for other religions and their followers as solemnly stated by the Second Vatican Council in its Declaration on the Relation of the Church to Non-Christian Religions, *Nostra aetate*.

ARTICLE 2

1. The Holy See and the state of Israel are committed to appropriate cooperation in combating all forms of anti-Semitism and all kinds of racism and of religious intolerance, and in promoting mutual understanding among nations, tolerance among communities and respect for human life and dignity.

2. The Holy See takes this occasion to reiterate its condemnation of hatred, persecution and all other manifestations of anti-Semitism directed against the Jewish people and individual Jews anywhere, at any time and by anyone. In particular, the Holy See deplores attacks on Jews and desecration of Jewish synagogues and cemeteries, acts which offend the memory of the victims of the Holocaust, especially when they occur in the same places which witnessed it.

ARTICLE 3

1. The Holy See and the state of Israel recognize that both are free in the exercise of their respective rights and powers, and commit themselves to respect this principle in their mutual relations and in their cooperation for the good of the people.

2. The state of Israel recognizes the right of the Catholic Church to carry out its religious, moral, educational and charitable functions, and to have its own institutions, and to train, appoint and deploy its own personnel in the said institutions or for the said functions to these ends. The church recognizes the right of the state to its functions, such as promoting and protecting the welfare and the safety of the people. Both the state and the

church recognize the need for dialogue and cooperation in such matters as by their nature call for it.

3. Concerning Catholic legal personality at canon law, the Holy See and the state of Israel will negotiate on giving it full effect in Israeli law, following a report from a joint subcommission of experts.

ARTICLE 4

1. The state of Israel affirms its continuing commitment to maintain and respect the status quo in the Christian holy places to which it applies and the respective rights of the Christian communities therein. The Holy See affirms the Catholic Church's continuing commitment to respect the aforementioned/status quo and the said rights.

2. The above shall apply notwithstanding an interpretation to the contrary of any article in this fundamental agreement.

3. The state of Israel agrees with the Holy See on the obligation of continuing respect for and protection of the character proper to Catholic holy places, such as churches, monasteries, convents, cemeteries and their like.

4. The state of Israel agrees with the Holy See on the continuing guarantee of the freedom of Catholic worship.

ARTICLE 5

1. The Holy See and the state of Israel recognize that both have an interest in favoring Christian pilgrimages to the Holy Land. Whenever the need for coordination arises, the proper agencies of the church and of the state will consult and cooperate as required.

2. The state of Israel and the Holy See express the hope that such pilgrimages will provide an occasion for better understanding between the pilgrims and the people and religions in Israel.

ARTICLE 6

The Holy See and the State of Israel jointly reaffirm the right of the Catholic Church to establish, maintain and direct schools and institutes of study at all levels, this right being exercised in harmony with the rights of the state in the field of education.

ARTICLE 7

The Holy See and the state of Israel recognize a common interest in promoting and encouraging cultural exchanges between Catholic institutions worldwide and educational, cultural, and research institutions in Israel, and in facilitating access to manuscripts, historical documents and similar source materials, in conformity with applicable laws and regulations.

ARTICLE 8

The state of Israel recognizes that the right of the Catholic Church to freedom of expression in the carrying out of its functions is exercised also through the church's own communications media. This right being exercised in harmony with the rights of the state in the field of communications media.

ARTICLE 9

The Holy See and the state of Israel jointly reaffirm the right of the Catholic Church to carry out its charitable functions through its health care and social welfare institutions. This right exercised in harmony with the rights of the state in this field.

ARTICLE 10

1. The Holy See and the state of Israel jointly reaffirm the right of the Catholic Church to property.

2. Without prejudice to rights relied upon by the parties:

a. The Holy See and the state of Israel will negotiate in good faith a comprehensive agreement, containing solutions acceptable to both parties, on unclear, unsettled and disputed issues, concerning property, economic and fiscal matters relating to the Catholic Church generally or to specific Catholic communities or institutions.

b. For the purpose of the said negotiations, the permanent bilateral working commission will appoint one or more bilateral subcommissions of experts to study the issues and make proposals.

c. The parties intend to commence the aforementioned negotiations within three months of entry into force of the present agreement and aim to reach agreement within two years from the beginning of the negotiations.

d. During the period of these negotiations, actions incompatible with these commitments shall be avoided.

ARTICLE 11

1. The Holy See and the state of Israel declare their respective commitment to the promotion of the peaceful resolution of conflicts among states and nations, excluding violence and terror from international life.

2. The Holy See, while maintaining in every case the right to exercise its moral and spiritual teaching office, deems it opportune to recall that, owing to its own character, it is solemnly committed to remaining a stranger to all merely temporal conflicts, which principle applies specifically to disputed territories and unsettled borders.

ARTICLE 12

The Holy See and the state of Israel will continue to negotiate in good faith in pursuance of the agenda agreed upon in Jerusalem on July 15, 1992, and confirmed at the Vatican on July 29, 1992 likewise on issues arising from articles of this present agreement, as well as on other issues bilaterally agreed upon as objects of negotiation.

ARTICLE 13

1. In this agreement the parties use these terms in the following sense:

a. *The Catholic Church and the church*—including, *inter alia*, its communities and institutions.

b. *Communities* of the Catholic Church—meaning the Catholic religious entities considered by the Holy See as churches *sui juris* and by the state of Israel as recognized religious communities.

c. *The state of Israel and the state*—including, *inter alia*, its authorities established by law.

2. Notwithstanding the validity of this agreement as between the parties, and without detracting from the generality of any applicable rule of law with reference to treaties, the parties agree that this agreement does not prejudice rights and obligations arising from existing treaties between either party and a state or states, which are known and in fact available to both parties at the time of the signature of this agreement.

ARTICLE 14

1. Upon signing of the present fundamental agreement and in preparation for the establishment of full diplomatic relations, the Holy See and the state of Israel exchange special representatives, whose rank and privileges are specified in an additional protocol.

2. Following the entry into force and immediately upon the beginning of the implementation of the present fundamental agreement, the Holy See and the state of Israel will establish full diplomatic relations at the level of apostolic nunciature on the part of the Holy See, and embassy on the part of the state of Israel.

ARTICLE 15

This agreement shall enter into force on the date of the latter notification of ratification by party.

Signed in Jerusalem, this 30th day of the month of December, in the year 1993, which corresponds to the 16th day of the month of Tevet, in the year 5754.

See also HOLY PLACES.

Bibliography

Ferrari, S. *Il Vaticano e Israele, dal secondo conflitto mondiale alla guerra del Golfo*, Bologna, 1991.

Flannery, A., ed. "Vatican II's Declaration on the Relation of the Church to Non-Christian Religions" (Nostra Aetate), no. 4.

Mendes, M. *Le Vatican et Israel*, Paris, 1990; *Le Saint-Siège et le conflit du Proche-Orient*, Paris, 1991.

Origins, 23, 30 (13 January 1994), 525–8.

Tincq, H. *L'Étoile et la Croix, Jean-Paul II et Israël*, Paris, 1990.

JUDGES DELEGATE. The judge delegate is a judge appointed by a pontifical commission to solve one or two litigations that are not in its normal field. This institution, still in force (CODE OF CANON LAW 1983, canon 1442) was at its highest point in the 12th and 13th centuries, due to the double effect of the extension of papal justice and the impossibility of treating everything at a central level. It played a key role in forming an inquest and in spreading "Romano-canonical" procedure. Its precedents may be found in the special tribunals the Roman emperors of the late empire were able to form (*cognitio extraordinaria*). Sanctioned by the Theodosian and Justinian codes, this practice was quickly borrowed by the papacy, but only for major matters (*causae majores*). In 419, the clerics of Valence sent the pope a written complaint about their bishop; the examination of the case (*provincialis delegatio*) was handed to the bishops of the province of Vienne; the same took place in Embrun in 463–6. GREGORY I's correspondence contains many examples that involved mostly underdeacons charged with administration of the papal PATRIMONY. At the end of the 9th century, the register of JOHN VIII contains others from the south of France; in 878, the pope even wrote a set of instructions on the procedure to be used by judges. It was during the Gregorian REFORM, however, that the conditions existed under which pontifical delegation took wing. Multiplying privileges of protection and confirmations of goods of ecclesiastic establishments, generalizing the appeal to the HOLY SEE, even for many minor cases, the pope became a means of redress. Ecclesiastical establishments tried to win lawsuits through questionable "surreptitious demands" on which he was misinformed. He had to use local judges. Originally charged with advising the pope, we see them later hand down sentences submitted for pontifical ratification. Delegations were already numerous under PASCHAL II; a few decades later, Bernard of Clairvaux and John of Salisbury portrayed a CURIA and cardinals already overwhelmed by cases. It was not until ALEXANDER III and INNOCENT III that firmer rules of intervention and procedure were established. The most important DECRETALS of Alexander III and his successors were collected by Bernard of Pavia around 1195 under the title *De judicibus delegatis* in the collection called *Compilatio prima*. Around 1230 they were reviewed and the decretals of Innocent III were added in the official compilation of GREGORY IX called Extra (*Corpus juris canonici*, ed. C. Friedburg, II, 158–83). There is more written there about the judges delegate than about the LEGATES or ordinaries.

The oldest testimonies concerned Italy and southern France. The first known delegations for the west of France (Nantes, Vannes, Angers) go back as far as 1067. Several years later, after repeated demands by the abbey of Marmoutier, GREGORY VII delegated the archbishop of Tours and the bishop of Angers. In the Netherlands and Rhenish provinces, there were few delegations, whereas the ecclesiastic provinces of Reims and Sens saw delegations multiply. Their history has been most studied for England. For a long time, as in the empire, Anglo-Norman royalty had tried to limit appeals; after 1137, this tendency reversed itself, even if Henry II worked to hinder the movement beginning in 1164 (Constitutions of Clarendon) after the exile of Thomas Becket. The number of collections of decretals specially compiled for England and the continental provinces of the Plantagenets show his failure. The bishop Roger of Worcester (1164–79) alone is known to have received more than 100 delegations. Alexander III willingly addressed the bishops of London, Hereford and Chichester, and the archbishop of Canterbury was a permanent delegate. The unequal diffusion of the delegations is illustrated by the known apportionment of those receiving decretals during the 12th century (a large percentage of these is made up of acts addressed to the judges delegate themselves): 434 in England, 156 for the Italian part of the empire, 133 for Capetian France, 39 for the Iberian peninsula, 13 for the German and 14 for the Burgundian portions of the empire, and 12 for Hungary-Dalmatia. Until around 1170 the delegates were usually bishops; after that more and more were deans, provosts, and abbots; lay delegates were quite rare (Arras, 1113; Plaisance, 1149). Except for rare exceptions (Noyon, 1252–61; Bruges, 1269–1301; York, 1279–96), it is difficult to know their methods of work in detail due to a lack of documentation, the victorious parties keeping only, at best, a record of the pontifical commission and the sentence in their archives.

The length of the procedure varied widely: in the province of Canterbury in the early 13th century, many trials lasted one to three years, but others dragged on for decades. Most of the time a primary procedure was held before the ordinary, and the archbishop was interrupted or restarted by an appeal of one party to Rome. The question, raised during the pontifical *Audientia* in the presence of the parties or their attorneys was put in the hands of one or several delegates, which the parties could challenge. The pontifical commission defined the case and the procedure to follow. The judges called the parties together, examined written proofs and witnesses, sought counsel, and reported debates and decisions to the pope. Their sentence, if there was one, was handed down to both parties. They could interrupt this procedure by an arbitrated compromise on the person of the judges. In the area of *spiritualia*, the business was usually about tithes, rights of burial, possession of parishes, altars, churches, and chapels. Slowly cases increased, involving inheritances, donations in wills, and very delicate matrimonial issues. Cases involving temporal matters developed in the 12th century (real estate, rights to use woods, fields, water; church debts). These interventions, sometimes accompanied by sentences of excommunication, developed in areas where civil power was weak, and engendered vigorous protests (as in 1164 by the count of Nevers) or limitations (from the 13th century by the king of France). The institution had its weaknesses. Even if sentences were rendered on behalf of the pope, the loser was often able to find a lapse in procedure that justified a new appeal. Also, burdened by other duties, the delegates did not hesitate, in turn, to delegate cases elsewhere. In 1129, in a case between Luxeuil and Saint-Benigne, they complained of the distance from Rome, the expenses, and the

inevitable "machinations" that resulted. These fears and bitterness found an echo in the satiric literature that criticized the corruption of the Curia. The most serious was undoubtedly the possibility of fraud in the statement made by one party to obtain the delegation (*tacita veritas, suggestio falsi*). In the final centuries of the Middle Ages, lay judges competed with ecclesiastical judges and limited the latter to purely religious matters at the moment when the development of the judicial organs of the Curia made the need for delegates less pressing. The institution survived but its field of increasingly limited intervention explains the lack of interest in its functioning and archives for world historians, who find the central portion of the Middle Ages to be rich material.

Dietrick Lohrmann

Bibliography

Brentano, R. *York Metropolitan Juridiction and Papal Judges Delegate, 1279–1296*, Berkeley, CA, 1959.
Guyotjeannin, O. "Les reliques de saint Éloi à Noyon: Procès et enquêtes du milieu du XIIIe siècles," Revue Mabillon, n.s.1 (1990), 57–110.
Herde, P. *Audientia litterarum contradictarum*, Tübingen, 1970, 2 vols. (formularies).
Holtzmann, W. *Über eine Ausgabe des päpstlichen Dekretalen des 12. Jh.*, Göttingen, 1945 (for statistics).
Lohrmann, D. "Papstprivileg und päpstliche Delegationsgerichtsbarkeit im nördlichen Frankreich zur Zeit der Kirchenreform," Monumenta juris canonici, Subsidia, 7 (1985), 535–50.
Naz, R. "Juge délégé," *DDC*, VI (1954), 216–18 (commentary on the code of 1917).
Sayers, J. E. *Papal Judges Delegate in the Province of Canterbury, 1198–1254*, Oxford, 1971.
Uruszxzak, W. "Les juges délégués du pape et la procédure romano-canonique à Reims dans la seconde moitié du XIIe siècle," Tijdschrift voor Rechtsgeschiedenis, 53 (1985), 27–41.

JULIAN THE APOSTATE. *(b. 331, d. 363).*

After the usurpation of Lutecia and the victory of Naissus, followed by the death of Emperor Constans II in November 361, definitively making Flavius Claudius Julianus, cousin of Constans II and last representative of the Constantinian dynasty, the only augustus, the pontifical situation was particularly critical. In effect, the resolutely pro-Arian policy of Constans II had disastrous effects on Rome, especially during the last years of his reign. Pope LIBERIUS (17 May 352–24 September 366), first exiled for his support for Athanasius of Alexandria, had weakened little by little, ending up approving the formula of the COUNCIL of Sirmium in 358, which marked a victory for the homoiousians led by Basil of

Ancyra. This "concession" allowed him to make a triumphal entry ("*quasi victor*," wrote Jerome) into Rome thanks to popular support, but the Church was then deeply divided between "Liberians" and partisans of FELIX, whom Constans had placed on St. Peter's throne during the time of Liberius' exile, and to whom the clergy had sworn fidelity. An uprising of the people forced Felix to resign quickly, but the situation remained tense and Rome was not represented at the councils of Rimini (summer 359) and Constantinople (January 360).

Although Julian, whose title of "lector" had been conferred during his stay in Macellum (344–51) had attended the liturgy of Epiphany in Vienne on 6 January 361, he soon showed his true self: beginning in November 361, he participated in pagan sacrifices and ordered the reopening of the temples. Though this apostate emperor never directly attacked the papacy, his three-year reign still contained numerous incidents. Born in Constantinople and exiled to Cappadocia for a long time, fervent about neo-Platonism and the doctrine of the "divine" Jamblicus, Julian showed no lasting interest in the West, despite his many military campaigns in Gaul, even in his pagan dimension. He never visited Rome, and the pagans in the city did not demonstrate any sympathy for him. A virulent anti-Christian polemicist, the emperor did not speak about the pontifical see in any of his many writings. It is true that his greatest work on this topic, *Against the Galileans*, written during the winter of 362–3, is only known to us in the extracts that Cyril of Alexandria gives in his refutation one century later. Julian seems to have been content to denounce the "hypocrisy" of Peter regarding the decisions of the Council of Jerusalem (Acts 15: 28–9). There are no more allusions in the *Caesars* or in the *Correspondence* of CONSTANTINE's nephew. The polemicist reveals himself, however, during the Christian controversies of the time (he names Photinus, in *Against the Galileans*, and even writes to him; he mentions the positions of Aetius, founder of the sect of Anomeans), but the losses due to fate or a voluntary silence have left little trace of the conflicts between the followers of Liberius and the partisans of Felix in Rome. We cannot forget that Julian wished to organize the pagan priests into a hierarchy strictly imitating that of the Church structures. It is, therefore, possible that Julian chose to be silent about the pontifical reality of the middle of the 4th century as he was silent on the aspects of Christianity of his time.

In practice, the religious policy of this emperor was not without effect. Sincerely wishing to avoid the bloody persecutions that make martyrs, Julian, zealous restorer of paganism, used deceitful indirect measures against Christians. He called back all the bishops exiled by Constans to their episcopal sees in order to increase confusion and make it (according to Ammianus Marcellinus so that "freedom that he appeared to give disintegrated into lawlessness and increased dissensions." He fully attained this goal in Antioch and in Donatist Africa: the Anomeans, for their part, became more powerful, but this same action permitted Athanasius to resume his position and functions beginning 21 February 362. The reign of the apostate emperor freed Liberius from worry by permitting him to get back a little prestige: in 362 he adopted the decisions of the SYNOD of Alexandria where Athanasius had regrouped the Nicaeans. The decrees of Rimini were broken and the devotion to the symbol of the Nicaeans served as a basis for reconciliation.

Julian did not directly obssess about the papacy and ordered no persecution of Peter's successor. Nevertheless, his short reign indirectly helped Liberius to reaffirm his authority, thus preparing for the decisive progress of the Church of the West under the direction of Damasus beginning in 366.

Jeanne-Marie Demarolle

Bibliography

Athanasiadi–Fowden, *Julian and Mellenism: An Intellectual Biography*, Oxford, 1981.

Bidez, J. *La Vie de l'empereur Julien*, Paris, 1930 (republished 1965).

Bouffartigue, J. *L'Empereur Julien et la culture de son temps, Études augustiniennes*, 133, Paris, 1992.

Braun, R. and Richier, J., ed. *L'Empereur Julien I: De l'histoire à la légende*, Paris, 1978, and *II: De la légende au mythe*, Paris, 1981.

Catabiano, M. "Un quindicennio di Studi sull'imperatore Giuliano," *Koinonia*, Naples (1983), 15–30, 113–32, and (1984), 16–31.

Gauthier, N. "L'expérience religieuse de Julien dit l'Apostat," *Augustinianum*, XXVIII (1987), 227–35.

Klein, A. *Julianus Postata*, Darmstadt, 1978.

Malley, W. J. *Hellenism and Christianity: The Conflict between Helenic and Christian Wisdom in the Contra Galileos of Julian the Apostate and the Contra Julianum of St. Cyril of Alexandria*, Rome, 1978.

JULIUS I. (*b. Rome, ? d. 12 April 352*). *Elected 16 February 337. Buried in the Calepodius cemetery on the via Aurelia. Saint.*

According to the *LIBER PONTIFICALIS*, he was of Roman origin and son of Rusticus. His papacy was characterized by caution and the wisdom with which he acted during the difficult years of the Arian crisis. The firmness he displayed in safeguarding the principles reinforced the authority of the head of the Roman Church, when even the Eusebians, opposed to Athanasius of Alexandria, called upon him for arbitration.

The beginning of his papacy coincided with the death of CONSTANTINE (22 May 337) and the dividing up of the empire, which changed the circumstances of ecclesiastical policy. Partisans and adversaries of Athanasius then sought his judgment. Constantine II authorized the bishops deposed by the Council of Tyre (July 335) to resume their seats; Athanasius, in exile in Treves was able to go back to ALEXANDRIA. The Eusebians—a name given by Athanasius and Pope Julius to the bishops regrouping around Eusebius of Nicomedia—sent him a priest, Macarius, and two deacons, Hesychios and Martyrios, to show him the illegality of Athanasius's returning to Alexandria, by presenting the pope with acts from the Council of Tyre. On the other side, Athanasius, who had had his orthodoxy proclaimed by an Egyptian council, had the synodal letter carried to the pope by priests from Alexandria, and to the three emperors. The two delegations met in Rome and the eastern DEACONS asked the Roman to intervene with the emperor for the convocation of a council. Hearing the question of the Eusebians, the pope, in answer to their demand, sent two of his priests, Elpidius and Philoxenus, east to carry letters of convocation to a future council in Rome (early 341). After having waited for a long time, his LEGATES returned bearing a refusal that, though filled with formulaic words of respect for the pope, threatened to break off relations if Julius continued to receive Athanasius, who had again been condemned at ANTIOCH (early 341).

In Rome during late 340 or early 341, the pope assembled a SYNOD of about 50 bishops, mostly from Italy, in the church of the priest Vitus who, with Vincentius also present, had been the legate of SILVESTER I to the council at Nicaea. According to Julius's testimony, some Eastern priests from Athanasius's entourage were also present. In this assembly, a particular duty fell to the Roman bishop. At his request, they proceeded to examine documents (*instrumenta*) from both parties. He asked Marcellus of Ancyra for a written profession of faith that was judged to be satisfactory by the council. Athanasius, having presented his defense, was recognized once again as the rightful and legitimate bishop of the see of Alexandria, which made Julius known, according to Hilary of Poitiers, as one of the primary defenders of those who had been oppressed by the Arians. With firmness rather than trials of the Easterners, the Roman bishop reminded everyone of the rules of ecclesiastical discipline in procedures of judgment and appeal, without condemning those who obviously had not respected them. It was his duty alone to pronounce judgment and to make it known to the eastern group by letter. His long letter, addressed to the eastern bishops, considered as the synodal of the council, has been completed preserved by Athanasius in the *Apology Against the Arians*. Appreciated for various reasons by posterity, it remains the earliest known pontifical letter and is, for this reason, a unique document. In this letter, Julius I laments the absence of the eastern group and explains that a council's sentence can be revised, thus sketching out the beginning of a hierarchy in the synods. He informs them of the illegality of the election of Gre-gory to the see of Athanasius. At the end of the letter he reminds them of a principle that permeates Church affairs, the PRIMACY of Rome: "You should have written us first of all . . . What I write, I write in the interest of everyone, and what I explain to you, we have received from the apostle Peter . . ." He ends with an exhortation for compassion and peace, but the Roman bishop was ignored, as confirmed by the council convened in Antioch in the fall of 341. Pope Julius I, with several Western bishops, addressed the emperor to ask that he convene a general council of both eastern and western representatives in order to settle the current problems, including the case of Athanasius. A council was held at Serdica (modern Sofia), in the fall of 343, to which the pope, although summoned, did not attend; he declared that he could not leave his Church, an excuse considered plausible (*bona et necessaria*) by Hilary of Poitiers. To represent him, he sent two priests, Archidamus and Philoxenus, and a deacon, Leo, who signed a letter to the churches of Mareota in his name; in any case, they played an unobtrusive role. In their synodal, the eastern bishops, meeting separately from the western ones, condemned Julius along with other priests because they had sided with Marcellus of Ancyra and Athanasius, whom they had condemned. On their side, the western contingent drew up a synodal with a series of disciplinary canons that maintained, in the case of an APPEAL to Rome, the manner of papal intervention to review the case, with the pope appointing judges for the appeal. These should be the bishops of the province neighboring that of the first judges. During Athanasius's visit to Rome, on the way back to Alexandria after his second exile in 349, the pope gave him a letter addressed to the priests, deacons, and people of Alexandria, congratulating them on the reestablishment of their bishop. In this letter he expressed his esteem for Athanasius, a letter inserted in the *Apology Against the Arians* and republished by Socrates. The bishop of Rome received, shortly thereafter, a letter of recantation from Ursacius of Singidunum and from Valens of Murcia who wrote him to express their submission. Julius consented to give them back control of their churches.

The *Liberian Catalogue* says Julius I constructed five churches. On the via Flaminia, the pope constructed the Valentinian basilica in the Valentine cemetery. Archeological digging in this area by O. Marrucchi has identified what is probably the first known *martyrium* and the construction of a building with a niche for the episcopal *cathedra*. For the basilica in the via Aurelia, at the third mile, in an area containing the tomb of CALIXTUS, digs have found a funerary zone with some Julian construction that seems to be a subterranean chapel. We cannot precisely locate where a first Iulii basilica might have been, mentioned in the *Liberian Catalog* as near Trajan's Forum, but he was the founder of a Iulii basilica, built across the Tiber, near Calixtus, which has been identified as the church of Julius and Calixtus (now Santa Maria in Trastevere) and which is corroborated by the Roman councils of 499 and 595. On the Portuensis, the *Liberian Catalog* mentions another basilica at the third mile: perhaps this is the Felicis basilica, now gone.

Elizabeth Paoli

See also HERESIES.

Bibliography

AAAS, Apr. III, ed. G. Henschenius and D. Papebrock, Paris-Rome, 1865, 82–6.

LP, I, 205.

Acta syn. rom., MGH AA, 12, 411.

Acta syn. rom., MGH. Ep. 1, 367.

Amore, A. "Giulio," *EC*, 6 (1951), 749–50.

Baümer, R. "Julius," *LTK*, 5 (1960), 1203.

Caspar, E. *Geschichte des Papsttums*, Tübingen, 1930, I, 131–65.

Catalogue libérien, ed. Duchesne, 10.

Chapin, J. *NCS*, 8 (1967), 51 *sq.*

Depositio episcoporum, MGH AA 9, 70.

Duchesne, L. *Histoire ancienne de l'Église*, Paris, 1910, II, 193 *sq.*

Ep. syn. Sardicensis ad Iulium, Hilaire, ibid., II, 9–15, *CSEL*, 65, 126–9.

Ep. syn. Sardicensis orient.ad African., Hilaire, *Coll. Antiar. parisin. (Fragmenta Historica)* II, 24, *CSEL*, 65, 63, 65, 67.

Falconi, C. *Storia dei Papi*, Rome-Milan, 1967, I, 393–9.

Fliche-Martin, III, 116–140.

Julius, *Ep. ad. Orient.*, Athanasius, *Apol. contra Arian*, 21–37, ed. Opitz, II, 1, 102–13 (PG, 25, 281–309); *Ep. ad Alex.*, Athanasius, ibid., 52–4, PG, 25, 344–8.

Pietri, C. *Roma christiana*, Rome, 1976, I, 22–5, 72–7, 86–95, 187–237, and II, 1694.

Quae Gestae sunt inter Liberium et Felicem episcopos, CSEL, 35, 1, 2.

Seppelt, F. X. *Papstgeschichte*, Munich, 1933, 14–18.

Ursace and Valens, *Ep. ad Iulium*, Hilaire, ibid., II, 6, *CSEL*, 65, 143–4.

JULIUS II. *Giuliano Della Rovere (b. Albisola, near Savona, 5 December 1443, d. Rome, 21 February 1513). Elected pope 1 November 1503, crowned 18 November 1503. Buried at S. Pietro in Vincoli in Rome.*

Julius II regrouped and consolidated the States of the Church. He adorned the capital of Christianity with the greatest works of art. But by using temporal and spiritual arms ceaselessly and by systematically double-crossing alliances, he behaved more like a lay prince than as a sovereign pontiff. This attitude, linked to displaying worldly glory, drew criticism from his contemporaries regarding the papacy and justifying the movement of radical reform launched by Luther during the next reign, that of LEO X.

The fortune of Giuliano Della Rovere was linked to that of his uncle, Francesco Della Rovere, who became Pope SIXTUS IV on 9 August 1471. Named cardinal in the same promotion as his cousin Pietro Riario on 15 December 1471 and given the title of the church of S. Pietro in Vincoli, Guliano, already bishop of Carpentras, received numerous other positions: the bishoprics of Lausanne (1472), Messina and Catania (1473), Avignon (1474), Coutances (1476), Vivers, then Mende (1478), Bologna (1483), Lodevi (1488), Savona (1499) and Verceil (1502), as well as the rich abbeys of Grottaferrata and Nonantola in Italy, St. Gilles-du-Gard in Provence, and Gorze in Lorraine.

The entry of Giuliano Della Rovere into world politics took place in 1474. Freed by the death of his cousin, Cardinal Pietro Riario, and from the rivalry between them, he was named by his uncle to the bishopric of Avignon, which was transformed into an archbishopric a year later. In 1476 the pope recalled Charles of Bourbon, a puppet of Louis XI who led the legation to Avignon, and gave that position to Guliano, who was clever enough to get the appointment confirmed by the king of France. Triumphantly, Giuliano returned to Rome, but found himself wrestling with the ambition of another cousin, Girolamo Riario, whom Sixtus VI wished to endow with a state by purchasing Imola. The banker to the papacy, Lorenzo the Magnificent, refused to accept the operation. His Pazzi rivals got together with Girolamo Riario and put together a plot against him, which he escaped, but which was fatal to his brother Guliano de Medici on 26 April 1478. War broke out between Florence and the pope and his allies, which included Louis XI. Cardinal Giuliano, LEGATE *a latere*, assumed an important role as negotiator in bringing peace in 1480 and preparing a new CRUSADE against the TURKS. Girolamo Riario's ambition, had brought about a war between the Holy See, Ferrara, and Naples; Giuliano actively participated in the defense of Rome and the liquidation of the conflicts with the Colonna that had bloodied the papal region. After the death of Sixtus IV in 1484, the Genoan Giambatista Cibo became Pope INNOCENT VIII, taking Giuliano Della Rovere as counselor in the war that continued between Rome and Ferrante of Naples, which finally ended in May 1492. However, at the death of the pope on 25 July 1492, Cardinal Roderigo Borgia was elected to the pontificate under the name of ALEXANDER VI. Until the death of the Borgia pope, Giuliano Della Rovere was part of his opposition. He accompanied the king of France, Charles VIII, in his march on Naples (1494), trying in vain to depose the pope when the French entered Rome. Retreating to France with King Charles VIII (summer 1495), Guliano stayed in his legation at Avignon where, however, he received Cesare Borgia when he, named duke of Valentino, was on his way to Louis XII with the DISPENSATION that would permit him to marry Anne of Brittany. When Alexander VI passed away (18 August 1503), a first CONCLAVE named Pope PIUS III, then, after his death, elected cardinal Della Rovere on November 1, who took the name of Julius II. The new pope attacked Cesare Borgia immediately, making him return the territories in the Romagna that he had taken with his father's help. Cesare was taken prisoner and transferred to Spain (spring 1504).

In the spring of 1505, Julius II undertook a massive building program designed to exalt his pontificate and the Roman See. He hired architect Donato d'Angeli Lazzari, called Bramante, to reconstruct the aging basilica of ST. PETER's in Rome. The architect had distinguished himself in Milan with projects done for Ludovico Sforza, and in Rome by the construction of the *tempietto* of S. Pietro in Montorio on the Janiculum. Julius II planned to place his own mausoleum in the basilica on top of the tomb of St. Peter and chose Michelangelo Buonarotti in March 1505 to oversee this project. The contract expired in April 1505 but was reinstated a year later, when the pope was placing the first stone of the new church. Julius II, convinced by Bramante that it was better to give priority to the building, stopped paying Michelangelo who, furious, left Rome. Other financial worries plagued the pope: He was preparing for a new military campaign to take back usurped pontifical territories.

On 22 August 1506, the pontiff himself rode at the head of an army that, by way of VITERBO and Orvieto, went through Perugia where Giampaolo Baglioni had taken power. This deployment of force was enough to make the tyrant yield in September 1506. Marching from there to Bologna, which he wished to liberate from the grasp of Giovanni Bentivoglio, the pope crossed the Appenine Mountains and rejoined French troops camped beside the city walls. On 11 November, after Bentivoglio fled, Julius II made a solemn entrance into the city's main square of la Romagna. He reconciled with Michelangelo, from whom he commissioned a colossal bronze statue of himself to commemorate his triumph over the Bolognese.

This policy of military intervention and sumptuous purchases was very troublesome. To get the money necessary, the pope benefited from the cleverness of his banker, the Siennese Agostino Chigi, who controlled the exploitation of the riches of the PAPAL STATE, especially those of the salt mines and alum mines. Although he severely prohibited SIMONY, the pontiff was devoted to organizing a regular growth of revenues to the chancellery by the selling of BULLS of privileges, dispensations, and INDULGENCES and by the confiscation of the property of dead prelates belonging to the court of Rome.

He forced Venice to give back the portions of the Romagna that it had no right to occupy. This whole operation could not have occurred without the participation of the greatest powers present in Italy—the empire, France, and Spain. Louis XII came to confront the rebellion of the people of Genoa (June 1506), which reached its high point in March 1507 with the massacre of French subjects. He attacked the city himself and forced it to surrender after a lightning-swift campaign (28 April 1507). The pope had possibly surreptitiously encouraged the rebellion of his countrymen.

In the Italian status quo, which involved France occupying the north around Milan, and Spain controlling the kingdom of Naples, having been ratified during the interview in Savona between Louis XII and Ferdinand of Aragon (June 1507), Julius II played an intermediary role by bringing together these two powers with the king of the Romans, Maxilimilian of Austria. This man who had proclaimed himself emperor had suffered a setback in February 1508 against Venice that had cost him, besides Verona, Padua, Vicenza, and Treviso, the largest part of Friulia and Istria. His resentment matched that of Louis XII, who was angry with the Venetians who occupied Brescia, Bergamo, and Cremona, previously part of the duchy of Milan. The king of Aragon wanted revenge for the ports of Apulia, which Venice had taken over: Otranto, Trani, Brindisi, and Gallipoli.

The pope pushed for a united campaign against Venice, from which he hoped to regain his own former possessions in Romagna: Ravenna, Cervia, Faenza, and Rimini. The agreement was concluded on 10 December 1509 at Cambrai. Joining this league in March 1509, Julius II excommunicated the Venetians (April 27). The French went off to battle and fought fairly substantial Venetian forces commanded by Niccolò Orsini, count of Pitigliano, and Bartolomeo Alviano at Agnadello on 14 May 1509. It was a stunning victory for Louis XII. The lands fell into his hands and Venice had to give back all the territories it had taken. This huge defeat, eclipsing Venetian power, left no counterbalance between France and the emperor in the north of Italy. Deeming this equilibrium worrisome, Julius II changed sides. He freed the Venetians from the imposed censures (February 1510) and, having made peace with them, joined the kings of Spain and England against the French and their ally, Duke Alfonso of Ferrari, who, after recruiting Swiss mercenaries, shut himself away in Bologna. The city was besieged by the French (October–December 1510), but Julius II was crafty enough to lure them away from Bologna, in order to take Mirandole (20 January 1511) after a memorable siege that he had directed himself. Then Bologna, poorly defended, surrendered (22 May 1511) to the French; the pope's nephew, Francesco Maria Della Rovere, duke of Urbino, commanding the papal troops, put the responsibility on the shoulders of Cardinal Francesco Alidosi, the pope's favorite, governor of the city. He got revenge on the prelate by putting him to death. This internal anarchy, linked to the threat against the pope posed by the schismatic council of Pisa, called by the French for the purpose of condemning the pope, made Julius take the offensive by calling another council at the LATERAN (18 July 1511). He formed a "holy league" against France made up of the papacy, Spain, Venice, and soon England and the Swiss cantons (October–November 1511). While these two COUNCILS denounced each other, and a violent campaign of pamphlets against the pope took place in France, Gaston de Foix, nephew of Louis XII, took the offensive, taking Bologna and Brescia, and confronting the Spanish whom he crushed at Ravenna on 11 April 1512. However, the young general was killed and the new French commander was incapable of defeating the allies of the pope. Jacques de Chabanne, marshall of La Palice, retreated as far as the Alps (28 June 1512), taking with him the fathers of the schismatic council who had taken refuge from Pisa to Milan. After emperor Maximilian rallied to the Lateran Council in December 1512, the victory of Julius II seemed to be complete. Besides the condemnation of the French, Julius had the council ratify the interdiction of simony, especially those practices that attempted to buy votes in the conclaves.

The pontiff died on 21 February 1513, just as the walls of St. Peter's were beginning to emerge from the ground. A gallery joined the Vatican Palace to the Belvedere, a villa for relaxation as well as a veritable archeological museum where famous pieces such as the Laocoon, discovered in January 1506, had been placed. In the SISTINE CHAPEL from March 1508 to October 1512, Michelangelo completed the admirable decoration of the vaulted ceiling, which traced human history from the creation of the world to the flood, from the fall and the annunciation of the redemption by prophets and sibyls. In the pontifical apartment, the brush of Raphael had placed *Parnassus*, the *School of Athens*, the *Dispute of the Holy Sacrament*, and the *Proclamation of the Decretals*, recalling the benefits brought to mankind by the great poets, philosophers, theologians, and jurists. The painter also depicted devotion to the Eucharist (in his *Miracle at the Mass of Bolsena*) and the condemnation of the keeping of wealth from the Church (*The Chastisement of Heliodorus*). This series, dealing with the triumphs of the Roman Church, would be completed under Leo X, with the evocation of the victory of holy Pope LEO against the barbarian king Attila, and the deliverance of St. Peter by the angel of the Lord—two transparent allusions to the victory of Julius II over Louis XII and to the liberation of the Papal States.

Ivan Cloulas

Bibliography

Brosch, M. *Papst Julius II und die Grundung des Kirchenstaates*, Gotha, 1878.
Cloulas, I. *Jules II*, Paris, 1990.
Duval, A. " Jules II," *Catholicisme*, 6 (1967), 1215–18.
Fusero, C. *Giulio II*, Milan, 1965.
Gilbert, F. *The Pope, his Banker, and Venice*, Cambridge, MA, 1980.
Klaczko, J. *Jules II*, Paris, 1898.
Kolsky, S. "Culture and Politics in Renaissance Rome: Marco Anotio A Hieri's Roman Weddings," *Renaissance Quarterly*, 40, (1987), 49–90.
Mollat, G. "Jules II," *DIC*, 8 (1925), 1918–20.
Patridge, L., and Starn, S. *A Renaissance Likeness: Art and Culture in Raphael's Julius II*, Berkeley, CA, 1980.
Picotti, G. B. *La Politica italiana sotto il pontificato di Giulio II*, Pisa, 1949; "Giulio II," *EC*, 6 (1951), 750–8.
Quilliet, B. *Louis XII*, Paris, 1986.
Schwaiger, S. "Julius II," *LTK*, V, 1960, 1204–5.
Shaw, C. *Julius II: Warrior Pope*, Oxford, 1993.

JULIUS III. *Giovanni Maria Ciocchi del Monte (b. Rome, 10 September 1487, d. Rome, 23 March 1555). Elected pope 8 February 1550, crowned 22 February. Buried at St. Peter's in Rome.*

Julius III, a pope with no pronounced personality, still managed to accomplish two important things: the reopening of the COUNCIL OF TRENT (second period) and the reconciliation with England.

Born in a family originally from Monte San Savino, his father died in 1504. Giovan Maria del Monte was raised by his uncle Antonio del Monte, auditor of the ROTA and archbishop of Siponto (Manfredonia). His training, at first by the humanist Raffaele Brandolini Lippo, included the study of law at Perugia and Siena. His uncle got him a position as a chamberlain and then, having been made cardinal in 1511, renounced his archbishopric of Siponto in his nephew's favor (1513), to which was added the bishopric of Pavia (1521–30, 1544–50). Honored with several duties by the CURIA, twice governor of Rome, Cardinal del Monte was liked for his affable manner and for his demonstrated abilities as an administrator. Taken hostage by the Imperials during the SACK OF ROME (1527), he barely escaped execution. After that, he was named vice-legate to Bologna and then auditor of the APOSTOLIC CAMERA, and then cardinal with the title of San Vitale on 22 December 1536. Having distinguished himself in the Reform Commission, he represented PAUL III as LEGATE and first president of the council at Trent (1545–47), and then at Bologna (1547–48); he shone as a brilliantly competent canonist more than for his theological knowledge.

The election of Julius III took place at the end of the longest CONCLAVE of the 15th century after that of PIUS IV (28 November 1549–8 February 1550, 71 ballots), due to contradictory pressures from Emperor Charles V and the king of France, Henri II. The choice of Cardinal del Monte was the result of a compromise between cardinals on two opposing sides. He took the name of Julius III, in memory of Julius II, who had raised his uncle Antonio to the dignity of cardinal.

His character is not very well defined, alternately jovial and choleric, inclined towards celebrations, hunting, theater, and banquets. Regular in his religious devotions and favorable toward reform of the Church, he aimed most often, in his indecisive political actions, toward peace and compromise. Despite his declared opposition to the NEPOTISM of his predecessors, he only halfheartedly resisted his family's demands, which followed him even to his deathbed. The most notable scandal of his pontificate was the mysterious fortune of Innocenzo del Monte. This debauched street urchin, former caretaker of his monkey, was adopted by his brother, covered with favors, and made cardinal at age 15 and put at the head of the SECRETARIAT OF STATE. His criminal life ended later in prison.

In 1550 two questions were suspended: the resumption of the council and the confirmation that the duchy of Parma belonged to the Farnese family (created for them in 1545), both actions predetermined in the electoral negotiating defined by the SACRED COLLEGE before Julius III's election.

Due to ill will on the part of France, he was forced to collaborate with Charles V, calling the council at Trent (therefore, on imperial land) for 1 May 1551 (BULL *Cum ad tollenda* of 14 November 1550). Henri II refused to recognize the council, whose ecumenical character he challenged; the French prelates were therefore absent. Work went slowly, delayed by waiting for the Protestant envoys, then by the impossibility of reaching an agreement with them. The authoritarian attitude of the president, Cardinal Marcello Crescenzio, also created serious tensions within the council. In six sessions (XI to XVI), three decrees on dogma were formulated concerning the sacraments of the Eucharist (defining "real presence" and "transsubstantiation"), on penance, and on extreme unction, accompanied by three decrees of reform with special emphasis on episcopal jurisdiction, the morals of the clergy, and the nomination of clerics for benefices. In March 1552, Elector Maurice of Saxony and the Protestant princes allied to Henri II went to war against the emperor; on 28 April the council announced the suspension of work, decided upon by the pope on the 15 April.

The question of Parma was linked to the council by the policies of Henri II. The concession of this fief was given by Julius III to Ottavio Farnese, but refused by Charles V, who said that Parma and Placenza belonged to the empire. Farnese then turned to France's support, allying himself with Henri II in March 1551, despite the warnings of the pope. Julius III then had to ask for the emperor's help against his vassal, whom he declared had forfeited his holding on 22 May. Farnese's first military successes, which devastated the territory of Bologna, the entry of French forces into Piedmont, the fear of a Gallican SCHISM, and the insufficiency of pontifical finances led Julius III to declare an armistice on 29 April 1552. The confrontation, continuing between the king and the emperor with the war of Siena, would last beyond Julius' death.

Julius III began work on serious Church reform measures, setting up a commission of six cardinals on March 1550, renewed after suspension of the council. He reduced the size of his court and gradually undertook reform of the abuses of DATARY, conclaves, penalties, the Apostolic Signatura, preaching, confession, the residence of bishops, convents, and others according to an ambitious program set forth to the CONSISTORY in a resounding speech on 16 September 1552. The bull of reform (*Varietas temporum*), ready for the most part at the beginning of 1555, was not published because of his death, but certain measures had already been applied, and the work begun would serve as a basis for that of the following popes.

While the Reformation was progressing throughout northern Europe, the pontificate was marked by the Catholic restoration in England. Between 1550 and 1552, severe measures had inclined the English Reformation toward more radical positions. Mary Tudor, ruling after Edward VI in 1553, reestablished the mass and, the following year, married Philip of Spain. The legation of the English cardinal Reginald Pole, long delayed due to the distrust of English opinion of Rome, and in particular by the question of former ecclesiastical properties, culminated with the absolution pronounced on 30 November 1554.

Julius III also showed himself favorable to the Society of Jesus (JESUITS): he confirmed the foundation in a bull on 21 July 1550 and extended its privileges, including the right to confer the title of doctor. The German College, created in 1552 for the training of German clergy, was given to the Jesuits to run.

The tribunal of the INQUISITION, equally confirmed, was strengthened against competition with lay jurisdictions.

Disappointing the humanists' hopes, the literary patronage of the pope was relatively limited, despite the reform of the University of Rome and the nomination of the humanist Marcello Cervini (the future pope MARCELLUS II) to head the Vatican Library. Without equaling Paul III, Julius III still gave a lot of attention to the arts: he preferred the musician Giovanni Pierluigi da Palestrina, he defended Michelangelo against his adversaries among those concerned with ST. PETER'S BASILICA, and consulted him for the construction of the splendid Villa Giulia. Vignole was his official architect.

The opinions of historians on Julius III are divided. Pastor insists on his will to reform but admits the feebleness of any concrete results. The importance of his work for that of his successors (Jedin) and his sincerity (Erdmann) permit some of them to count him among the reforming popes, but his lack of moral decisiveness and his mode of life connect him to the Renaissance popes (Ganzer).

Marc Smith

Bibliography

Baugmartner, F. J. "Henry II and the Papal Conclave of 1549," *Sixteenth Century Journal*, 76, no. 3 (1985), 301–14.

Burkle-Young, F., and Doerrer, M. L. *The Life of Cardinal Innocenzo del Monte: A Scandal in Scarlet*, Lewiston, NY, 1997.

Duval, A. "Jules III," *Catholicisme*, 6 (1967), 1218–19.

Erdmann, C. "Die Wiedereröffnung des Trienter Konzils durch Julius III," *QFIAB*, 20 (1928–29), 238–317.

Fliche-Martin, *XVII*, 105–45.

Ganzer, K. "Julius III," *Theologische Realenzyklopädie*, 17 (1988), 445–7.

Jedin, H. "Kirchenreform und Konzilsgedanke, 1550–1559," *Historisches Jahrbuch*, 54 (1934), 401–31; "Analekten zur Reformtätigkeit der Päpste Julius III und Pauls IV," *Römische Quartalschrift*, 42, (1934), 305–32, 43 (1935), 87–156; *Geschichte des Konzils von Trient*, 3, Freiburg, 1970.

Lutz, H. *Christianitas afflicta. Europa, das Reich und die päpstliche Politik im Niedergang der Hegemonie Kaiser Karls V. (1552–1556)*, Göttingen, 1964.

Pastor, 11 and 12.

JURISDICTIONALISM. This is an orientation that did not become a real judicial system until the 18th and 19th centuries. It wanted to regulate, especially in the various Italian states, and then in Italy after its unification, the relationship between the state and the Catholic Church, and the rapports between the political and ecclesiastical powers. It was a collection of rights, prerogatives and interests on the part of the state, more or less legitimate, distinct, and sometimes opposed to the rights and forms of intervention of the Church. Still, it should not be identified simply with other ideological or juridical models or with the methods of political and ecclesiastical policies of the Church from the end of the Middle Ages to modern times, like regalism in the Iberian peninsula, GALLICANISM in France, and JOSEPHISM in Austria, whose jurisdictionalism did contain elements of concession and inspiration.

In the second half of the 15th century, with the development of pontifical policy in the Italian peninsula, forms of protection against the interventions of Rome could already be found. This was a common point for different political systems: republican, seigniorial, and monarchic in Florence, Venice, Milan, and Naples, but it was not until later, after the COUNCIL OF TRENT that this orientation became definite against the growing sphere of influence that the Church and the papacy wished to possess along with the sector of local ecclesiastical institutions concerning aspects that dealt more or less directly with the ecclesiastical immunities and privileges and the presence of clergy in society. It is not due to chance that the first intense jurisdictional conflicts took place especially—but not only—in Spanish-controlled Milan between 1567 and 1568, after the publication of the BULL *In Coena Domini*. In it, Pius V fully asserted the traditional prerogatives and freedoms of the clergy, especially the right of ecclesiastical censures to override lay censures. This attempt at confrontation was greeted as others were under GREGORY XIII (1572–85), when he tried to generalize a system of apostolic visitors throughout the peninsula. These visitors, provided with broad powers, were to see that conciliar decisions were applied everywhere as coordinated by Rome. It was for this reason that, in the second half of the 16th century, almost all the Italian states created multiple magistratures where civil servants were placed to defend what they judged to be traditional rights of political power. After the institution of officials for heresy, charged with defending the subjects named by the Roman tribunal of the INQUISITION, Venice named a delegate for the monasteries that controlled the female monasteries with which the interests of the noble families were closely linked, as well as *in jure* consultants, among whom was Paolo Sarpi, famous because of the episode of the INTERDICT. In Naples a delegate for royal jurisdiction was named, assisted later in the 18th century under the Bourbons by an Ecclesiastical Secretariat. In Florence, Grand Duke Cosimo I created an auditor of royal law who would become secretary of royal law under the house of Lorraine rule. Lasting from the regency to the government of Leopold I, it represented an important phase of Italian jurisdictionalism during the ENLIGHTENMENT. On his own behalf, the pope responded with State interventions, under Gregory XIV, with the bull *Cum alias* (1591) that defended the right of ecclesiastical sanctuary and, under URBAN VIII in 1626, with the institution of the Congregation of Immunity. Jurisdictionalism expanded even more during the course of the 18th century into the political arena, drawing support from the Gallican tradition (already present with Sarpi), Belgian canon law (Van Espen), and Febronianism. The ecclesiastical policy of the enlightened despots would be strongly influenced by a distrust of the Curia due to the strength of the papal presence in Italy. In Naples, the hopes expressed in the *Istoria civile* by Pietro Giannone (1723) would be repeated by Minister Bernardo Tanucci, whereas in Joseph II's Lombardy and in Leopold I's Tuscany traditional jurisdictionalism took on new, more complex forms. On one side, that of Josephist state control, and, on the other, an ecclesiastical reformism, linked in certain ways (relationships between the grand duke and the bishop of Pistoia and Prato, Scipione de Ricci) to JANSENIST religious reform.

In the 19th century, after the Restoration, jurisdictionalism was reimposed in Piedmont. In the days before unity, the guardian of the seals, Siccardi, enacted an ecclesiastical legislation of the Josephist type (1850–5), which was later extended, with a few variations, to Tuscany and Naples (1859–60). The famous law of guarantees (1871) that the Italian state enacted after the occupation of Rome, but which was not accepted by the HOLY SEE, was a very partial renunciation by the state of its jurisdictional powers and a limited realization of Cavour's program, founded upon the separation of Church and state. However laws already on the books concerning liquidation of ecclesiastical properties (1866–7) and other polemics that sprang from them, as well as other legislative interventions from the left at the end of the century, especially under Francesco Crispi's government, contributed to the creation of powerful opposition forces between the liberal state and Italian Catholic society. These were not overcome until later, under fascism, with the 1929 concordat.

Mario Rosa

Bibliography

Capra, C. "*Il Settecento*," in D. Ssella and C. Capra, *Il ducato di Milano dal 1535 al 1796*. Turin, 1984.

Catalano, G. "Controversie giurisdictionali tra Chiesa e Stato nell'età di Gregorio XIII e Filippo II," *Atti dell'Accad. di Scienze, lettere e arti di Palermo*, series 4, 14 (1954–5), part II, 1–306.

Catalano, G., and Martino, F. *Potestà civile e autorità spirituale in Italia nei secoli della Riforma e della Controriforma*, Milan, 1984.

Enciclopedia Italiana, XVII, *sub voce* (by A. C. Jemolo).

Jemolo, A. C. *Chiesa e Stato in Italia negli ultimi cento anni*, new ed., Turin, 1963.

Jemolo, A. C. *Stato e Chiesa negli scrittori politici italiani del Seicento e del Settecento*, 2nd ed. published by F. Margiotta Broglio, Naples, 1972.

Lauro, A. *Il giurisdizionalismo pregiannoniano nel regno di Napoli. Problemi e bibliografia*, Rome, 1974.

Novissimo Digesto Italiano, VII, *sub voce* (by A. Piola).

Prodi, P. "San Carlo Boromeo e le trattative tra Gregorio XIII e Filippo II sulla giurisdizione ecclesiastica," *RSCI*, 11 (1957), 195–240.

Prosdocimi, L. *Il diritto ecclesiastico dello Stato di Milano dall'inizio della signoria viscontea al periodo tridentino (secc. XIII–XVI)*, Milan, 1941.

Rodolico, N. *State e Chiesa in Toscana durante la Regenza lorenese* (1737–65), Florence, 1910.

Rosa, M. "Giurisdizionalismo e riforma religiosa nella Toscana leopoldina," *Riformatori e ribelli nel '700 religioso italiano*, Bari, 1969, 165–213.

Rosa, M. "Politica concordataria, giurisdizionalismo e organizzazione ecclesiastica nel regno di Napoli sotto Carlo di Borbone," *Riformatori, op. cit.*, 119–63.

Schwarzenberg, C. "Sul giuridizionalismo veneziano nel '700," *Annali di storia del diritto*, vols. 10–11 (1966–7), 197–239.

Stella, A. *Chiesa e Stato nella relazioni dei nunzi pontifici a Venezia. Ricerche sul giurisdizionalismo veneziano dal XVI al XVIII secolo*, Vatican City, 1964.

Venturi, F. *Settecento riformatore*, II, *La Chiesa e la repubblica dentro i loro limiti 1758–1774*, Turin, 1976.

KEYS. The two keys seen, increasingly frequently, from the 13th century onward, on banners, money, and monuments, then above or behind the arms of popes, are those of St. Peter. They symbolize the power to bind or loosen, to close or open, granted by Christ to Peter, his vicar on earth. Transmitted to all of Peter's successors, they represent the authority of the pope over the Church and over the world, as well as his power to administer the benefits of the resurrection.

Symbols of Peter, the keys are seen in religious iconography starting in the 5th century. As emblem of the pope, they appear only during the pontificate of INNOCENT III, but from then on, they are abundantly represented, painted or sculpted, engraved or molded. The composition of their presentation varies: sometimes a single key, more often two, arranged vertically or, more often, crossed. In the figuration of arms, they surmount the family shield of the pope from the pontificate of CLEMENT VI on. One key is gold, the other silver; a cord of gules (red) links them.

The keys are placed on a shield. From the beginning of the 14th century, the two crossed keys constitute the arms of the papacy. The field of the shield is generally gules (red) and the cord is azure (blue). Most often the key placed in bend is gold and the one placed in bend sinister, silver; sometimes they are both gold, or, less often, silver. These arms are also those of the Church; as such, they are placed on numerous banners from the 14th century on. In the modern epoch, one must sometimes differentiate the arms of the Church from those of the papacy by color or by the position of the keys (gold/silver; straight/crossed), or by the color of the field of the shield (azure/gules or silver). But these subtle differences are hard to interpret, and the confusion between the two arms continues up to the present time.

Michel Pastoureau

Bibliography

Galbreath, D. L. *A Treatise on Ecclesiastical Heraldry.* Part I: Papal Heraldry, Cambridge, 1930, 6–16.
Heim, B. B. *Coutumes et droit heraldiques de l'Eglise*, Paris, 1949, 65–6 and 114–8.

KULTURKAMPF. In the period following the First Vatican Council (VATICAN I), there was an anti-Catholic policy in the recently formed German states as well as in the Austrian Empire, based on the 1867 compromise that the German empire (*Deutsches Reich*) accepted under the aegis of Prussia on 18 January 1871. This policy was known in Germany as the *Kulturkampf* (German for "combat for culture"); it was less of a religious persecution than a political policy.

The main architect of the *Kulturkampf* was Chancellor Otto von Bismarck, who was not personally hostile to Catholicism but was a product of the Prussian tradition, in which the evangelical church (which since 1818 had united followers of the Augsburg Confession—who were in the majority—and Calvinists, who formed the minority) was entirely compliant with the authority of the state. He supported the liberals who decided to do battle "for the freedom of culture and humanism"—a battle that was soon baptized *Kulturkampf* by Professor Rudolf Virchow. The offensive began in 1871, soon after the new Empire's first general parliamentary elections on March 3, conducted by universal suffrage, with all citizens represented. The Catholic party, the Zentrum, which had won 724,000 out of 3,890,000 votes cast, had 63 representatives out of 382 and became the second most powerful group in Parliament, after the Protestant liberal-conservatives (Freikonservative Partei, founded in 1866), the party supported by Bismarck, even though the new constitution had not yet mandated a parliamentary government, only the separation of powers.

In the beginning, the Zentrum was a Prussian Catholic party as conservative as the government party. It was among the political groups formed during the Frankfurt parliamentary session of 1848–49. Since 1852 there had been a Catholic parliamentary group (*Fraktion*) in the Prussian Landtag (diet) that included fifty-four deputies; in 1861, forty-eight Catholic deputies collectively adopted the name "Zentrum," because they were seated close to the center of the meeting hall. In 1862, they adopted a program with a Catholic orientation, conservative and pro-German, under the influence of lawyer Hermann von Mallinckrodt. The first article of this program was stated in these terms: "The essential foundation of a state rests upon the teachings and principles of Christianity," which explained this loyalty to the German Confederation (*Deutscher Bund*, under Austrian direction) and to national unity. The Austrian defeat of 1866 gave them severe problems of conscience in this respect. Finally, in December 1870, right in the middle of the Franco-Prussian War, the Prussian Catholic party changed into a German Catholic party, which was to keep the name Zentrum until 1945, and which immediately came into conflict with the Reich's government, that is to say, with Bismarck. He represented a fearsome political power because he also had the support of the two Catholic parties from southern Germany, the Bavarian Patriots and the Catholic People's Party from the grand duchy of Baden; thus, in the spring of 1871, the Zentrum became the core of the parliamentary opposition. Moreover, Bismarck suspected or pretended to suspect that an alliance had been formed by the enemies of the new state: Polish Catholics from the eastern provinces of the Empire (Poznan, Silesia, western Prussia) and residents of Alsace-Lorraine, recently annexed by the treaty of Frankfurt (May 1871). Bismarck accused the Catholics of wanting an alliance with Catholic Austria and of never having accepted the rupture of 1866, which doomed a unified Germany to being merely a Greater Prussia or at best, a Little Germany under Protestant control.

The electoral success of the Zentrum was a warning for the chancellor, who reacted immediately. Beginning in July 1871, he reversed the Catholic orientation of the Prussian Ministry of Religions, despite the importance of the latter since the annexation of the Prussian Rhine region in 1815 (the dioceses of Cologne, Trier, and Mainz were at that time part of Prussia). In December of the same year, the decrees by the chairman (*Kanzelparagraphen*) were disseminated as laws of the Empire, at the demand of the Bavarian government, in imitation of new Italian legislation. It was forbidden for clergy, in the exercise of their pastoral duties, "to bring up political affairs of the state in a manner that could disturb the public peace." Even a minor infraction would be punished by a prison sentence. The following year, school inspections in Prussia were taken out of ecclesiastical hands and given to the state. In 1872, Jesuits were forbidden to found establishments on territory anywhere in the German Empire.

In 1873, with the "May Laws," government restrictions began to interfere directly in the affairs of the Catholic Church. The training and appointment of clergy members was placed under state control. The administration of church properties was handed over to elected municipal commissions. Finally, in 1875, the Reichstag voted for a law according to which only marriages contracted before officials of the civil government were valid. They thus instituted a system of civil marriage, to the detriment of all religions—Catholic or Protestant—who lost their monopoly in this area. This law would indirectly permit divorce, as religious marriage was reduced to a symbolic ceremony with a religious aspect, which had to be preceded by a civil wedding. All these legal measures, particularly the Prussian legislation (which did not apply to German territory, due to the federal character of the Empire), were directed against the autonomy of churches and aimed, at the least, to reduce their influence. However, it was somewhat excessive to talk of "persecution of the believers of Germany" or "persecution of Christians" as Pius IX did. The legislation was not directed at believers—at any rate, not like the persecutions that had been organized in the days of the Roman empire, whose only goal had been to make Christians abandon their religion—but against the power of the Church as an institution. They were aimed at breaking that power, and making it subordinate to that of the state.

But these measures did not have the desired effect. The Church hierarchy took the lead in resisting, led by the bishop of Mainz. Descended from a family of Baltic barons, Wilhelm von Ketteler (1811–77) had first studied law and begun a career as a Prussian civil servant. Ordained a priest in 1844, he had been a representative to the parliament of Frankfurt in 1848 and one of the founders of the "Catholic club." Bishop of Mainz in 1850, he participated in the Vatican Council, where he was first an opponent and then a partisan of the dogma of papal INFALLIBILITY. From 1871 to 1873 he held a seat in the Reichstag, where he fought to soften anti-Catholic legislation and where he developed theses on Christian socialism, before publishing a work about the *Kulturkampf*. In February 1871, he had drawn up a plan for the Catholic party, which was adopted at the end of March under its Latin title, *Justitia fundamentum regnorum* ("Justice is the foundation of governments"). Contrary to Bismarck's expectations, the Catholics also received support from Protestant conservatives who rejected civil marriage and the control of schools by government inspectors. Besides, the chancellor was poisoning the political climate and abridging fundamental rights; the liberals, who had supported him on the confessional issue, began to worry. Politically, the campaign accomplished nothing. The Zentrum was far from being destroyed as a political force, since the number of its deputies continued to grow as fast at the Prussian Landtag, increasing from 58 to 97 by 1879, as at the Reichstag, where it went from 63 to 94 seats. Also, tensions within German Catholicism due to the proclamation of papal infallibility actually decreased rapidly. Bismarck had suffered a political defeat and, as a true statesman, instead of being obstinate, he attempted a reconciliation with the Catholic party. In foreign policy, the chancellor had always tried accommodation with powers he could not defeat, and in 1878 he took advantage of the death of PIUS IX, who had always been intransigent, to attempt a settlement with the Holy See. In a letter dated 24 March 1878 and countersigned by Bismarck as chancellor of the Empire, Emperor Wilhelm I congratulated LEO XIII on his election, which he had learned of indirectly from the king of Bavaria. This maneuver was indicative of the deplorable state of relations between the Vatican and Berlin, but it also shows that the two sides were ready to begin a dialogue. The letter also indicated that the emperor hoped the new pontiff would use his influence with the German Catholics to get them to cooperate with contemporary legislation that was in force.

The past could not, however, be erased with one stroke of a pen, since the Berlin government was not about to withdraw the measures it had taken against the Church. It demanded that the hierarchy submit to it, but the new pope could not accept these conditions, as he told the emperor in a letter dated 17 April 1878. He asked that the Prussian constitutional legislation be brought into conformity with Church laws. Nevertheless, he expressed his personal sympathy for Wilhelm I after the latter survived two attempts on his life, on May 11 and June 2 of that same year. At least direct communication had been established. It was Crown Prince Frederick-Wilhelm (the future emperor Frederick III) who answered on 10 June 1878, in a long letter also countersigned by Bismarck, for the old emperor was in no condition to write personally. After the usual polite phrases, the crown prince referred to Leo XIII's letter of April 17, and then spoke of the "millenary" quarrel between the Church and the Empire.

Berlin wished to put an end to the quarrel with the Holy See based on a "spirit of reconciliation" rather than merely an "agreement on principles." The confrontation had produced no results, and efforts were made to relax tensions and establish mutual confidence. The Vatican was as conscious of this as Berlin was, and both were ready to attempt this experiment. Leo XIII discreetly but efficiently tried to help Bismarck reach a compromise with the Zentrum, and the chancellor, little by little during the course of the 1880s, cut back on the most vexing portions of his laws aimed at the Church. However he

never capitulated in the areas of school inspection, civil marriage, and control of ecclesiastical appointments. In consequence, the problems between the Catholic Church and the Prussian State brought about by the *Kulturkampf* never ended, and repercussions would be felt throughout the history of the Federal Republic.

On the other hand, in the Austrian Empire (that is to say, following the 1867 Compromise, Cisleithania), the *Kulturkampf* took a much less dramatic form and therefore had much less serious consequences. As soon as Cisleithania had a constitution and a parliament (the Reichsrat), the Liberal party took power from 1868 to 1879, and Franz Joseph did not feel authorized to oppose the policies of his liberal cabinet. In January 1868, putting into effect the new Austrian Constitution (the "December laws"), the emperor named an Auersperg government that rushed to abolish most of the dispositions of the concordat of 1855, to the great sorrow of the nuncio Falcinelli, who could not stop the emperor from authorizing civil marriages nor from sanctioning new school laws. Civil and state control and the control of the schools were again in the hands of the state, as they had been before the revolution of 1848 and in the spirit of Josephist tradition. The new Austrian legislation established obligatory lay elementary schools, though teaching of the catechism could be done by priests at the schools. The parliament of Budapest voted in similar legislation, with the blessing of the primate of Hungary, Cardinal Simor, and all the clergy. Of course, Pius IX condemned these "abominable laws," but there was no diplomatic crisis between Vienna and the Vatican. When, in April 1870, Franz Joseph named Count Potocki (a Polish aristocrat from Galicia) president of the Austrian Council, the latter benefited from the consequences of the liberal laws of 1868, and purely and simply denounced the concordat of 1855 at a moment when relationships with the Vatican had deteriorated. Neither the emperor nor Cardinal Rauscher, archbishop of Vienna, nor the clergy had subscribed wholeheartedly to the dogma of papal infallibility. They gave the excuse that, since one of the partners had changed, the contracted agreement was null and void. Franz Joseph took this point of view with the Crown Council (the supreme executive body of the Austro-Hungarian monarchy) on 30 August 1870. But the solid attachment to the Catholic religion on the part of the dynasty and the majority of the inhabitants avoided an Austro-Hungarian *Kulturkampf* similar to the one Germany experienced.

Jean Bérenger

Bibliography

Buchheim, K. *Ultramontanismus und Demokratie. Der Weg des deustchen Katholiken im 19. Jahrhundert*, Munich, 1963.

Hahn, L. *Geschichte des "Kulturkampfes" in Preußen. In Aktenstücke dargestellt. Mit einer Uebersicht*, Berlin, 1881.

Lönne, E. *Politischer Katholizismus im 19. und 20. Jahrhundert*, Frankfurt-am-Main, 1984.

Ross, R. J. *The Failure of Bismarck's Kulturkampf: Catholicism and State Power in Imperial Germany, 1871–1887*, Washington, D. C., 1998.

Schmidt-Volkmar, E. *Der Kulturkampf in Deutschland 1871–1890*, Göttingen, 1962.

Von Ketteler, W. *Der Kulturkampf gegen die katholische Kirche*, Mainz, 1874.

Wallace, L. P. *The Papacy and European Diplomacy, 1869–1878*, Chapel Hill, N. C., 1948.

LAITY, MIDDLE AGES. Impious, uncultivated, and rapacious—this is the image of the lay world supposedly held by clerics during the Middle Ages. The image of two opposing groups prevailed for a long time, until recent research brought to light a different and more complex reality. Far from being in a state of silent subordination, the laity of the period knew how to get the clergy to respond to their initiatives. Thus, one could properly speak of a real "emergence of the laity" (A. Vauchez) without the problems of this "state of affairs" being resolved.

In speaking about the laity, the writers of the Middle Ages, following the usage of the Church Fathers, rarely used the term *laicus*, which is Greek for "noninitiated" and Latin for "common." They preferred the term *saecularis*, which is seen often. The layman was defined as one whose life, though recognized by the Church for its uniqueness and its value, was nonetheless defined by certain limits when compared with those of a priest or religious. His matrimonial status would keep him forever from that state of perfection that is virginity; his frequent lack of training would keep him from the study of literature, and especially of Latin, and, therefore, from access to the Scriptures; and finally, his worldly life, with all its temptations, would invite him to succumb to them. Thus he was removed from the spiritual realm, which he could access only through the mediation of a priest. The relationship between the two groups evolved throughout a long period based on a common belief in these ideas.

In an earlier period, the laity represented to clerics a world in need of conversion, even well after Western Europe was christianized. This can be explained by the fact that conversion was not just one simple action but had to be accompanied by a constant watch over the behavior of the newly baptized, an attitude amply illustrated by the advice of POPE GREGORY I the Great to the evangelizers of England at the beginning of the 6th century. But the enterprise of conversion takes a long time, and pastoral literature until the 15th century is full of complaints about the intractability and negligence of the faithful. With their limitations in mind, the LATERAN IV COUNCIL in 1215 had set very moderate minimal obligations (annual confession and communion for Easter). Nonetheless, the laity of the Middle Ages seem to have been very concerned about their salvation. They wished to participate in the spiritual riches of the clergy, first by putting their salvation in the hands of priests and religious, and then, more and more, by imitating the religious forms of piety. The laity would do so well that, by the end of the period, there were many more who had received religious training and could recite the Liturgy of the Hours (matins, lauds, vespers, etc.). Moreover, they also showed a real ability to create their own forms of devotion, whether in personal attempts to imitate Christ, or by initiating devotions to those whom they regarded as saints and who could be recognized as such by the Church.

Paradoxically, even the REFORM movements emphasizing asceticism that attracted some laity during this period reflect a high regard for the consecrated life. GREGORY VII was able to use the *patarini* ("ragpickers," a reform sect) of Milan in his fight against priests who were guilty of simony. For the laity, the Church offered ideas for an ideal Christian life. In the Carolingian era, theologians, among them Jonas of Orleans in his *De institutione laicali*, suggested a mode of living to members of the aristocracy and defined a Christian view of marriage as a consensual and indissoluble link of sacramental value.

Beginning in the 12th century, some specific activities of the lay world were restored that, in earlier centuries, had been fairly exclusively reserved to ascetics and monks. For warriors, the Church presented an ideal that consisted of channeling the use of violence and finding just causes for combat, such as the defense of the poor and priests and religious—who were forbidden to bear arms—as well as defending orthodoxy by fighting crusades against infidels and heretics. Those who worked saw their manual labor recognized for its ascetic value and its social usefulness, in all its different aspects. They therefore were able to live a holy life in the world. The laity were encouraged to do the corporal and spiritual "works of mercy" (Mt 25:35–46). Pope IN-NOCENT III in 1199 canonized the layman Homobonus of Cremona just two years after his death. A husband, father, and merchant draper, Homobonus had devoted his life to the service of the poor and the fight against heresy. The canonization of a layman was an exception to the more usual canonization, in that period, of bishops, clergy, or members of the aristocracy. Beguines and beghards (lay female and male members of ascetic and philanthropic communities) began in the 13th century and spread rapidly; however, some of their practices led to criticisms and censure by POPE JOHN XXII in 1317–18.

In the later Middle Ages, piety changed somewhat. For some there was an emphasis on the penitential or the eschatological. For others, like the English laywoman Julian of Norwich (1348–after 1416), author of *Revelations of Divine Love*, there was a desire to experience God and Christ's passion. This contemplative mysticism is found in several women of this period, Catherine of Siena (c. 1347–80) and Joan of Arc (c. 1412–31), for example. Virginity was again presented as the more perfect state. Marriage no longer seemed compatible with perfection. Whereas the century before had found a Christian use for marriage justified by procreation and the spiritual support that spouses could provide for each other, "virginal marriage" (marriage to Christ) was now exalted. The Middle Ages ended, for the laity, with an intense spiritual quest that would find its answer in reform, both Protestant and Catholic.

Catherine Vincent

See also OPUS DEI; REFORMATION; TRENT, COUNCIL OF; VATICAN I COUNCIL; VATICAN II COUNCIL.

Bibliography

Congar, Y. "Laïcat au Moyen Âge," *DS*, 9 (1976), 79–93.
Astell, A. W., ed. *Lay Sanctity, Medieval and Modern: A Search for Models*, Notre Dame, 2000.
Vauchez, A. *Les Laïcs au Moyen Âge*, 1987.

LANDO. *Lando (d. end of March 914). Elected pope in November 913, probably buried in St. Peter's in Rome.*

Lando's father, Tainus, was apparently born in Fornovo in Sabina. No pontifical acts have been preserved from his reign, which did not last more than six months, and only one judicial document, a dating from the 15th century (1431), tells us about this pope. Doubtlessly drawing from a rich inheritance from his father, he made donations to his natal diocese of Sabina, at Vescovio, in order to restore the S. Salvatore cathedral, destroyed at the end of the 9th century by SARACENS who were then pillaging Italy. The confirmation of episcopal rights is also found in this same document. It allowed the episcopal residence to return to Vescovio from Toffia, where it had been moved. The lack of additional information about this pope, who is certainly not of major importance, may also be explained by the situation in the city of Rome at this time. The papacy was completely dominated by the lord of the city, Theophylact, who as CHAMBERLAIN (*vestararius*) to the pope, controlled the management of all ecclesiastical possessions and, as leader and consul of Rome, also performed the most important governmental functions on the temporal level, as the head of the Roman militia and of the SENATE.

Harald Zimmermann

Bibliography

Zimmermann, H. *Papstregesten*, 6–7; "Lando," *LexMA*, 5 (1991), 1671.

LATERAN IV COUNCIL (1215). From the beginning of his reign, INNOCENT III was committed to curbing HERESY, pushing for a crusade to the Holy Land, and reforming the Church. On 19 April 1215, he issued a BULL proclaiming the universal COUNCIL announced in 1199 (*Vineam Domini Sabaoth*, Register XVI, 30) and the necessity of a crusade (*Quia major nunc*, XVI, 18). He broadened the call to cathedral and collegial churches, who were invited to send delegates, bursars, and invited kings, princes, and the rulers of city-states to attend on 1 November.

Attendance at the Lateran was considerable: ambassadors from Frederick, king of Sicily and elected king of the Romans, from the emperor of Constantinople, the kings of France, Hungary, Jerusalem, Cyprus, and Aragon; consuls from Italian republics, nobles involved in the Albigensian affair, procurators from English barons. There were a large number of delegates from cathedral and collegiate churches. Over 1,200 attended, including the five patriarchs of the East.

The written account by "An Anonymous Man from Giessen" provides a perspective on the course of the Council. Besides the three solemn sessions on the 11th, 20th, and 30th of November, the recorder specified the chronology of those dealing with the English crisis, aired as early as the 4th, with the primacy of Toledo on the 13th, the Albigensian heresy, from the 14th on; the imperial question was brought up on the 20th in accordance with the formal order required in a quasi-judicial session.

In his solemn homily on 11 November, Innocent III referred to the words of Jesus: "And he said to them: With great desire I have desired to eat this passover with you, before I suffer" (Luke, 22:5), the exegesis of which he made relevant in speaking of the triple "passage" to which the Church was called: physically, from one place to another "in order to free pitiful Jerusalem"; spiritually, from one state to another through reform; eternally, "from this life to the next and to glory." The final session on 30 November opened with a solemn profession of faith. Then general peace and the crusade were proclaimed, and ANATHEMAS pronounced, and Frederick von Hohenstaufen was named as candidate for the imperial crown and Otto of Brunswick was stripped of his rights; the barons and their allies in rebellion against John Lackland were excommunicated; Raymond of St. Giles was reduced to the condition of penitent and deposed; and Simon of Montfort was made count of Toulouse by a two-thirds majority vote. The Trinitarian thesis of Joachim of Flora and the "extravagant" one of Amaury de Bène were formally condemned. After the reading of the decrees, the *Te Deum* was sung, and the papal benediction closed the council.

The *Corpus lateranense* (decrees of the council) begins with the dogmatic document *De fide catholica*, a Trinitarian creed in three parts that are organically linked: God in his essence; the divine Persons and the common work of the Trinity; and the universal Church where Christ is both priest and victim. The Trinitarian faith of Nicaea (325), developed at the Council of Constantinople (381), on the procession of the Holy Spirit is theologically explained. In a dense formula, the Chalcedonian confession is affirmed: Jesus Christ, one person with two natures, true man with a body and soul. Following the eleventh council of Toledo, the Incarnation was proclaimed a work of the Trinity. The link between universal Judgment and Christ in his glory, between the resurrection of the body and the just reckoning of deeds, is affirmed vigorously. The creed of the Lateran IV is a development of the traditional formulation of the nature of the Church—sacrificial and eucharistic. Defined as such for the first time in a dogmatic document, this teaching presents an ecclesiology of communion with Christ's body and blood and the mystery of oneness. It lists the basic precepts of sacramental theology developed by Peter Lombard, Peter the Chanter, Stephen Langton and others. By the simple fact of professing the faith explicitly, the Lateran creed exorcised heresies in multiple forms, crystallized in the neo-Manicheaism of the Cathars and Albigensians. Renewing ALEXANDER III's decrees, and those of LUCIUS III, an anathema was declared against the Joachimite thesis. Peter Lombard's teaching was reaffirmed (c. 2). The measures of repression enacted in 1184 were continued and extended to the universal Church (c. 3).

The ecclesiastical unity achieved since 1204 rested on a unity of jurisdiction, linked to the rite held to be intrinsic to faith. Constantinople, "the ecumenical patriarchate," recognized the authority of Rome: "the Roman Church which has ordinary power over everything"(c. 7).

The pope would confer the *pallium* on metropolitans. In this way, the council affirmed a pyramidal conception of the Church, which was foreign to Orthodoxy. Several concessions of a pastoral nature (c. 9, 14, 53) could not hide the ideal goal: universal acceptance of the Roman rite.

Following the Lateran III Council, ecclesiastical government was developed and refined: church vacancies; the rights of devolution; procedures of election, calling of provincial SYNODS, correction of abuses, and procedure of inquiries. The council endorsed papal efforts to reform monastic life and to end abuses of privileges. Both canons regular and monastic orders were required to hold a triennial chapter (c. 12). The privilege *Vitam religiosam eligentibus* proposed a life for monks, nuns, and canons regular far stricter than what many of the ascetic lay movements of penitents and preachers had advocated.

The pastoral ministry presented by Lateran IV went beyond the formality of previous councils. It aimed at the edification of the faithful, prescribing the creation of auxiliaries to the bishop for preaching duties and confession (c. 10); the choosing of a *grammaticus* in each cathedral and a theologian in each metropolis; obligatory and free ecclesiastical teaching (c. 11, see also Lateran III Council, c. 18); and the preparation of candidates for the priesthood (27). The "Easter duty," confession, and the minimal obligation of yearly communion (c. 21), confirmed an already established usage. Similar pastoral concern inspired reforms concerning marriage: from 7th to 4th degree of consanguinity as an obstacle to marriage (c. 50); the publication of bans so as to prevent any clandestine marriage (c. 51); and procedures in matrimonial cases to help preserve the bond (c. 52). Canons 35–49 specified the forms of appeal as well as the case for revoking an interlocutory or comminatory sentence on appeal (36). Trial proceedings were to be recorded. The introduction of rational proof, accompanied by the rejection of ordeals and the institution of the position of court clerk, radically changed legal procedures. In the name of equity, canons 39–41 went beyond the civil law stipulating the need for legitimate possession and conservatory possession as well as proof of good faith.

The canonical legislation of 1215 had a serenity and a breadth unknown until then in conciliar decrees. It reflects the collections of DECRETALS as well as the decrees of Lateran III and the decretals of Innocent III. The teachings of Lateran IV for the most part survived until the Council of TRENT, and, together with the latter, formed the basis for the CODE OF CANON LAW OF 1917.

The document *Ad liberandam*, elaborated on the text on the crusade proposed in 1213. It called for various measures to mobilize the personnel and imposed a 20 percent tax on ecclesiastical revenues. It also specified that the crusaders were to meet at Brindisi and Messina on 1 June

1217, under the direction of the pope. It spelled out and amplified the methods for protection of parishes and their possessions, and proclaimed a general peace for four years so as to mobilize all the efforts of Christendom on behalf of the Holy Land. Finally, it promulgated the crusade indulgence, to which the council added "its prayers and blessings to open the way to salvation for the Crusaders."

Raymonde Foreville

Bibliography

Foreville, R. *Latran I, II, III, et Latran IV*, 1965 (*Histoire des conciles oecuméniques*), 6.

Garcia y Garcia, A. *Constitutiones concilii quarti Lateranensis una cum commentariis glossatorum (Monumenta juris canonici, ser. A, 2)*.

Gouvernement et vie de l'Église au Moyen Âge, London, 1979.

John the Teuton, *Compilatio quarta* (Canon Law).

"L'iconographie du XIIe concile oecuménique (Latran IV, 1215)," *Mélanges René Crozet*, 1966, 112–30.

Paris, M. *Chronica majora*, ed. Luard, II, London, 1874, 627 *ff.* in *Conciliorum oecumenicorum decreta*, 1st ed. 1962, 203–47.

Robb, F. "The Fourth Lateran Council's Definition of Trinitarian Orthodoxy," *Journal of Ecclesiastical History* 48 (January, 1997), 22–43

Small, C. "The Fourth Lateran Council of 1215: A Turning Point in the History of Medieval Europe," *Regligious Studies and Theology* II (1991), 66–78.

LATERAN V COUNCIL (1512–7). On 3 May 1512, a council called by JULIUS II convened in Rome's LATERAN BASILICA. The inaugural sermon by Giles of Viterbo, general of the Augustinian order, made a big impact on the audience. The speaker welcomed the advent of new times: the pope, who had defeated his adversaries, was now going to complete his exploits by assembling a reforming council and launching a new crusade against the infidels. In particular, Giles of Viterbo praised the benefits of councils, the only appropriate bastion against the threats posed by HERESIES, SCHISMS, and depraved morals: "O, happy the times that have seen these great assemblies, unhappy those who did not benefit from them!" In reality, it was not enthusiasm but rather pressure that had brought the pope to call this council. He had done so to counteract a council called by the king of France and supported by the emperor that had been meeting at Pisa since October 1511. The origin of this proceeding that threatened the pope's authority and Church unity was the political conflict caused by Julius II's changes in policy in 1510. Allied with Louis XII against the Venetians, until the latter suffered a crushing defeat at Agnadello (14 May 1509), the pope suddenly changed course and made peace with the vanquished, allying himself with Switzer-

land and the other major powers of Christendom to drive the French out of Italy. Louis XII's counterattack inevitably took place on ecclesiastical terrain. Not only did he revive all the Gallican principles, but the king, taking advantage of the anti-Roman sentiment that existed throughout the empire at the time, obtained Maximilian's support in convening a council. The plan was supported by five CARDINALS, who were personal enemies of Julius II, including two from Spain and one from Italy. A preparatory assembly was held in Lyon in the spring of 1511, raising again the conciliar themes of the preceding century. The council that was meeting in Pisa included six cardinals, twenty-four archbishops and bishops (including sixteen French ones), and several abbots, as well as theologians and jurists. On 18 July 1511, the pope officially condemned it. The following April, Julius II convoked his own council at the Lateran.

Before the latter even opened, the council at Pisa had its first difficulties. Threatened by a popular uprising, it had to move to MILAN in the spring of 1512, French military losses soon forced it to return to Lyon, where the "conciliabulum" ignominiously disbanded. Thus, the Lateran V Council attained its first objective, that of neutralizing its rival. But the pope and his council could not ignore the impetus for reform that the Pisa council had helped set in motion and that persisted even after the death of Julius II (21 February 1513). Pope LEO X, his successor, proceeded with the council.

Among the plans for reform that had motivated the Lateran Council, the most elaborate were those of the Spanish episcopate, presented to Leo X by two Italian priests, Tommaso Giustiniani and Vincenzo Quirini. The reform plans of Gian Francesco Pico della Mirandola were also brought up before the council. All of these projects were relatively conservative. All saw reform as a return to a more perfect former state. All the authors would have subscribed to the famous formula of Giles of Viterbo: *Homines per sacra immutari fas est, non sacra per homines*. The council brought together a good number of participants; 431 council fathers, in all, met in its different sessions, most often attended by approximately 100 at a time. It was relatively ecumenical, since one-third of the dioceses represented lay outside Italy. Even some members of the Pisan council ended up attending: A session dedicated to abjuring and pardoning the two most compromised cardinals took place in June 1513, and in turn the French prelates came to sit at the Lateran beginning in the fall of 1513. There was also an attempt by the pope to convince the Hussites—by conceding communion under both species—to send a spokesman to the council. The Lateran V Council had twelve sessions, stretching from 1512 until its conclusion on 16 March 1517. Whereas the five sessions held under Julius II were essentially occupied in combatting schism, the following ones, under Leo X, took up doctrinal and disciplinary matters. The texts approved by the council are far from insignificant. But fearful of reopening the conflict of authority with the pope, the council agreed to have its decrees published as papal BULLS.

Abandoning chronological order so as to present them in a methodical fashion, the works of the Fifth Lateran Council are as follows:

Doctrinal Work. Taking note of the invention of the printing press—greeted as a gift from God—and the possibilities it offered for the diffusion of culture, the council nevertheless denounced the dangers it could raise for faith and morality, and created a system of censorship for books and other printed texts under the authority of the pope, bishops, and inquisitors in the bull *Inter sollicitudines* on 4 May 1515. The council also ruled on a debate raised several years earlier at the University of Padua by Pietro Pomponazzi. Interpreting Aristotle, Pomponazzi held that the immortality of the individual soul is impossible to demonstrate and thus was a matter of faith. The council rejected this and affirmed that the immortality the soul is a philosophical truth; it also stated the principle that philosophy should never be independent from the lights of revealed truth (in the bull *Apostolici regiminis,* 19 December 1513).

Reform of the Curia and the Clergy. Universally sought, the reform of the Roman CURIA began under favorable auspices, judging by the remarks made by Cardinal Riario, dean of the SACRED COLLEGE. He asserted that he had always wanted this reform; it was urgent, he said, in order to eliminate any "cause for railing against us, particularly across the mountains and in foreign nations." Not to carry this out would be unpardonable since it depended only on those concerned with it, he maintained. Thus the council reminded the cardinals that they must lead exemplary lives and conduct their affairs with strict discipline; it warned them against the abuses of nepotism. As for the services of the Curia, a text suggested regulating its tariffs and tax system. As for the clergy in general, the council raised the minimum age for bishops to thirty (with possible exceptions made for persons as young as twenty-seven) and for abbots to twenty-two. It outlawed the commendam on principle (but listed multiple exceptions) and the accumulation of benefices (while allowing the acceptance of two nonconflicting benefices "for grave and pressing reasons"). To respond to the wishes of the bishops, the council restricted the EXEMPTIONS of the canons (bull *Regimini universalis Ecclesiae,* on 4 May 1515) and even the exemptions of religious clergy whose pastoral activity would be supervised by the ordinary of the diocese (bull *Dum intra mentis,* 19 December 1516). To these mild measures of clerical reform, the council would give a first blow on 19 December 1516, by agreeing to ratify the CONCORDAT that Leo X had just concluded at Bologna with the king of France. It was true that the council was most sensitive to the abolition of the Pragmatic Sanction of Bourges, this "impious text," the charter of Gallicanism. But by giving the king the right to appoint bishops and most abbots, this council reopened the door for most of the abuses it wished to abolish.

For the Christian People. The Lateran Council had no comprehensive plan for the Christian people but took circumstantial action. One harsh decree condemned blasphemers. Another dealt with a debate that had been troubling moralists for several decades by affirming the legitimacy of Monti di Pietrà, which did not (contrary to Cajetan's pronouncement in 1498) fall under the label of usury. The council's most important decree concerned preaching (the document *Munus praedicationis,* 19 December 1516): all preachers, including those belonging to religious orders, had to be examined by their superiors and approved by the local ordinary. Moreover, they were to teach only pure Church doctrine, based upon Scripture and the Church Fathers and doctors of the church with no other purpose than the saving of souls. In particular, eschatological preaching, which was attracting crowds during the early years of the 16th century, was condemned as the work of men "who raise terrors and threaten, who proclaim numerous misfortunes to be imminent . . . , who insist that these misfortunes are already here," and who support their assertions with fake miracles. The council forbade them "to state with any assurance a specific time for these misfortunes to occur, or the coming of the Antichrist, or the precise day of the Last Judgment." Besides these false prophets, however, the Church was also aiming at reformers who were too zealous in criticizing the hierarchy and the clergy: "They should abstain from criticizing the bishops, the prelates and other superiors in a scandalous manner, as well as their circumstances, for we see them denounce and attack them in public without prudence or restraint, even in front of laypersons, and criticize their actions openly, not even fearing at times to name them." This, the Council said, risked tearing apart the seamless tunic of Christ.

It is difficult to estimate fairly the effects of Lateran V. Luther's entry onto the scene, seven and one-half months after its closure, and the formidable acceleration of the reform process that resulted make the measures the council had planned seem very inadequate, even if they had been put into effect. In fact, the decrees of the Lateran would be stifled by the indifference of the pope, to whom the council, by giving their decisions the canonical form of bulls, had given all the responsibility for implementing them, and by the ill will of the Curia, which did not wish to refine its practices now that the danger was past. The most lasting achievement of this council was to put an end to conciliarist theories that held that the council's authority was superior to that of the pope.

Marc Venard

Bibliography

Bernorio, V. L. *La Chiesa di Pavia nel secolo XVI . . .* , 1971.

Christophe, N. P. and Frost, F., *Les Conciles oecuméniques. II. Le Second Millénaire*, Paris, 1988.

D'Addario, A., *Aspetti della Controriforma a Firenze*, 1972.

De La Brosse, O. et al., *Latran V et Trente*, 1975.

Fliche-Martin, XV.

Hefele-Leclercq, *Histoire des conciles*, VII, Paris, 1917.

Jedin, H. A History of the Council of Trent, I, trans. E. Grof, St. Louis, 1957.

Lemaitre, N. *Le Rouergue flamboyant: Le clergé et les fidèles du diocèse de Rodez, 1417–1563*, 1988.

Mansi, *Sacrorum conciliorum nova et amplissima collectio*, XXIII, 1759, 649–1002.

Minnich, N. H. "Concepts of Reform proposed at the Fifth Lateran Council," *AHP*, 7 (1969), 163–251; and "The Participants at the Fifth Lateran Council," *AHP*, 12 (1974), 157–206.

Minnich, N. H. *The Catholic Reformation: Council, Churchmen, Controversies*, Aldershot, 1993.

Minnich, N. H. *The Fifth Lateran Council (1512–17): Studies on Its Membership, Diplomacy, and Proposals for Reform*, Aldershot, 1993.

O'Malley, J. W. *Giles of Viterbo on Church and Reform. A Study in Renaissance Thought*, 1968.

Veissière, M. *Guillaume Briçonnet*, 1986.

LATERAN COUNCILS. The basilica of St. John Lateran in Rome has taken on a special significance in the history of the papacy. Quite early, it became one of the major centers for decisions since it was the Cathedral of the pope, who had a residential palace next to the BASILICA. Five conciliar assemblies met there, in a room that served as an *aula* reserved for the council and adjoining the basilica. Its construction was begun by LEO III (795–816), who had it sumptuously decorated with MOSAICS among which are found, in the center of the room, a representation of Christ, the Mother of God, and the apostles Peter and Paul.

The Lateran Council of 1112. The first conciliar meeting was ecumenical in theory but not in fact, which sets it apart from the next five meetings held in the Lateran. It was exclusively preoccupied with the settlement of the quarrel over INVESTITURES. After the death of Pope GREGORY VII in 1085, Emperor Henry IV had been able to think that he had total latitude in the choice and nomination of bishops. In spite of the revolt led by his sons, which forced him to abdicate, his son Henry V adopted the ecclesiastical policy of his father and was actually able, by 1111, to physically compel Pope PASCHAL II (1099–1118)—whom he captured—to accept imperial investitures for major benefices. Bowing to pressure in the opposite direction by prelates who held fast to the Gregorian REFORM, the pope had to backtrack during the council in 1112. The distinction between the two investitures, temporal and spiritual, as stated by the French canonist Yves of Chartres, opened the way for the compromise formulated ten years later by the concordat of WORMS, the first act of this type (1122).

Lateran I Council (18 March–6 April 1123). [9th Ecumenical Council]. Due to the fragmentary nature of sources and the total absence of surviving official minutes, we know little about the First Lateran Council other than its decisions, which were published as canons. The estimate of 997 participants, suggested by Pandulf in his biography of CALLISTUS II (1119–24), is surely exaggerated; the council probably had only around 300 participants. It published twenty-five canons, but some were merely reformulations of earlier decisions: for example, the dispositions banning SIMONY, and those maintaining the Truce of God begun in France by the Council of Le Puy in 987, generalized by the Council of Anse in 994, and expanded by URBAN II (1088–99) at Clermont in 1095. DISPENSATIONS were given to crusaders for the remission of penance for their sins, while the council condemned acts of pillaging committed against pilgrims on their way to Rome by decreeing the excommunication of the guilty parties. Other canons dealt with the administration of the sacrament of ordination and the various ways of granting ecclesiastical appointments. Finally on 28 March, the council fathers proceeded to canonize the former bishop of Constance, Conrad, who died in 976.

Lateran II Council (4–11 April 1139). [10th Ecumenical Council]. The origin of the Lateran II council was a dispute within the Church. After the death of Pope HONORIUS III (1124–30), sixteen CARDINALS, most of them French, chose INNOCENT II, the candidate of the powerful Frangipani family. But on 14 February 1130, twenty other cardinals elected Pietro Pierleoni [Petri Leonis], from a family of Jewish origin, who was supported by the king of Sicily, Robert II. The "ghetto pope," as he was nicknamed, took the name of ANACLETUS II, but was deposed, without abandoning his throne, by the combined intervention of St. Bernard and Emperor Lothair III, who had Innocent II crowned in Rome. The death of Anacletus II on 25 January 1138 left the field free for Innocent II, who called a "general SYNOD" the following year, qualified as *maxima* by the chroniclers of the time, which included perhaps 700 participants, a considerable number. The pope deplored the trouble brought to the Church by the SCHISM of Anacletus and gave his supporters back their *pallium*, staff, and ring. The greatest portion of the thirty canons of this council fit within the tradition of Gregorian reform, condemning once again usura (interest on a sum of money lent at 33⅓ percent), forbidding jousts or tourneys, invalidating marriage by priests (rather than merely judging them to be illicit), and forbidding monks to study secular disciplines such as law or medicine. Canon 28 confirmed the cathedral chapters' right to elect bishops, as religious orders did for their superiors, a starting point for the growing influence of chapters in the life of dioceses throughout the Middle Ages. Finally, the council excommunicated those who rejected the Eucharist and the baptism of babies, but was silent about the stand taken by Canon Arnold of Brescia, accused by his bishop before the entire assembly of the council of having maintained that no cleric or monk who had material possessions could be saved.

Lateran III Council (March 1179). [11th Ecumenical Council] After a fifteen-year period of relentless strife, Emperor Barbarossa finally consented, in a bitterly negotiated peace treaty signed in Venice, to stop supporting the ANTIPOPE CALLISTUS III and to return some confiscated Church possessions. The Venetian treaty made provision for the convening of a council. The Lateran Council, the third by that name, sanctioned the authority by the papacy that had been gained by the treaty. ALEXANDER III (1159–81) wanted to have this peace confirmed by the largest possible assembly of clergy: more than three hundred council fathers answered the invitation addressed to them. The council was held in three sessions, the 5th, 7th (or 14th), and 19th (or 22nd) of March 1179, ending in the publication of twenty-seven *Capituli* on various issues, with no internal homogeneity of purpose. In the hope of preventing future schisms, a majority (defined as two-thirds) of the cardinals was required to elect a pope, and the minimum age required to be an elector was set at thirty years of age. Other measures dealt with major concerns: the accumulation of stipends and benefices was limited, with no one able to hold several offices simultaneously; and a professor was to be named for each cathedral to ensure the instruction of clerics and indigent students. The council ruled more precisely on several heresies, striking first at the furnishing of arms or supplies to the SARACENS, punishable by excommunication, and then declared the Cathars ANATHEMA, as well as anyone having any dealings with them or sheltering them. On the other hand, according to a fairly reliable source, the council received a delegation from the "poor men of Lyons," a group of supporters of the former merchant Pierre Valdes, who presented his translation of the Bible and asked for approval of their sermons; though they did not get it, neither were they condemned.

François Jankowiak

Bibliography

Alberigo, G., ed. *Storia dei Concilii ecumenici*, 1990.
Foreville, R. *Latran I, II, III and Latran IV*, 1965 [*Histoire des Conciles oecuméniques*].
Fournier, P., and Le Bras, G. *Histoire des collections canoniques en Occident depuis les Fausses Décrétales jusqu'au Décret de Gratien*, 1931–32.
Fransen, G. "Papes, conciles généraux et oecuméniques," *Istituzioni ecclesiastiche della "Societas Christiana" dei secoli XI–XII*, Milan, 1975.
Fuhrmann, H. "Das ökumenische Konzil und seine historischen Grundlagen," *Einladung im Mittelalter*, Munich, 1987.
Gaudemet, J. *Les Sources du droit canonique, VIIIe–XXe siècles*, 1993.
Longére, J., ed. *Le Troisième concile de Latran (1179). Sa place dans l'histoire*, 1982.
Pacaut, M. *Alexandre III: Étude sur la conception du pouvoir pontifical dans sa pensée et dans son oeuvre*, 1956.

LATERAN PACTS. The agreements that sanctioned the "reconciliation" between the Church of Pius XI and the Italy of Mussolini were signed at the Lateran Palace, 11 February 1929, by the secretary of state of the Holy See, Cardinal Gasparri, and by the head of the Italian government, the fascists, Benito Mussolini. After more than half a century, they put an end to the "Roman question" begun by the annexation of the PAPAL STATES by Italy and by the occupation of the city of Rome on 20 September 1870. The "law of guarantees" that Parliament had approved in 1871 to assure the prerogatives of the pontiff and of the HOLY SEE and to normalize relations with the Italian state had never been accepted by Pius IX and his successors. However, the two sides had been engaged in the process of settling the conflict since the beginning of the century. Thanks to the first political alliances between moderate liberals and clerics and to the "silent reconciliation" that characterized the period of Giolitti (1901–14), the basis for an agreement between Italy and the Vatican had been established.

During WORLD WAR I unofficial relations intensified, and, despite firm Italian opposition to any presence by the Holy See at peace talks, a first step was effected by a meeting in Paris in June 1919 between the Vatican envoy Monsignor Cerretti and the president of the Italian council, V. E. Orlando. It was officially a disappointment, but, that same year, there was a definite entry of Catholics into public life—which they had avoided for almost fifty years—with the founding of the Partita Populare. After a brief and troubled existence, it would be used as a "hostage sacrificed to fascism" in exchange for a definitive ruling on the Roman question (Sturzo). On the eve of fascism, the church hierarchy, like the old ruling class, had to choose between respect for the law—which in bringing to power the classes that had emerged from universal suffrage would have changed the entire social basis of the state—and tolerance for the violence of the fascist paramilitary commandos—which, the Church thought, would end up reinforcing the groups in power. The Church could lean only toward a solution that would stabilize the existing social order and also reinforce the abandonment of the anti-Concordat prejudices of post-Unity liberalism, already begun in 1914. That is to say, the Church quickly understood that a union between the proletarian movement and the Catholic movement would not bring it everything that it was certain of getting by allying its own specifically conservative groups with the fascists. These would eliminate, in due time, the inflexible wing and the "liberal" wing of Mussolini's party which had implemented the reform of ecclesiastical laws in 1923–25—a reform drawn up by a government commission—clearly favorable to the Church. The terms had been officially "agreed upon" with the Vatican, during talks between the government and the clerico-fascists at the time of the 1924 political elections, and with the elimination, approved by the Vatican, of the Partita Populare. On the other hand, these actions could easily be seen in the context of politics of pre-fascist governments hostile to the populism of Sturzo. The Catholic question needed to be settled; it was the last ambiguity to eliminate on the way to an agreement with the papacy to formally resolve the Roman question, and thus consolidate and concentrate all the strengths of the middle class.

A turning point in ecclesiastical policy and legislation was Mussolini's speech of 3 January 1925. This was the effective beginning—on the topic of the relationship between the state and religious beliefs—of a political "restoration" that led to the agreements between Italy and the Holy See in February 1929. The foundations were those sketched out in 1914 by the nationalists, especially A. Rocco and L. Ferderzoni—and which Rocco himself had quickly proposed just before the march on Rome. These agreements were honored not so much in a truly "fascist" sense—as official fascist rhetoric would have it, as well as general anti-fascist polemic—but rather as a way to defend capitalist society and the existing social order. This was a time when the battle against the Risorgimento had long ago lost any hope for recovery of territory. The recovery of "temporal" power had taken on a different form and significance, much more concrete, complex, and modern than that expressed by Pius IX.

The negotiations that ended with the Lateran Treaty began in 1926. They lasted, due to the reciprocal hardening of positions between Mussolini and the Vatican, until 1929. On 11 February of that year, Mussolini and Cardinal Gasparri solemnly signed the protocols at the Lateran Palace. The CIVILTÀ CATTOLICA, which titled its commentary "The Hour of God," saw these accords as an instrument for the "religious restoration" of Italy. It praised the "renewal of an Italy once again Christian in its laws, its education, and its domestic and civil, private and public life." Pius XI seized this occasion to issue his famous statement about the restoration of God to Italy and Italy to God, as accomplished by the accords, and to applaud the new regularization of "religious conditions . . . altered, toppled, devastated" by liberal governments "obedient and submissive to the enemies of the Church."

The Lateran Pact of 1929 had three distinct parts: a "treaty," written to declare "the Roman question definitely and irrevocably ended and therefore eliminated"; a "financial agreement" aiming to fine-tune the financial relationships between Italy and the Holy See "following the events of 1870"; and a "CONCORDAT" intended to "govern the position of religion and the Church in Italy." The "treaty" created a state called VATICAN CITY and accorded it "full ownership as well as exclusive and absolute authority and independent jurisdiction" by the Holy See with all limitations, legal capacities, and endowments specified in the documents attached to the protocol. As a consequence, in this city-state, there would no longer be any Italian interference, and there would be no other authority except that of the Holy See. Also, all that was necessary was done to guarantee the public services and the security of the exterior perimeter of the "enclave" and the air space above it. For his part, the pope renounced any attempt to reestablish the Papal States and recognized the "Kingdom of Italy under the dynasty of Savoy, with Rome as capital of the Italian State." A capital whose "sacred character," incidentally, the concordat sanctioned and committed the Italian government to defend against any opposition that might occur. The concordat also placed the Catholic Church's people and institutions in a judicial situation that favored the religious interests of the citizens insofar as they belonged to the official state religion. It recognized the civil aspects of religious marriage and of the Church's judgments on marriage issues. It instituted the mandatory teaching of the Catholic religion at all levels of education and recognized the Church's jurisdiction over spiritual and disciplinary matters, with serious consequences such as loss of employment, civic disabilities, or ecclesiastical punishments for apostate priests, thus reestablishing a real "secular arm." The state was guaranteed review of the nomination of bishops—who also had to swear an oath of loyalty to the king—and of curates. Any political action on the part of Catholic Action was prohibited—a guarantee that clerics and members of religious orders would neither be part of that group nor active in any political party whatsoever. Mussolini's goal of blocking any further attempt at forming a "Christian" party was accomplished.

To these dispositions agreed to by the Church, Mussolini's regime added a series of unilateral dispositions (L. 24. 6, 1929; R.D. 28.2 1930; R.D. 30.10, 1930) authoritatively regulating the treatment of all other religious denominations (Protestants and Jews), who were not merely to be tolerated, but were "recognized." This established a great difference between the legal treatment of the Catholic religion and all others, as well as between citizens, who found themselves identified according to their denominational affiliations. The nomination of ministers of any religion had to be approved, and government permission had to be obtained before building any synagogues or chapels. There was also an entire series of clauses regulating religious organizations, and a special distinction was made on the subject of marriages. In 1938, these standards were expanded by "measures for defense of the Italian race" and by a series of other laws which, on top of persecuting the Jews, deprived them of a series of rights and freedoms, especially in matters of religion and culture.

Relations between the Church and the fascist regime remained essentially good during these two decades, framed by the concordat system, but neither side was able to completely achieve its goals: on the Church's side, restoring a "Catholic State" and, on the fascist side, that of "making the Church fascist." The only periods of crisis occurred between 1931 and 1938, after a series of polemics about Catholic Action. Encouraged by the privileges in the Lateran accords, the Holy See wanted to transform the group into a big "refrigerator" (De Felice) in which Catholic militants could hibernate. Protected in this way from the ideological pollution of the fascist regime, they could wait for a better time that would allow them to become the ruling faction and replace the fascist hierarchy, or, in the worst-case scenario, stand up to it since it had not been possible to "Catholicize" it. In additional accords between the government and the Holy See in 1931 concerning Catholic Action, the government was assured of the religious and diocesan nature of Catholic Action, as well as its close dependence upon the Church hierarchy.

But in early 1938, the fascists decided to renew hostilities against Catholic Action, bringing a new crisis with the Vatican. This crisis was much more serious than protests against racial legislation or the closer ties between Rome and Berlin; it was due to the reinstatement, beginning in 1934, of various Catholic lay organizations that seemed to present dangerous competition for the regime. In May 1935, a particularly astute informer of the secret police defined Church strategy in this way: "It is not a question of a political party," but of a "throng that, tomorrow, in a few hours, could become the most powerful political party in Italy, if the internal political situation would allow it . . . No party is able any longer to get new members or directors . . . Only Catholic Action . . . will be able to exercise political supremacy in a country in which the political opposition has become almost nonexistent. Whether this could actually happen or not is another question. The important thing is that all the Catholic leaders, from the Vatican down, believe it, and are working toward this goal."

Faced with the subsequent change toward totalitarianism imparted to the regime in the second half of the 1930s, referred to as "the *cultural revolution* of the lower classes," the Holy See was forced to act, by increasing its control over Catholic Action in order to "stave off the danger that closeness to and the consensus for the regime . . . would increase more and more and engage, particularly among the young, a process of effective fascization" (De Felice).

Convinced that the development of Catholic Action was only the preparation for structures destined to become the successor to fascism, as it would actually turn out, and now sure of not being able to use the Church as a "pillar" of the regime, Mussolini could only see the Church as an ideological enemy at the end of the 1930s, although he did not want matters to reach the point of an open confrontation such as the conflict then happening in Germany, which he judged to be "stupid and useless." He favored an insidious campaign of attrition that would intimidate the militants, make any action on their part difficult, and put them on the defensive. It did not take long for the Vatican to react. In the beginning of January 1938, the Jesuit Tacchi Venturi told Mussolini that Pius XI was threatening to excommunicate fascism and the regime. In August, an agreement put an end to all hostilities, though it did not end the conflict. In the middle of 1939, Mussolini obtained some normalization of the situation with the reform of the statutes of Catholic Action.

There were many who believed that the defeat and collapse of fascism, then of the monarchy, would also bring down the Lateran accords that had been one of the "glories" of the fascist regime, and one of the essential elements of the wide consensus enjoyed by Mussolini's Italy, both at home and abroad. Paradoxically, not only did the accords, remarkably, survive, but they found affirmation in the constitution of the postwar democratic republic that the fascist legal system itself had never given them. Following a heated debate and a vote that split the leftist workers' parties (communist party in favor, socialist party opposed), the constitutional assembly approved Article 7 of the Constitution recognizing that the state and the Church were "each in its own way" independent and sovereign. It also established that "their relations were regulated by the Lateran accords" and that modifications of the aforesaid accords, agreed to by both parties—that is, an agreement on modifications or on a new concordat—would not require a "Constitutional amendment or revision" (Article 138 of the constitution). The deep differences between the provisions of the Lateran accords and the principles of the constitution immediately posed the problem of a revision of the accords themselves in order to make them conform to these principles. But resistance by the Holy See, a relatively major factor, the very slowness and difficulty encountered in putting the Constitution into practice, as well as the ups and down of Italian politics, thwarted any parliamentary or political initiative in this direction.

However, by the 1960s the crisis of centrism, the opening to the left when the socialists became the majority party in the government, the pontificate of JOHN XXIII and the VATICAN II COUNCIL, as well as the reemergence of the constitutional plan contributed to put the problem of the state's relationship to religious denominations on the parliament's agenda.

A long and complex process began. In early 1984, under the first government directed by a socialist president, B. Craxi, an agreement was reached that dealt with modifications to the Lateran pact. Its form and content made it virtually a new concordat. From 1967 to 1983, no fewer than seven official plans for revision of the concordat (1969, 1976, 1977, 1979, 1980–81, 1982, and 1983) were proposed, as well as two plans for agreements with the Waldensian and Methodist churches, and another with the Union of Jewish Communities. Parliament discussed these on several occasions. Still, until 1984 it was not possible to resolve the fundamental problems concerning the relations between the state and the Church (ecclesiastical organizations and possessions, "nonreligious" activity of its various groups, religious instruction in the public schools, recognition of Church jurisdiction over marriages, etc.), which would have allowed a large political majority to approve a new concordat system. On the other hand, without any justification of a constitutional nature, the difficulties raised by revision of the concordat also blocked the conclusion of agreements with any other religious denominations. It was not until between 1984 and 1987 that the relationship between the state and the various religious denominations changed on a fundamental level and came to conform, though very belatedly, to constitutional principles. In the course of these three years the government arrived at the following:

—an agreement with the Catholic Church (18 February 1984), to modify the treaty of 1929, an additional protocol for this agreement (18 February 1984), and another approving the dispositions regarding ecclesiastical institutions and possessions (15 November 1984)—dispositions included in the law of 20 April 1985—all of which was completed by a ruling on its implementation (13 February 1987);

—an agreement between the Ministry of Public Education and the Italian episcopal conference on the teaching of religion in public schools (16 December 1985);

—a series of agreements applying article 8, line 3, of the constitution, with the Waldensian and Methodist churches (21 February 1987), the Italian Union of Seventh Day Adventist Churches (19 December 1986), the Pentecostal Assemblies of God (19 December 1986), and the Union of Jewish Italian Communities (18 February 1987). These agreements were approved by parliament, made into a special law, and concretely put into effect. A new group of accords with religious denominations began in 1992–93 with the preparation and signature of complementary accords with the Waldensian and Methodist churches (mostly concerning the system of financing), and new agreements with the baptist Church and the Evangelical Lutheran Church of Italy;

—concerning the Catholic church, in the following years, an agreement on the religious holidays recognized by the civil government on days other than Sundays, and another instituting a spiritual assistance service for state police were passed. Later some "sub-concordat" agreements between the parties (the Italian government, and the Holy See or the episcopal conference) would determine: (a) the academic degrees in ecclesiastical disciplines given by pontifical universities that could be recognized by the state; (b) modes of assistance for Catholics in the armed forces, hospitalized, in rest homes, or detained in penal institutions; (c) adequate dispositions for the application of Italian law to cultural possessions of religious significance that belong to ecclesiastical organizations or institutions and the appropriate procedures for the conservation of archives and libraries of these organizations and institutions.

To objectively judge the reforms of ecclesiastical legislation that occurred between 1984 and 1987, one cannot consider the agreements with the Catholic Church separately; they must be looked at in conjunction with agreements made with other denominations a fact that without question constitutes entirely new political and legal experience for the Italian system. Moreover, the changes in 1984 had at least formally accepted the transformations that had been occurring in society and in both civil and religious institutions for more than fifty years. Therefore, it is not possible to support the thesis that the 1984 accords were a modern reworking of the same principles found in the Lateran Treaty of 1929, in favor of the Catholic Church. In fact, the Treaty returned to the concordat model of the Restoration. In a number of its technical solutions it adopted the basic criteria of that model, in particular, the affirmation of the confessional nature of the state (confirmed explicitly by Article 1 of the Lateran Treaty that was overridden by the protocol added in 1984). This justified, on the one hand, the privileged condition assured for the Catholic Church by the treaty of 1929 and, on the other hand, the controls that the state had maintained over that same Church. Comparing the Lateran accords with the last concordats of the Restoration, the most famous specialist in civil ecclesiastical law, A. C. Jemolo, explicitly emphasized this continuity. He insisted, in fact, that the Austrian concordat of 1856 had been the definitive model for the treaty signed in 1929.

However, the 1984 accords with the Catholic Church are clearly different from this model. They rest, though with certain inconsistencies, upon three premises that can be summarized in the following way: (a) the absolute distinction between the civil and religious orders through the abrogation of the confessional principle of the "state religion" by Article 1 of the added protocol, and through the elimination of all state interference in Church life, and of all privileges for the clergy; (b) the commitment on the part of the Holy See to respect the sovereignty and independence of the state and to collaborate "in the promotion of man and for the good of the country" (art. 1)—concepts quite different for the Church and the state—(c) the valorization and application of constitutional principles concerning religious freedom, be it according to the rights of each to make free and concious choices in the matter of religion, or according to the guarantee of collective freedoms of churches and religious groups, traditionally called "ecclesiastical liberties"; (d) the cessation of the system (direct or indirect) of state financial support of the clergy and the Catholic church as well as the establishment of a system of self-financing for the religious.

The 1984 accords recognize the two different orders of the state and of the Church and the constitutional foundations on which their relations are based. They refer back to earlier accords, to different levels of competence, between the authorities of both parties, for the settling of particular questions. They also ensure that the accords might be adapted to changes in both societies. Since Vatican II, the CEI (Italian Episcopal Conference) has dealt with civil authorities, dealings traditionally reserved exclusively for the Holy See.

To conclude, other than the repeal of the principle of a state religion and the indirect modification of Article 23 concerning the canonical jurisdiction over clerics and members of religious orders, the Lateran treaty has remained unchanged and continues to apply to anything concerning the pontiff, the Holy See, and Vatican City.

Francesco Margiotta Broglio

Bibiligraphy

Berlingo, S., and Casuscelli, G. *Codice del diritto ecclesiastico*, III, 1993.

Botta, R. *Codice di diritto ecclesiastico*, 1990.

Cardia, C. *Stato e confessioni religiose. Il regime pattizio*, III, 1992.

Dalla Torre, G. *La riforma della legislazione ecclesiastica: Testi e documenti*, 1985.

Giustiniani, R. "Bibliografia degli Accordi Lateranensi," *Il diritto ecclesiastico*, 1934, 100 ff.

Lariccia, S. *Diritto ecclesiastico italiano, Bibliografia, 1972, 1974; Diritto ecclesiastico italiano e comparato, Bibliografia 1973–1979*, 1981; and *Diritto ecclesiastico*, III, 1986.

Long, G. *Le confessioni diverse dalla cattolica. Ordinamenti interni e rapporti con lo Stato*, 1991.

Margiotta Broglio, F. *Stato e confessioni religiose, 1/Fonti, 2/Teorie e ideologie*, 1976 and 1978.

Pollard, J. F. *The Vatican and Italian Fascism, 1929–32: A Study in Conflict*, Cambridge, 1985.

LATERAN PALACE. See **Residences, Papal; St. John Lateran**.

LATINITY. In the historical link between the popes and Latin, the following aspects can be distinguished: the linguistic character, natural or artificial, of the Latin used as the language of communication within the Church; the institutional evolution of Latin as the language of Church administration; the ethics of the choice of Latin as a pastoral language; and the cultural uses of Latinity outside the sphere of public prayer and other strictly religious activities. The brief comments that follow can only touch lightly upon each of these topics within a chronological framework.

After the first two centuries, during which most known pontifical texts were in the Greek language, the natural language of Christian communities belatedly became spoken Latin. Because the Roman west spoke Latin in its more cultured form, it was the language of oral and written communication used by the bishops of Rome. From the merging of traditional Latin and Christian Latin was born a new language, illustrated by two popes, each known for a distinct literary register. Under Emperor Theodosius, DAMASUS had brief and intense epitaphs engraved for elite Christians in impeccable verse. The following century, LEO I the Great carried a Christian eloquence destined for a much larger public to its highest point. The 5th century was thus one of synthesis between classical tradition and Christian renewal.

During the early Middle Ages (6th–9th centuries), which were apparently less suited to continuity, the popes emphasized the evangelical character of Christian Latinity through the voice of GREGORY I the Great. The "consul of God" (end of the 6th century) applied Augustine's lessons on preaching and used a modest but elegant Latin, good for instructing and persuading (if not for charming) the Roman crowds, whereas his correspondence reveals him to be a patrician who was master of all the registers of the language. To be Roman was to speak Latin, as Pope NICHOLAS I proudly proclaimed in the 9th century. This linguistic nationalism waned a bit by the year 1000, when Pope GREGORY V used Italian for the first time to speak to the baptized in the city. After that, the popes reigned over a city whose speakers used a language different from that of late Latin, which only remained alive in the circle of the *litterati*. The evolution of different Latinities, purely academic, bears the mark of this linguistic specialization. During the classic Middle Ages (10th to 13th centuries), the papal CHANCELLERY developed an even more hieratic style that accentuated and affirmed the reconquest of Roman ecclesiastical authority. This is how a new rhythmic form called the *cursus* prevailed, with strict rules for the placing of tonic accents at the end of pronounced vowels (*clausulae*), and highly artificial strictures concerning the order of words, according to whether a *cursus uelox* ("rapid cadence"), *tardus* ("slow"), or *planus* ("neutral") was desired. This formal structure does not stop very personal accents from appearing in the missives of GREGORY VII. The master of this form was John of Gaeta, first a papal chancellor, before taking the throne himself under the name GELASIUS II. In addition, these accentual constraints were reinforced and enriched by disyllabic rhymes at the ends of propositions (*cursus leoninus*): the papacy thus forged an ultra-educated Latinity, disdainful of European vernaculars, yet functional and harmonious according to the canons of medieval style.

This work, where the care for form is most obvious, took on a new liveliness and a different orientation during the beginnings of the Italian Renaissance. From the 14th and 15th centuries, the return to classical Latinity appeared in the Roman CURIA, especially on the part of the patron who had already founded the VATICAN LIBRARY, NICHOLAS V, as a method for achieving an image of intellectuality and an accompanying cultural legitimacy. Despite internal quarrels on Ciceronianism, the influence of the humanists from Petrarch through Erasmus by way of Valla, triumphed until the reign of LEO X, before a new sack of ROME (1527) led to a pious reaction in the papal court that ended the reborn cult of fine literature for half a century. The debate of the 3rd through the 5th centuries on the relationship between education and Ciceronian eloquence and Christian ministry was reviewed. Eleven centuries after Augustine, Pope PIUS IV charged his nephew Cardinal Charles Borromeo with the mission of creating a basic synthesis that legitimized the definitive return to *artes dicendi*, magnified by the mission of the *orator christianus*.

The second phase of the Counter-Reformation favored, amid the plastic arts later called the baroque, the supremacy of classic Latinity, for, using Sidonius Apollinaris' own terms, the new papal motto was "Wherever the language of Rome is spoken, the Empire is still standing." Catholic universalism, thus furnished with an eternal language, found a poet and patron in a former student of the Jesuits, URBAN VIII, the perfect figure of a "Ciceronian pope." The palace he built that bears his family name, *palazzo Barberini*, symbolized the second Roman renaissance and the final fusion of Christianity and the ancient languages.

To this internal evolution of the state of Latinity over the course of the centuries, correspond external changes due to the restrictions on collective transmission of the Christian message. The conversion and instructing of people of many languages required a series of concrete adaptations, however. Thus, Christian Latinity opened the way to literature in the vernacular languages of the Germanic countries (7th through 10th centuries) and then the Slavic ones (9th through 11th centuries). After a little hesitation, some popes authorized the translation of the Scriptures and prayers into these languages that existed along with Latinity. On the other hand, at the same time in the former Latin-speaking provinces the evolution of the language as spoken separated the native tongue of the illiterate masses from the traditional language of the Church (7th through 10th centuries), it was convenient to adapt to this linguistic revolution, which would ultimately result in the creation of the various Romance languages of Europe.

Michel Banniard

Bibliography

Banniard, M. *Viva voce, Communication écrite et communication orale du IVe au IXe siècle en Occident latin, L'Age Rhétorique*, 1992.

Brunholzl, F. *Histoire de la littérature latine du Moyen Âge, De Cassiodore à la fin de la renaissance carolingienne*, 2 vols., Paris, 1990–91.

Di Capua, F. *Il ritmo prosaico nelle lettere dei papi e nei documenti della cancelleria Romana dal IV al XIV secolo*, Rome, 1937–46.

Fumaroli, M. *L'Âge de l'éloquence. Rhéorique et 'res litteraria' de la Renaissance au seuil de l'époque classique*, Paris, 1980.

Janson, T. *Prose Rhythm in Medieval Latin from the IXth to the XIIIIth Century*, Stockholm, 1975.

Lentner, L. *Volkssprache und Sakralsprache, Geschichte einer Lebensfrage bis zum Ende des Konzil von Trient*, Vienna, 1963.

Manitius, M. *Geschichte der lateinischen Literatur des Mittelalters*, 3. vols., Munich, 1911–31.

Schanz, M., Hosius, G., and Krueger, G. *Geschichte der römischen Literatur bis zum Gesetzgebungswerk des Kaisers Justinian*, Munich, 1959.

[LAWRENCE]. *Antipope elected 22 November 498. Definitively deposed in March 507.*

A Roman priest known for his asceticism, Lawrence was elevated to the pontificate after the death of ANASTASIUS, at the same time as SYMMACHUS. The battle between these two rivals lasted almost seven years, during which Lawrence never gained the upper hand.

After the death of Anastasius, the clergy was divided into two factions. The largest, which met at the LATERAN Palace, included the majority of the clergy, who were hostile to the dead pope's policies toward the East, which seemed to some of them to sacrifice the purity of faith to the necessities of diplomacy. This group elected the deacon Symmachus as pope. That same day, 22 November 498, the other group, gathered around the *prior senatus* (the oldest of the senators) Festus, elected Lawrence. The partisans of each candidate brought this conflict before King Theodoric, who took Symmachus's side. Lawrence had to submit, and participate in the COUNCIL held on 1 March 499, under Symmachus's authority, to adopt a decree that excommunicated any priest, deacon, or cleric plotting to succeed any pope still living, and guaranteed a pardon to anyone who provided information about any such intrigue. Lawrence was probably the Coelius Laurentius, archpresbyter of the church of Sta Prassede, who was first among the priests to sign this decree. After that, Lawrence became, under unclear circumstances, bishop of Nuceria, in Campania. He was probably compelled to accept a see that took him far away from Rome, where his presence was unwelcome.

We know nothing of Lawrence's activities as a Campanian bishop, but his supporters remained active in Rome. In 501, Symmachus celebrated Easter according to Roman computations, which had not been used for a long time. His adversaries denounced him to the king, who called the pope and Lawrence to RAVENNA. Lawrence went to the court, and his supporters, foreseeing victory, took possession of all the churches in Rome. We do not know exactly what role Lawrence played in the organized plot against Symmachus, accused before the king of depleting the treasuries of the Church and leading a depraved life. When Symmachus, accidentally informed of the plot, returned to Rome, he was unable to enter the city and had to take refuge in ST. PETER'S. The absence of Symmachus did not help advance his case before Theodoric, who, influenced by Senators Fautus and Probinus, named a visitor, Peter of Altinum, to celebrate Easter in Rome in 502. But Lawrence's situation was not yet all that secure: the majority of bishops assembled at a council in Rome in the spring of 502 believed that Symmachus, elected according to the rules, could not be judged by either the king or a SYNOD and condemned Lawrence and Peter of Altinum for having illegally deposed a pope. In November 502, at the meeting of a council presided over by Symmachus, Lawrence was deposed from his episcopal see.

Nevertheless, Lawrence remained in Rome, where he had the support of part of the clergy and the Senate; this situation persisted for four years, preventing Symmachus from taking control over all churches. King Theodoric, irritated with Symmachus's actions, was more favorable to Lawrence and so did nothing to help reestablish order. The Eastern emperor, Anastasius, also seems to have preferred Lawrence in this conflict, where positions were for the most part determined by the question of the SCHISM of Acacius. But, little by little, Lawrence lost his supporters; it is known that in September 506, a deacon, Johannes,

defected. Another deacon, Dioscorus, faithful to Symmachus, succeeded in persuading the king that his interests lay in ending his support for Lawrence. In March 507, Theodoric sent the Senate a *praeceptum* commanding Festus to stop supporting Lawrence. At that time, Lawrence retired to his patron's lands, which he remained until his death on an unknown date.

Enmeshed in a conflict whose ramifications were mostly political, Lawrence never gained the upper hand. However, until his death, he maintained a reputation for asceticism and rigor that even his adversaries never tried to contest.

Claire Sotinel

Bibliography

LP, I, 260 and 44–46.
Anonymus Valesianus, 65, *MGHAA* 9, 324.
Lex data a Theodorico, Thiel, 695–6.
Pietri, C. "Aristocratie et société cléricale en Italie du Nord au VIe siècle," *MEFRA*, 93 (1981), 455–61.
Stein, E. *Histoire du Bas-Empire*, vol. 2, 1959, 134–9.
Symmachus, *Ep.* 1, 8, *Thiel*, 651.
Theodorus Lector, *Historia Ecclesiastica*, 2, 17, *PG* 86, 192; *Acta syn. rom.*, 1, 7, *MGHAA* 12, 410.
Victor Tonnenensis, *Chronica*, 497, 2, *MGHAA* 11, 192.

LEGATE.

Antiquity. The appearance of legates reflects the Roman pontiff's increasing secure jurisdiction over the entire Church and is a manifestation of this PRIMACY. Though relations between Rome and the local Churches were established early, there is no record of the creation of true legates before the beginning of the fourth century. The subscriptions from the COUNCIL of Arles (314) mention two priests and two DEACONS *ex Urbe Roma, missi ab Silvestro episcopo*. The information "sent by the bishop Silvester" is important. Nothing similar was noted for the other deacons or priests who signed the acts of the Council of Arles, where they were representing their bishop. The minutes simply say "*de civitate*." The four Roman *missi* were, therefore, a special case. They were "sent by Silvester," which means delegated. They probably did not have a special place at the council, nor did they play a particularly prominent role. But even had he gone himself, the bishop of Rome, who sent them, would not have had the place that later popes enjoyed when they attended a council. They were the "envoys" of Rome, thus ensuring the presence of the Roman Church at the councils whose sessions had been arranged by the emperor. In 325, at Nicaea, where Constantine had also called a council, there once again were two priests sent by the pope. They signed the acts immediately after Ossius and before all the other participants: *Victor et Vincentius presbyteri urbis Romae pro venerabili viro papa* *et episcopo nostro sancto Silvestro subscripsimus* (Mansi, *Ampl. Coll.* II, 692). At the council of Serdica (343–4), again called by the imperial power, Pope JULIUS I had himself represented by two priests, Vincent and Ianuarius, who signed the acts as *legati sanctae ecclesiae romanae* (Turner, *Ecclesiae occidentalis Monumenta iuris*, t.I, fasc. 2, pars 3, 1930, p. 546).

The expression (*missus*) . . . *e latere* appears in canon 5. By its imagery, this terminology emphasizes the tight, almost physical connection that attaches the *missi* to the pope. The qualifier *e latere suo* is not reserved just for papal legates. BONIFACE I (419–22) speaks about an envoy from Emperor Theodosius I who came *e latere suo* to Rome (JK 365, c.6) (cf. Caspar, *Gesch.* I, 1930, 380). The expression *legatus a latere*, which was to become a popular one, is not seen before 860 (NICHOLAS I; ph. Jaffé, *Reg. pont. Rom* 2682–83). It was reserved for legates with the rank of bishop. From the first decades of the fourth century, the necessity of calling upon legates for tasks that the pope could not take on himself would only become more essential later. Increasingly frequent recourse to the Holy See, as well as the desire of popes from the 4th and 5th centuries, from GELASIUS to LEO The Great, to fully wield their authority and extend their jurisdiction farther and farther multiplied the occasions to designate legates. The imperial Roman tradition provided many examples and a vocabulary based on references to legates from Caesar or from the provincial government. Pomponius (*ad Libro Xo ad Quintum Mucium* = D.1, 16, 13) had already defined their status: *Legati proconsulis nihil proprium habent, nisi a proconsule eis mandata fuero iurisdictio.*

The word "legate," taken from Roman legal language, appears frequently in the vocabulary of the councils of AFRICA at the end of the 4th and the beginning of the 5th centuries. The acts of the council at CARTHAGE on 25 May 419 mention *legati ecclesiae Romanae* (CCL. 149, 89). The presence of "legates" from bishops is often noted, or requested, in the African conciliar assemblies of this period.

The *commonitorium* of ZOSIMUS read at the Council of Carthage on 25 May 419, recalling the disposition of the council at Sardica (which he attributed to the council at Nicaea—a widespread mistake, and the reason the declaration of the letter to Pope CELESTINE from the council at Carthage of 424–5 [ibid. 171] said that no such thing had been found in the canons of Nicaea) made reference to a request addressed to "the bishop of the Romans" *ut a latere suo presbyteros mittat* (CCL. 149, 91). Moreover, the letter from this council to Pope Boniface (ibid. 159) cites the same passage. Among these legates, the "apocrisaries" represented the pope to the emperor of Constantinople. Their mission and their duties were defined for the first time in 452, in a letter from Pope Leo the Great (JK 487–9). Before the appearance of this letter, there was only sporadic mention of ambassadors (cf. for bibliography E. Pitz, *Pastreskripte im frühen Mittelalter*, 1990, 217, n. 27).

The growing influence of the papacy under the pontificate of GREGORY I (590–604) explains the importance that legates took on during that period (based on accounts of pontifical legations in the letters of Gregory the Great, cf. Chevailler-Génin, 369–76). A letter from the pope to the bishops of Sicily in 591 speaks of their necessity and their functions (*Ep.*I, 1; represented in numerous CANONICAL COLLECTIONS. This text is present in Gratian's DECRETUM, D. 94, c. 1). "It is very necessary" wrote the pope, "that, as our predecessors have already determined, all matters be entrusted to one and the same person and that, wherever we cannot be present, our authority should be represented by the one to whom we gave instructions about a certain matter." There follows the delegation of power for all of Sicily to a subdeacon. This province was entrusted to him so that he would act *vices nostras*, and to him the pope "entrusts the entire patrimony of the Church" in that region. The formulas of delegation were not always the same: *Quicquid disposuerit velut a me dispositum* (I, 49); *quae illi mandavimus, . . . ex nostra auctoritate exequatur et faciat* (XII, 11), etc. But the meaning is clear and clearly expressed in legal terms: the legate acts in the name of the pope, in his place, in the realm for which he has been given authority, whether on questions concerning internal Church life or relations in secular instances (apocrysaries, cf. *supra*; or relations with Queen Brunhilde, Reg. XIII, 7). To speak only about the first, Gregory's correspondence shows the variety of subjects handled: management of church possessions, reorganization of monasteries, control of the lives of clerics, resolution of conflicts, surveillance of episcopal elections, protection of Christians, and assistance for the most deprived. Any failure in their mission would expose them to the reprimands of the pontiff.

These "representatives on a mission" were sometimes given a precise and limited task; but more often they had general jurisdiction over any matter that might come up wherever they were, by virtue of a general delegation from the all-powerful Roman pontiff. Besides these occasional envoys, there were also "legates" sent long-term and quasi-permanently in some regions. This was true for the subdeacons Peter in Sicily (Reg. I to III, 40 *passim*), who was followed by deacon Cyprian (III, 58, to VIII, *passim*), the subdeacons Anthemius in Campania (during the entire pontificate of Gregory), Antoninus in Dalmatia (*Ep.* II, 20; III 9 and 22), John at Ravenna (Reg. III, 30; XI, 26; XII, 24; XIII, 17), and Sabinus at Rhegium (Reg. III to XIII *passim*). Those representatives sent permanently were often called *subdiaconus (Siciliae, Ravennae, regionarius)* or *rector patrimonii in Dalmatia (Sicilia*, etc.) Such *rectores* were found not only in suburbicarian Italy—the area around Rome—where they seemed to have had more authority than the *defensores ecclesiae* who already represented the pope there, but even in other regions (for example, in Dalmatia).

Jean Gaudemet

Bibliography

Chevailler, L., and Génin, J. C. "Recherches sur les apocrisaires: Contribution à l'histoire de la représentation pontificale (Ve-VIIIe siècle)," *Studi in onore di G. Grosso*, III, 1970, 361–461.

Pietri, C. *Roma Christiana*, 1976, (*BEFAR*, 224).

Pitz, E. "Papstreskripte im frühen Mittelalter, Diplomatische une rechtsgechichtliche Studien zum Briefcorpus Gregors des Großen," *Beiträge zur Geschichte und Quellenkunde des Mittelalters*, 14, Sigmaringen, 1990.

Middle Ages. The generic term "legate," like that of NUNCIO, first meant an envoy. Although the meaning of the term remained fluid and included various subcategories, CANON LAW in the 13th and 14th centuries refined the term to mean, generally speaking, a cleric representing the pope—sent, with or without power of jurisdiction, either to assure relations with a Church or a prince, or to act in place of the pope, but always with a commission and for a given area, often called a "province." In ST. PETER'S PATRIMONY, primary delegates of the pope often received the title of legate and gave their names to their districts, the "legations" of modern times.

Since ancient times, the pope's need for representation to the EASTERN CHURCHES and the emperor of Constantinople, and soon also to the various transalpine Churches, multiplied the appointments of papal envoys. In 343, the Council of Sardica brought up the case of deposed bishops, judged on appeal in the presence of special envoys from the bishop of Rome in his role as the successor of St. Peter (*e latere suo [missi] . . . habentes ejus auctoritatem:* the expression *e latere*, which indicates that the envoys were detached from the entourage, or the "flank" of the pope, would become popular). While the apostolic VICARS, seen as early as the 4th century pose yet another problematical example, stable papal representation to the imperial court of BYZANTIUM appears under the pontificate of PELAGIUS (556–61); the concept and the word "apocrisiarius" were borrowed from the patriarchs of the Eastern Church. Sometimes coupled with assistants or "*responsales*" whose permanence was less assured, they were also dispatched to the EXARCH of Ravenna. Gregory I had been an apocrisiarius to Byzantium. Once he became pope, he included multiple bits of information about this well-established practice in his correspondence; however, it began to decrease as ties between Byzantium and Rome became weaker.

The embassies of close collaborators and highly placed Lateran dignitaries, suburcarian bishops, priests with

Roman titles, *judices* from the pontifical palace, were, from the middle of the 8th century on, but not permanently, sent to the king of the FRANKS, soon to be the emperor of the West. These papal envoys, *nuntii* or *legati* (still sometimes called "apocrisiarii" until the reign of GREGORY VII), intervened with kings and emperors. Throughout the 10th century, pontifical legates could still play an important political role, even assisting and shaping Church government in France and Germania. The legates of Pope FORMOSUS attended the COUNCIL of Vienne in 892, legates from Agapitus presided over the synod of Ingelheim in 948, and legates from JOHN XII went to see Otto I in 960 and accompanied him to Rome where he was crowned in 962. But with the decline of the papacy, caught in local struggles and at best put under the tutelage of emperors, the use of legates declined. While a legate of JOHN XVIII resolved a conflict between the bishop of Orleans and the abbey of Fleury and consecrated the church of Beaulieu-les-Loches around the year 1008, Normandy, a rather unpleasant place during those times, did not—to the indignation of the local bishopric—welcome a single pontifical legate between 911 and 1055, the date on which a legate attended the deposition of an archbishop in Rouen, but essentially only as an observer.

Beginning with its foreshadowing under LEO IX, GREGORIAN REFORM gave not only a fresh start but new amplification to legations, an essential tool in the affirmation of papal power over highly reluctant Churches. The great names of the reform are immediately found here: Hildebrand (the future Gregory VII) under Leo IX (Council of Chalon in 1056), Cardinal Stephen under NICHOLAS II, Peter Damian under ALEXANDER II. From this time, the legate, accompanied by papal letters to the clergy he is going to visit—or rather intimidate—is presented as a delegate with full powers (*vicem nostram pleno jure commisimus*) whose jurisdiction, whatever his rank, overrides that of bishops. He can call SYNODS, depose bishops, and remodel the diocesan geography. As a legate beginning in 1075, Hugues (bishop of Die beginning in 1073, archbishop of Lyon in 1082–83) led a campaign to reform the episcopate in the kingdom of France, assisted, most often in Aquitaine, by the bishop of Oléron, Amat, a legate since 1074, calling councils that sometimes became unruly. Gregory VII nevertheless reversed the deposition pronounced by Hugues against the bishops of Reims, Sens, Bourges, and Tours. There were also legates to royal courts: two legates from Nicholas II, bishops from the kingdom of Arles, attended the coronation of Philip I, a type of ceremony they had not attended in France in 1017, 1027, and 1031.

The post-Gregorian papacy further strengthened the institution, and SCHISMS caused by antipopes were the occasion for multiple legations to various sovereigns and provincial Churches. For the twenty-second anniversary of ALEXANDER III's papacy, there were about sixty legations, meaning about 150 legates *a latere*, sent in twos and threes. Their duties expanded, too. Peter, cardinal-priest of Saint-Chrisogone, sent to France in 1174, reorganized the Paris schools, initiated the battle against the CATHARS, (which the legate Henry, cardinal-bishop of Albano, continued), and arranged a peace between the kings of France and England in 1177 (a necessary prelude to the CRUSADE). At the same time he settled various conflicts between bishops, the latter much better documented, in church charters, than his other activities. Legations thus became more and more politico-diplomatic at the same time that the Staufen dynasty began to send imperial legates to northern Italy when the emperor was forced to remain in Germany.

The great pontifical legations became an occasion for training through contact with the world, as well as an opportunity to prove oneself. Thus they began to represent an essential step in the career of a curialist, if sometimes an occasion for disgrace. Archbishops receiving the post of legate could see a confirmation of their role as intermediaries between the pope and a provincial Church. The practice fluctuated during the second half of the 12th century, but soon several dioceses had a legation *ex offiçio*, limited to their ordinary jurisdiction; this privilege, originating from the institution of apostolic vicars, was conferred on, among others, the archbishops of Canterbury, Salzburg, Cologne, Arles, Toledo, and Prague.

In the following century, canon law would call them *legati nati* or *creati*, as opposed to legate envoys—a pleonasm that designated clerics drawn from the pope's staff. Among the latter, there were the *legati a latere*, with considerable powers, also called *legati laterales, collaterales, derivati, emanentes, specialissimi*—all terms that indicate a privileged relationship with the pope. They were essentially—and soon exclusively—recruited from among the cardinals, with some special exceptions (in which case the apostolic CHANCERY speaks of *legatus cum potestate legati a latere*). There were also the *legati missi*, or just plain *legati*, with a briefer mission, and for whom the more specialized term *nuntius* (messenger, without jurisdiction) would very slowly develop over time. An exceptional form of legation was arranged for the NORMAN kingdom of Sicily, where the king himself based his leadership of the Church on permanent commissions set up by URBAN II in 1098 and PASCHAL II in 1117.

The phenomenon of the great legations reached its apogee in the first decades of the 13th century. The cardinal-bishop of Ostia, Ugolino, third cousin of INNOCENT III, and the future Pope GREGORY IX, was a legate in southern Italy in 1199, and in Germany in 1207 and 1209 before receiving two important legations in northern Italy (1216–19 and 1221). He fought against HERESY while coordinating the preparations for a crusade and trying to regulate the life of the communes (he was legate of the king of the Romans, Frederick II, at the same time). When relations with the emperor became adversarial, Gregorio da Montelongo (nephew of Innocent III and notary of the chancery, but only a subdeacon) rekindled the GUELPH resistance and directed the second Lombard League from 1238 to 1251 (after his legation, the pope gave him the post of patriarch of Aquileia). The legates were thus leaders of war, leaders of crusades (the bishop of Le Puy fulfilled this duty for Urban II in 1095), the heart of the antiheresy movement (Pierre de Castelnau and then Arnaud Amalric, assisted by a Roman in the Cathar territories). They could even become, as conceived by Innocent III, the support for a mistreated Christian monarch: the legate Guala, cardinal-priest of the title of Saints-Silvester and Martin, saved the throne of John Lackland in 1216–17, and of his young son Henry, threatened by the English barons and the son of the king of France. In 1225, the Roman cardinal-deacon of Sant'Angelo supported the regent of France, Blanche of Castille, while he also contributed to the "pacification" of the southern part of the kingdom and clashed with the University of Paris. The decades of affirmation of the pope's *plenitudo potestatis* were also the era of the superlegates.

Canon law naturally dealt with the nature of the powers of legates, which posed the crucial problem of the delegation of authority and representation of the person of the pope including representation in a physical sense. Beginning with Gregory VII, the legitimacy of the legates' actions was questioned; as discussed above, the pope had to moderate certain pronouncements by the zealous Hugues de Die. In the 12th century, some particularly crucial decisions had to be confirmed by the pope, less, it is true, to reduce the powers of the legates than to assure their more efficient implementation. Between 1230 and 1300, the DECRETALS of Alexander III and Innocent III in particular formed the initial basis for the theorization of the canonists, ending in a detailed and homogeneous body of doctrine, formulated in the *Decretals* of Gregory IX (Book I, title 30), the *Liber Sextus* (Book I, title 15), and in the works of decretalists like William Durand, who wrote a special treatise on the question, the *Speculum legati*, integrated into his *Speculum juris*. The legates *a latere*, papal representatives in the strongest sense of the term, were "popes" in a province, considered vastly superior to the "born" legates, who were still subject to appeal, and the legates *missi*, who were named for a specific mission. They saw themselves universally invested with a sort of omnipotence, covering any area and circumscribed only by space and time, but revocable at any time by the sovereign pontiff. "Popes" in the absence of the pope, they wore his insignia and enjoyed many of his privileges.

Beginning in the 11th century there were some references, difficult to interpret, showing legates with papal insignia and privileges: red clothing, a canopy or a horse with white reins, the cross carried before them (in the territory of their legations and, by special permission, everywhere outside the official pontifical residence), conferring blessings in solemn processions. Canonists and liturgists also fastened onto this issue. For certain decretalists, these privileges applied only to legates *a latere* on a mission overseas. The Roman *ordo* number 14 (beginning of the 14th century) showed the legate *a latere*, named in consistory, putting on his new clothing (purple with a BIRETTA) when he had left Rome, and taking it off before he reentered the city. But these forms of identification were shared by all cardinals at the end of the Middle Ages, even those outside legations, and they could, by special permission, be worn even by noncardinal legates. The pope and the legates *a latere* also shared the signature by *fiat* (followed by the initial of the surname) on PETITIONS submitted to them, whereas legates of lower rank (for example, the vice-chancellor of the Curia) signed them with the word *concessum*. From the 13th century on, we can see a real tradition of diplomacy developing from the actions of legates, who, when they did not call on writers or local notaries, made increasing use of the services of a small traveling chancery made up of personnel drawn from the pontifical chancery. The decrees made in this fashion are quite naturally in the same mold as pontifical decrees. Of greatest interest was the practice by which the decrees of a legation were registered: Formulated during the 13th century along the lines of a cartulary account-book, keeping track of the most important documents sent and received (like the "register" of Ugolino of Ostia), the register became a listing of letters sent, probably selectively, like that of the pontifical chancery.

Legates once again increased the scope their activities with the papacy in AVIGNON and the GREAT SCHISM. In the first case, the legation was the appropriate instrument to use in order to give the most extensive powers to the vicars charged with preserving or reestablishing pontifical authority in a turbulent Italy. From 1319 to 1334, the cardinal legate Bertrand du Poujet tried to bring the Italians back to order and obedience. He planned to make Bologna, taken in 1327, a military and administrative center to smooth the way for the pope to return to the peninsula, though he failed in the end. Archbishop of Toledo and primate of Spain from 1338, made cardinal-priest of the title of Saint-Clement in 1350, Gil Albornoz was even more energetic and a bit luckier, even if his long legation (1353–57 and 1358–67) was interrupted by a disgrace that replaced him briefly with the legate Androin de la Roche, abbot of Cluny, who assisted him afterward (1357–58 and 1363–68) before falling into disgrace himself (the pope had to threaten him with excommunication in order to make him return to Avignon). The pontifical decree nominating Albornoz in 1353 fully delegated to him the pope's powers, both spiritual and temporal (*vices nostras ac plene legationis officium committendo*) in a very well-defined territory: northern Italy (civil provinces and dioceses were specified), Tuscany, and the PATRIMONY (the kingdoms of Sicily, Corsica, and Sardinia were explicitly excluded). In it the usual statements about decrees and commissions may be found, but the emphasis is strongly placed on objectives of the legation that are both ecclesiogical and moral, with political implications: returning the region to peace and harmony (the legate would intervene *tanquam pacis angelus*, an image still being used in 1431 for the legate Nicolas Albergati), restoring by any means necessary the "freedom" of the Church, and watching over the salvation of souls as well as defending the provincial Churches.

As in the 12th century, the Great Schism was the occasion for an increase in the number of legations of a mostly diplomatic nature, as a continuation from the 1430s, when the main goals were to bring the pope closer to the national Churches, to prepare concordats, and find new sources of financial assistance. Pietro da Monte, former collector in England and bishop of Brescia, was thus sent as a legate to the king of France in 1442. The emblematic legate of this period was the German Nicholas of Cusa, mystic theologian and humanist, named legate to Germany and Bohemia in 1450, who tried to correct doctrinal and moral deviations, fought against superstitions, and preached INDULGENCES.

The legate was above all an expert in the art of diplomacy, which had become increasingly important and complex at the end of the Middle Ages. The legation was still a juridical tool in the service of a pragmatic goal, that of diplomacy, and sometimes of a moral goal, Church reform and the salvation of souls. The titles emphasize this which, used in a homogenous fashion (1467 for Castille; 1475 for France with the dispatching of Giulio Della Rovere, bishop of Modena; 1476 for the States of the duke of Burgundy) speak for the most important of the former *legati missi*, of *nuntii et oratores cum potestate legati de latere*. The time of the nuncios had arrived.

Olivier Guyotjeannin

Bibliography

Blet, P. *Histoire de la représentation diplomatique du Saint-Siège des origines à l'aube du XIXe siècle*, Vatican City, 1982 (*Collectanea Archivi vaticani*, 9).

Diplomatorio del cardinal Gil de Albornoz, 2 vols., Barcelona, 1976–81.

Figueira, R. C. "Legatus apostolice Sedis: The Pope's *alter ego* according to Thirteenth-Century Canon Law," *Studi Medievali*, III, 27 (1986), 527–74.

Glénisson, J., and Mollat, G. *Correspondance des légats et vicaires généraux, I, Gil Albornoz et Androin de La Roche (1353–1367)*, Paris, 1964 (*BEFAR*, 203).

Janssen, W. *Die päpstlichen Legaten in Frankreich von Schisma Anaklets II. bis zum Tode Coelestins III. (1130–1198)*, Cologne–Graz, 1961.

Kier, C. I. "Legatus and nuntius as used to denote Papal Envoys, 1245–1378," *Medieval studies*, 40 (1978), 473–7.

Lesage, G. L. "La titulature des envoyés pontificaux sous Pie II (1458–1464)," *MAH*, 58 (1941–6), 206–47.

Levi, G. *Registri dei cardinali Ugolino d'Ostia e Ottaviano degli Ubaldini*, Rome, 1890 (*Fonti per la storia d'Italia*).

Mörsdorf, K. "Gesandtschaftwesen," *LTK*, 4 (1960), 766–73.

Ollendiek, H. *Die päpstlichen Legaten im deutschen Reichsgebiet vom 1261 zum Ende des Interregnums*, Fribourg, 1976.

Pacaut, M. "Les légats d'Alexandre III (1159–1181)," *RHE*, 50 (1955), 821–38.

Riesenberger, D. *Prosopographie der päpstlichen Legaten von Stephan II. bis Silvester II.*, Fribourg-en-Brisgau, 1967.

Ruess, K. *Die rechtliche Stellung der päpstlichen Legaten bis Bonifaz VIII.*, Paderborn, 1912.

Sabeköw, G. *Die päpstlichen Legationen nach Spanien und Portugal bis zum Ausgang des 12. Jh.*, 1931.

Schieffer, T. *Die päpstlichen Legaten in Frankreich vom Vertrage von Meersen (870) bis zum Schisma von 1130*, Berlin, 1935.

Tillmann, H. *Die päpstlichen Legaten in England bis zur Beendigung der Legation Gualas (1218)*, Bonn, 1926.

Wasner, F. "Fifteenth-Century Texts on the Ceremonial of the Papal legatus a latere," *Traditio*, 14 (1958), 195–358.

Modern and Contemporary Eras. The transformation of temporary legations into permanent nunciatures did not make the post of legate disappear from pontifical diplomatic representation. In 1530, at the time when Pio di Carpi in France, Pimpinella in the empire, and Aleandro in Venice were consolidating modern nunciature, PAUL III sent Cardinal Lorenzo Campeggi to the empire, with the full powers of legates in medieval Christendom. His authority extended to all territories that were part of the empire, and to "Dacia, Norway, Bohemia, Livonia, Russia, Prussia, Austria, Burgundy, Flanders, Brabant, Holland, Zeeland, Frisia, Silesia, Moravia, and other adjoining areas." A special document gave him the power to absolve repentant heretics of all censures. He could also pronounce sentences of capital punishment against hardened malefactors. At the time when the nuncio Pio di Carpi arrived, a new form of legation was created in France: the chancellor of the kingdom, CARDINAL Antoine Duprat, had received a BULL as legate *a latere* allowing him to award pardons and indults that normally came from Rome. This time it was not permanent, for

upon his death the court at Rome refused to name a successor, in order not to deprive the Roman CURIA of the revenues gained from awarding such favors. But the popes still continued to use legates just as much to reinforce the diplomatic activity of the nuncios in the more important matters and during particularly critical times.

Following in the footsteps of LEO I the Great, Paul III and his successors had legates represent them in the three sessions of the Council of TRENT. The meetings of the diets of the empire were usually attended by papal legations. Similarly, the apostasy of the archbishop-elector of Cologne provoked GREGORY XIII to name Cardinal Madruzzo as legate; a short time later, Cardinal Gaetani received the same powers as legate when, by virtue of the Salic Law, France's crown went to Henry, the king of Navarre, a relapsed heretic. Despite the fiery warnings that he sent forth against the man from Béarn and all his followers, the cardinal legate Gaetani did not stop the latter from taking the throne of St. Louis, but not until he had rejoined the Church. And when, after the chaos of war, Rome had to reestablish relations with France in order to undertake a serious reform of ecclesiastical discipline in the kingdom, once again a legate, the cardinal of Florence was sent to Henry IV and his subjects. These were obviously entirely religious matters and involved exceptional circumstances. But in the following century, while the institutions of nunciatures functioned normally, in 1625, URBAN VIII did not hesitate to confer upon his nephew, Francesco Barberini, the dignity and powers of a legate *a latere* in an attempt to avoid war while handling the thorny question of the Valteline. And despite the futility of this mission, the cardinal vicar of Rome, Ginetti, was again sent as a legate *a latere* to Cologne, to wait on the ambassadors of the warring powers and mediate on behalf of the Holy See in the peace talks. But the presence of the pontifical legate in Cologne did not influence the parties in conflict to send their ambassadors to Cologne. Ginetti would return to Rome at the end of a totally fruitless stay in the Rhine metropolis. Thus, in 1639, when Urban VIII was trying once again to resume negotiations to end the Thirty Years War, he gave up on solemn and costly legations and sent special nuncios to add their efforts to those of the regular nuncios. This was perhaps the final step in the consolidation of permanent nunciatures. After this there was no more question of legations except for unusual events. It seems that, at this time, Richelieu had entertained the idea of a legation that would have sent him to the baptism of the dauphin, the future Louis XIV, as the delegate of Pope Urban VIII, who was supposed to be the godfather. Afterward the cardinal would have exercised the powers of a legate *a latere* over the Church in France. But when the cardinal of Vendôme represented CLEMENT IX at the baptism of the dauphin, he did not dream of such a future. The legation of Cardinal Chigi was rather unusual as well, bringing Louis XIV all the apologies of ALEXANDER VII after an attack against the king's embassy by the Corsican Guard. It was not until the revolutionary overthrow of the government and the need to reestablish the church that France was visited once again by a legate with even greater powers, perhaps, than any legate of Cristendom had ever possessed. Cardinal Caprara, not only was given power to validate marriages contracted by priests and members of religious orders during the revolutionary turmoil, as Cardinal Pole had done for Mary Tudor in England, but also to give the canonical appointment to bishops named by the first consul. It was Caprara who, in agreement with the government, set up four religious holidays that today are still official holidays in all French territories: Christmas, the Ascension, the Assumption, and All Saints' Day.

Since that time, legations are most often representations of pontifical participation in specific matters rather than the exercise of universal jurisdiction by the Roman pontiff. It is sufficient to remember the solemn legations that PIUS XI entrusted to his secretary of state, Eugenio Pacelli, received with high honors not only in Catholic states but also by the very secular French Republic. This anticipated the time when modern methods would permit the pope to go in person to the different places on the globe.

Pierre Blet

Bibliography

Barbiche, B., and de Dainville-Barbiche, S. "Les légats *a latere* en France et leurs facultés aux XVIe et XVIIe siècles," *AHP*, 23 (1985), 93–165.

Repgen, K. "Die Hauptinstruktion Ginettis für den Kölner Kongress (1636)," *QFIAB*, 34 (1954), 250–87.

Tizon-Germe, A. C. "Jurisdiction spirituelle et action pastorale des légats et nonces en France pendant la Ligue (1589–1594)," *AHP*, 30 (1992), 159–230; and "La représentation pontificale en France au début du règne d'Henri IV," *Bibliothèque de l'École des Chartes*, 151 (1993), 37–85.

LEGATIONS. See **Papal States.**

LEO I. (*b. ?, d. 10 November 461*). *Consecrated 19 September 440. Initially buried in the portico of St. Peter's in Rome, his remains were transferred to the interior of the basilica under Pope Sergius I (688).*

Originally from Etruria, Leo was, according to the *Liber pontificalis*, the son of Quintianus, about whom we know nothing else. After becoming pope, Leo spoke of Rome as his birthplace (JK 425), but it is impossible to ascertain if Rome was really his native city or if he considered it as such because he was its bishop. There is a record of him in the Roman clergy in the summer of 418: he would most definitely have been the acolyte Leo who delivered a letter to Bishop Aurelius of Carthage from the Roman priest Sixtus (the future SIXTUS III), defending himself against any suspicion of sympathy for the Pelagian theses.

Having become a DEACON of the Roman Church, Leo was entangled in the Nestorian controversy: he asked the monk Cassian from Marseilles—with whom he was on friendly terms—to refute the theses of Nestorius, the bishop of Constantinople, put on trial in Rome for his Christology. He received the dedication of the *De incarnatione domini contra Nestorium*, written by Cassian, who accused Nestorius of teaching about two Sons, probably before August 430, the date of the condemnation of the bishop of Constantinople by Pope Celestine, but without being able to determine what part Leo played in the debate.

Leo enjoyed a certain amount of influence with Pope Sixtus III, since in 439, according to Prosper of Aquitaine, he succeeded in persuading Sixtus to refuse the Pelagian bishop, Julian of Eclanum, permission to resume participation in Roman communion. In 440, he was on a mission to Gaul—surely with the permission of the court at Ravenna—to put an end to the conflict between the military leaders Aetius and the prefect of the pretorium Albinus. After the death of Pope Sixtus III, 19 August 440, Leo was elected, while absent from Rome, to take his place as pope. Brought back to Rome by a public delegation, he was consecrated bishop of the city on 29 September 440, after a forty-day vacancy of the pontifical see.

During the twenty-one years of his pontificate, Leo I represented permanence and authority at one of the most difficult moments for the Western Empire, which was coming apart under the pressure of the Barbarian invasions. Inheriting the ideas of his predecessors, he knew how to develop them into a system that glorified Christian Rome and defined the role of the pope, successor to St. Peter. This ideology may be seen in the many sermons and letters written by the pope, who produced more than 140 letters (the most substantial number until Pope Gregory the Great). For Leo, pagan Rome, whose providential role he acknowledged, had become, thanks to the see of St. Peter, the leader of the universe (Sermon 82). PRIMACY had returned to the Church, which had the honor of being the site of St. Peter's martyrdom and his tomb: The power that Christ had given to Peter—personally, unlike the other apostles—and the revelation that he alone experienced ("You are the Christ, the living Son of God") justified his position as head of the apostolic body that leads all the Churches: "Who would be so ignorant as to underestimate the glory of St. Peter and believe that there would be parts of the Church that would escape the solicitude of his government?" Peter's primacy was handed down to his successors, who were also in charge of all Churches *ex divina institutione* and who governed *plenius et potentius*.

On these ideological foundations Leo tried to consolidate and extend papal authority: In the West, he had the benefit of Emperor Valentinian I's support (d. 455) and that of his mother Galla Placidia, who certainly saw in the Roman Church a useful fortress against the Arian Germans threatening the Empire: in the East, where he had to deal with the force of imperial authority, with the great ecclesiastical metropolises, and with the monastic elements.

The Pope in the "Pars Occidentis." We know little about the activities of the pope in dealing with the Roman community. Ninety-seven sermons, evidence of his preaching, have been preserved, most concerning the liturgical cycle of Christmas and Easter. The pope also preached in special circumstances: for the feast days of Peter and Paul (June 29) whose martyrdoms were exalted, and of Lawrence, for the anniversary of his *natalis* (September 29). Adapted for use in the catechism, his sermons contain few speculative explanations, being devoted to the defense of orthodoxy—a battle against Manichaean HERESY and that of Eutyches—and especially to the Christological question, but also discussing the forms of charity and morality. We also know several measures taken by the pope concerning discipline and the liturgy, including the conditions for giving the veil to consecrated virgins and a modification of the canon of the mass. According to the *Liber pontificalis*, Leo also inaugurated the *custodes*, taken from within the Roman clergy and put in charge of watching over the confessions of St. Peter and St. Paul. He also began restoration work on the basilicas of ST. PETER's and ST. PAUL's, where the entire roof of the building had caved in: The *Liber pontificalis* credits him with additional work on the Lateran, as well as the foundation of a basilica dedicated to Pope Cornelius and a monastery near St. Peter's, perhaps dedicated to Sts. John and Paul.

The pope also played a role as protector of the city. In 452, when Attila began to march on Rome and Emperor Valentinian was unable to offer more than token resistance, he was sent as ambassador, along with two Roman senators, to the Goth chieftain, who abandoned his attack on the city; Prosper gives Leo the credit for this change of heart—undoubtedly due to an offensive by imperial troops in the East. In 455, after the assassination of both Valentinian and his successor, the pope was the only leader present in the city, which was threatened by the Vandals of Genseric. He interceded once again, this time with the Vandal king, and got him to spare the life of the Romans, but without being able to save it from fourteen days of pillaging.

In the struggle against the Manichaean heresy, the pope's control over religious life and the full weight of his authority in Rome, and all of Italy, became evident. He launched an inquisition against the Manichaeans; before January 444, he presided over an assembly of bishops, clerics, and notable Christians in Rome, with the responsibility of judging the Manichaeans' Elect after a scandal provoked by the sect, and he exhorted the faithful to denounce the ones they knew of. Manichaeans who abjured were allowed to atone, but the others were prosecuted to the full extent of the law and exiled, and their books were burned. The pope widened his intervention to all of Italy: in January 444 he invited Italian bishops to be vigilant against the hunted, fleeing Manichaeans (JK 405). He used imperial support to reinforce his actions: a statute issued by Valentinian III acknowledged the pontiff's authority by exiling the Manichaeans, taking away their civil rights and extending these actions to the entire Empire.

The pope took action, against other heretics as well, but at the local level he condemned the complacency of the metropolitan of Aquila toward the Pelagian clerics and required that he hold a council gathering together all the bishops under his jurisdiction (JK 416). The doctrinal role of the pope was not contested elsewhere in Italy: in 449 the metropolitan bishop of Ravenna, Peter Chrysologus, opposed the monk of Constantinople, Eutyches, condemned by his bishop, reminding him that it falls to the pope to decide questions of faith. In the summer of 451, shortly before the council of Chalcedon, Leo had no difficulty in getting Bishop Eusebius of Milan and his provincial council to approve his doctrinal letter (*Tome to Flavian*) defining Roman Christology.

Like his predecessors, the pope was careful to maintain ecclesiastical discipline and Roman liturgical customs in the name of the apostolic canons and the authority handed down to the see of St. Peter. In SUBURBICARIAN Italy, admission into the ranks of the clergy, the management of Church properties, and the administration of baptism all elicited letters from the pontiff containing detailed instructions (JK 402; 414–5; 417; 545); he also responded to problems submitted by metropolitans, like that of Aquila, confronted by the consequences of the invasions (JK 536), or by their suffragans, like those of Ravenna (JK 543).

In the rest of the *pars Occidentis*, difficulties due to the invasions limited papal action. Only one intervention is recorded, in Spain in 447, motivated by a letter from the bishop of Astorga, who reported to Rome that the Priscillian heresy had been reborn. In response, the pope sent him a detailed report on the errors of this sect and the *gesta* against the Manichaeans. Concerned with unmasking heretics, he asked the Spanish bishops to meet in general council to condemn them or, if circumstances didn't allow it, to at least hold a regional council in Galicia (JK 412).

In Africa—where only one part of Numidia and the two Mauritanias remained Roman, before falling under Vandal control in 455—Leo was able to assert Roman authority over local churches where it weakened: a hearing was held *uicem curae nostrae* on the unlawful ordinations, schismatic bishops, and reconciled heretics who had to send a profession of faith to Rome. Local condemnations were suspended through appeals to the Holy See in 446 (JK 410).

In Gaul, the pope successfully opposed any supra-metropolitan organization and the recurring claims of primacy by the Church in Arles. He vigorously denounced Hilary of Arles, who had assigned himself the role of metropolitan for all of Gaul, despite the privileges of the Holy See: Leo deprived him of all jurisdiction and stipulated that the ordinations of bishops should be overseen by the metropolitan of the province (JK 407). A statute passed by Valentinian III, proclaiming the primacy of the Holy See based on the dignity of Peter and the city of Rome, extended Roman primacy to the *pars Occidentis*. Bishops were forbidden to go against tradition and were told they must go to Rome if they were called, under pain of being forced to go there. Responding to the nineteen bishops of Gaul, who supported the reestablishment of the primacy of Arles, in the name of the antiquity of their see, the pope countered with, the rights of the see of Vienne and settled the question in May 450 by dividing it into two distinct jurisdictions, respectively controlled by the bishop of Vienne and the bishop of Arles (JK 450). Relations between the pope and the bishops in Gaul seem to have improved afterwards: Leo relied upon the bishop of Arles to see that his decisions concerning the paschal liturgy were respected (JK 477), and he responded immediately to questions and requests sent to Rome by the bishops of Gaul (JK 485–544). In the doctrinal area, the pope met with no opposition in Gaul: he sent Ravennius of Arles the letter noted above, defining Roman Christology and asking Ravennius to spread his message, (JK 451) and the agreement of forty-four bishops of Gaul. He associated the latter with the doctrinal victory won at the council of Chalcedon (JK 479–80); moreover, he gave Arles the role of relaying the letter to Flavian in Spain—a very pragmatic decision. As for the vicariate of Thessalonica, beginning in January 444 the pope confirmed *ex auctoritae sedis apostolicae* the privileges his predecessors had accorded the bishop of Thessalonica, as their representative, bidding all Illyrian prelates to obey him in everything concerning ecclesiastical discipline (JK 403–4). In January 446, illegal ordinations and abuses of power by Anastasios of Thessalonica led him to solemnly specify the rights and duties of the bishops of Illyricum. He guaranteed the rights of the metropolitans under Anastasios's control *ex delegatione nostra*; he disowned the latter for not having referred a serious case to Rome and reminded him that he did not have full *potestas*.

Major cases, which could not be handled in Thessalonica, must be reviewed on appeal in Rome (JK 441). On the doctrinal level, in the conflicts between Rome and the Monophysite party, the pope took care to warn the bishops of the vicariate of the orthodox position in 449 (JK 440) and in 457, at the time of the second Monophysite offensive (JK 525). The ambitions of the Church of Constantinople concerning Illyricum probably explain the pope's vigilance regarding this vicariate.

The Pope and the "Pars Orientis." Until 449, there is little evidence regarding Pope Leo's relationship with the *pars Orientis*. Having apparently maintained the same level of confidence his predecessors did in Bishop Cyril of Alexandria (JK 495), in July 444 he invited Cyril's successor, Dioscoros, in the name of the primacy of St. Peter's see over the throne of St. Mark, to conform to Roman customs on matters of discipline and liturgy (JK 406). In 448, the pope refrained from taking a position in the Christological controversy that arose again in the East, despite an approach to Rome by Eutyches, monk of Constantinople, who was very influential at the court of Theodosius II and who, as a confirmed opponent of the Nestorians, warned him against them (JK 418).

Beginning in 449, however, the East became the pope's dominant preoccupation: between 449 and 454, there were no fewer than seventy-one letters from Leo addressed to different instances of the *pars Orientis*, and between 449 and 451, four Roman legations were sent to Constantinople. These multiple interventions were provoked by an exacerbation of the doctrinal controversy—of which the pope seems to have originally underestimated the importance—between the supporters and the adversaries of the Christology of the two natures. Distance, communication difficulties, linguistic obstacles, and the absence of a permanent official Roman representative to Constantinople made it difficult for Rome to assess the situation when facing an imperial power subject to court intrigues crisscrossed by different religious currents, and driven by contradictory ambitions. The controversy surrounding Eutyches shows the difficulties of Roman intervention in the East: Eutyches, excommunicated and deposed in November 448 by the bishop of Constantinople, Flavian, for having refused to admit the two natures of Christ after the Incarnation, had appealed to Rome with the support of Theodosius II, whereas Flavian, worried about the Eutychian party's growing influence, asked the pope, on his own behalf, to confirm the ruling. But the actions of the pope, who had decided to support Flavian, were thwarted by the initiative of Theodosius II, who called an ecumenical council at Ephesus in August 449, "destined to reestablish unity, which had been troubled by several arguments," which changed the scope of the affair.

The pope accepted the imperial decision to convene a council in the East and sent three LEGATES (JK 424). However, in contrast to Pope Celestine's actions during the Nestorian crisis, he took a strong position on the faith. On 13 June 449, he wrote Flavian a letter that would become a reference on the doctrinal level just like the four ecumenical councils (*Tome to Flavian*) in which he proclaimed two natures in Christ—the divine nature and the human nature—each with its own characteristics but united in one single person, the Son of God; to affirm only one single nature after the Incarnation, as Eutyches did, was virtually to deny the hope of salvation; without hesitation, the pope condemned the latter by calling his profession of faith "scandalous" (JK 423).

The condemnation of Eutyches by Rome and the pope's support of Flavian were not able to block the victory of the Eutychians, supported by Theodosius and his entourage. The council that met at Ephesus, beginning 8 August 449, presided over by Dioscoros of Alexandria, was a total defeat for Rome, whose legates were unable to prevent the deposition of Flavian and the rehabilitation of Eutyches, which at the same time confirmed the Monophysite Christology. The great Eastern sees—Constantinople, Antioch, Jerusalem —fell into the hands of Eutychians who deposed, replaced, or exiled intransigent opponents, and opposed the publication of the *Tome to Flavian*.

Confronted by the victory of the Monophysites in the East, and threatened with a schism, the pope took on the role of defender of doctrinal rectitude and unity of the Church. He received the appeals of the deposed bishops; beginning in October 449, he denounced the "Brigandage of Ephesus" (*Latrocinum Ephesinum*), reversing all its decisions, and threatening to convene a general council in Italy (JK 437–9, 443–4). He expanded his intervention in the East (JK 445–8), and also in the West regarding Valentinian III and the imperial family, who supported his petitions to Constantinople (February 450). But Theodosius II refused to rescind his judgment, so the pope resigned himself to temporizing: he stopped referring directly to Brigandage, stating his acceptance of Flavian's successor Anatolios into communion with Romen (July 450; JK 452–3). However, he remained adamant on the doctrinal level: he required that Anatolios sign a profession of faith showing his aceptance of the *Tome to Flavian* and sent four more legates to the East to assess the new bishop's orthodoxy.

The success of the Roman demands was assured by a change in the situation. After the death of Theodosius II in July 450, the new emperor, Marcian, obviously wishing to see himself recognized as master of the *pars Occidentalis*, received the pope's envoys favorably. Beginning on 21 October 450, in a council at Constantinople, they received Anatolios's acceptance of the *Tome* of Leo and solemnly reaffirmed the Catholic doctrine that Christ is one person with two natures. After consolidating this first victory, the pope tried to reinforce his doctrinal and disciplinary authority in the *pars Orientis* by sending, two new legates after 9 June 451 to guide with Anatolios the reintegration of the bishops who had signed the Brigandage of Ephesus into Church communion (JK 463). However, this initiative was called into question by Emperor Marcian, who, wishing to affirm his power over the *pars Orientis* and to avoid too much intrusion by Rome into the affairs of the Eastern Churches, decided, in May 451, to call a new ecumenical council, to which the pope was invited. Despite reservations, the pope agreed (24 June 451) to send more legates to the East (JK 469), who, along with those sent previously, were to be his representatives to this council. A patristic dossier and precise instructions aimed at Dioscoros of Alexandria and maintaining pontifical authority were given to this Roman delegation.

At the council that met at Chalcedon beginning on 8 October 451 and presided over by the head of the Roman delegation, Paschasinus of Lilybea, the legates had a certain amount of success. They had Dioscoros of Alexandria deposed (and then exiled). They also were able, not without difficulties, to get Eastern bishops, led by Anatolios, some of whom were not sure about the *Tome to Flavian* (tainted, in their eyes, by Nestorianism), to allow the Roman document to be included in the council's profession of faith that recognized the unity of the person of Christ, with two distinct natures that remain so after the union. The deposed bishops were reinstated at Ephesus in the presence of the legates, and with their consent. But the Roman representatives did not succeed in completely defeating the demands of the Church of Constantinople: the latter was confirmed by a council composed of Eastern churchmen as equal to Rome in primacy and honor as the council of Constantinople had decreed in 381, for it was recognized as the New Rome, residence of the emperor and seat of the senate. In the name of this primacy, it also received privileges of jurisdiction over the dioceses of Thrace, Pontus, and Asia, as well as over the barbarian regions that were attached to them (Canon 28). This decision, which made official what was already an existing reality, also aimed to replace the principal of primacy based on the authority of St. Peter—tirelessly defended by the pope—with one established by political dominance. The legates protested in vain against this measure, which they insisted was against the canons of Nicaea, and refused to ratify it. After the council at Chalcedon, the pope continued to hold fast to the defense of Chalcedonian orthodoxy and the hierarchy of Churches, in the name of the unalterability of the canons of Nicaea.

Beginning in May of 452 (JK 481–3), despite the actions of the council fathers—of Anatolios and the emperor Marcian himself—the pope unambiguously rejected Canon 28, saying that the glory of Constantinople was a temporal glory. He expanded his intervention in the imperial capital to denounce the ambitions of Anatolios (JK 487–9). In an attempt to gain tighter control of the Church of Constantinople, he officially named his permanent representative to the imperial capital, Bishop Julian of Cos, as a delegate in *causa fidei* to the emperor and also offered support to several clerics dissatisfied with their archbishop. He only succeeded in getting a stiff, formal condemnation of Canon 28 from Anatolios (JK 509); on the doctrinal level, it wasn't until March 453, and at the insistence of Emperor Marcian, that the pope decided to formally approve the work of the council of Chalcedon (JK 490). Otherwise, he denounced the presence of followers of Eutyches in the clergy of Constantinople and the lack of sufficient cooperation by Anatolios in the fight against heresy. He succeeded in having measures taken against clerics and monks in Constantinople who were suspected of Eutychianism, but without total success in this matter. His relationship with the bishop of the New Rome remained marked by mistrust, and the latter ended up complaining about Rome's interference in the Church of Constantinople's affairs.

The pope's intervention in the rest of the *pars Orientis* was marked by the same zeal to preserve the faith of Chalcedon and defend Roman authority against the ambitions of Constantinople. In 453 he tried to get the support of the Church of Antioch, declaring that he would assume responsibility—in the name of the apostolicity of the see—for the privileges of this Church, not a contradictory offer, since the Roman legates to Chalcedon had ratified a sharing of jurisdiction between Antioch and Jerusalem (JK 495), departing from the canons of Nicaea. The pope wrote in the same vein to Theodoret of Cyr, whom he reminded of how the Holy See's support for his case after the Brigandage (JK 496). In 452 and 453, during the troubles that arose in Palestine when Monophysite monks drove Bishop Juvenal from his see of Jerusalem, the pope intervened to reestablish the authority of the council: he demanded that the emperor stop the troublemakers from doing any further harm (JK 486) and asked Empress Eudocia, initially favorable to the Monophysites, to separate herself from them and join those who opposed them (JK 499). He also was concerned with expounding Roman Christology: he sent a long letter to Palestinian monks about the faith, in which he strongly condemned the two opposing heresies of Eutychus and Nestorius and laid out the Roman doctrine of the Incarnation as a middle road between the two, which they must take (JK 500). In 454, when Juvenal was reinstated to his see, the pope took care to write him a letter affirming Chalcedonian orthodoxy and reminding him of the eminent dignity of his Church (JK 514).

The pope also situated himself as defender of the faith and the hierarchy of Churches with the see of Alexandria, where a Chalcedonian bishop, Proterios, had re-placed Dioscoros. Leo got him to accept the *Tome to Flavian* and to distribute this Roman document throughout Egypt (JK 505). Against the ambitions of Constantinople, the pope confirmed all the former privileges of the throne of St. Mark for the Egyptian bishops, considered as *subjecti* (JK 5050). However, he never hesitated to question, in the name of a tradition preserved by Rome, the paschal computation established by Theophilus of Alexandria—he asked Marcian "in the name of the truth of the sacrament and Church unity" to revise the Alexandrian system (JK 497). Upon the death of Marcian in early 457, doctrinal unity could be considered reestablished in the East thanks to the efforts of the pope and the emperor. The *Tome to Flavian* was distributed and recognized, and papal intervention in the realms of the liturgy and even discipline had been essentially been effective.

But these successes remained precarious and depended, for the most part, on the goodwill of the emperor. At the beginning of 457, the pope was once more forced to intervene in the East to defend Chalcedonian orthodoxy, without having the same degree of support from the new emperor, Leo. In March 457, after the massacre of Proterios by the Alexandrian Monophysites and his replacement by Timotheos Elure, head of the anti-Chalcedonian group, the pope asked the emperor several times to reinstall an orthodox bishop in Alexandria and to forbid any calling in to question of the Chalcedonian council (JK 521–4). He also warned different authorities in the imperial capital (JK 522–3, 527, 534, 538), as well as the bishops of the large ecclesiastical metropolis against heresy (JK 525–6). Worried about the Monophysite threat in Constantinople itself, he asked Anatolios to move the clerics who supported heretics some place where they could do no further harm (JK 529–31, 540), but without much success.

Strengthened by their victory in Alexandria, the Monophysites demanded a revision of the council of Chalcedon, and the emperor invited the pope to come East to discuss the question of faith. The pope refused, citing the invulnerability of the decrees of the council at Chalcedon and the peace of the Church (JK 532). He nevertheless agreed in May 458 to send two legates to Constantinople (JK 539–41), with a doctrinal letter—accompanied by a patristic dossier—explaining Roman Christology (the second *Tome* by Leo) (JK 542), but refused to permit them to discuss the faith of Chalcedon. At the same time, he supported the Egyptian bishops faithful to Chalcedon who had taken refuge in the imperial capital. (JK 530-533-537). Despite these steps, the pope was not able to impose his doctrinal authority on the *pars Orientis* without discussion. Without informing Rome, Emperor Leo I took the initiative in consulting the Eastern metropolitans about the opportunity to revise the council of Chalcedon and on maintaining Timotheos

Elure in Alexandria. It was not until the Eastern prelates had come forward against Timotheos Elure that he was driven out of Alexandria by imperial intervention and exiled. The pope could only support the Chalcedonian restoration, which remained shaky. Beginning in June 450, he wrote to the new archbishop of the imperial capital, Gennadius, a Chalcedonian, to warn him of an offensive by Timotheos Elure's supporters, who were plotting in Constantinople, and to remind him that no reconciliation could be made with the murderer of Proterios (JK 547). In August 460, he invited the new titular of the see of Alexandria, also a Chalcedonian, to uphold orthodoxy and to maintain close ties with Rome (JK 548).

In the course of a pontificate more than twenty years long, Leo tirelessly intervened, in the name of the Petrine principles, to make Roman authority prevail in matters of doctrine, discipline, and liturgy. He was able to establish his views in the *pars Occidentis* more than in the East, where an underestimation of the complexity of the situation and of political realities limited his effectiveness. But he knew how to acquire an influence over the great Eastern sees that was unknown to his predecessors—an influence that, on the doctrinal level, would be felt for the next century. As the last pope representing tradition during a troubled period, his energy, his tenacity, and his organizational abilities earned him the name "Leo the Great."

Christiane Fraisse-Coué

Bibliography

PL, 54–6; *PLS*, 3, 229–350.

Barclift, P. L. "Predestination and Divine Foreknowledge in the Sermons of Pope Leo the Great," *Church History* 62 (1993), 5–21.

Bardy, G. *Histoire de l'Élise* IV, Paris, 1945, 259–70.

Bartnik, C. "L'interprétation théologique de la crise de l'Empire romain," *RHE*, 63, 1968, 745–84.

Battifol, P. *DTC*, 9, 1926, 218–301.

Camelot, T. "Théologies grecques et théologie latine à Chalcédoine," *Revue des sciences phil., et théol.*, 35, 1951, 401–12, (*Das Konzil von Chalkedon*, I), Würzburg, 1951.

Caspar, E. *Geschichte des Papsttums*, I, Tübingen, 1930, 422–564.

Chavasse, A. *S. Leoni Magni R.P. tractatus septem et nonaginta*, cc 138–138A; French translation, R. DOLLE, *Saint Léon le Grand, Sermons I–IV*, SC 22, 49, 74, 200, Paris, 1949–73.

Conroy, J. P. *The Idea of Reform in Leo the Great*, 1981.

De Halleux, A. "Le décret chalcédonien sur les prérogatives de la Nouvelle Rome," *Ephem. Theol. Lovanienses*, 1988, 288–323.

Dekkers, E. "Autour de l'oeuvre liturgique de saint Léon le Grand," *SE*, 10, 1958, 363–98.

Deneffe, A. "Tradition und Dogma bei Leo d. Gr.," *Scholastik*, 9, 1934, 543–54.

Dominguez Del Val, U. "San Leo Magno y el Tomus ad Flavianum," *Helmantica*, 13, 1962, 199–233.

Dupuy, B. "Les appels de l'Orient à Rome du concile de Nicée au concile de Chalcédoine," *Istina*, 32, 1987, 361–77.

Galtier, P. *Saint Cyrille et saint Léon le Grand à Chalcédoine, Chalkedon* II, Würzburg, 1953.

Grillmeier, A. *Christian Church Tradition*, New York, 1965.

Guenther, N. Collectio Avellana, *CSEL* 35, 1.

Guillaume, A. *Jeûne et charité dans l'Église latine . . . , en particulier chez saint Léon*, Paris, 1985 (reedition).

Gundlach, W. *Epistulae Arelatenses, MGH*, III, Berlin, 1892.

Hofmann, F. *Der Kampf der Päpste um Konzil und Dogma von Chalkedon von Leo dem Großen bis Honmisda (451–519)*, 13–94.

Hudon, G. "La perfection chrétienne d'après les sermons de saint Léon," *Lex orandi*, Paris, 1959.

Hudon, G. *DSp.*, 9, 1976, 597–611.

Jalland T. G. *The Life and Time of St. Leo the Great*, London, 1941.

James, N. W. "Leo the Great and Prosper of Aquitaine: A Fifth-Century Pope and His Adviser," *Journal of Theological Studies* 44 (1993), 554–84.

Jouassard, G. "Sur les décisions des conciles généraux des IVe—Ve siècles dans leurs rapports avec la primauté," *Istina*, 4, 1957, 485–96.

Jugie, M. "Intervention de saint Léon dans les affaires intérieures des Églises orientales," *Miscellanea P. Paschini*, 1, Rome, 1948, 77–94.

Klinkenberg, H. L. "Papsttum und Reichskirche bei Leo der Große," *ZRGKA*, 38, 1952, 37–112.

Langärtner, G. L. *Die Gallienpolitik der Päpste um V. und VI. Jahrhundert*, Bonn, 1964.

Lauras, A. "Saint Léon le Grand et le manichéisme romain," *SP*, XI, *TU*, 109, Berlin, 1972, 203–9.

Lepelley, C. "Saint Léon le Grand et la cité romaine," *Revue des sc. relig.* 35, 1961, 130–50; "Saint Léon le Grand et l'Église mauritanienne," *Les Cahiers de Tunisie*, 15, 1967, 189–204.

Liber Pontificalis, Duchesne, 238–341.

MacShane, P. A. *La Romanitas et le pape Léon le Grand*, Paris, 1979.

Maier, M. O. " 'Manichee!' Leo the Great and the Orthodox Panoptican," *Journal of Early Christian Studies* 4 (1996), 441–60.

Schwartz, E. *Leonis pape Epistularum collectiones, ACO* II, 1–4, Berlin-Leipzig, 1932.

Sieben, J. H. "Leo der Große über Konzilium und Lehrprimat des römischen Stuhles," *Theologie und Philosophie*, 47, 1972, 358–401.

Silva Tarouca, C. *Textus et documenta*, theol. series., 9, 15, 20, 23, Rome, 1932–7.
Stockmeier, P. "Imperium bei Papst Leo dem Großen," *TU*, 78, Berlin, 1961, 413–20.
Studer, B. *TRE*, 20, 737–41.
Studer, B. "Una persona in Christo," *Augustinianum*, 25, 1985, 453–87.
Thullier, A. "Le primat de Rome et la collégialité de l'épiscopat d'après la correspondance de saint Léon avec l'Orient," *Nuovo Didascaleion*, 15, 1965, 53–67.
Tolland, T. G. *The Life and Times of St. Leo the Great*, 1941.
Ullmann, W. "Leo I and the Theme of Papal Primacy," *JTS*, 11, 1960, p. 25–51.
Vollmann, B. *Studien zum Priscillanismus* (Ep. 15), St. Ottilian, 1965.
Winkelmann, F. "Papst Leo und die Sog. Apostasia Palästinas," *Klio*, 70, 1988, 167–75.
Wojtowytsch, M. *Papsttum und Konzilie von de Anfägen bis zu Leo I. (440–461)*, Stuttgart, 1981.

LEO II. *(b. Sicily, ?, d. Rome, 3 July 683). Consecrated pope 17 August 682. Buried at St. Peter's in Rome. Saint and confessor (ancient cult, already witnessed in the martyrologies of Bede and Adon; by error, his feast day, 28 June, replaced that of the Translation).*

This pontificate lasted less than one year, but that did not prevent it from being filled with important events. Son of a certain Paul, Leo was not a newcomer to the city at the time of his election. Excelling in singing and psalmody, he came from the *scola cantorum* and had made his ecclesiastical career in Rome. The story of his life in the *LIBER PONTIFICALIS* tells of perfect harmony with the clergy and doubtless with most of the population. He built two churches and was quite attentive to the needs of the populace. But these were not his most important accomplishments. Sources tell us that Leo was also a very eloquent man, capable of speaking both Greek and Latin, skills he needed in order to continue the work of Agatho.

His predecessor had died on 10 January 681, and Leo was definitely elected during the same month. His envoys to the imperial court arrived the following 10 March during the COUNCIL being held then. Constantine IV refused to confirm Leo's election as long as he would not suscribe to the condemnation of HONORIUS I for his participation in Monothelitism. Negotiations lasted for six months after the council ended, on 16 September 681. The emperor wanted to condemn a pope so as not to intensify the resentment of the patriarchs who were being forced for purely political reasons to first defend Monothelitism and then to condemn all the patriarchs who had been faithful to the sovereign. The Romans used their position of strength as much as possible to counter these aims. A comprehensive compromise was reached. In exchange for the condemnation of Pope Honorius, ratified by a letter from Leo to the emperor (7 May 683), which would shock no one for eight centuries, Constantine accepted and confirmed the election of the pope, and was to receive a permanent aprocrisarius from the papacy at Constantinople. In addition, he agreed to send to Rome, for judgment, Macarius, patriarch of Antioch, and other obdurate Monothelitists condemned by the council, as well as to ratify the subordination of the archbishop of RAVENNA to the pope and to decrease the payments by the patrimonies of Sicily and Calabria to the imperial treasury (he reduced the number of base units or *anno-capita*, the delivery of wheat levies, and other taxes that the Roman Church found abusive).

After having received the acts of the council, Leo was able to translate them and send them for approval to the western churches by way of their kings. Thus, as an intermediary between the emperor and the kings, the pope asserted his authority as spiritual head of these churches without infringing on the prerogatives of the sovereigns.

Jean Durliat

Bibliography

JW, 1, 240–1.
LP, 1, 359–62.
Bertolini, O. *Roma di fronte a Bisanzio e ai Longobardi*, Bologne, 1971, 383–92.
CONTE, P. "Leo II," *LexMA*, 5 (1991), 1877.
Mansi, XI, 713–922; 1046–58.

LEO III. *(b. ?, d. 12 June 816). Elected pope 26 December 795, consecrated 27 December. Saint (local ancient cult, for example in Brittany in the tenth century; enrolled in Roman martyrology in 1673, feast day not celebrated in modern times).*

A Roman born of humble stock, Leo became a cleric very early and climbed the rungs of the ecclesiastical hierarchy at the Lateran one by one all the way up to becoming cardinal-priest of Santa-Susanna, with the status of *vestararius*, an important person in charge of guarding the sacred treasures and the pontifical wardrobe. His modest origins were assumed to be an obstacle to his chances to rise to St. Peter's throne, traditionally occupied by a member of one or another of Rome's great noble families. Therefore, it is thought that his rapid election (the same day as HADRIAN I's death) and consecration (the very next day) must have resulted from a maneuver by his supporters in the high echelons of the clergy to take the other contenders by surprise, which he did.

Whether or not his election was canonically correct, the new pontiff needed as much support as possible from outside the church to reinforce his legitimacy. That is certainly one of the motives that led him to send an embassy to the king of the FRANKS, Charlemagne, already very involved in Roman affairs since his intervention against the king of the LOMBARDS, Didier, as requested by Hadrian I in 774. Not content merely with an official notification of his election, Leo sent the keys to St. Peter's tomb and the banner of the city, asking him to send someone in return to receive an oath of loyalty from the Romans. Charlemagne's role as protector of the city and the PAPAL STATES could not have been more clearly drawn. The *missus* Charlemagne sent to Rome—Angilbert, the abbot of St-Riquier—was also the bearer of a message, both written and oral, that left no doubt that the king of the Franks firmly intended to fully assume his title as "patrician of the Romans": the pope was told to limit himself strictly to the spiritual domain that was his and carefully conform to canonical regulations on church discipline (perhaps a warning against providing arms to Charlemagne's adversaries)—in other words, to leave everything else in the king's control.

Despite this diplomatic support, the political situation in Rome rapidly worsened. The partisans of the aristocracy, quickly regrouping, plotted together and, more and more openly, led a hostile campaign against Leo III. Events escalated to the point where, on the morning of the feast of St. Mark 799 (April 25), as Leo made his way toward San Lorenzo in Lucina to lead a procession to ST. PETER's, the pope was pulled off his horse, beaten severely, and then locked up in a monastery on the Celian hill after his captors attempted to put out his eyes and cut out his tongue. Having succeeded in escaping, he fled to the duke of Spoleto (a Frank), and then went to Charlemagne at Paderborn for justice. The rebels also sent their own embassy, justifying their action with a full series of accusations against Leo III, including adultery and perjury. Charlemagne had the pope escorted back to Rome in late November 799, accompanied by a commission of inquiry to conduct an investigation. Seeing their report, which seemed to confirm the major charges, Charlemagne, at the end of the year 800, went in person to Rome, where Leo III welcomed him with unaccustomed pomp. In the month of December, a trial began at St. Peter's to allow the pope to defend himself against the charges against him. Leo III excused himself by taking an oath of purgation (whose text has been totally preserved) on 23 December, insisting all the while that he did so of his own free will and not by force.

The pope got his revenge two days later. In the course of the liturgical celebration of Christmas, in front of St. Peter's tomb, he crowned Charlemagne with an imperial diadem and had him acclaimed three times by the people using these words: "To Charles the Pious, Augustus, crowned by God, great and peace-loving emperor, long life and victory!" Then he knelt before him in homage, according to the traditional rite for emperors. Seen in the context of the time, and freed from the confines of the historical commentary that has followed, up to the present day, this initiative, from Leo III's point of view, was dictated by the "protective logic" that had guided the pope since his election. Obviously, the desire (stimulated by the "vacancy" of the Eastern Empire, ruled by a woman since 797) to realize the dream of restoring the Empire also motivated him, an idea that had been circulating in Rome and in Aachen for some time, and which found iconographic expression in the MOSAICS of the Lateran's *triclinium*. In any event, this gesture had long-term consequences beyond Leo III's lifetime. Following the attempt on his life, whose perpetrators were condemned for the crime of high treason, the relationship between the pope and the "new Constantine" continued just as before. Charlemagne commanded the pope regularly to look into specific matters of administration or ecclesiastical discipline, which Leo did with enthusiasm. Leo III nevertheless was able to impose his will in the more dogmatic controversy over the *Filioque* (809). The words "and of the Son" were in the creed from Nicaea-Constantinople that was then being used in France and Spain, but not in the text of the Greek and Roman churches. Conflict surrounding this question arose in Jerusalem between Frankish and Greek monks. When it was brought before the pope, he presented the case to Charlemagne, more out of courtesy and for information (since the Franks were involved) than as a consultation on theological grounds. The theologians of Charlemagne's court were obviously favorable to inserting the *Filioque*, and the emperor sent a message to Rome that he considered definitive. But Leo III refused to bend and reprimanded the impudence of the bishops across the Alps.

In his relations with Constantinople, he was also drawn into a conflict of some importance between the monk Theodore, abbot of the monastery of Studion, and the patriarch. The latter, a former high official of the imperial administration appointed in an entirely arbitrary fashion by Constantine VI, had provoked the anger of the Studite by reinstating the clerics who had supported the adulterous marriage of the *basileus*. Exiled, Theodore had appealed to the pope by asking him to call a disciplinary council. The situation was settled by the well-timed succession to the throne of a new emperor, which allowed Leo III to intercede for the reconciliation of the monk and the patriarch.

The death of Charlemagne (28 January 814) removed all of Leo III's protection. Conspiracies began again. A new plot against the pope's life was discovered and severely punished (sources tell of three hundred executions), which brought about a visit to Rome by the king of Italy, Bernard, son of Louis the Pious, and the dispatch of an embassy to the emperor to justify the pope's actions once again. When the pontiff died, the Roman countryside was torn by revolt.

François Bougard

Bibliography

JW, 1, 307–16; 2, 701–2, 743.

LP, 2, 1–28.

Amann, É. "Léon III," *DTC*, 9 (1926), 304–12.

Folz, R. *Le Couronnement impérial de Charlemagne, 25 Décembre 800*, Paris, 1964.

Hageneder, O. "Das *crimen maiestatis*, der Prozeβgegen die Attentäter Papst Leos III. und die Kaiserdrönung Karls des Groβen," *Aus Kirche und Reich. Festschrift für Friedrich Kempf*, ed. H. Mordek, Sigmaringen, 1983, 55–79.

Kerner, M. "Der Reinigungseid Leos III, vom Dezember 800. Die Frage seiner Echtheit und frühen kanonistischen Überlieferung. Eine Studie zum Problem der päpstlichen Immunität im früheren Mittelalter," *Zeitschrift des Aachener Geschichtsvereins*, 84/85 (1977–8), 131–60.

Llewellyn, P. "Le contexte romain du couronnement de Charlemagne. Le temps de l'Avent de l'année 800," *Le Moyen Age*, 96 (1990), 209–25.

Mordek, H. "Leo III," *LexMA* 5 (1991), 1977–8.

Noble, T. F. X. *The Republic of St. Peter: The Birth of the Papal State*, 680–825, Philadelphia, 1984.

LEO IV. (d. 17 July 855). *Elected pope at the end of January 847, consecrated 10 April 847. Buried at St. Peter's in Rome. Saint (figures in Roman martyrology, feast day not celebrated in modern times).*

Born of a Roman father, Leo was first educated in the monastery of St. Martin, near ST. PETER'S, before rising through the ranks of the clergy until he was named cardinal-priest of the church of SS. Quatro Coronati. His merits were so obvious and universally recognized that his election as pope was immediate, and occurred even before the funeral of his predecessor, SERGIUS II, who died on 27 January 847. Still, Leo had to wait two months before his religious consecration on 10 April (Easter) due to the fact that Lothair's constitution of 824 stated that the consecration could not take place until the emperor had ratified the election, and the ceremony had to be held in the presence of his *missi*. For reasons that are not clear (possibly fear of a threat from the SARACENS nearby, slow communications, or even a deliberate political gesture), Rome finally went ahead with the consecration without receiving word from the emperor. However, care was taken to avoid any break with him by repeated assurances of loyalty. Leo IV first had to make his faithful safe from the Saracen peril: In 846, St. Peter's had been sacked, as well as ST. PAUL'S OUTSIDE THE WALLS, and in 848 a new invasion was announced, which this time the Romans were able to contain. The pope had the murals of Aurelian restored and, in particular, left his name on two new fortifications. The most important surrounded St. Peter's and the immediate vicinity and was linked to the old wall by the CASTEL SANT' ANGELO and the bridge bearing the same name, an area that became known as the "Leonine City," and was consecrated as a religious edifice on 27 June 852. The other was the city of Leopolis, founded *ex novo* in 854 to serve as a refuge for the inhabitants of the neighboring center of Centumcellae (Civitavecchia), which was threatened by repeated coastal attacks. In these enterprises he was assisted by the emperor Lothair.

In his relationship with the FRANKISH power, Leo IV was able to maintain a real independence, though not without some mild friction with the sovereigns. It was under his pontificate that Lothair chose his son Louis II, who ruled Italy, to take over the empire. The pope consecrated Louis at Rome in April 850. By renewing, for the first time, Charlemagne's ceremony of 800, the young king laid claim to an illustrious heritage but also reinforced a sense of papal "rights" over the empire, which drew notice and comment. Louis II established a permanent *missus* to Rome, the subject of ongoing friction that is noticeable in the pope's correspondence. But the main subject of conflict was the case of Anastasius, promoted to cardinal-priest of San Marco by Leo IV himself in 848, who took refuge in northern Italy several months later, without anyone really knowing why, seemingly due to a rivalry of a personal nature with the pope. Leo IV excommunicated him twice, divesting him of his sacerdotal position, but Louis II, at least to judge by later events, seems to have given the fugitive his protection.

All the same, Leo IV took care to stifle any attempts toward autonomy on the part of the high clergy on the other side of the Alps, admonishing Hincmar of Reims several times. Finally, in the same vein, he showed his irritation with the patriarch of Constantinople, Ignatius, who had deposed the archbishop of Syracuse without notifying or checking with him (the archbishop had taken refuge in the East since 843 because of the Moslem presence in Sicily and had endeavored to become the successor to the patriarch Methodius, but Ignatius had prevailed). The aspiration to be the supreme arbitrator of the Church and to tolerate no interference found strong and efficient support in the publication of the pseudo-Isidorian *Decretals*, a collection of sometimes authentic, sometimes false canons assembled by a group of clerics in the diocese of Reims between 847 and 852, with the aim of guaranteeing the independence and power of bishops and of the Church in general against the abuses of temporal power. Leo IV also paid attention to the Church in Great Britain by sending a detailed response to questions of ecclesiastical discipline by the local episcopate, insisting, as his successors would during the second half of the 9th century, on the sanctity of marriage and the necessity of preventing rape.

François Bougard

Bibliography

JW, 1, 329–39; 2, 702–3, 744.

LP, 2, 106–39.

Amann, É. "Léon IV," *DTC*, 9 (1926), 312–6.

Herbers, K. "Leo IV.," *LexMA*, 5 (1991), 1878.

Viard, P. "Léon IV," *Catholicisme*, 7 (1975), 321–2.

LEO V. *(d. October 905). Elected pope at the end of July or the beginning of August 903. Probably buried at St. Peter's in Rome or at St. John Lateran.*

Leo V, whom sources sometimes erroneously identify as LEO VI, was a priest when he was elected pope at the end of the month of July or in early August 903. The note *natione ardeatinus, de loco qui appellatur Priapi*, which is found in several papal catalogs, is generally reported to refer to the city of Ardea, thirty-seven kilometers south of Rome, Priapi being the place where Leo was supposed to have served as a priest. According to the testimony of Auxilius, he seems to have been part of the "Formosan faction." His origins outside the Roman clergy contributed to the formation of a legend; we know the version in the *Vita Tugduali* that appeared in the 11th or 12th centuries, according to which Leo was a Breton pilgrim who had come to Rome, where he was unexpectedly elected pope. The legend moved the fictionalized events to the 10th century from the 6th, attributing them to St. Tutwal (Tugdual) of Tréguier, unexpectedly elected pope in Rome under the name of Leo. It was the title of *pabu* or *papa* that many Breton saints were given that gave rise to this confusion. It is not known if Leo V had any original policies, as it is impossible to attribute, with any certainty, any of his lost acts, promulgated for Bologna and the monastery of Reichenau, or confirming the metropolitan of MILAN to that post. He was pope only a short time, probably because he came from outside Roman clergy. At the end of the month of August, after thirty days as pope, he was overthrown and incarcerated by Christopher, a Roman cardinal-priest whose motivations remain obscure. He died in October 905. Later sources hesitate between the Lateran and St. Peter's as the site of his grave.

Klaus Herbers

Bibliography

JL, I, 444; II, 746.

LP, 2, 234.

Dümmler, E. *Auxilius und Vulgarius*, 1866.

Herbers, K. "Leo V," *LexMA*, 5 (1991), 1878–9.

Platelle, H. "Tutwal," *Bibliotheca Sanctorum* (1969), 723–4.

Vita Tugdualdi, ed. A. de la Borderie, *Les Trois Vies anciennes de saint Tudual*, Paris, 1877; *Histoire de Bretagne*, Paris, 1888.

Zimmermann, H. *Papstabsetzungen des Mittelalters*, Graz–Vienna–Cologne, 1968, 63.

LEO VI. *(d. beginning of January 929). Elected pope in mid-June 928. Buried in St. Peter's in Rome.*

Born into the Roman nobility, son of Christopher, who served as notary under Pope JOHN VIII, he was the cardinal-priest of Sta Susanna. He rose to the pontifical throne immediately after Pope JOHN X was deposed, thanks to the decisive influence of the senatrix Marozia who reigned over Rome at the time. He had been chosen because he was already quite old and his family belonged to Rome's anti-Formosan faction. No information about his brief pontificate has survived to this day except for one act. Based on information supplied by his LEGATE, Bishop Madalbert, just returned from Dalmatia, about the decrees adopted by a SYNOD that had met at Split slightly earlier, in this act the pope ended the quarrel over the rights of the metropolitan of Croatia by taking the side of the Dalmatian archbishop of Split against Bishop Gregory of Nin, who was transferred to Skradin. Leo VI soon died and was buried in St. Peter's.

Harald Zimmermann

Bibliography

Zimmermann, H. *Papstregesten* 911–1024 (J. F. Böhmer, *Regesta Imperii*, II/5), Vienna, 1969, 35 *ff*; "Die ersten Konzilien von Split im Raahmen der Geschichte ihrer Zeit," *Medioevo e Umanesimo*, 1982, 14; and "Leo VI," *LexMA*, 5 (1991), 1879.

LEO VII. *(d. beginning of July 939). Elected pope at the beginning of January 936. Buried in St. Peter's in Rome.*

Leo VII reigned as pope in Rome from the beginning of January 936 to the beginning of July 939. A native Roman, this cardinal-priest of San Sisto became pope thanks to Alberic II (932–54), the prince then ruling over Rome; nothing in the sources suggests that there was a canonical election. The pope and the prince were animated by the same desire for monastic reform, and it has even been suggested that Leo had previously been a Benedictine monk. In any event, the sixteen authentic pontifical ACTS that have survived from this pontificate were established for monasteries: the abbot Odo of Cluny received no fewer than six for his monasteries at Cluny, Déols, and Fleury. In 936, together with the prince, the pope had called upon him to introduce monastic reform to Rome and had given him the monastery of ST. PAUL'S OUTSIDE THE WALLS. Odo mediated once again in the quest for peace between Alberic and Hugo, king of Italy (926–48). Four pontifical acts were preserved for the Benedictine mother abbey of Subiaco, and we can deduce the existence of three other acts. At the request of their abbot, the reformist abbey of Gorze in Lorraine near Metz and the abbey of Fulda in Hesse, which benefited from the EXEMPTION, also received pontifical acts. Most of these privileges conceded to the monasteries only confirmed rights and properties. A reference to old Roman law (*lex romana*), handed down by the *Pseudo-Isidore*, makes one act particularly interesting. Established for Déols and destined to put an end to litigation between the abbey and the archbishop of Bourges over a donation in a will, Leo gave the *pallium* to Archbishop Adalgag of Hamburg-Bremen, and to Archbishop Frederick of Mainz the title of apostolic vicar to Germany. At the request of Frederick, the pope, using this same privilege, advised him to expel JEWS resisting conversion. From France, the pope received a visit from the chronicler Flodoard of Reims in 936, and the latter took advantage of his stay in Rome to do research on the history of the popes, recopying, for example, the epitaphs of pontiffs.

Harald Zimmermann

Bibliography

Antonelli, G. "L'opera di Cluny in Italia," *Benedictina*, 4, 1950, 19–40.

Chénon, É. *Une question de droit au Xe siècle*, Paris, 1899.

Lotter, F. *Der Brief des Priesters Gerhard an den Erzbischof Friedrich von Mainz*, Sigmaringen, 1975.

Zimmermann, H. *Papstregesten*, 911–1024, Vienna, 1969, 46–60; and *Das dunkle Jahrhundert*, Graz, 1971, 84 *ff*.

Zimmermann, H. "Rechtstradition in Papsturkunden," *Im Bann des Mittelalters*, Sigmaringen, 1986, 192–3; *Papsturkunden*, 2nd ed., Vienna 1988, 115–65; "Leo VII," *LexMA*, 5 (1991), 1879.

LEO VIII. (*d. Rome, beginning of March 965*). *Elected pope 4 December 963, consecrated 6 December 963. May be buried at St. Peter's in Rome.*

As soon as Otto the Great left Rome after his CORONATION as emperor, to fight Berengar of Italy, JOHN XII formed alliances with Adalbert, the son of Berengar, and with BYZANTIUM. Otto later returned to Rome and John XII, who had fled, was deposed on 4 December 963, at a SYNOD arranged by the emperor. From that time on, the Romans agreed neither to elect a pope nor to ordain him without the consent of the emperor. That same day, by triple acclamation, the synod elected as the successor to John XII the protoscriniarius (notary) Leo, a layman in the CURIA, on whom they had—against canonical rules—to confer all the orders at once. Roman by birth, originally from the region of Clivus Argentarius and son of the notary John, Leo owed his election as pope to the influence of Otto the Great and to those opposed to the Roman ruling families.

On 6 December 963, Leo was consecrated by the bishops Sico of Ostia, Benedict I of Porto, and Gregory of Albano at ST. PETER's. Barely several weeks later, a riot broke out against Otto and Leo. The emperor successfully quelled this riot, forcing the Romans to take an oath of loyalty and to deliver a hundred hostages, who were quickly freed at Leo's request. As soon as the emperor left Rome, Leo, unable to maintain his position, fled. John XII retook the city. The COUNCIL he presided over on 26 February 964, at St. Peter's, declared the imperial synod unlawful and deposed and excommunicated Leo. After the sudden death of John XII on 14 May 964, the Romans did not allow Leo to return. At the end of May of the same year, they elected as pope the deacon Benedict, an educator (*grammaticus*) who took the name of BENEDICT V. Once again, Otto and his forces marched on a Rome that, broken by famine, surrendered and handed over Benedict. Afterward, Leo VIII was solemnly reinstated on 23 June 964, and a synod, which Leo and the emperor presided over at the end of the month of June, decreed the demotion of Benedict to the rank of DEACON and his EXILE from Rome. From then on, Leo's papacy continued without incident until his death at the beginning of March 965. Three documents known under the name "false documents of investiture"—fakes prepared by the followers of Henry IV during the quarrel of the INVESTITURES CONTROVERSY—cite Leo as their author. These are the *Privilegium minus*, the *Privilegium majus*, and the *Cessio donationum*, which give the sovereign the right to choose the pope and to approve archbishops and bishops before their ordination, and which returned all the donations made to the Roman Church by preceding emperors and kings.

Rolf Grosse

Bibliography

LP 2, 250.

Die falschen Investiturprivilegien, ed. C. Märtl, Hanover, 1986; "Parteiungen und Papstwahlen in Rom zur Zeit Kaiser Ottos des Großen," *Römische historische Mitteilungen*, 8–9 (1964–66), 29 *ff*. (repr. in *Otto der Große*, 1976, 325 *ff*.); *Papstabsetgen des Mittelalters*, 1968, 88–95, 235 *ff*.; *Das dunkle Jahrhundert*, Graz, 1971, 150–3; "Leo VIII," *LexMA*, 5 (1991), 1879–80.

Wolter, H. *Die Synoden im Reichsgebiet und in Reichsitalien von 916 bis 1056*, Paderborn, 1988, 79–86.

Zimmermann, H. *Papstregesten*, Sigmaringen, 129–50; and *Papsturkunden*, I, 294–333.

LEO IX. *Bruno of Egisheim (b. 21 June 1002–d. Rome, 19 April 1054). Named pope at Worms in December 1048, elected at Rome 2 February 1049, and enthroned 12 February. Buried at St. Peter's in Rome. Saint and confessor (cult formed almost immediately, implicitly recognized by Victor III in 1087 at the translation of his relics; witnessed at Toul in 1091; Clement XIII adopted him as the patron saint of Benevento in 1762). Feast day April 19.*

Leo IX is considered the first pope of Gregorian RE-FORM. Third in a series of four German popes chosen by the emperor, he would remain in possession of the see of Rome, as did CLEMENT II, DAMASUS II, and VICTOR II. He was a representative of the imperial Church on ST. PETER's throne, without, however, being in the service of the emperor. His pontificate was marked by numerous initiatives. An ascetic and a gifted preacher, he had a personality that made an impression on his biographers and contemporary chroniclers.

The son of Count Hugo of Nordgau, Bruno was related by blood to the Salian dynasty (he was a cousin of Conrad II and of Henry III). He was sent while very young to the cathedral school at Toul, where he became a canon. After 1025, he was at the royal court; in 1026, he directed the city's military contingent for Conrad II's Italian expedition. He was in Italy when Herman of Toul died (1 April 1026) and the people of Toul demanded to have him as their new bishop, despite his youth. Consecrated on 9 September 1027, he managed the city's defense against the machinations of the Champenois count Eudes and participated in several embassies dealing with foreign relations in France, Burgundy, and the EMPIRE (1033). He rapidly became involved in the everyday life of the monasteries of his diocese and city, where he favored the expansion of the spirit introduced by William of Volpiano. After the death of Pope Damasus II in August of 1048, a Roman delegation went to Henry III and asked him to choose a successor. Bruno of Toul was thus designated in Worms in early December 1048, but he would not accept unless he was elected by the people of Rome, which was done 2 February 1049; his enthronement took place on 12 February.

The pontificate of Leo IX represents an important moment in the history of the Church, the papacy, and reform, as well as in the history of the 11th century. Certainly he was a bishop of the imperial Church, but elected by the clergy and the people of Toul, he kept his distance regarding lay intervention in episcopal elections. In Rome, he wanted to be chosen by the Romans and not just the man chosen by the emperor. He therefore began a bitter battle against all those who had yielded directly or indirectly to SIMONY. He also took as his own the principles of reform inaugurated by his predecessors, but required them to be put into practice by convening SYNODS outside Rome. He also began to deal with the question of NICOLAISM, but in a way that was not immediately challenging. Despite his strong desire for change, he remained influenced by the institutions of his native country and allowed lay control over the abbeys in the form of approval and intervention of families in abbatial elections.

Leo IX traveled extensively throughout his pontificate, going to Germany three times, to France and to Slovakia, and several times to northern and southern Italy. He presided over synods in Rome during Eastertide (1049, 1050, 1051, 1053), in Pavia, Reims, and Mainz in 1049, Siponto and Vercelli in 1050, and Mantua in 1053. During his first trip north in 1049, he demonstrated his authority, obtaining the submission of some Lotharingian princes who had revolted against the emperor. He showed himself to be particularly unyielding against bishops and abbots whose manner of election was suspect, requiring them to explain and justify themselves, and going as far as deposing or even excommunicating some of them. The detailed account of the synod of Reims in October 1049 by Anselm of St. Rémy illustrates precisely how things occurred at these meetings under Leo's direction. At Mainz, allied with Henry III, Leo IX was not able to act with equal vigor, because he knew the quality of the episcopate as it then existed under the emperor. In northern Italy, he met with serious resistance on the part of the Lombard bishops. Leo IX refused to acknowledge as null sacraments conferred by priests who had been consecrated by simoniacal or lying bishops. He also intervened on points of dogma, strongly condemning the theses of Berengar in April 1050 and the book on the Eucharist by Ratramme. Leo IX's travels and the effectiveness of the synods constituted a significant innovation. On the important issue of the election of bishops, he took several decisive actions: he reaffirmed the necessity for election by the clergy and the people, backed the elected bishops against the wishes of the king of France (Henry I), and forced simoniacs to yield or resign. The secondary consequences of simony would be the object of study and of violent attacks against Humbert of Moyenmoutier after the death of Leo IX.

In the course of his travels, Leo IX stayed in abbeys and gave them generous support. Within the empire, he sent forth-seven bulls to monasteries, including forty for Lotharingia (Lorraine) alone; he addressed seventeen to Burgundian abbeys and nearly seventy-two to Italian communities. He allowed that laymen could own churches, defended the monks against the bishops in Italy, confirmed property rights (these are the first pontifical confirmations of this type), and took many abbeys directly under his protection. He translated the relics of Rémy Reims in 1049, bishop Gerhard Toul, in 1050, bishop Wolfgang Ratisbonne, in 1052, which for many was the equivalent of CANONIZATION. His skills as a negotiator, already tested when he was the bishop of Toul, were also put to work in Lorraine, where he ended the rebellion of Duke Godfrey the Bearded against the emperor; in Reims, where he upheld the Truce of God; and in Moravia in 1052, in the Hungarian campaign of Henry III.

Leo IX was a decisive force in the reorganization of the CURIA, significant expanding the influence of the CARDINALS. He surrounded himself with a group of friends and advisers, some of whom had come from

Lotharingia (Lorraine) and shared his point of view: Halinard, archbishop of Lyon; Hugh of Salins, archbishop of Besançon; Hildebrand (the future GREGORY VII); Humbert, a monk from Moyenmoutier who became archbishop of Sicily and Cardinal of Silva Candida; Hugh Candidus, canon of Remiremont, who was cardinal-priest of St. Clement; Frederick of Ardenne, the archdeacon of Liège (the future STEPHEN IX); and Udon, bishop of Toul, beginning in February 1051. Humbert, Hugh, and Frederick were sent as legates to Spain and to Constantinople.

The CHANCERY had been progressively reorganized since the end of the 10th century. Leo IX turned its management over to Peter, then to Udon, and then to Frederick of Ardenne. Soon bulls took on a new solemn form, inspired by imperial diplomas: the first line in tall letters, written in ornate script, names and titles of witnesses and formulas of chancery, and then the date. To the monogrammatical *benevalete*, Leo IX added the *komma*, a sort of large period-comma, and, of special interest, the *rota*, a wheel that included a cross bearing the pope's name at its center and around it the pope's motto, which Leo IX always wrote in his own hand. Today it is seen as a symbol of Christ's mercy, redeeming the Earth (the wheel) with his Cross. Thus he gave the Curia added importance, which can be seen by the large number of bulls he sent out (there are about 180 of them).

Leo IX's pontificate was equally crucial to the relationship between Rome and Constantinople. The relations between the two Churches had become more and more tense. A letter, inspired by the patriarch Michael Cerularius to Leo of Achrida and sent to the bishop of Trani, contained violent words against hated practices of the Latin Church, especially the use of unleavened bread in the Eucharist. Leo IX, informed by Humbert of this letter, dictated a long memo of justification of the Roman Church but perhaps never sent it (end of 1053). A deferential letter from the patriarch led Leo to send a delegation of reconciliation consisting of Cardinal Humbert, and the librarian Frederick, the future Pope Stephen IX, in January 1054. The negotiations lasted a long time and ended brutally when Humbert laid a bull excommunicating the patriarch on the altar of the Hagia Sophia. By that time (July 1054), Leo IX was no longer alive. He can in no way be held responsible for the rupture that marked the end of a long quarrel, but due to his participation in the final dealings with the East, his name is most often linked with the beginning of this SCHISM.

Leo IX ended his pontificate amid political complications in southern Italy. The papacy had acquired some rights over Benevento; twice the pope had gone to southern Italy to hold synods and follow political developments there. Expansion by the NORMANS, which Byzantium was not able to control, worried him, and he asked Henry III for military support in 1053, meeting him in Pressburg (Slovakia). With several Swabian and Italian troops, the pope became involved in an expedition designed to liberate Benevento. He was not able to rendezvous with the Byzantine troops; the pontifical army was defeated and the pope was taken prisoner (Civitella, 18 June 1053). Leo IX had to undergo long negotiations and submit to the demands of his captors by granting them the conquered lands. He was not able to return to Rome until March of 1054. He died there on the following 19 April and was soon added to the litany of saints.

Michel Parisse

Bibliography

JW, 1, 529–49; 2, 709–10, 749.

Anselm, *Historia dedicationis ecclesiae sanct Remigli, PL*, 142, 1415–40.

Beumann, H. "Reformpäpste als Reichsbischöfe in der Zeit Heinrichs III: Ein Beitrag zur Geschichte des ottonisch-salischen Reichskirchensystems," *Festschrift Friedrich Hausmann*, ed. Ebner, H., Graz, 1977, 21–37.

Bloch, R. "Die Klosterpolitik Leos IX. in Deutschland, Burgund und Italien," *Archiv für Urkundenforschung*, 11 (1930), 176–257.

Bonizonis episcopi Sutrini liber ad amicum, MGH Libelli de lite, 1, 568–620.

Borgia, S. *Memorie istoriche di Benevento*, II, Rome, 1764.

Bröcking, W. *Die französische Politik Papst Leos IX: Ein Beitrag zur Geschichte des Papsttums im XI. Jahrhundert*, Stuttgart, *1872; and Die französische Politik Papst Leos IX.*, Stuttgart, 1889.

Brucker, P. P. *L'Alsace et l'Église au temps de S. Léon IX*, 2 vols., Paris, 1899.

Dalhaus, J. "Aufkommen und Bedeutung der Rota in den Urkunden des Papstes Leo IX.," *AHP*, 27 (1989), 7–84.

Desiderii Casinensis Dialogi, MGH SS, 30, 1143–46.

Garreau, A. *Léon IX, pape alsacien, réformateur de l'Église (1002–1054)*, Paris, 1965.

Goez, W. "Papa qui et episcopus. Zum Selbstverständnis des Reformpapsttums im 11. Jahrhundert," *AHP*, 8 (1970), 27–59.

Huyghebaert, N. "Saint Léon IX et la lutte contre la simonie dans le diocèse de Verdun," *Studi Gregoriani*, 1 (1947), 417–32.

Kehr, P. *Vier Kapitel aus der Geschichte Kaiser Heinrichs III.*, 1930 (*Abhandl. Akad. Wissensch., Phil hist. Klasse*, 3).

Krause, H. G. *Deutsches Archiv*, 32 (1976), 49–85.

Leonis Casinensis Chronicon, MGH SS, 7, 683–6.

Poncelet, E. "Vie et miracles du pape saint Léon IX," *Analecta Bollandiana*, 25, 258.

Santifaller, L. "Über die Neugestaltung der äusseren Form des Papstprivilegien unter Leo IX.," *Festschrift für H. Wiesflecker*, ed. A. Novotny and O. Pickl, Graz, 1973, 29–38.

Schieffer, R. "Leo IX," *LexMA*, 5 (1991), 1880–1.

Tritz, H. *Studi Gregoriani*, 4 (1952), 194–364.

Vita Leonis IX, ed. Watterich, 127–170, and *PL*, 143, 465–504.

Wolter, H. *Die Synoden im Reichsgebiet und in Reichsitalien von 916 bis 1056*, Paderborn, 1988.

LEO X. *Giovanni de' Medici (b. Florence, 11 December 1475–d. Rome, December 1521). Elected pope 9 March 1513, crowned 21 March. Buried at Santa Maria Sopra Minerva.*

Judgments made about this brilliant and ruinous pontificate were immediately contradictory and have varied little since then. Rarely has historiography been more subjective. On the one hand there are the historians who side with Sanuto, alive during the actual events, who like Pastor at the end of the 19th century saw Leo X as a lazy pleasure seeker, lacking in character and depth of mind, who understood nothing about the crisis of conscience that was beginning to shake the Christian world. On the other hand there are the scholars, most often Italians like Pennachini, Luzio, Nitti, Picotti, or more recently Berenci, who insist that, beneath this aristocratic indolence, there were strength and generosity, along with great political agility and skill. Each of these two visions has a solid foundation: a great lord raised amid luxury in all things—the material objects surrounding him and the refined culture that was taught to him—Giovanni de' Medici lacked neither perceptiveness nor true goodness, but used both with a certain remoteness rather like giving alms. He never was able to tell the difference, for example, between true poets and hacks, both of whom praised him, or to assess accurately a delicate political situation and determine what was just a temporary expedient or what was a long-term solution.

Leo X's reign, which began under favorable circumstances, took place without real difficulties. Francis I, victorious at Marignano, was easily handled and held in check thanks to the ruling on the painful question of the PRAGMATIC SANCTION. The council at the LATERAN ended after interminable sessions in a great triumph of pontifical power, but without finding any real solutions to any of the problems that were raised. The posting of Luther's theses was reduced to a mere distant phenomenon to be dealt with by excommunication, and the pretensions of Charles of Spain had been thwarted as much as possible without open conflict. Yet by the time Leo X died, the coffers of the Holy See, filled by JULIUS II, were empty, and the moral credit of the pontiff was equally ruined. However, viewing things in the best possible light, it can at least be said that during this very personal reign, full of events for which he always seemed to be able to find some sort of arrangement that suited himself and his family, Leo X was upset by only one catastrophe, the death of his favorite artist, Raphael.

The second son of Lorenzo the Magnificent and Clarice Orsini, young Giovanni received an education worthy of the Medicis, with Angelo Poliziano, Bernardo Michelozzo, Demetrius Chalcondyle, and Gregorio da Spoleto as his tutors. From infancy he was friends with his cousin Giulio, the future pope CLEMENT VII, and a young noble full of caustic wit, and Bernardo Dovizzi, later Cardinal Bibbiena. These two companions, whose characters were so different from his own, were true friends and almost brothers to him his entire life. At age eight he was named apostolic PROTONOTARY by SIXTUS IV; at thirteen he became a CARDINAL and left to study CANON LAW in Pisa, where he would become friends with the young Cesare Borgia. His father's death and the trouble stirred up by Savonarola's followers that resulted in the exile of the Medici family from Florence two years later forced the young man to take refuge at the court in Urbino, accompanied by his younger brother Giuliano and his cousin Giulio, and then to travel throughout Europe. Arrested in Rouen, he was expelled from France with no regard for his rank and dignity, and he returned to Rome in 1500 to live in the sumptuous Madama Palace, the Medici residence in the Eternal City. He spent a dozen or so years there until his elevation, an existence full of sophisticated pleasures, amassing, in particular, a magnificent collection of antiques. It was during this period that he acquired his attachment to poets and musicians, whom he would sometimes accompany himself, becoming accustomed to a classless association with real artists—and also hangers-on of all sorts, whom he continued to entertain after he became pontiff, at the expense of the Holy See. In this figure, whose taste remained that of a luxury-loving aristocrat, there is also evident a man with little real consistency in his ideas and no great vision. He allowed Raphael to sumptuously decorate the Stanza and the Loggia of the pontifical palaces and to arrange for the tapestries in the SISTINE CHAPEL, but he did not find the funds for, or give priority to, the great building project his predecessor had begun on ST. PETER'S BASILICA. When Bramante died in 1514, he gave Raphael and Sangallo the mission of continuing his work, without really giving them the material resources they needed. As for urban planning in the city of Rome, the pope was totally uninterested.

On 21 February 1513, Julius II died. Three weeks later, at the end of a CONCLAVE that was extremely brief, Cardinal de' Medici rose to the pontifical throne without any real opposition. By choosing this young thirty-eight-year-old lord who showed no emotion when viewing the votes, the SACRED COLLEGE hoped to achieve the double goals of placing on the throne of St. Peter a priest with pure morals, who would put an end to the scandals of the three preceding popes, and a person whose political and financial power—the Medicis had returned to Florence in 1512—would allow them to drive the Spanish and

French from Naples and Milan. His princely elegance, his attractiveness, and his magnificent lifestyle had seduced them.

In truth, the first acts of Leo X's pontificate were full of goodness and forgiveness. The "schismatic" cardinals were absolved and returned to their sees. The promotion of several men to cardinal, including his lifelong friend Bernardo Bibbiena, his two relatives Giulio de Medici and Innocenzo Cibo, as well as a compatriot, Lorenzo Pucci, strengthened the Florentine faction, while Louis XII was contacted to begin peace negotiations. The repugnance of Leo X to the French was notorious; however, he overcame it and was able to have the king ratify the canons of the Lateran council, whose eighth session opened on December 19. This was a diplomatic triumph, and ceremonies of obedience by various princes of Christendom took place in Rome with a pomp that anticipated a glorious pontificate.

A year and a half later, the victory of the new king of France at Marignano would upset the entire chessboard of Italian politics. It happened that Francis I needed the Holy See's help in dealing with the difficulties created within his kingdom by the application of the Pragmatic Sanction and the necessity for reforming the Church in France as quickly as possible, for it had almost been destroyed by the unending lawsuits that arose from the collation of benefices and from the election of bishops. Therefore, he accepted the proposed meeting with Leo X in Bologna in December 1515 to set up the framework for a concordat, to which the UNIVERSITY and the parlement in Paris were fiercely opposed a priori. The monarch and the pope worked in such close harmony that on 18 August of the following year, Leo X was able to sign the document, which was ratified six months later by the Lateran council, abolishing the Pragmatic Sanction. On 22 March 1518, after much hesitation, the French parlement, under threats of punishment and dissolution by Francis I, agreed to ratify the pontifical BULLS. With extreme dexterity, the pope had succeeded in maneuvering his way out of this very delicate situation with his prestige enhanced: the Pragmatic Sanction was ended, but the pontiff still was able to nominate candidates to a number of episcopal or abbatial sees by means of elections that were mere formalities. This total victory momentarily swept away the clouds that had gathered during the French presence in the north of Italy.

At the same time, using the pretext of the duke of Urbino's treason, Leo X sent his nephew Lorenzo to conquer the duchy, which was taken over bloodlessly in August 1516. Unfortunately, this devious maneuver was as poorly received by public opinion as it was by the Sacred College, where several members plotted a conspiracy, supported by Francesco Maria Della Rovere and Spain. It failed, and Cardinal Petrucci, the leader, was put to death, Cardinals Sauli and Riario were thrown in prison and

then freed, after the payment of an enormous sum, but the pope's reputation for goodness did not survive these events. Probably worried due to an imbalance in the Sacred College after all these troubles, Leo X decided to promote thirty-one new cardinals, an exorbitant number never seen before. Rome, Milan, Venice, Naples, France, Spain and, of course, Florence found they had new representatives of whom few were worthy of wearing the purple. Whereas the three previous promotions had given the rank of cardinal to eminent men like Thomas Wolsey, Adrien Gouffier de Boissy, Antoine Du Prat, and the most modestly qualified Jacques de Croÿ, the nominations of 1 July 1517, other than those of Thomas Cajetan and Giles of Viterbo (Canisius), were totally scandalous: Francesco Conti, Andrea della Valle, Pompeo Colonna, Silvio Passerini, Franciotto Orsini, Alessandro Cesarini, Paolo Cesi were named in an attempt to reconcile the irreconcilable clans of the Roman feudal system; Nicolo Pandolfini, Lorenzo Campeggi, Ferdinando Ponzetti, Lodovico de' Rossi, Francesco de' Medicis, Giovanni Salviati, Nicolo Ridolfi, and Ercole Rangoni were mostly from Florence and were related to the Medicis; Scaramuzio and Agostino Trivulzio for Milan, Giovanni Pallavicini and Bonifacio Ferreri for Genoa, Giovanni Piccolomini and Raffaello Petrucci for Siena, and Francesco Pisani for Venice presented a shocking contrast to the few foreign nominees like Adrian Florensz (the future HADRIAN VI), Raymond de Vich, Louis de Vendôme, and Alfonso of Portugal. The following year, the pope decided, for the sake of some balance, to name Albrecht of Brandeburg, Jean of Lorraine, and Erard de La Marck, three subjects of Emperor Maximilian.

From an assembly traditionally made up of twenty-four members, the Sacred College became a true court whose members had nothing ecclesiastical about them except their rank and titles. The pope himself lived in opulence and luxury, surrounded by 683 servants from the archbishop of the chapel to the elephant keeper, who cost the Holy See 100,000 ducats per year. For weeks, the pope would leave to go hunting, accompanied by 200 knights and the more vigorous of the cardinals. He organized concerts and theatrical shows written by his friends Bibbiena and Ariosto. To support such prodigious spending, they had to find expedient solutions expanding the rights of chancery and selling court positions and even the title of CARDINAL, as Sanuto's *Journal* suggests. A storm cloud of debt collectors, whose methods were as reprehensible as they were brutal, descended upon Christendoms, ultimately ruining the reputation of the pope and the entire papacy in the eyes of the faithful. Despite repeated warnings, especially from the young Jerome Aleander, Leo X, lost in a dream of elegance and pomp, changed nothing about his way of living, seeing the posting of Luther's theses at Wittenberg on 31 October 1517 as only a slight mental aberration that could be corrected by a simple excommunication of the guilty party. Opportunely seconded by Henry VIII, who had published a pamphlet against Luther, the pope granted him the right to the GOLDEN ROSE and the title of "*Defensor fidei*," and washed his hands of the problem.

The Lateran council's eleventh and twelfth sessions, which opened in December 1516 and March 1517, consecrated the Holy See's supremacy over metropolitan churches without dealing with any internal problems. The Pragmatic Sanction was abolished, with the regulars again under the control of diocesan clergy, in theory at least, and everyone was urged to display modesty, humility, and purity of morals. Once again the accommodating but indifferent temperament of Leo X had found a way to seemingly deal with things and achieve momentary calm, worrying little about the poisonous inheritance he was leaving for his successors. His basically good intentions were shown by the organization of an illusory CRUSADE. A league named the Brotherhood of the Holy Crusade was instituted for this purpose: it evaluated the cost and methods for this undertaking that no Christian prince really wanted, and mostly served as a pretext for levying new taxes. The conflict between Francis I and Charles V over the succession of Maximilian, beginning in 1519, did not help the situation, and the TURKS, already at Hungary's borders, made several raids without encountering any opposition in Calabria, Campania, and even at the mouth of the Tiber. It took the fall of Rhodes, reconquered five years later, and Vienna, besieged in 1529, for Christendom to finally take action.

At the time, Leo X had to maintain an equilibrium between the two candidates for the iron crown, to keep both of them from taking over Italy and usurping papal power. The pressures increased, especially from Charles of Spain, who did not hesitate to use double blackmail by threatening to reignite the revolt in Tuscany by using the Petrucci, lords of Siena, and threatening at the same time to form a coalition of Roman barons, especially the Colonna then in possession of the kingdom of Naples. During the same period, the pope's favorite nephew, the same Lorenzo who had helped him take over the duchy of Urbino in 1516, died of phthisis, leaving only a daughter, Catherine; his other nephew, Giuliano, whom Leo X hoped to place on the throne of Naples, also died, and he refused to risk the difficult task of reestablishing the political hegemony of the Medicis for Giuliano's son Ippolito, whose disgraceful tendencies had shown themselves quite early in life. There was only one way left open to him, that of annexing the rapid, abusive conquests of 1516 to the Patrimony of the Holy See. Urbino, Parma, Piacenza, and Reggio "belonged no more to the house of the Medici but only to the house of God," as the pope declared in CONSISTORY. This was not done with ease: Reggio and Modena belonged to the duke of Ferrara and were defended by the

fearsome Baglioni of Perugia, whom the pope had coldly decapitated, while hanging three feudal lords of lesser rank as an example. Milan, which had revolted against the government of Lautrec, to whom the regent Louise of Savoy refused to send any subsidy, opened its gates to Francesco Sforza, the son of Ludovico il Moro, accompanied by the troops of the marquis of Pescara. Once again, order reigned in the PAPAL STATES, and the French threat was staved; once again the pontiff had been able to get himself out of a disastrous situation, adroitly wavering between the two candidates for emperor and reestablishing the power, if not of the Medicis, at least of the Holy See, forming the basis of a policy called "Freedom for Italy" that HADRIAN VI and CLEMENT VII would follow, with less luck and skill.

At the end of this reign, when the worst had been avoided, only two periods of mourning would darken the atmosphere and strike the pope terribly hard, to the point of bringing to tears this man famous for his impassivity: the double blow of Leonardo da Vinci's death at Amboise and that of Raphael in Rome. The task of finishing the decorations of the Stanza was handed over to Giulio Romano and Luca Penni, while the reform of the university of Rome that Erasmus had advised in 1513 was carried out. Leo X also took it upon himself to restore his father's library, which had been pillaged by the followers of Savonarola: his cousin Clement VII would finish this project by appointing Michelangelo to supervise the building of the Lawrentan. Weariness and illness—a poorly cared-for fistula—caused the pope's death on 1 December 1521. For this man revered since childhood, who had received so many mostly obsequious dedications and homages, there was only a simple tomb in Santa Maria Sopra Minerva, without any inscription.

François Fossier

Bibliography

Berence, F. *Les Papes de la Renaissance*, Paris, 1966.

Conforti, C. *Leone X e il suo secolo*, Parma, 1896.

D'Amico, J. F. *Renaissance Humanism in Papal Rome: Humanists and Churchmen on the Eve of the Reformation*, Baltimore, 1983.

De Grassi, P. *Diarium*, ed. Doellinger, Vienna, 1882.

Ferrajoli, G. "La congiura contro Leone X," *Misc. della Soc. romana di stor. patria*, 1919, 35–46.

Gnoli, D. "Il Secolo di Leone X," *Rivista ital.*, 1 (1897), 74–93; 2 (1898), 625–50; *La Roma di Leone X*, Milan, 1938.

Guicciardini, F. *La Storia d'Italia . . .* ed. C. Paganiga, Bari, 1967.

Jovius, P. *Vita Leonis X et Adriani VI*, Florence, 1548–51.

Kolsky, S. "Culture and Politics in Renaissance Rome: Marco Antonio Alteris Roman Weddings," *Renaissance Quarterly* 40 (1987), 49–90.

Mollat, G. "Léon X," *DTC*, 9 (1926), 329–32.

Nitti, F. *Leone X e la sua politica*, Florence, 1892.

Picotti, G. B. *La Giovinezza di Leone X*, Milan, 1928.

Rodocanachi, E. *Le Pontificat de León X*, Paris, 1930.

Roscoe, G. *Vita e pontificato di Leone X . . .*, 1816, 12 vols.

Sanuto, M. *I Diarii*, Venice, 1878–1903.

Winspeare, F. *La congiura dei cardinali contra Leone X*, Florence, 1957.

LEO XI. *Alessandro de' Medici (b. Florence, 2 June 1536–d. Rome, 27 April 1605). Elected pope 1 April 1605, crowned 10 April. Buried at St. Peter's in Rome.*

From a collateral branch of the famous Florentine family, he was the son of Ottaviano de' Medici and Francesca Salviati. On his mother's side, he was the great-nephew of Pope LEO X and the second cousin of the grand duke of Tuscany Cosimo I. In 1560, he met Philip Neri, the founder of the Oratory; they became friends and under Neri's influence he was ordained as a priest on 22 July 1567. In 1569, Cosimo I named him as his ambassador to Rome, a position he fulfilled for fifteen years while ascending the ranks of the ecclesiastical hierarchy: made bishop of Pistoia on 9 March 1573, then archbishop of Florence on 15 January 1574, he was created cardinal by GREGORY XIII on 12 December 1583 and thereafter had himself called "the cardinal of Florence."

Held in Rome by his job as ambassador, this pious reformist bishop still exercised a remarkable pastoral influence in his successive dioceses by having his high-ranking vicars apply the Tridentine decrees. In 1575, he laid the first stone of the Chiesa Nuova in Rome. In May 1584, he finally made his entry into Florence, took the government of the diocese in hand, and called a SYNOD there in 1589. A trusted advisor to CLEMENT VIII, he was one of those who motivated him to lift the censures from the king of France, Henry IV, that had been pronounced against him by SIXTUS V in 1585. His absolution was solemnly pronounced on 17 September 1595. To seal this reconciliation, reorganize the wounded Church in France, divided by the troubles of the League, and introduce pontifical mediation between Henry IV and Philip II of Spain who were then at war, Clement VIII named the cardinal of Florence as his LEGATE *a latere* to France on 3 April 1596. Cardinal Alessandro left Rome on April 10, was welcomed by Henry IV in person at Montlhéry on 19 July, and received the act of ratification of his absolution from him on 19 September. The cardinal remained in France for more than two years, performing his mission of peace with zeal. He endeavored to restore religious life and ecclesiastical discipline, obtained spectacular conversions, presided over negotiations that ended on 2 May 1598 with the treaty of Vervins, but was not able to stop the promulgation of the Edict of Nantes. After having taken leave of Henri IV in early September 1598, he rejoined the pontifical court at Ferrara on 10 November. He became bishop of Albano (30 August 1600), and then of Palestrina (17 June 1602).

In the CONCLAVE that opened after the death of Clement VIII, Cardinal Alessandro was one of the *papabili* supported by the French delegates. His election to the throne, on 1 April 1605, despite the opposition of Spain, was a triumph for French diplomacy, especially because of the family ties that linked him to Queen Marie de Medicis. But he passed away due to pleurisy after a brief pontificate of only twenty-seven days, *ad summam Ecclesiae Dei foelicitatem ostensus magis quam datus*, as the inscription on the plaque on his TOMB erected by the Algardi in ST. PETER'S in Rome reminds us.

Bernard Barbiche

Bibliography

Barbiche, B., and S. "Un évêque italien de la réforme catholique légat en France sous Henri IV: le cardinal de Florence (1596–1598)," *RHEF*, 75 (1989), 45–59.

D'Addario, A. "Aspetti del governo spirituale del cardinale Alessandro de' Medici," *Aspetti della Controriforma a Firenze*, Rome, 1972 (*Publicazioni degli archivi di Stato, 77*), 243–327.

Jaitner, K. *Die Hauptinstruktionen Clemens' VIII. für die Nuntien und Legaten an den europäischen Fürstenhöfen, 1592–1605*, Tubingen, 1984 (*Instructiones pontificum Romanorum*), CCXXII–CCXXIV, 450–69.

Pastor, 25.

Ritter, R. *Lettres du cardinal de Florence sur Henry IV et sur la France (1596–1598)*, Paris, 1955.

LEO XII. *Annibale Della Genga (b. Genga, 22 August 1760–d. Rome, 10 February 1829). Elected pope 18 September 1823, crowned October 5. Buried in St. Peter's in Rome.*

The reign of Leo XII (five years and four months) probably does not occupy the position in Church history that it deserves: a pontificate of division, sometimes violent, having inherited from CARDINAL Consalvi the *politicante* diplomacy of the second half of the 18th century and the Napoleonic period. Leo XII steered the papacy in a new direction, one of inflexibility based upon affirmation and intensification of the notion of Church tradition. With Leo XII, between Lamennais and Metternich (to reuse the terms of R. Colapietra's dilemma), the Church of Rome suddenly favored the boldness of the former, without knowing how, or being able to, or perhaps even wanting to, renounce protection of the latter. Few portions of the early career of this future pope of the Restoration give us hints of his later rigidity.

The sixth child of Count Ilario and Countess Maria Luigia Periberti di Fabriano, Annibale Della Genga belonged to a family from Umbria's ancient feudal nobility, patricians in the city of Spoleto, with a Curia tradition. On his father's side he had distant relatives who included a cardinal and a prelate in the CURIA; on his mother's side, a bishop of Assisi. A younger son of a noble family, he was thus promised early to the Church. Entering the school at Campana d'Osino at age thirteen, by age eighteen he continued on to the Collegio Piceno of Rome, which took ecclesiastical students from the Marches. Ordained a priest at age twenty-three, in June 1783, he pursued his studies from 1783 to 1790 at the Academy for Ecclesiastical Nobles, reorganized in 1775 by PIUS VI to train the future prelates of the Curia. His predecessors there included the future cardinals Consalvi and Severoli, and Pacca was one of his fellow students. He won favor with Pius VI, who liked his elegant manners and his wit, and soon promoted him. From January 1790, he was a secret CHAMBERLAIN, a member of the pontiff's private secretariat. He gave the Latin funeral oration for Emperor Joseph II on 25 August 1790, and then was made a canon of ST. PETER's.

The last pontiff of the ancien régime assigned the "*carissimo, dilettissimo et amatissimo*" Della Genga to a diplomatic career. On 21 January 1794, he was promoted, at age thirty-three, to archbishop of Tyre *in partibus* and on March 14th, named NUNCIO to Cologne, where he took over from Pacca. But the French occupation of the left bank of the Rhine forced him to set up residence in Bavaria, first at Augsburg, then at Munich. For eight difficult years that also led him to Austria and Saxony, he tried with constancy and determination to safeguard the interests of the HOLY SEE in the complex maze of German politics and to face the after-effects of the incessant wars of the REVOLUTION in the territories of the empire, and the collapse and secularization of ecclesiastical principalities. In 1799, he went to see Pius VI in Florence to urge him, in vain, to march to the north.

The CONCLAVE of Venice disappointed him: he would have liked to have seen the unyielding Cardinal Leonardo Antonelli elected rather than the *politicante* Chiaramonti, PIUS VII.

But the "nuncio of Germany," though a friend of ladies and conversation and passionate about hunting, moved the religious and ecclesiastical reform of the Church in Germany to the forefront of his agenda, and worried less about the ruptures of political balance in the empire. Recalled to Rome, Della Genga left his post in December 1802 after refusing a diplomatic mission to St. Petersburg, in the throes of an attack of deep depression that he often experienced. Back in Rome, he was unemployed for more than two years. The cardinal secretary of state Consalvi was not fond of him: in addition to incompatibility of character and temperament, they were also separated by Della Genga's attachment to the memory of Pius VI and the ancien regime, allegiance to the ministry (while Consalvi remained a DEACON) and the pastoral

level, and differences in diplomatic style. However, Della Genga's knowledge of German politics earned him a second nomination on 23 September 1805, as special nuncio to the imperial legislature at Ratisbon, which he reached belatedly, due to war, on 16 June 1806, the day after the proclamation of the German Confederation (1 August), which sanctioned the disappearance of the Germanic Holy Roman Empire. Instead of passing a general CONCORDAT with the confederation as Napoleon wanted, the nuncio tried in vain to make individual concordats with Bavaria and Wurtemberg that would favor Rome. Called to assist the cardinal of Bayane in negotiations with the emperor, he met him in Paris on 18 November 1807 but encountered French resistance to the Continental System; he received his passports 10 January 1808 and returned to Rome, which was occupied by the troops of General Miollis on 2 February. For the next six years he withdrew to the abbey of Monticelli in Umbria sick and discouraged, preparing for death.

In spring 1814 the third episode of the future pope's diplomatic career took place. It was as brief as it was disappointing. Della Genga, who hastened to be with Pius VII, who had been imprisoned by Napoleon, (rejoining him at Cesena on or before 29 April), was one of the first prelates and the very first diplomat to approach the pontiff. Soon sent to Paris as temporary nuncio to Louis XVIII, who had been restored to the throne, on 30 April he was provided with instructions (drawn up with the help of the pope's *zelante* entourage, the prelates Sala, Rivarola, and Morozzo) that advocated the abolition of the concordat of 1801 and the associated articles, the suppression of the civil code of law and divorce, and the reestablishment of the former ecclesiastical discipline, and also sought the restitution of Avignon and the Venaissin county, and the support of France for the restitution of the Papal States, entreating the king not to sign an overly liberal constitution.

Leaving from Cesena on 7 May, Della Genga traveled in short stretches and did not arrive in Paris until twenty-two days later, on 29 May. In the meantime, the king had already set up the terms of the constitutional charter, published on 4 June, and the first treaty of Paris, signed by the Allies on 30 May, had annexed Avignon and the county to France, leaving the legations to Austria, and, in essence, the nobility to Murat. The nuncio barely had time to obtain his first royal audience when he was joined in Paris on 2 June by Cardinal Consalvi, who had been named secretary of state on 17 May and had left from Foligno at full gallop on 20 May, with plenary powers and more prudent instructions to negotiate a new concordat while first and last reserving power for the Holy See. Consalvi had little regard for Della Genga: "They should send him back to minimize the expense, since he's good for nothing"—but his letters remained courteous, it was the *zelante* Cardinal pro-secretary

Pacca who, from Rome, judged Della Genga "liquidated." Thus, after several months in a row with no position, the nuncio left Paris, sick and defeated; he returned to Rome on 10 December, and quickly went back to his solitude at Monticelli. Still, Della Genga found he was the first person named in the promotion of twenty-one cardinals created by Pius VII during the CONSISTORY of 8 March 1816. However, he was dismissed from Rome the very same day and made bishop of Senigaglia, in the Marches. Several months later, he handed in his resignation, for reasons of health (which Pope Pius VII accepted on 18 September) and retired to his property of Poreta, near Spoleto, where he regained his health little by little. Called back to the side of Pius VII, he was made, successively, pro-prefect of the Congregation of Ecclesiastical Immunity (9 May 1820) and then cardinal vicar of Rome (12 May 1820) and archpriest of the basilica of ST. MARY MAJOR (10 February 1821). Della Genga, a rather tall man with a profound expression and an imposing manner, emaciated by illness (a hemorrhoidal condition that weakened him for long periods), had matured through all his difficulties and periods of solitary meditation. Effectively the bishop of Rome, he showed a pastoral zeal that was narrow-minded and inflexible, assessing the spiritual problems of the city he wanted to transform into a "holy city," supporting his parish clergy, for whom he obtained, with great difficulty, places as consultants to the Curia.

The twenty-five-day-long conclave that began after Pius VII's death on 10 August 1823 put him on the side of the *zelante* faction, the group of the "ardent ones,"—called, ironically, "the party of the saints," by Stendhal and the "Italian party," by the Duke of Laval, the French ambassador, who were dedicated to the defense of the freedoms of the Church in contrast to state control. Metternich, who favored Consalvi, tried to unite a "party of the Crowns" (Austria, France, Spain, Naples, Piedmont, Bavaria, and the cardinals) and put together a minority block (with more than one-third of the votes) within the conclave. The voices of the *zelante* faction also united, after a short period of observation, in favor of Cardinal Severoli, bishop of VITERBO and former nuncio to Vienna from 1801 to 1817, whose opposition to the principles of JOSEPHISM and manifest hostility toward the policies of Consalvi could only displease the court of Austria. On the evening of September 21, when Severoli was about to attain the two-thirds majority required for election, an EXCLUSION was pronounced in his case through the intermediary of Cardinal Albani. Severoli then designated Cardinal Della Genga to his followers as a replacement. The reluctance of France to take on "the quarrels of Austria," and the determination and growing exasperation of the *zelante* party did the rest. On the morning of 28 September 1823, Annibale Della Genga was elected pope, receiving 34 out of 49 votes. The newly elected pope, after having tried to refuse the choice of the conclave by

reason of his health, took the name of Leo, which no pontiff had taken since 1605, in memory of LEO I the Great.

First considered lost amid the responsibilities of the papacy, Leo XII, who had called the holy bishop of Macerati, Vincenzo Maria Strambi, to be with him, slowly reestablished himself; symbolically he left the QUIRINAL for the Vatican, where the popes had ceased to live, and progressively imposed his authority. The very day of his election, he replaced Cardinal Consalvi with the venerable cardinal Della Somaglia (aged 79), as SECRETARY OF STATE preserving his independence from the start. Though the influence of Cardinal Severoli, who had made him pope, was strong until his death in September 1824, the *zelanti* cardinals (Pacca, De Gregorio, Galleffi, Rivarola, Cavalchini) who surrounded him at first, gradually, lost their influence. Overcoming the past and the ill will of his party, Leo XII called Consalvi back and gave him his political testament: "We will work together often; it is only that today we must not die," said the pope to him, naming him Prefect of PROPAGANDA on 13 January; but the cardinal died on 24 January.

Early on, Leo XII visited the poor cloistered at the monastery of Regina Coeli and at the mendicants' station at the baths of Diocletian. He celebrated the union of the throne and the altar with a *Te Deum* in honor of the victory of the French army against the liberals of Spain and placed an apostolic administrator in the diocese of Lyon to take the place of Cardinal Fesch. On 31 March 1824, he issued an unpopular edict restricting the activity of Roman night life.

On 3 May 1824, Leo XII published his first ENCYCLICAL, *Ubi primum*. Under the influence of Lamennais (welcomed at Rome with the utmost deference in the summer of 1824), the pope denounced "the system of indifference" that threatened Catholicism and expressed his unshakable conviction that the Church's mission was that of salvation, whose tradition and authority he reiterated forcefully. "Do not lose courage," he wrote. "We have certain prophecies, and when writing to you, we speak of the wisdom of the flawless past, not the wisdom of this century; of this wisdom that makes known to us, as we take it on faith, that there is but one single God, one faith, one baptism; and that there is no other name given to men on earth to bring about their own salvation, except that of Jesus Christ of Nazareth; which makes us teach that outside the Church there is no salvation." He called once again for a plan for religious restoration, founded on the union of the throne and the altar—"the secular princes," he wrote, "defend their own cause by defending that of the authority of the Church"—and on the authority of the Holy See—"in your setbacks, your doubts, and all your needs, resort to the Apostolic See: for God, according to St. Augustine, has placed the doctrine of truth in the see of unity." This search by the

Church for a more secure visibility took shape symbolically and practically in the renewal of the tradition of the HOLY YEAR. The BULL *Quod hoc ineunte saeculo* (24 May 1824), bearing the motto of his pontificate, *omnia in Christo instaurare*, "to restore everything in Jesus Christ" (Eph. 1:10), invited the faithful from "all parts of the world" to flock to Rome, to "the see of St. Peter," from which springs "the most abundant aids of reconciliation and of grace for salvation," and to seize "the lucky chance to work to restore everything through Jesus Christ by the beneficent expiation of all Christian people." Despite the obvious ill will of "Christian princes," the poverty of the papacy, and the lingering attacks of the Enlightenment, the Holy Year brought together 120,000 to 150,000 pilgrims in Rome in 1825. Over 90,000 were lodged at the hospice of the Trinity-of-Pilgrims: fewer than a thousand foreigners (two-thirds of them German or Swiss), and a huge majority of inhabitants of central Italy (Latium, Umbria, Abruzzi, Molise, the Marches, and southern Tuscany), who connected their pilgrimage to the gesture of reconciliation, which the pope extended the following year, in the form of a jubilee, to all Catholics.

In Rome and within the borders of the Papal States, the religious restoration took on the feeling of an essentially futile reactionary plan to return to the ancien regime. The reform of public administration and judicial procedure between 5 October 1824 and 21 December 1827 reversed the Consalvian reforms: restoration and extension of episcopal jurisdiction, reestablishment of the legal procedures of the ancien regime, protection of trusts, division of communal councils into two classes, noble and middle class. At the same time, the pope instituted a decrease of about one-fourth in fiscal levies and a congregation to revise the accounts (December 1828) in an attempt to contain expenses for the feeble Papal States. Secondary education was reorganized by putting into place a congregation on education (August 1824), and the ROMAN COLLEGE was returned to the Jesuits in September. A tentative and inefficient law tried to establish a "holy city" in Rome, whose better-provided-for parishes were reduced in number in November 1824, with a weighty and conservative moral order on pastimes, morals, and even dress. An edict on 20 November 1826, sent the Jews of Rome back to their *ghetto*. The pope took more energetic measures to control the widespread thievery in southern Latium: after the failure of the impractical measures of the *zelante* Cardinal Pallotta (May–June 1824), the rigorous policy of the delegate Benvenuti ended with the destruction of the main bands in the fall of 1825. A resolute battle began against liberal forces, especially in the Romagna: apostolic letters on 13 March 1825 renewed condemnations of the Freemasons and the *carbonari*; an unpopular vigilante commission was formed on 27 February 1826 to investigate the employees of the pontifical administration. The confrontation took a bloody turn: in Rome, two *carbonari*, Targhini and Montanari, were executed 23 November 1825, during the holy year, for attempted assassination within their own organization. The *zelante* Cardinal Rivarola, sent to the Romagna with full powers, after three months condemned 513 people on 31 August 1825. He was the victim of an assassination attempt 23 July 1826, after which the Invernizzi commission executed 5 people at Ravenna; 3 *carbonari* met the same fate in May 1828. The narrow-mindedness and restrictions of the *zelante* project threw the pope's government into an impasse created by an unrealistic restoration attempted through inept and despised repression.

It was in the domain of ecclesiastical policies (under the direction of Cardinal Della Somaglia until June 1828, then of the younger and more political Cardinal Bernetti) that Leo XII had the most substantive results. Alternating firmness and flexibility, trying to balance pastoral concern with unbending principles, worrying over new religious freedoms and maintaining a theological policy based on the notion of "Christian princes," pontifical diplomacy looked everywhere to consolidate the legal status of the Church as well as Church discipline. France's politics were dominated by the ecclesiastic-political quarrels of the Restoration. Under the influence of his unbending advisers (the *zelante* Marchetti and the Mennasian Ventura), Leo XII seemed at first to approve of the offensive led by Lamennais against royal GALLICANISM, but a change was seen in summer 1826 when Marchetti was dismissed. The Four Articles of 1682 were not officially censured, and the pope took a moderate line with the French episcopate during the crisis that arose due to the June 1828 ordinances on the JESUIT colleges and junior seminaries. Relations with Spain became difficult because of the pope's wish to reorganize the Church in the former colonies of the Americas that had rebelled and gained their freedom, while still keeping King Ferdinand content. A MISSION composed of Monsignor Muzi and young Mastai, the future PIUS IX, was sent to Chile in 1823, and a second one to Colombia; an autonomous ecclesiastical hierarchy was put in place in Colombia in 1827, and another in Brazil; new apostolic vicariates were created everywhere in the Americas. In the kingdom of Holland, to which Catholic Belgium had been reattached in 1814, the battle engaged by the episcopate against the state's creation of the college of philosophy of Louvain for training priests gave way to an attempt at conciliation: negotiations conducted by Cardinal Cappellari, the future GREGORY XVI, led to the signing of the short-lived concordat of 18 June 1827 and the formation of a new district of dioceses in Belgium and in Holland.

In Germany as in Switzerland, Rome tried to reorganize religious life using a structure of concordats and accords settled with great effort by Cardinal Consalvi with the princes or the cantons. Leo XII proceeded, little by little, to the division of DIOCESES (such as Hildesheim and Osnabruck to Hanover) and to the installation of bishops, cathedral chapters, and seminaries and protected the endowments of the clergy. But it was in England that pontifical diplomacy achieved its most splendid success: trying to establish relations, through Cardinal Consalvi, with the court and a portion of the British aristocracy on one hand, and the encouragement given to the campaign in Ireland beginning in 1825, led by O'Connell through the Catholic Association, on the other hand, led finally to the vote on the bill of emancipation of the Catholics that was approved by King George IV on 13 April 1829.

Leo XII had died two months earlier on 10 February, without having seen his work completed. The previous October, Chateaubriand had traveled to Rome to offer his respects to this "prince of great stature with a look at once serene and sad, dressed in a simple white cassock [who] stood in an almost unfurnished, shabby room [. . .] knew he was very sick and saw his decline with a resignation that was partially Christian joy." The "pontiff whose memory will never cease to be venerable and cherished by us," as Lamennais wrote in 1836 in the *Affaires de Rome*, passed away to relative indifference, which history has maintained: the last pope of the ancien regime, prisoner of an unshakable attachment to the old order of things and to a reactionary plan to reestablish the temporal Papal States and a holy city that went against all the wishes of the people and of the century. It was he, however, who caused the Catholic Church of the 19th century to begin the journey toward an uncompromising restoration of her discipline and traditions.

Philippe Boutry

Bibliography

Artaud De Montor, A. *Histoire du pape Léon XII*, Paris, 1843, 2 vols.

Colapietra, F. *La Chiesa tra Lamennais e Metternich: Il pontificato di Leone XII,* Brescia, 1963; "Il diario Brunelli del coclave del 1823," *Archivio storico italiano*, 120 (1962), 76–146; and *La formazione diplomatica di Leone XII*, Rome, 1966.

Daly, G. "Catholicism and Modernity," *Journal of the American Academy of Religion* 53 no. 4 (1985), 773–96.

Leflon, J. "Le pontificat de Léon XII," *La Crise révolutionnaire 1789–1846*, Paris, 1949, 379–408.

Schmidlin, I. *Histoire des papes de l'époque contemporaine*, 1, 2; *Léon XII, Pie VIII et Grégoire XVI (1823-1846)*, 1938–40, Paris, 1–137.

Terlinden, C. "Le conclave de Léon XII (2–28 septembre, 1823)," *RHE*, XIV, 1913.

Ugolini, P. "La Politica estera del Card. Tommaso Bernetti Segretario di Stato di Leone XII (1828–1829)," *ASR*, 112 (1969), 213–320.

LEO XIII. *Giacchino Pecci (b. Carpineto, diocese of Anagni, 1810–d. Rome, 20 July 1903). Elected pope 20 February 1878, consecrated March 3. Buried in St. Peter's in Rome.*

Leo XIII has gained a reputation unique in history: as the one pope of the 19th century who tried to understand his times and to use the pontifical MINISTRY less for pronouncing ANATHEMA than for defining the role of the Church in making irreversible changes. His pontificate cannot be summed up as simply the inverse to that of PIUS IX (1846–78); yet the juxtaposition of two such different temperaments and contrasting modes of conduct created the feeling that the Church was suddenly going from resistance to movement. Leo XIII's genius lay in a subtle alloy of flexibility and obduracy. He was the pope of the "hypothesis." Favored by the moderates and in particular by the French at the conclave, CARDINAL Pecci, CAMERLENGO since 1877, was elected in the third ballot. He was not a well-known figure in Roman circles.

Born in 1810, the sixth child of a prominent provincial family from Latium, Vincenzo Gioacchino Pecci entered the Roman college of the ACADEMY of Nobles and was ordained a priest in 1837. A young cleric in the household of GREGORY XVI (1831–46), he was careful, as he should have been, to "*fare una carriera*" and was put to the test in 1838 when nominated as delegate to Benevento, and then in 1841 to Perugia. In the exercise of sensitive administrative and judiciary functions in situations where liberal opinions were stifled by the *zelante* party, known as the Intransigents, Joachim Pecci succeeded in accomplishing his tasks while demonstrating the human qualities that earned him rare appreciation. His flair for diplomacy found a wider outlet in his position as NUNCIO to Brussels, where he was sent in 1842. In a young state led by a Protestant monarch, where liberals and Catholics had fought hand-in-hand for their freedom and together had drafted a constitution with no privileges for the Catholic Church, which Gregory XVI had long tried to ignore, the nuncio Pecci managed to gain credence with the king and affirm the authority of Rome. Still, his tact was unable to head off a conflict on the question of education, and he was recalled at the request of the king. The pope then appointed him bishop of Perugia. The administrator from Umbria had returned as a pastor. That same year, Pius IX (1846–78) succeeded Gregory XVI, to the joy of the liberals, who were nevertheless soon disappointed. Monsignor Pecci made his way through a tormented pontificate without changing. He was created a cardinal in 1853, but he never found favor with Pius IX or his entourage. Suspected of liberalism by the pope, he himself had certain reservations about the openly opinionated behavior of Pius IX. He preferred to remain silent at the Vatican I Council (1869–70). But the thirty-two years he spent at the see of Perugia were a time of maturation through reading and meditation, and the gradual refining of a personal point of view.

Cardinal Pecci had acquired, during his nunciature in Belgium, a certain knowledge of parliamentary and industrial Europe, through travels to Cologne, Paris, and London. Thus he had a sense of contemporary realities different from that of Pius IX, an emotional and pious cleric from an Italy that was still both rural and feudal. Cardinal Pecci was not a liberal. But his pastoral letters revealed, more and more, original concepts for his time that without going in the direction that Pius IX resisted with such stiffness and intolerance, tried to discern which positions the Church should take a stand on to confront the times. In 1864, the year of the *Syllabus*, Cardinal Pecci recognized that the defining characteristic of the times was "the separation of the two societies, civil and religious, with the religious being subordinate to the civil." He felt that it was not enough for the Church to continue to assert itself merely by rejection. His lucidity regarding his weaknesses and confidence in his strengths was balanced by a capacity for sympathy capable of creating the change everyone was waiting for when Pius IX died.

The most spectacular and rapid results of this change appeared in the diplomatic area. Since the taking of Rome in 1870, public opinion had been persuaded that the papacy had lost its authority in the material world and that it could only wield spiritual force. Leo XIII shows that the papacy did not need a state in order to exercise power. He refused to play the part of a martyr outside Italy, as Pius IX had, and compensated for his besieged position in the Vatican by acquiring a powerful diplomatic position in relations with other states. He drew from the huge resources of the Roman centralization that his predecessor had brought to its ultimate form. The nuncios represented an important intermediary between the sovereign pontiff and the public powers, the hierarchy, and the faithful. Through the channel of their influence, Leo XIII reached out to the minds and wills of Catholics and did not hesitate to sacrifice the Zentrum at the end of the *KULTURKAMPF* in Germany, to stop Albert de Mun in France from founding a Catholic party in 1885, or to replace bishops posing difficulties to the authorities, such as Bishop Mermillod.

This willingness to compromise extended past the narrow boundaries of Europe west of the Elbe. He looked for an opening into the Slavic world by sending a representative to the coronation of Alexander III in 1882 and by showing interest in the Christian churches of the EAST (ENCYCLICAL *Orientalium Dignitas*, 1894). Great Britain was honored by the elevation to cardinal of Henry Edward Manning in 1879, and a reconciliation was effected with the Anglican church in the years 1893–96 under the impetus of Lord Halifax and the abbé Portal, who attempted to resolve the question of ordinations; even

though this effort met with failure, Leo XIII confirmed their canonical invalidity in the encyclical *Apostolicae curae* on 16 September 1896. Relations of high mutual esteem were also established with the United States. Intractable on the Roman question, the papacy displayed an authority abroad that seemed calculated to impress Italy and continued to explore paths leading to an understanding. But the subtle diplomacy of Bismarck and the power plays after his disgrace put an end to the pope's aspirations: the conclusive signing of the Triple Alliance in 1882 and the reinforcement of Bismarck's plan in the Triplice put the Italian monarchy in a position of strength against the powers of central Europe. In France, the Ralliement proposed by the archbishop cardinal of Algeria, Monsignor Lavigerie (the episode of the toast of Algiers), on 12 November 1890 troubled many consciences and brought only a short period of peace. The Dreyfus Affair brought about increasingly violent anticlerical demonstrations. Outside Europe, the expansion of Catholicism to which Leo XIII was particularly devoted, in emulation of Gregory XVI, the missionary pope, sometimes clashed with the policies of world powers jealous of their dominion, notably in China.

Although the role of the papacy on the international scene was not always what Leo XIII had hoped, its presence as a moral and political force had been maintained and transformed. This success was due in large part to the novelty of Leo XIII's attitude in terms of doctrine. What he had introduced was a balance between the traditional rejections and adaptations that seemed to be needed. More than was readily apparent at the time, he confirmed the teachings of Pius IX on many issues. He strove against lay liberalism and declared the FREEMASONS anathema (encyclical *Humanum Genus*, 1884). He insisted on the dominant role of devotion in faith, especially devotion to the Virgin Mary, in nine successive encyclicals. In 1899, he consecrated the entire world to the Sacred Heart. But, for most of the chapters where the Church had become rigid with inflexibility, Leo XIII returned during the course of his pontificate and, with a rare sense of timing, enunciated the positive insights and critiques of Pius IX's SYLLABUS OF ERRORS. In this way, he took a stand in the political arena, on the basis of sovereignty (encyclical *Diuturnum Illud*, 1881), as well as positions on liberalism (encyclical *Immortale Dei*, 1885), on civil and political freedoms (encyclical *Libertas Praestantissimum*, 1888), and on the duties of the citizen toward the state (encyclical *Sapientiae Christianae*, 1890). Without denying the basis of existing doctrine, Leo XIII was able "to show hospitality toward all the legitimate triumphs of the human spirit" (G. Goyau). This attitude was also clear in the theological and intellectual domains. Leo XIII put religious instruction and the works of St. Thomas Aquinas back in the forefront, remarking, in reply to the demands of rationalism and the rivalry shown toward the Church by positivism, scientism, and relativism, that the Church had nothing to fear from confronting history, that her duty was to go back to her original roots, and that God "does not need our lies" (encyclicals *Æterni Patris*, 1879, and *Providentissimus*, 1893). Thus he created a biblical commission in 1902 and opened a portion of the documents preserved in the VATICAN ARCHIVES to researchers.

Nothing shows Leo XIII's mediatory position regarding education better than the encyclical *Rerum Novarum*, published 15 May 1891. The social climate of the 1880s, the development of anarchy, and socialism's growing influence on society led the pope to react both as a traditionalist and an innovator. He declared his opposition to socialism and the class struggle (encyclical *Quod Apostolici*, 1878) and reaffirmed the strength of the family as the base of society (encyclical *Arcanum*, 1880). But as a pastor who in 1875 had founded the "Gardens of St. Philip Neri," in Perugia, based on the model of the Catholic workers' associations organized in France by the brothers Robert and Albert de Mun and La Tour du Pin, he stated that the Church should declare herself in favor of a social order based upon justice. In 1878, he showed an unfailing interest in Catholic socialists, making friends of certain leaders, encouraging their conferences, defending their actions, including those regarding unions, and stimulating reflection. *Rerum Novarum* was the standard-setting synthesis of aspirations on various issues, affecting Catholics in the large industrialized countries of Europe. Of course it treated the worker's dilemma as primarily a moral issue. But Leo XIII was able to make the Church's voice heard on matters considered up to then as being outside the faith—questions of just pay, working conditions, the right of workers to organize, and the duty of employers to listen to them. The range and impact of the encyclical were considerable in the long term, precisely because its reception was not as unanimously enthusiastic as historians of the event have presented it. A work of perspicacity, drafted at a truly historic moment, the encyclical on "the workers' condition" was neither a catechism filled with dogma on a social issue nor the vector of a specific expression of ideology, as it would be interpreted especially in the Ultramontane areas. After an address to the pope by the Union of Freiburg in 1887, asking that Leo XIII convoke an international conference on labor legislation, which the pope seemingly refused in order not to upset the Italian government, in 1902 the International Association of Workers asked the pope to send delegates to its meeting in Cologne. Rome considered this compensation for the political ostracism Italy had shown it by vetoing its presence at the meeting of the International Association for Peace in 1899.

The last years of the papacy, as is frequently the case, were marked by a hardening on the part of Leo XIII, who seemed more concerned about security than innovation. The contrast between the great positive encyclicals of his pontificate and the later ones, like *Testem Benevolentiae* on 22 January 1899 (a condemnation of "AMERICANISM") and *Graves de Communi* in 1901 (voicing reservations about democracy) show the stiffening of the pope, who was influenced by the conservative atmosphere around Cardinal Masella. But his death in 1903 caused widespread emotion, due to the prestige the papacy had regained and the affection that Leo XIII had been able to win from social classes long ignored by the Church. A pope of moderation and acumen, Leo XIII had pointed the Church toward paths she could not avoid if she wanted to bring the Gospel to the contemporary world. Upon his death, the spiritual and moral leadership of Rome—devoted to the unity in diversity that seemed to have gone out of fashion in 1878—was maintained.

Philippe Levillain

Bibliography

Acta Leonis XIII (1878–1903), Rome, 1881–1905, 23 vols.

Boets, J. "'Totila campait dans les parages de Pérouse': Une hymne de Léon XIII en l'honneur de saint Herculanus, traduite par Léon Gezelle [en néerlandais]," *Ons Geestelijk Erf*, 63/2 and 64/1 (1989), 191–200.

Chevallier, P. *La Séparation de l'Église et de l'École: Jules Ferry et Léon XIII*, Paris, 1981.

Dante, F. "Cattolicesimo intransigente e cattolicesimo sociale nella seconda metà del XIX secolo: Il contributo di Matteo Liberatore alla *Rerum novarum*," *Studi e Materiali di Storia delle Religioni*, 53/2 (1987), 219–58.

D'Arros, J. *Léon XIII d'après ses encycliques*, Paris, 1902.

De T'Serclaes, C. *Le Pape Léon XIII*, 1894–1906, Bruges, 3 vols.

Filibero, M. *Leon XIII, los carlistas y la monarquía liberal*, 2 vols., Valencia, 1894.

Fogarty, G. P. "Leo XIII." in *The New Dictionary of Catholic Social Thought*, J. Dwyer, ed. Collegeville, 1994, 546–8.

Fulton, B. "The Revival of Church-State Hostility in France: The Affair of the Religious Decrees, 1879–80," *Journal of Religious History* 20 (1996), 20–31.

Gargan, E. T., ed. *Leo XIII and the Modern World*, New York, 1961.

Haywayd, F. *Léon XIII*, Paris, 1937.

Isensee, J. "Keine Freiheit für den Irrtum. Die Kritik der katholischen Kirche des 19. Jahrhunderts an den Menschenrechten als staatsphilosophisches Paradigma, *ZRGKA*, 104, 73 (1987), 296–336.

Joblin, J. J. "L'appel de l'Union de Fribourg à Léon XIII en faveur d'une législation internationale du travail. Son lien avec *Rerum novarum*," *AHP*, 28 (1990), 357–72.

Lefebvre-Pigneaux De Béhaine, E. *Léon XIII et le prince de Bismarck: Fragments d'histoire diplomatique*, Paris, 1898.

Leonis XIII Allocutiones, Epistolae et constitutiones, 1887–1911, Bruges, 8 vols.

Martina, G. "Il testamento politico di Leone XIII," *RSCI*, 40/1 (1986), 121–33.

Mitchel, J. J. "Embracing A Socialist Vision: The Evolution of Catholic Social Thought, Leo XIII to John Paul II," *Journal of Church and State* 27 (1985), 465–81.

Monetti, G. *Léone XIII*, Rome, 1942, 3 vols.

Pope, S. J. "Rerum Novarum," in *The New Dictionary of Catholic Social Thought*, 828–44.

Prud'Homme, C. *Stratégie missionnaire du Saint-Siège sous le pontificat de Léon XIII: Centralization romaine et défis culturels*, Rome, 1994.

Renault, F. "Aux origines du Ralliement: Léon XIII et Lavigerie (1880–1890)," *Revue Historique*, 570 (1989), 381–432.

Robles Munoz, C. "La Cum Culta de Leon XIII y el movimiento católico en España (1882–1884)," *Hispania Sacra*, 39 (1987), 297–348.

Spahn, M. *Leo XIII*, Munich, 1915.

Weber, C. *Quellen und Studien zur Kurie und zur vatikanischen Politik unter Leo XIII*, 1973.

LEONINE CITY. See Vatican City State.

LEPANTO (1571).

Lepanto may be seen as the victory of Christ, of technique and courage, or even a Pyrrhic victory. It was all of these at once, and more, judging by the repercussions of the event and the abundance of literature that arose from it. As a battle, however, it is assessed differently depending on whether one is on the side of the winners or of the losers, whether analyzing the military or psychological consequences, or considering it as a 16th-century war for Cyprus, or a millenary conflict between the Mediterranean West and East, strewn with great battles along their common border from Actium to Navarin.

Lepanto also marked the beginning of a technological revolution—the last great battle of galleys, which revealed the Ottoman Empire to be behind the times and provoked a violent but brief crisis in the empire of the sultan who, until then, had terrorized western Christianity.

The Origins of Lepanto. Lepanto, the pivotal point in a millenary conflict, involved the struggle between Catholic Christianity and the Ottoman Empire for control of the Mediterranean and the Balkans, which had been ongoing since the end of the 14th century. Until this date, the conflict had consisted of a long series of retreats and catastrophic defeats for the West. The glorious reign of Suleiman the Magnificent (1520–66) was the apogee of Ottoman military efficiency, with a long string of triumphs—from Belgrade (1521) to Rhodes (1522), from Mohacs (1526) to Preveza (1538), from Bude (1541) to Djerba (1560) and to Chio (1566)—not even mentioning the victories in Asia—barely punctuated by the standoffs that seemed like true miracles to westerners; the sieges of Vienna (1529), of Corfu (1537) and of Malta (1565).

Admittedly, the empire of Suleiman was beginning to show signs of weakness during the last decade of his reign, with the civil war that broke out in Anatolia between his last two sons and the interminable negotiations that took place with the shah, along with the considerable increase in corruption that hurt the efficiency of the state apparatus, also with a long series of poor harvests, which stimulated the black market, making the provisioning of cities difficult and favoring rebellions by farm workers. The final years of this glorious reign were gloomy: even the military expeditions, except Djerba, were at best only modest successes (Chio and the campaign of Szigetvar) and, at worst, humiliating reverses (Malta).

The international balance of power was also deeply affected by the abandonment by his French allies with the signing of the treaties of Cateau-Cambrésis and by the short-term elimination of an active foreign policy by France because of difficulties due to the Wars of Religion. This was exactly the opposite of the evolution taking place in the western camp. While Venice continued to reap the benefits of neutrality and saw its prosperity stimulated by the reestablishment of religious peace in the Holy Roman Empire at Augsburg (1555), the HOLY SEE had certainly emerged stronger due to its trials during the REFORMATION, and was doubly reinforced by the legitimacy that the Catholic nations had given it at the end of the Council of TRENT. Spain thus could, with the effacement of France and in defense of the true faith, fully play the role of the number one European power; the disaster at Djerba brought about the patient reconstitution of the Catholic King's naval power.

None of this, however, would have been possible without the election of PIUS V to ST. PETER's throne on 7 January 1506. A true example of the new generation of prelates of the Counter-Reformation, of modest birth and unshakable faith, and with a will of iron, the new pontiff, although only weakly supported by Spain during the CONCLAVE, would dedicate his pontificate to defending Catholicism and regaining what had been lost. His first actions prove this, in particular his concession, without bargaining, of the quinquennial subsidy, for the fight against the infidels, to Philip II upon his accession to the throne, and the provision of aid to Maximilian II during the campaign at Szigetvar. From 1566 to 1568, the Mediterranean remained calm. The efforts of Spain were turned toward recovery of the Netherlands, which required prudence, and therefore no official alliance was possible with the Holy See. The Ottoman Empire was also undergoing a period of internal stabilization with the accession to power of Selim II, the colonization of the state by the clientele of the Grand Vizier Sokullu Mehme Pastha, considerable difficulties with the grain harvest from 1566 to 1568 (which alone excluded any aggressive campaign), and, to ensure a transition without any hitches, the renewal of international accords, surrenders by western "friends," the secret accords made with Persia in exchange for the execution in 1562 of Prince Bayezid, and the resumption of negotiations with the emperor that ended in the signing of an eight-year truce in February 1568. Even though La Porte armed his fleet every year and spread rumors of expeditions against Malta, Cyprus, La Galite, or their outposts, requiring Venice to take up arms every spring, the Ottoman fleet barely made it past La Valona, and secret negotiations between Philip II and the sultan continued almost without interruption during these two years, each of the two sides intending to gain some time by keeping the other busy through the exchange of unofficial agents, Austrian ambassadors, and finally the new duke of Naxos, Joseph Nasi.

In 1569 a new Mediterranean conflict took shape. The revolt of the Moriscos of Grenada, a long and cruel civil war that shook the south of Spain for almost two years, obliged the sultan to promise aid, which was put off until a better time, but which saw the Barbary States come to the aid of those who shared their religion, permitting Uluç Ali, the beylerbey (provincial governor) of Algiers, to take Tunis in January 1569, a loss that would not be forgotten by Madrid. Difficulties in Yemen and Egypt, the failure of the Ottoman expedition to Astrakhan and Kazan in an attempt to open a new route to the Caspian and direct contact with the Uzbeks, enemies of the shah, turned the Ottomans' attention from Mediterranean Christianity for a while, but also made a rapid victory necessary, due to popular discontent. This would occur on Cyprus, the front position of Venice, which the Turks had coveted for a long time.

The Battle. The war in Cyprus, planned for in advance in Istanbul, with extensive armaments, the renewal of the alliance with France, the false assurances to the Venetian doge Marcantonio Barbaro, and the burning of the Venetian arsenal, was, from the beginning of the Turkish attacks against the Stato da Mar, a disaster for Venice. It clearly showed the dislike of the Greek population for la Serenissima, the lack of preparation for its defense, and the cowardliness of its admirals. Despite decades of enormous expenditures to strengthen the presidios, Nicosia and Kyrenia fell in September 1570, and only Famagusta resisted. In Crete and Dalmatia, the Venetian fortresses held, but Venice was on the defensive everywhere and underwent destruction and pillaging. Public opinion and, more importantly, Pius V were able to force Spain and Venice to reach an understanding, despite the strong reluctance of Venice due to bitterness over the withdrawal of the fleet of Andrea Doria at Preveza in 1538, and that of Madrid, due to the treaty signed separately by la Serenissima in 1540, and to the Spanish interests in Maghrib.

The Holy League was proclaimed on 25 May 1571, when the galleys of the pope and of the Spanish king had already brought aid to the Venetian fleet. Italy became enthusiastic about defending the forward bastion of Christianity; and participation in the planned expedition by the nobility of the peninsula was massive. But it took time to organize the counterattack: the legendary slowness of Spanish bureaucracy, with disastrous consequences at the time of Djerba and the Invincible Armada, this time favored the Holy League. When the Ottoman fleet set sail toward its winter bases after a rather fruitless campaign lasting several months, with heavy losses and a human booty difficult to manage, it was almost by chance that it found itself hemmed in by the coalition's fleet in the gulf of Lepanto, where discord had broken out between the admirals: Don John of Austria, head of the expedition; Sebastiano Venier, the captain-general of Venice; Marcantonio Colonna, captain of the pontifical galleys; and Gianandrea Doria and his private fleet, which had just been launched. The kapudan pasha, Muezzinzâde Ali Pasha, a poor sailor (he had replaced Piyale Pasha, the victor of Djerba, who had fallen into disgrace after his losses in the campaign of Cyprus) had an express order to attack the league's fleet.

Three days before the battle, the allied fleet had learned of the fall of Famagusta and the betrayal of the guarantees made to its defenders: this no doubt stimulated the ardor of the combatants. The skill of the admirals and the technological superiority of the Christians (especially the Venetian galleons, actual floating fortresses that cannonaded the Turkish galleys until they were almost completely destroyed), the removal of the stems on the Spanish galleys so that the artillery pieces could be fired more precisely, the considerable number of harquebusiers—these factors provided all that was needed on 7 October 1571. It was the largest naval battle of that era, with 170,000 participants divided nearly evenly between the two fleets, half being galley slaves, most of whom were chained—230 galleys on the Turkish side, and 208 galleys and 6 galleons on the Christian side. The fleets on each side were divided into three parts; the combat began early in the afternoon and ended at nightfall in a sea of blood and debris. The decisive moment was the death of the kapudan pasha barely an hour after the battle began, but combat continued fiercely until the Turkish fleet was almost totally destroyed and the 30 galleys of Uluç Ali, the beylerbey of Algiers, and a very experienced pirate, had executed a skillful turning maneuver and fled the scene.

The toll for the day reflected the fury of combat: 25,000 dead on the Turkish side, many of them valued captains, 8,000 wounded and prisoners, 15,000 slaves, mostly Greeks, freed; on the Christian side, 8,000 killed and 21,000 wounded.

The Consequences of Lepanto. When news of the victory reached Italy and then the rest of Europe, there was a general explosion of joy, even in the Protestant regions: the myth of Turkish invincibility had crumbled, the recapture of territory and ultimate victory seemed possible once again. This enthusiasm was expressed in an extraordinary number of festivals, pardons, lampoons, the building of monuments, and plans for a general crusade. In the Ottoman Empire on the other hand, after a brief moment of panic, what took over was the determination to overcome this setback. On 23 October, the news arrived in Istanbul. The next day, exceptional defense measures were put in place along the Ionian and Aegean coasts, and an unprecedented war effort was undertaken to rebuild a fleet of 250 galleys before springtime, with all the difficulties that construction *ab nihilo* of over 200 ships would involve, as well as the replacement of galley-rowers. All the sandjaks of Rumelia and Anatolia were forced to furnish men as part of their annual taxes. Uluç Ali, greeted as a victor when he returned with 30 galleys intact, was named kapudan pasha and put in charge of supervising the maritime rebuilding. La Porte also tried to minimize the extent of the disaster and would be able to do this thanks to the league. The heart of the empire was untouched, its power being, above all, worldly.

The euphoria of the victory evaporated quickly before the enormity of the losses and the sniping over the dividing of the booty, which reanimated old quarrels. Don John intended to attack the archipelago or attempt to retake a foothold on Cyprus, but the state of the fleet and bad weather stopped him. Philip II did not want to take an expedition to the Middle East, which was to the sole advantage of la Serenissima, who, while taking action against the Turkish outposts (with a loss at Saint-Maure in January 1572) had reopened secret negotiations with the Grand Vizier in order to reap the fruits of victory as quickly as possible, but the latter knew admirably well how to stall. The republic tried to reunite the league by agreeing to sacrifice Admiral Venier, whose shady character made a poor fit with submission to Don John on the altar of this understanding. On 10 February 1572, Philip II agreed to rejoin the league, but his heart was not in it because of the accumulated threats from the north: an alliance was being shaped between the Huguenots and Queen Elizabeth I (which would become the League of Blois on 19 April 1572), and the situation was more difficult than ever in the Netherlands (the insurrection of the Sea Beggars would begin in April). Finally, the death of Pius V on 1 May 1572 meant the loss of the league's greatest supporter. The interests of Venice and Spain seemed more divergent than ever. Before undertaking any campaign in the Levant, Philip II

ordered Don John to take Tunis or Bizerta and refused to countermand this decision until July, when protests were heard from Venice, the Italian states, and especially GREGORY XIII, whose financial support was crucial. The Venetian-papal fleet renewed its military operations, searching for the new Ottoman fleet under the command of Uluç Ali, which now had galleons whose archers had been replaced by harquebusiers. Uluç Ali twice broke off combat at Cerigo, on 7 and 10 August, when it became impossible to get around the Venetian galleons, whose firepower and mobility had been perfected over the winter. After joining the Spanish at Corfu on 1 September, the allied fleet, again under the command of Don John, twice let the Ottoman fleet escape (at Navarin and at Modon) and then failed to capture Navarin. The campaign of 1572 finished with a moral victory for the TURKS and sounded the death knell of the league. Venice, exhausted by three years of war and the interruption of trade with the Levant, tried harder than ever to make peace, through the mediation of the French ambassador, François de Noailles, bishop of Dax, while trying to regain at least its monopoly over trade with Cyprus. The conditions for the peace treaty of 7 March 1573, were very burdensome (ceding Cyprus, paying war reparations of 300,000 sequins, and agreeing to changes in the borders of Dalmatia), and these led to a flood of protests in Europe.

A new expedition by the Ottoman fleet took place in 1573, to protect the coasts from an attack by Don John. After its departure for the Levant, the Spanish fleet attacked La Galite, landing an army there on 9 October and two days later, occupying Tunis, whose inhabitants had fled. It installed a client of Spain, the hafside Mulay Muhammad under protection by a garrison of 8,000 men. Holding Tunis appeared impossible for Spain, especially since Philip II feared Don John's ambitions. Philip moreover, was also plagued by financial troubles (bankruptcy would be necessary in 1575). Abandoned to its own devices, the garrison at Tunis was not able to resist for long the Ottoman landing of 11 July 1574. With 230 galleys and 40,000 men, Uluç Ali took first La Galite on 25 August, and then the fortress of Tunis on 13 September, despite enormous losses that were compensated somewhat by the taking of thousands of prisoners. In Constantinople, the triumphal greeting for the kapudan pasha far eclipsed the defeat at Lepanto, especially since it was followed two years later by the temporary takeover of Morocco, but—ironically—this would be the last Ottoman naval victory for almost a century. The two opponents, summoned to other theaters of war—the north and the Atlantic for the Catholic king, the Persian succession for the sultan—would maintain positions they then held, thus deserting the Mediterranean and putting an end to a border dispute and arms race; a truce was signed in 1580.

Bruno Simon

Bibliography

Braudel, F. *La Méditerranée et le monde méditerranéen à l'époque de Philippe II*, Paris, 1966, 2, 383.

De La Gravière, J. *La Guerre de Chypre et la bataille de Lépante*, 2 vols., Paris, 1888.

Gollner, C. *Turcica: die Türkenfrage in der öffentlichen Meinung Europas im 16. Jahrhundert*, Baden-Baden, 1978, 3, 137 *ff.*

Hess, A. C. "The Battle of Lepanto and its Place in Mediterranean History," *Past and Present*, 57/XI, Paris, 1972, 53–73.

Lesure, M. *Lépante, la crise de l'Empire ottoman*, 1972.

Livet, G. *L'Équilibre européen de la fin du XVe siècle*, Paris, 1976.

LETTERS TO THE POPE. Devotion to the pope or, more generally, the expression of devotedness to the papacy has been manifested in a specific way since the pontificate of Pius IX in the form of material or spiritual offerings, often accompanied by written texts. Many religious congregations and private archives preserve such valuable documents. Although the documents are rather dispersed, there does exist an archive reserved for them at the Vatican Library. The collection is classified under *Indirizzi dei papi*. Serialization begins with the pontificate of Pius IX (1846–78) and continues up to John Paul II. There is no general catalog for the collection, and it is therefore difficult to know exactly how many conserved archival pieces it includes. Only the section dedicated to Pius IX has been indexed, at least for the years 1848–71. For these twenty-four years, it is estimated that there are more than 110,000 items, or more than forty million autograph signatures of faithful from the world over. In all likelihood, the letters have never reached these figures under another pope. Following the pontificate of Pius IX, Leo XIII (1878–1903), Pius X (1903–14), and John XXIII (1958–63) were the beneficiaries of a significant though hardly comparable movement expressive of support. Italy represents, at least until the pontificate of Paul VI, the source of the overwhelming majority of the letters. Next, in Europe, come France, Spain, and Austria. Asia, Africa, and the Americas make a showing for this same period, up to the Vatican II council, though essentially obliquely, through the medium of the European missions. Only the collection of letters to Pius IX, though still only partially examined, allows us, by its richness and diversity, to sort out some characteristics useful for guiding the analysis of what were and still are letters sent by Catholics to the pope.

Signatures. The quantity of the signatures serves as the gross indicator of a support both material (Peter's Pence) and spiritual (prayer) for the pope; the undersigned protest against the measures taken by the modern and secularized world, and adhere to the great Christian principles vigorously redefined by the supreme pontiff. But to limit the interest of the letters to the number of signatures gathered is insufficient. Not all of them have the same value: What meaning should be attached to the signatures of schoolchildren, who sign their names along with the whole class? What value should be assigned to the crosses marked by illiterate populations under pressure from the local priest, who himself has been pressured by his bishop to fill up the space at the bottom of the letter with as many marks as possible? In cases where men alone were allowed to sign on behalf of an entire family, should we adjust the total figure by adding the potential signatures of other family members? The interest of the letters does not boil down to a question of numbers. The texts and the iconography constitute their real value.

Adherence in a Matter of Principle Expiatory Offering. The texts of the letters have sometimes been written by an official author, the bishop of a diocese or a writer publishing in a periodical (*l'Univers* in France, *Civiltà Cattolica* in Italy). These letters, accordingly, are most often in printed form. They have been published in defense of the cause of the Catholic religion and that of the interests of the Holy See. Sometimes they exceed the limits of a single diocese, and they may even have been circulated in several countries. In such cases, their dissemination is linked to various factors: the name of the author (Louis Veuillot, for example) or the subject of the initiative (the consecration of the Church and the world to the Sacred Heart of Jesus in 1874). Other letters, less numerous, have been written by groups of people, usually religious congregations, but also people belonging to associations (the Society of St. Vincent de Paul, the Children of Mary, workers' circles, factory councils, etc.). Finally, there are individuals who have written to the pope on their own. They are mostly figures from the literary or political worlds, or members of the aristocracy. The texts of these letters often have a literary flavor. The current event that has prompted the letters is frequently evoked by means of learned biblical and historical metaphors; poems and canticles abound. The illustrations are carefully wrought and the bindings richly ornamented. Occasionally, a gift is sent with the letter: a sum of money, an object fashioned especially for the pope (a statue, purse, chalice, album, etc.), or a "spiritual bouquet" of works performed for the pope (the saying of rosaries, hours of silence, wholesome amusements, etc.) The handwritten letters have the character of an offering perhaps to a more marked degree than do the printed ones. The printed letters express adherence to politico-religious principles, whereas the handwritten letters have an expiatory dimension.

Support for the Papacy or Attachment to the Person of the Pope? The sending of many of the letters has been dictated by historical events (the fall of the temporal power) or by pontifical acts (encyclicals, affirmations of dogma, councils). Others have been sent for special occasions, a birthday or a jubilee (of priestly ordination, episcopal consideration, or enthronement as pope). In these cases, the authors are publicly demonstrating an attachment to the reality of the papacy by sending congratulatory telegrams or birthday presents to the pope himself. Is this an adherence to the papacy, or an attachment to the person of the pope? The two tendencies come together, particularly when the pope is charismatic (Pius IX, John XXIII) or inspires by his authority a renewal of the pyramidal vision of the Church (Pius IX, PIUS XII).

The letters may be, during troubled periods of history (wars, post-conciliar eras), the channel through which is expressed the confusion felt by Catholics confronted with upheavals in the world (BENEDICT XV, First World War; Pius XII, Second World War) or the Church (Paul VI, the post-conciliar era). During these unstable periods, Catholics instinctively turn toward the center, regroup themselves around the pope, and focus their gaze on Rome in order to rediscover there a kind of collective identity. Gripped with anxiety in the face of the secularization of society at the expense of the Church, they look in the vicinity of the pope for some reassurance that they belong to a Christian society. The letters are valuable documents through which the catholicity of the faithful identifies itself, constructs itself, defines its links with Rome and the world, and specifies the relations between Church and society that are proper to it.

Experience of Closeness, or of Universal Communion with the World? In the beginning, under Pius IX, the letters were ways of experiencing a kind of closeness with the head of the Church. The urgency of the historical situation drove Catholics to make it a duty to show themselves as coming to the side of the pope. Very quickly, this duty became a right and then a habit. Why miss a chance to send the assurance of one's prayers and warmest congratulations to the prisoner of the Vatican? Thanks to these letters, the pope was given the experience of a kind of universal communion with the world. Now that the popes, beginning with Paul VI, have become pilgrims of the whole world, the letters they are offered are, for them, ways of experiencing closeness with the people they have visited; their visit and the messages they deliver stand as the commemoration of a great event, the experience on the part of each of the faithful of a universal communion with the world.

Bruno Horaist

Bibliography

De Rossi, G. B. *La biblioteca della Sede Apostolica ed i catalogi dei suoi manoscritti: I Gabinetti di oggetti di scienze naturali, arti ed archeologia annessi alla Biblioteca Vaticana*, Rome, 1884.

Le Saint-Siège et la France, douze siècles d'histoire, exhibition, Vatican Library, 3 October to 15 December 1987.

Tamburini, F. "Il fondo 'Indirizzi de Pio IX' della Biblioteca Vaticana e alcuni documenti della intransigenza cattolica," *Miscellanea Biblioteca Vaticana*, 1, Vatican City, 197–227.

LIBER CENSUUM. This document's purpose was to report the revenues that the papacy received from its real estate properties. It shows the birth of a new institution, the APOSTOLIC CAMERA, and emphasizes the renewal of pontifical power following the Gregorian REFORM. The real estate patrimony of the Roman Church necessitated an accounting of her revenues from the very beginning. At the end of the 5th century, Pope GELASIUS took care of this task by drafting a *Polyptique*, which remained in use for four centuries. The turmoil of the 10th and 11th centuries brought about the loss of the most ancient documents, and it became necessary to wait until the Gregorian reform to witness an effort at administrative reorganization; the start of a new kind of registry of Church revenues, and the titles justifying them. The *Liber censuum* put together by Cardinal Cencius in 1192 was actually a series of works that illustrated a new conception of the papacy, which had appeared a century earlier, and gave concrete form to the prerogatives of the HOLY SEE and its historical rights, beginning with its past splendor and the uninterrupted series of popes since the apostle Peter. The *Collectio canonum* of Deusdedit (1087), the *Liber politicus* of the canon Benedict (1140?), the dossiers of the chamberlain Boson (1149–78) and, to a lesser extent, the *Digesta* of CARDINAL Albinus (1188) grew out of the same frame of mind. However these documents came into the hands of Cencius, it is clear, in any case, that the first three collections became an important part of the first *Liber censuum*. Chamberlain to Popes CLEMENT III and CELESTINE II, Cencius completed the work of the previous writers with other documents from the archives, especially three fundamental texts written in 1192 that shape the entire book:

(a) general census and rent table grouped by diocese, based upon territories extending throughout western Christianity: this central document takes up seven of the eighteen original volumes. Under the name of each diocese are listed all the establishments, communities, or strongholds that recognize the eminent domain of the Church and thus remit an annual rent, written beside the name and set by a juridical act spelled out a bit later in a cartulary.

(b) an *Ordo romanus*, which is a description of the religious ceremonies presided over by the pope on the occasion of FEAST days, showing the chamberlain's role alongside the pope and in the distributions of the *presbyterium*, payments to members of the CURIA; we also see an early version of the state of curial expenses.

(c) a pontifical history that serves as a link between the historiographic tradition of the LIBER PONTIFICALIS and this new book of the Apostolic Camera.

The eighteen books that made up the first *Liber censuum* of 1192 were divided in the following manner: a census table (books 1–7); two lists of bishoprics and monasteries directly under the Holy See's control (book 8); a mythical description of Rome, the *Mirabilia* (book 9); an *Ordo romanus* (books 10 and 11); two pontifical chronicles (books 12 and 13); and a cartulary (books 14–18).

The originality of this document was due less to the extent of the documentation gathered than to the astonishing organization that Cencius gave to it: the general format includes between the two most important parts the table of payments and the cartulary, the other elements of the compilation. Within each division, the documents were arranged to make it easy to consult, along with empty spaces left in the payment table and at the end of the cartulary chapters, foreseeing new listings. In effect, the collection was destined to grow within this functional frame adapted to the demands of the administration of wealth and the finances of the papacy and given to the Apostolic Camera. This book for the camera would define, for more than two centuries, the worldly rights of the papacy. Its history is linked to that of two major manuscripts that served in turn for listing the changes that occurred. The original *Liber censuum* of Cencius, identified by Paul Fabre, its first editor, is the manuscript *ms Vat.Lat.* 8486 in the VATICAN LIBRARY. The space that was left empty in the original document was quickly insufficient to contain the later additions made to it. As early as the beginning of the pontificate of Cencius, who had become pope under the name of HONORIUS III, five more books were added at the beginning and the end of the manuscript. By the end of the 13th century, it had grown to fifteen new books, including dossiers on several cities in the PAPAL STATES and on the lives of the popes. The copy made in 1228, the manuscript *ms Riccard.* 228 in the library in Florence, was kept updated together with the original and served to hold the listings for the Avignon period. In this way, the *Liber censuum* became one of the symbols of pontifical power. It is significant that in 1429, when the LEGATE of Pope MARTIN V received CLEMENT VIII's abdication at the end of the GREAT SCHISM, the ambassadors of the king of Aragon gave him, as a sign of complete submission, a TIARA and a copy of the *Liber censuum*.

Thérèse Boespflug

Bibliography

Fabre, P. *Étude sur le "Liber censuum" de l'Église romaine*, Paris, 1892.

Le "Liber censuum" de l'Église romaine, ed. P. Fabre and L. Duchesne, Paris, 1889–1910.

Montecchi Palazzi, T. "Cencius camerarius et la formation du 'Liber censuum' de 1192," *MEFRM*, 96 (1984), 49–93.

Pfaff, V. "Der 'Liber censuum' von 1192 (Die im Jahre 1192–1193 der Kurie Zinsflischtigen)," *Vierteljarhsschrift für Sozial- und Wirtschaftsgeschichte*, 44 (1957), 78–96.

Toubert, P. *Les Structures du Latium médiévale: Le Latium méridional et la Sabine du IXe siècle à la fin du XIIe siècle*, Rome, 1973, 1064–68.

LIBER PONTIFICALIS. The document known as the *Liber pontificalis* (a title that has existed since the 12th century, has been current since the 15th century, and was adopted and "canonized" by the editor L. Duchesne) was a collection of pontifical biographies, from PETER to HADRIAN II (867–72), sometimes ending with the story of the first part of the pontificate of STEPHEN V (886). The most reliable ancient manuscripts call it *Episcopale* or *Liber episcopalis in quo continentur acta beatorum pontificum Urbis Romae*, and in more recent manuscripts, it is called *Gesta* or *Chronica pontificum*. It was added to in several stages by Roman administrators; however, it was not an official document, but rather an unofficial instrument of pontifical propaganda. Rabanus Maurus (d. 856) was the first to attribute its beginning to Pope DAMASUS, probably on the basis of two apocryphal letters from Jerome and from Damasus that appear as a sort of preface (this attribution would be repeated by Martinus Polonus or Martin of Troppau, who continued the *Liber pontificalis* in the 13th century).

The notations all follow the same pattern: the name of the pope and of his father, mention of his native region or country, and of his profession before his accession to the pontificate; the duration of his pontificate in years, months, and days; several indications about the history of the pontificate (increasingly detailed as the pontificates approach modern times), followed by a listing of decrees concerning discipline and the LITURGY, a report on the administrative and leadership activities of the pope; and at the end (which was always the same), a count of ordinations of priests and DEACONS for Rome and bishops for the other Churches, the date (obituary or feast day) of his death, the place he was buried, and the duration of time the see was vacant.

The story behind the compilation of this document was established by L. Duchesne and is still regarded as valid, except for several minor subpoints and details. The *Liber pontificalis* can be broken down into two large parts: the first, which is called the "original section" or "ancient *Liber pontificalis*," was written in the 6th century (the Gothic period of Rome); after an interruption of about forty years at the end of VIGILIUS's pontificate, at the end of the 6th century, writing was resumed until the middle of the pontificate of Stephen V. Then the practice of writing biographies of popes was halted again, and until the 12th century it was deemed sufficient just to write down the episcopal succession, with a few brief chronological and biographical indications.

The "ancient *Liber pontificalis*" was edited two times, not far apart, but only the second is accessible to us in manuscript. This second edition furnishes pontifical biographies as far as Vigilius (537–55), to which were added several notices under the pontificate of PELAGIUS II. It is a reworking of a first edition written all at once by an author probably employed at the *domus lateranensis* under the pontificate of HORMISDAS (514–23); this first reworking continued, as far as FELIX IV (526–30), and then expanded by an eyewitness account of the years from 537 to 538, until the pontificate of SILVERIUS (d. 537). It is accessible only by restoration, through collations and cross-checking between the second edition, the sources used by the latter and known in other places, and two shortened versions of the ancient *Liber pontificalis*, the *Felician Abridgement* and the *Cononian Abridgement* (the former goes back to the pontificate of Felix IV, the second until the pontificate of CONON) (Duchesne, 47–113).

It is evident that the first *Liber pontificalis* was rapidly circulated, since it was used by Gregory of Tours in Gaul and by the Venerable Bede (several reworkings also from the 6th and 7th centuries are known). The ancient *Liber pontificalis* was then, at least until the notice of ANASTASIUS II (496–98), a document based on ancient sources that could be partially identified. Of these sources, the Church of Rome is certainly the one that has the most ancient records: the first episcopal catalogs for the city were begun in the second century, in the context of a theological polemic. The battle against the Gnostics led each Church to establish its episcopal successsion so as to ensure respect for its apostolic tradition and to assure authenticity of its teaching (using lists written by Hegesippus, Irenaeus, and Hippolytus, handed down by Eusebius of Caesarea); these lists provide practically no details about the pontificates, except, sometimes, a few chronological indications. On the other hand, the Church of Rome certainly had lists dating back to ancient times used for liturgical commemorations, of the type of *depositio episcoporum* included in the *Chronograph* of 354, which indicated the birthdays of the popes from 254 to 352 and their place of burial. This *Chronograph* also was put together from several chronological civil and religious documents: the *Liber generationis* of Hippolytus, a Roman chronicle up to the death of LICINIUS (323); the

Notitia regionum urbis Romae, which was the source for the first *Liber pontificalis*; and the *Liberian* (or *Filocalian*) *Catalogue* (from the name of Dionysius Furius Filocalus, the scribe of Pope Damasus). The latter catalog, all of which would be reused in the first *Liber pontificalis*, provided pontifical biographies from Peter to LIBERIUS (352–66). The listings, rewritten using ancient catalogs and added to from documents that, for the greatest part, based on legend, still furnished only summary information (date of accession to the pontificate and of death, duration of the reign, several brief biographical items). Their interest and historical value tend to increase beginning with the pontificate of MILTIADES (d. 314). Other catalogs, like that used in the 5th century by Optat of Milet and Augustine against the Donatist "innovators," or the one that chroniclers and church historians reproduced during the 5th century (Prosper, Hidace, Socrates, Sozomenes, Theodoret, etc.) were also used by the authors of the *Liber pontificalis*.

Furthermore, they also sought and used all sorts of other documents when writing the pontifical biographies. Some were archival documents, which lend a certain historical value to the information furnished. For ecclesiastical rulings they used collections of pontifical DECRETALS and rulings concerning either all the Latin Churches or the regions directly under the control of Rome after the middle of the 4th century, (called SUBURBICARIAN ITALY) or controlled by the Church of Rome itself. For governing activities and donations to the Churches, they used founding charters and charters of endowment, inventories and account books, and epigraphic documentation accessible to the editors at that time—*tituli* or dedication inscriptions. Others were apocryphal documents, including widely known ones such as hagiographic legends (notably those of Peter, CLEMENT, CALLISTUS, URBAN, CORNELIUS, CAIUS, SIXTUS, etc.), apocryphal canonical collections or pseudoepigraphs (like those from the SCHISM of LAWRENCE, in 501–6), and chronicles and ecclesiastical histories (like the *De viris illustribus* of Jerome, used in the listing for Peter). All these materials were reworked and rearranged by the authors of the *Liber pontificalis*, who often had a tendency to rewrite the past in light of contemporary events, and to bestow great antiquity upon recent institutions. This is a risk for any historical reconstruction; in this case, the pontifical chronicle presented by the *Liber pontificalis* of the 6th century was aimed at historically situating the claims of the see of Rome in matters of faith, discipline, and jurisdictional primacy (the fragments of the catalog rewritten in the 6th century by those who supported Lawrence against SYMMACHUS confirm that this type of document can constitute an instrument of propaganda). Nevertheless, despite the legendary character of a great part of the documentation used, the ancient *Liber pontificalis* remains an essential source of information for knowledge about the history of the BISHOPS of Rome until the 6th century.

The second part of the *Liber pontificalis* contains listings generally written by contemporaries of the respective popes. Despite the fact that these writers are often quite partisan because of their involvement in the story they are relating, the biographies obviously are much more complete and less questionable beginning in the 6th century.

Françoise Monfrin

Bibliography

LP, I–II, (1886 and 1892) (*BEFAR*); anastatic reprinting and III, ed. C. Vogel, Paris (1955 and 1957).

The Book of the Pontiffs, trans. Davis, R. (Translated Texts for Historians, Latin Series, 5; Liverpool, 1989).

LeClercq, H. "Historiens du christianisme," *DACL*, 6, 2 (1925), 2699; and "Liber pontificalis," *DACL*, 9, 1 (1930), 354–60.

The Lives of the Eighth-Century Popes, trans. R. Davis, (Translated Texts for Historians, Latin Series, 13; Liverpool, 1989).

The Lives of the Ninth-Century Popes: the Ancient Biographies of Ten Popes from AD 817–891, trans. R. Davis (Translated Texts for Historians, Latin Series, 20; Liverpool, 1995).

Vogel, C. "Le 'Liber pontificalis' dans l'édition de Louis Duchesne, État de la question," *Monseigneur Duchesne et son temps*, Acts from the colloquium organized by the EFR, 23–25 May 1973, Rome (1975), 99–140.

LIBERALISM. "Liberalism" is a concept whose meaning has changed over time; some would argue that it has disappeared from contemporary political, and even from the Catholic, vocabulary. One could seek it in vain in the official documents of the VATICAN II COUNCIL.

Since the 19th century, the papacy has not ceased to denounce liberalism in clear and firm terms. It has not withdrawn this condemnation—but there is a question as to exactly what it wants to denounce and condemn. The Church first used the word to target a modern revolution with two major characteristics: the emancipation of reason and the self-sufficiency of a society, forgetful of its debt to the Creator, which the Church saw as leading the world toward catastrophe; and the profound trauma caused by the incomprehensible fury of the FRENCH REVOLUTION, the sirens of modern society seducing Catholics who liked to think of themselves as liberals, various conflicts between the Church and modern states, and the economic materialism that pitted social classes against each other in the pursuit of material wealth. The ultimate explanation for this subversion, in the eyes of the Church, could only be the satanic action of the Prince of Darkness. Liberalism was the root of all the evils afflicting society: a leprosy or a plague, as Catholic publicists described it; a sin, as it was explained by a Spanish priest, Don Felix Sarda y Salvany, in 1884, in a book still in print that circulated around the globe and whose "sound doctrine" the CONGREGATION OF THE INDEX defended against detractors who were demanding the condemnation of its "integrist" errors. The spirit of VATICAN II reduced the power of this argument, but it did not defeat the opposition of principles that had accumulated over the years. Antiliberalism has deeply marked Catholic culture. Even when it is no longer easily seen, it remains, like a reflex, and will tolerate only a weak liberalism, full of restraint as foreign to liberal thought as it is to Catholic doctrine.

"Liberal" comes from Latin and is associated with both freedom and generosity, a dual meaning that leaves it open to interpretation, which will vary according to time and place. In the Middle Ages, the liberal arts were held in opposition to the mechanical arts and, more generally, to menial, or in other words manual work, which was prohibited on Sundays. At the end of the 18th century, liberal ideas in politics and economics began to spread, and they would go hand-in-hand during the July Monarchy. They would give rise to the neologism "liberalism," attributed to Maine de Biran (1818). The growing antagonism between Catholicism and liberalism explains the perception of a separation between the Church and freedom. In reality, the problem was the invention of modern freedoms and their relationship—of separation or continuity—to traditional freedoms, which created two radically different conceptions of freedom. LEO XIII explained the problem in his ENCYCLICAL *Libertas praestantissimum* (1888). Liberalism was first defined by comparing it to absolutism, on a continuum between the two poles of divine right and enlightened despotism. It was basically different from modern totalitarianism, even if it bore the seeds of it: the monarch was the supreme sovereign, depending only upon his own conscience and reason and recognizing no higher authority, beginning with that of the pope. In this sense, absolutism (a recent word, born during the French Revolution) supported European nationalism and announced that individualism was within everyone's grasp as set forth in the concepts of the rights of man and of democracy. The latter would also alternate between two poles: the sovereignty of the people and the sovereignty of the nation. In this new society, there would no longer be a divine order forming the basis for social order, but a social contract based upon the will of the individuals making the contract.

The French Revolution would sweep away absolutism and Catholicism in Europe—the throne and the altar—leaving liberalism on its own, with its own internal contradictions. What would leave the most lasting impression would be the opposition between 1789 and 1793, the middle-class revolution by right and social revolution by violence. From then on, a triangular game began where each of the adversaries would be menaced from two sides: the Church by anticlericalism from the right and left; the liberals by the growth of socialism and by the Catholic reaction; the socialists by the capitalist bourgeoisie and by religious alienation. From this situation, depending on situations and opportunities, grew alliances of two against one, despite insurmountable differences: necessity compels, but does not bind. For the Church, "freedom needs the compass of truth" (Bruno Chenu). For the liberals, freedom was left up to the conscience of each individual. If Christianity was a religion of freedom (*Veritas liberabit vos*), liberalism seemed to be both its realization and its negation, whereas socialism (especially in the rigid form of communism) would be felt as the dual negation of both truth and freedom. Though Christianity came first historically, this precedence has been of little help to it in the conflict of interpretations that has arisen over the basic values of Western modernity.

Through papal documents of the past two centuries, we can thus read on one hand the tension within the Roman Church, inflexible in its principles, yet welcoming to all men and on the other hand, the slow relaxation of this conflict as its religious influence waned. The language of exhortation without veto succeeded that of condemnation without appeal. But it is not necessarily possible to draw conclusions about modulations of doctrinal attitude based upon observed behavior. It should not be forgotten that PIUS IX, the pope of the *SYLLABUS*, chose as prime minister Pellegrine Rossi, whose teaching of economics at the Collège de France was inspired by liberal theses. Catholic criticism of liberalism therefore implies a double tension: religious and social. This can even be seen in the thought of Cardinal Billot, the favorite theologian of PIUS X, and dear to Charles Maurras also. For him, this term designates "a multiform doctrine that frees man more or less with regard to God, His laws and revelations and, as a consequence, frees civil society from any dependence with regard to religious society, that is to say, from the Church, which is the guardian, interpreter, and mistress of divinely revealed law." Applied to public life, this principle leads "through inevitable logic" to the unraveling of both civil society and the family. It engenders "the inhuman struggle for life and the giant scourge of modern life, which is the proletariat," for whom the only "freedom [that remains] is to die of hunger." According to *L'OSSERVATORE ROMANO*: "Before its principles on economic and political issues took concrete form, liberalism was a state of mind, which had come from an anthropology," whose orientation was to "make individual liberty the main thing for man." The danger that lay in wait for theologians was that of providing support for this "devastating relativism" and for a "totalitarian collapse of true liberalism," by restoring the Enlightenment in the name of a particular reading of the Gospel (2 November 1990,

article by M. Schooyans, written for a study in progress by the Congregation for the Doctrine of Faith). It is evident that Rome has not rejected the famous Article 80 of the *Syllabus*, condemning the idea that the pope "can and must reconcile himself to and come to terms with progress, liberalism and modern civilization." An ardent defender of Catholic liberalism, Marcel Prélot justified it without difficulty: "Liberalism in the 19th century is hostile to Catholicism. Dominated by the spirit of free enquiry, it oscillates between virulent anticlericalism and disdainful philosophism. It offers nothing to seduce a believer, whose religion will deter him from liberalism, just as this relationship—"authoritarian and closed"—would alienate liberals from it.

The debate could end in a theoretical standoff, and there would be no lack of authors to write about it, from the greatest authorities to simple satirists, condemning any effort to break the impasse. There precisely lies the difficulty in trying to loosen the knot while so many others are trying to tighten it, which explains the inextricable and interminable Catholic debate on liberalism. Some treat it as a massive totality to which one can only oppose the immutable truth and criticize all those who look for an angle or an opening to "get things moving." One must be "anti-liberal right down the line" if "one does not want to 'play the game' of liberalism," and it is this complaint that, at the Second Vatican Council, united the council minority with regard to the constitution *Dignitatis humanae* on religious freedom.

Whereas Catholic antisocialism and the various attempts at "Christian socialism" appear simple to grasp, Catholic antiliberalism shows itself to be a complex and deeply entrenched phenomenon with multiple aspects. Under Pius X, Father Emmanuel Barbier led the fight in his magazine *La Critique du libéralisme*, whose subtitle specifies "political, religious and social"; he had to justify the elimination of "economic" for a long time. Sixty years later, the Catholic encyclopedia *Catholicisme* lists three entries on the subject: "Liberalism," "Catholic Liberalism," and "Economic Liberation." Obviously, these are not all based on the same mindset. As for the different histories of liberal Catholicism, they are based on political liberalism, which has raised discussions that have essentially been about democracy and the republic. Histories of economic liberalism have usually been the work of social Catholics. Religious liberalism is symbolized by liberal Protestantism and Catholic MODERNISM. Social liberalism has been identified by its adversaries as "Christian democracy" or "Christian unionism" (interconfessional) and with the advanced positions of "Social Catholicism." There remains a nameless liberalism, the common denominator of all the others, the origin of a constellation of convertible terms: rationalism, naturalism, individualism, subjectivism.

Émile Poulat

Bibliography

Barbier, E. *Histoire du catholicisme libéral et du catholicisme social*, 5 vols., Bordeaux, 1923.

Billot, L. *Les Principes de 89 et leurs conséquences*, Paris, 1910 (repr. 1989).

Constantin, C. "Libéralisme catholique," *DTC*, 9 (1926), 506–629.

Jardin, A. *Histoire du libéralisme politique*, Paris, 1985.

Les Catholiques libéraux au XIXe siècles: Actes du colloque international de Grenoble, Grenoble, 1971, 1974.

Manent, P. *Les Libéraux*, anthology, 2. vols., Paris, 1986; and *Histoire intellectuelle du libéralisme*, Paris, 1987.

Morel, J. *Somme contre le catholicisme libéral*, 2 vols., Paris, 1876.

Prélot, M. *Le libéralisme catholique*, Paris, 1969.

Sardav y Salvany, F. *Le Libéralisme est un péché*, Paris, 1910.

Veuillot, L. *L'Illusion libérale*, Paris, 1866 (repr. 1986).

LIBERIUS. (*d. Rome, 24 September 366*). *Elected on 17 May 352. Buried in the cemetery of Priscilla on the via Salaria.*

Liberius succeeded Julius in May 352; the date of May 17 should be used rather than that of May 22, indicated in the Liberian catalog, because ordination in Rome always took place on a Sunday. His episcopate coincided with one of the decisive phases of the Arian conflict within the Church, when Constantius II, the sole emperor in 353 adopted a political policy that was openly favorable toward the Arians. In line with his predecessor, Liberius was a determined defender of Athanasius of Alexandria, and he offered a resistance so fierce that it was punished by exile. After ultimately submitting, he returned to his episcopal see. His faltering and his return to Rome have been judged severely. In any event, this controversial episode obviously distracted attention from the latter part of his episcopate, during which he worked to restore his authority as head of the Church.

At the beginning of his reign, in response to the letter from the East sent to his predecessor, to remind him of the chief accusations made against Athanasius, Liberius decided to call a SYNOD in Rome, to which Athanasius was invited. Before the summer of 353, despite the refusal of Athanasius, Liberius convened a council at which he had the Eastern act of accusation read, as well as a statement signed by eighty bishops defending Athanasius. He asked the emperor, then in Arles, for the *tricennalia* to call an ecumenical COUNCIL at L'Aquila. But once they arrived in Arles, his own LEGATES, including Vincentius of Capua and Marcellus, under pressure from Ursacius of Singidunum and from Valens of Mursa, all signed the condemnation of Athanasius, except Paulinus of Trevi. According to Sulpicius Severus, the emperor issued an edict, inviting the entire episcopate to condemn Athana-

sius. Liberius looked to Osius of Cordova for support, as well as to Fortunatus of L'Aquila and Caecilianus of Spoleto, sending them letters in which he encouraged them not to follow the example of Vincentius of Capua.

In 354, Liberius once again wrote to the emperor, in a letter delivered by Lucifer of Cagliari, to insist on convening a council, specifying that the debate should not be about the guilt of the man but about the faith of Nicaea. Liberius had decided "not to allow the episcopate of this city to be weakened for any reason, and he wanted to preserve the faith which had come to him as the successor to such great bishops, several of whom had been martyrs" (*Ep. Obsecro*). Early in the summer of 355, at Milan, Constantius brought together several hundred Western bishops and several Eastern ones. In a turbulent meeting, all of them signed the condemnation of Athanasius except Dionysisus of Milan, Eusebius of Vercelli, and Lucifer of Cagliari, who were then exiled. Liberius immediately wrote them a letter of encouragement, congratulating them (*Ep. Quamuis sub imagine*). Isolated and feeling threatened, he rejected conciliatory offers made to him by the emperor through his chamberlain Eusebius. The prefect of the city, Leontius, was then ordered to arrest Liberius discreetly, for fear of the reaction, due to his popularity. In secret, Liberius was taken to Milan early in the summer of 356; he maintained his resolute attitude in the presence of the emperor. According to the account of the audience pieced together by Athanasius, Theodoret, and Sozomenes, Liberius stated that the Nicene Creed must be signed and the exiles recalled before Athanasius's case could be examined. Refusing the extension of time granted to him as well as monetary assistance offered by the emperor, Liberius was immediately sent, without a trial, into exile in Beroea in Thrace, in the care of Demophilos. His archdeacon Felix was soon chosen to replace him as pope.

After two years of exile, he disavowed Athanasius. Four letters written in 357, collected by Hilarius in 360 in the *Collectanea antiariana parisina* (or *Fragmenta Historica*), trace the course of his weakening stance. They illustrate the evolution of the pope who, through progressive concessions, abandoned the courageous attitude he had previously maintained. The authenticity of these letters seems established, including even the first (*Ep. Studens paci*), which unlike the three others, had not been included in ancient canonical collections. This first letter was sent to all the Eastern bishops. In it Liberius explained it how, having received the letters they had sent to Julius, he had tried without success to summon Athanasius. He desired "to remain united with all the bishops of the Catholic Church (*uniuersis*)," and declared his readiness "to separate Athanasius from communion in the Roman Church." The second letter (*Pro deifico*), also addressed to the Eastern bishops, was basically an extension of the preceding one. Liberius reminded them that he had notified the court of the condemnation of Athanasius by a letter carried by Fortunatianus of L'Aquila, which he had signed as a profession of "Catholic faith," drawn up at Sirmium and submitted by Demophilos, and that he had done this "of free will." Following this letter, Hilarius, in a commentary, added the names of the bishops who had signed the first formulary of Sirmium (351), to which Liberius had just added his, thus implicitly rejecting the *homoousios* by labeling as "perfidy" what he had previously called "Catholic faith." The pope also sent a letter (*Ep. Quia scio*) to the leaders of the winning party asking them to intercede with the emperor. Finally, he addressed himself to Vincentius of Capua *(Ep. Non doceo)*—the same person he had reproached for his weakness at Arles—to suggest the calling of a synod in Campania and to remove him from exile.

The cohesion of these four letters, more than a comparative study of their style, argues in favor of their authenticity, against the hypotheses advanced by those who passed silently over Liberius's weakness in exile, when most of the episcopate, except for a small minority, had set the example for his submission to the emperor with their own. The testimony about Liberius's weakening was reported by his contemporaries several times—first, by Athanasius, whose refusal of the condemnation was the very reason for the pope's exile, and who wrote in the *Historia arianorum*, after recalling Liberius's resistance, that "having been banished, two years later he wavered, frightened by threats of death, and signed." He recounted this again, in the *Apologia contra arianos*, in an addition made after its first drafting in late 357 or early 358. An additional witness in the matter was the Roman author of the *Collectio Auellana*, a supporter of Liberius. In his *Chronicle*, Jerome, present in Rome in 358, reported that "defeated by the boredom of exile, he subscribed to the spitefulness of the heretics," and he renewed his accusation in the *De uiris illustribus*. We do not know, stated Hilary of Poitiers in the *Contra Constantium* in 360, if "Constantius committed a greater crime by exiling Liberius or by sending him back to Rome." The bishop of Poitiers, though a supporter of Liberius, did not list him among the victims of the imperial fury. Historians like Sulpicius Severus and Rufinus looked for plausible explanations that did not agree with the accounts of contemporary witnesses. Socrates and Theodoret no longer mentioned the signing of the formulary. Philostorgus restored the negotiations between the pope and the emperor with seeming truthfulness, but his story does not agree with that of his contemporaries.

Liberius, by accepting the condemnation of Athanasius and signing the first formulary of Sirmium, had made his return to Rome possible. The liberation of the bishop of Rome created a delicate situation for the Roman see, which Constantius solved by maintaining both bishops, Liberius and Felix, in agreement with the bishops who

met at Sirmium in 358, before whom Liberius signed a profession of faith prepared by Basil of Ancyra. During the second half of 358, Liberius returned to Rome where he was greeted with enthusiasm, "almost as a victor," according to Jerome. After attempting to resist, Felix, abandoned by the clergy, rejected by the people and the senate, left the city.

Until the death of Constantius in 361, Liberius abstained from participation in the great theological debates. The emperor, to assure discipline in the Churches, had a meeting of the episcopate at Rimini. Liberius was not invited to this meeting held in the summer of 359, and the Church of Rome was not represented there. All but seven of the Western bishops were present at this synod, which ended on 10 October 359. Leading them was Restitutus of Carthage. After having refused the "dated Credo"—formula drawn up at the council of Sirmium in 359—they agreed to meet with the Arian deputation and, contrary to their mandate, signed a formula even more accommodating than the one Liberius signed. The episcopal see of Rome was also unrepresented at the council of Constantinople, in January 360, which confirmed the formula of Rimini. Not having compromised himself with the episcopate that had failed a second time, Liberius's prestige and authority were partly restored, as the visit to Rome by Hilary of Poitiers after his return from exile showed.

After Constantius's death, during the reign of Julian (361–63), Liberius worked at reconciliation. Associating himself with the peace measures adopted by the synod that Athanasius presided over in Alexandria in 362, he appealed to the bishops of Italy *(Ep. Imperitiae)* asking them to pardon the bishops who had made mistakes at Rimini "out of ignorance," as long as they returned to the faith of Nicaea. The accession to the throne of Valens in the East (354) led the Eastern bishops to seek the support of the Roman pope, while the Western ones, with Valentinian, saw the Nicaean orthodoxy grow stronger. An Eastern embassy, in 366, met with Liberius in Rome and presented him with the decisions taken at the synod of Lampsaque (365) by the bishops who wanted to reestablish ties with Rome. Liberius required the legates to show their adherence to the Nicene Creed with their signature, and by also condemning other heresies. In a solemn meeting, where he presented himself as the spokesman for the Western episcopate, Liberius gave them a letter that certified the reestablishment of the union between the East and Rome, the guardian of the Nicaean orthodoxy. It was read at the Council of Tyane (367) when the Eastern bishops returned home. The peace to which he had contributed was temporarily reestablished.

Theological quarrels excepted, little is known of Liberius's activities in Rome. At an unspecified period during his episcopate, perhaps before his exile (as the allusion to the young age of Ambrose of Milan would suggest) he proceeded, in the month of December, to ST. PETER's at the Vatican to consecrate the virgin Marcellina, the sister of Ambrose, in the presence of a large crowd, and on this occasion he gave a speech whose words were reported by Ambrose in the *De Virginibus* (377). He embellished the tomb of St. Agnes and constructed a basilica near the *macellum Liviae* on the Esquiline, called the *basilica Liberii*, in which partisans for Ursinus, who supported him against DAMASUS, took refuge on 26 October 366. But we cannot with certainty attribute to Liberius the renovation plans dating from the middle of the 4th century for a cemetery in Ostia, nor those for a CATACOMB that may be St. Thecla's. He died on 24 September 366, according to the anonymous author of the *Gesta inter Liberium et Felicem* (he is mentioned on 23 September, by mistake, in the *Hieronymian Martyrology*). He was buried in the cemetery of Priscilla on via Salaria. There is no decisive argument designating him as the pope named in the epitaph from a cemetery of Priscilla found by J. B. De Rossi in 1883, which traces the life of a pope (*immaculatus papa*) who fought alone for the faith of Nicaea and died in exile.

Because of his weakness, the memory of Liberius has not left historians indifferent. He had already been misrepresented by the *LIBER PONTIFICALIS*, which made him, in the name of the Arian HERESY, the persecutor of the Catholic followers of Felix. In the 6th century, the *Gesta Liberii* came to the defense of his memory in a hagiographic narrative. From then on, the defenders of the innocence of Liberius and those convinced of his guilt countered each other's theses until the early 20th century. Through the many studies dedicated to him, we are able to appreciate more fully the pontificate of Liberius, without minimizing his errors, in the historic context of a troubled time.

Élisabeth Paoli

Bibliography

LP, I, 207–11.

Ambrose, *De virginibus*, III, 1–14, ed. Cazzaniga, 57–9.

Amman, E. "Libère," *DTC*, 9 (1926), 631–59.

Ammianus Marcellinus, *Rerum Gestae*, I, 15, 7, ed. Eyssenhardt, Berlin, 1871, 51–2.

Amore, A. "Liberio," *BS*, 8, (1966), 17–23.

Athanasius, *Hist. Arian.*, 35–41, ed. Opitz, II-1, 202–6; *Apol. Contro Arian.*, 89, 3–90, 2, ibid. 167–8.

Caspar, E. *Geschichte des Papsttums*, 1, Tübingen, 1930, 166–95.

Chapman, J. J. "The Contested Letters of Pope Liberius," *RB* (1910), 22–40, 172–203, 325–55.

Duchesne, L. "Libère et Fortunatien," *MAH*, 28 (1908), 31–78.

Feder, A. *Studien zu Hilarius von Poitiers*. I. "Die sogenannten 'Fragmenta Historica' und der sogenannte 'liber ad Constantium imperatorem,'" *AK. der Wissenschaften, Phil.-Hist. Klasse*, 162, Vienna, 1910.

Gesta Liberii, *PL*, 8, 1387–410.

Hamman, A. "Hilaire est-il témoin à charge ou à décharge pour le pape Libère?," *Hilaire et son temps: Actes du Colloque de Poitiers*, 1968, Paris, 1969, 43–50.

Hefele, C. H. *Histoire des conciles*, Paris, 1907, I, 2, 908–29.

Hieron. Martyr., *AASS, Noa.* II, *p. post.*, 259, 498, 524, 256.

Hilarius, *CSEL*, 65, see Index II, 278–9; *Contra Constantium*, 11, *PL*, 10, 587 ff.

Jerome, *Chron. a.* 354, *PL*, 27, 501; *De uiris ill.*, 97., *TU*, 14, 1, 47.

Leclercq, H. "Libère," *DACL*, 9, (1930), 497–530.

Liberius, *Epistulae*, cc 9, ser. lat., 121–4 and in Hilarius, *CSEL*, 65, 155–73; see Index, 278–79.

Liébaert, J. "Libère," *Catholicisme*, 7 (1975), 601–4.

Meslin, M. *Les Ariens d'Occident*, Paris, 1967, 38–42.

Monachino, V. "Il primato nella controversia ariana: Saggi storici intorno al Papato," Rome, 1959, 17–90.

Philostorge, *HE*, IV, 3, GCS 21, 60.

Pietri, C. *Roma christiana*, Rome, 1976, I, 237–68 and II, 1695.

Quae Gesta sunt inter Liberium et Felicem, *CSEL*, 35, 1, 1–5.

Rufin, *HE*, I, 27, *PL*, 21, 498.

Saltet, L. "La formation de la légende des papes Libère et Félix," *Bulletin de littérature ecclésiastique* (1905), 222–36.

Schwaiger, G. "Liberius," *LTK*, 6 (1961), 1015–16.

Seppelt, F. X. *Papstgeschichte*, Munich, 1933, 18–21.

Socrates, *HE*, II, 36–7, *PG*, 67, 301–24.

Sozomenes, *HE*, IV, 8–15, GCS 50, 147–57.

Theodoret, *HE*, II, 12–15, GCS 44, 122–31.

Zeiller, J. "La question du pape Libère," *Bulletin d'ancienne littérature et archéologie chrétienne*, 111 (1913), 20–51.

LIBRARY, VATICAN. See **Vatican Library**.

LINUS. According to the *LIBER PONTIFICALIS*, Linus, of Tuscan origin, succeeded ST. PETER, in Rome, from 56 to 67 A.D. At Peter's demand he advised women to come to church veiled. A martyr, he is said to have been buried in the Vatican, near the Apostle. Another legend, as fantastic as the indications in the *LIBER PONTIFICALIS*, says that Linus dictated the ACTS OF PETER. Missing in the *Liberian Catalogue* and the *Hieronymian Martyrology*, but found for a long time in the *Roman Martyrology*, he was no longer included in the Roman calendar of 1969. According to Irenaeus of Lyon (*Contre les hérésies*, III, 3, 3), which cites a Roman list from the time of Pope

ELEUTHERIUS, Linus received the position of bishop of Rome directly from the apostles themselves. He would have done so, according to Eusebius of Caesarea (*Ecclesiastical History*, III, 13; *Chronicle*, ed. Helm, 185), from 68 to 79—dates that correspond, within two or three years, to those postulated by historians today.

Jean-Marie Salamite

Bibliography

LP, 1, 121.
Liébaert, J. *Catholicisme*, 7 (1975), 807–8.
Pietri, C. *Roma christiana*, Rome, 1976, 1, 394.

LITERATURE. See **Image of Rome in Literature**.

LITURGICAL CHANT, ROMAN.

4th Through 12th Centuries. The recent progress of musicology, put at the service of history as a new auxiliary science, has made it possible to follow the formation and development of the liturgical chant of Rome, from its still visible ancient foundations, which go back to the 4th century. From the simple local or regional chant, it became, beginning in 750, the chant of the entire Carolingian empire. However, it became a hybrid on contact with the Gallican chant of the Frankish countries and was transformed into the Franco-Roman chant, the so-called "Gregorian" chant. It eventually returned to Rome in this form in the 10th century under the influence of various Ottonian sovereigns. Its pure ancestry, called "old Roman" (*alt-römisch, romano antico*) was gradually eliminated until its total disappearance at the beginning of the 13th century.

The Roman rite was only at the origin of one of many local or regional rites, all Mediterranean, of the later centuries of antiquity, before the early Middle Ages replaced them little by little with a single centralizing rite developed within intellectual circles of Austrasia between 750 and 800. The other rites of the western basin of the Mediterranean in the later centuries of antiquity were: the Milanese rite, around the capital of the Prefect of Praetorium Italy; the Benevetan rite in the south of Italy; the "rites" of Aquileia and of Ravenna are only variations on the Franco-Roman rite; the African rite, well documented by the works of Saints Cyprian and Augustine; the two Hispanic rites of Léon and Toledo; the different Frankish ("Gallican") rites. The liturgical chant of the popes was, therefore, only one among many.

Within the different parts of this repertoire, the chants of the Mass, the Eucharistic Sacrifice, should be differentiated from those of the Office, the seven Hours that mark off the day. Within the repertoire of the Mass itself, a distinction must be made between the chants of the Ordinary, on the one hand, which are identical for each Mass and which, in the order of the ceremony, are the *Kyrie*, the *Gloria*, the *Credo*, the *Sanctus*, and the *Agnus Dei*. Although they were included between the 5th century (*Gloria, Sanctus*) and the 11th (*Credo*), their historical interest is not very great because their generally very simple melodies were not written down, in spite of the fact that they appear very late in our documentation. On the other hand, the chants of the Proper appear in the very earliest manuscripts. They will serve as a base. The majority of these chants are specific for each mass. The Mass begins with the Introit, followed by the Gradual, the Tract, the Alleluia, the Offertory, and the Communion. From the old stock of the Roman repertoire (those composed before the 10th century) remain some 20 tracts; 100 offertories; 150 graduals, introits, and communions; and several hundred alleluias—a corpus of at least 600 pieces; a solid foundation on which to base serious historical research.

To date, only five complete manuscripts of ancient Roman liturgical chants have been found: three Graduals (Mass); Vatican lat. 5319 (beginning of the 12th century; a transcription by B. Stablein), Arch. Cap. S. Petri in Vat. F 22 [beginning of 13th century; originating from St. Peter; (unpublished)] and Bodmer C 74 (dated 1071; copied in the *scriptorium* of the titular church of St. Cecilia of Trastevere; facsimile by M. Lutolf), and two antiphonaries (office), Arch. Cap. S. Petri in Vat. B 79 (12th and 13th centuries; originating from St. Peter; unpublished) and London, British Library Add. 29988 (second half of 12th century; attributed by Dom Jean Claire to the Holy Cross-of-Jerusalem basilica; unpublished). The oldest sources of the Franco-Roman chants in the mass are classified under two categories: manuscripts without musical notation and those with musical notation. The six oldest of the first group, which date from the 8th and 9th centuries, have been published by Dom Hesbert; the oldest of the second group, particularly the manuscripts of St. Gall, and of Einsiedeln, Laon, and Mont Renaud, which date from the 10th century, have been published in facsimile in the *Paleographie musicale* of the Solesmes monks. This tripartite group forms the essential basis of any work on the liturgical chant of Rome. To exploit this documentation, it should be noted that the ancient liturgical chant was based on "three tenors which form the three-chord major of the pentatonic scale without semitone: $G \, A \, C \, D \, E$" (Dom J. Claire); in the clearest cases, each melody can be brought back to one of these three tenors, or major chords, of C, D, and E. In addition, experience has shown that while the C and E chords are very well represented in the Roman chant, the D chord is absent from the oldest stratum of the Roman liturgy, but is well represented in non-Roman liturgies. It can, therefore, serve as a dating and placement component. It should be pointed out that because the oldest strata of the Roman chant are contemporary with patristic typology,

948

frescoes, CATACOMBS, sarcophagus, and Paleo-Christian basilicas, a comparison of all these elements very often clearly shows the existence of synchronism and allows the development of a chronology.

The influence that the synagogal cult of the sabbath might have had on the Roman liturgy has been exaggerated. In reality, analogies between the structure of the latter and the preface of the Mass are very elementary. If, indeed, in both cases, there are readings, chants, and prayers, they are not the same, they are not in the same place, their number is not the same, and their significance is different. The importance given to psalmody in the cult is of Christian origin. The importance of ancient hymnody has been equally underestimated; it played a greater paraliturgical than liturgical role, strictly speaking. Nothing remains of a hypothetical Roman hymnodal repertoire, which is supposed to have existed up to the 5th century. On the contrary, Rome, partial to the psalter, only accepted the use of hymns in the liturgy at a very late date: not before the 12th century—like Lyons. The Roman liturgical chant, as far back as one can go, was psalmic.

The oldest chants of the Roman mass are the chants between the Readings, that is the Tract and the Gradual. The fact that two chants remained between the Readings—the Alleluia is not a chant between the Readings, but a chant added on later to the chants between the Readings—proves that three Readings existed in the beginning. There was then the following sequence: Reading (1) (prophet); Chant 1 (today, the Gradual); Prayer 1; Reading 2 (apostle); Chant 2 (today, Tract or Alleluia); Prayer 2; Reading 3 (Gospel). Only the last two Readings survived after the 6th century; the prayers can still be seen during the Easter vigil and on Saturdays of Ember days. These chants are sung by a soloist while the faithful listen in silence.

The oldest stratum conserved from the Roman liturgical chant consists of three chants in C, all of which have the same melody or tone. They are three Old Testament canticles of the Easter vigil, *Cantemus Domino* (Ex 15), *Attende caelum* (Dt 32), and *Vinea facta est* (Is 5). These chants are the lyrical continuation of the reading that precedes them and from which they are taken: the most ancient Roman chant arises from the reading. The Easter vigil, *mater omnium sanctarum vigiliarum* (St. Augustine,) was the primitive Easter mass, before the Sunday morning mass, which was no doubt created in the 5th century. During this vigil, the catechumens, who at that time were adults, received baptism, confirmation, and communion for the first time, after a baptismal preparation lasting three weeks, even before the creation of Lent. These three chants were well suited to this purpose: the first (Ex 15) alluded to the historical Easter, the journey out of Egypt, and the crossing of the Red Sea, foreshadowing the baptism, which liberates from the slavery of

sin. The other two evoked the rejection of Israel, the putting to death of Christ (Is 5), and the calling together of the nations, the new Israel, in conformity with the most ancient typology. The tract *Sicut cervus* (Ps 41, an illustration of the decoration of the baptistry of the Lateran built by Constantine), which is not a canticle but serves as a processional chant to the fonts during Easter night, should be added. Its melody is practically the same as the three *cantica*, apart from a few minor details. Thus, one seems to go back to a time when in Rome, there was only one tone used for everything.

Psalmody appears almost immediately as a psalm without refrain, sung entirely by the soloist. Traces remain of at least 20 of these psalms without refrain, which have only survived during Lent and on Saturdays of Ember time. Everywhere else they have been replaced, first by the responsorial psalms, apparently introduced in Rome by Pope CELESTINE I (422–32), then by the Alleluia, from St. Gregory the Great (590–604). These chants are of two types. The majority of them are "rising canticles" (Ps 119 to 133) and form the key signature of the old "Lent" of three weeks, previous to the 40-day Lent, which was only introduced between 350 and 384. The chant of these psalms is, therefore, prior to 384. They all share the same melody in C, which is derived from the chant of the canticles. The second group also has the same melody, but in D. They form the key signature of Holy Week. This is a Gallican import dating from the creation of the *Schola cantorum*.

When the faithful were capable of responding to the soloist with a small refrain or *responsio*, thanks to progress of catechesis, a new liturgical genre was introduced: the responsorial psalm. Its first appearance in the West seems to have been at Milan, where it was introduced by St. Ambrose (337/9–97), based on the model in vogue in some Eastern Centers. It is probable that Rome imitated this innovation during the reign of Celestine I. The majority of these pieces are in C, like all the old stratum of Roman psalmody. Some are also in E which is another Roman mode, but equally in D, under three forms: retransposed in G (Graduals of the 8th mode), D finishing in G (Graduals of the 7th mode), and Graduals finishing in A (Graduals in II A). These last groups are Roman borrowings from the Gallican liturgy. These melodies become more numerous and more diversified the further one advances in time.

The *Schola cantorum* (c. 461–520) appears between the death of St. Leo the Great (440–61), who knew nothing of it, and 520, the date of the introduction, during the Lenten feria, of the 26 psalmic communion chants, which represent the final stratum of Lenten composition. The rest, Offertories and Introits, were in existence before. The *Schola* then seems to have been created closer to 461 than to 520. It is no doubt the fruit of a synthesis of all the old soloists of titular churches and basilicas of

Rome who contributed their repertoire and their "grand airs" —personal vocalization or melismata. Its role is diverse.

The *Schola* is responsible for the shortening of the psalm without refrain, transformed into a Tract, like the refrain of the responsorial psalm, reduced to a single verse and metamorphosed into a Gradual. At the same time it ornamented their melodies, which at the beginning consisted of a simple recitation on one tenor, articulated at the middle and penultimate logical distinction of the text through a melisma (a characteristic vocalization).

The *Schola* has equally introduced melodies in D, which came from still unidentified Gallican repertoires. From specialists to specialists, such a borrowing is facile, while it has been impossible in the repertoire of the soloist with a popular refrain.

For the first time, chants were created which no longer had any link with the Readings; it is a veritable rupture which led, in addition, to the diversification of the rites. The Offertory accompanies the offertory procession, before the canon was no doubt created in the 5th century. It is formed of two parts: an *offertorium*, a psalmic verse to which was added progressively, one, two, and sometimes three *versus*, psalmic verses. The principal characteristic of the Offertory is its centonisation (the use of fragments of multiple verses of the same psalm) and its very elaborate ornamentation. The verses were suppressed from the 10th century. The Alleluia was added to the chants between the readings without being a chant, and consists of the agglomeration of elements of different times: acclamation (*allelu-*), *iubilatio* (vocalization on the syllable *-ia*) and one, then sometimes several, verses. The melodies are often arrived at through reuse of the ancient melodies of Tracts, Graduals, and Offertories. The Alleluia, without doubt, was created in the 5th century for Easter Sunday, to which it had been reserved for a century. It was then extended to Easter time, from which it emerged only on the intervention of St. Gregory the Great, and spread throughout the liturgical year, with the exception of Lent when it was never again used. The Introit, created during the 5th century to accompany the entrance of the clergy, consists of one antiphon, which serves as a refrain to a psalm whose verses are chanted until the clergy has entered the sanctuary. Its melodies are generally simple: in the ornate genres (the *Schola* is the preeminent style) a simple melody is an indication of late creation. Finally, in relation to the Communion, it seems that at the beginning, Ps 33 was chanted at all masses to accompany the communion of the faithful. From the chant of the Ordinary, this chant then passed into the Proper and took its present form in the 6th and 7th centuries. It is exactly like the Introit on which it must have been created. It is chanted until all the faithful, who so desire, have taken communion.

The repertoire was practically completed while the liturgical year was still developing, because of the creation of new feasts, temporal as well as sanctoral. Several stratagems were employed: (1) the use of tones (use of a single melody on which a great number of texts are adapted; this was the case for the Alleluia and for some late Graduals), (2) reuse (on the creation, under GREGORY II [715–31] of masses for the Thursdays of Lent, until then aliturgical, no new piece with the exception of the gradual *Tollite hostias* was composed; the period of composition was finished); (3) the creation of nonpsalmic pieces (a clear phenomenon for the sanctoral and the last Sundays after Pentecost); and (4) borrowings from foreign repertoires (particularly long non-psalmic offertories derived, no doubt, from the Gallican chant). Adding new verses in a very characteristic melodic style also lengthened Alleluias and Offertories. In the 8th century, the Roman chant was completed, but it did not find new inspiration.

The initiative in the birth of Gregorian chant was not the papacy's, but Pepin the Short's (751–68), followed by his son Charlemagne (768–814), who desired a single liturgy in a single Empire. For the prestige as well as in the desire for unification, they had cantors (the music was not yet been written down) and manuscripts brought from Rome. Metz, along with scholars at the palatine chapel at Aix, played a very important role in this process, particularly under Chrodegang (d. 766). The sovereigns expected their cantors to copy the Roman melodies exactly (600 for the Mass, 2,000 for the Office!). As this was materially impossible and the Frankish cantors were very attached to their own repertoire, a hybridization (spontaneous) between the Roman chant ("old Roman") and the Gallican repertoire occurred, unbeknownst to the sovereigns. The combination of the Roman melodic line with the traditional Frankish ornamentation produced a new chant, Franco-Roman, known as the "Gregorian chant." Shortly thereafter, the first musical notations were invented to facilitate its memorization and diffusion. In addition, Charlemagne, desirous of imitating the *basileus* in every way, had ordered his cantors to adopt the framework of the *octoechos*, which made it obligatory to harmonize the entire repertoire into eight modes, each defined by the final note and the psalmodic tenor: four final notes, each with two tenors, makes eight modes. In order to do this, the Roman melodies had to be contorted, lowering or raising tenors as required. The change from a system based on tenors (the C, D, and E major chords) to a system based on the final notes led to major complications until the discovery at Solesmes, around 1960, of the original tenors. In any event, the birth of the "Gregorian" chant is evidence of the intellectual advances in Austrasia, the decline of the western basin of the Mediterranean, and of the vitality of the Frankish liturgical chant, which was able to fit into the Roman mold by transforming and revivifying a Roman chant that had ceased to renew itself.

The Franco-Roman chant, born in Austrasia, spread rapidly throughout Europe. The Milanese chant was marginalized—and thoroughly contaminated from the beginning of the 10th century. When a Milanese piece and a Gregorian piece have the same text and a similar melody, it is always the Milanese—under duress—that copied the Gregorian. It was the price of survival. On the other hand, the Beneventan rite was first contaminated then destroyed. The two Hispanic rites, in their turn, were abolished by the Spanish sovereigns with the help of the Cluniac monks at the behest of GREGORY VII around 1074. At the end of the 11th century the Gregorian chant had practically become the sole liturgical chant of the Latin Church.

Because of the influence exerted on the papacy by the Ottonian sovereigns, manifested by a series of German popes (1046–57), the Gregorian chant invaded Rome, in its turn, at the same time as the Romano-Germanic pontificate. As of 1071 it had already thoroughly contaminated some Roman manuscripts, as an analysis of the Gradual of St. Cecilia of Trastevere shows. The cosmopolitanism of the chapters of regular canons of some great Roman basilicas, such as the LATERAN, hastened the movement. These ecclesiastics, accustomed to singing á la Gregorian in their countries of origin, continued this practice even in Rome. On the other hand, St. Peter's Basilica seems to have remained attached to the Roman tradition, no doubt because members of its chapter were recruited from the autochthon nobility. Pope NICHOLAS III (Captain Orsini) delivered the final blow between 1277 and 1280, suppressing the Roman chant and imposing the Franco-Roman liturgy (the missal and the breviary *secundum ordinen Romanae Curiae*) and its chant, the "Gregorian" chant.

Philippe Bernard

Bibliography

Bernard, P. "Sur an aspect controverse de la reforme carolingienne: 'vieux-romain' et 'gregorien,'" *Ecclesia Orans*, 7 (1990), 163–89.

Cattin, G. *La monodia nel Medioevo*, 2e ed. Turin, 1991.

Claire, J. *Revue gregorienne*, 40 (1962) and 41 (1963).

Etudes gregoriennes, 15 (1975) and "Le Cantatorium roman et le Cantatorium gallican," *Orbis musicae*, 10 (1990–1), Tel Aviv, 50–86.

Graduale Triplex, Solesmes, 1979.

Hesbert, R. J. *Antiophonale Missarum Sextuplex*, 2nd ed. Rome 1967.

Lutolf, M. ed. *Das Graduale von Santa Cecilia in Trastevere*, 2 vols., Cologne-Geneva, 1987.

The New Grove Dictionary of Music and Musicians, ed. S. Sadie, 6th ed., London, 1980.

The New Oxford Dictionary of Music, II, The Early Middle Ages to 1300, ed. R. Crocker and D. Hiley, Oxford, 1990.

Paleographie musicale of the Solesmes monks, 1888 and foll. (facsimiles of St. Gall, mss 339 and 359, Einsiedeln 121 and Laon 239.

Stablein, B., and Landwehr-Melnicki, M. *Die Gesänge des altrömisschen Graduale Vat. Lat. 5319*, Börenreiter, 1970.

Talley, T. *The Origins of the Liturgial Year*, 2nd ed. Collegeville, 1991.

Vogel, C. *Medieval Liturgy. An Introduction to the Sources*, Washington, 1986.

See also HYMN.

LITURGY.

7th Through 15th Centuries. Until the 6th century, there was no organized missal in Rome, nor any liturgical centralism. Prayers and formulas were left up to the inspiration of each celebrant, and were often deficient. To aid the celebrant, single, loose sheets called *libelli missae* began to be written and were placed under the nose of the priest at the desired moment. The perfectly unwieldy nature of these *libelli missae* soon led liturgists in Rome to compose practical missals, organized logically into an easy-to-use volume, that celebrants only had to open in order to find the desired mass. This is when Roman liturgical genius shone: the pope, bishop of Rome, only celebrated mass in public and with convocation of the people (the Roman STATIONS) about 20 Sundays per year, in addition to the days of Lent and certain important feast days. Roman liturgists, therefore, had the idea of writing a practical missal for the pontiff's personal use, containing only the formularies for the masses called "stational." This strictly papal missal was born around the year 625 and was called afterwards the "Gregorian Sacramentary," because it was wrongly attributed to Pope Gregory: this is the "Type 1 Gregorian" of liturgical historians. For liturgical use in the parishes of Rome, the "titles," where mass is celebrated practically every day of the year, they wrote (at almost the same time) another missal, a parish missal, much fuller and built on an entirely different base. This was the "Gelasian Sacramentary," named as such because it was wrongly attributed to Pope Gelasius I. Thus, as astonishing as it may seem, there were two concurrent Roman liturgies during the 7th century, one for the use of the pope, and the other for daily use by the parishes. Around the year 680 a very minor event took place, which was rich in unforeseen consequences: one of the monks serving in ST. PETER'S BASILICA had for use the papal missal, the Gregorian stational. Wanting to use it at the altar, but noticing that it was quite incomplete for current usage, he took the initiative to fill in the missing portions by adding to it the daily liturgy that was missing, beginning with the 32 non-stational Sundays, for which he borrowed the formulas, and other things, from the old parish Gelasian. Thus the "Gregorian of St. Peter's" was born, also called the "Type 2 Gregorian." The success of the PILGRIMAGE to Rome explains how numerous prelates from Merovingian Gaul got the idea of taking a copy of the parish Gelasian and the Type 2 Gregorian back to their home country as a souvenir. The liturgists of Gaul, of Milan, and of Visigothic Spain had, for a long time, written out their own liturgies, "Gallican," "Ambrosian," and "Mozarabic" (also called "Visigothic"), all of great richness. Visigothic liturgy, the sister of Gallican liturgy, claimed to have been created by four illustrious Spanish bishops during the 7th century, St. Ildephonse, St. Eugene, St. Julian of Toledo, and St. Isidore of Seville. Ambrosian literature had depended upon the prestige of Saint Ambrose of Milan since the end of the 4th century.

"National" liturgies shared the same fate as the Churches that saw them created. In 8th-century France, the old Gallican liturgy was moribund. Founder of the Carolingian dynasty, crowned king of the FRANKS in 754 by Pope STEPHEN II personally, Pepin the Short had the idea of reunifying religion on the Roman liturgical basis, as when Roman chant was introduced to Metz by St. Chrodegang. The Frankish liturgists did not have to look very far for Roman books because there were at hand numerous copies of the old Gelasian and the Type 2 Gregorian. An anonymous monk from the abbey of Flavigny, near Dijon, took on the task, around 765, of fusing the two texts, while trying not to lose anything from either. A voluminous compilation was the result, called the "8th-century Gelasian," which was practically imposed on his new kingdom by Pepin. Copies rapidly multiplied, but changing and growing, augmented by formulas borrowed from the defunct Gallican liturgy, so that this fat hybrid missal, destined to promote unanimity, was rather, once again, the cause of great diversity. Wanting to find a remedy, Charlemagne asked Pope ADRIAN I to send him a copy of his papal missal, the Type I Gregorian, purely Roman, with no interpolations or modifications, transcribed from the fairly authentic one that was kept in the Lateran palace. A little before 791, the copy arrived at the palace in Aix-la-Chapelle (Aachen). The Carolingian liturgists, like their long-ago predecessor at St. Peter's in Rome, immediately noticed that 32 Sundays and a goodly number of other celebrations were missing. Charlemagne then ordered one of his followers, Benedict of Aniane, a former Visigoth count and a reformer of Benedictine monachism, to write a supplement to fill these gaps. Drawing deeply from the various versions of the Gelasian of the 8th century, and not shrinking from reproducing certain formulas from the Gallican liturgy and also several Visigothic pieces, he masterfully compiled a substantial supplement, which he added to the papal Gregorian, to which he also made a few minor changes: thus the

"Gregorian Type III" was born, and promoted around 800 to the status of official missal for the Carolingian Empire; originally papal, but now mingled with non-Roman elements, it was also called the "Romano-Frankish rite." This was the common basis for all future missals.

Spread throughout all the dioceses in the immense Carolingian Empire, the Romano-Frankish missal quickly adapted itself and flourished. It only contained Roman saints' days and ignored the good old saints of the Frankish lands, including, among others, St. Denis of Paris, St. Irenaeus of Lyon, St. Leonard of Limoges, and St. Léger at Autun. The diocesan liturgists then began to fill in this lacuna, and literally stuffed the Romano-Frankish original list with countless celebrations of local saints, not to mention ceremonies then unknown to Rome, such as Candlemas, Ash Wednesday, Palm Sunday, and Rogation Days. The religious orders that appeared since the 11th century did their part as well, and added to the liturgical variety, spreading proper rituals beyond their dioceses, injecting their own spirituality into the preexisting liturgies. The Cluniac monks order, at first very distinctly employing the Empire formulas, drew inspiration much more widely during the middle of the 11th century, using Roman practices and enriching them. The Cistercians rejected the pomp of the Cluny celebrations, putting the accent on individual prayer; they influenced, more or less directly, the liturgies of other orders, like the Carthusians, who were also influenced by the old Lyonnais liturgy. The Latin medieval liturgy then offered once again, an incredible diversity, with the names of the dioceses or orders for which they had been written beginning to appear in the titles of the liturgical books, which revealed, in their way, the historical tradition or the spiritual specificity of each; hence the "Parisian rite," "Rite of Lyon," and the "Dominican rite" are spoken of.

Toward the end of the 9th century, a new type of liturgical book appeared in Frankish territory, which was unknown to Rome and perfectly distinct from the missal: it was called a "pontifical," a ritual for the use of bishops for ceremonies other than mass such as for confirmation, ordinations, crowning kings, dedicating churches, etc. Rudimentary at the beginning, the pontifical suddenly developed into something extraordinary when, around 960, an anonymous Benedictine from the abbey of St. Alban in Mainz put together everything he could find in the way of rituals, ceremonies, and canonical texts, and compiled an enormous volume designated by the name "Romano-Germanic Pontifical." This masterwork, infinitely precious for having preserved texts that, without it, would have disappeared forever, was soon an extraordinary success; very rapidly copied, it spread almost wholly through the dioceses of Europe. The liturgy still followed political trends, but this time it was in the Empire-to-Rome direction. The Ottonian influence over

Italy, the establishment in 962 of what was going to become the Holy ROMAN EMPIRE, brought numerous prelates to Italy; they brought with them their Romano-Frankish missals and the Romano-Germanic pontifical. All these books were immediately adopted in Rome itself. The old Roman liturgy, which shone with such brightness 100 years earlier, was replaced without striking a blow by the Franco-Germanic creations. Compared to the ancient ritual of Rome, "Roman of Rome," these hybrid books became "Roman" when adopted by Rome. As usual, they were not long in evolving and "Romanizing" themselves: the pontifical was adopted, revised, and modified according to local needs. The same was true for the Romano-Frankish missals, multiplying throughout every parish in Rome and in all the Italian dioceses, where celebrations unknown in other areas crept in.

In the 12th century the diversity of missals used daily in Rome and in all Christianity was extreme. The final centuries of the Middle Ages were based upon this legacy, with no liturgical centralization; finally certain pontifical or parapontifical initiatives received a better reception, which prepared for a return to unity. The Gregorian reform had already made a few points: ALEXANDER II and GREGORY VII intervened to decree the suppression of Hispanic liturgy, not exempt from risks of doctrinal deviation; the same movement saw the ending of the old Celtic liturgies of Scotland and Ireland. From the 13th century on, the pontifical reservation of CANONIZATION and the institution by the pope of new universal celebrations imposed liturgical texts written in Rome for that occasion upon all Christianity. But most of the celebrations still escaped unification. Even in Rome there was no unity. During the pontificate of INNOCENT III the liturgy of the pontifical chapel won over the traditional one of the Lateran. Around 1210, the pope had his liturgists compile new books, destined for usage by the CURIA: almost simultaneously, a new missal appeared, with a new breviary, a new pontifical, all three "following the uses of the Roman Curia." Evidently these were Frankish and Germanic books that had been rethought, recast, and remodeled according to local evolution. They were quickly known, appreciated, and copied outside Rome, in Italy. In the dioceses, the evolution of the episcopal recruitment could go in their favor, when the new bishop was a former curialist. They were, therefore, imposed in 1337 in AVIGNON during the papacy's stay there. On the other hand, since 1223, they had been adopted by St. Francis of Assisi for his new order, the Franciscans; swarming through all Europe, they were among the most active agents of its spreading. However, globally, the diffusion of liturgical works used by the Curia was slow and timid; it hardly accelerated until the printing press.

The second initiative, with even heavier consequences, came around 1295 from the celebrated canonist and liturgist, the bishop of Mende Guillaume Durand. Noticing that the pontifical of the Curia was clearly insufficient for his diocese and that many ceremonies that he must celebrate were not in there, he surrounded himself with an enormous amount of documents and compiled, for his own personal use, a new and voluminous pontifical, very complete and totally practical: that was the key to its success. Many bishops adopted it. It even progressed to Avignon, where, very peacefully, it was used in parallel with the pontifical of the Curia. The return of the papacy to Rome in 1378 introduced it to the Eternal City, where it ended up taking the place of its rival. When in 1485 Pope INNOCENT VIII decided to give the first printed edition of the pontifical, he decided to only print Guillaume Durand's pontifical, but gave it the title "Roman Pontifical." Thus it remained basically in use throughout the entire Latin Church until VATICAN II. At the end of the 13th century, Guillaume Durand wrote: "Nothing should be sung or read that was not canonized by the Holy Roman Church, approved expressly or tolerated by it." Nevertheless, in actuality, the papacy of the final centuries of the Middle Ages could still act on this issue only step-by-step; still it had the basis, doctrinal and practical, for a liturgical unification, which was put into effect only after the COUNCIL OF TRENT.

Robert Amiet

Bibliography

Cabié, R. *Histoire de la messe des origines à nos jours*, Paris, 1990 (*BHC*, 23).

Gy, P. M. "La papauté et le droit liturgique aux XIIe et XIIIe siècles," *The Religious Roles of the Papacy Ideals and Realities, 1150–1300*, ed. C. Ryan, Toronto, 1989 (*Papers in Mediaeval Studies*, 8), 229–45; *La Liturgie dans l'histoire*, Paris, 1990 (reprinting of articles).

La liturgia: panorama storico generale, under the direction of S. Marsili, Casale Monferrato, 1978.

Martimort, A. G. *L'Église en prière: introduction à la liturgie*, 4th ed., Paris, 1983, 4 vol.

Senn, F. C. *Christian Liturgy: Catholic and Evangelical*, Minneapolis, 1997.

Vogel, C. *Introduction aux sources de l'histoire du culte chrétien au Moyen Âge*, Spoleto, 1966; reed. Turin, 1975; posthumous ed. by W. G. Storey and N. K. Rasmussen, under the title *Medieval Liturgy: An Introduction to the Sources*, Washington D.C., 1986.

Since the Council of Trent. Among the Roman CONGREGATIONS created by the BULL *Immensa aeterni Dei* (22 January 1588), was one "*pro sacris ritibus et caeremoniis*" dedicated to the reform of liturgical books following the prescriptions of the COUNCIL OF TRENT, but also with making the Church's liturgy more uniform. Beginning in 1588, the congregation launched an inquiry into the necessity of such a reform. Except for the reception of the new "Roman missal" (1570) and the breviary (1568), the impetus quickly sank into inertia and the congregation, for the next three centuries, only served to answer multiple questions about details and to favor the extension of the worship of saints. Still, some learned men tried to go back to the sources of the liturgy. In the 16th century, Melchior Hittorp (1525–84) was one of the first to compare ancient texts in a book of prayers. His work, *De divinis catholicae Ecclesiae officiis ac ministeriis varia vetustorum aliquot Ecclesiae Patrum ac scriptorum*, (Cologne, 1568) would be called the "prototype of a body of liturgical works." In the 17th and 18th centuries, the erudite works followed one another, among which we must mention J. Morin (d. 1659) and his commentators on the sacraments of penance and order (Paris, 1651 and 1655); J. Mabillon (d. 1707) and his *Museum italicum* (Paris 1687–89); Louis Thomassin (1619–95), author of the three volumes of *Vetus et nova Ecclesiae disciplina* (Paris, 1688); and of course the *De antiquis Ecclesiae ritibus* of Dom Martène (d. 1739). There was a substantial evolution of liturgy during this time period; there were several local initiatives, particularly in France. In answer to the directives of Pope PIUS V (the bulls *Quod a nobis* and *Quo primum*), the Church of France had, without difficulty, adopted liturgical reform during provincial synods. In 1745 on the other hand, the promulgation of the Roman pontifical caused several differences between Rome and France. Several dioceses looked elsewhere to improve the liturgical books. Some, taking into account the Roman missal, went to ancient books. Following the breviary of Henri of Villars (Vienne, 1678), there was a reduction of breviaries and missals belonging to dioceses (Besançon, Lodève, Paris, Meaux, etc.). These are what would later be called "neo-Gallican liturgies." Evidence of a real movement of independence from Rome, these initiatives met with very little opposition from the pontiffs. Under BENEDICT XIV, a commission on liturgical reform was unable to accomplish much after several years of labor (1741–47). In the ENCYCLICAL *Auctorem fidei* (18 August 1794), PIUS VI did not hesitate to condemn the liturgical intentions of the JANSENIST SYNOD of Pistoia. The decisions made by this assembly (and already applied in Germany during the *Aufklärung*) tended to favor the participation of the faithful: utilization of the country's language for the ordinary of the mass, recitation of the canon aloud, relative purification of the liturgy.

After the confusions of the revolutionary years, no reform succeeded in unifying the diversity of the diocesan liturgies. Not even the pious intention of the "organic articles" added to the concordat of 1801: "A liturgy and a catechism for all Catholic churches in France" (no. 39). A "period of hunger," as Dom Cabrol would write of it.

In January 1840, Dom Prosper Guéranger (1805–75) published the first volume of the *Institutions liturgiques*. Two volumes would follow to set forth the liturgical prin-

ciples in which the author—a staunch ultramontane—called for liturgical unity using the Roman ritual and for the recognition of pontifical omnipotence in liturgical matters. Although unfinished, the *Institutions* made reference to the very sources of traditions, but had little practical effect on the religion of the people. Ordained a priest in Tours in 1827, Prosper Guéranger reestablished Benedictine life in France by founding the abbey Saint Pierre de Solesmes (in Sarthe); approved in 1837 by GREGORY XVI, this community achieved the liturgical principles of its founder. The writings of Guéranger would cause a major change of opinion among the French high clergy. This explains the reactions of the archbishop of Toulouse, Monsignor d'Astros, and the bishop of Orleans, Monsignor Fayet, before the first condemnation, in 1843, by the archbishop of Paris, Monsignor Affre. After 1841, Dom Guéranger still undertook the publication of another Summa on a large scale: *L'Année liturgique* (9 volumes, 1841–66). His work was not done in vain. In his battle against the inroads of Gallicanism, PIUS IX mandated the missal, the breviary, and the Roman ritual (encyclical *Inter multiplices*) in March of 1853. Less than ten years later, almost every French diocese had renounced any particularism, directly adopting the Roman liturgy. Still, some situations remained a source of conflict in France, England, Belgium, and Germany. The influence of Dom Guéranger and the abbey of Solesmes was also felt in the area of Gregorian chant and sacred music. New schools for playing the organ brought a breath of fresh air: those of the Belgian Nicolas-Jacques Lemmens or the Frenchman César Franck. Despite interesting compositions, European polyphonic music has largely remained outside the liturgical renewal.

A certain elite group of college professors, in many publications, was going to answer the expectations of Dom Guéranger. The knowledgeable editor of the *LIBER PONTIFICALIS*, Monsignor Louis Duchesne (1843–1922) taught at the Catholic Institute of Paris, then at the Ecole pratique des haute études, before becoming director of the French School in Rome (1895–1922). His work on the *Origines du culte chrétien* (Paris, 1888) inspired many other works of liturgical erudition. Victim of the modernist controversy, Monsignor Pierre Batiffol (1861–1929) left behind, after his rectorship of the Catholic Institute of Toulouse, a *Histoire du Bréviaire* (1893, reworked in 1911) as well as one volume of *Leçons sur la messe* (1919). Initiated by Dom Cabrol and Dom H. Leclercq, a *Dictionnaire d'archéologie chrétienne et de liturgie* was begun in 1903. The movement was not limited only to France. Catholic Germany tried makeshift simplifications of the liturgy, but ones supported by real references to tradition: the works of Johann-Adam Moehler (1796–1836) were reflected by the liturgical apostolate of the Belgian community of Beuron, and the mother abbey Maria Laach, as in England, wishing to re-Christianize the kingdom, the OXFORD MOVEMENT provoked a real liturgical renaissance of the Anglican Church.

It was Dom Guéranger who first used the expression "liturgical movement," but since then, it designates all the efforts of theologians, historians, and pastors who have prepared the great liturgical reform that the Fathers of the Second Vatican Council wanted. This evolution found its impetus in several decrees by PIUS X at the beginning of the century. Through songs by the assembly and a renewal of Gregorian chant, this pontiff wished to heighten the participation of the faithful in the liturgical mystery (*motu proprio Tra le sollicitudini* of 22 November 1903). Pius X was also the pope of "frequent communion" (1905), giving a strong momentum to eucharistic worship, in response to the expectations of many bishops and of the movement begun since Beuron by Dom Van Caloen. Through a reform of the breviary and psalter, the same pontiff returned Sunday to its former position of importance (bull *Divino afflatu* of 1 November 1911).

The decisive initiative came from the Belgian abbey of Mont-César and, above all, the intervention of Dom Lambert Beauduin (1873–1960)—encouraged by Cardinal Mercier—during the Eucharistic congress held in the city of Malines in 1909. The plan for a translated missal for the faithful was discussed. The appearance of the review of *Questions liturgiques* (1910), later *Questions liturgiques et pastorales* (1919), extended the views of the reformers to the clergy in the parishes: to allow the greatest number possible of the faithful to participate in the mystery celebrated in Church liturgy. The famous *Missel des fidèles* by Dom Gaspart Lefebvre (a monk from Saint-André-les-Bruges) also had many editions and translations of its own.

In the period between the two world wars, the liturgical movement found a more theological foundation in the German abbey of Maria Laach, through the work of Dom Odo Cassel (1886–1948) on the theology of the mysteries: *Le Mémorial du Seigneur* and *Le Mystère du culte* (both published in 1932). The work of Romano Guardini (1885–1968) had a similarly strong influence: *The Spirit of Liturgy* (1918, translated into French in 1929). In Austria, Pius Parsch (1884–1954) developed a large popular movement by publishing many tracts and brochures: the *Volksliturgisches Apostolat*. From then on, a "liturgical pastorate" was discussed. In France, the movement found excellent "testing laboratories" within the youth movements (Boy Scouts, Catholic Action). We must also emphasize the prophetic action led by Father Paul Doncoeur, a Jesuit (1880–1961) in his many writings for the magazine *Études* and by the doctrinal and liturgical teachings he did with the cadets and then the older branch of the French Boy Scouts, which he founded. In all these movements, the accent was placed on participation—a "living liturgy," as Father Doncoeur called it: mass as a dialogue,

use of the vernacular language, improved quality of Latin and vernacular hymns. In 1936, two Dominicans, Fathers Maydieu and Louvel, organized a dialogue mass for the friends of the review *Sept* in Notre Dame de Paris cathedral: with an altar that "faced the people," Bible readings that were repeated in French, the Introit and Gradual were even translated. The liturgical movement found determined supporters among the Dominicans for the publications of *le Cerf* (which may be seen in the impact of the issues of *Fêtes et saisons*). It was at their institution, in Paris, that the first meeting of the Center for Liturgical Pastorate (CPL) was held on 23 May 1943, with Dom Lambert Beauduin surrounded by the Dominicans Pius Duployé and Aimon-Marie Roguet, Father Doncoeur and the Toulousan Aimé-Georges Martimort. Theologicans, historians, and pastors all added convergent efforts at that time. The work of Fathers Congar, Chenu, Dalmais, Daniélou, Gy, Pierre Jounel, Henri de Lubac, Dom Botte, Dom Capelle, Father Louis Bouyer, and the erudite writings of Monsignor Michel Andrieu must be mentioned. The fruits of this research are found in the review of the CPL (*La Maison-Dieu*) and its collection of works *Lex Orandi*. The CPL would organize national sessions for priests, encouraged by several bishops including the one in Chartres, Monsignor Harscouët (1874–1954). The other countries of Europe also developed many initiatives of their own. In Germany, attempts to use the language of the region did not occur without distress. In Holland, Italy, and Spain, the movement toward liturgical pastorate would be felt more after 1945.

The liturgical movement was, for the most part, confirmed by Pope PIUS XII personally. In his soul, this pope was more of a reformer than people were willing to admit. In 1948 Pius XII set up a commission on liturgical reform within the Congregation of Rites. Beginning in 1951 the paschal vigil was again celebrated at night. Four years later, an entire group of offices for Holy Week were reestablished. The encyclical *Mediator Dei* (20 November 1947) detailed the progress toward the use of vernacular languages in liturgy, while emphasizing the excesses of some liturgists. In 1955 the encyclical *Musicae sacrae disciplina* would mislead some due to the preference given to Latin, the traditional symbol for Church unity. JOHN XXIII would continue the work of Pius XII by putting out, in 1960 and 1961, a series of simplifications of liturgical rubrics. His major enterprise still remains the convocation of an ecumenical council (25 January 1959).

Prepared for in 1960 by a commission of 60 members, the constitution *Sacrosanctum concilium* was the consecration of the whole liturgical movement. The first topic discussed by the Fathers of the Second Vatican Council (15 general congregations between 22 October and 13 November 1962), the definitive text was approved by 2,147 favorable votes (four votes against), and announced by Pope PAUL VI on 4 December 1963. After reviewing the general principles of restoration of the liturgy, the constitution successively addressed the mystery of the Eucharist (c. 2), the other sacraments and the sacramentals (c. 3), the liturgical Hours (c. 4), the liturgical year (c. 5), sacred music (c. 6), and finally, sacred art (c. 7). An exercise of the sacerdotal function of Christ transmitted to his Church, the liturgy is a participation in the heavenly liturgy. For that, the council's text insists forcefully on "full participation, conscious and active" by all the faithful (no. 14). The key word of the constitution, "participation," must be made easier by more access to Biblical texts, the possibility of using the language of the country (no. 36), the possibility of adapting the liturgy "to the temperament and traditions of different peoples" (no. 37), a responsibility conferred upon the conferences of the bishops, for renovation of all the rites and liturgical books.

Propelled by the drumbeat of the *consilium "ad exsequendam Constitutionem de sacra liturgia"* (25 January 1964), working under the fervent leadership of the Lazarist Annibale Bugnini (1912–82), the application of the council's directives was regulated by several documents: the *motu proprio Sacram Liturgiam* (25 January 1964), the instruction *Inter oecumenici Concilii* (25 September 1964), the decree *Ecclesiae semper* (on concelebration and communion of both kinds, 7 March 1965), a second instruction on liturgy *Tres abhinc annos* (4 May 1967), and finally another on the worship of the Eucharistic mystery *Eucharisticum mysticum* (25 May 1967). In six years, the *consilium* accomplished a remarkable amount of work, increasing the typical publications of liturgical books: adding other Eucharistic prayers to the Roman Canon (23 May 1968), a new pontifical for ordinations (19 March 1969), a new *ordo missae* (3 April 1969), a Roman calendar (9 May 1969), a baptismal ritual for infants (15 May 1969), a new *ordo* of readings for the mass (25 May 1969), a ritual for funerals (15 August 1969), a ritual for religious profession (2 February 1970), the volumes of the "Liturgy of the Hours" (1971), and the ritual of the sacrament of penance (1974), which would set the stage for many abuses of interpretation of the opportunity for "general absolution."

This departure slowed somewhat after the disgrace of Monsignor Bugnini, named apostolic nuncio to Iran. The Church liturgy in the 1970s saw the consequences of applying things too rapidly. Under the pretext of "adaptations," the feeling of the most noble, "sacred" liturgy of the Church were flouted on many occasions, provoking violent if not schismatic reactions (Monsignor Lefebvre). There can be no justification for that. Wounded, the liturgy of the Latin Church, 30 years after the conciliar constitution, tried to return to the first intentions of the reformers, the quality of celebrations.

Jean-Michel Fabre

Bibliography

Bouyer, L. *Dom Lambert Beauduin*, Tournai, 1964.

Braga, C. "La preparazione della Costituzione *Sacrosanctum concilium*," *Mens concordet voci. Mélanges . . . Martimort*, Paris, 1983, 381–403.

Bugnini, A. *La riforma liturgica—1948-1975*, Rome, 1983.

Combe, P. *Histoire de la restauration du chant grégorien d'après des documents inédits*, Solesmes, 1969.

Doncoeur, P. "Cinquante années de renaissance liturgique (1903–1953)," *La Maison-Dieu*, 40 b (1955).

Duployé, P. *Les Origines du Centre de pastorale liturgique (1943-1949)*, Mulhouse, 1968.

Fontaine, G. "Présentation des missels diocésains français du XVIIe au XIXe siècles," *La Maison-Dieu*, 141 (1980), 97–166.

Gozier, A. *Dom Casel*, Paris, 1968.

Gy, P. M. *La Liturgie dans l'histoire*, Paris, 1990 (4th part).

Haquin, A. *Dom Lambert Beauduin et le renouveau liturgique, témoignages et souvenirs*, Paris, 1973.

Johnson, C. *Dom Guéranger et le renouveau liturgique: une introduction à son oeuvre liturgique*, Paris, 1988.

Jossua, J. P., and Congar, Y. *La liturgie après Vatican II. Bilan, études, prospectives*, Paris, 1967.

Jounel, P. "L'évolution du Missel romain de Pie IX à Jean XXIII," *Notitiae*, 14 (1978), 246–58; "Les missels diocésains français du XVIIIe siècles," *La Maison-Dieu*, 141 (1980), 91–6.

Jounel, P. "Genèse et théologie de la constitution *Sacrosanctum concilium*," *La Maison-Dieu*, 156 (1983), 7–23.

Koenker, E. B. *The Liturgical Renaissance in the Roman Catholic Church*, Chicago, 1954.

Le Deuxième concile du Vatican, 1959–1965, EFR, 1989.

Le rôle de G.-B. Montini—Paul VI—dans la Réforme liturgique, Istituto Paolo VI, Brescia, 1987.

Leclercq, H. "Liturgies néo-gallicanes," *DACL*, 9 (1930) 1636–1729.

Martimort, A. G. *L'Église en prière, Introduction à la liturgie*, Paris, 1961; new ed. Paris, 1983–4 (4 vol.).

Martimort, A. G. "Du Centre de Pastorale Liturgique à la Constitution liturgique de Vatican II," *La Maison-Dieu*, 157 (1984), 15–31; "La Constitution sur la Liturgie de Vatican II," *La Maison-Dieu*, 157 (1984), 33–52.

Martimort, A. G. *Mirabile laudis canticum. Mélanges liturgiques*, Rome, 1991.

Rasmussen, N. K. "Liturgy and Liturgical Arts," in *Catholicism in Early Modern History: A Guide to Research*, ed. O'Malley, J. W., St. Louis, 1988, 273–97.

Roguet, A. M. "Le Centre de Pastorale Liturgique," *Mens concordet voci. Mélanges . . . Martimort*, Paris, 1983, 371–80.

Rousseau, O. *Histoire du movement liturgique*, Paris, 1945.

Vinck, H. "Enquête faite en 1588 sur la nécessité d'une réforme des livres liturgiques," *Question Liturgiques*, 56 (1975), 113–25.

Winninger, P. "Le culte public, le movement liturgique, musique et chant sacrés," *Histoire du droit et des institutions de l'Église en Occident*, 18, Paris, 1984, 337–71.

LOMBARDS. For centuries, an Italian perspective essentially dominated historical research on the Lombard problem. In effect, although the peninsula had been overrun in the 5th and 6th centuries by numerous peoples called "BARBARIANS" (Visigoths, Vandals, Herules, Sciri, Ostrogoths), none of them stayed as long as the Lombards, a Germanic people. For five centuries, from 568 (the year the king Alboin, at the head of the Lombards, crossed the Julian Alps to invade Italy) until 1077 (when the principality of Salerno was conquered by the NORMANS), political entities whose dominant elite could be called "Lombards" existed on the peninsula. During this period, the two first centuries (568–774) saw a Lombard monarchy dominating almost all of northern Italy, Tuscany, and, nominally, two other Lombard political entities that occupied large portions of the central southern portion of the peninsula: the duchies of Spoleto and Benevento. When Charlemagne, in 774, defeated the last two kings, Didier and Adelchis, and took over their kingdoms, he was not thinking about annexing the Lombard kingdom to the Frankish one. He took the title of King of the Lombards, which he handed down to his son Pepin. Based on this action, it may be observed that domination of Italy was thus identified with domination of the Lombard people. At the same time, a process was completed that could be called the "geographical assimilation" of the Lombards into Italian territory, due to which the name "Lombardy" was given to a large portion of the plains of the Po River (especially the northwest.) All these considerations on the actual penetration of the "Lombards" into Italian territory are necessary for a fair perception of the problematic negative image that most historical criticism has given them from the end of the Middle Ages until the early 20th century.

The people who arrived in 568 following Alboin were mostly pagan, and those who converted to Christianity joined the Arian HERESY. What is more, their entry into the zone of the Romanized world was very late (the end of the 5th century, when they installed themselves in the formerly Roman Pannonia). It followed that their integration into what had been the "heart" of the Roman Empire, meaning Italy, was extremely difficult and without the transition that had been the characteristic of other peoples (like the Goths, the Franks, and even the Vandals) who had lived for a long time within the confines of the empire and even served in its army. The arrival of the Lombards therefore caused the total replacement of the dominant social classes. What was left of the Roman senatorial aristocracy—after the disasters of the Gothic war (535–53)—was eliminated and the greater majority of the lands passed into the hands of the invaders. The definitive destruction of this social class brought about the irreversible disappearance of a climate thanks to which the cultural flowering of late antiquity had been possible. Moreover, the arrival of the Lombards destroyed the political unity of the Italian peninsula, previously achieved by the Roman conquests of the 2nd and 3rd centuries before Christ—a unity that Italy would not totally recover until the end of WORLD WAR I, exactly 1,350 years after the arrival of Alboin. To all this must be added the observation that the Lombards, given their positions on religious matters, appeared to the Church—particularly to the Church of Rome—as a real threat to her survival.

Thus, the flight of several of the most prominent bishops of northern Italy before the dreaded arrival of these new barbarians was memorable: the patriarch of L'Aquila took refuge in the islands of the nearby lagoon, where Grado was founded, and the archbishop of MILAN emigrated to Genoa, which was still in the hands of the Byzantines. Several letters of Pope GREGORY I the Great have remained famous for their portrayal of this era. They reflect the anguish (and almost eschatological feeling) evoked by the approaching armies of King Agilulph and the duke of Spoleto, Ariulph, as they reached the walls of Rome. This profound hostility on the part of the Church of Rome would wane, only to reappear later, in relatively less dramatic circumstances, expressing the pope's persistent fear of a neighbor who was too invasive. This was basically the catalyst for of the intervention by the Pippinides, and then the Carolingians, on the Italian political scene. In 739, Pope GREGORY III established the first contacts with Charles Martel. Then in 774, Charlemagne as noted above, eliminated the independent Lombard kingdom. The final developments in the alliance between the papacy and the FRANKS led to the coronation of Charlemagne in Rome as Emperor of the West in 800. These facts traditionally represented a sort of symbol of Italy's emergence from the darkest period of the early Middle Ages and its turn toward the rebirth of Europe. To summarize, tradition has made the appearance of the Lombards coincide with an important historic rupture that brutally severed Italy from antiquity and cast it into the dramatic shadow of the Middle Ages. This viewpoint, especially due to the fact that the majority of the written sources were pontifical in origin, has been progressively revised and enriched, thanks to the development of research.

On one hand, there has been an increase in knowledge about the various aspects of the severe crisis facing society in the aftermath of the Byzantine-Gothic war. This civilization was no longer in a condition to offer any real resistance to these new invaders—and sometimes did not even want to try. The ancient administrative structures and urban organization to which the Lombards dealt the final blow had in reality been dying for some time. On the other hand, progress in archaeological research has allowed the history and the civilization of the Lombards to be better understood, including their identity within the Germanic world during the half-millennium that preceded their coming to Italy. During this period, they left the lower basin of the Elbe—they are mentioned by Tacitus and Velleius Paterculus (A.D. 1st century)—for Pannonia, where they settled during the end of the 5th century. For the following phase, their establishment in Italy, the information gleaned from archaeological research has also been of primary importance, to the point of encouraging a re-reading of the written sources. Thus it has become possible, by looking at both types of sources, to arrive at a reading of history "from the Lombard side" and to reach the basic conviction that if their arrival in Italy was a traumatic event for the Romans, it was one for the Lombards as well. Their civilization was based on a seminomadic, tribal model that preserved a unique ethnic aspect, including military identity, social hegemony, and the role played by lineage. Now it was brutally confronted by an entirely new set of problems.

Among these the principal one was the necessity of becoming attached to a land whose political and administrative structure had been based for centuries upon cities, whose role, though now in crisis, had been reinforced during late antiquity by the territorial government of the Church, which rested on the bishops. The latter lived in the cities, and, from there, controlled a precise extra-urban territory (the diocese), with no gap between episcopal authority and any other. This system underwent adjustments after the arrival of the Lombards. During this period, certain cities acquired an importance unknown during the Roman period (this was the case in Pavia, which had become the residence of the Lombard kings, as well as Cividale, Siena, Lucca, and Spoleto). The interior spaces of the cities themselves, as recent archaeological digs have shown (Milan, Brescia, Verona), were considerably remodeled. Great monasteries were founded far from cities (Bobbio, Farfa, San Vincenzo al Volturno). But the principle of the city as a pivotal territory remained. The more general problem of the "settlement" of the Lombard people was linked to this. As a consequence, the possession of land became a newly fundamental source of wealth for them. The union of the use of arms and real estate led to the formation of new kinds of aristocracies. These created new forms of social differentiation, which were reinforced, with the christianization

of the 7th century, by stronger and stronger ties with ecclesiastical society.

Another great problem for the Lombards was their passage from an ethnocentric society to a multiethnic society. Although the ties of blood were strong, the Lombards, who were few in number, found themselves confronted by diverse elements: the immensity of the territory they needed to divide between them, the number of Roman people (although this was greatly reduced compared to the past), and the simultaneous presence of "scraps" of other Germanic populations (surviving Goths, Swabians, Bavarians, Thuringians, and others, who followed the Lombards during their invasion). Another far-reaching problem was that of the confrontation between one civilization (Lombard) based on oral communication, and another (Roman) based on the use of written documents, and therefore basically "stronger" in preserving memory. All this presaged a process of cultural assimilation (loss of the Germanic language, abandonment of typical types of arms, clothing, and ornaments, absorption of the Latin modalities of the Christian religion), for which there are accounts and evidence beginning in the late 6th century.

The complexity of relations between ethnic identity, cultural forms, social usages, and modes of political domination can already be seen rather clearly during the time of King Rothari (636–52), author of the famous code published in 643. Written in Latin, it took on a double aspect. On one hand, it glorified the memory and ethnic tradition of the Lombards (as expressed in the genealogy of Rothari, accompanied by a mythical recital of the Lombard national origins); and on the other hand, it showed a willingness to organize civil life and criminal law according to criteria that applied to all of conquered Italy, which then became a multinational kingdom and not just a simple region of armed colonization. Between those two moments, the affirmation of ethnicity and bloodlines, and that of a public territorial sovereignty, it is difficult to say if a balance was achieved. Still, we can conclude without a doubt that the effort accomplished by the sovereigns of the 8th century, beginning with Liutprand (712–44), who had taken the significant first name of Flavius, toward political unification of Italy under the Lombard crown (elimination of the Byzantine enclaves and control of the duchies of Spoleto and Benevento) had very different connotations than those at the end of the 6th century.

It was aimed toward creating a political unity, cemented by the *sodalitas* between the warrior and ecclesiastical aristocracies under the tutelage of the king, an example of military strength united with religious piety—an evolved conception that, with all its idiosyncrasies, bore within it many points in common with the synthesis that would be developed by the Carolingians.

Federico Marazzi

Bibliography

Cilento, N. *Italia meridionale longobarda*, Naples, 1971.

Diacre, P. *Historia Langobardum*, ed. G. Waitz, *MGH SS Rerum Langobardicarum et Italicarum*, 1878 (French trans. F. Bougard, 1994).

Hallenbek, J. T. "Instances of Peace in Eighth-century Lombard-papal relations," *AHP*, 18 (1980), 41–56.

I Longobardi, dir. G. C. Menis, Milan, 1990.

Longobardia, ed. S. Gasparri, Udine, 1990.

LUCIUS. *(b. Rome ?–d. 5 March 254). Consecrated 26 June 253. Buried in the catacomb of Callistus.*

Lucius is one of the lesser-known popes of the 3rd century. Originally from Rome (*natione Romanus* according to *LP*, I, 153 = *MGH, GPR*, I, 32) he succeeded Cornelius, dead at Centumcellae (Civitavecchia) during the persecution by Trebonianus Gallus, possibly in June 253. His ordination date is given as 26 June, if we can be sure of the chronological information deduced from ancient sources (according to the *Liberian Catalogue, MGH, AA*, 9/1, 75, where it is necessary to correct the number of years and months: three years, seven months, and ten days; on the other hand, *LP* I, 153 = *MGH, GPR*, I, 32, gives the correct information: eight months and ten days).

According to the *Liberian Catalogue* and the LIBER PONTIFICALIS, after a short exile he returned to his community. It is not known whether his wanderings were due to persecution or to the troubles caused by the crisis in the year 253, which saw, in short-lived succession, Trebonianus Gallus associated with Volusian, and Emilian and Valerian associated with Gallian.

Under his episcopate, the SCHISM of Novatian was worrying the authorities in Rome and CARTHAGE, despite the condemnation handed down by the SYNOD of Rome called by CORNELIUS. Cyprian warned his colleague about the attitude of bishop Marcian of Arles (*Epist.*, 68). Moreover, two questions that would later concern his successor STEPHEN were becoming serious, that of the Iberian bishops who had abjured the faith and whom the faithful were rejecting (Cyprian, *Epist.* 67) and that of the baptism of heretics.

Lucius was buried on 5 March 254 (*LP*, I, 153 = *MGH, GPR*, I, 32). According to the *Liber pontificalis*, he was a victim of imperial power (*martyrio coronatur a Valeriano capite truncatus est*). Cyprian of Carthage called him a *beatus martyr* (*Epist.*, 68), as did Cornelius, although there is no evidence that he was martyred. His body was laid in the papal crypt in the cemetery of Callistus on the Appian Way (*MGH, AA*, 9/1, 70), where his epitaph was found (*ICUR*, IV, 10645).

Michel Christol

Bibliography

Turner C. H. "The Papal Chronology of the Third Century," *JThS*, 17 (1916), 343–5.

Vogel, C. *LP* (reed. 1957), III.

LUCIUS II. *Gherardo Caccianemici, his mother's surname (b. Bologna ?–d. Rome, 15 February 1145). Elected pope 12 March 1444. Buried at Rome, in St. John Lateran).*

Gherardo probably chose the name of Lucius in memory of LUCIUS I, who was commemorated in prayer several days before his consecration. He first belonged to the prominent congregation of canons regular of San Frediano of Lucca (or, according to other sources, of Santa Maria of Reno). In 1123, CALLISTUS II created him cardinal-priest with the TITLE of Santa Croce, which had a regular chapter. In 1125 and 1126, he was a LEGATE of HONORIUS II in Germany. He intervened in the election of the king of Germany, Lothair III, to whom he later brought the papal confirmation, and supported that of Norbert of Xanten to be archbishop of Magdeburg. During the double pontifical election of 1130, Gherardo was part of the group of cardinals who sided with INNOCENT II against the ANTIPOPE ANACLETUS II.

A collaborator of Innocent II, the cardinal of Santa Croce held many positions in the course of the next few years. In 1130, 1130–1, and 1135–6, Gherardo again represented the pope as legate to Germany. In addition, he was rector of the pontifical possessions of Benevento, which was how he established a relationship with Roger II of Sicily, the ally of Anacletus. During talks with Lothair III in 1137, Gherardo, together with Cardinal Guido di Santa Maria in Via Lata and chancellor Aimeric, tried to impose on Monte Cassino the direct submission required by Rome. The abbey was forced to stop obeying Anacletus. During the same year, Gherardo participated with Guido, Aimeri, and Bernard of Clairvaux in a delegation that negotiated the end of the SCHISM at Salerno, in the presence of Roger II.

It is known that the supporters of Anacletus recognized Gherardo as the principal supporter of Innocent II without finding anything to criticize about his personal conduct. For his contemporaries, he was the model of the impeccable cleric. Among his friends were Bernard of Clairvaux, and Archbishop Gautier of Ravenna as well as Peter the Venerable, the abbot of Cluny. That Gerhoh of Reichersberg called him a "pillar of the Roman Church" and dedicated to him as well as to other cardinals his *Libellus de ordine donorum Sancti Spiritus*, which reveals both the political importance and the intellectual interests of Gherardo. In 1144, after Aimeric's death, he became CHANCELLOR and librarian of the CURIA. A short time later, he succeeded CELESTINE II on Peter's throne.

As his predecessors had done, Lucius II took the side of the empress Matilda in the competition for the English royal crown. He recognized the vassal status of Portugal in relation to the HOLY SEE, planned under Innocent II, without releasing the country from its dependence on Castile. Concerning the Sicilian question, Lucius II tried to negotiate a compromise between the two camps. Still, the interview he had in June 1144 with Roger II of Sicily at Ceprano was fruitless; the pope sought the restitution of the Norman conquests in the duchy of Capua, which Roger refused. It is possible that the cardinals had pushed him to adopt a tougher attitude toward Sicily. Roger II's sons then threatened the PAPAL STATES and made it as far as Rieti; Lucius II withdrew and negotiated a seven-year truce. The Sicilian sovereign kept possession of the conquered territories but promised not to attack Benevento or any other papal possessions. Lucius II was ready to make overtures to Roger II, from whom he hoped to obtain support against the Romans rebelling against his authority, who wanted to set up an independent republic. The movement was mostly carried on by merchants and artisans, whereas the greater part of the urban nobility remained neutral. Lucius II was able to obtain a temporary submission of the Senate, set up by the rebels. But after that, the latter required the termination of all pontifical governmental prerogatives. The pope would retain only ecclesiastical taxes and voluntary tributes. The aristocrat Giordano Pierleone, one of Anacletus's brothers, led the rebellion as a patrician. He wanted to drive out the pontifical prefects. Roger II did not come to the aid of the papacy, because he had never obtained full recognition of his kingship. Lucius II sent a desperate appeal for help to the king of Germany, Conrad II. But the pope died before receiving a response. Exposed in the front lines during the capital battles, he was struck by some thrown rocks with fatal consequences. The creations of cardinals by Lucius II show that he was favorable to innovative currents. Among those he raised to the dignity of the cardinalate we find the English theologian Robert Pulleyn, who later became chancellor, and the French Carthusian Jourdain de Ste. Suzanne.

Karl Schnith

Bibliography

JL, 2, 7–19.

LP, 2 385–6.

PL, 179, 819–938.

Horn, M. "Lucius II," *LexMA*, 5 (1991), 2162.

Maleczek, W. "Das Kardinalskollegium unter Innocenz II. und Anakelt II.," *AHP*, 19 (1981), 27–78.

Schmale, F. J. *Studien zum Schisma des Jahres 1130*, Graz–Cologne, 1961.

Swietek, F. R., and Deneen, T. M. "Pope Lucius II and Savigny," *Analecta Cisterciensia*, 39 (1983), 3–25.

Watterich 2, 278–81.

Zenker B. *Die Mitglieder des Kardinalkollegiums von 1130 bis 1159*, Dissertation, Wurzburg, 1964.

LUCIUS III. *Ubaldo Allucingoli (b. Lucca ?–d. Verona, 25 November 1185). Elected pope 1 September 1181. Consecrated September 6. Buried at Verona.*

The son of Orlando Allucingoli and a native of Lucca, he played a decisive role in Alexander III's legitimatization by crowning him at Ninfa on 20 September 1159. He was close to the Cistercian order; Bernard of Clairvaux had personally received him. Thus no one was surprised by his ascetic way of life, in accordance with the precepts of St. Benedict's rules, nor by his wishing to encourage Church reform by imposing strict rules. He served popes who defended an unwavering conception of the Church's juridical prerogatives, especially in relation to the empire, and who tried to strengthen the internal government of the Church by taking disciplinary measures. By requiring that curial decisions be based on Roman law and forbidding the return to the customary practices stipulated in GRATIAN'S DECRETUM when they were in conflict with canon law, he took actions that had great consequences for the future.

In 1138, INNOCENT II created him cardinal-deacon of Sant'Adriano, and then in 1141, cardinal-priest of Santa Prasseda; in 1158, HADRIAN IV raised him to the position of cardinal-bishop of Ostia and Velletri. In 1156, together with the future Pope ALEXANDER III, he had negotiated the treaty of Benevento with the kingdom of Sicily: during the troubled pontificate of Alexander III he came to occupy a central position in the CURIA, which he would retain.

In September 1181 Ulbaldo was elected pope. Throughout his reign, Lucius III pursued the same political policies as his predecessor. The most burning question was that of the return of the Curia to Rome, which required a conciliation with the Roman commune as well as with the SENATE, or else strong support from a temporal power. An initial attempt at reestablishing pontifical authority over Rome by making several concessions, but without instituting the generous payments of former times, failed. The pontifical stay in the Eternal City, which had been negotiated on the basis of this compromise, lasted only from 2 November 1181 to March 1182. It appeared that only imperial power could help the pope attain a solid position in his own episcopal see. Open conflict with the Romans resumed over Tusculum, formerly placed under papal control by Frederick Barbarossa, under condition of maintenance of imperial rights, rebuilt after its destruction in 1173, and again attacked by the Romans on 28 June 1183. Lucius III then appealed to Christian, the archbishop of Mainz, imperial legate, and succeeded in obtaining helpful support from him. But the latter died of a raging fever on 25 August and had to be replaced. Previously, on June 25, the emperor had finally reconciled with the LOMBARD league by signing the peace of Constance, thus opening new vistas for his Italian policy as he was decisively increasing his political options regarding the papacy.

The pope was assured of the goodwill of the Norman sovereign: it was with this outlook that he had, in 1183, raised the Sicilian abbey of Montreale to the rank of archbishopric, which the king had founded in the hopes of establishing a lineage. But concerning external politics, the main concern of the pontificate of Lucius III was the entente with Frederick Barbarossa, especially since increasingly urgent calls for assistance were coming from the Holy Land to Rome. Two meetings on this subject took place with the emperor and his plenipotentiaries in Verona during the fall (mid-October and early November) and winter (mid-December) of 1184 that were of great significance. The different parties were also trying to arrive at an agreement on the still pending question of implementation of the peace of Venice (1177).

The predominant issue was the question of the inheritance of Matilda, which the countess of Canossa had willed to the Roman Church upon her death in 1155. This bequest was being challenged. The juridical difficulty of the affair lay in the fact that Matilda was able to freely dispose only of her allodial properties but not of her imperial fiefs. The papacy had given its portion of Matilda's inheritance to the empire while reserving the Roman Church's property rights, but it had not established a clear distinction between a fief and an allodium; this was the basis for the quarrel, which was nearly insoluble because of the confusion surrounding the status of these properties. Frederick Barbarossa should have had to give up possession of this inheritance *salvo omni juri imperii* in accordance with the treaty of Venice. But these lands, as well as other territories disputed between the two parties, remained the object of bitter negotiations. The emperor proposed to give up his claims in exchange for payment of rent to the pope and the cardinals, or have recourse to arbitration; but no agreement could be reached.

At the same time, there was still the question of the coronation of Frederick's son. The emperor wished to have the latter crowned emperor in his own lifetime to avoid eventual takeover attempts of the type made against the imperial crown by the Hohenstaufen dynasty. Lucius III was not able to grant this wish, which would have led to the installation of a hereditary empire, thus limiting the options of the papacy. In Verona, moreover, he learned of the engagement of Henry VI, celebrated on 19 October, to Constance of Sicily, the aunt of King William II. It was still impossible, in the fall of 1184, to determine exactly the problems of any future succession, even if the pope had been totally informed about the situation, as the support he gave to the abbey at Monreale proved. On the other hand, the succession itself, despite

the contract of marriage agreed to at the time of engagement, depended upon the right of the Norman nobility to a free election. Nevertheless, it was the link between the Germanic Empire and the kingdom of Sicily that—independently of any ambition for imperial succession of an eventual *unio regni ad imperium*—opened the way to the juridical pretensions of the Hohenstaufens and to new political alliances with southern Italy, seriously limiting the papacy's possibilities for action. The kingdom of Sicily was, of course, a fief of the Holy See, and as a result, the king was a vassal of the pope. However, this situation did not give the state the right to determine succession by escheat, so settlement of the succession was left to the discretion of the king of Sicily according to the CONCORDAT of Benevento (1156). In return, Lucius III had demanded that Henry the Lion, the duke of Saxony, who had been condemned by the emperor, be able to return from exile to his former lands; Frederick Barbarossa allowed this on 19 October. The pope was trying to play the English card against him, and at the same time to destabilize the position of the Hohenstaufens in their internal politics. It is still debated whether, pressed by the cardinals, the pope agreed to the Sicilian engagement.

As for internal Church affairs, there was still the ever-present problem of the sacraments conferred during the SCHISM of Anacletus by the latter, as well as his successors and followers. The question was not settled at Venice with regard to the lower ranks, and it had been revived by the decisions of the Lateran III Council in 1179, which had nullified these ordinations. The pope appears to have been hesitant on this point, and almost disposed to grant the affected clerics the dispensation that Barbarossa wanted for them. But according to the account of the chronicler Arnold of Lübeck, the cardinals' influence prevailed and within a day succeeded in requiring that the definitive decision could only be made in general COUNCIL. The SYNOD planned for Lyon, probably for tactical reasons—the meeting of prelates held in Verona had all the required conciliar characteristics—was never held.

At the same time, another conflict appeared between the Church and the empire, based on the double election to the metropolitan see of Trier in 1183, resulting from a confused electoral procedure. Participation by lay members and acceptance of the one they had proposed had separated the two parties; moreover, the majority of the cathedral chapter had refused to recognize Volkmar, who had been elected thanks to his popularity with the people. The partisans of the defeated candidate, the chapter provost Rudolph of Wied, had brought the matter before the emperor. The latter canceled the election, and Volkmar, who remained convinced of the legitimacy of the initial proceedings, resigned. Rudolph was then elected archbishop by his followers, who only represented a minority, and invested by Barbarossa. This matter touched directly upon a question that had been a sensitive one since the INVESTITURES controversy—the influence of lay members in ecclesiastical elections. Volkmar had therefore appealed to the pope. Barbarossa was insisting that his candidates be invested, whereas the timid Lucius III was biased against Volkmar's supporters, in particular because of the announcement of the tough attitude of Henry VI. Because of his precarious position at Verona, the pope was unable to resolve this conflict, which continued to occupy his successors. Independently of any ecclesiastical political concerns, this seemed an ideal occasion for refusing the coronation of Henry VI. Thus, the negotiations at Verona ended in failure. It was only on the subject of the campaign against heresies and collaboration in this area between temporal and spiritual powers that they were able to arrive at any sort of agreement. Together with the emperor, who enforced the ecclesiastical sanction of excommunication by banishment, Lucius III published, on 4 November 1184, the BULL *Ad abolendam* (*Decret. Greg.IX*, 5, 7, 9), against heretical movements, which had been growing larger and larger for some time. Beside the Cathars, the Patarines, the Humiliati, and the Waldensians, a number of lesser-known movements were named. In effect, the accusatory procedure was eliminated, and the refusal to swear the required oath was considered sufficient to serve as proof.

These measures designed to consolidate the campaign against heresies were the main contribution of Lucius III to the internal reform of the Church. In other areas, his actions were less significant. His personal inclinations led him to favor the monastic orders. He only rarely changed the dispositions of his predecessors, as in the case of lifting the interdict against the kingdom of Scotland. As to CANONIZATIONS, he continued to delegate that procedure to the Curia. During his pontificate the hermit Galganus (d. 1181) and the bishop Bruno of Segni (d. 1123), were canonized and the investigation into the life of archbishop Piero of Taranto (d. 1174) was begun.

Ludwig Vones

Bibliography

JL, 431–92, 725, 766–9.

LP, 2, 450.

PL, 202, 1067–1380.

Mann, E. A. "Lucius III," *DTC*, 9 (1926), 1058–62.

Petersohn, J. "Kaiser, Papst und praefectus Urbis zwischen Alexander III. und Innocenz III.," *QFIAB*, 60 (1980), 157–88.

Pfaff, V. "Die deutschen Domkapitel und das Papsttum am Ende des 12. Jahrhunderts," *Historisches Jahrbuch*, 93 (1973), 21–56; and "Sieben Jahre päpstlicher Politik: Die Wirksamkeit der Päpst Lucius III., Urban III., Gregor VIII.," *ZRGKA*, 67 (1981), 148–212.

Schmidt, U. "Lucius III.," *LexMA*, 5 (1991), 1262–3.

Watterich, *Vitae*, 2, 650–2.

MAGISTERIUM. The magisterium is the power and authority to teach in Christ's name. It is deemed authentic and true because it is drawn from and practiced in the name of Jesus Christ. This authentic magisterium of the Church is INFALLIBLE throughout, including the concrete formulations by which authority declares that a particular doctrine is considered infallibly defined if it is manifestly established (The CODE OF CANON LAW of 1983, c. 749, § 3).

Depending on how it is practiced, we distinguish *extraordinary magisterium*, also called solemn magisterium, which is realized in a solemn form, for example, in an ecumenical council where the pope speaks *EX CATHEDRA*; and *ordinary magisterium*, or the current forms of teaching. Ordinary magisterium may be universally applied to the whole Church.

Authentic magisterium is the responsibility of the Roman pontiff, the College of Bishops, and the particular councils when they act as pastors of the Church, rather than as private persons. Authentic infallible magisterium is solemn and extraordinary when it is done by the Roman pontiff and the ecumenical council, who proclaim, using a definitive document, a doctrine that must be upheld as a truth of faith or morals. The magisterium of a council is equally infallible when it reproduces what the previous magisterium has defined. The magisterium of the College of Bishops is also infallible (a group that is spread throughout the world and united with the Roman pontiff) when they agree on a point of doctrine that must be considered as definitive. Guided by this ordinary and universal magisterium, God's people are infallible in their *sensus fidei*, because they accept the true word of God, not human words. The conditions of teaching *ex cathedra* by the pope are rarely mentioned, although the pope can and does exercise both ordinary and universal magisterium. The teachings of VATICAN II are considered as part of the ordinary and universal magisterium.

The Degrees of Adhesion to the Magisterium. In the case of an infallible magisterium (c. 749), the faithful have an obligation to accord the pope, the vicar of Christ, a total acquiscence in regard to faith and morals and to avoid any doctrine that might oppose the teaching (c. 750). The simple authentic magisterium of the Church regarding faith and morals does not ordinarily take on the definitive character of canon 749 and does not require the acquiescence of belief of canon 750, but it remains a teaching given by virtue of the commandment of Christ (Luke 10:16, Mark 16:15–16): Therefore, it deserves respect and consideration.

When it is a question of the noninfallible magisterium of the pope and the College of Bishops, the faithful owe this doctrine "a submission of intellect and of will" (c.752), for it is based upon witnesses of the divine truth. The quasi-integrality of the documents of Vatican II falls in this category. A simple, purely external adhesion does not suffice: There must also, and especially, be internal adhesion of the intellect and the will.

Sacred truth can be furthered by scholars in the sacred discipline, but they must always show respect and reverence (*obsequium*) for the magisterium, the ultimate arbiter. This duty of *obsequium* is a limitation on the rights of scholars to free research (c. 218). Consequently, freedom may be exercised only in areas where no definitive resolution has already been pronounced.

There is no freedom of opinion regarding doctrine defined by the magisterium. Any personal opinion that might oppose authentic magisterium falls outside the true faith and is not protected by any right. Theologians have no right to spread errors, and the faithful have the right to receive the faith in completeness and integrity.

The relationships between the magisterium and theologians have been defined in the following terms: "While having different gifts and functions, the living magisterium of the Church and theology have by definition the same goal: that of keeping the People of God in truth which frees them and thus providing a 'light to the nations.'" This activity of the ecclesiastical community merges the theologian and the magisterium. The latter teaches the doctrine of the apostles authentically and, drawing support from theological works, refutes objections to and deformations of the faith, proposing instead, with an authority drawn from Jesus Christ himself, developments, explications, and new applications of revealed doctrine. Theology, on the other hand, acquires, through reflection, a deeper knowledge of the Word of God as contained in Scripture, and faithfully transmits it through the living tradition of the Church, under the leadership of the magisterium; it tries to enlighten the teaching of revelation as interfaced with reason and gives it an organic and systematic form (Congregation for the Doctrine of Faith, instruction *Donum veritatis*, 24 May 1990, no. 21).

It is the responsibility of the diocesan bishop to defend the integrity and unity of faith and the holiness of morals by any methods that seem appropriate to him, while at the same time preserving freedom in regard to truths that can possibly be developed further (c. 386, § 2). This is accomplished through a thorough analysis that includes a development of the truth, but still *eodem sensu eademque sententia*. The diocesan bishop has several different means at his disposal, including providing norms on the teaching of religion in the schools (c. 804, § 2), and exercising vigilance regarding books and other publications (c. 823–31).

A just penalty is prescribed when someone, neither heretic, schismatic, nor apostate, is found teaching of a doctrine condemned by the Roman pontiff or an ecumenical council, or "rejecting with obstinacy" a teaching mentioned in canon 752, which, after a warning from the apostolic see or from the Ordinary, is not retracted (c. 1371, 1°).

The faithful are obliged to accept with religious devotion and a submissive spirit (c. 753) the teachings of conferences of bishops, local councils, or individual bishops.

This magisterium of the bishops deals only with faith and morals given in the name of Jesus Christ (Vatican II, dogmatic constitution *Lumen gentium*, no. 25). It implies communion with the magisterium of the pope, so that it is finally "a bishopric that is one and undivided and which, thanks to this internal cohesiveness of the Church, the universal multitude of believers keeps a unity of faith and of communion" (VATICAN I, dogmatic constitution *Pastor Æternus*). However, since bishops do not, in this case, enjoy a full guarantee of truth, the faithful are not expected to show absolute and unchanging assent, which has four characteristics: obedience of the intellect, which means that it is not enough just to conform the practice to the teaching in question; intellectual judgment, which makes simple silent assent insufficient; an internal act of positive adhesion to what the master teaches; and certain assent, with a relative and conditional certitude.

It is possible, in certain cases, that reasons may justify a suspension of judgment, of considering as true the opposite of what is proposed, but even in this case, the faithful are obliged to follow the norms of prudence and charity regarding the pastors, for the edification of the People of God.

If the faithful are required to subscribe, through Christian obedience, to what the bishops as pastors (representatives of Christ) declare to (c. 212, § 1), they must also observe all the constitutions and decrees made by the legitimate ecclesiastical authority in order to deepen the truth and forbid erroneous opinions, *a fortiori*, when these decisions emanate from the Roman pontiff or from the College of Bishops (c. 754). This obligation has been frequently repeated, for example by PIUS IX (letter *Tuas libenter*, 21 December 1863; encyclical *Quanta cura*, 8 December 1864); LEO XIII (letter *Testem benevolentiae*, 21 January 1899), PIUS X (decretal *Lamentabili*, 3 July 1907); PIUS XII (encyclical *Humani generis*, 12 August 1950). The decrees of the Roman congregations exercise a particular authority, especially when they deal with faith. The mission of the Congregation for Doctrine and Faith it is "to promote and guarantee the doctrine of faith and morals in the entire Catholic world" (JOHN PAUL II, apostolic constitution *Pastor bonus*, 18 June 1988, art. 48). By examining these doctrines, it follows one of the procedures (ordinary or extraordinary) set forth in its ruling (*Nova agendi ratio in doctrinarum examine*, 15 January 1971). A new ruling was announced by John Paul II (apostolic constitution *Pastor bonus*). The congregation speaks with the author of the errors whom it wishes to reprove, asking him or her to more clearly explain the positions advocated by them, or to rectify them. Competent ecclesiastical authority decides on how public the reprobation and eventual sanctions will be, for example, the retiring of the mandate to teach theology in Catholic institutions.

Although simply authentic magisterium implies religious obedience, it must fulfill the conditions set forth previously: "This religious submission of intellect and will is due to the unusual manner of the authentic magisterium of the Roman pontiff, even when he is not speaking *ex cathedra*." This assent must be given, taking into account "the spirit and the intention shown by the Roman pontiff" (Vatican II, dogmatic constitution *Lumen gentium*, no. 25).

Vatican II indicated three criteria for this religious submission of intellect and will:

1. The nature of the document: an encyclical being more important than an allocution, for example. However, the fact that the pope sometimes uses Roman congregations to propose a doctrine should be taken into account. This was the case, for example, with the instruction

Donum vitæ to the Congregation for Doctrine and Faith (22 February 1987).

2. The frequent repetition of doctrine. This fits a doctrine into a continuum with the entire previous magisterium, as solemn as it is ordinary (Vatican II, dogmatic council *Lumen gentium*, no. 21), which is still not the same thing as a pious exhortation in a homily.

3. The method in which the pope expresses himself: the exceptional solemnity indicates the will to proclaim a doctrine, as for example, in the case of the encyclical *Humanae vitae*: "This is why, having attentively examined the documentation which has been submitted to Us, after deep reflection and assiduous prayers, We now maintain, by virtue of the mandate the Christ has given Us, to give our response to these serious questions" (PAUL VI, encyclical *Humanae vitae*, 25 July 1968, no. 6).

As for encyclicals, one must not underestimate what they say simply because they do not require definitive assent. The popes "are not using the supreme power of their magisterium in them. That which is taught by ordinary magisterium, is also based on the words 'He who listens to you, listens to me'" (Pius XII, encyclical *Humanae generis*).

Also, when the pope expressly shows judgment through his actions on a matter that was previously controversial, everyone understands that the matter is no longer considered an open question for theologians (Ibid.) It can happen that the bishops, united in a council, limit themselves to exercising a simply authentic magisterium—as was the case with Vatican II. The obligation to accept such teaching is a serious matter for all the faithful, even when the teaching is not imposed as definitive and unchangeable.

The ecclesiastical authority is not the only one to exercise a magisterium in the Church. In fact, all the faithful participate, each in his or her own manner, in the unique mission of evangelization, of proclaiming the truth of Christ to the world. This common function of all the faithful, by virtue of the common sacrament they have received at baptism, has no public character. The laity are particularly appropriate for transmitting the Christian doctrine in temporal structures. They are called to render testimonials to Christ, "especially in the management of temporal things" and "in the accomplishment of secular responsibilities" (c. 225, § 2). They act in their own name and under their personal responsibility, without engaging the Church, because they have no mandate to speak with that authority.

The Moral Judgment of the Church on Temporal Matters. The ecclesiastical hierarchy also has the right to make a moral judgment on questions of a temporal nature. It is just, proclaimed Vatican II, that the Church "may everywhere and at all times preach the faith with an authentic freedom, teach its social doctrine, accomplish

without hindrance its mission among men, making a moral judgment, even on matters that involve the political domain, when the fundamental rights of the person or the saving of souls requires it. The means, the only means, it may use, are those which are in accord with the Gospel and the welfare of all men" (pastoral constitution *Gaudium et spes*, no. 76).

The hierarchy may judge the conformity of actions and temporal institutions with moral principles and "declare itself on the subjects concerning what it required for safeguarding and promoting things of the supernatural order" (the decree *Apostolican actuositatem*, no. 24). These are the themes on the public rights of the Church. These principles were taken up by the general legislation of the Church, in the first canon of Book III on the function of teaching within the Church. The context is not that of relationships between the hierarchy and the faithful but of the relationships between the Church and the world—fundamental rights of the individual and the saving of souls. This formula applies to all men, not just to Christians. Thus judgments of a moral nature that the hierarchy formulates on temporal realities are not an attack on the freedom of the faithful in the temporal domain but rather an attempt to enlighten the faithful so they may illuminate all mankind; the value of these judgments depends on the intention shown by the authority making them. The formula is as follows: "It behooves the Church to announce at any time and place the moral principles concerning society, as well as to pass judgment on any human reality, as required by the fundamental rights of the individual and the saving of souls" (c. 747, § 2).

These judgments are not temporal judgments—though they deal with temporal questions—and are even less political interventions. "The Church in no way wishes to involve itself in the government of earthly realms. It also reserves no position for itself other than that of being of service to all men" (decretal *Ad gentes*, no. 12). In these interventions, the Church is trying to make sure that temporal matters do not interfere with the accomplishment of her mission and the saving of souls, "which must always be the supreme law for the Church" (c. 1752).

Offenses Against Ecclesiastical Magisterium. These are enumerated in canon 751, which refers to HERESY or stubborn negation of a truth of divine and Catholic faith that should be believed; apostasy, or total withdrawal from the Catholic faith; and SCHISM, or refusal to obey the Roman pontiff and to live in communion with him and the members of the Church. The general law allows for excommunication *latae sententiae* for all those who commit any of these three offenses (c. 1364 § 1), offenses that, in order to be considered committed, must have been public and have had a social repercussion (c. 1330). This censure does not apply to those who are born and have been raised in separated ecclesiastical communities (directory *Ad totam Ecclesiam*, 14 May 1967, no. 19). It cannot apply to minors.

He who holds a church office loses it, *ipso iure*, if he commits these offenses (c. 194 § 1, 2), offenses that also make him unsuited for receiving holy orders (c. 1041, 2) or for continuing to exercise any order legitimately received before (c. 1044, § 1, 2). Authors of such offenses are banned from receiving a religious burial, except if they have shown signs of repentance before their death (c. 184 § 1, 1).

The opinions that the Church may condemn are not all of the same magnitude. Other than heretics, they may be classified as "in error." The opposite doctrine must clearly be held for certain. An affirmation close to heresy must be made against a prime truth of the faith. A reckless doctrine without sufficient grounds separates itself from the general teachings of theologians. A scandalous opinion, "offending pious ears" is not always false, but it should not be taught without due caution.

Dominique Le Tourneau

Bibliography

Basevi, C. "Comisión Internacional de Teología, Tesis. sobre las relaciones mutuas entre el Magisterio Eclesiástico y la Teología," *Scripta Theologica*, 9 (1977), 215–41.

Berti, C. M., Meo, S. M., and Toniolo, H. *De ratione ponderandi documenta Magisterii Ecclesiastici*, Rome, 1961.

Blystal, L. "Obsequium: A Case Study," *The Jurist*, 48 (1988), 559–89.

Choupin, L. *Valeur des décisions doctrinales et disciplinaires du Saint-Siège*, Paris, 2d. ed., 1913.

Congregation for the Doctrine of Faith, Instruction on the Ecclesiastical Vocation of the Theologian *Donum veritatis*, 24 May 1990.

De Aldama, J. A. "Origen de las fómulas dogmáticas," *Estudios Eclesiásticos*, 43 (1968), 5–14.

Fagiolo, V. "Il Munus docendi: I canoni introduttivi del Codex e la dottrina conciliare del Magistero autoritative della Chiesa," *Monitor Ecclesiasticus*, 112 (1987), 10–42.

International Theological Commission, Theses on the Relationship of Ecclesiastical Magisterium and Theology, 6 June 1976 (French text in *La Documentation Catholique*, 58 [1976], 658–65).

Marin Sola, R. *Evolución homogénea del dogma católico*, Madrid, 1952.

Montan, A. "La funxione de insegnare della Chiesa," *La normativa del Nuovo Codice*, Brescia, 1983, 135–76.

Morales, J. "Nota histórico-doctrinal sobre las relaciones entre Magisterio eclesiástico, oficio teólogico y sentido popular de la fe," *Scripta Theologica*, 2 (1970), 481–99.

Nau, P. "Le magistère pontifical ordinaire au premier concile du Vatican," *Revue Thomiste*, 62 (1962), 341–97.

Nicolau, M. "Magisterio ordinario en el Papa y en los Obispos," *Problemas del Concilio Vaticano II. Visión teológica*, Madrid, 1963.

Sesboüé, B. "La notion de magistère dans l'histoire de l'Église et de la théologie," *L'Année Canonique*, 31 (1988), 55–94.

Sobanski R. "Les canons 753 and 754: Questions choisies," *Studia Canonica*, 33 (1990), 285–98.

Sullivan, F. A. *Magisterium: Teaching Authority in the Catholic Church*, New York, 1983.

Urrutia, F. J. "La réponse aux textes du magistère pontifical non infaillible," *L'Année Canonique*, 31 (1988), 95–115.

MALACHY, PROPHESIES OF. See **Prophesies of Malachy**.

MARCELLINUS. *(b. ? Rome–d. 24 October 304). Elected pope in 296. Buried in the cemetery of Sta. Priscilla, on the via Salaria.*

Marcellinus followed GAIUS in 296. He was born in Rome (according to *LP*, 1, 161 = *MGH*, *GPR*, 1, 41). His pontificate began in a time of peace, but ended when the great persecution was beginning.

In effect, since the edict on tolerance of Gallian, times had been favorable to the development of Christianity; this period is called, significantly the "short peace of the Church." The communities converted new followers, as Eusebius of Caesarea says, writing that Christians could be found even in the highest levels of administration (Eus., HE, VIII, 1). In the imperial palace, Prisca, wife of Emperor Diocletian, and Valeria, her daughter, showed strong sympaties for Christianity; servants of high rank, like the great chamberlain Dorotheus, had even been won over.

The persecution began in 303 and intensified the following year. Four edicts punctuated this development. The first, promulgated in 303, ordered that churches should be destroyed throughout the empire and the sacred books burned, and that believers should be relieved of their positions, honors, and privileges. In Italy as in AFRICA, the edict was applied very rigorously because the administration of these regions had been given to Maximian Hercule, who was made augustus by Diocletian. Consequently, the library of the Roman Church, also containing its archives, was destroyed. That same year two other edicts aggravated the persecution: one ordered the imprisonment of clerics and the other the torture and punishment of those who refused to recant. Finally, in 304, the final edict ordered all subjects of the empire to make sacrifices to the gods of the state. In Italy and in Rome there were many martyrs.

The attitude of Pope Marcellinus has resulted in controversy. The LIBER PONTIFICALIS mentions that, led before several pagan altars, he sacrificed by offering incense ("*ad sacrificium ductus est, ut turificaret, quod et fecit,*" *LP*, 1, 161 = *MGH*, *GPR*, 1, 41). Nevertheless, this same source adds that several days later he was executed on 24 October 304. Eusebius (*HE*, VII, 32) indicates that he was removed from his community by the persecution. Whatever happened, the treason of Pope Marcellinus became commonly mentioned in the polemics that the Donatists later made against the Catholic Church. Actually, they had, it is believed, access to sources from that time relating the affair; in particular they had obtained an ecclesiastical document used by Petilian of Constantine at the beginning of the 5th century (PCBE, 1, 858) to show that Marcellinus was an example of betrayal of the faith. This theme was long-lived: it is found in the "acts" of the Council of Sinuessa, a polemic made at the beginning of the 6th century, at the time of the election of Pope SYMMACHUS, by his adversaries.

As a result, the judgments by historians have varied. Le Nain de Tillemont impugned any doubts about the firmness of Marcellinus. Louis Duchesne, not without euphemisms, wrote that "for a person of this importance, it was rather distressing, at such a time, to die in bed." Others note a "short-lived weakness" (J. Zeiller) or a weakening followed by a reconciliation (E. Caspar). Another scholar notes that Marcellinus was "dead during, but it seems not due to, the persecution" (H. Marrou). They, therefore, are hesitant about the reality of his martyrdom: his name is absent from the list of *depositio episcoporum*, a list of Roman bishops preserved in the calendar of 354 (*MGH*, AA, 9/1, 70). The *Liberian Catalog* (*MGH*, AA, 9/1, 75) mentions the persecution that took place during his pontificate, adding simply that it ended after seven years, six months, and twenty-five days, on 24 October 304. It must have been almost impossible for the Roman community then to give him a successor. Pope MARCELLUS I, who followed him, was not elected until 308.

Michel Christol

Bibliography

LP, 1, 161 = *MGH*, *GPR*, 1, 42.

Amann, E. *DTC*, 9, 2, 1999–2001.

Frend, W. H. C. *Martyrdom and Persecution in the Early Church*, Oxford, 1965, 477–505.

Lebreton J., and Zeiller, J. *De la fin du IIe siècle à la paix constantinienne*; Fliche-Martin, 2, Paris, 1943, 159–60, 419, 463–67.

Simon M., and Benoit, A. *Le Judaïsme et le christianisme antique, d'Antiochus Epiphane à Constantin*, Paris, 1968, 135–8.

Testini, P. *Archeologia cristiana*, I, Rome, 1958, 254–60.

Vogel, C. Le *Liber Pontificalis*, (reed. 1957) III, 75–6.

MARCELLUS I. *(d. January 309). Elected in May or June 308. Buried in the cemetery of Sta. Priscilla on the via Salaria.*

The brief reign of Marcellus I is only poorly known and is full of uncertainties. Some scholars have even wanted to merge Marcellinus and Marcellus's two reigns (Th. Mommsen, who presumed a vacancy of almost five years between Marcellinus and EUSEBIUS); but G. B. De Rossi and L. Duchesne have spoken definitively in favor of the distinction; a precise discussion on this question based upon available texts may be found in the *DACL*, 1757–60.

Pope Marcellinus died on 24 October 304, during the persecution by Diocletian, after which there was a three-year and four-month vacancy. Elected bishop by the Roman clergy, the priest Marcellus was installed in May–June of 308 (*LP*, I, 164) during a serious time of crisis for the Church. This crisis was because of the long interregnum due to uncertain political circumstances (the retreat of Diocletian and usurpation by Maxentius), to persecutions, and especially to the schisms that followed them.

The history of Marcellus's reign is obscure. According to sources (*LP*) and an epitaph dictated by Pope DAMASUS I sixty years after Marcellus's death (A. Ferrua, *Epigrammata Damasiana*, Vatican City, 1942, 181), it seems that three concerns dominated it: (1) the reorganization of the Church of Rome, where he reestablished (or brought to a total of twenty-five) the presbyterian "titles" (or urban churches) with priests responsible for the preparation of converts for baptism, (2) the preparing of the *lapsi* for penitence, and (3) the preparation of Christians for entombment and the administration of the cemeteries (*LP*, I, 74; *Marcellus . . . XXV titulos in Roma constituit, quasi diocesis propter baptismum et poenitentiam et sepulturas martyrum*). He had probably prepared for this reorganization as priest-vicar (*vice episcopi*), if it is true that during the throne's vacancy he had directed the Church administration. He also oversaw the opening of a new cemetery near the CATACOMB of Sta. Priscilla at the third mile marker of the via Salaria (*LP*, I, 164). Mentioned by the *Gesta Liberii*, the cemetery of Novella had been renovated (cf. G. B. De Rossi, *Roma sotterranea*, I, 189) in a slightly different position, to the left of the via Salaria (according to O. Marucchi, *Nuovo Bull. Arch. Crist.*, 1903, 205, 227; 1908, 61).

Marcellus's main task was to take care of the "renegades" (*lapsi*), Christians, many of whom, as it seems, had abjured their faith during the persecutions. This problem began with the persecution of Decius in 250. When the persecution died down with the arrival of Maxentius, the *lapsi* demanded to return to the Church unconditionally, that is, without doing any penitence. This led a group of them to press their cause, while the rigorists who, surrounding Pope Marcellus, believed strongly in discipline and demanded first and foremost a penitent atonement. Because of the large number of *lapsi*, the dissension grew heated; there were even bloody fights in the streets. Fond of public decorum, Maxentius made the bishop of Rome responsible and condemned him. According to some he was immediately sent into exile. According to the *Liber pontificalis* I, 165–166), he was first sent to the *catabulum*, where he maintained the stables, the beasts of burden, and the carts of the *cursus publicus*, and from there perhaps went into exile, where he died in January 309. As the Damasian epitaph indicates, the body of Pope Marcellus (he is called a *rector*, a word used exclusively for popes) was brought back to Rome and buried in the cemetery of Sta. Priscilla (De Rossi-Duchesne, *Hieronym. Martyrol.*, 9) and honored on January 16, a date furnished by the *Depositio episcoporum* of the *Chronograph of 354* (where we must change *Marcellini* to *Marcelli*).

After 314, Pope SILVESTER I, the second pope to follow Marcellus, had a basilica constructed in the cemetery, where his tomb was later placed, and the Damasian epitaph added at a still later date. It remained there until the 9th century; the body of the saint was then transferred to a *titulus* on the via Lata. This *titulus* appeared for the first time in the form of *ecclesia Marcelli*, in a report from the prefect Symmachus of Rome to the Emperor Honorius, who told of the consecration of Pope BONIFACE I in this church on 29 December 418 (*Coll. Avellana, Ep.* 14, 6, *CSEL*, 35, 60; *LP*, I, 228 no. 1). A little later the *Passio Marcelli* was written (*Acta sanctorum*, January, II, Antwerp, 1643, 3–14). In any case, the *titulus Marcelli*, founded by a Marcellus who was confused with the pope became, in 595 the *titulus sancti Marcelli*. We should note that this *titulus* of the via Lata (today's via del Corso) could correspond with the position of the *catabulum*, the stable for the imperial post, where according to some the bishop of Rome had been persecuted. Restored by HADRIAN I (780–5), the church was enriched during the 9th century at the time of the transfer of the holy relics. Burned in 1519, it was rebuilt by LEO X.

Marcel Le Glay

Bibliography

Barnes, T. D. *Constantine and Eusebius*, Cambridge, Mass., 1981, 38 and 303ff.

Caspar, E. *Geschichte des Papsttums von de Anfängen bis zur Höhe des Weltherrschaft, I, Römische Kirche und Imperium romanum*, Tübingen, 1930, 43–54, 97–101.

Duchesne, L. *Hist. anc. Église*, 2, Paris, 1907, 92–7.

Kirsch, J. P. *Die römischen Titelkirchen im Altertum*, 1918.

Lebreton J. H. and Zeiller, J. 2, Paris, 1935 (Fliche-Martin), 472.

Pietri, C. *Roma christiana*, 2 vols., Rome, 1976, 491–561.

MARCELLUS II. *Marcello Cervini (b. Montepulciano, 6 May 1501–d. Rome, 1 May 1555). Elected pope on 10 April 1555, crowned the same day. Buried in St. Peter's of Rome, then in the Vatican Grottoes.*

This noble soul, as Pierre de Nolhac called him, is the pope whose short pontificate was immortalized by the Mass of Pope Marcellus. This masterpiece by Palestrina, celebrating his memory, was not published until 1567. Historians are divided in their opinions on the time of its composition. Some say that it was done at the express wish of the pope himself. Others place it seven years after his death, when the Council of TRENT had given musicians some freedom.

Cervini served as secretary to Pope PAUL III and the young cardinal Alexander Farnese. He was raised to the purple at age thirty-nine in December 1539. He left Rome to be a LEGATE *a latere* at the courts of King Francis I and the emperor Charles V. He had other legations before the one that made him, along with Reginald Pole and Cardinal del Monte, the future JULIUS III, one of the presidents of the Council of Trent in 1545.

The decrees on justification and the residence of bishops were partially his work. In Bologna in 1548, he wanted to have the council's decisions printed out for Angelo Massarelli, as was done. In Rome after 1548, he was the head cardinal of the library. The Vatican Library owes many of its manuscripts and printed books to him. He especially loved the Greek manuscripts, and imposed order over his collection. We know that, for a time, the lending of manuscripts outside the Vatican was stopped. He wanted to rediscover the traditions of the ancient Church. The stela of HIPPOLYTUS of Rome, found in an excavation, was preserved by him. It can still be seen at the entrance to the Vatican.

The famous men who worked for him must also be mentioned: Angelo Massarelli; cardinals Bernardino Maffei and Guglielmo Sirleto; and Onofrio Panvinio, whom he induced to leave profane history for that of the popes. He knew how to use industrious editors like Gentien Hervet, Guillaume Postel, Paulus Manutius, and printers like Antonio Blado and the Juntes. He himself spent time in the company of poets and humanists and theologians, including Angelo Colocci, Annibale Caro, Latino Latini, the Lascaris, Sadoleto, Bembo and Giovio, Giberti and Commendone, Aleandro and Morone, Campegio, Rodolfo Pio di Carpi, and Gasparo Contarino, who were his friends and correspondents. His works and his literary tastes were second only to his religious zeal. His relationship with St. Ignatius of Loyola and his first companions show his spirituality. Laynez and Salmeron, Jesuit theologians, knew him at Trent. In contact with the founder of the JESUITS he showed himself to be a man of prayer. He was a cardinal who made his associates confess and receive communion regularly. He wanted a reformed Church.

At the CONCLAVE on 10 April 1555, the integrity of Cervini's life, holy zeal for reform, and the ardor of his piety caused the thirty-nine cardinals to vote unanimously for him. It was almost midnight when he thanked them for electing him, but said he did not want to change his name (ONOMASTIC); he would be called Pope Marcellus II. The bishop elect of a diocese in Calabria, which he renounced, and then of Reggio Emilia, and finally the administrator of Gubbio, he was a cardinal-priest and had never wished to be a bishop. The dean of the SACRED COLLEGE, the future Pope PAUL IV and archbishop of Chieti, Gian Pietro Carafa, quickly sent the ceremonialist of the conclave to his palace to look for the pontifical ornaments. He celebrated mass in the SISTINE CHAPEL and consecrated Cervini bishop using the formulas of Patrizi's ceremony. The new pope wanted to be crowned the same day. He put on the TIARA in ST. PETER's. The first of the cardinal-deacons presented him to the people. Cervini explained to the ambassador of France that he wished to save the 10,000 or 20,000 gold pieces that another CORONATION would have cost, with a procession of entry into the Lateran. Half this sum would be given to the poor, and the other half would help the Vatican treasury, which was then in distress. He was, therefore, a generous and economical pope.

His other virtues appeared soon thereafter. Most members of his family were to remain in Montepulciano. His two nephews, aged fifteen and thirteen, were in Rome. He had them take off the purple clothing that they had been forced to wear. According to custom, he appointed other relatives as chamberlain of SANT'ANGELO and commander of the papal guard. His first actions showed that he was the reforming pope the Church had been waiting for. The Roman CURIA would be purified from all scandal. He got busy regulating various offices from that of the Signatures and those of the CONSISTORIES and PENITENTIARY. He had no patience for spongers. His only BULL extant today, dated 14 April, impressed the regular clergy. After the first ten days of his pontificate, illness stopped him from pursuing his task. He died the morning of the 22nd day of his papacy.

Marc Dykmans

Bibliography

Bignami-Odier, J., and Ruysschaert, J. *La Bibliothèeque vaticane de Sixte IV à Pie XI*, 1973, 402.

Devreesse, R. *Le Fonds grec des origines à Paul V*, 1965, 328–30.

Dorez, L. "Le cardinal Marcello Cervini et l'imprimerie à Rome," *MAH*, (1982), 289–310; *La Cour du pape Paul III*, Paris, 1932.

Dykmans, M. "Quatre lettres de Marcel Cervini cardinal-légat de Charles-Quint en 1540," *AHP*, 29 (1991), 113–71.

Hudon, W. V. *Marcello Cervini and Ecclesiastical Government in Tridentine Italy*, DeKalb, 1992.

Lutz, H. "Marcellus II," *LTK*, 7 (1962), 3–4.

Palma, M. "Cervini (Ricciardo)," *DBI*, 24 (1980), 111–3.

Palmarocchi, R. "Marcello II," *EC*, 8 (1952), 17–9.

Paschini, P. "Un cardinale editore," *Miscellanea . . . Luigi Ferrari*, Florence, 1952, 383–413.

Pollidori, P. *De vita, gestis ac moribus Marcelli II*, Rome, 1744.

MARINUS I, also MARTIN II. *(b. Gallese, ?–d.c. May 884). Elected pope in December 882 (after the 15th). Buried in St. Peter's in Rome.*

His brief reign was, in large part, a reaction against the policies of JOHN VIII. A cleric since the age of twelve, Marinus climbed the rungs of the ecclesiastical ladder one by one by establishing himself as a specialist from the East. In 860 he assisted as subdeacon at Rome's welcome for the ambassadors of Emperor Michael III, who were then attempting to settle the quarrel over images and the awkward case of the patriarch Photius. In 866 Pope NICHOLAS I sent him on a legation to Constantinople, this time as a deacon, to deal with the Bulgarian affair: Rome and Constantinople were at odds over the religious leadership of this newly converted country (the embassy was a failure, the pontifical representatives being turned back at the border of the Byzantine states). In 869, finally, Marinus was part of HADRIAN II's legates sent to preside over the eighth ecumenical COUNCIL of Constantinople, which saw Patriarch Photius deposed in February 870. A little while later, he was made bishop of Cerveteri. His knowledge of the Eastern problems and the Bulgarian situation had given Marinus a certain celebrity. This was why King Boris made him one of his candidates for the position of archbishop of Bulgaria, although in vain, for Pope Hadrian II had used the canonical impossibility of translating bishops from one see to another in order to keep him.

Under Pope JOHN VIII, Marinus continued to display his diplomatic talents. He was sent once again to the East in 880 and 881, whereas in 882, on Italian soil, he intervened with the bishop of Naples, Athanasius, to ask him firmly not to trade with the SARACENS, simply for his own personal ambition. At this time, Marinus was also made treasurer for the Holy See.

In December 882, Marinus succeeded John VIII, who had been assassinated on December 15. Ironically, less is known of his pontificate than of his previous career, but it is clear that, on most levels, his policies were different from those of his predecessor, although the initiative for changes in orientation did not always come directly from Rome. In BYZANTIUM, Photius had regained his patriarchal see, having been recognized by John VIII in 880. Supported by Emperor Basil, he opposed the election of Marinus, denouncing it as invalid, that is, according to ecclesiastical custom, Marinus as a bishop should not have been eligible because a vote in his favor would have meant exchanging one episcopal see for another. The conclave chose to ignore this rule. Instead, the electors argued that since the office of treasurer of the Holy See was usually given to an archdeacon, Marinus, at the time of his election, was "rather more" of an archdeacon than a bishop.

Pope Marinus I rehabilitated Formosus, the main person responsible for the conversion of the Bulgarians, who later fell into disgrace and was excommunicated by John VIII. Formosus regained his title of cardinal-bishop of Porto, and partisans were also returned to grace.

Finally, according to a custom that had long been a tradition for Roman pontiffs, Marinus I tried to find support from the emperor of the West. The principal political concern for the papacy was the designs the duke of Spoleto, Guy, had on making the lands of the Patrimony his, even Rome itself, so he could take over the empire from Charles the Fat. In the spring of 883, Charles met Marinus at the monastery at Nonantola, near Modena; the pope demanded concrete protection for the Papal States, thus reminding the emperor of his traditional responsibilities to the Church.

François Bougard

Bibliography

JW, 1, 425, 2, 704.

LP, 2, 224.

Amann, É. "Marin Ier," *DTC*, 9/2 (1927), 2476–7.

Fliche-Martin, VI, 439–41, 498.

Herbers, K. "Marinus I," *LexMA*, 6 (1992), 294.

Maisonneuve H. "Marin Ier," *Catholicisme*, 8 (1986), 681–2.

Majarelli, S. "Marino I," *EC*, 8 (1952), 162–3.

MARINUS II, also MARTIN III. (*b. ?–d. the beginning of May 946*). *Elected pope at the end of October 942, buried in St. Peter's in Rome.*

Marinus II, often erroneously called Martin III beginning in the 12th century, was pope in Rome from the end of October 942 until the beginning of May 946. A native of Rome, and the cardinal-priest of San Ciriaco, he was probably elected pope thanks to the influence of Alberic II (932–54) who then reigned over Rome as its all-powerful prince.

According to the chronicle written at that same time by Benedict of Mont-Socrate, the pope did not dare do anything without checking with Alberic. Only eight authentic pontifical acts of Marinus II have survived, mostly confirmations of property addressed to abbeys or Italian bishops' churches. Later acts allow us to de-

duce the existence of five lost pontifical diplomas. The only act that has any great importance is the concession, renewed in 946 after Pope LEO VII, of the appointment as apostolic vicar of archbishop Frederick of Mainz (937–54), which gave him, beyond the German borders, a field of influence enlarged to Gaul. The context for this was probably the renewal of the quarrel between the Carolingians and the Capetians over the French city of Reims, a quarrel in which the German church and the king of Germany, Otto the Great (936–73), quickly intervened by taking the side of Archbishop Artaud, who, after having been deposed, had petitioned Rome in 943 to be relieved of his obligations. From the German kingdom, the pope received visits from Bishop Ulrich of Augsburg in 942 and Abbot Hadamar of Fulda in 943; these two visits, beside religious motives, had political goals. The pope must have also been in contact with and have received tributes, St. Peter's pence, from England, as the Roman treasury record found in 1883 seems to show. The Cluniac Abbot Baldwin of Monte-Cassino was recalled to ST. PAUL's-OUTSIDE-THE-WALLS in 945, which contributed much to the diffusion of ecclesiastical and monastic reform in Rome. Two abbeys received the distinction of a pontifical privilege. If we believe a later tradition, Marinus II was buried in ST. PETER's.

Harald Zimmermann

Bibliography

Herbers, K. "Marinus II," *LexMA*, 6 (1992), 294–5.

Zimmermann, H. *Papstregesten*, 72–4; *Das dunkle Jahrhundert*, Graz, 1971, 84 ff; *Papsturkunden*, Vienna, 1988, 172–91.

MARK. (*b. ? – d. Rome, 7 October 336*). *Elected on 18 January 336. Buried in the cemetery on the via Ardeatina. Saint.*

His papacy only lasted eight months according to the records (all in agreement) of the *Chronique* by Eusebius, rewritten by Jerome, and of the *Liberian Catalog*, under the consulate of Nepotianus and Facundus in 336. We cannot account for the two years indicated by the LIBER PONTIFICALIS, which indicates the beginning of the term of his successor, JULIUS I, as 337. Of Roman origin, the son of Priscus, according to the *Liber pontificalis*. Mark decided that the bishop of Ostia would consecrate the bishop of Rome, and would wear the PALLIUM. St. Augustine of Hippo, in 411, told of the privileged status of the bishop of Ostia, "the first of the three bishops" who consecrated the pope, but no text before the 6th century mentioned the *pallium*, which Caesarius of Arles and Pope VIGILIUS spoke of then as a well-known ecclesiastical insignia.

Mark left a reputation mostly as a builder: he constructed two churches and created a cemetery. In a part of town near the center monuments, *iuxta Pallacinis*, near the via Lata, the pope founded a church mentioned in the *Liber pontificalis*. A contemporary epigraphic record confirms the existence of a *titulus de Pallacine* whose lector had a shortened name (Antius, for Amantius?) and who was buried with a Petrus in 348 in the cemetery of Priscilla. The archaeological digging by A. Ferrua in 1949 confirmed the existence of a Christian establishment in the 4th century, destroyed by a fire in the 5th or 6th century and rebuilt. He also constructed, outside the city, via Ardeatine, a cemetery basilica, *in coemeterio Balbinae*, in which he was buried. In the 4th and 5th centuries, the inscription of a *fossor* named Felix speaks of the existence of a *basilica in Balbinis* with surrounding porticoes covered with tiles (*locum sub teglata*). This church bore, in 499, the name of *titulus Marci*, and was represented by the two priests Cyprianus and Abundius at the Roman council that was held *in basilica Petri Apostoli* (St. Peter's of the Vatican). A church *tituli sancti Marci* was well represented at the Roman COUNCIL of 595 and Pope GREGORY II designated it as a *basilica sancti Marci*. Mark died on 7 October 336, according to the *Liberian Catalog*, the *Depositio espicoporum*, and the *Hieronymian Martyrology* (which placed it as 6 October). He was buried in the cemetery on the via Ardeatina which he had prepared during his lifetime (*quem ipse fecit insistens*). The Damascene inscription composed for an untitled Marcus, and whose locale was not stated, was probably not that of the pope. The letter to Athanasius attributed to Pope Mark, inserted in the pseudo-Isidorian DECRETALS also has no characteristics of authenticity.

Élisabeth Paoli

Bibliography

AASS, Oct. III, 886–903.
ICUR, n.s. 4, 12458 (Thiel 2143).
LP, I, 202–4.
Acta syn. rom., 1, 7, *MGH*, AA 12, 413.
Augustine, *De unico baptismo*, 16, 27 and 30, *CSEL* 53, 28 and 31; *Brev. Coll.*, III, 16, 29, *CSEL*, 53, 78.
Caspar, E. *Geschichte des Papsttums*, Tübingen, 1930, I, 131–42.
Catalogue libérien, ed. Duchesne, 9.
De Rossi, G. B. *Roma sotterranea*, Rome, 1864, I, 226; III, 8–13 and 180–1.
Depositio episcoporum, *MGH* AA IX, 70.
Ferrua, A. *Epigram. Damas.*, 50, Rome, 1942, 200–1.
Ferrua, A. "La basilica di Papa Marco," *Civiltà Cattolica*, (1948), III, 503–3; *Rivista di archeologia cristiana*, 25 (1949), 8 ff. and 14 ff.
Gregorius, *Decretum*, *MGH*, *Ep.*, 1, 366.
Kirsch, J. P. *Die Römischen Titel Kirchen im Altertum*, Paderborn, 1918, 87–90.
Krautheimer, R. *Corpus basilicarum Christianarum Romae*, Rome, 1962, 2, 218 ff.
Le Clercq, H. "Marc de vico Pallacine (Saint)," *DACL* 10, 2 (1932), 1741–9; "Marc," *ibid.* 13, 1 (1937), 1198–9.
Martyrologie hiéronym., AASS, Nov. II, p. post., 540, 543, 544.
Monachino, V. *La cura pastorale a Milano, Cartagine, Roma, nel IV secolo*, Rome, 1947, 282 ff.
Picard, J. C. "Études sur l'emplacement des tombes des Papes," *MERA*, 81 (1969), 725–82.
Pietri, C. *Roma christiana*, Rome, 1976, I, 21–2, 72, and II, 1696; "Appendice prosopographique à la Roma Christiana (311–440)," *MEFRA*, 89 (1977), 394.
Seppelt, F. X. *Geschichte der Päpste*, I, Munich, 1954, 86.
Symmachus, *Ep.* 1, 9, ed. Thiel, 653.
Vieillard, R. *Recherches sur les origines de la Rome chrétienne*, 1941, 150 ff.

MARSHALL OF THE CONCLAVE. See Conclave.

MARTIN I. (*b. Todi, ?–d. Cherson (Sebastopol), 16 September 655). Consecrated pope 5 August 649, deposed 17 June 653. Buried at Cherson. Saint and martyr (ancient cult, prior to Adon's martyrology).*

The only "Byzantine" pope died in exile, the last of all the popes venerated as martyrs, the first to be elected by the Roman nobles and consecrated without confirmation by the emperor or the exarch. He dared to oppose the decisions of a regional COUNCIL to the imperial will. Such a pontificate could not fail to make its mark upon the epoch.

Born at Todi, in a family of Tuscan nobility, Martin had been the apocrisarius of the pope to Constantinople, evidence of a brilliant career in the Church of Rome, and possessed a good knowledge of both Greek and of the most burning issue of the time, that of monothelitism. The Romans, therefore, must have known what they were doing. Martin was elected fifty-two days after Theodore's death and consecrated immediately, without waiting for confirmation of this choice by the emperor or the exarch. This is why he remained, for the court at Constantinople, "the one who had been the apocrisarius in the Imperial City" and not the legitimate pope of Rome. Theological quarrels and distinctions of protocol were all the more freely expressed because, seen only by Byzantine Italy, the situation did not seem desperate since the LOMBARDS, divided, seemed peaceful.

As soon as he was elected, Martin carefully called a Lateran SYNOD of bishops under his jurisdiction (5–31 October 649) to condemn the monothelitism professed by the Church in Constantinople and the *Typos* of 648, which outlawed any Christological discussion. Prelates from Byzantine Italy were there, as well as representatives of Byzantine AFRICA, an integral part of the Western patriarchate. The occasional presence of Eastern observers gave this synod the appearance of a special council, but it was only a metropolitan council called by the person in charge of southern Italy, then in Byzantine control, as the councils of 646 had been provincial councils. His truly original act was to arrange for the presence of Maximus the Confessor and the Greek monks, who took an active part in the organization and discussions. They laid out what was probably the clearest condemnation of monothelitism and of the *Typos*. At their request the synod also issued two versions of the documents, in Latin and in Greek; and so Rome found itself at the forefront of the anti-Constantinople movement. They even asked Martin to name an apostolic visitor for the patriarch of Jerusalem, temporarily unable to run the administration himself.

In Rome, Martin's position remained strong until 653. The exarch of RAVENNA, Olympius, put a stop to the meeting of the Lateran synod and questioned Martin, but was unable to stop him. In fact, the opposite occurred: he got closer to the pope and named himself emperor before perishing in a battle against the SARACENS. But Constans II Pogonatus sent a former exarch, Theodore Calliopas, with a large army. This time the pope was taken, on 17 June 653, and returned to the capital. The Roman nobility, unable to oppose them, withdrew their support for their bishop; there was no move in his favor during his arrest, his trial, or his condemnation.

Back in the capital, ill after a particularly trying three-month voyage, Martin waited another three months before his trial on 20 December 653. It was obvious by then that the emperor was interested in religious affairs only from a purely political point of view. Martin was found guilty of the crime of high treason for the support he gave to the usurper Olympius, and he was condemned to death. The sentence was commuted to life imprisonment at the request of the patriarch of Constantinople, Paul, who himself was ill and died soon thereafter. In the prison of Diomedes, Martin dictated a memoir in Greek, sent in the form of a letter to a certain Theodore, "spondee" of Hagia Sophia, to give his point of view to his followers. This document was used by the editor of a Greek life whose translation, adapted to the taste of a learned man of the 9th century, became the only available source for the West.

This often-violent attack on the court seems to have fallen into the emperor's hands; he decided to remove this religious opponent who was weakening the monothelitist side. Martin was exiled to faraway Cherson in the spring of 654 and seems to have died there on 16 September 655, although the Greeks celebrate this on 13 May, and place his death in the year 656. Illness, starvation, and isolation caused his death. In his final letters to friends in Constantinople, he complained of being abandoned by his Church, which had even found a successor while he was still alive.

After his death, Martin was considered a martyr in the West. Several miracles were attributed to him, and he became the symbol for clerical resistance to heresies and abuses of secular power. In the East, the emperor forbade his rehabilitation by the third council of Constantinople (680–1) because he was condemned for high treason, but clerics saw in him a defender of the faith and veneration of him lasted a long time, especially during the iconoclastic quarrel.

Jean Durliat

Bibliography

JW, 1, 230–4, 2, 699–740.

LP, 1, 336–40.

PL, 87, 105–212, 129, 591–604.

Bertolini, O. *Roma di fronte a Bisanzio e ai Longobardi*, Bologna, 1971, 337–50.

Conte, P. "Martin I," *LexMA*, 6 (1992), 341

Peeters, P. "Une vie grecque du pape Saint Martin I," *Analecta Bollandiana*, 51 (1933), 225–62.

Riedinger, R. "Papst Martin I. und Papst Leo I. in den Akten der Lateran-Synode," *Jahrbuch der österreichischen Bysantinistik*, 33 (1983), 87–9.

MARTIN II. See **Marinus I**.

MARTIN III. See **Marinus II**.

MARTIN IV. *Simon de Brie (b. Mainpincien, France, Seine-et-Marne, com. Andrezel, c. 1210–20–d. Perugia, 28 March 1285). Elected pope on 22 February 1281, enthroned on 23 March, buried in the cathedral of S. Lorenzo of Perugia.*

A relatively unknown Frenchman, obliging and too devoted to Charles of Anjou, elected at Viterbo, he lived mostly at Orvieto, which he left for Montefiascone when troubles broke out there, or for Perugia, when he received the submission of Charles and where he died. Martin IV never succeeded in making his entry into a hostile Rome, and in several years he had completely undone the entire fragile construction accomplished by his predecessor Nicholas III, who had known how to deal with the ANGEVINS.

Simon de Brie was, according to tradition, from a family of lesser nobles from the Ile-de-France destined to serve the king of France; brother of one of Louis IX's advisers, he studied at the University of Paris before being named archdeacon and chancellor of the cathedral chapter of Rouen, and then treasurer of the prestigious royal chapter of St. Martin of Tours (in honor of this saint and protector, he took the pontifical name of Martin IV, after an ONOMASTIC confusion, which had counted

Popes MARINUS I and MARINUS II, since the 9th and 10th centuries, as Martin II and Martin III). In 1260 he became guardian of the seals of the king of France, which meant he was chancellor without having that title. The following year, URBAN IV made him cardinal-priest of the see of Saint-Cecilia; thus, he naturally played an important role in Franco-pontifical diplomacy. He was LEGATE to France for CLEMENT IV and GREGORY X and negotiated the accords between the HOLY SEE and Charles I of Anjou, brother of the king who was recognized in Italy as protector of the pope and the GUELPHS against the last Staufen. However, Charles soon became determined to create a Mediterranean monarchy.

When Nicholas III, who had tried to thwart the Angevin ambitions, died, the CONCLAVE was dominated by this political question. When the cardinals met at Viterbo, the Orsini relatives of the dead pope had obviously consolidated their positions at the CURIA, in Rome and in that region. The conclave lasted six months and only one energetic action by Charles of Anjou and his Aldobrandeschi partisans was able to guide the choice toward his candidate Simon, with the help of a pro-Angevin portion of the Curia (including one influential NOTARY, Benedetto Caetani, the future BONIFACE VIII, whom the new pope raised to cardinal on 12 April 1281). The choice of the conclave of 1280–1 was also assisted by less commendable means: Charles peremptorily replaced the podesta of Viterbo, Orso Orsini, with Riccardello Annibaldi, a member of a family that had already opposed the Orsinis under ALEXANDER IV; two cardinals were arrested, and Cardinal Matteo Rosso, nephew of the dead pope, was not permitted to attend the conclave.

As soon as he was enthroned, Martin IV reacted vigorously against the Orsini nepotism, and began substituting a Franco-Angevin clan for them, less skilled in business; in the Romagna, he replaced a nephew of his predecessor with a Frenchman from Charles's followers, the famous canonist Guillaume Durand, as his vicar general. Beginning on 10 March 1281, Martin IV received the post of Roman senator, which his predecessor had included in the papacy, but he gave it away to Charles of Anjou, and "Sicilian" garrisons went to take control of several areas of the PAPAL STATES. As he had done from 1268 to 1278, Charles had himself represented in Rome, as a pontifical vicar, by royal vicars, until the Romans, in revolt, elected Giovanni Cenci as captain and defender on 22 January 1284, forcing the pope to recognize this new city government (We find, besides Annibaldo Annibaldi, beginning in August 1284, Pandolfo Savelli, who was co-senator for the pope during Nicholas III's report in 1279.) But Angevin expansionism, after having assured, with an iron hand, its grip on southern Italy and Sicily tried to consolidate its positions in the rest of the peninsula and looked toward the Balkans. These aims were supported by the pope, to the detriment of a fragile union with the Greek Church and the idea of a CRUSADE. In July 1281 the sovereign pontiff ratified the alliance concluded at Orvieto between Charles, Venice, and the pretender to a Latin Empire reconstituted in the East, Philippe de Courtenay; on 19 November the pope excommunicated Emperor Michael VIII Palaeologus, giving Charles's undertaking the designation of a crusade against the Byzantine Empire. Charles, who could count on support from the lords of Epirus and of Thessaly, as well as some Serbs and Bulgarians, had several skirmishes in 1282 but postponed all large actions until 1283. Faced with an Angevin threat, the Byzantine emperor made contact with the king of Aragon, Pedro III, who laid claim to the Sicilian succession to Manfred, a Staufen, as his son-in-law, and with Genoa, Venice's traditional rival. The Angevins were quickly driven out of Sicily by a revolt begun at the Sicilian Vespers (30 March 1282), mostly financed by the *basileus*. The rebels offered the island to the pope, who refused to receive their oaths of loyalty and excommunicated and then deposed Pedro III (18 November 1282, and 21 March 1283), who had disembarked at Palermo and accepted the crown before consolidating his successes in a naval victory at Naples in June 1284. The pope then negotiated with King Philip III of France and offered the crown of Aragon to his son: this was the beginning of the disastrous crusade of Aragon in the summer of 1285, whose end neither Charles of Anjou, dead on 7 January 1285, nor Martin IV, dead almost three months later, would see.

It is important to note here that everything took place on the level of feudal rights: Aragon was supposedly a fief of St. Peter because its king had given homage to INNOCENT III, and Martin IV intervened as a feudal lord against his kingdom-vassal. It was still at the feudal level, despite the expressly declared wish of Charles of Anjou, that the "lease" of the Angevin kingdom of southern Italy was given to the pope upon his death and in the absence of his heir Charles of Salerno, the future Charles II, a captive of the Aragonese. The unconditional support given to Angevin projects had other disastrous consequences. Beginning in 1283, the successor to Michael III, Andronikos II, broke the union of the Greek and Latin churches, achieved with much difficulty at the COUNCIL of Lyon in 1274; the Ghibellines of Romagna, supported in secret by the enemies of the Angevin, brought the province to the boiling point, and it was pacified only with difficulty by Nicholas III.

Martin IV showed his attachment to the king of France, whom he had served, by beginning the instruction for the process of canonization for Louis IX, the future St. Louis. He also intervened in other kingdoms: he supported King Alfonso X of Castille against his sons who had revolted, and maintained good relations with King Rudolph of Germany who, out of the Italian wasps' nest, dedicated himself to his kingdom across the mountains. The pope tried to speed up the collection of the tithe for a crusade. Protecting the Friars Minor (Franciscans), he caused serious troubles: the bull *Ad fructus uberes* on 13 December 1281, basically gave the brothers the right to preach and hear confessions on the authority of the minister general and the provincial ministers, to the detriment of the ordinary and the secular clergy. These issues fraught with so many thorny problems vexed his pontificate and those of his successors.

Olivier Guyotjeannin

Bibliography

LP, 2, 459–65.
Potth. 1756–95, 2132.
Amann, E. "Martin IV", *DTC*, 10–1 (1928), 194–8.
Backes, M. *Kardinal Simon de Brion*, 1910.
Olivier-Martin, F. *Les Registres de Martin IV*, 1901–35.
Paravicini Bagliani, A. *I testamenti dei cardinali del Duecento*, 1980 (*Miscellanea della società romana di storia patria*, 25), 37–8.
Roberg, B. "Martin IV," *LexMA*, 6, 341–2.

MARTIN V. *Odone Colonna (b. Genazzano [province of Rome], 1368–d. Rome, 20 February 1431). Elected pope November 11 and crowned 21 November 1417. Buried at St. John Lateran in Rome.*

The pontificate of Martin V put an end to the GREAT SCHISM OF THE WEST. Practically, the conciliar crises were not finished, but the physical return of the sovereign pontiff to Rome marked the beginning of the papacy's modern history, the renewal of the pontifical monarchy in the bosom of a temporarily reunited Christianity.

Odone Colonna was the second of seven children of Agapito of the branch of the Colonnas of Genazzano and of Caterina Conti. Considered the most intelligent of his siblings, he was destined for an ecclesiastical career: though he probably attended the University of Perugia, we do not know his university degree. Already a PROTONOTARY under URBAN VI's pontificate, he was named cardinal-deacon of the see of Saint-George in Velabro on 12 June 1405, by INNOCENT VII. In 1408 he abandoned the party of GREGORY XII, the successor to INNOCENT VII, and joined the cardinals who were meeting in Pisa to elect ALEXANDER V. Upon the latter's death, he was among the electors of JOHN XXIII. Strengthened by his family's position, whom he favored already in many different ways, he saw his support sought after by John XXIII when the latter, in difficult circumstances during his pontificate, tried to consolidate his position in Rome. In 1410 and 1411, the pope gave the cardinal's brothers a confirmation of their recent acquisitions, thus putting the family in a prosperous position that it had not had until then, even if it could not yet pretend to rival the branch of the Colonnas of Palestrina.

At the Council of Constance Colonna supported John XXIII, and when the latter fled (21 March 1415), he joined him at Schaffhausen but refused to follow him any farther. Returning to Constance, he became a witness for the prosecution and signed the deposition of his former protector. On 8 November 1417, fifty-three electors (twenty-three cardinals and thirty delegates of the five nations represented at the council) met in a CONCLAVE. Despite the difficulties presented by the method of scrutiny adopted the preceding October 11 (the elected person had to receive two-thirds of all the votes, not only of the cardinals, but in each of the five groups), the choice fell upon Odone Colonna on 11 November 1417, the feast of St. Martin, whose name the new pope adopted. Because he was only a deacon, two days later he was ordained a priest, consecrated a bishop, and crowned on November 21. The Christian princes approved the newly elected pope without difficulty, except in France and Aragon. In France, the government of Charles VI still waited until 13 April 1418 before giving him their support. Count Jean IV of Armagnac, who took a hostile position toward Martin V for a long time, did not make a definitive submission until 1430. King Alfonso V of Aragon, unhappy with the pope's support for the Angevin party in the succession to the kingdom of Naples, continued to protect the antipopes BENEDICT XIII and then his successor CLEMENT VIII until 1426, when he forced the latter to abdicate and finally recognized the pope in Rome.

The newly elected pope found himself immediately confronted by the problems that would dominate his pontificate: the reform of the Church, her leaders and her members, and the reestablishment of pontifical authority over the territories of the Church in Italy. For the reform of the Church, a commission of cardinals and of delegates chosen by the pope immediately after his coronation went quickly to work. As they could not reach an agreement, Martin V took the initiative at the end of January 1418 to plan reform, where he put some order in the nominations for benefices, prescribed rules for university degrees and the deportment of prelates, limited the possibilities of accumulating titles, and eliminated several obvious abuses in the fiscal practices of the Roman CURIA. This plan was adopted in the session of the council (21 March 1418). The pope negotiated agreements separately with each of the nations (*concordata*, that is to say CONCORDAT), assuring the conciliar decree by adapting it to local circumstances for a period of five years (with the exception of England, with whom the agreement was perpetual). Still remaining was the lasting wish expressed by the conciliar assembly even before the pontifical election, for a general council that would meet periodically. This unanimous desire was made a reality by the decree *Frequens* of the 39th session (9 October 1417), which provided for a new council less than five years after the end of the one at Constance, a second seven years after the close of that one, and another every ten years thereafter. Thus, on 19 April 1418, Martin V proclaimed his intention of calling the next council to be held in Pavia. The opening took place on 23 April 1423, but an epidemic of plague forced the assembly to move to Siena where the debates began again in July. Discussions on the subject of papal authority, the fear of Aragonese influences opposing the pope, and the plans of France all convinced Martin V to abstain from appearing, and to close the assembly as quickly as possible. The dissolution was pronounced on 26 February 1424 after an extremely forceful intervention by the pope against the Pisans, accusing them of wanting to prolong the council out of a spirit of pure cupidity. Before separating, the fathers decided that the next council would meet in Basel. The pope was so convinced of his powerlessness to lead such a hostile assembly that the permanent threat of a council and, therefore, the questioning of papal authority became an efficient weapon used by the princes to obtain all sorts of favors from the HOLY SEE.

The reform of the Church's leaders, that is to say of the Roman Curia above all, remained a serious problem for Martin V. The pope certainly tried to apply the recommendations of Pisa and Constance (reductions in taxes and officers, high moral standards, internationalization of personnel, and exclusion of laypersons). The BULL of dissolution of the Council of Siena had set up a commission of cardinals charged with gathering opinions on Church reform: it ended in the constitution of 13 April 1425, issued by the CHANCERY the following 16 May. If it was easy, because of the reunion of the different obediences, to conserve an international character in the Curia for some time, which it did not have again until the 20th century, the reduction of offices and the suppression of financial transactions regarding positions and benefices were fruitless. Those with positions, and even those with benefices, had often given the papal treasury advances of money that it was impossible to repay. The popes of various obediences as well as Martin V himself had often needed to avail themselves of this form of credit. Resistance was much too strong and the rights acquired much too important for anyone to consider radical reforms. And though the addition of the former Avignon personnel improved the functioning of the Roman offices, the curialists remained mediators involved between the center and the periphery. Martin V resisted the pressures of his family with difficulty, and he gave his relatives favors that went against the rules that he himself had set up, but if he tolerated corruption, it was in lesser proportions than his successors.

The restoration of papal power in Italy had become vital after the hard blows struck against the finances of the Holy See by the reductions of the taxes on benefices, particularly in the kingdom of France where the revenues had been cut by half due to the great misery caused by the Hundred Years' War. Once he had pronounced the closing of the Council of Constance (22 April 1418), the pope left the city on 16 May. During a journey whose final destination (Italy or Avignon) was kept secret until the middle of summer, he successively visited Geneva, Turin, Milan, and finally, in November, Mantua. Unable to go to Bologna, which had dismissed its papal legate in 1416, or to Rome, occupied by Neapolitan troops, Martin V went to Florence in February 1419. There he ensured the support of Joanna II in exchange for her recognition as queen of Naples (a fief of the Holy See) and, by a secret bull in November 1419 that established obstacles to any Aragonese pretensions, and with her agreement, admitted the house of Anjou to be her legitimate successor. The pontifical ambassador to Naples, Giordano Colonna, the pope's own brother, was given many honors and fiefs. The queen gave Benevento and Pontecorvo back to the pope while waiting to pull the Neapolitan troops out of Rome and those in other zones occupied by a captain in her pay, Muzio Attendolo Sforza.

Martin V finally reentered Rome on 25 September 1420. In the meantime, with the support of Joanna II and the Florentines, and lacking any power to subdue him by force, the pope held talks with Braccio da Montone who had, at the expense of the Church, hacked out a state for himself in the center of Italy (26 February 1420). Braccio gave back the duchy of Spoleto and the Tiber valley with its possessions but obtained the vicariate of important communes in Umbria in exchange for the payment of a fee to the APOSTOLIC CAMERA. Braccio was still powerful, and to come to the aid of the Aragonese party in Naples, he crossed through the Papal States, sacking them. In 1423, Martin V, who knew how to be patient, renewed his vicariate but got l'Aquila to revolt against him; Braccio administered that province, while Filippo Maria Visconti occupied his lands in the Romagna. Finally the pope, who borrowed from all sides, raised an army under the leadership of the Colonna family and the son of Muzio Attendolo, Francesco, which defeated Braccio near l'Aquila on 2 June 1424. Braccio died three days later, and in the two months that followed, all his possessions fell into the hands of the Roman pontiff.

In Bologna, in 1419, Martin V was able to reestablish his nominal authority in exchange for sufficient autonomy and payment of a fee, but the following year the accord was broken. This time the pope used force, besieging the city, which surrendered on 14 July 1420. The commune's government was ensured by the papal legate. The pope was happy to remove the ruling families from the communal administration and to take over their possessions in the county. A new revolt in 1428 was ended in September 1429 by an agreement that gave the county of Bologna a greater autonomy in its administration. An understanding was concluded at Ferrara, with Filippo Maria Visconti giving the Holy See Imola and Forlì, and in 1429 Martin V used the internal conflict of the members of the Malatesta family to his own benefit, making them give up a few more lands in the Romagna to the temporal sovereignty of the Holy See. To complete this restoration of papal authority, Martin V limited his objectives: he rarely tried to modify the traditions of local governments but only required formal recognition of his authority and the payment of a fee. In exchange, he favored the influence of local oligarchies over the communal power. As for his military enterprises, they were mostly accomplished with the help of his family, the Colonnas, but also those he had been able to win over, such as the lord of Urbino, Guidantonio da Montefeltro, to whom he had given his own niece in marriage. In exchange, he received fiefs and positions. This Colonna domination of the pontifical government had risen to such a point that at the end of the pontificate, Martin V's successor could only hope to get rid of them by using the support of their rival faction, the Orsini family.

Not wishing to give the SACRED COLLEGE the role of the official registry office and, therefore, control over papal authority as certain fathers at the council of Constance would have wished, Martin V exercised extreme caution in his choice of cardinals. He waited until 24 May 1426, almost nine years, for his first promotion of fourteen new cardinals, with two reserved *in pectore*. Besides the powerful prelates recommended by a sovereign who was often their relative (the archbishop of Rouen, the uncle of the king of England, the cardinal of Lusignan) we find in the list the faithful servants of the Roman Curia: Antonio Casini, bishop of Siena, but long the treasurer of the Apostolic Camera; Louis Alemand, long vice chamberlain and nephew of François de Conzié; Giuliano Cesarini, auditor of the ROTA; the brilliant Domenico Capranica, close to the Colonna of Genazzano; Prospero Colonna, who followed his uncle to the see of St. George in Velabro; Ardicino della Porta, the consistorial advocate and corrector of the apostolic letters. The second promotion (8 November 1430) included Juan Casanova and the bishop of Saint-Malo.

Martin V took a minor part in the conciliar debates on the subject of the Hussites and, even if the decrees of condemnation were supported by his authority, his personal role was certainly not a large one. The care for defending pontifical prerogatives was stronger in him than the will to engage in discussions for which he was not well prepared. However, despite the respect he always showed for the major decisions of the council during which he had been elected, he never failed to remember the obstacles he needed to overcome. The Polish ambassadors at Constance, unhappy with the decision made by the pope on the subject of the Falkenberg libel, had appealed it to the future council. Martin V replied with a document, unpublished, dated 10 May 1418, in which he affirmed that no one could, in matters of faith, appeal a decision by the

pope. In 1427 he intervened on behalf of Bernardino of Siena. He had been denounced to him because of excesses he engaged in to demonstrate his devotion to the holy name of Jesus, for whom he devised the form of a trigram (the letters YHS in writing pierced by a sun with twelve rays). After a public debate held before the pope, the latter passed a sentence favorable to Bernardino (early June 1427). This polemic was due in large part to the rivalries between the religious orders because Bernardino's fiercest opponents were the hermits of St. Augustine. Worried about accusation of partiality, Martin V gave the latter the relics of St. Monica on 17 April 1430, kept until then in the church of Santa Aurea of Ostia, so that they could take them to the church next to their convent of Sant'Agostino in Rome.

Even more astonishing to most historians is the pope's attitude toward Jews. He abolished vexatious measures taken against them by BENEDICT XII: in 1422 and 1429 he forbade violent accusations against them. Especially, he forbade the baptism of children of less than age twelve against the will of their parents, under pain of excommunication *ipso facto*.

Martin V was not a man of the Renaissance. The few bits of information that can be gleaned from his library show that he was not very curious about new things and was still anchored firmly in the medieval past. He showed little interest in books, quite different from most of the popes of the Great Schism and from his successor, EUGENE IV. The artistic choices of the pope, those in which we might assume he took a personal part, reveal a person linked to tradition. His return to Rome, although late, marked the renewal of construction. Besides the maintenance and restoration of the great basilicas (ST. PETER's, ST. JOHN LATERAN), the Pantheon, and the Capitol, Martin V and his entourage were especially interested in the great cycles of paintings. These reveal a profound tie with medieval tradition, in particular with early Christian art. Even the choice of the places for artistic interventions is revealing: the route for the procession which led to the Lateran for the *possesso* and that of the pilgrims who visited the basilicas, and the places associated by tradition with the Colonnas. Martin V may be found there, in the sort of political artistry of the great pontiffs of medieval theocracy.

Those in favor of the council that the pope was supposed to convene in Basel applied so much pressure that Martin V ended up publishing the bulls of convocation on 14 February 1431. Stronger from his earlier experiences, he named the young cardinal Giuliano Cesarini his legate *a latere* and president of the assembly with the power, if needed, to change the meeting place of the council. One week later, on 21 February 1431, the pope died of apoplexy. His body was transported to St. John Lateran, whose archpriest he had remained since 1411. In 1445, probably initiated by his nephew Cardinal Prospero Colonna, a bronze plaque made in Florence that represented the pope on his deathbed was placed on his tomb at the foot of the confessional where it may still be found today. The portrait is attributed to Donatello and the rest of the work to Simone da Firenze.

François-Charles Uginet

Bibliography

Caravale, M., and Caracciolo, C. *Lo Stato pontificio da Martino V a Pio IX*, Turin, 1978.

Dykmans, M. "D'Avignon à Rome, Martin V et le cortège apostolique," *BIHR*, 1968, 201–308.

Fink, K. A. *LTK*, 7, 1962, 118–19.

Maddalo, S. "Identità di una cultura figurativa"; Finocchi Ghersi, L. "Le residenze dei Colonna ai SS. Apostolici"; Manfredi, A. "Note per la recostruzione della biblioteca di Martino V," Frehberg, A. "Osservazioni sul nepotismo di Martino V"; Schwarz, B. "L'organizzazione curiale di Martino V e i problemi derivanti dallo Scisma"; Esch, A. "La tomba di Martino V e i registri doganali di Roma," in *Alle origini della nuova Roma-Martino V (1417–1431)*, documents from the colloquium of Rome (2–5 March 1992).

Mollat, G. *DTC*, 10, 197–202.

Picotti, G. B. *EC*, VIII, 225–8.

MARXISM AND THE PAPACY. For almost a century and a half, from the encyclical *Qui pluribus* of PIUS IX (9 November 1846) to *Centesimus annus* of JOHN PAUL II (1 May 1991), the Catholic Church has persisted, without any discontinuity whatsoever, in denouncing the perils and damages toward mankind of the doctrine that has come from the thoughts of Karl Marx as well as the applications of it. The spectacular collapse of most of the communist regimes between 1989 and 1991 was greeted by many observers, even non-Christian ones, as the well-founded confirmation of this nonviolent battle (*CA*, 23) led by the words of the pope and by the blood of the martyrdom of men and women who maintained their dignity and their faith (*ES*, 107). A chronology, however tedious it may be, of this rejection without compromise allows us to explicitly detail the official statements in this regard:

Pius IX: encyclical *Qui pluribus* of 9 November 1846; address *Quibus quantisque* of 20 April 1849; encyclical *Nostis et Nobiscum* of 8 December 1849; address *Singulari quadam* of 9 December 1854; encyclical *Quanto ficiamur maerore* of 10 August 1863; encyclicals *Quanta cura* and *Syllabus* of 8 December 1864.

Leo XIII: encyclicals *Quod Apostolici muneris* of 18 December 1878; *Immortale Dei* of 1 November 1885; *Libertas praestantissima* of 20 June 1888; and *Rerum novarum* of 15 May 1891.

Pius XI: address to the world on 13 December 1924; encyclicals *Miserentissimus Redemptor* of 8 May 1928;

Quadragesimo anno of 15 May 1931; *Caritate Christi* of 3 May 1932; *Acerba animi* of 29 September 1932; *Dilectissima Nobis* of 3 June 1933; and *Divini redemptoris* of 19 March 1937.

Pius XII: encyclical *Summi pontificatus* of 20 October 1939; Christmas message in 1942; decree from the Holy Office on 1 July 1949; and radio messages to the entire world on 23 December 1949 and Christmas Day 1955; encyclical *Ad apostolorum principis* of 19 June 1958.

John XXIII: decree from the Holy Office on 4 April 1959, encyclical *Mater et Magistra* on 15 May 1961.

Paul VI: encyclical *Ecclesiam suam* on 6 August 1964; VATICAN II Council; document *Gaudium et spes* of 7 December 1965; encyclical *Populorum progressio* of 26 March 1967; apostolic letter *Octogesima adveniens* of 14 May 1971.

John Paul II: encyclical *Laborem exercens* of 14 September 1981; instructions to the Congregation for the Doctrine of the Faith *Libertatis nuntius* on 6 August 1984 and *Libertatis conscientia* of 22 March 1986; encyclicals *Sollicitudo rei socialis* of 30 December 1987 and *Centesimus annus* on 1 May 1991.

All these texts, implicitly or explicitly, condemn Marxism under all the different names used to represent the same relationship: communism, socialism, Bolshevism, Marxism, and Marxism-Leninism.

In 1846 when Pius IX spoke of "the execrable doctrine called communism," even before the publication of the *Communist Party Manifesto* by Karl Marx and Frederick Engels in 1848, the pope was aiming at a group of doctrines that were developing within the growing socialist movement, and a group of clandestine movements that called for the proletarian and communist revolution. The objective of Marx and Engels during these same years consisted of penetrating one of these revolutionary societies in order to become an inspiration and impose their way of thinking. In 1849 Pius IX put the faithful on guard against those who would let themselves "be tricked by the promoters of actual maneuvers" by consenting "to conspire with them for the wicked systems of socialism and communism."

In 1891, Leo XIII, in *Rerum novarum*, only used the concept of "socialism," which at that time meant a doctrinal body able "to be considered basically as one" and he denounced "well-defined doctrines that formed an organic whole" (*QA*), largely inspired by the thoughts of Marx. When, forty years later, Pius XI tried to make a point on the "social question," he clearly distinguished between socialism and communism. In the meantime, two "revolutions" had taken place: the Russian revolution and the Mexican revolution. The former effected a geopolitical transfer of center of influence; the Marxist political leader Lenin, with great deftness, made Moscow (proclamation of the 3rd International) the new center of world socialism in place of Berlin and the German Social-Democratic party. He simultaneously discredited the 2nd International to some extent, as represented by socialist parties who had compromised with the nationalism of 1914 and WORLD WAR I. Nevertheless, the communism and socialism of the 1930s were rooted in the same source: Marxism (even if afterward communism only admitted one "orthodoxy" relating to the theories of Marx through Marxism-Leninism). After having recalled "the impious and unjust nature of communism," which showed itself to be "savage and inhuman" wherever it took power, Pius XI concluded his attentive examination of the evolution of socialism in these well-known terms: "religious socialism, Christian socialism, are contradictions: no one can be both a good Catholic and a true socialist" (*QA*).

It was the Spanish Civil War, a fundamentally ideological and religious war, which would push Pius XI to devote an entire encyclical to "Bolshevik and atheist communism." Published five days after *Mit brennender Sorge* denouncing the errors and evils of Nazism, *Divini redemptoris* on 19 March 1937, made a similar analysis of the theoretical errors and the practical wickednesses of Marxism:

The doctrine of modern Communism, which is often concealed under the most seductive trappings, is in substance based on the principles of dialectical and historical materialism previously advocated by Marx, of which the theoreticians of Bolshevism claim to possess the only genuine interpretation. [. . .] Such, Venerable Brethren, is the new gospel which Bolshevistic and atheistic Communism offers the world as the glad tidings of deliverance and salvation! It is a system full of errors and sophisms. It is in opposition both to reason and to Divine Revelation. It subverts the social order, because it means the destruction of its foundations; because it ignores the true origin and purpose of the State; because it denies the rights, dignity and liberty of human personality. [. . .]. For the first time in history we are witnessing a struggle, cold-blooded in purpose and mapped out to the least detail, between man and "all that is called God." [. . ..]. See to it, Venerable Brethren, that the Faithful do not allow themselves to be deceived! Communism is intrinsically wrong, and no one who would save Christian civilization may collaborate with it in any undertaking whatsoever.

In the middle of WORLD WAR II, in his Christmas message of 1942, Pope Pius XII repeated this condemnation of all socialism, communist or not, whenever it drew inspiration from Marxism. Ten years later, the growth of power of Communist parties took place within democracies with an ancient Christian tradition, and Marxism in particular was at the highest level ever in the intellectual circles of these same countries. Pius XII rejected any new idea of compromise: "We reject communism as a social system by virtue of Christian doctrine and we particularly wish to affirm the foundations of natural law. For the same reason, we reject the opinion according to which a Christian today should regard communism as a phenomenon or a stage in the course of history, like a necessary 'moment' in evolution and, as a result, accept it as if it were decreed by Divine Providence" (*RM*, Christmas 1955).

In the international context of a peaceful coexistence that could not hide an ideological competition and a continued persecution of the faith in Communist countries, Paul VI (*ES*, 1964) and Vatican Council II (*GS*, 1965) added to previous warnings the reference to "the Church of silence":

These are the reasons which compel us, as they compelled our predecessors and, with them, everyone who has religious values at heart, to condemn the ideological systems, which deny God and oppress the church-systems, which are often identified with economic, social and political regimes, amongst which atheistic communism is the chief. It could be said that it is not so much that we condemn these systems and regimes as that they express their radical opposition to us in thought and deed. Our regret is, in reality, more sorrow for a victim than the sentence of a judge. (*ES*, 101)

The "coexistential dialogue" cannot take place when one of the discussants physically suppresses the other: "The Church of Silence, for example, speaks only by sufferings, and with her speaks also the suffering of an oppressed and degraded society, in which the rights of the spirit are crushed by those who control its fate" (*ES*, 103).

John XXIII evoked, in 1963, the possibility of "certain meetings regarding practical directions that until now seemed inopportune or sterile" between the Church and "movements that have a direct bearing either on economic and social questions, or cultural matters or on the organization of the state, even if these movements owe their origin and inspiration " from "false philosophical theories on the nature, origin and finality of the world and of man" (*PT*, 159–60). For this dialogue to be possible, these movements would had to have undergone a considerable evolution in their political orientation, removing them from their initial theoretical references, to be "in agreement with the healthy principles of reason" and to answer "the just aspirations of the human being." Catholics, for their part, should be "faithful to the principles of natural law," follow "the Christian doctrine of the

Church," and obey "the directives of ecclesiastical authority." It could not be a question of communism, as Paul VI would recall one year later (*ES*, 105–9) and during the 1960s and 1970s, when the Marxist strategy of entry into the Catholic Church in Latin America took place, under the cover of the label of "theologies of liberation." On the level of theory, the rejection of Marxism was still very clear:

Any Christian who wishes to live his faith in a political activity which he thinks of as service cannot without contradicting himself adhere to ideological systems which radically or substantially go against his faith and his concept of man. He cannot adhere to the Marxist ideology, to its atheistic materialism, to its dialectic of violence and to the way it absorbs individual freedom in the collectivity, at the same time denying all transcendence to man and his personal and collective history; nor can he adhere to the liberal ideology. . . . (*OA*, 26)

As for the historic evolution of a living Marxism ending in different levels of interpretations ("active practice of class struggle," "collective exercise of political and economic power," "socialist ideology based upon historical materialism and on the denial of everything transcendent" or even "rigorous method of examining social and political realities"), "it would be illusory and dangerous to reach a point of forgetting the intimate link which radically binds them together, to accept the elements of Marxist analysis without recognizing their relationships with ideology, and to enter into the practice of class struggle and its Marxist interpretations, while failing to note the kind of totalitarian and violent society to which this process leads." (*OA*, 33–4).

He did not state his understanding of the non-communist socialism, which had noticeably evolved when compared with its historic roots tied to Marxism; it was enough to think of the formal denial with reference to Marx the German Social Democrat party had offered during its meeting at Bad-Godesburg, to understand what John XXIII was trying to say in *PT*. Paul VI furnishes a cautious attempt at interpretation:

Now this historical current takes on, under the same name, different forms according to different continents and cultures . . . Careful judgment is called for. Too often Christians attracted by socialism tend to idealize it in terms that, apart from anything else, are very general: a will for justice, solidarity and equality. They refuse to recognize the limitations of the historical socialist movements, which remain conditioned by the ideologies from which they originated. Distinctions must be made to guide concrete choices between the various levels of expression of social-

ism . . . Nevertheless, these distinctions must not lead one to consider such levels as completely separate and independent. The concrete link which, according to circumstances, exists between them must be clearly marked out. This insight will enable Christians to see the degree of commitment possible along these lines, while safeguarding the values, especially those of liberty, responsibility and openness to the spiritual, which guarantee the integral development of man. (*OA*, 31)

In 1984 John Paul II reiterated the total incompatibility of Marxism with Christianity. Speaking against a certain "theology of liberation," John Paul II in 1991 concluded, after the fall of communism in the countries of Central and Eastern Europe:

In the recent past, the sincere desire to be on the side of the oppressed and not to be cut off from the course of history has led many believers to seek in various ways an impossible compromise between Marxism and Christianity. Moving beyond all that was short-lived in these attempts, present circumstances are leading to a reaffirmation of the positive value of an authentic theology of integral human liberation. Considered from this point of view, the events of 1989 are proving to be important also for the countries of the Third World, which are searching for their own path to development, just as they were important for the countries of Central and Eastern Europe. (*CA*, 26)

This systematic and ultimately successful triumph over Marxism by the papacy did not proceed from a sectarian viewpoint focusing mainly on one current, one vision of the world, or one form of power with totalitarian tendencies. Simultaneously, the papal magisterium denounced and rejected LIBERALISM with similar energy "that at its very root . . . is an erroneous affirmation of the autonomy of the individual in his activities, his motivation and the exercise of his freedom" (*OA*, 35). Pius XI did not hesitate to denounce the false opposition of these two ideologies in order to show how much socialism is based historically on liberalism and results from it: "Workers were already prepared for this propaganda by the religious and moral abandonment in which they were left by the liberal economy . . ., it is not astonishing that in a mostly de-Christianized world, communist error flourishes" (*DR*).

In fact, from Pius IX to John Paul II, the criticism of Marxism is only one aspect of the rejection of a vision of man and the world that is usually called "modernity," and which has been, fundamentally, the opposite of Christianity for more than two centuries: "For his real shape as a creature, having his beginning and ending in

God, the false portrait of a man whose conscience is autonomous has been substituted, the out-of-control ruler of himself, irresponsible toward his peers and towards his society, with no other destiny than that on earth, no other goal than to enjoy his possessions, no other law than that of fact and the undisciplined satisfaction of his desires" (*RM*, Christmas 1949). That was essentially the same conclusion John Paul II reached in 1991, when he analyzed the anthropological error of "socialism":

> The atheism of which we are speaking is also closely connected with the rationalism of the Enlightenment, which views human and social reality in a mechanistic way. Thus there is a denial of the supreme insight concerning man's true greatness, his transcendence in respect to earthly realities, the contradiction in his heart between the desire for the fullness of what is good and his own inability to attain it and, above all, the need for salvation which results from this situation (*CA*, 13)

Jean-Luc Chabot

List of abbreviations:
QA: Quadragesimo anno (encyclical of 15 May 1931)
DR: Divini Redemptoris (encyclical of 19 March 1937)
RM: Radio messages of Pius XII
PT: Pacem in terris (encyclical of 11 April 1963)
ES: Ecclesiam suam (encyclical of 6 August 1964)
GS: Gaudium et spes (document of 7 December 1965)
OA: Octogesima adveniens (apostolic letter of 14 May 1971)
LN: Libertatis nuntius (instruction on 22 March 1984)
CA: Centesimus annus (encyclical of 1 May 1991)

Bibliography

Chabot, J. L. *La doctrine sociale de l'Église*, 2nd ed., 1992; *Histoire de la penseé politique (XIXe–XXe siècle)*, 1988.

Chambre, H. *Christianisme et communisme*, 1959.

Cottier, G. *Le Conflit des espérances*, 1977.

De Laubier, P. *La Penseé sociale de l'Église catholique*, 1984.

Guerry, E. *Église Catholique et communisme atheé*, 1960.

Lazzarotto, A. S. "Christians and Marxists Building a Common House in Europe," *Tripod* 58 (1990) pp. 61–6.

Piettre, A. *Marx et marxisme*, Paris, 1959; *Les Chrétiens et le socialisme*, 1984.

MASS, PAPAL: LITURGICAL OBJECTS. A number of liturgical objects are unique to the papal mass.

Asterisk. The asterisk is a liturgical object used in the papal liturgy until VATICAN II COUNCIL. It consisted of a circle of gold, 12 cm. in diameter, elevated by the eight curved arms of a star with, at its center, a raised precious stone that allowed the object to be grasped. This was placed, as a perforated cover, over the consecrated host placed upon a gold paten; it held the sacred species during the long procession that the cardinal-deacon made from the papal altar of the confessional of ST. PETER's to the papal throne under the pulpit at the back of the apse to bring communion to the pope during solemn masses.

Fistula. A very ancient object for the Roman liturgy whose use was little by little reserved only for the pope, the straw was used for reception of consecrated wine, the Blood of Christ. It was used by the pope to drink without drinking directly from the chalice in all the solemn masses except the one on Maundy Thursday. This straw was a tube 50 cm. long, made of gold encrusted with diamonds and emeralds. It was brought to the pope, with the chalice, by the cardinal-bishop assisting him and carried back to the altar by the deacon, who in turn drank the precious blood that remained in the chalice. This rite was abolished after the Vatican II Council.

The "Incarnatus est" cloth. The *Incarnatus est* is an altar cloth sewn four centuries ago and exclusively used for the papal altar for solemn services of the sovereign pontiff at ST. PETER's in Rome. It is a linen cloth bordered with golden lace, large enough to cover the entire altar of the confessional under the canopy of Bernini. Its special characteristic is its composition of thirteen equal pieces joined by golden lace in which some see the symbolism of the twelve apostles and St. Paul, joined by Christ. This altar cloth was first placed on the altar, but then folded back halfway in its length. During the singing of the *Credo*, two pontifical subdeacons came up and opened it, precisely at the moment when the choir came to the phrase "Et incarnatus est," which is how it got its name. The cardinal-deacon then put the communion cloth over it and prepared the holy vases for the celebration of the offertory by the pope. When it was used for papal vespers services, its unfolding was done during the singing of the *Magnificat*.

Joel-Benoit D'Onorio

Bibliography

Battandier, A. "Les ornements du souverain pontife," *Annuaire pontifical catholique*, 1907.

MASTER OF THE SACRED PALACE. The ancient title borne until 1968 by this cleric, member of the pontifical court, was *Magister Sacri Palatii apostolici*. Today, he is officially called Theologian of the Papal Household.

The most ancient writers traced this position to the pontificate of HONORIUS III (1216–27), who first gave it to St. Dominic. Studies effected during the course of the 20th century have shown that its origin was actually later than this. It is linked to the creation, by INNOCENT IV, in 1244–5, of a *studium generale Romanae Curiae* or *Sacri Palatii* in the ranks of the pontifical court, which was then in the city of Lyon. This *studium* would follow the court wherever it went and was charged with teaching theology, CANON LAW, and civil law.

The first masters (*magister* was the title given to professors in medieval universities) who taught theology came either from the secular clergy or the regular clergy. Beginning in the 14th century, the position became exclusively restricted to DOMINICANS and has remained as such until the present day. Along with this duty, the master of the Sacred Palace received the privilege (confirmed once again by LEO XII in 1824) of conferring the ranks of Doctor of Philosophy and Doctor of Theology, even after the *studium Sacri Palatii* was dissolved at the beginning of the 16th century. The position also survived the suppression of the court because the bearer of this title had, in the meantime, received other duties as well. First of all, it is probable, even though there is no written proof of this, that the master of the Sacred Palace was, from the beginning, a consultant of the pope's on matters of doctrine, including trials for HERESY judged directly by the HOLY SEE. Then, in 1456, CALLISTUS III gave the master of the Sacred Palace the task of designating the preachers apostolic. He had to review the text of their sermons with these preachers, and, eventually, admonish these speakers, even when they preached to the pope, if they proposed erroneous beliefs on matters of faith.

This role as controller of writings regarding orthodoxy was expanded finally, after the use of the printing press became widespread in Italy. From 1515 to 1925 it was the master of the Sacred Palace who granted permission to print all works published in Rome. Beginning in 1625, the authors living in Rome who wished to publish their works outside the borders of the PAPAL STATES were required to ask for authorization from him.

The province of the master of the Sacred Palace over questions of doctrine explains how, beginning in the 17th century (but probably, for certain matters, even before that), the men who received this title had been members by right of certain organs of the Roman CURIA and of the vicariate of Rome.

In the course of the reform of the ancient pontifical court pronounced in the *motu proprio Pontificalis domus* of 28 June 1968, Paul VI changed the title of the master of the Sacred Palace into one that better matched his actual duties (Theologian of the Papal Household), preserving all his traditional duties. The bearer of this title, therefore, continues to be the legal consultant for the Congregation for the Doctrine of the Faith, titular prelate of the Congregation for the Causes for Sainthood, and, in general, consultant for the pontifical Biblical Commission.

Agostino Borromeo

Bibliography

Catalano, G. *De Magistro Sacri Palatii Apostolici libri duo . . .* , Rome, 1751.

Creytens, R. "Le *Studium Romanae Curiae* et le maître du Sacré Palais," *Archivum Fratrum Praedicatorum*, 12 (1942), 5–83.

Del Rè, N. *La Curia romana, Lineamenti storico-giuridici*, 3rd ed., 1970 (*Sussidi eruditi*, 23), 90, 328, 357.

Fontana, V. M. *Syllabus magistrorum Sacri Palatii Apostolici . . .* , Rome, 1663.

Hilgers, J., *Der Index der verbotenen Bücher in seiner neuen Fassung dargestellt und rechtlick-historisch gewürdigt*, Freiburg im Breisgau, 1904.

Loenertz, R. "Saint Dominique écrivain, maître en théologie, professeur à Rome et maître du Sacré Palais d'après quelques auteurs du XIVe et Xve siècles," *ibid*, 84–97.

Reusch, F. H. *Der Index der verbotenen Bücher. Ein Beitrag zur Kirchen- und Literaturgeschichte*, 2 vols., Bonn, 1883–85.

Taurisano, I. *Hierarchia Ordinis Praedicatorum*, Rome, 1916, 29–63.

Tavuzzi, M. *Prierias: The Life and Work of Silvestro Mazzolini da Prierio, 1456–1527*, Durham, N.C., 1997.

Tosi, A. *Lo stato presente o sia la relazione della Corte di Roma già pubblicata dal cav. Lunadoro . . .* , 2 vols., Rome, 1765. I, 109; II, 217–20.

Zucchi, A. *Roma Domenicana, Note storiche*, 4 vols., Florence, 1938–43, III, 66–77.

MEDALLIONS, PAPAL. A medallion is a metal disk, originally cast using the lost wax method and retouched by the engraver. It was later almost exclusively produced using instruments and machines invented for the manufacture of coins: stamps, balancers, and presses, and the unit became closer and closer in size to a large coin (about 30 mm). One of the first medallion makers to use this method was the Venetian Vittore Gambello "Camelio," working at the Roman Zecca during LEO X's pontificate in 1515–6. The manufactured medallions were certainly more quickly finished, but lost some of the relief and modeling. Due to the multiplication and a sort of systematization, the creative vein dried up late in the 16th century.

The front bears the profile of the patron or the honored person, while the back is ornamented with various motifs. In the beginning, these served to identify the person on the front in a symbolic or allegorical manner: a reference to a character trait, or social status, finished with a motto or descriptive label. Later, they alluded more and more to events in which the patron had taken part. An art born in the second third of the 15th century in certain

Italian aristocratic circles, it spread rapidly and was favorably received by the Roman pontiffs, who often came from the same social backgrounds and shared the same cultural values. Collectors of antiques, Maecenas inspired by humanism, the popes attracted goldsmiths, casters, chiselers, and engravers to Rome who, with their intaglios, cameos, and medallions contributed to regaining papal Rome's status as *caput mundi*.

From the very beginning, a master dominated this art, Pisanello, and, though he did not work for the papal court, we can be certain that his work was known there. The medallion representing the embassy of John VIII Palaeologus, coming to ask for help against the TURKS in 1437–8, must have made an impression on the minds of the participants of the council in Ferrara-Florence, among whom was Tommaso Parentucelli, a doctor of theology, the future NICHOLAS V, because the first dated papal medallion (1455) was precisely a casting honoring this pope. Created by Andrea Guaccialotti, certain stylistic details were inspired by Pirandello's style (a truncated bust, framed by a descriptive label, the ground line from the scene on the back). Also, in 1453, Constantinople had fallen, and Nicolas V decided to lead a new CRUSADE. The back of this medallion, therefore, was decorated, not with St. Peter's successor depicted as a fisher of men, but with the bishop of Rome showing the way from the deck of a ship, the Church, whose mast is a cross topped by a pennon.

The papal medallion, therefore, served from the beginning to support a specific ideological program. As the transitory and chance inheritor of the throne of St. Peter, the pope could not reproduce the thought patterns of an aristocratic group anchored in the world (a taste for emblems and mottoes) even if he sometimes yielded to it. A priority was given to the illustration of Church ideals (religious messages, portrayals of the PAPAL STATE, moralistic allegories), which made the main theme an unworldly one.

This path was, however, less narrow than it appeared, because it was added to according to the tastes of the artists, encouraged by the numerous collectors swept up in this fad: the entire papal court. Since PAUL II, a somewhat indiscriminate collector, the papacy encouraged artists to produce works for it, and Rome saw the famous ones flock to her. Vasari reported that, thanks to the reputation acquired by Valerio Belli, the Vincenza, the art of the medallion "has a crowd of masters flocking to it now: before the SACK OF ROME, from Milan or elsewhere, they had become so numerous that it was astounding" (Book VII). In this area as in others, 1527 brought many material damages, but the fashion did not die out. Benvenuto Cellini, goldsmith already noticed by members of the papal court, offered his services to CLEMENT VII and was officially hired in 1529. Two medallions mentioned in his *Memoirs* showed the perfection of various ways of honoring papal Rome. One of them, dedicated to peace, depicted Fury loaded down with chains, clearly identified by the label *Clauduntur Belli Portae*; the second showed the episode where Moses struck the rock, *Ut Bibat Populus*, a commemoration of the digging of a well at San Patrizio at Orvieto.

Until the end of the 16th century, medallion makers from every part of Italy prospered in Rome and made it renowned as the center of the medallion making. Attracted to Rome by JULIUS II, the goldsmith Caradosso, originally from the province of Como, portrayed Bramante's plans for the façade of ST. PETER'S. Inspired mostly by ancient art, the prolific Valerio Belli (he did 150 different designs) worked for Clement VII and PAUL III. The Castelbolognese G. Bernardi took over for B Cellini at the Zecca of Rome in 1534, and Leone Leoni of Arezzo, an enemy of Cellini, chose the readying of the papal city's defenses as the theme of his illustration. Gianfederigo Bonzagna, called Federigo of Parma, joined Alexander Farnese in Rome to take care of the commission from Pope Paul III, and then his successors, from PAUL IV (1555–9) to GREGORY XIII (1572–85). His compatriot Lorenzo Fragni followed him to the court of GREGORY XIII and SIXTUS V, as well as the Florentine Domenico Poggini, in order to commemorate in metal the numerous works of art of these two pontiffs (bridges on the Tiber and the Paglia, St. Gregory's chapel in Naziance; the restoration of aqueducts, the erection of the obelisk of ST. MARY MAJOR, the fortification and arming of the port of Civitavecchia).

Certainly, with time, some of these engravers succumbed to the ease of systematically using one idea, such as the fantastic medals of G. Pozzi from Milan, working at the end of the 16th century and creator of a gallery of portraits from St. Peter to ALEXANDER V (1410). However, thanks to the plentiful supply of events and causes interesting Christianity and the papacy, most of them knew how to vary their themes and express their artistic qualities best. Even the Paduan Giovani Cavino, in a rather conventional narrative style, tried to illustrate contemporary history by celebrating the hope, born from the marriage between Mary Tudor and Philip II, of seeing England return to the Catholic Church. More skillfully, the jeweler of Milanese origin, Giovan Antonio de Rossi, adapted his style of engraving to the desired subject: mannerist for the Adoration of the Shepherds, for Pius IV, or for the thanksgiving to God for exterminating the arrogant (the Huguenots, French Protestants) for PIUS V; more serious but still as precise and efficient for celebrating the governing and architectural activities of PIUS IV: the fountain of Acqua Pia in Rome, the gate to the meat market. This artistic "overconsumption" brought about a decline in some of the Roman medallion art, and the medallion became, more and more, a sideline for engravers who specialized mostly in coining money, and much less a field of expression open to artists from other fields such as painters, sculptors, casters. Portraits and descriptive scenes took on the artistic styles of coins where the currents of the baroque, classicism, and realism may be seen; we find the signatures of Mola, Bernii, the Hameranis, Gerbara, and Girometti.

The reasons for and implications of this frenzied collecting of medallions are noteworthy, and two complementary factors must be taken into account. The first is tied to the origin of the object, which was to be a social emblem to flatter the personality of the patron. Numerous popes of the 15th to 16th centuries belonged to the great Italian families, and they had all the same tastes. The best example is PAUL II, chastised by Cardinal Ammannati in 1468 for having placed several medallions in the foundations of each of the buildings he had constructed (the Palazzo Venezia, the apse of St. Peter's) to commemorate the monument itself as well as to ensure the posthumous glory of their patron. Following the example of ancient Roman emperors, Paul II even had the lead tiles of the church of St. Paul's Outside the Walls in Rome stamped with his name as well as with the motif of one of Pisanello's medallions that he owned. Such practices, at first employed by laypeople like Francesco de Carrara and Sigismondo Malatesta, were later used by SIXTUS IV on the ponte Sisto, and especially by Julius II. For the placing of the first stone of the new basilica at the Vatican on 18 April 1506, two gold medallions valued at fifty and eleven ducats, and others of less valuable metal, were placed in a sealed container, and buried. Caradosso had chosen to illustrate the back with the building itself, under construction, and the motto: "*Instauratio Basilice Apostolorum Petri et Pauli per Iul. II pont. Max.*" Afterward, the practice became routine and lost some of its original meaning; each of the medals with an architectural theme had, as their primary goal, being a record of the urban history of the popes.

The second factor was of a somewhat institutional nature. It was, in fact, linked to the exercise of the pope's duties within Rome itself. Since the 16th century (although we do know of several attempts made before that time, such as the medallion of the engraver Emiliano Orfini (?) commemorating the meetings of the consistory of 1466–7, which condemned the king of Bohemia George Podiebrad, who had participated in the Hussite HERESY), the ruling pontiff has had a medallion struck bearing his effigy, adorned on the back with an illustration of the principal event of the past year. It could consist of simply evoking a purely religious act: the washing of the apostles' feet by Christ (an ordinary medallion) or could deal with an exceptional subject with political connotations. Such might be the battle of LEPANTO in 1571 or the speech on peace PAUL VI gave at the United Nations in October 1965 (his fourth annual medallion, by

L. Minguzzi). Social issues included the commemorative illustration of the encyclical *Rerum Novarum* (15 May 1891), which proclaimed in modern times the Church's teaching on labor and social justice (the 15th medallion of LEO XIII). Medallions are used also to commenorate the HOLY YEARS. The first jubilee medallions were covered with varied themes, but during the 1520s, Valerio Belli immortalized the gesture of ALEXANDER VI opening the Holy Door, ornamented also with the Cross, the Veronica or its guardians Peter and Paul; a representation of the Father opening the Pearly Gates of Heaven, duplicated on Earth below by the pope opening the Golden Door of St. Peter's in Rome; a line of pilgrims crossing the threshold of the same door, following the pope, as a sign presaging the salvation of the just, this motif commemorating the main liturgical act of the jubilee was presented on expensive medallions (gold or silver) offered by the pope to important people welcomed on this occasion or, more rarely, to several deserving, distinguished members in the crowd of pilgrims. It is also found on the small medallions distributed to the pilgrims at the four basilicas, St. Peter's, ST. PAUL'S OUTSIDE THE WALLS, ST. JOHN LATERAN, and ST. MARY MAJOR, as a reminder of the INDULGENCES acquired on that occasion.

At the same time, as a parallel, there were a series devoted to precise needs such as the prizes for the academies, awards for outstanding merit, or those put out by the assessor cardinals during Holy Years, by the CAMERLENGO during vacancies of the Holy See, and by the religious orders with the permission of the Curia. Official art diversified them to excess in order to satisfy the spiritual and social needs of the various categories of the population. This, along with the fact that the repertoire of themes had become more and more narrative, leading to a standardization of the motifs, and a lessening of the number that attempted to be esthetically innovative, was inevitable. It remains true, however, that the papal medallion gallery is one of the most varied and most regular that exists. Two facts bear witness to this. First, since 1870, the papal medallion makers have been able to issue a symbolic annual medallion, with restrictions only affecting the subject commemorating certain ritual practices (such as the Washing of the Feet). Second, it should be noted that PIUS VII had given an order, in 1801, to acquire, from master engravers or their descendants, the dies used to strike the papal medallions over the course of past centuries. Until then the exclusive property of the artists, these original tools had remained in their possession, and the engravers had even kept their privilege of making additional castings for their own benefit. The purchase of the collection of casting molds and tools accumulated by the Hamerani "dynasty," papal engravers of over 748 medallions, became the nucleus of the collection of the Numismatic Cabinet of the Vatican, begun by LEO XIII in 1824. This organ has the official duty of maintaining the record of medallions issued by the papacy from MARTIN V to the present. A true chronicle, the papal medallion is, therefore, an historic document of major importance for the image that the papacy has of itself, even now when the medallions are made in the workshop of the Italian government.

Jean-Luc Desnier

Bibliography

Bartolotti, F. *La medaglia annuale dei Romani Pontefici, da Paolo V a Paolo VI, 1605–1967*, Rimini, 1967.

Bascapé, G. C. "Introduzione alla medaglistica papale," *Rivista italiana di Numismatica*, 69 (1967), 169–82; 72 (1970), 175–228.

Berni, B. *Le medaglie degli Anni Santi*, Barcelona, 1950.

Foerschner, G. *Papstgeschichte auf Medaillen, Historiae o. sacrum decus*, Frankfurt, 1978 (*Kleine Schriften des Historischen Museums Frankfurt am Main*, 11).

Gallamini, P. "Christian devotional medals, XVIIth, XVIIIth and XIXth Centuries (Part I)," *Medaglia*, 24 (1989), 35–78.

Panvini Rosati, F. *Medaglie e Placchette italiane dal Rinascimento al XVIII secolo*, Rome, 1968.

Pollard, J. G. *Medaglie italiane del Rinascimento, nel Museo Nazionale del Bargello*, Florence, 1984–5 (I, 1400–1530, II and III, 1530–1640).

Roma 1300–1875. L'arte degli anni santi (Exposition in Rome, Palazzo Venezia, from December 1984–April 1985), Milan, 1985.

Weiss, R. *Un umanista veneziano: Papa Paolo II*, Rome and Venice, 1958 (*Civiltà veneziana*, Saggi, 4).

Whitman, N. T. "The First Papal Medal: Sources and Meaning," *The Burlington Magazine*, December 1991, 820–4.

MEDIA, COMMUNICATION, AND THE VATICAN.

Problems related to information in the modern sense of the word began to face the papacy when its temporal power came to an end. At that time, other publications rapidly followed the official bulletin *Diario di Roma*, during 1848–9: The *Gazzetta di Roma*, the *Monitore romano*, and then the *Giornale di Roma* (between 1849 and 1870), and between 1848 and 1852, *Il Costituzionale romano* and the first periodical called *L'Osservatore romano*. Both of the latter, which were unofficial publications, took openly conservative positions. In 1861 *L'Osservatore romano* began to appear, at the wish, and with the support, of the papal government, which nevertheless did not own the newspaper. Although it was never to become the official organ of the Holy See, even after it was bought back by LEO XIII and later established in the Vatican in 1929, *L'Osservatore romano* did in fact take on official functions after the demise of the official bulletin. The motto appearing on the first page, "*Nostre in-*

formazioni" ("our information"), is nevertheless official. Controlled by the SECRETARY OF STATE'S office, the newspaper has always been managed by laypeople and has enjoyed a certain autonomy, depending on the papacy and the newspaper management in question.

With PIUS XI, the papacy showed itself to be clearly more sensitive to the question of information. Directed by JESUITS, VATICAN RADIO was founded in 1931. From the time of WORLD WAR II, and immediately after the war, the radio developed programs addressed to the countries of the Eastern bloc, and thus became an important intermediary for the HOLY SEE, often profiting from the considerable latitude that its unofficial nature allowed it.

A number of projects and initiatives came into being under Pius XI's papacy. To broadcast the news of missions, the international agency Fides was created in 1927. In 1935, the papal representation in China founded the agency Lumen, which established a religious news brief, even in Chinese. In 1931, publication of a Spanish version of *L'Osservatore romano* in Argentina was planned, as was, in 1940, the establishment of ties of the same kind between the Vatican and the United States. The increase in initiatives such as the establishment of a press review in the Secretary of State's office, illustrated magazines published in the Vatican, or the world fair on the Catholic press from around the globe held in the Vatican in 1936, show that there was a clear awareness of the growing importance of information. In the same vein, the under secretary (*sostituto*) in the Secretary of State's office, Giovanni Battista Montini, the future PAUL VI, created *L'Osservatore romano's* press service in 1939. Preceded by atttempts under Leo XIII's papacy, the daily paper's information bureau was to be replaced by the Holy See's press room, as a consequence of the increase in religious information during the time of VATICAN II.

The attention the papacy paid to information and the interest the Vatican and the Church stirred up in the press developed at the beginning of PIUS XII's papacy. The first television experience for the Vatican took place in 1947, but the Vatican Television Center, which produces and broadcasts programs—although without its own broadcasting station—was not instituted until 1983. The Papal Commission for Educational and Religious Films was founded in 1948; it was to undergo a number of transformations up to the time of the creation (1964) of the Papal Commission for Social Communication (which in 1988 became the Pontifical Council for Social Communication). The press's interest in the papacy was notably increased beginning with JOHN XXIII, and especially with Vatican II, which in turn dedicated a decree to the instruments of social communication; starting in 1967 a world day of social communication was celebrated.

The pontificate of Pope John Paul II saw an extensive development in the use of the media as a means of evangelization and of carrying the message of the Holy See. Archbishop John Foley, president of the Pontifical Council of Social Communications since 1984, oversaw the expansion of the council's activities, including the development of a Vatican web site (www.vatican.va), an Internet-based Vatican Information Service (VIS), the extensive use of television and radio, and the issue of a number of letters concerning such topics in modern communications as pornography and ethics in advertising.

Giovanni Maria Vian

Bibliography

Accattoli, L. "La figura di Paolo VI nell'opinione pubblica italiana," (*CEFR*, 72), 209–24.

Agostino, M. *Le Pape Pie XI et l'opinion (1922–1939)*, Rome, 1991 (*CEFR*, 150).

Arató, P., and Vian, P. *Paulus pp. VI. 1963–1978. Elenchus bibliographicus*, Brescia, 1981 (*Pubblicazioni dell'Istituto Paolo VI*, 1), 239–40, 384–5, 591.

Bourdarias, J., Chevallier, B., and Vandrisse, J. *De Paul VI à Jean Paul II. Les fumées du Vatican*, Paris, 1979, 241–85.

Bresso, P., and Traniello, F. "Il Concilio Vaticano II nella stampa communista italiana," (*CEFR*, 113), 405–41.

Conzemius, V. "Paul VI dans l'opinion publique allemande," (*CEFR*, 72), 225–55.

Cornet, A., Dumoulin, M., and Stelandre, Y. *Extra muros. Les réactions de la presse belge à trois voyages de Paul VI (Jérusalem-ONU-BIT) 1964–1969*, Brescia, 1993 (*Saggi*, 2).

Dulles, A. "Vatican II et les communications," *Vatican II. Bilan et perspectives vingt-cinq ans après (1962–1987)*, III, Montreal and Paris, 1988 (*Recherches*, 17), 515–33.

Favasseur-Desperriers, J. "L'image de Vatican II à travers la chronique de l'abbé Laurentin," (*CEFR*, 113), 379–403.

Garofalo, S., ed. *Dizionario del Concilio Ecumenico Vaticano Secondo*, Rome, 1969, 109–20.

Gerest, C. "L'immagine di Giovanni XXIII in Africa: il caso della Costa d'Avorio," *Giovanni XXIII transizione del Papato e della Chiesa*, ed. G. Alberigo, Rome, 1988, 123–50.

Gritti, J. "L'image de Paul VI et de son pontificat en France," *Paul VI et la modernité dans l'Église*, Rome, 1984 (*CEFR*, 72), 185–207.

Gritti, J. *Jean XXIII dans l'opinion publique*, Paris, 1967.

Guasco, M. "L'Ufficio giornali," *La figura e l'opera di Federico Alessandri*, Ancona, 1991, 28–38.

Laurentin, R. "L'information au concile," *Le Deuxième Concile du Vatican (1959–1965)*, Rome, 1989 (*CEFR*, 113), 359–78.

Levillain, P. *La Mécanique politique de Vatican II. La majorité et l'unanimité dans un concile*, Paris, 1975 (*Théologie historique*, 36), 146–8.

Marazziti, M. "Cultura di massa e valori cattolici: il modello di 'Famiglia cristiana,'" *Pio XII*, ed. A. Riccardi, Rome and Bari, 1984, 324–6.

Marazziti, M. *I papi di carta. Nascita e svolta dell'informazione religiosa da Pio XII a Giovanni XXIII*, Genoa, 1990 (*Terzo millennio*, 25).

Nobécourt, J. "Le Monde *et le personnage de Paul VI*," (*CEFR*, 72), 257–71.

Paola VI e i problemi ecclesiologici al Concilio (Pubblicazioni dell'Instituto Paolo), Brescia, 1989.

Barriod Valdés, M. "El Papa Paulo y la prensa chilena," 450–1.

Busquets Sindreu, P. "La información de la prensa española en la 2a y 3a etapa conciliar," 517–29.

Carbone, V. "L'azione direttiva di Paolo VI nei periodi II e III del Concilio Ecumenico Vaticano II," 68–70.

Conzemius, V. "La presse suisse et les interventions de Paul VI dans les travaux du concile," 530–44.

Fink, E. "Die Leitung des 2. Vatikanischen Konzils durch Paul VI. im Spiegel der deutschen katholischen Presse," 470–85.

Fogarty, G. "American journals and Paul VI at Vatican II," 547–59.

Grootaers, J. "L'opinion publique en Belgique et aux Pays-Bas face aux événements conciliaires de 1963 et 1964," 431–49.

Levillain, P. "L'opinion publique et Paul VI pendant la seconde et la troisième période de Vatican II," 274–85.

Levillain, P., and Uginet, F. C. "L'opinion publique française et les interventions de Paul VI au deuxième concile du Vatican (IIe et IIIe période)," 452–69.

Pieronek, T. "Le pape Paul IV vu par la presse laïque polonaise durant la deuxième et al troisième période du concile," 507–13.

Skoda, F. "Il giudizio dei sovietici sul Concilio Vaticano II e su Paolo VI," 545–6.

Turowicz, J. "Paul VI, le concile et la presse polonaise," 514–6.

Vian, G. M. "Gli interventi di Paolo VI nel secondo e terzo periodo (1963–1964) del Vaticano II nella stampa italiana," 496–506.

Yarnold, E. "Paul VI at Vatican II: the second and third periods. The British and Irish Press," 486–95.

Ruszkowski, A. "Décret sur les communications sociales: succès ou échec du concile?" (*Recherches*, 17), 535–62.

Vian, N. *Anni e opere di Paolo VI*, Rome, 1978, 127–8, 183–4.

White, R. "Les mass media et la culture dans le catholicisme contemporain: le sens et l'importance de Vatican II," (*Recherches*, 17), 563–93.

MEDIATION. See **Arbitration, Papal.**

MILAN. The importance of Milan, capital of the Transpadane region since Augustus, named *colonia Aelia* since Hadrian, was confirmed during the late empire in both the political and religious spheres. Following Diocletian's reform, the city was, several times during the 4th century, the administrative capital of the *Pars Occidentalis* as well as an imperial residence, and it benefited from the vicissitudes of Rome as well as from the temporary weakening of certain northern cities (Aquileia, Ravenna, Pavia). It was especially during the second half of the 4th century that Milan appeared to reach its highest point, when—and this was a significant event—the combination of the imperial presence and a strong personality at the head of the episcopate took place: this was notably the case during the long episcopacies of Auxentius (355–74) and of Ambrose (374–97).

Given the administrative and political situation of northern Italy at the end of the 3d century, and the rank claimed by the first recorded Milanese bishop, Merocles, who designated himself at the Council of Arles of 314 as bishop "of the province of Italy," we may suppose with a fair amount of accuracy that the episcopal see was founded during the course of the second half of the 3rd century, perhaps due to the "little peace" of the Church under Gallienus. The bishops who followed after the year 340—Protasius, Eustorgius I, and Dionysius—were engaged in the defense of the Nicene faith, beside Athanasius and other Italian bishops, notably Eusebius of Vercelli and Lucifer of Cagliari, thus founding a tradition of orthodoxy of which Ambrose would later make use. But in 355, Dionysius was exiled to Cappadocia, and the emperor Constantine II, who favored the Arian party, put a Cappadocian priest adhering to that doctrine in charge of the see of Milan. Somewhat dimmed in Milanese memory for his reputation of HERESY, it is nevertheless certain that due to his long pontificate, Auxentius, who benefited from imperial support, made a strong mark on the Milanese Church. Some of the achievements for which Ambrose is given credit could be attributed to Auxentius, especially the adoption of certain Eastern traditions into the liturgy, and perhaps the construction of the new episcopal church, the *basilica nova* (St. Thecla). Sliding into the Arian party surely brought a weakening of Milan's relationship with Rome, a relative isolation from the Padane and Adriatic regions and from southern Gaul, where the Ligurian city had extended its influence before: toward the regions of northern Italy and Pannonia, where Aquileia then took over as the link with St. Peter's see. Milan also became, at this time, the center of a powerful heretical stronghold, thanks to relationships with several Illyrian sees (Sirmium, Musa, Singidinum) and to the proximity of the Gothic troops (Arian for the most part) stationed on the *limes*. Ambrose was elected in a very unexpected way after Auxentius' death, in 373, in the controversy of a difficult succession because of the division of the Milanese community.

Quickly, the former governor of Emilia-Liguria worked to restore the Nicene orthodoxy to Milan and in the regions where the city traditionally had some influence, which he tried to extend as far as possible, not without creating a situation of rivalry with Rome. The interventions of the bishop took place in the three western provinces of Italy, the Gauls and Illyricum, and they concerned Church government, rulings on doctrinal conflicts, and pastoral matters. Ambrose, therefore, exercised a *de facto* power that went far beyond his metropolitan jurisdiction. In local government he endeavored to perfect the standards of life for the community. Paradoxically, conflicts with civil authorities, favorable to Arianism during Justinian's regency, assured him the support of the majority of the Milanese people. Then, during the reigns of Gratian and Theodosius, over whom he exercised an undeniable influence, he benefited from a political and religious climate once again directly favorable to him. The miraculous discoveries of relics permitted him to organize the cult of saints and the liturgical year by controlling popular piety, which may be seen in the new buildings (the *basilica ambrosiana*, now S. Ambrogio, and *basilica romana*, now S. Nazaro, in which Ambrose had relics of the apostles placed, thus showing his attachment to the tradition of Rome in material form). He was probably also the one who built a new octagonal baptistry (S. Giovanni alle Fonte) close to the cathedral, whose function we know quite well thanks to his baptismal catechesis. Above all, he deepened, during the theological and political conflicts that shook the last third of the century, reflection on the definitions of the spheres of competence of religious and civil authorities—a distinction that had remained vague because this tended to enhance the independence of the Church in relation to the civil authority, while still claiming the good will if not the protection of the latter. Between Eusebius of Caesarea, insensitive to the dangers of too tightly linking the interests of the Church and those of the empire, and the witnesses to the fall of Rome (in which some, like Augustine, saw the ontological frailty of man), Ambrose marked a major step in the elaboration of the foundations of political theology in the West.

The death of Theodosius (395), and then of Ambrose (397) almost coincided with the great waves of barbarians attacking Italy. The city still had several years of peace and prosperity under the episcopacy of Simplicianus (397–400/401; construction of San Simpliciano). In the beginning of the 5th century, the threat of Alaric and the raids of Radagaisus plunged the city into insecurity and cut it off from its traditional supporters to the north and the east, in southern Italy, in Pannonia, and in Noricum. It was the beginning of the decline of Milanese political and religious power. In 403, the imperial court went back to Ravenna, whereas on the religious map, Aquileia grew more powerful in the north, and Rome reasserted its authority. In the middle of the century, the sack by Attila in 452 and the creation of the patriarchate of Ravenna (Peter Chrysologus, 425–50) were new causes of further weaknesses. In the last third of the century, Milan found itself in the center of the barbarian torment, especially during the conflict that opposed Theodoric to Odoacer. Nevertheless, the episcopacy of Lorenzo I (about 489–510/512) was the occasion of a relative increase in prosperity, despite the Goths who were ravaging Italy. The action of the bishops did not seem to extend farther than the city itself. Their funeral eulogies, written by Ennodius of Pavia, suggest mostly pastoral and charitable actions, and perhaps several reconstructions of religious buildings.

In the middle of the 6th century, the bishop Datius left his city to beg for imperial assistance and died without ever being able to return to it. The three bishops who followed him were caught up in the quarrel of the Three Chapters, which cut northern Italy off from the Roman communion. This episode coincided with the arrival of the Lombards who, after having crossed the Isonzo in 568, occupied Milan in April 569. Many of the clergy, including the bishop, took refuge in Genoa. This abandonment also coincided with the disappearance of the ancient administrative and religious region of Liguria, which became Neustria, and whose capital was, from then on, Pavia.

Françoise Monfrin

Bibliography

Lansoni, F. "Le diocesi d'Italia dalle origini al principio del sec. VII (a. 606)," 2, Vatican City, *Studi et Testi*, 35 (1963).

Milano capitale del Impero romano (286–402 c. C.), Milan Palazzo Reale, 24 January–22 April 1990.

Picard, J. C. "Le souvenir des évêques, Sépultures, listes épiscopales et culte des évêques en Italie du Nord des origines au Xe siècle," *BEFAR*, 268 (1988).

Pietri, C. "Roma Christiana, Recherches sur l'Église de Rome de Miltiade à Sixte III (311–440)," *BEFAR*, 224 (1976).

Storia di Milano, I-II, Milan (1953–4).

MILITARY ORDERS. The military orders arose in the 12th century in the context of the CRUSADES and of the Gregorian REFORM, in a nobiliary society in which chivalry was exalted by the Church and in an ecclesiastical society in which papal primacy was establishing itself. The orders consisted of groups of regular soldiers whose primary calling was to defend the Holy Places (Templars), wage war against the "infidels," SARACENS, and Prussians (Iberian and German orders), and assist pilgrims and crusaders (Hospitallers, Teutonics, etc.), though their character grew more and more frankly military.

The boundaries distinguishing them are therefore hazy. On the one hand were the actual hospitaller orders, some of whom may on occasion have developed subsidiary military tendencies (for instance, the order of St. Lazarus, or the more regional order of St. James of Altopascio, known as the Knights of Tau, in the diocese of Lucca). On the other hand there were the confraternities, some verging on orders, in which members of the laity, men and sometimes women, were grouped together under a religious rule in a sort of ascetic mobilization against HERESY and the enemies of the Church; such was the Militia of Jesus Christ, founded in 1233 in Parma (approved by GREGORY IX on 22 December 1234, with a rule approved by the same pope on 24 May 1235) to fight both the Cathars and the GHIBELLINES (the experiment ended in 1261, when they were siphoned into the Militia of the Glorious Virgin Mary, also known as the Gaudenti). But in spite of the ambiguous terminology, the confraternity of the Knights of the Holy Sepulcher, which, at least from the 14th century, brought together pilgrims who had received knighthood at the church of the Holy Sepulcher in Jerusalem, cannot be counted as a military order.

Like the hospices and infirmaries, which were either isolated or, sometimes, grouped together as orders, the military orders—the "Militia of Christ," which combined the old ideal of the monastic struggle against Evil with that of armed chivalry—were at the origin of the ascetic "institutions of perfection." There is no better evidence for this than the early official names, for example, the Brothers of the Militia of the Poor Knights of Christ, who soon took the name Templars because, having settled on the site of the ancient Temple of Solomon in Jerusalem, they put themselves at the disposal of the Latin patriarch of Jerusalem in order to protect the Holy Sepulcher by force of arms. St. Bernard sublimated the movement, in a sense, by giving it perfect theological and moral expression (*Liber de laude novae militiae* [1128–36]). Although they took the same vows as religious, (chastity, obedience, and poverty; later, married knights were admitted to the order of Santiago), the brothers had to follow a rule that allowed some accommodation in practice (life in the world, engaging in combat, eating meat). Hence the frequent success of the rule of canons known as the Rule of St. Augustine, which was adapted bit by bit in ways that often gave it a Cistercian character, even if the Cistercians did not take supreme control of the order; the rule of the Teutonico, on the other hand, was somewhat under Dominican influence.

Another peculiarity contributed to their individual character. The orders made a clear distinction between "knights" (*milites*, a small elite) and "sergeants" (employed as squires, *armigeri*, sometimes also as craftsmen or servants, *famuli*), as well as including a third category, that of the priests, non-combatant clerics who were often known as "chaplains." In many cases, the orders were associated with convents of women dedicated to prayer and care of the sick. The major orders developed a firmly hierarchical structure. The basic cells, called "commanderies," "preceptories," "bailiwicks," or simply "houses," combined monastery-barracks, chapel, cemetery, sometimes a "hospital," and often a farming center. They were grouped into geographical areas known as "priories," then "grand priories" or "langues." The government of the order was in the hands of a "master" (called in later years a "grand master"), who resided at the "convent," the order's headquarters, and was assisted by grand officers.

The conditions in which the military, or rather military-hospitaller, orders came into being explain their privileged ties to the papacy, especially in the case of the major international orders. The orders founded by the Spanish and Portuguese monarchies were more particularist. The Teutonic knights, for their part, very soon developed an independent way of operating, even incurring Rome's anger when their territorial policy caused them to clash with the new Slavic or Lithuanian states, on their way to becoming Christian. Their rules were approved in Rome; EXEMPTION was normal, as was exoneration from the TITHE. No fewer than 113 acts and letters addressed by HONORIUS III (1216–27) to the Teutonics alone have been preserved.

This quite original situation had many strange consequences. Independent, and very soon contemptuous of the crusaders passing through the region but also competing with one another, the major orders of the Holy Land saw their responsibility called into question when the defense of the Roman East became difficult. Despite their origins in the movement toward apostolic poverty, they accumulated a huge fortune in land and chattels; their pattern of geographical settlement made the Templars bankers to popes and kings. The loss of Acre in 1291 forced those orders still in the Holy Land into a reconversion, at least a partial one. The Teutonics, already well entrenched on the German borders, devoted their energy to building a regular state, on the margins of the empire. But it was most of all the Templars who paid the price for the pervasive animosity toward the orders. Their dramatic end, under CLEMENT V, was hastened by a papacy that preferred not to let itself be outflanked by the king of France. Aside from the Teutonics, who suffered serious reversals at the end of the Middle Ages, the orders were put under strict supervision in the 14th and 15th centuries. The papacy took a keen interest in the reform of the Hospitallers (thanks to which we have an extremely rich inquiry in 1373 by GREGORY XI on their material situation). The Iberian military orders, too closely involved in dynastic disputes, were taken in hand by the sovereigns with the approval of the Holy See: so began their mutation into essentially honorary societies of nobles, which entered, with their specific religious inspiration, the company of the many princely orders, created outside the Church, at the end of the Middle Ages.

Appendix.

List of the principal medieval military orders (in chronological order by date of creation):

Hospital of St. John of Jerusalem. Originated as a hospice founded around 1070 by merchants from Amalfi. It was placed under papal protection by PASCHAL II on 15 February 1113, and it took on an increasingly military character despite its continuing to operate hospices and perform charitable works. Fighting in both the Holy Land and Spain, it withdrew successively to Acre at the fall of Jerusalem in 1187, to Limassol (Cyprus) at the fall of Acre in 1291, to Rhodes (taken from the Greeks) in 1309, and to Malta (given by Charles V) when the TURKS seized Rhodes in 1522.

Temple. Founded in Jerusalem by a knight of modest extraction from Champagne, Hugh de Payns, around 1119. The rule of the order, probably directly approved by HONORIUS II, was recognized at the regional council of Troyes in 1128, and the first grand pontifical confirmation was handed over by INNOCENT II on 29 March 1139. The Templars withdrew to Cyprus after the fall of Acre. In the wake of accusations (of sacrilege, idolatry, and homosexuality), Clement V ordered an inquest in 1307 and, in response to Philip the Fair's arrest of the French Templars, had all the members of the order seized on 22 November 1307. The order was abolished at the council of Vienne (BULL of 22 March 1312). Its possessions were transferred to the Hospital, except in the Iberian Peninsula (bull of 2 May 1312), where they were recovered by local orders already in existence or created for that purpose.

St. Lazarus. Founded around 1120, the order took in lepers and non-lepers tending the former. Under the influence of the Templars and Hospitallers, it followed the Rule of St. Augustine. It became increasingly military in character, especially at the beginning of the 13th century, and took part in the defense of the places in the Holy Land. To make good the casualties, in 1253 a decision was reached, with papal approval, to choose a knight who was not a leper to head the order. After 1291, the order abandoned all military activity.

Aviz (or Evora). Founded by Alfonso Henriquez, king of Portugal, in 1147, the "Novo Ordem" did not take the name Aviz, where it gained possessions and built a fortress, until around 1215. It followed the Benedictine rule, under Cistercian influence, and for at least a century was merely a Portuguese offshoot of the Calatrava order, existing under the rule of the same papal bull of confirmation of 1164. The order declined from the 14th century on and was incorporated into the crown in 1561.

Calatrava. Created in 1164, the order takes its name from a fortress given to the Templars by Alfonso VII of Castile in 1147. Judging that they could not defend it, the Templars handed it over to Sancho III in 1158. Raymond, the abbot of the Cistercian monastery of Fitero, agreed to take it over with some of his men and some Toledan crusaders, who made up a confraternity. In 1164, this became affiliated with the Cistercian order and received a rule (pontifical confirmation of 25 September 1164). In 1187, the affiliation became full incorporation, under the control of the abbot of Morimond (pontifical confirmation of 4 November 1187). The fortress was lost in 1195 and recovered in 1212, but the order moved into another fortress, called Calatrava-la-Nueva. In 1440, EUGENE IV changed the vow of chastity to a vow of conjugal chastity for the knights (confirmed by PAUL III in 1540). In 1489, INNOCENT VIII transferred administration of the order to King Ferdinand the Catholic (confirmed by a bull of ALEXANDER VI 19 March 1492).

Santiago (or St. James of the Sword). Originally a confraternity founded in 1170 by the king of León under the name Brothers of Cáceres. In 1171, with the agreement of the archbishop of Santiago, it adopted the name St. James, the national patron saint, and then a rule derived from that of the Templars. Recognized by Cardinal Giacinto (the future CELESTINE III) in 1172, the order was confirmed by ALEXANDER III on 5 August 1175. In 1316, the king of Portugal placed the Portuguese commanderies under the aegis of an autonomous order, called Sao Tiago da Espada. The administration of the order was personally entrusted to the Spanish monarchy by Alexander VI (19 March 1492; the union with the crown was proclaimed perpetual by HADRIAN VI on 4 May 1523).

Montegaudio (Mons Gaudii, also known as Monsfrag or Hospital of the Holy Redeemer). An order detached from Santiago in 1173 by Rodrigo Alvarez, a nobleman of León, who sought a more ascetic life and gave it a Cistercian rule (the order was placed under the direct control of the abbey of Cîteaux in 1175). The foundation was confirmed by Cardinal Giacinto (later Celestine III) and then by Alexander III (bull of 5 May 1180). In 1196, the Temple took over the castle-seat of the order (Alfambara), and with papal approval the rebels joined Calatrava in 1221.

Alcántara. An order founded in 1176 under the name San Julián del Pereiro, or order of Trujillo. It was first Castilian, and then Leonese from the time of its installation in 1218 at Alcántara. Confirmed by Alexander III on 29 December 1176, it followed first the Cistercian rule and then that of Calatrava, when it was affiliated with that order in 1218. The order was incorporated into the crown in 1501.

Teutonics (Hospital Our Lady of the Germans of Jerusalem). Originally a hospital for German pilgrims and crusaders founded by knights from Bremen and Lübeck in 1189 or 1190 at the time of the siege of Acre (bull of CLEMENT III, 6 February 1191). It did not became a true military order until 1198, and Innocent III approved it on 19 February 1199. Besides engaging in actions in the Holy Land, it soon intervened politically in the empire and militarily in the Prussian, Pomeranian, and Baltic lands, where it took over the objectives of the less important orders (Sword Bearer, Dobrin), which it absorbed. In time it became a regular state, but it was weakened by the defeat of Tannenberg (1410) and the treaty of Thorn (1466), which established the Lithuanian-Polish power of the Jagiellonian dynasty.

St. Thomas of Acre. The only English military order, founded in circumstances similar to those surrounding the foundation of the preceding order. These hospitaller canons regular, who may have been established by Richard Coeur de Lion himself, quickly declined. An attempt was made to revive the institution by giving it a more definite military character, following the rule of the Teutonics (confirmation of GREGORY IX, 5 February 1236). After 1291, the order wavered between Cyprus and London, choosing the second as its definitive home for the second half of the 14th century, when it lost its military calling.

Alfama. A Catalan order, founded in 1201 by Peter II of Aragon in honor of St. George, the monarchy's patron saint (who appeared in the sky over the battle of Huesca in 1095). It first received simple episcopal approval. Then on 15 May 1372 Gregory IX approved the Rule of St. Augustine, influenced by the observance of the Hospitallers. The union with Montesa was approved by BENEDICT XIII on 24 January 1400.

Sword Bearers. (*Swertbrudere, officially Fratres Milicie Christi de Livonia*). Founded in Riga in 1201, under Cistercian influence, by North German knights to protect missions and the newly converted, the order was approved by INNOCENT III on 12 October 1204. The rule was influenced by that of the Templars. The knights formed a state in Livonia and Latvia, warred with the Estonians, and suffered heavy reversals under the Lithuanians in 1236. The survivors were taken in by the Teutonics on 14 May 1237.

Mercedarians (Ordo Beate Marie Virginis de Mercede). Founded in Barcelona in 1218 by Pedro Nolasco for the ransom of prisoners of the Muslims, the order was placed under the Rule of St. Augustine and approved by GREGORY IX (17 January 1235). In the 13th century, it developed a secondary military calling, which it abandoned definitively in 1317, when the brother knights joined the order of Montesa.

Faith of Jesus Christ. An ephemeral order founded in France in the years 1218–21 to accompany the crusade against the Albigensians. An imitation of the Templars, it was placed under the protection of the cardinal legate Conrad of Urach and recognized by HONORIUS III (bulls of 7 June and 16 July 1221). On achieving their mission in 1229, the knights were returned to the order of Santiago; the non-combatant brothers were definitively attached to the Feuillants in 1261.

Dobrin (Fratres Militiae Christi de Livonia contra Prutenos). Founded in 1228 at the latest by the bishop of Prussia and confirmed by Gregory IX (bull of 28 October 1228) on the model of the Sword Bearers. In 1235, the order was incorporated with the Teutonics with pontifical approval (bull of Gregory IX, 14 May 1236).

Star (or Cartagena, or St. Mary of Spain). Founded in 1272 by Alfonso X of Castile to support his naval exploits, it was incorporated into the Cistercian order and placed under the administration of the abbey of Grandselve. Stricken almost immediately by the king's naval defeats, it was incoporated into the order of Santiago.

Montesa (Our Lady). Founded by James II of Aragon to recover the Templars' patrimony. After hesitations on the part of CLEMENT V, the foundation was approved by JOHN XXII (10 June 1317). The order was incorporated into Cîteaux by John XXII in 1321. Having rejoined the order of Alfama in 1400, it was incorporated into the crown in 1502.

Christ. Founded in 1318 by Deniz, king of Portugal, to recover the possessions of the Templars. It received formal approval from John XXII at the same time as the rule of Calatrava (15 March 1319). Its incorporation into the crown was approved by JULIUS III in 1551.

Bethlehem (Our Lord). The only order directly created by the medieval papacy. It was founded on 19 January 1459 by PIUS II to defend the Aegean islands against the Turks, and was given the statute of the Hospitallers. Forced to retreat to Naples, it disappeared after some twenty years of existence.

Olivier Guyotjeannin

Bibliography

Boockmann, H. *Der deutsche Orden*, Munich, 1982.

Demurger, A. *Vie et mort de l'ordre du Temple, 1118–1314*, Paris, 1985.

Die geistlichen Ritterorden Europas, ed. J. Fleckenstein, Sigmaringen, 1980 (Vorträge und Forschungen, 26).

Hiestand, R. *Papsturkunden für Templer und Johanniter*, Göttingen, 2 vols., 1972–84.

L'Enquête pontificale de 1973 sur l'ordre des Hospitaliers de Saint-Jean de Jérusalem, I, L'enquête dans le prieuré de France; ed. A.-M. Legras, Paris, 1987.

Linage Conde, A. "Militari (Ordini)," *Dizionario degli Istituti di perfezione*, 5 (1978), Rome, 1978, 1287–99 [with reference to particular accounts].

Lomax, D. W. *Las ordenes militares en la península iberica durante la Edad media*, Salamanca, 1976.

Luttrell, A. *The Hospitallers in Cyprus, Rhodes, Greece and the West (1291–1440)*, London, 1970 (*Variorum Reprints*).

Sainz de La Masa Lasoli, R. *La orden de San Jorge de Alfama*, Barcelona, 1990.

MILITARY ORDINARIATES. The Church's spiritual service to armies has a long history. Clerics celebrated mass in the camps of CONSTANTINE's army (Eusebius, *Vita Constantini* II, c. 12). A letter of Pelagius (556–61), included in the DECCATUM OF GRATIAN's (D. 63, c. 15), indicates that such service was offered in peacetime.

Military chaplaincy in France. The first capitulary of Carloman (742) mentions CHAPLAINS, that is, bishops whose right of jurisdiction derived from the king, and who, with priests assisting them, formed groups that were canonically and legally autonomous. This autonomy soon disappeared, but the military orders had a chaplaincy endowed with special powers by the pope.

The title of chaplain first turns up in connection with a certain Roger, who died in 1180 during the reign of Louis VII. The Grand Almoner (a title that appears in 1543) was bishop of the armies and appointed the military chaplains. BENEDICT XIV decided that the post of Almoner of France called for episcopal dignity.

The Grand Almonry and military chaplaincy were suppressed in 1790. Napoleon restored them on 6 January 1806 in favor of his uncle, Cardinal Fesch. Under the first Restoration, an ordinance of 1 October 1814 completed on 24 July 1816 reorganized the chaplaincy. Louis-Philippe modified it in less liberal fashion (ordinance of 30 September 1830) and the Restoration suppressed it. It was reestablished under Napoleon III (decree of 17 June 1857).

After the defeat of 1871, the law of 20 May–3 June 1874 restored the chaplaincy. PIUS IX clarified the status of the French military chaplains (*brief Quo catholico nomine*, 6 July 1875). The 1874 law was abrogated by the law of 8 July 1880, complemented by the decree of 27 April 1881 and, in connection with military hospitals, by a decree of 25 November 1889. The chaplaincy of the navy was suppressed by a decree of 6 February 1907. This ruling was modified by the decree of 5 May 1913, which made the appointment of chaplains a prerogative of the Ministry of War. A letter from the SECRETARIAT OF STATE to Cardinal Luçon (14 September 1913) stresses that chaplains were answerable to the local bishop in spiritual matters. Other dispositions granted chaplains special wartime powers. The CONSISTORIAL CONGREGATION appointed two inspectors as proper ordinaries of priests and seminarians chosen by the civil authority as volunteer soldiers or chaplains.

On 22 August 1914, the Ministry of War authorized the sending of volunteer chaplains to the armies. WORLD WAR I accelerated this liberalization. After the war, the government, in agreement with the Holy See, created the position of chaplain-inspector of the Army of the Rhine (decree of 13 May 1921). The Holy See also granted chaplains special powers during WORLD WAR II.

Cardinal Verdier had received the title "delegate of the Holy See for the French infantry and air force." A decree issued by the apostolic NUNCIATURE (18 April 1940) gave Msgr. Audrain the title "military vicar." Cardinal Suhard assumed this title at the end of the war for the entire French forces. The troops stationed in Austria and Germany came under a special statute (Consistorial Congregation, decree of 16 December 1946).

The Consistorial Congregation organized the vicariate to the French forces (decree *Obsecundare votis*, 26 July 1952) and then the provision of religious services to the armies (decree *Vicariatus castrensis*, 28 March 1964). It modified the vicariate, which office from now on was to be separate from any episcopal see (decree *Arduum gravissimumque*, 15 April 1967). In conformity with the decree *Christus Dominus*, no. 43 of the council of VATICAN II, the military vicar is a member of the CONFERENCE OF BISHOPS. The President of the Republic recast the civil arrangements regarding ministers of religion attached to the armed forces (decree of 1 June 1964). Mention should also be made of the general chaplaincy of prisoners of war, founded in June 1940 by Fr. Jean Rodhain, which became Secours Catholique (Catholic Assistance), and the general chaplaincy of labor deportees.

Military ordinariates. In Spain, the first text on the subject was an order under which, in 1535, Emperor Charles V sent a secular priest to each company. At the request of Philip IV, Pope INNOCENT X granted the king's armies permanent exemption in wartime from the jurisdiction of the territorial ordinaries (brief *Cum sit majestatis tuae*, 26 September 1645). Jurisdiction was entrusted to the head chaplains. But the brief had no practical effect. CLEMENT XII granted full exemption, in peace and war, for seven years (brief *Quum in exercitibus*, 4 February 1736): he personally assumed jurisdiction over the armies and delegated it to a vicar general. Benedict XIV extended it for seven years (brief *Quoniam in exercitibus*, 2 June 1741). Even though the formal concession was not renewed, the actual practice of exemption was retained. At the request of Charles III, Pope CLEMENT XIII delegated all powers to the patriarch of the Indies (brief *Quoniam in exercitibus*, 10 March 1762). The concession was extended by successive popes, from 1768 to 1869. The government of Pi y Margall abolished the military vicariate (decree of 21 June 1873), but it was reestablished under the Restoration. The previous regime was reinstituted by the apostolic letters of 9 December 1920, and then extended from PIUS X to PIUS XI (brief *Quae catholico nomine*, 1 April 1926). The brief was not renewed in 1933 under the secular republic, which dissolved the corps of military chaplains (law of 30 June 1932). The Church reorganized the corps provisionally

during the civil war (brief published 28 February 1937) and the state reinstated it at the war's end (law of 12 July 1940). The situation was made official by "the agreement between the Holy See and the Spanish state on the jurisdiction over and the religious assistance to the armed forces (18 October 1950), later revised by "the agreement between the Spanish state and the Holy See on religious assistance to the armed forces and the military service of clergy and religious" (3 January 1979).

In the United States, the military chaplaincy was established by an act of Congress at the time of the War of Independence (29 June 1775). The first Catholic chaplain was appointed on 26 January 1776. The chaplaincy was dissolved after the treaty of Versailles, at the end of 1783. However, in 1791 the President authorized the appointment of military chaplains, who numbered sixty-four when the country entered the Great War. The Act of National Defense created the post of chaplain in chief (1920). Powers were granted to the military chaplains by the Holy See (1 July 1947), and the military vicariate was established on 8 September 1957. There have been chaplains in the navy since an act of Congress of 27 March 1794. On 3 May 1910, the Holy See set up a military vicariate for Chile, and then, during the First World War, a military ordinary for Italy (which became a vicariate on 6 March 1925) and a military vicariate in Belgium. The CODE OF CANON LAW of 1917 makes clear that questions regarding military chaplains must be decided by the Holy See (c. 451 § 3). Concordats settled the question with Poland (5 February 1919; after the vacancy in 1947 the military ordinariate was reestablished on 21 January 1991), Lithuania, Germany (20 July 1933 and 19 September 1935), Austria, and Portugal.

A vicariate was reestablished in Peru (15 May 1943) and then in Colombia (13 October 1949), Indonesia (25 December 1949), Brazil (6 November 1950), Philippines (8 December 1950), Canada (17 February 1951), South Africa (17 May 1951), Great Britain (21 November 1953), Netherlands (16 April 1957), Argentina (8 July 1957), Belgium (7 September 1957), Dominican Republic (23 January 1958), Austria (21 February 1959), Bolivia (19 March 1961), Paraguay (20 December 1961), Uganda (*ad instar*, 20 January 1964), Germany (31 July 1965), Portugal (29 May 1966), El Salvador (25 March 1968), Australia (6 March 1969), New Zealand (28 October 1976), Kenya (24 January 1981), Ecuador (30 March 1983), and Korea (*ad instar*, 22 November 1983; formally, 23 October 1989), Venezuela (31 October 1995) Croatia (25 April 1997), and Hungary (18 April 1999).

Other arrangements have been made, by convention with Bolivia (29 November 1958), by agreement with Paraguay (26 November 1960), by concordat with Colombia (2 July 1975), and by agreement with Peru (26 July 1980).

Juridical framework. The first broad framework law was outlined in the instruction *Sollemne semper* (23 April 1951), which brought the military vicariate into the common law of the Church. The Holy See thereby recognized a widely shared need on the part of the faithful calling for particular attention and organization.

Vatican II had called for initiatives better adapted to the realization of "particular pastoral activities" (decree *Presbyterorum Ordinis*, no. 10). The result was a reorganization of the vicariate, which became the military ordinariate (apostolic constitution *Spirituali militum curae*, 21 April 1986). By using the cumulative jurisdiction as a pastoral tool, the Holy See showed its desire to meet the spiritual needs of a group of the faithful who would not otherwise have had ready access to all the means of salvation.

The military ordinariate resembles a diocese but differs from one on a number of points; among other things, the bishop who is the military ordinary no longer has a titular see.

The statutes issued by the Holy See for each ordinariate complement the framework law and must not call into question agreements with states. The military ordinariate answers to the Congregation for Bishops or the Congregation for the Evangelization of Peoples. Its prelate is subject to a quinquennial report and "AD LIMINA" VISITS.

The following belong to the ordinariate and come under its jurisdiction: those faithful who are in the military and those required by civil laws to work in the military; their families (spouse, children—even those who have reached the age of majority—living at home, parents, servants living in their home); students at military schools and patients at military hospitals, retirement homes, etc., and their staff; any member of the faithful who carries out a regular function entrusted to him by the military ordinary or with his consent.

This jurisdiction is personal, ordinary, and proper, cumulative with that of the diocesan bishop, since the members of the ordinariate remain members of the particular Church in which they make up part of the people of God by virtue of their domicile or rite.

The apostolic constitution *Spirituali militum curae* does not give a specific definition of the military ordinate, and merely states that it constitutes a particular ecclesiastical circumscription. Its conciliar origin, its objectives, and its constitution have prompted some writers to see the ordinariate as having a number of features in common with the personal PRELATURE.

Dominique Le Tourneau

Bibliography

Annuario pontificio per l'anno 2000, 1114–22.

Arrieta, J. "El Ordinariato castrense (notas en torno a la constitución apostólica *Spirituali militum curae*)," *Ius Canonicum*, XXVI (1986), 731–48.

Badré, J. "Le Vicaire aux Armes," *La charge pastorale des évêques*, Paris, 1959, 353–7.

Baura, E. *Legislazione sulle ordinariati castrensi*, Milan, 1991.

Bonnet, M. *"L'Ordinariat militaire ou Ordinariat aux Armées," Les Cahiers du droit ecclésial*, 3 (1986), 63–74.

Coppola, R. "Lettura della '*Spirituali militum curae*" in prospettiva di norme per uno statuto dell' Ordinariato militare in Italia," *Monitor Ecclesiasticus*, 511–19.

García Castro, M. "Convenio entre la Santa Sede y el Estado español sobre la jurisdicción castrense y asistencia religiosa a las Fuerzas Aramadas," *Revista Española de Derecho Canónico*, 5 (1950), 1101–71; (1951), 265–301; "Jurisdicción eclesiástica castrense. Ultimos documentos relativos a la misma," ibid. (1951), 695–771.

Ghirlanda, G. "De differentia praelaturam personalem inter et Ordinariat militarem seu castrensem," ibid., 219–51.

Gutiérrez, J. L. "De Ordinariatus militaris nova constitutione," *Periodica de re canonica, morali et liturgica*, 76 (1987), 189–218.

Instruction *Sollemne semper*, 23 April 1951, *Acta Apostolicae Sedis*, 43 (1951), 562–5.

Jean Paul II, apostolic constitution *Spirituali militum curae*, 21 April 1986, *Acta Apostolicae Sedis*, 78 (1986), 481–6.

Le Tourneau, D. "La juridiction cumulative de l'ordinariat aux armées," *RDC*, 37 (1987), 171–214; "La nouvelle organisation de l'Ordinariat aux Armées," *Studia Canonica*, 21 (1987), 37–66.

Martínez Fernández, L. "La asistencia religiosa católica a las fuerzas armadas y a regulación del servicio militar de clérigos y religiosos," *Revista Española de Derecho Canónico*, 42 (1986), 23–45.

Militum cura pastoralis, Vatican (since 1987).

Pugliese, A. *La cura Castrense*, Turin, 1953; *Storia e legislazione sulla cura pastorale alla Forze Armate*, Casale, 1956.

Schouppe, J. P. "Les Ordinariats aux Armées dans la Constitution Apostolique 'Spirituali militum curae,'" *Ephemerides Theologicae Lovanienses*, 64/1 (1988), 173–90.

Seco Caro, C. "La provisión del Arzobispo castrense en el Derecho Eclesiástico español," *Las relaciones entre la Iglesia y el Estado. Estudios en memoria del profesor Pedro Lombardia*, Madrid-Pamplona, 1989, 491–510.

Service d'Histoire, Archives et Documents du Vicariat aux Armées françaises, *L'Aumônerie militaire française*, Paris, 1960.

Tammler, U. "Spirituali militum curae" Entstehung, Inhalt, Bedeutung und Auswirkungen der apostolischen Konstitution vom 21. April 1986 über die Militärseelsorge," *Archiv für Katholisches Kirchenrecht*, 155 (1986), 49–71.

Tovar Patrón, J. *Los primeros subditos de la jurisdicción castrense* española, Bilbao, 1964.

Tozzi, V. *Assistenza religiosa e Diritto ecclesiastico*, Naples, 1985.

Viana, A. "Los ordinariatos militares en el contexto del Decreto 'Presbyterorum ordinis' no. 10," *Ius Canonicum*, 28 (1988), 721–49.

Viana, A. *Territorialidad y personalidad en la organización eclesiástica. El caso de los ordinariatos militares*, Pamplona, 1992; "La pertenencia del Ordinario militar a la Conferencia episcopal," *La synodité. Actes du VIIIe Congrès international de droit canonique*, Paris, 1992.

MILTIADES (or MELCHIADES). *(b.?–d. Rome, 10 or 11 January 314). Elected 2 July 311 (or 310). Buried in the cemetery of Calistus on the Appian Way. Saint.*

Of African origin, according to the *Liber pontificalis*, Miltiades, along with Silvester, was part of Marcellinus's clergy. The catalogs do not agree on the dates of his taking charge or on the death of this Marcellinus. If we use the consular dates given in the *Liberian Catalog*, he became pope on 2 July 311 (*cons. Maximiano VIII*) and died 10 or 11 January 314 (*Volusiano et Anniano cons.*). The length of his episcopate varies: three years, six months, and eight days according to the *Liberian Catalog*, four years for Eusebius of Caesarea and Gerona; and four years, seven months, and eight days according to the *Liber pontificalis*. Succeeding another EUSEBIUS, who was pope in 309 or 310 after a vacancy difficult to verify as to length, Miltiades' accession to the papacy could also be dated 310.

The pontificate of Miltiades coincided with the events that gave birth to the peace of the Church. After the victory of Emperor Constantine at the Milvian bridge on 28 October 312, the policy of tolerance illustrated by the edict of Milan in February 313 established new ties between the papacy and the emperor. It does not seem as if Miltiades had any influence whatsoever on these events. Church property, taken away during the time of persecution by Diocletian (303), was restored under Maxentius (306–12), and the Church of Rome, through her intermediaries, the deacons Cassianus and Strato, took possession of the places and properties that had previously belonged to her. Miltiades' activities as pastor are only known through two liturgical and disciplinary decrees according to the *Liber pontificalis*. He forbade fasting on Sundays and Thursdays, and he prescribed that a portion of the bread consecrated by the bishop (*fermentum*) be distributed at various churches of Rome.

His pontificate was marked by his role in the Donatist quarrel. Associated through the emperor with the conflict that divided the Church in Africa, he showed an amount of tact in this matter that distinguished him from being just a simple executor of imperial orders.

After the contested election of the bishop of Caecilianus to the see of CARTHAGE in 311–2, the Donatists presented a letter to the proconsul of AFRICA, Anulinus, asking him to submit their quarrel for the arbitration of the bishops of Gaul. Constantine then sent a letter to Pope Miltiades that is the first known letter from an emperor to a pope: "Constantine Augustus to Miltiades, bishop of the Romans, and to Mark." The emperor deplored the fact that a problem he considered "of very little importance" could provoke so much agitation and, to settle it, he wished Caecilianus to appear in Rome accompanied by ten bishops from each of the two sides to be heard there, in the presence of Miltiades, with three bishops from Gaul whom he had already named. In order to instruct the pope, he sent with this letter a copy of the documents that Anulinus had sent him. The recommendations at the end of the letter were very clear: "I bear so much respect for the legitimate catholic Church that I do not wish you to tolerate any public schism or dissension, wherever it may be."

In this African conflict where the judgment of the Gauls was sought, the bishop of Rome was able to transform the tribunal of arbitration over which Constantine had asked him to preside, into a true council. In response to his letter, Miltiades called fifteen bishops from various regions of Italy, who joined the three from Gaul in the presence of the two adversaries, Caecilianus and Donatus of *Casae Nigrae*. They met during the first few days of October in the "house" of Fausta, the empress's residence in the Lateran (*in domum Faustae in Laterano*) in a synod that lasted three days, 2–4 October 313. Donatus was not able to sustain his accusations against Caecilianus and was convicted of having broken the rules of the discipline by rebaptizing apostates and ordaining lapsed bishops. At the end of the third session, Pope Miltiades pronounced the final judgment (*sententia*), reported by Optatus of Mileva: "Since Caecilianus was not accused by those who came with Donatus, as they had announced, and that he had not been convicted on any point by Donatus, I think (*censeo*) that he should be retained in his right to ecclesiastic communion, in his rank and in his position." The acts of this council were sent to Constantine and carefully preserved until the synod of Carthage in 411, where they were produced. The judgment of Miltiades was poorly received and the pope died soon afterward, without knowing about the appeal sent to Constantine by the Donatists, in late 313. Rumors spread and one century later, at the end of the synod of Carthage in 411, the Donatists went as far as to accuse him of having handed over the Scriptures (*crimine traditionis*). He and two of his deacons, Cassianus and Strato, had been charged under Macentius with reclaiming the

MINUTANTE

Church property taken away from the prefect of the city during the time of persecution. Augustine of Hippon several times loudly defended his memory, praising the wisdom and the moderation of the pope whom he called the "father of the Christian people."

Miltiades died on 10 or 11 January (*III* or *IV id. Ianuarius*) of the year 314 according to the concordance of the dates established by the *Liberian Catalog* and the *Depositio episcoporum* as well as the *Hieronymian Martyrology*, which also mentions his *depositio* on 2 July; this error can be explained by confusion between the date of his death and that of his ordination as bishop. He was buried at the cemetery of Calistus, on the Appian Way, in a place that has not yet been located, despite the discovery in 1852 by J. B. De Rossi in this cemetery of a vast chamber, located not far from the crypt of the popes, which he gave the name of Miltiades' *cubiculum*.

Élisabeth Paoli

Bibliography

LP, I, 168.
Amman, E. "Miltiade," *DTC*, 10, 2 (1929), 1764–5.
Amore, A. "Miltiade," *BS*, 9 (1967), 488–91.
Augustine of Hippo, *Ep* 43, 4, 14 and 16, *CSEL*, 34, 2, 87, 96 and 98; *Ep* 53, 3, 154; 88, 3, 409; 89, 3, 421; 105, 8, 601; *Ad Donat. post. coll.*, 13, 17, *CSEL*, 53, 115: 15, 17, 117; *Breviculus coll. cum Donat.*, III, 12, 24, *CSEL*, 53, 72; III, 17, 31–3, 80–3; III, 18, 34, 83–4; *Contra Ep. Parmeniani*, I, 5, 10, *CSEL*, 51, 29; *De unico baptismo*, 16, 27–8, *CSEL*, 53, 28–30.
Caspar, E. "Die Römische Synode von 313," *ZKG*, 46 (1928), 333–46; *Geschichte des Papsttums*, I, Tübingen, 1930, 110–13.
Congar, Y. M. *Augustin, Traités antidonatistes* I, *Bibliotheca Augustiniana*, 28, 1963, 725–6.
De Rossi, G. B. *Roma sotterranea*, II, Rome, 1864, 195–210, pl. XXII.
Depositio episcoporum, *MGH*, AA, 9, 70.
Eusebius of Caesarea, *HE*, X, 18–20, *SC*, 55, 108–9.
Eusebius of Caesarea and Jerone, *Chron.* a. 308, *PL*, 27, 493.
Frend, W. H. C. *The Donatist Church*, Oxford, 1952, 142–50.
Gesta Conl. Carth., III, *Cap.* 319–22, CC, 149A, 36.
Hieronym. Martyr., AASS, Nov. II, p. *post.*, 34, 347, 427, 641.
Instinsky, H. U. "Zwei Bichofnamen Konstantinischer Zeit. 1. Miltiades von Rom," *Römische Quartalschrift*, 55 (1960), 203–6.
Lamirande, E. *Augustin, Traité antidonatistes, V, Bibliotheca Augustiniana*, 32, Paris, 1965, 725–6.
Leclercq, H. "Miltiade," *DACL*, 11 (1933), 1199–203.
Liber Genealogus, MGH, AA, 9, 196.
Liberian Catalog, ed. Duchesne, 9.
Mardouze, A., and La Bonnardière, A. M. *Prosopographie chrétienne du Bas-Empire, I, Afrique* (303–533), 1982, s.v. Caecilianus 1, 165 ff., Donatus 5, 292 ff.
Optatus of Mileve, *Contra Parmenianum Donat.*, I, 23–4, 25, *CSEL*, 26, 26–8.
Pietri, C. *Roma christiana*, Rome, 1976, I, 4–14 and 159–68 II, 1696.

MINUTANTE. The *minutanti* (plural) were the employees of Roman congregations in charge of keeping a record of documents. The Latin translation, *informatores* (or the English "editors"), better shows their real role, codified only recently by the reform of the CURIA in 1908 (*Normae peculiares*).

The work of the *minutanti*, with whom the *aiutanti di studio* are also classified, consists of studying documents, summing them up, and filing them. They attend weekly meetings of the congregations (*congresso*) to present reports and their opinions and to edit and send documents. The texts of 1908 also define the qualifications for this job (a doctorate in theology or in canon law) and the methods of selection (a competitive test). In practice, co-optation from Rome's ecclesiastical universities plays an essential role.

Responsible for one sector of business, by subject or by country, the *minutanti* are at the center of a network of information and influence decisions, alternately playing the role of secretaries or consultants. Taking an oath of secrecy, they are nevertheless easier to access than are the heads of the dicasteries. For these reasons, they are sought-after by those who habitually deal with the Curia.

If the careers of the majority of the *minutanti* take place within the pontifical government, for a number of them, particularly in the Congregation for the PROPAGATION OF THE FAITH and at the SECRETARIAT OF STATE, the exercise of this function serves as preparation for the highest responsibilities. Without making a long list of the *minutanti* who later became cardinals, NUNCIOS, or prefects of congregations, we can name PIUS XII, formerly a *minutante* to Ecclesiastical Affairs in 1905, and PAUL VI, a *minutante* to the Secretariat of State where he shared space in 1925 with the future secretary of state (Tardini) and the prefect of the Holy Office (Ottaviani).

The ruling of the Curia in 1968 made the *minutanti* the highest class of all the minor officers. It retained the requirement for a thesis (*laurea*) in theology or canon law as a condition of employment, but foresaw accepting "an equivalent title"; it still requires the knowledge of Latin, Italian, and a "modern language." The introduction into the hierarchy of the rank of "office chief" (*capo d'ufficio*), (an immediately superior level), relativizes the importance of the *minutanti* a little. Vatican II Council proposed the internationalizing of the recruitment of *minutanti* and of giving a priority to candidates proposed by the ecclesiastical conferences "with equivalent competence."

Claude Prud'Homme

Bibliography

Annuaire pontifical, Paris, 1898–1939.

Annuario Pontificio, Vatican City.

La Gerarchia cattolica, Tipografia vaticana, Vatican City.

Martin, V. *Les Congrégations romaines*, Paris, 1930.

"Normae peculiares" (1908), *Pie X, Actes Encycliques . . .*, IV, s.d . . .

"Règlement général de la Curie romaine," *DC*, 1968, 693–715.

MISSAL, TRIDENTINE. During the course of the Council of TRENT, the bishops worried about a certain number of abuses that had been introduced into the celebration of mass. These concerned the gestures and attitudes of the celebrant or the faithful, as much as the formularies, that hinted of superstitions or were otherwise not compatible with Christian faith. The best solution appeared to be the publication of an official missal, reformed according to the ancient customs of the Roman Church and mandatory for all Christianity. They thus revisited a concern that had existed throughout the 16th century in several regions (Germany, Italy, and Spain). The problem was examined during the third session of the council, beginning in the summer of 1562, but the work was never finished: PIUS IV was in a hurry to close the council, and liturgical reform was tabled. The bishops, in their final session (4 December 1563), turned the task of publishing the new liturgical books, breviary, and missal back over to the pope.

We do not know the details of the work done by the commission established by Pius IV, which was enlarged by his successor PIUS V. We know, however, that an essential role was played by the erudite humanist Guglielmo Sirleto, who had already advised the council fathers and who, in the meantime, had been made a cardinal. The first book finished was the breviary, which came out in the fall of 1568 from the presses of the Stamperia del popolo romano of Paolo Manuzio. The missal followed in the summer of 1570 (after 29 July); for this, Pius V had chosen another printer, Bartolomeo Faletti (who died before the job was finished, and the work appeared under the name of his heirs), who worked with a Venetian typesetter, Giovanni Varisco.

The new missal left little initiative to the celebrant in the choice of formulas, determined by the *Rubricae generales*, or in the manner of enacting the rites, regulated by the *Ritus servandus in celebratione missae*. The two documents, printed in the front of the volume, were imposed upon the priest, as was the CALENDAR that accompanied them. This calendar, identical to the one in the breviary,

corresponded to the contents of the missal, which was, in fact, an innovation. The commission had reduced the calendar drastically, leaving only 120 feast days on specific dates—those that had existed in Rome before the 11th century, but with the feast days of saints of the Greek Church added.

The missal chosen as the foundation of the new liturgical book was the ancient Roman missal, *Missale secundum consuetudinem curiae Romanae*, which had been most widely used until then, thanks to its adoption by the Franciscan order in particular. Some consideration was given to restoring it to its original purity; however, many embellishments added during the course of the Middle Ages, such as the last Gospel or certain offertory or communion prayers, were retained. In addition to the Ordinary of the mass and the temporal and sanctoral cycles, the missal included a Common of the saints, made up of whole formularies and not of multiple pieces from which the celebrant could choose; a collection of votive masses much smaller than the number known at the end of the Middle Ages and into which many formulas had been inserted; and finally, there was a small appendix of benedictions.

The bull *Quo primum tempore* of 14 July 1570, printed at the very beginning of the volume, dictated a very strict manner for using the missal. It was made mandatory in all churches and chapels; only the dioceses and religious orders whose liturgy could be proved to be at least 200 years old were authorized to retain their own. The obligation to use the missal began one month after the promulgation of the bull for the priests of the CURIA, three months later for all of Italy, and six months for countries located on the other side of the mountains. Such a schedule was, in fact, impossible to enforce, incompatible with the technological constraints of typography during this period and with the privilege of ten years granted to the printer, who was not about to give up a third of his rights of reproduction (this privilege expired after 1573, but before that date the rights of reproduction were only given to Jacques Kerver of Paris, and to Christopher Plantin of Anvers). It took a long time before the new missal was able to be used in every place of religious observance, but the results were obtained and the missal imposed in the entire Latin Church, with the exception of several dioceses (Lyon, Milan) and religious orders (Carthusian, DOMINICANS) that were able to prove 200 years of uninterrupted tradition.

The bull *Quo primum* forbade any modification of the published text. In reality, the printing of the missal—despite the time that had passed since the Council of Trent—had been too hasty, and the commission was still working on it. The editions of 1571 included numerous corrections of details. It was also necessary to change the missal to take into account many requests. The Congregation of Rites, founded by SIXTUS V in 1588, had the job of channeling the resulting momentum at the same time as it prescribed what should be in the different rubrics. In the following centuries, several innovations were introduced such as the prescription of the preface of the Trinity for ordinary Sundays (1759), the three masses for the observance of All Souls (1915) and the preface for the dead (1919), the restoration of the Easter Vigil and the offices for Holy Week (1951–5), and the mention of the name of St. Joseph in the Canon (1962). The calendar was enriched over the years by the introduction of many feast days of saints (145 until the reform of 1970), which again upset the relationship between the celebration of events of Christ's life and that of the saints to the benefit of the latter.

However, despite some changes, the same Tridentine missal was in use for over four centuries, until the publication in 1970 of a new reformed missal, which was also issued by a council (VATICAN II), prepared by a commission of experts, and promulgated by a pope (PAUL VI) who wished to see the council's decisions accomplished.

Louis Duval-Arnould

Bibliography

Ducal-Arnould, L. "Notes sur l'édition princeps du Missel tridentin," *Memoriam sanctorum venerantes: Miscellanea in onore di Monsignor Victor Saxer*, Vatican City, 1992, 269–84; "Nouvelles recherches sur les premirès impressions du Missel tridentin (1570–1571)," *De l'histoire de la Brie à l'histoire des réformes. Mélanges offerts au chanoine Michel Veissière.*

Frutaz, A. P. "Contributo alla storia della riforma del Messale promulgato da san Pio V nel 1570," *Problemi di vita religiosa in Italia nel Cinquecento. Atti del convegno di storia della Chiesa in Italia (Bologna, 2–6 sett. 1958)*, Padua, 1960, 187–214.

Jounel, P. "L'évolution du Missel romain de Pie IX à Jean XXIII (1846–1962)," *Notitiae*, 14 (1978), 246–58.

Jungmann, J. A. *The Mass of the Roman Rite: Its Origins and Development*, 2 vols., Dublin, 1986.

Schmid, J. "Studien über die Reform des römischen Breviers und Missale unter Pius V." *Theologische Quartalschrift*, 66 (1884), 451–83, 621–64; "Weitere Beiträge zur Geschichte des römischen Breviers und Missale," ibid., 67 (1885), 468–87, 624–37.

MISSIONARY CHILDHOOD. See Holy Childhood, Pontifical Society of the.

MISSIONARY UNION, PONTIFICAL. The Missionary Union of the Clergy (its original title) was founded in 1916 in Parma, Italy, by Father Paolo Manna of the Foreign Missions of Milan. Its aim is "to develop in the priests, and through them in the faithful, the spirit of prayer and zeal in favor of missions." According to JOHN PAUL II, it has "as its immediate and specific goal the sensibility and missionary training of priests and religious . . . It aims to promote the other works, of which it is the soul" (apostolic letter *Redemptoris missio*, 7 December 1990).

The Missionary Union was approved in 1916 by a rescript of the Congregation of PROPAGANDA FIDE, to which it was attached in November 1919 (this later became the Congregation for the Evangelization of the Peoples). BENEDICT XV played an important part in its diffusion, writing to the bishops: "Know that our desire is to see instituted in all the countries of the Catholic world the pious work called 'Missionary Union of the Clergy'" (encyclical letter *Maximum illud*). The Congregation of Propaganda Fide promulgated its statutes at the same time as it organized the cooperation of the Missionary Union of the Clergy with the Work of the Propagation of the Faith and the Work of St. Peter the Apostle (instruction *Ut universa*, 4 April 1937).

Beginning in 1949, the Union extended membership to religious men and women. Its name was changed to the Missionary Union. Later its membership was extended to deacons, catechists, and other leaders of communities. Members of the Missionary Union must aid missions through prayer, by encouraging the love of missions, and by organizing "mission days" to stimulate the zeal of the faithful. In 1967 the Union was organized in five countries.

"The objective of the Pontifical Missionary Union is the missionary training and information of priests, of members of religious institutes or societies of communal life or secular institutes, of candidates for the priesthood and the consecrated life, as well as other persons engaged in the pastoral ministerium of the Church. In short, the Union addresses all those men and women who are called to guide and inspire the people of God" (*Statutes of the Pontifical Missionary Union*, 26 June 1980, chap. II, art. II, IV, note 23). It is certain that the success of the other pontifical missionary initiatives depends in large measure on the vitality of the Union.

Dominique Le Tourneau

MISSIONS.

Middle Ages. The direct intervention of the papacy in the missionary area was not obvious until the time of GREGORY I the Great. His predecessors had been interested in the conversion of pagans and in the return of heretics to the Church, especially through letters that they addressed to princes and bishops. It was Pope Gregory who, influenced by a meeting with Angle slaves, decided to send Augustine, the prior of the Benedictine convent of Mont-Coelius, into the kingdom of Kent, where the presence of a Frankish princess, the wife of

King Ethelbert, assured him of a favorable welcome (596). Augustine baptized the king and made many conversions. The pope then established a diocese at Canterbury, and designed a missionary doctrine advocating the christianization of places and practices compatible with a belief in Christ, foreseeing the future organization of England where EVANGELIZATION was just beginning. In fact, a cathedral was built in York in 627, and the missionaries from Rome were able to prevail over the hostility of the Celtic-Roman Britons toward the Anglo-Saxon invaders. Pope VITALIAN strengthened the links between Christian England and Rome by sending a new metropolitan, Theodore of Tarsus, and a group of monks (668). England is the first example of a christianization by Rome that spread even into rural areas of the country due to the conversion of the rulers, whose people followed their example. Nevertheless, this example was difficult to follow in Germany. English and Irish missionaries tried to convert the still pagan Germans, but when St. Willibrord converted the Bructeres, the Saxons exterminated them; it was necessary to obtain the protection of the Frankish kings, who tried to extend their influence to Germany. Willibrord continued his apostolate with the Frisians. Pope SERGIUS made him a legate, with the title of archbishop, and Pepin II, called the Younger or Pepin of Herstal, gave him his support. St. Boniface was also given authority over northern Germany by the pope in 719; he had successes in Hesse and was appointed bishop (722) and then archbishop (732), becoming archbishop of Mainz in 751. He obtained the support of Charles Martel and Pepin III, the Short, to evangelize Thuringia, and organize there, as well as in Bavaria, a network of dioceses and monasteries in the Roman and Frankish style. Bavaria had earlier been visited by missionaries sent from Rome, like Vivilo at Passau. Duke Theodo had asked Rome in 715 to send LEGATES to install the Church in his duchy, but the work was not completed until Boniface.

The initiative then passed to the Frankish kings. The conversion of Saxony (772–804) was the work of Charlemagne, who used armed forces there for that purpose. The Saxon dioceses were attached to those of Cologne and Mainz. It was also the German bishops who tried to bring the Danish and Scandinavian peoples to the faith; Popes PASCHAL I and GREGORY IV merely gave powers to archbishops Ebbon and Ansgar, who had only minor success. Rome did not directly intervene in the conversion of Norway and Denmark, which took place thanks to England and Ireland as well as Germany, and would not be complete, in Sweden, until the 12th century.

Beginning in the 7th century, Rome was preoccupied with the evangelization of the Slavs in the Balkans, for whom Emperor Heraclius had asked the pope for priests. The creation of a metropolis at Salone by MARTIN I (649–53) began the conversion of the Croats, but the Slavic world became more accessible after the destruc-

tion of the empire of the Avars. In the south, difficulties arose because iconoclastic emperors took Illyricum from Rome and transferred it to the patriarch of Constantinople, and the Byzantine influence ran against that of the Germanic emperors. The khan of the Bulgars, Boris, wrote to Pope NICHOLAS I to ask for a patriarchate that would enable him to escape from BYZANTIUM; the pope sent him Bishop Formosus, who was very successful with Boris. But the Byzantines regained the upper hand. The prince of Moravia, Rastislav, asked Constantinople for missionaries, and Cyril and Methodus created a Slavonic liturgy that HADRIAN II approved, which set up Sirmium as a metropolis for Methodus. This time, the Germans fought the influence of Methodus (who died in 885), brought Moravia back to the Church of Germany, and had STEPHEN V outlaw the use of the Slavic language (which would assure the success of the Byzantine missionaries in the Balkans and in Russia, where the German missionaries also went). The missionary efforts of the German bishops brought about the conversion of the duke of Bohemia, which in turn brought the conversion of the duke of Poland. This ruler, Mieczko I, appealed to Rome and obtained a bishopric independent of the German metropolises, which assisted in converting the Poles. Rome acted in much the same manner when a Hungarian chieftain, already baptized by the bishop of Passau (who asked for his see to be made a metropolitan and Hungary to be attached to it), placed himself under papal protection: it was a papal legate who gave St. Stephen the royal crown bestowed by the emperor, and an independent bishopric was created at Vesprim (around 1006), and then a metropolis at Esztergom. During the preceding century, in 925, another legate of the pope had crowned the first king of Croatia, Tomislav, thus assuring the conversion of the Croats and their return to Latin Christianity.

The evangelization of the Slavs along the Elbe was left to the initiative of the neighboring bishops, whose efforts coincided with those, not totally disinterested, of the Saxon, Danish, or Polish princes. The Abodrite state, at the beginning of the 12th century, was on the verge of declaring its independence as a Christian state; a pagan reaction overthrew it, without Rome being called to intervene. EUGENE III, giving the war that the neighboring princes wished to undertake against the Wends in 1147 the INDULGENCE of a CRUSADE, in a way, legitimized the use of force as a method to encourage the conversion of the latter.

The popes of the 13th century tried to separate the evangelization of the Baltic peoples from the neighboring princes' appetites for conquest, in the hope of obtaining the conversion of the first by persuasion alone. A bishopric in Prussia, another in Estonia, and a third in Livonia were created with no exterior dependency. HONORIUS III refused to give the archbishops of Bremen the authority they asked for over these territories. The early successes obtained by these archbishops allowed the creation of small Christian enclaves, but the attacks by pagans led the prelates to ensure the defense of their flock by militias made up of soldiers such as the Swordbearers, under the authority of the vicar of the Holy See in Livonia at the beginning, who later became archbishop of Prussia, Livonia, and Estonia and, in 1255, archbishop of Riga. Having been defeated by Alexander Nevsky, the Swordbearers' order was combined with the Teutonic Knights headquartered in Prussia, who maintained the feeling of a permanent "crusade" in the Baltic countries and probably slowed the Prussians' and their neighbors' devotion to the Christian faith. INNOCENT IV thought he would have more success with the Lithuanians whose prince, Mindaugas, accepted baptism and a crown in 1251, but he returned to paganism. Prince Gedymin, in the 14th century, made contact with JOHN XXII who invited him to convert and authorized the construction of churches at Vilnius, but Lithuania was torn between the Latin and Russian influences and its conversion was only achieved by the marriage of Prince Jagiello to Jadwiga of Poland (1386).

To ensure the conversion of these people, it was necessary to first convert their princes, who were attracted to the freedom of pagan cults; thorough christianization was mostly the doing of monks, especially Cistercians in the northern countries. The papacy would not have a truly missionary group until the appearance of the mendicant orders. The first land they found to work in was the land of the Coman Turks (Ukraine and Rumania today); it was a Hungarian protectorate and the zeal of the Hungarian Dominicans allowed the conversion of the Comans, but GREGORY IX wanted to affirm the independence of the Coman bishop and took this group under his protection (1228). This Christianity disappeared under repeated attacks by the Mongols, but the Franciscans quickly resumed the missionary task "with the Tartars." It was in Comania that William of Rubruck hoped to settle when he took the trip that led him to Mongolia (1254). After that, Franciscans and Dominicans, with exceptional powers given to them by the pope in his bulls *Cum hora undecima* and soon grouped within their orders in special congregations (*Fratres peregrinantes pro Christo*), evangelized the Mongols, including the nomadic tribes and their subject peoples. The exchanges of ambassadors with the khans were chances for the popes to invite them to be baptized and to place some priests with them, obtaining several conversions among the princes themselves. Supported by merchants who traveled throughout Mongol Asia, they reached China, India, and Ethiopia.

The successes obtained by Franciscan John of Montecorvino in China led CLEMENT V to create an archbishopric of Khanbaliq (Peking) for the entire Tartar Empire. JOHN XXII created another one at Sultanieh for the Mongol Empire of Persia and India. Some bishoprics were set up in Ts'iuan xiau, Almaligh in Turkestan, and Quilon in the south of India. In addition Franciscan and Dominican missionaries established communities and centers following the Latin rite, of which several still existed in the 15th century. The black plague and the ravages of Tamerlane slowed these efforts; the conversion of the Mongol leaders to Islam or to Buddhism put an end to the hopes of Rome for the conversion of the Mongols and the peoples they had conquered.

The papacy was also led to work with Christians belonging to the Eastern Churches, with whom the crusades had made new contacts, with a view of achieving a unity of faith. Leo II, the Armenian prince of Silesia, wishing to obtain a royal crown, negotiated a true concordat with the pope, recognizing the primacy of the pope (1198–9). Coming to the LATERAN Council, the Maronite patriarch acted in the same manner (1215). INNOCENT IV, preparing for the council at Lyon in 1274, sent messengers to the leaders of the Eastern Churches to ask them for their professions of faith; the Dominicans in Jerusalem were already at work on bringing the churches together again. As a result, missionaries were told to promote union as well as to preach to the infidels; they obtained new members of the Roman Church, notably the catholicos of the Chaldeans, Yahballaha III. They also tried to have the faithful of these churches give up their dogmatic differences, as well as practices, although they recognized that a diversity of rites was possible. A particular effort was made in Armenia where the Latin school met with great success: some Armenians, wanting to follow the Latin practices, founded a religious order using the Dominican observances, that of the Uniters (1356). Finally, a rupture occurred within the Armenian church, whose bishops declared themselves still united with Rome.

The Council of Ferrara-Florence, (1438–47), which met to cement the union with the Greeks, seemed to EUGENE IV like a chance to unite with all the Eastern Churches. He sent his ambassadors, mostly Franciscans, to the leaders of the Armenian and Syrian Churches, to the Maronites and Chaldeans of Cyprus, and the Ethiopians of Jerusalem because they could not join those of distant countries, and the *Decreta* of the council proclaimed that unity had been achieved. Still, on the local level, divergences continued to surface and small communities wanted to be attached directly to Rome. The pursuit of union of these Churches, not only by declarations of principles, but by expanding the points of doctrine whose expression divided Christianity, was the objective of this missionary effort which, since the early 13th century, was really the responsibility of the papacy (cf. the actions of Ramon Lull).

At the end of the Middle Ages, a new field of evangelization opened, however, not with the Muslims: the popes understood how resistant this group was, where all preaching was forbidden. If bishops had been named for Morocco, it was to serve the community of Christian mercenaries working for the king of this country. The discovery of the Canary Islands opened up a new field of action for the missionaries, and here again the papacy wished to take part. CLEMENT VI put a Spanish prince in charge of the kingdom of the Canary Islands and gave him the mission of bringing the natives to the Christian faith (1344). An effort to do this was made and a diocese created. Some religious workers were martyred there in 1360. John of Bethancourt received an INDULGENCE to conquer the Canaries: the possibility of converting the natives was still there and, with the creation of the diocese of Rubicon (1404), the conversion of the Canaries began and continued throughout the 15th century. The papal strategy remained that of setting up new "plantations of faith" in independent states whose princes would have the courage to allow Christianity to take its place there, with no question of submission to foreign domination.

Jean Richard

Bibliography

Addison, J. T. *The Medieval Missionary. A Study of the Conversion of Northern Europe*, New York, 1936, repr. 1976.

Christianity of Britain, 300–700, M. W. Barley and R. P. C. Hanson, eds., Leicester, 1968.

Dvornik, F. *Byzantine Mission among the Slavs*, New Brunswick, N.J. 1970.

Goodman, M. D. *Mission and Conversion: Proselytizing in the Religious History of the Roman Empire*, Oxford, 1994.

Haendler, G., and Stoekl, G. *Geschichte des Frühemittelalters und der Germanenmission*: *Geschichte der Slavenmission*, 2nd ed., Göttington, 1976 (*Die Kirche in ihrer Geschichte*, II).

Heidenmission und Kreuzzugsgedanken in der deutschen Ostpolitik des Mittelalters, H. Beumann, ed., Darmstadt, 1963 (*Weg der Forschung*, 7).

La conversione al cristianesimo nell'Europa dell' alto medioevo, Spoleto, New York, 1967, 2 vols. (*Atti delle settimane*, 14).

Latourette, K. S. *A History of the Expansion of Christianity*, 7 vols., 1937–1945.

Les Missions des origines au XVIe siècle, Paris and Monaco, 1956 (vol. 1 of *Histoire universelle des missions catholiques*, directed by S. Delacroix).

Richard, J. *La papauté et les missions d'Orient au Moyen Age (XIIIe–Xve siècles)*, Rome, 1977 (*Collection de l'École française de Rome, 33*).

Schieffer, T. *Winfrid-Bonifatius und die christliche Grundlegung Europas*, new ed., Darmstadt, 1972.

Sullivan, R. E. *Christian Missionary Activity in the Early Middle Ages*, Aldershot, 1994.

Vincke, J. "Coninzios de las misiones cristianas en las islas Canarias," *Hispania sacra*, 12, 1959, 197–207; "Kanarien," *LTK*, 5, (1960), 1276.

Modern Era. In the 16th century, the papacy was not very interested in missions. This may appear paradoxical during the great European expansion, when the Portuguese and the Spanish were opening up new worlds destined to be christianized, but when the Portuguese took possession of the coasts of AFRICA in the 15th century, the papacy was involved in the GREAT SCHISM and then with the Muslim danger represented by the Turkish advances into Europe (the taking of Constantinople on 29 May 1453). The latter remained the dominant obsession of the 16th century, at which time the European divisions got worse and Christianity began tearing itself apart during the Reformation.

These reasons may explain why the popes did not take charge of the task of christianizing the newly discovered lands of the two great colonial powers of the time. It was inconceivable for Rome to directly take charge of the material aspect of EVANGELIZATION and the problems of recruiting, travel, and maintenance of the men to do this. Even more important, they were still living within the mental framework of a Christianity whose princes took care of the spiritual needs of their subjects. This model would explode with the mounting rivalries between the European powers and the colonial expansion of the Protestant states. Finally, where the 16th century was the great century for invention and experimentation in evangelization, with the Franciscans and the Dominicans in the Americas and the Jesuits in Portuguese Asia (the death of St. Francis-Xavier at the gates to China in December 1552), the 17th and 18th centuries were those for the consciousness of and debates about Christian expansion and the meeting of cultures.

The legal officials of the missions of the 16th century were the Portuguese "*padronao*" and the Spanish "*patronato*" accorded by the popes. In the previous century, MARTIN V conceded the temporal and spiritual jurisdiction over the lands newly conquered by the Portuguese to Henry the Navigator. EUGENE IV and then NICHOLAS V renewed these privileges. In 1493, ALEXANDER VI separated Spanish and Portuguese possessions with the bull "of demarcation" (modified by the treaty of Tordesillas, 7 June 1494), which obligated the rulers to the evangelization of the new subjects of their empire. The bull *Universalis Ecclesiae* of 1508 gave the patronate its legal form: the monarch held all powers that were not directly linked to sacerdotal function. The king awarded all BENEFICES, even those of bishops. The pope could not intervene except with the king's accord. In exchange, the ruler paid all the expenses for evangelization and also the living expenses for the clergy, construction and maintenance of churches, and other expenses. Under these conditions, the popes would not do anything in lands under Spanish or Portuguese jurisdiction except to award spiritual privileges, set up new bishoprics or new divisions in the religious orders, and remind the rulers of their evangelization duties. The idea of a "mission" and of the missionary responsibility of the ruling pontiffs did not arise, therefore, until the final third of the 16th century. It did not specifically appear in the Council of TRENT (1545–63), but after 1546, the council fathers were concerned about the ignorance of Christians, due to the introduction of "abuses" in the liturgy, dogma, and beliefs. The challenge posed by the Protestant Reformation, its origins and beliefs, and the necessity of combating its ideas, thus brought about assiduousness toward the mission, that is to say, the defense and propagation of the Catholic faith.

The principal missionary creation of the council was the *Catechism of the Council of Trent*. Developed beginning in 1561, it appeared during the pontificate of PIUS V, at the end of 1566, in Latin and in Italian. If it was not the first such work of its kind (catechisms were widespread in Spain by 1540), it was still a simple doctrinal form, destined to be published, abridged, copied, and translated for all the countries of the world.

The period during which the popes cared the most about the missions dated from the reign of Pius V (1566–72) until that of URBAN VIII (1623–44). Their initiatives in this domain were the expression of their wish to apply the decisions of the Council of Trent. The attempts of Pius V to establish a special NUNCIO for the Spanish Americas, a commission of cardinals to study ways of combating heresy in Germany, and another for the propagation of the Catholic faith in the world, were responding to a general need for efficiency. At this same time, the popes set up permanent nunciatures in each Catholic state and multiplied the appointments of cardinals. Even more important, it was the need to combat Protestantism that led the popes to favor the missionary effort. The Jesuit Peter Canisius, the apostle for Germany, focused the pope's attention on a method designed to reduce the effects of the Reformation and to bind the Catholic people more firmly to Roman dogma. With the German cardinals he organized the *Congregatio germanica*.

After the Council of Trent, new "Indias" were discovered: ignorance, paganism, the "abuses" in Christian lands, and misconduct and incompetence of clergymen in Europe itself. Protestantism advanced, especially in the 17th and 18th centuries, when Holland and England diminished Portugal's, and then France's, empires to their own benefit.

At the end of the 16th century and the beginning of the 17th, the Dutch gained a foothold in Portuguese Asia. In Japan they collaborated in the persecution unleashed against the Catholics beginning in 1614. In 1629, English colonists were responsible for the breakdown of the first Huron mission in Canada. London and Amsterdam were also the chief locations for the printing and publication of heretic, schismatic, and antireligious books. The artisans of the anti-Latin reaction in the Eastern Churches found their logistical support in Wallachia and Russia. In 1616 in Leiden, a *New Testament* appeared in Arabic followed, in 1632, by a *Pentateuch*. At about this same time (1628), a Calvinist took over (temporarily) the patriarchal see of Constantinople.

The idea of the mission remained tightly attached to fighting Islam and to organizing a crusade to free the Christian pockets in the East and reunite them with Rome. This state of mind was shared by Ignatius of Loyola (1491–1556), Father Joseph, the "eminence grise" of Richelieu (1577–1638), and by the ruling pontiffs. CLEMENT XI made the final appeal for a crusade in 1715. CLEMENT VIII sent Discalced Carmelites to Persia in 1603 to take care of the local Christians and to work toward a behind-the-scenes alliance with Shah Abbas against the Ottomans. GREGORY XIII founded the Greek College (1576) and the Maronite College (1584) in Rome, and the Illyrian College in Loreto (1581) to train Eastern clergy destined to return to their native countries or to hold rites for the Levantine Christians who had taken refuge in Italy. From Lepanto (1571) to Kahlenberg (1683), the Muslim danger came primarily from the Turks, but Catholic priests encountered Islam in Africa, India, and as far away as the emperor's court in China. Still, because of the Portuguese and Spanish patronates and their proximity, the Protestant countries and Muslim coasts of the eastern Mediterranean were, for a long time, the main direct field of action for the papacy in terms of missions.

From Pius V to Urban VIII, the missionary efforts of the popes were also the product of an enormous spiritual outreach that filled the Catholic world during this time, for which the propagation of the faith throughout Europe and in distant "idolatrous" lands was an absolute priority. Beginning in 1540, the bull of PAUL III approving the founding of the Society of Jesus (Jesuits) established the link between the special vow of obedience to the HOLY SEE taken by the JESUITS and their availability for any activity to spread the faith, with the Turks, the other "infidels," or the "heretics." Francis Borgia and Peter Canisius were among the inspirations for the measures taken by Pius V in favor of missions. Some Discalced Carmelites were among the initiators of the measures taken by Gregory XV. The Capuchins were sent out into the world by Father Joseph, named prefect of missions for Rome in 1625, during the time of the privileged alliance between Urban VIII and Richelieu's France. In 1664 the Seminary of the *missions étrangères* was founded in Paris, supported by the confraternity of the Holy Sacrament.

The interest in missions found a wide audience. The first treatises on missiology, such as those of the Jesuit Acosta (*De procuranda Indorum salute*, 1584) or of the Carmelite Thomas of Jesus (*De procuranda salute omnium gentium*, 1613) served as manuals for the generations that followed. At the same time, in Paris, the first *Lettres Indiennes* appeared, narratives about foreign missions whose success in bookstores popularized the heroism of the evangelizers. Francis Xavier, the apostle to the Indias and Japan, was canonized in 1622. Missionary vocations increased. Pious laypersons flocked to support the initiatives with their money and their power.

It was in this context that Gregory XV, who had been a student at the Jesuit College, founded the Congregation for the Propagation of the Faith on 6 January 1622. Pius V and GREGORY XIII had already convened some short-lived commissions of cardinals dealing with apostolates, and Clement VIII had set up a congregation "*de Propaganda Fide*," functioning from time to time until the death of its prefect, Cardinal Sartori (April 1602). Gregory XV, however, permanently established a congregation, giving it a "constitution," its own income, and numerous privileges.

The congregation, composed of a dozen cardinals, was presided over by a cardinal-prefect. Frequently attending meetings for the first few years, the popes participated more and more infrequently after Urban VIII. The most important member was its secretary. Among those who held this position were Francesco Ingoli (1622–49), Urbano Cerri (1675–9), and Stefano Borgia (1770–89). A general meeting was held each month. The cardinals specialized, more or less in one geographic sector or in a given domain. During the 18th century, "special congregations" were held to examine more complex questions and propose solutions.

The congregation had no territorial limits to its responsibility, which theoretically extended to the entire world. In reality its freedom of action was more restricted wherever an "infidel" sovereign held power, like the Ottoman sultan or the emperor of China, and in lands under Portuguese, Spanish, or French jurisdiction. It also had latitude on all that concerned the spreading of the faith, but it was not always able to influence bishops and the superiors of religious orders who defended their rights, privileges, and concepts in this area. Finally, a conflict over spheres of influence occurred between it and the Congregation of the Holy Office, which had its own commission of theologians to answer the doubts of missionaries on questions of dogma. In 1658, ALEXANDER VII reserved this domain for the latter, which demonstrated that it was incapable of making rapid decisions and taking into account the very complex realities of areas outside Europe. Yet, in 1719, CLEMENT XI created a Congregation for the Correction of Eastern Books, more dependent this time upon that of the Propaganda than on that of the Holy Office.

The search for information was, from the beginning, a permanent occupation for the congregation. However, missionaries only rarely responded to the numerous demands for detailed reports. Consequently, the cardinals went to the nuncios, the consuls of Christian states, or even to simple individuals in order to get the necessary information. They also made countless expensive apostolic visits, often with indeterminate results. The lack of information led them, in many cases, to postpone decisions, and condemned them, at times, to powerlessness or to contradictory responses. Issues generally examined by the congregation were jurisdictional conflicts between rival missionary orders or between missionaries and local clergy. Theological or liturgical questions mingled with quarrels on the rights and privileges of each. On the other hand, demands of all sorts flooded the secretary's office: requests for supplementary workers, for books printed by the Propaganda, for admissions into colleges, for indulgences, alms, and so forth. In addition to managing ordinary things, the Propaganda was able, for two centuries, to be constantly working on certain big projects.

It had always stated its wish to increase recruitment, training, and discipline of the missionary clergy. In fact, the secretaries often showed signs of distrust or even opposition to the great missionary orders. They reproached the regulars, either showing intemperate zeal for earning the martyr's crown, or leaving for missions in order to "enjoy a greater freedom and shake off the yoke of obedience" (report of Urbano Cerri, 1678). Their superiors were supposed to be fooled as to their real aptitudes, or to send their worst members in order to rid themselves of them. The congregation preferred to send missionaries they had recruited and supported, and who were entirely devoted, rather than religious men who had ties to their own order, but it had neither the money nor the means carry out such an ambition. The project, brought up several times, to use diocesan priests was not successful. "Regarding secular priests, no one suggests any, and those who offer themselves are not very good prospects" (Urbano Cerri). In 1706, the congregation sent an appeal to the Italian clergy to recruit diocesan missionary priests, with the idea of opening a college for them in Rome, but met with no success. From 1642 to 1678, the number of missions reporting directly to the congregation increased from 50 to 100, but the effort faltered, and institutions in its service, like the seminary for foreign missions in Paris, had a recruitment crisis beginning late in the century.

Several times, the popes recommended that the religious orders train missionaries, especially by teaching various languages. From its beginning, the Propaganda participated in the founding of missionary colleges through either subsidies or decisions. It granted privileges to the priests who went there to study. The reign of CLEMENT XI (1700–21) was another great time of initiatives, probably in order to combat the decrease in vocations. These colleges, however, suffered from chronic recruitment problems as well as those with management due to the religious orders' lack of enthusiasm for such duties. Also, the teaching methods of the time could only partially respond to the practical needs of the mission.

Dissatisfied with European missionaries, the cardinals had always wished for a native clergy to take shape. Besides the advantage they counted upon, that the congregation would not have to pay for their upkeep, the missionaries who came from the country itself "despite the persecutions of the Infidels, understand the language, know the country and, having friends and family there, would not be forced to run away as has happened in Japan, China and Ethiopia . . . which are now entirely abandoned" (Urbano Cerri). In 1627, Urban VIII established the Collegio Urbaniano for the Propagation of the Faith. Several cardinals set up about thirty scholarships for young men sent from all over the world. In fact, most of them were from northern and eastern Europe and the provinces of the Ottoman Empire; students from countries farther away were rare. From 1700 to 1815, 635 students completed training. Upon admission, they took an oath to consecrate themselves to the missions in their home country once they had finished their studies. The living conditions in Rome and the length of time required for their studies (seven years or more) made their reintegration difficult once they returned home. Nevertheless, they played a considerable role in the spreading of Catholicism, even if some of them became the theoreticians of the anti-Latin reaction in the Eastern rites. In reality, the colonial authorities and the European missionaries were not successful in developing native-born clergy in the Americas or Asia. The native bishops found it difficult to exert their authority and the priests, deprived of the Church's resources, lived with their families, which made it easy to bring accusations against them.

Another important aspect of the activities of the Propaganda was the publishing and distribution of books. From the beginning of the 16th century, Rome was interested in the liturgical books of the Eastern Churches. After the Council of Trent, this interest grew with the desire to keep to the traditional rites by purging them of any trace of "abuse" or of "heresy" (see the decisions of Clement VIII regarding the Union of the Ruthenes, 1595). The Propaganda went to work on publishing books in different languages, destined to be distributed free of charge to priests working in missions. The polyglot printing company created in 1627 had already put out sixteen different works by 1633. In 1677 it was printing in forty-eight different languages. It printed the Holy Scriptures, liturgical works (missals, breviaries, rituals), books of devotions (e.g., *Imitation of Christ*), and some controversial ones, as well as pedagogical works (the *Annamite Dictionary* by Alexander of Rhodes in 1651), and catechisms. These

works were not strictly orthodox. Their linguistic quality was not always satisfactory, but they were useful for the teaching of foreign languages in Europe during the 18th century, and formed the basis of a written culture in many countries. The first initiatives of Pius V clearly show the desire for autonomy of religious power from the political regimes. At the end of the 16th century voices were raised to denounce the system of the *encomienda* imposed upon the Indians, and raised again against the enslavement of blacks as obstacles to evangelization. The divorce between the colonials' interests and those of the missions became clearer and clearer. The bull of Urban VIII excommunicating those who owned Indian slaves in 1640 was renewed one century later by BENEDICT XIV. The cardinals of the Propaganda were always aware of the shortcomings of the colonial regimes and tried to separate missionary activity from it. But this policy often conflicted with European preoccupations with the papacy, which was not able to divorce itself from the support of temporal authorities. This gave France a virtual patronate over all the Christian regions and missions in the Ottoman Empire.

The states' opposition to the initiatives of the Propaganda and the hesitations of the pope sometimes created a real imbroglio that hurt the evangelization work and increased the crisis of the missions during the 18th century. In their assigned country, the missionaries often showed fierce nationalism and often sought help from the local temporal powers and merchants. In the "infidel" territories such as China and Persia, they could only maintain themselves with the prince's good will.

If the papacy was led to oppose the authority of Spain in the countries under its patronate until the concordat agreed upon by BENEDICT XIV in 1753, it was especially in Portuguese Asia that the conflicts multiplied from the middle of the 17th century to the middle of the 19th, transforming it into intense European rivalries in that part of the world.

From the beginning, political conflict was mixed with another great source of problems for the popes: the question of Chinese and Indian rites. In fact, the first report unfavorable to the Jesuits' actions under the Portuguese patronate in China was sent to Rome by the Dominican Morales, who came to the continent from the Spanish Philippines; it was based upon rivalries between the two Iberian states (1631).

The actions of the congregation grew out of its observation that the fortunes of the Portuguese empire were declining and almost ceased to exist around 1650. Some young Christian communities fell under the domination by Protestants (Dutch) or Muslims. Some dioceses and parishes were left vacant for long periods. The missionaries were often left on their own with no resources. From 1640 to 1670, Portugal, which had regained its independence, had no diplomatic relations with the Holy

See, which thus was unable to fill vacant sees. This is why the Propaganda, still determined to reinforce its control over the regulars and to favor the emergence of a local clergy, was led to reduce the extent of the patronate by taking away the apostolic vicariates (1659) where Portugal's authority was only theoretical. Some French priests from the seminary for foreign missions were sent in as missionaries and apostolic vicars in Tonkin, Cochinchina, and in China. Independent from the great religious orders and the colonial powers, they were directly obedient to the Propaganda, abstained from all political action, and favored the creation of a native clergy. In fact, the emissaries from Rome did not hesitate to work for France, which had more and more of a presence around the Indian Ocean. In 1677–8, the Propaganda required an oath of obedience to the apostolic vicars from all missionaries, which was contested by all the regulars and the Portuguese authorities. The latter replied by demanding an oath of allegiance to the crown, whereas Louis XIV forbade his subjects to submit to this formality, condemned by the Sorbonne in 1686 as being against all French freedoms. Confusion was total in the countries involved. Despite the attempts at reconciliation by INNOCENT XI and ALEXANDER VIII, the jurisdictional quarrel only occasionally subsided during the 18th century. At the request of Protestant England and Holland, the Propaganda took away the lands of the bishops of the patronate to keep them from falling into Portuguese hands.

In 1701, Clement XI sent Millard de Tournon to India and China, with the title of legate, in order to settle the problems of discipline and the business of the rites, without previous agreement with John V of Portugal. The prelate traveled on a French ship, and legislated from Pondichery. Expelled from China in 1707, he was confined by Portuguese authorities to his residence at Macao under surveillance until his death in 1710, without ever submitting. His successor Mezzabarba, sent in 1720, recognized the patronate by passing through Lisbon, and compromised, which reduced his authority and handicapped him from the beginning. We can, therefore, see how the "padronao" kept the Holy See from applying its decisions in the famous question of the Chinese and Indian rites. This debate, which continued for a century, was between the partisans of two options, which were, however, not all Jesuits on one side and their enemies on the other. One side wanted the adaptation of Christianity to certain mental and social basic givens (the cult of ancestors of the Chinese, deemed purely "civil," the caste system in India, the Chinese and Indian revulsions toward certain sacramental rites). The others opposed this, sniffing out superstition in the Chinese "civil" rites, rejecting the Chinese and Indian morality and social organization as un-Christian. The responses of the Propaganda and the Holy See to questions on these points were at first cautious and equivocal (1645, 1656, 1669), but under the

pressure of uncontrolled European public opinion, Rome was forced to renege. The affair became heated with the arrival of the apostolic vicars (1684 and 1693). Poorly received by the Jesuits of the patronate, they declared themselves in opposition to any adaptation, and once again submitted the question to Rome. This affair of the rites, which owed as much to European quarrels as it did to a knowledge of the Chinese and Indian realities, was added to the complaints about the Jesuits' lax ethical theories and probabilism. Already in his fifth *Provincial*, Pascal presented the practices of the Jesuits in China as proof of their relaxed morals. Beginning in 1676, the debate took place in public in a series of publications coming from the two sides in order to win over Rome to their side. The Jesuits themselves contributed, through their writings on the Chinese rites, to their offensive action against the Jansenists, making it a general theological, moral, and political question. They furnished arguments to free thinkers, who demanded autonomy for the secular, contested the chronology of the Scriptures, and favored a natural morality without any grounding in the supernatural.

Under these conditions, the Holy Office judged according to the current theology, taking into consideration the distrust of the time for "superstitions" and the debates taking place on the efficacy of grace alone for salvation or the need for good works. In 1704 Clement XI made a decree condemning the Chinese rites, but torn between the necessity of defending a certain conception of Christianity in Europe itself, in the middle of the Jansenist crisis, and the desire not to sacrifice the missions, he tried to stall for time by keeping the decision secret in order to calm public opinion. In 1710 the Inquisition confirmed the decree of 1704, and the decisions taken by Tournon in 1707. These decisions were still not known in the Far East in 1715. Mezzabarba's LEGATION was to allow them to be quietly put into effect, but this only added to the confusion by allowing exceptions. Under CLEMENT XII, from 1735 to 1741, the entire affair was reexamined. In the bull *Ex quo* (1742), Benedict XIV condemned the Chinese rites and all those who looked for loopholes in order to avoid conforming to the prohibitions. The same decision concerning the Indian rites appeared in the bull *Omnium sollicitudinum* in 1744. At that time, the Jesuits, attacked from all sides, were no longer able to oppose the Roman decrees, while the relationship between Rome and Portugal relaxed.

These condemnations were doubtlessly not the main things responsible for the failure of the missions in Asia. In fact, the experiment of adapting Christianity was based upon equivocations and misunderstandings. In China, the neo-Confucians of the imperial court had already become disenchanted with the Christian religion and had pulled away from it, well before Benedict XIV's bull, which did not definitively settle the question in any event. In 1790, the problem was again brought up by the missionaries, but it was not until 1933 that the pope decided definitively by approving the conservation of Chinese rites.

The latter part of the 18th century saw the rise of skepticism, along with a decrease in religious vocations and in the missionary spirit. The "reductions" in Paraguay were abandoned in 1759 and in 1768. The suppression of the Jesuits (21 July 1773) further accentuated this crisis. Several thousand Jesuit missionaries expelled from the possessions of Portugal (1759), France (1764), and Spain (1767) would not be replaced. The apogee of the crisis came during the revolutionary period (the Propaganda was disbanded from 1808 to 1813). It took the creation of the Institute of the Propagation of Faith (Lyon, 1822) to see the great Catholic expansion begin during the 19th century.

Bernard Heyberger

Bibliography

Cerri, U. *État présent de l'Église romaine dans toutes les parties du monde écrit pour l'usage du Pape Innocent XI par Mgr Urbano Cerri, Secrétaire de la congrégation de Propaganda Fide*, Amsterdam, 1716.

Delacroix, S., ed., *Histoire universelle des missions catholiques*, 1, Paris, 1956; 2, 1957.

De Vaumas, G. *L'Éveil missionnaire de la France d'Henri IV à la fondation du séminaire des Missions étrangerères*, Lyon, 1942.

Gadille, J. "Mission chrétienne et cultures," *RHE*, 85, 3–4, 1990.

Jacqueline, B. "Mission et Missions" (17th century), *DS*, X; "Les réveils missionnaires en France du Moyen Âge à nos jours, XIIe–Xxe," *Actes du Colloque de Lyon, 19–31 mai 1980*, Lyon, 1984.

Metzler, J., ed., *Sacrae Congregationis de Propaganda Fide Memoria Rerum*, I/1, I/2, II/3, Rome, 1973.

Contemporary Era. The rupture of the union of Latin Christianity during the 16th century, the emergence of ways of thinking that freed men from ecclesiastical authority, and the rise of the nation state pushed the papacy to become more directly involved in missionary activity. Conforming to the spirit and doctrine of the Council of TRENT, Rome tried to take the mission into its own hands, in the name of the theology of the pope, vicar of Christ on earth. The centralization of the missionary activity for the benefit of the papacy would, from then on, characterize Roman policy. It took shape in 1622 with the creation of the Congregation for the Propagation of Faith. During the 17th and 18th centuries, papal policy was occupied by distant endeavors that raised great hopes but failed or obtained only very modest results in AFRICA (Congo, Ethiopia) and in Asia (Japan, India, China). The definitive condemnation of the Malabar and Chinese rites by BENE-

DICT XIV in 1744 and the suppression of the Jesuits by CLEMENT XIV in 1773 showed the powerlessness of the papacy to impose its strategy and authority on the missions.

Conversely the 19th century saw a constant strengthening of the control the pontiff exercised over the exterior missions. The latter took precedence over interior missions, spreading in Africa, Asia, and Oceania, while specialized religious orders increased. The progressive disappearance of territories under Iberian patronates and the refusal to extend the concordat in the new French colonies, with the exception of Algeria, gave Rome an unprecedented freedom to act, with the missionary personnel showing a very strong attachment to the pope.

The Congregation of Propaganda especially put this new development to good use. But it was not the only one to oversee the direction and regulation of the missions *ad gentes*. The Congregation of the Holy Office, beginning in 1658, reserved for itself any doctrinal questions, and enlarged the domain of its interventions. The specialized congregations, especially the one for Rites, also increased their decrees, often at the request of the missionaries themselves. The missionary activity thus was the object of a regulation that would have led to a paralyzing Romanization if the hypertrophy of the ecclesiastical right had not tolerated a multitude of exceptions taking into account the "circumstances of the time and place" in the mission countries, at least temporarily. In this context, the interest of the pontiffs in missions was constant, from Gregory XVI (1831–1846), prefect of the Propaganda before rising to the see of St. Peter, to John Paul II. But the direct and personal interventions were limited to questions considered to be essential. First of all, they attempted to provide spiritual and material support for the faithful. They then reminded missionaries of several fundamental principles which constantly guided missionary policy: training a native clergy, establishing a complete Church with an ordinary hierarchy (but not necessarily native-born), independence of the mission (which did not exclude an appeal to the secular arm), and seeking local financial support. In the 19th century, the training of the local clergy was the main priority confirmed in the instructions from the Propaganda or the apostolic letter that Leo XIII wrote on the founding of seminaries in India (*Ad Extremas*, June 24, 1893). In the 20th century, Benedict XV (*Maximum Illud*, November 30, 1919) and Pius XI (*Rerum Ecclesiæ*, February 28, 1926) resolutely proclaimed the supranationality of the missions and undertook the drawing up and signing of powers that symbolized the consecration to Rome, by the pope himself, of six Chinese bishops (1926), then, from 1927 to 1939, of Japanese, Vietnamese, African, and Madagascan bishops. After having seen a historically necessary stage in colonization for many peoples, without ever taking any official position, the papacy distanced itself from it. If PIUS XII renewed appeals for a mobilization in favor of the missions, his encyclicals gave priority to native resources, emphasized a respect for all cultures, incited the missionaries to accelerate the training of Catholic elites, of clerics capable of running their Churches, and of laypersons prepared to exercise responsibilities in the city (*Evangelii Præecones*, 2 June 1951), including "political freedom" (*Fidei donum*, 21 April 1957).

Beginning in the 1960s, decolonization, the sensitizing of Christians to underdeveloped countries, and criticisms of Western domination modified the approaches to the mission. At the same time, the VATICAN II COUNCIL called by JOHN XXIII insisted on the missionary responsibility of "all God's people" and advocated a dialogue between religions. Nevertheless, the traditional distinctions between the older forms of Christianity and the mission countries, called young Churches, did not disappear, and the papacy continued to exert a specific authority through pontifical travels, begun by PAUL VI, and its doctrinal and pastoral interventions. JOHN PAUL II reaffirmed, in his encyclical *Redemptoris missio* (7 December 1990) the necessity for a mission *ad gentes*; but he also encouraged efforts in favor of *inculturation*, that he defined in these terms: "By inculturation, the Church embodies the Scriptures in diverse cultures and, at the same time, introduces people and their culture into its own community" (no. 52). The question of the mission, its foundations, its goals and its limitations thus remains at the heart and center of Catholicism.

See also PROPAGANDA FIDE; MISSIONARY UNION, PONTIFICAL.

Claude Prud'Homme

Bibliography

Comby, J. *Deux mille ans d'évangelisation*, Paris, 1991.
Delacroix S. dir., *Histoire universelle des Missions catholiques*, 4 vols., Paris, 1956–1959.
Metzler, J., ed., *Dalle missioni alle chiese locali (1845–1965), Storia della Chiesa*, XXIV, Milan, 1990.
Ohm, T. *Les Principaux Faits de l'histoire des missions*, Tournai, 1961.
Yates, T. *Christian Missions in the Twentieth Century*, Cambridge, 1994.

MITER, PAPAL. See **Tiara**.

MODERNISM. In its religious and Catholic usage, "modernism" is a late term, appearing in Italy at the beginning of 1904 and recognized by Pope PIUS X in his ENCYCLICAL *Pascendi*, which denounced the moral danger that the Church was placed in by the modernists' profane novelties of language and false knowledge.

The term, therefore, refers to one of the major internal conflicts that occurred in Church history; however, in comparison, it had none of the scope of the Protestant Reformation, which split western Christianity in two, nor the duration of the Jansenist controversy. With one papal encyclical and several rather strict disciplinary measures, everything seems to have been settled. After a bit of agitation and floundering, the Catholic hierarchy showed that it had the situation well in hand.

Still, it was, for the Catholic Church, a trauma that has not been fully overcome. In 1958, the future Cardinal Henri de Lubac anonymously published some correspondence dealing with the controversy.

Since then, historians, especially in France and Italy, but also in the United States, have continued to work to tell the story as if nothing had happened, or to evoke this crisis as a limited incident, localized, without any real importance or any great consequences in the course of events. On their side, theologians have often simply sidestepped the subject rather than explain it. Many contemporary Catholics flinch at the idea of a new modernism, for closely related to the word modernism is the word MODERNITY.

In one sense, western modernity can be defined as a "permanent revolution" against which the Church instinctively resisted. Modernity involved the transformation of everything; how could traditional religion be an exception? It could neither stay out of things, turning inward; nor abandon itself to modernism, a destroyer of identity. Thus, Catholic modernism developed as a part of a general modernism that the Catholic Church could condemn but not escape. The Church was in the eye of the storm: the first confrontation was brutal, and then a new approach began. Without joining modernity, the Church became familiar with it, sometimes being drawn in beyond the limits it thought acceptable, which occasioned periodic shake-ups.

The word modernism, therefore, has a double meaning which leads to misunderstandings of whether it is meant in the ecclesiastic (very narrow) sense of doctrinal errors rejected by the Catholic MAGISTERIUM or in the more generalized sociological sense of a cultural process affecting the entire contemporary world.

"They are changing our religion." How many times have we heard this observation? In fact, a lot of energy has been expended so that things went in the opposite direction, to convince those around us that they must resist these undertakings. All this display is part of the history of modernism, but it is only ripples on the surface, hiding movements deep underneath that are more difficult to see. Nothing is more mysterious than change; much more inseparable from continuity than we believe, it is often affected very little by the violence that attempts to change its course.

You cannot change people easily. The religion of a country, like its language, changes unconsciously but surely within its very permanence, through the simple renewal of the generations and their preoccupations. We know what divides us; by the evidence that remains, we can reconstruct what divided our ancestors at the beginning of the century. We have only a rather confused concept of the global changes that have occurred between their time and ours and that have affected us. The words of language are our greatest resource: useful but fragile, it is enough to use them and see the effect. The meanings of words are similar to the value of money: the face value remains constant, but that in no way guarantees its purchasing power or its exchange rate.

Sociologists quickly speak of secularization, without making us understand what this notion includes, or its importance. We can examine outward evidence—the development of science, industry, technology—but this assumes and shapes a state of mind, a new form of rationality. Here we get at the heart of things: this reason sees itself as autonomous, positive, enterprising, quantifiable, experimental, emancipated from authority and tradition; nothing should escape its emancipated examination. With patience and tenacity, it edifies and furnishes a representation of the universe—both heaven and earth—very different from the biblical story the Church has made the basis of its teaching and which western culture has deeply absorbed.

Thus, little by little, the question narrows and becomes more dramatic: not without unforeseeable social reactions does one touch the foundations of a culture and the authority that legitimizes them. This new rationality is given a name by the Church: *rationalism*. Watching it work, the German sociologist Max Weber (1864–1920) defined it as a "disenchantment (*Entzauberung*) of the world." Applying it to the Bible, the German Protestant exegete Rudolf Bultmann (1884–1976) advocated the "demythologization" (*Entmythologisierung*) of the New Testament and worked to replace "Christianity in the ranks of ancient religions."

Faced with this agenda, the reaction is one of anxiety: how far to go? This, we quickly see, is not the way to ask the question, which becomes: Where do we begin? By the "negation of the supernatural," they would say in the 19th century or, in a more vivid way, by the "death of God." In effect, what the historians or scholars say is of little significance. God, who is part of any holy history, is not a character in the new one, which relies upon documents, because science does not recognize the supernatural, which cannot be taken hold of, and which has no laws. There is neither history nor knowledge for a modern mind, except phenomena and experience, within the limits of verifiable and constructive reasoning. The methodical doubt of Descartes has given way to methodical atheism: in his encyclical *Pascendi* (1907), Pius X denounced it as a typically modernist error.

Marcel Gauchet took up Max Weber's thesis from a larger perspective: *Le Désenchantement du monde, crise moderniste* (Gallimard, 1985) begins with the birth of Christianity—a religion that broke away from all previous religions, from the "dawn of religion"—and became whole in a series of stages up to the present. Spread over two millennia, this is not the end of religion, but the end of an era: Born in a universe in which everything was religious, Christianity awoke the need to abandon this, was frightened by its own demands, and, in the end, not without difficulty or false starts, ended up making itself a universe that was no longer religious. A nonreligious Christianity—is not this a contradiction in terms? Rather than engage in a verbal dispute on the malleable definition of the word "religion" across the centuries, or in abstract speculation (how is this conceivable?), or even in a symbolic reminder (the figure of Dietrich Bonhöffer, a German Protestant theologian who was a victim of his opposition to Nazism), it is better to view things from a historical perspective. The path followed for 100 years is not simply a cemetery of positions that were defended and then abandoned, but a shaping of the spirit that was slowly transformed: reading from the Bible, representation of the world, the miracles of Lourdes, the place and role of the Church; many examples abound. Catholicism has passed from the time when, even though disobeyed, Christian principles ruled the world, to the current situation when the world holds pockets of Christian life. If "religion returns," as they say, it will not be that of former days, but a religious belief that emerges from another world, our own.

One may easily suppose that this transformation would not occur without grave problems, open to reflection and, therefore, not without debates as to their conclusion, because everything will not be acceptable to all. But it has not been able to take place without confronting problems that today have been dried up, which then appear even more fearful because no one was seriously prepared for them—not ecclesiastical authorities or Catholic groups. The *modernist crisis* was, under their influence, a hypertension in the Catholic intellectual circles, a heating up of the circuit, a circuit break heavy with consequences.

This historical modernism—that of the beginning of the century and the "crisis"—is part of the vast array necessary to comprehend it. It is a phenomenon of Catholic terrain, belated in relation to Protestantism or the bitter quarrel between the "orthodox" and the "liberals" is its equivalent and its precedent. This is neither an exclusively French phenomenon nor exclusively clerical, but it is true that the French clergy found themselves on the front lines. We will not rehash a story that has been often, if not always well, told: we will simply recall several essential features and evoke several influential figures. These men, of unequal intellectual and spiritual stature, found themselves, for various reasons, at the heart of the crisis. They were not all "modernists" in the sense of that time, but they were not acquitted of the suspicion of being so.

Since the Renaissance and especially since the EN-LIGHTENMENT, the criticism of Christianity in the name of reason is a classic commonplace. At the end of the 18th century, this issue was taken up by the new sciences that flourished in the following century: the comparative history of religions at first; then prehistory, geology, and paleontology; finally archeology, history, and philology. The study of fossils pushed the origin of man back farther and farther; the theory of evolution revisited the problem of creation; digs in the Near East revealed civilizations that we knew little about, sometimes not even that they had existed, and questioned the historic value of the Old Testament. The critical methods of history were applied to the texts of the Bible, to early Christianity, to doctrinal formulations, to hagiographic records, etc. Revelation and divine inspiration wore away: the sacred writings were treated as documents written by humans, viewed according to common rules of authenticity and veracity.

We do not really take into account today what this revolution represented, the fever for knowledge that stimulated it, the avalanche of data that it produced; we understand even less the climate of battle and passion that was part of it. The end of the 19th century, in France, brought the "lay laws," the great moments of secularism and anticlericalism, and the separation of Church and State (voted in 1905).

From this renewal and enrichment were born what is called in France the "religious sciences," where religion stops being individual belief and becomes the object of detached, positive study. Research enhances teaching: the chairs in the College of France, one section (1886) at the École pratique des Hautes Études. Chair against chair: the specialists in religious science oppose the professors on the faculty of the theology department. The symbol of this conflict, for a long time, was Ernest Renan (1823–92), Hebraist, a seminary student in his youth, whose work had distanced him from the faith of his childhood.

On the Catholic side, the reaction took place in a diffuse manner and on contradictory positions that ranged from rejecting everything to a great openness. The handicap would be long and hard to recover from: the law on the freedom of secondary teaching would contribute to this, soon followed by the creation of five Catholic institutes (in Paris, Lyon, Lille, Angers, and Toulouse). The end of the century would be a moment of great intellectual movement, in the clergy as well as in lay circles. This openness was not without risks of diverse types. First came polemics in Catholic newspapers or magazines and denunciations to ecclesiastical authorities, followed by the intervention by these authorities, accusations and rep-

rimands; termination of jobs, dismissal from teaching, bans from writing; putting publications in the Index; canonical sanctions going even as far as excommunication. Finally, there were crises of conscience whose outcome could be a loss of faith and an exodus from the clergy.

To present a gallery of figures from the center of this movement makes the historian run another risk: that of setting up a prize list or a martyrology. It is more interesting to illustrate the variety of positions that were taken by several of the more visible figures.

First, two names. Maurice d'Hulst (1841–96), the first great rector of the Catholic Institute of Paris, who could not foresee "modernism," but whose sympathy and support would go out to those he had called "the broad school." And then, the one that everyone recognizes as "the father," Louis Duchesne (1843–1922), whose prudence and piety kept him on this side without, however, sparing him any difficulties, but whose penetrating look hid neither problems nor their gravity. Historian of the ancient Church (up to the 6th century), he had a brilliant career in the great government establishments—Hautes Études in Paris, the director of the French School in Rome from 1895 until his death—crowned by election to the Académie Française in 1911. His oldest students, split between the right and left wings, would find themselves in the front lines of the crisis.

One other place should be reserved for Eudoxe-Irénée Mignot (1842–1918), archbishop of Albi in 1900, the only intellectual in the French episcopate of the time who closely followed the movement of ideas and the evolution of the exegesis. Relying on his vicar general, the canon Louis Birot (1863–1936), he spared neither his pain nor his aid: "He was one of those who await the triumph of truth without impatience. His death left a vacuum in the French Church, which was not particularly noticed. He has not been replaced." He was a bishop in whom the modern spirit was in harmony with the "ancient virtues," wrote Loisy, the protagonist of the crisis, for whom he felt a "great friendship."

Among the characters, three positions are designated: in the middle, the *modernist*, (condemned); to its left, an evolution that pronounced itself to be *rationalist*; to its right, an opposition that wanted to be *progressivist*. Rationalism was the natural end result of a radical religious crisis. It had several forms and nuances. The philosopher Marcel Hébert (1851–1916), who was the teacher of Roger Martin du Gard, the novelist who wrote *Jean Barois*(1913), based his work on Kantian idealism in order to profess a spiritualist symbolism. Albert Houtin (1867–1926), historian of contemporary Catholicism, refused to be fooled by "the ecclesiastical lie" that brought fear, ignorance, and interest with it. Joseph Turmel (1859–1943), historian of dogmas, professor at the great seminary of Rennes where, as a student, he had lost his faith, considered it as a calling and, under multiple pseudonyms, never stopped settling his accounts with the Church until his belated excommunication in 1930.

Before calling it modernism, it was *Loisyism*. Alfred Loisy (1857–1940) was far from occupying this middle position by himself, but his work and his personality dominated it. A personality much discussed from his own lifetime to the present; abundant and irregular work, very marked by its time. A student of Duchesne, a professor dismissed from the Catholic Institute of Paris in 1893, he covered the interpretation of the Old and New Testaments. Very aware of the lack of high-level ecclesiastical studies and the seriousness of the problems raised by rationalist criticism, he thought at first that it was possible to refute Renan. He assimilated this destructive situation very early and never gave up trying to make everything fit for himself. In 1902, he published a small book that set things on fire: *L'Évangile et l'Église* [The Gospel and the Church], a book which some found admirable and others found subversive. Against the German Protestant historian Adolf Harnack, he showed the continuity of the Gospel to the Church, but, critics said, dissolved the link between Jesus and the Gospel. In 1907 he was the author targeted by the decree *Lamentabili* by the Holy Office, soon after followed by the encyclical *Pascendi*, much more all-encompassing. Refusing to submit to it, he was formally excommunicated in 1908. The following year he was named to the chair of religious history of the College of France where he was joined in 1921 by Edouard Le Roy (1870–1954), mathematician and philosopher, disciple of Bergson, and friend of Teilhard de Chardin, and whose book *Dogme et Critique* had been condemned in 1907. He later progressed outside of Christianity, still considering himself faithful to his vocation and to the tradition from which he came.

Not all those who thought they were modernists had as tormented a fate. Many passed through the storm, neither denying Loisy nor following him. Those who, wanting to be progessivists, thought a reconciliation was possible between science as practiced and deep faith, met a different fate. At their head, Father M. J. Lagrange (1855–1938), DOMINICAN, founder of the Biblical School of Jerusalem in 1890, of the *Revue biblique* in 1892, and of the collection "Études bibliques" (Biblical Studies) in 1920; Monsignor Pierre Batiffol (1861–1929), the almoner of Péguy at the College of Sainte-Barbe, rector of the Catholic Institute of Toulouse, dismissed in 1908, and historian of the ancient Church; Father Léonce de Grandmaison (1868–1927), Jesuit, founder of the *Recherches de science religieuse* in 1910. The original figure of Father Lucien Labethonnière (1860–1932), orator and philosopher, friend of Maurice Blondel (1861–1949) until a misunderstanding that occurred between them; put on the Index in 1913, condemned to silence, submitted, maintaining his intellectual prestige and his spiritual radiance intact.

As the pivot between the two groups, Abbé Henri Bremond (1865–1933), former Jesuit, successor to Duchesne in the Académie française and very attached to Loisy, left unfinished a monumental *Histoire littéraire du sentiment religieux en France depuis le XVIIe siècle* [Literary History of Religious Feeling in France Since the 17th Century] 11 volumes long. The cultural intermediaries added to the action, like Lucien Lacroix (1854–1922), bishop of Tarentaise, and Paul Sabatier (1858–1928), Protestant historian of Saint Francis of Assisi.

The movement was far from being limited to these thinkers. In the seminaries, among Catholic youth, new ideas fermented: it was altogether a social action, Christian democracy, republican regime, the modern world, biblical exegesis, a maelstrom of aspirations and hopes where it was uncomfortable—to those involved as well as their superiors—to find oneself. Parallel to modernism that seemed easy to avoid, a "social modernism" developed whose diverse character and many forms invited hardening. Two countries were sanctioned: France (the dissolution of the Sillon of Marc Mangnier in 1910, denunciation of the Social Weeks) and Italy (dissolution in 1904 of the central organization of Catholic Action, a long conflict with don Romolo Murri, leader of the Catholic youth, until his excommunication in 1909). Still, the strongest opposition, before which Pope PIUS X would retreat, came from Catholic Germany, which rose up in an impassioned response when Rome imagined it saw modernism in its *Reform Katholizismus*.

In this climate, the intellectuals worked and published as much as they could. Among those most involved in this crisis outside France, few would be considered in the front lines: in England, two spiritual leaders, Father George Tyrrell (1861–1909) and Baron Friedrich von Hügel (1852–1925), polyglot and cosmopolitan; in Italy, Antonio Fogazzaro (1842–1911), the novelist, and Don Ernesto Buonaiuti (1881–1946), historian of Christianity, excommunicated in 1925.

At the time of his death in 1903, LEO XIII was the pope with the outstretched hand. From his first encyclical, PIUS X denounced those who had refused that hand, and the apostasy that was leading mankind to its ruin. The condemnation of modernism followed this line. In fact, to read them well, the decree *Lamentabili sane exitu* (3 July 1907, 65 propositions) and the encyclical *Pascendi domini gregis* (8 September 1907) owed everything to French writers: no name was given, but the modernism being targeted was French first. The encyclical began with a sketch of seven faces: the philosopher, the believer, the theologian, the historian, the critic, the apologist, and the reformer. It defined the system as "the collector of all heresies." It took seven steps intended to prevent "the spirit of novelty" from growing in the clergy, completed in 1910 by an anti-modernist oath.

The condemnation of modernism seems to have encouraged integralism. In reality, the future went to "progressivism": the teaching in the papal Biblical Institute in Rome contributed to it through its program and its methods; the encyclical of PIUS XII, *Divino afflante* (1943) legitimized it. Soon, people spoke of a "Christian progressivism" in a wholly different way, as an advanced form of social modernism. Still, in Rome, under PIUS XI and later under Pius XII, the spirit of modernism and the fear of a neo-modernism were permanent. The encyclical *Humani generis* (1950) was a memorable example of this. The most dangerous man during these years was Father Teilhard de Chardin.

Emile Poulat

Bibliography

Boland, A. *La Crise moderniste hier et aujourd'hui. Un parcours spirituel*, Paris, 1980.

Daly, G. *Transcendence and Immanence: A Study of Catholic Modernism and Integralism*, Oxford, 1980.

Goichot, É. *Henri Bremond, historien du sentiment religieux*, Paris, 1982.

Dom Inda, J. P. *Un prêtre béarnais, Édouard Tauzin (1874–1925) dans les remous de la crise moderniste*, Pau, 1980.

Montagnes, B., ed., *Exégèse et obéissance. Correspondance Cormier-Lagrange (1904–16)*, Paris, 1989.

Nineteenth-Century Religious Thought in the West, ed. N. Smart et al., Cambridge, 1985.

Poulat, A. *Histoire, dogme et critique dans la crise moderniste*, Paris, 1962; 1979, 2nd ed.; *Modernistica. Horizons, physionomies, débats*, Paris, 1982; *Critique et Mystique, Autour de Loisy ou la conscience catholique et l'esprit moderne*, Paris, 1984; *Monseigneur Duchesne et son temps*, Paris-Rome, 1975 (colloquium at the French School of Rome for the 50th anniversary of his death).

Rivière, J. *Le Modernisme dans l'Église*, Paris, 1929.

MODERNITY. This word does not belong to the tradition of Catholic language. It is not found in any papal or conciliar dictionary, not even in the Second Vatican Council where it was never written or spoken. It does not appear in Latin, even as a new word. It is a relatively recently minted French word: in the middle of the 19th century it designated anything that was modern; in the middle of the 20th century, it designated the period that valued the modern and, therefore, defined itself according to that concept. It was forged from the Vulgar Latin *modernus*. There is a considerable amount written about the adjective "modern," an area of conflict between rival conceptions of man and history. For someone skilled at highly precise chronology, to date when "modern times," "modern civilization," and "modern society" (expressions which do not overlap) occurred, to mark the exact beginning and end (that is, to link them with an event), is a hopeless task. They must be considered as fluctuating entities, useful for dealing with and thinking about our society and its movement, and improper anywhere other than western Europe.

The quarrel between the *antiqui* and the *moderni* during the Middle Ages, that of the ancients and the moderns, finished during the classic age of the 17th century: an affair of generations. With the ENLIGHTENMENT, in the 18th century, it changed. It was not between the young and the old, but between philosophers and theologians, enlightened minds and traditional ones, reason and faith. Thus today we are able to speak of *postmodernity:* a temporal word to show that "faith" and "reason," formerly so often invoked, only possess slight credibility, much less than previously. After that, the word was defined: modernity was and is *post-Christianity.*

If this future that we are heading toward has neither name nor face,—it is possible to understand the reactions of the Catholic church to the pretensions of modernity: its principles could only lead to catastrophe. Catholic doctrine remains anathema to liberalism, to naturalism, rationalism, the self-sufficiency of man, the closing-in of the world upon itself, and to the authority of conscience in the latter instance. Between enlightened modernity and Roman Catholicism, there has been, since the beginning, a conflict of principles, sometimes tempered by a commonality of interests, sometimes pushed to a test of strength, a real *KULTURKAMPF.* Catholic criticism does not go after the modern as a new thing opposed to previous times, but as an attitude, a modernity that took hold in Europe before going after the rest of the world. In this sense, it represents an unprecedented development of the relationship between the Church and the world, an appealing notion but an ambivalent one since St. John and St. Augustine. The empirical world of phenomenology is overlaid by the dramatic one of theology: creation, fall and redemption, grace and sin, the forces of evil and the seductiveness of idols. Running away from the world and presence in the world are the two poles of the commandment: "Be in the world without being of the world."

It is easy to see that Catholic discussion of this world and its modernity is singularly complex and quickly becomes difficult to follow, to the point that, even among Catholics and theologians, many get lost. The concept of modernity and the destruction of Catholic discourse is familiar. We are less sensitive to its division in two parts, however classic. It is made up of two registers or alternative modes, incapable of expressing the same thought: to condemn false modernity, to recover true modernity. Either you are modern and, therefore, I cannot be, or I am modern and you are falsely modern. This is what Benigni, a confidential aide of PIUS X, explained unceasingly: "Both the modernist and the antimodernist are modern, and both at the same time, absolutely like a doctor and a patient who are in the same hospital." Maritain, in his *Antimoderne* (1922), made the interplay even more complicated: "What I call antimodern here could just as easily have been called ultramodern . . . . Catholicism is as antimodern by its unshakable attachment to tradition as it is ultramodern by its determination to adapt to the new conditions springing up in life in this world."

The Catholic process of modernity is only one chapter, however substantial, of a much broader and varied criticism that it has never stopped accumulating. From its beginnings, explains Jean Baudrillard, it has taken "a liberal middle-class tone which has marked it ideologically ever since" (*Encyclopaedia universalis*). Péguy is a witness to this, according to whom "the modern world is corrupting": also sensitive to its double nature, he railed against socialists who stirred up things, using the word modernity, which they denounce using the terms bourgeois and "capitalist." As for the Church's process of modernity, this can be observed in the popes' battle against the Enlightenment and the Revolution. It was in this vein that PIUS VI, condemning the civil constitution of the clergy in the BRIEF *Quod aliquantum* (10 March 1791), was able to revile "this freedom of thinking, of speaking, of writing and even of printing with impunity, on religious subjects, anything that the most uncontrolled imagination can suggest, [. . .] this equality and liberty without restraints which seems to stifle reason, the most precious gift that nature has given to mankind and the only thing that distinguishes him from animals." This conflict would culminate symbolically in 1864 with the *SYLLABUS* of PIUS IX, a collection of 80 propositions of "the principal errors of our time." The final one was stated in this way: "The Roman Pontiff can and should be reconciled to and adapt to progress, with liberalism and modern civilization." This proposition led to endless criticisms. In Rome, they were asking: Why should the pope be the only one to come to an understanding with a society that has emancipated itself from the Church and has never stopped attacking it? We would notice only that Pius IX avoided the word "modern" used in French and English by the translators and instead chose "recent civilization."

LEO XIII thought in much the same way and treated this theme in 1877 and 1878 in two pastoral letters that preceded his election to the see of St. Peter, *The Church* and *Civilization*. He shows an acute awareness of the awkwardness of language and of words that mislead due to equivocal meanings. Civilization of our time, "separated from the Church and from God," only aims to "supplant Christianity." So, "there can be no peace with this illegitimate thing whose only tie to civilization is the name, and which is the treacherous and implacable enemy of legitimate civilization." He discerns "the signs of a growing barbarism" born of a corrupt civilization and which makes him shiver, because the only true civilization is a Christian one.

In 1903 his successor, Pius X, saw the shadow of the antichrist fall over the earth; since 1887 he had denounced "this modern Christianity," which wanted to subject the Church "to the needs of the times" and sacrifice "the primitive honesty of its laws." At no moment until now has this basic discourse been denied or modified: it allows only adjustments and modulations that can change its tone. The relationships change, relax, but the quarrel remains: we are learning to live with it.

The Second Vatican Council was not "the council that opened the way to the modern world," an open door to the "modernization" of the Church. That was neither its outlook nor its concern. In its acts, "modern" is used five times, without any significant meaning, and it is useless to search for "modernism" or "modernity." On the other hand, the council turned down the heat on the great cultural challenge that had continued from PIUS VI until PIUS XII: to change into a pastoral youthfulness that would make the Church more attractive. Its message of 8 December 1965 said it all: from the entire world, it could hear "an immense and confused clamor" rising toward it; it saw a multitude of anxious and questioning looks directed toward it. It answered without hesitation: what you are searching for, we have. . . .

The following day, Paul VI, in his speech to the council, was more circumspect: "Lay and profane humanism has appeared and has, in a certain way, defied the council. The religion of God who was made Man has encountered the religion (because it is one) of Man who has made himself a God." Neither shock nor ANATHEMA followed: the council took the Good Samaritan as its example . . . The theocentric cult of man had no ties in modernity with the anthropocentrism of the lay culture.

Twenty-five years from that time, in word and in deed, would JOHN PAUL II teach otherwise? The "fundamental link of the Gospel with man" that he spoke of to UNESCO on 1 June 1980 remains the center of open debate on modernity. Pope John Paul II has made the challenges of the modern world one of the recurring themes of his long pontificate. Indeed, his first encyclical, *Redemptor Hominis* (1979), on redemption and the dignity of the human race, began a long standing concern with the effects of modern culture on the human person. This consideration of modernity's pervasive influence has been seen from a variety of perspectives, in *Laborem Exercens* (1981), *Sollicitudo Rei Socialis* (1987), *Centessimus Annus* (1991), including capitalism and social progress; and in *Veritatis Splendor* (1993), *Evangelium Vitae* (1995), and *Fides et Ratio* (1998), offering teachings on moral and ethical dilemmas raised by technology, personalism, contemporary philosophy, and a host of moral theological issues (abortion, contraception, pornography, euthanasia, and cloning) that are part of the tapestry of modern times. Less preoccupied with waging a war on modern civilization, John Paul II—a philosopher and ethicist before his election—has sought to call attention to the obligations of contemporary society to understand fully the many dimensions and risks inherent in modernity and to make responsible, ethical decisions rooted not in profit or expediency but in law, natural law, and above all in the Gospel.

Émile Poulat

Bibliography

Aron, J. P. *Les Modernes*, Paris, 1984.

Baudrillard, J. "Modernité," *Encyclopaedia universalis*, 12, 1985.

Bouveresse, J. *Rationalité et cynisme*, Paris, 1985.

Chesneaux, J. *De la modernité*, Paris, 1983.

Corbin, A. *Archaïsme et modernité en Limousin au XIXe siècle*, 2 vols., Paris, 1975.

Daly, G. "Catholicism and Modernity," *Journal of the American Academy of Religion*, 54 (4), 1985, pp. 773–96.

Domenach, J. M. *Approches de la modernité*, Paris, 1986.

Lyotard, J. F. *La Condition postmoderne*, Paris, 1979.

Lyotard, J. F. *Le Postmoderne expliqué aux enfants*, Paris, 1986.

Maritain, J. *Antimoderne*, Paris, 1922.

Messine, P. *Liberté, égalité, modernité*, Paris, 1985.

Nicholls, W., ed., *Modernity and Religion*, Toronto, 1987.

Parsons, T. *Le Système des sociétés modernes*, Paris, 1973.

Poulat, É. *Catholicisme, Démocratie et Socialisme*, 1977 *Église contre Bourgeoisie*, Paris, 1977.

Simmel, G. *Philosophie de la modernité*, 2 vols., Paris, 1989–1990.

MONASTICISM.

Antiquity. Monasticism, a new form of martyrdom, tried to give man, or woman, back his unity; after a first upsurge, a growth crisis led the West to organize monastic life around a Rule. Rome and its bishop played an important and misunderstood part in this evolution. Monasticism was born in the 3rd and 4th centuries. For a long time it was believed to have been a specifically Egyptian phenomenon, because it appeared in this region earlier than in others and spread progressively into the rest of the Roman world. On the contrary, monasticism is obviously a unique phenomenon linked to Church life. Deeply disturbed by the persecutions and even more, perhaps, by the official position of Christianity following the great persecution, the first monks reacted by retreating to the desert, later called the white martyrdom, rather than the bloody martyrdom.

Linked to martyrdom, monasticism did not evolve from asceticism, which had been a facet of Christianity since its origin; it assimilated Christian asceticism, but went much further because the basis of monasticism is the *peregrinatio*, the departure that causes the faithful to abandon their country, family, friends, and worldly goods. The person that practices this attains the absolute poverty of the emigrant; he expects everything from God. This may relate to the biblical theme of the exile of Abraham and the Promised Land (Gen. 12:1), but also to the evangelical parable of the rich young man (Matt. 19: 21). With asceticism, combined with chastity and obedience, the *peregrinatio* was the origin of the three evangelical vows that defined medieval monasticism: poverty, chastity, and obedience. The goal of the monk or nun is to achieve an inner unity by turning only to God without a care for the rest of life. He or she attempts to become a new person and lead an angelic life; this we see relatively early in Rome.

Monasticism is, therefore, a local and autonomous phenomenon whose spread was independent of the travels of famous easterners, as supposed previously. The voyage to Rome of Athanasius, the bishop of Alexandria exiled to the West from 339 to 346, was not the origin of monasticism in the City nor in Italy, even if propaganda from this visit may have played a role in its development. The *Life of Anthony* written by the same Athanasius after 356 was a masterpiece, rapidly translated into Latin, which contributed to making monastic life known, but monasticism developed in Rome independently.

Monasticism first appeared in Rome in the second half of the 4th century. The City was one of the centers of its development in the West, but not the oldest. Monastic life was also witnessed in Gaul, in Spain, in AFRICA, and in northern and southern Italy. Our knowledge of this comes from the presence of great writers who were Fathers of the Church, Jerome and Augustine. The bishop of Rome played an important role, that of vigorous supporter of the monastic movement, as was the case with LIBERIUS, DAMASUS I and, later, ANASTASIUS I, or observing it with cautious reserve, SIRICIUS.

Jerome stayed in Rome from 382 to 385 with Pope DAMASUS I, who held him in high esteem. He is our principal witness to monasticism in Rome. His text is, however, difficult to use because he hardly differentiates the ascetic who retires to his own home to pray, fast, and remain chaste, from the monk proper, solitary or coenobite (living in a community), who has abandoned everything. Jerome affirms that monasticism was unknown in Rome in the aristocracy and looked down upon by the people (Ep.127: 5) until a period when Marcella, born around 330, was a young widow (c. 345–50?). The bishop of Alexandria had spoken to her about Anthony during his lifetime, around 345. Marcella refused to remarry, led an ascetic life, and then gathered some friends around her in her palace in a study circle that Jerome led later, between 382 and 385. She then retired to a property in the countryside which was a monastery for her: *suburbanus ager vobis pro monasterio fuit* (Ep. 127: 8). Lea, another Roman woman of Jerome's circle, belonged to the order of widows (*de secondo ordine castitatis*), but she went to live in a community; Jerome notes that she instructed her companions and that she was the superior *monasterii princeps mater (?) virginum* (Ep. 23). She therefore belonged to a community, probably in Ostia because after her death she was buried there. Asella was presented as a virgin consecrated by Jerome (Ep. 24), but another witness, Palladus, an eastern bishop taking refuge in Rome, reports that he had consecrated her himself twenty years later, in 405, in a monastery (HL 41, 4).

Monastic life also touches the rest of the population. Jerome severely criticizes those he calls *remnuoths*, adding "a detestable brood" (Ep. 22, 34). These are monks who live in small groups, work to earn their living, and only obey themselves. Jerome also sketches scathing portraits of men who live alone, begging, leading an austere and studious life; he names several, like Antimus and Sofronius, which proves they really existed. They were probably the type of pneumatic monks that are better known in the East, but who also existed in Rome: there are "men with the braided hair of women, . . . the beard of a he-goat, with black coats and bare feet"; the women "change clothes, adopting a masculine dress; they cut their hair, . . . dress in hair shirts and hooded cloaks, as if they were returning to infancy." Behind this satiric attack we see the appearance of monks, driven by the Holy Spirit, who wish to lead an exemplary life, as a new person. At this same time we find this type of monk at CARTHAGE, where Augustine, more tactfully recognized that among them there were honest men. For Jerome, they were only fakers and hypocrites.

The observations of Augustine several years later, in 387–8, are perhaps more interesting. In Rome he knew monasteries directed by experienced men where monks lived in communes by working for their living; they fasted and "live in Christian love, holiness and freedom" (*De moribus Ecclesiae catholicae*, I, 33, 70). "And this was not only with men but also with women; many virgins and widows live together and earn their living by spinning and weaving. Very old and virtuous women lead them, not only to oversee their morals and reprimand them, but also to cultivate their mind" (ibid.).

We can look in vain for traces of these monastic establishments. We find several funerary inscriptions near St. Lawrence for *sacrae virgines*, but it is difficult to use them to prove the existence of a monastic community. For a long time it was believed that a monastery from the time of Constantine stood beside the basilica of St. Agnes Outside the Walls, but this was known only through a later addition to the acts of the martyr Agnes, dated from the 5th century. Still, in 1901 a plaque of white marble in the apse of the building bearing the funerary inscription of *Serena abbatissa*, dead in 514 at age 85, was discovered. This *forma* could be the first evidence, in the 5th century, of a monastery for which there is no sure record

until the 9th century. Still, no proof exists of a community at an earlier date. Around St. Paul's Outside the Walls, numerous inscriptions are found for *sacrae virgines* including a *Petronia abbatissa* (6th century?) but, as at St. Lawrence, it is difficult to establish the existence of a monastic community that did not appear until the end of the 6th century with GREGORY I the Great.

Informal monasticism, pneumatic, aristocratic circles, *cenobia* of the Egyptian type recorded only at the end of the 4th century—these traces may appear deceptive regarding early monasticism, but Rome is nonetheless one of the poles of its development. The role of the papacy is found in two different areas: the mission and the organization of monasticism. Eusebius of Vercelli may have been the first in the West, according to Ambrose (Ep. 63, 66) to impose monastic life on the clerics of his *presbyterium*. These priest monks led a communal life; they had a dormitory because there were "little beds of the monastery, resembling the ideal life of easterners" "*monasterii lectulos, instar orientalis propositi*" (Sermon 56, 3–4). Eusebius made monastic life known to the youth of his city. Ambrose indicates that these deeds occurred before 355, the date of his exile in the East: "With Saint Eusebius, resistance had been nourished by monastic training and he placed the acceptance of hardships within the strictest observances" (*Haec igitur patientia in sancto Eubsebio monasterii coaluit usu, et durioris observationis consuetudine hausit laborum tolerantiam*, Ep. 63, 71.)

Two indications link this curious personage to the Roman Church. We know from Jerome that he was originally from Sardinia and that he came to Rome where he was integrated into the Roman clergy as a lector (*De viris illustribus*, 96). Ambrose writes that he became bishop of Vercelli, although he was totally unknown before his arrival. Eusebius, therefore, had been sent by the Church of Rome to take over the direction of the community. He continued this missionary work by sending out his own disciples to evangelize the northern and western portions of northern Italy (Novaro, Ivrea, Tortoni, Turin). Everywhere, Eusebius integrated the mission into monastic life, but the monastic vocation of Eusebius predates his stay in Rome, as Ambrose (Ep. 63, 68) notes that Eusebius left his homeland and his parents and preferred the *peregrinatio* to his own domestic ease. "*Eusebius sanctus exivit de terra sua, et de cognatione sua, et domestico otio peregrinationem praetulit*." We have here probably the most ancient trace of monastic life in the West. Pope JULIUS I, bishop of Rome, around 350, was able to recognize the quality of this vocation, attach this man to himself, and finally send him on a mission. His successor, LIBERIUS, also knew how to use him in the fight against Arianism. The popes Liberius and DAMASUS I supported the ascetic movement as well as monasticism, but the development of the latter provoked a more and more vigorous agitation among Christians. Jerome's case is a typical one, as he is both the witness and victim of demonstrations when Blesilla died. He tells, in a letter dated November 384, that the monks were considered responsible for the death of this young noblewoman because of numerous fasts they had imposed upon her: "This detestable brood of monks, what are we waiting for to eject them from the city, or stone them, or throw them into the waves?" (Ep. 39, 6). The marginal aspect of "pneumatic" monasticism was surely responsible for this sort of opposition, as the excess and deviations of this first anarchic monasticism make it hard to tell the saints from the trend followers and the simulators. The crowd and the authorities found it difficult to put up with "a style of life that combines begging with an insistent apostolate" (Ch. Pietri, p. 641). This real crisis happened at the same time the popes were trying to normalize the customs of the Roman Church and to spread these practices throughout the West (Siricius, Ep. 1; Innocent, Ep. 2). It was, therefore, quite normal that they also tried to regulate monastic life. Siricius showed his distrust regarding certain monks named above; they viewed it as systematic hostility, but it was not, for Siricius was careful to respect the monastic *propositum* and wanted to include the monks with the clergy. Even better, INNOCENT I tried to recruit the priests into the monasteries (Ep. 1 and 6). There was still some reluctance with ZOSIMUS, who condemned promotions made too rapidly (Ep. 9, 1) and CELESTINE I, who suspected some monks of southern Gaul, the *palliati*, of doubtful behavior and doctrine (Ep. 4, 1).

The most austere Roman nobles, the *zelanti*, and a large number of monks defended monasticism and orthodoxy. Pammachius, a senator friend of Jerome's, became a monk, and founded a *xenodochium* at Portus; he was in touch with a holy man, the priest Domnio; they set up a community and their action provoked quite a bit of agitation. The Jovinianus affair also occurred at this time. This monk with no clerical responsibilities seems to have been completely admirable, despite the defamatory allusions made by Jerome. Nothing exists to cast doubt on his moral stature or the integrity of his asceticism. He only denied that there was a hierarchy of states and affirmed that marriage was of equal merit with virginity. His *Commentarioli*, published shortly before 392, provoked violent reactions in Christian circles. After reading this book, some monks and adjuncts abandoned the monasteries and married. The *zelanti* led a campaign against Jovinianus, appealing to Jerome who published, in 393, a violent pamphlet *Contra Jovinianum*; finally they intervened with Pope Siricius who called a council at Lateran in late 392. The decree of excommunication that followed (Siricius, Ep. 7) was sent to Milan where Jovinianus and his friends had moved to plead their cause with Ambrose and the emperor. They were condemned there, also, by a council that met at the request of the bishop of Milan, and exiled from there several years later.

Rome began to legislate in favor of monasticism. A true reform gradually put in place a new type of monastic life: regular monasticism. The first attempt was made in Rome by Jerome who, beginning in 384, proposed normalizing the Roman monks according to the Egyptian model in his famous letter to Eustochium (Ep. 22). Once he had moved to Bethlehem, he translated the rules of Pachomius in 404 for use by the Latin monks in the East, and his work was very well received in the entire West. In 397, Rufinus of Aquileia, back from the Holy Land, had already proposed to the monks of Italy who had taken him in to translate the rules of Basil. Finally, Augustine and Cassian created an original work, writing first a set of monastic rules, the *Praeceptum*, and second, some works, institutions and conferences, from which a set of monastic rules would later be derived. From these mother-rules, the West would draw inspiration for the orders that would be the heart of monastic life. This profound transformation occurred mainly in Africa and in Provence, but Rome and Italy also participated.

From then on, regular monasticism developed in Rome and its surrounding areas. SIXTUS III (432–40) established a well-documented monastery *in catacumbas* (*LP*, I, 234) at St. Sebastian (?), and LEO I the Great (440–61), founded the *monasterium major* dedicated to John and Paul at the Vatican (*LP*, I, 239); Hilary (461–8) founded the first monastery *intra urbe Roma, ad Luna*, (*LP*, I, 245) near St. Peter in Chains. In all, five or six monasteries definitely existed by the end of the 5th century. Rules multiplied in the West during the 5th and 6th centuries. In the Italian peninsula the Rule of the Master appeared in the 6th century, and then that of St. Benedict, the Rule of Eugippius, and that of Paul and Stephen. Benedict first lived in Subiaco, not far from Rome, and then at Monte Cassino. This spiritual master was said to have been steeped in the Roman culture and in Latin laws. Benedict's biographer was, by the way, GREGORY I the Great, who belonged to a great Roman family and who founded in Rome, in his family home on the Celian in 587, a great monastery that he placed under the Rule of St. Benedict. Gregory was the first to make this Rule known, which would not become dominant until much later. After becoming pope, he founded about ten more monasteries in Rome. Western monasticism was then in full growth. Rome, fortunate due to its location, was an ancient center for the development of monasticism, but it played a relatively small role in its beginnings, which we know thanks to writers attracted to the city. On the other hand, the intervention of the popes was decisive in the development and regularization of monastic expansion. This influence increased over time, and began to extend over the entire West.

Jacques Biarne

Bibliography

Ambroise, *Sermo* 56, *PL*, 17, 719–21; *Lettres*, *PL*, 16.

Augustine, *De moribus ecclesiae catholicae*, Bibl. Aug. 1; *De opere monachorum*, Bibl. Aug, 3.

Biarne, J. *Les Origines du monachisme en Occident*, thesis in 3 vols., Paris, 1990; "Les origines du monachisme en Occident (IVe-Vie siècles)," *L'Information historique*, 54, 1992, 53–9.

Chitty, D. J. *The Desert a City: An Introduction to the History of Egyptian and Palestinian Monasticism Under the Christian Empire*, Birkbeck Lectures for 1958–9, Oxford, 1966.

Danielou, J., and Marrou, H. I. *Nouv. Hist. de l'Égl.*, I, Paris, 1963.

Desprez, V. *Règles monastiques d'Occident, IVe-Vie siècles, d'Augustin à Ferréol*, Paris, 1980 (*Vie Monastique*, 9).

De Vogüe, A., and Neuville, J. *La Règle de Saint Benoît*, 6 vols., S.C. 181–6, Paris, 1971–7.

De Vogüe, A. *La Règles du Maître*, 3 vols., S.C. 105–7, Paris, 1964–5.

De Vogüe, A. "Regola," *DIP*, VII (12983), col. 1415–34.

Ferrari, G. *Early Roman Monasteries*, Rome, 1957 (*Studi di antichità cristiana*, 23).

Fontaine, J. "La romanité de saint Benoît: vocables et valeurs dans la *regula benedicti*," *Rev. Et. Lat.*, 58 (1980), 403–27.

Franck, K. S. *Frühes Mönchtum im Abendland*, Zurich, 1975.

Gribomont J., and Miquel, P. "Monachisme II–III," *DS*, 10 (1980), col. 1536–57.

Guillaumont, A. *Aux origines du monachisme chrétien. Pour une phénoménologie du monachisme*, Bëgrolles, 1979 (*Spiritualité orientale*, 30).

Jerome, *De viris illustribus*, Richardson, *TU*, 14–1896.

Jerome, *Lettres*, ed. Hilberg, *CSEL*, 54, 1912; ed. and trans. J. Labourt, *Univ. of Fr.*, 8 vols., 1949–63.

Lanne, E. "Peregrinatio," *DIP* (*Dizionario degli istituti di perfezione*), VI (1980), 1424–32.

LeClercq, J. *Études sur le vocabulaire monastique du Moyen Âge*, Rome, 1961 (*Studia anselmiana*, 48).

Lialine, C. "Monachisme oriental et monachisme occidental," *Irenikon*, 33 (1960), 435–59.

Lorenz, R. "Die Anfänge des abendländischen Mönchtums im 4. Jahrhundert," *ZKG*, 77 (1966), 11–61.

Pietri, C. "Appendice prosopographique à la Roma christiana (311–440)," *MEFRA*, 89 (1977), 371–415.

San Benedetto nel suo tempo, Atti del 7° Congresso internazionale di Studi sull'alto Medioevo, Spoleto, 1982.

Verheijen, L. *La Règle de saint Augustin*, 2 vols., Paris, 1967.

Villegas F., and De Vogüe, A. *Eugipii Regula*, *CSEL*, 87, 1976.

Middle Ages. In the West, monasticism was spectacularly successful in the 7th century after a somewhat hesitant beginning. The arrival of Columbanus gave it a boost. There were more and more monasteries being founded in every country, and advancements across the Rhine as the Frankish conquest progressed and missionaries arrived. In the middle of the 8th century, Boniface's tenure was marked by the creation of several great centers, the most remarkable being the one at Fulda. The Carolingian period was a time for monasticism to assimilate. Pepin the Short and Charlemagne took great areas of territory into their kingdom and under their control, including monasteries and their adjuncts, and used them as if they belonged to the crown, naming the abbots and abbesses, giving these positions to the faithful who sometimes accumulated posts, leaving religious life under the direction of deans and provosts. Religious life was uncertain, with distinctions no longer clear between those who were canons and monks, where no one knew exactly when a monk should be considered as a canon, with a similar situation for the nuns, reformed by Benedict of Aniane.

This man, who had begun his work in Aquitaine, was invited by Louis the Pious to help him get teaching texts ready at the very beginning of his reign. In 816 and 817, after studying the ancient texts, two institutions defined the practices to be followed in order to stay aligned with traditional rules. Monks found themselves strongly ordered to follow St. Benedict's Rule and it alone. The politics of the rulers, the ambitions of the great, and the shocks of invasions dealt mortal blows to monasticism in the 9th century and brought about the disappearance or the ruin of a very large number of these foundations, and the decline of regular life.

The 10th century began with a slow recovery, growing stronger in the regions that suffered the least destruction, in Burgundy at Cluny, in Lorraine at Gorze and Treves, then at Verdun and Stavelot. Thanks to the return of regular abbeys, the rebuilding of patrimonies and the reestablishment of discipline, the return to monasticism was strengthened during the second half of the century, and then accelerated a bit everywhere, to the point that the number of establishments of all sorts, abbeys and priories, and canonical centers, doubled in less than a century. The return of peace and the beginnings of prosperity were favorable to the great monasteries, which were economic and intellectual centers. Libraries were reconstituted and writings multiplied. New centers of inspiration appeared little by little, Marmoutier and Fleury, Fécamp, Saint-Victor of Marseille, and in Italy the hermit movement resurrected the asceticism of the regulars. The monks reached the apogee of their long history in the West, dominating all areas. They were powerful enough to consider themselves, and be regarded as, perfect beings, "immaculate lambs." The evolution as such led to the development of the Cluniac movement, so strong that it was able to separate itself from episcopal control. At Fleury-sur-Loire, whose customs were beginning to spread throughout the entire empire, the abbot Abbon formulated the hierarchy of the monastic order. At Cluny, for the first time, a customary was drawn up, revised, and developed. England was touched by the movement on the continent during the last third of the 10th century and three reformer prelates there wrote a "concordance of the rules." The Holy Roman Empire, where monasticism developed later, was not reached by the spirit of reform until after 1050, whereas Italy saw the influences of Vallombrosa and the Camadoli.

The papacy was not directly involved in monastic life. This was not due to a lack of interest, it simply had not been appealed to because the monasteries were still mostly under the control of the founding aristocracy or sovereigns. The bulls issuing from Rome were mostly addressed to bishops and archbishops. Still, several great centers had privileges and possessions confirmed. Ten or so houses in all were thus favored, such as Cluny, Saint-Denis, and Farfa or Fulda, to cite a few. The great bull of GREGORY V in favor of Cluny (997) listed in detail the dependencies of the Burgundian monastery, and then gave it the episcopal exemption that it had long requested. At Fleury they also dreamed of asking the papacy to recognize its superiority as a royal French abbey and a great center of historical writing.

From eremitical reflection came the contestation of traditional monasticism, surrounded by its riches and intellectual superiority. At the end of a long period of progress, the movement of regular canons was born, made official by a BULL given by URBAN II at Rottenburg. At that time, there were already many foundations of canons who lived a quasi-monastic life. Thereafter, papal involvement was no longer unusual. After the pontificate of LEO IX, however, the number of bulls ceased. The pontiff, of Alsatian origin, had shown his interest in monastic life and during his journeys he transferred relics and blessed churches. In the Saint-Remi abbey of Reims, he presided over a SYNOD on the application of anti-simoniacal principles. In the empire, he did not infringe upon monastic traditions, which left an important part of the initiative to the families of the founders in electing the superior, like that of the solicitor. The momentum given to monasticism by Leo IX did not slow; more and more frequently the new monastic orders looked to Rome. Whereas the regular canons were set up at various cathedrals, the monks embraced the Benedictine Rule. Thus the Cistercians were were born. Abbeys for men and women were founded at Chaise-Dieu, then Grandmont, and Fontevraud.

It is impossible to name all the new orders; these new foundations were no longer dependent on great Benedictine abbeys, dominated and controlled by them, but individual creations which set themselves up in networks, thanks to similar customs. After Cîteaux, but also to take up a more ancient idea, the new orders had the habit of sending their leaders to an annual meeting called the general chapter. From then on, the papacy found itself relating to superiors acting on a vast scale instead of the multiplicity of houses that were formerly independent. Instead of having to deal with abbeys in a regional context or under the authority of a patron, it found mostly collectivities, for example, Cluny, Citeaux, and Prémontré. From then on, the demands for privileges could be made to Rome on behalf of an entire order, and, in the opposite direction, bulls of grants were addressed to a group.

Beginning with the pontificate of HONORIUS II, and even more with the pontificates of INNOCENT II and EUGENE III, we see more and more monasteries sending representatives to Rome to ask for general and detailed confirmations of their holdings, established on the basis of archives brought all the way to Italy. Thus a completely new form of documentation made its appearance and constituted an unequaled archivistic collection. The practice continued to grow, and popes such as ALEXANDER III, LUCIUS III, and CELESTINE III put forth a quantity of these very large repetitive bulls, the most recent adding a fine distinction, or a new gift, to the former. The papacy specifically distinguished small cases that could be handled on a small bit of parchment and that could be written in a small segment, with no paleographic embellishments, neither rota nor *Benevalente*, and without a list of signatures of cardinals. In the great bulls, the pope systematically introduced the clause of regularity, by which the beneficiary house would promise to remain faithful to the monastic order or the canonical order, defined as the first group following St. Benedict's Rule and the second following that of St. Augustine, and to remain attached to a given institution that represented the chosen custom: the institutions of Citeaux, Chartreux, Grandmont, Camaldoli, or Arrouaise, Prémontré, Saint-Ruf, and others. This step demonstrated the will, shown by the CURIA, to establish some order over the monastic and canonial expansion, which increased dramatically in the 12th century. The LATERAN IV COUNCIL, however, recognized no more than three rules: St. Benedict, St. Augustine, and St. Basil.

The pontifical intervention in monastic life had been spurred by the Gregorian reform, which among other matters dealt with abbatial elections and the management of parishes. The Curia could not always rule alone on conflicts between the monasteries, thus LEGATES as representatives of the pope traveled throughout the West. Besides Leo IX, other popes traveled: Urban II made a long voyage in France and many abbeys took heart during his visit. Because of schism, Innocent II also traveled, but it was Alexander III especially who remained away from Rome for a long time, in French territory. On these occasions, the pontiffs spent time almost exclusively with all the monastic and canonial orders.

The monastic influence was also more strongly felt in Rome because of the recruitment of several pontiffs who personally knew monastic life, thus Leo IX had reformed several houses, Hildebrand (GREGORY VII) had been consecrated at Cluny, and the former prior of Cluny became Urban II. Later, a Cistercian became Eugene III. With the crusades monastic orders of the knights were formed, including the Templars, Hospitalers, and Teutonics, each eventually receiving papal blessing.

Since Carolingian times, the papacy had been involved in the life of the dioceses as well as the monasteries. The 12th century saw the papacy consider monasticism in its totality and not just as an agglomeration of independent cells.

Michel Parisse

Bibliography

Dubois, J. "Les Orders religieux au XIIe siècles selon la Curie romaine," *RB*, 78 (1968), 283–309.

Knowles, D. *The Monastic Order in England*, 2d ed., Cambridge, Eng., 1963.

MONUMENTALITY AND ROMAN URBANISM (1848–1922). From 1848 to 1922, Rome had two politically distinct periods, bringing about different monumentalities: the last years of the temporal power of the papacy, which was happy just to preserve the past, and then after 1870, Rome the capitol, during which the new Italian government attempted to leave its mark on the city. After 1922 the fascist period began, which considerably remodeled the urban scene and increased the construction of monuments in the honor of the Duce or in the service of the regime.

The Final Years of Temporal Power. The buildings symbolizing papal or communal power were, in 1850, mostly inherited from the past. The political power was represented by the QUIRINAL, the home of the pope-king; military power was incarnated by the Castel Sant' Angelo, and religion's power was symbolized by the imposing mass of the basilica of SAINT PETER's and the square that was used for gatherings and the most majestic ceremonies. As for the capitol, it marked the heritage of the civil power of the *Urbs*, the municipal power. The Quirinal, the Castel Sant' Angelo, and especially the capitol were the first places occupied during the revolutionary troubles (1848–9, 1859).

Spread over most of the Roman territory, numerous palaces were then the sites of congregations, tribunals, and governmental institutions (Montecitorio, the palace of the Propaganda Fide). This city, still largely a repository of the past, covered with green parks even within its walls, organized by a network of streets and avenues mostly dating from the Renaissance, and with a relatively small population, gave contemporary travelers the feeling of a frozen, or even dead, city: in any case, a city detached from the 19th century's movement, outside the industrialization and urban growth and whose image, still symbolically very strong, was in total contrast with reality.

Still, the ruling pontiffs were not inactive during the first half of the 19th century. The Napoleonic period, during which Rome had fed the emperor's ambitions, had been dominated by the activity of the prefect de Tournon, who began numerous archeological digs permitting the restoration of ancient monuments, as well as construction of the ascent to Pincio and the reorganization of the Piazza del Popolo. For this, PIUS VII and Consalvi had the Pincio finished by G. Vladier in 1820; R. Stern and Camporese were in charge of restoration of the new ancient ruins like the arches of Titus or of Septimius Severus, the pyramid of Caius Cestius, and the aqueduct of Claudius and the Pantheon. Under LEO XII, the huge work of reconstructing the basilica of SAINT-PAUL-OUT-SIDE THE WALLS, destroyed by a fire in 1823, began. The work was handled by L. Belli and L. Poletti and elicited a lively debate on the nature of the restoration. A cattle market was also built outside the Porta del Popolo, thus avoiding having the cattle pass through the city. If GREGORY XVI was considered as a great maecenas—which was fair because around 50 architects were at work in Rome during his papacy—the main operations were those of traditional interventions. Archeological digs of the temple of Antoninus and Faustinus, a part of the Julian basilica, and restoration of the Porta Maggiore were done. Many palaces, churches, and gardens were also improved: the Lateran palace, the Monte di Pietà, and the gardens of the Quirinal and of the Vatican, the villa Celimontana. Gregory XVI was also involved in the modernization of the hospitals and the completion of the new cemetery of Verano.

During the first years of the papacy of PIUS IX, the projects of reform only marginally included the architectural aspects. Several projects for public housing were begun, but the main problem was that of finding jobs. Public works could partially reduce unemployment, which explains the inauguration of the fortification work around Rome. The restoration of Pius IX first allowed the repair of damages due to fighting (like the gate of San Pancrazio in 1854). Then, work was begun along classic lines: archeological digs, religious architecture, and the renovation of a certain number of historic places in the capital. Saint-Paul-Outside-the-Walls was finished, work was done on San-Lorenzo-Ouside-the-Walls, on Saint Agnes on the Nomentana, and on Santa Maria di Trastevere. Digs in the CATACOMBS gave birth to Christian archeology. The piazza Navona was paved, an access road linked the Trastevere with the Janiculum, and the Porta Pia was restored.

A bit of modernity was beginning to filter in to these Roman projects: an increased intervention in the area of services and infrastructures, modernization of the techniques and materials used. A new asylum was built on the Lungara, and the hospitals of San Giacomo, Fatebene-fratelli and Santo Spirito were redone—for these, architect Franco Azzuri made use of the latest European techniques—and a barracks was built at Castro Pretorio. With gas lighting, the city began to change its look. The first metal truss bridges were built across the Tiber (Ponte Rotto, 1853, and the San Giovanni dei Fiorentini, in 1863). This touch of the modern was not the result of a change deep within the city, but simply that of its economy or its activities. Finally, like many other European cities, the first decisive changes were linked with the appearance of the railroad. In 1867, the central train station of Termini was begun by architect S. Bianchi, replacing the stations of Porta Portese and Porta Maggiore. This construction greatly influenced the area surrounding it and, under the joined pressures of demographic growth, lack of housing, and speculation in real estate investments, new apartment blocks were built. The most interesting and best-known example was that of Monsignor de Mérode who bought (privately) some properties along the via Nazionale and had middle-class *palazzi* constructed there.

Intervention by the Papal State remained weak, and its main contribution of rulings on the remodeling of the *Urbs* was the "*Regolamento edilizio e di pubblico ornato per la città di Roma*," put into effect in 1864. Architecturally, the most representative monuments built during the pontificate of Pius IX were the tobacco factory in Trastevere, built by A. Sarti; the column of the Immaculate Conception in the Piazza d'Espagna (L. Poletti); and finally, the dedication of the new fountain of Acqua Pia Marcia, in Piazza Termini.

The city penetrated by the Piedmontese on 20 September 1870 had changed little since the Renaissance, and nothing in its structure or its organization would allow its rapid transformation into a modern capital.

The Piedmont Challenge. For the Piedmontese who arrived in Rome, there was a double task: to make Rome a viable capital, capable of accommodating government, government workers, an army, and new population, and to transform the capital of Catholicism into the capital of Italy. The spatial reorganization of Rome was done after UNITY, under the double auspices of the negligence of the authorities and of real estate speculation. Because Monsignor de Mérode had begun real estate operations in the area around the Quirinal and the train station before the arrival of the Piedmontese, this area of expansion was not abandoned after 1870. On the contrary, it is striking to note that the great orientations of the ruling pontiffs of the Renaissance, in particular by SIXTUS V, were renewed

and completed by the commune of Rome. The via XX Settembre—along which the great Italian ministries would be built—adopted the axis of the upper city of the 16th century. Even more remarkable was the participation of the great princely Roman families in real estate speculation, with no regard for their political sympathies (Caetani, Di Carpegna, Doria Pamphili, Pallavicini). Beginning with De Mérode, a former minister of war to Pius IX who, after 26 February 1871, signed an agreement with the Commune of Rome for the area of the via Nazionale, all the advantages were for the prelate, who was selling the properties belonging to him at high prices, and leaving the city of Rome the job of taking care of the area. Other similar agreements, disastrous for Rome's finances, were signed for the Esquiline quarter of town.

Besides the Prati di Castello, an area behind the Vatican, speculation was also heating up. A consortium of landowners, composed of international banks, had bought the land at the prices of agricultural lands, and was proposing to build, if they had the support of the commune, which was considerable.

Two weeks after the abolition of the *asse ecclesiastico* on 19 June 1873, the first regulatory plan for Rome was handed to the mayor of Rome. In reality, this plan suggested as new residential areas, all those that had already been approved separately and which had already been partially built during the direction of the train station. Only the Prati was not approved. But L. Pianciani, mayor of the city, understood that the city was going to have to play not only the role of an organizer but also the financial role, which would allow it to get back part of its deficit. He decided, therefore, that from then on, the commune would prepare these areas before reselling them to the promoters. All the speculators allied themselves against this reform and the municipal council was in the minority. The regulatory plan of 1873 was rejected.

The following decade saw the government occupied with the fate of Rome and two agreements were signed between the State and the city, while speculation ran amok. The regulatory plan of the capital would then be sent to the government and the supplying of public utilities conceded for all the works of the plan, with a required contribution by the owners of the areas concerned, in order for the commune to construct several public buildings like the Supreme Court building. The second regulatory plan proposed in 1883 was along the same general lines as that of 1873 (Esquiline, Castro Pretorio, Celio, Testaccio) and added, at last, the Prati.

During this period, the great Roman families sold and speculated on properties which were among the most beautiful in Rome: the villa Ludovisi was divided into lots and sold, as were the villas Massimo and Spithover. This period of Italian unity was, for Rome, that of lost chances: to preserve the historic center, to preserve the marvelous villas scattered about the *Urbs'* periphery, to control the development, so many opportunities that slipped away.

The monuments of Rome, the capital, therefore had to allow for new uses as well as celebrating the new capital and the history of unified Italy. The problem of a "national style" was crucial, with its most ardent defender being Camillo Boito. In Rome, the definition of this style was difficult because architects with different styles had been active during the preceding years: a neoclassical style (L. Carimini, V. Vespignani, A. Busiri Vici, F. Azzurri) and newcomers, ardent defenders of an eclectic style, historically influenced, and, according to them, capable of better portraying the cultural genealogy of Italy. Finally, several artists like E. Basile, from Sicily, used the "liberty" (or *floreale*) style; others, more daring, like G. De Angelis, tried to use iron and glass (the Bocconi stores on the Corso, the Policlinico, the military hospital).

In the early days, the king moved into the Quirinal and the different ministries had to take over ancient, confiscated convents, which was not very practical. Quickly, the construction of the Ministry of Finances and of the Supreme Court were moved to the top of the list. Soon these were followed by the War Ministry, and then, along the via Nazionale, the Belle Arti building (P. Piacentini), the Bank of Italy (G. Koch), and finally the Piazza Esedra (G. Koch). The Policlinico and an entire series of ministries along the via XX Settembre were built, filling the area from the historical center to the Portia Pia.

There were competitions held to design some buildings and there were also some extremely long and passionate debates: the Supreme Court, finally built in the neo-Baroque style by G. Calderini, the construction of Parliament (E. Basile), and the monument to Victor-Emmanuel (G. Sacconi). The latter belonged to a second category, that of commemorative monuments with other function than that of glorifying the heroes of unification and their precursors. Rome covered itself, in the years between 1870 and 1911, with a forest of statues, the result of private generosity, as well as that of the Roman commune and the Italian State. A certain number of competitions were held by the State: in 1881 for a monument to Victor-Emmanuel, in 1883 for a monument to Garibaldi, in 1884 for Quintino Sella, and in 1886 for Marco Minghetti. It was not until 1890 that a competition for one for Mazzini—a rather vague person for the Piedmontese monarchy—was held. Public subscriptions permitted the construction of a monument by Giordano Bruno to the philosopher Nicolà Spedalieri and to a hero of the Roman Republic, Angelo Brunetti, called Ciceruacchio. The monuments to Victor-Emmanuel and to Giordano Bruno were those that caused the most publicly opinionated debates. There were no less than two competitions, several hundred projects, and almost 30 years passed before the

enormous mass of white stone was finally erected in honor of the father of the country. After Giuseppe Sacconi died while working on it, a triumvirate took over, composed of M. Manfredi, G. Koch, and P. Piacentini, who finished the colossus. Begun—without the quadriga (chariots)—in 1911, it was not totally finished until 1921, and by then the Tomb of the Unknown Soldier had been added to it.

Finished in 1889, the statue of Giordano Bruno in the Campo dei Fiori, the work of the freemason sculptor Ettore Ferrari, incarnated all the Roman anticlericalism at the end of the century. Its inauguration caused demonstrations and confrontations between the partisans and the detractors of this work. Finally, this period also saw the construction of several churches of very different styles such as Santa Chiara (L. Carimini), S. Gioacchino (R. Inganni), and Sacro Cuore del Suffragio (G. Gualandi). The Rome of 1922 had become an Italian capital. Still, the Piedmontese construction had trouble imposing itself with the competition from the religious and ancient heritage. The entire monumental policy of Mussolini attempted to skirt the recent successes and rejoin the ancient grandeur, for the greater glory of his regime, and to bring modern Rome closer to the Vatican by linking the two with the via della Conciliazone.

Catherine Brice

Bibliography

Accasto, G., Fraticelli, V., and Nicolini, R. *L'architetture di Roma capitale*, Rome, 1971.

Architetture e urbanistica, Catalogue de l'exposition Roma Capitale, Venice, 1984.

Frutaz, A. P. *Le piante di Roma*, Rome, 1962.

Insolera, I. *Roma. Immagini e realtà dal X al XXe secolo*, Bari, 1980.

Piacentini, M. *Le vicende urbanistiche ed edilizie di Roma dal 1870 ad oggi*, Rome, 1952.

Spagnesi, G. *L'architetture a Roma al tempo di Pio IX*, Pomezia, 1974.

MOSAICS. An art that consists of juxtaposing small elements, most often quadrangular in shape, made of stone, marble, glass, or terra cotta, called "tessera," in such a way as to make geometrical designs or pictures. These tessera are sealed in place by a fixing mortar that may be applied to the ground to make a pavement (pavement mosaic), on the sides of walls (a parietal mosaic), or on ceiling vaults. The last two types mentioned are the ones found most frequently in the buildings constructed at the behest of popes. Mosaics have often been characterized as a quintessentially Roman art because the capital of the empire was the center of the most active dissemination of this art to all the provinces of the Roman world, bringing them its techniques, models, ornamental repertoire, and often even its artists in the form of itinerant workshops. This Roman art concept also takes into account the fact that this term also came from the expression "the Roman Apostolic and Catholic Church," for it is true that mosaics were one of the favorite artistic languages of the papacy, at least since the peace of the Church. In fact, from the simple quantitative point of view, we can say that the surfaces covered in mosaics in the churches of the Christian world are more important works of art than those that have come from the ruins of the ancient world. However, this accumulation of evidence has little significance as to the specific actions of the popes in this area, even if the message of faith conveyed through these images has always depended, basically, on the teaching of Peter and his successors. The question could be better assessed if we try to show how the popes, by the support they gave at different times to the mosaic art, and especially in Rome itself, by their orders, rendered it, practically until the middle of the 18th century, the classic "Christian art."

Early Development of the Use of Mosaics. In order to understand the exceptional strides that led mosaics to be considered the exclusive expression of choice of artisans working for the popes, we must briefly recall the reasons for this success. Although examples of painting, can be found in the catacombs during the early days of Christianity, the art of mosaics had advantages that painting did not. The first was of a practical nature: its apparent unalterability due to the strength of its constituent parts made it the covering that best resisted the crowds of faithful, rubbing and pressing against the walls of the church. The second advantage was the more determining factor: the use of tessera of glass, and the perfecting of the technical procedure allowed the manufacture of a glass tessera that covered a thin leaf of gold (an invention that first appeared during Nero's time, but did not really spread until the 5th century) gave it the primordial quality of being an art of lights. Our modern lighting, with its implacable steadiness, makes us forget that these mosaics were destined to be seen in the half-darkness of sanctuaries, in the flickering light of thousands of tiny flames, which made the colorful array of glass paste and gilded bottoms glisten. It has often been said that the atmosphere created by these vibrations of colors had an effect that could be characterized as magical, but it should also be said that since God was the light that illuminates the darkness of the world (e.g., John 1:5; 3:19,) there was a particular sort of match between the language of the mosaics and the message of faith.

Among so many other examples, we must mention the mosaics of St. Mark's church in Rome, work done under GREGORY IV (828–44), in which Christ, surrounded by the pope, St. Mark (the Evangelist), Pope Mark, St. Felicissimus, Pope AGAPITUS I (535–6), and St. Agnes, holds

the Bible open, where you can read the words *Ego sum Lux*. A very durable technique, the art of lights, mosaics was therefore better than painting, the ideal artistic method for expressing the truths of an eternal faith. In this sense, this religious art very early became a "catechism in pictures" for the use of the small and humble, and, to reprise the saying of St. Gregory the Great: *Quod legentibus scriptura, hoc idiotis picture* (*Lib.* IX, *Epist.* 209). Mosaics, "painting in stone," according to the traditional expression, was for simple souls what writing was for those who knew how to read. Or, to use the terms of one of the first historians of mosaics, P. Le Viel: "The holy pontiffs, often great philosophers, felt that the impression on the senses and the effect on the imagination would act upon ordinary Christians as well as on idolaters." In certain cases a mosaic itself became holy. Take, for example, the mosaics of the apse of St. Clement's church in Rome (12th century), whose inscription speaks of the image of Christ on the cross placed in the center of the dome: it explains that, among the squares that make up the body of the Lord, they inserted two teeth from St. James and St. Ignatius. The mosaic thus became a reliquary as well as a sacred expression of faith.

Finally, the idea of the continuity of traditions of the Church, of which the pope is the guardian, found, in mosaics, a particularly well-suited "vector." From the beginnings of the Christian era to the 18th century, the technique of mosaics never varied and the repertoire of ornamental forms remained, for the most part, unchanged. This form of sacred art, handed down using a tradition shaped in Rome, allows us to understand the special characteristics of Christian mosaics, which are restoration, redoing them according to ancient plans, and even the transposition of new materials from older mosaics, which were used by the popes. As much as pagan art was ready to destroy and replace a mosaic with another one, so the Christian version was the object of constant restorations, to the point that these "masterpieces of respect" were often veritable "patchworks" on which successive centuries had left their mark. One of the most striking examples was the mosaic in the cupola of ST. JOHN LATERAN where Christ's head stands out distinctively from the style of the figures surrounding him, due to its archaic construction. But this difference may be better understood if we remember that this head was considered, since the beginning of the Middle Ages, as "miraculously preserved." Among the remnants of the first mosaic, somewhat destroyed, it appeared mysteriously intact during the 13th century to the mosaicist Jacopo Torriti, sent by Pope NICHOLAS IV to redo the vault. The artist would have had less difficulty obeying the orders of the pope, who wanted this face put back in place without modification, if he had assembled, on a slab of marble, according to the ancient technique, some "*emblemata*" put together separately and then inserted them in place. Even in the second restoration that the mosaicists of LEO XIII did in 1884, the "miraculous" figure was treated in such a way as to suggest the expression of the faces at the end of the 4th century, of which it is a distant reflection. Another example shows this desire for continuity: the mosaic of "Christ among the Doctors," given by JOHN PAUL II to UNESCO in Paris in 1980, is a work full of history, although quite modern. The scene was borrowed directly from one of the religious tableaux from the arch of St. Mary Major, which goes back to the pontificate of SIXTUS III (432–40); the tessera are cubes of glass made in 1727 by the papal studio at St. Peter's in Rome; and the frame of gilded bronze, poured for PIUS VI in 1796, had the coat of arms of John Paul II added to it.

Pagan Imagery and Christian Symbolism. Still, even if it has remained the expression of a tradition, papal mosaics have not been an essential "conservative" art, or more exactly, its conservatism was constantly renewed by novel interpretations aiming to give images a Christian feel, which improved them. First, we must emphasize that paganism had accumulated an exceptional wealth of images, especially mythological ones, which were obsolete with the triumph of Christianity. What remained were purely ornamental decorations or scenes less stamped with their pagan origins, which could be reused with just a few semantic changes; for the workrooms in charge of the new mosaic overlays in the churches were the same as in the past, and papal orders could not totally obliterate the knowledge of a culture, or an imagination, of which these artisans were the descendants. That is the reason why we see that, until the end of the Middle Ages at least, a large part of the ancient imagery is the basis or the web upon which new, truly Christian images were embroidered. Certain motifs were preserved as they were, such as the branches of flowers and fruits escaping from great kraters in the angles of the vaults, which were so often used in the mosaics of the late imperial time, especially in Africa: they continue to symbolize the profusion and abundance of goods, but here, it is those the Christian will enjoy in the afterlife. We must mention, among others, the mosaic of Pope PASCHAL I (828–44) on the ceiling of Santa Maria in Domnica in Rome, where the pontiff is shown at the feet of the Virgin, under a garland of flowers and fruits interlaced by a ribbon, doubled by a band studded with gems, both absolutely identical to some motifs in pagan pavements from the 4th and 5th centuries.

Much the same at St. Clement's, the foliage whose spirals are peopled with profane scenes (little cherubs riding dolphins, fighting with geese, etc.) could be, at first glance, in the pagan style. But, superimposed on the Dionysian background design is the Tree of Life, marked by the cross placed over its center, which explains its significance, sheltering the fathers of the Latin Church in an enjoyable companionship where St. Gregory and St. Am-

brose occupy spaces next to those of the harvesting "putti." The most striking thing is not that the 12th century artist used ancient motifs, probably borrowed from a previous mosaic whose spirit he respected, if not its letter, but that he recopied a pagan motif by deforming it, because he did not understand it: at the feet of Christ, a deer is surrounded by an enigmatic arabesque in which we see the legendary scene taken from Roman bestiaries, where the deer, devoured by a serpent, is reborn to a new life. Drawn by the more current image of the thirsty deer that wants a drink of fresh water, the artist unconsciously altered the motif by replacing the serpent with an ornamental curl. In other cases, an exegete guided the mosaicist, making him accompany a scene with a few explanatory words; thus, at Santa Maria in Trastevere, the classic theme of the bird in the cage is depicted with the saying *Christus Dominus captus est in peccatis nostris* as if they felt at the time of INNOCENT I (1130–43), who had this mosaic redone, that this scene inherited from pagan times needed to be explained so that it could be truly understood. We find recovery of a repertoire and semantic deviations in the dove, the bird of Venus, which became the sign of the apostles in the 12th century on the cross of St. Clement and was the emblem of INNOCENT III (1198–1216) in the mosaic restored for the pontiff at St. Peter's in Rome, before becoming the symbol of the Holy Spirit that we know today. John Paul II had it again copied in mosaic form, but with an olive branch so that it became the symbol of universal peace that he gave to the United Nations in 1979. If we go from individual motifs to group subjects, we see that the choice of images is inseparable from the personality of the pope who ordered them; it is the reflection of his personal, family, or, most often, theological preoccupations, or even political in many cases. We can show, for example, how much the mosaics of the St. Zeno chapel in the church of St. Praxedes in Rome, done around 820 on the order of Paschal I in honor of his mother Theodora, were marked by his personality, his antique-loving tastes, and his desire for Roman "*renovation.*"

In the church of St. Mary Major, Émile Mâle had already detected echoes of the Council of Ephesus, and the details of the scenes relating to Epiphany that were the exact illustration of the sermons of Pope LEO I the Great, who may have been the direct inspiration for the choice of scenes for the triumphal arch. Some clearly political resonances have been seen in certain mosaics from the 12th century, where the presence of the Virgin is not without significance in the scenes of the emperors' investitures. Sometimes, papal authority brought forth simple legends in order to give them an easy-to-decipher political significance. Such was the miraculous healing of Constantine, attacked by leprosy and saved by Pope SILVESTER I's baptism, which appears several times in order to remind the holders of political power that they are nothing without the ruling pontiff. A mosaic with this scene was placed on the triumphal arch of the ancient basilica of St. Peter's in Rome. At the time of the Investiture Controversy, notably in the fight of Alexander III (1159–81) against Frederick Barbarossa, the scene was redone at the insistence of the pope. It was seen on the portico of St. John Lateran, around 1170, and even in the Saint-Maximus basilica at Riez (Alpes-de-Haute-Provence) in a similar political context, probably right after the Lateran Council in 1179, where it reminded them of the attitude of submission of the first emperor, who converted when he received his salvation and his power from the hands of St. Peter's successor. Paleo-Christian and medieval mosaics have, therefore, been much more that an art of ornamentation perpetuating ancient traditions: They served to edify simple souls who found the images spoke to them of the various teachings of the Church, but they were also an arm in the service of the papal ideology. Whether the mosaics were Roman in style, or Byzantine, or Venetian, according to the strength or weakness of the workshops of the capital of the Christian world, they were original, because the mosaicists who created them were directed by the pope. Entry into modern times allows us to verify this essential characteristic.

The Renaissance and the Modern Period. Due to the encouragement of Gregory XIII (1572–85), there was a renaissance of Roman mosaics. The pivotal year was 1578 when the workshop in Rome had no more workers capable of executing the grandiose plans of the pope. He was therefore forced to ask the Republic of Venice to lend him "four artists, among the best you have in the field of mosaics," but it was with the intention of creating a new, stable workshop in Rome, which would allow him to be free of any dependence on Venice. Having inherited the Byzantine traditions, and strengthened by a technical mastery in the field of glass making, Venice had always been the great rival, with numerous, powerful workshops. By encouraging a large-scale program (the "Gregorian" chapel), which could have important extensions, Gregory XIII found enough work to maintain a permanent workshop. Given the quality of the results (the mountings were by Girolamo Muziano) after two years of work, the workshop began work recovering the walls of the "Clementine" chapel in St. Peter's and then, under Clement VIII, they began the mosaics on the vault of the main cupola, a gigantic work that required no less than a dozen workers who labored on this until 1612.

This order definitively launched the workshop of St. Peter's, whose mosaic work sites were continuously busy until 1757. In 1727, the workshop was given a proper building and took the name of "*Studio vaticano dal mosaico*," with a superintendent as its leader who, at that time, was the famous mosaicist Pietro Paolo Cristofari,

one of the most fecund artists among all those who would later be called "Sanpietrini." This papal workshop was the breeding ground where all the European nations during the 18th century got their mosaicists who, in turn, created French, English, and Russian workshops, among others, which progressively disappeared. Only the Studio del Vaticano still survives today. Its development was also due to the fact that the orders did not end when the recovering of the basilica was complete. In a second phase, the Vatican workshop was given the task of changing all the altar paintings into mosaic murals. The first one to be done in mosaic form was the *St. Michael Archangel* of the chapel bearing the same name (around 1627), but the copy was vigorously criticized by purists because of the brilliant reflections brought about by the use of multicolored glass cubes as the medium.

It took until 1731 for the movement to become irreversible. At this date, an Italian chemist, A. Mattioli, perfected a procedure for manufacturing cubes using powdered marble, linseed oil, and colored pigments. It was then possible to make up to 15,000 different hues, this number later expanding to 28,000. This was the long-dreamed-of means for mosaicists to imitate the nuances created by painters. The workshop plunged into the systematic copying of all the canvases in the basilica. The president of Brosses, traveling in Italy in 1739–40, marveled at these masterpieces that time could no longer destroy: "The best thing they are doing now is to remove all the paintings from the chapels of St. Peter's that the humidity had completely ruined, replacing them with mosaic copies, the most beautiful that anyone has ever seen."

This was a new period of intense activity for the Studio del Vaticano. From 1731 to 1822, all the canvases of St. Peter's were copied in mosaics. Among the masterpieces from this time are the immense *Transfiguration of Christ*, from Raphael's painting, done between 1759 and 1767, which required six of the workshop's mosaicists, and the *Martyrdom of St. Petronilla*, a copy of the painting by Le Guerchin. The action of Pope Clement XI to speed up these orders was decisive. The insertion of religious subjects into profane ones was unnoticeable. The portrait of Pope Clement XII with Cardinal Corsini at his side by P. P. Cristofari is one of the papal orders done for the great Roman families. They could also count on the restoration of ancient works discovered during archeological digs to furnish some work. In particular, the unearthing of Hadrian's Villa in Tivoli by the teams of Cardinal Marefoschi in 1780 allowed the "Pope's Museum" to be remarkably enriched, but the pavements acquired at great cost were heavily restored, and the director of the Académie Française wrote: "When it all will be repaired, half the work will be modern, [. . .] the substitution was done in such a way that only the pope can stand it." This restoration work and these copies, which pandered to an antique-loving style favored by the tastes of collectors for the pontiffs (especially BENEDICT XIV, to whom Monsignor Furietti dedicated his *De musivis*, the first work on mosaics, in 1751), were soon not enough to keep the "Sanpietrini" busy.

Many private workshops were already working in Rome to supplement a growing demand for small generic mosaics, which foreign visitors bought: we see country scenes, scenes with animals, and especially views of the main monuments in Rome. To avoid this competition, the "Reverend Fabric of St. Peter's" decided to also add compositions of a profane nature to its repertoire. It was also pressured by the fact that a new technique had begun to be used by mosaicists. It was based on a perfecting of Mattioli's invention and consisted of making, from the malleable paste he had created, some *smalti filati*, or elements similar to spun glass in colors, no longer cubes or quadrangles, but able to take any desired shape for the artist. The mosaicist was then able to make a sort of tiny puzzle, whose joints were almost invisible. Thereafter, it was possible to imitate painting, not only in the pictures for altars, destined to be viewed from a certain distance and which still used classic tessera (a technique called *mosaico in grande*), but also on smaller surfaces, which could be admired as closely as possible (a technique called *mosaico minuto*). This new possibility gave the papal workshop other outlets. It began to produce views of St. Peter's in large numbers, and admirable tables bearing a series of figured medallions. For example, we know of the table called "Achilles' Shield," decorated with scenes from the *Iliad*, which LEO XII gave to King Charles X of France.

In the area of small pieces, the workshop also excelled in medallions, like the portrait of PIUS VII, which had the quality of miniatures from the 18th century, or in the decoration of objects encrusted with mosaics like the snuff box that the same Pius VII gave as a gift, on the occasion of Napoleon's coronation, to his brother Joseph Bonaparte. The large orders that produced all the altar images in the sizes of the original paintings were also renewed in the form of copies in a reduced size, which the pope gave to his illustrious guests. An example is the masterpiece of miniaturization by the mosaicist Aguati, a *Descent from the Cross* copied from the famous painting by Caravaggio, or the *St. Michael Archangel*, a smaller version of the mosaic drawn from the painting by Guido Reni, which was, for a long time, part of Josephine de Beauharnais's collection. The time of mosaics on walls being in complete accord with architecture seemed to have passed. We have a record of this when Pope PIUS IX had the restoration of St. Paul's Outside-the-Walls with a series of 258 medallions in mosaic, representing portraits of his predecessors, which ten artists from the studio did around 1847. Despite the placement of these portraits on the façade, it was still in a painterly tradition. A late attempt (in 1896) to associate the life of the papal court to the

themes of the mosaics from the workshop of the Vatican was doomed. There are hardly any of this type except the one by B. Barzotti representing LEO XIII receiving three cardinals on the terraces of the Vatican, and whose effect is rather mediocre. Since the end of the 19th century, the Vaticano studio has no longer shown any originality in its work. In any case, the workshops of Ravenna, or even those of the school at Spilimbergo seem to be much more lively, and if they cannot rival the technical perfection and the immense variety of colors of the materials accumulated by the papal workshop, they are more creative and more open to contemporary art.

If we look at the general evolution of the art of papal mosaics, we must recognize that as much as it was the expression of a living, active faith, an imagination constantly enriched by new interpretations of the ancient repertoire and by theological or political reflections on the Gospel message or on the mission of the Church in the world (that is to say, from the origins of Christianity until about the middle of the 18th century), it knew how to remain lively and inventive. After it succumbed to the temptations of painting, it could only imitate its rival. Perhaps the mosaicists of the Vatican, who had earned the coveted title of *pittori di mosaico*, lost their soul to it.

Henri Lavagne

Bibliography

Bulletin d'information de l'Association internationale pour l'étude de la mosaïque antique, 1968–91.

De Brosses, C. *Lettre familières sur l'Italie*, Paris, 1930.

De Rossi, G. B. *Musaici cristiani e saggi di pavimenti delle chiese di Roma anteriori al secolo XV*, Rome, 1873–99.

Grabar, A. *Les Voies de la création en iconographie chrétiénne*, Paris, 1979.

Ladner, G. B. *Die Papstbildnisse des Altertums und des Mittelalters*, 3 vols., Vatican City, 1941–82.

Lavagne, H. *La mosaïque*, Paris, 1987.

Lavagne, H. "Triomphe et baptême de Constantin," *Journal des savants*, 1977, 164–90.

Le Viel, P. *Essai sur la peinture en mosaïque*, Paris, 1768.

Mâle, E. *Rome et ses vieilles églises*, Paris, 1950.

Matthiae, G. *Le chiese di Roma dal IV al X secolo*, Rome, 1962.

Nilgen, U. "Maria Regina, ein politischer Kultbildtypus," *Römische Jahrbuch für Künstgeschichte*, 19 (1981) 1–33.

Oakeshott, W. *The Mosaics of Rome from the Third to the Fourteenth Century*, London, 1967.

Petochi, D., Alfieri, M., and Branchetti, M. G. *I mosaici minuti romani dei sec. XVIII e XIX*, Rome, 1981.

Sand, G. *Les Maîtres mosaïstes*, Paris, 1993.

Walter, C. "Papal Political Imagery in the Medieval Lateran Palace," *Cahiers archéologiques*, 21 (1971), 109–36.

MOSCOW. See **Third Rome (Moscow)**.

MOVIMENTO CATTOLICO. The term *Movimento cattolico* appeared in Italy beginning in the 19th century (a heading bears this title in the CIVILTÀ CATTOLICA in 1871). Bearing the same name was the official publication of the *Opera dei congressi*, the first organization for all of Catholic Italy, from 1880 to 1904. The term refers to the "movement" or activity of Catholics in Italian society. In the 1950s, this expression was chosen by historians of both Marxist and Catholic leaning. For the former, it was the totality of Italian forces under the control of the papacy, and for the latter, the *Movimento* encompassed all the Catholic attitudes, in particular that of the laity, regarding the ruptures in Italian society due to bourgeois and liberal changes. The latter definition may be used to characterize the *Movimento*, whereas the first puts the accent on its deeper meaning: the closeness to and influence of the HOLY SEE. From 1861 to 1919, and the founding of the Italian People's Party and direct entry of Italian Catholics into politics, Catholics began to take an active role in society. Historians of various tendencies agree that the existence of the *Movimento*, however, extends beyond 1919. Its evolution may, therefore, be examined up to the present.

Beginnings and Nonpolitical Phase. Within the framework of a unified Italy, the first organized Catholic movement was created. It was dominated by the continuing current of thought that rejected the *Risorgimento* and unity as expressions of lay ideology, encouraged by the firm positions taken by PIUS IX and LEO XIII, forbidding any Catholic participation in Italian political life. The "compromised" Catholics, heirs of various secular currents of the 18th century, saw the national process as a political phenomenon that did not affect the religious sphere. Obeying papal directives, the Italian Catholics organized into militant groups favoring popular action and organization. The first notable group, the *Opera dei congressi*, was founded in Florence in 1875 after a preparatory congress in Venice in 1874. The *Opera*, structured into regional, diocesan, and parish committees, added to its title, in 1881, *e dei comitati cattolici in Italia*. It was inspired by German and Belgian models, but had very specific aspects because of its proximity to the Holy See.

The Roman question was foremost on the list of the *Opera*'s preoccupations, and influenced its political inflexibility, in particular during the presidency of Paganuzzi (1889–1902). It brilliantly led actions that were educational, social (rural banks, workingmen's societies), and editorial (a Catholic press) that were outside the political realm. The ENCYCLICAL *Rerum novarum* (1891) gave a strong impetus to the work, but left the political question open (*non expedit* of Leo XIII—creation of a Catholic party in the Italian institutional structure). The serious political and social crises of 1898 made a strong impact on many Catholics and accelerated political reflection. We see a "clerico-moderate" tendency appear, agreeing to collaborate under certain conditions with the liberal state (this tendency ended much later, in 1913, with an electoral agreement with the governmental party, the famous Gentiloni pact). On the other hand, the priest Romolo Murri wanted a popular opening for the movement, and he launched a Christian Democratic platform in 1899. This led Leo XIII to set limits for such a movement in the encyclical *Graves de communi* (1901). Murri tried, during the presidency of Grosoli (1902–4) to influence the work in the direction of his ideas (in particular, on freedom). He was not far from success when PIUS X, obsessed by this evolution, which coincided with the MODERNIST crisis, decided to suppress the *Opera* in 1904. Consequently, the pope greatly changed the thrust of the *Movimento* by the encyclical *Il fermo propositio* (1905), which created three autonomous branches. The leadership of the *Movimento* was decisively returned to the Holy See. Romolo Murri left the Church and was excommunicated in 1909. The *Movimento*, though battered, regrouped under Giuseppe Toniolo (1845–1918), whom Maurice Vaussard, in 1920, hailed as the only great leader that Italian lay Catholicism had known. Toniolo, a fervent Christian and a prominent sociologist, remained an emblematic figure in the *Movimento*. In his many writings, especially in a *Treatise on Social Economy*, he was able to establish ties between Catholic doctrine and a social renovation that he felt was indispensable, out of respect for humanity. This professor from the University of Pisa was one of the principal inspirations of the *Movimento* during this early period.

Diversification of the Movement. In 1919, with the agreement of BENEDICT XV, the Italian People's Party (PPI) was founded under the impetus of Don Sturzo, while, slowly, Catholic Action took shape, soon becoming the "apple of [Pius XI's] eye." The difficult fascist period, which led to the disappearance of the PPI, has been read in various ways by the historians of the *Movimento*. Some regard it as a gray period of minimal activity and compromise, which centered on religious values. The pontificate of PIUS XI may also be seen as a waiting phase, one of survival for a movement that kept its distance from political action. In any case, after 1945, there was an extraordinary blossoming of various actions that emerged from the *Movimento*. We see a certain continuity of inspiration and a continuation of the characteristics of the Italian movement. This was expressed politically by the powerful Christian Democrats (DCI). This pivotal party of the Italian Republic, rooted in the Italian people, mixed a taste for management with a desire for deep social reforms and a concern for the family. There were many debates, as there were during the entire history of the *Movimento*, and we see two tendencies distinguishing themselves for further study.

The DCI accomplished, during the years after the war, reforms that profoundly changed Italian society. State planning and intervention were used in certain sectors and, in the agrarian area, the reforms undertaken fit well with the policies of the *Movimento* that quickly impacted on the peasant economy and reforms "for social utility." The same remark may be applied in the associative area. The *Coldiretti*, for example, defended small rural farms, economically and culturally. In the world of the working man, a characteristic response had been made to the great question of organizing into large corporations. The debate had been lively at the beginning of the century about the creation of worker's syndicates. The creation of the CIL in 1918 resolved nothing, because the fascist experiment obliterated everything soon afterward. The attitudes of the Holy See toward Italy had long been ambivalent. Also, in 1944, when all the Italian collectives had united under the Pact of Rome, the Catholic workers were invited to join the ACLI (*Associazioni cristiane lavoratori italiani*), with the goal of reorganizing workers to promote Christian principles in religious, moral, and cultural domains. The *circolo* was the place to take action and hold meetings, allowing workers to affirm their identity. It was not until 1950 that an independent union, the CISL, was created to act within the framework of democratic unions.

On the intellectual front, the FUCI (Federation of Italian Catholic University Students) continued action taken vigorously since 1896. This federation of intellectuals, marked by the thoughts of Tonolio and Contardo Ferrini, in line with the Holy See, became of capital importance during the presidency of Igino Righetti and the ecclesiastical adviser G. B. Montini (1925–33), later Pope PAUL VI. Under the impetus of the latter, the FUCI was inspired by German and especially French thought (particularly that of Jacques Maritain).

Through great editorial action, the federation tried to form elites. After 1933, the creation of the *Movimento laureati* continued the actions of the FUCI. Important names illustrate this association, which continued its rise after 1945 in another political and religious realm. The ministry of the future Paul VI in the FUCI was, for him, a determining step in his reflections, and we see here, very concretely, the new links between the *Movimento* and the papacy. All in all, the *Movimento cattolico* kept the constituent and common characteristics that make it so original in European Catholicism. Nevertheless, over the decades changes have occurred. In the 1960s, the Christian Democrats, with the support of JOHN XXIII, engaged in dialogue with the leftist parties. The CISL, again became interested in joining the other unions. The ACLI progressively grew less religious, while the FUCI saw a rapid evolution in the 1970s, confronted by other types of organizations claiming to be Catholic. With the advent of the 21st century, the *Movimento* has had to adapt in response to new circumstances, yet many insist on the necessity of clearly maintaining its Christian identity in Italian society, while offering a lay Catholic response to the social issues of contemporary Italy.

Marc Agostino

Bibliography

Dizionario storico del Movimento cattolico in Italia (1860–1980), 5 vols., Turin, 1981–4, ed. by F. Traniello and G. Campanini.

Il movimento cattolico e la società italiana in 100 anni di storia, Acts of the Colloquium of Venice on the Catholic Movement, Rome, 1976.

Mayeur, J. M. *Catholicisme social et démocratie chrétienne*, Paris, 1986.

Vaussard, M. *L'Intelligence catholique dans l'Italie du XXe siècle*, 2nd ed., Paris, 1921.

MUSEUMS, VATICAN. The history of the formation of the diverse and rich collections joined together under the name "Vatican Museums" is inseparable from that of the pontiffs. The origin of these collections may be found at the beginning of the 16th century during the pontificate of JULIUS II (1503–13). A great lover of works of art, he took the interior court of the small palace called "del Belvedere" which INNOCENT VIII (1484–92) had built on a hillside overlooking (to the north) St. PETER'S BASILICA and the palace of the Vatican, and filled it with ancient marbles. Until PAUL III (1534–49), this collection was ceaselessly enriched. From JULIUS III (1550–5) to PIUS IV (1559–65), the pontiffs improved it. Several masterpieces were there that are known worldwide including the *Apollo* and the famous *Torso* to which the addition of the word *Belvedere* was made, the grouping of the *Laocoön*, the two twin colossal statues of the *Tiber* and the *Nile*, the *Ariadne Asleep* that was then thought to be—and would continue thus for a long time—a *Cleopatra Dying*, and so forth.

The pontificate of the austere PIUS V (1566–72) brought this action to a complete halt. The pontiff believed that such monuments profaned the apostolic palace. Numerous statues were taken from the Vatican and only the fierce opposition of influential members of the CURIA stopped it all from being systematically dispersed. GREGORY XIII (1572–85) and SIXTUS V (1585–90) observed the same inflexibility, which continued through 17th century. It was not until the pontificate of CLEMENT XI (1700–21) that the remainder of the collection came out of oblivion. The erudite Francesco Bianchini added a group of pagan and Christian inscriptions to it. Then a project was begun to open a Museo Ecclesiastico; this initiative faltered, but the initial impulse had been given. CLEMENT XII (1730–40),

BENEDICT XIV (1740–58), and CLEMENT XIII (1758–69), surrounded by learned men like Venuti, Vettori, and especially Winckelmann, developed the research and the collection of ancient objects (sculptures and inscriptions, vases and coins, etc.), many of which were given to the Apostolic Library, which opened a Museo Sacro in 1756, and a Museo Profano in 1767.

CLEMENT XIV (1769–74) demonstrated this renewed interest in enriching and displaying the Vatican collections in magnificent fashion. In 1770 the pontiff acquired the Fusconi and Mattei collections. Behind this initiative we find Giambattista Visconti, whom the pope had named commissioner for antiquities and who was soon charged with building a real museum to display these two collections. From 1771 to 1773, the architects Alessandro Dori and then Michelangelo Simonetti built a monumental ensemble in which Visconti presented the marbles acquired by the pontiff. The former courtyard of the Belvedere (today the Cortile Ottagono) where the statues brought in from Julius II to Paul III still stood, was rearranged and encompassed by a quadruple vestibule on one side (the east), two great galleries on the other side, the double Animals Room (to the west) where the *Tiber* and the *Nile* were installed, and the Gallery of Statues and Busts (to the north) where the "*cosidetta*" *Cleopatra Dying* was displayed. The Museo Clementino was born and would soon be enlarged. In effect, Pope PIUS VI (1775–99) augmented the work of his predecessor. By new acquisitions and by an active policy of excavations, the collection was enriched. New buildings were constructed under the auspices of Michelangelo Simonetti. From 1776 until 1784, we see, grafted onto the Animals Room of the Museo Clementino, several prestigious additions such as the Room of the Muses (where today we find the *Belvedere Torso*); the Rotunda, in the center of which the great porphyry basin from the Domus Aurea of Nero is displayed; the Greek Cross Room, which had the two great sarcophagi made of porphyry of Constance (the daughter of Constantine) and of St. Helen (the mother of Constantine); and finally the monumental staircase by which one accessed what afterwards was named the Museo Pio-Clementino.

Beginning in 1785, a second round of work was undertaken, which lasted until 1793 and to which the architect Giuseppe Camporese, successor to Simonetti (d. in 1787) and Filippo Aurelio Visconti, who followed his father (d. in 1784) as commissioner of antiquities, devoted themselves. They set up the Candelabra Room and the pavilion "dei Quatro Cancelli," which became the official entrance of the museum as well as sheltering the famous Bige Room. In addition to this enormous effort to present these examples of ancient sculpture, the first Picture Gallery (Pinacoteca) of the Vatican was set up and installed in the expanded part of the Candelabra room (where the tapestries are today) thus joining the gallery of Geographic Maps built between

1578 and 1580 by Ottaviano Mascherino, originally decorated by Ignazio Danti. These were barely completed when all this work seemed to be irremediably ruined by the vigorous expansion of the young and hungry French republic. Article 13 of the treaty of Tolentino (19 February 1797) stipulated "the completion, as promptly as possible" of one of the clauses of the armistice of Bologna, which specified the transfer to Paris of 100 major works of art that a commission of experts was appointed to select. The Museo Pio-Clementino and the brand new Vatican Picture Gallery were heavily raided. Among other masterpieces, the following left for France: the *Laocoön* and the *Apollo Belvedere*, the *Nile* and the *Tiber*, the *Torso*, and paintings by Raphael, Caravaggio, Guercino, as well as 500 of the most precious manuscripts, numismatic collections, and cameos, which were taken from the Apostolic Library. Still, despite the vicissitudes of his papacy, PIUS VII (1800–23) pursued with energy, tenacity, dedication, and ambition the path trod by his two predecessors. With the assistance of his inspector general of fine arts, the sculptor Antonio Canova, the pontiff decided to found his own museum. Once again, acquisitions and digs made it possible to gather rich groupings of ancient marbles: almost 1,000 busts and sculptures were installed from 1807 to 1810 by Canova in the long gallery along the eastern edge of the cortile della Pigna, which became the Museo Chiaramonti.

By a fortunate turn of events, the restitution in 1816 of many of the works taken earlier to Paris made another exemplary accomplishment possible: in 1822 the gallery of Braccio Nuovo was opened, thanks to architects Raffaele Stern and Pasquale Belli. In it, on the southern side of the cortile della Pigna, the masterpieces of monumental statuary returned from Paris after the treaty of Vienna were displayed, placed in fifty-six niches evenly spaced on both sides of an exedra or throne next to the *Nile*, back from its exile, but unfortunately separated from its twin the *Tiber*, which remained at the Louvre where it still may be seen. Later, this gallery was enriched with one of the most famous statues of all the Vatican museums: the statue of *Augustus*, discovered in 1863 in the Villa Livia at Prima Porta. On the other side of the cortile della Pigna, after their return from Paris in 1816, paintings were collected in the Borgia apartments (which today contain a part of the collection of modern religious art) where the Pinacoteca Pius VI had wanted was recreated and expanded.

Although the Vatican museums made no notable acquisitions during the pontificates of LEO XII (1823–9) and PIUS VIII (1829–30), the reign of GREGORY XVI (1831–46) was one of the most fruitful: four new museums were founded under this pontiff. Two were put in the LATERAN Palace: one picture gallery and a museum of ancient sculptures called, from its founding in 1844, Museo Gregoriano Profano. Two others were situated in the Vatican itself, in the north wing of the cortile della Pigna. The first was the Museo Gregoriano Etrusco, begun in 1837. Collections of Etruscan antiquities and Greek ceramics from Etruria, previously separate, were brought together again and then considerably increased by acquisitions and the results of recent digs like those of Todi (the famous *Mars*), Cerveteri, and others. The second was the Museo Gregoriano Egizio, opened two years later in 1839; Egyptian and Egyptian-influenced pieces scattered throughout the Vatican or in other Roman museums (in particular those of the Capitol where, under Benedict XIV, the Egyptian-style antiquities of Hadrian's Villa had been installed) were all reunited in this new museum. The recent discovery by Champollion and the birth of Egyptology had just promoted Egyptian artifacts from the rank of "curiosities" to that of historic documents and, Egypt being fashionable, the architect Giuseppe Fabris thought up an astonishing Egyptian décor for this museum (columns, throated cornices, etc.) that were finished off by an amazing hymn to the reigning pontiff written in hieroglyphics by the Barnabite Egyptologist L. Ungarelli, the first director of this museum (research at the end of the 20th century made it possible to rediscover these interesting accomplishments).

Besides the foundation in 1854 of a Christian museum at the Lateran Palace, balancing the profane one of Gregory XVI, the long tumultuous pontificate of Pius IX (1846–78) made no major changes in the museums themselves. It was the same during the pontificates of Leo XIII (1878–1903), Pius X (1903–14), and Benedict XV (1914–22). After this long hiatus, the pontificate of Pius XI (1922–39) made a brilliant mark in the history of the Vatican museums. Pius XI wanted to respond to a triple need: to further enrich the collections, to make them more and more accessible, and to watch over their maintenance. In 1926, an ethnological museum was founded (and temporarily installed in the Lateran Palace), containing the 40,000 objects and documents sent from every part of the globe to illustrate the great missionary exposition that had been held in 1925 in the Vatican. In 1932, the architect Luca Beltrami constructed a special building to house the Vatican Picture Gallery, ending the many moves it had made during its stay within the Vatican. That same year, a new and monumental entrance to the museums was inaugurated, opening onto the viale Vaticano, allowing easy, direct access for an eager and large audience (400,000 visitors in 1925). Architect Giuseppe Momo and the founder, Antonio Marsini, designed a magnificent layout articulated around the impressive double helix staircases with a sumptuous bronze handrail. In 1933, finally, the Bureau of Scientific Research was installed, completing the restoration laboratories instituted since 1923. These were the initiatives that ushered Vatican museums into the modern phase of their history, by opening them fully to the world, on the human as well as on the technical level.

Although the pontificate of Pius XII (1939–58) held no spectacular achievements (except—as an anecdote—the restoration in 1957 of the Laocoön group, whose original right arm was returned to it, fortunately found and skillfully identified by Ludwig Pollak at the beginning of the century), it was not so for that of John XXIII (1958–63), and especially for that of Paul VI (1963–78). In 1963, on the initiative of John XXIII, construction was begun on a large new museum to hold three collections that had been displayed in the Lateran Palace until then: the ancient sculptures put there by Gregory XVI in 1844 and called the Museo Gregoriano Profano; the paleo-Christian antiquities assembled by Pius IX in 1854 and called the Museo Pio-Cristiano; and the ethnological artifacts collected in 1926 under Pius XI, which then became the Museo Missionario Etnologico. The building, done in an avant-garde style by brothers Fausto Lucio and Vincenzo Passarelli, was opened in 1970. In 1973, Paul VI began two new museums. The first, to which the pontiff attached particular importance, was the Collezione di Arte Religiosa moderna, with sculptures, paintings, and other works of art illustrating religious sentiment in contemporary art. It was located in the Apostolic Palace itself: the Borgia rooms and the apartments of Alexander VI (1492–1503), which were connected to ancient sites located beneath the Sistine Chapel. The other is the Museo Storico, which has two sections: one contains carriages, sedans, and automobiles used by the popes, housed in a huge underground room constructed under the Giardino Quadrato; the other section, which has been in the Lateran Palace since 1985, includes an iconographic collection of the popes, part of the picturesque objects having gone out of usage in ceremonies ("SEDIA GESTATORIA", fans, sedan chairs, etc.), the uniforms of the military groups dissolved in 1968, and a collection of antique arms.

We could not end this brief look without mentioning actual life in the museums of the Vatican under Pope John Paul II. In 1989 the Museo Gregoriano Egizio was totally renovated to celebrate the 150th anniversary of its founding; the Museo Gregoriano Etrusco was enlarged; and the scientific research laboratories were modernized and expanded. Under his pontificate major art exhibitions were undertaken. Many masterpieces from the Vatican museums traveled to the United States of America and to Japan. Beginning in 1981, and completed in 1995, the frescoes of the Sistine Chapel were cleaned and restored. Only a rare few were privileged enough to be able to gaze at the few statues that Julius II had grouped in the little courtyard of the Belvedere. Today more than 2 million visitors a year come to admire one of the richest collections of art and cultural treasures in the world, which has been assembled by the munificence of popes over more than five centuries.

Jean-Claude Grenier

Bibliography

Pietrangeli, S. *I Musei Vaticani—Cinque secolie di storia*, Rome, 1985.

NAPOLEONIC EMPIRE. See **First French Empire and the Papacy.**

NATION. See **Churches, National, in Rome.**

NATIONAL CLERIC. The post of national cleric of the Sacred College was first created at the time of establishment of the College of Cardinals of the Roman church, councilors and electors of the papacy, during the Third Lateran Council. The council was held in 1179 during the papacy of ALEXANDER III (1159–81).

There were three national clerics: one Germanic, one French, and one Spaniard (before the Anglican Schism there was also an Englishman), who with the prior agreement of the College of Cardinals, were appointed by their respective sovereigns. They were clerics of the Sacred College and for the consistories assisted the secretary of the Italian consistorial congregation. The secretary was appointed by the pope and has sometimes been wrongly referred to as the Italian national cleric.

In principle the national clerics took turns in the performance of their duties. They stood beside the consistorial advocate for the postulation of the PALLIUM. During his one-year period of service, the national cleric had to be prepared for all eventualities. He was called on to perform various duties, for example, chapel services for deceased cardinals, the NOVENDIALS of dead popes, and the Corpus Domini procession, and he accompanied the cardinal CAMERLENGO on his way to and from the Sacred College. The national cleric could not be a family member of the pope or of a cardinal or prelate (Constitution of Pope PAUL III, 19 June 1546). Furthermore, he had to be tonsured and celibate.

National clerics were entitled to receive gifts in kind: bread, so-called Cardinal's salt, a candle twice per year from the pope on 2 February, and from the Sacred College, for Corpus Christi. Upon the death of a cardinal, the cleric received five gold ducats, plus 50 ducats at the time of his appointment (at least such was the case when the post was first created).

Bernard de Lanversin.

Bibliography

Lacroix, P. *Institutions de la France à Rome*, 1892.

NAVY, PAPAL. The origins of a papal fleet of ships go back as far as the 8th century. This may be explained by the proximity of Rome to the sea, and by the necessity of defending itself against attacks from outside the PATRIMONY acknowledged as belonging to the Church by Charlemagne (in 774) and expanded by his successors: in the center of Italy between the Tyrrhenian Sea, from Corneto to Terracina, and the Adriatic, from RAVENNA to Ancona. During the Middle Ages, the naval forces serving the Roman Church were responsible for surveillance and security of the coasts, safeguarding the provisioning of Rome provided by the ports of Latium since Roman times, and linking all the Churches in communication with the Roman see. In the 9th century, the first concern of the popes regarding the seacoasts was defending their territory against the incessant attacks by the SARACENS. The completion of the walls around the Leonine city in 852 was done as a result of a devastating raid in 846, with the constant support of Byzantine ships; their victory in 849 near Ostia was commemorated by Raphael. In 915, Pope JOHN X led a large force against the Saracens, who were entrenched along the Garigliano River. They were driven from Italy.

The objectives of the popes during the 9th and 10th centuries were to reinforce the defense of Ostia; to set up a flotilla of heavy galleys under the command of a naval prefect; and to maintain, not without difficulty, the alliance with the people of Amalfi who were constantly tempted to cooperate with the Saracens. Nevertheless, on the Tyrrhenian side of its patrimony and the maritime province, the Church of Rome had to rely upon the good will of the coastal lords, lay or ecclesiastic, and soon, upon that of the communes at Ancona and at Civitavecchia; the latter was granted special statutes in the 11th century codifying its maritime franchises. They also, more and more, had to rely upon the Genoese, who received trade privileges in exchange for providing security and for assistance with travel, notably due to an agreement negotiated in 1166 by Cardinal Stefano Borgia.

Thus it became customary for the papacy to rely upon Genoese services, in the form of transportation by sea, for destinations outside Italy troubled by war and by schism. GELASIUS II, in 1118, sailed first from Gaeta to Genoa and then, on a ship from Ostia, from Civitavecchia to Marseille via Pisa and the Ligurian coast. Three years later, INNOCENT II fled to France by sea, and 40 years later ALEXANDER III made some difficult crossings: in 1162 he arrived at Hyères and then at Montpellier thanks to five Genoese and Pisan ships; his return in 1165, begun at Narbonne with the assistance of the knights of St. John of Jerusalem, was intercepted by the Pisans, begun again at Maguelonne, and finally finished at Ostia and Rome in winter, by way of a detour through Messina and with the loan of five galleys by the king of Sicily.

Until then, the sea had essentially, on the Tyrrhenian side, played a defensive role, first against Islam and then as a way of avoiding perils within Italy. At the end of the 12th century, the papacy inaugurated, if this could be said appropriately, an active maritime political policy. The cause was the progresses made in papal power, particularly striking under INNOCENT III, when his area of influence extended from the Tyrrhenian to the entire Mediterranean, because of the fourth CRUSADE. At times, pontifical fleets were mentioned, armed partially with money from the Holy See and under its command, sailing under its banner and often overseen by a LEGATE (a latere). From 1195 on, Innocent III had a ship built to carry grain to the Holy Land to the Hospitalers and the Knights Templar, who kept the vessel for their own use in the fourth crusade, whose ships were furnished by the Venetians, paying just the participants' fees and then repaying themselves at the expense of the Byzantines. The fifth crusade benefited from obvious pontifical support because it was putting into effect a decision made by the Fourth Lateran Council. Both maritime sides of the Papal States were asked to contribute; Ancona played a role unlike previous times, by arming eleven vessels, with Ostia and especially Civitavecchia equipping nine, including the admiral's ship, intended for the two cardinals heading the operation. These ships differed little from the types used in the West. The Holy See did not stop its efforts during the 13th century, which was not without difficulty, for Frederick II was trying to cover himself with glory,

and because the pope's ships had to not only confront an emperor in revolt, but also a crusader. When HONORIUS III and GREGORY IX fortified Ostia and Civitavecchia, the main menace was not the Saracens; it was a united group of Christians who defeated the 32 galleys in the service of the pope at La Meloria in 1241. Once more, it was Genoa that INNOCENT IV asked for ships that would allow him to make the quite difficult crossing from Civitavecchia to France (1244). In this effort, the Genoese navy took turns with that of the Angevin king of Naples, who owed support to his papal protector. At the end of the century, in 1290, 20 galleys were armed to serve the pope, this time at Ancona, with a large number of transport vessels, with the goal of bringing help to suffering Acre; but the pontifical navy was only able to evacuate the survivors of the siege to Cyprus in 1291.

The move of the Roman court to AVIGNON between 1305 and 1376 did not relieve the pope from his naval problems. The crusade was still a constant mission. The pacification of the Papal States, necessary before the pope could return to Rome, required a large naval contingent. The correspondence of the papal legates Gil Albornoz and Androin de la Roche (1353–68) in Romagna and in the Marches of Ancona show a lot of activity involving the reprovisioning of grains, wine, and salt under the papal administration's direction, at Rimini, Fano, and especially Ancona. Included in the documentation are licenses, safe-conducts, permits, applications, and exchanges of letters with Venice. As this proceeded in 1351, we find a Genoese captain, Raffaele Roverini, at the head of the papal fleet, and there is a record of Albornoz's thanks to the Doge in Venice for the construction of a galley and the furnishing of materials for other ships at Ancona. Later, in 1370, after Albornoz, the papal treasury paid for the repair of a galley in Ancona including raw materials, Venetian workmen, and the purchase of 220 oars from Venice. Perhaps this was for the *Galea grossa*, which, during the same year, was the "capitane" of the 23 boats the pope brought from Marseille to Italy. This was a slow crossing, full of unforeseen difficulties, by way of Toulon, Saint-Tropez, Fréjus, Antibes, La Turbie, Nice, Villefranche, Sansteva, Albenga, Genoa, Portofino, Portovenere, Porto Pisano, and Piombino. It was impossible to land at Civitavecchia, in the hostile hands of the prefect of Vico, and they were forced to go back up the coast to Corneto. It was from this place that the huge galley from Ancona, escorted by six armed papal galleys, took the pope back up the lower Rhone River to Avignon. The same vessel, at Marseille on 2 October 1376, headed up the 14 Provençal, Castilian, Genoese, and Pisan galleys that finally brought the pope and his followers back to Rome. Once more, the "bark of St. Peter" had difficulties at sea, landing at Portofino after a great storm during which the passengers, through a vow to and the intercession of St. Cyricus, were saved;

Pope Gregory had to go from one galley to another three times before disembarking at Ostia.

Once the SCHISM began, the Avignon successors of Gregory XI also made use of the sea. In 1387 CLEMENT VII had five galleys and another vessel, because the chamberlain François de Conzie had contracted for 19 ships three years earlier. A new supplier was then found: Seville. During these years, the court at Avignon paid part of the naval expenses of Louis of Anjou for his Neapolitan ventures, and of the Duke de Bourbon for his undertaking in northern Africa (14 galleys in 1392–3). BENEDICT XIII added additional expenses for taking Civitavecchia away from Boniface; the city's captain put financial conditions on his surrender. The ports on the Tyrrhenian coast benefited from the political position promoted by Cola di Rienzo in the middle of the 14th century, to free navigation on the Tiber from the tolls exacted by the lords whose domains lay along the river. Regulated in 1384, 1416, and 1461, the sea tax demonstrated the need to patrol an increased marine traffic. Between Monte Argentario and Terracina, ships were assessed an *ad valorem* payment of 4 percent, to which Rome added a 2.5 percent tax for the ports of Ripa and Ripetta near Trastevere. At the mouth of the Tiber, Ostia controlled the movement of the sailing barges (*sandalae*), whose regularity is attested to in literature (the poems of Buccio) and in the archives of the APOSTOLIC CAMERA; a system of safe-conducts with an increase of more than 50 percent shows a large geographic extension of control (130 safe-conducts between 1422 and 1434). Maritime surveillance was handed over in 1398 to Gaspar Cossa, the brother of the future JOHN XXIII, who reorganized the Roman navy. At that time, the correspondence of Francesco di Marco Datini shows evidence of the large number of pilgrims for the jubilee of 1400 who arrived by sea due to the safety provided by the vigilance of the papal fleet.

After the middle of the 15th century, the navy of the Papal States benefited from the restoration to power of the Roman pontiff, if judged by the developments at Ancona and Civitavecchia. Ancona possessed a large, deep waterfront (almost 700,000 square meters), well sheltered, in a favorable geographic position in the center of the Adriatic coast, with the possibility of successfully challenging Ragusa. The formation of its *Maritime Statutes* (1385) had defined this role, the cartographic work of Grazioso Benincasa (in the middle of the 15th century) had shown its prominence, and the strengthening of its fortifications by Antonio Sangallo showed its power (16th century). Ostia and Civitavecchia also took control, Ostia of the city with riverside access to Rome, and Civitavecchia of the route via the seacoast. This safeguarded the pope's freedom: for this reason, EUGENE IV was able, in 1434, to escape an uprising via the Tiber, and to take a ship at Civitavecchia toward Porto Pisano. One

hundred years later, Clement VII was able to assure Charles V that Civitavecchia, 72 kilometers from Rome, "was the port without which he would not feel secure." From NICHOLAS V to PIUS II, great architects worked at the site. Bramante, Sangallo, and Michelangelo made it a powerful fortress, enclosed by walls 12 meters high and 6 to 8 meters thick, flanked by towers 16 to 23 meters tall, all in all an impregnable urban enclosure. To adjust for silting, the harbor was deepened an additional two meters under LEO X; its total surface area (around 130,000 square meters in the 16th century) held a small permanent fleet of from 6 to 12 galleys with sufficient security when the winds from the southwest did not blow too hard. There was much activity at Civitavecchia, on the increase thanks to the exportation of alum from Tolfa beginning in 1462, whose port was used by the papal fleet for its diplomatic and military missions. Among the first missions was the commissioning, in 1437 in Venice, of four galleys to carry the *basileus* John Palaeologus, coming at the pope's expense, to negotiate the union of the two Churches. Of two other notable examples, one is the trip HADRIAN VI made in 1522; the papal fleet (four galleys and a brigantine), reinforced by 54 Spanish galleys, took the new pope from Tortosa to Civitavecchia in about two months, with almost daily stops. The other is the naval parade in 1533 during the meeting between Clement VII and Francis I at Marseille; among the 78 galleys that accompanied the pope, 12 were the pope's, and another four belonged to the order of St. John.

The renewal of the crusades brought about several efforts during the 14th century, one in 1334 when three papal galleys under Piero Soggifanti, joined by about 30 French, Italian, and Byzantine vessels, defeated the TURKS at the entrance to the Sea of Marmara. Ten years later, Zaccaria Centurione was serving the pope with his ships under the direction of the *condotta*. This system continued until LEPANTO with the construction of ships being under direction of the Church of Rome. At the time of the crusade of Varna (1444), a cardinal had gotten 10 galleys from Venice that were destined to patrol the Dardanelles. One month before the fall of Constantinople, NICHOLAS V sent 18 galleys and 2 sailing ships to aid the city. After the disaster, his efforts and those of his successor, CALIXTUS III, left records in the Vatican archives of the rational organization of a considerable naval force. Nicholas V devised a plan on 15 May 1455, and put a commission of cardinals in charge of its accomplishment. In the fall, the archbishop of Tarragona, Pedro Urrea, was the papal legate at the head of the expedition. The naval organization was accompanied by an activity whose actions and expenses were registered by the chancellery and the Apostolic Camera under the control of the *depositarius* Ambrosio Spanocchi. The forests of the patrimony contributed to this effort; the wood and all the metal and textile materials, the fittings and the arms, bought from several sources, especially Genoa, Calabria, and Lombardy, were on their way to the shipyards of Ostia and Rome where several master shipbuilders and fitters waited, including some from Ancona, Gaeta, Capua, Messina, Genoa, and even Barcelona and France. To these expenses of construction were added the commissioning of vessels equipped according to contracts from the *condotta* on almost every page, for example, in Register 25 of the *Diversa Cameralia* for 1455–7. They even hired some pirates, at the risk of having to denounce their violent undertakings later. In 1457, a law with 46 articles "for the good management of the galleys of His Holiness" was necessary. The total effect of such a disparate navy was impossible to determine. Most of it set sail in the summer of 1456 with Asia Minor as its destination, specifically to the Genoese base at Chios.

The mediocre results of this experiment did not halt the renewal of similar attempts, of lesser scope and to lesser effect. A MEDALLION, made by an unknown person, shows PIUS II seated on the deck of a ship in Ancona, tiara on his head, holding in his left hand a banner with a cross on it, his right hand lifted in blessing. Ancona armed three vessels in 1471, built eight in 1502, and six in 1509 to fight the Turks and the pirates infesting the Adriatic. The lack of security was widespread on every coast of Italy. With the assistance of the Knights of Rhodes (soon to be of Malta), later the *Cavalieri di San Stefano*, a "sea guard" was set up beginning in 1486 under INNOCENT VIII and ALEXANDER VI, and in 1499 six vessels in two squadrons patrolled the area between Terracina and Monte Argentario under the command of captains responsible for assuring the safety of the large numbers of pilgrims expected to arrive for the jubilee of that year. Putting Ostia and Civitavecchia on the defensive was also a response to this need.

The strength of the papal navy in the 16th century was due less to its ships, reduced by several galleys (between 12 and 30 according to the circumstances), brigantines, and other vessels, than to the valor of his captain-generals, linked to the Holy See by a *condotta*, and to the pivotal role that it could maintain on the international level. The names of Andrea and Antonio Doria, of Bernardo Salviati, and of Gentile Virginio Orsini show both the quality of the choices and the esteem surrounding the sought-after position of commander of the armed navy of the pope. This prestige, despite certain failures, came from the coordinating role of the Holy See in the fight against the Turks beginning around 1530, when it was feared they might even take hold of Italy. The resounding success of Lepanto corresponds to the intensity of the anxiety felt during the decades that preceded it.

Michel Mollat

Bibliography

Becatti, G., and G. *Ostia*, Rome, 1954.

Carlisse, C. *Storia di Civitavecchia*, Florence, 1898.

Favier, J. *Les Finances pontificales à l'époque du Grand Schisme d'Occident 1378–1409*, Paris, 1966.

Guglielmotti, A. *Storia della Marina Pontificia nel Medio Evo dal al 1489*, 2 vol., Florence, 1895.

Mollat, G., and Glénisson, J. *Correspondence des Légats et Vicaires généraux*, I (1363–7), Paris, 1964.

Natalucci, M. *Ancona nel Medioevo, Cita di Castello*, 1966.

Palermo, L. *El Cardenal Albornoz y el Colegio de España*, Congresso de Estudios Albornocianos, 1969, Bologna, 1972.

Palermo, L. *Il porto di Roma nel XIVe–XV secolo. Struttura socio-economische et statuti*, Rome, 1979.

Palermo, L. *Il Quattrocento a Roma e nel Lazio*, catalog from the exhibition, Ostia, 1980.

Paschini, P. "La flotta di Calliste III," *ASR*, vol. LIII–LV, 1930–2.

Schniedt, G. "I Porti italiani nell' alto medioevo," *La Navigazione-mediterranea nell' alto medioevo, XXXVa Settimana del Centro italiano di Studi sull' alto medioevo*, I, 129–259, Spoleto, 1978 (with maps and charts).

Usini-Viri, A. "L'Arsenale di Civita Vecchia di Gianlorenzo Bernini," *Palladio, Rivista di Storia di Architettura*, 3 (1956), 127–36 (charts and photos).

NEOGUELPHISM. See **Unity, Italian.**

NEPOTISM. The word "nepotism" was first used in the 17th century as a collective term designating relatives of popes who enjoyed significant favoritism. The term later became a more generalized designation for the many benefits distributed by other celibate dignitaries of the Catholic Church. Eventually, in its modern usage, the term came to encompass the broad, inappropriate influence that persons in power granted to relatives or close associates. In this sense, today the term belongs in the category of corruption, but not so under different historical conditions. This qualification is not a historical apology for the phenomenon—presenting nepotism apologetically prevents one from understanding it, just as quickly condemning it does. A measured cultural and social historical evaluation must take into account four theoretical points of view.

1. Networks of social relations always structure human interactions, and familial relationships are an important basis for such networks. The process of filtering candidates to office positions through the sieve of social networking should be considered the rule, regardless of how official norms might make this seem.

2. In the premodern era, cultural norms placed less value on equality of opportunity and on the division of public and private life than on the moral duty to care for one's own family. For Thomas Aquinas, such behavior was piety and as such a virtue of justice (STh 2 II, q. 101). Thus, even the nepotism accorded to the Italian prelate and controversialist Roberto Bellarmino (1542–1621) was not a stain on his holiness, but a compliment to it!

3. What social scientists call nepotism's welfare function—supplying material benefits to the favored—seems corrupt by modern standards, but in the premodern era it was considered a legitimate and even expected contribution to a family's status, under the condition that similar chances remained open to other families. From the 15th through the 18th centuries and beyond, most popes and cardinals belonged to an extensive network of aristocratic families from central and northern Italy.

4. Thomas Aquinas always emphasized that when presented with equally virtuous candidates, one should give preference to relatives when assigning offices, because one could expect more reliable service from them (STh 2 II, q. 63). In a time when no professional bureaucracy with an abstract devotion to duty existed and officeholders were guided by personal loyalties, one could hardly pass over the guaranteed loyalty nepotism provided. Hence, in Rome, nepotism also served a decisive governmental function and over time became a quasi-institution.

Similar to the way relatives and friends close to Jesus played important roles, the relationship between church office and family was considered self-evident in early Christianity. We know that episcopal sees could be inherited before Constantine's reforms made these offices even more attractive. During the eastern schism with VICTOR I (189–199), Polykrates of Ephesus explicitly referred to being the 8th member of his family to hold the same episcopal office. By examining the world of the Roman bishops more closely, one discovers a similar situation. Even Gregory the Great came from a family that had already placed two popes on the throne. On one hand, the affairs of the community would be served best by bishops from certain highly positioned families. On the other, since the late 5th century there have been prohibitions on dispersing church moneys to relatives. In 494 a Roman synod issued the decisive decree that in the future, Church income would be distributed equally among the bishop, the clergy, the church buildings, and the poor. After the 6th century the vow of celibacy was meant in part to prevent relatives of church officers from inheriting church income and property.

In the Middle Ages, nepotism increased amid aristocratic family dynasties. One cannot separate the governmental function of nepotism in the service of kings, bishops, and abbots from the welfare function it had for aristocratic families (the occasional blood feud that was fitting for a bishop to revenge his father and predecessor supports this). In the 8th century, after a series of eastern popes, a clearly aristocratic papacy installed itself in Rome. These popes ruled with their families' help in a way typical of the Middle Ages, when no other options existed. If the papacy fell prey to rival aristocratic families, it did not matter if the family served the papacy or the papacy served the family. Thus, for the wide-ranging reform movement during the time of LEO IX (1040–54), the freedom of the church meant, first of all, freedom from rival parties of Roman aristocracy, but aristocratic rule and nepotism could not be disbanded. On the contrary, these practices reasserted their governmental function. The more the popes were entangled in multiple political conflicts, the more they relied on blood loyalty to rule, especially when they came from a family rich in power and skilled in battle. Even for INNOCENT III (1198–1216), avoiding support of his own family would have meant handing himself and the church over to other nobles. Thus he entrusted his family with powers, set them up with church benefices, raised them to cardinals, and used the laymen among his relatives as army commanders and in politically motivated marriage arrangements. His cousin, GREGORY IX (1227–41), became pope, and this cousin's nephew was Pope ALEXANDER IV (1254–61). Criticisms arose during the reign of INNOCENT IV (1243–54) because he employed nepotism not only for the purpose of governance, but also used the pope's *plenitudo potestatis*, which became fully developed under his rule, to enrich his family with church benefices. A "foreign" pope had to create a reliable environment of relatives and compatriots; for example, GREGORY X (1271–6) supported himself with relatives from his hometown, Piacenza. Even the nepotism of NICHOLAS III (1277–80) served not only to enrich his own family—the house of Orsini—which caused Dante to condemn him to the inferno, but also to secure his threatened hold of the Holy See. All these examples stand out but are in no way exceptional. In secular affairs, the presiding custom was that a relative of the pope became the justice minister, or seneschal, of the Curia. When BONIFACE VIII (1294–1303) installed his favored relatives as provincial governors, but assigned the exercise of these offices to deputies, he was simply exploiting an office for the sake of sinecure.

In Avignon, nepotism's welfare function of distributing benefits held the upper hand over its governmental function, which would have placed relatives there to protect the residence of Avignon and to create a loyal following in southern France. Military commands as a pretext for enrichment, money presents, and magnificent weddings at the church's expense were as common as later in the Renaissance and Baroque eras—in addition to the ordinary distribution of benefices to relatives.

Sometimes, those favored by the nepotism of Avignonese popes were assigned tasks in distant regions of the Italian Papal States. With the Great Schism, and afterward with the reconciliation and stabilization of the papacy, nepotism's governmental function became as indispensable for rival popes as it would be for their Roman successors beginning with Pope MARTIN V (1417–31), who was lucky to have in his family (the Colonna), dependable relatives ready to come to his aid. In addition to entrusting positions to favored cardinals, nepotism extended to secular favors, including assigning relatives to hold strategic fortified outposts and to serve as high commanders in the Papal States' army, ensuring relatives family estates in the Papal States and fiefdoms in the kingdom of Naples, and establishing lands for the benefit of their families.

The Renaissance papacy represented a new high point for nepotism in its functions of governing and granting benefits—and not only due to the piquant details of the Borgia family. One must recall that every pope in the 15th century paid homage to nepotism, even the humanist PIUS II (1458–64). During the Renaissance, when INNOCENT VIII (1484–92) and ALEXANDER VI (1492–1503) rose to the papal throne, children of popes again made an appearance in Rome. In the time of SIXTUS IV (1471–84), with the expansion of the college of cardinals and the formation of factions of cardinals who had received papal favors, it became easier for relatives of former popes to get elected pope themselves. Thus, as in the Middle Ages, one again finds popes of the same family: EUGENE IV and PAUL II; CALIXTUS III and Alexander VI; Pius II and PIUS III; Sixtus IV and JULIUS II; LEO X and CLEMENT VII. Ultimately, modern power politics and Catholic reform changed this, and the last attempt by a grandchild of PAUL III (1534–49), Alessandro Farnese, to be elected pope proved not in keeping with the times—despite three tries.

The brutal family politics of the Borgia served to subdue and modernize the Papal States, a process that Julius II (1503–13) could continue without the help of relatives. Nepotism's governmental function seemed to have come to an end. The corresponding welfare function of granting benefits only increased, however, with favored persons receiving principalities cut out from the Papal States, a practice that reached its high point with the establishment of the Farnese dukedom, Parma-Piacenza, in 1545. The ban by Pius V in 1567 could not prevent later families favored by nepotism, like the Barberini in the 17th century, from similar projects. After all, to what other end would a papal uncle dispose of the *plenitudo potestatis*? No larger political opportunities existed then beyond the granting of rich estates and high aristocratic titles in the Papal States as well as in the kingdom of Naples, and nepotism no longer had any function for actual governance. Between the 15th and 17th centuries, nepotism's function of providing welfare permitted social mobility, which was not legitimate in the Middle Ages and so was far less common. Unlike ancient and medieval family dynasties, who planned and achieved no shift in social status due to having a relative in the papacy, most papal families rose in social status between the time of Eugene IV (1431–47) and that of ALEXANDER VIII (1689–91), as a result of nepotism. City patricians and even poor petty aristocrats did not manage to become ruling princes of Europe like the Farnese, but families like the Borgia, Piccolomini, Cibo, Boncompagni, Peretti, Aldobrandini, Borghese, Ludovisi, Barberini, Pamfili, and Ottoboni continued to rise in the European high aristocracy.

Between 1538 and 1692 a kind of institutionalized system of nepotism existed. At first glance, one could dismiss the claim that such nepotism had a governmental function for the state and see it as merely an ideological legitimation of its primary function of distributing and acquiring benefits. This is especially true if one has an understanding of the papal system of government. On second glance, however, one can observe nepotism's active governmental function, though not by looking to its official capacities. On one hand, a papal nephew of ecclesiastical quality would be routinely named cardinal and with a papal brief, appointed Sopraintendente dello Stato Ecclesiastico, a kind of viceroy ruling over the secular affairs of the papacy with wide-ranging but exactly circumscribed powers. As head of the secretaries of state, he was the correspondence liaison with papal diplomats and provincial governors in the position of cardinal legate. In addition, he was the prefect of the most important of the administrative congregations, the Consulta and the Congregazione del Buon Governo. In military and financial dealings, his signature would appear again and again. Other relatives were granted secular positions such as the offices of general and admiral of the church, the commander of the papal guards, or governorships, such as that of Benevento. These offices were pure sinecures. In these positions, the favored collected revenues and their employees executed the work.

In case of the Sopraintendente, things were somewhat more complicated. The official function of this position, comparable to prime minister in the manner of a Richelieu, was only fully realized by the nephews of weak popes, such as Cardinal Ludovisi under GREGORY XV. Most limited themselves to producing signatures and acting as representatives, like Cardinal Borghese under PAUL V. The pope ruled in direct cooperation with the secretaries of state and of the congregations. Attempts to change this—made by Francesco Barberini under URBAN VIII—were not successful. One could easily conclude that the favored cardinal remained limited to a position of pure beneficence; this meant he could accumulate huge amounts of church income, 150,000 scudi and more, mainly from commendatory abbeys, and with this money he could acquire investments, especially property. With the privilege of *"Facultas testandi"* such property could be transferred over time to the family fortune. This impression is deceptive, however. There was, throughout, a governmental function for the cardinal nephew. First, to govern by means of mere letters of the Sopraintendente signified a modernization of papal administration, a transition from the age of the certified original document to the age of record keeping. Such letters were binding by law but could be revised, whereas letters written by the pope, such as bulls and briefs, were considered absolute documents that set down an irreversible law. Second, this arrangement permitted the pope a formal distance from everyday business and an ability to play the role of a neutral *padre comune* over competing parties in international politics as well as in the micropolitics of the Curia. The management of social networks, especially of family clientele, without which no governance was possible in eras before the development of bureaucracies, lay in the hands of the cardinal nephew. He was thus often referred to as Cardinal Padrone, the chief of the papal and family clientele, because here governmental function and the distribution of benefits were closely tied together.

Allegedly, this was a reason for the long life of the system, since the actual affairs of office no longer required relatives. In the 17th century they were transferred to the secretary of state, who was raised to the position of cardinal. The system of nepotism was revoked in 1692 by INNOCENT XII in a papal bull that all cardinals swore to uphold. This dissolved many offices filled by relatives who had enjoyed special favor. An income limit of 12,000 scudi, which corresponded to the traditional idea of the average income of cardinals, was imposed on those who had risen to cardinal through nepotism. The papal financial crisis created in part by excessive nepotism under Urban VIII (1623–44) generated these reforms. In contrast to the Fifth Lateran Council, which had declared in 1514 that the care of relatives was still commendable practice, the Council of Trent in 1563 expressly forbade nepotism for cardinals and bishops (XXV de ref:1), in an act of great rigor—though the holders of papal plenary power did not feel bound by it.

Nepotism, as an institutional system, had disappeared by the 18th century, but as a support for relatives according to the law of "Pietas," it lasted well into the 20th century. It often does not require the intervention of a papal uncle; the mere existence of such a relationship would raise a nephew's chances. Under autocratic popes like PIUS VI (1775–99), LEO XIII (1878–1903), and PIUS XII (1939–58), the weakening of the church bureaucracy to some extent led to the establishment of an informal parallel government of those enjoying family favoritism. But in the end, the disappearance of the church as a state and the internationalization of the Curia greatly reduced the possibilities for nepotism.

Wolfgang Reinhard

Bibliography

Emich, B. *Bürokratie und Nepotismus unter Paul V (1605–21)*, Stuttgart, 2001.

Grisar, J. *Päpstliche Finanzen, Nepotismus und Kirchenrecht unter Urban VIII*, Miscellanea Historiae Pontificiae 7/14, Rome, 1943, 205–366.

Hallman, Barbara McClung. *Italian Cardinals, Reform, and the Church as Property, 1492–1563*, Berkeley, Calif., 1985.

Reinhardt, V. *Kardinal Scipione Borghese 1605–1621*, Tübingen, 1984.

Reinhard, W. "Nepotismus," *Zeitschrift für Kirchengeschichte* 86 (1975), 145–85.

Reinhard, W. *Papstfinanz und Nepotismus unter Paul V (1605–21)*, 2 vols., Stuttgarte, 1974.

Sfondrato, C. *Nepotismus theologice expensus* [1692].

Williams, George L. *Papal Genealogy: The Families and Descendants of the Popes*, Jefferson, N.C., 1998.

NICHOLAS I. *(b. Rome, early 9th c., d. Rome, 13 November 867). Elected pope on 24 April 858. Buried at St. Peter's in Rome. Saint (early cult attested in the 14th century, included in the Roman Martyrology).*

Descended from a Roman family of modest origins, Nicholas I in his youth served the *patriarchum* of ST. JOHN LATERAN in the pope's entourage. He became subdeacon under LEO IV (847–55) and counselor to BENEDICT III. Somewhat in the background up to that time, he was chosen by Emperor Louis II to take Benedict's place. No sooner was he elected than the Tiber overflowed, claiming a large number of victims. The pope opened a hospice near ST. MARY MAJOR, where the stricken were taken in. Following that episode, he turned his attention to the blind, the crippled, and the paralyzed so that, in the words of the *LIBER PONTIFICALIS*, "there was not in the whole city a single poor person who did not benefit from the good deeds of the holy pontiff." He also strove to defend Rome against the SARACENS, rebuilding the port of Ostia and setting up a sizable garrison in that city. Yet the pope's actions extended far beyond the boundaries of Rome to embrace the whole of Christendom.

Nicholas in fact was a source of moral authority toward which the Carolingian kings turned when they were in trouble. In 858, Charles the Bald asked him to intervene in his conflict with his brother Louis the German, who in spite of his oaths had invaded the French kingdom of the West. Charles appealed to Nicholas again in 862, when his two sons, Louis and Charles, rebelled against him in Aquitaine. The pope also intervened with vigor in the matter of the divorce of Lothair II, king of Lorraine. His wife, Teutberga, not having given him an heir, Lothair wanted to divorce her and marry his mistress, Walrade, by whom he had a son. The archbishops of Trier and Cologne were prepared to annul the marriage, but Queen Teutberga appealed to the pope. Invoking the sanctity of marriage, Nicholas I excommunicated and deposed the complaisant archbishops and announced to the bishops of Lorraine, who, in Metz, had proclaimed Lothair's second marriage valid, that they would suffer the same penalties. When Lothair's brother, Louis II, invaded Rome, the pope took refuge in ST. PETER'S and stood his ground. The bishops of Lorraine surrendered, and Lothair agreed to take back his first wife. On 30 October 867, shortly before his death, Nicholas I sent the clergy of Germania a letter reminding them of his uncompromising position.

The pope asserted his PRIMACY over the Western Church. He refused to bow to the demands of the Breton princes, who wanted to transform the diocese of Dol into an archdiocese at the expense of the metropolis of Tours. He went to the aid of Bishop Rothad of Soissons in his conflict with Archbishop Hincmar of Reims. Rothad was acting in response to the publication of the "False Decretals" in Reims and Le Mans, which strengthened the power of both bishops and pope to the detriment of that of the metropolitan archbishops. After the Rothad affair came that of the clergy appointed by Ebbo, Hincmar's predecessor, who had been deprived of their posts by the archbishop of Reims. The pope called for a reexamination of their case, in particular that of Wulfad, a candidate for the archdiocese of Bourges. This gave rise to an important exchange of letters between the pope and Hincmar: the latter, while declaring himself faithful to Rome, defended the rights of the metropolitans and their authority over their suffragans. Similarly, Nicholas took action against the archbishop of RAVENNA, whom tradition painted as a rival to the bishop of Rome. The pope reproached Archbishop John, after which John seized Rome's lands in the region around Ravenna. Excommunicated, he was forced to present himself and explain his actions at the Lateran, and Nicholas visited Ravenna shortly thereafter. John finally submitted to the Roman SYNOD of 18 November 862. Nicholas wrote many letters to Ado, archbishop of Vienne, calling him to order on matters of doctrine as well as supporting him against the bishop of Tarentaise. In 863, at the COUNCIL of Rome, he reminded the assembly that the metropolitans must hold regular synods, not be too accommodating to princes, and along with the bishops concern themselves with the religious education of the LAITY. The council's final canon pronounced, "If anyone defy the dogmas, the orders, the interdictions, the sanctions, or the decrees soundly promulgated by the head of the Apostolic See, whether it

have to do with the Catholic faith, ecclesiastical discipline, the reprimand of the faithful, the punishment of the wicked, or interdictions concerning imminent or future evils, may he be ANATHEMA."

Nicholas was determined to make this claim to overall authority prevail in the same way in the East. Ignatius, the patriarch of Constantinople, who had been deposed by Emperor Michael at the urging of his minister Bardas, was replaced by a well-educated high official, Photius, who within a week was given top command. Ignatius's supporters, especially the Studios monks, rebelled against Photius and were persecuted. At this point Nicholas I intervened. The Roman LEGATES whom he sent to Constantinople and who sided with the emperor were stripped of their authority, and in 863 a Roman synod demanded that Photius surrender his see to Ignatius. Nicholas asked Anastasius, the Greek-speaking abbot of Sta Maria in Trastevere who was his secretary for the East, to propound to the emperor the papal teaching concerning the government of the universal Church: "The Church of Rome welcomes within herself and includes what God has prescribed to the universal Church to welcome and contain . . . We have the right to convoke not only the monks but also the clerks of any diocese whatsoever when that is necessary and the situation of the Church demands it. As long as we are there, we shall perform the task that is entrusted to us, we shall follow in our predecessors' footsteps, and we shall bear like a burden the care of all the churches, and the one who will give us strength is our Lord Jesus Christ." At this juncture, the Bulgarian prince Boris, who had converted to Christianity (862), conceived the idea of organizing an autonomous church. When Photius refused, he turned to Rome. The pope, pleased to exert his influence again in Illyricum, which, before the iconoclastic controversy, had been part of the Western patriarchate, sent two bishops to Boris, Formosus of Porto, who would become pope in the late 9th century, and Paolo di Piombino. In a "Letter to the Bulgarians," Nicholas addressed Boris's questions on the differences between the Eastern and Western Churches: the Sabbath rest, dietary matters, the marriage of priests, the preeminence of Rome, etc. On learning that Boris was in negotiation with Rome, Photius summoned a synod calling for a sentence of excommunication against the pope. Some consider this "Photian council" of 867 as marking the date of schism between the Churches of Constantinople and Rome. Nicholas's reaction was to affirm that "the first see can be judged by no one," and to buttress his claim he appealed to the wisdom of the theological scholars of the West, of whom Hincmar was one. The deposing of Photius on 25 September 867 after a palace revolution and, later, Nicholas's death would put a temporary halt to the conflict between the two Churches.

When Nicholas I died, many people realized that one of the greatest popes of the age had passed away. Thus

Regino of Prüm wrote at the end of the 9th century: "Since Blessed Gregory, no bishop raised in the city of Rome to the pontifical see can be compared to him. He ordered kings and tyrants with such authority as though he were master of the world. He showed himself humble, gentle, pious, and benevolent toward bishops and religious priests who observed the Lord's precepts, but terrible and extremely rigorous toward the impious and those who strayed from the right path."

To many, Nocholas's claims seemed new. Nicholas loudly proclaimed the full powers of Peter's successor, at a time when the Carolingian kings' authority was beginning to weaken. "Christian emperors," he said, "need pontiffs in order to gain eternal life, and pontiffs, in their turn, need to have recourse to the laws of empire, but only for the working out of temporal affairs." Congar writes of Nicholas's pontificate: "Nicholas's conception of papal power is that of a pastoral monarchy. Nicholas was aware that his duty was to exercise a supreme magistrature of justice, peace, and unity. To that end, he had to redresss deviations having to do with faith, conduct, and regular procedure. He carried out this mission without faltering, whether it was a question of the freedom of ecclesiastical elections or of marriage among the nobility, or the integrity of his authority when threatened by that of the metropolitans (Hincmar), or by the intervention of the Byzantine emperor in the designation of a patriarch (Photius) . . . If Nicholas prefigures GREGORY VII, it is not so much because he claimed the power to depose kings as because he was anxious to confer on the ecclesiastical order its full independence and, as they would say in the 11th century, its liberty."

Pierre Riché

Bibliography

JW, 1, 341–68; 2, 704, 745.

LP, 2, 151–72.

MGH, Epist., 6, 257–690.

PL, 119, 753–1212.

Congar, Y. *L'Ecclésiologie du Haut Moyen Âge*, Paris, 1968, 210, 224.

Dvornik, F. *Le Schisme de Photius, histoire et légende*, Paris, 1950.

Fliche-Martin, VI, 367–95, 469–83.

Lapôtre, A. *Études sur la papauté du IXe siècle*, I, Rome, 1978.

The Lives of the Ninth-Century Popes: the ancient biographies of ten popes from AD 817–891, trans., R. Davis, Liverpool 1995.

NICHOLAS II. *Gerard (b. Lorraine or Burgundy, d. Florence, 27 July 1061). Elected pope in Siena on 6 (?) December 1058, enthroned in Rome on 24 January 1059. Buried at Sta Reparata in Florence.*

Bishop of Florence from the attested date of 1045, he is said to have been connected originally with the Lorraine-Burgundy reform movement that reached Rome in the wake of LEO IX. However, his hypothetical adherence to the reform order of Cluny is not admissible. After the death of STEPHEN IX in Florence in 1058, members of the Roman aristocracy hastily nominated Bishop John of Velletri as pope, under the name BENEDICT X—this without asking for the participation or the consent of the reform group that had built up around Hildebrand (later GREGORY VII) and Peter Damian. The cardinals, who had fled Rome, and Hildebrand, who was returning from a legation to the German court, met in Tuscany to elect as pope Bishop Gerard of Florence, with the assent of Duke Godfrey of Lorraine and Tuscany and on the advice of the German court. Godfrey and his troops escorted the new pontiff into Rome, and he was crowned in ST. PETER's basilica; shortly before that, in early January 1059, a synod held at Sutri in the presence of the imperial chancellor, Guibert of Parma, had pronounced the banishment of Benedict X, who had hurriedly left Rome. In the imperial city, power now lay in new hands: henceforth, families that for the most part came from Trastevere and were linked to the reformers made up the ruling class, which, united with the reformed papacy, eclipsed the heretofore dominant ancient Roman NOBILITY. For example, one of Hildebrand's partisans, John Tiniossus, took over as city prefect. From this time, too, the influence of the Pierleoni and Frangipani families came to the fore. Measures designed to restore the condition and dignity of the Roman Church were ineffective. The reform group only gradually won key positions and cardinals' posts in the city, its greatest successes being in densely populated areas like Trastevere. Nevertheless, suburbicarian dioceses were conferred exclusively on advocates of reform. Nicholas II promoted to bishops's sees in central Italy a long line of Florentine collaborators, who were continually called upon to form his entourage and thus create a sort of counterweight to the Roman reform group, to which he was anxious not to become completely subordinate.

Benedict X's SCHISM had demonstrated the dangers that hung over the task of reorganizing the Roman Church, besides laying bare the attitude of the traditional ruling elites, who refused to be ousted from their posts—including that of the bishop of Rome—without protest.

For this reason, circles close to Nicholas II prepared to use the Lateran synod, held in April 1059, to strengthen and develop what they had gained. The famous decree of 1059 on papal election stipulated that the pontiff must first of all be chosen by the cardinal bishops with the support of the cardinal clerics, then by the rest of the Roman clergy and people. Where circumstances demanded, the election of a cleric not belonging to the Roman Church would be permitted, and, if need be, the election could also take place outside Rome; the newly chosen pope would thus possess complete pontifical authority even without proper enthronement. In essence, the decree introduced a higher element of hierarchy into papal election while decisively reducing the influence of the rest of the clergy and, above all, of the lay element—first and foremost of the Roman nobility. This quite revolutionary innovation in electoral canon law was clearly the logical response to the events, as well as to the power struggles and interests of various groups, in the years 1058–9. As for the rights of Emperor Henry IV in the papal election, they were referred to only in a restrictive, vague fashion: the young emperor was guaranteed *debitus honor* and respect—though these were described as concessions on the part of the pope—but only rights obtained from the Apostolic See after negotiation would be confirmed to his successors. A big step had been taken toward the juridical and formal emancipation of the papacy, which both escaped outside influences and, in the present instance, eluded the emperor's right of participation in his function as *patricius*. Other synodal decrees strengthened provisions against the marriage of priests, against SIMONY, and against the possession of more than one church at a time. Clergy attached to a church were obliged to live in community (*vita communis*). In response to the controversy aroused by Berengar of Tours's symbolical and spiritualist Eucharistic doctrine, Berengar was made to sign a profession of faith drawn up by Humbert of Silva Candida. At subsequent synods, in 1060 and 1061, action was taken to spread and entrench the goals of the reform. Unlike his itinerant predecessors, Nicholas II and his chief collaborator Hildebrand, now archdeacon, relied on the support of LEGATES appointed to see to the reorganization of the Church. Accordingly, the pope increasingly sent out cardinals and external bishops such as Peter Damian, Anselm of Lucca, and Dodon de Roselle, whose task, aside from their political missions, was to propagate the spirit of reform among the local and national Churches of western Europe.

On the advice of Hildebrand and Abbot Desiderius of Monte Cassino (the future VICTOR III), Nicholas introduced into southern Italy a momentous political change that eventually led to the recognition of the Norman princes Robert Guiscard and Richard d'Aversa. Up to that time, they had been considered usurpers, who held their principalities only by right of conquest. Now that the pope had granted them their lands in fief, the Church found itself propelled into the suzerainty of a vast domain. It was at this time that notions about temporal power and about relations with the secular powers began to be used in the context of the Church and the papacy. In August 1058, at a synod held by the pope at Melfi, the NORMANS swore loyalty and promised at future papal elections to guarantee the *Cathedra Petri* to the reform group's candidate. At the same time, an opening appeared for the papacy, whereby it gained influence on the ecclesiastical organization of southern Italy, so far largely determined by BYZANTIUM. The alliance with the Normans had the long-lasting effect of strengthening the reformed papacy; it was put to the test in 1059, when, with the help of Norman forces, siege was laid to Benedict X's refuge of Galeria.

A special problem for the Roman papacy was constituted by the rich Lombard clergy, imbued with its prerogatives, and, first and foremost, by the Ambrosian Church of Milan, which had its own liturgy. In 1059, the conciliatory Peter Damian and the Milan-born Anselm de Baggio (later ALEXANDER II) were dispatched to Milan to intervene in the bloody conflict between the populist Pataria movement and the upper clergy, fiercely proud of its nobility; there the pope was to appear as a figure of authority, an arbiter who kept his place firmly above both parties. In this instance, the reform projects were hardly realized, even though the demands of the Patarenes, at least concerning the way of life of the clergy, were comparable to those put forward by Nicholas II's reformers. Still, Archbishop Guido of Milan declared himself ready to come and justify himself in a Roman synod.

The mission entrusted to Cardinal Stephen of S. Crisogono in 1061 probably consisted of explaining to the German government the change of policy toward the Normans and the growing severity of the measures taken against simony and NICOLAISM; however, not only was the legate not heard, he was not even granted an audience with Archbishop Anno II of Cologne, who was responsible for Italian imperial policy. It was a shocking insult, barely veiling criticism of the pope. A synod of German bishops even declared null and void the papal decrees concerning church reform and broke off relations with Nicholas. Thus, a serious conflict was on the horizon when Nicholas II died in Florence, where he had preserved his episcopal see even while pope, and where he is buried.

Tilmann Schmidt

Bibliography

Hägermann, D. "Zur Vorgeschichte des Pontifikats Nikolaus II," *ZKG*, 81 (1970), 352–61.

Jasper, D. *Das Papstwahldekret von 1059. Überlieferung und Textgestalt*, Sigmaringen, 1986 (*Beiträge zur Geschichte und Quellenkunde des Mittelalters*, 12).

Krause, H. G. *Das Papstwahldekret von 1059 und seine Rolle im Investiturstreit*, Rome, 1960 (*Studi Gregoriani*, 7).

Somerville, R. "Cardinal Stephan of St. Grisogono: Some Remarks on Legates and Legatine Councils in the 11th Cent.," *Law, Church, and Society: Essays in Honor of Stephan Kuttner*, Philadelphia, 1977, 157–66.

Stürner, W. "Das Papstwahldekret von 1059 und seine Verfälschung," *Fälschungen im Mittelalter*, Hannover, 1988 (*Schriften der MGH*, 33, 2), 157–90.

Violante, C. "Il vescovo Gerardo—papa Niccolò II e le communità canonicali nella diocesi di Firenze," *Bolletino storico pisano*, 40/41 (1971/72), 17–22.

Zema, D. B. "The Houses of Tuscany and Pierleone in the Crisis of Rome in the 11th Cent.," *Traditio*, 2 (1944), 155–75.

NICHOLAS III. *Giovanni Gaetano Orsini (b. Rome, ca. 1210–20, d. Soriano, near Viterbo, 22 August 1280). Elected pope on 25 November 1277, enthroned on 26 December. Buried at St. Peter's in Rome.*

The successor of three eminent popes, INNOCENT V, HADRIAN V, and JOHN XXI, who died too soon to reap the results of the pontificate of GREGORY X (d. January 1276) and the COUNCIL of Lyon of 1274, Nicholas III responded with vigor when faced with a political situation in Italy that was troublesome, despite the liquidation of Frederick II's sons. He was confronted with interminable negotiations with the Holy Roman emperor, Rudolf of Habsburg, whose coronation was, from 1273, the central issue of territorial disputes with the papacy (and who died, uncrowned, in 1291); and with the insatiable territorial appetites of Charles I of Anjou, brother of the late French king, Louis IX, and founder of the ANGEVIN dynasty. In his desire to carve out a Mediterranean empire, Charles was satisfied neither with the kingdom of Sicily, enfiefed to him by URBAN IV in 1263 and where he rid the territory of the Hohenstaufen in 1266–8, nor with the post of senator of Rome, granted him for two years by CLEMENT IV in 1268 and which even jeopardized the union with the Greek Church and the difficult rapprochement with Constantinople, Greek once again from 1264. To the solution of these delicate problems Nicholas applied himself with an energy and ability that led some to compare him with INNOCENT III, who had worked on a comprehensive plan aimed at restoring the independence of the PATRIMONY OF ST. PETER. But in Nicholas's case, his pontificate of less than three years was too brief to bear fruit, especially as his actions were almost immediately undone by his successor, MARTIN IV.

John XXI died unexpectedly, and after a good six months the cardinal electors finally chose for this herculean task an elderly man: like all his predecessors from the past quarter-century (with the exception of Innocent V), Giovanni was over fifty when elected, probably nearly sixty. But the electors had also chosen a noble Roman of the best lineage as well as a cardinal long experienced in CURIA affairs. A member of the powerful, multi-branched Orsini family ("sons of Ursus/Orso"), which had already produced Pope CELESTINE III, Giovanni was the son of Matteo, also named Rosso, Orsini;

his mother, Perna Gaetana, came from the family of the dukes of Gaeta. Matteo first came to public notice (against his brother Giacomo Napoleone) as one of the leaders of the GUELPH party of Rome but also as a friend of Francis of Assisi (he joined the order of lay tertiaries). Made senator of Rome in 1241, Matteo also fought the Colonna, taking from them the fortress surrounding Augustus's mausoleum. In 1244, his son Giovanni, the future Nicholas III, was appointed by INNOCENT IV cardinal deacon of S. Nicola in Carcere Tulliano, and followed the pope to Lyon. Under ALEXANDER IV, he increasingly gained the reputation of a disinterested cardinal living off his patrimony, devoted to his studies and the repression of HERESIES, which earned him the appointment of grand inquisitor; under Urban IV, in 1263, he was named protector of the Franciscans. But he was also a skillful negotiator who encouraged the kings of France and England to sign a peace treaty in 1258. In 1262, Urban IV gave the cardinal's hat to Giovanni's nephew Matteo Rosso Orsini (later chief of the Orsini, summoned to take part in fourteen CONCLAVES) and strengthened Giovanni's dominant position at the Curia: in 1263, Giovanni was named rector of Sabina, and it was from his hands that in 1265 Charles of Anjou received investiture of the kingdom of Sicily. A genuine Orsini party was emerging at the Curia: besides an ally, Cardinal Giacomo Savelli, rector of the Patrimony in Tuscia (later HONORIUS IV), there was Matteo Rosso as legate for Tuscany, while another nephew, the layman Bertoldo Rosso, served as Giovanni's vicar in his rectorate before becoming *podesta* of Lucca in 1262 and doing battle at Tagliacozzo. Giovanni skillfully made himself recognized as a man of compromise, not too Angevin, moderately Guelph. The oldest cardinal in 1276, he swung the election of the Portuguese Pope John XXI, who was not politically minded enough to escape being dominated by Cardinal Orsini, whom in 1276 he named archpriest of ST. PETER'S in the Vatican. In this capacity, Giovanni increased the number of canons of St. Peter's from twenty-two to thirty. It was symbolic of the regional power of the Orsini family that when Giovanni was elected to the conclave in 1277, at VITERBO, the city *podesta* was his nephew Orso Orsini.

Cleverly avoiding any frontal attack, when extending the investiture of Sicily on 24 May 1278 Nicholas III did not renew Charles's ten-year post as senator of the city of Rome or his position as vicar of Tuscany. He reduced the senatorial post to one year and even laid down that in future no emperor, king, prince, or exterior baron should be named to it except with the explicit agreement of the Holy See (constitution *Fundamenta militantis ecclesiae* of 11 July 1278). In fact, the position was entrusted to the pope himself, who delegated to it members of the LAITY—his own brother Matteo, then a Colonna, and then a Savelli. He entrusted Tuscany to a nephew pending the emperor's coronation. He actually dealt with Rudolf up to November 1279. Already by 1274, Rudolf had relinquished the EXARCHATE, the duchy of Spoleto, and the Marches of Ancona and promised to confirm all the Church's privileges; following the example of Innocent III, Nicholas sought to recover Romagna, which Rudolf had called "the garden of the empire." As he made his authority felt in Romagna, the pope strove for the pacification of that turbulent region, relying on the aid of two of his nephews, the cardinal bishop of Ostia, Latino Frangipane Malabranca, LEGATE, and Bertoldo Orsini, rector. In 1279, according to the chronicler Tolomeo of Lucca, a DOMINICAN writing around 1317, the pope purportedly intended to divide the Empire into four: the kingdom of Germania, now hereditary, under Rudolf; the kingdom of Arles, under the Angevins; and two new kingdoms, Tuscany and Lombardy, to be carved out of the old kingdom of Italy. Although concrete evidence of his intention is lacking the pope was clearly seeking to bring Charles and Rudolf together in a lasting peace, sanctioned by the marriage of Clementia, Rudolf's daughter, to Charles "Martel" of Anjou, the grandson of Charles I.

Nicholas III also devoted much energy to the CRUSADES. He tried to accelerate the raising of funds decided on at Lyon, to appease tensions between France and Aragon as well as in Hungary and to send a mission to the Mongols in the long-nourished hope of an alliance against the Muslims. Favoring the mendicant orders, in particular the Franciscans, he gave his approval to the Poor Clares and confirmed the Franciscan rule (constitution *Exiit qui seminat* of 14 August 1279); his family and personal history led him to give a fairly strict interpretation of poverty in the debate that would shortly tear apart the order. He appointed several mendicants to head dioceses and named four to membership of the SACRED COLLEGE, at the promotion of cardinals of 12 March 1278—two Franciscans and two Dominicans, his nephew Latino, at that time a Dominican prior in Rome, and the theologian Robert Kilwardby (also promoted were his brother Giordano Orsini and Giacomo Colonna, who would be removed under BONIFACE VIII in 1297). In Rome, Nicholas was responsible for important additions to the Vatican—a papal RESIDENCE of which, along with the VATICAN GARDENS, he is the true founder and which he preferred to the old Lateran Palace. He also saw to the restoration of St. Peter's basilica and the papal chapel of St. Lawrence. He is buried in the Orsini chapel of St. Peter, symbolic of a nepotism that was both a tool of government and a method of promoting the family. Soon after his death people would condemn the pope's favors to the "little bears," favors which earned him a place in DANTE's hell, among those guilty of SIMONY (*Inferno* XIX, 70–2): "E veramente fui figliuol de l'orsa / cupido si, per avanzar li orsatti / che su l'avere e qui me misi in borsa."

Olivier Guyotjeannin

Bibliography

Amann, E. "Nicolas III," *DTC*, 11-1 (1931), 532–6.
Demski, A. *Papst Nikolaus III*, Münster, 1903.
Heft, J. L., SM, "Nicholas III (1277–1280) and John XXII (1316–1334): Popes in Contradiction?" *Archivum Historiae Pontificiae* 21 (1983), 245–7.
Gay, J., and Vitte-Clémencet, S., *Les Registres de Nicolas III*, Paris, 1898–1938.
Potth., 1719–56, 2132.
Roberg, B. "Nikolaus III," *LexMA*, 6 (1992), 1170–1.
Sternfeld, R. *Der Kardinal Johann Gaetan Orsini (Papst Nikolaus III.), 1244–1277: ein Beitrag zur Geschichte der römischen Kurie im 13. Jhdt*, 1905 (*Historische Studien*, 52).

NICHOLAS IV. *Girolamo Masci (b. Lisciano [near Ascoli Piceno], 30 September 1227, d. Rome, 4 April 1292). Elected pope on 15 then 22 February 1288, enthroned the same day. Buried at St. Mary Major.*

The first Franciscan pope, of modest origins (his father was described as a scribe or clerk), Nicholas was elected after a vacancy of nearly eleven months. Like his predecessors, he faced a Rome in which the great noble families were pitted against each other (he tended to favor the Colonna), as well as a southern Italy rife with problems: here, out of feudal duty and political realism, he supported the ANGEVINS, whom the Aragonese had hounded out of Sicily but who were solidly entrenched on the Peninsula. His Franciscan origins are scarcely visible in this problematic context, save in the vigorous encouragement he gave to the Eastern missions.

Most likely a doctor of theology, the new pope had a long career with the Friars Minor. In 1272, he was elected provincial of Dalmatia, and in that same year GREGORY X sent him on a mission to BYZANTIUM, where he worked to bring about the union of the Latin and Greek Churches that would be proclaimed at the COUNCIL of Lyon in 1274. In this latter year, he succeeded St. Bonaventure as general of the order, being appointed on 12 March 1278 cardinal priest of the title of Sta Pudenziana by NICHOLAS III, a great friend of the Franciscans (he retained, notwithstanding, the direction of the order until 1279). MARTIN IV next promoted him to the rank of cardinal bishop of Palestrina, a diocese that Nicholas tended with care. These successive posts did not exclude diplomacy. John XXI asked him to negotiate peace between France and Castile, and Nicholas III, just before his death, was planning to send him on a mission to King Rudolf. When a CONCLAVE was held on the death of HONORIUS IV, in that pope's new "palace," the hostile factions could not agree on an acceptable candidate. A scorchingly hot summer followed, which caused the death of six cardinals and led others to leave Rome for less unwholesome RESIDENCES. Cardinal Girolamo was the only one to stay in Rome. On their return, the cardinals unanimously voted for him, on 15 February 1288, but out of humility the Franciscan cardinal refused the election, which had to be repeated on 22 February. The new pope took the name Nicholas IV, allegedly to pay homage to Nicholas III, who had raised him to the cardinalate.

Nicholas IV's problems were those of his predecessors: like Martin IV and Honorius IV (but without the former's prejudices), he supported the Angevin dynasty, now weakened, as opposed to a house of Aragon that was in full ascendancy and seemed all too ready to take up the aspirations of its Hohenstaufen forebears. Negotiations with Rudolf of Habsburg, king of Germania, languished until the king's death in 1291, when the pope turned his full attention to the conflict among France, Aragon, and Sicily. Forging a Franco-Castilian alliance, he played Alfonso III (king of Aragon since 1285) against his brother, James II (king of Sicily). Like his predecessor, he broke the treaties that allowed Charles of Salerno, son of the deceased Charles I of Anjou, to regain his freedom and by virtue of which he had abandoned the island of Sicily to the Aragonese James II (treaties of Oléron, 25 July 1287 and Champfranc, 28 October 1288). On 29 May 1289, Nicholas received Charles's homage and crowned him, as Charles II, king "of Sicily, Apulia, and Calabria." But James II, well established on the island of Sicily and heedless of the pope's repeated condemnations, threatened the mainland of Italy with his attacks, and on his brother's death in June 1291 became king of Aragon, with the pope powerless to prevent it. The solution to the conflict would have to wait.

Nicholas IV clearly favored the Colonna, whose possessions at Palestrina had no doubt influenced him: among the six cardinals he created in a promotion of 16 May 1288 were one Colonna, Pietro (but also Napoleone Orsini); he appointed several Colonna governors or rectors in the PATRIMONY OF ST. PETER (Landolfo Colonna in the duchy of Spoleto, Giovanni in the Marches of Ancona, Stefano in Romagna); and in 1290, he made Giovanni Colonna sole senator of Rome (as to his predecessors, that post had fallen to the pope, who delegated to it a member of the laity). At the CURIA, too, there was the rise of the future Boniface VIII, a cardinal priest whom Nicholas IV in 1291 named cardinal bishop after his skillful negotiation of the peace between France and Aragon (his relation Loffredo Caetani was to be senator of Rome). With his bull *Coelestis altitudo* of 18 June 1289, Nicholas IV increased the prerogatives of the SACRED COLLEGE as well as its revenues, which were managed by a Chamber distinct from the APOSTOLIC CAMERA (*Camera Collegii*).

In May 1291, Acre, the last Christian stronghold in the Holy Land, fell to the Muslims, and within a few months the last Latin settlements had fallen with it (only Cyprus and Armenia remained Christian). Yet even before that date, Nicholas IV was systematizing his predecessors' efforts (Honorius IV had revived the study of Oriental languages in Paris), among them the appeal to the mendicants. In 1289, the pope sent the friar Giovanni da Montecorvino to the court of the Great Mongol Khan, whose empire stretched as far as the north of China (Giovanni would be named archbishop of Beijing in 1307), in the hope that the ruler would become a convert and an ally against the Muslims. Other Franciscans were sent into the Balkans and the Near East, while the pope strove to unite the Latin Church and the dispersed Christian Churches, in Ethiopia, Georgia, and—with most notable success—Armenia.

The pope divided his stays among Rieti, Orte, Orvieto, and Rome. In Rome, he had a palace—his favorite residence—built near the basilica of ST. MARY MAJOR, and he restored the apse both of that church and of ST. JOHN LATERAN. Because such renowned artists as Pietro Cavallini, Arnolfo di Cambio, and Giacomo Torriti were working in Rome at the time, Nicholas has sometimes been portrayed, with a degree of exaggeration, as a patron of the arts.

Bibliography

Barne, G. "Nikolaus IV.," *LexMA*, 6 (1992), 1171.

Franchi, A. *Nicolaus papa IV, 1288–1292*, Rome, 1990.

Langlois, E. *Les Registres de Nicolas IV*, Paris, 1887–93.

Potth., 1826–1915, 2133.

Ryan, James Daniel. *The Interrelation of the Oriental Mission and Crusade Activities of the Papacy under Nicholas IV, 1288–1292*, Ann Arbor, Mich., 1972–73.

Schiff, O. *Studien zur Geschichte Papst Nikolaus IV*, Berlin, 1897 (*Historische Studien*, 5).

Teetaert, A. "Nicolas IV," *DTC*, 11–1 (1931), 536–41."

[NICHOLAS V]. *Antipope, enthroned on May 1328, repudiated on August 1330: d. 16 October 1333.*

The story of the antipope Nicholas V is but one episode in the struggle between JOHN XXII and Emperor Louis IV of Bavaria. After eliminating his rival Frederick of Austria (the battle of Mühldorf, 28 September 1322), Louis had invaded Italy, had himself crowned king of Italy in Milan (1327), and entered Rome (1328), where he had himself elected emperor by an assembly of Romans (11 January 1328) and crowned at ST. PETER'S by the bishops of Aleria and Castello, who had rebelled against the Holy See. Another assembly was held in the emperor's presence on 18 April, in St. Peter's square; under the influence of Marsilius of Padua, the author of *Defensor pacis*, this assembly pronounced the deposition of John XXII, accusing him of HERESY.

Louis had no cardinals at his disposal to replace him. He ordered the Roman clergy to appoint a college of thirteen delegates, which proceeded to elect a Friar Minor, Pietro Rainalducci, also known as Pietro di Corbara; summoned once again to St. Peter's, the people ratified this choice (12 May 1328), apparently without enthusiasm. At once, the candidate was brought into the cathedral and put on the throne; ten days later he repeated the imperial CORONATION.

Little is known of Pietro Rainalducci's personality, his contemporaries having painted contradictory portraits of him. Was he of humble origins, or related to the Colonna? Was he a saintly man, truly poor, an obedient religious, a great preacher consumed with a zeal to save souls? Or was he a hypocrite, hiding beneath apparently virtuous practices a sensual, avaricious, and debauched nature, one always on the lookout for honors? He had been married for five years before separating from his wife, against her wishes, in order to embrace the Franciscan order. For at least some time, he had lived in Rome, at the monastery of Ara Caeli.

Louis of Bavaria gave him the name Nicholas V. This was a political decision, for the name linked him to the Franciscan pope NICHOLAS IV, and especially to NICHOLAS III, the author of the bull *Exiit qui seminat* of 1279: this document, which defined the rules of Franciscan poverty, had been torn to pieces by John XXII, and a SCHISM thereby provoked in the order of the Minors, whose minister general, Michael of Cesena, came to lend his support to Louis of Bavaria's side.

Thus it was chiefly among the Friars Minor, especially those in Italy, that Nicholas V recruited his supporters, finding further support in the other mendicant orders—the Augustinians and, to a lesser extent, the DOMINICANS. However, the ideal of poverty was hardly practiced by the so-called pope, who surrounded himself with a court and an ADMINISTRATION in the image of those of AVIGNON, including a CHANCERY, an APOSTOLIC CAMERA, a PENITENTIARY, and even a SACRED COLLEGE with as many as nine members.

The illusion created by the antipope in Italy, thanks to imperial protection and Franciscan propaganda, did not last long. Louis of Bavaria's power in Italy was without foundation: as early as August 1328, he had to quit Rome, along with Nicholas. The latter wandered a little in the PAPAL STATES, finally rejoining the emperor, who had settled in Pisa (January 1329). There, he renewed the sentence deposing John XXII and proceeded to deface a dummy fashioned in his likeness (19 February). But the political situation in the country forced Louis to leave Pisa (April 1329). Abandoned by the emperor and most of his supporters, Nicholas was taken in by Count Bonifacio de Donoratico and went into hiding in his castle of Burgaro and then in Pisa itself. Negotiations were opened with John XXII, who, in exchange for a formal oath, proposed to his rival absolution, safety, an annual pension of three thousand florins, and exemption from all authority other than that of the HOLY SEE. The antipope accepted:

on 25 August 1330, he was received in Avignon, recanted, and was pardoned. He was assigned to a residence in the papal palace and died there forgotten by all.

Louis Duval-Arnould

Bibliography

Baluze, É. *Vitae paparum Avenionesium*, ed. G. Mollat, II, Paris, 1928, 196–210.
Frutaz, A. P. "Rainallucci (Rainalducci), Pietro, antipapa," *EC*, X, Vatican City, 1953, 505–6.
Mollat, G. *The Popes of Avignon, 1305–1378*, New York, 1963.

NICHOLAS V. *Tommaso Parentucelli (b. Sarzana, 15 November 1397, d. Rome, 25 March 1455). Elected pope on 6 March 1447, crowned on 19 March.*

His father was the Pisan Bartolomeo, a doctor of medicine who was forced for political reasons to take refuge in Sarzana, the birthplace of his wife, Andreola. Tommaso studied arts at the University of Bologna but for lack of money was forced to find employment in Florence, where he worked as a tutor to children of Rinaldo degli Albizzi, and then at the house of Palla Strozzi. Back in Bologna, he studied theology, and upon completing his course at twenty-two, he entered the service of Niccolò Albergati, bishop of that city, whom he accompanied on his foreign missions and with whom he stayed when the bishop became cardinal and took up residence in Rome. At Cardinal Albergati's death, EUGENE IV named Tommaso vice-CAMERLENGO (1443) and, the following year, bishop of Bologna. He was twice sent on a mission to Germany; on his return from the second legation, as a reward for his skill in reconciling the League of Princes with the pope, the latter gave him the cardinal's hat (16 December 1446). He became pope on 6 March 1447, elected unexpectedly by the eighteen cardinals present at the CONCLAVE. On 19 March, he was crowned under the name Nicholas, chosen out of gratitude to his protector, Cardinal Albergati.

A skilled diplomat, Nicholas V succeeded in ending the schism between Rome and Avignon with the dissolution of the COUNCIL of Basel and the surrender of the ANTIPOPE FELIX V (7 April 1449), thanks especially to the collaboration and mediation of the French king, Charles VII, who had returned to the bosom of Rome during the summer of 1448. Honorable conditions were offered the lapsed pope: he was appointed cardinal of the title of Sta Sabina, pontifical LEGATE, and vicar for life for the States of Savoy. The last antipope in history retired to the château of Ripaille, on Lake Geneva, where he died on 7 January 1451. The council, which had moved to Lausanne, pronounced itself dissolved on 25 April, after recognizing Nicholas V as sole legitimate pope. The promulgation of three BULLS (1449) mitigated the consequences of the past—that is, the censures pronounced on the adherents of the council of Basel were annulled, the benefices granted by the council were confirmed, and several cardinals appointed by Felix V were admitted to the SACRED COLLEGE. Some important figures had already been promoted in the College, on 20 December 1448—among them Latino Orsini, Alain de Coétivy, Nicholas of Cusa, and his half-brother, Filippo Calandrini.

Before the happy conclusion to the conciliar period, there had been a flurry of diplomatic activity to force Frederick III to bend the knee to Rome. Negotiations culminated in the signing of the concordat of Vienna (17 February 1448), which was ratified in Rome on 19 March. The agreement offered a partial solution to the knotty question of the conferral of benefices. The pope was guaranteed all benefices that the previous constitutions of John XXII and BENEDICT XII had reserved to the Holy See. But he no longer had the right to nominate bishops and abbots, who would be appointed in free elections, though the pope could revoke those if they had taken place in contravention of canonical rules.

The celebrations for the 1450 jubilee set a magnificent crown on the newfound unity of the Church. Thanks in particular to the relative calm in the papal territories, an extraordinary crowd of pilgrims flocked to the holy city, not only demonstrating the strength of the pope's spiritual power but also greatly helping to restore the papal finances. Notable among the solemn ceremonies at the time was the Franciscan Bernardino of Siena's canonization (24 May), the process for which had begun under Eugene IV. This was an event eagerly anticipated by the masses of Italian faithful, inspired as they had been by itinerant Franciscan preachers.

Nicholas's efforts to enhance religious life would not end with the jubilee year. Using the indulgences associated with the jubilee as a means of attracting the masses and as a pretext for extending his influence, he sent papal legates out into the most important Christian countries. They were to restore not only the authority of the Holy See but, first and foremost, respect for orthodoxy in religious life, which had gradually fallen into neglect. Thus Nicholas of Cusa traveled to the German lands, Bohemia, and neighboring countries, John Capistrano to central Europe, and Cardinal Guillaume d'Estouteville to France. These three legations did not achieve all the results desired. Nicholas of Cusa only partly succeeded in raising the moral standard of the German clergy, by eliminating SIMONY and concubinage and restoring respect for hierarchical order in the monasteries. Despite his unusual eloquence, Capistrano's mission did not have a lasting effect. Finally, Cardinal d'Estouteville, to whom fell the difficult task of abrogating or at least softening the Pragmatic Sanction fared no better: the French clergy, which met in Bourges in July 1452, largely supported the Sanc-

tion, to the great satisfaction of Charles VII. On the other hand, the pontiff's authority was strengthened with the coronation of Frederick III, the last emperor to be crowned in Rome (19 March 1452). On that occasion, the pope's dignity outshone, with extraordinary splendor, that of the emperor, which was henceforth badly compromised and rendered meaningless. This ceremony, which Frederick had ardently desired, brought no change in the status quo and no real benefits to the new emperor, nor did it increase his prestige in the eyes of his contemporaries.

With regard to papal politics in Italy, Nicholas V was clever enough to profit from the healthy balance that had been achieved among the powers in the Italian peninsula, and at first managed to remain neutral. No sooner had he been elected than he hastened to confirm the agreements signed by Eugene IV and Alfonso of Aragon. Next, he sought to gain the favor of the king of Naples by recognizing his claims to ecclesiastical benefices and dispensing with the traditional oaths and acts of homage demanded of the king as a vassal of the Holy See. In actual fact, as far as benefices and fiscal matters were concerned, Nicholas's whole strategy was aimed at reconsidering papal claims in light of the princes' interests, in exchange for their support of the temporal policy of the papacy. His chief preoccupation was the consolidation of the PAPAL STATES: to this end he instigated a policy of alliances with the other Italian powers, thus placing himself on an equal footing with them. He resumed relations with Florence, in dispute with Rome since the time of Eugene IV, and especially with Milan, where Duke Filippo-Maria Visconti had died in a conspiracy just a few months after Nicholas's election. In his will, the duke had named the king of Aragon as his heir to the duchy of Lombardy, thus threatening the equilibrium of the peninsula. While Milan was proclaiming itself the Ambrosian republic (1447–50), other pretenders joined the ranks—France, and especially its ally Francesco Sforza, who counted on his rights as a relation of Visconti's, whose daughter he had married. Venice immediately sided with Aragon. The pope, for his part, kept a neutral stance, even though in fact he had supported Sforza from the start, financing him with 35,000 gold crowns (the amount officially given as the price of the city of Iesi, held by the *condottiere*) in order to maintain the status quo. Nicholas made a first attempt at agreement by convening a meeting in Rome: Florence had formed an alliance with Sforza, and there was fear of French involvement in the Italian crisis (meanwhile, Constantinople had fallen into the hands of the Turks [1453], a development that made the union of Christian forces all the more necessary). In 1454, the peace of Lodi was signed between Venice and Milan, and the following year saw the formation of the Italic League, which the pope, irritated at first at being excluded from the peace talks, was the last to join. The situation in Italy reverted to what it had been before Visconti's death, and the pope finally felt free to apply in the papal territories a policy of reestablishing pontifical authority over local autonomies. To that end, he favored consolidating the oligarchies, both communal and seignorial, which had already been set up in the different regions and cities of the Papal States. This had been done largely through the concession of the apostolic VICARIATE (as in the case of Federico da Montefeltro, Sigismondo Malatesta in Rimini, and Autario Ordelaffi in Forli) and by giving the oligarchies financial and organizational autonomy with the aim of "consolidating the interested submission of the city patriciates." In Rome, too, the municipal class was put under increasing if not very noticeable pressure, which gradually reduced its margin of independence. With regard to the Roman barons, Nicholas acted impartially. He enhanced in equal measure the economic power of the leading Roman aristocratic families, first among them the Colonna and the Orsini. This caused discontent among the houses of the lesser NOBILITY, which were more and more subject to the great overlords, and at times even openly revolted against the pope. The conspiracy of Stefano Porcari may be seen in the context of reaction to papal politics. He belonged to the class of merchants that made up the dominant group at the time when Roman communal life was at its most splendid. Imbued with ideas of republican freedom and, consequently, opposed to the complete subjection of the municipal class to the pope and also to the tight papal control of the government of the community, Porcari, along with a small group of conspirators, prepared an attack on the Vatican, to be followed by a general revolt of the Roman people. He was discovered and arrested on 6 January 1453, and hanged three days later. This incident in fact had no repercussions on the political life of Rome, henceforth very closely linked to that of the CURIA.

As far as the city of Rome is concerned, recent historiography has viewed the pope's city planning project (actually realized only to a very small extent) as another aspect of Nicholas's centralization policy. The plan concerned two areas: the old city that grew up around the Capitol, whose palaces Nicholas wanted to rebuild; and the Borgo, that is, the area surrounding the Vatican where the Curia service buildings would be erected. Important fortifications were planned, especially for CASTEL SANT'-ANGELO, as was the rebuilding of ST. PETER'S and the enlarging of the Vatican Palace. A patron of the arts, Nicholas V commissioned frescoes from Fra Angelico and his pupil, Benozzo Gozzoli. He was also a bibliophile and lover of literature, who summoned humanists and scholars to his court to translate the Greek authors, both classical and patristic, into Latin. The VATICAN LIBRARY may well consider Nicholas V its founder because of the huge number of manuscripts he acquired and had copied: at his death, he left around twelve hundred Greek and Latin manuscripts. For all these reasons, both political and cultural, one may think of him as the first Renaissance pope.

Anna Esposito

Bibliography

Aubenas, R., and Richard, R. *La Chiesa e il Rinascimento (1449–1517)*, 2nd ed. P. Prodi, Turin, 1972 (*Storia della Chiesa dalle origini ai nostri giorni*, 15), 19–51.

Burroughs, C. "Below an Angel: An Urbanistic Project in the Rome of Pope Nicholas V," *Journal of the Warburg and Courtauld Institutes*, 45 (1982), 94–124.

Caravale A., and Caracciolo, A. *Lo Stato pontificio da Martino V a Pio IX*, Turin, 1978 (*Storio d'Italia*, ed. G. Galasso, 14), 65–76.

Cessi, R. "La congiura di Stefano Porcaro," *Studi romani*, Rome (1956), 65–112.

Da Bisticci, V. *Le Vite*, A. Grecoet I. Florence, 35–81.

Manetti, G. *Vita Nicolai V summi pontificis*, ed. L.A. Muratori, Milan, 1743 (*RIS*, III, 2).

Mollat, G. "Nicolas V," *DTC*, 11/1 (1931), 541–8.

Platina, B. *Liber de vita Christi ac omnium pontificum*, G. Gaida, Città di Castello, 1913–32 (*RIS*, III, 1), 328–39.

Prodi, P. *Il sovrano pontefice. Un corpo e due anime: la monarchia papale nella prima età moderna*, Bologna, 1982, passim.

Sforza, G. *Ricerche su Niccolò V. La patria, la famiglia, la giovinezza di Niccolò V*, Lucca, 1884.

Soranzo, G. *La Lega italica 1454–1455*, Milan, 1924.

Tafuri, M. *Cives esse non licere. La Roma di Niccolò V e Leon Battista Alberti: elementi per una revisione storiografica*, Rome, 1984, 13–39.

Towes, J. B. "Formative Forces in the Pontificate of Nicolas V (1447–1455)," *The Catholic Historical Review*, 54 (1968–9), 261–84.

Vasoli, C. "Profilo di un papa umanista: Tommaso Parentucelli," *Studi sulla cultura del Rinascimento*, Manduria, 1968, 69–121.

von Pastor, L. *Storia dei papi dalla fine del Medioevo*, It. trans. A. Mercati, I, Rome, 1910, 323–578.

Westfall, C. W. *In This Most Perfect Paradise: Alberti, Nicolas and the Invention of Conscious Urban Planning in Rome, 1447–1455*, University Park, Penn., 1974.

NICOLAISM. In the letters to the Churches of Ephesus and Pergamum in the Book of Revelation, the "Nicolaitans" are described as a sect abhorrent to Christ. Like the Balaam of apocryphal legend, they "put a stumbling block before the people of Israel, so that they would eat food sacrificed to idols and practice fornication" (Rv 2:6, 14–15). St. Irenaeus (ca. 130–ca. 200), one of the Fathers of the Church, believed, mistakenly, that the Nicolaitans, *qui indiscrete vivunt*, appeared with Nicholas, a proselyte of Antioch and one of the first seven deacons of the Church of Jerusalem (Acts 6:5). According to Epiphanius of Salamis (ca. 315–403), Nicholas advocated a married priesthood (*Panarion haer.*, chap. 5), and the historian Eusebius of Caesarea (ca. 260–ca. 340) considered the Nicolaitan HERESY an ephemeral movement that, according to some accounts, practiced free love (Clement of Alexandria, *Strom.* 3, 4, 25–6, quoted in *Ecclesiastical History* III, 3, 29). The 6th-century *Decretum Gelasianum* pronounced an ANATHEMA upon Nicholas after Simon Magus and before other heretics and schismatics (*JK*, 700). On account of the biblical reference to fornication and in light of these patristic writings, the term nicolaism was used by the reformers of the late 11th and of the 12th century to stigmatize infractions of the law of clerical celibacy that was imposed on Western clergy in major orders, from the rank of subdeacon. These infractions were often associated with SIMONY (the buying and selling of orders and ecclesiastical positions), a term that was more widespread than nicolaism. The latter term, therefore, turns up only rarely in papal letters and declarations, and only once in those of GREGORY VII (1073–85) (*JL*, 5005).

Cardinal Humbert of Silva Candida introduced the term into medieval disputation when quoting the writings of Epiphanius against the Greeks. In a letter written in 1053 to the Studite monk Nicetas, he rebuked him for favoring the marriage of priests and declared that "the accursed deacon Nicholas, the prince of that heresy, came straight from hell." Against Nicetas, he compiled some of the first papal and conciliar decisions in favor of celibacy. The 1054 excommunication of the patriarch Michael Cerularius by Humbert and the other papal LEGATES includes in the list of Greek heresies the accusation that "like the Nicolaitans, they authorized and encouraged carnal marriages of the ministers of the Holy Altar." It was perhaps Humbert's influence that led Pope NICHOLAS II (1059–61) in 1059 to write the preface to a synodal letter referring to the decisions of the COUNCIL held in Rome in April of that year "on the heresy of the Nicolaitans conceiving the marriage of priests, deacons, and all members of the clergy" (*JL*, 4404). Shortly after that, in a tract against clerical intemperance, Cardinal Peter Damiani wrote that "married priests are called Nicolaitans because of a certain Nicholas, who originated this heresy" (*Ep.* 112). At the end of the 11th century, the term was taken up by the German Gregorians Manegold of Lautenbach—who quotes Peter Damian's report (*Lib. ad Gebehardum* 68–70, 76)—and Bernold of St. Blasien (*Libelli* 1).

It was in the 12th century that there appeared some of the most violent attacks specifically against the Nicolaitans. Abbott Rupert of Deutz (ca. 1075–1129/30) recounts the story according to which the deacon Nicholas instituted the custom, clearly disapproved of in the Book of Revelation, of exchanging women (Rv 2:6, 15). In the next generation, the canon regular Gerhoh of Reichersberg (1093–1169) waged a lengthy campaign against the evils that had long plagued the Church, praising the papal reforms of the 11th century. Summing up the general opinion, he wrote that "the Nicolaitans and simoniacs are like grapes on the vine of the world, not of the Church; before LEO IX [1049–54], they virtually invaded the vine of Christ and, in defiance of the law, took women even as they served the Church. They used the Church and the income she procures for their own ends. Afterward, the popes who, under divine injunction, readily wielded the sickle, showed that these grapes had never been part of the vine of Christ even if certain popes had once tolerated them, no doubt because they were not yet ripe. But the vine of the world is now ripe; it has been in large measure harvested by popes who have borne it away from the city of God and placed it in that of the devil." After marriage, Gerhoh points the finger at concubinage: nicolaism implies both, Nicholas being "the foremost fornicator among the clergy." He takes up the 12th-century idea that the marriage of clerics is null and void. Among his many writings, the subject is dealt with principally in *Ad Innocentium papam* and *Commentarius in Psalmos*.

While the term nicolaism is used in only a few, mainly polemical and scholarly writings, clerical marriage and concubinage were condemned by all kinds of reformers between the 10th and 12th centuries. Abbots Odo of Cluny (926–42) and Abbo of Fleury (988–1004), of the monastic orders, as well as bishops such as Atto of Vercelli (924–64), Ulrich of Augsburg (924–73), and Fulbert of Chartres (1007–29) proscribe it in no uncertain terms. A bishop or priest was generally held to be linked to his see or benefice and therefore could not be joined to a woman. The argument according to which the hands that touch the body of Christ in the Eucharist must not touch a female body was also increasingly put forward. In the Rome of the first reforming popes, carnal transgressions on the part of the clergy were vehemently condemned by Cardinal Peter Damian (in particular *Ep.* 31, 112).

Even before this period, popes intervened. At the SYNOD of Pavia (1022), convened jointly by Pope BENEDICT VIII (1012–24) and Emperor Henry II (1002–24), the pope gave a long speech against clerical marriage and promulgated seven canons. One of the main objectives of the synod was to oppose the alienation and hereditary transfer of the Church's landholdings (*MGH, Const.*, I, 34). But Gerhoh of Reichersberg correctly placed the beginning of the papal campaign in the reign of Leo IX. That pope legislated equally strictly against clerical marriage and simony at councils held in Rome, northern Italy, France, and the German lands. According to Peter Damian, Leo IX decreed in 1049 that all the "priests' prostitutes" should be reduced to the status of serving maids (*ancillae*) at the Lateran Palace, a measure he urged should be applied in other dioceses (*Ep*. 112). At the council of Rome in April 1059, Pope NICHOLAS II (1058—61) decreed that no one should attend a mass celebrated by a priest who was known for a certainty to have a concubine or wife (*JL*, 4405–6). In Milan and other places in northern Italy, the Patarenes launched an aggressive, largely secular campaign against married priests and simoniacs; they were in contact with Rome and in particular with the archdeacon Hildebrand. Once he was pope—under the name GREGORY VII (1073–85)—the latter often used the Roman councils held during Lent and in November to legislate against clerical debauchery, which he battled vigorously through his legates and in letters. He urged the laity, especially in the German lands, to refuse the sacraments when administered by clerics in a state of sin (*JL*, 4931–3, 1948). These penal sanctions and pressures were accompanied by the deliberate promotion of a communal clerical life that conformed to canon law, one that could both offer a social life to celibates and serve as a model for the whole clergy. Leo IX believed that it was the duty of the episcopal chapters to preach the message; he wrote to the canons of Lucca that "if God rids your Church of married priests, these priests will once again become chaste and pure and the goods of the Church which they squandered by leading unruly lives will be returned for the use of men who live together in accordance with canon law" (*JL*, 4254). At the end of the 11th century, the development of canons regular obeying the Rule of St. Augustine received wholehearted encouragement from Pope URBAN II (1088–99), who accorded them an esteem equal to that for the monks (*JL*, 5459). The canons regular living "according to the apostolic model of the Church" (Acts 2:43–7) constituted, in effect, a counterexample to the "heresies" of the deacon Nicholas and of Simon Magus.

Throughout the Middle Ages, the struggle to promote the celibacy of the clergy was pursued by reforming popes and bishops. The different canons promulgated at the Lateran councils—I (1123), canon 7; II (1139), canons 6–8; III (1179), canon 11; and IV (1215), canons 14 and 31—are the best source concerning the decisive developments between Urban II and INNOCENT III (1198–1216).

Herbert E. J. Cowdrey

Bibliography

Amann, E. "Nicolates," *DTC* 11 (1930–2), 499–506.

Denzler, G. *Das Papsttum und der Amtszölibat*, Stuttgart, 1973–6 (*Päpste und Papsttum*, 5/1–2).

Grégoire, R. *La vocazione sacerdotale. I canonici regolari nel Medioevo*, Rome, 1982.

Mirbt, C. *Die Publizistik im Zeitalter Gregors VII.*, Leipzig, 1894.

NOBILITY, PONTIFICAL. See **Nobility, Roman.**

NOBILITY, ROMAN.

Up to Gregory the Great. The concept of nobility (*nobilitas*) in Rome is ambiguous, since it is not truly based on a juridical reality. At the end of the republic, Cicero used it to define the group of former consuls, to which he belonged, and extended it to their families; in roughly the same sense, Sallust declared that the nobility passed down the consulate from hand to hand. Under the empire, the term could be applied both to the group of families that dominated the SENATE and, more broadly, to the Senate and the whole senatorial order; indeed, Ammienus Marcellinus divided the free society of Rome into just two parts, the nobles and the people. No distinction between these two meanings will be made here.

The senatorial order consisted, on the one hand, of the senators, who were members of the assembly, and, on the other, of their spouses and descendants, male and female. From Hadrian's time, these individuals were recognized by the title "clarissimi," the one most often used in inscriptions. Their dignity (*dignitas*) derived from this title. In the first three centuries, the term implied both the possession of property equal to or greater than a million sesterces in value, together with various advantages and privileges like exemption from property tax or from the obligation to receive guests at one's domain, and monopoly of access to the highest administrative and military posts. It also carried with it various obligations: *clarissimi* were forbidden to marry women who were former slaves (women were forbidden to marry former male slaves), to work in the theater, or to own ships for commercial profit—all rights and duties that determined the rank and respectability of *clarissimus*. A senator had to live in Rome or the surrounding area, even if he came from the provinces. This rule was modified during the 3rd century, but the senator still was subject solely to the city authorities if a civil action was brought against him. At least a portion of his property had to be in Italy. This set of rules was characteristic of a social class that tried to maintain as best it could the traditions of the ancient *nobilitas*, the achievements of its ancestors, and an ethic reaching back to remote origins. It is worth noting that new members of society coming from outside Rome very quickly fitted into the existing pattern, readily adopting its prejudices, ways of thinking, and ideology.

Profound changes affected the status of the senators in the reigns of Diocletian and, later, CONSTANTINE. The senators became subject to the property tax, and then also were obliged to make a contribution in gold, the *gleba*, based on the size of their landholdings; at the same time, the number of members of the assembly was increased from six hundred to two thousand, thanks to many newcomers from the provinces who were entitled to live outside Rome. This hardly seems to have affected the number of actual Roman senators regularly attending assembly sessions. The emperor, who no longer made Rome his capital, was obliged to give the assembly more local initiative. Soon, indeed, because of the foundation of Constantinople and the establishment of a second Senate in that city, Eastern recruitment was in practice stopped; from the reign of Constans II, the Roman Senate concerned itself only with the West.

We have scant information as to the undoubtedly limited number of Christians among the *clarissimi* through the end of the 2nd century. Tradition cites the name of Flavia Domitilla, the wife of a cousin of the emperor in Domitian's reign. More certain are the testimonies of the early 3rd century, in particular that of Hippolytus, who reproached his rival, Pope CALLISTUS, for allowing *clarissimae* to live with slaves or Christian freemen in concubinage instead of lawful wedlock so that they could keep their rank. Conversions certainly became more frequent after Gallienus's edict of tolerance. Around 270, Porphyry speaks again of noble, wealthy women who give their assets to the Church and the poor. It is interesting that all these examples concern women of the aristocracy, especially widows able to dispose of their fortunes as they please. With a few exceptions, the men seem to have been more reluctant to abandon the ancient cults, those of the family Lares and the ancestors in particular. Constantine's conversion caused certain taboos to be lifted, and in fact the first convincing testimonies from the Roman nobility date from his time and that of his sons. Acilius Severus was the first consul, in 323, and the first prefect of Rome, in 325, who might be considered Christian; it is true that he was of Spanish origin. We are far better informed about the case of Junius Bassus, son of Constantine's prefect of the praetorium, who was also named Constantine, in 318–32. He died while holding the post of PREFECT OF THE CITY in 359, according to the inscription on his famous sarcophagus in the Vatican Grottoes, which notes that he was then a "neophyte," that is "recently baptized" (not necessarily "a Christian of fresh date"). The most sophisticated aristocratic family of the 4th century was that of the Anicii. Prudentius refers in passing to the "generous Anicius" who was the first Christian of the line, and what is known of the family shows that it was already largely Christian by the mid-4th century; the conversion of this first member of the family may date back to Constantine's reign. For this reason, some historians have thought, though without absolute certainty, that he was Sectus Anisius Paulinus, prefect of Rome in 331.

We know more about the genealogy of the Caeionii. It appears that the first to be converted were the two sisters of the praetorium prefect in 335, C. Caeionius Rufius Volusianus, known as Lampadius. One of these, Albina, had two daughters, both Christian. While the prefect remained pagan, his two nieces, Marcella, a widow, and

Asella, a virgin, led an exemplary life in their house on the Aventine; their cousin, Pammachius, son of Albina's sister, was also unmarried. All Lampadius's children remained pagan, but two of his sons married Christian wives, and once again it was the women whose embrace of Christianity carried the day. Around 400–3, when, according to Jerome, the old pagan pontiff Caecina Albinus, one of Lampadius's sons, was surrounded by his Christian grandchildren, all of the pontiff's family had been converted except his eldest son; at the same time, the pontiff's nephew, Volusianus, was likewise the only pagan of his branch. It therefore seems that from the middle of the century fathers tried to maintain tradition for the sake of their principal heir, leaving the other children to the influence of their wives. Questions of imperial politics may have played a role in this development. But too hasty a generalization should not be made on the basis of this family, though it does provide a highly significant example.

There was thus, over the century, a progressive conversion of the great Roman senatorial families, though that fact should not be overestimated. Pagan and Christian senators confronted each other in the great debate on the altar of the goddess Victory in 382–4; that was occasion for Symmachus to assert, not without reason, that the pagans retained the majority when the assembly was deliberating and voting. If Ambrose claimed the opposite, that was no doubt because he included those senators who lived in the provinces and did not actually take their seats in the Roman CURIA. The majority changed sides after Eugenius's defeat in 394 and in the early years of the 5th century.

It is in connection with this evolution that relations between the pope and the group of Christian senators become clearer. Strange as it may seem, sources do not show any contact between the two sides in Constantine's time, so secretive were Pope SILVESTER'S actions. Later, from the time of DAMASUS'S pontificate, relations grew closer. Jerome shows how the women on the Aventine, led by Marcella, exchanged more and more letters, and even held interviews, with the pope, who reportedly knew how to flatter widows, virgins, and high-born ladies (he was nicknamed "ear-tickler of matrons"). It was Damasus who forwarded to Ambrose and the court of Milan the Christian senators' counter-petition. The Theodosian era marks the triumphal phase of conversions among the aristocracy a change that had enormous consequences.

Constantine and his family had enriched the Roman Church with unheard-of prodigality. At his bidding, the great basilicas of Rome and its surroundings had been built and decorated. Among these was the basilica of the Lateran, close to which the pope's residence had been established—on a lot that had belonged to Empress Fausta. Each of these structures he furnished with lands, revenues, and sacred gold objects, all described minutely in the *Liber pontificalis*. Thus the pope became custodian of impressive capital assets and, in Damasus's time, did not hesitate to solicit and accept donations and legacies made to the Church by senators or their widows. The pagans were quick to criticize the pomp surrounding him; but it was by way of a personal ironical gibe that one of the most prominent pagan aristocrats, Pretaxtatus, declared that he would convert to Christianity at once if he could be bishop of Rome and benefit from all the advantages that went with the office. Thus the BENEFACTION of the converted nobles "took over from an imperial beneficence exhausted by Constantinian largesse." In 401–2, a prefect of Rome called Longinianus had a BAPTISTRY built at his expense near the titular church of Sta Anastasia, in Velabro. A little earlier, the famous praetorium prefect Petronius Probus arranged for his family mausoleum to be built in the very apse of ST. PETER'S. But this dramatic gesture was halted for a time by the catastrophes accompanying Alaric's sieges and the SACK of Rome in 410.

After Julian's death appeared the new official titles for the members of the senatorial order: simple *clarissimi* for those not embarked on a career or who were just starting out, *spectabiles* ("worthy of respect") for those who had been promoted to proconsul, *illustres* ("illustrious") for those who had reached higher echelons. This last group profited from their increased influence and by around 440 were indeed the only true members of the assembly. After 410, if there certainly remained some pagans among the Roman nobility, they were in a definite minority and soon became the exception. Such a change in the span of a half-century foreshadowed political rapprochement between the BISHOP OF ROME and the assembly. This can already be seen between 384 and 386, when, following a preliminary inquest held by the Roman prefect in cooperation with the pope, Emperor Valentinian II ordered that decisions to rebuild the basilica of ST. PAUL'S OUTSIDE THE WALLS be communicated to the Senate. In 408–9, the Roman prefect Pompeianus consulted INNOCENT I before sending for Etruscan haruspices to save Rome from Alaric's siege; the affair had no repercussions. The threat of danger brought about a rapprochement on several occasions. During the winter of 409, Innocent agreed to join an embassy of senators bound for Ravenna to plead Rome's cause before Emperor Honorius. In 452, LEO the Great accompanied the praetorium prefect Trygetius on a mission to Attila, who had just invaded Italy. After the death of Pope ZOSIMUS in 417, the rivalry between two candidates BONIFACE and EULALIUS was marked by serious uprisings. The Christian senators, like the people, were certainly far from unanimous, but once order was restored and Boniface had been recognized thanks to the emperor's final vote, the Senate took an active part in the decision. A message from the emperor was read in the Curia, and the prefect of the city had the assembly approve the solution.

The fall of the Western Empire and the invasion of the BARBARIAN king Odoacer in 476 paradoxically brought about a decided strengthening of the influence of the Senate and its principal members. In 483, Pope SIMPLICIUS feeling his end draw near, turned to the Senate to ensure a peaceful succession, and an assembly of clergies and senators prepared the election of FELIX III: presiding over it was the praetorium prefect Basilius, head of the powerful Decii family, who acted on the emperor's orders. Felix's successor, GELASIUS, corresponded with members of the Roman nobility: Andromachus, a Christian who wanted to keep the Lupercalian feast; the Jew Telesinus, who converted; and John, father of the future pope VIGILIUS, who consulted him on Eutychianism. But in Theodoric's reign, the schism between Rome and Constantinople caused relations to break down by sowing division among the senators and thus weakening the aristocracy vis-à-vis the pope. Certain highest-ranking senators served as ambassadors between the bishop of Rome and Emperor Anastasius—Faustus Niger, and later the *caput senatus* Festus. In 525, with the resumption of the struggle with the emperor and the executions of Boethius and SYMMACHUS, Theodoric forced Pope JOHN I to journey to the East to see the emperor; the pope was accompanied by four patricians, among them two members of the Decii family, the former consuls Theodorus and Importunus.

Even in these periods of crisis, collusion between the pope and at least part of the aristocracy was undeniable. Moreover, the Senate was closely linked to pontifical elections throughout the period. But at the same time, the pope was making an effort to take real control of the patrimony of his Church and break free of the influence that certain aristocratic benefactors maintained, or had maintained, over him. He managed to put a stop to transfers of property and the traffic in ecclesiastical possessions, resisted the pressure of the aristocracy, and gained far better control over the Church's riches and the power these conferred. The members of the aristocracy ceased to maintain Roman places of worship, preferring to devote themselves to the founding of monasteries and churches on their great domains.

The Byzantine reconquest was followed from 536 by a gradual decline in the senatorial assembly. Rome was under siege four times, passing from hand to hand during the long, atrocious Byzantine-Gothic war, which lasted until 552. Many senators left Rome and Italy; some settled in Constantinople every time Rome changed masters; the survivors' properties were often confiscated. Soon only a handful of senatorial families remained. The result was a considerable diminishing of the Senate, along with a rise in the power of the pope and clergy. The church's landholdings once again grew as a result of donations and legacies from senators or their widows. The assembly more and more came to resemble the municipal council of a city of moderate demographic importance, or a civilian council assisting the pope alongside the clergy, for the pope had to keep a closer eye on affairs than before.

It is worth noting that until 483 the bishop of Rome was not a member of the aristocracy; he came from a more modest background and started his ecclesiastical career when very young, climbing the ladder sometimes as high as the diaconate. This type of career pattern varied as historical circumstances changed. The first pope to be elected from a family of the *clarissimi* seems to have been Felix III; later, a prime example was Vigilius, who likewise had not followed a civilian career but had taken orders long before becoming pope. Fifty-three years after that, in 590, there was another example, in the election of a senator who was a member of the assembly and who had even been promoted to the prefecture of Rome, in 573, before retiring to papal administration: this was Gregory the Great.

It was this pope, the last one of the 6th century who bore witness to the total eclipse of the Senate in a homily he gave in 593, while Agilulf's Lombard army was drawing near to Rome on a forced march: "To what has this city come which not so long ago seemed mistress of the world . . . Where is the Senate? the people? The Senate is diminished, the people have disappeared, Rome, now empty, has been burnt." The assembly is mentioned for the last time in 603, when Gregory was presiding over the ceremony to receive the images representing the emperor Phocas and his wife: the portraits were acclaimed at the Lateran Palace "by all the clergy and the Senate." We shall cite Ernest Stein's comments on this episode: "The fact that on that occasion the Senate merely appears to be a group of laymen joining in the clergy's celebration, that it is not deliberating under the presiding prefect of Rome or a *prior senatus*, that it is not it but the pope who makes the decision concerning the imperial icons, all this is one more proof that the Senate of Rome had ceased to be the institutional and administrative organism that Justinian had wished to preserve." Its disappearance at that time is confirmed by a passage in Agnellus, who points out that after the Lombard invasion "the Roman Senate gradually disappeared, and as a consequence the freedom of the Romans was suppressed." Only the pope remained to represent Roman society as a whole, henceforth consisting solely of the clergy and the people. Italian epigraphy corroborates this brutal end. The last *spectabiles* and *illustres* date from 571, even if the terms *clarissimus* and *clarissima* can still be found describing isolated individuals throughout the 7th century.

André Chastagnol

Bibliography

Chastagnol, A. *Le Sénat romain à l'époque impériale. Recherches sur la composition de l'Assemblée et le statut de ses membres*, Paris, 1992; "Le sénateur Volusien et la conversion d'une famille de l'aristocratie romaine au Bas-Empire," *REA*, 58, 1956, 241–53, repr. in A. Chastagnol, *L'Italie et l'Afrique au Bas-Empire. Scripta varia*, Lille, 1987, 235–47.

Piétri C. *Roma christiana. Recherches sur l'Église de Rome, son organisation, sa politique, son idéologie de Miltiade à Sixte III (311–440)*, 2 vols., Rome 1976; "É vergétisme et richesses ecclésiastiques dans l'Italie du IVe siècle. l'exemple romain," *Ktèma*, 3, 317–37; "Aristocratie et société cléncale dans l'Italie chétienne au temps d'Odoacre et de Théodoric," *MEFRA*, 93, 1981, 417–67.

Stein, E. "La disparition du Sénat de Rome à la fin due VIe siècle," *Académie royale de Belgique: Bulletin de la Classe des Lettres*, 25, 1939, 308–22; *Histoire du Bas-Empire*, I: *Del'État romain à l'État byzantin (284–476)*, Fr. trans., 2 vols., Paris, 1959; II: *De la disparition de l'Empire d'Occident à la mort de Justinien (476–565)*, Paris, 1949.

From the Middle Ages. The families that dominated the Roman region in medieval times and up to the dawn of the modern era were hardly numerous. There is a long tradition of these families, but it is not free of inaccuracies or approximations. Yet their ties to the papacy have long served as a backdrop to papal history. Depending on the place and time, the *nobiles* were a complex group the contours of which were imprecise in juridical terms. This was especially true in central Italy in the Middle Ages, where communes and seigniories gave rise to a fluid social diversification which the popes had to reckon with before they were able, in the early 16th century, to impose the undisputed authority of a monarchical type of state. Henceforth the papacy became the source of new nobiliary fortunes, small and large. Still, it was not until the mid-18th century that the pope produced the official catalog of the Roman nobility. This was the period when the papacy was beginning to hand out titles without lands attached, its immediate objective being both to repay a service rendered and to satisfy the social vanity of the faithful or of friends or relations. The custom has continued up to our own day and has never explicitly been abolished.

It is difficult to pinpoint the origin of the great feudal families that would dominate the social and political history of Rome until the end of medieval times. The most numerous ones had ancient urban roots (the Annibaldi, Boccamazza, Capocci, Orsini, Savelli, etc.), with others coming from towns in the *districtus Urbis* and having, in the beginning, no seignorial privileges (the Conti, Caetani). But this was not an exclusively urban and communal aristocracy because of the ever-growing influence on its destiny of the CURIA and the Angevin monarchy. These two entities allowed the aristocratic families of the Roman region to enjoy wealth and power that their counterparts of northern and central Italy never possessed.

In the middle of the 12th century, the Roman "barons" (*magnates, barones*) formed a tightly knit group of families, clearly separate from the other noble groups (*milites, nobiles viri*) and conscious of its own power. This distinctiveness was recognized by the Curia and impressed itself on the collective imagination. A hundred years later, in the mid-13th century, five or six families can be recognized as standing out in this group on account of the importance of their territorial possessions and the key posts they held in perpetuity in the communal offices of Rome, in the SACRED COLLEGE, and in the Curia, and which enabled them to wield influence not only with the pope but also with the Italian communes and the European monarchies. These were the Annibaldi, Colonna, Conti, Orsini, Savelli, and, at the end of the 13th century, Caetani. The rise of these houses caused the great aristocratic groups of the 12th century (the counts of Tusculum, the Pierleoni, Boboni, Corsi, Frangipani, etc.) to disappear or enter into severe crisis. No longer were they able to hold their own on the Roman stage, since the other families had taken over every mechanism of enrichment and of the distribution of power set in place by the Curia from the time of the pontificate of INNOCENT III. The Angevin monarchy, anxious to strengthen its influence in Rome and central Italy, also drew these families into its orbit; through large concessions of fiefs and through marriages, it inaugurated a process of "southernizing" the great Roman lineages that would last until the dawn of the modern era. The end of the 13th century was, for the group as a whole, a period when the autonomy of the various branches (the Orsini had as many as eight) was reinforced, each one trying to attract the favors of the popes, who, from 1277 to 1303, were almost all Romans. For their part, the popes handled the baronial caste with care, in order both to ensure their tranquil possession of Rome and its district and to have at their disposal an army whose loyalty would be guaranteed by ties of blood and close friendship. The absence of the popes throughout the whole Avignon period deprived the barons of their traditional opportunities for expansion and caused increased fighting among the lineages: between the Colonna and the Orsini, among the Colonna, the Anguillara, and the Savelli, and even among the various branches of the same family. This was the period that saw the beginnings of the rivalry between the Orsini and the Colonna that would polarize the aristocratic Roman struggles up to the beginning of the 16th century. The strengthening of the power of the communes, in the absence of the papacy, led to the barons' being excluded from communal positions during the urban revolutions of the 14th century, specifically under the regime of the *banderesi* (*gonfalonieri*). This ex-

clusion was confirmed in 1363 in the constitutions drawn up by Cardinal Albornoz, which remained the basis of communal Roman legislation up to the end of the ancien régime. Not until the popes returned definitively to Rome did the barons once again play a leading role. New political circumstances often obliged the popes to look for support from one faction in order to keep the Roman city government, or even that of the Papal States, under control, insofar as the barons were also captains able to provide troops. For instance, for his political restoration, MARTIN V relied to a large extent on help from the Colonna of Genazzano and their clientele, whom he rewarded liberally. At the end of his pontificate, the power held over the papal government by the pope's relations had become such that it provoked a forceful reaction from EUGENE IV, who, for his part, was obliged to rely on the Orsini to break free of the Colonna. Thus the conflicts of the preceding century were revived.

From the end of the 12th century, the popes had tried to use the feudal system as a means of control over these restless families, on whom they systematically imposed the obligations of exclusive loyalty and liege homage in return for their many *castra* in Latium and elsewhere. In doing so, they cut the ties potentially binding fief holders to the emperor, who was always on the alert to regain papal territory. But when the struggle between the pope and the emperor became open and violent, this attempt at isolation was quickly overtaken by a cross-split between the pope's supporters and the emperor's (the GUELPHS and the GHIBELLINES). Adherence to one of the two parties relegated feudal loyalties to the background, and it often happpened that some of the pope's vassals, for instance the Di Vico, who long held the prefecture of Rome, would head up the Ghibelline forces in order to fight the papal troops. Traditionally, but with certain exceptions, the Colonna supported the empire and the Orsini the pope. This latent opposition would continue a loose hold into the modern era, when the Colonna were considered the chiefs of the Spanish side, and the Orsini ("Ursins") as heading the French faction. The ceaseless private wars between the two families had their epilogue, at least for historiographers, in the pontificate of JULIUS II. When he, though not gravely ill, was said to be facing certain death, the barons rushed to Rome at the head of their troops to confront the cardinals, reportedly about to go into conclave. At the Capitol, with Pompeo Colonna as spokesman, the chiefs of the leading families staged a passionate assertion of Roman liberty against clerical tyranny, which had grown even harder to bear since the representatives of the leading Roman families had been banned from the Sacred College. The Capitoline magistrates were about to demand that the cardinals make firm pledges for the future when news arrived that the pope had recovered. The revolution ended with a pact that was the answer to the communal authorities' prayer: on 18

August 1510, an agreement was signed by the Colonna, the Orsini, and their baron peers guaranteeing that henceforth, to avoid disturbing the coming conclave, they would live in peace for the great good of all. This truce calling for perpetual peace—the so-called *Pax Romana*, according to the words on the medal that Julius II had minted on that occasion—which might well have suffered the fate of so many other truces, effectively put an end to the great confrontations between the families, though not an end to the rebellion of individuals against papal authority, for instance, that of Ascanio Colonna at the time of the so-called salt war (1541). Julius II tried to soothe passions by designating the heads of the Colonna and Orsini families spokesmen of the Roman nobility so that they would forever hold the rank of assistants to the papal throne. This epilogue was no doubt written in the destiny of the ancient Roman nobility, whose survival had largely depended all along on the wealth and influence derived from close participation in the spiritual and temporal government of the papacy.

For a long time, the families in Latium had owed their considerable fortunes to their close family ties with the pope. Many *castra* had been granted to the Boveschi, Orsini, Conti, and so on as early as the 12th and 13th centuries. The rise of the Caetani relations of BONIFACE VIII, which was achieved partly at the expense of the Colonna, was one of the leading causes of the movement that culminated in the Anagni coup (1303). The long Avignon papacy and the Great Schism put a temporary halt to the "NEPOTISM" practiced by popes of Roman origin long before the term had been coined. And if it was a Roman, Martin V Colonna, who took up the ancient tradition once again, few of his successors could resist it. Some would try, more or less successfully, to carve out a territorial principality for their relations, tied to the Holy See by the tenuous link of vassalage. The luckiest would be the Farnese. Their duchy of Castro and Ronciglione, established in 1537, was forcibly retaken by the pope in 1649, but the duchy of Parma, conferred on Pier Luigi Farnese in 1545, would finally be lost to the papacy at the death of the last male descendant of the family in 1731. This very prevalent nepotism, which allowed certain families to gain access to the milieus of the sovereign dynasties, was no longer possible from the mid-16th century on, either because of a change in mentality or because the Italian political map was becoming less fluid. According to the logic of the absolute power they held from now on, the popes were content to give their relations key government posts and huge benefices as well as granting them important fiefs on papal lands, without any prejudice to sovereign authority. In doing so, they brought new members into Roman vassalage in a more lasting way. Claiming in their domain an authority equal to the emperor's, from the 16th century on the popes liberally handed out princely and ducal titles, both for the ancient fiefs and for

recently granted ones. The new beneficiaries, almost none of them of Roman origin, thoroughly merged with older families by means of alliances, often appointing substitute heirs to revive illustrious names whose male representatives had disappeared. This new influx dried up, however, after nepotism was officially suppressed. Except for CLEMENT XIV Rezzonico and PIUS VI Braschi, the 18th-century popes showed little inclination to bring their own families into the Roman aristocracy, whose demographic decline nevertheless was certain. Nor was the situation of the urban nobility any better.

One of the idiosyncracies of Italian history, especially that of central Italy, is the coexistence of two types of nobility: that of the *castra* and that of the cities. The latter nobility had no jurisdiction over the population, but, claiming descent from a chivalrous and military tradition, it led a life comparable to that of the feudal nobility, though it was distinct from that group. Usually well versed in the law, it played an important part in the debates among communal authorities. In 16th-century Rome, this class combined the upper urban bourgeoisie, that of the *popolo grasso*, made up of the new landowning families of the great estates in the Roman Campagna, with the agricultural entrepreneurs (the *bobacterii*) and the leading merchants. This nobility strove constantly to seize the first city posts, either during the period of communal autonomy or when the pope became in fact the sovereign arbiter of the Capitoline institutions. In the 18th century, under the pressure of diminished social mobility and perhaps for reasons of etiquette—a motive never to be underestimated in Rome, a city of solemn and extremely spectacular ceremonies in which all the elites were involved—the need was gradually felt to make a definitive, fixed list of the Roman nobles, henceforward clearly distinct from the rest of the population.

On 12 January 1746, Benedict XIV issued the constitution *Urbem romanam*. This decreed that a register (an *Albo*, commonly known as the *Libro d'oro*) was to be drawn up, and deposited in the Capitol, containing the names of 180 families whose forebears had held the posts of senator, conservator of the Capitol, or prior of the *Caporioni* (district heads), and whose descendants thereby made up the order (*ceto*) of the noble Roman citizenry. Among these families, he picked sixty who, under the heading "LX conscripted nobles," were to make up the patriciate, or first rank of the nobility, and appointed them himself. When one of these families died out, four scrutineers would be drawn by lot from among these same *patrizii coscritti*, and could make a choice only from among the families already listed in the *Albo*, at the rank of simple nobles. These last were to be chosen in the same fashion, provided the postulant could prove he had a hundred years of nobility on both sides of his family. Nobility of the second rank was extended to all the descendants; the distinction of conscripted noble was personal and transmissible by custom, though not by right, to the eldest male of the family. Families of reigning popes were to be admitted unconditionally into the ranks of the nobility. This organization left out the feudal nobility, which had been excluded from civic posts since the 14th century.

Under the ROMAN REPUBLIC, all noble titles were abolished, and the *Libro d'oro* was burned during a solemn ceremony at the Capitol on 17 July 1798. But this was a mere interlude not to be repeated during the Napoleonic period. The abolition of the feudal regime, negotiated from 1816 to 1818 in the provinces regained by the pope in 1814 (*provincie di primo recupero*), caused the baronial jurisdictions gradually to disappear. The aristocracy, which had reluctantly agreed to the suppression of its jurisdictional privileges and whose membership in the Sacred College was waning, remained very largely removed from those public posts notoriously monopolized by the clergy. Its relations with the papacy, at least up to 1870, chiefly touched questions of protocol concerning positions and ranks at the papal COURT. In the chirograph of 2 May 1853, PIUS IX called for the inclusion in the *Libro d'oro* of the nobility at the Capitol of all the princely and ducal families in Rome that henceforth could be chosen to make up the LX patrician families as members died out. The Heraldic Capitoline Congregation created as a result of this chirograph deferred to the pope's wishes in its deliberation of 17 January 1854, further deciding to include among the Roman patricians the heads of families that had produced a pope. The newly included ancient members of the feudal nobility constituted a separate group, that of the Roman princes and dukes ("ceto dei principi et duchi romani"). Their existence was later recognized by the *Consulta araldica* of the kingdom of Italy with the privileges of TITULATURE that derived therefrom (in particular, the custom of prefixing a name with *Don*).

With the ending of papal temporal power, the situation of the Roman nobility was frozen. The kingdom of Italy recognized the old papal titles but had put an end to the use of "golden books" of municipal nobilities, while continuing nonetheless to make substitutions in the Roman patriciate. The pope continued to deal with those who had not compromised themselves with the new governments, but stopped updating the *Libro d'oro*, which thus remained fixed as it was in 1870, save for the insertion of relations of the new popes. The most fervent members of the nobility, those who had remained faithful to the Roman pontiff and whom people called the "black nobility," continued to lend their support to the pope, whether by actively holding court posts or by serving as intermediaries in financial dealings where the Holy See needed an accommodating cover. The patriciate was convened regularly by Pius IX and his successors, up to PAUL VI. The only ones to be excluded, until the reconciliation be-

tween Italy and the Holy See, were the heads of families who had accepted public posts in the new kingdom or, in a general way, individuals whose conduct was judged not to conform to the rules of Catholic morality. Paul VI, responding in 1968 to the patricians' New Year's wishes, announced that he was putting an end to their existence as a constituent body in the papal court. Among other things, this meant the loss of membership in the Tribune of Honor, opposite that of the diplomatic corps, in official ceremonies. Three months later, the *motu proprio Pontificalis domus* (28 March 1968) abolished all the positions in the papal household traditionally reserved for Roman families. The only ones to be retained were the two assistant princes to the throne, Aspreno Colonna and Alessandro Torlonia, who, apparently, will have no successors.

In the Middle Ages, and frequently in the 14th century, on grand occasions the pope and the emperor conferred the title of Palatine Count of the Lateran—an explicit reference to the palace over which they both claimed to have jurisdiction. In addition, the pope granted the order of Knight of the Golden Militia (*Militia aurea*), a purely honorific chivalric order. The concession did not always include transmission of the title, but did confer hereditary nobility. Soon attached by right to certain positions at the papal court, the title could be conferred by cardinal legates, by bishops assistant to the throne, by certain other prelates, and, from the 16th century, by Duke Sforza Cesarini. The privileges that went along with the title of Palatine Count included the right to create apostolic NOTARIES, legitimize bastards, and concede family coats of ARMS. A large number of people who lived outside the PAPAL STATES received the title of count in this fashion. In 17th-century France, there were precise tariffs for registering this type of title. In 1815, to give some credibility to an honorific title that had been distributed too broadly, PIUS VII reserved the granting of the title of Palatine Count to the pope alone, separating it definitively from the Order of the Golden Militia, except when expressly mentioned in the nominating brief. It was at this time that the title of Roman count became current, a title that did not mean that the bearer was a member of the Roman nobility. But already in the 18th century the popes were granting foreigners principalities, duchies, and marquessates that were purely honorific (though not baronetcies, for fear of offending the great feudal vassals): for example, the Ripert d'Alonzier were created marquesses in 1741 and confirmed in 1789. At the time of the Restoration, the fashion for papal TITLES flourished with the triumph of UTRAMONTANISM, and there was total confusion between the title of Roman count and a traditional noble title. With Paul VI (1963–78), the custom practically disappeared, even though it was not explicitly abolished, and JOHN PAUL II may have resorted to it in favor of a compatriot at the beginning of his pontificate. Papal titles were generally decried by purists of nobiliary law, who most often saw them as merely a surreptitious way of having oneself admitted into the national aristocracy, or of getting at bargain price an upgrading in title that otherwise would have been difficult to achieve. True, only rarely did the popes grant titles *motu proprio* to nationals of countries outside the Papal States (the best known exceptions being officers in the service of Pius IX). The granting of honorific titles in almost every case was carried out at the request of an intermediary, whence the reputation for venality that papal titles have gained, one they by no means always deserve.

The French, champions of the papacy in the 19th century, seem to have benefited the most from the papal prerogative. Ancient families had recourse to the pope to obtain high-sounding titles: that of prince for the Polignac in 1820 and the Clermonts-Tonnerre in 1911; that of duke of Pavese for a junior branch of the Rohan-Chabot in 1907; that of duke for the Pimodan in 1860; that of count for the Haute-clocque in 1857.

Others, and they are the most numerous, were anxious to affirm or confirm a noble status. Among these were honorable officials of the Republic of France such as the ambassador to the Holy See, Poubelle, who, when he left Rome in 1898, was given the title of Roman Count by LEO XIII. In the absence of an official list, the most likely estimates give a figure of four hundred for the number of papal titles granted to French citizens between 1820 and 1920. The French Chancery recognized them only very reluctantly under the Restoration and virtually stopped doing so under the Second Empire. In Italy, titles conferred by the pope in his States before 1870 were ratified under the laws of the new kingdom. Titles granted to Italian nationals after that date could be ratified based on the LATERAN PACTS (1929), up to 1946. Spain, too, was a country of choice for papal titles, which were especially sought-after since—except for the interim republican period—the government readily recognized them even if they did not include a Spanish place name, as was often the case. Catholics of the United States have tried to obtain a title even though their federal constitution forbids them to use one. By a curious chance, the last name in the official list of members of the Roman nobility published by the Holy See is Rose Fitzgerald Kennedy, the mother of the president, who was created countess in her own right by Pius XII in 1951.

François-Charles Uginet

Bibliography

Ameyden, T. *La storia delle famiglie romane*, with notes and additions by C. A. Bertini, Rome, n.d. (1915) [critical ed. of a 17th-c. ms. that remains fundamental].

Boutry, P. "Nobiltà romana e Curai nell'età della Restaurazione," in *Signori, patrizi, cavalieri nell'età moderna*, ed. M. A. Visceglia, Bari-Rome, 1992, 340–422 [important bibliography for the end of the 18th c. and the 19th].

Caffarelli, G. P. *I principi e duchi romani dalla feudalità all'inserimento nel patriziato e nella nobiltà romana*, in *Rivista araldica*, LXXVI, 1978, 161–78.

Carrocci, S. *Baroni di Roma. Dominazioni signorilli e lignaggi aristocratici nel Duecento e nel primo Trecento*, Rome, 1993.

Colonna di Stigliano, C. *L'ultima corte pontificia, Rivista araldica*, LXXXV, 1988, 67–83 [last official list of the Roman nobility, drawn up by the Holy See in 1964].

d'Alboiusse, L. *Un cahier blanc. Noblesse pontificale*, Paris, 1958.

Pasini-Frassoni, F. "Considerazioni sui titoli nobiliari e sugli ordini equestri pontifici," *Rivista del Collegio araldico*, June 1914.

Pietramelara, G. *Il libro d'oro del Campidogli*, 2 vols., Rome, 1893–7.

Tosi, M. *La società romana dal feodalesimo al patriziato (1816–1853)*, Rome, 1958 [posthumous work, partly unfinished but useful for the modern era].

Williams, George L. *Papal Genealogy: The Families and Descendants of the Popes*, Jefferson, N.C., 1998.

NOBLE GUARD. An army corps responsible for the protection of the pope that also serves as his honor guard. On 11 May 1801 PIUS VII, who was reorganizing his court, accepted the proposal of Marquis Costaguti for the creation of a guard whose members would be chosen from among the ranks of the NOBILITY in the PAPAL STATES. This entailed reviving the cavalry (*cavalleggeri*) and the *lance spezzate* that had been abolished three years earlier, a number of whom had found positions in the two newly created companies. The name of the new body was inspired by an analogous institution in the Spanish court. Other than antechamber and sentinel service within the PALACE, the noble guards were to surround the pope during ceremonies and in his travels. An exempt (colonel) commanded the detachments and rode on horseback alongside the pope's carriage. The noble guards were soon accompanying papal representatives while on extraordinary missions to foreign courts, particularly to carry the golden ROSE or the birettas for new cardinals residing outside Rome. The guards received a salary and were listed on the papal family roster. Dissolved during the French occupation of the papal territories, the corps was reconstituted in 1813 in order to receive Pius VII on his return to the Papal States. On 17 February 1824, LEO XII decided that it would henceforth be formed of a single company, instead of the two previous ones under the command of two captain commanders, who shortly thereafter were replaced by one captain commander, seconded by a coadjutor with the right of succession. Until 1901, the commanders were recruited alternately from the Barberini and Altieri families. The vexillary of the Roman Church, who until 1798 was a captain of the cavalry became captain of the noble guard, and the company stored and cared for the *vexillum* (BANNER) of the Church.

Service in this corps was considered honorable work for the younger sons of the noble families of the Papal States in the 19th century: the young Giovanni Mastai (the future PIUS IX) wanted to enlist, but was discouraged for health reasons. The regulations expected the applicant to produce proof of nobility, to guarantee a set personal revenue, and, if he were married, to assure that his wife had a dowry greater than 25,000 lira. The nobility of the family could be proved by the holding for at least sixty years, of the title of patrician of one of the cities of the Papal States, whose civil administrations were well known as an undeniable sign of nobility status by the Order of Saint Stephen (Tuscany) or that of Saint John of Jerusalem (Order of Malta). The taking of Rome in 1870 greatly reduced the responsibilities of the noble guard, which nevertheless continued to maintain daily service within the Vatican itself, and even maintained a stable until the papacy of PIUS X. But membership in the corps took on a symbolic character of inflexible attachment to the Holy See and of the rejection of the new political state of Italy. Under LEO XIII and Pius X, a good number of those in charge of Catholic works in Rome were noble guards, not counting all those who lent their names for real estate operations occurring in the administration of the Patrimony's building projects. The Secretary of State Merry del Val and the commander Camillo Rospigliosi were the inspiration behind the regulation of 1912. Rospigliosi called for stricter conditions for admission into the corps: the family's nobility was to be at least 100 years old, and the wife's minimum dowry was doubled. One other innovation, aimed at increasing the number of honorific charges distributed by the pope throughout the Catholic world, was the admission of noble guards born in regions outside the former Papal States, as long as they could meet the same criteria of nobility and fortune. This honor guard, which was abolished in 1918 allowed a noble guard of Spanish origin to be sent to Vienna to carry the cardinal's biretta to the nunccio while Italy was at war with Austria.

By the *motu proprio Pontificalis domus* (28 March 1968), PAUL VI retained the noble guard, henceforth called the honor guard of His Holiness, but excluded it from the pontifical chapel. And finally, on 14 September 1970 (in a letter to the secretary of state), he announced that all branches of the pontifical armies would be abolished, with the exception of the SWISS GUARD. Some of the former noble guards became GENTLEMEN OF HIS HO-LINESS. The others, if they had not publicly demonstrated opposition to the abolishment of their service, retained certain material advantages connected to their former status (access to banking services and to Vatican City stores). Some regrouped, privately, in the association called *Compagnia delle lance spezzate*, whose survival is linked to that of its members.

The noble guard's archives have remained in the Vatican. They contain the daily reports of the antechamber service since the time of Gregory XVI, as well as the evidence presented by candidates for admission into the corps.

François-Charles Uginet

Bibliography

Colonna di Stigliano, C. "L'ultima corte pontificia," *Rivista araldica*, LXXXV, 1988, 67–83 [a list of noble guards in 1970].

Trezzi, G. *La Guardia nobile del corpo di Sua Santitá*, Rome, 1922.

NORMANS OF SOUTHERN ITALY AND SICILY. Probably in the year 999, a group of Norman pilgrims returning from the Holy Land helped the prince of Salerno repel a Saracen incursion. Over the following decades, the authorities of southern Italy called on Norman mercenaries for aid. In 1030, a group of these mercenaries was given the town of Aversa; in 1062, the commander of the group seized Capua, the capital of a Lombard principality. Another group, established in 1041 in Melfi by the Byzantines, conquered Apulia (Bari, 1071). Robert Guiscard, who became duke of Apulia in 1057, along with his brother Roger also seized Calabria (Reggio, 1060) and Muslim Sicily (Palermo, 1072). Roger's son, the count of Sicily, Roger II, inherited the duchy of Apulia in 1127, had himself crowned king in 1130, and succeeded in uniting the south. Ruled by him, his son, and his grandson until 1189, the kingdom at that time passed to Tancred of Lecce (1190–4), who fought Emperor Henry VI, married to Constance, the daughter of Roger II. Henry VI and Constance governed the kingdom until their deaths (1197 and 1198).

The special, often inimical relations between the Normans of Italy and the pope have several origins. The most obvious one is geographic: in the 12th century, the PAPAL STATES' only neighbor to the southeast was the Norman kingdom of the Two Sicilies. Now owing to the false DONATION OF CONSTANTINE but also to the privileges of Otto I (962) and Henry II (1020), the pope had dominion over the "duchy of Benevento," which formerly had covered most of southern Italy. Moreover, the Norman states were established during the Gregorian Reform, so that the pope, who at that time was arrogating to himself temporal rights, was able to find aid and refuge in southern Italy during his warring with the em-

NORMANS OF SOUTHERN ITALY AND SICILY

peror. Third, the position of the church in these regions was unique, especially in conquered Sicily, where it was the counts who erected the cathedrals. Lastly, the monarchy had a very Eastern conception of power, which enabled it to dictate to the Church in a manner hardly compatible with contemporary Church law. Accordingly, the pope's relations with his southern neighbors had a dual character: they intermixed political problems and religious questions, and, depending on the actual power of the rulers of southern Italy, they were sometimes very close and sometimes extremely loose.

In 1038, Emperor Conrad II made Rainulf count of Aversa; in 1047, Henry III invested Rainulf and Drogon with Aversa and Melfi respectively, as had been the emperors' custom since the 10th century with the Lombard princes of the south. By the mid-11th century, however, the Normans had became notorious pillagers. To escape them, in 1051 Benevento gave itself over to the pope, and the city henceforth became a papal enclave in Norman territory. LEO IX decided to get rid of the invaders, but they defeated him at the battle of Civitate (in the north of Apulia, 1053); taken prisoner, the pope was forced to recognize the Norman conquests.

When, in 1059, NICHOLAS II found himself confronted by an antipope, he resolved to appeal to Richard d'Aversa. Assuming the role of the emperor, he received the oath of fealty from Richard and from Robert Guiscard and invested them with the standard of the conquered territories: officially, the Norman leaders were loyal subjects of the pope, whom they had to provide with a census report and assistance. The alliance worked tolerably well. Even though, in 1061, ALEXANDER II owed his installation entirely to Richard's support, the latter ravaged the papal territory while other Normans were advancing in the Abruzzi; in 1073, conversations between GREGORY VII and Robert Guiscard led to a rupture, whereas the pope invested the prince with Capua; and Robert Guiscard's conquest of Salerno (1077) resulted in his excommunication. Yet, in the midst of his war with Henry IV, Gregory VII came south and in 1080, in Capua, received the oath of fealty of Robert Guiscard and of Jordan of Capua. When the emperor besieged him in Rome in 1084, he appealed to Guiscard, who entered the city and sacked it. Gregory VII died in Salerno in 1085, and his successor, VICTOR III, spent almost all his brief pontificate in the south. The struggle of the reform popes with the emperors pushed them into alliance with the Normans, and numerous reform councils were held in southern Italy. On the other hand, the Normans' subordination to the pope was highly theoretical: the Norman rulers claimed to hold power only by grace of God and never referred to papal investiture; in actual fact, the pope was dependent upon their armies.

Relations between the two powers changed after the death of Robert Guiscard, whose successors, Roger

(1085–1111) and William (1111–27), confronted with baronial revolt, tended to be weak. URBAN II, who spent a good part of his pontificate in southern Italy, invested Duke Roger in 1089 and held councils in Troia (1089, 1093) in an attempt to bring the warring Normans under control by means of the truce of God (his successors did the same in 1115 and 1120). In Sicily, from 1080 on, Count Roger I created dioceses on his own initiative, and in 1098 Urban II promised him not to send LEGATES onto the island without his assent, and even allowed him to act (on his orders) as a legate himself. The counts of Sicily lost no time in extending the scope of this agreement, which was the origin of the privilege of legation claimed in Sicily by the Spanish kings in the modern era.

In 1127, HONORIUS II challenged Roger II of Sicily, who took the title Duke of Apulia and had himself crowned in Salerno like the Lombard princes of old; yet the pope was still obliged to invest him, in 1128. In 1130, Roger sided with ANTIPOPE ANACLETUS II and the royal title conferred on him by an assembly in 1130 was recognized by that antipope, who promised him Beneventan support, a recognition that was no longer personal but dynastic. After Anacletus's death, and in the face of Roger's successes (he now also dominated Apulia and Naples), INNOCENT II recognized him in his turn and invested him at Mignano in 1139. Until the death of William II (1189), the pope had scarcely any opportunity to intervene politically in the kingdom: William I swore loyalty only to the vanquished HADRIAN IV, in 1156, and William II did not swear loyalty to CLEMENT III until 1188, after he had reigned for twenty-two years; the kings were crowned without the authorization of the pope. Political relations were dictated by the attitude of the monarchy. It was after Roger II raided Benevento that CELESTINE II was forced to renew the agreement of 1139. In 1144, after fruitless negotiations between Roger and LUCIUS II in Ceprano, a military clash ended in a seven-year truce, which in fact determined the frontier between Sicily and the Papal States, and in 1148 Roger gave military aid to EUGENE III.

Nonetheless, in the religious sphere, Roger II "dispensed ecclesiastical offices as he did positions at his palace," as John of Salisbury put it. Accordingly, for a long time the popes refused the ordination of bishops who had not been elected according to canon law; the question was settled in 1150 in Ceprano with Eugene III. Relations were soured yet again at the beginning of the reign of William I of Sicily (1154–66), when Hadrian IV supported the great revolt of 1155–6 and the Byzantine invasion. The reaction of the victorious king led to the CONCORDAT of Benevento (1156). The pope invested William I and recognized the Norman conquests in the Abruzzi. And he agreed to an ecclesiastical anomaly in the kingdom: in Sicily, APPEALS TO THE POPE and papal legations were forbidden; they were authorized on the

1053

mainland (in fact, no more legates were sent there) except in the city where the king resided; the king would oversee episcopal elections and have the power to reject any candidate considered a traitor, an enemy or simply "odious." Political relations improved when the pope led the war against Frederick Barbarossa: allied to the pope, the kingdom was represented at the negotiations held in Venice in 1178.

Things suddenly changed once again at the end of the 12th century. In 1184, LUCIUS III allowed a marriage between Constance, daughter of Roger II, and Henry VI, son of Frederick Barbarossa, and their right to succeed William II, who was childless. But at the king's death (1189), it was the count of Lecce, Tancred, Roger's grandson, who gained the throne. In 1192, he was obliged to sign the concordat of Gravina with CELESTINE III. This was not as aberrant a concordat as that of Benevento, for the pope would once again be able to send legates and hold councils in the Continental part of the kingdom, and the king could no longer forbid him to ordain a bishop judged "odious." Accordingly, when, after Tancred's death (1194), Henry VI and Constance took control of the kingdom without requesting papal investiture, the pope sent a legate whom the sovereigns repudiated, pointing to the old custom, and the legate had to take refuge in Benevento. Similarly, they refused to recognize an archbishop elected without their assent. Yet, during a troubled time, Constance had to swear loyalty to the pope and, in 1198, allow the kingdom to return to general canon law: the king's agreement with respect to elections was put on the same level as papal confirmation. In the same year, before her death Constance named INNOCENT III regent and tutor of her son, King Frederick II, then four years old.

During the first years of his pontificate, the pope strove to govern the kingdom, which was being fought over by several factions: he dispatched numerous legates; in 1202, he appointed the Frenchman Gauthier de Brienne (Tancred's son-in-law) and his own cousin, the marshal Jacques, captain and master justiciary of Apulia and Terra di Lavoro respectively, thus making them practically viceroys on the Continent. In actual fact, however, up until 1220 power was in the hands of local authorities.

It is clear that relations between Rome and the kingdom bordering the Papal States to the southeast were complex, close, and often conflict-ridden (they would become more so under Frederick II). On the political level, the pope's right of investiture was counterbalanced by the Normans' military superiority. On the ecclesiastical level, this land, in which the bishops depended politically and economically on the monarchy, still partly eluded the general law of the Church in the 12th century, even though the Norman rulers of the 11th century had been the principal military supporters of the pope at the time of the Gregorian Reform.

Jean-Marie Martin

Bibliography

Chalandon, F. *Histoire de la domination normande en Italie et en Sicile*, Paris, 1907, 2 vols., repr. New York, 1960 and 1969.

D'Alessandro, V. *Storiografia e politica nell'Italia normanna*, Naples, 1978.

Deer, J. *Papsttum und Normannen*, Cologne-Vienna, 1971.

Fodale, S. *Comes et legatus Siciliae*, Palermo, 1970.

NOTARY, APOSTOLIC. The term *notarius* originally referred to a person capable of setting down a speech in *notae* (tachygraphic summaries) the moment it was delivered, or of drawing up a detailed report of a speech. In the Roman Empire, notaries were public writers or clerks in the service of private persons or public bodies. The Church also had its notaries. Today, little credit is given to the claim of the *LIBER PONTIFICALIS* that CLEMENT I (88–97) created seven regional notaries of the Church of Rome. On the other hand, a reference to such notaries at the time of Popes FABIAN (236–50) and JULIUS I (337–52) seems to have foundation. In contrast to the "pope's notaries" (*notarii papae*), who answered to the papal CHANCERY, from the 13th century on the term apostolic notary (*notarius apostolicus, auctoritate apostolica*) meant a notary to whom the Holy See had granted jurisdictional power to act as a public officer and in that capacity, to draw up documents in an authentic form. These notaries were appointed to service in the Roman Curia itself, particularly the ROTA (*notarii palatii apostolici*), in the offices of the Papal States, and in various parts of Christendom, chiefly the episcopal curias (officialities). In 1216, Rainerius of Perugia observed in his *Ars notaria* that the post of notary could be granted by the pope or by the emperor (*Bibliotheca Juridica Medii Aevi*, ed. A. Gaudenzi, II, Bologna, 1892, 64–5). It is not clear whether the power of the apostolic notary by that time extended to the *ubique terrarum*. A few decades later, Pietro da Unzola wrote explicitly that a notary appointed by apostolic authority could "ubicumque . . . suo officio uti et instrumenta conficere" (Rolandinus, *Summa totius artis notariae*, Venice, 1546, 407). In fact, during the second half of the 13th century, apostolic notaries were practicing in England, and there were some in France, Germany, and, later, Spain. In that century they were known as *sanctae Romanae ecclesiae auctoritate notarius publicus*, and, from the 14th century, *publicus auctoritate apostolica notarius*. The appointment of an apostolic notary (*officium tabellionatus*) could be carried out at the papal CURIA or *in partibus*, by those entitled to make a certain number of such nominations (apostolic LEGATES, bishops, ecclesiastical or lay dignitaries). Candidates had to take an examination determining their level of education (*liter-

atura), their writing skill, and their morals. In the 13th century, those presenting themselves at the Curia were questioned by the pope's CHAPLAINS, and from the 14th century generally by the vice-chancellor. The candidate was required to be a tonsured cleric or to have received minor orders, to be unmarried, and to be more than twenty-five years old (M. Tangl, *Die päpstlichen Kanzleiordnungen von 1200–1500*, CXXXIII, 329). However, there were frequent exceptions. Married men were often admitted *cum unica et virgine*, as were priests, and sometimes the age requirement was waived. On the other hand, the examination *in partibus* was often entrusted to an ecclesiastical dignitary, never a layman. Once appointed, the apostolic notary was sworn in. Until recently, the function of notaries *auctoritate apostolica* continued, especially in ecclesiastical bodies, and more frequently in Italy than elsewhere. In lay circles, it always coexisted with the notaries appointed *auctoritate imperiali*.

Paulius Rabikauskas

Bibliography

Barraclough, G. *Public Notaries and the Papal Curia*, London, 1934.

Baumgarten, P. M., *Von der Apostolischen Kanzlei*, Cologne, 1908 (7–68: "Die päpslichen Notare im dreizehnten, vierzehnten und fünfzehnten Jahrhundert").

Cheney, C. R. *Notaries Public in England in the Thirteenth and Fourteenth Centuries*, Oxford, 1972.

Costmagna, G. "Il notariato nell'Italia settentrionale durante i secoli XII e XIII," *Notariado publico y documento privado: de los origenes al siglo XIV*, II, Valencia, 1989, 991–1008.

Fournier, P. *Les Officialités au Moyen Âge*, Paris, 1880.

NOVATIAN. Novatian was an eminent member of the Roman clergy at the time of the Decian persecution, carried out against all the Christian communities of the Roman Empire in 250 and 251. He had been ordained priest by Pope Fabian and was renowned for his theological scholarship. In the period between FABIAN'S martyrdom (20 January 250) and the election of CORNELIUS who became pope on 6 or 13 October 251, Novatian played an important role in the Roman *presbyterium*. Two letters preserved in the correspondence of Cyprian of Carthage (*Ep.* 30 and 36) are attributed to him. They were written in the name "of the priests and deacons living in Rome," at a time when a severe crisis, growing out of the persecution, was raging in AFRICA: the question was whether or not to reintegrate the *lapsi*, those who had denied the faith, succumbed under persecution, and wished to return to the bosom of the Church. Cyprian, who had left his see

out of prudence and thereby incurred blame in some quarters, was opposed to erratic initiatives and undisciplined behavior. The letter written to him by Novatian was stern but measured: it proposed waiting until a bishop was appointed in Rome who would "attend to the *lapsi* with authority and wisdom" and maintained that it was important "to settle the matter . . . after having deliberated it in common with the bishops, the priests, the deacons, the confessors, and the laypersons who have remained faithful" (Cyprian, *Ep.* 30). Letter 36, also generally attributed to him, shows, for its part, restraint and also repugnance in the face of the extreme attitudes of certain members of the African Christian community. It was in this period of Novatian's life that he produced the treatise on the Trinity (*De Trinitate*), said to be the first theological work in Latin from within the Roman Church. His role in the development of Latin theology is a significant one. It remains perfectly orthodox and undoubtedly helped to enhance Novatian's great renown within the Roman Christian community.

The decisive moment in Novatian's life occurred at the time of the election of Pope Cornelius, whose ordination took place on 6 or 13 March 251 (*Liberian Catalogue, MGH, AA*, 9/1, 75). Some members of the community refused to recognize it and rallied behind Novatian. He was quickly supported by three Italian bishops, "rustic and very simple men," as Cornelius, their rival, put it disparagingly in a letter to Fabian of Antioch that was preserved by EUSEBIUS of Caesarea (ECCLESIASTICAL HISTORY VII, 43).

Pitted against Cornelius, Novatian gathered together the rigorists to the *lapsi* and presented himself as their pope. His followers described themselves as the "pure ones," or *katharoi*. They urged that the Church refuse to pardon the apostates, for sins against God cannot be forgiven by the Church, according to Matt. 10:33: "But whoever denies me before others, I also will deny before my Father in heaven."

A Roman SYNOD excommunicated Novatian. But from then on a relentless conflict arose between Novatian and his dissenting Church on the one hand and the Catholic Church on the other. The schismatics' pamphlets portrayed Cornelius as an apostate who had obtained a certificate documenting that he had sacrificed to the gods. The schism immediately spread, to Carthage, where the community was already divided by Novatian's activities, to Antioch, and, finally, to Gaul and the Christians of the West. A good description of the actions of his envoys in Africa appears in letters sent from Rome by Cornelius to Cyprian, which are preserved in the latter's correspondence: "They go from door to door and locality to locality," the bishop of Carthage wrote, alarmed at the aggressiveness and ceaseless activity of Cornelius's adversaries. Cornelius, on the other hand, as portrayed by the pen of a cleric as well nurtured on classical culture as Cyprian, appears as the ideal bishop, the "best of princes" for the Church of Rome (*Ep.* 55).

Cyprian's support was invaluable in the western part of the empire. The Marcian affair, which blew up after Cornelius's death, exemplifies his relentless vigilance. On learning from Faustinus of Lyon that Marcian of Arles had gone over to Novatian's side, Cyprian put pressure on Pope STEPHEN, encouraging him in no uncertain terms not only to excommunicate Marcian but to arrange for a new bishop to replace him: "We must [. . .] keep inviolable the respect due our predecessors, the blessed martyrs LUCIUS and Cornelius. We ourselves honor their memory; but it is much rather you, beloved brother, who must honor it and defend it with the weight of your authority, you who are their successor and hold their place" (*Ep.* 68). Furthermore, other letters (*Ep.* 59 in particular) and a systematic work, the treatise *On the Unity of the Church*, reveal the fundamental importance of the see of Rome in the universal Church.

In the East, the spread of the schism was checked when Cornelius succeeded in winning over Fabius of Antioch (Eusebius, I *EH* VI. 43) and when a council led by DIONYSIUS of Alexandria brought all the Churches of this part of the Roman world into Catholic unity.

Like Cornelius, who was exiled at Centumcellae (Civitavecchia) during the persecution ordered by Trebonius Gallus, Novatian was banished from Rome. Cut off from his faithful, he followed the example of other bishops separated from their flock by writing them instructions or pastoral letters, the rigorist tone of which allows them to be dated easily within his writing as a whole. In the list of his works provided by Jerome (*De viris illustr.* 70, *PL* 23, 681), some are identifiable: the *Treatise on Jewish Foods*, another *On Spectacles* (in French) and one *On the Benefit of Chastity* (in French) the last two being included in the body of Cyprian's works. These writings make clear that he never abandoned austerity or rigorism in his teaching, which frequently invoked tradition. In the 4th and 5th centuries, nuclei of rigorists were still loyal to him in various regions of the West.

Michel Christol

Bibliography

Amann, E. *DTC*, 11, 1, (1930) 815–49

Daniélou J., and Marrou, H. *Des origines à Grégoire le Grand* (*Nouvelle Histoire de l'Église*, I, ed. L. J. Rogier, R. Aubert, M. D. Knowles), Paris, 1963, 229–37.

Fliche-Martin, II, Paris, 1943, 192–7, 409–15.

Lebreton J., and J. Zeiler. *De la fin du IIe siècle à la paix constantinienne*.

Novatien, A. D'Alès, *Étude sur la théologie romaine au milieu du IIIe siècle*, Paris, 1924.

Testini, P. *Archeologia cristiana*, I, Rome–Paris–Tournai–New York, 1958, 241–2.

NOVEMDIALES. According to the arrangements drawn up by GREGORY XV (1621–3) for papal funerals, the ceremonies prior to the interment of the pope, whose body was exposed to view at St. Peter's, were to last for nine days (*Novemdiales*). The office was celebrated for the first six days in the canons' choir and for the last three in the confession of St. Peter, where the catafalque was raised at a height of more than 65 feet/20 meters and was decorated and surrounded with a thousand candles. Five absolutions were sung by different cardinals at the end of these three solemn masses. On the final day, the pope's funeral oration was given by a prelate appointed by the cardinals. Inhumation followed.

This novena, intended to show the Christian world in mourning and to draw heavenly grace upon the illustrious deceased, has been simplified. The supreme pontiff is now interred on the third day. And today it is no longer only the chapter of St. Peter's and the Sacred College who follow the religious ceremonies but the people of God throughout the diocese of Rome, the entire Catholic Church by actual or intended participation, and the Eastern Churches.

Philippe Levillain

Bibliography

De funere Summi Pontificis, Vatican City, 1978.

Del Rè, *La Curia romana. Lineamenti storico-giuridici*, 4th ed, Rome, 1998.

Regolamento generale della Curia romana, Vatican City, 1999.

NUMBERING. See **Onomastics, Pontifical.**

NUNCIATURE. The nunciature is the institution *par excellence* of the diplomacy of the HOLY SEE and the place where that diplomacy finds its fundamental expression. It arose from the first vicariates (*Vicarii apostolici*), attested toward the end of the 4th century, and from the APOCRISARII. From the 9th century on, high-ranking members of the clergy, the LEGATES, were sent out on special, supposedly temporary, missions, mostly of a diplomatic nature. In the 11th century, the custom arose of assigning CARDINALS to the most important local political authorities. These legates *a latere* were given huge powers and were presumed to contribute to the external prestige of the papacy and the influence of the Church, in particular the Roman Church. With the growth of secular monarchies in the 16th century came a need for a stable system of diplomatic representation to be established. As early as 1488, under the pontificate of INNOCENT VIII (1484–92), the republic of Venice had instituted a permanent ambassador to the Holy See, while in 1500 ALEXANDER VI (1492–1503) reciprocally accredited

Bishop Angelo Leonini of Tivoli as permanent *nuncius*. Similar connections were set up with the Spain of Ferdinand the Catholic, who attached an ambassador to Rome in 1482. Alexander VI sent Don Francisco des Prats, apostolic PROTONOTARY, as *collector et nuncius* to that country. Bishop Jean Ferrari of Arles was given the same assignment to the French king in 1500. But it seems to be from the pontificate of LEO X (1513–21) that the definitive institution of nunciatures as agencies of permanent representation, deliberately distinguished by that definition from legations, should be dated. Since then, the criterion has remained unchanged. The pope believed the prestige of the Church would be enhanced by steady diplomatic activity, aimed at effectively settling the religious struggles that were tearing Western Christendom apart. Remodeling the structure of the nunciatures and reaffirming their legitimacy in 1584, GREGORY XIII (1572–85) made the thirteen existing nunciatures into an important tool of the Catholic REFORM that began as a result of the council of TRENT. After the treaty of Westphalia (1648), powerful anti-Roman currents somewhat diminished the influence of the nunciatures until the Congress of Vienna (1815), which inaugurated a veritable rebirth of papal diplomacy in general and of the nunciatures in particular. The establishment of exceptional diplomatic exchanges with Turkey and then Russia, by means of extraordinary missions, was followed after the First WORLD WAR by the institution of new nunciatures, first in Latin America and in the European countries born of the peace of Versailles and then, after the Second WORLD WAR, in the states of the Middle and Far East. For the most part, these exchanges took the form of an apostolic internunciature, administered by a pronuncio of ambassadorial rank (from 1965) but not enjoying the precedence that fell by right to the nuncios, the recognition of whom presented some difficulties in the case of non-Christian countries.

A kind of class distinction operated likewise between the different nunciatures. The qualification of first-class nunciature was reserved for the oldest Vatican representations (Paris, Vienna, Madrid, and Lisbon), although nunciatures accredited to the governments of the leading nations of the world are today on the same footing. Nuncios delegated to these capitals are usually promoted to the rank of cardinal when their mission ends, the cardinal's BIRETTA being bestowed by the relevant head of state by virtue of a privilege granted *ab antiquo* by the Holy See to the Catholic sovereigns of these states. Acting on a request from certain VATICAN II council fathers, PAUL VI (1963–78), in his apostolic CONSTITUTION *Sollicitudo monium ecclesiarum* of 24 June 1969, explained in detail the functions of papal legates (in the broad sense), who henceforth were to be subject to the dispositions of canons 362 to 367 of the CODE OF CANON LAW of 1983. The Code did not, however, modify in a major way the functioning of an institution that includes some 170 representations and whose mission presupposes both flexibility of organization and marked local autonomy.

Philippe Levillain

List of Apostolic Nunciatures [170].

—Albania, Algeria, Andorra, Angola, Antigua and Barbuda, Argentina, Armenia, Australia, Austria, Azerbaijan

—Bahamas, Bangladesh, Barbados, Belarus, Belgium, Belize, Benin, Bolivia, Bosnia and Herzegovina, Brazil, Bulgaria, Burkina Faso, Burundi

—Cambodia, Cameroon, Canada, Cape Verde, Central African Republic Chad, Chile, China (Taiwan), Colombia, Congo (Republic of the), Congo (Democratic Republic of the), Cook Islands, Costa Rica, Croatia, Cuba, Cyprus, Czech Republic

—Denmark, Dominica, Dominican Republic

—Ecuador, Egypt, El Salvador, Equatorial Guinea, Eritrea, Estonia, Ethiopia, European Community

—Fiji, Finland, France

—Gabon, Gambia, Georgia, Germany, Ghana, Great Britain, Greece, Grenada, Guatemala, Guinea, Guinea-Bissau, Guyana

—Haiti, Honduras, Hungary

—Iceland, India, Indonesia, Iran, Iraq, Ireland, Israel, Italy, Ivory Coast

—Jamaica, Japan, Jordan

—Kazakhstan, Kenya, Kiribati, Korea, Kuwait, Kyrgyzstan

—Latvia, Lebanon, Lesotho, Liberia, Liechtenstein, Lithuania, Luxembourg, Libya

—Macedonia, Madagascar, Malawi, Mali, Malta, Marshall Islands, Mauritius, Mexico, Micronesia, Moldova, Mongolia, Morocco, Mozambique

—Namibia, Nauru, Nepal, Netherlands, New Zealand, Nicaragua, Niger, Nigeria, Norway

—Pakistan, Palau, Panama, Papua New Guinea, Paraguay, Peru, Philippines, Poland, Portugal

—Romania, Rwanda

—Saint Kitts–Nevis, Saint Lucia, Saint Vincent and the Grenadines, Samoa, San Marino, São Tomé and Principe, Senegal, Seychelles, Sierra Leone, Singapore, Slovakia, Slovenia, Solomon Islands, South Africa, Spain, Sri Lanka, Sudan, Suriname, Swaziland, Sweden, Switzerland, Syria

—Tadjikistan, Tanzania, Thailand, Togo, Tonga, Trinidad and Tobago, Tunisia, Turkey, Turkmenistan

—Uganda, Ukraine, United States, Uruguay, Uzbekistan

—Vanuatu, Venezuela

—Yemen, Yugoslavia

—Zambia, Zimbabwe

NUNCIO

Bibliography

Biaudet, H. *Les Nonciatures permanentes jusqu'en 1648*, Helsinki, 1910.

Blet, P. *Histoire de la représentation diplomatique du Saint-Siège. Des origines à l'aube du XIXe siècle* [*Collectanea Archivi Vatican*, 9] Paris, 1982.

Cardinale, I. *Le Saint-Siège et la diplomatie. Aperçu historique, juridique et pratique de la diplomatie pontificale*, Paris-Tournai, 1962.

De Echeverria, L. "Les représentations pontificales," *Concilium*, 147 (1979).

d'Onorio, J. B. *Le Pape et le gouvernement de l'Église*, Paris, 1992.

d'Onorio, J. B. *Le Saint-Siège dans les relations internationales*, Paris, 1989.

Dupuy, A. *La Diplomatie du Saint-Siège après le IIe concile du Vatican*, Paris, 1981.

Fernandez, J. "Don Francisco des Prats, primer nuncio permanente en España (1492–1503)," *Anthologia Annua*, Rome (1958), 67–154.

Graham, R. A. *Vatican Diplomacy*, Princeton, 1959.

Le Tourneau, D. "Les légats pontificaux dans le Code de droit canonique de 1983, vingt ans après la constitution apostolique *Sollicitudo omnium Ecclesiarum*," *Année cononique*, 23 (1989).

Oliveri, M. *Natura e funzioni dei legati pontifici nella storia e nel contesto ecclesiologico del Vaticano II*, Vatican City, 1982.

Richard, P. "Origines de la nonciature en France," *Revue des questions historiques, 28 (1905)*.

Annuario pontificio per l'anno 2000, 1399–1425.

NUNCIO. The language of Caesar and Cicero used the word *nuntius* to mean the messenger who bears news. The Bayeux tapestry, which offers thousands of visitors a year the illustrated story of the conquest of England by William of Normandy, bears a subtitle *nuntii Wilelmi*, "William's nuncios." The picture shows two armed horsemen galloping, lance in hand; they are the messengers of Duke William. Some ten years later, the same term crops up in the register of GREGORY VII, this time to describe not messengers but the pope's delegates, sent to France invested with the most extensive powers. Used afterward coupled with other terms—nuncio and LEGATE, nuncio and spokesman, orator, nuncio, and collector—the word nuncio came to refer exclusively to the pope's ambassador to governments and particular Churches. Today the apostolic nunciature represents the final stage of a long evolution, by no means linear. From the first centuries, the pope was represented by bishops, priests, and deacons, even then described as "legates," in the COUNCILS held at a remote distance from Rome. In the 6th to 8th centuries, the Roman see had a permanent representative at the court of Constantinople, called the *apocrisarius*, who could be regarded as an ancestor of the modern nuncios. In the Middle Ages, CARDINAL legates *a latere* traveled throughout Christendom, armed with great powers to reestablish ecclesiastical discipline and good relations among Christian princes. In the same period, agents of more modest rank entrusted with missions limited by particular sets of circumstances were sometimes described as "nuncios," "nuncios and legates," or "nuncios and ambassadors."

In the 15th century, legates, often called "legate envoys" because they did not have either the high rank or all the powers of the legates *a latere*, the *oratores*, the spokesmen or ambassadors, or the collectors of the APOSTOLIC CAMERA were sent out on various types of missions, some diplomatic, some specifically ecclesiastical, which most often combined political mission and spiritual duties. Sometimes their task was to defend the jurisdiction of the Church and the Holy See against encroachments of the nascent modern states; sometimes, to persuade the Christian rulers to band together against the threat offered by the TURKS; or, again, to defend the authority of the Roman pontiff against the claims of the council of Basel. Meanwhile, in Italy the states of Venice, Milan, and Florence, among others, were fighting to affirm and extend their authority in the peninsula. The Roman state had to protect itself from its neighbors' ambitions, and by the end of the 15th century, large numbers of papal envoys were dispatched to defend and promote the temporal interests of the Papal States, or even of the papal family. It is in this period and geographical area that historians usually place the origins of modern diplomacy.

It is somewhat pointless to debate whether the permanent nunciatures originally followed the example of the permanent embassies of other states or whether they sprang from the COLLECTORS entrusted by the pope with diplomatic missions. Basically, the permanent NUNCIATURE was the means whereby papal representation adapted to the demands of the modern state, a task which up to that time had been carried out by temporary envoys of various ranks. As head of the universal Church, where he had to maintain the purity of the faith and the rigor of discipline, head of Christendom, which had to be defended against the ambitions of the Ottomans, and, finally, head of the PAPAL STATES, which had to be protected from its neighbors, the pope had many reasons to send out agents to princes and Christian peoples, and to maintain these envoys at their courts. Over the years, their repeated and sometimes prolonged missions were made permanent. It is safe to say that by around 1530 permanent nunciatures existed in Spain, France, Venice, and the Holy Roman Empire. It is somewhat problematic to bring this date forward by about thirty years, as some have suggested. For it is precisely between 1520 and 1530 that the Lutheran crisis, and the decision to convene a council calling for peace in Christendom, made the need for a permanent pontifical diplomat in the great Christian courts all the more pressing. In fact, it was on the eve of the third session of the council of TRENT that PIUS IV welcomed the petition of the dukes of Tuscany and Savoy and in 1560 established the nunciatures of Florence and Turin, both nuncios having as their principal task to ensure the participation of the bishops of those duchies in the third Tridentine session. And before the century was finished, the demands of the Catholic Reform would bring about the creation of the nunciatures of Cologne and Lucerne, while that of Brussels would be inaugurated at the beginning of the next century. Thus, in the early 1600s we see a permanent nunciature in the empire, in France, Spain, Portugal, and Poland, in Savoy, Florence, and Venice, and in the Swiss cantons. The nuncio was the pope's ambassador to these princes or republics and at the same time a pontifical magistrate, as a BRIEF of URBAN VIII puts it, invested with a spiritual authority over these rulers' subjects. The situation was rather different in Naples and Flanders, where the pope's representative resided not at the court of a sovereign prince but at that of a governor subordinate to the Spanish king. His diplomatic role therefore tended to be slight as compared with his duties respecting the local Church. Somewhat in a category by itself was the situation of the nuncio of Cologne, who was accredited not only to a prince elector, the archbishop of Cologne, but to a series of states whose rulers were both vassals of the emperor and, as prince bishops or prince abbots, subject to the pope by special right. This was also the case of the apostolic delegate to Malta, who resided in that island at the court of the grand master of the order.

Since it is impossible to list here all the particularities of each of the nunciatures, we shall describe the two extreme models, the nunciatures of Spain and France.

Of all the representatives of the Holy See, the Spanish nuncio was the one who preserved to the fullest extent the heritage of the legate *a latere*. Indeed, in all aspects of his charge he exercised the immediate jurisdiction of the Roman pontiff. All the nuncios of the classical age, except for the nuncio in France, were named by the pope "nuncio with the powers of legate *a latere*." For none of them was this an empty formula, and least of all for the Spanish nuncio. His nominating brief laid out the extent of his powers: to institute canonical visits to the patriarchal, primatial, metropolitan, cathedral, and collegial churches, the monasteries and convents, and to confirm or modify their status. He could criticize the diocesan and religious clergy as well as fulminate against those under sentence of excommunication or INTERDICT. While respecting the right of bishops to start proceedings, he could terminate proceedings in civil, criminal, matrimonial, and beneficial matters. He conferred ecclesiastical benefices granted at the pope's behest, where the income did not exceed twenty-four gold ducats. He legitimized bastards to allow them to inherit and take holy orders and, to the same end, removed the impediments of deformity and *publicae honestatis*. In the matrimonial area, he waived the impediments of consanguinity and affinity in the third degree. Finally, he granted various kinds of permissions and indulgences. These powers were not peculiar to the Spanish nuncio, and other nuncios were given powers that the Spanish nuncio did not possess.

In Spain, the nuncio's powers were such that the nunciature had a tripartite administration: 1) the chancery supervised jurisdiction of grace, gave out dispensations, indults, and privileges, and above all, conferred benefices; 2) the tribunal received appeals against the sentences of episcopal curias and other local tribunals; and 3) the collector received the fees that the Apostolic Camera continued to charge in Spain.

The activity of these nunciature tribunals has often been oveshadowed by the diplomatic activity of the representatives of the Holy See. The nuncios' correspondence with Rome is filled with their efforts to restore peace in a Europe at war or to defend the jurisdiction and rights of the Holy See when threatened by the claims of royal jurists or by episcopalist tendencies, whereas the activity of the nuncios' tribunals has only rarely left traces in their dispatches to the Secretariat of State.

The French nunciature presents a special case but one that is also of singular interest, if only because it has been the object of misunderstandings on the part of historians. While other nuncios were described in their brief of nomination as "nuncio with the powers of legate *a latere*," *nuncius cum potestate legati de latere*, the nuncio in France was described merely as *nonce*. The difference could seem to have arisen as a result of the legal formalities imposed by the Parlement of Paris on the legate's exercise of power. This French limitation on the nuncio's prerogatives has misled many historians, who have regarded a nuncio without jurisdiction as merely a papal ambassador to the king and even as an ambassador of the pope as temporal ruler. This was certainly what the parliamentary legislators wanted to reduce him to, but they did not succeed. In 1641, the nuncio Scotti clearly defined the nuncio's juridical situation in France, as recognized by the pope, the bishops, and the king himself: "The nunciature of France is held in an esteem of which everyone is aware, not for jurisdiction, which it does not practice as do the other royal nunciatures, but because the nuncio resides at the court of a great monarch, His Most Christian Majesty, the elder son of the Church, and because he is at the same time apostolic delegate to such a powerful and flourishing kingdom." Being nuncio to the king was a diplomatic post, at once political and religious, for the nuncio spoke with the king about the interests of religion just as about the interests of the states and Christendom. He was apostolic delegate to the kingdom of France, that is, to bishops, doctors of the Sorbonne, and priests and religious just as to the faithful of Christ's Church.

Nothing better shows the ecclesiastical significance of the nuncio's mission as papal representative than the task incumbent on him, in France as elsewhere, to carry out the canonical inquiry on candidates named by the king to dioceses in the kingdom. The French parliament tried in vain to prevent him from carrying out this task. In the 18th century, despite all the usurpations the king's judges were able to perpetrate at the expense of the Church's authority, the manual of expeditionary bankers at the Roman Curia made it clear that bulls confirming appointments to dioceses and consistorial abbeys were sent from Rome "only on the strength of documents drawn up in Paris before Monsieur le Nonce." Whether this referred to the exercise of a jurisdiction or simply to an informational role, the fact remains that in France, as in the other Christian kingdoms, where sovereigns usually had the right to appoint bishops, the nuncio guaranteed control prior to the canonical installation in CONSISTORY. And if the choice were inadmissible, it was up to him to explain to the sovereign that a new nomination should take place. But it was advisable to warn of such a nomination in advance.

It appears, therefore, that at the beginning of the modern era nuncios essentially carried out the tasks incumbent on them today. When study is restricted to individual periods, an evolution in the nuncios' function becomes apparent. It is true that they were sometimes absorbed in political questions, such as questions of peace and war. The nuncios of the second half of the 14th century filled their dispatches with their concern for the survival of the Papal States. During the Thirty Years' War they devoted volumes to the question of the proper title to be granted to the Dutch plenipotentiaries to the peace conference.

Many changes have taken place since the establishment, over time, of the permanent nunciatures. The fourteen nunciatures in existence at the end of the 18th century in the Catholic states have grown to over a hundred today, representing the pope in most of the nations of the world. Even states with only a tiny Catholic minority maintain diplomatic relations with the Roman see. And it is not among the least of the paradoxes inherent in certain situations that a state with a large Catholic majority can be content with an apostolic delegation that is officially ignored by the civil authorities. More numerous are the governments that, while welcoming diplomatic representation of the Holy See, fail to give the nuncio all the prerogatives granted him by the two congresses of Vienna, of 1815 and 1964, that is, to be the dean of the diplomatic corps. In this case, the nunciature is under the direction of a pro-nuncio. Never does the diplomatic function vis-à-vis the government exclude the ecclesiastical function vis-à-vis the faithful, the bishops, and the priests of the country concerned. The new CODE OF CANON LAW even emphasizes that the latter function is the principal role of the contemporary nuncio. Nuncio to the Most Christian King and apostolic delegate in the French kingdom, wrote Scotti in 1641. To make the ties uniting the Holy See and the particular Churches ever stronger and more effective (canon 364), to fulfill a diplomatic mission to states according to the norms of international law (canon 365)—these are the two essential functions, the twofold representation, of the contemporary nuncio. From the time when LEO the Great sent Julian of Cos to the court of Constantinople, in order to make his own presence felt in some fashion by the emperor and to ensure communications with the Eastern Churches, the style and *modi operandi* have certainly changed; but the principles and goals remain substantially the same.

Pierre Blet

Bibliography

Baudet, H. *Les Nonciatures apostoliques permanentes jusqu'en 1648*, Helsinki, 1910.

Blet, P. "Le nonce en France au XVIIe siècle. Ambassadeur et délégué apostolique," *Revue d'Histoire diplomatique*, 88 (1974), 233–58.

Claeys-Bouuaert, F. "Légat du Pape," *DDC*, 6 (1957) 371–7.

De Marchi, G. *Le Nunziature apostoliche dal 1800 al 1956*, Rome, 1957.

Deutsches Historisches Institut, *Nuntiaturberichte und Nuntiaturforschung*, Rome, 1976–.

Halkin, L. E. *Les Archives des nonciatures*, Brussels-Rome, 1968.

Histoire de la représentation diplomatique du Saint-Siège, des origines à l'aube du XIXe siècle, Vatican City, 1982 (*Collectanea Archivi Vaticani* 9).

Karttunen, L. *Les Nonciatures apostoliques permanentes de 1650 à 1800*, Geneva, 1912.

Naz, R. "Nonce apostolique," *DDC*, 6 (1957), 1014–15.

Olivieri, M. *Natura e funzioni dei legati pontifici nella storia e nel contesto ecclesiologico del Vaticano II*, Turin, 1979.

Wojtyska, H. D. *Acta nuntiaturae polonae* I, Rome, 1990 [includes chronological list of the nuncios in Poland; the author gives all editions of the correspondence of contemporary nuncios].

O

OATH OF FIDELITY. See **Profession of Faith and Oath of Fidelity**.

OBELISKS OF ROME. Between the end of the 1st century B.C. and the middle of the 4th century A.D., the emperors had an indeterminate number of obelisks brought from Egypt for erection in Rome. From the late 14th to the mid-18th century, some 20 of these monuments were dug out from among the ruins of imperial Rome. Thirteen of them were raised once again on the squares and in the gardens of modern Rome, 11 of them on the initiative of various popes.

SIXTUS V, during his brief pontificate (1585–90), had four obelisks erected in four years:

—in 1586, that of the piazza of St. Peter's in front of the Vatican basilica (no epigraph: date and Egyptian origin problematic; brought to Rome under Caligula around 40 B.C. to adorn the *spina* of the Circus Vaticanus);

—in 1587, that of the piazza dell'Esquilino in front of the apse of ST. MARY MAJOR (no epigraph; brought to Rome probably under Titus a. 80 B.C. to frame the door of Augustus's mausoleum with its twin, which stands today on the piazza del Quirinale);

—in 1588, that of the piazza of St. John Lateran (Karnak, Thutmosis III [1458–25 B.C.] and Thutmosis IV [1401–1390 B.C.]; moved a. 335 B.C. to ALEXANDRIA by CONSTANTINE, who intended it for Constantinople; finally brought to Rome by Constans II, who had it placed in 357 on the *spina* of the Circus Maximus);

—in 1589, that of the piazza del Popolo (Heliopolis, Sethi I [1294–79 B.C.] and Rameses II [1279–13 B.C.]; brought to Rome under Augustus, who ordered it raised in 10 B.C. on the *spina* of the Circus Maximus).

INNOCENT X (1644–55) erected the obelisk on the piazza Navona in 1650 (brought from Egypt without epigraph; decorated in Rome a. 85 B.C. with hieroglyphic texts praising Domitian's legitimacy as emperor and in-

stalled in the sanctuary of Isis and Sarapis in the Campus Martius).

ALEXANDER VII (1655–67) erected the obelisk of the Piazza Sta Maria sopra Minerva in 1667 (Saïs, Apries [589–70 B.C.]; brought to Rome under Domitian ca. 85 B.C. to decorate the temple of Isis in the Campus Martius).

CLEMENT XI (1700–21) erected the obelisk of the Piazza della Rotonda in front of the Pantheon in 1711 (Heliopolis, Ramses II; brought to Rome under Domitian a. 85 B.C. to decorate the temple of Isis in the Campus Martius).

PIUS VI (1775–99) was responsible for the erection of three obelisks:

—in 1786, that of the Piazza del Quirinale (twin to the one Sixtus V ordered raised in 1587 on the Piazza dell'Esquilino);

—in 1789, that of the Piazza della Trinità dei Monti (brought from Egypt without epigraph, decorated in Rome a. 275 B.C., on Aurelian's initiative, with hieroglyphic texts reproducing those of Ramses's obelisk on the Piazza del Popolo, which was then on the *spina* of the Circus Maximus; Aurelian intended it to adorn the hippodrome in Sallust's gardens);

—in 1792, that of the Piazza di Montecitorio (Heliopolis, Psammeticus II [595–89 B.C.]; brought to Rome under Augustus and erected in 10 B.C. on the *horologium* of the Campus Martius to serve as a gnomon).

PIUS VII (1800–23) in 1822 erected the obelisk of the gardens of Monte Pincio (brought from Egypt without epigraph, decorated in Rome a. 135 B.C., on Hadrian's initiative, with hieroglyphic texts commemorating the death and deification of his favorite Antinous and installed on the latter's tomb in the gardens of Adonis on the Palatine).

The two obelisks of the Villa Celiomontana and the Viale delle Terme di Diocleziano (Heliopolis, Ramses II; brought to Rome under Domitian a. 85 B.C. to decorate the temple of Isis in the Campus Martius) were not erected by popes. The first was put up in 1813 by a private individual, Ciriaco Mattei, during the vacancy of papal temporal power, the second in 1887.

The erection of these obelisks is an integral part of the monumental and artistic history of papal Rome and must be included among the numerous initiatives taken by the popes to embellish their capital. It is worth remembering not only the architects, who managed to move and raise these often colossal monoliths (e.g., Domenico Fontana, responsible for erecting the obelisks of Sixtus V, among them that of the piazza of St. John Lateran, which, 105 feet/32 meters high and weighing over 550 tons/500 metric tons, is certainly the largest ever raised), but also the artists involved. They produced some of their masterpieces on these obelisks, giving free rein to imagination and fantasy in the conception and realization of the bases (fountains, monumental sculptures, etc.) supporting the structures (e.g., Bernini and his famous Fontana dei Quattro Fiumi for the obelisk on the Piazza Navona, or his no less well-known elephant for that on the Piazza Sta Maria sopra Minerva). The installation of these obelisks therefore makes for a precious and original testimony as to the personality of certain popes and the spirit of their respective times.

While striving for his own glory, Sixtus V (whom some have taxed with "megalithomania") intended the obelisks to illustrate the triumph of Roman Christianity over pagan Rome and over all exotic and barbarous cults—as attested by the ritual with which the monuments were exorcised before being consecrated to the CROSS, or, more simply, by the triumphant dedications Sixtus ordered inscribed on their bases. Subsequently, as people and ideas evolved, the erecting of an obelisk became a pretext for some act of munificence on the part of a ruler toward his subjects (the quest for beauty of realization, the combination of fountain and obelisk, etc.). For the pontiff, the interest of the antiquarian replaced the enthusiasm of the crusader: the long, detailed notices inscribed on the bases of the obelisks of Pius VI and Pius VII show, above all, their interest in these monuments as witnesses of the history of their city and, beyond that, as witnesses of a yet more remote and mysterious past.

Jean-Claude Grenier

Bibliography

D'Onofrio, C. *Gli Obelischi di Roma*, Rome, 1965.

Iversen, E. *Obelisks in Exile: The Obelisks of Rome*, Copenhagen, 1968.

OBSERVATORY, VATICAN. The beginnings of the Vatican Observatory (the *Specola vaticana*, the seat of the official Pontificio Osservatorio Astronomico) are linked to questions concerning the measurement of time,

or, more precisely, the redefining of the CALENDAR, rather than the study of space. Around 1579, Pope GREGORY XIII (1572–85) gave orders for a tower 231 feet/73 meters high to be built on the present papal territory of Vatican City, which was at first called the Tower of the Winds (*Torre dei venti*) or Gregorian Tower. It was from the so-called Calendar Room at the very top of the structure, which contained a meridian (*meridiana*), that, according to tradition, the scientist Ignazio Danti persuaded Gregory and the assembled astronomers of the need for revising the computation of the days of the year, by demonstrating how the equinox regularly occurred around the eleventh day of March. The calendar was duly revised and promulgated a year later by the BULL *Inter gravissimas*. Later, since calendar reform, the task for which it had been exclusively conceived, was completed, the room was turned into a library, under the pontificate of URBAN VIII (1623–44), until CARDINAL F.-S. De Zelada, who had been appointed librarian in 1780, decided in 1784 to restore the memorable place to its earlier useful purpose by dedicating it to more active scientific research. G. Calandrelli, then professor of astronomy at the Roman COLLEGE, dissuaded him, arguing that the tower was poorly placed to carry out observations of the heavens. Nonetheless, at the request of Msgr. F. L. Gilii, PIUS VI (1775–99) agreed in 1789 to the creation of a meteorological center devoted to study of the climate of Rome and the surrounding area. He arranged for the restoration of the tower rooms and appointed Msgr. Gilii director of the "Specola Pontificia Vaticana," the observatory's first official name, in 1797. Under his leadership, regular activities were carried out, but they came to a halt when he died in 1821. A fresh start came in 1888, when, during the sacerdotal jubilee of LEO XIII (1878–1903), the Italian clergy presented the pontiff with a collection of scientific instruments assembled by Fr. Denza, founder of the Italian Meteorological Society. Leo XIII wanted to turn the instruments over to science and ordered them moved to the abandoned Tower of the Winds, the administration of which he entrusted to Fr. Denza and his aide, the Oratorian G. Lais. At a meeting of the Permanent Committee for the Establishment of a Complete Cartography of the Sky in Paris in 1889, the scientists assigned the Vatican Observatory a declination area defined by the points + 55 degrees and + 64 degrees. The photographic work, which was carried out with a camera with an equatorial mounting of 13.26 inches'/34 centimeters' aperture and 11.25 feet/3.43 meters of focal length, was entrusted to G. Lais, then vice-director of the Observatory. These directions were confirmed in the *motu proprio Ut mysticam* of 14 March 1891, by which Leo XIII gave the Observatory its definitive statutes and entrusted it with extensive missions covering not only astronomy and astrophotography but also meteorology, geophysics, and seismology. At

Denza's death, in 1894, the Observatory was confined to meteorological tasks, which were directed by the Augustinian A. Rodriguez.

In 1904, PIUS X (1903–14) appointed as president of the institution Archbishop Maffi of Pisa, who was shortly afterward raised to the purple. The archbishop asked the Jesuit J. G. Hagen, then professor at Georgetown and director of the Observatory from 1906 to 1930, to rethink and reform totally its organization and aims. Emphasis was once again placed on astronomy, leading in 1928 to the production of a *Catalogue astrographique* in ten volumes that recorded some 500,000 positions and sizes of stars. Under the direction of another JESUIT, J.W. Stein, Hagen's assistant from 1906 to 1910, the problem of modernization was posed as well as the transfer of some of the Observatory instruments to an area less subject to nocturnal illumination than the city of Rome and one more convenient for observation and measurement. In 1931, PIUS XI (1922–39), greatly interested in the question, allowed the Observatory to use the terrace of his summer residence at Castel Gandolfo, which soon sported a huge visual refractor and a four-lens telescope, provided by the German firm Zeiss, which was inaugurated on 29 September 1935. From there, the Observatory carried out research on the structure of meteorites and of the galaxy. In 1954, a more powerful telescope was installed that provided the scientists of the astrophysics laboratory with detailed information on the spectrochemistry of space. These results contributed greatly to ensuring the credibility of the Vatican Observatory, which in the early 1980s acquired a research unit at Tucson, Arizona, that functions in continuous liaison with the administrative center at Castel Gandolfo.

François Jankowiak

Bibliography

Annuario pontificio per l'anno 1991, Vatican City, 1991, 1740–1.

Lais, G. "La Specola Vaticana," *Atti della Pontificia Accademia N. Lincei*, 32 (1879), 239–47.

Stein, G. "Cinquanta anni di attivit à della Specola Vaticana (1891–1941), "*Mémoires de la Société astrologique italienne*, 15 (1942), 41–6.

Stein G., and Junkes, G. *La Specola Vaticana nel passato e nel presente*, Vatican City, 1952.

OFFENSES AGAINST THE POPE. The legislation in force—that of the CODE OF CANON LAW of 1983—outlines the following cases:

Physical violence against the person of the Roman pontiff (c. 1370 § 1) is punished by excommunication *latae sententiae* (of general reach) reserved to the Holy See. It must be a physical violence, not just verbal, that is to say, one which requires a visible action, intentional, se-

riously detrimental to the one it affects: an attack on his body, his freedom, or his dignity, in violation of the "principle of the canon" (which applies as well to bishops, clerics, and religious orders, considered in § 2 and 3 of the same c. 1370), which was in the Code of Canon Law of 1917 (c. 119) and which derived its name from c. 15, *Si quis suadente diabolo*, of the Second Lateran Council (1139), excommunicating *ipso facto* those who would use violence against a priest or a monk; an excommunication *latae sententiae* created by a general law thus became, for the first time in the Church, a *nominatim* excommunication, a true canonical punishment. If the author of the deed is a cleric, a condition that would be considered an aggravating circumstance, another punishment (a censure or an expiatory punishment) could be added to the excommunication, including revoking his clerical status, according to the gravity of the offense.

The offense of assassination (c. 1397) is punished in the same way as the offense of physical violence, even if the murder is not accompanied by the above-mentioned violence.

Recourse to an ecumenical council or to the College of Bishops against an action by the Roman pope (c. 1372) is expressly forbidden (c. 333 § 3) due to the fact of PAPAL PRIMACY (c. 331). Such recourse would imply negation, in at least an implicit sense, of the primacy of the pope and would thus be tainted with *saporem schismatis*.

This recourse must be made against a document that truly comes from the Roman pontiff, and not from a congregation, a tribunal of the Roman CURIA, or from one of the institutions that assist the pope in governing the Church (c. 360), unless the action by the Curia was taken by special and express mandate from the Roman pontiff or was approved by him in specific form, for then it would become a true pontifical document. The recourse must be aimed at a document of the pope's as supreme head of the Catholic Church, and not as ruler of Vatican City, and it may be a document on any matter: legislative, judicial, or administrative. The punishment is a censure *ferendae sententiae* of specific, indeterminate, and preceptive reach (excommunication, INTERDICT or SUSPENSION for a cleric; excommunication or interdict for a layperson). It would involve any person, independently of his rank or his duties, ecclesiastical or civil.

Formal refusal to submit to the Roman pontiff or to communicate with the members of the Church, which is under his leadership (c. 751), in other words, the offense of schism. For it to be a true offense, there must be an obvious action that brings about social consequences, defined as that which is perceived as such by a third party (c. 1330). Its author would be excommunicated *latae sententiae* (c. 1364 § 1), which would not be applied to a minor who had not yet reached age 16 (c. 1323 1°), nor to baptized people who were born during the schism (c. 11). If the author of the offense is a cleric, he could also be assigned an expiatory punishment *ferendae sententiae:* interdict, removal from office, or of favors, privileges, etc. that he had received and of their use (c. 1336, 1°, no. 1–3). In case of prolonged obstinacy or a particularly serious scandal, other punishments could be added, including revoking his clerical status (c. 1364 § 2), which would not include a dispensation from the law of celibacy (c. 291).

Dominique Le Tourneau

OLDEST DAUGHTER OF THE CHURCH.

The expression "Oldest Daughter of the Church," applied to France in reference to its conversion to Catholicism earlier than the other nations of western Europe, seems to be of fairly recent origin; it appears in neither the Littré (1865) nor in the Larousse *Grand Dictionnaire universel du XIXe siècle* (1872). This leads us to believe that it is a late modification of the title "Oldest Son of the Church" used for the first time by ALEXANDER VI in reference to Charles VIII on 19 January 1495, and attributed to the Very Christian Kings up to the time of Charles X. These two names translate old prerogatives that have been expressed in different words throughout the centuries.

The origin of privileged ties that connect France to the papacy go back to the baptism of Clovis, the first Germanic king who, at the end of the 5th century, professed Christianity in union with the see of Rome, while other invaders from Gaul and the Roman empire adhered to the Arian HERESY. In the 8th century, relations between the FRANKISH kingdom and the papacy were tightened. In 751, pope ZACHARIAS recognized Pepin the Short with the title of king in the place of the last Merovingian, and had him blessed by his LEGATE, saint Boniface. In 755 and 756, Pepin, at STEPHEN II's appeal as he was being threatened by the LOMBARD king, led two military expeditions into Italy, ending with the conquest of the EXARCHATE OF RAVENNA, which was handed over to the pope and became the PATRIMONY OF ST. PETER, later to be called the Papal State. Finally, to thank the king and his sons, pope PAUL I, brother and successor to Stephen II, gave them St. Petronilla as protector, the Roman martyr considered by legends of the time to be the daughter of ST. PETER. The pope had her body taken from the CATACOMB of Domitilla and transferred to a mausoleum next to the Vatican basilica, henceforth called "chapel of the Frankish kings." After the building's destruction in 1544, the mortal remains of the saint were placed in a chapel in the right nave of the new basilica.

The papacy's alliance with the French monarchy thus sealed in the 8th century was to be confirmed regularly by a number of acts. In modern times, the epithet "Elder Daughter of the Church" appears in political treaties, in official documents, and in the works of sacred orators; it has taken the form "Elder Daughter" when applied to a queen (Catherine de Medici is so called in a letter from the nuncio Prospero Santacroce in 1564). And, the glory of the sovereign flows out over his kingdom: GREGORY IX declared to Saint Louis in 1239 that "the kingdom of France was placed by God above all peoples," and in 1562 we find the expression "elder kingdom of the Church," which might be seen as an early version of the present wording. The mass celebrated every year on 31 May in honor of St. Petronilla in St. Peter's Basilica in the presence of the French ambassador and the French colony is, still today, reminiscent of the Holy See's secular predilection for France.

Bernard Barbiche

Bibliography

Lecler, J. "Le roi de France, fils aîné de l'Église. Essai historique," *Études*, 214 (1933), 21–36 and 170–89.
Martin, J. *Le Vatican inconnu*, Paris, 1988, 129–40.

ONOMASTICS, PONTIFICAL.

Sources. The oldest list of bishops of Rome comes from Irenaeus of Lyon (Adv. haer. III, 3, 3). After those of the "founders" of the Christian community, Peter and Paul, there follows a list of twelve names: Λινος (LINUS), Ανενκλητος (ANACLETUS), Κλημης CLEMENT I), Εναριστος (EVARISTUS), Αλεξανδρος (ALEXANDER I), Ξυστος (SIXTUS I), Τελησφορος (TELESPHORUS), Ὑγινος (HYGINUS), Πιος (PIUS I), Ἀνικητος (ANICETUS), Σωτηρος (SOTER), and Ἐλευθερος (ELEUTHERIUS). Then follow the extremely valuable accounts of nomenclature provided by EUSEBIUS of Caesarea's *Ecclesiastical History* (*LP* I, V) and the *Liberian Catalogue* of 354. The latter was meant to pass as a precise chronography providing a continuous succession of popes, together with consular dates and (fictitious) imperial synchronisms (*LP*, VI–X). "LIBERIUS" divides the name Anencletus into two, Cletus and Anacletus.

The custom of recording in writing the date of ordination and the day of death goes back to 235. Beginning in the 4th century, the tradition of lists gains in accuracy and historical certainty. The earliest preserved manuscripts of the *LIBER PONTIFICALIS* date from the 7th to 8th centuries; legend ascribes them to Pope DAMASUS (366–84) (*LP* I, 48ff.). The *Liber pontificalis* was altered and completed several times, so that different editions show divergences as to the succession of the popes and their legitimacy.

On a certain number of points, the list of popes in *Pseudo-Isidore* differs from *LP*; it omits Linus and Cletus, changes spellings, and stops after GREGORY the Great (with only one addition, GREGORY II). The CULT of the first bishops of Rome, the holy POPES-MARTYRS, developed especially thanks to the efforts of the popes of the Gregorian REFORM (Bernold of Constance, d. 1100, *Micrologus*). Of the medieval historians of the papacy, Martin of Troppau (Martin the Pole, d. 1278), frequently uncritical, had the greatest influence. Bartolomeo Sacchi, known as Platina (d. 1481), wrote the last pontifical history of the Middle Ages, following his own criteria; his system of numbering is at variance with that of the *LP*. The *ANNUARIO PONTIFICIO* (1912) in its unofficial lists adopts the Roman principle of the uniqueness and legitimacy of each pope; the lists are based mainly on the series of medallions at ST. PAUL'S OUTSIDE WALLS and the research of Theodor Mommsen, Louis Duchesne, and Angelo Mercati (d. 1955); the uninterrupted succession of "legitimate" popes has been abandoned in more recent editions.

Choice of Name and Adoption of Ordinal Number: Origins.

The earliest Roman lists consist mainly of Greek names, but there are also some Roman ones; the names of Greek divinities and Roman emperors are included. There are no descriptive appellations or double names among the first fifty; the Roman names are taken from the repertory of *praenomina* as well as of *nomina gentilicia* or *cognomina*, without evidence of any principle governing the choice of name. In early times, the attribution of the name Peter to Simon (Mt 16:18) or the double name of Saul-Paul (tantamount to a change of name) was not regarded as warranting the use of a double name; that practice did not develop until later, and was adopted as a way of making a theological point (Peter Lombard, *PL* 191, 1303; Bernard of Clairvaux, *Opera*, VIII, *Ep.* 238 *Ad papam Eugenium prima*). The first pope to have a double name was JOHN II Mercury (533–5); most likely he thought it unfitting for a Christian to retain the name of an ancient divinity (unlike DIOSCORUS [530] and others). In the case of JOHN XII–Octavian (955–64), it is not known whether John is the actual name of this descendant of the Tusculani (he was a nephew of JOHN XI) or his pontifical name. The systematic change of name came to be well attested only from the end of the 10th century. In 983, Pietro da Pavia changed his first name to JOHN (XIV), no doubt out of deference to the apostle Peter; a few years later, Pietro Os Porci, otherwise known as SERGIUS IV (1009), followed suit. By taking a new name, the two familiars of Otto III, Bruno of Carinthia (GREGORY V) and Gerbert d'Aurillac (SILVESTER II), abandoned their "barbarian" first names, and they were also the first to emphasize the theological and intentional aspect of the step: Bruno linked himself with Gregory the Great, the renowned Doctor of the Church, and Gerbert d'Aurillac with the pope of the DONATION OF CONSTANTINE and the council of Nicaea (325). It was not until after the pontificate of Sergius IV (1009) that the change of name be-

came an actual rule (though not a written one). Only a few antipopes did not manage to adopt a pontifical name (THEODERIC, 1100–2; ALBERT, 1102). Just two elected popes took office under their own names (HADRIAN VI, MARCELLUS II); two others modified their names with ironic intent (Enea Silvio Piccolomini–PIUS II; Giuliano della Rovere–JULIUS II).

Beginning in the 6th century, it became necessary to distinguish popes of the same name by means of a numeral. PELAGIUS II (579–80) was the first to take on the epithet *junior*, doubtless borrowed from the tradition of the Roman emperors and consuls. In the 7th and 8th centuries, the appellation *junior* for a pope who succeeded another pope of the same name either directly or after a few years' interval became common. To distinguish a third pope of the same name, the Curia first adopted the formula *papa secundus junior* (GREGORY III, STEPHEN III), but that frequently caused confusion. The ordinal number appears for the first time under Gregory III, but it was used only sporadically. The custom of distinguishing the popes by a Roman numeral did not become the rule in registers until the 10th century; later, the practice was extended also to the metal BULLS (LEO IX) and FISHERMAN'S RINGS, whereas the emperors did not begin to be distinguished by numbers until the reign of Otto II.

Contested Ordinal Numbers.

Contemporary sources and papal histories show frequent divergences in numbering, resulting from confusions, name divisions, or additions and deletions due to quarrels over legitimacy. The names listed below are particularly problematic:

1. **Donus.** Pope Donus II (after BENEDICT VI) (e.g., Platina no. 139) is imaginary. The name comes from a confusion between BENEDICT VII's title *domnus* ("lord") and the Roman name Donus (*LP* II, XVIII, and 256).

2. **Felix.** The numbering of popes named Felix presented little problem in the Middle Ages; according to the *LP*, it went as follows:

FELIX I (*Romanus*), 268/9–274, *LP*, no. XXVII, 70ff.

FELIX II (*Romanus, Mart.*), 355–65, *LP*, no. XXX–VIII, 84ff.

FELIX III (*Romanus, ex patre Felice*), 483–92, *LP*, no. L, 92ff.

FELIX IV (*Samnius*), 526–30, *LP*, no. LVI, 106ff.

Beginning in the 6th century, a host of confusions led to Felix II being venerated as a martyr (Döllinger, 1890; Kirsch, 1925). Duchesne makes him an antipope (*LP* LXXIV ff.); the *Annuario pontificio* excludes him from the list of legitimate popes, and the *motu proprio Mysterii Paschalis* of 1969 from the list of martyrs. Since FELIX V (Amadeus of Savoy) also is considered an antipope, the number of pontiffs named Felix recognized by Rome is reduced to three.

3. **Stephen.** In 752, the electors first chose a priest named Stephen (*quendam presbiterum Stephanum*), but

he died before being consecrated bishop, which explains why there is no mention of him in *LP* (LP I, 440); as a result, the successor of ZACHARIAS, who was elected that same year, was designated STEPHEN II (*LP* I, no. XCIII, 440ff.). Frederick of Lorraine, elected in 1057, is therefore correctly called *Stephanus Nonus Papa*. From the 16th century on, however, some respected historians have defended the legitimacy of the pope chosen in 752 (Panvinio, Baronius). He remained listed in the *Annuario pontificio* until 1960, so that the whole series of Stephens is off by one. At the present time, there has been a return to the medieval numbering, which is more correct (cf. *Annuario pontificio*, 1981, 11).

4. **John**. In the Middle Ages, the numbering of the popes named John, from JOHN I (523) to JOHN XIV (983), posed few problems, since the deacon John who in January 844 replaced the deceased GREGORY IV was not usually included. But from 1100 a tradition grew, based on a false interpretation of *LP*, according to which John XIV was succeeded by a second pope of the same name, so that the numbering was off by one. As the disputed pope John Philagathos was included under the name JOHN XVI, Peter of Spain in 1276 took the name JOHN XXI (not JOHN XX). The numbering adopted by historians of later centuries varies depending on their interpretation of the sources and their opinion of the candidates' legitimacy. Platina includes both the John of 844 ("Pope JOAN," after Gregory IV) and the "repeat" John XIV among the legitimate popes; accordingly he assigns the numeral XXII to Peter of Spain. Likewise acknowledging the existence of a "repeat John XIV," Baldassare Cossa in 1410 adopted the name JOHN XXIII. But doubting Baldassare Cossa's legitimacy in his turn, Angelo Roncalli in 1958 took the numeral XXIII. The legend of Pope Joan (also called Jutta, Gilberta, Agnes, Glancia, etc.), usually assigned to the 9th century, goes back to Martin of Troppau (1277) and was introduced into the pontifical historiography of the Curia by Platina (Herbers, 1988).

5. **Marinus/Martin**. Because later traditions mistakenly listed MARINUS I (*LP* II, no. CX) and MARINUS II (*LP* II, no. CXXXI) under Martinus, in 1281 Simon de Brie took the name MARTIN IV. MARTIN V (who likewise chose the name with reference to Martin of Tours) followed this numbering, which has remained unchanged until today.

Ritual and Function of the Change of Name. For candidates with non-Christian first names, the change of name means the renunciation of paganism and the recognition of Christianity and the Christian saints; this holds true for the early examples (from John II to Silvester II) and also, in a certain way, for the *electi* of later periods who had non-Christian first names (for instance, Pius II, LEO XII, PIUS XI). In the age of the Theophylacti and Crescenzi, the pontifical name denoted membership in a family of origin and, by extension, gentle birth (John, Benedict). It was not until the period of the popes of the Gregorian REFORM (11th–12th centuries) that the professed name took on the character of a sovereign's name emphasizing the holy function of the one who bore it. By adopting a new name, the pope distinguished himself from all other European sovereigns, who changed theirs only in exceptional cases (e.g., Charles IV, d. 1378, whose first name was Wenzel). In the era of the Gregorian reform it was, according to the sources, chiefly the *electores*, in particular the archdeacon, who seemed to intervene in the choice of name. One example is the influence apparently exercised by Hildebrand (the future GREGORY VII) on the choice and change of candidates' names, from VICTOR II to VICTOR III. URBAN II provides the first instance of a personal choice (*Urbanum illum placere vocari*—Pietro da Monte Cassino, *Chron.* IV, 2). In a few other cases, the reasons were most likely subjective (e.g., for ALEXANDER II, who linked himself to the church of S. Alessandro Maggiore of Lucca). The change of name at that time was closely tied to the Gregorians' Petrine ideology. The papacy brought up to date and extended earlier traditions, going back to the 10th century, which insisted on the real presence of Peter and the direct participation of the Prince of the Apostles in the election (*Ordo Romanus* XXXVI, ed. Andrieu, IV, 204). In the *Benedictio pape de episcopo facti*, the cardinal bishop of Ostia explicitly recalls the PRIMACY of Peter (ed. Andrieu, I, no. XXXIV, 259). The enthronement in St. Peter's (or in another church dedicated to him) and the adoption of the name of the preceding successors of Peter illustrate the role of Petrine ideology and the importance attached to Roman authority as symbolized by the saint's KEYS. From this it can be seen that the change of name was also intended to express Roman primacy and a centralizing conception of the papacy. Moreover, the ritual of the change of name fits into the general context of the adoption of imperial insignia (*cappa rubra, laudes, ferula*, throne, processions, distribution of coins, etc.). Since that time, the ritual has been carried out in three stages: 1) the deliberation between the electors (and others) and the elected candidate, immediately after the vote (these consultations are assumed, as they are not attested by the sources); 2) the proclamation of the new pope, wearing his cloak *coram publico*, under his new name; 3) the solemn enthronement under the *nomen proprium*, marking the beginning of unlimited pontifical sovereignty.

From the 13th century, change of name was above all a matter of the candidates' personal, subjective choice (for instance, Pius II, 1458: *interrogatus quo nomine vellet notari, Pio respondit*). Nevertheless, the advice or wishes of certain electors or friends were permitted. Because of the sanctity of his office, it behooved the pope to keep the reasons for his choice secret; the sources reveal the new popes' reasons only in a few isolated cases (BENEDICT XII, Pius II). This silence has given rise to much speculation in anecdotes and pontifical legends. John XXIII (A. Roncalli, 1958), who was the first to recall his personal motivations in the *Acta*, was an exception (*AAS* 50, 1958, 878ff.). The pope used his personal first name only when he wanted to speak as a private individual, in private, and with his family; the custom was often invoked by the popes when they were on the point of DEATH (examples in Krebsius). The death of the pope likewise was announced using his baptismal name. At the bottom of the text of the PETITIONS, the pontifical confirmation is made using the initial of the private first name (e.g., E. in the case of Pius II, after his first name, Enea). Popes who resigned (CELESTINE V) or were deposed were also referred to by their baptismal names (for instance, JOHN XXIII–B. Cossa by Martin V, 1417, Nov. 21: Bibl. apost. Vat., Reg. Lat. 192: *Baldassar, in eadem obediencia succedens et Johannes XXIII nominatus*).

Motive and Significance. When the Theophylacti and Crescenzi were in power, the choice of papal name chiefly followed a genealogical principle which soon appeared suspect, to the point that even close relatives avoided it. It was not until after 1500 that the custom was occasionally reverted to (PIUS III, CLEMENT VIII). The Reform popes followed in the theological and political footsteps of Gregory V and Silvester II and chose names of legendary or historical predecessors from before the *saeculum obscurum* (10th century), taking them principally from the earliest lists. This explains the remarkable frequency of the numeral II: out of a total of 27 candidates (including those who were not recognized at a later stage) who succeeded one another between 1046 (the council of Sutri) and 1145 (the assassination of LUCIUS II), 16 popes bear the numeral II. Four others similarly took the names of predecessors who had already had successors of the same name: Leo IX, STEPHEN IX, Gregory VII, SILVESTER IV.

What sources did the Gregorian reform popes draw on to create an image of their real or supposed predecessors (cultural traditions, conciliar decisions, juridical collections)? We do not know. Note that the names of only 24 candidates out of the 27 coincide with those of the collection of the pseudo-Isidorean *Decretals*. Subjective or incidental factors may have played a part, though a secondary one, in the choice of name: a saint's day that fell on the day of election (Stephen IX, Lucius II, and perhaps NICHOLAS II); a biographical link with the name of a church (Alexander II); an etymological reason (especially for the names Victor, Honorius, Urban, and Paschal). In many cases, the subjective motivations are fairly mysterious. After this period (more exactly, from Landon, 913–14), there are no more new names, so that the numeral I disappears until 1978 (JOHN PAUL I).

Whereas, between 1145 and 1159, the popes broke strikingly with the tradition of Gregorian names (EUGENE III, ANASTASIUS IV, HADRIAN IV), the popes of the Hohenstaufen era and the period from the end of the conflict between the papacy and the Staufen up to INNOCENT V (1276) returned to one exclusive source, that of the names of the Gregorian popes (Alexander, Victor, Paschal, Callistus, Innocent, Lucius, Urban, Gregory, Clement, Celestine, Honorius); here, not infrequently, the name of profession expressed a current political design (ALEXANDER III, GREGORY IX).

At the end of the 13th century, the choice of name was often made independently of any ecclesiological or political consideration. John XXI (Peter of Spain) no doubt chose this name in memory of Cardinal Giovanni Gaetano Orsini; NICHOLAS IV, as a memorial to his protector NICHOLAS III. HADRIAN V and Nicholas III recalled the patron saint of the churches they had presided over as cardinals; MARTIN IV, the patron saint of Tours. For CELESTINE V (Pietro del Morrone), etymology was most probably the determining factor. In the 14th century, John, Boniface, and Benedict, names from the *saeculum obscurum* that had lost their negative connotation, reappeared. For the Avignon popes, recalling their French predecessors amounted to a kind of politically motivated agenda: Clement IV for CLEMENT V, Innocent V for INNOCENT VI, and URBAN IV for URBAN V. During the GREAT SCHISM, the French side took the names of Avignon popes (Clement, Benedict) while the Roman side looked back to the most illustrious representatives of a Roman idea of universal sovereignty (BONIFACE IX, INNOCENT VII, GREGORY XII). In 1415, MARTIN V broke with tradition by choosing the name of the saint of the day, thus renouncing political motivation. The period of the Renaissance popes saw a craving for originality and individualization: the numeral II, which had become rare, reappeared (Pius II, PAUL II, Julius II), and the memory of pagan heroes was explicitly invoked (ALEXANDER VI's enthronement speech alluded to Alexander the Great, and the satires against Julius II recalled Julius Caesar.).

From the 16th century, the name chosen has invariably been inspired by the principle of *pietas*: PAUL IV, GREGORY XIV, CLEMENT X, INNOCENT XI, INNOCENT XII, CLEMENT XII, CLEMENT XIII, BENEDICT XIV, CLEMENT XIV, PIUS VII, PIUS VIII, and PIUS XII took the names of those predecessors who had raised them to the cardinalate. JULIUS III, PAUL V, and GREGORY XV chose the name of the pope who had launched them on their curial CAREER. CLEMENT VIII, LEO XI, INNOCENT X, ALEXANDER VII, and INNOCENT XIII chose the name of the pope who had actively supported their family. PAUL IV, PIUS V, SIXTUS V, and ALEXANDER VIII adopted the names of those predecessors whose nephews had contributed to their election. Taking a predecessor's name not only was a way of giving symbolic thanks but also implied the wish to be faithful to a spiritual heritage. Hence the stereotypical, conservative character of pontifical names in the modern era. Julius, Marcellus, and Sixtus were chosen once; as for the others, the choice of names over the roughly four centuries from the council of TRENT to VATICAN II boils down to nine: Paul, Pius, Gregory, Urban, Innocent, Clement, Leo, Alexander, and Benedict. In the 17th and 18th centuries, the name Clement takes the lead, and then, until 1958, the name Pius. John XXIII (A. Roncalli, 1958) was the first to take the name of a medieval pope, thus symbolically emphasizing the end of the "papacy of the Piuses." His successor PAUL VI's choice was a subjective one, inspired primarily by a theological consideration. John Paul I was the first pope in history to adopt a double name, but his choice still obeyed the principle of respectful *pietas* toward his predecessors. The pontifical name of JOHN PAUL II invokes the memory of his three immediate predecessors.

List of popes named John (names, dates)	*LP, Annuario pontificio*	Platina
J. Tusculanus, ex patre Constantino, 523–6	J. I, no. LV	J. I, no. 55
J. qui et Mercurius, 533–5	J. II, no. LVIII	J. II, no. 58
J. Romanus, 561–74	J. III, no. LXIII	J. III, no. 63
J. Dalmatinus, 640–2	J. IV, no. LXXIIII	J. IV, no. 74
J. Syrus, 685–6	J. V, no. LXXXIIII	J. V, no. 84
J. Grecus, 701–5	J. VI, no. LXXXVII	J. VI, no. 87
J. Grecus de patre Platone, 705–7	J. VII, no. LXXXVIII	J. VII, no. 88
J. quidam diaconus, 844	[not entered]	J. VIII (Pope Joan), no. 106
J. Romanus ex patre Gundo, 872–82	J. VIII, no. CVIIII	J. IX, no. 110
J. Tiburtinus, 898–900	J. IX, no. CXVIII	J. X, no. 119
J. of Ravenna, 914–28	J. X, no. CXXV	J. XI, no. 126
J. Romanus, ex patre Sergio papa, 931–6	J. XI, no. CXXVIII	J. XII, no. 129
J. Romanus Octavianus, 955–64	J. XII, no. CXXXIII	J. XIII, no. 134
J. bishop of Nani, 965–72	J. XIII, no. CXXXVI	J. XIV, no. 137
J. Pietro da Pavia, 983–4	J. XIV, no. CXL	J. XV, no. 142
[J. XIV repeated]	[not entered]	J. XVI, no. 143
J. Romanus ex patre Leone, 985–96	J. XV, no. CXLI	J. XVII, no. 144
J. Philagathos, 997–8	[J. XVI, antipope]	J. XVIII, no. 146
J. Sicco, 1003	J. XVII, no. CXLIIII	J. XIX, no. 148
J. Fasanus, 1003/4–1009	J. XVIII, no. CXLV	J. XX, no. 149
J. Romanus, germanus Benedicti, 1024–32	J. XIX, no. CXLVIII	J. XXI, no. 152
	J. XX omitted	
J. Petrus Hispanus, 1276–7	J. XXI	J. XXII, no. 194
J. Jacques Duèze, 1316–34	J. XXII	
J. Baldassare Cossa, 1410–15	[antipope]	J. XXIII, no. 203
J. Angelo Roncalli, 1958–63	J. XXIII	J. XXIV, no. 214

Bernd-Ulrich Hergemöller

Bibliography

Herbers, K. "Die Papstin Johanna, ein kritischer Forschungsbericht," *Historisches Jahrbuch der Gorres-Gesellschaft*, 108 (1988), 174–94.

Hergemöller, B. U. *Die Geschichte der Papstnamen*, Münster, 1980; "Die Namen der Reformpäpste (1046–1145)," *AHP*, 24 (1986), 8–47.

Hofmann, J. "Die amtliche Stellung der in der ältesten römischen Bischofliste überlieferten Männer in der Kirche von Rom," ibid., 109 (1989), 1–23.

Kramer, F. "Über die Anfänge und die Beweggründe der Papstnamenänderungen im Mittelalter," *Römische Quartalschrift für christliche Altertumskunde und für Kirchengeschichte*, 51 (1956), 148–88.

Krebsius, J. F. *De nominum immutatione potissimum in religiosorum professione atque pontificum Romanorum inauguratione*, Leipzig (1719).

Poole, R. L. "The Names and Numbers of Medieval Popes," *English Historical Review*, 128 (1917), 465–78.

See also the bibliography under LIBER PONTIFICALIS.

OPUS DEI. Opus Dei is a Roman Catholic organization made up of priests and lay men and women who belong, in varying degrees, to the personal prelature governed by its own bishop. Its purpose is to sanctify its members through the exercise of their professional lives which are, as the Constitution of Opus insists, to be lived out in society at large. It is open to all Catholics, though there is a special emphasis on attracting the intellectual and professional elite to "the Work," as its members refer to it (opus dei means "the work of God").

The prelature was approved by Pope JOHN PAUL II in the course of an audience granted to the Cardinal Prefect of the Congregation of Bishops on 5 August 1982. It was announced on 23 August of that year, though the news was not made public until 28 November. It was on this day that the constitution was formally approved, and also, in the apostolic letter *Ut Sit*, that the personal prelature was created. The legal documents were, however, not handed over to the then head of Opus Dei, Alvaro del Portillo, until 19 March 1983, in the organization's Roman church of San Eugenio. This act brought to an end, at least for the time being, the long and often controversial juridical development of Opus Dei within the Church. An official of the congregation revealed that the status now achieved had been proposed to the founder of Opus Dei, Msgr. Josemaría Escrivá de Balaguer, by Pope PAUL VI as early as 1969, but it had at that time apparently not been regarded as a suitable solution.

Pope Paul himself had created the category within the Church of personal prelatures, in *Ecclesiae Sanctae* of 1966. He was responding to a suggestion contained in Vatican II's Decree on Priestly Life and Ministry that there should be structures equivalent to dioceses, but without geographical boundaries. The idea behind this new form of "diocese" was the realization that there were groups of people—military personnel or gypsies, for example—for whom geographically-based structures did not make sense. Whether the status of a personal prelature will prove to be a satisfactory solution for Opus Dei remains to be seen. Thus far it is the only example.

The juridical problem for Opus Dei is that it does not regard itself as a religious order. Indeed, though there are similarities with traditional religious orders, it certainly does not fit that category, chiefly because it includes members of both sexes and of varying status. There are differing levels of membership. The highest rank are the numeraries, who may be either clerical or lay; the lay members may be of either gender. All these members are bound to the prelature by "fidelities," which are similar in effect, if not in name, to the vows traditionally taken by members of religious orders. Members who are numeraries normally live in Opus Dei communities and are required to support the community, and Opus Dei in general, through their earnings. Although there seems to be at this level no particular distinction between the male and the female numeraries—both, for instance, are expected to be equally accomplished academically—the female numeraries have a particular responsibility for the maintenance of the Opus Dei houses. There is even a special category of female numeraries, the "auxiliaries," whose task is explicitly to clean and undertake other domestic work on behalf of the male numeraries.

In addition to those who live in Opus Dei communities there are members who take the same fidelities as the numeraries, but for some reason continue to live in their own homes. These are the "oblates" (technically, "aggregati"). Supernumeraries also live at home. They do not take the same fidelities and can marry and raise children, but their spiritual needs are met by priests of the prelature, and they live, as far as they can in their own circumstances, according to the spirituality of the organization. Finally there are "cooperators," who are not, strictly speaking, members, and who need not necessarily even be Catholics, who associate themselves with the work of the organization.

While there are ways in which the clergy can associate themselves with the work and spirituality of Opus Dei, ordained priests may not join. It is numerically a mainly lay organization, and its clergy constitute only a small proportion of the total. They are selected from among the numerary members, all of whom receive a theological education. Those men thought particularly suitable are asked to accept ordination within the prelature. They receive all their religious formation, both academic and spiritual, within Opus Dei. Although it presents itself as a lay organization, priests hold all its major posts, from the prelate and others in the central government down to the regional level. The prelate, who holds office for life, is elected by a general congress that includes lay members, drawn from a special category within the numeraries, that of elector, a position also held for life. Women do not take part directly in the election, though they have roughly parallel structures to those of the male numeraries. This division reflects a cardinal principle of Opus Dei, that the male and female sections of the prelature should not mix.

Apart from promoting the sanctification of its members, it is unclear what Opus Dei undertakes as an organization. It commonly operates by setting up a trust, or a series of trusts, in a region, and these may engage in "common works" such as business undertakings that are the responsibility of Opus Dei itself to manage and staff, and, where appropriate, from which to profit. More frequently, however, undertakings that appear to belong to Opus Dei fall into the category of "cooperative works." Cooperative works are wholly owned not by Opus Dei itself, but by a group of its members, and, strictly speaking, they have no legal ties to the organization itself. The most notable examples of the common works are the University of Navarre at Pamplona, Spain, and the

Athenaeum of the Holy Cross, situated in Rome's historic center. Examples of the cooperative works are the schools, publishing houses, broadcasting stations, press agencies, television production and distribution companies, and magazines that were listed in a document forwarded to the Congregation of Bishops in 1979. As is clear from that document, though numeraries may work in a variety of different professions, Opus Dei as such has a particular interest in education and in media-related activities.

The membership of Opus Dei was given in that same document as 72,375, scattered through eighty-seven countries. In the Vatican's yearbook, *Annuario Pontificio*, for 2000, the figure of 81,954 was given as the total of lay members of the organization. In the *Annuario* the number of priests is given as 1,780, with a further 344 preparing for ordination. The priests are, of course, all numerary, or full, members. No analysis of the lay membership is available. Presumably it includes supernumeraries as well as numeraries, but it may also include the more loosely associated cooperators. Opus Dei runs 1,654 churches and pastoral centers. The largest groups are in Spain and Mexico.

History. The founder of Opus Dei, José Maria (the two forenames were eventually run together) Escrivá, was born in Barbastro, in northeast Spain, on 9 January 1902. He was the second of six children, three of whom died young: his elder sister Carmen survived, as did his youngest brother Santiago. His father was a partner in a struggling textile business, and when this collapsed in 1915 the family moved to Logroño, where he became partner in a clothes shop. José Maria entered the seminary in Logroño in 1918, but a year later transferred to the seminary in Zaragoza: he was ordained on 25 March 1925, a few months after his father's death had left the family in straitened circumstances. Two years later he moved to Madrid, and it was in Madrid on 28 October 1928, while he was making a retreat, that, it is claimed, he conceived of the idea for Opus Dei, though the original concept seems to have been some time in taking shape. He was at this time supporting himself by working as a chaplain, while also giving spiritual direction to some of the Madrid clergy. He persuaded his mother to move to the Spanish capital from Logroño, and to invest her small inheritance in a residence for male students of law and architecture. Escrivá built his apostolate around this all-male group, though in 1930 he decided that his organization should also have a women's section.

The development of his organization was interrupted by the Spanish Civil War. At the end of 1937 Escrivá had to flee Spain, returning almost immediately to the headquarters of the Nationalist forces in Burgos. From then on Opus developed rapidly, and was closely associated with the national Catholicism of the Franco regime. This can readily be appreciated from the pages of Escrivá's major work of spiritual guidance, *Camino* ("The Way"), a small book of 999 maxims which reached its final form in this period. He had by this time gathered a number of followers, and they were already arousing a degree of hostility. They were, however, defended by the Bishop of Madrid (Escrivá had moved back there), and it was from the Bishop of Madrid that he sought, and obtained in March 1941, the status of a "pious union" for his fifty or so members.

Two years later Escrivá decided to establish, in addition to the male and female wings of his organization, an association of priests to care for their spiritual welfare. He took this step because he was dissatisfied with the spiritual guidance that might be imparted to them by clergy who had not been immersed from the very beginning of their formation in the Opus Dei ethos. But for there to be an association of priests, the approval of the Vatican was needed. Under the title of the Sacerdotal Society of the Holy Cross it received this approval on 11 October 1943, but only two years later Escrivá was seeking further changes. Once more he sent his second in command, Alvaro del Portillo, to negotiate a new status with the Vatican. In 1947 The Apostolic Constitution *Provida Mater Ecclesia* established within the Church the category of secular institutes. Members of such institutes were to wear no special form of religious dress, or to take public vows. They were to pursue their vocation through their chosen trade or profession. This seemed a suitable formula for Opus Dei, and on 24 February, only three weeks after *Provida Mater Ecclesia*, it became the first secular institute to be recognized as such. Two months later Escrivá was raised to the rank of domestic prelate, entitled to be called "Monsignor." The headquarters were moved from Madrid to Rome, to a building in viale Bruno Buozzi that had once been the Hungarian embassy.

This move to the administrative center of the Catholic Church reflected Opus Dei's expansion around the world. In addition to its several houses in Spain, new ones had been opened in Portugal (1945), England (1946), France and Ireland (both 1947), and Mexico and the United States (both 1948). The concept of what it meant to be a member had also been broadened. Hitherto all members had been in the category defined above as "numeraries." In 1947, with its establishment as a secular institute, Escrivá created the category of supernumeraries for those who were married and also, at least from the constitution of 1950, for diocesan priests who might wish to join. These constitutions governed the organization until 1982 when, as has been seen, a new status was negotiated and a new constitution enacted. It was the 1950 constitution that enshrined the degree of secrecy which has become associated with Opus Dei: the constitutions themselves were to remain secret; members were to wear no sign of their adherence, or to reveal the names of members. Alvaro del Portillo solicited from the Vatican permission even to keep the full constitution secret from bishops within whose dioceses Opus Dei was operating, unless it had a fully established center in the diocese.

By the mid-1950s Escrivá had become disillusioned with the status of the secular institute, which brought the organization under the aegis of the Congregation for Religious. The congregation, in his view, was encouraging other secular institutes to assimilate themselves increasingly to the model of a religious order. The search for a new status was begun. His preferred solution was that of a "prelatura nullius," but this rather anachronistic proposal was rejected by both JOHN XXIII and Paul VI. The status of personal prelature was eventually conferred in 1982 by Pope John Paul II, a man more sympathetic to the organization than were his predecessors.

By that time Msgr. Josemaría Escrivá de Balaguer, Marques de Peralta (a title he had petitioned for from the Spanish government in 1968), was dead. He died in the Rome headquarters of Opus Dei on 26 June 1975. The cause for his eventual canonization was actively, and promptly, promoted by the organization he had founded. He was beatified by Pope John Paul II on 17 May 1992 amid considerable controversy about the appropriateness of Escrivá's elevation, the speed with which it had been achieved, and the process by which it had been accomplished.

Controversies. Opus Dei has been dogged with controversy almost from its beginnings. The earliest complaint was about its apparent secrecy. There is no doubt that Escrivá urged "discretion" from his members. At least in recent years, the organization has become rather more open about its constitution and its membership, though the fact that its members wear no external sign of belonging to "the Work," or declare their allegiance in their publications or in cooperative activities or businesses which they run, is still regarded with suspicion by many in the Church. There is still much confusion about the degree of responsibility that Opus Dei has for the business activities of its members, a matter that becomes especially acute when such businesses fail, as has happened in a small number of high-profile cases.

But perhaps the greatest cause of concern has been methods of recruitment. In December 1981 the archbishop of Westminster, Cardinal Basil Hume, issued guidelines on recruitment to be followed by the organization in his diocese. According to these, no one under 18 should be permitted to make any long-term commitment to Opus Dei; minors wishing to do so should discuss the issue with their parents; no undue pressure should be exercised on members to prevail upon them to stay in the organization, and that they ought to be allowed to choose their own spiritual directors; and any initiative by Opus Dei should be clearly be labeled as such.

Opus Dei has also been criticized for its political stance. It is commonly perceived to be a right-wing movement within the Catholic Church, one not unsympathetic to totalitarian regimes. The clearest evidence of this is seen in Spain in the 1950s and early 1960s, when a surprisingly large number of Opus Dei members held senior positions in the government of the country or in other significant national posts. But not only has it been seen as politically right-wing, it is also regarded as theologically conservative. That this should be so is not, perhaps, particularly surprising. As has been noted, the spirituality of its founder was forged in the context of Spanish national Catholicism. Moreover, it tends to recruit from the more conservative stratum of society. In response, however, members of the organization claim that, with its insistence on the role of the laity in the Catholic Church, Opus Dei was a precursor of the theology of Vatican II.

Michael Walsh

Bibliography

Artigues, D. *El Opus dei en España*, Paris, 1971.

Bernal, S. *Msgr. Josemaría Escrivá de Balaguer: A Profile of the Founder of Opus Dei*, Dublin, 1977.

Bowers, F. *The Work: An Investigation into the History of Opus Dei and How it Operates in Ireland Today*, Swords, Ire., 1989.

Carandell, L., *Vida y milagros de Mons. Josemaría Escrivá de Balaguer, fundador del Opus Dei*, Barcelona, 1975.

Casanova, J. V. *The Opus Dei Ethic and the Modernization of Spain*, Ph.D. thesis, New York, New School of Social Research, 1982.

Escobar, M. J. *Opus Dei génesis y expansíon en el mundo antecendentes sobre el polémico proceso de Beatificación de su Fundador*, Santiago, Spain, 1992.

Escrivá de Balaguer, J. *The Forge*, London, 1988.

Escrivá de Balaguer, J. *The Way*, Dublin, 1985.

Estruch, J. *Saints and Schemers: Opus Dei and its Paradoxes*, New York, 1995.

Fuenmayor, A. de, et al., eds. *El itinerario jurídico del Opus Dei: historia y defensa de un carisma*, Pamplona, Spain, 1990.

Gondrand, F. *At God's Pace: A Biography of Josemaria Escrivá de Balaguer Founder of Opus Dei*, London, 1989.

Hertel, P. *Geheimnisse des Opus Dei*, Freiburg, Germany, 1995.

Hertel, P. "*Ich verspreche euch den Himmel*," Düsseldorf, Germany, 1985.

Hutchison, R. A. *Their Kingdom Come: Inside the Secret World of Opus Dei*, London, 1997.

Le Tourneau, D. *What is Opus Dei?* Cork, Ire., 1987.

Messori, V. *Opus Dei: una investigacíon*, Barcelona, 1994.

Mettner, M. *Die katholische Mafia: kirchliche Geheimbünde greifen nach der Macht*, Munich, 1995.

Moncada, A. *Historia oral del Opus Dei*, Barcelona, 1987.

Moreno, M. A. *Opus Dei, anexo a huna historia*, Barcelona, 1976.

Moreno, M. A. *El Opus Dei, creencias y controversias sobre la canonización de Monseñor Escrivá*, Madrid, 1992.

O'Connor, W. *Opus Dei an Open Book*, Cork, Ire., 1991.

Ombres, R. "Opus Dei and Personal Prelatures," *Clergy Review*, 70 (1985), 292–5.

Rocca, G. *L'"Opus Dei": appunti e documenti per una storia*, Rome, 1985.

Rodriguez, P., et al., eds. *Mons. Josemaría Escrivá de Balaguer y el Opus Dei*, Pamplona, Spain, 1985.

Schützeichel, H., ed. *Opus Dei, Ziele, Anspruch und Einfluß*, Düsseldorf, Germany, 1992.

Soto, F. *Fascismo y Opus Dei en Chile: estudios de literatura e ideología*, Barcelona, 1976.

Steigleder, K. *Das Opus Dei—eine Innenansicht*, Zürich, 1983.

Tapia, M. del Carmen, *Beyond the Threshold: a Life in Opus Dei*, New York, 1997.

Thierry, J. *Opus Dei: A Close-Up*, New York, 1973.

Vázquez de Prada, A. *El fundador del Opus Dei*, Madrid, 1983.

Walsh, M. *The Secret World of Opus Dei*, London, 1989.

West, W. J. *Opus Dei Exploding a Myth*, Crows Nest, Australia, and London, 1987.

Ynfante, J. *Opus Dei así en la tierra como en el cielo*, Barcelona, 1996.

ORDERS, PONTIFICAL. The *ANNUARIO PONTIFICIO* states that nominations are made directly by the pope by apostolic letter.

—*Supreme Order of Christ*. Instituted by JOHN XXII (1316–34) on 14 March 1319.

—*Order of the Golden Spur*. The exact date of foundation is not known. Restored by PIUS X (1903–14) on 7 February 1905. One class.

—*Ordine Piano*. Instituted by PIUS IX (1846–78) on 17 July 1847, reformed by PIUS XII (1939–58) on 11 November 1939 and 25 December 1947. Four classes: knights of the Collar (*di collare*), knights of the Grand Cross, commanders "with plaque" (*con placca*) and commanders, knights.

—*Order of St. Gregory the Great*. Founded by GREGORY XVI (1831–46) on 1 September 1831, reformed by Pius X on 7 February 1905. Classes (civil and military): knights of the Grand Cross, commanders "with plaque" and commanders, knights.

—*Order of Pope St. Sylvester*. Formed on the model of the Milizia Aurata by Gregory XVI on 31 October 1831,

reformed by Pius X on 7 February 1905. Three classes: knights of the Grand Cross, commanders "with plaque" and commanders, knights.

—*Equestrian Order of the Holy Sepulcher of Jerusalem*. Founded in the Middle Ages to guard the HOLY PLACES of Jerusalem, more specifically Christ's tomb. The order was reorganized on two occasions by Pius IX, in 1847 and 1868, and then by LEO XIII in 1888. Pius X reserved the title of Grand Master for the supreme pontiff, and PIUS XI combined it with the Work for the Preservation of the Faith in Palestine. In 1940, Pius XII entrusted the spiritual patronage of the order to a cardinal, who assumed the title of Grand Master of the Order, and dissociated the order's historic center at Jerusalem from its central seat, henceforth in Rome. By an apostolic letter published under the FISHERMAN'S SEAL on 25 December 1957, the same supreme pontiff significantly extended the domain of the order of Pius IX by joining to it the Collar of Gold, with the explicit intention of reserving this decoration for heads of state or those who exercise an extremely important authority. In that same letter, he decided that the Supreme Order of the Militia of Our Lord Jesus Christ and the Order of the Golden Militia or the Militia of the Golden Spur would be conferred on those of extraordinary merit. The contemporary extension of diplomatic relations held by the Holy See implied a reexamination of the question of the equestrian orders. Henceforth, they would be conferred only on particularly solemn occasions, and only on high-ranking persons on the express condition that they profess the Christian faith—or certain eminent places of international scope and of interest to people of all nations. JOHN XXIII (1958–63) approved the statutes of the order in a BRIEF of 8 December 1962, which was followed by one from PAUL VI (1963–78) on 8 July 1977 giving them "sovereign approval." In the *motu proprio Equestres ordines* of 15 April 1966, Paul VI recalled that for various reasons the Roman pontiffs had instituted, modified, or developed the equestrian orders, designed to express their esteem, affection, and gratitude to statesmen and those remarkable in other ways who were worthy of being honored.

The *Croce per Ecclesia et Pontifice* and the "Benemerenti" Medal are honorific distinctions created by Leo XIII (1878–1903).

Philippe Levillain

Bibliography

Annuario pontificio per l'anno 2000, 1372–3.

ORDINATIONS, ANGLICAN. The question of Anglican ordinations is pivotal in the relations between the Catholic Church and the Anglican communion. The declaration of nullity contained in the BULL *Apostolicae curae* issued by LEO XIII on 13 September 1896 is a major document in this area; it confirmed a practice that was established when the Anglican Church first came into being, and that remains unchanged despite the development of ECUMENISM in the 20th century.

Under Henry VIII (1509–47), the central issue was the rupture with Rome, after the king proclaimed himself Supreme Head of the Church of England. He had no desire to found a new church or to reform the faith of his Church; and, during his reign, orders were invariably conferred using the Roman pontifical. Nevertheless, the "schismatic" situation he had created encouraged the penetration into England of Lutheran, Calvinist, and Anabaptist arguments, especially since Thomas Cranmer, the archbishop of Canterbury who had annulled Henry VIII's marriage to Catherine of Aragon, did not conceal his sympathies with certain of them.

The shift to Protestantism essentially took place during the reign of Edward VI (1547–53). The king had surrounded himself with advisers imbued with Protestant thinking, who drafted a new ordinal, which was published in 1550 and slightly revised in 1552. Whereas, under Henry VIII, the clergy had been ordained according to the Roman pontifical, the new ordinal of 1550–2 was the one adopted under Edward VI, from March 1550 to July 1553.

Queen Mary abolished the ordinal when she came to power in 1553. But after her death, during Elizabeth's reign (1558–1605), it was put to use again, and a new hierarchy was instituted, with the new archbishop of Canterbury, Matthew Parker at its head; he was ordained with the Edwardine ordinal by the four bishops who had remained outside the reconciliation of 1553.

Various problems arise in connection with the question of the historical origins of Anglican ordinations. Even the historical authenticity of Parker's ordination has been called into question. The ceremony was long shrouded in mystery. The silence surrounding it throughout Elizabeth's reign contributed to the growth of a legend, the "Nag's Head story," according to which the ordination was in fact enacted amid revelry at a tavern whose sign was a horse's head. The legend persisted until to the end of the 19th century.

Apart from the question of the genuineness of Parker's ordination, there arises another problem, with respect to the tradition of the indivisible Church: the problem of the validity of the ordination, which depended on the powers of those ordaining on the one hand and on the ordinal used on the other. The point can be made that whereas two of the four ordaining bishops had been ordained with Edward VI's ordinal, the other two had been ordained with the Roman pontifical under Henry VIII, and the chief ordaining bishop, William Barlow, was one of these two; in the view of the Catholic Church, therefore, his power to confer was valid. There remains, then, the question of the ordinal used.

The new ritual introduced in Edward's VI's time included important modifications of the Roman ritual. Without going into detail, it should suffice to say that the formulas of ordination employed no longer made precise reference to the order being conferred (diaconate, presbyterate, episcopate), at least until 1662; at that date the Anglican authorities, aware of a lacuna in their ritual, elaborated the text on this point. Still, the use for more than a century of a formula considered incomplete by the Catholic Church, and which was originally intended as a sign of rupture by the Anglican Church, caused a break in the apostolic succession. Furthermore, the Anglican ritual of priestly ordination suppressed a medieval custom of the Latin Church, that of the *porrectio instrumentorum*. In this ritual, the ordinand touched the paten and the chalice, the instruments of the Eucharistic sacrifice, a gesture that referred to the sacrificial character of the mass. But in the absence of explicit reference to the "power to consecrate and offer the sacrifice," the omission of the ritual in question could, in the eyes of some theologians, give rise to at least a degree of doubt, especially since the sacramental doctrine expressed elsewhere by the Anglican Church diverged on some fundamental points from that affirmed in the Church (for example, the notion of the real presence). Finally, the desire to break with Rome, as evidenced by the creation of the new ordinal and a new hierarchy, seems hard to reconcile with the intention to do what the Church does, a condition traditionally required for a sacrament to be valid.

The practice adopted by the Catholic Church with respect to Anglican ordinations was determined during Mary Tudor's reign, and the first pontifical documents relating to the question date from that time. Chief among them are part of the BULL *Praeclara carissimi*, issued by PAUL IV on 20 June 1555, and the BRIEF of 30 October 1555 addressed to Cardinal Pole, whom JULIUS III had sent to reorganize the Church of England and, in particular, to correct the faults he might find in the Anglican hierarchy. Both these documents advocated the reordination of ministers who had not been ordained according to "the form of the Church." Members of Edward VI's clergy therefore arranged to be reordained according to the old Latin rite, to ensure their reintegration; and after the documents were published, many Anglican ministers who had converted to Catholicism were reordained unconditionally.

The third pontifical document having explicitly to do with Anglican ordinations is CLEMENT XI's decree of 17 April 1704. It was written in response to the request of the Anglican bishop John Clement Gordon, a convert to Catholicism, that he be given orders according to the Roman rite. This was an opportunity to pose the question as to whether the ordinations he had previously received were valid. His case was studied in light of an inquiry on the question of Anglican orders carried out in 1684–5.

This inquiry had eliminated the objection regarding the *porrectio instrumentorum* and had based its conclusion on the deficiency of the forms in force between 1551 and 1662, that is, on the interruption of the apostolic succession—even if "the form as it was reformed under Charles II [1660–85] was valid." These conclusions served as the basis for the study of the Gordon case. The grounds for nullity put forward at the time were tied not, as was believed at the end of the 19th century, to Parker's ordination, but to the inadequacy of the form that had cut the bishop off from the legitimate succession of the English and Scottish bishops. Consequently, declared Clement XI, Gordon should receive *ex integro et absolute* all orders, particularly priestly orders, and if he had not been confirmed, he should first receive the sacrament of confirmation.

The custom of reordaining Anglican ministers who had converted to Catholicism therefore belongs to a tradition dating back to the very beginnings of the Anglican Church and has been followed since that time, especially in the second half of the 19th century, under the influence of the OXFORD MOVEMENT.

The Oxford Movement was inaugurated in 1833 by the first of Newman's tracts (between 1833 and 1841 he published ninety tracks, whence the name Tractarians, given to his followers). The improvement sought to develop the idea of union. Eager to return to early Christianity by ridding Anglicanism of the influence of Protestantism, the Tractarians stressed certain elements (the importance of dogma, the divine constitution of the Church, the sacraments, the liturgy, etc.) that played a part in bringing them closer to Catholicism. Several of them—notably Newman in 1845 and Manning in 1851—converted to Catholicism. These individual conversions, however, were not in line with the thinking of the movement, whose vision was of a corporate union. During the 1860s, the unionist trend broke out of the narrow framework of the Tractarian movement and spread to numerous High Church groups. All this intense activity could not but help draw attention to the question of Anglican ordinations. Indeed, the problem of their validity did not arise only in connection with cases of individual conversion: corporate union implied that it had already been resolved. The partisans of union were so aware of it that they favored clandestine reordinations. The very fact that these ordinations often led to individual conversions shows that Anglicans not only attached great importance to their priesthood but also harbored doubts as to the validity of their orders.

This evolution coincided with the period leading up to the VATICAN I council, which some Anglicans (including Pusey) saw as a possible instrument of the desired union. The contacts Pusey formed at the time with several French bishops, especially Bishop Darboy and Bishop Dupanloup, seemed to him harbingers of hope; the Bollandist Victor de Buck, then playing an active role as intermediary, ventured to tell Pusey that one of the conditions of reunion the Anglicans might obtain would be conditional reordination. This eventuality left Pusey somewhat disappointed, since it cast doubt on the authenticity of the Anglican priesthood. But the disappointments piled up. First, Fr. de Buck had to put an end to their talks, on the order of the superior general of the JESUITS. Then the terms of the pope's invitations to attend the council seemed to Pusey to imply a kind of rejection. Indeed, in his announcement of the council and his concomitant appeal for unity, PIUS IX addressed, on the one hand, the Eastern bishops who were not in communion with the Holy See, and on the other, "Protestants and other non-Catholics." For Pusey, this distinction was tantamount to denying the Anglicans the apostolic succession and thus ruining all hope of corporate reunion.

Despite these difficulties, which the definition of papal infallibility only reinforced, the question sprang up again under the next pontificate.

On the one hand, the unity of the Christian Church was a matter dear to the heart of Leo XIII, as is especially clear in the letter *Praeclara gratulationis* of 20 June 1894, issued on the occasion of his jubilee. This text, which is a general call to unity, came at a time when a debate had begun between Anglicans and Catholics, precisely on the question of ordinations. The debate originated in an initiative born of the friendship between Lord Halifax, one of the last great Tractarians, and the French Lazarist Fernand Portal. Keen to awaken public opinion to the idea of union, the two men made the topic of Anglican ordinations an opportunity for exchanges between Anglicans and Catholics. As it happened, the question of such ordinations quickly became the kernel of a controversy that in the end led Rome to make an important decision.

The "Anglo-Roman campaign" was launched early in 1894, when Portal, in collaboration with the Anglican Puller and under the pseudonym Fernand Dalbus, republished in a booklet on Anglican ordinations two articles that had appeared the previous year. The authors decided that the rite of ordination of bishops was valid, but that ordinations of priests were invalid (and that the apostolic succession was therefore interrupted) because the ritual of the *porrectio instrumentorum* was absent. One cannot help but think that Portal was using a clever tactic here namely, that of having invalidity rest solely on a ritual which, in itself, could be thought of as secondary: the arguments put forward in favor of validity could thus retain all their force, and it would be easy to arrive at a conclusion that Portal was careful not to draw himself. His tactic immediately produced results. Fr. Louis Duchesne, to whom he sent his article without delay, entered the arena wholeheartedly, at least for a while: having expressed his support to Portal in a letter, which the Lazarist hastened to disseminate in England, Duchesne published an article, on 15 July 1894, in his well-known

Bulletin critique; he came out in favor of the validity of Anglican ordinations, which aroused huge enthusiasm among the Anglicans but hostile reactions among the English Catholic hierarchy, especially on the part of the archbishop of Westminster, Cardinal Vaughan.

The repercussions of the debate and the measures taken by Portal in Rome itself prompted Leo XIII to intervene. First came a consultation, during the autumn of 1894, in which several experts (among them Louis Duchesne) were called upon to draw up a report on the question. Next was the meeting of a commission, which held twelve sessions between 24 March and 11 May 1896. Presided over by Cardinal Mazzella assisted by Merry Del Val, it consisted first of six and then of eight consultors. The champions of invalidity were the principal members, whom the Benedictine Dom Gasquet had been gathering around him since September 1895 to study the question of orders: besides Gasquet himself, Canon Moyes, from the chapter of Westminster, and Fleming, a Franciscan. The Spanish Capuchin Llaveneras, consultant to the Holy Office, also joined the group. Among the champions of validity there were shades of opinion. If Duchesne (at least at the outset of the debates) and De Augustinis (professor of theology at the Gregorian University in the United States) were clearly for validity, Gasparri considered the orders doubtful. Fr. Scannell, a Catholic priest in a parish in Kent, known to be friendly to the Anglicans, apparently did not have a fixed opinion on the specific question of orders. Mazzella was against Anglican participation in the sessions, but Duchesne and Gasparri were authorized by Cardinal Rampolla to consult Puller and Lacey, who were in Rome while the commission was at work.

The commission took into account the results of recent research, stimulated by the reopening of the debate: The bull *Praeclara carissimi* of 20 June 1555 and the brief of 30 October 1555, discovered by Gasquet in February 1895; a new study, also by Gasquet, in 1896, of the conclusion of the Gordon case (arrived at by an explicit declaration of the Church, in the form of a decree of Pope Clement XI, and not, as was generally believed, by a simple decision of the Holy Office); and, especially, the results of research done by the Anglicans themselves (published in 1896) concerning the reordinations during Mary Tudor's reign of members of Edward VI's clergy (works by Howard Frere) and of Anglican ministers who had converted to Catholicism (works by Brown). These discoveries, which established the "very great antiquity" of the custom of reordination, undoubtedly helped to undermine the position of one such as Duchesne: in the end he seems to have come round to expressing doubt as to the validity of the ordinations, thus joining with the positions of Gasparri and Scannell, while Gasquet, Moyes, Fleming, and Llaveneras declared themselves for invalidity.

These conclusions served as a basis for the work of the cardinals' commission, which inherited the dossier and pronounced its decision on 16 July 1896, with the pope presiding: it ruled that the new inquiry on the question of Anglican orders showed no need for a revision of Church practice in this area. In the opinion of the champions of reconciliation, this formula had at least the merit of not publicly declaring the orders invalid and of leaving the door open for a work of reconciliation, once the architects of union got over their disappointment. But Cardinal Vaughan believed he was speaking for English Catholics when he stressed that the whole campaign discouraged individual conversions among Anglicans. He therefore insisted that the pope should solemnly declare the ordinations invalid. It may be that his point of view was a determining factor in the decision finally reached by Leo XIII: on 13 September 1896 the bull *Apostolicae curae* was promulgated, whose text, prepared by Merry Del Val with the assistance of Gasquet, solemnly proclaimed the nullity of Anglican ordinations.

In the 20th century, the problem of Anglican ordinations reappears in a new context: the development of ecumenism, sanctioned by the VATICAN II council (1962–5)—in particular in the Decree on Ecumenism, promulgated on 21 November 1964—which set forth ecumenism as a requirement, calling for attention and effort on the part of every member of the Church. Henceforth, when the term "dialogue" has been used, it no longer refers only to individual contacts but to official meetings between representatives of separated Christian confessions and, as regards Anglicanism, between the pope and the archbishop of Canterbury, since the latter has presided over the Anglican communion since it was constituted at the first Lambeth conference in 1867.

This evolution had begun in the years following the First World War, at the time of the "Malines Conversations," so named because of the city in which they took place, the episcopal see of Cardinal Mercier. In Great Britain, even before the first of these meetings, at the 1920 Lambeth conference, 252 Anglican bishops had launched an "Appeal to All Members of Christianity," signed by the archbishop of Canterbury; in this appeal they declared their readiness, the terms of union having been settled in other respects, to accept what the leaders of the other Churches might judge was necessary for bringing about recognition of the ministry of the Anglican clergy. At the second Malines meeting, in 1923, the "modalities of rectification" admitted by the Lambeth conference were studied, and Msgr. van Roey, vicar general of cardinal Mercier, voiced the idea of a conditional laying-on of hands, first for the archbishop of Canterbury by the pope or his LEGATE, and then by the archbishop for his suffragans. According to the terms of the debates it seemed possible to think "the Anglican bishops would have no difficulty accepting whatever element of the ordination ritual the Roman Church deemed necessary to remove all doubt in everyone's eyes, about the validity of their ministry." Henceforth, efforts at reconciliation between Anglicans and Catholics were headed in that direction, without discussion of the validity of ordinations being explicitly reopened. The doctrinal debate that was intensified by the development of the ecumenical movement reinforced this trend.

Vatican II, in its desire to be more pastoral than doctrinal in a formal sense, captured, defined, and developed a deep ecumenical openness. As far as Anglicanism is concerned, the "dialogue" set in motion by the ecumenical movement is marked principally by two major encounters: the meeting in Rome in March 1966 between Pope Paul VI and Archbishop Michael Ramsey, the hundredth archbishop of Canterbury; and that in May 1982 between John Paul II and Archbishop Robert Runcie during the PILGRIMAGE made by the pope to Canterbury to retrace the steps of Augustine, sent as a missionary to the British Isles by Gregory the Great. Since then, Dr. Runcie has made an official visit to Rome from 29 September to 2 October 1989; and more recently, on 25 May 1992, the new archbishop of Canterbury, George Leonard Carey, paid a unofficial visit to the Vatican.

The two summit meetings of 1966 and 1982 also mark two stages in the setting up of a structure to serve the reconcilation between Anglicans and Catholics, the ARCIC (Anglican Roman Catholic International Commission). The first commission, ARCIC I, which had been preceded by a preparatory commission, worked from January 1971 to March 1982 on the three topics it considered essential: Eucharist, the ministries, and authority. The second commission was set up in May 1982, at the time of the Canterbury meeting, its main agenda being to study obstacles to the mutual recognition of ministries.

The growth of the ecumenical movement has thus been accompanied by a broad, bilateral discussion of doctrine, which has helped change the approach to the question of Anglican ordinations: agreement on this question is no longer a prerequisite for union but rather one element of a global reflection.

This doctrinal review might lead to renewed discussion of the question of orders. The sharpest point of Leo XIII's argument was that the Anglican ordinal of 1552 was in fact the expression not only of a defective doctrine of the Eucharist and the priesthood but also of a conscious intention to break away (from the Roman Church). If this disruptive intention is replaced by a common desire to work toward restoring unity, the context is obviously changed. Moreover, if the common discussion between Anglicans and Catholics were to issue in doctrinal agreement, then Anglican rituals regarding future ordinations might be considered sufficient. The only problem remaining would be the reintegration of the bishops transmitting the sacrament of orders into the apostolic succession. Such was the argument developed in 1985 by Cardinal Willebrands, prefect of the Secretariat for Christian Unity.

The terms of the report of ARCIC I, which was presented on 31 March 1982, encouraged the belief that agreement had been reached "on the essence of the Eucharistic faith as regards the sacramental presence of Christ and the sacrificial dimension of the Eucharist, and on the nature and the goal of the priesthood, of ordination, and of the apostolic succession." However, the "evaluation" of this report revealed that it sometimes smoothed over ambiguities and misunderstandings. Moreover, the Anglican communion's decision to accept the priesthood of women (in 1991, according to official Anglican sources, there were 1,342 women priests, including 3 bishops, and 1,942 women deacons, for the whole of the Anglican communion) highlights the existence of divergences, precisely with regard to the ministerial priesthood and the Eucharist. This question does constitute a stumbling block, but at a moment when Anglicans are beginning to change their stance on another fundamental point, that of the primacy of Rome: certain experiences within the Anglican communion (the development of the role of the archbishop of Canterbury and the Lambeth conferences) have led to recognition that, while the diversity of local Churches is to be respected, the service of the faith requires some kind of primacy. Dr. Runcie expressed this point when he visited JOHN PAUL II in 1989: "The example of Gregory, that is, a primacy of unity and mission—which is likewise embodied for us in the ministry of his successor John Paul II—is starting to find a place in Anglican thinking." As for the respect for diversities, he drew its limits: "Realism and honesty lead me to admit that the initiative taken by certain Anglican provinces to allow women to enter the priesthood and the episcopate appears to the Roman Church to exceed these limits."

Brigitte Waché

Bibliography

Aubert, R. *Le Saint-Sige et l'union des Églises*, 1947, Brussels.

Bivort de La Saudée, J. *Anglicans et catholiques, 1893–1933*, 1949, Paris.

Cren, P. R. "Approche de l'anglicanisme," *Lumière et Vie*, 12 (1963), 5–29.

Fouilloux, E. *Les catholiques et l'unité chrétienne du XIXe au XXe siècle*, 1982, Paris.

Hughes, J. J. *Absolutely Null and Utterly Void: The Papal Condemnation of Anglican Orders*, 1968, London.

Irenikon, the whole collection.

La Documentation catholique, especially 1982, 497–514; 1985, 867–82; 1986, 354–5; 1987, 320–1; 1988, 663–9; 1989, 933–40; 1992, 633–4.

Ladous, R. *L'abbé Portal et la campagne anglo-romaine, 1890–1912*, 1973, Lyon; *Monsieur Portal et les siens*, 1985, Paris.

Marchal, L. "Ordinations anglicanes," *DTC*, 11, 1154–93.

Marot, H. "Les ordinations anglicanes," *Lumière et Vie*, 12 (1963), 87–116.

Neveu, B. "Mgr Duchesne et son mémoire sur les ordinations anglicanes," *The Journal of Theological Studies*, 29 (1978), 443–82.

Rambaldi, G. "La memoria di Mgr L. Duchesne sulle ordinazioni anglicane ed un suo esame critico contemporaneo," *Gregorianum*, 62 (1981), 681–746; "Leone XIII e la memoria di L. Duchesne sulle ordinazioni anglicane. Note di contesto con documenti," *AHP*, 29 (1981), 333–45; "Relazione e voto del P. Raffaele Pierotti, o.p., Maestro dell S. Palazzo apostolico, sulle ordinazioni anglicane. Note introduttive ed edizione del testo," *AHP*, 20 (1982), 337–88; "Il caso di coscienza di Leone XIII sulle ordinazioni anglicane," *Civiltà Cattolica*, 140 (1989), 3, 28–42; "Una memoria inedita del Barone Friedrich von Hü gel sull'unione cattolici e anglicani," *AHP*, 27 (1989), 419–32.

Waché, B. *Mgr Louis Duchesne, historien de l'Église, directeur de l'École française de Rome*, 1992, Rome; the question of Anglican ordinations is treated in V, 329–401: "Duchesne et la question de l'unité de l'Église."

ORGANIZATIONS, INTERNATIONAL, THE HOLY SEE AND.

As the central government and supreme authority of a universal Church the HOLY SEE has close ties with a large number of international, that is to say, in the government, organizations established on a permanent basis and able to express their own will, juridically distinct from that of the states that comprise them. The active role played by the supreme pontiff in the multilateral diplomacy for which the United Nations offers a privileged setting cannot be overstated. But this role, which in any case is a recent one, must be precisely defined on account of the personal union (to use the traditional language of the law of nations) of the Holy See with the VATICAN CITY STATE. Even though it is carried out among states and enforces intergovernmental agreements, the Holy See's international action is not usually imputable to the (highly special) state of which it is the established organ. If, since the LATERAN PACTS (1929), the Apostolic See has a territorial seat, designed to guarantee and symbolize its independence, its international identity is independent of that seat: this identity was taken for granted at the time of the *Respublica christiana* and since then has never been overshadowed (under the regime of the Law of Guarantees, from 1870 to 1929, the popes continued to sign treaties, exercise the right of active and passive legation, and give arbitrations, even though they had been deprived of all temporal power). The Holy See freely decides, case by case, in which capacity, that of the universal Church or that of the symbolic State, it plays its part in the life of nations. The first is by far the more frequently invoked, without this duality of function raising problems of principle.

More delicate are the doctrinal questions faced by successive pontiffs owing to the emergence of international organizations in the 20th century, and particularly of general organizations with a universal mission. As we shall see, they have found growing favor with Rome. Nonetheless, pontifical encouragement has never implied that the Holy See should participate directly in the activities of such international organizations. The relations established between the Holy See and these diverse organizations vary enormously in form and range.

Pontifical Encouragement of the Growth of International Organizations. The Holy See manifested interest in international organizations at a very early stage. It viewed sympathetically institutions such as the International Association for the Protection of Workers, at which it was represented from the beginning (1900), and especially the International Labor Organization, created by the treaty of Versailles, whose statutes, especially as expressed in the preamble, harmonized well with the SOCIAL TEACHING of the Church as formulated by LEO XIII in the encyclical *Rerum novarum* (15 May 1891).

About the League of Nations the papacy had more reservations. In his *Message to the Warring Nations and Their Heads* (1 August 1917), BENEDICT XV hoped for a transformation of international relations to replace "the material force of arms [with] the moral force of the law" through a reduction of armaments and obligatory arbitration, duly sanctioned. Although excluded in advance from the coming peace conference, he approved President Wilson's Fourteen Points of 8 January 1918—the last of which foresaw the creation of a "General Society of Nations"—before defending the idea of a universal organization: "It is greatly to be desired that all states, putting aside reciprocal suspicions, join together to make one society, or better, one family, both for the defense of their individual liberties and for the maintenance of social order." Benedict XV added: "To the Nations united in a League founded on Christian law, the Church will faithfully lend its active and urgent support for all their enterprises inspired by justice and charity" (encyclical *Pacem Dei munus pulcherrimum*, 23 May 1920).

The League of Nations, which Catholic circles readily viewed as an organization of socialist or masonic inspiration, offered nothing that would warrant such support. The Holy See took note of that. In his first encyclical, *Ubi arcano Dei* (23 December 1922), PIUS XI deplored the powerlessness of the new institution to "impose on all nations a sort of international code adapted to our age, analogous to that which in the Middle Ages governed that veritable Society of Nations known as Christendom."

The repeated failures of the League of Nations clearly were not calculated to dispel the pontifical prejudices. However, a definite turning point was reached during the pontificate of PIUS XII. No sooner had he been elected than, in a strikingly new voice and with unprecedented vigor, the pope defined the teaching of the Church on the rebuilding of world society. He stressed the positive role for peace that a renewed universal organization could play. His inaugural encyclical, *Summi pontificatus* (20 October 1939), underlined the need to establish a "new world order" far removed from the "shifting sand of changing and ephemeral rules dictated by collective or individual selfishness." On 10 November 1939, Pius XII clarified his thought by praying for an "organization which, because it would respect the rights of God, [could] ensure the mutual independence of peoples great and small, impose fidelity on agreements loyally consented to, and, thanks to everyone's efforts toward the welfare of all, safeguard the sound liberty and dignity of the human person" (reply to the new minister of the Republic of Haiti). A few weeks later, in his Christmas message, among "the fundamental points of a just and lasting peace" he ranked "the constitution of juridical institutions designed to guarantee the loyal and faithful application of conventions and, in the case of acknowledged need, to review and correct them" (speech to the SACRED COLLEGE, 24 December 1939). Other declarations followed, in which the pope indicated his interest in the proposals for world organization drawn up by the great powers on 7 October 1944 at Dumbarton Oaks.

Nevertheless, these proposals, and the United Nations charter (signed at San Francisco on 26 June 1945) that resulted from them, hardly matched the views of the Holy See on the ideal international society. According to the teaching of Pius XII, who was transposing into this area the traditional doctrine of the church on political society, the peoples of the world formed a natural community which God commanded should be organized into a society founded on the principles of order and justice, for the international common good. To this end, a supreme authority, deriving its competency neither from contract nor from delegation but from inherent right, should constitute a kind of world government, which would be placed over all nations in a "real and effective" manner (Christmas radio message, 24 December 1944) and would have full power to use means of constraint to safeguard peace.

The United National charter was not so ambitious. Aside from the fact that the new body was neither universal nor obligatory, it left states free to hold on to spheres of concern to them; and it gave the permanent members of the Security Council, that is, the great powers, a right of veto that would quickly prove paralyzing. Pius XII did not hide his disappointment: "No clearsighted and dis-

cerning mind, after the disillusionments and, to say the least humiliating lessons of the postwar period, will be inclined to overestimate the immediate and concrete possibilities of this world tribune" (reply to the new minister of El Salvador, 28 October 1947). In spite of everything, he continued to give encouragement to the strengthening of the world organization as though to the accomplishment of a missionary duty: "No one, among those whose hearts are set on fighting for a worthy peace, should cease to use this possibility—however limited it may be—of reaching the conscience of the world from such a lofty and visible place, even though countless indications seemingly would have us believe that the words of these courageous people are doomed, sooner or later, to become simply 'a voice in the desert'" (ibid.); "We wish to see the authority of the UN reinforced, mostly in order to obtain the general disarmament so close to Our heart" (Christmas radio message, 24 December 1956).

The position of the Holy See vis-à-vis the UN was forcefully reaffirmed and clarified by Pius XII's successors. In the encyclical *Pacem in terris* (11 April 1963), JOHN XXIII expressed "the sincere wish that the United Nations may, through its structure and its means of action, eventually succeed in proving equal to the greatness and nobility of its task." Since governments no longer seemed capable of ensuring the common good, the moral order demanded the establishment of a universal public authority; to this necessity the United Nations was bringing the beginnings of a response which Christians had the duty to improve, notably in order to ensure better protection for the rights of persons and peoples.

For his part, PAUL VI tried, from the time of his accession, to express the "very high esteem" in which the Holy See held the world organization. Receiving its general secretary, U Thant, on 11 July 1963, he paid homage to this "instrument of brotherhood among nations." And he voiced his appreciation very overtly by paying an official visit to the institution's headquarters in New York on 4 October 1965. On that occasion he declared: "We bring to [your] organization the support and the approval of Our recent predecessors of the Catholic hierarchy, and of Ourselves, persuaded, as We are, that it represents the path toward a modern civilization and the attainment of world peace . . . We are tempted to say that your characteristic feature reflects, as it were, in the temporal order what our Catholic Church wishes to be in the spiritual order: unique and universal. One can conceive of nothing more elevated, on the natural plane, in the ideological construction of humanity." This praise was echoed shortly thereafter, in the pastoral constitution *Gaudium et Spes* (7 December 1965), which insisted on the value of the work of international institutions: "[They] are certainly worthy of the human spirit. They seem to be the first rough sketches of the international bases of the whole human community for solving the most important questions of our age: to promote progress in all places on earth and to prevent war in all its forms."

The trend was maintained after Paul VI. As "universal pastor," JOHN PAUL II invited governments to work with the UN, which he visited in his turn (2 October 1979). He hoped that it "will ever remain the supreme forum of peace and justice, the authentic seat of freedom of peoples and individuals in their longing for a better future." A few weeks later, speaking of human rights, he did not hesitate to refer to the United Nations charter (14 January 1980). This can be seen as confirmation that the Holy See considers the objectives and values proclaimed by the UN as being in harmony with those inspiring the activity of the Church, whether they have to do with improving the human material and spiritual condition and the defense of human rights or with the search for peace and a better understanding among peoples. Today more than ever, it is imperative to deal with the immense problems facing humanity (disarmament, development, the environment, population, public health, education and culture, etc.) in a global setting that permits dialogue among all members of the international community.

For this reason, the specialized agencies of the United Nations enjoy the sympathy of the Holy See. Moreover, because their activities are less directly affected by political opposition, successive popes have looked on them more favorably than on the UN as a whole. Paul VI's visits to the International Labor Organization (ILO) in his jubilee year, in 1969, and to the Food and Agricultural Organization (FAO) the year after, were seen by everyone as a testimony of this sympathy, as was John Paul II's visit to the United Nations Educational, Scientific, and Cultural Organization (UNESCO) in 1980. For some time, in fact, these agencies, and others like the World Health Organization (WHO), had received unequivocal encouragement from the Holy See—for example, the FAO, which Pius XII congratulated on having realized the Creator's wish by providing the destitute with their daily bread (speech of 8 December 1953), and, above all, the ILO, whose activity won John XXIII's solemn approval in the encyclical *Mater et magistra* (15 May 1961).

No less remarkable, if at first more surprising, is the encouragement given to regional organizations. Even as he was advocating a universalist form of international society, Pius XII lent his firm support to the rebuilding of EUROPE. A few days after sending his personal representative to the congress at The Hague (7–10 May 1948), during the earliest stage of the European Movement, he spoke in favor of a "European union" (2 June); and on 11 November, before the delegates of the European Union of Federalists, he insisted on the urgent need for "the great nations of the continent, with their long history full of memories of glory and power," to "set aside their former grandeur and stand together in a higher political and economical unity." The welcome he gave, in 1950, to the Eu-

ropean Iron and Steel Community, his disappointment, in 1954, over the failure of the European Defense Community, and the hope he evinced at the signing of the treaties of Rome instituting the European Economic Community and Euratom (25 March 1957) even gave rise to talk of a "Vatican Europe," denounced, particularly in France, by enemies of the Christian Democrats.

Pius XII's successors followed the path he had set. Symptomatic of definite approval for European federalism was Paul VI's accreditation of an apostolic NUNCIO (the nuncio to Brussels) to the European Communities (10 November 1970). As this is the form of representation normally used by the Holy See in its relations with states, it has been inferred by some that the supreme pontiff saw the communities, because of their supranational character, as a nascent federal state rather than as a gathering of international organizations. For his part, John Paul II expressed his approval of regional groups set up with free popular consent. He gave on this issue a much applauded speech at Strasbourg before the European Parliament (11 October 1988). Attentive to all forms of regionalism, the preceding year he had visited the Organization of American States (OAS) in Washington.

Participation of the Holy See in the Activity of International Organizations. There is a distance between a doctrinal position favorable to the organization of international society and membership in international organizations. Aside from greetings and visits, the payment of financial contributions (for the fight against malaria, for example, or the preservation of monuments in Nubia), and participation in certain international conferences (such as the Conference on Security and Cooperation in Europe), the Holy See's ties to international organizations with general and political powers have always been subject to debate. No doubt strong arguments can be made for its presence in their midst, based on the Church's overall responsibility to provide for the life of the spirit, on its natural role as conciliator, or again, in the case of the UN, on the partial coincidence of its temporal missions with those of that international body; furthermore, participation by the Holy See in the activity of international organizations is in harmony with the universality of the Church and the oft-proclaimed essentially supranational character of papal diplomacy. Nonetheless, it is necessary to take into account the highly singular position of the Holy See in the international order. By the terms of article 24, paragraph 1 of the Lateran pacts, the Holy See is bound to observe neutrality vis-à-vis the political powers: "The Holy See, as regards the sovereignty that is its due even in the international domain, declares that it intends to remain and will remain uninvolved in conflicts that arise between the other states and in international meetings convened to deal with them, unless the parties in litigation unanimously appeal to its mission of peace, in which case it will take every opportunity to exercise its moral and spiritual authority."

This disposition, and the firm intention of Pius XII to remain aloof from purely political matters, for a long time justified a strict guardedness on the part of the Holy See. All forms of participation in an organization like the UN, where from the outset ideologies of all kinds found fertile soil for confrontation, seemed out of bounds. Yet in the 1950s, a remarkable development took place. Pius XII had shown his interest in the United Nations Relief and Rehabilitation Administration (UNRRA), created in 1943, as well as in the International Refugee Organization (IRO), which would become a specialized agency of the United Nations before being replaced by the UN High Commissioner for Refugees in 1952. From the beginning, the Holy See was a member of the executive committee of the High Commissioner's program (and was also associated, as an observer, with the work of the Inter-Governmental Committee for European Migrations). From 1956 on, it sent a representative to the Economic and Social Council of the UN, where it would play a unique role: as the embodiment of the universal Church, the Holy See has (since 1977) been associated in a consultative capacity with the work of the five regional economic committees, and not only with the one concerned with Europe, to which the Vatican belongs geographically; it should be emphasized, too, that juridically it has never been the Vatican City State but the Holy See itself, that is to say, the central government of the Church, that is represented at the UN (the misunderstanding, possibly caused by certain official UN documents, was cleared up in October 1957 by an exchange of notes at the highest level).

The Holy See took a new step under the pontificate of Paul VI with the appointment, in April 1964, of a permanent observer to the United Nations and, three years later, to the Office of the United Nations at Geneva. Although it is not a member, the Holy See is thus associated with UN activities: it can attend meetings, receive the official documentation, and freely circulate notes and documents; in practical terms, all it lacks is the right to vote, since voting would obviously be incompatible with its neutrality.

The same desire for openness is evident in the relations of the Apostolic See with regional organizations. Not only does it send representatives to the European communities, as we have seen, but it takes a direct part in certain activities of the Council of Europe and its subsidiary or connected bodies. Since 1974, the Holy See has accredited to the council a special envoy with the functions of a permanent observer (the nuncio to Paris) and a delegate of the special envoy residing in Strasbourg; this envoy represents the Holy See at the Council for Cultural Cooperation and the Permanent Conference of Ministers of Education, in which it has enjoyed the right of membership since joining the European Cultural Convention in 1962. At the OAS, the Holy See is similarly represented by a permanent observer (as it is at the Inter-American Economic and Social Council and at the Council for Education, Science, and Culture). For a long time, the Holy See has been developing organic relations, or ties of close cooperation, with numerous intergovernmental organizations in the social, cultural, scientific, and technical areas, including several specialized institutions of the United Nations. Chief among those institutions having long-standing ties with various Catholic organizations is the International Labor Organization. Beginning in 1926, a Jesuit priest held a post in the permanent secretariat of the ILO, with informal Vatican approval; the Holy See, however, has had official relations with the organization only since 1967, when its permanent mission, with observer status, was established at the Office of the United Nations in Geneva. It is represented in similar fashion at the FAO, in Rome, to which, in 1948, it sent its first observer accredited to an international organization; at the WHO and its regional bureau for Europe (through its Geneva mission), since 1967 (though it was invited, in 1949, to attend the assembly sessions); and at UNESCO, since 1952, (the nuncio to Paris acting as observer), following an initial, official form of collaboration. It also has a permanent observer at the World Tourism Organization, of more recent date.

The Holy See has full membership in other organizations, where it is represented by a permanent delegate who is entitled to speak and vote. In its desire to play a part in building peace and fostering development, it was one of the founders of the International Atomic Energy Agency, set up in 1957 under the authority of the UN with the aim of promoting peaceful uses of nuclear energy. In the same spirit, it was an original participant in the United Nations Conference on Trade and Development and in the United Nations Industrial Development Organization; both these agencies were set up by the UN General Assembly (in 1964 and 1966), with the status of subsidiary bodies, to redefine the rules of international economics. The Holy See is also a contributing member of the United Nations Development Program.

The Holy See likewise has long been a member of technical organizations, in which it represents the Catholic Church or the Vatican City State (the distinction here being somewhat dependent upon circumstances). Following the Lateran pacts, the "Vatican" took its place among administrative groups that later became specialized institutions of the United Nations, such as the Universal Postal Union and the International Telecommunication Union (constituted under its present name in 1932). Today it belongs to the European Conference of Postal and Telecommunications Administrations and is a party to the Intelsat and Eutelsat agreements relating to international and European organizations governing satellite telecommunications. It has joined the Bern and Paris Unions that are part of the World Intellectual Property Organization, and is a member of the International Wheat Council (as a 100 percent importing country) and the International Institute for the Unification of Private Law. Similarly, the Holy See belongs to various organizations like the International Committee of Military Medicine and Pharmacology, the Latin Union, the United Nations Fund for the War against Drug Abuse, the (World Heritage) Committee, and the International Center for the Study of the Preservation and Restoration of Cultural Property (as associate member).

Finally, mention should be made of the important connections the Apostolic See maintains with nongovernmental organizations, that is, organizations established by private initiatives. A party to the Geneva conventions of 1949, it has official relations with the International Committee of the Red Cross (through its permanent observer at the UN office in Geneva); since it became a member at the first Geneva convention in 1868, when its object was to help the wounded with spiritual aid, it has suppported the Red Cross's actions on several occasions and firmly defends its universal vocation. In different capacities, the Holy See is represented in a numerous other non-governmental organizations of an artistic, cultural, social, scientific, and, of course, religious character. The *Yearbook of International Organizations* lists more than one hundred of these, of which a random sampling shows the International Confederation of Free Trade Unions, the International Astronomical Union, the International Confederation of Societies of Authors and Composers, the International Touring Alliance, the International Union of Family Organizations, the World Medical Association, and the International Technical Committee for the Prevention and Extinction of Fire—all illustrating, as it were, the presence of the Church in every sector of international life.

Jean-Pierre Machelon

Bibliography

Acta Apostolicae Sedis (Commentarium officiale), Vatican City.

Annuario pontificio, Vatican City.

Arès, R. *L'Église catholique et l'organisation de la société internationale contemporaine (1939–1949)*, Montreal, 1949.

Bertoli, P. "Le Saint Siège et les organisations internationales," *La Revue des deux Mondes*, 15 May 1961, 198–203.

Cardinale, I. *The Contribution of the Holy See to World Peace in the Areas of Diplomacy, Development and Ecumenism, in the Vatican and World Peace*, Boston, 1970.

Cardinale, I. *The Holy See and the International Order*, London, 1977.

Cardinale, I. *Le Saint Siège et la diplomatie*, Paris–Tournai–Rome–New York, 1962.

Casaroli, A. "Le Saint-Siège et la Communauté internationales," *La Documentation Catholique* (1975), 309–18.

Chenaux, P. *Une Europe vaticane? Entre le plan Marshall et les traités de Rome*, Brussels, 1990.

Chevailler, L., Lebvre, C., and Metz, R. *Le Droit et les institutions de l'Église catholique latine de la fin du XVIIIe siècle à. 1978*, Paris, 1982 (especially 403–22).

de La Briére, Y. *L'Organisation internationale du monde contemporain et le Saint-Siège*, Paris, 1927–30 (3 vols.).

de Riedmatten, H. "Les catholiques et les organisations internationales," *Actes de la première Conférence mondiale catholique de la santé*, Brussels, 1958, 515–25.

de Riedmatten, H. "Présence du Saint-Siège dans les organismes internationaux," *Concilium*, 58 (1970), 67–82 (other editions in several languages).

de Riedmatten, H. "Le catholicism et le développement du droit international," *Requeil des cours de l'Académie de droit international*, 151-III (1976), Leiden, 1978, 115–62.

d'Onorio, J. B. ed., *Le Saint-Siège dans les relations internationales*, Paris, 1989.

Gallina, E. *Le Organizzazioni internazionali e la Chiesa cattolica*, Rome, 1967.

Graham, R. *Vatican Diplomacy*, Princeton, 1959.

Köck, H. F. *Die Völkerrechtliche Stellung des Heilingen Stuhls*, Berlin, 1975.

La Documentation catholique, Paris.

L'Attività . . . della Santa Sede, Vatican City.

Lucien-Brun, J. "Le Saint-Siège et les organisations internationales," *Annuaire français de droit international*, 10 (1974), 536–42.

Machelon, J. P. "Pie XII, l'Europe et les institutions internationales," *Pie XII et la Cité*, Paris–Aix-en-Provence, 1988, 201–17.

Mayeur, J. M. "Pie XII et l'Europe," *Relations internationales*, 28 (1981), 413–25.

Minnerath, R. "Le Saint-Siège et les relations internationales," *Encyclopaedia Universalis, Symposium, Les Enjeux*, II, 1477–85.

Russo, F. "Le Saint-Siège et les organisations internationales," *Études*, 345 (1976), 15–31.

Vellas, P. "1968–1978: dix ans de diplomatie vaticane," in *Mélanges Dauvilliers*, Toulouse, 1979, 809–29.

Yearbook of International Organizations, Munich–New York–London–Paris.

OSSERVATORE ROMANO. The Holy See's daily newspaper, founded in 1861, appears every day except Sunday and the feast days of the Vatican CALENDAR (the evening edition is dated the next day). The paper, which is published in Italian (papal texts are published in the original language and if need be translated into Italian), includes six weekly editions (English on Monday, French on Tuesday, Italian on Thursday, Spanish and German on Friday, Portuguese on Saturday) and a monthly edition in Polish.

The column on the first page, with the descriptive heading "Nostre Informazioni" (Our News), is the only official section of *L'Osservatore*, which is the Vatican's sole newspaper. Drawn up by the SECRETARIAT OF STATE, it provides a list of papal AUDIENCES and appointments together with communiqués relating to the activities of the pope and the Holy See. In addition, the newspaper publishes, immediately and in full, papal texts and information on the Holy See and the Catholic Church throughout the world; it also provides international news from a very broad perspective and publishes articles of cultural, Italian, and local interest. Only ten pages in all, it is without doubt the slimmest of reference newspapers and the one with the smallest print run (in 1994, fewer than 12,000 copies for the daily, around 50,000 for the weekly editions, and about 40,000 for the monthly). Its unique character makes it a first source for the modern and contemporary history of the papacy and the Church.

It is no accident that the paper began its life just when the temporal power of the papacy was declining. This was in fact the period when the first newspapers in the modern sense of the term, especially Catholic newspapers, were multiplying throughout Europe in a climate of lively confrontation with violently anticlerical publications. Moreover, the trend was toward the ending of the pope's temporal power and the beginning of the Roman question. The first of the series of newspapers was the famous *Diario di Roma* (1717–1848), which was succeeded by the *Gazzetta di Roma* (1848–9), the *Monitore romano* (1849), and the *Giornale di Roma* (1849–70), all of which followed the same official line as their predecessors. Other reactionary, clerical papers were the French-owned *Il Costituzionale romano* (1848–9) and a periodical that would later become a daily, *L'Osservatore romano* (1849–52).

Unconnected with the previous titles, despite its having the same name, *L'Osservatore romano* was born on the initiative of a Forlí lawyer, Nicola Zanchini, and a Bologna journalist, Giuseppe Bastia, who had settled in Rome after the annexation of a major part of the Papal States to the kingdom of Italy. The two refugees were able to realize their idea because it accorded with a project of the papal government, as represented by the minister of the interior, Marcantonio Pacelli (grandfather of the future PIUS XII), to found a political newspaper parallel to the official *Giornale di Roma*, and because the founders were able to obtain private financing. Accordingly, 1 July 1861 saw the first edition of *L'Osservatore romano*, which the papal government had first thought of calling *L'Amico*

della Verità (The Friend of Truth). Below the paper's name, the subtitle "political and moral newspaper," later definitively replaced by "political and religious daily," defined the paper's vocation and recalled the dual objective that inspired it. Then, in the edition of 1 January 1862, two quotations, which still appear today, were added to the title to emphasize its polemical character and devotion to the faith: *Unicuique suum* (To each his own) and the evangelical *Non praevalebunt*, an allusion to the gates of hell, that is, to the forces of evil.

The paper, which was privately funded, was supported in various ways by Pope PIUS IX from the outset. Its two founders were also its first editors (1861–6), their successor being the marquess Augusto Baviera. Baviera was PIUS IX's godson, an officer of the NOBLE GUARD, and a journalist. He had become a co-owner of the newspaper in 1863, then sole owner in 1865 and editor from 1866 to 1884. An editor in the modern sense of the term and an excellent observer of the Roman milieu, Baviera was able to give the paper its individuality and maintain relative autonomy with regard to governmental directives; he was also the first journalist to sit in on the workings of a COUNCIL. In fact, *L'Osservatore romano* followed every stage of the VATICAN I council from the moment it was announced: from his seat in the Vatican basilica, the director took shorthand notes of all the proceedings in the council sessions and reported them in the column "Cose interne" (Internal Affairs).

Immediately after the capture of Rome on 20 September 1870, the official organ, *Giornale di Roma*, disappeared and *L'Osservatore romano* had to suspend publication. The paper reappeared, however, the following 17 October, when it took over the functions of the *Giornale di Roma* and therefore adopted a more official line. The events of Baviera's last years as editor accentuated this trend. The marquess handed over *L'Osservatore romano* to the Société générale des publications internationales in Paris: an intransigent Catholic group, it controlled newspapers in several European capitals, and in Rome had founded the *Journal de Rome* (1881–5), which initially enjoyed the support of LEO XIII but later contested that pope's moderate thinking. Baviera edited the *Journal de Rome* and *L'Osservatore romano* at the same time, but in 1884 the marquess Cesare Crispolti became owner and editor. Later, when the *Journal de Rome* had gone out of business, Leo XIII acquired *L'Osservatore romano* once and for all for the Holy See, and the paper took on the character of an official newspaper.

During the last fifteen years of the century, the newspaper began to increase its print runs, while its prestige grew in parallel fashion. To replace Crispolti (1884–90), Leo XIII turned to Giovanni Battista Casoni (1890–1900), a Bologna lawyer and journalist, with the intention of ensuring direct control of the publication for himself. Under the leadership of Giuseppe Angelini (1900–20), another journalist, the involvement of the popes, especially BENEDICT XV, in *L'Osservatore romano* grew. From 1911, the paper went from the initial four pages to six, the fourth page for several years being devoted almost entirely to advertising; for a time, the paper included a serial as well as a column devoted to art, sports, and the theater. The newspaper's ideological line naturally followed that of the Holy See. Thus, the articles in *L'Osservatore romano*, which also published the text of pontifical interventions, focused chiefly on the Roman question and paid particular attention to Italian news. In the area of international politics, from 1911 on the paper commented coldly on the Italian colonial adventure that led to the occupation of Libya. During the FIRST WORLD WAR, it took an impartial stance, as witnessed by the seventy-odd articles written or inspired by the cardinal secretary of state, Pietro Gasparri. The international column was made up of dispatches from the press agency Stefani, published, the paper made clear, according to "a program of strict impartiality," "simply by way of information for its readers and without taking the slightest responsibility for the news they contain or making them its own in any way."

In 1920, Count Giuseppe Della Torre was appointed to edit *L'Osservatore romano*. A journalist and leading spokesman for Catholic organizations, he remained in this post for forty years (until 1960), working with distinguished editors and collaborators, several of whom came from intellectual Catholic movements unconnected to fascism, such as Federico Alessandrini and Guido Gonella. When the VATICAN CITY STATE was established following the LATERAN PACTS, *L'Osservatore romano* left the center of Rome, where it had occupied nine successive offices since its founding and moved in late 1929 to premises inside the Vatican. This move coincided with an increase in prestige and readership and was motivated as well by a shortage of free arenas in the fascist Italy of the time. The paper's average print run reached its peak, around 60,000, sometimes rising to over 100,000. This period saw the beginning of perhaps its best-known column, "Acta diurna" (since 1984, this has once again been the title of a column, unsigned). Here Gonella gave an attentive, critical account of the international political scene: between 1933 and 1940, he published over a thousand articles based on information which at the time only the Vatican, in its independent position, could make public, some of which were highly successful and far-reaching in their impact. The independence of *L'Osservatore* resulted in the fascist regime's setting ever greater obstacles in the newspaper's path after Italy entered the war, so that it had to reduce its print runs significantly and then stop publishing any information on the war.

While Della Torre was editor of *L'Illustrazione Vaticana*, between 1930 and 1938 (a periodical which De Gasperi, then at the VATICAN LIBRARY, worked on under a pseudonym), the illustrated weekly *L'Osservatore romano della domenica* had begun publication, in 1934; from 1951, it was entitled *L'Osservatore della Domenica*, and from 1979, it was reduced to a simple insert. Shortly before it first appeared, in 1931, the idea of a non-Italian edition of *L'Osservatore* had been launched in Argentina, but it came to nothing. In 1939, the SUBSTITUTE at the Secretariat of State, Giovanni Battista Montini, the future PAUL VI, created the Holy See's first press office in liaison with the Vatican daily. On his initiative, in 1942 the Vatican published a new illustrated magazine, the monthly *Ecclesia*, which lasted until the 1960s. In the postwar period appeared the first weekly editions of the daily paper, Italian in 1949 and French at the end of the same year (the French was first published in France, then from 1951 at the Vatican). In 1951, the Spanish edition came out in Buenos Aires, thanks to a private initiative; it was not published at the Vatican until 1969. These were followed by the English edition in 1968, the Portuguese in 1970, the German in 1971 (printed in Germany since 1986), and, from 1980, a monthly edition in Polish.

In 1960, Della Torre was succeeded by Raimondo Manzini, a former member of the society of St. Paul, a secular institute founded in Milan in 1920. He was a journalist of great ability who had, among other things, edited the Bologna Catholic daily *L'Avvenire d'Italia* for over thirty years. But he was also a leading figure in politics, having served as deputy of the constituent assembly and undersecretary of state at the presidency of the Council of Ministers. Manzini headed *L'Osservatore romano* at the time of VATICAN II and for almost the whole of the pontificate of Paul VI. During those years, when the paper had a circulation of 30,000, he brought in new contributors, some of them famous. For example, the column entitled "Bailamme" was given prestige by bearing the name of the respected journalist Giuseppe De Luca. At the beginning of 1978, Valerio Volpini, an intellectual and writer, replaced Manzini. He redesigned the newspaper's layout to good effect. The front page of the extraordinary editions announcing the papal elections of Cardinals Albino Luciani and Karol Wojtyla in 1978, was designed by Giacomo Manzù. Since 1984, Mario Agnes, former president of the Italian Catholic Action, has been editor. Under his leadership, the newspaper, which after Paul VI's pontificate made a prudent retreat from Italian politics, has once again embraced polemics, not sparing the Catholic world. Agnes has had to deal with other changes of presentation, including those connected with the introduction of new technology and the restructuring of the Vatican Press. *L'Osservatore* consists of some thirty editors, almost all of whom are laymen (there are no women), as well as seventy administrative and technical employees who, since

1937, have been supervised by Salesians. The paper's annual deficit in 1993 was close to 6.5 billion lire (plus 1 billion for the German edition, which is economically independent).

In 1961, for the newspaper's centenary, Cardinal Montini, wrote a celebrated article which was not without irony and was interesting in many ways. The future Paul VI was sensitive to the problems of newspaper publishing because of family tradition and personal interest, and unusually familiar with the Vatican daily paper and its mechanisms. In his article he described the problems of an organ of the press with limited means and having requirements that are highly unusual for a journal of opinion, and quite specific in the context of the Vatican. Nonetheless, as he confronted these problems Montini recalled the positive experience and unique role of the Vatican's newspaper during the SECOND WORLD WAR. With its location, its function, its network of reporters and collaborators, its authority and freedom, and its heritage and experience, *L'Osservatore romano* can become a newspaper of the first rank, Montini concluded—a remark that is still valid for our day.

Giovanni Maria Vian

Bibliography

Albertazzi, A. "Casoni, Giambattista," *DBI*, 21 (1978), 398–403.

Anichini, G. "Illustrazione vaticana," *EC*, 6 (1951), 1638.

Bongioanni, G. *Don Bosco in Vaticano*, Vatican City, 1990.

Borzomati, P. "'L'Osservatore Romano,' negli anni della guerra fredda," *Studium*, 88 (1992). 81–96.

Cavili, F. "Nel centenario dell'*Osservatore Romano*," *La civiltá cattolica*, 112 (1961), III, 140–52.

Dalla Torre, G. *Azione cattolica e fascismo*, Rome, 1964 (*Minima*, 2).

Dalla Torre, G. *Memorie*, Milan, 1965.

De Luca, G. *Bailamme ovverrosia pensieri del sabato sera*, Brescia, 1963.

Gonella, G. *Verso la 2a guerra mondiale, Cronache politiche. "Acta diurna" 1933–1940*, Rome-Bari, 1979.

Huetter, L. "Ecclesia," *EC*, 5 (1950), 36–7.

Ignesti, G. *Laici cristiana fra Chiesa e Stato nel Novecento, Profili e problemi*, Rome, 1988, 253–327.

Ignesti, G. "La Chiesa e gli Stati nel secondo dopoguerra attraverso *L'Osservatore Romano*," *La figura e l'opera di Federico Alessandrini*, Ancona, 1991, 77–86.

Lai, B. *Finanze e finanzieri vaticani tra l'Ottocento e il Novecento, Da Pio IX a Benedetto XV*, Milan 1979, 95–100, 246–50.

L'attivit à dela Santa Sede, Vatican City.

Lazzarini, A. "L'Osservatore Romano," *Vaticano*, ed. G. Fallari and M. Escobar, Florencce, 1946, 631–52.

Leoni, F. "*L'Osservatore Romano*," *Origini ed evoluzione*, Naples, 1970.

Levi, V. *L'Osservatore Romano*, in *Le Vatican et la Rome chrétienne*, Vatican City, 1975, 365–8.

L'Osservatore Romano. Special issues published on the newspaper's anniversary, 31 May 1936 (no. 75), 1 July 1961 (no. 100), 13 December 1981 (no. 120).

Malgari, F. "Dalla Torre del Tempio di Sanguineto, Giuseppe," *DBI*, 32 (1986), 49–53; "Alessandrini, Federico," *DBI*, 34 (1988), 49–52.

Malgeri, F. *La Stampa cattolica a Roma dal 1870 al 1915*, Brescia, 1965, 18, 142–6, 159–62, 221–2.

Merril, J. C. *The Elite Press: Great Newspapers of the World*, New York–Toronto–London, 1968, 232–9.

Merril, J. C. and Fisher, H. A. *The World's Great Dailies: Profiles of Fifty Newspapers*, New York, 1980, 230–8.

Montini, G. B. *Le difficoltà dell' "Osservatore Romano,"* published as a supplement to the issue of 1 July 1961 and reproduced with a commentary by N. Vian in *Notiziario*, 17 (1988) of the Paul VI Institute, 17–20; the same issue also reproduces, with commentary, the presentation of *Ecclesia*, 7–10.

Sandmann, F. *Die Haltung des Vatikans zum Nationalsozialismus im Spiegel des "Osservatore Romano" (von 1929 bis zum Kriegsausbruch)*, Mainz, 1965; It. trans. *"L'Osservatore Romano" e il nazionalsocialismo (1929–1939)*, Rome 1976 (*Collana di storia del movimento cattolico*, 38).

Soderini, E. *II pontificato di Leone XIII*, II, Milan, 1933, 75–81.

Zazinovic, C. *L' "Osservatore Romano" negli ultimi dieci anni dello Stato Pontificio*, Rome, 1943.

OSTPOLITIK. Literally, policy toward the East. The term, used here to describe the diplomatic dialogue between the Holy See and the USSR and its satellites, was borrowed from the policy adopted by Chancellor Willy Brandt in the early 1960s to defend the interests of the Federal Republic of Germany vis-à-vis the Soviet Union. The first successful achievement of the Holy See's *ostpolitik* is thought to be the protocol of agreement signed with Yugoslavia on 25 June 1966. The election of Cardinal Wojtyla as JOHN PAUL I's successor on 15 October 1978 testifies to the peculiar character of Vatican *ostpolitik*; to gain sufficient living space for the Church, and to participate in "the erosion of the system" (Hélène Carrère d'Encausse).

This *ostpolitik* has consisted in renewing connections in a gradual and pragmatic way with a group of countries in which Catholicism had been systematically muzzled (Romania, Bulgaria, Albania) or even periodically persecuted (Hungary, Poland, Czechoslovakia). After some initial hesitation, but with his diplomatic experience in Poland and Lithuania between 1917 and 1920 to back him up, PIUS XI had abandoned the idea of negotiating a concordat with Bolshevik Russia in order to preserve the interests of Catholics, especially the UNIATES of Ukraine. But the Holy See never gave up exploring ways in which to establish dialogue with the Orthodox and Soviet authorities, and this was notably the object of the mission entrusted to Msgr. d'Herbigny in the 1930s. In 1937, Pius XI condemned communism in his ENCYCLICAL *Divini Redemptoris*. The SECOND WORLD WAR and the cold war caused PIUS XII to conceive a real phobia for Bolshevism and impelled the Holy See toward an Atlantist policy. The persecuted Churches became known as the Churches of Silence. Communications between them and Rome were rare or nonexistent. Numerous dioceses were vacant or else governed by a capitular vicar chosen under state control. Seminaries had declined and were under surveillance, and religious orders and congregations were decimated. Except in Poland, the teaching of catechism was strictly subject to bureaucratic control. The foremost representatives of the hierarchy (Cardinal Wyszinski in Warsaw, Cardinal Mindszenty in Budapest, Bishop Beran in Prague) had been thrown into prison or deported, so as to "mortify in humiliating fashion the morale [of the] Catholic communities."

Thinking about the kind of diplomacy to be conducted with respect to the people's democracies, and especially the USSR, hung over the last years of Pius XII's pontificate. And it is not unlikely that the principle of a "duty mission" vis-à-vis the Churches of Silence, involving, on the part of the Holy See, "many negotiations, many steps, and many efforts" (PAUL VI) as called for by G. B. Montini, contributed to his being removed from the CURIA in 1954.

The 20th Communist Party Congress (1956) and the beginning of the Khrushchev era, the election of Cardinal Roncalli in 1958—he had, among other things, served as nuncio to Bulgaria—and the convocation of a twenty-first ecumenical COUNCIL (VATICAN II) favored détente between the Holy See and the Western communist world, opening the path to the Vatican's *ostpolitik*. During the Cuban crisis of 1962, JOHN XXIII appealed to the American and Soviet leaders to exercise responsibility and brought a humanitarian touch to a conflict with appalling prospects. In 1963, the pope received the Adjoubeis, the son-in-law and daughter of Nikita Krushchev. On 11 April of that year, the encyclical *Pacem in terris* advised the faithful "never to confuse the error with the one who is mistaken" nor to identify historical movements with the doctrines that have given rise to them. The Vatican II council (1962–5) was the occasion of a test between the Catholic Church and the communist countries, which greeted this doctrinal consultation with a mixture of skepticism and interest. The Soviet government authorized the Russian Orthodox Church to send delegates to the council, and one Soviet representative, in the person of M.

Mcedlov, was dispatched to Rome to follow the proceedings. The people's democracies varied in the manner in which they delivered passports to the bishops invited to Rome. The Polish government was generous; Hungary, Czechoslovakia, and Yugoslavia raised obstacles. Nonetheless, on 5 February 1963 the Soviet authorities freed Bishop Slipyj, the metropolitan of the Ukrainians of Lviv; on 9 October he arrived in Rome, and two days later he addressed the assembly for twenty minutes, longer than the limit set by council rules. The Yugoslavian authorities, for their part, allowed Cardinal Seper, archbishop of Zagreb, to take part in the council. The strength of Vatican II lay in the fact that it offered freedom of expression, if only for a short time, to conciliar fathers whom the communist states kept continually under observation and against whom they could take retaliatory measures.

The *aggiornamento* announced by John XXIII in 1959 and made explicit in his subsequent interventions clearly implied that Vatican II would not be a council of condemnation. The communist world could, officially, take this avowal as a confession of weakness. But Vatican II made a rigorous strict distinction among atheism, MARXISM, and communism, thereby allowing for consideration of the freedom of the conscience and its relationship to systems of government. In spite of heavy pressure, atheism was not condemned by the council.

It was during the Vatican II council that Bishop (later Cardinal) Agostino Casaroli, then secretary of the CONGREGATION for Extraordinary Ecclesiastical Affairs of the Church, traveled to Hungary and Czechoslovakia (May 1963) with a view to finding ways of settling the plights of Cardinal Mindszenty and Msgr. Beran. The man who would become JOHN PAUL II's secretary of state (from 1979) thus set in motion a "policy of small steps" that consisted of travels embarked upon without fanfare, exchanges of views without press coverage, and observations upon which each side could reflect. In conformity with Paul VI's principles concerning the apostolic duty belonging to the successor of Peter, the aims were simple: recognition of the authority of the supreme pontiff over the Catholics in the countries concerned; restoration of the hierarchy in the dioceses by virtue of the right of the Holy See to appoint bishops; reestablishment of communications between Rome and the bishops. These canonical demands implied the acceptance of a revitalization of parishes, seminaries, vocations, and so on that went against the spirit of the cold war and in fact foreshadowed that of HELSINKI. This *ostpolitik*, inspired by a "diplomacy of faithfulness" (André Dupuy), was also a policy of significant competition. The agreement signed with Yugoslavia in 1966 led to a regime of "separation"—the exchange of representatives of a diplomatic sort in August 1971, preceded by a visit of Marshal Tito to the Vatican on 29 March 1971. That same year, Cardinal Mindszenty agreed to leave the United States embassy in Budapest for Vienna and to be relieved of his duties (5 February 1974). Before that, a similar negotiation undertaken in Prague (1965) concerning Bishop Beran, who was made cardinal and replaced by Bishop (later Cardinal) Tomasek as apostolic administrator, had met with failure. But the Holy See continued its attempts at dialogue with the Prague authorities in December 1970, March 1971, November 1972, and January 1973, as a result of which two bishops and two apostolic administrators were appointed in March 1973. On 1 December 1977, symbolically, as it later proved, Paul VI received in AUDIENCE the first secretary of the united Polish Communist party, Edward Gierek. The supreme pontiff indicated in his speech that "the Catholic Church was not asking for privileges, but only for the right to be Herself and the possibility of carrying out unhindered the activity that belongs to Her by Her constitution and Her mission."

The *ostpolitik* entrusted by Paul VI to Bishop, later Cardinal, Casaroli had mixed results. John Paul II seems to have wanted to substitute, from 1978 to 1985, a principle of more direct intervention than that of the "small steps" followed by his secretary of state. Perestroika opened up new horizons, as did the fall of the Berlin Wall in 1989. In all this, the *ostpolitik* of the Holy See played a not insignificant role. Since the collapse of the Soviet Union and the Warsaw Pact, the chief aims of the Holy See in Eastern Europe and Russia have been in forging relationships with the post-Communist governments (most notably the Russian Republic) and promoting ecumenism with the Orthodox Churches.

Philippe Levillain

See also CONCORDAT; THIRD ROME (MOSCOW); UNIATES.

Bibliography

Carrère d'Encausse, H. "Paul VI et l'Ostpolitik," *Paul et la modernité dans l'Église*, EFR, 1984, 546–54.
Dupuy, A. ibid., 555–7.
Morozzo Della Rocca, R. *Le Nazioni non muoiono*, Bologna, 1992.
Riccardi, A. *Il Vaticano e Mosca*, Rome, 1992.
Cardinal Silvestrini, A. "L'Ostpolitik de Paul VI," *Paul VI et la vie internationale*, Brescia, 1992, 112–28.
Zubov, A. "Uno squardo dall'Est sulla Ostpolitik vaticana," *Le Città di Dio, Limes*, 3 (1993), 163–73.

OXFORD MOVEMENT. The Oxford Movement was the name given to a spiritual revival within the Church of England, which originated and remained centered at Oxford between 1833 and 1845. The university not only gave its name to the movement, but also provided all its leaders and most of their followers. Since nation, church, and university were intimately linked, what affected one affected the others as well; hence the significance of the Oxford Movement for the religious life of England in the 14th century.

The acknowledged leaders were John Keble (1792–1846), Richard Hurrell Froude (1803–36), John Henry Newman (1801–90), and Edward Bouverie Pusey (1800–82). All four were fellows of Oriel College and were endowed with exceptional talents. Newman, however, was the heart and soul of the movement and remains the preeminent figure of its history.

The movement's aim was to restore to the Church of England the high ideals of the 18th century, in sharp contrast to the liberalism and worldliness that pervaded it in those times. Emphasis was placed on the divine origin of the church; the apostolic succession of its hierarchy; a return to primitive Christianity, as exemplified in the writings of the early fathers and councils; the administration and reception of all seven sacraments, especially the Eucharist; the essential role of dogma in theology, with the Book of Common Prayer as the rule of faith; and, not least, the independence of the church from the state.

Contingent factors rendered such a revival desirable and mature. Several enactments of Parliament were judged by Anglicans to be subversive of the established order of the church in England including the law that allowed dissenters and nonconformers to hold public offices from which previously they had been barred (1827); the bill of Catholic Emancipation that canceled the penal laws still remaining in the statute book (1829); and the Reform Act of the House of Commons, which appeared to give greater legislative power to radicals and others hostile to religion (1832). This fear of subversion culminated in 1833 when the government attempted to suppress ten Irish dioceses; this was seen by the churchmen as an unwarranted interference by the secular powers.

Keble denounced the king, the cabinet, the godless Parliament, and the nation as being guilty of what for him was tantamount to national apostasy. His cry of alarm came from the pulpit of the university church of St. Mary; it deeply moved and disturbed his audience and had immediate repercussions throughout the university. This sermon, which was preached on 14 July 1833, marks the beginning of the Oxford Movement.

The aims of the movement were chiefly realized through the dissemination of a series of anonymous pamphlets entitled simply *Tracts for the Times*, which began publication in 1833. The majority were the texts of Newman's Sunday sermons at St. Mary's, which were attended by an increasingly attentive and avid audience, most of whom were destined for the ranks of the Anglican clergy in the immediate future. Newman's influence, as charismatic head of the Oxford Movement, was prodigious. The *Tracts* set out to demonstrate spiritual continuity of the Church of England with the Catholic Church of antiquity. Publication continued uninterrupted for nine years, while the pamphlets became longer and denser in content.

At this juncture the leaders were all convincingly anti-Roman and anti-papal, even if they stated that Catholicism contained some elements of good. The Anglican church alone, however, had discerned and followed the right road, the *Via Media,* avoiding the superstitious aberrations introduced over the centuries by the Roman church, and the destructive excesses of the 16th-century Protestant reformers. Where Anglicanism was at risk was in its toleration of Protestantism and neglect of its authentic Catholic heritage. The Church of England was neither Roman nor Protestant; it was simply Catholic and should have recognized its roots and insisted upon its basic ecclesial rights. In 1839, during the long summer vacation, Newman dedicated his time to a study of the Monophysite heresy, with special attention to the position of the Donatists vis-à-vis Rome. For the first time he began to entertain doubts about the impregnability of his own position.

Tract XC, the last, was published on 27 February 1841. In it Newman attempted to show that the Thirty-Nine Articles of the Anglican Church (approved in 1562 and inspired by the *Confessio Augustana,* therefore anti-Roman in expression and intent, or so it had always been supposed), were (on the contrary) perfectly compatible with the Catholic faith and in no way constituted a repudiation of the apostolic and early church. Having submitted the articles to a severe critical analysis, he noted that even if the intention of the reformers had been to exclude the Catholic faith, by divine providence they had not succeeded in doing so. Any believer could subscribe to the articles in good conscience.

The reaction in Oxford was immediate: the *Tract* was condemned by an overwhelming majority. War was declared on the movement by the university authorities, whose members were already suspected of moving toward the Roman church, despite their disavowals. Most of the Anglican bishops followed suit and the damage to the prestige and influence of the Oxford Movement was incalculable. Newman retreated from the heat of controversy and retired to the parish house of Littlemore, five miles from the city. There he began the spiritul odyssey that finally, on 9 October 1845, brought him into the fold of Roman Catholicism. Others had preceded him in this conversion, and others followed his example. That date signaled the end of Oxford as the center of revival within the Church of England.

Tract XC was the apex of the Oxford Movement; everything else either led up to it or away from it. Its influence endured, especially in the realm of liturgy and worship, which came to play a larger role in the life of the Church of England. The clergy became more zealous in the performance of their duties and more ecclesiastically minded. The Oxford Movement reintroduced religious community life, a natural consequence of the ideals it propagated. Its contribution to scholarship was also of considerable and lasting benefit, and included collections such as the *Library of the Fathers*, and the *Library of Anglo-Catholic Theology*, its direct offspring.

Charles Burns

Bibliography

Church, R. W. *The Oxford Movement—Twelve Years 1833–1845,* 1891.

Dawson, C. *The Spirit of the Oxford Movement*, London, 1933.

Ker, I. *John Henry Newman*, Oxford, 1989.

Liddon, H. P. *Life of E. B. Pusey*, 4 vols., 1893–7.

Newman, J. H. *Apologia pro Vita Sua*, 1864.

O'Connell, M. R. *The Oxford Conspirators: A History of the Oxford Movement 1833–1845*, London, 1969.

P

PACTS, LATERAN. See **Lateran Pacts.**

PAINTING. From the 16th to the 18th century, Rome was widely considered to be the artistic capital of Europe, an almost obligatory stopping place in a painter's career. The abundance of works preserved there and the reputation of many of them as incomparable models gave Roman art exceptional importance. Certain popes played a decisive role in making Rome the artistic center it became, their interest in painting manifesting itself above all in the modern era.

Although painting was one of the means of artistic expression patronized by the popes, it was not the art form they favored the most. They undoubtedly appreciated its advantages (relative speed of execution, moderate cost) but could not think of it as a monumental art capable of spanning the centuries. Every modern pope made the point that the Roman Empire had left behind buildings and statues which still bore witness to its power, whereas with rare exceptions, which certain popes (LEO X, CLEMENT VIII, and PIUS VI) found of particular interest, Roman paintings and frescoes had disappeared. This awareness of the transitory nature of painting relative to the history of the Church impelled the popes to have the paintings in ST. PETER'S copied in MOSAIC from the end of the 17th century, a number of them already having been severely damaged by humidity. Several pontiffs (notably SIXTUS V and ALEXANDER VII) encouraged urban-planning works, and the majority were eager to mark their reigns by building churches, fountains, and palaces far more than by commissioning the works of painters. Moreover, only rarely were Rome's main artistic projects not directed by architects or sculptors; the best-known figures responsible for carrying out papal commissions were architects like Fontana, Maderno, and Bernini, while even architect-painters like Pietro da Cortona did not play as important a part.

Still, painting held a far from negligible place, essentially from the second half of the 15th century, thanks to the commissions of the humanist popes, NICHOLAS V, PIUS II, SIXTUS IV, ALEXANDER VI, JULIUS II and Leo X. The great works sites for the replanning of Rome, especially in jubilee years, and the work at the Vatican (in particular the building of the SISTINE CHAPEL and the redesign and enlargement of the palace) afforded painters vast fields of action, while the fame of two of the artists employed by the HOLY SEE, Raphael and Michelangelo, helped to give painting a larger role within the framework of a cultural policy. Up until the end of the 19th century, the Vatican frescoes were studied by artists just as seriously as were the ancient statues preserved in Roman palaces, and no foreign traveler failed to go and admire them. Rome's artistic fame was enhanced in the 17th century with the emergence of a new shrine of classical art, the Carracci gallery at the Farnese Palace. By encouraging painting and multiplying their commissions, the 17th- and 18th-century popes sought to enhance and prolong the prestige of the center of international artistic culture that was Rome. It is worth noting that the most illustrious convert to Catholicism of the 17th century, Queen Christina of Sweden, collected paintings avidly and settled in Rome.

While painting thus contributed to the prestige of the papacy, it also served to reinforce that of the popes and their families. The Medici were the last to furnish popes for several generations, for despite their ambitions, neither the Farnese in the 16th and 17th centuries nor the Albani in the 18th and 19th managed to do so. The CARDINAL NEPHEWS therefore had only the relatively short length of a pontificate in which to set up a new family foundation for the next several generations. Eager to be assimilated into the old Roman families, they made many prestigious alliances, acquired a sizable territory, built and decorated magnificent palaces as well as villas near the city or in the *Castelli romani*, and accumulated works of art—principally works of antiquity, but also paintings. The great pontifical families of the Renaissance, the Medici and the Farnese, were the inspiration for most of the new families of popes of the modern era in their pursuit of prestige. One is struck by the achievements of Cardinal Ludovico Ludovisi, whose uncle, GREGORY XV, reigned only two years, and who himself died in 1632 at the age of thirty-seven: he assembled one of the largest collections of antiquities preserved in Rome, as well as numerous paintings, and also commissioned Domenichino to execute the frescoes at S. Andrea della Valle and Guercino to paint the casino in his villa. The families of popes who enjoyed long reigns possessed the most important collections of paintings in Rome (those of the Farnese, Aldobrandini, Barberini, Pamphili, Albani, Corsini, etc.).

It would be reductive, however, to consider painting solely as an element of a cultural policy or a policy of prestige, for it was a weapon in the Counter Reformation's mission of religious reconquest. The council of TRENT (Trent, XXV, c. 1) reaffirmed the legitimate place of painting in churches. Only one pope, BENEDICT XIV, produced a text on the problem of images, in his letter *Sollicitudini nostrae* of 1745, but numerous reflections on painting emanated from the circles around the popes: from Agucchi, secretary of BRIEFS under Gregory XV, from Giulio Mancini, physician of URBAN VIII, and from Cassiano del Pozzo, secretary to Francesco Barberini. A few dominant themes recur in these writings and helped point the way for pictorial creation. The pedagogical role of paintings is constantly stressed: artists are enjoined to be scrupulously faithful to the texts they illustrate (Holy Scripture or the lives of the saints) and to produce compositions that are clear and easily interpreted. They are asked to edify the spectator and collaborate in his or her conversion:

"The paintings that depict the mysteries of our redemption instruct the people, helping them to keep the articles of the faith in their minds and to guard them diligently. Thus great profit is to be drawn from sacred images, not only because they tell of Christ's gifts and blessings, but also because, having before their eyes the miracles and salutary examples God has granted them through the agency of his saints, the faithful are better able to give thanks to God and to conduct their lives in imitation of the saints, and are moved to adore and love God and practice devotion" (Trent, XXV c. 1).

Emphasis was therefore placed on a kind of painting capable of arousing pity and terror in the spectator. The choice of paintings executed in mosaic at St. Peter's is highly revealing with respect to these requirements: not content to reproduce the works already there, the popes got rid of the least expressive ones and added copies of those Roman paintings most praised for their expressiveness—Raphael's *Transfiguration*, Domenichino's *Last Communion of St. Jerome*, and Guido Reni's *Crucifixion of St. Peter*. The exigencies of pedagogical painting also had stylistic consequences: according to Denis Mahon, the circle around Gregory XV is responsible for the change of manner in a painter like Guercino, having brought pressure to bear on him to produce works that were easier to interpret and more dignified. The variety of roles assigned to painting was naturally reflected in the different sites in which the popes made use of it. As heads of the Church and heads of state, they set painters to their task in the great public works sites of Rome; as heads of families, they acted as private patrons, on a larger scale than the prelates and Roman nobility but in the same places—the churches under their patronage, their palaces and villas. The principal public works sites were those of the great basilicas, St. Peter's first and foremost, but also ST. MARY MAJOR, ST. JOHN LATERAN, S. Croce in Gerusalemme, and ST. PAUL'S OUTSIDE THE WALLS. Even before the nave of St. Peter's was completed under PAUL V, the popes had seen to it that the basilica was adorned with altarpieces. Under GREGORY XIII and especially Clement VIII, artists like Nebbia, Muziano, and Pomarancio provided scenes from the life of ST. PETER, and the cupola was decorated with mosaics after cartoons by Cavaliere d'Arpino. The most important commissions were carried out in the 17th and 18th centuries, often in the years preceding the jubilees; for instance, in 1624 Guercino painted his *Death of St. Petronilla*. The most famous paintings in St. Peter's were executed during the time of Urban VIII: Domenichino's *Martyrdom of St. Sebastian* and Lanfranco's *Christ Walking on the Waters*, both commissioned in 1625, as well as Poussin's *Martyrdom of St. Erasmus* of 1629. The commissioning of works continued up to the 18th century; CLEMENT XII and, especially, Benedict XIV, having decided not to have several late 16th-century canvases reworked in mosaic, turned to contemporary artists. Executing an altarpiece for St. Peter's was regarded by most painters as a consecration of themselves or their work, by the implicit honor; only Poussin, though warmly praised by Bernini and Urban VIII, felt that he had failed.

If St. Peter's was the most prestigious works site for 17th- and 18th-century painters, the second half of the 16th century saw most painters at work in the great basilicas. St. John Lateran was for the most part decorated under Sixtus V (the benediction loggia, the Scala Santa) and Clement VIII (the frescoes, in the transept under the direction of Cavaliere d'Arpino). At St. Mary Major, Sixtus V had a chapel built in 1586 and decorated with frescoes under the supervision of Nebbia. Following his example, Paul V built the Pauline chapel, in which most of the painters living in Rome worked between 1611 and 1615 (both the earlier generation, Baglione, Cigoli, and Cavaliere d'Arpino, and the new, Reni and Lanfranco).

In the 17th century, Lanfranco, who enjoyed the favor of Paul V, adorned the chapel of the Blessed Sacrament at St. Paul's outside the Walls during the preparation for the jubilee of 1625. In the 18th century, Corrado Giaquinto painted the ceiling of the church of S. Croce in Gerusalemme, in 1744, at the request of Benedict XIV, who had had the church rebuilt.

The popes directed other painters' work sites in their Vatican, Lateran, and Quirinal palaces. The chief Vatican commissions were carried out during the 15th and 16th centuries. Earlier, Nicholas V had called upon Fra Angelico to decorate his chapel and upon Piero della Francesca for his apartments. SIXTUS IV commissioned Melozzo da Forlì to decorate the VATICAN LIBRARY with frescoes, and Botticelli, Perugino, Signorelli, and others to paint the walls of the Sistine Chapel. Under Julius II and Leo X, Michelangelo painted the ceiling of the Sistine Chapel, and Raphael the *Stanze* along with a section of the loggias. This work of decoration continued throughout the century (Michelangelo's *Last Judgment* was executed under PAUL III; the *Sala Regia* was begun under Paul III and completed under Gregory XIII, with Perino del Vaga, Daniele da Volterra, Salviati, the Zuccaros, Vasari, Beccafumi, and others working on it; and the Library was decorated in Sixtus V's reign under the direction of Guerra and Nebbia). In the 18th century, the opening of the Pio-Clementine Museum was the occasion for an important commission for painted ceilings, carried out largely by Anton Raphael Mengs. The other papal palaces were also extensively decorated, as was the Palazzo dei Conservatori at the Capitol.

These examples make it possible to appreciate the extent of the projects initiated by the popes in their role as bishop of Rome or head of state. In a more personal way, they also turned to painters to decorate the churches under their patronage. The pope responsible for most commissions of this sort was Urban VIII. From the very beginning of his pontificate, he charged Bernini with rebuilding the church of Sta Bibiana (the saint's body had just been discovered) and had it decorated with frescoes by Agostino Ciampelli and Pietro da Cortona. One of the places in which the ostentatious character of the pope's patronage and that of the Barberini family most clearly appears is the church of the Capuchins, Sta Maria della Concezione. Urban VIII's younger brother, Antonio Barberini, was a Capuchin; upon being made cardinal, he decided to rebuild the church of his order. With the pope contributing to the undertaking, many patrons were eager to commission altarpieces, including Emperor Ferdinand II. The Capuchins had repeatedly to plead for decoration that was not too sumptuous, thereby allowing the pope to turn down several offers of help. Nonetheless, both Urban VIII and his brother called on the most celebrated painters to provide the altarpieces. Among them are works of the major painters of the Bologna school (Guido Reni with his *St. Michael Triumphing over the Demon*, Lanfranco, Domenichino) as well as painters of the new generation (Pietro da Cortona, Andrea Sacchi, and others). The quality of the paintings was such that several were recast in mosaic in St. Peter's.

The pontifical families thus showed their munificence as they turned to the best painters of the day to embellish the churches, but their palaces were just as much the object of their attention. The painters were commissioned using immense decoration in fresco (a technique that ensures the longer life of works), to celebrate the family annals, which reached their apogee in the records of the pontificate. One example is in the *Salotto Dipinto* in the Farnese Palace, decorated in the years following the death of Paul III; Salviati and then Zuccaro covered the walls with paintings depicting both the military exploits of the early Farnese and the most prestigious actions of Paul III's pontificate. The Barberini Palace is doubtless the place where painting was most obviously used to glorify a pope and his family. Most of the rooms of the apartments on the second floor were adorned with painted ceilings, notably by Camassei and Sacchi, and the ceiling of the main salon especially was given over to the glorification of the Barberini with Pietro da Cortona's vast fresco, *The Triumph of Divine Providence*, executed between 1632 and 1636. This is the largest continuous work ever executed outside a church. The composition was painstakingly worked on by Francesco Bracciolini, a protégé of Urban VIII and secretary to his brother; the principal theme of the fresco is Divine Providence's pointing to the three bees of the Barberini arms, which are shown on a giant scale. The fresco praises the virtues of the supreme pontiff and the achievements of his reign, to such an extent that Domenichino wrote that he thought the ceiling more suited to a secular ruler than a pope.

Besides their prestigious palaces, various popes, and especially their nephews, also built villas on the outskirts of Rome or in the *Castelli*. Here, decorative painting is less extensive, though far from nonexistent. Pietro Aldobrandini, nephew of Clement VIII, engaged a whole crew of artists, including Cavaliere d'Arpino, at the Villa Aldobrandini in Frascati. The two principal pupils of the Carracci were commissioned to decorate the casinos in the villas of nephews of the popes, atop the Roman hills. In 1614, Guido Reni painted an *Aurora* for Cardinal Scipione Borghese (in what is now the Palazzo Pallavicini-Rospigliosi on the Quirinal), and in 1624, Guercino painted, another, for Cardinal Ludovico Ludovisi's villa on the Pincio. Comparison of the two frescoes, each of which is considered a masterpiece, was a ritual for all travelers up until the 19th century.

The leading collections of paintings in Rome were put together, at least in the beginning, by nephews of the popes during their uncles' reigns. It is difficult to tell what arises from personal taste and what belongs to the desire for ostentation, yet we know that certain cardinals stopped at nothing in order to accumulate paintings. Cardinal Pietro Aldobrandini took advantage of the capture of Ferrara in 1598 to seize Titian's *Bacchanals*, part of the d'Este collection (today, two of these are in the Prado in Madrid, one in the National Gallery in London). Cardinal Scipione Borghese also acquired several works from the d'Este collection. In 1607, he ordered Cavaliere d'Arpino thrown into prison and confiscated his collection of paintings (105 canvases, including a number of Caravaggios)—which did not prevent the Borghese from continuing to employ the artist at St. Mary Major and the Quirinal. He also had Domenichino arrested so as to force the artist to sell him a *Hunt of Diana* commissioned by Cardinal Aldobrandini. Guido Reni, who had left Rome in 1612, was also threatened with imprisonment if he did not return to paint the fresco demanded of him. These extreme methods were certainly not generally employed, but they bear witness to a veritable passion for painting that would stop at nothing.

The extent of the commissions should suffice to underline the influence exerted by the Holy See on pictorial creation. A regular effort extending over more than three hundred years helped make Rome the chief center of European painting. Still, the popes were not content to give their artists work; they also strove to improve their status and, in certain cases, to encourage changes of style.

Most of the artists who worked in Rome between the 16th and the 18th century were not of Roman origin. Some were born in the Papal States—the Bologna school naturally comes to mind—but the majority came from other Italian, even European, states. In most cases, there was a spontaneous movement of artists attracted by the profusion of work sites and by the large number of collectors living or sojourning in Rome; these artists, furthermore, came to complete their training through exposure to antiquity and the works of the great masters. From the 16th century, access to the papal collections was fairly easy. Sixtus IV had given the "Roman people" statues that hitherto had been in the Lateran and then had been moved to the Palazzo dei Conservatori. The Belvedere had also been largely open to artists since Julius II's reign. In 1733, Clement XII founded the Capitoline Museum, which was enlarged under his successors, and Clement XIV and Pius VI founded the Pio-Clementine Museum at the Vatican. These important collections of the works of antiquity, together with Raphael's frescoes, served to establish universal norms of artistic beauty; they played their part in attracting large numbers of painters to Rome, which remained the mecca for all disciples of ideal beauty up until the end of the 19th century.

The paintings acquired by cardinal nephews played a similar role at various stage. For instance, Titian's *Bacchanals*, acquired in 1598 by Cardinal Aldobrandini,

were little known until two of the paintings passed into Cardinal Ludovisi's collection in 1621. They were then widely copied as models, leading to a restoration of Venetian influence on painting in Rome and influencing the work of Pietro da Cortona and Poussin.

The popes also played a more direct role by calling upon artists whose works brought about a renascence in artistic creation; there is no need to emphasize the consequences of the summoning to Rome of Raphael and Michelangelo by Julius II. At times a division of tasks took place: the popes turned to the most prestigious artists, while their intimates, occasionally even their nephews, encouraged the avant-garde. While Clement VIII was handing out important commissions to the most prestigious of the mannerist painters, Cavaliere d'Arpino (the dome of St. Peter's, the decoration at the Palazzo dei Conservatori), Cardinal Pietro Aldobrandini was ordering from Guido Reni, then twenty-six years old, a *Crucifixion of St. Peter* for S. Paolo alla Tre Fontane (today at the Pinacoteca at the Vatican). Paul V also turned to artists of established reputation in his public commissions, while his nephew, Cardinal Scipione Borghese, bought a work by Caravaggio that had been turned down by the commissioners, the *Madonna of the Palafrenieri*. The Barberini likewise did not hesitate to employ in their palace the representatives of opposing trends: Andrea Sacchi painted there his *Divine Wisdom* (1629–33) with as much sobriety as Pietro da Cortona painted his *Divine Providence* (1632–6) with movement. At that time too, Cassiano del Pozzo, secretary to Francesco Barberini, became the leading patron of Poussin.

The popes were certainly not the only ones to employ avant-garde artists in Rome. At various stages, the latest trends were encouraged by other families—Cardinal del Monte patronized Caravaggio, Cardinal Farnese brought Annibale Carracci to Rome, and Cardinal Albani commissioned Mengs to decorate his villa—but only rarely did an artist of high repute not enjoy the patronage of the pope or of his circle at one time or another.

Furthermore, the popes took an interest in the status of artists, and in the teaching of painting and making available a body of lore about it. One instance of this is their support of the Academy of St. Luke. This was founded by two briefs, one of Gregory XIII in 1577, most likely at the request of Muziano, the other of Sixtus V in 1588; however, it opened its doors only in 1593, under Federico Zuccaro's direction. Its difficult beginnings brought it the successive support of Clement VIII, Paul V, Gregory XV, and Urban VIII, each of whom helped it financially but also took care to draw up new regulations. CLEMENT X modified the statutes again in 1675, and CLEMENT XI began a competition for painters, the *concorso clementino*, in 1702. This last pope also founded an academy of painting in Bologna, the *Accademia clementina*. The popes who showed interest in the Academy were also those who supervised the leading Roman work sites and whose families held the largest collections. Patronage of the Academy was a not insignificant element of the cultural policy of the Holy See. It provided a means of keeping artists living in Rome under supervision and at the same time of encouraging the teaching of painting. It fell to the Academy to give rise to a truly Roman school that would reduce the dependence on artists from elsewhere. Close associates of Popes Gregory XV and Urban VIII, Agucchi and Giulio Mancini, helped establish the principle that remained in force until to the end of the 18th century: painters, in imitation of the First Maker, were to represent ideal beauty. This tenet, reformulated by Bellori, would have a lasting influence on the other European academies, among them that of Paris, which joined with the Academy of St. Luke in 1676. However disappointing the works produced by many painters of the Academy, the popes nevertheless had made of it a durable and prestigious institution.

The continuity of the popes' encouragement of painting is striking. From the early Renaissance until Pius VI, there was a practically uninterrupted flow of commissions, and most important, works on the whole were preserved. What happened in France at that time, when works were often painted over or destroyed in the next generation, did not not happen in Rome. The controversy that raged with the completion of Michelangelo's *Last Judgment* prompted several popes (PAUL IV, PIUS IV, Pius V, and even CLEMENT XIII, in 1762) to have the figures draped, but despite strong inducements, no pope resolved to destroy the work. The feeling for tradition that inspired Church policy impelled the popes to follow the artistic policy of their predecessors as a model. Even their portraits followed Raphael's archetypes, the portrait of Julius II and that of Leo X with two cardinals. This respect for tradition sometimes caused Roman painting to ossify, but it also brought about periodic returns to the source, causing a regeneration of European painting at the end of the 16th and in the second half of the 18th century.

Christian Michel

See also ARTISTS, FOREIGN, IN ROME.

Bibliography

Abramson, M. C. *Painting in Rome during the Papacy of Clement VIII (1592–1605)*, Ph.D., Columbia University, 1976.

Barroero, L. "La pittura a Roma nel Settecento," in A.a. v.v., *La pittura in Italia. Il Settecento*, Electa, 1990, I, 383–463.

Beldon-Scott, J. *Images of Nepotism: The Painted Ceilings of Palazzo Barberini*, Princeton, 1991.

Blunt, A. *Guide to Baroque Rome*, London, 1982.

Boespflug, F. *Dieu dans l'art*, Sollicitudini nostrae *de Benoît XIV et l'affaire Crescence de Kaufbeuren*, Paris, 1984.

Chastel, A. *The Sack of Rome*, Princeton, N.J., 1983.

Haskell, F. *Patrons and Painters: A Study in the Relations between Italian Art and Society in the Age of the Baroque*, London, 1963.

L'Accademia nazionale di San Luca, Rome, 1974.

L'Arte degli Anni santi a Roma 1300–1875, Rome, 1984–5.

L'Arte per i Papi e per i Principi nella Campagna Romana; Grande Pittura del '600 e del '700, Rome, 1990.

Le Bianco, A. "La pittura del Cinquecento a Roma e nel Lazio," in A.a. v.v., *La Pittura in Italia. Il Cinquecento*, Electa, 1987, II, 457–71.

Mahon, D. *Studies in Seicento Art and Theory*, London, 1947.

Mâle, E. *L'Art religieux de la fin du XVIe siècle, du XVIIe siècle, et du XVIIIe siècle*, Paris, 1951.

Mancini, F. *Considerazioni sulla Pittura (c. 1620)*, ed. A. Marucchi and L. Salerno, Rome, 1956.

Paleotti, G. *Discorso intorno alle imagini*, Bologna, 1582.

Pollak, O. *Die Kunsttätigkeit unter Urban VIII*, Vienna, 1927–31.

Schleier, E. "La pittura a Rome nel Seicento," in A.a. v.v., *La Pittura in Italia. Il Seicento*, Electa, 1988, II, 399–460.

Titi, F. *Studio di Pittura, Scoltura ed Architettura nelle chiese di Roma, 1674–1763*, ed. B. Contardi and S. Romano, Florence, 1987.

The Vatican Collections: The Papacy and Art, New York, Chicago, and San Francisco, 1983.

Venuti, R. *Descrizione topografica e istorica di Roma moderna*, Rome, 1764, rpr. 1977.

Zuccari, A. *I Pittori di Sisto V*, Rome, 1992.

PALACE, APOSTOLIC. The pope's ordinary residence. The plural "apostolic palaces" or "sacred palaces," customary in Italian, has long been used to refer not only to the residences of the Vatican, the QUIRINAL, and Castel Gandolfo, but also to all the staff attached to the PAPAL FAMILY as well as the numerous employees of the associated services and the members of the armed guards. In the 15th century, this complex organization was placed under the authority of the majordomo or prefect of the apostolic palace. Many of the posts that were created have lasted from the mid-1500s until today. Accordingly, we have quite a good idea of those who, in one post or another, were included in the budget of the papal household. In the 19th century, when the Papal States were in economic difficulties, these posts were reviewed. In 1824, LEO XII set up a committee consisting, among others, of the majordomo, the quartermaster general, and the grand equerry to manage the day-to-day administration of the palace and its staff. Funds came from the public treasury and from the rental of premises belonging to the apostolic palaces.

Dependent on this committee, at least for their maintenance, were the secretary of state and all the autonomous secretaries, all secretaries of the congregations of cardinals, members of the papal chapel and the secret antechamber, the officers of the DATARY, the VATICAN LIBRARY and the ARCHIVES, the maintenance staff of the papal palaces and gardens, and the palatine army corps. One statistic, from 1842, cites the figure of 1,418 people answerable to the Prefecture of the Apostolic Palace. Under PIUS IX, this complex organization was streamlined and on 1 November 1848 handed over to the secretary of state, Cardinal Antonelli, who then assumed the title of Prefect of the Apostolic Palace, thereby surpassing the majordomo and becoming palatine cardinal. In 1870, when the temporal government was nearing its end, the Apostolic Palace had to provide for the maintenance of the papal court and household, the SACRED COLLEGE, all the ecclesiastical congregations, the nunciatures and legations abroad, the armies (NOBLE GUARD, PALATINE GUARD, SWISS GUARD, GENDARMES), the SECRETARIAT OF STATE and the secretariats attached to the Apostolic Palace, the museums and galleries, the facades of the major BASILICAS, the stables, and the pensions of former members of the court. The Italian government, which had seized the Papal States, proposed paying out a "civil list" equivalent to that of the "mandate of the Prefecture of the Apostolic Palace" written into the old papal budget. Pius IX refused and survived—very well, as it happened, thanks to Peter's Pence. Cardinal Antonelli, in his function as prefect of the apostolic palace, took over the administration of Peter's Pence, thereby becoming the sole administrator of the revenues of the Holy See. This situation was handed down to his successors until 1880, when the new secretary of state, Cardinal Nina, asked to be relieved of the prefecture in everything that had to do with managing life at the Vatican. It was at that time that a new body was created, the Administration of the Property of the Holy See. The Prefecture of the Apostolic Palace once again became autonomous under a cardinal's authority, and no longer was concerned with financial management. Nevertheless, in 1892 it was placed once again under the supervision of the committee responsible for the Administration of the Property of the Holy See, merging with it in 1894 and eventually disappearing from the lists of papal agencies. PIUS X drew a fresh distinction between administration and prefecture, placing both, however, under the sole direction of the secretary of state, Cardinal Merry del Val. After the LATERAN PACTS and the creation of Vatican City, the various structures were profoundly modified. The Prefecture of the Apostolic Palace as it existed at the end of Pius IX's pontificate is now dispersed among the

Administration of the Patrimony of the Holy See, the Secretariat of State (administrative section), the Prefecture of the Papal Household, and the *Governorato*. The expression "Apostolic Palace" survived for a few more years, for the sake of designating the survivors of the "college of procurators of the Sacred Apostolic Palaces" (of whom there were four in 1993), that is, a corps of lawyers allowed to defend certain causes before the apostolic TRIBUNALS (the Rota and a section of the administrative legal department of the Signatura).

François-Charles Uginet

Bibliography

Lay, B. *Finanze e finanzieri vaticani tra l'Ottocento e il Novecento da Pio IX a Benedetto XV*, Milan, 1979, 45–47, 64, 92, 134, 221.

Moroni, G. *Dizionario di erudizione storico-ecclesiastica*, 23, Venice, 1844, 113–25; 50, Venice, 1851, 202–3.

PALACE, PONTIFICAL, OF MONTECAVALLO AT THE QUIRINAL. See **Quirinal (Pontifical Palace of Montecavallo)**.

PALATINE. The adjective used to describe a person or institution attached to the apostolic palace, that is, the papal residence. In the modern and contemporary era, the word applies above all to important individuals who are housed in the palace ex officio, or to administrations that have established their headquarters there in order to attend to the more pressing aspect of their service of the pope. The palatine CARDINALS of the modern era are the CARDINAL NEPHEW, the secretary of state (and secretary for interior affairs under GREGORY XVI), the secretary of briefs to princes, the datary, the secretary of memorials, and the librarian. The best-known palatine prelates are the majordomo, the MASTER OF THE SACRED PALACE, the secret almoner, the master of the chamber, and the auditor of His Holiness. Palatine cardinals and prelates belong to the PAPAL FAMILY and have special seats near the pope in the PAPAL CHAPEL. Their almost daily physical proximity to the pope led to their being, at certain epochs, his intimate advisers. All these distinctions, including the title "Palatine," were abolished by the *motu proprio Pontificalis domus* (28 March 1968).

The denomination "palatine" as applied to institutions answerable to the pope came into use at the end of the 19th century and has always shifted in meaning. Sometimes it designated those administrations formerly dependent on the prefect of the Apostolic Palace (Administration of the Property of the Holy See, MUSEUMS), sometimes institutions headed by a cardinal who was not *stricto sensu* part of the Roman CURIA (VATICAN LIBRARY, VATICAN ARCHIVES, FABRIC OF ST. PETER'S), or sometimes subsidiary institutions of more or less ancient origin (Special Administration of the Holy See, *Acta apostolicae sedis*, Vatican Polyglot Press, Vatican Publishing House, L'OSSERVATORE ROMANO, etc.). As the Curia underwent partial or broad reform, the palatine administrations were transformed into offices integrated into the Curia, or attached to the *Governorato*. The remainder, together with a few from other departments and newly created offices, joined together to form what the constitution *Pastor bonus* (29 June 1989) calls "institutions connected with the Holy See," this time deprived of the title palatine. These are, in the order given in the ANNUARIO PONTIFICIO, the Vatican Archives, the Vatican Library, the Vatican Press Room, the Vatican Printing Press (formerly Polyglot Press), *L'Osservatore romano*, the Vatican Publishing House, VATICAN RADIO, the Vatican Television Center, the Fabric of St. Peter's, and the Apostolic Almoner.

François-Charles Uginet

PALATINE GUARD. The Palatine Guard of Honor is an armed corps responsible for protecting the pope; it also serves as his honor guard. It originated from the civil guard created in 1796, disbanded in 1799, and reestablished by PIUS VII. In 1816, a company was created within the civil guard and called the Prima Compagnia Granatiera Scelta; in 1847 it was renamed Compagnia Palatina, and then Guardia Palatina, thus indicating service to the Papal Palace. The military bodies disbanded in 1849 (the civil guard was one of them) and were reorganized after the pope's return to Rome. In a dispatch dated 14 December 1850, the secretary of state gave regulations to a Palatine honor guard in which the old Palatine Guard and the urban militia were combined. The new corps was not disbanded until 1870. It included two companies of 60 men each. The regulations that followed brought the contingent up to two batallions of volunteers that, until their recent disbanding, constituted a force of some 500 men. Like the Noble Guard and the Swiss Guard, the Palatine Guard provided antechamber services in addition to those of an honor guard in pontifical CHAPELS. It was recruited from among the lower middle classes and the master artisans of Rome. PAUL VI disbanded it (letter to the secretary of state, 14 September 1970), stipulating that its former members, with their uniforms taken from them, might be employed in another of the Holy See's volunteer services. Currently united in an association, the former guards occasionally help maintain order in the basilicas during large papal ceremonies. They continue to enjoy material advantages, like access to the Vatican stores.

François-Charles Uginet

Bibliography

Usai, M. *La Guardia palatine d'onore*, Rome, 1942.

PALLIUM. See **Vestments, Pope's Liturgical**.

PANTHEON. Consecrated to all the gods, as its name indicates, the Pantheon was originally a temple designed to exalt the divine charisma of the emperor Augustus, whose statue Agrippa had planned to set up alongside those of Venus (the goddess from whom Augustus's family claimed descent), Mars (the father of Romulus), and the *Diuus Iulius* (the name given to Caesar, Augustus's father, after the initiation of a cult in his honor). This accounts for Agrippa's decision to erect the temple in the middle of the Campus Martius, at the spot called *palus Caprae* ("Goat's marsh"), where according to legend the mysterious disappearance and implicit apotheosis of Romulus had taken place. The temple was dedicated in 27 B.C., at a time when Augustus was no longer encouraging deifying homage to his person; the decision was accordingly made to place the statues of Augustus and Agrippa at the entrance to the temple, not inside it.

After Domitian's restoration of the building, it fell to Hadrian to rebuild the Pantheon in its entirety, between 118 and 125. The previous temple was razed (traces of it have been found beneath the entrance of the new temple), and the new sanctuary was given a northerly orientation (not a southerly one like the old building). The original dedicatory inscription was retained (*M[arcus] Agrippa co[n]s[ul] tertium fecit*) and two recesses created in the vestibule to house the statues of Augustus and Agrippa. But first and foremost, the new Pantheon was conceived as a combination of a traditional temple, with octostyle facade and pediment, and an imposing rotunda supporting a gigantic dome 142 feet/43.30 meters in diameter, pierced with an oculus 29.5 feet/9 meters in diameter. The distance from the oculus to the floor of the rotunda being equal to the diameter of the dome, one can say that the temple was conceived as a sphere (clearly in the image of the cosmic sphere) enclosed in a cylinder. The seven chapels arranged in a circle around the rotunda are presumed to have contained statues of the seven planetary divinities, though this is not certain. What is certain, however, is that the disc of light projected into the rotunda when the rays of the sun passed through the oculus reinforced the cosmic symbolism of the structure. Restored in 202 by Septimius Severus and his son, the future emperor Caracalla, the temple, from the time it was built, became a model for the architects of the empire; one example is the sanctuary built in imitation of it at Pergamum in Asia Minor, in 150, dedicated to Zeus Asklépios. Closed, as were all the pagan places of worship, by a decree of Honorius around 400, the

Pantheon became a Christian church like other temples during the period of the Byzantine rule of Rome. BONIFACE IV consecrated it to *Sancta Maria ad Martyres* in 609, perhaps in a desire to exorcise the former temple, dedicated to all the gods, by referring to the multitude of Christian martyrs. In later years, the church was chiefly known as Santa Maria Rotonda.

After Constans II despoiled the Pantheon of its gilded bronze roofing in 663, GREGORY III replaced the roof with one of lead in 735. Ever after, it was a constant concern of the popes as well as of the city of Rome to renew the covering, as is proved by the many coats of arms and inscriptions dating from the 15th century on that have been found on the plates of lead. Probably from the 12th century, the temple's unique architecture, originally intended to express Hadrian's cosmic pantheism, served for the staging of theatrical productions of the Christian cult: for instance, on the feast of the Assumption, the oculus was used with the help of machinery, to enact the Virgin's ascent into heaven. We also know the extent to which the successive architects of the new ST. PETER'S profited from this prestigious model. The papacy assumed the right both to restore the monument (in 1663, ALEXANDER III replaced two columns on the front porch) and to complete it (in 1270, a small campanile was built in the middle of the facade, and in 1627, it was replaced by two small matching campaniles, which were not removed until 1882). It also felt free to pillage its bronze (from the end of the 16th century, SIXTUS V, and then CLEMENT VIII and URBAN VIII carried off huge quantities for the beautification of pontifical Rome). Yet the city of Rome always claimed a right of intervention, even ownership, with regard to the Pantheon, and from the Renaissance on, the monument was transformed into a mausoleum of the glories of Italy (Raphael, Perino del Vaga, Giovanni da Udine, Annibale Carracci, and Flaminio Vacca are among those buried there).

Unlike many other classical Roman monuments, the Pantheon only rarely served as a pawn in the struggles between rival factions of the Roman nobility, doubtless because of its early consecration as a church. (Only the Crescenzi, whose palace was adjacent, were able to lay claim to it for a brief period.) But it did provoke a permanent struggle of influence between the papacy and the city. After 1870, the Pantheon was chosen as the resting place for the kings and queens of Italy (Victor Emmanuel in 1878, Umberto I in 1900, Margherita in 1926), and the LATERAN PACTS consecrated it as the king of Italy's "palatine basilica" (1929), thus putting an end to the age-old rivalry of which it had been the object.

Gilles Sauron

Bibliography

Coarelli, F. "Il Pantheon, l'apoteosi di Augusto e l'apoteosi di Romolo," *Città e Architettura nella Roma imperiale* (*Analecta Romana Instituti Danici*, suppl. X), Rome, 1983, 41–6.

De Fine Licht, K. *The Rotunda in Rome*, Copenhagen, 1968.

McDonald, W. L. *The Pantheon: Design, Meaning and Progeny*, London, 1976.

PAPAL STATES.

8th to 13th Centuries. The birth date of the "States of the Holy See" can be placed in the 8th century, even if the expression, when applied to that period, runs the risk of creating multiple misunderstandings. Before that, the Church of Rome and its bishop, like all the Churches, had a PATRIMONY or, more precisely, patrimonies; these, however, were nothing more than a gift in land, a source of revenue that gave rise to no exercise of sovereignty, even if there were hints that the authority of the pope—who was the successor of Peter as well as a key figure in the empire—was spilling over into the public domain. The "States" developed with a certain tenacity, albeit in fits and starts and in the absence of a preconceived plan; after a long period of constitution extending from the 8th to the 16th century, they reached the point where they formed an essential element in Italian geopolitics, until their dissolution in 1870 and the final resolution of the question in 1929. Consequently, their historiography has long been dominated by pro and con polemics, and influenced to a greater or lesser extent by the vigorous challenge, in the 12th century with Arnold of Brescia and in the 13th with broad layers of the Christian population, who were more receptive to the HERESIES of "apostolic poverty," to the idea that the Church—and particularly the vicar of Christ—should hold no temporal goods and exercise no wordly power. As we know, the quarrel arose again in the 16th and 17th centuries, and then in the 19th the framework of the Risorgimento. The polemic was nevertheless not without fruit, and on each occasion it gave rise to new historical research; in 1861, for example, it caused the prefect of the Vatican Archives, Augustin Theiner, to publish the first of the three large folio volumes of the *Codex diplomaticus dominii temporalis Sancte Sedis*, in which he hoped to document, from the Donation of Quierzy to the 16th century, both the legitimacy of and the long papal experience in administering the States. His introduction is still worth reading; in it, he declares he is using French (as opposed to the Latin of his other prefaces) so as to be better understood by "a few Statesmen."

Hindered by falsification, marred by several lacunae, and threatened by anachronisms and lexical misinterpretations, the prehistory of the States of the Holy See has been reconstructed thanks to a number of studies undertaken, especially in Germany, on the Carolingians, but also in recent decades thanks to a better approach to the relations between Rome and Byzantium in the 7th and 8th centuries. Even if shadowy areas remain, a broad picture can be drawn of an evolution that in the second half of the 8th century led a supreme pontiff, who had long been the principal source of authority and interventions in the area of the "administration" of Rome (not unlike a number of Western bishops at the time), to act as a substitute for the Byzantine (that is, imperial) public authority that was faltering totally in the surrounding areas. The first duke of Rome, a delegate of the exarch of Ravenna, was named in 592; the last cited appeared in 756: there are a number of indications that he was already in the orbit of the pontifical power (the uncle of Pope HADRIAN I was a duke, then a dignitary of the Roman Church; the duke from 756, Eustathius, was later noted to be in one of Pope STEPHEN II's embassies). With no official recognition, the duchy of Rome thus dissolved into the "Patrimony" of St. Peter, while papal correspondence, from GREGORY III to ZACHARIAS, saw a blossoming of expressions (*populus peculiaris sancti Petri, terra* [or *terre*] *sancti Petri, respublica Romanorum*) that translated the Pope's taking hold of effective and exclusive public authority over the city of Rome and its surrounding areas. This zone, often defined as "from Acquapendente to Ceprano," roughly covers present-day Latium; in the 13th century, this early kernel of the Papal States was still called *ortus deliciarum Ecclesiae* by the papal CHANCERY.

Act two followed almost immediately thereafter, with the entry on the scene of the FRANKS, the new protectors against, and replacements for, the LOMBARDS (774), and even promoted to universal empire (800). Neither of the two parties was without ulterior motives for its actions: for the papacy, it was a matter of getting recognition for previously Byzantine territories appropriated from the Lombards, taking the peninsula in a wide swath of territories, from south of Rome to the Po delta; for the Frankish sovereign, it was a matter of making a few rather gratuitous promises, and then not allowing the kingdom of the Lombards or the imperial authority to be carved up. The question was all the more complicated since the texts of the royal, and then imperial, "donations" have been very poorly transmitted to us. The donations of Pepin (754) and Charlemagne (774, renegotiated in 781) are known only through the *LIBER PONTIFICALIS*, the partiality of which one can imagine. The least uncertain element, other than the restitution of the most recent Lombard conquests, is the demarcation of the northern boundary of a zone of pontifical influence: quite generous, it begins at Luni, clears the Apennines, crosses the plain of the Po, and encompasses the old EXARCHATE OF RAVENNA, Venetia, and Istria. Louis the Pious's diploma in 817 (*Ludovicianum*), doubtless interpolated, appears to have brought the line farther south; passing through Orvieto and Peru-

gia, it still encompassed cities like Bologna, Ferrara, and Comacchio; the emperor thus confirmed the passage under Frankish authority of Emilia, Tuscany, and a large piece of the old Lombard duchy of Spoleto (from as early as 781, there are records of surveys carried out for defining the boundaries of the "Roman Sabina," which was pontifical, and of the rest of the duchy). In compensation, theoretically, the pope managed to get not only the previously confirmed Corsica recognized, but also Sardinia and Sicily; but most noteworthy, although this significant concession was quickly denied by his successors, was that for the first time the emperor recognized the pope as an independent public authority, as expressed in a set of terms as strong as *jus principatus, ditio*. In 824 (*Constitutio romana*), Lothair reacted and established a kind of pontifico-imperial condominium on "the lands of St. Peter"; in practice, it was widely ignored, but it did furnish a basis for the imperial claims of the Ottonians, the Salians, and the Staufen. This restrictive definition was renewed at the time of the restoration of the empire by Otto I, in 962 (*Ottonianum*), who returned (with no practical impact) to the expanded borders of 774 and, after the interlude of Otto III, by Henry II in 1020. The plot had already come to a head, with moveable borders and mutual demands, and, with a few added ingredients, was not really resolved until the 13th century.

The history of borders recognized, "given," or "restored" to the papacy is one thing; that of the exact limits of the authority and of the means of government is another. Ninth-century sources are sorely lacking, although they suggest an effective exercise of justice, with the Lateran Palace as its center, and, from the time of Hadrian I, active minting of papal COINS. A few documentary hints, like a comparison with the other European principalities, do shed enough light to give the 10th century, or, more precisely, the decades from 900 to 950, a face of its own: it was a period less of anarchy than of restructuring on the part of the great secular house that dominated the papacy at that time; Theophylact (who combined direction of finances and direction of the army, with the double title of *dux* and *vestararius*, from 904 to 924), his daughter Marozia (924–32), and, after her eviction, his grandson Alberic II (932–54), finally failed, but their efforts were soon taken up again, with less brilliance, by various descendants, the Crescenzi and the counts of Tusculum ("Tuscolani"). In control of the papal see and the palace, they scoured from the area of SARACENS and set up a true principality. Their control was thwarted by the imperial reformatory papacy, and later by the popes of the Gregorian REFORM, but the territorial revenues remained: as P. Toubert has pointed out, between the end of the 8th century and the middle of the 10th, the old Byzantine *ducatus romanus* to which its borders were limited constituted a true territory, and remained the only true "State" of the Holy See until the time of INNOCENT III, and one in which the popes became "silent apprentices of power."

From the middle of the 11th until the middle of the 12th century, the reforming papacy reinforced the legal concepts relating to the defense of the Patrimony, stiffened inalienability and "claims," and then made broad use of the DONATION OF CONSTANTINE and of the imperial acts. But, caught among the real difficulties of governing territories where public authority was divided among a scattering of lordly dynasties, the nearly permanent conflict with the emperor and his ANTIPOPES, as well as with the NORMANS, whose help was sometimes doubtful and always self-interested, it registered a loss of authority over a number of surrounding territories, up to the time of the Roman revolt of 1143, which showed the fragility of the pontifical power over Rome itself. The great local dynasties dominated the area around Rome: "Tuscolani" in Campagna (immediately to the south of Rome), who controlled the coastline and the Via Appia, the counts of Ceccano on the outer edges of the Norman kingdom, and the counts Ottaviani in Sabina. Difficulties were compounded with the inclusion of Matilda of Canossa's inheritance, scattered among Tuscany (but quite dense to the north of Siena, and all around Lucca), the Tusco-Emilian Apennines, and the plain of the Po from Emilia to the delta (the papacy's definitive possession of which, followed by a number of reenfeoffments for the parts farthest from the center, did not take place until the years 1210–20).

It was during the following period that administrative tools were patiently forged which allowed control to be regained, leading to the constitution of a true State, a monarchy among monarchies. Not without difficulties, threatened by the politics of the reintroduction of imperial power that ran through more than a century, from Frederick I Barbarossa to the dissolution of the inheritors of Frederick II (1155–1266), the popes began—with HADRIAN IV and EUGENE III—a patient politics of territorial structuring around land acquisitions, and especially of a complex network: administrative and judiciary, castral (*castra speciala Sancte Romane ecclesie*, of which Hadrian IV bought about twenty) and feudal (beginning in the 1150s, great lords like Jonathan of Tusculum, Odo of Poli, and the counts of Aquino and Calmaniare entered into a relationship of personal dependence vis-à-vis the pope). As elsewhere in the West, the concept of "subject" was rediscovered, and the popes, further supported by their moral authority, launched broad campaigns for collective oaths of fealty to be sworn by the communities of inhabitants, who early on had been poured into the mold of vassalage. The compilation of the *LIBER CENSUUM* was only one of the elements in the development of a written administration and of surveys.

Firmer on its foundations, the papacy again took up its "claims," and with greater vigor. In 1159, Hadrian IV addressed a statement of claims to Frederick I which was still rather timid, as it laid claim only to the duchy of Spoleto, Ferrara, Sardinia, and Corsica. CELESTINE III claimed the duchy of Spoleto, but also the Marches of Ancona. With the death of Emperor Henry VI, the first phase of the Italian implantation of the Staufen came to an end, and Innocent III maneuvered among the pretenders, not without undergoing setbacks, in order to get the papal claims recognized. Otto of Brunswick, in Neuss, "confirmed" to the pope not only the territory from Radicofani to Ceprano, but also the old EXARCHATE of RAVENNA and the Pentapolis, the Marches of Ancona, the duchy of Spoleto, the lands of Countess Matilda, the county of Bertinoro (confirmed to Egen by the young Frederick II, at the time under pontifical tutelage, in 1213). Once again in question at the time of the battle against the last Staufen, this increase also failed to correspond to the true facts, since the pontifical power was unable to absorb everything. The Patrimony was notably enlarged around the initial kernel, taking in lands integrated into the "Patrimony of St. Peter in Tuscany," but also the duchy of Spoleto, the Marches of Ancona, the ephemeral Massa Trabaria (integrated into the Marches, and then into the Romagna). But it would not be until the third quarter of the century that Romagna was ceded to the pope by Rudolf of Habsburg (December 1275); here, as previously in the Marches of Ancona, papal authority was imposed only with difficulty, and not without multiple vicissitudes, on aggressive feudal landowners and on cities jealous of their independence: Bologna recognized only a token papal authority, with no system of taxation, no justice, and tiny military requisitions.

The popes of the 12th and 13th centuries pursued and enlarged their predecessors' politics of state construction, which was in no way upset by the tendency of the Roman popes to favor the implantation of their families, "NEPOTISM" being also a means of reinforcing governmental structures, though one that occasionally led to nearly definitive alienations of *castra* (as with Celestine III in favor of the Boveschi and the Orsini, CLEMENT III in favor of the Sclari, Innocent III and GREGORY IX in favor of the Conti, NICHOLAS III in favor of the Orsini, (something that now seems shocking, etc.). The provinces, with the rather fluid details of their geographies, were entrusted to great clerks, called rectors. Although they were primarily judges, both spiritual and temporal, they could also be named as LEGATES; their recruitment evolved throughout the pontificates, but for the most part they were clerics (over 90 of the approximately 150 known from 1198 to 1304); flanked by vicars and a veritable provincial court, under GREGORY X they had treasurers assigned to them depending directly on the APOSTOLIC CAMERA. The popes developed an impor-

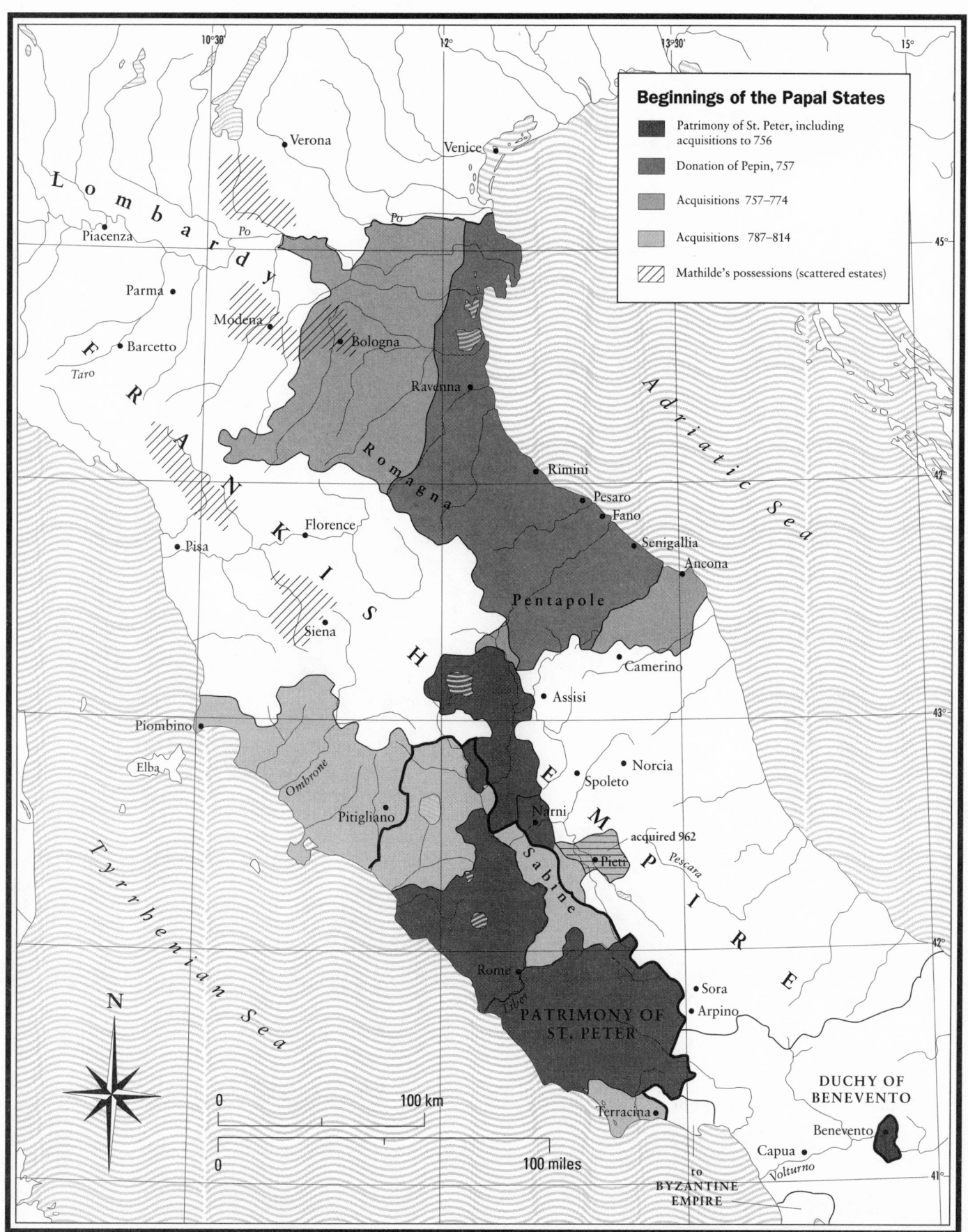

Beginnings of the Papal States

Patrimony of St. Peter, including acquisitions to 756

Donation of Pepin, 757

Acquisitions 757–774

Acquisitions 787–814

Mathilde's possessions (scattered estates)

Lombardy

Verona

Venice

Piacenza

Po

Parma

Modena

Barcetto

Taro

Bologna

Ravenna

Romagna

FRANKISH

Florence

Pisa

Rimini

Pesaro
Fano

Senigallia
Ancona

Adriatic Sea

Pentapole

Siena

Camerino

Piombino

Assisi

Norcia
Spoleto

Elba

Ombrone

Pitigliano

Narni

acquired 962

Pietri

Sabine

Pescara

EMPIRE

Rome

Sora

Arpino

Tyrrhenian Sea

PATRIMONY OF
ST. PETER

DUCHY OF
BENEVENTO

Terracina

Benevento

Capua

Volturno

to
BYZANTINE
EMPIRE

N

0   100 km

0   100 miles

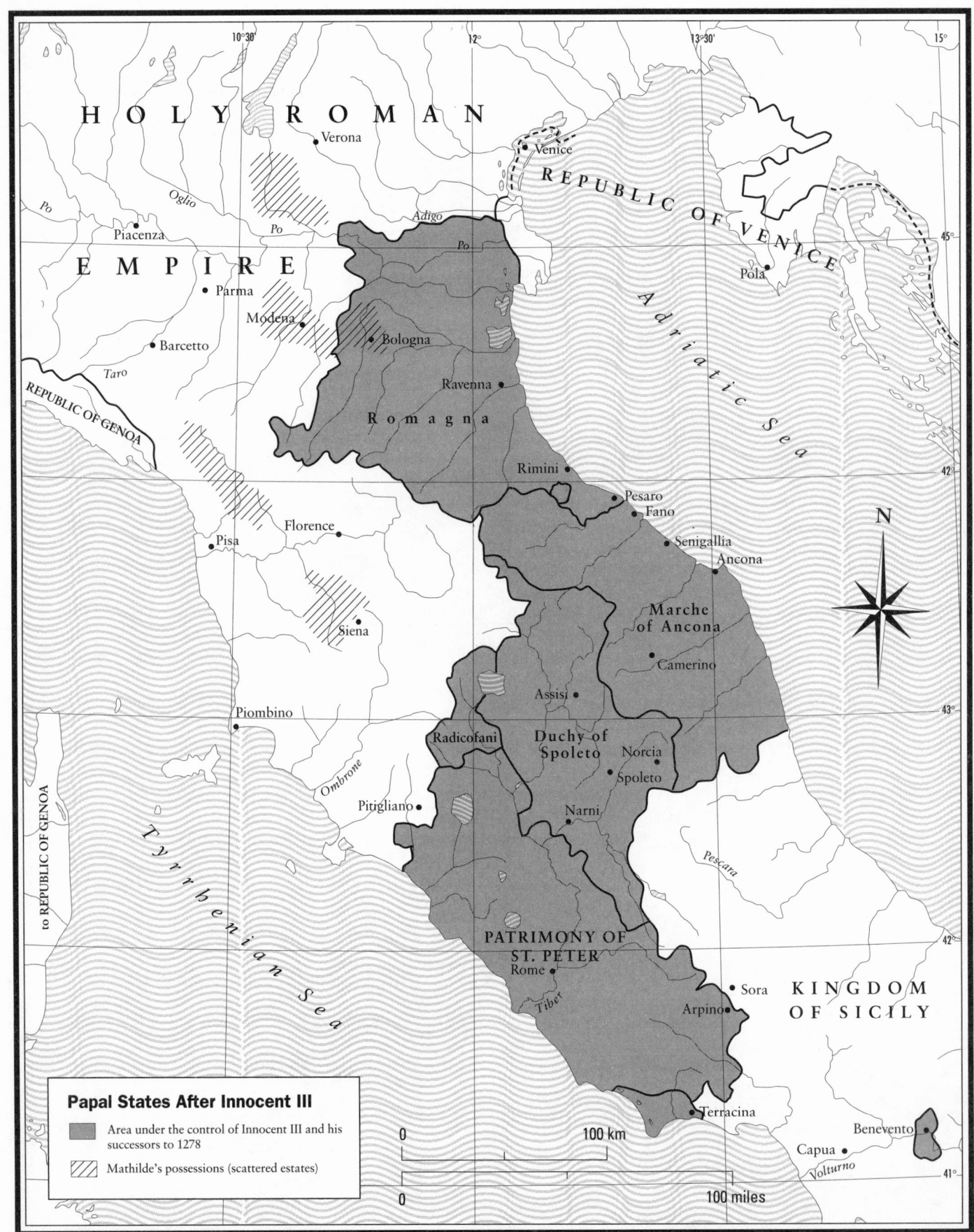

Papal States After Innocent III

Area under the control of Innocent III and his successors to 1278

Mathilde's possessions (scattered estates)

HOLY ROMAN

EMPIRE

REPUBLIC OF VENICE

REPUBLIC OF GENOA

to REPUBLIC OF GENOA

Verona

Venice

Pola

Piacenza

Parma

Modena

Barcetto

Bologna

Ravenna

Romagna

Rimini

Pesaro

Fano

Senigallia

Ancona

Florence

Pisa

Siena

Marche
of Ancona

Camerino

Piombino

Assisi

Radicofani

Duchy of
Spoleto

Norcia

Spoleto

Pitigliano

Narni

Pescara

PATRIMONY OF
ST. PETER

Rome

Sora

KINGDOM
OF SICILY

Tiber

Arpino

Terracina

Benevento

Capua

Volturno

Adriatic Sea

Tyrrhenian Sea

Po

Oglio

Po

Adige

Po

Taro

Ombrone

N

0   100 km

0   100 miles

tant legislative activity, often promulgated after great parliaments (such as at Viterbo under Innocent III): this led to the great codification of BONIFACE VIII, who decreed three constitutions of administrative "reform" (*Romana mater ecclesia* in September 1295 for the Campagna and the Maritima; *Licet meum* in January 1300 for the Patrimony of Tuscany; *Celestis patrisfamilias* in September 1303 for the Marches of Ancona). Introduced from above, papal authority was strengthened from below. Patient work in developing the *castra speciala*, difficult negotiations with the local dynasts and with the ever-rowdy communes (who often obtained important concessions in the domain of justice and in the choice of "podestas," such as Spoleto in 1247 and 1295), made possible the federation of a constellation of lords and communities within a veritable State, where waved the *vexillum sancti Petri*. It should also be noted that even before the decisive upswing in taxation in the AVIGNON period, the Patrimony did not furnish the papacy with more than a modest portion of its revenues: perhaps 25,000 florins per year under Boniface VIII, according to D. Waley's estimation; that is, one-tenth of the total income.

Olivier Guyotjeannin

Bibliography

Galasso, G., ed. *Storia d'Italia*, VII-2, *Comuni e signorie nell'Italia nordorientale e centrale*, Turin, 1987 (contributions from G. Arnaldi, P. Toubert, and D. Waley on the Papal State from its origins to the beginning of the 15th century, 1–320, with bibliography).
More, J. C. "Pope Innocent III, Sardinia, and the Papal State," *Speculum*, 62 (1987), 81–101.
Noble, T. F. X. *The Republic of St. Peter: The Birth of the Papal State 680–825*, Philadelphia, 1984.
Partner, P. *The Lands of St. Peter: The Papal State in the Middle Ages and the Early Renaissance*, London, 1972.
Waley, D. *The Papal State in the Thirteenth Century*, London and New York, 1961.

15th to 19th Centuries. The solution to the crisis brought on by the GREAT SCHISM OF THE WEST was found in the COUNCIL of Constance, thanks to the combined efforts of the emperor, the SACRED COLLEGE, the bishops, and the members of the council who represented the "national" clergy and the great universities. This collective, not to say collegial, participation took the form of a conclave in which not only cardinals but also representatives of the council, divided into national groups, took part. There was no precedent for such a singular arrangement, nor was it ever repeated: it also had the advantage, quite in line with previous tradition, of making the pope the representative of all Christendom. This ecclesiological view of the pontifical figure was nevertheless colored by the view that supreme power was exercised by the college of cardinals and the conciliar assemblies, who were sup-

posed to be meeting periodically. MARTIN V, and especially EUGENE IV, resisted such constraint to the best of their ability by seeking the support of the sovereigns against the conciliar assemblies and by surrendering a portion of the papal prerogatives to those sovereigns. Recent historiography (P. Prodi) has convincingly suggested this struggle as the point of departure for the evolution of the pontifical state in modern times, allowing us better to understand the internal contradictions that this political anomaly retained until its extinction.

At what point did the lands belonging to the Church become the Papal State? The 14th century certainly paved the way for a more rational organization of a complex mosaic of possessions whose status varied considerably. The efforts of Cardinal Albornoz to reorganize the Italian lands, and the enormous financial sacrifices of the Avignon popes to ensure their possessions on the other side of the mountains, were nearly brought to nothing at the beginning of the 15th century. With patience and the assistance of his brothers, Martin V, in the context of a highly favorable international political situation, took charge of restoring papal authority. That possession of an autonomous state would be the primary guarantee of its independence in the new European system of states was a consciously held attitude of the papacy from the middle of the 15th century. The formation of this state was of course not immediate, and there is no shortage of historians who emphasize that the centralization of papal government was so imperceptible, and underwent such repercussions, that it was barely achieved before the end of the 17th century. However, the conversion of the PATRIMONY OF ST. PETER into a state was noticed by contemporaries as early as the 15th century, particularly Laurenzo Valla, whose 1440 refutation of the Donation of Constantine emphasized the recent developments in papal tyranny, personified under Eugene IV by Cardinal Vitteleschi. For Valla, it was not the Church that sought to ensure the possession of a territory by force, but the pope. And a few years later, Enea Silvio Piccolomini, the future PIUS II, theorized not only on the supreme pastoral power of the pope, but also on his capacity for governing in the temporal sphere, for uniting in his person the spiritual authority and the temporal authority, he thereby avoided conflicts between the two spheres. The national Churches of the subsequent period would not fail to draw a lesson from such principles. And in his notes on the council of Basel, the same Piccolomini reported the favorable opinion given by him, in contrast to others, regarding the papal election of Duke Amadeus VIII of Savoy. According to him, such a choice assured the new pope of the support of his close relations in defending the Church against those who might wish to subjugate it. For, he said, "the Roman pontiff without the patrimony of the Church is nothing more than the slave of princes and kings." We see here the newly acquired importance of the Patrimony of St. Peter as a guarantee of papal independence, and even the foundations of the nepotism of which Pius II was one of the first to be guilty.

In the 15th century, and until the beginning of the 19th, a distinction was made between lands that were "immediate subjects" (*immediate subjectae*) and those that were "mediate subjects" (*mediate subjectae*): the former were often large autonomous communes or territorial units in which a papal representative resided but which were administered by their own rules, the latter were removed from the authority of papal representatives, and public power was exercised in them by a vicar or a feudatory who had direct contact with the pope. The same commune or the same land could pass from one status to the other depending on circumstances, especially in regions bordering on the large territorial principalities of the peninsula. The unity of the pontifical territory found its ideal framework in the so-called Egidian constitutions (from the name of Cardinal Gil [*Egidius*] Albornoz), put in place in the 14th century, but the effect of which, at the time, was not of long duration. They divided the Italian lands of the Church into six principal districts (the Marches of Ancona, the duchy of Spoleto, Romagna, the Patrimony of St. Peter in Tuscany, Campagna and Maremma, and Benevento), which underwent a number of modifications up until the 19th century. In each of the provinces, a rector represented pontifical authority: he was supposed to be assisted by a parliament made up of representatives of the clergy, of the nobility, and of the cities, as well as a treasurer dependent on the Apostolic Camera but whose district did not always coincide with that of the rector. The parliament never functioned except in the Marches of Ancona, and the crisis of the papacy during the Great Schism hardly favored the permanent installation of papal authority. Circumstances intervened which entailed the withdrawal of some zones from the jurisdiction of the rector in order to place them under the authority of a cardinal legate, that is, a figure supposed to represent the pope in person and who communicated directly with him. Such was the case, for example, for Bologna (first in the second half of the 14th century, and for good beginning in 1429), and then for Perugia under the pontificate of Martin V. The powers of these legates were often challenged by the communal autonomies, and it was not until nearly the 16th century that they truly acquired a local political role.

By the end of the 15th century, the situation had changed very little since the time of Martin V's pontificate. A significant amount of land was still *mediate subjecta*, that is, subject to the authority of vicars or of great feudatories capable of counteracting the authority of the pope. Practically speaking, the communal autonomies excluded the papal representative from government. Some popes, especially SIXTUS IV della Rovere, even created new seigniories that tended to enlarge the indirect domain. It was only in Rome that we see a progressive decline in communal authority to the advantage of the pope, who appointed the governor and the most important local functionaries. In short, until to the end of the century, the lands of the Church retained their composite reality, characterized by a burgeoning development of the local autonomies and thereby favoring an extraordinary season of the arts in the lordly courts (Ferrara, Urbino).

Charles VIII's descent into Italy opened an era of intervention on the part of the primary monarchies of the Continent, who fought with one another over their predominance in Europe. Cesare Borgia's attempts to carve out for himself a State in Romagna during the pontificate of his father, ALEXANDER VI, were brought to nothing by JULIUS II. The latter succeeded in taking back for the Church Ferrara and all the lands of Romagna, the possession of which was contested by Venice (1510). Two years later, he would secure recognition of the rights of the papacy over Parma, Piacenza, and Reggio. Francis I's intervention upset these acquisitions for a time, but the final victory of the Imperials would confirm the position of the Holy See on the political map of Italy. The end of the Renaissance saw the last great concessions by the pope in favor of near relations: in 1546, PAUL III gave his son, Pier Luigi Farnese, Parma and Piacenza, elevated to the status of duchies; the Church thus lost them forever, her rights never being recognized by the powers of the 18th century, when the Farnese family's male line died out. But after Paul III, with varying degrees of willingness, the popes were subjected to Spanish domination. This domination became definitive in 1557 at the end of a disastrous war that forced PAUL IV to accept the conditions of Philip II. And the situation was confirmed by the treaty of Cateau-Cambrésis (3 April 1559), which left the field open to the Spanish in Italy. The Papal State became a second-class state. The religious crisis, especially in the German lands, was transformed into a means of permanent blackmail against the Holy See. Henceforth, the independence of the Papal State and the problem of the Italian balance of power would never fail to weigh on the pope's decisions. And even if the powers had no desire to change the situation on the peninsula, they hoped to influence the pope in such a way that he could be used for their own ends. Whence the struggles during conclaves, the importance in Roman life of diplomatic representatives, and the more or less overt attachment of a large part of the Sacred College and the prelacy to one party or another.

Beginning in the second half of the 16th century, the popes attempted above all not to lose by prescription the vaunted rights of the Church on lands given in hereditary concession to families. The weakening of Spain at the end of the century even left the field open for the recuperation of Ferrara, upon the death of the last duke of the house of Este in 1597, and then for that of Urbino, in 1625, even before Francesco Maria della Rovere passed away (1631). The particular conditions for the return of Ferrara and Urbino to the pontifical domain saw the land of the former made into a legation, and that of the latter entrusted to a governor from the ranks of the cardinals. Recuperation of the enclave of Castro and Ronciglione, raised to a duchy by Paul III for Pier Luigi Farnese's heirs, was settled in 1649, at the end of an economic and military war that lasted nearly ten years. This latter operation set what were almost the definitive boundaries of the Papal State until the end of the 18th century.

In this framework, which was stable from then on, administrative centralization was strengthened through the slow assimilation of local autonomies; despite the fracas of declarations, timid efforts toward assimilation can be followed from the time of the pontificate of PIUS V (1566–72). But it was only in 1704, for example, that the subjects of the Roman barons were finally brought under the jurisdiction of the Congregation for Good Government, whose responsibility in fiscal matters over the totality of the State had been established twenty years earlier. Ties between the ruling class, a class regularly reinforced by the families of successive popes, and the great feudal landowners were so tight that the efforts of rigorist popes at the end of the 17th century were unsuccessful until after nepotism had been done away with once and for all and the venality of a certain number of offices had been suppressed.

The 18th century, marked by the realization that the Papal State lagged economically behind the rest of Europe, was also the century in which the political role of the supreme pontiff was more or less deliberately ignored by the other powers. The positions taken by Pope CLEMENT XI in favor of the Bourbons in the war of the Spanish succession were at the origin of an armed conflict with Emperor Charles III, who had had no scruples about invading the papal land of Comacchio, on the borders of the republic of Venice. The poorly equipped and badly commanded papal army was quickly routed, and the invasion of the territory of the ecclesiastical state forced the pope to sign, in 1709, a humiliating peace treaty that provisionally confirmed the transfer of Comacchio. The rights of the papacy over Parma, and over Naples and Sicily, were not mentioned in the treaty of Utrecht in 1713, just as no guarantee was foreseen for the Catholics in the lands ceded to England (Minorca) and Prussia (Gelderland). Diplomatically, a deep rift was opened between the traditional methods of papal diplomacy (threats and exhortations, excommunications and appeals) and the real forces capable of upholding them. Rome gave up military defense against the great powers. At the time of the war of the Austrian succession, the Papal State was crossed by the troops of the warring factions, and Spanish and Austrians went so far as to wage a

battle under the walls of Velletri without the pope having any power to intervene (1744). The general peace that characterized the second half of the century allowed successive pontiffs (from BENEDICT XIV to PIUS VI) to devote themselves with greater care to the better management of a Papal State that had no dearth of either ferment or new initiatives on the part of prelates as well as of common citizens and men of letters. Despite the exuberance, at the end of the century the Papal State appeared to observers to be on the verge of collapse, so far was its reality from that of the rest of Europe.

The consequences of the French Revolution for the institutional framework of Rome were suspended until the time of the armed intervention of the Directory in Italy. The only exception was Avignon and the Comtat Venaissin, which proclaimed the demise of the pontifical authority and then voted to be annexed to France (12 June 1790). After the conquest of Milan in 1796, General Bonaparte successively occupied Bologna, Ferrara, and Ravenna and announced his intention to descend on Rome. First stopped by an armistice signed at Bologna, the French troops, fearing the assistance the papal government was seeking in Austria and England, occupied Ancona and then Perugia. The treaty of Tolentino (19 February 1797) put an end to the invasion, but the pope had to cede Avignon and the Comtat Venaissin to France, as well as Bologna, Ferrara, and Romagna, and to pay an enormous tribute for which a great part of the silver in Roman churches was melted. The assassination of General Duphot in the French embassy in Rome (28 December 1797) was the pretext seized upon by the Directory for occupying Rome, where a provisional government, proclaimed on 15 February the following year, declared the fall of the temporal power, the protection of the pope and of religion, and the arrival of the Republic. The same day, Pius VI was led away a prisoner, first to Tuscany and then to Valence, where he died on 29 August 1799. In September 1798, the troops of the king of Naples put an end to the Roman Republic and occupied the city while the English were at Civitavecchia and the Austrians replaced the French in the Legations and in the Marches. General opinion held that the Papal State had been wiped off the map, just as the republic of Venice had been.

The defeat of the Austrian forces and the election of a new pope (PIUS VII) allowed a restoration of papal authority, and thus of the Papal State, under the suspicion-laden protection of Austria and Naples. A period of calm, characterized essentially by the reforms introduced into the administration by the pope and the secretary of state, Consalvi, in order to confront a dramatic situation, was ensured by the drawing up of the concordat with France and by Pius VII's trip to Paris to crown Napoleon Bonaparte emperor. But Napoleon's hegemonic designs quickly led to a *de facto* occupation of Ancona in 1805, of Civitavecchia in 1806, of the

Marches in 1807, and finally of Rome in 1808, where it would not be until eighteen months later that a State Council would be created to "recast the constitution." After the abduction of the pope by French troops (5–6 July 1809), the Council governed under the watchful eye of the Paris government until 17 February 1810, the date of the *senatus consultum* that united Rome and the Papal State with the French Empire. The northern provinces had already been annexed to the kingdom of Italy, while Umbria and Latium were directly attached to the empire and divided into two departments: that of the Tiber, with Rome as its administrative center, and that of Trasimeno, whose administrative center was Spoleto. Rome was proclaimed the second capital of the empire and became the title of the hereditary prince. At the moment when the fate of the French forces was being decided in the north of Europe, Murat, king of Naples, sent Neapolitan troops into Rome (25 November 1813) to replace the French garrison, and in January 1814 he installed a "governor general of the Roman States." The liberation of the pope by Napoleon (10 March 1814), accompanied by a complete recognition of his sovereignty, destroyed Murat's plans. Pius VII returned to his capital on 24 May 1814, intent on reclaiming his States.

The restoration of the old pontifical state almost in its entirety had not been attained in the sense that the redrawing of lines on the map of Europe had caused a number of smaller states to disappear, in both Italy and the German lands. But favorable circumstances were not wanting: Murat's adventurous behavior, the divisions among powers, the skill of Cardinal Consalvi, and, above all, the very nature of the sovereign and of his rights, which some Christian and conservative monarchs could not treat as those of just any prince of the Rhine. Finally, Pius VII found himself with a territory which was that of the 18th century with the exception of Avignon and the Comtat Venaissin, the loss of which the pope did not fail to protest solemnly (4 September 1815), although the protest was not renewed. The history of the restored Papal State is inextricably linked to the history of the liberal movement and to the formation of Italian unity. When the revolution broke out in Paris in 1830, the Roman government, completely intent on the restoration and on the preservation of positions it had lost during the previous decades, appeared singularly isolated in the context of Europe. And the pontificate of GREGORY XVI, a pope who, though reactionary, was superior in a number of ways, pointed out the lack of comprehension, if not the condemnation, of the whole system of papal government. The day after his election (2 February 1831), uprisings in the States of central Italy and the cities in the northern part of the Papal State brought on armed intervention from Austria in Bologna and Ancona. France was worried, and demanded the evacuation of the Legations and the delivery, in the name of the great powers, of a memo-

randum informing the Holy See of a series of reforms to be undertaken: the admission of laypersons to public functions, a judicial reorganization based on a *motu proprio* of 6 July 1816 (organic law on the "organization of public administration") that had never been applied, the organization of representation from the provinces, elected municipalities, the creation of a state audit office. Some reforms went into effect only following a new armed intervention by Austria in the Legations and by France in Ancona, after a first return of papal troops to the Legations had stirred up new troubles. The disdainful opposition to change that had characterized the pontificate of Gregory XVI was overturned by the election of his successor, PIUS IX.

The numerous reforms enacted by the new pope only made the situation of the Papal State, and especially that of Rome, more unstable. In November 1848, his prime minister, Pellegrino Rossi, was assassinated, and at the end of the month Pius IX secretly reached Gaeta, where he was received by Ferdinand II of Naples, the thorn in the side of the Italian liberals. While the secretary of state was appealing to the chanceries to ask for the assistance of the states that had signed the treaty of Vienna, the Romans, after trying to get the pope to return, convoked a constituent assembly that proclaimed the Republic on 9 February 1849. At the end of one stormy session, the constituent French National Assembly decided on military intervention, not without the ulterior motive of precluding a maneuver by Austria, which had victoriously freed itself from the Piedmont attack on the battlefield of Novara. The French general Oudinot entered Rome on 3 July 1849, but the pope did not return to the city until 12 April 1850, after abandoning all the concessions from the first part of his pontificate and giving his support to an authoritarian police government. The French troops stationed inside Rome ensured its independence, just as the Austrian army controlled the Legations, which it did not evacuate until 1859. This state of siege highlighted the precariousness of the permanence of a temporal domain. Such a problem, which had had few repercussions on public opinion at the beginning of the century, was now becoming a complex international issue for which Catholics mobilized and sought to exert pressure on their respective governments. In Rome, the violent events of 1849 persuaded the pope to refuse all compromises on the temporal question and to accept only the advice of the intransigents.

From the time of the congress of Paris (1856), the political unity of Italy begins to seem concretely realizable. Austria, which occupied a large part of Italy's territory, was pushed back in 1859 to the northeast of the peninsula, and ended up losing it in 1866 after being beaten at Sadowa by Bismarck's troops. The Austrian departure from the territories of the Legations in June 1859 gave rise to the reconnection, acknowledged by the great pow-

Papal States in the 16th Century

■ Papal territory ca. 1500

■ Claimed or controlled by the Papal States by 1512

1506 Date of acquisition by Rome, where known

1506 Date of autonomy or independence from Rome

REPUBLIC OF VENICE

DUCHY OF MILAN

DUCHY OF MANTUA

Verona

Venice

Po

Mantua

Piacenza

Duchy of Parma 1512 *1545*

Parma

Taro

Barcetto

Modena

Duchy of Modena 1512 *1527*

Duchy of Ferrara *1598*

Bologna

Massa *1527*

REPUBLIC OF GENOA

Republic of Bologna 1506

Ravenna

Romagna 1504

Rimini

San Marino Papacy recognized independence 1631

Adriatic Sea

Pesaro
Fano

Senigallia

Ancona

Duchy of Urbino *1625*

Camerino

Florence

REPUBLIC OF FLORENCE

Pisa

REPUBLIC OF PISA

Siena

REPUBLIC OF SIENA

Ombrone

DUCHY OF PIOMBINO

Piombino

Republic of Perugia 1506

Assisi

Marches

Spoleto

Narni

Norcia

Pitigliano

PAPAL STATES

Pescara

Rome

Tiber

Sora

Arpino

KINGDOM OF NAPLES

Terracina

Benevento

Capua

Volturno

Tyrrhenian Sea

N

FRANCE

Montauban

Orange

Rhône

Arles

Durance

Aix

Mediterranean Sea

0   100 km

0   100 miles

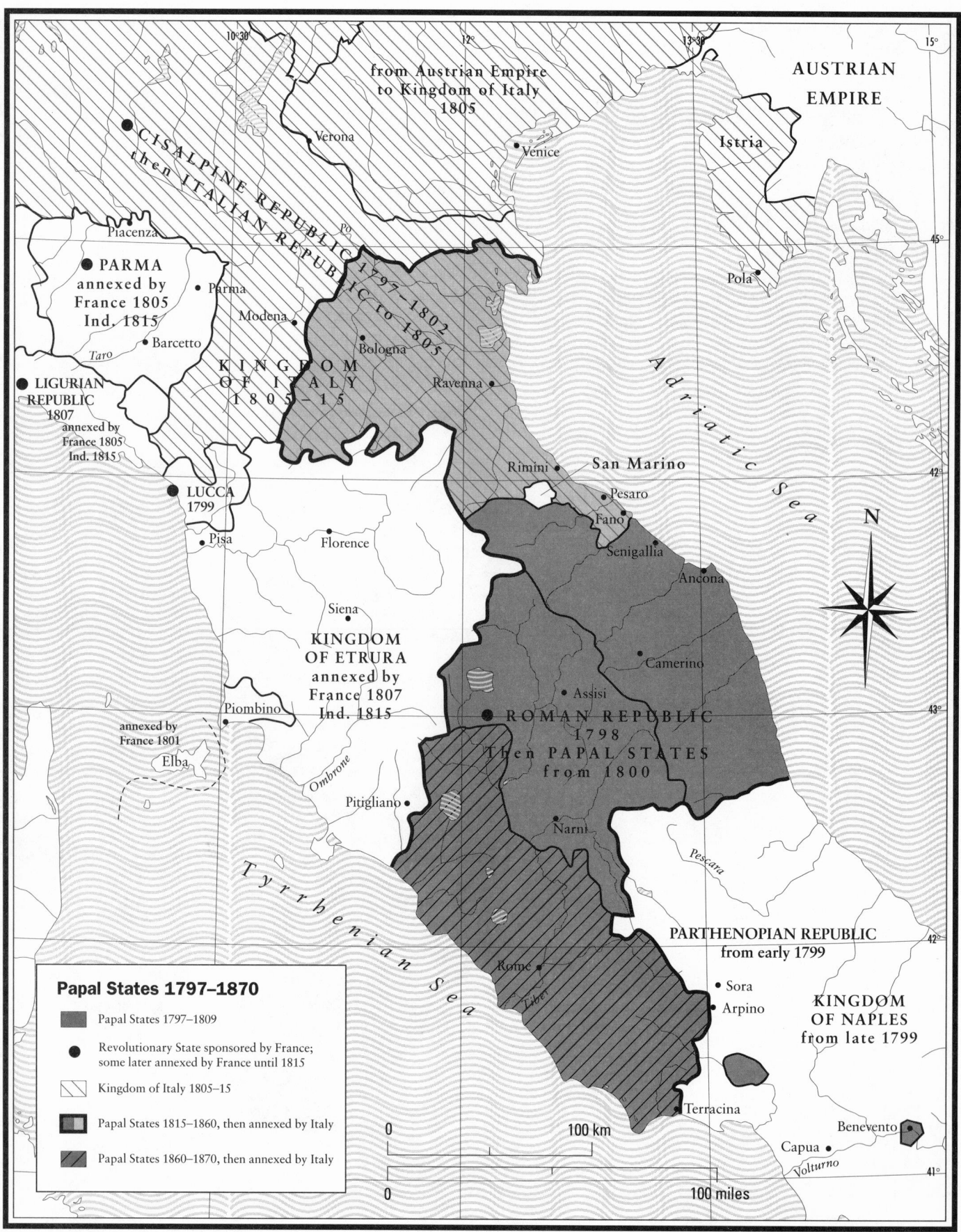

AUSTRIAN EMPIRE

from Austrian Empire
to Kingdom of Italy
1805

Istria

Verona

Venice

Pola

CISALPINE REPUBLIC
then ITALIAN REPUBLIC 1797–1802
IC to 1805

Piacenza

PARMA
annexed by
France 1805
Ind. 1815

Parma

Modena

Barcetto

Taro

Po

Bologna

Ravenna

KINGDOM
OF ITALY
1805–15

Adriatic Sea

LIGURIAN
REPUBLIC
1807
annexed by
France 1805
Ind. 1815

LUCCA
1799

Pisa

Florence

Rimini

San Marino

Pesaro

Fano

Senigallia

Ancona

N

Siena

KINGDOM
OF ETRURA
annexed by
France 1807
Ind. 1815

Camerino

annexed by
France 1801

Elba

Piombino

Assisi

ROMAN REPUBLIC
1798
Then PAPAL STATES
from 1800

Ombrone

Pitigliano

Narni

Pescara

Tyrrhenian Sea

Rome

Tiber

PARTHENOPIAN REPUBLIC
from early 1799

Sora

Arpino

KINGDOM
OF NAPLES
from late 1799

Terracina

Benevento

Capua

Volturno

Papal States 1797–1870

■ Papal States 1797–1809

● Revolutionary State sponsored by France;
some later annexed by France until 1815

▨ Kingdom of Italy 1805–15

▨ Papal States 1815–1860, then annexed by Italy

▨ Papal States 1860–1870, then annexed by Italy

0   100 km

0   100 miles

ers, of Romagna to the kingdom of Sardinia in March 1860. Umbria was lost a few weeks later, and at the end of the year the Marches fell in their turn, after the Sardinian army had crushed the pontifical Zouaves at Castelfidardo (29 September). And when the young kingdom of Italy was constituted in 1861, it was clear that only France kept the Papal States from being totally occupied. From that time on, they were reduced to Rome and the Patrimony of St. Peter, the borders of which were defined only by an agreement between the French general and the Italian general who found themselves face to face on the terrain itself.

Italy took the initiative. On 27 March 1861, the young National Parliament met in Turin and proclaimed Rome the capital of the kingdom. And when attempts to come to a direct understanding with Pius IX failed, the royal government proposed that Napoleon III be its intermediary with the pope. The emperor, who had to reckon with the internal situation in France as well as with the international importance of the matter, tried to avoid the problem. Finally, a compromise formula was found: it was the convention of 15 September 1864, to which both France and Italy subscribed without the pope's being consulted. By the terms of this convention, Italy agreed not to attack what remained of the pope's territory; France was to withdraw its troops gradually over a period of two years; and the Italian government was to allow the creation of an international papal army. An invasion of Roman territory by Garibaldi volunteers in 1867, encouraged behind the scenes by the Italian government, was repelled at the gates of Rome, at Mentana, by a French expeditionary body that had just disembarked in Civitavecchia, joined by the pope's regular troops (3 November 1867). This energetic stance on the part of the French government was a direct blow to the determination of the Italian government, convinced of the legitimacy of its claims to Rome. Nevertheless, the Italian government could not count on a general insurrection by Romans in favor of the new kingdom, as had been the case in other regions: the apathy of the masses echoed interparty divisions. The Franco-Prussian war extricated the Italian government from its difficulty. Preparations for the conflict had led French diplomacy to request a military alliance with the Italians against Prussia: the price demanded (or rather the inadmissible condition that would enable the Italians to avoid making a negative reply) was abandonment of Rome. Napoleon III refused to pay the price and ended up facing the army of the Confederation of North Germany and its allies alone. His defeat put an end to the Second Empire. The pope's temporal power survived him exactly sixteen days.

On 20 September 1870, Italian troops entered Rome through a breach opened by artillery in a section of the Aurelian walls, near Porta Pia and bordering a property belonging to the Bonaparte family (the present-day seat of the French embassy to the Holy See). The royal army was supposed to avoid useless violence. After symbolic resistance, to which Pius IX quickly put an end, there were sixteen victims. The Italian troops had received an order to stop at the entrance to the Leonine city, that is, they were not supposed to cross the Ponte Sant'Angelo. The threatening demeanor of the population of the Borgo persuaded the secretary of state, Antonelli, to allow them to go as far as the Vatican Palace, where the pope had locked himself in. After the plebiscite that reconnected Rome and Latium to Italy (2 October), the Papal State ceased to exist. The Law of Guarantees, which ensured the independence of the pope, gave him no sovereignty over the land left under his control. Hope for a restoration was held out for a while by the conviction of a few that the Catholic powers would force Italy into a settlement. Such was far from the case. Nevertheless, a few voices were raised in Germany during the World War I suggesting punishment of Italy by reconstituting a micro-State for the pope with an opening to the sea. These suggestions were remembered at the time of the negotiations for the Lateran Pacts.

François-Charles Uginet

Bibliography

Caravale, M., and Caracciolo, A. *Lo Stato pontificio da Martino V a Pio IX*, Turin, 1978 (*Storia d'Italia* under the direction of G. Galasso, 14).

Coppa, F. J. *Cardinal Giacomo Antonelli and Papal Politics in European Affairs*, Albany, N.Y., 1990.

Prodi, P. *The Papal Prince: One Body and Two Souls: The Papal Monarchy in Early Modern Europe*, New York, 1987.

PAPISM. The term has chiefly been used, pejoratively, since the Reformation to denote total submission to the pope as head of the Church. In a more moderate sense, "papism" is akin to "ultramontanism," according to which the pope's jurisdictional primacy and dogmatic infallibility represent the superiority of the spiritual (*sacerdotum*) over the temporal (*regnum*). This opposition has continued throughout the history of the papacy. Every history of the popes invariably begins with the Jew Simon, the son of Jonah, whom Jesus surnamed Peter (in Aramaic *kepha*, or rock) and thus placed him at the head of his closest followers, the apostles: "You are Peter, and on this rock I will build my church, and the gates of Hades will not prevail against it" (Mt 16:18). The surname rapidly became Peter's true proper name and in the end completely supplanted his original name.

Peter was neither the founder nor the head of the Christian community in Rome. Yet his stay in Rome and his death there are generally acknowledged to be historical facts. We have little reliable information on the leaders of the Roman Church over the first two centuries.

The government of local Churches, originally collegial, gave way to a monarchical episcopate, but in Rome this development was slower than elsewhere. Among the Roman bishops, specific consciousness of reponsibility over the Churches outside Rome and Italy does not appear until the 3rd century. From that time, in fact, the bishop of Rome often took on the role of arbiter when the local Churches could not settle differences by themselves. Nevertheless, that is a long way from indicating a claim to primacy on the part of the bishop of Rome.

It was chiefly reference to Peter as founder of the Roman Christian community that caused the episcopal see of Rome to be thought of as the center of the Western Church, and, later, of the Eastern Church as well. But other factors came into play. "Beyond the obvious cultural, ideological, and political eminence of the city and the aura surrounding the 'head' of the Empire, the unrivaled role played by Rome in the West seems to have been a determining factor in the development of the theological basis for instituting the bishop of Rome" (N. Brox).

As it evolved, theological thinking came to justify Jesus' having instituted the papacy by referring especially to Mt 16:18–19 and to Jn 21:15–17. Even though Jesus' words have little historical authenticity, a synthesis of all the biblical passages referring to Peter makes clear that the apostle held a privileged place. But we cannot conclude therefrom that Peter was appointed to lead the universal Church. It is not possible to speak of the papacy in the strict sense of the term until the middle of the 3rd century. If the example of VICTOR I (188–99) and the controversy over the dating of Easter still cause us to hesitate, it is an established fact that STEPHEN I (254–7), during the conflict over the validity of the baptism administered by heretics, justified his decisive position by referring to the Petrine succession and, basing his arguments on Mt 16:17–18, claimed a preeminence that not all the Churches recognized. At issue here, however, was not a fundamental debate on the PRIMACY and the episcopate, but at most a case of rivalry between the Roman and African Churches: on that occasion, the *Sedes romana* was simply demanding acknowledgment of its traditional authority. The ecumenical COUNCIL of Nicaea (325) brought the three sees that enjoyed primacy, Antioch, Rome, and ALEXANDRIA, back to an "old custom." Even Augustine, bishop of Hippo (d. 430), was still unaware of the absolute primacy of the bishop of Rome, soon to be drawn as a conclusion from the reading of Mt 16:18.

Though LEO I (440–61) was not present at the council of Chalcedon (451), he nevertheless exerted through his theologians a decisive influence on its Christological definitions. Leo was the first bishop of Rome to claim primacy of jurisdiction (*plenitudo potestatis*) over the universal Church, by virtue of his being heir to the power of Peter (*vicarius Petri*). But he encountered sharp resistance from the Eastern Church, which upheld the principle of the patriarchate, according to which Antioch and Alexandria were the Eastern patriarchates and Rome the sole patriarchate of the West. During the period of the great invasions, Leo I's political activities increased the prestige of the papacy. A little later, GELASIUS I (492–6) interpreted the notion of Roman primacy in the light of the famous theory of the two powers. The temporal and the spiritual were to be considered on the one hand as two quite distinct domains, but on the other as completely indissociable since both emanated from Christ, the temporal being, however, always subordinate to the spiritual. From this theory, SYMMACHUS, (498–514) drew a conclusion that was to have far-reaching effect: the holder of the episcopal see of Rome can be judged by no one (*prima sedes a nemine iudicatur*). By instituting the title "servus servorum Dei," GREGORY I (590–604) expressed the notion of ministry as attached to the pontifical office. This bishop, imbued with awareness of his responsibilities, was so animated by missionary spirit that he succeeded in spreading Christian teaching among the Arian Lombards and Franks, and even among the Angles. In the 7th century, Scottish, Irish, and Anglo-Saxon monks were still making the long journey to the Continent in order to evangelize, to reform, and, it should be borne in mind, to "romanize," that is, bind the Churches to Rome.

The conversion of the Franks to Christianity around 500 under the leadership of Clovis resulted a few centuries later in the creation of the Christian kingdom of the Franks, whose emperor, Charlemagne, was crowned by Pope LEO III on Christmas Day, 800, and vowed as a *patricius Romanorum* to protect Rome and the Papal States. In the 11th and 12th centuries, this imperial coronation served as a basis for the idea that the Byzantine Empire had passed to the Franks and then to the Germans by the grace of the papacy.

The so-called Gregorian reform, named after GREGORY VII (1073–85), represented first and foremost an ecclesiological turning point, since the pope henceforth would play an important new role in the government of the universal Church. If the popes of the first millennium had, with a few exceptions, confined their attention to the ecclesial communities of Rome and the Roman ecclesiastical province, from the 11th century on their duties spread to lands well beyond Italy and other neighboring European countries.

The numerous conflicts between certain popes and the highest temporal authorities (emperors and kings) grew out of Gregory VII's conviction that pontifical power alone emanated directly from God, whereas the emperor and king were subordinate to the pope and owed him obedience. As one might expect, this pope claimed primacy within the Church. Gregory's other grand design was to ensure the freedom of the Church vis-à-vis the temporal powers, especially in purely ecclesiastical matters such as the investiture of a bishop (the INVESTITURE CONTROVERSY).

In the 13th century, these theological principles, along with others, were recast as juridical formulas. The canonical collections that were made during the time of GREGORY IX and BONIFACE VIII were combined with the DECRETUM completed in 1134 by Gratian, a monk who taught in Bologna, to form the *Corpus iuris canonici*, which remained in force until 1918.

From the middle of the 12th century, the Romans continually tried to shake off the power the pope wielded over their city and, like the cities of northern Italy, to become self-governing. These efforts had only short-lived success over the next two centuries. The most tragic episode concerned the tribune of the people Cola di Rienzo (d. 1354). It is noteworthy that both the Roman city government and the college of cardinals were known as SENATE.

Under INNOCENT III (1198–1216), the papacy, after violent conflicts with the temporal rulers, especially the Staufen emperors Frederick I Barbarossa and Frederick II, claimed supreme sovereignty over the Church and the world. Beginning with that pope, it became customary to call the bishop of Rome not only *vicarius Petri* but also *vicarius Christi*. Boniface VIII (1294–1303) declared in the bull *Unam sanctam* of 18 November 1302 that the pope had two swords, one spiritual and the other temporal, and that the king wielded his own temporal sword solely "on the order and with the permission" of the spiritual authority. The spiritual power established the temporal power and also revoked it, if necessary: "It is absolutely necessary to the salvation of all human creatures," so went the terse formulation, "to submit to the bishop of Rome." Having reached the pinnacle of power, this pope fell all the lower; as one of his contemporaries neatly put it, "He came to power like a fox, reigned like a lion, and died like a dog." In the end, political reality had triumphed. This would be made abundantly clear when the popes, having been heavily dependent on the kingdom of France, in particular on Philip IV the Fair, took up residence for several decades in Avignon (1309–77). At that time, the papacy lost much of its political influence on the nascent national states, and its religious authority was also impaired. The centralism of the CURIA and its niggling fiscality inflicted greater damage on the Church itself.

Scholars like Marsilius of Padua and William of Ockham shook the papal theocracy to its foundations by denying any biblical basis to the papal primacy and claiming the council as the highest authority of the Church. At the diet of Frankfurt (1338), Emperor Louis of Bavaria published a law declaring that it no longer belonged to the pope to take part in the election of the emperor since imperial dignity was universal and imperial power came directly from God. The pope's return from Avignon was followed by two papal SCHISMS, and then a third after the synod of Pisa (1409), whereupon the only solution to the decades-long crisis (1378–1417) appeared to lie in a return to the former constitution of the Church. The conflict between the two extremes, papism and conciliarism, became more turbulent at the council of Constance (1414–18) and, to an even greater degree, at the council of Basel (1431–49). At first, it seemed as though the papacy was in an inferior position with respect to the council, but it reasserted itself, though in constant fear of a resurgence of conciliarism. It was largely because of these endless disputes that the ecumenical council of TRENT (1545–63) was so late in taking place and that the Reformation unleashed by the Augustinian friar Martin Luther, devoted to the radical attacking of "the Roman papacy, work of the devil," was able to spread ever wider. The Roman pontiffs, full of enthusiasm for the Renaissance and humanism but tepid in their zeal for the evangelical renewal of the Church, misjudged the gravity of the times and bore their share of responsibility for the rupture of the unity of the Western Church.

Most of the decrees issued at the council of Trent have to be seen as a tardy reaction to the Lutheran Reformation. In its wake, the papal centralism that had taken shape beginning in the high Middle Ages expanded both in practice and on the canonical level. In particular, it manifested itself in the leadership of the Church (the nunciatures were Rome's external representation), in the liturgy (the breviary and missal were standardized), and in CANON LAW. With "battle lines drawn" (*acies ordinata*), the Church was able, it is true, to emerge relatively unscathed by the dangers born of absolutism and the ENLIGHTENMENT. But on the other hand, the Church failed to respond to the demands of the era, which was in a state of flux. The movement of the national Churches in France (GALLICANISM), in Germany (Febronianism), and in Austria (JOSEPHISM) set strict limits on the desires and actions of the pope, especially in the areas of school and family. Only in the Papal States could the pope still reign as an absolute monarch.

Beginning in 1798, the FRENCH REVOLUTION, which brought in its aftermath the secularization of ecclesiastical possessions, not only led to the decline of the Ancien Regime and the imperial Church but also placed the Papal States in constant peril. The Congress of Vienna (1814–15) raised once again the issue of a religious restoration even extending to the restitution of the PAPAL STATES, and it strengthened the opposition of the pope to the movement toward Italian unity and, more generally, modern currents of thought (democracy, liberalism, socialism), condemned by GREGORY XVI in the encyclical *Mirari vos* (1832) and by PIUS IX in the encyclical *Quanta cura* (1864) and its annex, the *Syllabus errorum*. The council of VATICAN I, (1869–70), by proclaiming the dogmas of the primacy of jurisdiction and of the infallibility of the pope, created dissensions within the Church and provoked reactions of rejection outside it. The permanent loss of the Papal States that followed Italian unification in 1870 threw the papacy back on its spiritual authority alone. Nevertheless, Pius IX, a pope of narrowly conservative ideas, sought to compensate for the loss of his temporal power by making excessive spiritual demands, which provoked fresh conflicts with the nation-states. The struggles known in Germany and Switzerland as KULTURKAMPF ended with the Church asserting itself in its domain, but reinforced the anticlerical trends favoring greater separation between Church and State.

Only with LEO XIII (1878–1903) was the papacy little by little able to make a connection with its era, as the social ENCYCLICAL Rerum novarum (1891) demonstrates. It is clear, too, from the number of circular letters (forty-six encyclicals in all) written by him, that this pope saw the encyclical as a publishing instrument well suited to positive teaching.

At the beginning of the twentieth century, when the forces of "MODERNISM" were striving to reduce the growing gap between faith and theology on the one hand and science and culture on the other, the papacy felt compelled to take the strongest possible counteraction. PIUS X (1903–14), a man of great personal piety, was easily influenced in matters of Church policy; with the Ancien Regime as model, he sought to restore the close cooperation between Church and State that existed before the Revolution. That is why he violently condemned the radical separation between Church and State achieved in France in 1905. All attempts from within at opening up the Church and its theology were severely repressed. From 1910, anyone aspiring to the care of souls or to teaching was obliged to take an antimodernist oath committing him or her to uncritical acceptance of Church tradition.

BENEDICT XV (1914–22) put an end to this shameful hunting down of modernists, which was mainly led by a prelate of the Curia, Umberto Benigni, in an atmosphere of excessive zeal and intrigue. During the First World War, Benedict XV's proposals at the time of the peace talks were stillborn. At Pentecost, 1918, the Codex iuris canonici came into force, the first juridical CODE valid for the whole Catholic Church. In his encyclical on the missions, Maximum illud (1919), the pope called for respect for the different cultures of the MISSION countries, thus breaking with the latinization that had been customary up to that time.

PIUS XI (1922–39) strove on the basis of CONCORDATS to guarantee the diverse national Churches an original status. In 1929, the Lateran pacts at long last settled the "Roman question," which had for decades hung over relations between the Vatican and the Italian government. A concordat was promulgated in 1933 between the Holy See and the Reich under Adolf Hitler, but it turned out to be a two-edged sword. The encyclical Mit brennender Sorge of 1937 publicly aired the grievances hitherto usually presented through diplomatic channels, and denounced the anticlericalism of the National-Socialists. In an even stronger manner, the pope stigmatized Bolshevik Russia for its hostility to Christianity and the Church.

The Second WORLD WAR and its unspeakable consequences marked the long pontificate of PIUS XII (1939–58). Anxious, as head of the Catholic Church and temporal ruler of the Holy See, to observe strict neutrality, the pope remained silent when human rights were massively violated and even while the genocide of the Jewish people was being perpetrated. Before becoming pope, Pacelli had been a wise diplomat in the service of the Church and a theologian of broad culture; his positions on almost all the urgent questions of his time had shown the way to be followed. With him ends the "Pian era," inaugurated by Pius IX and characterized by a strong attachment to Church tradition.

In contrast to his immediate predecessors, Pope JOHN XXIII (1958–63) exercised his lofty responsibility by placing emphasis on the pastoral rather than the dogmatic. This is strongly apparent in his encyclical letters on social problems (Mater et magistra, 1961) and on peace (Pacem in terris, 1963). Among the great merits of this pope, who was widely respected beyond the Church, was the convening of the council of VATICAN II (1962–5), of which he lived to see only the first session.

Pope PAUL VI (1963–78) brought the council begun by his predecessor to a satisfactory end and then had to work through the difficult phase of the carrying out of the conciliar decrees. His efforts and achievements in the area of the general renewal of the Church were unfortunately eclipsed by the encyclical Humanae vitae (1968), criticized for the rigid position it adopted on methods of birth control, and by another encyclical, Sacri caelibatus (1967), also rejected by many because of the uncompromising way it upheld the obligation of celibacy.

JOHN PAUL II, who has reigned as supreme pontiff since 1978, is the first Pole to sit on the throne of St. Peter in Rome; from the beginning, he has shown an extremely conservative attitude in theological and canonical matters. The ecumenical movement seems to be suspended, as far as the Catholic Church is concerned. On the other hand, there is no mistaking the exceptional interest and intense commitment manifested by this pope with regard to all the serious social problems of our times, especially in the developing nations. By means of his various TRAVELS to many countries, John Paul II has borne witness to the universality of the Catholic Church.

Georg Denzler

[PASCHAL] *(d. ca. 692). Antipope elected in 687.*

Nothing is known about him except his tortuous attempts to be elected pope, yet his story is highly instructive about contemporary social and psychological conditions indispensable for attaining the highest religious office in the West. He was archdeacon under CONON (686–7). When that pope died, he became the candidate of the Roman clergy. He was anxious above all to defend his own interests, even if it meant agreeing to the election of an "Oriental"—in fact, a "foreigner"—as long as he was a member of the diocesan clergy. Knowing that Conon's days were numbered, Paschal obtained the support of the exarch, John Platyn, in exchange for a promise of a hundred pounds of gold. The imperial administration supported his candidature against THEODORE, the candidate of the *militia*. He occupied a section of the papal palace of the Lateran, but, feeling that his chances were nil, again appealed to the exarch of RAVENNA, who thereupon recognized SERGIUS, the "third man," as the only one who could resolve the dilemma between two utterly similar candidates. Paschal was accused of magic and spent the last five years of his life imprisoned in a monastery.

It is clear that at the end of the 7th century rival factions were continually at loggerheads, using every means at their disposal—including extortion—to gain control of a prestigious post; the exarch still tried to intervene, in the name of the emperor, but to no avail.

Jean Durliat

Bibliography

JW, 1, 243.
LP, 1, 369–72.
Bertolini, O. *Roma di fronte a Bisantio e ai Longobardi,* Bologna, 1971, 399–401.
Schwaigerd, G. "Paschal," *LexMa,* 6 (1992), 1753.

PASCHAL I. *(b. 24 January 817, d. 17 May 824). Elected pope on 25 January 817. Buried in Sta. Prassede.*

His cursus before his election to the papal throne was fairly unusual. He had risen to subdeacon when LEO III appointed him abbot of St. Stephen's monastery, near St. Peter's, where he distinguished himself by his pious care of pilgrims. The experience of being in charge of a monastery the chief function of which was to aid foreigners may have marked Paschal as a particularly able candidate for a papacy that was deeply involved on the international level. No sooner had he been elected than Paschal sent Louis the Pious an embassy led by the *nomenculator* Theodore; its purpose was to complete the agreement with the FRANKS begun by STEPHEN IV and devoted to settling relations between the pope and the emperor. This document has come down to us only in 12th-century editions (the canonical collections of Deusdedit and Anselm of Lucca), but it is generally believed to be authentic. It contains a confirmation of Charlemagne's territorial concessions, as well as a series of guarantees of help on the emperor's part should the boundaries of the pope's domains be threatened. These guarantees, however, in no way compromised papal independence in internal Roman affairs.

Nothing is known of the relations between pope and emperor during the six years of Paschal I's pontificate. In 823, Lothair came south to Italy to take possession of the kingdom granted him by his father, Louis, and Paschal invited him to Rome to be crowned emperor. This was a highly significant act from the pontifical point of view, since it expressed the pope's approval of the ascent of the third generation of Carolingians to the imperial throne. Lothair's coronation took place on 5 April 823, Easter Day. But Lothair's presence in Rome also represented an opportunity for those forces in the city and the Roman province who sought to engage in political dialogue with the emperor. Among them was the abbot of Farfa, a monastery traditionally linked to the Carolingians, which was engaged in dispute with Rome over the territorial control of Sabina. He persuaded the emperor to pronounce against papal attempts to make Farfa subject to a tribute, which would have deprived the abbey of the full possession of its lands and made it a mere custodian under papal license. Some have seen this journey of Lothair's as a victory for Paschal, who sought to establish personal relations with the ruler; others have seen it as reflecting a desire on Lothair's part to reaffirm the emperor's role as supreme arbiter of Roman affairs, as would be shown when Lothair presided over a judgment of the dispute between Farfa and the pope. In any case, on this occasion it appears that a group hostile to Paschal took action in Rome. Consisting of members of the aristocracy and of the Lateran, the group sought to take advantage of the emperor's presence to weaken the political role of the pontiff. The latter reacted as soon as Lothair left Rome: two high dignitaries of the Lateran, the *primicerius* Theodore and the *nomenculator* Leo, were accused of *laesa maiestas* with regard to the pope and were blinded and executed. Others were likely exiled. On hearing the news, Emperor Louis appointed a commission to go to Rome to clarify the situation. The pope tried to prevent the investigation by sending LEGATES to Louis in order to assure him that he had had nothing to do with the murders. Nevertheless, the emperor's commissioners made their way to Rome, where they forced Paschal to pronounce a *purgatio per sacramentum*, or public oath of disculpation, before an assembly of twenty-four bishops. Not long after this, the pope died, and Louis and his son were unable to learn the truth. Paschal's funeral took place in a highly tense atmosphere, so tense that his body could not be entombed in St. Peter's. The *LIBER PONTIFICALIS* is silent on the events of 823 and 824, which have come down to us through "Frankish" sources.

Paschal's whole official biography is devoted to depicting a pope who busied himself with enhancing the splendor of Rome and its monuments. The only episode mentioned, one that could be described as "news in brief," concerns the fire that broke out at the *schola Anglorum*, near the Vatican, one night in 817 or 818. The pope personally led the fight against the flames, then supervised the rebuilding of the school in wood, according to the taste of the *Angli*. This gesture of cultural sensitivity can undoubtedly be accounted for by his former activity as abbot of the monastery of St. Stephen, which brought him in contact with foreign communities in Rome.

Like Leo III, Paschal wanted the embellishment of Rome to be a pontifical initiative. Three churches, Sta Prassede, Sta Cecilia, and Sta Maria in Domnica, contain well-preserved mosaics executed during his reign, in which Paschal's monograms and portraits are clearly visible. All this activity obviously provoked conflicts with the Roman aristocracy. Moreover, it is probably not coincidental that, roughly at the time of the clash with the abbot of Farfa, the *Liber pontificalis* recorded donations by the pope to the bishop of Foronovo and to the abbot of S. Salvatore Maggiore near Rieti, each of whom was competing with Farfa for the control of Sabina. We can conclude that Paschal I's conception was of a profoundly autocratic pontificate and that he was supported in this thinking by a large section of the clergy and also, at least until 823, by the emperor. Indeed, within certain limits, the latter profited from a political situation in Rome that was controllable owing to a "strong" pope.

Federico Marazzi

Bibliography

JE, 1, 318–20.

LP, 2, 52–68.

MGH, Ist., 5, 68–71, 528 and 605; *MGH, SS*, 2, 621 and 627–8; *MGH, SS, In usum schol.*, 6, 145–6 and 161–4; *MGH, Cap.*, 1, 352–5.

PL, 98, 579–88; 102, 1085–93; 106, 405–28.

Brezzi, P. *Roma e l'Impero medievale*, Bologna, 1947.

Duchesne, L. *Les Premiers Temps de l'État pontifical*, Paris, 1898.

Krautheimer, R. *Rome: Profile of a City*, Princeton, 1980.

Llewellyn, P. *Rome in the Dark Ages*, London, 1971.

Matthiae, G. *Pittura romana dell'Alto Medioevo*, Rome, 1965, 2nd ed. M. Andaloro, Rome, 1987.

Mordek, H. "Paschal I.," *LexMA*, 6 (1992), 1752.

Noble, T. F. X. *The Republic of St. Peter: The Birth of the Papal State*, 680–825, Philadelphia, 1984.

PASCHAL II. *Rainero (b. Bieda di Galeata, near Ravenna, d. Rome, 21 January 1118). Elected pope in Rome on 13 August 1099, consecrated on 14 August. Buried in St. John Lateran.*

Of modest family background, at a very young age he joined an unidentified monastery, thought to be Benedictine. Commissioned by his abbot, he had already spent some time in Rome when GREGORY VII named him abbot of S. Lorenzo fuori le Mura and, around 1078, CARDINAL priest of S. Clemente (to succeed the excommunicated cardinal Hugo Candidus). URBAN II entrusted Rainero, his faithful supporter, with the important Spanish legation (synodal activity in Toulouse and in Léon, 1090). After Urban's death (29 July 1099), Rainero was elected pope on 13 August 1099, at S. Clemente, under the name Paschal II. The same day he took possession of the Lateran, and on 14 August, he was consecrated in ST. PETER'S by the cardinal bishop of Ostia, assisted by five cardinal bishops. Paschal lacked the strong personality of a leader, being anxious and hesitant when it came to making decisions. Obviously, monastic modesty does not fully account for his resistance to being raised to the papal throne. His pontificate rested on foundations established by his predecessors Gregory VII and Urban II and found its supporters in certain individuals influenced by the Gregorian REFORM. He was less a pioneer than a successor and inheritor.

Shortly after his enthronement came the news that Jerusalem had been captured in the First CRUSADE. Paschal showed the keenest interest in the crusading movement. In 1105, he gave his blessing to the campaign of Bohemond of Tarento, prince of Antioch, against the Byzantine Empire, mistaking what was only a personal expedition for a genuine crusade. The highly political Byzantine emperor, Alexius I, initiated talks concerning the union of the Churches, such as were held under Urban II. They failed, however, because Paschal had set as a prior condition the recognition of Roman primacy. In Germany, Paschal at first leaned on his Gregorian supporters in the southwest, his LEGATE Bishop Gebhard III of Constance and the monks of Hirsau. The position of the ANTIPOPE CLEMENT [III] (Guibert of Ravenna) had been markedly weakened in the last years of Urban II's pontificate. With the help of the NORMANS, Paschal managed to hound him out of the areas immediately surrounding Rome. When Clement [III] died on 8 September 1100 in Civita Castellana, other antipopes came forward to take his place—Thierry (1100), ALBERT (1101), and SILVESTER IV (1105). But they found few supporters and could be eliminated in short order.

Emperor Henry IV (1056–1106) no longer championed these antipopes and sought peace with Paschal. Thenceforth, the quarrel was narrowed down once and for all to the question of investiture. As Henry refused to give up royal investiture with ring and crozier, the rival positions hardened. Paschal saw this investiture as a form of SIMONY. At the SYNOD in the spring of 1102, he reiterated the prohibition of investiture and the excommunication pronounced against Henry IV and his counselors. In 1105, he encouraged Henry V's revolt against his own father, the emperor, and released him from his oath of loyalty. But the pope was soon disillusioned, because Henry V, once he had become king (1106–25), showed the same obstinacy as his father, insisting on his right to investiture. At the synods of Guastalla in 1106, Troyes in 1107, Benevento in 1109, and the Lateran in 1110, the pope repeated the rigorous prohibition of investiture. In the meantime, a solution to the conflict was taking shape thanks to the principle of distinguishing between the spiritual and the temporal aspects of investiture. Ivo of Chartres in particular, and his pupil Hugh de Fleury, had developed the distinction in the *Tractatus de regia potestate et sacerdotali dignitate*, written after 1102 and dedicated to the king of England. The INVESTITURE CONTROVERSY, which pitted King Henry I of England (1100–35) against Archbishop Anselm of Canterbury, was settled at the diet of London (August 1107): The king renounced traditional investiture, but retained the right to demand loyalty and homage from the bishops before their ordination and insisted on being present at their election.

A similar practice had been introduced in France, although there was no treaty legalizing it. Under the pontificate of Urban II in spite of the serious differences that became apparent during the matrimonial conflict of King Philip I (1060–1108) and on the question of investiture, there had been no final rupture. Paschal did not renew the title of legate for the intransigent Gregorian, Archbishop Hugh of Lyon: because of his rigid attitude, Hugh had met with spirited resistance in the matter of investiture and primacy, even within the French episcopate. With Paschal's authorization, Hugh went away for some years on a crusade to the Holy Land. On 2 December 1104, at a synod held in Paris, Philip I obtained absolution for his matrimonial conflict. The reconciliation made it easier to settle the question of investiture, which had come to a head once more with the appointments of bishops to the dioceses of Beauvais and Paris. Bishop Ivo of Chartres served as intermediary. The growing political influence of Louis VI, Philip I's son and successor, encouraged the tacit settlement of the dispute. The pope's journey to France in 1107 marked an important turning point in the relations betweeen the papacy and the Western sovereigns, even if no agreement was reached with Germany. The coalition between the papacy and the French court at Saint-Denis (30 April to 3 May 1107) was the visible sign of the peace. In France, not only did investiture with crozier and ring cease from that time on, but the king, unlike his counterpart in England, no longer insisted that bishops swear loyalty and homage, and was satisfied with requiring an oath of fidelity. France and the papacy had come together again, bound by a friendly alliance which lasted some two hundred years and constituted from the beginning a kind of offensive against the German king.

At Châlons-sur-Marne (most likely toward the middle of May 1107), Paschal II had a violent confrontation with Henry V's legation, led by Archbishop Bruno of Trier. The German demand for the right of royal investiture was fiercely rejected. The synod of Troyes that followed (at the end of May 1107) confirmed this rejection and, as at Guastalla a year before, renewed the ban on investiture; at the pontifical synods of Benevento (1108) and Rome (1110), the penalties for clergy who had taken part in such investiture ceremonies were further reinforced. In 1110, Henry V took the road to Italy to have himself crowned emperor and close the Investiture Controversy. In order to avoid future conflicts, Paschal proposed a radical solution to the king at Sutri on 9 February 1111: at the imperial coronation Henry would renounce investiture and the pope would order the bishops to renounce the possessions they had received from the empire, as well as their regalia. The king agreed to the treaty even though it seemed unrealistic. The arrangement, now put into writing, was read out on 12 February during the coronation mass at St. Peter's in Rome and caused an uproar among nobles, clergy, and laity. The liturgical ceremony was interrupted. The king withdrew his assent to the treaty, and the pope refused to crown him. The talks came to naught. The king then had the pope and his cardinals arrested and left Rome with them the following night. Two months of detention (during which he was honorably treated) and the imminent danger of Silvester's election as pope, his consideration for the sufferings of the other prisoners, and the threat of the ravages of war propelled the pope into agreeing to the privilege of Ponte Mammolo (12 April 1111): Paschal granted the future emperor (not the king in general) the investiture of bishops who had been elected canonically, freely, and without resort to simony, with crozier and ring (before ordination). In the pope's name and on his express orders, sixteen cardinals took an oath on the act, to which was added a codicil stipulating that the pope would not avenge himself for the wrong suffered by him and his followers, and that he would never excommunicate Henry V. On 12 or 13 April, Maginulf (the antipope Silvester IV) was obliged formally to desist and swear obedience to the pope. After that, the emperor's coronation took place on 13 April 1111 in St. Peter's. Pursued by the indignant Gregorians and even accused of HERESY, Paschal that summer considered abdicating. At the Lateran synods of 1112, he withdrew the *privilegium*, indirectly, and then in 1116 he retracted it expressly by renewing the prohibition of investiture. To the end of his life, the pope avoided banishing the emperor, though he had to confirm several synods in France and Germany that had made that decision.

The last years of his pontificate were troubled and clouded once again by partisan fighting in Rome. On the emperor's initiative, and through the mediation of Abbot Pons of Cluny, among others, fresh negotiations were begun in March 1116. From the fall of that year, Paschal remained under the protection of the Pierleoni in Trastevere, but he left Rome and its environs when Henry V decided in 1117 to come to Rome. No meeting took place. In April 1117, in Benevento, Paschal pronounced the excommunication of Archbishop Maurice of Braga, because at Easter he had celebrated the solemn coronation of Henry V and had crowned Empress Matilda, Henry's wife. Seriously ill and at the end of his strength, Paschal was certainly over sixty years old when he died at CASTEL SANT' ANGELO during the night of 21–2 January 1118, shortly after his return to the besieged city. As St. Peter's was in rebel hands, the pope was buried in the Lateran basilica. Despite serious reversals, the Germanic Holy Roman Empire would, in its turn, find a solution to the investitures question, as had France and England. That Paschal's pontificate eludes firm delineation, already attested by the reactions of his contemporaries is apparent in recent research, which is unable to agree in its judgments.

Georg Schwaiger

Bibliography

JL, I, 702–74.
LP, II, 296–310; III, 134, 143–56.
MGH, Const., I, 134–52, 564–74.
PL, 163, 31–148.
Blumenthal, U. R. *The Early Councils of Pope Paschal II, 1100–1110*, Toronto, 1978; "Paschal II and the Roman Primacy," *AHP*, 16 (1978), 67–92; *Der Investiturstreit*, Stuttgart, 1982; "Bemerkungen zum [verlorenen] Register Papst Paschalis II.," QFIAB, 66 (1986), 1–19.
Blumenthal, U. R. "Paschal II.," *LexMA*, 6 (1992), 1752–3.
Cantarella, G. M. *Ecclesiologia e politica nel papato di Pasquale II*, Rome, 1982.
Hüls, R. *Kardinäle, Klerus und Kirchen Roms, 1049–1130*, Tübingen, 1977.
Morris, C. *The Papal Monarchy: The Western Church from 1050 to 1250*, Oxford, 1989, 134–62.
Schwaiger, G. "Kirchenreform und Reformpapsttum (1046—1124)," *Münchener Theologische Zeitschrift*, 38 (1987), 31–51.
Servatius, C. *Paschalis II. (1099–1118)*, Stuttgart, 1979; "Zur England-politik der Kurie unter Paschalis II.," *Festschrift für Alfons Becker*, Sigmaringen, 1987, 173–90.

[PASCHAL III]. *Guido of Crema (b. Rome, 20 September 1168). Antipope elected on 22 April 1164, consecrated on 26 April 1164.*

Born of noble stock in Lombardy, Guido of Crema was one of the SACRED COLLEGE's staunchest supporters of the agreement with Emperor Frederick Barbarossa and, following the double election of 1159, one of the most enthusiastic defenders of the ANTIPOPE VICTOR IV against ALEXANDER III. After Victor's death he succeeded him under the name Paschal III (April 1164). Like his predecessor, he was recognized solely by the emperor and, far from unanimously, by the Germanic episcopate as well as by some bishops in the kingdom of Italy. In fact, the imperial chancellor Rainald of Dassel promoted his appointment in order to prevent the moderate imperialists from taking advantage of Victor's death to side with Alexander III. Similarly, Rainald worked to strengthen loyalty to Paschal in Italy and throughout the empire. At the diet of Würzburg (June 1165), Frederick, on his chancellor's advice, swore never to abandon Paschal or to support his rival. He enjoined the bishops of the German lands to swear likewise, but could not prevent several of them from doing so with reservations, while others, in particular the metropolitan of Salzburg and his suffragans, refused to take the oath and became dissident. A similar scene was played out in England, where King Henry II Plantagenet had opposed Alexander III as a result of the conflict between the king and his archbishop of Canterbury, Thomas Becket. Even though the king's representatives had sworn that their master was loyal to Paschal, they were not believed. Nonetheless, that did not prevent the emperor's party from pursuing the struggle with the utmost vigor and grandly exalting the authority of the emperor and the glory of the HOLY ROMAN EMPIRE. The result was that Paschal III proclaimed Charlemagne's canonization at a magnificent celebration in Aix-la-Chapelle at Christmas 1165 (solemn recognition of relics).

Following the same dynamics, the emperor in 1166 prepared another military expedition to Italy to force Lombardy and Tuscany to submit once and for all, and to establish Paschal in Rome, where Alexander had taken up residence again the preceding November. At first, despite strong resistance in Rome itself, it looked as though the campaign was succeeding. The German army seized the city, and Alexander III fled. In June 1168, Paschal III was enthroned, and proceeded to crown the new emperor. But a few days later a terrible epidemic ravaged the imperial army, turning into a disaster what up to that time had been one of the most brilliant operations of the century. Without troops, Frederick once again reached the German lands. The peninsula, where the Lombard cities leagued together against him, began to elude his grasp. Lacking support, Paschal III also was forced to flee the capital. He returned, however, at year's end and remained there until his death, on 20 September 1168, whereupon his cardinals elected antipope CALISTUS III to succeed him.

Marcel Pacaut

Bibliography

JW, 2, 426–9.
LP, 2, 410–21.
Fliche-Martin, IX–2.
Schaiger, G. "Paschal III." *LexMA*, 6 (1992), 1753–4.
Watterich, 2, 537–78.

PASSPORT, VATICAN. VATICAN CITY STATE is the juridical personification of the Church, by virtue of the incontestable sovereignty granted to it, including in the international domain, by the terms of the LATERAN PACTS of 1929. As such, it is entitled to give those of its nationals traveling abroad a regular Vatican City passport (article 19). This "ordinary" passport is distinct from the "diplomatic" passport granted by the cardinal secretary of state to members of the diplomatic staff of the papal representations abroad, independently of their original or present CITIZENSHIP. The ordinary passport, however, indicates and serves as proof of Vatican citizenship only in the case of those holders who are of Italian origin. In addition to these two categories of document is the "service" passport (*passaporto di servizio per l'estero*), which is signed by the SUBSTITUTE and granted by the SECRETARIAT OF STATE to other employees of these diplomatic missions. It should be noted that this passport is granted whatever the holder's nationality, and does not in itself confer Vatican citizenship. Like the diplomatic passport, to be valid it requires a visa of the Italian authorities permitting free circulation and passage across Italian territory.

Philippe Levillain

Bibliography

Beales, A. C. F. *The Catholic Church and International Order*, Harmondsworth, 1941.
Cardinale, I. *Le Saint-Siège et la diplomatie. Aperçu historique, juridique et pratique de la diplomatie pontificale*, Paris-Tournai, 1962.
Corsini, V. *Diritto diplomatico consolare*, Milan, 1958.
de La Brière, Y. *La Condition juridique de la Cité du Vatican*, Paris, 1931.
d'Onorio, J. B., ed., *Le Saint-Siège dans les relations internationales*, Paris, 1989.
Zielewicz, Z. *La Situation internationale du Saint-Siège*, Lausanne, 1917.

PATRICIANS, ROMAN. See **Nobility, Roman**.

PATRIMONY OF ST. PETER. The expression "Patrimony of St. Peter" (*patrimonium sancti Petri*) serves to denote the complex of temporal possessions and rights retained by the Holy See in medieval times, an era when the patrimonies of cathedrals and abbeys were generally considered to be the personal property of the patron saint of the see or establishment.

Before the 8th century, when the pope came to exert public authority over Rome and the region surrounding it, the term "patrimony" designated a domain or group of domains belonging to the Church of Rome. CONSTANTINE's restitution of Church possessions is evidence that these existed before the confiscation, even if we know very little about them. Nor is much known of the ways in which they were administered in the 4th century: what documentation there is concerns the possessions of the churches of Rome rather than of the Church of Rome. Like the patrimonies of the great senatorial families, and actually more modest than those, the patrimony "of Peter" was extremely dispersed throughout Italy, from the Alps to Calabria (according to the calculations of Charles Pietri, the possessions in central Italy must have covered an area roughly a hundred times that of present-day Vatican City), Sicily, and other provinces of the empire. Technically, the term *patrimonium* means a territorial grouping of landholding units which were entrusted to *conductores*—half farmers, half managers—on the basis of short-term contracts, and entrepreneurs who gave the lands over to the care of peasant farmers (*coloni*). GREGORY I's correspondence gives some lovely testimonies on the organization of the patrimonies, however difficult they may be to interpret: each one was entrusted to a *rector* or *defensor*, appointed before the tomb of St. Peter, who centralized revenues, though no written evidence has come down to us of what must have been a fairly diversified administration, obviously inherited from antiquity. Beyond Continental Italy, there was a "patrimony of Corsica," a "patrimony of Sardinia," a "patrimony of Gaul" (concentrated around Arles), and a "patrimony of Sicily." This last, both rich (probably covering one-nineteenth of the surface of the island) and essential to Rome's grain supply, was confiscated by the *basileus*, along with the patrimony of Calabria, in 732–3, and thus lost forever to the papacy. A probable response to this serious loss was the appearance, attested shortly afterward in central Italy, of the *domuscultae*, carefully structured landholding units, of which the pope was more than a simple landowner and over which he wielded public authority in many ways. Yet even before these developments, the patrimonies outside central Italy had suffered grievously from the ravages of war, the collapse of the empire, and, especially, the invasion of the LOMBARDS.

Byzantium's response to the invasion was to organize the defense of Italy around the EXARCHATE OF RAVENNA and, from the end of the 6th century, to create within it a duchy of Rome (*ducatus romanus*). Having passed solely into the hands of the popes during the 8th century, under the new name of "Patrimony of St. Peter," and viewed as an extended Latium, from Aquapendente to Ceprano, it became the hard core of the future Papal States. The term "patrimony" so began a new career. Henceforth, along with expressions like *terra* [land] *sancti Petri*, and with artful ambiguity, it designated sometimes this initial hard core and sometimes the whole ensemble of territories subject to the popes' temporal authority or claimed by them as such.

Olivier Guyotjeannin

See also PAPAL STATES.

Bibliography

Noble, T. F. X. *The Republic of St. Peter: The Birth of the Papal State 680–825*, Philadelphia, 1984.

Partner, P. *The Lands of St. Peter; the Papal State in the Middle Ages and the Early Renaissance*, London, 1972.

PATRONAGE, PAPAL. Despite the decline of its empire, Rome, thanks to its monuments, was able to keep its prestige as a city unique in all the world. Its luck lay in the conversion of CONSTANTINE and the patronage that followed: The emperor installed great BASILICAS on all his properties and at the Lateran built the bishops' palace. After that, the tradition had been set. However poor and lacking in power the BISHOP OF ROME was, he had a somewhat permanent goal: to maintain the city's rank as capital of all Christianity, to restore it after destructions and pillages, and to beautify it to attract even more pilgrims. The basilicas located outside the walls were redone: San Lorenzo in the 6th century by PELAGIUS II, and S. Agnese fuori le Mura in the 7th century by HONORIUS I, who was a great builder. Inside Aurelian's wall, Christian buildings multiplied, while the ancient monuments disappeared little by little. There is hardly any Roman church that does not have a medieval origin, even if later transformations make this hardly visible, as at ST. JOHN LATERAN where only the mosaics of the apse, off center, remain visible. During its difficult relationship with the east, Rome again was lucky that the quarrel over images made Byzantine artists move west, maintaining the art of frescoes and mosaics and enabling the growth of a truly Italian school with Cavallini, Torriti, and Rusuti. The exile to AVIGNON did not stem this outpouring, since the papal patronage redirected itself to this new city with the construction of the popes' Palace and the decoration of it, sometimes by Italian artists like Simone Martini, whom BENEDICT XII called to work there.

Upon the return from Avignon, the popes found a desolate city, full of monuments falling into ruin. It was their actions, based upon an uncontested rule and the riches of all Christianity, to which Rome owes its splendor. The artistic patronage by the popes is not without its ambiguity and its front line with "good government" often appears unclear. The duties of the temporal sovereign were metamorphosed by the religious dimension of the city, which had to attract, welcome, and convert. This justified the inclusion of the useful, even the necessary, along with the formal beauty. Despite suspicions that compared the splendor of appearances with the austerity of beliefs, the patronage may be understood as a play of mirrors. The magnificence reflects the power of the State that must be seen as a reflection of the truth it contains. This patronage was, however, neither linear nor single-minded. It had strong points, weak points, a decline. The creative and prodigal popes, drunk on temporal power, were followed by the humble and conservative ones, believers in austerity and counting the Church's every penny, finishing, restoring, maintaining with no motive of personal glory. The Renaissance between the 15th and 16th centuries was marked by the seal of extravagant monarchs, SIXTUS IV, INNOCENT VIII, JULIUS II, LEO X, PAUL III, and SIXTUS V. After an eclipse, and the resultant examinations of conscience, the Baroque age spread, born from a lucid and reasoning concept of the role of art. PAUL V Borghese, URBAN VIII Barberini, ALEXANDER VII Chigi were the protagonists on whose coattails the entire 18th century followed *mezza voce*. But at the head of a State that became ever poorer due to a lack of a coherent economic policy, the popes were not prepared to confront the changes of a world that was becoming laicized. The suppression of ANNATES by revolutionary France signaled the beginning of a patronage that, thanks to the effort of PIUS IX, survived until Italian unity. Contemporary popes continued the tradition while adapting it to the narrowness of their domain.

Though the popes did not neglect their States, assuring their defense and their development—the fortress of Civitavecchia, Castelfranco in Emiglia, and of Lazaret of Ancona—it was Rome that took most of their attention. The urbanization of the Renaissance included the construction of avenues to make travel to the center of the city easier for the crowd of pilgrims, many of whom entered by the Flaminia gate in the north. From there, the two "tridents," one the Piazza del Popolo, and the other at the end of Sant' Angelo bridge where the via Giulia ended, were created by Julius II to lead directly to the VATICAN. The pattern of streets set at right angles to each other, established under Sixtus V to link the basilicas was, in the same spirit, set up for the easy movement of parades and processions, spectacles that were an important part of the life of the Church. The taste for large-scale buildings appeared in the creation of places intended as suitable for stopping to admire views, like that of the Capitol designed by Michelangelo and Bernini's colonnade in front of ST. PETER'S. The fountains show the modification of the useful to include the magnificent, as well as the interest the popes took in them: Sixtus V and the Acqua Felice, Paul V and the Acqua Paola, INNO-CENT X and the Fountain of the Four Rivers at Piazza Navona; and finally, the Trevi fountain, begun by CLEMENT XII and finished by BENEDICT XIV, the most famous and the most grandiose; it was the last.

The triumphant Church showed what it was capable of in the rebuilding of St. Peter's, from 1454, the date of the first project, to the completion of the façade in 1614: a long, sweeping approach that merged all the differences into one continuity; changes of architects, changes of plans, including the abandonment of a layout like the Greek cross that Michelangelo wanted in favor of the Latin cross shape, which was better for containing the crowds that were expected. The cupola was an unequaled architectural feat: The desired effect of grandeur was achieved and remains today. Julius II left nothing of the Constantinian basilica. This extreme dislike of the past, which was seen as faith in the modern style, may be seen in the restoration of the major basilicas, redone to the taste of the day: for example, the redoing of the nave of St. John Lateran by Borromini. The glorification of temporal power went along with it. The papal palaces, the QUIRINAL, the Vatican, and even the Lateran, though unused, were less renovated than they were enlarged so that they would compare with those of foreign powers. The Quirinal, which had become the permanent residence of the ruling pontiff in 1592, got its current look between the 17th and the 18th centuries. The Vatican shows the successive interventions of popes, who have not stopped redoing it even today, with no fear of clashes of style. The decoration speaks less of grandeur than of riches. Paintings have taken over not only the walls, but the vaults that replaced the coffered wooden ceilings (the SISTINE CHAPEL, Michelangelo's masterpiece; loggia and rooms by Raphael). Sculpture was everywhere. Despite the criticism of the Reformation, the popes kept the images whose teaching value they knew well. Through them, a reflection of their taste and of the message they wished to make known, the popes displayed the spirituality of the Church.

The choice of artists was dictated by the origins and family attachments of the ruling pontiff. The Florentines were in the forefront. They were also the grandest, if you include Raphaël, who also passed through Florence during his career. This precedence lasted until the 18th century with Clement XII Corsini. Despite the controversial results of the Beneventin patronages of BENEDICT XIII, the patronage still showed in the sense of quality, as in the protection of Canova by Pope Rezzonico. In the search for excellence, the popes did not exclude foreign artists. CLEMENT XIV in 1772 gave the job of decorating the Papyrus Room to Anton Raphaël Mengs and Christopher Unterberger. There were popes fond of the French like Urban VIII and Benedict XIV. The status symbol of fame was an order from St. Peter's (paintings by Vouet, Valentin, Poussin, Subleyras, or sculptures by Slodtz and Thorvaldsen), or an order for a painted portrait: EUGENE IV (Fouquet), Urban VIII (Vouet), INNOCENT XI (Velasquez), Benedict XIV (Subleyras), CLEMENT XIII (Mengs); or sculpted by Bouchardon (Clement XII), Verschaffelt (Benedict XIV), and Hewerson (CLEMENT XIV).

In their role as protectors of the arts, the popes were interested in institutions like the Academy of St. Luke, the congregation of the *Virtuosi al Pantheon*, the *Accademia del nudo* with which they maintained the supremacy of Rome, and to spread out the works of art, they created a chalcography that long rivaled those of Paris and Madrid. More importantly, they created MUSEUMS dedicated to conservation, education, and enjoyment. To prevent the despoiling of their States, the popes bought art. In 1734 Clement XII founded the Museo Capitolino beginning with the antiques of Cardinal Alessandro Albani and in 1769, Benedict XIV created the Pinacoteca with collections of Sacchetti and Pio di Savoia paintings. Last of all, Clement XIV and Pius VI established the Museo Pio-Clementino at the Vatican to receive the finds from contemporary archaeological digs.

Olivier Michel

Bibliography

Fagiolo, M., and Madonna, M. L. *Roma 1300–1875, la città degli Anni Santi.*, Milan, 1985.

Haidacher, A. *Geschichte der Päpste in Bildern*, Heidelberg, 1965.

Pressouyre, S. *Rome au fil du temps*, Boulogne-sur-Seine, 1973.

PAUL (ST. PAUL THE APOSTLE). *Saul, known as Paul (b. Tarsus in Cilicia, ca. 15 B.C., d. Rome, ca. 67–8).*

Paul merits a place alongside the popes only by virtue of the founding role attributed to him very early by the Church of Rome. This view of things is paradoxical, since his apostolate and activities in Rome are clouded in almost total obscurity. The Acts of the Apostles, which describe the preaching of the apostle as an irresistible thrust from Jerusalem to Rome, end with his arrival in the capital, whereas the Pauline Epistles treat the Roman mission merely as something in the planning stage. The figure of Paul as founder, or rather co-founder, of the Church of Rome is a retrospective construction that exalted his martyrdom in the imperial city and conceived of his personality and vocation as complementing those of Peter, from the moment the Christian religion won Roman society and then the Roman state.

Saul, to use his Hebrew birth name, was born at Tarsus into a family of the diaspora involved in the trading or manufacture of textiles. Familiar with the roads of the Anatolian plateau, they had emigrated to Macedonia, along the Via Egnatia, and later settled in Corinth and Ephesus. They were people of standing, particularly well integrated into the empire, who had received Roman citizenship in return for certain political services rendered during the civil wars or the internal conflicts that shook Tarsus until the beginning of the 1st century. However, we do not know the apostle's Latin family name, which was conferred by an emperor (most likely Julius) or proconsul.

The young Saul had the benefit of polyglot and multicultural education. He read the Bible in Hebrew, but also the Greek Septuagint and the commentaries (*targum*) in Aramaic. He knew Latin and was capable of writing the Epistle to the Galatians according to the rules of judiciary eloquence. Although untrained in philosophy or rhetoric, he had attained a good level of Greek culture. But he had also been touched by Stoicism and Platonism filtered through synagogal teaching and Hellenistic Jewish literature: the wisdom and apocalyptic writings exerted a major influence on him. In Tarsus, which was a fairly large, bustling university town, he learned the methods and repertoire of the popular philosophical sermon, the diatribe. His apprenticeship ended with time spent in a school of the Pharisees in Jerusalem, which turned him into a remarkable controversialist. His teacher is believed to be Gamaliel, a particularly open-minded individual, who was already convinced of the final Resurrection.

The end of his period of apprenticeship, his conversion, and his first two missions can be established around two chronological points: the proconsulate of Gallio in Corinth, in 51, during the course of which Paul's first European journey came to an end; and his flight from Damascus, which Vitellius besieged during his expedition against the city when it was held by the Nabataeans, in the spring of 37—Paul fled three years after his conversion.

The conversion took place in 34, after the popular uprising and the lynching of Stephen, which Saul is said to have witnessed. From 34 to 37, he retreated into the desert, and then he began to preach in Damascus and visited the Church of Jerusalem. Next, he withdrew to Cilicia, where Barnabas sought him out to encourage him to take part in the evangelization of Antioch in Syria. It was Barnabas again who initiated him in the great missionary journeys, first to Cyprus, Barnabas's homeland, around 45, and then in southern Asia Minor, in a rather wild region that was not far from Tarsus and had close economic ties to that city. At this time, the apostle took a Latin surname, Paul, which evoked both his Hebrew name (by assonance) and the patronage of the proconsul of Cyprus, to whom he had begun his mission. He then acquired his independence, at the cost of a break with Barnabas, and looked for a field of action. Forced to avoid the province of Asia, he made his way to Europe and preached in Macedonia, and then in Corinth in the years 48–51. The

founding of the Church of Ephesus and that of the Pauline Churches in western Phrygia, around Colossae, constitute a third stage, after the apostolic conference that took place in Jerusalem in 51, fourteen years after Saul first visited it.

Having become a missionary through conversion following a mystical experience, Paul was a charismatic like all the apostles of his generation. All of them justified their vocations by a personal call from Christ; relations were therefore difficult within the first Christian communities, which broke up into many tiny groups. Tensions and personal disputes are at the heart of the Epistles to the Corinthians, the Galatians, and the Colossians, sent by Paul between 53 and 55 in an attempt to impose the principle of complementary and independent missions against Jewish missionaries of strict observance. These Epistles attest that the relations between Peter and Paul went through successive phases without any true cooperation between the two. From the time of his conversion, Paul conceded to Peter the teaching authority of one who could transmit the words of Jesus: it was for that reason he had spent two weeks with Peter in 37. Fourteen years later, in 51, he recognized in Peter one of the "Columns of the Church," alongside James (whom he named in first place) and John; he bowed to their decision in his conflict with the faithful of Antioch, after the arrival of a judaizing countermission. Peter and the others accepted his gospel, "without adding anything to it," admitting the special origin of his apostolic calling. The Acts of the Apostles go further, reporting that Peter actively supported Paul's arguments by downplaying the importance of circumcision and by opposing James during the conference commonly known as the "first council of Jerusalem;" Paul, however, took no active part in it, and in all likelihood did not attend.

For Paul, the essential point of the meeting in Jerusalem was a sharing of the apostolic field between Peter and himself: he was entitled to evangelize the pagans, while to Peter went the conversion of the Jews; the Christian mission was to function like a *koinônia* (translated as "communion"), that is, in Greek, a structure of participation based on a principle of parity. The classic image of a two-headed Church has its origin in the Epistle to the Galatians, which represents Paul's personal, retrospective point of view at a time when he saw his apostolic authority contested in the Churches he had founded and when Peter's activities were competing with his own in Corinth. There was actually no division of the mission countries; throughout the Christian tradition, inaugurated by the ACTS of the Apostles at the end of the 1st century, Peter comes across, just as much as Paul, as the apostle of the pagans.

Yet Paul wanted to thrust him into the judaizing Christians' camp when he imputed to him the responsibility for his rupture with the Church of Antioch, which had been his missionary base until 51. Whereas Paul promoted the union of Jews and Greeks at the same Eucharistic feast, despite kosher rules, and refused to apply to converts from paganism the marginal status that the synagogues reserved for proselytes, Peter abandoned his previous liberal positions while visiting Antioch and began to eat apart with the observant Jews. In this, he represented the majority opinion at Antioch, for after a public debate Paul was obliged to quit the city for good. Henceforth, Peter was considered the true founder of the Church that Paul had played a part in creating. In 51, his teaching authority was already evident, and Paul's still had to assert itself. On the disciplinary level, Paul was ill served by his passionate stances, whereas Peter emerged as the forger of a middle way.

The image of Paul as the "apostle to the gentiles" also deserves some qualification. True, all the Churches he founded were situated in Roman colonies (Antioch in Pisidia, Iconium, Lystra, Philippi, Corinth) or provincial capitals (Antioch of Syria, Thessalonica, Corinth, Ephesus). But the few Latin names associated with him appear only later, and his Epistles from the 50s, steeped as they are in the Old Testament and differing so widely from the speeches "for Greeks" rewritten in the Acts of the Apostles, were obviously addressed to people more or less familiar with the Bible—hellenized Orientals and Greeks sympathetic to Judaism. It was Jews converted in Corinth and Ephesus who brought Paul's thinking to Rome, by disseminating there his Epistle to the Romans, written in 54. This is a true doctrinal treatise, which represents the totality of his thinking and arrives at an ecumenical, unitary, and autonomous conception of the Church, one arising from Jewish and pagan converts at the same time.

Paul was thus welcomed by certain Christian groups in Rome when he was transferred to the capital, in the spring of 58, to reply to an accusation of sacrilege made by the Jerusalem religious authorities. He appealed to the emperor. Taking advantage of the fairly flexible conditions of his detention, he preached in Rome for two years, at the end of which he was freed, either because the accusation was found to be false or because the court was inundated with cases.

The Roman tradition has preserved no trace of his preaching. Later, Paul summoned to Rome the most faithful of his "collaborators," that is, all the Greeks—Timothy, Luke, Titus, the Macedonian Epaphroditus (if the Epistle to the Philippians is assigned to this period)—and the Asians Demas, Tychieus, and Onesiphorus. The pastoral Epistles, which are certainly apocryphal, also mention a small Latin nucleus consisting of Crescens, Pudens, and Claudia, later joined by Eubulus and LINUS, the second pope. The meetings with Peter were reinvented by Roman hagiography. The Acts of Paul, written in Asia at the end of the 2nd century, never name Peter although

they do include the account of the martyrdom in Rome; the Acts of Peter, for their part, introduce Paul only in the later Latin translation and never suggest any common activity.

The association of the two apostles is a peculiarly Roman idea, which appeared at the end of the 1st century. Around 90, CLEMENT of Rome named them both martyrs, and, a little later, Petrine circles rehabilitated Paul's person and writings in the second Epistle written under the name of Peter. Still, if both apostles died a martyr's death in the capital, it was not on the same date or in the same circumstances. According to the pastoral Epistles, Paul was rearrested in the East following a violent controversy in Asia, and once again transferred to Rome. But the context had changed: Nero's evolution toward an Oriental type of despotism from 62, the growing influence of the astrologers and the catastrophes that had struck the city from 64 to 68 all together are sufficient to account for a condemnation that the chroniclers place in 67 or 68. The Acts of Paul, which gives a long account of his martyrdom, makes much of accusations of subversion and magic.

Tradition preserved the memory of his place of execution, on the route leading out of Rome to Ostia, even as Paul's group was dispersing and his personality fading. But by the end of the 2nd century, the Romans were venerating in their city the "trophies" of the two "founders," Peter and Paul—in other words, their tombs; the two were associated in the same commemorative feast day, 29 June. Paul's importance in Rome thus results from a christianization of the cult of the hero, since in ancient times every community spontaneously organized itself around its founders' tombs. According to Eusebius, it was also to honor him as a "savior" that Christian artists repainted his portrait, giving him the banal countenance of a Semite but the bearing of an itinerant philosopher complete with toga, sandals, and the scroll of the Law.

Thus Paul the thinker was restored. Clement of Rome was the first to develop the theme of the philosopher-"herald" of God, on the Stoic model, hinted at in the Pastorals and at the end of the Acts of the Apostles. In the 4th century, the period of the conversion of the Roman elite, a forged apocryphal correspondence between Paul and Seneca made its appearance. Paul the intellectual thus became the symbol of a Christian culture more open to classical values.

The association of the two apostles also served as evidence of the unity of the Church, which brought together converts from Judaism and those of pagan background. In order to promote an ideal of concord beyond the dissensions stressed by pagan polemicists, Jerome and Augustine turned to the Epistle to the Galatians to affirm the equality of the two apostles who symbolized two cultures. The theme was exploited in the 4th century in the decoration of catacombs, basilicas, and sarcophagi, representing Paul as a pendant to Peter in a style of composition also showing an aesthetic preoccupation with symmetry.

Yet Paul gained nothing from this, for he remained in Peter's shadow. His portrait appeared later than that of Peter; the commemorative basilica of St. Paul's Outside the Walls was built by Theodosius, and not by Constantine as was that of the Vatican; and it was originally a modest building, before it acquired the sumptuous decoration described by Prudentius. Paul's emergence in Rome became a historical necessity, but he had not been one of its popular saints.

Nevertheless, this emergence does crown, even if posthumously, a sustained effort of penetration into the heart of the Greco-Roman world. And therein lies one of Paul's incontestable successes. Preaching first in Syria on the frontiers of the empire, then on the limits of Hellenism in Asia Minor, and then on the outskirts of the city among those sympathetic to JUDAISM, he managed from the time of the Ephesus mission of 51–4 to use the ancient city's network of roads and to gain recognition as an intellect of the first order whose trenchant theological teachings would impose themselves down through the generations.

Marie-Françoise Baslez

Bibliography

Baslez, M. F. *Saint Paul*, Paris, 1991.

Bornkamm, G. *Paul*, New York, 1971.

Dunn, J. D. G. *The Theology of Paul the Apostle*, Grand Rapids, Mich., 1998.

Farmer, W. R. *Peter and Paul in the Church of Rome: The Ecumenical Potential of a Forgotten Perspective*, New York, 1990.

Fitzmyer, J. A. *According to Paul: Studies in the Theology of the Apostle*, New York, 1993.

Jewett, R. *Dating Paul's Life*, London, 1979.

Kereszty, R. "Peter and Paul and the Founding of the Church in Rome: Forgotten Perspectives," *Communio* 15 (Summer 1988) pp. 215–33.

Murphy-O'Connor, J. *Paul: A Critical Life*, Oxford, 1996.

Pietri, C. *Roma christiana*, Paris-Rome, 1976.

Sanders, E. P. *Paul*, Oxford, 1991.

PAUL I. (*d. 28 June 767). Elected pope on 29 May 757. Buried at St. Peter's, in Rome. Saint (cult attested from the 14th century).*

STEPHEN II was succeeded by his brother Paul, who had played an active political role during his pontificate; he was a DEACON. For the first time in many years, the election was disputed: the creation of the PAPAL STATES was awakening ambitions, and the Romans were not all agreed on what policy to follow. In announcing his election to Pepin III, Paul placed himself resolutely under Frankish protection. But the king believed he had done his duty by the papacy and wanted to intervene as little as possible in Italian affairs; moreover, he no longer enjoyed the title of patrician, which Stephen II had given him.

Paul's policy was not one likely to consolidate peace with the king of the LOMBARDS, Desiderius. Even though there were no signs that the latter had the same territorial ambitions as his predecessor, Aistulf, the pope persistently warned Pepin against him. But in vain: Pepin let Desiderius reestablish his authority over the duchies of Spoleto and Benevento, which Stephen II had sought to have placed under Frankish protection. In order to gain Spoleto, the Lombard king crossed the Pentapolis, which he ravaged. Returning in 758, he passed through Rome, and in a meeting with Paul, he merely promised to give up Imola if the FRANKS freed the Lombard hostages they were holding. Pepin had to send his brother Remi, bishop of Rouen, and Duke Auchaire, in late 759, to reestablish peace between Paul and Desiderius. Despite a few frontier incidents, the situation grew more peaceful beginning in 761–2. Once again, the pope had to include among his enemies the emperor, who refused to see part of his Italian provinces disappear from his grasp.

Throughout his pontificate, Paul feared a Byzantine invasion, the threat of which he may have exaggerated, and the conclusion of an alliance between Constantine V and the king of the Lombards. The emperor's chief concern was to consolidate his authority in Campagna. He also sought to convert the Franks to iconoclasm, as they did not share the pope's liking for the veneration of images, scarcely developed in their kingdom. Constantine V was eager to begin diplomatic relations with Pepin, and they exchanged ambassadors, but the Franks invariably allowed the pope's representatives to be present at these discussions. At Easter, 767, Pepin convened a synod at Gentilly at which a debate took place on the Trinity and the cult of images, but the Greeks were unable to bring the Franks around to their point of view.

Paul also had to face the opposition of the archbishop of RAVENNA. At the very beginning of his pontificate, he had freed Archbishop Sergius, whom Stephen had imprisoned in Rome, and forced him to recognize his right to appoint functionaries and raise taxes: sources at Ravenna report that Sergius had to promise to hand his Church's treasury over to the pope. Afterward, Sergius acted as the exarch's successor and exercised temporal power in the EXARCHATE and the Pentapolis, much like the pope in Latium. In Rome, there was order. It is true that the pope ruled with a fist of iron, and his biographer acknowledged that the prisons held many condemned to death; Paul's injustices were at the origin of the troubled times that ensued after his death.

Paul arranged for the bodies of saints to be transferred from the Roman CATACOMBS, where they were exposed to looting. In his family home on the Via Lata, the pope founded the monastery of S. Silvestro in

Capite for the benefit of refugee GREEK monks. Here, he placed the bodies of three popes venerated as saints: DIONYSIUS, STEPHEN I, and SILVESTER. To please Pepin, who had a special veneration for St. Petronilla—St. Peter's daughter, according to legend—Paul in 757 transferred her body into one of the rotundas at the south end of St. Peter's.

Jean-Charles Picard

Bibliography

JW, 1, 277–83; 2, 701.

LP, 1, 463–7.

MGH, Epist., 3, 507–58.

Bertolini, O. *Roma e i Longobardi*, Rome, 1972.

Duchesne, L. *Les Premiers Temps de l'État pontifical*, Paris, 1911.

Noble, T. F. X. *The Republic of St. Peter*, Philadelphia, 1984.

Schwaiger, G. "Paul I.," *LexMA*, 6 (1992), 1823.

PAUL II. *Pietro Barbo (b. Venice, 23 February 1417, d. Rome, 26 July 1471). Elected pope on 30 August 1464, consecrated on 16 September 1464.*

A member of a rich merchant family and destined for a life in business, he embarked on an ecclesiastical career under the influence of his maternal uncle, who became Pope EUGENE IV. Beginning as apostolic protonotary and archdeacon of the cathedral chapter of Bologna, he was appointed bishop of Cervia in 1440 and, in the same year, cardinal deacon of the titular church of Sta Maria Nova, which NICHOLAS V exchanged in 1451 with S. Marco (in fact, sources generally refer to him as cardinal of S. Marco, or of Venice). Highly influential during the pontificates of Eugene IV, Nicholas V, and CALLISTUS III, he was named bishop of Vicenza in 1451, and then of Padua in 1459, an office he resigned the following year. His relations with PIUS II, in contrast, were marked by conflict, but his popularity at the CURIA and in Rome, a result of his generosity and munificence, betrayed no sign of this. After Pius died, he succeeded him unexpectedly at the first ballot, on 30 August 1464. He was enthroned on 16 September and took possession of the Lateran in one of most lavish ceremonies Rome had ever witnessed.

At the start of the conclave, all the cardinals had sworn to an eighteen-point electoral pact defining the steps the future pope would take toward Church reform. In particular, the pact called for the convening of a general council within three years and for strengthening the role of the cardinals in Church government. After consulting a number of canonists, among whom were Andrea de Barbatia and Teodoro de' Lelli, Paul II presented the SACRED COLLEGE with a new pact which substantially modified the previous agreement and was finally accepted with some reservations.

Accordingly, from the first few months of the pontificate everyone expected a reorganization of the Sacred College with a nomination of new cardinals, but it did not take place until September 1467. Among the newly promoted cardinals, a few names stand out—the pope's nephew Pietro Barbo, Oliviero Carafa, and Francesco Della Rovere, the future SIXTUS IV. In November of the following year, Paul named other members of his family, Battista Zeno and Giovanni Michiel. The new pontiff's tendency to absolutism showed itself particularly in his domestic policy, where he upheld the temporal authority of the Holy See vis-à-vis unruly vassals. In June 1465, in the wake of a quick and successful military campaign in Tuscia, he rid himself of the Anguillara family, which had been trying to create an independent domain since the pontificate of Nicholas V. He thus won control of a vast stretch of the Patrimony region, and later extended it to Tolfa, an important center for the mining of alum. The domains of Sigismondo and Roberto Malatesta at Cesena and Rimini were more difficult to restore to direct Church rule. The return of Cesena to the Holy See was made possible thanks to the support for Paul II of its leading citizens, who realized that their economic interests would not be compromised by a change of overlord. But in the case of Rimini, the pontiff was forced to deal with Roberto Malatesta, supported by the league of Milan, Florence, and Naples, and to confirm him as a vassal of the Holy See representing not only Rimini but a much wider territory (1470).

In Rome, Paul II initiated a revision of the municipal statutes in 1469. The purpose of the undertaking was to define precisely the respective areas of competence, especially juridical competence, of the communal administration and the papal government, since over time the areas had become confused, to the detriment of the *juridictio* of the commune. Paralleling these measures, which favored the Roman municipal class, was an interest in the development of city planning around the Capitol, the "center of communal life." Here, in 1455, as cardinal, the pope had begun the building of the imposing Palazzo di San Marco (today the Palazzo di Venezia) alongside his titular church. From 1466, he began to reside there permanently, amassing priceless collections of art and antiquities. Paul II, who had a liking for festivals and celebrations, also won the Romans by his promotion of carnivals; and for the first time, the Jews, who so far had been confined to a funding role, were allowed to take part in the games. Ecclesiastical ceremonies were invariably conducted with matchless pomp. Paul usually took part in them wearing the tiara, the symbol of the pope's temporal power, in order to underline the preeminence of the pontiff in the hierarchy of the Church. The proceedings of 1466 against the *Fraticelli della opinione*, a heretical sect vowed to poverty that at the time was spreading in the Marches and the area around Rome, together with the many treatises the case produced, have recently been reconsidered in the light not only of Church opinion and interests, but also of the anticonciliar opinion in the Curia, supported by such figures as Cardinals Jean Jouffroy and Bessarion, or Bishop Sanchez of Arevalo.

Paul II also took measures to stem the growth of the papal bureaucracy. Shortly after his election, he abolished the college of the seventy apostolic abbreviators, instituted by Pius II, which was made up largely of humanists. The Curia's displeasure, expressed through the intermediary of numerous members of the Roman Academy—among them Pomponio Leto, Bartolomeo Platina, and Callimaco Espediente—grew so lively and polemical that the pope feared he would have to face a real conspiracy. His violent reaction—he abolished the Academy and had his chief opponents, including Platina, hauled off to trial (1468)—was, according to the latest historiography, based on his suspicion that the humanists were in collusion with Mehmet II. The trial found no fault with the academicians, who were acquitted of all charges in 1469. In actual fact, if Paul mistrusted the study of classical authors and, more generally, humanist culture, he was certainly not an enemy of ancient culture, as witness his restoration of various monuments of antiquity and his archaeological and numismatic collections. Moreover, he had the distinction of having encouraged the introduction of printing in Rome, in 1467.

In the area of Italian politics, Paul II relied on the support of Venice, with which he nevertheless often clashed, sometimes violently, and of Florence, abandoning the traditional alliance with Milan and Naples. The instability of the Italian situation was aggravated by the death of Francesco Sforza (1466), who was succeeded by his son, Galeazzo Maria, whereupon was created a climate of uncertainty in the already complex political life of the peninsula. Indeed, Venice tried to take advantage of the situation by sending its *condottiere* Bartolomo Colleoni against Florence, which had allied itself with Naples and Milan in 1467. The peace signed the following year in Rome, on Paul's initiative, among all the Italian powers proved extremely fragile and was ruptured shortly afterward, when the question of the Malatesta cities arose. A general alliance was drawn up in Rome in December 1470, which Paul II intended as a re-creation of that of Lodi; but it too was short-lived, having been signed in an atmosphere of panic as news came that the island of Negroponte (ancient Euboea), the last Venetian outpost in the East, had fallen into Turkish hands (July 1470).

The crusade against the Turks, into which were poured the revenues from the Tolfa ALUM mines, had been a cherished objective of Paul's from the beginning of his pontificate. Even though he did not succeed in uniting the Christian forces in strong opposition to Mehmet II, for years he gave large subsidies to Hungary, Christendom's last bulwark, and to the Albanian *condottiere* George Skanderberg, who mounted a heroic resistance to the enemy forces. But at Skanderberg's death in January 1468 almost the whole of Albania fell into the hands of the TURKS. The leader who might have been able to stop them was the king of Bohemia, George of Podebrady. But he was suspected of sympathy for the Hussite HERESY, and Paul II had initiated proceedings against him. In the end, although Cardinal Carvajal had advised against it, the pontiff adopted a conciliatory attitude toward the Bohemian king and suspended the proceedings. Still, the king brushed off all attempts at negotiation and refused to send ambassadors, with the result that on 23 December 1466 the pope excommunicated him and declared him and his descendants stripped of the title of king. Podebrady's response was to appeal to the general council, particularly in order to win the king of France, Louis XI, over to his cause. Solicited by the pope, the king of Hungary, Mathias Corvinus, declared war on Podebrady on 31 March 1468. At first, fortune smiled on the Bohemian troops, and the Hungarian king was obliged to sign a truce in February 1469. The war having been resumed at the pope's desire, Corvinus had himself proclaimed king of Bohemia. This did not solve the problem, and hostilities began afresh with yet more violence but without decisive results. Though peace talks were taking place in Rome, and though Podebrady seemed to have decided to recognize the PRIMACY of the Roman Church and Paul II as the vicar of Christ, he died on 22 March 1471 without having regularized his relations with Rome.

During the pontificate of Paul II, relations between the Holy See and the king of France, Louis XI, were likewise ridden with conflict. The king claimed that the oath of obedience he had sworn to Pius II, providing for the abolition of the Pragmatic Sanction of Bourges, had fallen out of force upon that pope's death. Thanks to the activity of his royal agents, Cardinals Jean Jouffroy and Jean Balue, Louis XI managed to equivocate and to extract certain concessions from Paul, such as a cardinalate for Balue; it seemed, therefore, that he intended to abolish the Pragmatic Sanction, which aroused the protests of the University of Paris and of Parliament. Balue fell into disgrace before the king and was accused of treason in favor of Charles the Bold, and Paul II had to negotiate in order to save him from being put to death. So in his relations with France, Paul II achieved no significant results, and on several occasions, he was even threatened with a general council. On the other hand, the pope had excellent relations with Emperor Frederick III. The emperor came to Rome in 1468 to try to persuade the pope to hold a general council in Constance, but to no avail, thereby giving fresh proof of the feebleness of the imperial authority. In the last months of his life, Paul attempted to reconcile the Church of Russia to Rome by encouraging the marriage of Ivan III, grand duke of Russia, and Zoe, daughter of Thomas Palaeologus, the despot of the Peloponnese, who had fled to Rome, where he died in 1465. Paul did not live to see the conclusion of these negotiations. He died unexpectedly in the evening of 26 July 1471, at a little over fifty-three years of age.

Anna Esposito

Bibliography

Amann, E. "Paul II," *DTC*, XII/1 (1933), 3–9.

Ammannati Piccolomini, J. *Epistulae e commentarii*, Frankfurt, 1614.

Andrews, A. "The 'Lost' Book of the Life of Pope Paul II by Gaspar of Verona," *Studies in the Renaissance*, 17 (1970), 7–45.

Canensi, M. *De vita et pontificatu Pauli II*, ed. G. Zippel, Città di Castello, 1904–11 (RIS/2, III, 16), 65–176.

Dunston, A. J. "Pope Paul II and the Humanists," *The Journal of Religious History*, 7 (1973), 287–306.

Gaspare Da Verona, *De gestis tempore Pontificis Maximi Pauli II*, ed. G. Zippel, Città di Castello, 1904–11 (RIS/2, III, 16), 1–64.

Jedin, H. "Sanchez de Arevalo und die Konzilsfrage unter Paul II.," *Historisches Jahrbuch*, 73 (1954), 95–119.

Macek, J. "Le mouvement conciliaire. Louis XI et Georges de Podebrady. En particulier dans la période 1466–1468," *Historica*, 15 (1967), 5–63.

Medioli Masotti, P. "L'Accademia romana e la congiura del 1468. Con appendice di Augusto Campana," *Italia medievale e umanistica*, 25 (1982), 189–204.

Miglio, M. "Vidi thiaram Pauli papae secundi," *Storiografia pontificia del Quattrocento*, Bologna, 1975, 121–53 (the whole volume contains important references to Paul II).

Monfasani, J. "The Fraticelli and Clerical Wealth in Quattrocento Rome," *Renaissance Society and Culture: Essays in Honour of Eugene F. Rice, Jr.*, New York, 1991, 177–95 (on the treatises concerning the Fraticelli trial in 1466).

Pastor, 4.

Platina, B. *Liber de vita Christi ac omnium pontificum*, ed. G. Gaida, Città di Castello, 1913–32 (RIS/2, III, 1), 363–98.

Weiss, R. *Un umanista veneziano Papa Paolo II*, Venice-Rome, 19–58.

PAUL III.

PAUL III. *Alessandro Farnese (b. Canino ?, end of February 1468, d. Rome, 10 November 1549). Elected pope on 13 October 1534. Buried at St. Peter's in Rome.*

Farnese, a name that sounds a fanfare, immediately evokes the qualities associated with the Renaissance papacy: power, skilled diplomacy, a deep-seated desire for reform, and, at the same time, outrageous pomp and shameless NEPOTISM. It has often been said that PAUL III's pontificate "marks a turning point in the history of the papacy in that it definitively oriented the office in favor of a profound reform of the Church and thus broke with the tradition of the popes of the Renaissance" (M. Pacaut, *Catholicisme*, X, 926). To make this claim is to forget everything the Medici popes, LEO X and CLEMENT VII, had attempted in that direction in the twenty years leading up to the Farnese pope's election. It is to credit Paul III with a spiritual strength that would have proved singularly ineffectual if political circumstances had not been in his favor. And it is to see his reign of barely fifteen years as bringing not only a restoration of papal authority but a complete upheaval in the government of the Church, something that did not take place until the very end of the century. One thing is certain, however: the era of the medieval Church was coming to an end and that of the Church militant was beginning; it is no coincidence that the Society of Jesus saw its rule confirmed by the bull *Regimini militantis ecclesiae* of 27 September 1540 and that the Roman INQUISITION was instituted two years later. War did not necessarily entail victory, any more than nepotism automatically carried with it bad choices, or pre-conciliar talks result overnight in radical reform. Paul III's life was threaded through with these half-disappointments and hard-won successes, these diplomatic balances haphazardly obtained and constantly under threat. The portraits of him painted by Titian two years before his death (Naples, Capodimonte Museum) show us not so much the head of the Church as a worried old man, too skilled a politician to deceive himself as to the lasting quality of his legacy, and plagued by the memory of a mass of iniquities and opportunistic decisions of which he was unsure, in the end, whether they had been absolutely necessary or even fitting. He did not see the completion of the huge palace erected to the glory of his family. He did see his son murdered, his grandchildren tear one another to pieces, and his grandson's wife, the illegitimate daughter of Charles V, thwart his plans. He saw Protestantism spread like a plague without finding a way to stop it, the TURKS advance a little farther west every day, and, above all, the absence in the SACRED COLLEGE of many who, after his death, could stand up to dangers of which he himself was all too aware.

Origins. Whatever Paul may have said or caused to be written by scribblers in his employ such as Alonso Cano, his family origins remain obscure. It is not even certain whether he was born in Canino, in the province of Viterbo, or in Rome, where his grandfather Ranuccio was in fact senator under MARTIN V. Tradition has it that he received a refined literary education from Pomponius Laetus, knew Greek, and learned music, an accomplish-

PAUL III

ment his sister Giulia was able to add to the list of his already considerable charms. Yet a study of his library raises doubts as to his actual culture. Unlike that of his nephew Cardinal Alessandro, his learning seems to have been no more than a veneer, indispensable for one who hoped to shine at the court of ALEXANDER VI—of which his sister, married to an Orsini for the sake of form, was the chief ornament—and, after that, the court of Leo X. The future pope did not receive major orders until late. Although Alexander VI named him cardinal of the title of SS. Cosma e Damiano on 20 September 1493 and then conferred on him the diocese of Corneto and Montefiascone (his homeland), and, finally, the rich diocese of Parma in 1509, he produced a constant scattering of illegitimate children. The two eldest of these, Pierluigi (the future duke of Parma) and Paolo, were legitimized by JULIUS II, and Costanza and Ranuccio later, in 1518, by Leo X. INNOCENT VIII appointed him apostolic PROTONOTARY, and Alexander VI named him treasurer of the APOSTOLIC CAMERA and LEGATE to VITERBO to receive Charles VIII. Leo X and Clement VII showered him with benefices at Benevento, Soana, Anagni, Forlì, and Sora and made him their legate to Charles V before naming him suburbicarian bishop of Frascati, Palestrina, Porto and Santa Ruffina, Ostia, and Velletri.

Nevertheless, it appears that he underwent a conversion around 1513, under the influence of Bartolomeo Guidiccioni, whom the cardinal, then forty-five, chose to administer his diocese at Parma and to organize a reform synod in 1519. If he still maintained a luxurious style of life and showed a certain want of scruple in political affairs, henceforth Alessandro managed to restrain himself in the moral sphere and concentrate all his activity on diplomacy. Of this he had become a master, notably in the delicate transactions with the emperors, where on several occasions he saved Leo X from making serious mistakes in statecraft. When HADRIAN VI died, he already pictured himself on the papal throne, and the election of CLEMENT VII in 1523—actually a difficult one—was a humiliation. Furthermore, he did not enjoy the same influence with the new pope, who rejected his advice, pursuing a zigzagging policy that led to the catastrophic SACK OF ROME in 1527. Yet Cardinal Alessandro remained hugely popular within the Curia and in his diocese, an advantage that stood him in good stead when he was appointed suburbicarian bishop of Ostia in 1524. However, he had to wait another ten years for the death of the Medici pope before he himself could accede to the chair of St. Peter. This took place on 13 October 1534 after a two-day conclave, voting unanimously, when he was sixty-seven years old.

Pontificate. As soon as he was elected, the pope proceeded to create new cardinals, including his two grandsons—Alessandro, Pierluigi's son, who received the CHANCERY, and Guido Ascanio Sforza, the son of

Costanza, who was put in charge of the Apostolic Camera two years later. Pierluigi was named *gonfaloniere* of the Church in 1537 and then hereditary duke of the fiefs of Parma and Piacenza in 1545. The duchy of Camerino (later exchanged with the duchy of Castro) went to his second son, Ottavio, who in 1538 had been forced to marry Margaret of Austria, the illegitimate daughter of Charles V and the widow of Alessandro de' Medici. The third son, Orazio, was made prefect of Rome. All this created a climate of disappointment and resentment.

Such flagrant nepotism was not, however, a sign that interest alone would govern his choices, for in a second series of appointments, on 21 May 1535, men of deeply spiritual qualities were named, such as Cardinal John Fisher, executed the following year by the king of England, Cardinal Du Bellay, Cardinals Girolamo Ghinucci and Giacomo Simonetta, and finally, Gasparo Contarini, the former Venetian ambassador to Rome and friend of Vittoria Colonna. It is also worth noting that the diocese of Parma, even though part of the PATRIMONY OF ST. PETER, was being threatened on the frontiers of the Holy Roman Empire, and that there existed a very real need to cement temporal and spiritual policies by family ties. Paul III, perfectly aware of these problems, made many journeys in the Patrimony of St. Peter during the first years of his reign, especially to Perugia, Loreto, Bologna, Ferrara, and Rimini. He repeatedly called for a council, which Henry VIII and Francis I both refused. And he embarked on a third series of nominations which added to the Sacred College such figures as Jacopo Sadoleto, Reginald Pole, the great-nephew of Edward IV (Henry VIII had Pole's mother beheaded in reprisal), Marcello Cervini, the future Marcellus II, Gregorio Cortese, the reformer of the Benedictines, and two Neapolitans, Gian Pietro Carafa, the future PAUL IV, and Giovanni Morone, friend of the "spirituals" or "Catholic evangelicals."

Charles V, returning in April 1536 from his Tunisian expedition flushed with victory over Cherredin Barbarossa and the freeing of twenty thousand Christians, pronounced in consistory a long indictment of Francis I. It was a vain attempt to make the pope give up his policy of neutrality and cede to him the Milanese territory, whose duke, Francesco Sforza, had died. However, the Turkish threat became acute, and in late June the Ottomans invaded Apulia, while Venice, too, lost Corfu to the Turks. Milan and Savoy had become pawns in a struggle between the Holy Roman Empire and France, which had brought the imperial forces up to the gates of Villafranca in July 1537. The need for peace and a holy alliance against the Turks became urgent. Paul III's efforts to promote this met with success when he lured Charles V with the prospect of the throne of Constantinople. At Nice on 18 June 1538, he managed to conclude a ten-year truce between the belligerents, coupled with the promise to go to war against Henry VIII, pronounced schismatic three years before. Nine months later the truce broke down, and the Turks won another victory over the Venetian fleet commanded by Admiral Doria at Prevesa, and occupied Buda and the upper Danube. The Protestants refused to take part in such a crusade without solid guarantees of concessions in religious matters, and the prospects of a council were thereby postponed indefinitely.

It was at this point that St. Ignatius of Loyola came to prominence, in whom the Church found the animating spirit it needed for the Counter Reformation. Since 1535, he had been dedicating himself, together with his companions, to religious renewal and the service of neighbor. In the bull *Regimini militantis ecclesiae*, promulgated on 27 September 1540, Paul III approved the Society of Jesus and thus gave it a powerful impetus. The year before that, Henry of Saxony and Joachim II of Brandenburg had embraced Lutheranism, and the reports of the NUNCIOS sent to the German lands, Aleandro, Morone, Poggio, and Mignarelli, were alarming. A colloquy between Catholics and Protestants, the first of its kind, had opened at Speyer 18 April 1540, and then was moved to Hagenau and later to Worms. Here the legate Tommaso Campeggio represented the pope before being replaced by Contarini, whose gentle, conciliatory manner was ill suited to the ruthless debates led by Melanchthon, Bucer, and Pistorius at the diet, henceforth assembled at Regensburg. The basis for the conference was a "Regensburg Book" consisting of twenty-three articles, "whose moderation of form," to quote P. Richard, "had been calculated in such a way as to avoid offending the Protestants; the editors had emphasized the non-controversial articles and toned down the differences to the point of misunderstanding."

On 3 May 1541, Contarini sent the text of conciliation to Rome, but the majority of the consistory rejected the agreement as tendentious, and, to avoid hurting the legate's feelings, the cardinal nephew wrote him that the Holy Father neither approved nor rejected the text. As for Charles V, Nicholas Granvella advised him to publish the articles as imperial law and to promulgate an edict of tolerance until the next diet or national council was held. But when Paul III announced in his bull of 12 May 1542 the convening of the council of Trent, then in the bull of 21 July the reestablishment of the Inquisition, he was met not only with the hostility of Francis I, who threatened to create a schism, but also with the indecisiveness of Charles V, who still dreamed of a peaceful agreement between the two factions and the restoration of religious unity in the empire. A meeting between the pope and the emperor at Busseto in June 1543 was followed by a treaty of alliance designed to create an army to crush the alliance of German Protestants known as the Schmalkaldic League. But at first, all it accomplished was to give the emperor an easy victory over the Protestant rulers and permit a rap-

prochement among the emperor, the king of France, and the king of England, sealed by the peace of Crépy of 17 September 1544. This was a veritable snub to the pope, who now found himself in the same situation as Clement VII twenty years earlier. Nevertheless, he was able to put a good face on events and take advantage of the general peace to announce forthwith the convening of a council, at Trent, on 13 December 1545. Paul III appointed Cardinals Giammaria Del Monte (future JULIUS III), Marcello Cervini (future MARCELLUS II), and Reginald Pole as his legates to preside at the council. Two of them would succeed the Farnese pope, and Del Monte would reconvene Trent in 1551, to continue the enterprise begun by Paul III. With the council, in any case, Paul III had seized the initiative from Charles V in ways often frustrating to the emperor. The legates, though under some strict orders from the pope, were not always able to carry through on them. The "imperial bishops" at Trent, those generally taking their cue from Charles, were a strong force that advocated more radical reforms than the bishops of the "papal party." An imperial diet, held in Augsburg in September 1547, ended in complete failure, and painful transactions ensued between defenders of orthodoxy like Johann Pflug, Helding, the coadjutor of Mainz, the Carmelite Eberhard, the Spanish prelates Soto and Malvenda, and advocates of the Reform led by Agricola, preacher to the Elector of Brandenburg. A doctrinal formula known as the Augsburg Interim, consisting of twenty-six articles, was finally promulgated by Charles V in terms vague enough to please everyone. Ceremonies, ornaments, and all the sacraments as well the principal feasts were retained to satisfy the Catholics; on the other hand, communion under both species and the marriage of priests were henceforth permitted. No mention was made of purgatory, the communion of saints, or the virginity of Mary. The whole text represented such a compromise that it scarcely won respect anywhere except in Bavaria, and it displeased the pope, who felt the emperor was encroaching on his prerogatives. Paul III was strengthened politically by the convening of the council and by the dissensions that were tearing apart the Holy Roman Empire. Without forming an actual alliance with Francis I, who in any case would die two years later, a few months after the death of Henry VIII, the pope was able to rally the malcontents and secure the support of the faction hostile to Hispano-imperial hegemony.

In March, 1547, there was an outbreak at Trent of a disease later identified as typhus. Panic seized a few of the bishops, who began to demand appropriate action. Fearing an epidemic the council fathers, after bitter debate, voted by a two-thirds majority to move the council to Bologna, a decision pleasing to the pope and infuriating to the emperor. On 10 September 1547, Pierluigi, the duke of Parma and the pope's son, was assassinated at Piacenza by the thugs of Ferrando Gonzaga, ally of Charles

V. It was a hard price to pay for the reversal of the alliances, and the pope was all the more affected since his favorite grandson, Ottavio, left Rome to join the emperor's side and thus hold on to his heritage of Parma, which his irritated grandfather wanted to give to young Orazio, betrothed to Diane of France. The pope's final two years were marked by stubborn resistance to the insults heaped on him by those on the emperor's side and by despair at the ruin of his beloved Farnese family, still a political tool of great importance. With Cardinals Alessandro and Ranuccio at his side, the pope continued to the end to govern the Church, which owing to him had regained its strength and credibility. Even though he finally decided to suspend the council sessions on 13 September 1549, he attempted to compensate on the spiritual plane for what he had failed to do on the temporal. He died on 10 November 1549 in Rome after a bout of pneumonia and was buried in the magnificent tomb built for him in St. Peter's by Giacomo Della Porta; Romolo Amaseo gave his funeral eulogy in the form of an *Itinerarium Pauli III*.

Church Government and Reforms. Besides handing out promotions and favors unmistakably marked by nepotism, throughout his pontificate Paul III persevered in a campaign of reform. This consisted not only in the renewal of the Sacred College but in the approval of new religious orders, the promulgation of bulls, and, of course, the supervision of deliberations of the council. In all, the Holy Father appointed 71 cardinals, holding consistories almost every two years over the length of his pontificate. The first appointment concerned only his two grandsons; in the second, six months later, 7 prelates were promoted (Nicolaus Schomberg, Girolamo Ghinucci, Giacomo Simoneta, John Fisher, Jean Du Bellay, Gasparo Contarini, and Mario Carraciolo *in petto*). In the third, of 22 December 1536, 11 were named (Gian Pietro Carafa, Giovanni Ciocchi Del Monte, Ennio Filonardi, Jacopo Sadoleto, Cristoforo Jacovazzi, Charles Hémard de Denonville, Ridolfo Pio da Carpi, Reginald Pole, Ludovico Borgia, Girolamo Aleandro, Nicolo Caetani). In the fourth, of 18 October 1538, only the archbishop of Compostela, Pietro Sarmiento. In the fifth, of 20 December 1538, Juan Alvarez de Toledo, Pedro Manrique, Robert de Lenoncourt, Ippolito d'Este, and Pietro Bembo. In the sixth, of 19 December 1539, Federico di Campo Fregoso, Uberto Gambara, Pietro Paolo Parisio, Marcello Cervini, Bartolomeo Guidiccioni, Ascanio Parisano, Enrico Borgia, Jacopo Savelli, and Michele de Silva. In the seventh, of 2 June 1542, Gian Girolamo Morone, Pomponio Cecchi, Roberto Pucci, Tommaso Badia, Gregorio Cortese, Cristoforo Madruzzo, Gasparo d'Avalos, Francisco Mendoza de Bobadilla, Bartolomeo d'Albuquerque, Georges d'Armagnac, Jacques d'Anebault, Otto Truchsess Wadburg, Andrea Cornaro, Francesco Sfondrati, Durante de Durantibus, Girolamo Capodiferro,

and Tibertio Crispi. In the ninth, of 16 December 1545, at the start of the council of Trent, Pietro Pacecco, Georges d'Amboise, Ranuccio Farnese. In the tenth, of 27 July 1547, Charles de Lorraine and Giulio della Rovere, and in the 11th, of 8 April 1549, Girolamo Veralli, Jacopo Angelo de' Medici, Roberto de Ferraris, and Bernardino Maffei. All these choices show not only a systematic recruitment but a shrewd diplomatic balance among the various nations. There is a clear predominance for Spain in 1538, a gradual eliminating of the Florentine party (aside from Savelli and Pucci), who were suspected of bearing allegiance to the Medici, and a steady recruiting of humanists—Sadoleto, Du Bellay, then Georges D'Amboise for France, Contarini, the bibliophile Pio da Carpi, the epicurean Gambara, creator of the Villa Lante, Aleandro, Pietro Bembo, Marcello Cervini for Italy—as well as leading spiritual figures such as Fisher, Pole, Ghinucci, and Simonetta at the beginning, and then Guidiccioni, Morone, Fregoso, Cortese, Sfondrati, and Pacecco.

Paul III approved a number of new religious orders and supported the reform of some older ones—the reform of the Augustinians, headed by Girolamo Seripando, and the approval of the Theatines, under the influence of Cardinal Carafa, the Barnabites, the Capuchins—in spite of the apostasy of their vicar general, Bernardino Ochino—the Somaschi, the Hospitallers founded by John of Avila, the Ursulines of Angela Merici, the Angelicals of Ludovica Torelli, and of course, the Society of Jesus, approved by the special bull *Regimini militantis ecclesie* of 27 September 1540. The second important bull was that reestablishing the Inquisition, at the request of Cardinal Carafa, the future PAUL IV, who was appointed to head it along with six other cardinals and who put it to cruel use. The bull, *Licet ab initio* dated 15 July 1542, gave rise to what later became known as the Holy Office. Finally, several bulls were successively issued to convene the council, which was constantly being postponed—the first at Mantua on 2 June 1536, the second at Vicenza, and the third at Trent on 13 December 1545. Various reform commissions had previously been instituted, as early as November 1534. One consisted of Cardinals Sanseverino, Piccolomini, and Cesi for the reform of morals, another of Campeggio, Grimani, and Cesarini for the administration of the Patrimony of St. Peter. A third commission, this time made up of five cardinals and three bishops, was appointed on 23 August 1535. This commission produced a series of ordinances that were published under the title *Edictum reformationis generalis* on 11 February 1536 and reissued a year later in the memorandum *Consilium delectorum cardinalism et aliorum praelatorum de emendenda Ecclesia* of 29 March 1537. Its application was entrusted to Cardinals Carafa, Contarini, Ghinucci, and Simonetta, who first of all tackled the reform of the DATARY, while Cardinals Campeggio, De Cupis, Cesarini, and Ridolfi took on the reform of the ROTA, the Penitentiary, and the Chancery, whose new dispositions were registered by the bull of 12 May 1542, together with simplified regulations. Likewise, Ghiberti, bishop of Verona, Ercole Gonzaga, bishop of Mantua, and several cardinals took steps to reform the morals of their clergy, in particular regarding the obligation of residence. Finally, a series of dioceses was created in Portugal, Cape Verde, Peru, and Mexico to allow for the work of evangelization. All these measures, mostly ineffectual, had little effect on the work of the fathers of the council from 1545 on.

Patronage of the Arts. At first, Pope Farnese, like the Medici popes before him, was content to lead an ostentatious life surrounded by players, dancers, and buffoons, and to give sumptuous parties, the dates of which were not always compatible with his functions as pope. For example, on the day of his enthronement, he organized a ceremony in honor of the baptism of his great-grandchildren, for which he was quickly reproached, in particular by Aretino (Pietro Bacci [1492–1556]). Later, Paul III was intent on the embellishment of Rome. He tried to expedite the clearing of the Capitol to allow for the erection of the equestrian statue of Marcus Aurelius, and of the Palatine, where the famous *Orti farnesiani*, or Farnese Gardens, were created; he supervised the completion of Michelangelo's frescoes in the SISTINE CHAPEL and the so-called Pauline chapel at the Vatican and engaged Vasari for those of the Chancery Palace. He was also eager to continue JULIUS II's urban planning enterprise by razing a large number of dilapidated buildings, creating new streets like the Via Paolina and the Via del Babuino, and enlarging the squares—beginning with the one in front of the enormous palace he had built by Sangallo. Likewise, he put much effort into the restoration of the sanctuary of Loreto and of the Madonna della Quercia, had ramparts put up at Perugia, had the University of Rome rebuilt, and had a new university established in Macerata. Paul III has been seen as a man of letters, a collector of antiques, paintings, books, and art objects; aside from his passion for medals, however, it appears that the Farnese collections, now housed in Naples, should be credited to him rather than to his grandfather.

François Fossier

Bibliography

Accame, P. *L'Elezione del papa Paolo III*, Finalborgo, 1907.

Annibali, *Notizie storiche della familia Farnese*, Montefiascone, 1817.

Battistella, A. *Il S. Offizio e la riforma religiosa in Bologna*, Bologna, 1911.

Bini, T. *Lettere inedite di G. Guidiccioni*, Lucca, 1855

Brieger, T. *G. Contarini und das Regensburger Konkordenwerk des Jahres 1541*, Gotha, 1870.

Capasso, C. *La Politica di papa Paulo III e l'Italia*, Camerino, 1901.

Capasso, C. *Paolo III*, Messina, 1925.

Carabelli, G. *Dei Farnesi e del ducato di Castro e Ronciglione*, Florence, 1863.

Cherubini, L. *Bullarium romanum*, I, Luxembourg, 1742.

Ciaconius, A. *Vitae et res gestae pontificum romanorum . . .*, 3, Rome, 1677.

Ditrich, F. *Regesten und Briefe des Kardinals G. Contarini*, Brunswick, 1881.

Dorez, L. *La Cour du pape Paul III*, Paris, 1932.

Edwards, J. *Paul III. oder die geistliche Gegenreformation*, Leipzig, 1933.

Ehses, S. "Kirchliche Reformarbeiten unter Paul III. vor dem Trienter Konzil," *Römische Quartalschr.*, XV (1901).

Friedensburg, W. *Karl V. und Papst Paul III.*, Leipzig, 1932.

Friedenburg, W. *Nuntiaturberichte aus Deutschland*, I–IV and VIII–X, Gotha, 1892–1909.

Gualano, E. *Paulus papa III nella storia di Parma*, Parma, 1899.

Jedin, H. *A History of The Council of Trent*, I, London, 1957.

Jovius, P. *Historie sui temporis*, Florence, 1552.

Kannengiesser, P. *Die Kapitulation zwischen Kaiser Karl V. und Papst Paul III. gegen die deutschen Protestanten 1556*, Strasbourg, 1888.

Laemmer, H. *Monumenta vaticana historiam ecclesiasticam seculi XVI illustrantia*, Fribourg, 1861.

Le Palais Farnèse, Rome, 1979, 3 vols.

Lupo Gentile, M. *La politica di Paolo III nelle sue relazioni colla corte medicea*, Sarzana, 1906.

Marchal, L. *DTC*, XII, 1

Müntz, E. M. *Histoire de l'art pendant la Renaissance*, Paris, 1889–95, 3 vols.

Odorici, F. *Pier Luigi Farnese e la congiura piacentina del 1547*, Milan, 1863.

Pacaut, M. *Catholicisme*, X (1985).

Panvinio, O. *Pontificum romanorum vitae*, Cologne, 1626.

Pastor, XI and XII, Paris, 1925–9.

Richard, P. *Le Concile de Trente* (vol. IX of *L'Histoire des conciles* by Hefele), Paris, 1930.

von Drüffel, A. "Karl V. und die römische Kurie," *Abhandl. der königl. Akademie der Wissenschaften in München*, XIII, XVI, XIX (1869–82).

Wolf, G. "Das Augsburger Interim," *Deutsche Zeitschrift für Geschichtewissenschaft*, II (1898).

PAUL IV. *Gian Pietro Carafa (b. Capriglio, 28 June 1476, d. Rome, 18 August 1559). Elected pope on 23 May 1555. Buried at Sta Maria sopra Minerva.*

Gian Pietro belonged to a noble and influential family of the kingdom of Naples. His uncle, Cardinal Oliviero

Carafa, enabled him to embark on an ecclesiastical career, and in 1505 gave up his own diocese of Chieti in his nephew's favor. The young bishop was successively entrusted with diplomatic missions to Naples, England, and Spain. After this last mission, in 1518 (which reinforced his anti-Spanish sentiments, inherited from family tradition), he was promoted to the archdiocese of Brindisi, which he held along with his diocese of Chieti until 1524.

In that year, he gave up all his benefices and joined the congregation of religious clergy called "Theatines" (from the Latin name for Chieti), which he had just founded along with St. Cajetan of Thiene. Created cardinal by PAUL III on 22 December 1536, he was chosen as a member of the cardinals' commission that in the following year presented the pope with the famous plan for general Church reform known as *Consilium de emendenda Ecclesia*. A tireless partisan of energetic action against all forms of heterodoxy, he was one of the leading spirits behind the creation of a cardinals' commission specifically aimed at stamping out HERESY. With its creation, in 1542, Paul III in fact was instituting the Roman INQUISITION. Cardinal Carafa was part of this new body from the outset and became one of its most influential members.

At the conclave of 15 May 1555, after the premature death of MARCELLUS II, Cardinal Carafa hardly seemed a likely candidate, despite his having been promoted to archbishop of Naples in 1553 and his being dean of the SACRED COLLEGE. Yet when it became clear that neither of the two sides sharing the Sacred College (imperial and French) would succeed in putting forward a candidate, in the end he was elected unanimously, on 23 May. The new pope-elect chose the name Paul IV in memory of the pope who had raised him to the purple.

In spite of his seventy-nine years, the new pope was still in full possession of his physical and intellectual faculties. Ascetic and cultivated (the legend of his alleged insensitivity in matters of art has recently been demolished), sincerely animated by zeal for the reform of the Church, Paul IV was rigid and uncompromising by nature. Moreover, he lacked political experience. His blind confidence in his nephew, Carlo Carafa, proved disastrous for the success of his papacy. Carafa was an able and intelligent man, but ambitious and of doubtful morality. Unwisely, Paul IV had named him cardinal only two weeks after he was elected. When, at the end of his pontificate, the pope discovered the maneuverings and malfeasances of which his nephew was guilty, he reacted with extreme severity. He stripped him of all his offices and condemned him and his two brothers to leave Rome within twelve days.

But it was too late. From the very outset of his uncle's office, Carlo Carafa had been wily enough to take advantage of his uncle's anti-Habsburg bias to push him into an alliance with France and war against Spain. This latter conflict ended in the defeat of the papal forces by the Spanish army, a defeat sanctioned by the peace of Cave (12 September 1557).

The tensions with Spain were not offset by any success of the pope's policies in other regions. For example, Paul IV's efforts to prevent the German Protestant states from being formally recognized by the emperor after the peace of Augsburg (25 September 1555) were useless because of his intransigence. The pope's attempts to halt the progress of Protestantism in Poland, France, and England—where, after Mary Tudor's death in 1559, Anglicanism had been reestablished—met with no better fate.

Paul IV was more effective in the ecclesiastical domain. It might have been expected that a pope so impelled by fervent enthusiasm for reform would reconvene the council of TRENT, which had been suspended in 1552. But in a way he mistrusted the council, which seemed to him incapable of bringing about effective religious renewal. He accordingly preferred to set up, to that end, in 1556 a general congregation initially made up of sixty-two members, and later enlarged and divided into three sections. Since the new agency was slow in producing the desired plan for general reform, the pope ended by carrying out a series of partial measures. He reformed the Datary (the abuses of which had long been a source of bitter criticism), abolished the cardinals' right of recourse to benefices, imposed more strictly the obligation of residence, bound religious to strict observance of cloistered life, condemned simony and concubinage, and, more generally, strove to restore public morality, especially in Rome. He was particularly scrupulous in the choice of cardinals and bishops, although his circumspection in the appointment of bishops sometimes caused serious delays, so much so that in October 1558 at least fifty-eight sees remained unfilled.

Paul IV threw his energies especially into the repression of heresy—which is scarcely to be wondered at, given his extremist mentality. The Roman Inquisition was given increased powers and its activity broadened. Now no one was beyond its grasp, as is shown by the example of Cardinal Giovanni Morone, a man of great merit. Suspected of heresy (an accusation of which he was subsequently completely cleared), he was thrown into prison in CASTEL SANT'ANGELO in 1557 and brought to trial. The circulation of suspicious writings was another special concern of the pope's, who in 1559 published the first pontifical Index of forbidden books. The condemnations it contained were so severe that after Paul's death the Index had to be toned down and modified.

The excessive rigor of Paul IV's government caused general discontent in Rome. At his death, on 18 August 1559, riots broke out and the Palace of the Inquisition was stormed, and the statue of the pope erected on the Capitol was thrown into the Tiber.

Agostino Borromeo

Bibliography

Aubert, A. "Alle origini della Controrirorma: studi e problemi su Paolo IV," *Rivista di storia e letteratura religiosa*, 22 (1986), 303–55.

Aubert, A. *Paolo IV Carafa nel giudizio dell'età della Controriforma*, Città del Castello, 1990.

De Maio, R. *Alfonso Carafa, cardinale di Napoli (1540–1565)*, Vatican City, 1961 (*Studi e testi*, 210), passim.

De Maio, R. *Riforme e miti nella Chiesa del Cinquecento*, Naples, 1973, 93–139.

Fenlon, D. *Heresy and Obedience in Tridentine Italy: Cardinal Pole and the Counter Reformation*, Cambridge, 1972, *ad indicem*.

Fichtner, P. S. "The Disobedience of the Obedient: Ferdinand I and the Papacy, 1555–1564," *The Sixteenth Century Journal*, 11 (1980), 25–34.

Firpo, M. "Filippo II, Paolo IV e il processo inquisitoriale del cardinal Giovanni Morone," *Rivista storica italiana*, 95 (1983), 5–62.

Firpo, M., and Marcatto, D. *Il processo inquisitoriale del cardinal Giovanni Morone. Edizione critica*, 5 vols., Rome, 1981–9, *ad indices*.

Lutz, H. *Christianitas afflicta. Europa, das Reich und die päpstliche Politik im Niedergang der Hegemonie Kaiser Karls V. (1552–1556)*, Göttingen, 1964, *ad indicem*.

Pastor, 14.

Santosuosso, A. "An Account of the Election of Paul IV to the Pontificate," *Renaissance Quarterly*, 31 (1978), 486–98.

Scaduto, M. *L'epoca di Giacomo Laínez (1556–1565)*, 2 vols., Rome, 1964–74 (*Storia della Compagnia di Gesù in Italia*, 3–4), *ad indicem*.

Simoncelli, P. *Il caso Reginald Pole. Eresia e santità nelle polemiche religiose del Cinquecento*, Rome, 1977 (*Uomini e dottrine*, 23), *ad indicem*.

Tacchella, L. "Paolo IV e la nunziatura in Polonia di Luigi Lippomano, *Dalla Chiesa antica alla Chiesa moderna. Miscellanea per il cinquantes imo della facoltà di Storia Ecclesiastica della Pontificia Università Gregoriana*, ed. Fois, S. J., V. Monachino, S. J., F. Litva, S. J., Rome, 1983 (*MHP*, 50), 231–60.

Veny Ballester, A. *Paulo IV, cofundador de la Clerecía Religiosa (1476–1559). Trayectoria ejemplar de un papa de la Controreforma*, Palma de Mallorca, 1978.

PAUL V. *Camillo Borghese (b. Rome, 17 September 1552, d. Rome, 28 January 1621). Elected pope on 16 May 1605. Buried at St. Mary Major.*

For many, the name Pope Paul V Borghese still calls to mind two things: the rise of an exceptionally long-lived family to the summit of society in papal Rome, and a dramatic conflict with the republic of Venice. However, it seems that one of the longest pontificates of the age of the Catholic Reform (1605–21), beginning in the context of the Franco-Spanish rivalry at the heart of Catholic Europe and ending at the dawn of the Thirty Years' War, deserves a less polemic and fuller vision of its development and mixed record.

Born in Rome to the jurist Marcantonio Borghese, the doyen of the lawyers of the CONSISTORY, and Flaminia Astalli, Camillo Borghese belonged to a Sienese family that had settled in Rome in PAUL III's reign, and, through his mother, to the Roman NOBILITY. After studying philosophy at the University of Perugia and law at the University of Padua, where he obtained his doctorate, the future Paul V embarked on a prelate's career in Rome. Taking his father's place as consistorial lawyer, he became successively chief clerk of both tribunals of the Signatura, vicar of the basilica of ST. MARY MAJOR, and vice-legate of Bologna (1588). In 1590, thanks to Pope GREGORY XIV Sfondrati, he obtained the post of general auditor of the APOSTOLIC CAMERA, which his father had acquired for his elder brother Orazio (1553–90), who had died prematurely. The accession of Pope CLEMENT VIII Aldobrandini (1592) was decisive for the young prelate's future. Chosen in 1593 to be ambassador extraordinary to King Philip II of Spain, on his return he was promoted to the SACRED COLLEGE on 15 June 1596 at the age of forty-four. He was first named bishop of Iesi, in the Marches (1597–99), and then in 1603 cardinal vicar (and effective bishop) of Rome. Staying aloof from the squabbles between the Spanish and French factions in the Curia (although he had received a pension from Spain since his ambassadorship), reserved in his judgments, and precise in the performance of his duties, he very soon impressed those around him as a *papabile*. But Cardinal Borghese was only fifty-three when Clement VIII died (1605), and at the CONCLAVE he saw himself passed over in favor of Cardinal Alessandro de' Medici, the former LEGATE to France.

LEO XI de' Medici's extremely brief reign (1–27 April 1605) immediately occasioned the opening of a new conclave (8–16 May). Once again it was dominated by opposition between the Spanish and French factions in the Curia and by Clement VIII's powerful cardinal nephew, Pietro Aldobrandini. One after another, the candidatures of the JESUIT Bellarmine, the Oratorian historian Baronius, and Cardinals Sauli and Pierbenedetti were thrown out until general agreement was reached on the name of Cardinal Borghese. Elected in the following session, he took the name Paul V, in memory of Paul III Farnese, his family's erstwhile protector.

Following the grand tradition of 16th-century NEPOTISM concerning close relations of the pope, the new pontiff's first concern was to further the fortunes of the Borghese family. His nephew Scipione Caffarelli (1576–1633), the son of his sister Ortensia, joined the

Sacred College on 18 July 1605 and at less than thirty carried out the duties of prefect of the Consulta, secretary of briefs, and secretary of state, replacing at the head of the papal government the preceding pontiff's CARDINAL NEPHEW, Pietro Aldobrandini. He was promoted successively legate of Avignon, prefect of the tribunal of the Signatura, prefect of the Congregation of the Council, archbishop of Bologna (1610–12), protector of the Santa Casa of Loreto, of the Holy Roman Empire and of Flanders, of the DOMINICAN and Camaldolese orders, and archpriest of ST. JOHN LATERAN and then of ST. PETER'S. He was pensioned by both France and Spain, and his annual income rose from around 80,000 Roman crowns in 1609 to 150,000 in 1612. In 1614, he acquired, for 280,000 crowns, the fiefs of Montefortino and Olevano together with vast landholdings in the Roman Campagna, and began construction of the grand Borghese Palace and the admirable Villa Borghese. Paul V's second nephew, Marcantonio Borghese, became head of the new Borghese line. In 1610, he acquired the principality of Sulmona in the kingdom of Naples and in 1613 the fief of Morlupo, and in 1620 he became general of the Church of Rome. While the Papal States' public debt increased from twelve to eighteen million crowns during Paul's pontificate, the Borghese family rose to the rank of the old Colonna and Orsini clans, rapidly surpassing in wealth and power the families of Popes SIXTUS V Peretti and Clement VIII Aldobrandini.

Yet it would be a mistake to see nepotism as amounting in practice to no more than a family's rise in the world. Although he surrounded himself with close relations following the example of his predecessors and of the secular rulers of his own times, Paul V jealously held on to his authority and his prerogatives, restricting his nephew to the role of "chief minister," which fifty years later would be merged with the originally modest post of secretary of state. On the other hand, the pope's generous PATRONAGE of the arts, along with that of his nephews, helped attract a growing number of artists and intellectuals to Rome and played a role in increasing the city's growth and influence. Paul V's pontificate is also marked by a number of grand projects in ARCHITECTURE and urban planning which enhanced the image of the capital of Catholicism. For example, from 1607 to 1617 the Borghese pope completed the new St. Peter's basilica in the Vatican—the facade of which bears his name—and, against Baronius's advice, destroyed the remains of the former Constantinian basilica. He also built the Pauline chapel (*Paolina*) in the basilica of ST. MARY MAJOR, where he would be buried opposite his predecessor Clement VIII. It was on his orders, too, that the Archives of the Holy See were moved to the Vatican, and that a new aqueduct carried the waters of Lake Bracciano (*acqua Paolina*) to areas on the right bank of the Tiber (Trastevere).

Paul V's religious policy grew out of the spirit of the council of TRENT and has its place in the mainstream of the Catholic Reform. The pope rigorously saw to the application of the council decrees, especially those concerning episcopal residence and the monastic cloister. He approved the Capuchin rule (1616) and that of the new Congregation of the Oratory of the future Cardinal de Bérulle. On 20 June 1614, he published a new Roman breviary. He also canonized St. Frances of Rome (29 May 1608) and St. Charles Borromeo (1 November 1610) and beatified the greatest saints of the Catholic Reform of the preceding century, Ignatius of Loyola, Francis Xavier, Philip Neri, and Teresa of Avila. In the mission field, he expanded the Jesuit and Franciscan MISSIONS in New France (Canada), the Congo, Abyssinia, and Paraguay.

Under Paul V, the Holy See's politics adhered to the broad guidelines laid out in Clement VIII's pontificate, namely neutrality vis-à-vis the rival ambitions of France and Spain, appeal for the unity of the Catholic princes against the Turkish threat in the Mediterranean, and prudent attempts to call into question Protestant positions in central and western Europe. Yet the sixteen years of the Borghese pope's pontificate saw little change in the confessional division of Europe. In the aftermath of the Gunpowder Plot (November 1605), the conspiracy to overthrow the Protestant monarchy of James Stuart (James I), the situation of the English Catholics deteriorated further, and they were forced to swear new oaths of allegiance. In Russia and Poland, an attempt to support the pretender Dimitri (1605–6) met with total failure, while threats of schism hung over the Uniate Catholic Church in Ruthenia and Ukraine. As a result of the growing confrontation of the Catholic and Protestant kingdoms, the German lands were caught up in a cycle of civil and religious wars launched by the Bohemian Hussite revolt and the Prague defenestration (23 May 1618). Paul V himself vigorously backed the efforts of Emperor Ferdinand II of Austria, but his experience of the appalling Thirty Years' War was confined to the first Catholic successes, notably in the battle of the White Mountain (8 November 1620), which led to the restoration of Catholicism throughout Bohemia and Moravia.

The Holy See's conflict with Venice (1604–7) was waged in a more general context, that of the clash between the Tridentine Church's theocratic proclamations and the interests of the monarchies and national and regional powers, as shown by France's attempts at the time to block publication of the decrees of the council of Trent. Before Paul V's election, Venice had promulgated two laws (January 1604 and March 1605) subjecting all new construction of convent buildings to state authorization and prohibiting the donation or sale of secular property to the Church. At the same time, Venice brought to trial two members of the clergy, an action that called into question the principle of Church immunity, emphatically affirmed by the council of Trent, by which clergy were to be tried exclusively by ecclesiastical courts. Strict disciplinarian and skilled jurist that he was, the Borghese pope on 17 April 1606 threatened to place the city under an INTERDICT. But Venice refused to give in, developing through its Servite theologian Paolo Sarpi the case for the independence of the state in temporal affairs. The interdict came into force twenty-four days later and met with vigorous resistance on the part of the Venetian government, which forbade its publication, canceled out its effects (abetted by the foot-dragging of the Roman episcopate and clergy), and, on 14 June 1606, banished the Jesuits once and for all from its territory. Little by little, Rome's decrees were defeated. Meanwhile, the Catholic states and then the Holy See grew fearful lest Venice go over to the Protestant side. But, in the end, Henry IV's France offered its mediation, which was entrusted to Cardinal de Joyeuse. After laborious negotiations, he arranged for the lifting of censures, the freeing of imprisoned religious, and a public reconciliation (21 April 1607). If Venice did not quite win the day, Paul V's rigidity found itself, for the first time on Italian soil, pitted against the adamant opposition of the secular power.

The 1607 compromise thus serves to illustrate the strength of the resistance, both confessional and political, to the proposal for Catholic reform that emerged from the council of Trent. While the Borghese pope's pontificate to a large extent strengthened, within the Church and without, the dynamics of the Catholic Reform, it also made it possible to measure the limits of and the new constraints on papal authority on the eve of the age of absolutism.

Philippe Boutry

Bibliography

Borghezio, G. *I Borghese*, Rome, 1954.

Castronovo, V. "Scipione Borghese Caffarelli," *Dizionario biografico degli Italiani*, XII (1970), 620–4.

de Magistris, C. P. *Primordi della contesa fra la Republica veneta e Paolo V*, Turin, 1907.

Della Pergola, P. *Galleria Borghese. I dipinti*, Rome, 1955–9, 2 vols.

de Olarra Garmendia, J., and de Larramendi, M. L. *Correspondencia entre la nunciatura en España y la Santa Sede. Reinado de Felipe III (1598–1621)*, Rome, 1960–7, 7 vols.

de Stefani, L. *La nunziatura di Francia del cardinale Guido Bentivoglio. Lettere a Scipione Borghese cardinal nipote e segretario di Stato di Paolo V*, Florence, 1863–70, 4 vols.

Grendler, P., *Roman Inquisition and the Venetian Press, 1540–1605*, Princeton, N.J. 1977.

Hammermayer, L. "Grundlagen der Entwicklung des päpstlichen Staatssekretariats von Paul V. bis Innocenz X. (1605–1655)," *Römische Quartalschrift*, LV (1960), 157–202.

Heilmann, C. H. "Die Entstehungsgeschichte der Villa Borghese in Rom," *Münchner Jahrbuch der bildenden Kunst*, III/24 (1973), 97–158.

Hibbard, H. *The Architecture of Palazzo Borghese*, Rome, 1962; "Scipione Borghese's Garden Palace on the Quirinal," *Journal of the Society of Architectural Historians*, XXIII (1964), 163–92.

Linhartova, M. *Epistulae et Acta Antonii Caetanii (1607–1611)*, Prague, 1932–6, 4 vols.

Marchal, L. "Paul V," *DTC*, XII-1 (1933), 23–37 .

Monaco, M. *Le finanze pubbliche al tempo di Paolo V (1605–1621). La fondazione del primo banco pubblico in Roma (Banco di Santo Spirito)*, Lecce, 1954.

Ostrow, S. F. *Art and Spirituality in Counter-Reformation Rome: the Sistine and Pauline Chapels in S. Maria Maggiore*, Cambridge and New York, 1996.

Pastor, 25 and 26.

Reinhard, W. *Nuntius Antonio Albergati (1610 mai–1614 mai)*, Munich-Paderborn-Vienna, 1972, 2 vols.

Reinhard, W. *Papstfinanz und Nepotismus unter Paul V. (1605–1621). Studien und Quellen zur Struktur und zu quantitativen Aspekten des päpstlichen Herrschaftssystems*, Stuttgart, 1974, 2 vols.; "Ämterlaufbahn und Familienstatus. Der Aufstieg des Hauses Borghese, 1537–1621," *Quellen und Forschungen aus italienischen Archiven und Bibliotheken*, LIV (1974), 328–427.

Reinhardt, V. *Kardinal Scipione Borghese (1605–1633). Vermögen, Finanzen und sozialer Aufstieg eines Papstnepoten*, Tübingen, 1984.

Roca de Amicis, A. "Studi su città e architettura nella Roma di Paolo V Borghese (1605–1621)," *Bollettino del Centro di studi per la storia dell'architettura*, 31 (1984), 1–97.

Tygielski, A. *Acta Nuntiaturae Polonae 28—Franciscus Simonetta (1606–1612). I—21.VI.1606–30.IX.1607*, Rome, 1990.

van Meerbeck, L. *Correspondance des nonces Gesualdo, Morra, Sanseverino, avec la Secrétaire d'État pontificale (1615–1621)*, Brussels-Rome, 1937.

van Meerbeck, L. *Correspondance du nonce Decio Carafa, archevêque de Damas (1606–1607)*, Brussels-Rome, 1979.

Wittstadt, K. *Nuntius Attilio Amalteo (1606 september–1607 september)*, Munich-Paderborn-Vienna, 1975.

Wright, A. D. *The Early Modern Papacy: From the Council of Trent to the French Revolution, 1564–1789*, London, 2000.

PAUL VI. *Giovanni Battista Montini (b. Concesio, Brescia, 26 September 1897, d. Castel Gandolfo, 6 August 1978). Elected pope on 21 June 1963; crowned on 30 June 1963. Buried at St. Peter's in Rome.*

Cardinal Montini's election to the papal throne on 21 June 1963 is a direct result of the VATICAN II council. The eighty cardinals who met in CONCLAVE gave their votes to the archbishop of Milan (then sixty-six years old) because a large majority of them considered him the person most suited to guide safely to port the enterprise that JOHN XXIII had launched in 1959. Voting took place after a confused and at times tumultuous first session of the council (11 October to 8 December 1962). Cardinal Montini seemed a moderate capable of keeping an even balance between the conservatives grouped behind one section of the CURIA and the progressives determined to carry out John XXIII's proposed *aggiornamento*. He also obviously possessed clear-sighted authority, which was manifest during the first session, an authority respectful of the duties assigned to the council fathers and of their right to freedom of expression. Cardinal Montini had been SUBSTITUTE SECRETARIAT OF STATE from 1937 to 1952 and pro-secretary of state from 1952 to 1954 (a post he shared with Msgr. Tardini) under the pontificates of PIUS XI (1922–39) and, especially, PIUS XII (1939–51), with whom he enjoyed a relationship of noted confidence. His experience in the Curia was undoubtedly indispensable in the confrontation between the council and the central Church government. Some votes, it seems, had already been cast in his favor in the conclave of October 1958 even though he was not a cardinal (which, canonically, was not essential). If he had been elected in 1958, would Archbishop Montini have chosen the name Paul or Pius (XIII)? Above all, would he have convened a council? It was the crossroads of destiny. But the fact is that he had applauded John XXIII's decision, had spoken out forcefully to the faithful of his diocese about its promise for the Church in the pre-preparatory and preparatory years (1959–62), and had some very clear ideas on the work that it was the conciliar assembly's task to carry out in the last half of the 20th century.

The Vatican II council—its completion, the implementation of its sixteen documents (see VATICAN II, list), and their echo in the world—punctuates the chronology of a pontificate that was inaugurated in confidence but ended in the incomprehension and general indifference of public opinion, in which Paul VI was never actually popular. The pope was respected, even admired, during the council, for which he was responsible from 1963 to 1965. His detractors were in the minority and largely ignored, except in circles without influence on opinion. The future council pope, to whom John XXIII had given an apartment in the Vatican in 1962 and of whom it was said that "Good Pope John" knew (and had hoped) he would succeed him, gave the conciliar Church its international image, of which the visit to the United Nations (October 1965) was the most spectacular manifestation. The unexpectedly powerful image of a Catholic Church reflecting on its innermost nature and its relations with the modern world, and the person of the pope who led it, became fused into one, even if Paul VI struck many as an enigmatic supreme pontiff, at once diplomatic and firm. The publication of the ENCYCLICAL *Humanae Vitae* (29 July 1968) relating to the ends of marriage, a text that Paul long meditated over, opened up a brutal rift between the pope and the world in a clash of Christian ethics, papal authority, and individual practice. The disappointment caused by the encyclical at the very heart of the Catholic world and the attacks of which it was the target heralded a "crisis" in the Catholic and Roman Church—a post-conciliar crisis—of a magnitude which affected Paul VI's pontificate from 1970 until its end. The pope faced the crisis with patience and determination until 1974. The last four years of his pontificate were marked by a personal anticipation of the end of his reign and by the "cross" (to adopt the expression used by Paul VI in his conversations with Jean Guitton) of the prospect of a SCHISM represented by the remonstrances of Archbishop Lefebvre, a former council father, which were not only insistent and hostile but had the advantage of gaining a certain audience.

The historiography of Paul VI's pontificate is therefore somewhat polemical. It is articulated around two comparative poles of reference: that of the pontificate of John XXIII, whose profound intuitions and manifest intentions some believe Paul VI tarnished; and that of JOHN PAUL II, who set the Church once more on the path of a restoration that others thought Paul VI should have undertaken more decisively from 1970 on. It opposes an open ecclesiology in favor of a normative ecclesiology, placing Paul VI's pontificate in an unstable position in relation to a Church "shaken" (to use E. Poulat's word) by the council, in the face of which, some believe, Paul did not know whether he should be John XXIV or Peter II.

The Istituto Paolo VI, founded in 1979, arranges colloquies and round tables which, thanks to an exceptional (albeit partial) archival source, allow a better grasp of the formation and actions of a pontificate situated at the juncture between the Church in council and the Church of post-conciliar times. The image of the pope that emerges is not precisely the one remembered by public opinion—an opinion invoked largely by those who criticize Paul's pontificate as compared with that of his predecessor and that of his successor. This image is not as well known. It makes possible a more rigorous approach, from the inside, to the most complex pontificate of the 20th century.

A Patrician Education. Giovanni Battista Montini's family is known to have been settled in Brescia, in the plain of the Po, from the 1400s. In the following century the city became known as the richest in Lombardy after MILAN. (It was also famous for having produced, in the

12th century, one of the most zealous opponents of the Church's temporal power, Arnold of Brescia, who was burned at the stake in Rome in 1155.) It was around this city that the Montini gradually gained influence, as professional notaries, jurists, and physicians. Giovanni Batista Montini belonged to a family with many branches extending from the town to the country in a provincial city whose industry took shape in the 18th and 19th centuries (woolen and linen cloth; sawmills; foundries and arms factories) and whose artistic bent manifested itself very early, expressing in that way its true wealth. The boy was educated by his father, Giorgio Montini, a lawyer, and his mother, Giuditta Alghisi. Both parents were devoted followers of Roman Catholicism in the climate of post-unitary Italy, that is to say, at the time of the interdict of PIUS IX (1846–78) forbidding Catholics to participate in political life through the exercise of the vote (*Non expedit*, 1871). When Giovanni Battista was born, his father was in the public eye as the province's representative in the Catholic Movement (*Movimento cattolico*), an organization Catholics seeking to uphold their convictions in the area of social action through good works, encouraged by the encyclical *Rerum novarum* (15 May 1891). In 1895, Giorgio Montini became, with the agreement of the hierarchy, a member of the local municipal council, an administrative body that allowed Catholics to band together and defend their interests in a local setting. He very soon was promoted to leader of a Catholic party in Brescia.

Giovanni Battista Montini (from early childhood he was "Battista" to his family) was frail in health, a reality that was to weigh heavily on the first years of his life as it did on the last. He was placed with a wet nurse—a bourgeois tradition that brought with it the advantage of a sheltered country environment. His early education was at the Cesare Arici college, run by the JESUITS and founded in 1882. There he attended the meetings of the Sodality of Sta Maria della Pace, which was inspired by the spirituality of St. Philip Neri (1515–95, canonized in 1622), whose apostolate of charity developed in Rome almost throughout the 16th century, having as its vision a restoration of a Christian way of life. Battista's character was perceived as difficult as a result of the tremendous effort such an education demanded of him, owing to his weak constitution and the separation from his ever-watchful family. He appeared distant to some, studious to others, at any rate generally taciturn. Removed from school on one occasion, he had to skip examinations in 1910 and 1911. After a stay in the country in the spring of 1911, his family decided to withdraw him from the college for good and have him continue his education at home as a free candidate for the secondary school final examinations.

This sheltered adolescence, which gave no definite shape to his future, did not necessarily incline Giovanni

Battista Montini to religious vocation. The milieu in which he spent his youth offered a wide range of prospects, to which the example of his forebears (active in the liberal professions and politics) bore witness and which his own intellectual, though hardly scholarly, curiosity kept open. Montini could see that to be truly committed in the world called for a strength of character that he would have to exercise in a way suited to his own character, which was slow to develop. In his family, defense of the Church was undertaken through writing, through civic administration, and through piety. These were the natural expressions of a kind of lay service that promoted and took charge of "good works." It was a service peculiar to the Catholic Movement but typically Brescian, presenting Catholic culture as a spiritual enterprise in the service of the faith, in an Italy driven by an archetypal struggle between a Church charged with obscurantism and a modern Church of which Rome would remain the center. In May 1907, the Montini family went to Rome. Battista was ten years old. PIUS X, four years into his reign, received them in AUDIENCE. Giovanni Battista Montini touched the threshold to which he would be called in 1963 as Peter's successor, at the age of sixty-six.

Monastic Vocation and Pastoral Vocation. Next to nothing is known of the origin of Montini's vocation. It seems to have been inspired by contact with a French Benedictine community that settled in Chiari (15.5 miles/25 kilometers from Brescia) in 1910 after various relocations. Montini regularly attended religious services at the abbey and stayed at Chiari on several occasions. The community followed a strict observance, that of the Rule of St. Benedict of Nursia, founder of the abbey of Monte Cassino in the early 6th century. It combined austere communal life, where followers sought perfection in the practical humility of days spent in regular prayer and work under the direction of a superior, with a desire to be examples in order to promote the proclamation of God's glory. It was hierarchical, communal, and designed to produce sanctification through prayer and reading. Through the rapture of its liturgical ceremonies, it offered Montini a perfect synthesis of the tradition of authority inherited from his education, the perfectibility of faith in meaningful prayer for the world, and the discipline of an enclosed place that nourished Catholic culture. Was he dissuaded from a monastic vocation by the abbot (Dom Christophe Gauthey)? Whatever the case, the Benedictines of Chiari did encourage him to find his way to a priestly vocation. In this area, it is not possible to talk about influences. But mention should be made of two fathers, Bevilacqua (who joined the Sta Maria della Pace sodality in 1906 and was ordained priest in 1908) and Caresina, who joined later and was Montini's confessor until 1959. Upon close look, one can see a link between the temptation of monastic life and the secular vocation inspired by the spirituality of St. Philip Neri, a link established by Montini's Brescian roots: the living of an exemplary life of service in the Church, in humility, whether interior or in action. There were also influential encounters with contemporaries of his own generation, for example, Lionello Nardi (who joined the seminary at Brescia in 1913), Francesco Galloni, a young priest appointed to the parish of Piave di Concesio in 1914, and Andrea Trebeschi, who confided in Montini about his own vocation in the same year. With his friends Bevilacqua, Caresina, and Trebeschi, Montini in November 1914 introduced the idea of a traveling library in a small journal called *Numero unico*. In June 1916, he sat for his *maturità classica*. He was nineteen.

His field of action widened during the First WORLD WAR. In 1918, he joined the Manzoni Association, made up of students of high-school age as well as university students and founded to defend freedom of teaching. He got in touch with Msgr. Pini, chaplain of the Italian Catholic University Federation (FUCI). With his father's help, he launched the review *La Fionda* (The Sling), affirming his commitment to live the faith more openly. In it, he published articles under various pseudonyms (such as Nino Tom). On 18 January 1919, on the Via Santa Chiara in Rome, Don Luigi Sturzo made an "appeal to all men who are strong and free." When the September legislative elections came around, Catholics who had responded to the appeal thus became actors in a political life supported by their options expressed within the framework of a political party, the Italian People's Party (PPI) or "Populars." Avowedly non-confessional, the PPI declared itself independent of the ecclesiastical hierarchy and was against fighting for the temporal power of the papacy. Its work was to mobilize Catholics in favor of Christian social action, through the exercise of the vote, at the heart of a society ravaged by an apparently victorious war for a united Italy.

On 29 May 1920, although he had received no formal seminary education, Montini was ordained priest through the good offices of Bishop Gaggia of Brescia, who between November 1919 and May 1920 helped him receive minor and major orders leading to priestly ordination. He spent several weeks before his ordination at the seminary of Brescia, and was granted a dispensation (the 1917 CODE OF CANON LAW stipulated that candidates had to be twenty-four years old to be ordained priest). It was clear to all that his vocation had an urgency about it, that he was someone whose very existence was tormented by a desire for a demanding life in a kind of complicity with the supernatural.

Service of the Holy See. On 10 November 1920, Montini arrived in Rome, where the bishop of Brescia had arranged for him to continue his studies. He moved into the Lombard College and registered with both the Gregorian University (run by the Jesuits) and the State University of La Sapienza. This double *cursus* was not in any way exceptional, especially since Montini was given great freedom. He continued to collaborate on *La Fionda* and developed a taste for literary writing, as attested by the publication of some short stories. In the quasi-solitude of a university life oriented toward religious studies and literature, Montini seemed to be searching for a synthesis. It was offered to him in October 1921 by Msgr. Pizzardo, substitute at the Secretariat of State, after a conversation encouraged by a friend of his father's who had excellent relations with Cardinal Gasparri, the secretary of state. To Montini, Msgr. Pizzardo opened the narrow doors of the Pontifical Academy for Noble Ecclesiastics, the training school for Vatican diplomacy. This opportunity should be seen in the political context of the time. Parliament had been dissolved in the spring of 1921 by Giolitti, who was faced with a serious crisis (strikes, the onset of fascist violence) and was attempting to broaden the majority coalition elected in November 1919 by universal suffrage and proportional representation. The Populars (*I Populari*), led by Don Sturzo, were showing deeply rooted support (107 deputies instead of 100), but still were not able to exercise a decisive influence. The Socialists were on the decline. The Communists showed 16 deputies, while the Fascists were making noticeable gains, with 35 deputies (Mussolini, the candidate for Milan, had won only 1,164 votes in November 1919). On 4 July, a conservative government, led by the ex-Socialist Ivanoe Bonomi, was formed with the participation of the Populars. In this climate, the Curia's choice is understandable: a gifted, serious, and highly recommended young priest, from a political family—part of the Italian Christian Democratic lay tradition—singularly well suited to forge links between the Holy See and modern society in the aftermath of the First World War, which had left the Holy See, despite all its efforts, in a marginal position. But the prospect of a diplomatic career did not satisfy Montini's innermost needs or coincide with the service of the Church to which he had been called.

It is a noteworthy trait of his personality that he never followed without apprehension the institutional paths imposed on him, by birth, status, or unavoidable chance. He sat for the requisite examinations (at the Gregorian and La Sapienza) and traveled abroad, to Austria and Germany, usually seeking out the hospitality of Benedictine monasteries. On 9 December 1922, he was granted his doctorate in canon law from the law faculty of the seminary of Milan, where he had registered, *pro forma*, in November. On 4 January 1923, Msgr. Pizzardo informed him of various possible NUNCIATURE positions, and in May of that year Montini was sent to Warsaw as nunciature attaché. This was a key observation post in the context of the Holy See's preoccupations vis-à-vis a Russia undermined by Bolshevism. PIUS XI, who was elected on 6 February 1922, had served as nuncio to Warsaw and had specific ideas on the need to maintain contacts with Russia and to safeguard religious freedom, in particular by exerting influence in neighboring states. Poland, where Catholicism was the majority religion, was hierarchical, messianic, and loyal to Rome, and represented a complex territory. Should the Church negotiate a concordat with that country or with Russia, so as to offer wider protection to the UNIATES (Ukraine), the Lithuanians, and the Russian Catholics? The Roman Curia favored a special relationship with Poland, as a rampart. But the Holy See had in mind a possible recognition of Russia in exchange for a concordat guaranteeing liberties in Bolshevik territory. The nunciature, under Msgr. Lauri, was well supplied with personnel. Its principal mission was to reorganize an ecclesiastical hierarchy that had been dispersed among three countries up until 1920. Here Montini was given bureaucratic tasks. He asked to be returned to Rome, at the same time taking advantage of the opportunity to explore Poland (Cracow, Poznan, Czestochowa, etc.). On 2 October 1923, his wish was granted. Was this due to his father's influence, invoking his son's health as ill adapted to a severe climate? Or did Msgr. Lauri feel that his attaché had no aptitude for the business at hand? We do know that for a second time Giovanni Battista Montini was haunted by thoughts of the monastic vocation. His meeting with Ildefonse Schuster, the abbot of ST. PAUL'S OUTSIDE THE WALLS, a Benedictine liturgist and the future archbishop of Milan, gave new life to an option from which he had once again been dissuaded.

Thus it was as chaplain of the Roman Circle of the Italian Catholic University Federation (FUCI) that Montini was appointed by Msgr. Pizzardo, even as he finished his studies at the Pontifical Academy for Noble Ecclesiastics. The position would offer him a blessed route along which to pursue his vocation. This was the time of Mussolini's rise to power, which the Holy See watched closely (the dissolution of the Chamber of Deputies in 1924; the split in the Italian Popular Party among the optimists who believed Mussolini could be controlled, the independents, and the supporters of an alliance with the Socialists; the assassination of the Socialist leader, Matteotti, in June). In this torrid climate, the FUCI embodied a kind of young people's Christian group along the lines of the Catholic Movement, fit to provide cadres for the affirmation of catholic ideals. It was because he appreciated this kind of living Catholicism in Italy that Mussolini would enter the negotiations leading in 1929 to the LATERAN PACTS, even if he did use it to tame the Church.

Montini strove, successfully, to direct the Roman Circle toward greater religious and cultural depth. Parallel with these efforts, on 24 October 1924 Msgr. Pizzardo arranged a position for him at the SECRETARIAT OF STATE,

in the section for Ordinary Affairs dealing with internal matters of the Holy See (first as a minor official; as *minutante* in April 1923). From this bureaucratic position, he gradually made his way up the administrative hierarchy, coming into contact with young curialists who were destined to play an increasingly important role—Domenico Tardini, Alfredo Ottaviani, Antonio Bacci. His secretariat position guided him as to his course of action within the FUCI. The Holy See did not want Catholic Action to appear to have ties to the Italian Popular Party (PPI). Conversely, the leaders of the FUCI did not want to receive orders from the Holy See. And in the often violent confrontations between members of the FUCI (who were few in number) and young Fascists, it soon became necessary to interpose a spirit of intellectual and cultural vigilance for the long term. In this spirit, Giovanni Battista Montini resurrected the review *Studium* and encouraged the creation of *Azione fucina*.

In the August 1930 issue of *Azione*, he published an in-depth analysis of the the position of Italian Catholics in the context of Fascism ("Catholics and Culture"). Montini's position consisted in preventing Catholics from going over to Fascism by encouraging the formation of intellectual cadres, that is, a militant Catholic elite totally devoted to the service of the Church and prepared to defend the absolute ideal of Christianity within society. His position can be summed up as one midway between neutrality toward Fascism and anti-Fascism, and had the difficult objective of preventing Catholics from being distributed into right-wing positions (clerico-Fascists) and in left-wing positions, and of grouping them instead around the "autonomous identity of Catholic laity" (Andrea Riccardi). The influence of the DOMINICAN Bevilacqua played a role in this thinking. However, Montini's ideas clashed with those of Don Guiseppe De Luca, who at the same time was championing an infiltration of Catholics rather than a specifically militant approach, in order to end the rift between sacred and profane culture and restore the traditional unity of Italian culture. From 1926 on, Montini opposed all attempts at hibernation on the part of Catholic Action, taking the position that it was totally incompatible for its leaders to belong to any other movement (in this case Fascism). The Fascist police paid particular attention to the assistant of the FUCI, following his preaching and the positions he took in the organization's publications. One police report (16 December 1931) pointed out that in fact Montini's main position consisted in making a clear distinction between those Catholics who were declared and unshakeable anti-Fascists and those who were at least tolerant of Fascism. If Montini welcomed the Lateran pacts, which provided a juridical basis for the freedom of the Church (although Fascism did not express respect for the moral force of the faith of the Italian people), he feared that the treaty would result in over-confidence in the triumph of truth owing to external circumstances and a loss of religious identity on the part of Italian Catholicism through internal pacificism or opportunism. He paid close attention to the conflict between Mussolini and Catholic Action (which the Duce wanted to suppress in the wake of the Lateran pacts) between 1929 and 1931 and to the "Second Conciliation" (2 September 1931), through which the Holy See and the government each compromised over Catholic Action, and which he regarded as a "dangerous form of courtesy" that went beyond the 1929 treaty. The FUCI was replaced by "university associations" under the strict aegis of Catholic Action, with the agreement that the Church would ensure that its leaders did not adhere to the PPI. The FUCI was unable to hold its national congress until 1932, and then under close police supervision.

On 12 March 1933, Msgr. Montini's resignation was announced in *Azione fucina*, in an anonymous article containing a letter from Msgr. Pizzardo. The latter had been appointed secretary for Extraordinary Affairs after Cardinal Pacelli became secretary of state, replacing Cardinal Gasparri (7 February 1930). Msgr. Montini had remained at Ordinary Affairs with the title of *primo minutante*. But his job had increased in volume owing to the new secretary of state's personal style, more active and punctilious than that of his predecessor. Montini's extra duties at the secretariat of state were offered as an explanation for his resignation. However, Montini's correspondence with his parents shows that he had little enthusiasm for his curial post. The position he had taken within the FUCI since the crisis of 1929–31 was looked on with increasing disfavor by certain Roman authorities, especially the new cardinal vicar Francesco Marchetti Salvaggiani, who had appointed to the chaplaincy of the Roman Circle a certain Msgr. Ronca. It was noted that the FUCI assistant had advised the Circle chaplains "not so much to preach as to converse: a brotherly dialogue, filled with deep conviction, not academic or rhetorical, laying itself open to the irony of the young." Also, that he was skeptical about plaster statues and "the useless, tasteless profusion of candelabras, feathers and flowers . . ." Problems ensued when a collection was published of the course in religion Montini gave to FUCI students, *Via di Christo* (August 1931). The authoritarian guidelines established by Msgr. Ronca at the Roman Circle displeased Msgr. Montini, who confided in Msgr. Pizzardo about the matter. The Holy See has an intense dislike of this kind of conflict. There was pressure within the Curia to bring about his resignation, with the help of the Jesuits at the Gregorian, who had recently founded an institute of religious culture and spirituality targeted to young people. His resignation was probably encouraged by Pius XI, who nevertheless continued to hold his collaborator in high esteem. Meanwhile, Cardinal Pacelli had him under his protection, as the future was to reveal.

In the period from 1933 to 1954, Msgr. Montini placed himself at the service of the Curia. The commitment was somewhat relative, however. Appointed prelate *referendarius* at the tribunal of the Apostolic Signatura, he informed his father that it was merely a way to fill empty seats. He continued to take part in *Studium*. But in December 1937, after Msgr. Pizzardo had been named cardinal, Msgr. Montini became substitute and, as such, a member of the Consistorial Congregation and that of the HOLY OFFICE as a consultor. His reputation as a man of intelligence, culture, affability, and influence spread. The natural result was that he came in rather close contact with Pius XI, and his workload became very heavy. Friendship with Msgr. Tardini, whose career paralleled his own (at Extraordinary Affairs), was strengthened. On 2 March 1939, Cardinal Pacelli succeeded Pius XI, becoming PIUS XII. The new pope preferred to work in solitude and in authoritarian fashion. As his secretary of state he named Cardinal Maglione, who would die in 1944. But it was with the new secretary of state, Msgr. Tardini, and Msgr. Montini that Pius XII carried out his duties as supreme pontiff at the heart of the Curia. Msgr. Montini enjoyed the pope's complete confidence, even though his inclinations had not changed (the autonomy of Catholics; the preference for a CHRISTIAN DEMOCRACY which would not be a Catholic monopoly), and he was sensitive to the new theological and liturgical trends the pope had condemned in his encyclical *Humani generis* in 1950. The Roman party ("Il Partito romano," to cite A. Riccardi) tried to oust him in 1948. Nonetheless, in November 1952 Pius XII appointed Msgr. Tardini and Msgr. Montini pro-secretaries of state. And on 12 January 1953, in consistory, the pope took the unusual step of alluding to the refusal of his two helpers to accept promotion to cardinalate, in this instance in the Curia. Was this a case of humility on Msgr. Montini's part? Of fundamental disagreement between Msgr. Tardini and Pius XII, as the latter revealed to John XXIII in 1959? The stay in Milan would permit Msgr. Montini to work out his synthesis.

The See of St. Ambrose (November 1954 to June 1963). A few days after Pius XII appointed him to the archbishop's see of Milan, that of St. Ambrose and St. Charles Borromeo, Msgr. Montini wrote to Fr. Bevilacqua confiding his "dismay," his "bewilderment," his "feeling of abandonment," and the "temptation to faintheartedness that overcame him" (*Notizario*, 3 May 1981). Today, the appointment is still subject to manifold interpretations. Did Pius XII name his loyal collaborator bishop in a symbolic Italian diocese (Achille Ratti, the future Pius XI, had held the post in 1922) to give him a pastoral experience that would ready him to be made his successor? Yet Pius XII never held a consistory after that of 12 January 1953. Was it a result of the pope's illness?

Probably. But did Pius XII listen to those curialists who disapproved of Msgr. Montini's advocacy of a thaw in relations with the Soviet Union in order to improve the situation of the Churches in Eastern Europe—a way of thinking that, in a different climate, would produce Paul VI's *ostpolitik*—which clashed head-on with the pope's obsessional anticommunism and the Atlanticism of the Holy See? Finally, did Pius XII give in to these objections after a disciplinary incident? This was the resignation of Mario Rossi, head of the Italian Catholic Youth Action, who was a close friend of Msgr. Montini's and who had come up against Luigi Gedda, president of ICA (Independent Catholic Action). Montini had not informed the pope of this resignation, perhaps in the hope that he might change his mind (April 1954). The rumor of the resignation spread, feeding the notion that the pro-secretary of State was conducting a personal political campaign.

On 12 December 1954, Msgr. Montini was ordained bishop in St. John Lateran. Pius XII, who was ill, was unable to officiate and sent a message—which caused a stir and corrected the rumors of disgrace—that was broadcast during the ceremony. On 6 February, Montini entered Milan, after a few stops between Rome and the Lombard capital. "Cold and damp" was how Milan struck the new archbishop, who found himself faced with a city of 3.2 million people. The curialist came into a diocese that was the largest in Italy. It consisted of a laity with complex social stratifications and its own associative structures, a clergy split among a large number of parishes, a seminary, a Catholic university (Sacro Cuore), and a diocesan curia. Moreover, Milan boasted its own liturgy, a tradition rooted in its sense of itself as a second Rome, the capital of resistance to the barbarians, the Arians, the Germanic Holy Roman Empire, the Reformation, and the Illuminati (G. Rumi). Giovanni Battista Montini, who had never been a parish priest, bishop, or NUNCIO, found himself, at fifty-seven, head of the archdiocese of Milan and about to discover what it was like to have the care of a very singular local church. It was a decisive confrontation. On the one side was his mystical vocation, his status as a diocesan priest (at the FUCI) determined to develop an autonomous Catholic culture (not without political aims), and his familiarity with the workings of the central government of the Church. On the other side was a modern civilization which had produced industrial suburbs and a diverse secularized society, one with a solid democratic tradition inspired by Turatti's socialism and which furnished Ambrosian Catholicism with a wide variety of channels of expression—the university, publications, and the media. To this lay, industrial Milan, Montini gave his complete pastoral attention, all the while retaining his specific Catholic culture and remaining alert and listening, whether through audiences, visits, or reading. Here he learned the principle of action in all circumstances—*fare qualche cosa*, the direct relation between spirituality and history. Here he became a mystic through disposition, and a man of action through will. And here too was achieved, in orderly fashion and in humility, that blending of the mystical and the will to action that was to weigh heavily on the final years of his pontificate.

Montini's episcopate in Milan had two phases. The period from 1954 to 1959 (the year of John XXIII's project for a council) saw the deepening of his initial vocation. John XXIII created him cardinal at the consistory of 15 December 1958, making the gesture that had been expected of Pius XII. From 1959, Cardinal Montini prepared the Vatican II council. In this, he was aided by Don Carlo Colombo, his theological adviser and a member of the Preparatory Theological Commission, and by Msgr. Giovanni Colombo and Fr. Bevilacqua. He was appointed to the Central Commission in November 1961. He took a background position, although in several pastoral letters he wrote of the hopes he placed in John XXIII's resolve to hold a council. But at the first session of Vatican II, it became known that John XXIII had arranged for him to take up residence at the Vatican. Was the speech given by the pope on 11 October largely inspired by him? "To study and expound this authentic doctrine in a manner that responds to the needs of our times" corresponds perfectly with Cardinal Montini's concerns. Yet the program drawn up by the council was not to his liking, as he said soberly in a speech on 2 December 1963, which drew much attention. Yet his proposal, together with that of Cardinal Suenens, archbishop of Mechelen, to organize the council's work on the axis of a reflection of the Church on herself (*ad intra*) and on the world (*ad extra*) placed him in the position of leader.

The "Aggiornamento" According to Paul VI (1963–5). The conclave to choose John XXIII's successor ended on 19 June 1963. In attendance were 80 cardinals. The new pope had to receive 54 votes. Cardinal Montini was apparently elected after six ballots (beginning 20 June), that is, on the second day of voting, after he had collected votes in his favor in the first round from European cardinals (in particular French and German) and Americans. But Cardinals Siri (archbishop of Genoa) and Suenens also received votes. On 21 June, Giovanni Battista Montini was elected, probably by 60 votes, and chose the name Paul (*Vocabor Paulus*). Was this in memory of PAUL V Borghese (1605–21), who had rigorously implemented the decisions of the council of Trent and had canonized St. Charles Borromeo? Yet it was also under Paul V that Galileo received his first condemnation. In any event, the new pope refused to be known as John XXIV or Pius XIII and, first and foremost, chose the name of the missionary apostle. One analyst of Paul VI's pontificate was to note, in 1966: "Rarely, perhaps, did a pontificate begin in such thankless conditions, as the one chosen in the conclave of

1963; rarely had the KEYS of Peter weighed so heavily: a predecessor who had died in apotheosis, without having seen the consequences of his initiatives, leaving in motion the huge machine of the body politic of the Church but before the council fathers had actually been given direction in which to proceed, save for the recommendation, open to the widest or narrowest interpretation, expressed by the term *aggiornamento*; authority exercised over four and a half years through a day-to-day empiricism, today's turn of the rudder correcting, where necessary, what was perhaps excessive or inadequate in the momentum of the preceding day; an exceptional grace of improvisation, serenity, and confidence in the help of the Holy Spirit in every situation."

Paul VI's first acts were carried out under the calming influence of continuity. On the very evening of his election to the chair of Peter, the pope confirmed Cardinal Amleto Cicognani in his position as secretary of state, whose duties in conducting the council were fundamental. The next day, in an ALLOCUTION to the cardinals in the SISTINE CHAPEL, he declared: "The most important part of our pontificate will be taken up with the continuation of the Vatican II ecumenical council, toward which the eyes of all persons of goodwill are turned." But on his CORONATION day, 30 June, *L'OSSERVATORE ROMANO* published a letter addressed by Cardinal Montini to his priests on Palm Sunday which, contrary to usual practice, had not appeared in the *Rivista diocesana di Milano* and which bore a significant title: "What We Cannot Expect from the Council." From the very first day, "closely watched precisely because of the luster that had surrounded Cardinal Montini's name," Paul VI was eager to show that he would take over John XXIII's inheritance in such a way that all the promises it held out for the Church would be preserved. Three months after the opening of the new conciliar session, the pope seized every opportunity to declare his solidarity with his predecessor.

He took pains to see that his style had the same simplicity. He made the same gestures, taking over from Pope John as he visited the poor, the humble, the sick, prisoners. But along with this desire for identification, which also was a search for his own identity, toward the end of the summer on three occasions Paul VI gave the council the first impressions of his own personal stamp. Eight days before Vatican II resumed, in a speech directed at the members of the Curia, he announced an indispensable reform of that institution and invited his listeners to acknowledge its rightness in their hearts. On 6 September, in an allocution to members of the Thirteenth Italian Week of *aggiornamento*, he laid out the broad outlines of his conception of the term, its basis, and its dynamic, as a prelude to his speech of 29 September before the council.

The new pope's thinking seemed much more straightforward in the speech of 6 September than in the one inaugurating the second session, which was more diplomatic. It is therefore worth quoting the most revealing passage: "Today, this glorious word [*aggiornamento*] constitutes an entire program. The Vatican II council, as we all know, has adopted it, indicating by it its aims of reform and renewal. It would be wrong to see in this adjective describing the highest and most characteristic manifestations of the life of the Church an unconscious but injurious weakening toward the pragmatism and activism of our times, to the detriment of the inner, contemplative life, which must take first place in the scale of our religious values. This first place remains, even if in practice the apostolic demands of the kingdom of God in the contingencies of active life require that, in the use of our time and strength, we give a preferential place to the practice of charity to our neighbor. Furthermore, let no one think that this pastoral solicitude which the Church sets at the head of her program today, which absorbs her attention and demands her care, signifies a change in attitude with regard to the widespread errors already condemned by the Church, for example, atheistic Marxism. To attempt to apply salutary, urgent remedies to a contagious and deadly disease does not mean changing one's opinion about it, but striving to fight it, not in theory but in practice."

With these remarks, Paul VI revealed in luminous fashion the role he was assigning to the council. The passage from one pope to the other was a passage from enthusiasm to realism—from an *aggiornamento* of fervor to an *aggiornamento* of lucid resignation. Dismissing both the prophets of doom and the heedless progressives, the pope summoned the council to the sanctifying mission of the Church and its eschatology—a new approach, since heretofore the council had always situated itself within two periods of history, the present and the past. He restored pastoral action to its state of contingency and linked it to the permanence of doctrine of which he implicitly claimed to be the guardian. He refused to admit a facile separation of theory and practice, declaring that they possess no truth or force except in their profound union. Finally, between 30 August and 16 September, Paul VI proceeded to carry out a gradual reorganization of the council that would lead to a procedural reform, promulgated on the eve of the second council session.

The second session of Vatican II was the one in which the pope remained silent. The institution of moderators, a reform designed to streamline discussions—a discreet gesture by means of which Paul VI began to force the council toward its end—did not have the legitimate results that might have been expected. The moderators' powers were annoyingly vague in relation to those of the presidential council. Whatever part they played in the formulation of the five questions by means of which, on 30 October, the fathers were invited to give their opinion on the principles of collegiality, "what was striking [was] the responsibility the fathers [had just] recognized and taken upon themselves." Vatican II was strengthening its lead over the papacy, a position it had maintained since 1962, and "in all respects, that day of 30 October deserves to be considered as the one on which [the council] came of age." "Never, in a phenomenology illustrated by the memories of Constance and Basel, had the pendulum seemed so eager to move in such a direction."

At the end of the session, Paul VI effectively took charge of the council again, just when the assembly was beginning to lose its breath, that is, after the voting of 30 October. As the months went by, he would guide the council to its conclusion in three ways: by means of spectacular gestures like his TRAVELS to symbolic places, where the pope was both the council's messenger and its scout; by means of teachings promulgated as part of the proper exercise of his authority, through the use of the encyclicals that gave Vatican II an unmistakable orientation; by means of pronouncements made during the council's actual workings, even proclamations *motu proprio* at the assembly tribune. At the fourth session, a raised seat placed in the middle of the presidential table served as a sign that the pope, whether present or not, was responsible for supervising and giving direction to the works of the council. In his closing speech at the end of the second session, when he described the discussions that had just taken place on the question of collegiality, the pope was careful to remind the council that the college of bishops could not be an independent body, let alone one to rival the papacy, which was supreme.

The debate on collegiality, central to the third session, was complicated because it was here that collegiality took its first steps, within the framework of the council. This occurred on two levels, the ecclesiological level and the immediate practical level. The two overlapped, as the press was quick to note. Paul VI, determined with his diplomat's temperament to bring together the majority and the minority of Vatican II, took control over the third session. In this, he was helped by the media and the weight of public opinion, which was looking for action to come out of the proceedings of the council. To everyone's surprise, he partially presided over the general congregation of 7 November, just when Vatican II was starting to grapple with the schema on missions—his doing so provoked a variety of comments. The complexity of Vatican II obliged the media to give drier or more polemical information and to devote much space to the pope's trip to India, his message to the pan-Orthodox conference in Rhodes, and his gesture of giving up the TIARA to benefit the poor. Within two days of the closing of the third session, the press was still stressing Paul VI's determining role. Who deserves credit for the majority? Among others, the pope, who had tirelessly brought people together, personally revised the smallest details, and, while doing

so, always refused to curb the council's creative freedom. In rejecting the request for a vote in the third session on the Declaration on Religious freedom, Paul VI wanted, according to numerous analyses, to help the council give the matter further thought.

Nevertheless, a rupture occurred at the very end of the third session. It was caused by Paul's claim, on the morning of 21 November 1964 at ST. MARY MAJOR, that Mary was the "Mother of the Church." In their debate on the chapter devoted to the Virgin in *De Ecclesia*, the council fathers had not retained the word "Mother." In an article published in *Le Monde*, Oscar Cullmann judged the pope's change of terminology to be in the worst possible taste. H. Fesquet, in his analysis, implied that the pope had almost had to force Cardinal Bea's hand. The disappointment of the Germans, the English, and the Protestants was profound. The pope's long, fervent passage on the Virgin in his closing speech was presented as disconcerting.

With the fourth session, the pope's influence on Vatican II would be affirmed by a series of gestures and actions that were decisive for the spirit of the council. This was acknowledged by the fathers themselves, sensitive to the images reflected back to them of a Church far larger than its extraordinary assembly. The fourth session is, together with the first, the most famous session of Vatican II. There are several reasons for this. First, John XXIII's plan of January 1959, which over the course of time excited phenomenal public interest, was about to enter history. The commentaries offered over four years on the relationship between majority and minority, on papal authority, on the relations with the other Churches in particular and the world in general had given material for deep reflection.

Paul agreed to be photographed on numerous occasions, and many pictures show him surrounded by individuals he received in audience. From 3 to 31 October 1965, he gave the *Corriere della sera*, a non-confessional Milan newspaper noted for its interesting cultural page (page 3), seventeen interviews in which he adopted an unparalleled freedom of tone. The pope was making a personal contribution to religious information through the lay press in a country where such information was plentiful and free, except in the confessional newspapers, which still showed a marked spirit of prudence and reverence. Yet Montinian courtesy and a concern for variety of opinion were governed by a sense of the symbolic which was to express itself in the closing session of Vatican II, on 8 December 1965, and which was preceded by some spectacular gestures. To general astonishment, Paul VI announced at the opening of the session that a Synod of Bishops would be instituted "in accordance with the council's wishes." Vatican II thus inaugurated the phase of post-conciliar delegation just when it was getting into achievement mode. That very afternoon, the pope, followed by all the council fathers, made an impressive penitential procession from the BASILICA of Sta. Croce in Gerusalemme to ST. JOHN LATERAN. On the following day, seated at the table of the presidency of the council, he inaugurated the 128th general congregation and made it clear that the term "synod" had an ecumenical meaning since it also meant the institution surrounding the Eastern patriarchs. The pope also read a telegram addressed to him by Patriarch Athenagoras I expressing his "wishes for a happy and grand closure [of the council's] work, for the good of the whole Church of Our Lord Jesus Christ."

On 5 October, as the council in Rome debated a new chapter of schema XIII, interpolated during the recess, devoted to "the life of the political community," Paul VI was at the United Nations in New York, where, before the General Assembly, he gave the famous speech the first sentence of which has remained in many memories: "As we commence our address to this unique world audience . . ." He spoke of the UN as an "aula magna." The Holy See was entering the concert of nations in a spectacular way. And it was impossible not to contrast this speech about the dignity of humankind, unity and peace, ending with an appeal for "conversion," with Nikita Krushchev's admonishments, shoe-banging and all, of 1959. The *Zeri i popullit* of Tirana could claim that the pope had gone to the UN to defend the cause of American imperialism, but this charge was not echoed. At the close of the session, the cameras caught a warm, relaxed conversation between the pope and the Soviet minister for foreign affairs, Andreï Gromyko, who declared shortly afterward that he had listened to the pope's remarks with "concentrated attention." *Time*, a priori against the papacy, laid down arms, and in France, *Le Canard enchaîné*, basically anticlerical and antipope, went so far as to say, under Morvan Lebesque's byline, "I like the fact that this old man believes in the assembly of peoples while ours [General de Gaulle] gets on his high horse and sneers at it as a 'Thingumabob.'" Only later was it learned that Paul VI, with his acute pessimism, believed that because of the war in Vietnam, world peace was as much in danger in 1965 as it had been in 1940, and that he was using his speech to try to prevent the Americans from bombing Chinese nuclear installations.

On 6 October, the council fathers were to discuss chapter V of schema XIII: On the Establishment of Peace and the Community of Nations. Cardinal Alfrink, general chaplain of the armies of the Netherlands and international president of Pax Christi, opened the session (two other speakers listed before him having withdrawn) and criticized the passage on the balance of terror, inserted at the request of some American and British bishops. In the text, this balance was seen, "for lack of another solution," as the factor making possible "a certain stability in the human community." To which Paul VI had the day before opposed the cry "Never again war, never, never, never again . . . !" The debate got bogged down. At noon, the council heard that the pope's plane had landed in Rome. At 12:52, Paul VI entered St. Peter's basilica, which had been open to guests since 11 A.M. As the pope made his way to the presidential table, applause drowned the melodic chant of "Tu es Petrus." Cardinal Liénart thanked the pope for having associated the council with his trip and voiced the hope that the United Nations speech might be inserted into the Acts of Vatican II.

The culminating point of Paul VI's popularity had not yet been reached. This was to happen on 8 December 1965. But if one recalls that Vatican II still faced two months of debates, it is easy to see the conditions in which the council fathers had to reach their decisions. As each conciliar text was promulgated, the pope spoke and the media took up his words and made much of them. On 28 October 1965, at the promulgation of the Declaration on Non-Christian Religions (approved by 2,221 *placet* against 88 *non placet*), Paul VI evoked the memory of John XXIII, elected pope seven years before on that same date. It was a notable coincidence, which called upon the memory of Vatican II in an atmosphere of holy respect for his predecessor's initiative, apart from any comment on the consequences of the project and its effect on the role played by the supreme pontiff within the Church. On 18 November, at the promulgation of the Decree on the Apostolate of the Laity (a vote approved by 2,305 *placet* and 2 *non placet*), Paul VI announced the beginning of the canonical processes of beatification of Pius XII and John XXIII. The gesture invited a survey of modern pontifical holiness in the light of Vatican II. Prolonged applause greeted his initiative. Vatican II still had eighteen days to go. Five general congregations took place.

In view of all these symbolic gestures, it is easy to understand why the formula "the pope and the council" dominated commentary on the conciliar discussions. Not that these lacked liveliness, whether the subject was religious liberty, the priesthood, the question of the Jews (and non-Christian religions), or, especially, schema XIII, on the relations between the Church and the modern world, discussion of which took up the final meetings of the council. Yet the severe crisis that shook Vatican II when it came to the passage devoted to marriage, directly linked to the question of birth control, was too close to the end of the council (16 November to 6 December 1965), too complex, too limited in comparison with the far-reaching perspectives traced by the texts that were voted on, to concern a public opinion with respect to which the news reporters themselves were in trouble.

The papal commission created by Paul VI in June 1964 to study problems relative to population, family life, and birth was weighing upon the *modi* formulated by the fathers, as well as the chapter voted on, in its new version, on 17 November 1965. On 24 November, four papal *modi* were introduced. Moreover, the pope kept for himself the question of the regulation of births. Only *L'Avvenire d'Italia* reported the news, at the instigation of the Holy See. The debate centered on doctrinal continuity with Pius XI and Pius XII. The council had to acknowledge that it could not settle the argument. That could be done only by the pope's magisterium, taking into account the future constitution *Gaudium et Spes* promulgated on 7 December 1965 (2,309 *placet*, 75 *non placet*). The day before, 251 had declared themselves opposed to schema XIII in plenary congregation. But on 6–7 December 1965, *L'Osservatore romano* published the *motu proprio* entitled *Integrae servandae*, which turned the Holy Office into the Congregation for the Doctrine of the Faith by quoting 1 Jn 4:18: "Perfect love casts out fear." In a highly significant manner, Paul VI announced the reform of the Curia confirmed in 1963, and the most unpopular member of the council, Cardinal Ottaviani, wept publicly, a fact that received not a little notice and comment.

The closing of Vatican II, on 8 December, was preceded four days before by an ecumenical celebration at St. Paul's Outside the Walls. Even though journalists, who had publicized it, were not admitted, the liturgical ceremony was heavily covered. It was in this same basilica that John XXIII had announced the plan for the council, in 1959. It was there, too, that Paul VI had bid "adieu" to his non-Catholic brothers, marking the road traveled between an ecumenical council in the Roman Catholic tradition and the ecumenism of the Vatican II council. The date of 8 December, the feast of the Immaculate Conception, was also that of the ending of the first session. The central place of the veneration of Mary, debated heatedly at the time of the schema on the Church, was solemnly reaffirmed. At an open-air ceremony on a bright and balmy day, in which a huge crowd took part around the leading protaganists of Vatican II, Paul VI placed the council in the perspective of the past, present, and future "of the Church of Christ," that is, of the tradition the vitality of which Vatican II was demonstrating, *in situ juxta sedem Petri*. Addressing his words to the whole of humanity, he gave seven different speeches: to rulers, to thinkers and scientists, to workers, to artists, to women, to the sick, and to the young. To Jacques Maritain, *coram publico*, was entrusted the message directed to intellectuals. The pope blessed the first stone of the parish church about to be built on the outskirts of Rome in honor of the council. And five bishops representing the five parts of the world came before the Gospel to sing the "Acclamations." Christian unity, a faithfulness to the Gospel keenly aware of modern sociology, to which the Christian message, reinvigorated by Vatican II, was to refer, confidence in the relations between intelligence and faith—all this was said and understood in these terms. The *signa temporum* that

Vatican II had wanted to retain in the constitution *Gaudium et Spes* were, on 8 December, now made manifest.

Vatican II dispersed in joyful spirits and full confidence regarding the future of its work, which would fall to the post-conciliar committees and to the pope to put into effect.

The Post-Conciliar Test (1968–78). The publication of the encyclical *Humanae vitae* very soon created a deep and lasting rift in Paul VI's pontificate. The conditions under which it was drawn up—in two stages: 1965–7, when certain passages of the constitution *Gaudium et Spes* concerning marriage were suspended, and 1967–8, the year Paul VI resolved to confirm the 1930 encyclical *Casti connubii*—were obliterated by the text itself.

Later, specialists explained the context in which the encyclical was drawn up. But their analyses had no effect on a public opinion shocked by the intervention of papal authority in an area as sensitive as that of sexual morality. There was not a second's doubt that the pope had wanted this encyclical or that he had taken a decisive part in the writing of it. Never had a papal document appeared that seemed so thoroughly to express the dogmatic authority of a pope of whom no one, once the council was over, had expected such an exercise of that authority. The relationship with the encyclical of 1930 was not established, nor that with Pius XII's many speeches on the question. But even if they had been, the history of Pius XI's pontificate was largely unknown and, since Hochhuth's play *The Deputy*, Pius XII had been demonized. The date of the encyclical was unfortunate. The year 1968 saw an outburst of criticism and anarchy, reaching Europe from the United States. The generation born after the Second WORLD WAR questioned the authority of civil leaders, authority which had ties with the history of postwar reconstruction. (In France, General de Gaulle was seventy-eight, in Italy the Christian Democrats had been in power every year since 1946, in Germany the CDU had been in power since 1950, etc.). They also questioned an elitist parental culture. They opposed militancy whether on the part of the Church (Catholic Action) or of politics (political parties and trade unions), and were inspired by a revolutionary vision deriving from an exotic, that is, antibolshevik, Marxism. These were so many elements of a moral crisis expressed at every level by permissiveness. The encyclical *Humanae vitae* was summed up as a condemnation of contraception, which it did denounce. It seemed not to matter that this condemnation was not formulated as a principle but stated as a natural consequence of real love, celebrated in language recalling that of the Song of Songs, that is, as a consequence of the total, creative communion within and by the couple. It seemed not to matter that the encyclical was a warning cry to the Christian laity, giving them an exemplary mission correlative to their insertion within the people of God, whom the work of the council had made the foundation of the modern Church. The encyclical was received as an ethical norm established by the magisterium of Rome, not as a spiritual undertaking.

Humanae vitae was compared to the explosion of Hiroshima, though to varying degrees. The council fathers saw in it a problematic negation of the consensus worked out in Vatican II. Even though the debate on schema XIII had ended with a constitution that reflected compromise rather than unanimity, the council majority constituted in 1965 burst apart. The maximalists and pragmatists, who in 1964 had defended the principle of the diaconate for married men, now favored a more flexible position on the Church's part or else silence on the part of the magisterium to allow a pastoral action, and joined forces in condemning the timing of the encyclical. Cardinal Alfrink recalled that "encyclicals are never infallible." In Germany, the Catholic writer Heinrich Böll declared that the encyclical would be ignored. In France, *Le Monde* spoke of a "primitive mentality." Readers were reminded that the Church had never understood the first thing about the physical dimension of human love. Even those organs of the press and movements sensitive to the views of Paul VI spoke of fatal incomprehension, disappointment, and disarray. Still, French Catholic Action added in a communiqué of 4 August, "We are deliberately dismissing all disputes based on the opinion of a majority or a minority."

On 16 September, *France-Soir* published a French public opinion poll which showed that for 36 percent of those questioned Catholics ought to follow the papal directives and that for 50 percent of those questioned Catholics could ignore them. The Anglo-Saxon countries, in which Catholics were a minority and naturally disposed in favor of Roman authority, and from which many birth control pressure groups had gone to Rome, were confused. To their opponents, the encyclical gave the impression of being a matter of law, whereas it was evident that it laid down a standard, or norm, to live by. A law is to be obeyed, whereas a norm tends to inspire practice without imposing an obligation on the conscience. The distinction, incomprehensible to the Anglo-Saxon mentality, confounded the analysis, reduced the text to the level of the prescriptive and the binding, and undermined the authority of Rome.

We here enter a complex phase of the reception of the council, that of the levels at which it was received, or of the depth to which the work accomplished by the doctors and guardians of the faith is accepted in the Christian life of the people of God. Numerous analyses have been made of the process by which a council is received, analyses which differ depending on national Churches and the character of societies. They are conducive to a periodization which determines the relationship between the informational aspect (the reception of kerygma), "which contains a formal or juridical canonical aspect," and the actualization of the council in the life of the Church by its translation into actions and into ways of living, through liturgy and the spiritual and ethical life.

Traditionally, until Vatican II, reception of kerygma depended on a formalization *ad extra*—for example, the catechism of the council of Trent, the 1917 Code of Common Law—of a collection of conciliar texts produced by the Church *ad intra*. John XXIII's announcement in 1959 of the plan for a council and a reform of the 1917 Code was based on that principle. But Vatican II had taken place in the full public eye. No longer was information passed along traditional channels; bishops and theologians were often only one such channel. Advances in the liturgical domain had been made before the debate on the intimate nature of the Church. The structure of the council's work as defined by Cardinal Suenens (and Msgr. Montini and others) in December 1963 had set up a conciliar relation between the work *ad extra* and that *ad intra*, around the two poles represented respectively by *Gaudium et spes* (schema XIII) and *Lumen gentium*.

One part of the reception of kerygma came in 1983 with the publication of the new CODE of CANON LAW. But before that had come the promulgation of the Constitution on the Sacred Liturgy in 1964, the decrees on the means of social communication, ecumenism, religious freedom, and so on, and above all the constitution *Gaudium et Spes* (1965), in short, sixteen documents that took into account praxis and opened up to a praxis. The curial reform of 1967 achieved a synthesis between *praxis pietatis*—entrusted to the episcopates according to the principle of subsidiarity, to the post-conciliar committees, and, henceforth, to the Roman Curia, and transcending national boundaries—and a necessary *didachè*, that is, theology as a necessary reflection on that reality. It must be acknowledged that the *praxis pietatis*, recorded by a number of documents, was still normative once the council had ended. The council's authority had made it popular by virtue of the abundant questions freely raised in the course of discussion, notably during the debate on schema XIII. But as certain council fathers acknowledged in private, this popularity did not conform with the vision of Vatican II.

Many members of the laity, and also priests, expected an immediate solution to problems of personal life: divorce, birth control, clerical celibacy, means of active participation in the life of the Church, information, and so on. With the encyclical *Humanae vitae*, Paul VI closed Vatican II, which until then had been seen as rather an open council. Invoking the idea of "Understand me and accept," he asked for adherence to the profound spirit of Vatican II on a subject that harked back to

Church tradition in the matter, and with that he seemed to rob the term "pastoral," which had conditioned the council from its very beginning, of all meaning. And the encyclical caused the work of the council to be seen as mixed, to the point where good and bad texts were distinguished.

Was it an open council or a closed one? The debate was to widen until the extraordinary synod of 1985 celebrating the twentieth anniversary of the closing of Vatican II. Some zealous anti-conciliars had voiced their opinions throughout the council, Cardinals Siri, Ruffini, and Tisserand, for example. But just after Vatican II, noting that the consensus Paul VI had desired had meant that the wishes of the minority were taken into account, certain voices were raised to assign a counter-reformist character to the council's pastoral work and to encourage a literally submissive reception of the council. All these analyses counted less in the eyes of public opinion than did the perception that there was a general crisis in the Catholic Church: lack of respect for the spirit of the encyclical *Humanae vitae*; a crisis of the clergy, with the decline of priestly vocations in Western Europe; the dispersal of the Catholic vote and the crisis of the Christian democratic parties and movements; a spectacular crisis in the Church of the Netherlands, perceived since 1964. Once dispersed, the council fathers—bishops and theologians—could no longer take responsibility for Vatican II. The review *Concilium*, created in 1967 to maintain the spirit of the council, saw the departure of a certain number of eminent members of the editorial committee in 1969, such as Frs. de Lubac, Daniélou, and Karl Rahner, who favored the creation of the review *Communio* that same year in a spirit of defense of the Church's authority.

The term "crisis of the Church" appeared in 1970. That was the year Archbishop Lefebvre made public the positions that he had gradually been tried out in private since 1964. The movement based on the question "To be Catholic, must one become Protestant?" was radicalized from 1972, expanding to a systematic critique of the work of Vatican II, even though he had approved most of its texts. R. Witgen's work *The Rhine Flows into the Tiber* presented the documents of Vatican II as the fruits of a Franco-German collaboration that dominated the Third World through economic power and was supported by a revolutionary type of anti-curialist movement. According to Witgen, Vatican II was inspired by the spirit of the French Revolution: collegiality = egality; religious freedom = liberty; ecumenism = fraternity. *La Pensée catholique* argued in its review of the book that one could go further: Vatican II was a reply to the centuries-old effort of Protestantism and Freemasonry—to define man. Suspended *a divinis* in July 1976, Archbishop Lefebvre finally asserted in reply that Vatican II was "a schismatic council."

In a general sense, if the heritage of Vatican II is subject to multiple evaluations, that is true primarily for Western Christianity, for which the experience of its twenty-first council was one of different positions confronting one another, unlike the experience of the *Syllabus* and Vatican I. By contrast, as was evident at the extraordinary synod of 1985, the young Churches and especially the African Churches testified that for them Vatican II was the equivalent of the council of Nicaea. Yet Paul VI himself, noting the crisis to which Archbishop Lefebvre's attitude gave spectacular resonance, observed in June 1972 that the council had not brought about the hoped-for springtime of the Church and that, taking advantage of certain rifts, the fumes of Satan had penetrated the Church. The speech was directed against Archbishop Lefebvre. But it caused joy among the traditionalists, who were mustering their forces, and among other anxious conservatives.

Even before his election as pope, Giovanni Battista Montini had been seen as a Hamlet figure by certain curialists adamantly opposed to what others judged to be the leading direction of reconciliation, the direction welcomed by the council. Now even the moderate, pro-Vatican II circles saw him as a vacillating Hamlet. In reality, it is clear that the latent schism the traditionalists hoped for was forcing the pope to find a post-conciliar unity leaning to the right, after having thrust it toward the moderates and the maximalists against the conservatives. That accounts for the audience granted to Archbishop Lefebvre in 1977. Less attention was paid at the time to the fact that a left-leaning anti-conciliar movement was on the rise. It argued that Vatican II had proposed more or less significant changes (in the area of the liturgy, for instance, or relations with other religions) that, far from transforming the system of authority, had actually strengthened it.

Paul VI's international travels, which the media followed closely—he made nine in all—ended in 1970 with the *peregrinatio* to the Far East. In mid-journey he stopped in Hong Kong, at the gates of China, to which he addressed his message of 4 September 1970. By means of the HOLY YEAR of 1975, which was a necessary one, the pope tried visibly to make the spirit of Vatican II breathe through a centuries-old institution the meaning of which eluded the masses and they responded accordingly. "The holy year," the pope had said in 1975 in celebrating its inauguration for his Roman diocese at the Lateran, "is the moment when we are called on to decide what we wish to be, to define for ourselves what we are, not from the point of view of the civil state, but from that of life itself." To this spiritual inspiration by means of an act of devotion closely linked to Church tradition and to remembered unity they responded with a disorderly anti-conciliarism, which it was obvious Rome under Paul VI could not control. On several occasions, the pope alluded to his death. He responded to the political and theological reception of the work of Vatican II by retiring into little-noticed years of mysticism. At his death, on 6 August 1978, he left behind the image of a struggle between the council fathers and the supreme pontiff, of a council closed in 1965, and of a "shaken Church," to adopt Émile Poulat's expression. His funeral in St. Peter's Square roundly contradicted that image. The pope's coffin, laid on the ground with the Bible placed upon it, and surrounded by a commemorative representation of the council (council fathers, experts and observers, auditors), made an appeal for humility and unanimity with respect to the historic role the pope and the participants of Vatican II had played in a resolutely modern Christianity.

Philippe Levillain

See also OSTPOLITIK; VATICAN II.

Bibliography

Acerbi, A. "Chiesa, cultura e società nell'itinerario intelletuale di G.-B. Montini," *Problemi di storia della Chiesa dal Vaticano I al Vaticano II*, Rome, 1988, 391–428.

Acerbi, A. *Chiesa e democrazia da Leone XIII al Vaticano II*, Rome, 1991.

Actes et documents du Saint-Siège relatifs à la Seconde Guerre mondiale, 12 vols., Vatican City, 1965–81.

Adornato, G. *G.-B. Montini. Religione e lavoro nella Milano degli anni' 50*, Brescia, 1988.

Antonetti, N. *La FUCI di Montini e Righetti. Lettere di I. Righetti ad A. Gotelli*, Rome, 1979.

Bendiscioli, M. "Paolo VI," *Dizionario storico del movimento cattolico in Italia*, 2, Turin, 1982, 448–53.

Boyer, C. "Le pape Paul VI," *Esprit et Vie* (1978), 689–95.

Chiron, Y. *Paul VI, le pape écartelé*, Paris, 1993.

Colombo, G. "Papa Paolo VI ed il Concilio Vaticano II," *Vita e Pensiero*, 46 (1963), 535–41.

Colombo, G. *Omaggio a S.E. Mons. Carlo Colombo*, H. C., 1991.

Colombo, G. *Ricordando G.-B. Montini arcivescovo e papa*, Brescia, 1989.

Comblin, J. "El pontificado de Pablo VI," *Mensaje*, 273 (1978), 609–15.

Cremona, C. *Paolo VI*, Milan, 1991.

Cripa, R. "Paolo VI e la cultura contemporanea," *Coscienza*, 8/9 (1978), 13–4.

Detta, P. "Paolo VI e gli studi ecclesiastici," *La Civiltà cattolica*, 21.4.1979, 131–41.

Dorn, L. A. *Paul VI. Der einsame Reformer*, Graz, 1989.

Durand, J. D. *L'Église catholique dans la crise de l'Italie (1943–1948)*, Rome, 1991.

Fappani A., and Molinari, F. *G.-B. Montini giovane*, Turin, 1979.

Ford, J. T., ed. *Religious Liberty: Paul VI and Dignitatis Humanae*, Symposium sponsored by the Istituto Paolo VI and the Catholic University of America, Washington, D.C., 3–5 June 1993.

Fouilloux, E. "Paul VI," *Universalia* (1977), 445–6.

Garrone, G. M. *La Profession de foi de Paul VI*, Paris, 1969.

Giuntella, P. "Il Papa del dialogo," *Il Mattino*, 5.8.1988.

Gonella, G. "Amico Maestro," *Studium*, 74 (1978). 449–60.

Guasco, M. "Scritti e ricerche sul giovane Montini," *La Rivista del Clero italiano* (1981), 178–84.

Guelluy, R. "Le magistàre 'ordinaire' de Paul VI," *Revue théologique de Louvain*, 4 (1978), 407–16.

Guitton, J. *Dialogues avec Paul VI*, Paris, 1967.

Guitton, J. *Paul VI et l'année sainte*, Paris, 1975.

Guitton, J. *Paul VI secret*, Paris, 1979.

Hebblethwaite, P. "From G.-B. Montini to Pope Paul VI," *JEH*, 37/2 (1986), 309–20.

Hebblethwaite, P. *Paul VI: The First Modern Pope*, London, 1993.

Levillain, P. *La Mécanique politique de Vatican II*, Paris, 1975.

Macchi, P. "Adesso viene la notte," *La Prealpina*, 6.8.1988.

Manathodath, J. *Culture, Dialogue, and the Church: A Study on the Inculturation of the Local Churches According to the Teaching of Pope Paul VI*, New Delhi, 1990.

Moro, R. *La Formazione della classe dirigente cattolica (1929–37)*, Rome, 1979.

Neves, L. M. *Paolo VI. Profile di un pastore*, Milan, 1989.

Paoletti, D. *La testimonianza cristiana nel mondo contemporaneo in papa Montini*, Rome-Assisi, 1991.

Paul VI: Coscienza universitaria, Rome, 1930. *L'Église et les conciles*, Paris, 1965. *Documents pontificaux de Paul VI*, 17 vols., Saint-Maurice, 1967–80. *Vous les prêtres du Christ*, Paris, 1969. *Face à la contestation*, Paris, 1970. *Lettere a un giovane amico. Carteggio di G.-B. Montini con A. Trebeschi*, Brescia, 1978. *Scritti Giovanili*, Brescia, 1979. *Colloqui religiosi*, Brescia-Rome, 1981. *Giovanni XXIII e Paolo VI, Saggio di Corrispondenza (1925–62)*, Brescia-Rome, 1982. *Discorsi e scritti sul Concilo 1959–63*, Brescia-Rome, 1983. *Saggio di corrispondenza (1923–77)*, Brescia, 1985. *Lettere ai familiari (1919–43)*, 2 vols., Brescia-Rome, 1986. *Al mondo del lavoro (Discorsi e scritti 1954–63)*, Brescia-Rome, 1988. *Una rara amicizia, G.-B. Montini e M. Rampolla del Tindaro. Carteggio 1922–44*, Brescia-Rome, 1990. *Interventi nella Commissione Centrale Preparatoria del Concilio Ecumenico Vaticano II*, Brescia-Rome, 1992.

Paul VI et la modernité dans l'Église, École française de Rome, Rome, 1984.

Paulus PP.VI 1963–78. Elenchus bibliographicus. Colle-

git Pal Arato. Demmo refudit, indicibus instructionis Paolo VI, Brescia, 1981.

Poulat, É. *Église contre bourgeoisie*, Tournai, 1977.

Poulat, É. "Paul VI," *Universalia* (1979), 620–1.

Publications of the Istituto Paolo VI (Brescia). *Notiziario* (Istituto Paolo VI), 26 issues since 1979.

Riccardi, A. *Il "Partito Romano." Nel secondo dopoguerra (1945–1954)*, Brescia, 1983.

Riccardi, A. *Roma "Citta sacra"? Dalla Concilazione all'operazione Sturzo*, Milan, 1979.

Rouquette, R. "Paul VI héritier de Jean XXIII," *Études*, 219 (1963), 245–59.

Roy, J. *L'Année sainte de Paul VI*, Paris, 1974.

Sorge, B. "In memoria di Paolo VI," *La Civiltà cattolica*, 2.9.1978, 350–9.

Storman, E. J., ed. and trans. *Towards the Healing of Schism: The Sees of Rome and Constantinople: Public Statements Between the Holy See and the Ecumenical Patriarchate 1958–1984*, New York, 1987.

Vian, N. *Anni e Opere di Paolo VI*, Rome, 1978.

Wolff, R. J. "G.-B. Montini and Italian Politics 1897–1933: The Early Life of Pope Paul VI," *The Catholic Historical Review*, 71 (1985), 228–47.

PAVILION. The basilican pavilion, also known as *ombrellino* or *gonfalon*, is the emblem of the papacy and the Roman Church. It represents the supreme pontiff's temporal power. It has frequently appeared on banners since the 13th century, but the pope has used it only rarely, as a timbre or crest above his coat of ARMS (a few examples exist from the time of MARTIN V). Shaped like a half-opened sunshade, it is of two colors and patterned with alternating red and yellow stripes (in heraldic parlance, *gyronny gules and or*); the staff is gold. At first used alone, from the 14th century on it often appeared together with the two KEYS, embossed on the staff in crosswise position.

When the HOLY SEE is vacant, the cardinal CAMERLENGO places the pavilion above his own shield, and sometimes on his seal, to show that papal jurisdiction has not ended with the death of the supreme pontiff. At certain times the SACRED COLLEGE, the APOSTOLIC CAMERA, and various papal institutions have used the pavilion as a heraldic or paraheraldic emblem. Similarly, from the late 15th century, certain families that had given a pope to the Church introduced the pavilion into their coats of arms (the first to do so were the Borgia). Later, the pope himself rewarded other families for services rendered to the papacy by granting them the privilege of placing the pavilion in their shield.

Originally, the pavilion was most likely a dais or baldachin that was placed over the pope's head as a sign of respect and power. Each major BASILICA kept one with which to welcome the supreme pontiff. As time went on, the pavilion became an emblem of dignity, to be used in many non-liturgical ceremonies, and then simply a paraheraldic badge. Between reigns, the pavilion thus replaced the tiara on coins minted by the pontifical *Zecca*. The earliest example dates from 1521. Thereafter, the pavilion became, among its other uses, a specific emblem of *sede vacante*, appearing with or without the two keys.

Michel Pastoureau

Bibliography

Galbreath, D.L. *Papal Heraldry*, 2nd ed., London, 1972, 27–37.

Heim, B. B. *Coutumes et droit héraldiques de l'Église*, Paris, 1949, 66–9.

PELAGIUS I. (*d. 3 March 561*). *Consecrated on 16 April 556. Buried at St. Peter's, in Rome.*

Pelagius was the son of a certain John, described as a *uicarianus* (no doubt employed at the vicariate either of the praetorium or of the city). In the winter of 535–6, as a deacon of the Church of Rome, he accompanied Pope AGAPITUS to Constantinople, the pope having been sent on an embassy to Emperor Justinian by the Gothic king Theodahad. Shortly before the pope's death (22 April 536), Pelagius was named *apocrisarius* to Constantinople. It was as a simple Roman priest that, together with five papal legates who had served in a preceding embassy, he took part in the council held in the imperial capital from 2 to 4 June 536, under Bishop Menas, to confirm the work of restoring Chalcedonian Christology undertaken by Agapitus. There Pelagius signed the confirmation of the deposition of Anthimus, ex-bishop of Constantinople, as well as Pope HORMISDAS's earlier condemnation of the leading Monophysites, Severus of Antioch and Peter of Apamea.

Pelagius sided with VIGILIUS, who became pope in March 537 and had the support of Empress Theodora, against the former pope SILVERIUS. Opposed to Anthimus's rehabilitation, Silverius had been condemned for high treason and sent into exile in Lycia. Pelagius tried, in vain, to oppose Justinian's decision to bring Silverius back to Italy to be retried.

As *apocrisarius* to Pope Vigilius, Pelagius was embroiled in all the affairs agitating the Eastern Churches. He took steps to have a pro-Chalcedonian, Paul, abbot of Taba, chosen as bishop of Alexandria; but because the bishop had exceeded his powers he was obliged, probably in 538–9, by Justinian's order and along with the metropolitans of Antioch, Jerusalem, and Ephesus, to proceed to his deposition and to replace him with the monk Zoile.

Pelagius was also in the thick of the Origenist controversy. Some Palestinian monks who opposed Origen of Alexandria and admired Theodore of Mopsuestia urged Pelgius to have the emperor condemn certain propositions drawn from the writings of the Alexandrian doctor. Pelagius is believed to have seen this as an opportunity to checkmate the bishop of Caesarea in Cappadocia, Theodore Askidas, protector of the Origenists and his rival for imperial favor; he intervened effectively with Justinian, who, before February 542, issued an edict condemning the Origenist *capitula*, although Pelagius cannot be held solely responsible for instigating the emperor's decision. Eager for revenge and backed by Empress Theodore, who favored the Monophysites, Theodore Askidas, then persuaded Justinian to further the restoration of religious unity by acceding to the grievances formulated by the Acephales against the COUNCIL of Chalcedon. They had accused the council of tolerating praise of Theodore of Mopsuestia (Nestorius's teacher), of accepting Theodoret of Cyrrhus, who had denounced the anathematisms of Cyril of Alexandria, and of declaring orthodox the letter written by Ibas of Edessa to Maris the Persian criticizing Cyril's affirmation that "there is only one nature of the divinity and the humanity in Jesus Christ." After 542 and before the end of 545, Justinian published an edict condemning the person and writings of Theodore of Mopsuestia (who had died in the peace of the Church) and certain writings of Theodoret against the Alexandrian anathematisms, as well as Ibas's letter to Maris. Thus began the so-called Three Chapters controversy, which struck serious blows at papal authority and in which Pelagius played a significant part.

Pelagius returned to Rome, where in Vigilius's absence—he had been called to Constantinople to sign the condemnation of the Three Chapters—he was in the forefront of affairs. He used the considerable fortune he had acquired in the East to help the Romans, who in 546 were facing famine while the city was under siege to the Gothic king Totila. He also tried, without success, to negotiate a truce with Totila. After the sack of Rome (17 December 546) he successfully interceded with the king on behalf of the Romans and the Senate. Totila then sent him, along with the Roman advocate Theodorus, on an embassy to Justinian to negotiate peace, but Pelagius was forced to return to Italy without having won his case, as the emperor refused to come to terms.

Parallel with these activities, Pelagius took part in the controversy raised by Justinian's edict against the Three Chapters. With the Roman deacon Anatolius, he sent a letter (which has been lost) to the Carthaginian deacon Ferrandus in which he denounced the edict as a Monophysite maneuver against the council of Chalcedon and asked to be given the African Church's point of view. In his reply, Ferrandus urged the Roman clerics to struggle for the upholding of the decrees of Chalcedon and to reject all decisions that did not emanate from the Catholic Church itself.

But Pope Vigilius agreed to condemn the Three Chapters in his *Judicatum* of 11 April 548, which Pelagius, who was in Sicily at the time, read, though there is no way of knowing whether or not he supported the pope's decision. In any case, after Justinian condemned the Three Chapters a second time (edict of July 551), Pelagius, now back in Constantinople, rallied to the side of Vigilius, who by then had withdrawn the *Judicatum* and, despite pressure from the emperor, had refused to subscribe to the condemnation. After 23 December 551, Pelagius remained with the pope, who, feeling threatened, took refuge in Chalcedon in the basilica of St. Euphemia; he was driven from there by force, together with another Roman cleric, Tullianus, before February 552.

After Easter, 553 (20 April), Pelagius served as intermediary between Vigilius and the bishops who were meeting in Constantinople on Justinian's order to condemn the Three Chapters. He supported the pope's refusal to sit in council, and together with seventeen bishops and two other Roman clerics he signed the *Constitutum de tribus capitulis*, which the pope addressed to the emperor on 14 May 553. This prohibited any interference with the Chalcedon documents, which Pope LEO had approved in their entirety, forbade any attack on the memory of Theodore of Mopsuestia—while anathematizing propositions attributed to him—and prohibited the condemnation of Theodoret of Cyrrhus as well as of Ibas of Edessa and his letter to Maris, both of whom had been received by the council of Chalcedon. With this signature, Pelagius sided with Vigilius in opposing the decisions made in parallel fashion by the fifth ecumenical council of Constantinople, which declared anathema the person and writings of Theodore of Mopsuestia, the writings of Theodoret "against the orthodox faith," and the letter of Ibas (June 553).

But Vigilius finally yielded to the emperor's urgings (December 553) and agreed to denounce the Three Chapters (February 554). This time Pelagius parted company with the pope, who threatened to condemn him. He drew up a *libellus* (now lost), called a *refutatorium*, against Vigilius and, at the request of the Roman deacon Sarpatus, another *libellus* concerning the disputed passages in the letter of Ibas. Refusing to conform to the decisions of the fifth council and those of the pope, Pelagius was driven into exile in various places. In prison, he wrote a six-part work, *In defensione trium capitulorum* (incompletely preserved), inspired by Facundus of Hermiane, in which he praised Theodore of Mopsuestia, defended Theodoret, and analyzed the letter of Ibas of Edessa, stressing that, through them, it was the authority of the council of Chalcedon that their opponents sought to destroy. He denounced the fickleness and venality of

Pope Vigilius as well as the pernicious influence of the Roman clerics surrounding him.

When the pope died in Syracuse (June 555), the emperor recalled Pelagius from exile and named him to succeed Vigilius, on condition that he cease to defend the Three Chapters. He returned to Italy, probably leaving the Roman deacon Sarpatus in Constantinople as *apocrisarius* (JK 1035).

Chosen by Justinian to represent a doctrinal position that he had opposed, Pelagius met with a hostile reception in the West. The Churches of AFRICA, which favored the Three Chapters, included him in their censure of Vigilius, and in Rome he was accused of being responsible for the pope's death. Not until 16 April 556 was he consecrated, by two bishops and a presbyter from Ostia; it is not clear whether the bishop of that city, the usual consecrator of the pope, had abstained deliberately, or whether the see was vacant.

The new pope strove to calm things down. In Rome, with the aid of the patrician Narses, he organized a procession from St. Pancrazio to St. Peter's in the Vatican and swore that he had done Vigilius no wrong. It was probably also at the time of his accession that he published an encyclical letter to the people of God in which, without mentioning the fifth council of Constantinople, he proclaimed his fidelity to the four ecumenical councils, in particular that of Chalcedon, declared that he would accept Theodoret of Cyrrhus as well as Ibas of Edessa, and issued an anathema against whoever thought otherwise (JK 938).

Until 558–9, Pelagius worked hard to forge a policy of reconciliation. He minimized the importance of the Three Chapters controversy and the part he had played in it. He avoided mentioning the fifth ecumenical council and proclaimed his adherence to Chalcedon. He required no personal adherence to the condemnation of the Three Chapters, and if he regarded as schismatic anyone not in communion with the Apostolic See, he had no immediate sanctions in mind.

In Gaul, where rumors and writings were calling him into question, Pelagius tried to gain the support of Bishop Sapaudus of Arles (JK 940–1). But in December 556, at the insistence of King Childebert, he had to write a profession of faith (JK 942). When this seemed insufficient, he sent the king a second, more explicit one (February 557), in which he proclaimed his fidelity to the four ecumenical councils and to Pope Leo's *Tome*, insisting on recognition of the two natures after the union in the person of Christ (JK 946). On the same date, he confirmed Sapaudus as vicar of the Apostolic See in Gaul (JK 946) and asked the king to ensure that the traditional privileges due the bishop of Arles were respected (JK 945)—though he was unable to prevent the encroachment of royal power on Sapaudus's rights (JK 948).

In Italy at the same period, Pelagius avoided a direct attack upon the Churches of MILAN and Aquileia, whose bishops, supporters of the Three Chapters, were ignoring the new pope. On 16 April 557, he wrote to certain bishops in Tuscia Annonaria who were making clear that they refused to name him during the mass; in it, he referred to them as *dilectissimi fratres*, but he warned them that they could not be in universal communion if they were not in communion with the Apostolic See, and he invited them to return to unity (JK 959). He managed to rally certain bishops by 559.

Pelagius seems to have relied on the reorganization of the Church, which was made necessary by the ravages of war and the extended absence of the pope in Italy. He also relied on the control of episcopal elections and the placement of a clergy of confidants in order to defeat his opponents.

Nonetheless, his policy of appeasement did not meet with the success hoped for, and from the winter of 558–9, Pelagius had to invoke the authority of the fifth ecumenical council in an attempt to wear down resistance, and even to call on the use of troops to bring his obdurate opponents to heel.

In Gaul, where his profession of faith was found unconvincing, some bishops refused communion with Rome. Pelagius was attacked in connection with the writings he had produced as deacon in defense of the Three Chapters (his letter to Ferrandus?). He felt constrained to send Sapaudus of Arles a letter in which he referred to Augustine and his *Retractationes* and declared that henceforth the sentence of the general council, received throughout the world, must prevail over his past writings and the opposition of a few. He also issued a warning to the dissidents and suggested that Sapaudus repress abuses (JK 978).

During the same period in Italy, Pelagius could no longer ignore the schisms in Aquileia and Milan, whose bishops had espoused open resistance. The new bishop of Aquileia, Paulinus, who had been ordained by the schismatic bishop of Milan, had taken the title of patriarch. In February 559, Pelagius denounced the bishop's cordination (*execratus non consecratus*), which had been carried out in defiance of the canons and moreover by a prelate who had withdrawn from communion with Rome (JK 938). He called on the patricians John and Valerian for help, urging them to seize the two leaders and send them under strong guard to Constantinople (JK 1011–2). With Valerian shilly-shallying, Pelagius wrote an indignant letter denouncing the effrontery of Paulinus, who had disputed the legitimacy of the fifth council of Constantinople and claimed to judge its decisions in a synod. The pope accused the two "pseudo-episcopi" of trying to revive the controversy over the Three Chapters which four thousand bishops had settled once and for all. He once again demanded that they be sent to Constantinople so that an extended schism would be avoided; as for those who doubted the legitimacy of the condemnation of the Three Chapters, they must turn to Rome for enlightenment (JK 1018). Further, Pelagius had cause to fear lest his policy of reconciliation create an ambiguous situation, since some were wondering whether or not it was necessary to sever communion with the schismatics (JK 994).

At this time, Pelagius was still recommending indulgence toward those schismatics who wished to show repentance (JK 996 and 971). But to the representatives of the emperor, who were more mindful of public peace than of papal injunctions, he recalled that obstinate schismatics must be dealt with by the law (JK 1019 and 1024). On several occasions, he called, though without much success, for their intervention against the rebels. He could no longer tolerate that Italian bishops under his jurisdiction should affect to ignore him (JK 1036 and 1037) or vacillate in the fight against the schismatics (JK 1027). He also asked the bishop of Ravenna to excommunicate, within ten days, all clerics who persisted in the schism (JK 1032).

In spite of these coercive measures, Pelagius did not succeed in stamping out the schisms of Milan and Aquileia, which lasted until the pontificate of JOHN III in the case of Milan and until the beginning of the 7th century in the case of Aquileia. In Emilia, Pelagius also continued to be challenged by bishops who harked back to a letter he had sent to Italy when he was deacon and which, in a brief missive to the *illustris* Symeon, he declared a forgery (JK 972). As for the opposition to the fifth council manifested in Africa and Illyricum, it was smoothed over or crushed thanks to the emperor's efforts.

Beyond these preoccupations with controversy, Pelagius tried, as his correspondence attests, to restore ecclesiastical discipline and to set clear rules for the election of abbots and straightforward procedures for trials involving clergy, and on several occasions, he prohibited simoniacal practices. He also settled matters of morals concerning the laity and saw to it that laypersons in need received help. One example is his call on Sapaudus of Arles to come to the assistance of the Romans who had taken refuge in that city and to ship provisions to Rome. Pelagius also strove to restore Roman ecclesiastical possessions and enhance their value; he supervised the administration and prohibited the transfer of Church landholdings, and forbade the laity to interfere in their management. Pelagius died on 3 March 561; his epitaph celebrates him as the *rector apostolicae fidei* who fought for the unity of the faith and of the Church.

Christiane Fraisse-Coú

Bibliography

Batiffol, P. "L'empereur Justinien et le Siège apostolique," *Cathedra Petri*, Paris, 1938, 286–317.

Caspar, E. *Geschichte des Papsttums*, II, Tübingen, 1993, 286–304.

Duchesne, L. "Vigile et Pélage. Étude sur l'histoire de l'Église romaine au milieu du VIe siècle," *Revue des questions historiques*, 36 (1884), 369–440; *L'Église au VIe siècle*, Paris, 1925, 225–38.

Pelagius, *Epistulae*, Montserrat, 1956; *In defensione trium capitulorum*, ed. R. Devreesse (*Studi e Testi*, 57), Rome, 1932.

PELAGIUS II. *(b. Rome, ?, d. Rome, 7 February 590). Elected pope in August 579, ordained on 26 November 579. Buried at St. Peter's, in Rome.*

Pelagius II was pope during one of the most difficult periods of the Lombard invasion of Italy. He left behind some writings, the most important of which are the three letters concerning the question of the Three Chapters.

Pelagius was born in Rome, his father's name, Unigild, revealing his Germanic origins. He succeeded BENEDICT I at a time when the Lombards were pressing so hard on Rome that he was unable to inform Constantinople of his election and as a result was ordained without having waited for imperial authorization.

No doubt at the beginning of his pontificate, he appointed the deacon Gregory *apocrisarius* to Constantinople. According to John the Deacon, the 9th-century biographer of the latter, Pelagius often discussed Church affairs with GREGORY.

For Pelagius, the political situation was extremely troubling: writing in 580 to the Frankish king Arvarius, he complained that he was under the authority of an idolatrous prince, meaning Lombard domination. We have also, thanks to John the Deacon, a letter written by the pope to Gregory, begging him to sue for the emperor's help, both military and material.

In religious matters, after his predecessor John's successful approach to the Milanese, Pelagius tried in his turn to secure the return of the Christians of Venetia to the Roman communion. He dispatched to Aquileia two messengers carrying a brotherly letter inviting Bishop Elijah to renounce his errors. When Elijah refused, he repeated the attempt, developing arguments—more ecclesiastical than theological—to demonstrate the futility of defending the Three Chapters, and seeking especially to exalt the unity of the Church and to denounce as inauthentic the texts cited by his adversary. Despite the help which, according to tradition, Gregory gave him in drawing up the third, and longest, letter, Pelagius failed in his approach to the schismatics.

Amid all these difficulties, Pelagius had little opportunity for construction. However, he designed the crypt of ST. PETER'S, causing the apostle's tomb to be covered with plates of silver. And on the Via Salaria, he erected a basilica in honor of St. Hermes, which was still included in the 7th-century itineraries but later disappeared. He began the reconstruction of the Julian basilica dedicated to the Holy Apostles, but did not live to see its completion. Pelagius died on 5 February 590, during the epidemic of the plague then ravaging Rome.

Claire Sotinel

Bibliography

LP, 65, 309–11.

Amann, E. "Pélage II," *DTC*, 12 (1933), 669–75.

Leclercq, H. "Pélage," *DACL*, 13-1 (1937), 1222–4.

Pelagius II, *Ep. ad Gregorium diaconum, MGH, ep.* II, 440–1; *Ep. III ad episcopos Istriae, ACO*, IV, 2, 105–36; *Ep. II ad Aunarium Autussiodorensem, MGH, ep.* III, 448–50.

PENALTIES, ECCLESIASTICAL. According to the 1917 CODE OF CANON LAW, "an ecclesiastical penalty is the privation of some good, imposed by legitimate authority, for the correction of a delinquent and punishment of a crime" (c. 2215). The former is known as a medicinal penalty; the latter, as an expiatory one.

Medicinal Penalty. The censure is a medicinal penalty. The baptized individual (i.e., the subject of canon law, who must be at least sixteen years of age, according to c. 1323.1 of the Code of 1983) who has committed an offense and who is contumacious (contumacy being duly confirmed after at least one warning, in the case of penalties *ferendae sententiae*, and after the delinquent has been given a suitable time for repentance, according to c. 1347 § 1) is deprived of various spiritual goods or goods related thereto until he or she ceases to be contumacious and is absolved.

The censure is remitted upon absolution, provided the guilty individual is no longer contumacious, that is, has repented sincerely and has made or promised to make suitable reparation for the damages or scandal he or she may have caused. Absolution in that case may not be refused.

Its medicinal character means that a censure cannot be imposed in perpetuity or left for an indefinite time to the will of a superior.

The salvation of souls being the supreme law of the Church (c. 1752), canon 1335 allows the suspension of censures that forbid celebration of the sacraments or sacramentals or the exercise of acts of governance.

There are three types of censure: excommunication, INTERDICT, and SUSPENSION (cc. 1331 to 1335).

1. The interdict is a censure "whereby certain sacred acts are forbidden to the faithful, who nevertheless remain in communion with the Church" (c. 2268 of the 1917 Code). According to canon 1332, the person who is interdicted (whether by a penalty *ferendae sententiae*,

meaning an imposed penalty, or *latae sententiae*, that is, one incurred automatically or declared by a sentence or decree) is forbidden to have any ministerial participation in the celebration of the mass or other public worship, may not celebrate the sacraments or sacramentals, and may not receive the sacraments. If the interdict has been imposed or declared, the individual concerned who acts against these dispositions must be removed from the liturgical ceremonies in question. Alternatively, they must be interrupted, unless there is serious reason against that course of action.

The following give rise to an interdict: *a*) physical violence against or assassination of a bishop (cc. 1370 § 2 and 1397); *b*) the attempt on the part of a layperson to celebrate the mass (c. 1378 § 2.1.); *c*) or to give sacramental absolution or hear confessions (c. 1378 2.2); *d*) false accusation before an ecclesiastical superior of the offense of solicitation on the part of a confessor (c. 1390 § 1; *e*) the attempt by a religious who is not a cleric of perpetual vows to contract a marriage, even a civil one (c. 1394 § 2). In cases *a*), *c*), and *d*), if the delinquent is a member of the clergy, he is also suspended.

2. Suspension (cc. 1333 to 1334) is a censure that can be used only against clerics. Its limits are determined by law or precept, or in the sentence or decree imposing the penalty. The law or precept may establish that after the condemnatory or declaratory sentence the delinquent cannot validly exercise acts of governance. Only the law may establish a suspension *latae sententiae*.

Suspension prohibits the exercise of all or part of the acts of either the power of orders or the power of governance, or the exercise of all or part of the rights or powers inherent in an office. But this prohibition never affects the offices or power of governance not under the one who instituted the penalty, or the right of residence connected to an office, or, if the penalty is *latae sententiae*, the right to administer the goods pertaining to an office. Suspension carries with it the obligation to restore what would have been collected illegitimately, even in good faith.

The causes of suspension are *a*) physical violence against or assassination of a bishop (cc. 1370 § 2 and 1397); *b*) an attempt on the part of a deacon to celebrate the mass (c. 1378 § 2.1); *c*) an attempt on the part of a deacon or a priest lacking ministerial faculties to give sacramental absolution (c. 1378 § 2.2); *d*) ordination by a bishop without legitimate dismissorial letters, with the consecrator being forbidden to ordain for a year and the one who received orders being suspended for an indeterminate time (c. 1383); *e*) falsely accusing a confessor of solicitation (c. 1390 § 1); *f*) an attempt at a marriage, even a civil one (c. 1394 § 1).

A suspension *ferendae sententiae* is provided for *a*) the simoniacal celebration or reception of a sacrament (c. 1380); *b*) solicitation by a confessor in the act of or on the occasion of or under pretext of confession (c. 1387); *c*) concubinage and other grave faults against the sixth commandment of God (c. 1395 § 1).

Other offenses also entail suspension: *a*) lodging a recourse to the ecumenical COUNCIL or college of bishops against an act of the Roman pontiff (c. 1372); *b*) trafficking in mass offerings (c. 1385); *c*) a slanderous denunciation made to an ecclesiastical superior or any other attack on the good reputation of another (c. 1390 § 2).

3. Excommunication is a "penal sanction of positive ecclesiastical law with a specifically medicinal end, set up in response to extremely grave offenses, the indivisible effects of which consist in an interdiction of the exercise of rights and duties in conformity with the prescriptions of the code, such that they constitute an (almost) total exclusion from the spiritual goods of the Church" (Borras, *L'Excommunication*), without, however, severing the individual's communion with the Church, which derives from baptism and which imprints an indelible character on the soul.

Causes. — Excommunication applies to exceptionally grave offenses, of which there are nine; for certain of them, which are extremely grave, the excommunication can be lifted only by the Apostolic See.

a) The excommunication *latae sententiae* is reserved to the Apostolic See in the following cases: 1) profanation of the consecrated species (c. 1367), an offense that consists in scornfully throwing away the consecrated host or wine, or removing or retaining them for a sacrilegious purpose (on 4 June 1999, the Pontifical Council for the Interpretation of Legislative Texts replied to a query with the following authentic interpretation of canon 1367: the word "abicere" in the official Latin text of the canon cannot mean only "throwing" the sacred species but any action posited out of serious and voluntary contempt for the sacred species); 2) acts of violence against the person of the pope, or his assassination (cc. 1370 § 1, 1397); 3) absolution of an accomplice in a sin against the sixth commandment of God (c. 1378 § 1), that is, in a matter of chastity; 4) ordination of a bishop without papal mandate (c. 1382), an offense committed equally by the ordaining bishop and by the one who is ordained a bishop; 5) direct violation of the sacramental secrecy by a confessor (c. 1388 § 1), an offense that occurs when the confessor expressly reveals the sins heard in confession or the identity of the penitent, whether by naming the penitent or by designating the penitent in such a way as to make identification easy.

b) An excommunication *latae sententiae* not reserved to the Apostolic See may be imposed in the following cases: 6) apostasy (c. 1364 § 1); 7) heresy; 8) schism; 9) procured abortion (c. 1398), that is, abortion directly and knowingly sought after, provided, however, that the result was obtained. This offense is committed by all those who participate in that act (nurse, anesthesiologist, surgeon,

etc.). It exists regardless of the manner in which elimination of the fetus was achieved and regardless of the stage of its conception (Pontifical Commission for the Authentic Interpretation of the Code of Canon Law, reply, 23 May 1988).

c) An excommunication *ferendae sententiae* may be imposed 1) on anyone who is not a priest yet attempts to celebrate the Eucharist (c. 1378 § 2.1 and § 3), or 2) similarly attempts to grant sacramental absolution or to hear a confession (c. 1378 § 2.2 and § 3); 3) for violation of the seal of the confessional on the part of an interpreter or other person who, in one way or another, has, by means of the confession, acquired knowledge of the sins revealed in a confession (c. 1388 § 2).

d) Some censures *ferendae sententiae* also carry with them possible excommunication 1) for the baptism or education of children in a non-Catholic religion, on the part of Catholic parents (c. 1366); 2) for lodging a recourse to an ecumenical council or the college of bishops against an act of the Roman pontiff (c. 1372); 3) for profiting illicitly from mass stipends (c. 1385); 4) for making a calumnious denunciation or other attack against the good reputation of another (c. 1390 § 2).

Effects. — Canon 1331 specifies the rights of which the individual incurring excommunication is deprived.

a) If the penalty is *latae sententiae*, 1) the excommunicated individual may not take an active part as a minister in the Eucharistic sacrifice or other public worship; 2) is forbidden to celebrate the sacrament or sacramentals and to receive the sacraments; 3) may not hold ecclesiastical offices, ministries, or positions of any kind, or exercise acts of governance. The non-penal effects are 4) the inability to obtain indulgences; 5) the need for an authorization from the local ordinary in order to be present at the marriage of the individual under censure.

b) If the penalty is *ferendae sententiae* or declared *latae sententiae*, its effects are aggravated: 1) an individual who claims the right to participate actively in the mass or other public worship must be removed; or else the liturgical action must be interrupted, barring a serious objection; 2) forbidden acts of governance are posited invalidly and no longer only illicitly; even though it is not an act of governance, a priest's solemnizing a marriage is likewise invalid if the priest has been excommunicated, according to the dispositions of canon 1109 (but every priest may validly absolve from all censure or sin a penitent in danger of death); 3) the individual may not enjoy the privileges previously granted; 4) may not validly obtain an honor, office, or other ecclesiastical position; 5) may not appropriate the revenues of such positions or of any pension that might have been received from the Church. The non-penal effects are as follows: 6) the individual is ineligible to vote in elections to an ecclesiastical position; 7) is ineligible for valid admission to an association of the faithful; if already a member, he or she must be dismissed; 8) cannot be admitted to communion.

Since excommunication and interdict deprive the offender of the help of the sacrament of reconciliation, it can be difficult for him or her to have to remain in a state of grievous sin until the censure is remitted. For that reason the confessor in this situation may remit, in the internal or sacramental forum, the undeclared *latae sententiae* censure of excommunication or interdict; on the condition, however—on penalty of falling under censure once again—that within one month the offender turn to a competent superior or a priest possessing appropriate powers (for instance, the canon penitentiary alluded to in c. 508).

The Expiatory Penalty. According to the 1917 Code (c. 2286), the principal and direct aim of this penalty is the expiation of the offense, that is, public reparation of the affected social order, in such a way that the remission of the penalty does not depend on the cessation of contumacy on the delinquent's part, but rather that the penalty should cease by itself (that is, through its completion) or by an act of grace on the part of the superior, who is qualified to dispense such a grace. The penalty may be imposed in perpetuity, for an indeterminate time, or for a determinate time.

Canons 1336 to 1338 list the principal expiatory penalties, besides those that may have been provided for by law. These are: *a*) prohibition (to which clergy and religious may be subject) from living in a given place or territory; *b*) compulsory residence in a given place or territory (to which diocesan clergy may be subject and, within the limits of their constitutions, religious), with the consent of the diocesan bishop of that place; *c*) privation of a power, an office, a function, a right, a privilege, a faculty, a favor, a title, or an insignia, even merely honorary, that is subject to the power of the superior deciding on the penalty (the privation of the power of orders is not possible, nor of academic degrees); *d*) prohibition (not entailing nullity) from practicing what is enumerated under *c*), or from doing so in or outside a given place (this expiatory penalty is the only one capable of being *latae sententiae*); the rule given in canon 1335 for censures should be observed; *e*) penal transfer to another office; *f*) dismissal from clerical state.

Penal Remedies and Penances. These may also be used, according to the terms of canon 1312 § 3. The penal remedy is a moderate canonical measure of a preventive nature, set up to prevent offenses; it is therefore not a penalty in the strict sense of the term. It may take the form of a warning or a rebuke.

A penance is semi-penal in nature, since it is designed to replace or augment a punishment. The legitimate authority imposes on the repentant offender the performance in the external forum of a work of religion, piety, or charity, instead of the penalty that he or she deserved or a penalty imposed and remitted by absolution or dispensation. Such public penance can never be imposed for an occult offense.

Dominique Le Tourneau

Bibliography

Borras, A. *L'Excommunication dans le nouveau Code de droit canonique: essai de définition*, Paris, 1987; "Appartenance à l'Église, communion ecclésiale et excommunication. Réflexions d'un canoniste," *Nouvelle Revue théologique*, 110 (1988), 801–24; *Les Sanctions dans l'Église*, Paris, 1990; "De excommunicatione in vigenti codice," *Periodica de re morali, canonica, liturgica*, 79 (1990), 713–32.

Gerosa, L. *La scomunica è una pena? Saggio per una fondazione teologica del diritto penale canonico*, Fribourg (Switzerland), 1984; "Ist die Exkommunikation eine Straße?" *Archiv für katholisches Kirchenrecht*, 154 (1985), 83–120.

Jacquemet, G. "Excommunication," ibid., IV, Paris, 1956, 877–87.

Jombart, É. "Censure pénale," *Catholicisme*, II, Paris, 1949, 801–4; "Interdit," ibid., V, Paris, 1962, 1880–4.

Kotzula, S. "Zur Exkommunikation im CIC/83. Eine Definitionsmöglichkeit vom Comuniobegriff her," *Archiv für katholisches Kirchenrecht*, 156 (1987), 432–59.

Marzoa, A. *La censura de excomunnión. Estudio de su naturaleza jurídica en los siglos XII–XV*, Pamplona, 1985.

Sanchis, J. "Sulla natura e gli effetti della scomunica," *Ius Ecclesiae*, II (1990), 633–61.

PENITENTIARY, APOSTOLIC. One source dates to the late 1100s a reference to a cardinal who "receives confessions in the name [in place] of the pope" (*cardinalis qui confessiones pro papa recipit*), thus for the absolving from CENSURES and for the granting of DISPENSATIONS reserved to the Holy See, in conformity with the recently established doctrine that the power to dispense came from the lawgiver, and so from the pope. The title *poenitentiarius* seems first to have appeared in the reign of HONORIUS III (1216–27), and acquired the qualifier *maior* or *generalis* under CLEMENT V (1305–14), when penitentiary chaplains (*minores*) were appointed to help him in his task. Around 1246, Hugues de Saint-Cher was described as a *poenitentiarius summus*. When pilgrims started to flock to Rome encouraged by BONIFACE VIII (1294–1303), who granted them a plenary indulgence for the HOLY YEAR 1300, it became necessary to flesh out the institution. The function continued after the pope's death, thus ensuring continuity and a long life for the Penitentiary, even if the "minor" chaplains of today are attached administratively to the major BASILICAS of Rome.

Moreover, the internal workings of the office of the Apostolic Penitentiary remained remarkably stable over the centuries, notwithstanding some essential rearranging and reorganization. As the tribunal of the internal forum, the penitentiary had as his counterpart a tribunal for the external forum, from which was born the tribunal of the ROTA, probably begun during the pontificate of LUCIUS III (1181–5). In the 13th century, mention is made of *correctores*, of *scriptores*, of *distributores*, and of a guardian of the seals (*sigillator*). On 13 April 1338, BENEDICT XII (1334–42) added the function of a "doctor expert in canon law." A century later, to the day—13 April 1438—EUGENE IV (1431–47) created a position of general administration entrusted to a regent (*reggente*), whose task it was to sign requests and examine the most important petitions. The post of datary (*datarius*), authenticating the date of PETITIONS, is attested for the pontificate of ALEXANDER VI (1492–1503). After ordering the suppression of the Penitentiary and dismissing cardinal penitentiary himself (23 April 1569), PIUS V (1566–72) reconstituted it less than a month later (17 May), severely limiting the competence of the cardinal penitentiary in the external forum and instituting, among other offices, the position of theologian (a privilege reserved to the Society of Jesus) and another of canonist. Thus three colleges of minor penitentiaries were created to serve the Roman basilicas: the FRANCISCAN friars minor at ST. JOHN LATERAN, the DOMINICANS at ST. MARY MAJOR, and the JESUITS at ST. PETER'S. BENEDICT XIV (1740–58) initiated another reform in April 1744 (the constitution *In Apostolicae*, in which PIUS XI saw the "fundamental charter of the Penitentiary"). Thereafter the organization of the Penitentiary was not modified until the reform of PIUS X (1903–14), which definitively restricted the cardinal's powers to the internal forum (essentially covering questions of conscience and set the ordering of relations between man and God), and that of BENEDICT XV (1914–22), whereby the granting of indulgences was transferred from the Holy Office by delegation to the Penitentiary (25 March 1917). This configuration served as a basis for the APOSTOLIC CONSTITUTION *Quae divinitus Nobis* promulgated by Pius XI (1922–39) on 25 March 1935, and then for that of PAUL VI (1963–78), which stipulated that the major cardinal penitentiary be assisted by a regent, a theologian, a canonist, and three advisers.

The constitution *Pastor bonus*, which brought about a general reform of the Roman CURIA (28 July 1988) in conformity with the options retained by JOHN PAUL II, confirmed the entrusting to the Penitentiary of all questions concerning the area of the internal forum, leaving to the Congregation for the Doctrine of the Faith the right to pronounce on any questions of dogma that might arise through the examination or granting of indulgences.

With its home in the palace of the Chancery (Piazza della Cancelleria) in Rome, the Penitentiary meets under the presidency of the major cardinal penitentiary, holds regular sessions, and publishes in-depth doctrinal studies on precise problems of canon law. A "tribunal for consciences" (J.-B. d'Onorio), the Penitentiary is the first apostolic tribunal in precedence, even though no one resorts to it except in order to be granted a grace, and not to file suit following a true judicial procedure. Significantly, the CODE OF CANON LAW of 1983 refers to it only occasionally, reinforcing the ambiguous nature of the institution, which some consider archaic and no longer having a place in the conception of a "modern" Church government.

Philippe Levillain

Bibliography

Annuario pontificio per l'anno 2000, 1295.

Chouët, P. *La Sacrée Pénitencerie apostolique*, Lyon, 1908.

d'Onorio, J. B. *Le Pape et le gouvernement de l'Église*, Paris, 1992.

Göller, E. *Die päpstliche Pönitentiarie von ihrem Ursprung bis zu ihrer Umgestaltung unter Pius V.*, Rome, 1907–11.

La Curia romana nella Costituzione Apostolica Pastor Bonus, Rome, 1990.

Naz, R. "Pénitencerie," *DDC*, VI (1957), 1327–34.

van Hove, A. *De rescriptis*, Mechelen, 1936.

PERSECUTIONS. The Church of Rome and its bishops were not spared during the persecutions suffered periodically by Christians in the ROMAN EMPIRE until the reign of CONSTANTINE. True, owing to pious legends that grew quickly and have been popularized up to our own day by works of romantic fiction and the cinema, spreading the improbable image of Christians huddled in the CATACOMBS and of arenas perpetually stained with the blood of the faithful, the number of martyrs has been multiplied to excess. Yet the Roman community, though in general less severely tested than certain others (especially in the East), did pay a heavy price to the persecutors. Local in character, the first actions against the Christians in Rome—and in Rome above all—struck a community that, having established itself in the imperial capital, attracted the particular attention of the pagan authorities. From the 3rd century, whenever Christians were harried on the strength of edicts that held sway throughout the empire, the Roman Church was a particular target, since its bishops, as purportedly the successors of Peter, were now beginning to affirm their spiritual and dogmatic authority over the other Churches.

The Persecution of Nero and the Martyrdom of Peter. During the reign of Claudius (41–54), the presence of Christians in Rome is attested for the first time, and the first persecutions were visited on their community. The pagan historian Suetonius notes that in the year 49 of our era the emperor "expelled from Rome some Jews who were constantly stirring up trouble at the instigation of Chrestus." Christians were thus included in a stricture aimed at the Jews, pagan opinion making as yet no distinction between them. The imperial edict that obliged Aquilas and Priscilla to leave Rome for Corinth (Acts 18:2) was only partially enforced, according to Dio Cassius (*Hist.*, 60, 6): when Paul the apostle was arrested in Jerusalem and appealed to Caesar, he was sent to Italy (in 57/8) and greeted by "brothers" on his arrival in Rome (Acts 28:15), where, during the course of his first two-year stay, he preached with some success, converting Roman Jews but also pagans.

In 54, Claudius was succeeded by Nero, at whose instigation the first persecution was unleashed. The incident is reported by Tacitus in his *Annals* (XV, 40) in connection with the great fire that ravaged the city in 64. According to the historian, the rumor spread that the emperor himself had hired arsonists to further his urban-planning projects. To avert suspicions—whether justified or not—Nero accused the Christians of the crime. The first arrests, with confessions extracted under torture, were soon followed by "a multitude of others." "Convicted not so much of the crime of arson as of hatred of the human race," the Christians were sentenced to penalties reserved for common criminals (to being hurled to wild animals, to burning, to crucifixion). But in a refinement of cruelty that appalled even certain pagans, Nero transformed these tortures into spectacles offered to the crowd in his gardens between the Tiber and the Vatican Mount: "They took pleasure in covering Christians with the skins of beasts, so that they would be torn to pieces by the teeth of dogs; or else they were tied to crosses or coated with inflammable material and, when the light had faded, they lit up the darkness like torches."

Among the martyrs—if not in 64, then in the years following, during which the persecutions continued—was the apostle PETER, who had recently arrived in Rome, from which he probably dictated his First Epistle, addressed to his brothers in the East, recommending to the Christians, "For the Lord's sake accept the authority of every human institution . . ." (1 Pt 2:13–17). His message, to avoid all provocation, which echoes the teaching of Jesus (Mt. 22: 15–22), is proof that the disciples of Christ were not animated by subversive feelings with regard to the empire. But, recognized by the Roman Community as their spiritual guide, Peter was already marked out for vengeance by the pagan authorities. Like Paul, who had come back to Rome and was once again under arrest, Peter was therefore associated with the great number of the elect who were martyred in the city, as in the report several decades later by CLEMENT of Rome in his *Epistle to the Corinthians*, in which Clement refers to an event

that can only be connected with the persecution of 64. Like other victims of this persecution, Peter, as Tertullian reports (*Scorpiace*, XV, 4), suffered death on the cross, as Christ had foretold him (Jn 21:18).

The Persecutions of the 2nd Century. Nero, who unleashed the first fury against them in Rome, had chosen the Christians as scapegoats because their growing numbers and visibility had already made them the target of a lively aversion on the part of opinion in the capital: this is the explanation put forward by Tacitus and Suetonius, whose testimony in this area reflects contemporary sentiment particularly accurately (end of the 1st to the beginning of the 2nd century). The Romans, and especially those who lived in the city, a cosmopolitan capital that attracted representatives of all nations and sects, were rather tolerant of the religious beliefs of the peoples under their dominion—including those of the monotheistic Jews—since they respected national religions as being venerable provided they did not go counter to the laws of the empire. Christianity, on the other hand, struck them, in Suetonius's words, as a "new superstition," whose adherents, whether they had formerly been Gentiles or adherents of JUDAISM, had denied the god or gods of their ancestors and become apostates and atheists. Furthermore, since they refused to worship either the protective divinities of Rome and the empire or the emperor himself, they also appeared lacking in the values of good citizenship, as we know from accounts by Pliny the Younger of the procedure carried out against them in Bithynia in the early 2nd century. Without giving the stories his personal credence, Pliny also reports the crude accusations of infanticide and incest that were spread about among the people, attributing to the Christians the "abominations" mentioned by Tacitus and, a little later, by Tertullian.

For all that, were the Christians the object of a special law providing a juridical foundation for persecution? Certain historians, basing their argument on a highly ambiguous expression of Tertullian's, the *institutum neronianum*, claim that Nero legislated against the followers of Christ. But this alleged law, and any other legislative text in this area, was unknown to Pliny, who questioned Trajan on the subject, as the latter attests in his reply. The intermittent occurrence of the persecutions during the first two centuries—which took the form of pogroms attacking local communities in spasmodic fashion, or else of legal proceedings brought against high-ranking individuals—unmistakably shows the absence of any specific legislation; and the imperial rescripts, sometimes seized upon by the local authorities, as were those of Trajan and Hadrian, merely reiterated that Christians must not be prosecuted automatically and could be condemned only when their accuser demonstrated that they were acting unlawfully. The normal juridical arsenal was quite sufficient to put Christians to death once the legal machine was set in motion. Brought before a court following an accusation (sometimes even despite the law, an anonymous denunciation), or arrested and judged in the wake of unrest for which, although they were its victims, they were held responsible, they were interrogated about their faith and often tortured. If found guilty, if not of having committed the crimes they sometimes confessed to under torture then at least of practicing a religion the judges considered unlawful or subscribing to a superstition "unreasonably and immoderately" (Pliny, *Ep.* X, 96), they were left with a choice between apostasy and martyrdom.

The few testimonies available concerning the Christians of Rome illustrate the process. After the peaceful period following the death of Nero (68), persecution revived under the reign of Domitian (81–96), who is presented by the whole of Christian historiography as the second persecuting emperor. According to Dio Cassius (*Hist.* LXVII, 14), two individuals under the city's watchful eye, the consul Flavius Clemens, a cousin of the emperor, and his wife, Domitilla, along with many others were accused of atheism: some, like the consul, were put to death, others, like Domitilla, were banished to an island. The chief accusation brought against them surely marked them as Christians; this was confirmed later by EUSEBIUS of Caesarea in his *Ecclesiastical History* (III, 18, 4) and by St. Jerome, who tells in one of his letters (*Ep.* 108) that pious visits were made in his day to the cell on the island of Pontia where Domitilla was exiled and "suffered a long martyrdom."

In spite of this revived persecution—and at a time when there was arising an apocalyptic movement violently hostile to Rome, calling down plague, famine, and the sword on the city "set on the seven hills," the new Babylon—Clement, bishop of Rome (ca. 89–ca. 97) carried on the Petrine tradition; in his *Letter to the Corinthians*, he prayed for those in authority, "who have received from God the glory and honor in which they stand," and enjoined Christians to submit to them. He himself may have been martyred, if a somewhat late tradition is to be believed. In any case, a few years afterward, according to Irenaeus of Lyon (*Adv. haereses* III, 3, 3), another bishop of Rome, the seventh, TELESPHORUS, suffered "a glorious martyrdom"; in the absence of chronological indications in the ancient listings of bishops, the date has to be set approximately during the reign of Hadrian (117–38).

Until the end of the 2nd century, the Christians of Rome remained in a precarious situation, at the mercy of denouncers even though their loyalty to the state did not falter and the Antonine emperors did not personally seek their persecution. Thus, in the reign of Antoninus (138–61), Hermas, brother of Bishop PIUS (the second successor to Telesphorus after HYGINUS), enumerates in his work known as *The Shepherd* the tortures recently endured (between 140 and 150) by large numbers of believers, without concealing that certain others, out of weakness or fondness for the things of this world, denied Christ, an unpardonable sin in his eyes. In his turn, Justin in his *Apology* notes the condemnation of three Christians by Urbicus, the prefect of the city (ca. 155): one was denounced by a member of the city police and condemned to death along with two "brothers" who had dared to protest to the tribunal against a sentence that they claimed hardly conformed to the pious emperor's intentions. Justin, who expected at the time to be arrested himself, was denounced ten years later by the pagan philosopher Crescens, who, according to the apologist Tatian, was jealous of his colleague; he was condemned by the prefect Rusticus (*Acta Iustini*) sometime during the reign of the emperor-philosopher Marcus Aurelius (162–80). Under the latter's son and successor, Commodus (180–92), Christians were persecuted again. According to the antipope HIPPOLYTUS of Rome, Callistus, a rich Roman's slave, was denounced by the Jews and, despite his master's protests, condemned to the Sardinian mines, where he encountered other martyrs; around 190, the emperor's concubine, Marcia, who may have been a Christian herself, intervened on behalf of these Christians: having obtained from Pope VICTOR (189–99) a list of the condemned prisoners, she was granted a remission of their sentence by Commodus. In this way, Callistus was able to return to Rome, where he took orders before being chosen to lead the community (around 217–22). On the other hand, his contemporary the Christian philosopher Apollonius was refused clemency: as Eusebius of Caesarea recounts it (*EH*, V, 21), he was denounced by his own slave and brought before Perennis, the well-known prefect of the praetorium (between 183 and 185); highly perplexed by such a trial, the prefect dispatched the accused to the Senate, before which Apollonius was able to put forward his own defense, the *Apologia*, preserved in doubtless altered form in the *Acta Apollonii*. Perennis attempted to save the philosopher, inviting him to retract before the assembly; only retraction could ensure his acquittal, since the desire the Senate tended to be that there "should be no Christians." Apollonius was condemned to be beheaded.

The General Persecutions (3rd Century to the Beginning of the 4th Century). The first half of the 3rd century announced the coming of even more difficult times for the Roman community as well as all the Churches. True, the emperors who presided over the fate of the Roman world at that time, those of the Severan dynasty and their first, often short-lived successors, tended on the whole toward tolerance, some of them even practicing a syncretic worship that did not exclude Christ. Owing to this relative calm, the Roman community acquired a number of converts. Yet at the same time the danger that had begun to threaten all its frontiers made necessary a mobilization of all the forces of the empire. Now the Christians, whose number had grown, in some cases adopted a more intransigent attitude than did the leaders of the various Churches, in believing, like Tertullian in his treatises, that the followers of Christ should abstain from all civil or military service to the pagan state. Such declarations, which encouraged desertion, were of a kind to strengthen the authorities in their feeling that Christians were traitors to the empire and to support the emperors in their tendency to take general measures against them. At the end of his reign, Septimius Severus (193–211), according to the testimony of the *Augustus History* (*Severus* 17), "forbade under severe penalty what had been forbidden to the Jews, and took the same decision with regard to the Christians," thereby forbidding Christian proselytism just as Jewish proselytism had long been forbidden. The edict apparently did not halt the pace of conversions, despite the persecution he unleashed in certain regions (notably AFRICA). In any case, Rome seems to have been completely spared, Eusebius reporting (*EH* V, 28, 8) that a Christian by the name of Notalis had confessed to his faith after being arrested, without being condemned to death. On the other hand, after the accession to power of Maximinus Thrax (235–8), a new edict was enforced and harassment begun "against the heads of the Church": the bishop of Rome, Pontian (230–5), and the illustrious doctor Hippolytus were sent to the mines of Sardinia, where, according to the *Liber pontificalis*, their ill treatment soon brought on their deaths. In his absence, Pontian had been replaced as bishop of Rome by ANTERUS, who died before him, perhaps as a martyr himself. With the accession of Philip (244–9), who corresponded with Origen and was said to be a secret Christian, peace became a reality. Pope FABIAN, who succeeded Anterus, was authorized to bring back from Sardinia the body of their predecessor, St. PONTIAN.

Emperor Decius, who came to power after Philip (249), immediately found himself faced with a catastrophic military situation. To achieve the sacred union of all the inhabitants of the empire around the power of the emperor and the gods of Rome, he enforced a policy of systematic repression of all "dissidents." According to a general edict, the inhabitants of the empire—from 212, every Roman citizen—were required to demonstrate their adherence to pagan worship by making a sacrifice, under the supervision of the local authorities. First among those who refused, at the cost of their life, in Rome was Bishop Fabian, who was martyred on 20 January 250. His example was followed by several members of his clergy, such as the priest Moses, who died in chains, and numerous members of the laity, some of whom, like Calocerius and Parthenius, executed in the summer of 250, belonged to the imperial household. However, as we know from the account of Bishop Cyprian of Carthage, many others apostasized, whether by sacrificing or by fraudulently obtaining certificates of compliance attesting that they had obeyed the emperor's orders.

The death of Decius (251) brought about a truce which allowed the Christians of Rome to appoint a successor to Fabian in the person of CORNELIUS. The truce was short-lived, since the new emperor, Trebonius Gallus, rekindled the persecution in order to calm public opinion, which was blaming the Christians for the terrible epidemic of PLAGUE then raging throughout the empire. The new bishop of Rome was arrested; but the faithful, emboldened by the previous trial, massed in front of the tribunal that was to pass judgment. Owing to this demonstration of faith, Cornelius received a relatively merciful sentence of exile to Civitavecchia, where he died in 253. His successor, LUCIUS, was scarcely elected when he too was banished from Rome, to which he was later recalled following the death of Trebonius. By their heroic resistance, the bishops of Rome had given a witness that began to have an effect on some of the pagans, who had been seized with pity or disgusted by the massacres. On the other hand, by the stance he adopted in the delicate question posed by the reconciliation of the *lapsi*, the Christians who had weakened under testing, Cornelius reinforced the moral authority of the see of Rome over the other Churches: a rigorist faction had sprung up around the priest Novatian, who was opposed to the election of Cornelius and had assumed the leadership of a dissident community that called itself the Church of the saints and the pure. Cornelius, who disapproved of both this extreme severity and the excessive laxity preached in Africa by a certain Novat, joined forces with Cyprian of Carthage in having the repentant *lapsi* admitted to reconciliation, after a penitence commensurate with their offense.

A few years of calm ensued. But eventually Emperor Valerian (253–9), who had to fight on every frontier of an empire besieged by the barbarians, took up the suggestions of his counsellor Macrian, an adherent of the Eastern cults who was violently opposed to Christianity and who denounced the political and economic power of the Church. A first edict of August 267 obliged bishops, priests, and deacons, on pain of exile, to sacrifice to the gods of the empire, and also prohibited Christians, on pain of death, from celebrating their rituals and visiting the catacombs. A second edict ordered an immediate sentence of death against clergy who disobeyed the emperor's orders and, for high-ranking laity, transportation for life or forced labor with confiscation of goods. The Roman Christian community, whose real or supposed wealth tempted the impoverished imperial exchequer, was one of those most severely tested: in August 258, Pope SIXTUS II and his deacons met their deaths, among them Lawrence, whose Passion represents him being slowly burnt on a gridiron for having refused to deliver up the treasure of the Church.

The disappearance of Valerian, taken prisoner by the Persians in 259, in the midst of a dramatic situation forced his son and successor, Gallienus (253–68), to issue an edict—the first official declaration in this area—proclaiming tolerance with regard to Christians, to whom their places of worship and cemeteries were restored: the measure implied a recognition of ecclesiastical property but did not make Christianity a legal religion. The resulting truce was to last forty years, scarcely interrupted by a few isolated hostile actions. Thanks to the peace, imperial power was even led to acknowledge the spiritual authority of the bishop of Rome: when Aurelian was confronted with the conflict between two bishops—Paul of Samosata, who had been deposed for HERESY, and his newly elected successor—for entitlement to the episcopal church, the emperor in 272 ordered that the church be handed over to the one who was in communion with the episcopal see of Rome. This "little peace of the Church" fostered the movement of conversions throughout Roman society and the beginning of smooth coexistence at the local level between the pagan and the Christian communities.

Diocletian's institution of the tetrarchical system, whereby from 293 the tasks of government and of defense of the empire were to be divided between two Augustuses and two Caesars, made possible the restoration of the empire but set in motion great tribulation for the Church. Essentially totalitarian, the new regime, which founded its legitimacy on a political theology by linking the rulers to the race of Jupiter and Hercules, could not long tolerate Christianity, especially since a few acts of insubordination were flaring up among the Christian soldiers. In the end, it was the Caesar Galerius who, according to the accounts of Lactantius and Eusebius of Caesarea, managed to overcome Diocletian's last hesitations. The first edict, of February 303, put judicial impediments in the way of the Christian laity and ordered the churches and holy books destroyed: the library of the Roman Church and its archives perished accordingly. Two more edicts, of a few months later, called for imprisonment for members of the clergy and, next, obliged them to sacrifice on pain of torture; and a fourth edict, in the spring of 304, extended these measures to all the faithful. The persecution created a number of apostates, especially among the newly converted, who were ill prepared by the "little peace" to stand up to these threats, but also thousands of victims: Rome was subjected to the cruel repression imposed by the Augustus Maximian in the territories under his authority; according to the Passions that have preserved the names of the martyrs—which are not always trustworthy—it was at this time that Sts. MARK and MARCELLINUS were put to death, as well as St. Agnes. As for Pope Marcellinus, he died on 24 October 304, "carried off": Eusebius notes (*EH* VII, 32, 1), "by the persecution": however, Donatist schismatics later charged him with momentary weakness under pressure, a charge possibly confirmed by the absence of his name in the *Depositio episcoporum*. Maximian's abdication in 305 brought the persecutions in Rome to a halt, and their ending was officially sanctioned in 311 by Galerius's edict of tolerance: deploring the folly and obstinacy of the Christians, that emperor nevertheless declared their cult licit. But already from 306 Rome had benefited from the policy of appeasement adopted by the usurper Maxentius to ensure his power. The battle of Milvian Bridge, on 28 October 312, which eliminated Maxentius, whom Christian polemicists later wrongfully ranked among the persecutors, made his rival Constantine the master of Rome. Tolerant and very well disposed to Christianity, the new emperor set in motion throughout the West a policy of favors and largesse toward Christianity of which the Church of Rome was a chief beneficiary: by giving Pope Miltiades, in 313, responsibility for settling the African conflict between the "Catholics" and the rigorist Donatists on the question of the *lapsi*, the emperor showed himself sensitive to the moral prestige henceforth recognized as attached to the see of Rome.

Except for the brief interval during which Julian the Apostate once again carried out a policy hostile to the Church, the era of pagan persecutions was well and truly ended. The Church of Rome emerged from the test crowned with the glory of its martyrs and confessors: close to a dozen of its bishops had, through their sacrifice, borne witness to the faith they held, in an unbroken tradition, from the founder, the apostle Peter, thus playing their part in strengthening the spiritual and dogmatic authority of what was hence forth the papacy.

Charles Piétri

Bibliography

Davies, P. S. "The Origin and Purpose of the Persecution of AD 303," *Journal of Theological Studies*, NS 40 (1989) pp. 66–94.

Frend, W. H. C. *Martyrdom and Persecution in the Early Church*, Oxford, 1965.

Grégoire, H. *Les Persécutions dans l'Empire romain*, 2nd ed., Brussels, 1964 (hypercritical).

Griffe, E. *Les Persécutions contre les chrétiens aux Ier et IIe siècles*, Paris, 1967.

Lane Fox, R. *Pagans and Christians*, New York, 1986.

Lee, A. D. *Pagans and Christians in Late Antiquity: A Source Book*, New York, 2000.

Lepelley, C. *L'Empire romain et le christianisme*, Paris, 1969.

Moreau, J. *La Persécution du christianisme dans l'Église romaine*, Paris, 1956.

PETER (ST. PETER THE APOSTLE). With Simon Peter, Simon Cephas, or "the Rock," Roman Christianity was born. True, the history of the MISSION to Rome did not begin with him: very early on, converted Jews (those whom Paul salutes at the end of the Epistle to the Romans) heard and preached the Gospel in the capital. Yet Peter was the reputed founder of the Church of Rome, which through him held a special place in the communion of the small communities scattered over the vast territory of the ROMAN EMPIRE. The first testimonies referring to this Church, from the time of Ignatius of Antioch (two generations after the apostles), already describe it as the one presiding over the spirit of love, or *agapé*, knitting Christians together in the unity of the one faith. It is this Church close to Peter (*propinqua Petri*), notes an African in the 3rd century, that since the 4th century has been called the "Apostolic See," signifying the excellence of its PRIMACY.

This great movement in human history, and especially the personality of the one who initiated it, astonished pagan observers, who were fond of creating grandiose images of their founder-heroes: Celsus, in the 2nd century of our era, and even more the philosopher Porphyry in the next century, while noting the progress of Christianity, would not venture to consider how much this progress was due to a personality so different from contemporary standards of social or cultural glory. Judging from Christian testimony, they saw Peter as a Jewish "pilgrim" (a resident alien in Rome), coarse and uncultivated.

Simon, who belonged to the same generation as his Master, came from a family of Bethsaida, a Jewish town near Galilee, on the shore of Lake Genesareth, built on pagan land east of Jordan, more than 62 miles/100 kilometers north of Jerusalem; as in all the borderlands of Aramaean Judaea, the little local synagogue had undergone Greek influences. While his father's family names came from the Semitic tradition (Jonah, Johannes), Simon, his brother Andrew, and Philip, the original deacon of Bethsaida, had Greek names. Simon knew Scripture (by heart, like all the sons of the Covenant), even though he probably had not attended rabbinical school (cf. Acts 4:13). He also had at least a rough knowledge of the common language of the Hellenistic East as well as that of his own region in western Palestine, which was more hellenized than Judaea.

Simon moved to the province of Galilee, to Capernaum, a few dozen kilometers from his birthplace on the shores of the same lake, where he settled and married (Jesus went to his home to visit his mother-in-law: Mt 8:14). There he chose the humble life of a fisherman (Mk 1:10), working with his brother Andrew and with James and John, the sons of Zebedee (Lk 5:10), and living off the harvest of his nets, cast from his boat into the waters of Lake Genesareth (Lk 5:2).

But it was a time of messianic hopes, heightened by Roman domination, and Simon was not one to be content with a life of laborious routine. That he was an impulsive, generous man we know from numerous passages in the Gospels and the Acts of the Apostles. Thanks to his brother Andrew, he heard the teaching of the last prophet, John the Baptist (Jn 1:35), who, the evangelist explains, recognized Jesus, in Andrew's presence, as the "Lamb of God."

When, from the shore of the lake, Jesus called Simon and Andrew, as they were casting their nets, to "fish for people," the two brothers—Simon being the first—rowed their boat to shore and followed the Master (Mt 4:18; Mk 1:16). Simon, the first of the disciples to be chosen, was the one given first place, in the synoptics, in the lists of "the twelve" who witnessed Jesus' preaching and Passion (Mt 10:1; Mk 3:16 and 16:7; Lk 6:14). These three Gospels, and even that of John, so fond of evoking the unnamed disciple "whom Jesus loved," give Simon Peter's words and acts a privileged place with a few phrases or strokes of the pen. When Jesus sends two boats out onto the lake for a miraculous catch, Peter is the first of the companions, all of whom are exhausted by the fruitless search, to declare that he will let out the nets on the Master's orders. Once ashore, with the boats weighed down by a prodigious haul, he throws himself at the Lord's feet and, in a gesture on fire with faith and awe, implores him to go away from him, for he is a sinful man (Luke 5:1–11).

In another episode, "Lord, if it is you, command me to come to you on the water": Matthew tells of the courage of the first disciple, who set sail on the lake a second time in spite of the storm, saw his Master on the far shore, and began to walk on the rolling waves in the foolhardiness of his faith. Again, Peter says to the Lord, "Explain this parable to us" (Mt 15:15), and asks, "If another member of the church sins against me, how often should I forgive?" (Mt 6:12 also Luke 17:4). He is the mouthpiece of the disciples, the twelve, and even more, the representative of the faith. When the Lord comes to the area north of Batanea, near Caesarea, and asks the disciples, "Who do you say that I am?" it is Simon who answers, "You are the Messiah, the Son of the living God." Jesus' response is to choose him: "Blessed are you, Simon son of Jonah . . . And I tell you, you are Peter, and on this rock I will build my church" (Mt 16:17–18). The Aramaic *kepha*, a common word for rock, was transcribed into Greek as *kephas* (or in Syrian *kepha*) and is usually interpreted as *petros*, Petros, Petrus, or Peter. Contemporary exegesis, in its extreme and sometimes artificially ingenious way of trying to recapture the actual words used by Jesus in his preaching, includes, at least in the earliest version, the sentence giving Peter this authority and creating the group of the twelve, the witnesses of the paschal faith. Parallel with this, Luke recalls how, shortly before he is arrested, Jesus encourages the first of the twelve, Peter again, to strengthen his brothers (Lk 22:32). The Gospel according to John cites another traditional saying of Christ's, after the Resurrection: when Peter exclaims, "Lord, you know that I love you," Jesus says to him, "Feed my sheep" (Jn 21:16–18).

Peter is one of the privileged witnesses. At the time of the Passion, he is the only disciple identified in the Gospel accounts: the one who is sent to prepare the last Passover (Luke 22:8), the one who is rebuked for sleeping during the night of Gethsemane, the one who strikes the high priest's servant come to arrest Jesus, the one who denies him three times when a servant girl questions him in the courtyard of the high priest Caiphas, giving an example of weakness but also of repentance amid bitter tears (Mt 26). After Golgotha, when Peter hears that the crucified body has disappeared, he is the first to get up and run to the empty tomb, where he sees only the linen cloths (Luke 24:12). Later, he is given an even more exalted primacy: the risen Christ, declares Paul (1 Cor 15:5; also Lk 24:34), appeared to Cephas, and then (but only that second time) to all the twelve (except Judas).

When the disciples have returned from Galilee and are together in the upper room in the holy city, Peter (henceforth he is known by this name only, in the Acts of the Apostles) takes on the leadership of the group to decide who should replace Judas (Acts 1:25). Peter acts and sounds like a teacher when, just after Pentecost, he declares that the Scriptures have been fulfilled in Christ crucified: "God has made him both Lord and Messiah" (Acts 2). Pastor of the first Church, he heals a lame man near the Beautiful Gate (Acts 3); he sets before the priests and scribes the cause of the Gospel (Acts 4); he also chastises, punishing Ananias and Sapphira when they break the laws of the community by lying (Acts 5). According to the Acts, his prestige takes on so much authority that people bring the sick to have his shadow fall on them as he passes by (Acts 5:15).

While a Church was gradually taking on permanent shape in Jerusalem under James's leadership, Peter left on a mission to Samaria, Lydda, Joppa, and Caesarea, the pagan capital of Palestine. In its description of the acts of the first apostles, Scripture gives special emphasis to the conversion of a centurion, Cornelius, of the Italian cohort, a Roman citizen. Told from the apostle's point of view, before he baptized the centurion and all his household, the story is intended to serve as an exemplar: Peter, who has come from Jerusalem as head of the Judeo-Christian mission (before PAUL, the missionary to the Gentiles), converts the first pagan and sketches the practice of the young Church surrounding the conversion of new believers who are outside Jewish law, in exempting them from the dietary obligations imposed on observant Jews (Acts 10). As Acts has him explain, Peter believed he had been entrusted with the mission to the pagans. But James's resistance and that of the Judeo-Christians of Jerusalem, haughty defenders of Jewish law, gave him pause. He compromised as best he could after pointing out the way—so much so, that when he was in Antioch,

he attracted the disapproval of Paul, who reproached him for forcing pagan converts to Judaize (Gal 1; Acts 15). Paul's attitude as apostle of the Gentiles no doubt swept away Peter's last prudent scruples. For a time, he extended the radius of his mission; in 44, he was arrested and providentially freed from his chains. He left Jerusalem for good and, as Acts tells it, "went to another place" (Acts 12:17).

The biblical account stops here, throwing a veil of obscurity over all the activity of the apostle until his arrival in Rome. Later Roman chronicles (4th–5th century) give Peter barely a few months between the Ascension and the arrival in the capital, a distortion of fact doubtless intended to encapsulate the whole period of the apostolate. In fact, this period extended over more than a decade (if Origen as well as the historian Eusebius of Caesarea and John Chrysostom, who was from Antioch, are to be believed). At Antioch, and possibly at Corinth, Peter took on the role of founder. As Jerome notes, with evident anachronism of vocabulary, the apostle was the first bishop of that eastern metropolis. He evangelized the land of the Galatians, Pontus, the province of Asia, and Bithynia. In any case, he knew the diaspora of these communities, addressing to them the first letter ascribed to him. Throughout this time of missionary travel, Peter probably used the methods made illustrious by Paul, who often covered the same provinces (except Pontus); in this first letter, Peter seeks to strengthen the faith of those whom he has evangelized along the way. Although there is little likelihood that he actually wrote the letter, surely he inspired the text, which was written in Rome (shortly before 64?) by Silvanus (often identified with Silas, a longtime collaborator of Paul's). On the other hand, the second letter, attributed to Peter in spite of its obvious debt to apostolic teaching (for instance, to the Gospel according to Mark), belongs to a much later period.

"Through Silvanus . . . I have written this short letter . . . Your sister Church in Babylon . . . sends you greetings," declares the First Epistle of Peter. This final salutation is evidence that Peter had reached Rome well after 58 (the period when Paul was preaching to the Roman Christians without making any mention of Peter), probably after Paul's two-year imprisonment in the capital (60–2?). Almost nothing is known of Peter's apostolate in Rome save the essential: there he bore witness as a martyr. The year is uncertain. The first pontifical account associates Peter's glorious death with Paul's on 29 June, in the year 55. This chronology (similar to that of the accounts of the 5th or of the 6th century, which suggest 57 and 58) does not fit with the few guide marks already mentioned. On the contrary, many indications suggest that Peter's martyrdom took place in the time of Nero, in the twelfth, thirteenth or even fourteenth year of his reign (perhaps in 67?). Certain parallels support this calculation: a remark by Jerome that the apostle was martyred two years after Seneca, who died in 65; better still, the observation of CLEMENT of Rome, at the end of the 1st century, that the martyrdom took place in the year when Nero journeyed to Greece, in 67 according to Dio Cassius. We can certainly place Peter's martyrdom (and even more surely, Paul's) after (if not during) the first persecution carried out against the Christians by a Roman emperor, in 64, during the great fire of Rome: in the years immediately after the first massacre, which had served to deflect popular anger onto scapegoats during the conflagration, the Christians were identified as "enemies of the human race" and easily brought before the law. The nature of the apostle's suffering is known only through a tradition, the first witness of which, Tertullian, in the early 3rd century, refers to the testimony of John announcing to Peter the kind of death "by which he would glorify God": crucifixion, which, out of humility, he asked to suffer head downward.

All these testimonies should have rendered empty the polemic, begun by Luther and continued up to the twentieth century, disputing Peter's arrival in Rome. The critics' intent was to deal a decisive blow to Roman ecclesiology, which presents the bishop of Rome, the pope, as the direct successor of Peter, *vicarius Petri*, as certain ancient texts already describe him. In fact, this radical hypothesis hardly holds up before the long series of ancient testimonies: here it is sufficient to recall the reference to Babylon (i.e., Rome) in the letter inspired by Peter; some thirty years later (in 96), Clement of Rome, in a letter addressed to the Corinthian community, counts Peter and Paul among the Roman martyrs, as do Ignatius of Antioch in addressing the Christians of Rome and Bishop Dionysius of Corinth around 165–70. In the 2nd century, when the great Churches were attempting to refute the Gnostics, who claimed to possess a secret tradition regarding the faith, they published lists of the doctors who taught the truth of the Gospel from the beginning, in an uninterrupted succession; the Roman list had the advantage of exceptional authority. Irenaeus of Lyon, who taught in the last third of the century, drew up a Roman list at the head of which he placed Peter and Paul (*Adv. haer.* 3, 3, 1). In the same period, the historian Hegesippus lists the generations that ensured that in every city the chain of truth continued unbroken, and always included the two apostles. The historians Iulius Africanus and Hippolytus (a Roman cleric who brought the list of learned doctors to a total of 235) repeat the same testimony. The writer of a first chronicle of the urban Church (the *Liberian Catalogue*) arranged the episcopal list of Rome in the order already followed by Irenaeus, counting Peter as Rome's first bishop.

Also noteworthy are the testimonies supplied by the Roman liturgy, even though these are late. The Roman Church's first book of feast days (its definitive compilation dates from the end of MARK's pontificate, in 336; see

LP, I, 11) gives Peter two feast days. The first one cites 29 June as the feast of both Peter and Paul, noting that the celebration was instituted in 258. As is usual in this text, which lists all the feast days of the Roman sanctorale, it indicates the particular spot in the cemeteries where pilgrims can venerate the memory of the two martyrs: for Paul, near the road to Ostia; for Peter, *ad catacumbas* (a "combe," or hollow, near the Appian Way, whose name eventually came to mean a type of cemetery, the CATACOMB). The most plausible explanation of this unexpected siting (the Vatican seems a more likely place for Peter) is that the "catacomb" (today S. Sebastiano) was in some obscure way connected with the apostle and was used at a time when the building work at ST. PETER's at the Vatican made it impossible for pilgrims to pray near the tomb. In any event, pilgrims had for some time been venerating the apostles' memory on the Appian Way, leaving written testimony of their visits on the walls of a room largely open to the combe. They commended themselves or their dead loved ones to Peter and Paul, begged for their intercession in a prayer addressed to both apostles, and carried out near them the ritual of the *refrigerium*, taken from pagan burial ritual. The pagans would offer their dead refreshment in the form of a banquet near the tomb, accompanied by plenty of wine; the dead would receive some of the leftovers. The Christians changed the meaning of the ritual, since they did not seek to appease or refresh the dead but to invoke for their benefit the help of two saints, dead to the world but gloriously alive in paradise. When St. Peter's basilica became accessible to pilgrims' visits and the prayers of the community, the feast of 29 June was moved for good to the Vatican.

The Roman Church's book of feast days notes another feast, on 22 February, with a rather unusual notice: the feast of the CHAIR OF ST. PETER (in Latin, *Natale Petri de cathedra*). Furthermore, contrary to the usual practice, the writer does not localize the cult. Apparently, he makes no reference to a physical relic; in the 4th century, the Christians of Rome would have been hard put to come up with furniture for purposes of holy instruction; it was only much later, in the Carolingian period, that they filled in this gap with a *cathedra*, for which Bernini created a sumptuous case and which was placed in the apse of St. Peter's. Does the word *cathedra* suggest, as T. Klauser believed, the seat left vacant for the dead in pious family ceremonies? The German scholar recalled that the date chosen for the Christian feast coincided with that of the *caristia*, the pagan ritual celebrated each year with a feast for the absent dead. In reality, the hypothesis strains the meaning that had been attached to the word *cathedra* in Christian vocabulary for at least a century. Cyprian, bishop of Carthage in the mid-3rd century, designated Rome the *cathedra Petri*, the chair of Peter; far from representing a learned doctor's chair, it symbolized the whole body of the doctrine of salvation handed down by the Master's disciple, and at the same time the exceptional revelatory function entrusted to Peter. Thus, the Roman Church invited the faithful to celebrate Peter's feast by taking into account his magisterial qualities and his preaching, because of the apostolic tradition that he had founded and that later was entrusted to Rome.

At the beginning of the 4th century, the Church chose the date of a pagan family festival, as the Roman clergy frequently did in order to establish a Christian celebration over against one of the ancient religion. Moreover, the choice is understandable. Peter the Apostle is the most prestigious of these *patres*, these fathers (who instituted Tradition), the "pope" par excellence (if by this is understood the paternity of the founder, using a term that later on evokes the solicitude of the bishop of Rome). At the time (i.e., 336), St. Peter's basilica was not yet completed. As a result, the book of feast days called for all the Roman communities to mark the anniversary in the places where they usually met to celebrate the liturgy.

The celebrations of the apostles' feasts were at their most brilliant with the completion of the basilica built *ad corpus*, near the body of the apostle. Yet the Roman community gave other examples of its enthusiasm by producing a certain conception of Peter that vigorously illustrated the place of the apostle in the spirituality and ecclesiology of the city. The devotion hardly relied on the hagiographical literature: the apocryphal Acts of Peter were not written by Roman hands (cf. Apocryphal Acts of Peter and of Paul). There were strict rules against the trading of relics, according to which symbols were to be used to give some material support to the pilgrims' petitions to the martyrs. But the entire scholarly literature exalted the apostle's role and celebrated his prerogatives—in the letters of the popes (especially their solemn preambles), in the exegetical treatises, in particular the commentary on the pericope of Matthew (16:18), in homiletics, and even in poems and hymns. For example, near the basilica of the apostles on the Appian Way (at the site called *ad catacumbas* described above), Pope DAMASUS (366–84) placed a poem invoking, though not explicitly, the memory of the two apostles linked to the place; but he asserted forcefully that Rome had the right to claim Peter and Paul as citizens because it was there that they shed their martyrs' blood. Notable here is one of the characteristic features of a eulogy that exalts Peter while associating him with Paul, and at the same time proclaims his Roman-ness. A few examples must suffice, such as the titles bestowed on the apostle by patristic literature, in Rome, in the West, and, finally, in the East. All writers acknowledged him as a doctor for the universal Church. He enjoyed primacy in the college of the apostles (*primus: archàgos*), *summus discipulus*, as the Spanish poet Prudentius said in the 4th century (*Contra Sym-*

machum 2, 2). In the confession of faith, he has the *primatus*, declared Ambrose of Milan (*De incarnatione* 4, 32). In the 3rd century, an African (the anonymous author of *De aleatoribus*) recognized that he serves as the vicar of Christ. But especially in the 4th century he acquired a new title, which Roman legal language charged with a host of political and imperial connotations: he was *princeps* of the Church (as Augustus was of the empire), *princeps apostolorum*, as the pontifical letters added in the late 4th century. At the beginning of the next century, Pope ZOSIMUS bestowed a weightier title on the apostle, *caput auctoritatis* (head of authority), and his successor Boniface called him *rector summus et pastor perpetuus*.

This vocabulary surely evokes the idea of a lawgiver, invested with peculiar authority to found, in Rome and in the whole Church, unity of faith and discipline through the strength of a tradition handed down from the Master to the first disciple. The entire literature of this eulogistic tendency stressed the ties binding Peter to Rome, not only through martyrdom but also through the work of apostolate he accomplished there. All that the literature retains of the hagiographic elaboration is the episode of the struggle with Simon Magus, a conflict that was intended to purify the city and deliver it from the curses attached to it since the anathema hurled against the new Babylon. Associated in this work of purification was the other Roman apostle, Paul, whose teaching and apostolate reinforced the action of Peter. Peter and Paul formed a kind of couple, as though they were twins, true brothers who, in the unity of the faith, founded the new Rome—those whom Pope LEO, well into the 5th century, contrasted with the fateful pair, who by Romulus's murder of Remus established ancient Rome and its idolatrous past.

Echoing the themes of this ecclesiology, a learned and clerical discourse, is the more naive testimony of artists working from the late 3rd century on extremely humble objects; these were the painters of the catacombs, the sculptors of the sarcophaguses, and, later, those who covered church apses with mosaics. In their way, they reflected the same conception of Peter. In the era of the expressionistic style that was dominant under the tetrarchy (284–312), they gave him a face. They showed the head of a man who bore the traces and sufferings of a rough maturity: a thick head of hair, worn low on the brow, a short beard, an air of impetuous and decisive strength. The image remained in Christian iconography, and evokes rather well the fisherman of the Gospels.

The first examples of apostolic imagery often showed Peter as a learned man, accompanying a praying figure, teaching a disciple, or sitting in the college of the apostles, usually on his Master's right hand. But they also included a representation taken from the Gospels which was for a long time the only historical portrayal, created in Roman studios and principally employed as a decoration for sarcophaguses: next to a cock perched on a column, the apostle touches his chin in a gesture of pained protest, while with a gesture of his hand Christ warns of the triple denial. The artists singled out a scene they wanted to use as an example demonstrating the possibility of and the need for repentance: *primus amator et negator*, as Augustine of Hippo would put it later (*Sermons* 295 and 296).

At or about the same time (in any case, at the beginning of the 4th century), a more symbolic imagery appeared, based on typology: Peter was presented, in the New Covenant, as a figure already sketched in the Old, that of Moses. He is the new Moses, that is, the leader of the new chosen people. Like his predecessor in the desert of Exodus, he strikes the rock with his staff and a spring gushes forth (symbolizing the living water of baptism), which quenches the soldiers' thirst (since the faithful belong to Christ's militia). This representation adorned medallions, appeared on catacomb walls, on the alcoves of sarcophaguses, and on the base of engraved or decorated goblets, and, in Rome and in the West, which borrowed the image from the Roman studios, illustrated a symbolism forcefully celebrating the primacy of Peter. This symbolism dominated the imagery for nearly a half-century, even producing some further illustrations inspired by the same typology. In the second half of the 4th century, it was replaced by another symbolism: the image of the *Traditio Legis*. Artists used this image to decorate the apses of churches, and thus in the context of a somewhat official art; but they also employed it for more modest objects, including sarcophaguses. Here too they never strove for historical accuracy, but placed the scene beyond human history, representing Christ, Peter at his right (most often), and Paul. The Lord hands (*traditio*) the scroll of the new law (*legis*) to Peter, who receives it with a gesture of his veiled hands, following a ritual of the aulic liturgy that obliged the subject to receive the gifts of the emperor with this sign of respect. The image illustrates the investiture of the Prince of the Apostles, his role in the Church, and thus the place of Rome, his Church, in the *oikoumenè*.

Charles Piétri

See also EXCAVATIONS IN ST. PETER'S.

Bibliography

Caragounis, C. C. *Peter and the Rock*, Berlin and New York, 1989 and 1990.

Cullmann, O. *Pierre, disciple, apôtre et martyr*, Neuchâtel, 1953.

Epigrammata, 20, ed. Ferrua, Vatican City, 1942, 142.

Farmer, W. R. *Peter and Paul in the Church of Rome: The Ecumenical Potential of a Forgotten Perspective*, New York, 2000.

Grant, M. *Saint Peter*, London, 1994.

Kereszty, R. "Peter and Paul and the Founding of the Church in Rome: Forgotten Perspectives," *Communio*, 15 (Summer 1998) pp. 215–33.

Lietzmann, H. *Petrus und Paulus in Rom*, Berlin (2nd ed.), 1927.

Meyendorff, J., ed. *The Primacy of Peter: Essays in Ecclesiology and the Early Church*, Crestwood, N.Y., 1997.

O'Connor, D. W. M. *Peter in Rome: The Literary, Liturgical, and Archeological Evidence*, New York and London, 1968.

Perkins, P. *Peter: Apostle for the Whole Church*, Minneapolis, 2000.

Piétri, C. *Roma christiana*, I. Rome, 1976 (*BEFAR*, 224).

Ray, S. K. *Upon this Rock: St. Peter and the Primacy of Rome in Scripture and the Early Church*, San Francisco, 1999.

Rimoldi, A. "L'apostolo San Pietro," *Analecta Gregoriana*, 98, Rome, 1958.

Wiarda, T. *Peter in the Gospels: Patterns, Personality and Relationship*, Tübingen, 2000.

PETER'S PENCE. See Finances, Papal.

PETITIONS. In the 12th and 13th centuries, the custom developed of presenting a written request in order to obtain a pontifical deed. Corporations and universities sometimes sent whole scrolls of petitions (*rotuli*). In the 16th century, the form of the petitions came to be governed by strict rules. They had to be written on a sheet of paper approximately the size of the European A4 format (11.69 in. × 8.25 in.), but across the longer dimension. The text consisted of two blocks, known as the corpus and the clauses. The corpus contained a general statement of the facts, ending with a description of the relevant request. The clauses laid out specific demands of a more technical nature, such as dispensation from reading the plan to the pope (*et quod transeat sine alia lectione*), dispensation from examination in Rome (*cum commissione examinis ad partes*), or expedition in the form of a brief. The writing was often very hasty; erasures were severely frowned on, but crossings-out were permitted. The language was codified by the extremely strict rules of the curial style. To address the pope, the formula *Beatissime pater* was used; alternatively, the pope was referred to as *sanctitas vestra*, invariably abbreviated to *s.v.* with the *s* written in round calligraphy. The petitioner was referred to in the third person as *devotus orator*, or if female, *devota oratrix*.

These restrictive rules explain why the writing of petitions was often entrusted to specialists, and why the 13th century saw a burgeoning of writings on formulas, usually more officious than official. Once the petition had been looked over, the Chancery added a series of annotations, which concluded with the written authorization of the corpus and clauses and the addition of the signature, which was appended by the pope, the chief clerk, or the vice-chancellor. Next, the datary added the current date and the petition was recorded, ready to serve as the basis for the drawing up of a deed.

There were certain special forms of petition. By means of a second petition, known as a *reformatio*, it was possible to request a modification to a petition that had already been agreed on. In matters not concerning the rights of a third party, the pope could pronounce the validity *solo signatura*; in this case, the signed petition became equivalent to a deed, and there was no need to draw up a sealed document. Sometimes treated as display items, the petitions were written on parchment and the recipient had them illuminated.

Thomas Frenz

See also DATARY, APOSTOLIC.

Bibliography

Fabian, F. *Prunkbattschriften an den Papst*, Graz, 1931 (Veröffentlichungen des Hist. Seminars der Univ. Graz, 10).

Katterbach, B. *Inventario dei registri delle suppliche*, Vatican City, 1932; *Specimina supplicationum ex registris Vaticanis*, Rome, 1927 (Subsidiorum tabularii Vaticani, II extra).

Moyse, G. "Les suppliques médiévales: Documents lacunaires, documents répétifs," *Informatique et histoire médiévale*, Rome, 1977 (Collection de l'École française médiévale, 31), 55–72.

Schmitz-Kallenberg, L. *Practica cancellariae apostolicae saeculi XV exeuntis*, Münster, 1904.

Verger, J. "Que peut-on attendre d'un traitement automatique des suppliques?" *ibid.*, 73–8.

[PHILIP]. *Antipope elected on 31 July, deposed on 1 August 768.*

The rivalries among members of the Roman aristocracy, which encouraged the LOMBARDS to invade Rome, made it possible for the priest Philip to become pope for a day. After the partisans of the *primicerius* Christopher and their Lombard allies had come to Rome and seized the antipope CONSTANTINE, the priest Waldipert, who represented the interests of the Lombard king, Desiderius, took advantage of the fact that Christopher had not yet arrived in Rome to install on the papal throne a man he thought safe, that is, in favor of an alliance with the Lombards. He sought out the chaplain of the monastery of S. Vito, a priest by the name of Philip, and had him acclaimed pope by a group of Romans. Brought to the LATERAN, Philip was installed according to the regulations. But the *primicerius* Christopher arrived in Rome the same night: he announced that he would not set foot in the city as long as Philip was at the Lateran, and a dignitary of the papal palace escorted Philip back to his

monastery. No harm was done to him; the belief must have been that he was not in league with Waldipert. The latter was not so fortunate: a few days later, he was seized at his refuge in ST. MARY MAJOR and murdered.

Jean-Charles Picard

Bibliography

JW, 1, 284.
LP, 1, 470–1.
Duchesne, L. *Les Premiers Temps de l'État pontifical*, Paris, 1911.

PHOTOGRAPHY. The arrival of photography in Rome, around 1840, in the form of the daguerrotype, was greeted with enthusiasm and with apprehension—enthusiasm for the invention, apprehension for the fate of the craftsmen, painters, and engravers, who, not unreasonably, feared competition from the new method of reproduction. However, GREGORY XVI himself was not above acquainting himself with the process during an excursion to Tivoli, where, on 2 October 1845, in the Academy for Noble Ecclesiastics, he allowed himself to be photographed, alone and with his court, by the Jesuit father Vittorio Della Rovere. PIUS IX had his picture taken in the Quirinal Gardens on the day of his coronation (21 June 1846). In those days, Rome already contained numerous photographers who were experimenting with the new processes, among them the calotype, first used in 1843 by the Frenchman Victor Denis. But it was the rapid spread of collodionized negative plates that popularized the new art in a city offering a wide field of action to all aficionados of images.

The papal government first took an interest in the regulation of the photographic industry when the Chalcography section of the Apostolic Camera, which provided engravings of all sorts, was suffering the economic effects of the new procedure. Before deciding on ways to protect the traditional arts, the authorities asked the nuncios of Vienna and Paris to gather information on the Austrian and French regulations in the matter. The answers merely reinforced the application of legislation on artistic property, that is, the prohibition on reproducing a work of art without its creator's authorization.

It was not long before photography acquired legitimacy in the papal administration. In 1857, the FABRIC OF ST. PETER's commissioned Carlo Baldassare Simelli to provide a series of photographs documenting the cracks in the basilica's dome. Emboldened with this first success, Simelli began to specialize in artistic photography. To him, we owe the illustrations for Xavier Barbier de Montault's *Antiquités chrétiennes de Rome du Ve au XVIe siècle*, probably the first archaeological work to make use of photography. Parallel with this activity in documentation as well as with the great vogue for portraits, many "artistic" photographs were in circulation that claimed to replace expensive live models but which the papal censor simply regarded as obscene. To attempt to manage a situation that seemed to be spinning out of control, the cardinal vicar of Rome, Patrizi, on 18 November 1861 published an edict strictly regulating the photographic profession and providing severe penalties for both the creators and the sellers of forbidden photographs and the complying models. A third of the fines was reserved for the informant, as was customary. From then on, written permission to possess a camera had to be obtained from the MASTER OF THE SACRED PALACE.

These draconian measures did not prevent a scandal the following year, when the pope, the Sacred College, and a number of foreign rulers received photomontages in which the dethroned queen of Naples, Sophia of Bavaria, was shown in seductive poses in the company of Pius IX, Cardinal Antonelli, and Msgr. Pacca. The affair, probably organized by Roman "patriots" opposed to the Neapolitan monarchs accused of encouraging banditry in their former states, was taken extremely seriously by the papal police, who uncovered the guilty parties and had them jailed. In 1863, a priest who was an amateur photographer was imprisoned in the ecclesiastical jails for having made and circulated pornographic photographs.

Another priest, Antonio D'Alessandri (1818–93), was the first to be appointed "pontifical photographer" and, at least until 1870, to be granted the exclusive right to take portraits of the pope. To him, we owe large numbers of portraits of Pius IX and the members of his court as well as of photographs of the principal military events of the time (the Anzio military camp, battlefields of Mentana and Castelfidardo). After the ending of temporal power, D'Alessandri seems to have lost his title of official photographer. It was not until 1887 that Francesco De Federicis, who had already published a *Gerarchia cattolica illustrata*, a collection of portraits of prelates and papal dignitaries, gained permission, after numerous requests, to photograph the pope. He could thus use the title "photographer of H. H. LEO XIII," and it was he who, on the occasion of the 1888 jubilee, inaugurated the custom of photographing groups of pilgrims received in audience by the pope. His intention, which was to make an album to offer the supreme pontiff as a souvenir of that exceptional year, was the origin of a custom destined to last.

De Federicis was one of the first to think of employing cinematography to document Pope Leo's pontificate. In fact, it was in his studio, in 1900, that there was developed the film of the first movie that Giuseppe Filipini succeeded in making of Leo XIII, featuring the pope being carried in his SEDIA GESTATORIA along one of the Vatican galleries. The next day, the pope attended a showing of the film in the SISTINE CHAPEL. De Federicis himself filmed several sequences of the pope, and from then on

was known as "papal photographer and cinematographer." Apparently, the title did not imply an absolute exclusivity of reproduction of the pope's portrait. Aside from the fact that certain foreign photographers were welcomed at the Vatican, Giuseppe Felici, another pontifical photographer, was noted as an assiduous presence during Leo XIII's reign. His success in the world of the Vatican was due in part to the sizeable reductions in prices that he granted to ecclesiastics and seminarians. It seems certain that from the time of the pontificate of PIUS X, Felici, and after him his descendants, had a *de facto* monopoly on photographs of the pope.

Besides taking portraits, the official photographer's job was to record on film the personalities and groups received in audience. It was only with PIUS XII, after the Allies entered Rome, that the pope allowed himself to be photographed with his visitors. The custom took off spectacularly under JOHN XXIII. PAUL VI did not lag behind, authorizing a photographer from *L'Osservatore romano* to take pictures concurrently with the representative of the Felici firm and to commercialize his production in the same way. This was no small matter in business terms, since the photographers' skill allows them to include, in just one picture, the pope and all those he is greeting. The sale of these pictures is assured by a highly efficient service that offers them to pilgrims, at very reasonable price, during the reception following the audience.

François-Charles Uginet

Bibliography

Becchetti, P. *La fotografia a Roma dalle origini a 1915*, Rome, 1983.
Mostra della fotografia a Roma dal 1840 al 1915. Catalogo, Rome, 1953.

PILGRIMAGE.

Antiquity. The term *peregrinus*, in antiquity, usually meant the stranger far from home. In Jewish and Christian spirituality, it also meant the believer exiled on this earth. The origin of the modern meaning of the word "pilgrim" is to be found in an ancient practice, derived from JUDAISM, of voluntary exile to holy places. However, in late antiquity, and from the 6th century until the CRUSADES, the word was ambiguous. For Christians, the first and great pilgrimage was to the Holy Land, the land made sacred by divine acts. But pilgrims also journeyed to see the bodies of saints and martyrs and even, from the 4th century on, living people who were considered models of virtue, particularly the monks of Egypt or, later on, the holy stylites.

The Church of Rome, hallowed by the number and quality of its martyrs, also benefited from its position as prestigious political capital, even when the emperor stopped residing there, from the end of the 4th century. This prestige was reinforced by the apostolic tradition, and the Church's efficient episcopal organization made Rome the most important center of pilgrimage in the West.

Pilgrims came to Rome above all to venerate the tombs of the martyrs. Even before the Peace of the Church, the sanctuary on the Appian Way was visited by pilgrims who left behind graffiti honoring Peter and Paul. After CONSTANTINE's victory, not only did Christianity become the official religion, but in Rome the generosity of the imperial family within fifty years had established a prestigious setting in which to welcome the faithful who came for the cult of the saints: the basilica on the Appian Way, the basilica of ST. PETER's at the Vatican, where the many graffiti show that pilgrims visited the apostle's tomb throughout the construction, and at the tombs of St. Paul on the Via Ostiensis, St. Lawrence on the Via Tiburtina, and St. Agnes on the Via Nomentana.

The organization of the cult of the SAINTS, which the Church carried out in the 4th and 5th centuries, made it possible to offer pilgrims better accommodations as well as greater opportunities to visit the tombs. By organizing the tombs, entering saints' names in the canon of the mass, and elaborating a ferial calendar, the ecclesiastical authorities recognized certain devotions to the saints, thereby encouraging the pilgrims to stop at each of the great Roman cemeteries in turn and extending the sanctorale to almost every month of the year. Thus, with the exception of the essential periods of the baptismal and Easter liturgies, pilgrims could visit Rome at every season.

While we know that the faithful flocked to the tombs in great numbers, it is more difficult to find out who those were who made a journey in order to do so. However, thanks to epigraphy and some documentation scattered in the patristic literature, it is possible to pinpoint some of them. They were either humble pilgrims from places not far from Rome who were making a devotional journey, or else distinguished personalities, both lay and clerical, who, generally, came to Rome for other reasons and for whom the pilgrimage was a "travel bonus."

Before the 4th century, it is rare to find a Christian traveler clearly identified. Around 140, the Gnostic Marcus was in Rome seeking a wider public for his teachings. At the same time, Irenaeus passed through the capital on his way to Lyon. Around 216, a Syrian by the name of Abercius died in Rome in the course of a journey, as his enigmatic funerary inscription explains: "I am the disciple of a holy pastor [. . .] He it is who has sent me to Rome to contemplate the sovereign majesty / And to see a queen clothed and shod in gold / I saw a people who bore a shining seal." If the text is interpreted in a Christian light, Abercius came to visit a living community, not to venerate the dead. If it is not possible to speak of pilgrimage in

these cases, the faithful who came to the Appian Way were true pilgrims. The 183 names deciphered from inscriptions give evidence of popular peregrination (surnames are used rather than aristocratic titles), in family groups, mostly male. Only four clerics left their names (two priests and two faithful *servus dei*, an extremely vague term). A few graffiti are of non-Roman origin, one referring to Urbino and Fiesole and the other to Benevento. Several names are traditionally African, but it is impossible to tell whether the visitors came directly across the Mediterranean.

Several 4th-century texts suggest pilgrimages that have become ordinary manifestations of faith. Ambrose of Milan describes three processions bound for the Appian Way and heading for the tombs of St. Paul and St. Peter on 29 June. Prudentius describes the feast of St. Hippolytus around 400, noting that the participants came from Picenum, Etruria, and Campania. Behind the poetic names can be seen the outlines of a vast regional pilgrimage. A little later, Paulinus of Nola declares that he himself comes to Rome each 29 June from his diocese in Campania. Around 370, the young Jerome, living in Rome at the time, goes every Sunday with friends, fellow students, to venerate certain saints' tombs. In 387, John Chrysostom describes in general terms the "emperors, generals, and consuls" who come to worship at the tombs.

The *Lausiac History*, which recounts the lives of certain monks in Palestine and Egypt, mentions a number of pilgrims to Rome. Serapion the Simonite traveled with one of Origen's disciples and died in Rome during his peregrinations. Philonomus the Galatian went to Rome on foot to pray at St. Peter's *martyrium* besides making a great pilgrimage to Alexandria and Jerusalem. In that same era, Augustine severely criticized certain pilgrim monks who, under pretext of piety, were by means of their journeys eluding the rule of obedience (*De opera monachorum*). Some Western clerics also visited Rome, for example, Paschasius, the deacon of Rouen, who accompanied Paulinus in 398 for the feast day of 29 June, and Bishop Achilleus of Spoleto, who came to Rome in 419 on ecclesiastical business and took the opportunity to acquire some relics of St. Peter, which he subsequently placed in the cathedral of his city. We know that in the 5th century Rouen cathedral was on the route of an organized Roman pilgrimage, thanks to an inscription in which Achilleus invites the passerby to venerate the new relics and offers encouragement in the journey to Rome. The Illyrian bishop Nicetas of Remesiana came to Italy in 400 and 403. On his first journey, he went to Rome, although not especially to venerate the saints: at least, the letter written by Paulinus of Nola describing the journey does not speak of a pilgrimage.

The emperors, who no longer resided in Rome, combined their journeys with a pious visit. According to Augustine, Honorius visited St. Peter's in 404, and in the 5th century Valentinus met Pope LEO on a visit to the Vatican basilica. In the 6th century, when Theodoric, king of the Goths, came to Rome, he showed the greatest respect for the holy tombs, even though he was an Arian. For their part, the pilgrims were often responsible for the diffusion of Roman relics. The role played by Achilleus of Spoleto has been mentioned. Around 589, Gregory of Tours dispatched his deacon Agilulf, who brought back relics of Paul, Lawrence, and Pancras. He also knew an Angevin deacon, one Magnebod, who had been given the same mission by his bishop.

At the beginning of the 7th century, a Milanese priest named John was sent by Queen Theodelinda to find relics for the basilica she was constructing in Monza. To judge by the diffusion of Roman relics, crowds of visitors, half of them commisioned agents and half missionaries, must have come to see the holy tombs.

But clearly, throughout this whole period, the true pilgrims remained anonymous, and the well-known visitors to Rome were never solely pilgrims, and sometimes not pilgrims at all.

For all that, pilgrimages came to be better and better organized, as can be gathered from the effort made to welcome the pilgrims. Pope HILARUS (461–8) created a veritable neighborhood for them next to S. Lorenzo fuori le Mura, complete with monastery and thermal baths. On the same site, Pope SYMMACHUS (501–22) built small lodgings for the pilgrims. This same pope put up a similar complex, consisting of baths and lodgings, beside St. Paul's. The first monasteries at St. Peter's were installed as early as the 5th century. The sites of the tombs were made ever larger to accommodate the crowds of visitors. And in the 7th century, the earliest itineraries show that pilgrimage had become an institution. With their lists of saints to be venerated in Rome, they served as visitors' guides, like those that had long been in use for the Holy Land and those that would come later for great Western cities such as Milan. At the end of the 6th century, hagiography took up the theme of pilgrimage to Rome, a sign of its popularity. In certain lives of the saints, the Roman pilgrimage is not only an act of devotion—apparently not yet penitential in nature—but also a kind of obligatory step in the acquisition of holiness, perhaps already a gauge of the saint's orthodoxy and sense of the unity of the Church.

Claire Sotinel

Bibliography

Guyon, J. "Le pèlerinage à Rome dans la basse Antiquité et le haut Moyen Âge," *Pèlerins de Rome, Visages de Rome*, II, Centre Saint-Louis-des-Français, Paris, 1976.

Hunt, E. D. *Holy Land Pilgrimage in the Later Roman Empire AD 312–460*, Oxford, 1982.

Pietri, C. and L. "Le pèlerinage en Occident à la fin de l'Antiquité," in J. Celini and H. Branthomme, *Les Chemins de Dieu*, Paris, 1982.

Saxer, V. "Pèlerinage aux apôtres Pierre et Paul," *DS*, XII, 1, 909.

Middle Ages. Together with Jerusalem and Santiago de Compostela, Rome was indisputably one of the three great places of pilgrimage in medieval times. Thronged in the late Middle Ages, when the commemoration of martyrs was at its height, it suffered something of an eclipse after the Carolingian period and then regained its popularity in the 14th and 15th centuries, thanks especially to the institution of jubilee years. The evolution of its popularity among the faithful can be summed up as a transition from devotion to relics to a quest for INDULGENCES, although the second motivation certainly never effaced the first.

The history of pilgrimage belongs to the history of forms of devotion in general, at a time when the Christian's earthly life was presented as a journey, a true *peregrinatio*, that gave the making of the actual journey its whole spiritual value. More particularly, its history is also that of the city of Rome, which throughout this period rose to become the capital of the Christian world as a result of the strengthening and centralizing of papal power.

In the days of the barbarian kings, continuing a custom known to have been practiced in the preceding centuries, travelers came to Rome in ever greater numbers to venerate the relics of the martyrs, as was characteristic of the piety of the time. The chief object of their devotion was the foremost martyr, St. Peter, of whose TOMB at the Vatican the city was the proud possessor. GREGORY the Great rearranged the site to facilitate the celebration of the mass there. As the destination next in importance, the pilgrims made their way to the Via Ostiensis and the tomb of St. Paul. Virtually contemporary with that of the Vatican, this basilica was nevertheless less sumptuous, proof of a certain precedence already granted Peter. Yet the relics preserved in Rome were not limited to those of the two great figures of the Church. There were also those of a long list of martyrs, which was the pride of the city and largely explains its popularity among the faithful. In the early Middle Ages, these relics were still kept in the cemeteries and CATACOMBS, which formed a kind of vast sanctuary on the city outskirts. This site soon became dangerous during the troubled era of the Gothic wars, followed by the repeated sieges of Rome by the Lombards. Under pressure of events, up until around the mid-9th century the precious relics were moved inside the Roman basilicas, where they were henceforth venerated.

Drawn by this veritable museum of relics, the faithful came from all parts of the Christian world—from the

East, but above all from the West, in particular from the newly converted BARBARIAN peoples, the FRANKS, Frisians, and Saxons. It should be noted that in this they were following the example of the great, the kings and bishops. These were readily throwing themselves into the enterprise, whether to seal their new adherence to the orthodox faith, like Sigismund, the Arian Burgundian king, after his conversion by St. Avitus, bishop of Vienne, or through devotion, like St. Ouen, bishop of Rouen, who left for Rome at the age of seventy-six, or St. Amandus, the apostle of Flanders. And for their part the Scots monks were careful to include Rome in their long journeys on the Continent, for example Benedict Biscop, Willibrord, Boniface, and Wilfrid. Wilfrid even visited the city on three occasions, the last time at seventy years of age and on foot! The pope's role in the christianizing of England, especially that of Gregory the Great, and the ensuing privileged ties henceforth maintained with the Roman see, explain how this pilgrimage became a major factor in the religious life of the country. The English remained loyal to it up until the end of the Middle Ages, as witnessed by the account written by the mystic Margery Kempe at the beginning of the 15th century.

The crowds of visitors were welcomed in hospices or monasteries in Rome or the surrounding area. Some, however, slept beneath porticoes. Around the 9th century, or even earlier, appeared the *scholae*, inns designed especially to take in specific national groups. Four of these groups are known to have been the best represented among the Roman pilgrims: the Franks, the Frisians, the LOMBARDS, and the Saxons. The Saxons' *schola* took up practically a whole city quarter. These establishments continued to serve their purpose throughout the period.

As they moved about the city, the pilgrims were guided by itineraries, which first appeared in the 6th to 7th centuries, doubtless based on earlier models. The earliest guides consisted of little more than a somewhat bare listing of the sites and the relics contained therein. Their model was one of the earliest guides, the *De locis sanctis martyrum*. The most detailed of them, the *Notitia ecclesiarum*, added geographical directions. Another, the *Einsiedeln Itinerary*, had the original idea of offering the pilgrim eleven ways to cross the city, most of which began at the present-day Ponte Sant'Angelo, a central landmark in the Roman topography of the time. As in the other booklets, most of the monuments mentioned in the guide belong to the city's Christian past, but a few notations deal with classical antiquity. No doubt these responded to a more touristic interest the visitors must have had. In this connection, we know that the Roman tour owners invited the foreign pilgrims, for a fee, to climb to the highest point to view the surrounding countryside.

Yet the chief object of the pilgrims' stay in Rome was always the priceless evidence of the beginnings of Christianity. They tried to acquire a concrete reminder of their visit to the martyrs, something they could keep and show on their return home. The gesture had a different meaning depending on the pilgrim's social standing. Men of the Church coveted part of the city's spiritual treasure. They took advantage of the practice, initiated in Rome later than in the East—Gregory the Great was still objecting to it in the 6th century—of cutting up saints' bodies for distribution. In this way they acquired fragments for their churches, abbeys, and cathedrals, for example on the occasion of a dedication. Disseminated everywhere in the West, these relics sanctified the various places, made concrete the communion with the first generations of Christians and the see of Peter, and, in turn, encouraged local pilgrimages. Monarchs, conscious of the prestige attached to these objects, did not lag behind. If they could not make the journey themselves, they sent embassies to Rome to find bones for them. And it is well known that some clerics, fired by enthusiasm, did not hesitate to commit pious larceny in order to avoid coming back empty-handed. More simply, as happened with the vast majority of humble pilgrims, people had to content themselves with objects that had been in contact with the tombs. Nor did the high-born disdain these souvenirs. For instance, Theodelinda, queen of the Lombards, received from Gregory the Great flasks containing oil from the lamps that burned before the tombs of more than sixty martyrs. Sometimes the relics were pieces of metal or material, the *brandea*, according to Gregory of Tours's account, recorded by a witness: "If the pilgrim wishes to take away with him some blessed memento, he tosses upon the tomb a small piece of stuff [. . .] He keeps watch, fasts, and prays devoutly [. . .] Wondrous to relate, if the supplicant's faith is sound, the piece of stuff, having been withdrawn from the tomb, is so filled with divine virtue that the one who withdrew it knows that he has obtained the desired favor."

In this way, veneration of the relics of Roman martyrs spread throughout the West, and along with it grew the custom of placing relics beneath church altars. Envoys of princes and bishops returned laden also with liturgical books suited to these devotions. The Carolingians further emphasized the trend, thereby contributing to the diffusion of Roman liturgy in all parts of the empire. Further, churches had to be adapted for these devotional purposes, and here again Rome seems to have served as a model. Patterned after the arrangement at ST. PETER's basilica, a semicircular confessional area was adopted in many sanctuaries built in the Merovingian and Carolingian eras. This allowed pilgrims to move freely and have access to the space around the tombs. Traces of such confessionals can still be seen, despite frequent restorations and archaeological excavations.

The early Middle Ages also saw another type of pilgrim, one who made the journey to Rome as a penitential discipline. Under the influence of Irish missionary monks, the practice of the penitential tariff was introduced on the Continent, whereby an appropriate penance was established for the expiation of each sin. In the books regulating penance then in force, provision was often made in the case of the most serious sins for the faithful to be sent to Rome on pilgrimage and there to seek pardon. It was a way of temporarily getting rid of undesirable individuals, but also proof of the recognition of the power to bind and loose entrusted to Peter and his successors. Thus the pope appears as the only one entitled to decide on certain "reserved cases" sent him by the bishops. This explains how Jonas of Orleans could write, in the 9th century, that "penitence is synonymous with going to Rome." Still, the Carolingian authorities soon had reservations concerning these practices, which helped discredit both the pilgrimage and its prestigious destination on account of the doubtful elements thereby introduced into groups of pilgrims. Imperial laws attempted to curb the practices, so great was the danger of perdition, the opposite of the goal desired. Even monks and nuns were forbidden to go on penitential pilgrimages, since this kind of devotional act was becoming increasingly incompatible with the discipline their vows demanded. Later, too, spiritual writers like Peter Damian in the 11th century recommended such pilgrimages to religious only in the form of interior spiritual exercise. Moreover, the custom had arisen among the faithful of appealing directly to the pope in serious cases, and thereby bypassing the local authority. To avoid these abuses and prevent encroachment on the bishops' prerogatives, in the early 1100s the custom grew of defining cases of "direct reservation" for which there was automatic recourse to the pope: incest, murder, rape, sacrilege, parricide, sodomy, assassination of a cleric, SIMONY, and so on. But penitent pilgrims, who still flocked to Rome without end, helped discredit the image of this pilgrimage, which from that time was viewed with a great number of reservations.

Whether made strictly out of devotion or as a penance, pilgrimage to Rome seems not to have held the same importance for the Christian conscience in the 10th to 12th centuries as it did in the first few hundred years of the medieval era. Several circumstances explain the phenomenon, though there is no quantitative data to prove it. The INVESTITURE CONTROVERSY between Church and Empire did little to encourage pilgrimage on the part of the German faithful. It also aroused antipapal feeling, eventually disrupting the earlier unanimity regarding the City of the Apostles. Furthermore, Rome was soon outshone by other destinations more in keeping with the devotion of the time. First in importance was the pilgrimage to the shrine of St. James (Santiago) in Galicia, encouraged by the Spanish Reconquest and the revival of "apostolic" spirituality, for which the Christian ideal is to be found in the *vita apostolica* described in the Acts of the Apostles. The routes to Santiago de Compostela were well known

and dotted with shrines, themselves containing prestigious relics. Yet even more, the faithful were drawn to the adventure to the Holy Land, to that earthly Jerusalem they would have liked to see metamorphosed into the Celestial City. The pilgrims viewed this journey as a way of entering personally into the Passion of Christ in the very places where he had suffered, even as they meditated on the mystery of his incarnation and on his earthly life in its most concrete dimensions.

But Rome was not entirely deserted by pilgrims. It still received famous visitors such as Canute the Great, king of Denmark, in 1027, and the duke of Aquitaine, William V the Great, who came every year. Clergy from all over Europe were also drawn to the City of the Apostles at the time of the Gregorian reform. There they fulfilled their "AD LIMINA" VISITS or came to ask for papal arbitration. One example was Geoffroy, abbot of the Trinity of Vendôme, whose twelve journeys demonstrated his adherence to Gregorian ideas. Sometimes it was a penitential pilgrimage, as in the case of the simoniacal clergy of Milan, who came on the injunction of Peter Damian. And countless humbler visitors came whose names have been lost to history.

Evidence that pilgrims were still coming regularly to Rome, the guide literature continued to flourish, even as it introduced a few changes. Now entitled *Mirabilia urbis Romae*, the booklets no longer confined their attention to the places where relics were preserved. They also covered Rome itself, the avowed one and only capital of Christendom. They recommend a single itinerary to pilgrims, the one followed by the papal processions at the enthronement of a pope. The descriptions of monuments are embroidered with anecdotes illustrating Providence's hand in Rome's fortunes from antiquity up to Christian times. The glory of Rome thus was given another dimension in texts that conjured up history but also added some occasional tales. A more eloquent and original narrator, Master Gregory, an English cleric who traveled between the mid-12th century and the early 1200s, even dares evince a critical view of these tales. For example, he questions the credence to be placed in the ridiculous talk about the famous rider on the Lateran piazza, said to be Constantine. He identifies the equestrian statue, now at the Capitol, as that of Marcus Aurelius. He even dares impart to his readers the excitement he felt on seeing profane works of art, in particular a statue of Venus in Parian marble. The tone here becomes more personal, and the curiosity of a humanist before his time honors classical antiquity in its own right, not only in its foreshadowing of Rome's Christian destiny.

The waning enthusiasm for the CRUSADES and the increasing difficulties faced by expeditions to the Holy Land were no doubt the reasons behind a fresh surge in pilgrimages to Rome during the 13th century. The movement began in Italy, where many of the faithful paid several visits during their lifetime to the apostles' tombs. Others followed in their footsteps, from all over the Christian world. The routes they took are better documented than the early ones. And their journeys were easier, thanks especially to the construction of bridges. Meandering over the plains, the great axes met at the crossing of the Alps. The French and English used the Great St. Bernard or Mt. Cenis passes, while the Scandinavians, after a stay at the abbey of Reichenau, preferred to go by way of the central Alps. The Brenner pass was most often taken by the Germans coming from Innsbruck. From the high Middle Ages, the pilgrim routes had been furnished with hospices and inns organized by charity. No doubt the most famous of these was the hospice run by a community of canons regular founded by St. Bernard of Menthon at the pass that bore the name Montjoux before being called after the saint. The great Italian cities—Turin, Vercelli, Pavia, Piacenza, Lucca, Siena, and others—also played their part. Montefiascone and Viterbo marked the last stages of the long trek before the Eternal City revealed itself to pilgrims looking down from the top of Monte Mario.

If they were to obtain help on the journey, the pilgrims had to be readily identifiable. The pilgrim to Rome, like his counterparts on other routes, wore a costume consisting of cape, hat, and stout staff, all decorated with badges—in his case, the KEYS of St. Peter—one adapted to the conditions of the journey but also marking him out to other Christians. He also carried with him safe-conducts or letters of recommendation, especially for the benefit of the religious authorities. Likewise, on his return he had to produce written proof that he had indeed reached his destination.

The last two centuries of the Middle Ages saw crowds of pilgrims descending on Rome in sporadic fashion, depending on whether or not it was a jubilee year. Yet even apart from those years of exceptional grace, the city retained an extraordinary power of attraction. The risks of the journey and the effort it represented continued to give it a penitential meaning. Furthermore, the piety of the age, which delighted in the accumulation of good works with a view to salvation, found Rome an exceptionally fertile field. In fact, even before 1300, years of indulgences were granted following visits to Roman places of worship. Pilgrims came to see the shrines in ordinary years, and their visits even increased considerably with the passage of time. One relic seems to have surpassed all others in the pilgrims' devotions, which were highly Christocentric: Veronica's veil, on which Christ left the imprint of his features, and for which a special exposition was organized each Sunday afternoon at St. Peter's.

The guidebooks enthusiastically took up the theme of these treasures, which they knew the faithful were eager to see and of which, if the writings are to be believed, Rome furnished examples at every step. Guides were pro-

duced in greater numbers than in preceding centuries, and their production was further amplified by the advent of printing, which soon made wide distribution possible. Latin was abandoned and replaced by the vernacular languages, while the guides followed a pattern fairly close to that of modern guidebooks, even as they reflected their readers' main preoccupations. F. Rapp describes one such, written in German and published in the 15th century, in Rome itself, by Stephen Planck. It consists of three sections. The first is devoted to the history of Rome, from its founding by the Trojans up to Constantine's famous DONATION to Pope Silvester. The second describes the seven principal churches of Rome as well as the graces that can be obtained by visiting them. The third section lists "the indulgences and graces of all the churches and all the relics to be found therein." Some of the guides, whose subject matter is limited to these last, were therefore called *Libri indulgentiarum*. But the inclusion of brief historical descriptions shows a continuation of the development begun in the 12th to 13th centuries toward an interest in the city's ancient past. Motivations of a touristic nature eventually joined devotional ones for the more cultivated travelers, who came to admire the former imperial capital quite as much as the seat of Christianity. The currents of humanism, which arose during the 15th century in Italy and other nations, nourished the movement.

Whether mingled or not with other interests, the age-old devotional act of pilgrimage was thus still very much alive in the late Middle Ages. And Rome once again became the most popular destination for pilgrims, as it had been at the very beginning of the period, for somewhat different reasons. The evidence is both direct and indirect: the huge success of the jubilee years, especially those of 1300 and 1450, but also the marked attachment of pilgrims to St. Roch, the pilgrim from Montpellier who died of the PLAGUE in Tuscany after praying at the tomb of St. Peter. And yet the appearance, among certain 15th-century thinkers, of ideas less favorable to pilgrimage should not be forgotten. By that time, not everyone agreed on its spiritual significance. Whereas the practice of the "vicarious" pilgrim (one who traveled in another's place, for a fee) or the custom of the penitential pilgrimage had long filled the routes with unsavory individuals, now there was general condemnation of the "walkers of God" as impostors or ne'er-do-wells in disguise. Jean Gerson and the author of the *Imitation of Christ* both expressed reservations concerning pilgrimage and recommended that it be spiritualized. To this end, the chancellor of the University of Paris drew up a spiritual transposition of the pilgrim's journey, thus echoing Peter Damiani, several centuries earlier in his address to the monks. He broke the journey into daily stages of seven leagues, each of which the spiritual pilgrim would mark by reciting a *Pater noster*, that is, seven times a day, as well as at the hours of matins and vespers, for fifty consecutive days. Then the pilgrim would, in spirit, visit the Seven Churches of Rome, for seven times seven days, and hear mass in a church near his home. During all this time, he would fast, practice abstinence, and give the cost of the journey in alms. Finally, he would return by the same route, repeating his devotional exercises for fifty days. Whereupon, Gerson concludes, "he would gain more than if he had [gone to Rome] in body" (examples quoted by A. Vauchez in *Pèlerins de Rome*). At the end of the Middle Ages, the interior journey had therefore become, for spiritual writers, the Christian's true pilgrimage—which did not prevent thousands from taking the road to Rome!

Catherine Vincent

Bibliography

Chelini, J., and Branthomme, H. *Les Chemins de Dieu*, Paris, 1982.

Dupront, A. *Du sacré: croisades et pèlerinages, images et langages*, Paris, 1987.

Geary, P. *Le Vol des reliques au Moyen-Âge*, Paris, 1993.

Labande, E. R. "O Roma nobilis . . . ," *Villes, bonnes villes, cité et capitales*, Tours, 1989, 141–51.

Pèlerins de Rome, Paris, 1976, "Visages de Rome," II.

Rapp, F. "Les pèlerinages dans la vie religieuse de l'Occident médiéval aux XIVe et XVe siècles," *Les Pèlerinages de l'Antiquité biblique et classique à l'Occident médiéval*, Paris, 1973, 119–60.

Saxer, V. "Le pèlerinage aux apôtres Pierre et Paul jusqu'en 800," *DS*, XII-1, 909–18.

Sigal, P. A. *Les Marcheurs de Dieu*, Paris, 1979.

Sumption, J. *Pilgrimage, an Image of Medieval Religion*, 1975, 217–56.

Taviani, H. "Les voyageurs et la Rome légendaire au Moyen Age," *Voyage, quête, pèlerinage Sénéfiance*, 2 (1976), 7–23.

Modern and Contemporary Era. The "pilgrimage society," understood as the complex of actions, interactions, and developments having as its point of focus the pilgrim and his itinerary—as described notably in such recent research as that of Alphonse Dupront—suffered a decline in the modern era (14th to 18th centuries) that was marked but relative. In fact, it retained signs of vitality that became manifest from the second half of the 19th century in what contemporaries called a "renaissance" of pilgrimages, based on a heightened frequency of theophanies (apparitions, mostly Marian). In the last years of the 20th century, it took on a more particular and novel cast thanks to the numerous TRAVELS of the pope—occasions of pilgrimage on the part of a head of Christianity who, following the recommendations of VATICAN II, is intent on recognizing the "signs of the times" (*signa temporum*) and sees them as reference marks for the Church as a whole.

The custom of pilgrimage to Rome soon became established around two major and at times intermingled motivations. The first was the visit to the bodies of the saints (the *limina Apostolorum*), psychologically supported by participation in the immaterial and immortal glory which they possessed and offered the believer and which was orchestrated by the architectural wonders of the two major BASILICAS of ST. PAUL'S OUTSIDE THE WALLS and ST. PETER'S. The second was the opportunity to pay homage to the person of the pope, an important aspect of contemporary pilgrimages. In 1300, BONIFACE VIII (1295–1303) proclaimed a HOLY YEAR coupled with plenary INDULGENCE for those making the journey to Rome (as over 20,000 did); it marked an epoch in that it started a dynamic of pilgrimage that became the target of an ever-growing surge of criticism. This came, as early as the end of the 14th century, from the champions of the new, more interior piety (*devotio moderna*), who were followed by the humanists—such as Chaucer, Erasmus, and Rabelais—who stigmatized pilgrimages as "odious, useless journeys." Next, the Protestant reformers, from Luther to Pierre Viret, denounced the "false piety" they believed arose from an act that did little to elevate the soul. And in their *Encyclopédie*, the partisans of the ENLIGHTENMENT saw in pilgrimage nothing but a "misplaced act of devotion." This intellectual crisis of the pilgrimage idea left an undeniable mark on the modern period, notably on the numbers of visits to local shrines. The *peregrinatio romana* was relatively spared, thanks to the establishment of the first ROMAN CONFRATERNITIES and hospitality groups devoted entirely to receiving, lodging, and caring for the "roumieus" (*romei* in Italian).

There was also another essential form of the journey to Rome: the judicial pilgrimage, carried out, on order, to fulfill a penance imposed for an offense. Pilgrimages to Rome included the obligation to go to the pope to ask for absolution for such an offense. So numerous were these sorts of pilgrimages that the pope had to set up a Penitentiary to hear pilgrims' confessions (14th century) and soon to surround this major Penitentiary with minor ones charged with providing *litterae de universis*—pilgrimage certificates, so called because, not being directed to any particular individual, they served as proof that the interested party had performed his or her penance. The custom of judicial pilgrimages dwindled in the 16th century, especially with the turmoil of the Reformation. The use of pilgrim's garb as a cover for begging or licentiousness was reproved by successive edicts dated August 1671, January 1686, and August 1738. These obliged the pilgrim to obtain, before departure, an authorization from the bishop of the diocese, among other administrative papers.

The jubilee years 1575 and 1600 marked a noticeable renewal of the pilgrimage to Rome, a clear even if distant consequence of the Tridentine REFORM of the Church, which had raised the status of the saints to the rank of "living members of the body of Christ." PAUL III Farnese (1534–49), with the help of St. Philip Neri, caused various areas of the city to be relaid out to accommodate the anticipated crowds of pilgrims, and approved the foundation of the Gonfalon, the Holy Cross of St. Marcello, and the Holy Trinity of the Pilgrims. The Santa Casa of Loreto had a growing influence in the 16th and 17th centuries: Montaigne visited it in 1581, Descartes between 1623 and 1625. This current of activity saw the institution of national hospices (*Pii Stabilimenti*) intended for natives of countries or provinces that were not yet provided with them, for example, St. Yves-des-Bretons, St. Nicholas-des-Lorrains, and, above all, St. Louis des Français, a hospice which also engaged in some diplomatic activity. A great many guides for the pilgrims' use were produced, following a travel plan set up in the *De mirabilibus civitatis Romae* of N. Roselli (1314–62). The *Itinerarium urbis Romae*, the work of the Franciscan Mariano da Firenze published around 1517, came out in several successive editions. It presented the first Christians as the "heroes of Rome," besides including the sites of pagan antiquity that contributed to the glory of the city. The Church adopted, in part, a similar strategy of dispersion in the 17th century, causing many bones or simple fragments from the CATACOMBS to be moved into the various Roman churches. CLEMENT XI (1700–21), for his part, extended the plenary indulgence to visitors to ST. JOHN LATERAN and ST. MARY MAJOR. Henceforth the complete itinerary included an obligatory stop at the four major BASILICAS.

A more touristic aspect, at first difficult to separate from the religious one, was the only one to draw secular visitors of the 18th and 19th centuries (as in the case of Goethe, whose *Wanderjahre* leaves no doubt on this point). Peter's successors soon found themselves having to defend the authenticity of the pilgrimage enterprise, which they did by means of regulation. In modern CANON LAW, individual pilgrimage survives as a form of penance (c. 2313§ 1 of the 1917 CODE OF CANON LAW). One instruction issued by the CONGREGATION of the Council, dated 11 February 1936, ordered that pilgrimages have no appearance of a journey of tourism or a pleasure trip, and that the organization of pilgrimages be made the responsibility of the ecclesiastical authority, which would be required to approve all initiatives taken in this direction. The same authority—in theory, the ordinary of the area—should appoint an organizer and a spiritual director for each pilgrimage. Finally, the price of the journey must be within the range of all incomes, and the fixing of its amount be free of all profit motive; the technical management of the pilgrimage was entrusted to laypersons under the control of the ecclesiastical authority. The VATICAN II council, in its CONSTITUTION *Sacrosanctum Concilium*, warmly commends "the pious practices of the Christian people, provided that they be in conformity with the law and the norms of the Church" (§13). Positive canonical law (CODE of 1983, cc. 1181 to 1185) has in no way altered this somewhat suspicious view of pilgrimage. This view conceives of it as a spiritual exercise that doubtless may be very beneficial but carries with it a risk of worldly distraction or distortion of its aim, something the Church authorities constantly fear as the predictable result of popular and, moreover, large-scale piety. The particular reverence in which the tomb of JOHN XXIII (1958–63) is held has not inspired actual criticism. Nor has the form of DEVOTION TO THE POPE whereby, for most people, the general AUDIENCE or the BENEDICTION *urbi et orbi* is the culminating point of the pilgrimage to Rome.

Restoring and reviving pilgrimage's true dimension, this time by example, was one of the important features of the activities of PAUL VI (1963–78), essentially on the occasion of his historic TRAVELS in the Holy Land in 1964, and has been an especially important feature of the activities of JOHN PAUL II. The truly itinerant character of the latter's pontificate, complete with some sixty apostolic travels undertaken in the space of fifteen years, helps keep alive the theme of a pilgrim pope. Beyond the abiding pastoral dimension, analogous to that of a bishop's AD LIMINA VISIT throughout his diocese—in this case, the entire Catholic world—John Paul II's desire has been to add a personal exemplary lesson, a representation of every Christian's path to God, of which the supreme pontiff implicitly furnishes a model. Whenever he leaves Rome on a trip, in fact, the pope makes a local pilgrimage, on which he gives an appropriate homily, thus building up a fairly voluminous body of preaching. The choice of sanctuaries has fallen for the most part on sites of Marian apparitions (Lisieux, rue du Bac, Lourdes, Czestochowa), the Portuguese site of Fatima being especially favored. In connection with this last site, John Paul II has explicitly linked the help he received following the ASSASSINATION ATTEMPT of 13 May 1981 to the apparitions of the Virgin to the three young shepherds, from 13 May to 13 October 1917.

François Jankowiak

Bibliography

Boutry, P. "Espace du pèlerinage, espace de la romanité. L'Année sainte de la Restauration," *Luoghi sacri e spazi della santità*, Turin, 1990.

Dansette, A. *Histoire religieuse de la France contemporaine*, 2 vols., Paris, 1948–51.

Deffontaines, P. *Géographie et religions*, Paris, 1948.

de Sivry, L., and Champagnac, M. *Dictionnaire géographique, historique, descriptif, archéologique des pèlerinages anciens et modernes, et des lieux de dévotion les plus célèbres de l'Univers*, Abbé Migne, 2 vols., Paris, 1850–51.

Dupront, A. *Du sacré. Croisades et pèlerinages, images et langages*, Paris, 1987.

Kötting, B. *Peregrinatio religiosa*, Munich, 1950.

Laurentin, R. *Lourdes, histoire authentique*, 6 vols., Paris, 1961–64.

Marcel, G. *Homo viator, Prolégomènes à une métaphysique de l'espérance*, Paris, 1944.

Miller, K. *Itineraria romana*, Stuttgart, 1916.

Nolan, M. L. and S. *Christian Pilgrimage in Modern Western Europe*, Chapel Hill, 1989.

Oursel, R. *Pèlerins du Moyen Âge. Les hommes, les chemins, les sanctuaires*, Paris (2nd ed., 1978).

Plongeron, B. ed., *La Religion populaire dans l'Occident chrétien. Approches historiques*, Paris, 1976.

Richard, J. *Les Récits de voyages et de pèlerinages (Typologie des sources du Moyen Âge occidental*, 38), Paris, 1981.

Romani, M. *Pellegrini e viaggiatori nell'economia di Roma dal XIV al XVII secolo*, Milan, 1948.

van Cauwenbergh, E. *Les Pèlerinages expiatoires et judiciares*, Louvain, 1922.

PIUS I. *(140, d. 155).* Even though the *Liberian Catalogue* places him after Anicetus, Pius I has to be listed as the ninth successor of PETER, immediately after HYGINUS; this is in fact the place assigned him by the *LIBER PONTIFICALIS*, Irenaeus, Hegesippus, Eusebius of Caesarea, and Jerome. All say that his episcopate lasted fifteen years, and the dates given for Hyginus's pontificate make it necessary to identify these years as those from 140 to 155. He is described as an Italian from Aquileia and the brother of Hermas, the author of the well-known *The Shepherd*, written during this pontificate. During these fifteen years, Rome was agitated by important doctrinal questions: the gnosticism of Valentinus, who came to Rome under Hyginus, and of Marcion, who arrived from Asia around 140, was spreading, posing a threat to the Church. In July 144, Pius headed a synod of priests that banished Marcion from the Church; this forceful decision underlined both the danger of heresy and the fact that Rome had become the most important center of Christianity in the Roman world. Pius also knew the Christian philosopher and apologist Justin, who taught in his home. Although Pius is said to have been martyred (feast, 11 June), this is not supported by any documentary evidence, or by the presence of his tomb at the Vatican, near that of Peter.

Jean-Pierre Martin

Bibliography

Amann, E. *DTC*, Paris, 1935, XII, 2, 1612–13.
Eusebius, *EH*, IV, 11, 6; 11, 7; V, 6; 14.
Irenaeus, *Adv. Haeres.*, III, 3, 3; 4, 3.
Weltin, E. G. *NCE*, 1967, XI, 393.

PIUS II. *Enea Silvio Piccolomini (b. Corsignano, Siena, 18 October 1405 d. Ancona, 14 August 1464). Elected pope on 27 August 1458, crowned on 3 September. Buried in the chapel of S. Andrea at St. Peter's in Rome, transferred in 1614 to the church of S. Andrea della Valle.*

Pius II was the son of a failed Sienese nobleman, Silvio, and Vittoria Forteguerri. At eighteen, he studied law in Siena, although he was more drawn to humanistic culture. With his studies behind him (1432), he entered the service of cardinals and bishops as secretary and companion, and was sent on missions to Italy and abroad. He accompanied Domenico Capranica to the COUNCIL of Basel, Nicodemo della Scala to the diet of Frankfurt, Bartolomeo Visconti (although the failure of a plot to capture EUGENE IV put him in a compromising position), and Niccolò Albergati to Burgundy (peace of Arras, 1435). Albergati also sent him to Scotland to the court of James I. On his return to Basel, where Cardinal Giuliano Cesarini made him secretary and abbreviator of the council, he defended the conciliar theses and began to attract notice owing to his oratorical skill and knowledge of the law. When Eugene IV was declared deposed (1439), Enea Silvio attended as *ceremoniarius* in the conclave at which Amadeus of Savoy (FELIX V) was elected antipope, and became his secretary. He was sent to the diet of Frankfurt (1442), where Frederick III (who had declared himself neutral in the conflict between the pope and the council) crowned him poet laureate and offered him a post in the imperial chancery.

In the German lands, his "conversion" to obedience to Rome as against the antipope gradually ripened and his life changed decisively. Appointed ambassador to Rome, he made amends; censure was remitted, and he obtained the pardon of Eugene IV. In March 1446, he was ordained priest in Vienna. In 1447–48, with the aid of the pontifical LEGATE G. Carvajal, he was able to end German neutrality (by concordats with the princes and with Vienna). Appointed bishop of Trieste by NICHOLAS V, he sent to the rector of the University of Cologne an *Epistula retractationis* in which he confessed to the error he had committed in following conciliar theory and explained the reasons that had brought him to obedience to Rome. Transferred to the diocese of Siena (1449), he was ordered by Frederick III to arrange his marriage with Eleanor of Portugal and to obtain for him the imperial crown. In exchange, Enea Silvio received the title of prince and counselor of the empire.

After the fall of Constantinople in 1453, Nicholas V announced a CRUSADE. Enea Silvio (who in 1444 had been shaken by the defeat of Varna and by the death of Cesarini) several times undertook to preach the war against the infidels. After the emperor enjoined him to pledge loyalty to CALLISTUS III (1455), he remained in Italy, where he used his considerable skill to end a dispute between Siena and Iacopo Piccinino. Appointed cardinal of the title of Sta. Sabina (18 December 1456), he remained close to the pope as an adviser on relations with the Germans.

On the death of Callistus III, Enea Silvio was elected with the support of the duke of Milan, the king of Naples, Cardinal Barbo (who won for him the favor of the Italian cardinals to the detriment of d'Estouteville, the French candidate), and Cardinals Borgia and Colonna. The international situation was extremely tense. The TURKS were exerting greater and greater pressure; internal conflicts were erupting in Poland, Bohemia, Hungary, the German lands (among the great houses and between Frederick III and the elector princes), and England (with the Wars of the Roses); in France, tensions existed between the duke of Burgundy and Charles VII, who was angry with the pope, especially on account of d'Estouteville's defeat and the question of the kingdom of Naples; in Italy, the ANGEVINS clashed with the Aragonese, and rivalries continually mounted among the seigniories. Though his health was failing prematurely, Pius II's energy and political skill remained intact. Central to his political intention was the crusade. Besides its obvious aim of containing the Turks, it was designed to restore prestige to the pontifical authority. This holy war might enable Europe to forget its dissensions and regain political and religious unity.

The pope convened a diet at Mantua, but on 1 June 1459, the appointed opening day, no one turned up. The first session could not take place until September. The rulers and nobles were more preoccupied with their own problems than with the war against the infidels. Only Francesco Sforza traveled to Mantua, most of the delegations being made up of figures of the second rank. Venice and Florence were concerned for their trade and issued no more than vague promises. Despite everything, after renewed appeals and separate discussions with the various legations, Pius II proclaimed a three-year crusade (January 1460) and imposed the tithe.

In the Italian political arena, Pius II played the role of mediator and peacemaker among the different states. He granted investiture to Ferrante of Aragon, who had supported him at the time of the conclave. Jean of Anjou, championed by the king of France and aided by the Orsini of Tarento and Piccinino, had won the victories of Sarno and San Fabiano over the Neapolitan, papal, and Milanese forces. But he was defeated at Troia by Alessandro Sforza (1462). Sigismondo Malatesta, who had defied excommunication to launch several attacks against the Papal States, was vanquished at sea by Cardinal Forteguerri and on land by Federico di Montefeltro (1463). In Rome, a band headed by Tiburzio and Valeriano di Maso was broken up. Appealing to republican ideals, it operated in agreement with Piccinino, the Savelli, the Colonna, the Anguillara, and possibly the Angevins.

In the international domain, the pope strove to reinforce papal authority and establish the agreement necessary for the realization of the crusade. After lengthy negotiations first with Charles VII and then with Louis XI, and thanks to the manipulations of Cardinal Jouffroy, he obtained the abolition of the Pragmatic Sanction of Bourges. Nevertheless, the king, who had hoped for a change of policy on the Neapolitan question, later reestablished "Gallican liberties" against "Roman usurpations."

In the German lands, Cardinal Bessarion, the legate to the diets of Nuremberg, Neustadt, and Vienna (1460, 1461), was unable to prevent war between the Wittelsbachs and the Hohenzollern or to persuade the rulers to support the crusade, and returned to Rome sick and disheartened. Sigismund of Tirol had to be excommunicated owing to his warring against the bishop of Brixen, Nicholas of Cusa (their differences were not resolved until 1464). Also excommunicated was the archbishop of Mainz, Diether von Isenburg, who had taken up leadership of the German party opposed to the pope. In each case, the role of Gregory von Heimburg was an important one. An old enemy of Pius II, he too had been excommunicated and declared a heretic following his violent libels against the pope. He appealed to a future pope and to a council, and it was only after the intervention of Francisco of Toledo and of R. von Rudesheim that Diether, abandoned by the elector princes, submitted to the pope (1463). A trial for perjury and heresy (cut short by the death of Pius II) was also begun against George of Podebrady, king of Bohemia, who was playing a double game. On the one side, he swore obedience to the pope, who in 1462 had refused to accept the *Compacta* agreed upon by the council of Basel, while on the other he supported the ultraquists.

There remained the increasingly serious problem of the progress of the Turks (who were at Lesbos, near Lepanto, in Morea, and in Bosnia) and the crusade. A new opportunity arose. In 1462–3, at Tolfa, a potentially lucrative discovery of ALUM had been made. Moreover, Cardinal Carvajal had persuaded Frederick III to make peace with the Hungarian king, Mathias Corvinus; George Skanderberg and Philip of Burgundy had promised to help; Venice, where Bessarion had gone, had decided to enter the war and had joined in a league with Mathias Corvinus and Philip of Burgundy. But the Italian cities (including Florence and Naples, and Milan, which had seized Genoa and Savona), impelled by reciprocal mistrust and rivalries, did no more than make promises and evade the issue. The duke of Burgundy, at Louis XI's instigation, did likewise. Against his cardinals' advice, and even though he was seriously ill, Pius II therefore decided to lead the crusade. He hoped by setting an example to win over the others. Having left Rome on 18 June, he reached Ancona, exhausted, on 19

July, only to find that the promised vessels and troops had failed to turn up. He died on the vigil of the Assumption.

His heart was placed in the cathedral of S. Ciriaco, and his body was interred in Rome in the chapel of S. Andrea at St. Peter's, and then moved to S. Andrea della Valle.

The life and writings of Pius II were a faithful mirror of his times. The characteristic trait of his personality is to be found in a perfect correspondence between his culture and his actions (even his first name was intended to recall *pius Aeneas*). On the one hand, he was a fighter and a man of the world, a diplomat, politician, and pontiff; on the other, he was a writer, a poet, a humanist, a lover of books and of *otium*, and an ironic and astute observer. Without ever losing sight of his career, he invariably succeeded in reconciling his private interest with that of the institutions within which he had to operate. He used humanism to serve his politics and even his religious undertakings.

Although no stranger to NEPOTISM, he usually gave his support to those worthy of it. That was the case with respect to the children of his sister Laudomia Tedeschini (Antonio became governor of Rome, married Maria, Ferrante's natural daughter, and received the duchy of Amalfi and other possessions; Francesco, later PIUS III, became cardinal of Siena; Andrea and Giacomo received small fiefs, and one of them married Agnese Farnese, the aunt of Paul III, and the other, in a second marriage, a Colonna; it was the case also with respect to his cousin Niccolò Forteguerri and to Iacopo Ammannati, the apostolic secretary who was taken in by the Piccolomini family, both of whom became cardinals, as well as with respect to his cousin Gregorio Lolli.

Pius II was a prolific author. As a young man, he wrote two licentious works (*Cinthia*, around 1427, and *Historia de Eurialo et Lucretia*, in 1444), but he devoted his talents chiefly to books of a historical nature having to do with events he had lived through personally, countries he had visited, and personalities he had known. Principal among these are *De gestis Basiliensis concilii* (1440), which reappeared later in *De rebus Basileae gestis* (1550); *De curialium miseriis* (1444); *De viris aetate sua claris* (1440–50); *Historia Gothorum* (1453); *Historia Bohemica* (1458); *Historia Friderici imperatoris* (1452–58); and a *Cosmography*, of which he wrote only *Europe* (1458) and *Asia* (1461). The *Commentarii* are particularly interesting. They are autobiography in thirteen books (1462–63; 1464; Vat. Reg. Lat. 1995 with autograph corrections, Rome, Corsin. 147 dated 12 June 1464; ed. 1584 by F. Bandini Piccolomini), erroneously attributed to the copyist Johannes Gobelinus, in which he describes his life before his pontificate (book 1) and sets forth his political and religious engagement. The writer gives a well-calculated image of himself, as he would wish it to go down to posterity. The *Epistola a Maometto* (around 1462) may be apocryphal. The speeches, letters, and bulls, often written in his hand, are numerous. Noteworthy among the bulls are *Vocavit nos Pius* (13 October 1458), a convening of the rulers to Mantua; *Ecclesiam Christi* (16 January 1460), a proclamation of the crusade; *Execrabilis* (17 January 1460), a condemnation of appeal to a council; *Bulla retractationum* (26 April 1463) against antipapal doctrines; the bull of the crusade (22 October 1463), written before he left for Ancona; and *Ineffabilis summi providentia Patris* (1 August 1464), on the hypostatic union of the blood shed by Christ.

With Nicholas of Cusa and D. Domenichi, Pius planned a reform of the diocesan clergy and the religious orders (though because of the difficulties of the era he was unable to put it much into effect). He canonized St. Catherine of Siena, defended the Jews and the blacks against abuses, and combated usury. He disappointed the expectations of those who hoped finally to have found a patron of letters. The life he had lived and his humanistic culture ensured that he knew "the hirelings of the pen" only too well and had no need of literate secretaries for the editing of documents. Above all, he was almost completely without resources of his own and had no desire to use Church revenues for other purposes. The only writers he truly respected were Flavio Biondo, whose *Storie* he summarized, and G. A. Campano, to whom he entrusted the revision of the *Commentarii*. He arranged for numerous volumes to be written and illuminated for the pontifical library, and for the repair of the fortifications of the towns in the Patrimony of St. Peter. In Rome, he restored several churches as well as the Aurelian walls, and built the benediction loggia and the chapel of S. Andrea at St. Peter's, as well as the pope's loggia and the Palazzo Piccolomini delle Papesse in Siena. He devoted himself particularly to the village of his birth, which was reconstructed by B. Rossellino and raised to the rank of a diocese under the name Pienza.

Paola Piacentini Scaccia

Bibliography

Aenae Silvii Piccolomin . . . Opera inedita descripsit . . . I. Cugnoni," *Atti dela R. Accademia dei Lincei, Mem. cl. Scienze mor., store. e filol.*, 3rd ser., 8(1882–3), 319–686.

Aeneae Sylvii Piccolominei . . . Opera quae extant omnia . . ., Basel, 1551.

"Atti del Convegno storico Piccolominiano, Ancona, 9 maggio 1965," *Atti e memorie Dep. Storia Patria per le Marche*, 8th ser., 4/2 (1964–5), Ancona, 1966.

Aveseni, R. "Una fonte della 'Vita' di Pio II del Platina," *Bartolomeo Sacchi il Platina (Piadena 1421 – Roma 1481). Atti Conv. intern, studi per il V centenario (Cremona, 14–15 Nov. 1981)*, Padua 1986, 1–7.

Bianchi, R. *Intorno a Pio II: un mercante e tre poeti*, Messina, 1988.

Brosius, D. "Breven und Briefe Papst Pius' II," *Römische Quartalschrift*, 70 (1975), 180–224; "Das Itenerar Papst Pius' II," *Quellen und Forsch. aus italien. Archiven und Bibliotheken*, 55–6 (1976), 421–32

Diener, H. "'Fridericus Dux Austriae Hernesti filius': aus 'De Viris illustribus' des Enea Silvio Piccolomini," *Römische historische Mitteilungen*, 28 (1986), 185–208.

Enea Silvio Piccolomini Papa Pio II. Atti del Convegno per il 5° centenario della morte e altri scritti, ed. D. Maffei, Siena, 1968.

Gabel, L. C., ed. *Memoirs of a Renaissance Pope: The Commentaries of Pius II*, abridgment translated by F. A. Gragg, New York, 1962.

Le vite di Pio II de G.A. Campano et B. Platina, ed. G. C. Zimolo, Bologna, 1964 (RIS/2. III, 3).

Paparelli, G. *Enea Silvio Piccolomini (Pio II)*, Bari, 1950. Pastor, 3.

Piccolomini, E. A. "De codicibus Pii II et Pii III deque Bibliotheca Ecclesiae Cathedralis Senensis," *Bulletino senese di storia patria*, 6 (1899), 483–96.

Pii II . . . *Orationes politicae et ecclesiasticae . . .* , ed. G. D. Mansi, Lucca, 1755–7.

Pio II e la cultura del suo tempo, I Convegno Internazionale di Studi umanistici, Pienza, Montepulciano, Chianciano, 24–28 luglio 1989, Milan, 1990.

Scarcia Piacentini, P. "I codici," in AA.VV, *Il costo del libro*, in *Scrittura, bibliotheche e stampa a Roma nel Quattrocento, Atti 2° seminario, 6–8 maggio 1982*, Vatican, 1983, 364–7 and passim.

Strnad, A. "Personalita, famiglia, carriera ecclesiastica di Giovanni Hinderbach prima dell'episcopato," *Il Principe Vescovo Giovanni Hinderbach (1465–1486) fra tardo medioevo e umanesimo. Convegno Trento, 2–6 october 1989*.

Totaro, L. Pio II nei suoi Commentarii . . . , Bologna, 1978 (bibliog.).

Voigt, G. *Enea Silvio de' Piccolomini . . .* , Berlin, 1856–63.

Wolkan, R. *Der Briefwechsel des Eneas Silvius Piccolomini*, Vienna, 1909–18.

PIUS III. *Francesco Tedeschini Piccolomini (b, Siena, 9 May 1439 [?], d. Rome, 18 October 1503). Elected on 22 September, crowned on 8 October 1503. Interred in the chapel of S. Andrea at St. Peter's in Rome, transferred in 1614 to the church of S. Andrea della Valle.*

Pius III was the son of Nanni Tedeschini (whose name is shown on the family tomb at Sarteano), a jurist, who may have been related to the family of the counts of Sarteano. His mother, Laudomia Piccolomini, was the sister of PIUS II, who gave his family his name and coat of arms. With his uncle's help, Francesco studied law and liberal arts in Ferrara, possibly in Vienne (1451), and then in Perugia, where he completed studies in canon law and obtained his degree. The recipient of many benefices and prebendaries, he was made archbishop of Siena, cardinal deacon of S. Eustachio (1460), LEGATE for the Marches, and then vicar of Rome and the Papal States when Pope Pius II left for Ancona (1464). Under the subsequent popes, in particular during the pontificate of ALEXANDER VI, he preferred to reside at some distance from Rome. Nevertheless, he was able to win that pope's confidence and respect and to be given certain responsibilities, such as the administration of Fermo and Pienza, the legation to the diet of Regensburg (1471), and that to Charles VIII of France, who was on his way to Naples and who refused to receive him (1494).

At the conclave of 1503, in which thirty-seven cardinals took part, Cardinal D'Amboise's attempts to have himself elected failed in the face of opposition from Giuliano della Rovere and the Spaniards. After a month of deliberations, a decision was made to choose a "compromise" pope. But the exhausting ceremonies surrounding the ordination and coronation, followed by an operation on his leg for gout, brought about Pius's death and prevented him from making good on the electoral capitulation to which he had committed himself or intervening in the problems of the PAPAL STATES and of Rome, where the Colonna and the Orsini had formed an alliance against Cesare Borgia's abuses of power. Contrary to what was supposed, Pius was not poisoned. He was interred at St. Peter's, near the tomb of Pius II, his remains later being moved to S. Andrea della Valle. A lover of art, he assembled a collection of books and sculptures in the Piccolomini Palace in Rome (today the church and convent of S. Andrea della Valle). In Siena, he founded the cathedral *libreria* (1492) to house his own library and that of his uncle; in 1503–9, Pinturicchio decorated it with scenes from the life of Pius II. He also commissioned Michelangelo to create statues for the sanctuary (1501). He was no great politician, his prudence and generosity (for instance, to Cesare Borgia) at times causing him to be accused of weakness and lack of ability. Yet his culture, his exemplary conduct, and his honesty (he refused to practice nepotism) had aroused real hope for the prompt reform of the CURIA, at all levels, and the restoration of peace throughout Christendom.

Paola Piacentini Scaccia

Bibliography

Bandini, D. "Gli antenati di Pio III," *Bullett. Senese Storia Patria*, 73–5 (1966–8), 239–51.

Pastor, III, 1932, 465–79 and passim.

Piccolomini, P. "Il pontificato di Pio III secondo la testimonianza di una fonte contemporanea," *Arch. Stor. Italiano*, 5th ser., 32 (1903), 102–38.

Strnad, A. "Francesco Tedeschini Piccolomini: Politik und Maezenatentum im Quattrocento," *Römische his-*

tor. Mitteilungen, 8–9 (1964–6); "Pio II e suo nipote Francesco Tedeschini Piccolomini," *Atti Convegno storico Piccolominiano, Ancona, 9 maggio 1955, Atti e Memorie Dep. Storia Patria Marche*, 8th ser., 4 (1964–5), 35–84.

Ugurgieri Della Berardenga, C. *Pio II Piccolomini con notizie su Pio III . . .* , Florence, 1973, 504–22.

PIUS IV. *Gian Angelo de' Medici (b. Milan, 31 March 1499, d. Rome, 9 December 1565). Elected pope on 26 December 1559, crowned on 6 January 1560. Buried at Sta Maria degli Angeli, Rome.*

Pius IV's pontificate is marked by the third and final period of the council of TRENT and by vigorous efforts toward Church reform, carried out with the help of the CARDINAL NEPHEW, St. Charles Borromeo. The pope's name is more particularly linked to the *Professio fidei tridentina*.

Gian Angelo de' Medici was born to a Milanese family, and the kinship with the Medici of Florence on which he prided himself was imaginary. His father, a physician, was ruined by the defeat of Marignano and died in 1519. The youth studied law at Pavia, in materially difficult conditions, and when his family had regained prosperity after 1521, he transferred to Bologna, where he was admitted to the doctorate *in utroque* in 1525. He entered the service of the CURIA in 1527, and his promotion was gradual, linked to that of his brother Gian Giacomo, a soldier and the head of the family. After serving in several capacities in the PAPAL STATES and being sent on missions with the papal ARMIES, Gian Angelo was appointed archbishop of Ragusa on 14 December 1545, and at the same time received major orders; he was made a CARDINAL on 8 April 1549.

His training and experience made him far more of an expert in law, administration, and finance than a theologian. A cardinal of the second rank, he remained a man of simple tastes and style, with a preference for peasants' food and scant tolerance for Roman ceremonial. Strong and vigorous in character (he was a tireless walker), he could also act as a skilled diplomat, both affable and conciliatory. His private life was not above reproach: he fathered three illegitimate children.

His election as pope came at the end of the longest CONCLAVE of the century (5 September to 26 December 1559). The balance of power between the cardinals supporting France and those supporting Spain was held by a third group, that of Cardinal Carlo Carafa, made up of cardinals appointed by PAUL IV. The electoral capitulation, which the future pope promised ahead of time to uphold, provided for the reconvening of the council.

His pontificate opened with the sensational trial of the Carafa, who had made themselves the object of general opprobrium by abusing their position under Paul IV. Cardinals Carlo and Alfonso, as well as Giovanni, duke of Paliano, and members of their entourage were arrested in June 1559, accused of theft, violence, and assassination (including that of Giovanni's wife), abuse of power, lèse-majesté, and felony. Carlo and Giovanni were sentenced to death and their possessions confiscated (3 March 1561).

Despite the reluctance of secular rulers, Pius IV was firmly resolved to reopen the council. The first general congregation took place on 15 January 1562. Nine sessions (XVII to XXV) saw the promulgation of the fundamental decrees: five doctrinal decrees on the practice of communion, the sacrifice of the mass, the sacrament of orders, marriage, and finally purgatory and the cult of the saints. The reform decrees concerned first of all the parochial clergy: its recruitment, its formation, its morality and dignity, and its revenues. The Tridentine ideal of the priest thus was given lasting definition. One fundamental institution was created, that of the seminaries (15 July 1563). The final reform decrees concerned more specifically bishops and cardinals (their selection, the obligation of residence, episcopal visits, suppression of the accumulation of benefices, their style of life) and the discipline of the religious. Before they dispersed (4 December 1563), the fathers solemnly confirmed all the preceding decrees, thereby affirming the much-questioned unity of the three periods of the council.

Pius IV confirmed the council decrees as a whole (BULL *Benedictus Deus*, 25 January 1564) and instituted a commission responsible for seeing to their application, the future Congregation of the Council. The bull *Injunctum nobis* (13 November 1564) defined the *Professio fidei tridentina*, a public profession of faith and oath of obedience to the Church of Rome that would henceforth be demanded of all priests and ecclesiastical beneficiaries, and extended to superiors of orders as well as university professors.

The pope finished the work of the council on those points still outstanding. The so-called *INDEX librorum prohibitorum* of Trent, which reduced the excessive number of books forbidden by Paul IV, was published on 24 March 1564 (bull *Dominici gregis custodiae*). The Roman CATECHISM, the all-encompassing statement of Catholic doctrine, prepared by the council, drew up, was completed but would not be published until after Pius's death. The same was true of the reform of the BREVIARY and of the missal.

Pius IV threw much energy into Church reform. In 1560, he welcomed to Rome his nephews Frederick and Charles Borromeo along with many other relatives (in particular the Serbelloni and Hohenems or Altemps). Charles, his favorite, was made a cardinal at the first promotion, on 31 January, and archbishop of Milan on 7 February; then he was made LEGATE of Bologna and Romagna, with responsibility for governing the Papal States, and the pope's private secretary in his capacity as cardinal nephew; and he received numerous other positions and favors. His uncle's chief counselor, he gave proof of his intelligence and his extraordinary gifts for administration as well his piety and modesty, without, however, immediately abandoning the ostentatious way of life attached to his rank. After his brother's death in 1562, he began to lead a life of exemplary austerity and took an extremely active part in Pius IV's efforts at reform. In June 1564, the two men set an example of reform *in capite* by sharply curtailing their way of life, a requirement imposed on all cardinals. In 1565, Charles left Rome for his diocese of Milan, where he would carry out his pastoral duties indefatigably: Pius IV, once the council had come to a close, sharply recalled the prelates to the duty of their place of residence. The bull *In principis apostolorum sede* (17 February 1565) revoked all privileges contrary to the decrees of Trent. The Roman Seminary was founded and entrusted to the JESUITS.

With varying success, Pius IV strove to persuade the Christian states to accept the Tridentine decrees. The question of communion under both species, solicited by Emperor Ferdinand I, had been handed over to the pope by the council. On 16 April 1564, it was conceded to a large part of the empire. On the other hand, Ferdinand did not obtain the married priesthood, in particular because of Philip II of Spain's ferocious opposition. Protestantism, meanwhile, continued to make progress in Europe, and the rupture with the Catholic Church was complete: The wars of religion broke out in France in 1562, and England slipped irrevocably from Rome's grasp.

Pius IV was a patron of the arts rather than of letters. The *Noctes Vaticanae* organized by Charles Borromeo avoided discussion of secular literature and concentrated on religious topics. The Venetian printer Paolo Manuzio, the son of Aldo, was invited to set up his business in Rome, but in order to publish texts the revision of which had been provided for by the council.

Employing the architects Pirro Ligorio and Sallustio Peruzzi, the pope was responsible for several buildings at the Belvedere, in particular the Casina, also known as the Villa Pia, and the geographical gallery of the Terza Loggia. Michelangelo was commissioned to adorn the church of Sta Maria degli Angeli. Pius IV also added new fortifications to CASTEL SANT'ANGELO, extended the Leonine wall to the Borgo Pio, created streets, restored the aqueduct of the Aqua Virgo, and erected the Porta del Popolo and the Porta Pia.

Marc Smith

Bibliography

Constant, G. "Pie V," *DTC*, 12 (1935), 1633–47.

Fliche-Martin, XVII, 173–222.

Herre, P. *Papsttum und Papstwahl im Zeitalter Philipps II.*, Leipzig, 1907.

Jedin, H. *Geschichte des Konzils von Trient*, 4, Fribourg, 1975.

Pacaut, M. "Pie IV," *Catholicisme*, 11 (1988), 253–4.

Paschini, P. *Cinquecento romano e Riforma cattolica*, Rome, 1958.

Pastor, 15 and 16.

Rezzaghi, R. "Cronaca di un conclave: l'elezione di Pio IV (1559)," *Salesianum*, 48 (1986), 539–81.

Susta, J. *Die Römische Kurie und das Konzil von Trient unter Pius IV.*, Vienna, 1904–14, 4 vols. (collection of documents).

PIUS V. *Michele (Antonio) Ghislieri (b. Boscomarengo, near Alessandria, 17 January 1504, d. Rome, 1 May 1572). Elected pope on 7 January 1566, crowned on 19 January. Interred first at St. Peter's in Rome, his body was transferred to St. Mary Major on 9 January 1588. Canonized on 22 May 1712 (feast on 5 May, then 30 April).*

Long recognized as the pope of the Counter Reformation, Pius V is known today in France as the Integralists' pope. In Italy and Spain, on the other hand, his name is associated with the battle of LEPANTO and with the ROSARY, and in English-speaking countries with the INQUISITION. Though he comes to light as one of the most original of the 16th-century popes, he is famous rather than truly understood.

As a pope who identified completely with his function, which was close to that of the absolute monarchies in the making, he helped organize a pontifical power that was strong and coherent, yet still harbored medieval dreams of CRUSADE and of a united Christendom. These contradictory sides expressed one man's massive effort to respond to the anguish of his time.

The 222nd pope marked the attainment to the papacy of bureaucrats, for whom birth and family were no longer essential qualifications. He was in fact born in the countryside, to a peasant family rich enough to send him to the DOMINICANS for his schooling. Having entered the order at fourteen, he climbed all the rungs of a career open to an intellectually gifted friar, becoming priest (1528), preacher, and finally teacher of philosophy and theology in his order (1528–44), in which capacity he had already defended papal authority, badly undermined by the SACK OF ROME.

His life was to be a Dominican, but the *nec plus ultra* of a Dominican, in the context of the rise of the REFORMATION, was to be an inquisitor. Around 1546, he began a career in the newly created HOLY OFFICE; the zeal he exhibited in Como and Bergamo earned him the notice of Giampetro Carafa (the future PAUL IV), who appointed him commissary general of the Inquisition in Rome in 1551. His Roman career took off rapidly from that point: bishop in 1556, CARDINAL in 1557, Grand Inquisitor in 1558. The little Dominica became the "cardinal of Alessandria," an efficient and feared bureaucrat, linked to the Carafa clan. The ascent of PIUS IV to the papal throne (1559–65) put a temporary end to his activities, and from 1560 he found himself in relative disgrace.

He devoted his energies at this point to his diocese of Mondovi. The technocrat became an effective and sincere agent for pastoral reform. He battled with the duke of Savoy in order to safeguard ecclesiastical freedoms, reformed the religious, and, following Charles Borromeo, gave special protection to the new Clerics Regular of St. Paul (the Barnabites), founded in 1553, whose lectures he attended early on. Their aim, to create a clergy specializing in pastoral work, was not an original one, but their taste for dramatic liturgies, spectacular street missions, and public penitential exercises profoundly influenced the spirituality of the future pope. He thus found himself in contact with the strictest and most advanced milieus of the pre-Tridentine Catholic Reform. He stayed attached to the Carafa family during the council of TRENT and thereafter remained loyal to it, choosing as datary Marcantonio Maffei, a Theatine, and as secretary of state Cardinal Reumano, men close to Paul IV. The promotion of several family members to the cardinalate, such as Antonio Carafa, would strengthen the close connection.

Michele Ghislieri's surprise election, after three weeks of an undecided CONCLAVE, was due to the rallying of the Borromeo family to one of the candidates approved by Spain. The election signaled a victory for those who wanted an austere and pious pope, one capable of exalting the priesthood, of acting decisively and energetically against the Reformation, and of carrying out the decisions of the council without delay or favor.

Obsessed by HERESY and SCHISM, Pius V was the only pope to take his seat regularly in the Holy Office. Determined to combat Calvinism, he first of all strove to reestablish Catholicism in Scotland, which had been Presbyterian since 1560, by supporting Mary Stuart. After that queen had fled to England, he attempted to stir an uprising of the English Catholics. He hoped at one stroke to solve the Anglican question and that of the revolt in the Low Countries, by excommunicating Elizabeth I and releasing her subjects from their oath of loyalty (30 March 1570). As it turned out, these harsh measures did a disservice to English Catholicism, by dividing it, casting suspicion on its loyalty, and attracting to it a ruthless persecution.

In the Low Countries, the pope limited himself to sending the duke of Alba a blessed sword, but in France he sent money and armies to wage war with the Huguenots. The growth of the NUNCIATURES and the establishment of the JESUITS throughout Europe accompanied the effort toward Catholic reconquest. Even more, perhaps, the balance in the Mediterranean was a question that haunted Pius V. For more than a century, a constant preoccupation of papal politics had been to create an alliance of Christian rulers to fight against the TURKS, who were now

about to seize Malta (1566). The popes' ritual request was invariably answered by an offer of goodwill on the part of the rulers, but little in the way of concrete action. Only when the Turks, taking advantage of the burning of the Venetian arsenal (1569), gained mastery of the Adriatic and then seized Cyprus did an effective Holy League take shape under the pope's leadership (19 May 1571). Finally funded ($\frac{1}{6}$ by the pope, $\frac{3}{6}$ by Spain, and $\frac{2}{6}$ by Venice), and given spiritual support by great rogatory processions in Rome, the alliance produced an imposing fleet (208 galleys, some 20 to 30 warships, 1,850 cannons). It was placed under the command of one of the greatest contemporary captains, Don Juan of Austria, who on 14 August 1571 in Naples received from the pope's hands the baton and standard of the crusade: each man believed this crusade would be the last before Christ returned to Jerusalem. On 7 October, before Lepanto, the greatest naval battle of the century ended with the destruction of the Turkish fleet—a brilliant victory, but one without aftermath, owing to the divisions within Christendom and the death of Pius V on 1 May 1572.

If Pius V thought he was living the end of time, he was no war leader; faced with the ill will of the secular states, he was powerless. This he was quick to realize, for his promotions to the cardinalate were perfectly balanced between France (Jérôme Souchier, Charles d'Angennes, Nicolas de Pellevé) and Spain (Didacus Spinoza, Gaspar Cervantes, Gaspar Zuñiga). He seems to have been one of the first popes to confine his energies to the Church itself. He wanted above all to be the patron of the Catholic Reform, of the purification of the Church. As bishop of Rome, either in person or through others he visited churches, chapters, hospitals, and prisons, examined confessors and ordinands, and made compulsory the wearing of ecclesiastical dress. This arsenal of reform was not new, but was applied rigorously and methodically, with no loopholes remaining.

The religious clergy were treated in the same way. The original rules were reestablished and enclosure strictly imposed. Two new congregations received approval: the Barnabites and the Brothers of the Misericordia (Hospitallers of St. John of God). If the Dominican order was favored, it was not favored to excess (3 cardinals out of 21, as compared with 1 Franciscan—Felice Peretti of Montealto, the future SIXTUS V—and 1 Cistercian).

Pius V's pontificate marked a new stage in the material and moral purging of Rome, through the expulsion of prostitutes and the hounding of debauchery, and, even more, through religious if not ethnic purification: the Jews were made to live in ghettos, the aim being to force them to convert. The pope also strove to erase all traces of pagan and ancient art; the Apollo Belvedere was saved only by the protests of several humanist cardinals. It was his predecessor, Pius IV, who caused provocative artists' nudes to be veiled, but under Pius V Rome became like the-world-as-a-monastery through which pilgrims had to pass before being shown into the forecourt of paradise, with its artistic and religious splendor.

Pius V helped build a new image of the papacy. The council had entrusted the pope with the task of reforming the CURIA, and the result was the creation of the Congregations for Bishops and of the INDEX, as well as the reorganization of the PENITENTIARY in 1569. Under Pius V, the Congregation for Bishops became a singularly active turntable for doubtful decisions sent in from all parts of the Christian world. From that time on, the Holy See would intervene directly in areas previously handled by the bishops, such as the liturgy.

The CATECHISM of the council, which appeared in 1566 with its approval, was a collective work, largely written under the preceding pope. The BREVIARY (1568) and the MISSAL (1570), for their part, were directly linked to Pius V. While these were imposed only in dioceses unable to demonstrate that their LITURGY was more than two centuries old, they were nevertheless presented as universal models of the Catholic liturgy, to be studied and copied. The power of Rome would gradually iron out local liturgical peculiarities, in the name of the very principle that presided over the compilation of the new books: to use only the best texts. That meant eliminating redundancies and bad Latin, unifying the body of Christian believers to fit it for resisting the attractions of Reformation simplicity, and convincing by means of the beauty, the splendor, and the force of standardized rituals. The liturgy certainly gained in quality and in dignity by its imitation of Rome, but local liturgical specialists lost their freedom; in the Christian world as a whole, the creative capacity diminished some decades later, and quickly left to wither a liturgy that was more and more removed from the culture.

The pope had become the master of the Catholic liturgy because others had recognized his capacity. The personal prestige of the popes at the end of the century was immense. The piety of Pius V was known throughout Rome. People could behold the pope praying and weeping before the Blessed Sacrament, could see him making the pilgrimage to the Seven Churches with a reduced escort, were familiar with his personal austerity and the simplicity of his private life, and knew his family influence was limited to that of his CARDINAL NEPHEW, Michele Bonelli, a fellow Dominican.

Pius V was the first pope to exercise his pontificate as a priest rather than a sovereign. He aspired to be the supreme priest of all Christians, thus building up the image of the modern papacy. With him, the Catholic response to the Reformation was, more than ever, clerical and hierarchical; it was the effective application of a pastoral ideal that had reached its apogee, the search for cohesion indispensable for the reconquering of positions lost in the Old World and for the evangelization of the New.

Nicole Lemaitre

Bibliography

Anderson, R. *St. Pius V: A Brief Account of His Life, Times, Virtues and Miracles*, Rockford, Ill., 1978.

Hirschauer, C. *La Politique de saint Pie V en France, 1566–72*, Paris, 1922.

Jedin, H. "Pio V," *EC*, 9 (1952), 1498–1500.

Lemaitre, N. *Saint Pie V*, Paris, 1994.

Pastor, 17 and 18.

San Pio V e la problematica del suo tempo, Alessandria (Casa di risparmio), 1972.

Wright, A. D. *The Early Modern Papacy: From the Council of Trent to the French Revolution 1564–1789*, London, 2000.

PIUS VI. *Giovanni Angelo Braschi (b. Cesena, 25 December 1717, d. Valencia, 29 August 1799). Elected pope on 15 February 1775, simultaneously ordained bishop and crowned on 22 February. Buried at St. Peter's in Rome.*

The pontificate of Pius VI, among the longest in history, was also one of the most turbulent. It took place at a time of great crisis for the Catholic Church, which, having suffered the attacks of the *philosophes* of the ENLIGHTENMENT, found itself plunged into the turmoil of the FRENCH REVOLUTION.

Braschi came from an old Romagna family, perhaps of Swedish origin, that had belonged to the urban aristocracy since the early 17th century. He was the eldest of the eight children of Count Marco Aurelio and Anna Teresa di Conti Bandi di Cesena. Educated by the JESUITS, he soon obtained his degree *in utroque iure* (1735). He studied law at the University of Ferrara under the tutelage of his maternal uncle Giovanni Carlo Bandi, at that time auditor of Cardinal Tommaso Ruffo, the papal LEGATE of the province, to whom shortly thereafter he was appointed secretary. In 1740, on the death of CLEMENT XII, he followed Ruffo to Rome for the conclave, and he never again returned to his birthplace. In fact, the new pontiff, BENEDICT XIV, named Cardinal Ruffo dean of the SACRED COLLEGE and suburbicarian bishop of Ostia and Velletri, and Braschi became his auditor. He thus succeeded his uncle, who had been promoted to the rank of bishop.

In his new post, Braschi had to administer two dioceses. He also played a role in the protection of Velletri when a battle took place there, in 1744, between the Austrians and the Spanish during Don Carlos de Bourbon's conquest of the kingdom of Naples. His good relationship with the latter encouraged the pope to entrust him with overseeing certain jurisdictional disputes that had arisen between Rome and Naples. He was appointed secret CHAMBERLAIN as a reward for the fruits of his diplomacy. On Cardinal Ruffo's death, in 1753, he became Benedict XIV's private secretary and, finally, canon of

St. Peter's and referendary of the Signatura. It was only then that he received major orders and was ordained priest (1758). He also enjoyed the favor of the new pope, CLEMENT XIII, who recommended him to his nephew, the new cardinal Carlo Rezzonico, who made him his auditor and secretary. It was in this capacity that he witnessed the controversy between the Church and the princes on the Jesuit question, though he took no clear-cut position himself; this fact played a role in his future election to the papal throne. The important post of treasurer of the APOSTOLIC CAMERA (tantamount to a ministry of finance) had repercussions on his future activity. He was called to it in 1766, at the height of an appalling food shortage that had struck the Papal States and all Italy. He attempted to stabilize the financial administration and to boost the economic life of the country, an effort he would pursue during his pontificate. On 26 April 1773, Pope CLEMENT XIV named him cardinal of the title of S. Onofrio and, immediately after that, granted him the post of commendatory abbot of the Camaldolese monastery of S. Gregorio al Celio and of that of Subiaco, which he left for the long and arduous conclave of 1774–5. Thanks to the support of France and despite the opposition of Portugal, he was elected pope. The choice of the name Pius was not a random one: at a time when the role of the Church was being radically redefined in society, he decided to take as his mentor Pius V, who had rigorously applied the precepts of the council of TRENT, had created the Congregation of the Index, and, most important, had put together the Holy League against the TURKS that had triumphed at the battle of Lepanto.

The beginnings of his reign signaled a break with the conciliatory spirit of his predecessor. His first ENCYCLICAL, *Inscrutabile divinae sapientiae*, promulgated on Christmas Day 1775, severely condemned the ideas of the Enlightenment. No distinction was made among them, modern thought being presented as a work of the devil. Modern thought was charged with spreading atheism and with seeking to destroy the traditional harmony between the states and the Church, something that would carry with it grave consequences for the whole of society. At the same time, as always happened in periods of crisis and of aggressive reaction from ecclesiastical institutions, the pope reinstituted harsh measures against the Jews. The policy adopted during the first years of curtailing any attempt to create independent and centrifugal forces within Catholicism was uncompromising but shrewd. Without aligning himself openly with pro-Jesuit positions, at least in the early stages, the pope tried, in effect, to induce those ecclesiastical groups opposed to the Jesuits and in favor of the Jansenists to accept Catholic unity in a rigorous respect for papal authority. Nevertheless, this increasingly clear affirmation of the absolutism and of the PRIMACY of the pope led at first to isolation and then to open warfare against the Jansenists, who had now

also arrived at radical positions. His goal being Catholic militancy and mission, the pope supported the birth of a new journal, the *Giornale ecclesiastico di Roma*, which became the official organ of the papacy and one of the most effective expressions of Pius VI's policy of Catholic reconquest. It reflected the progressive radicalization of the struggle on the ecclesiological and disciplinary plane, which would erupt in violence, of tone and of polemic, during the period of the Revolution. Moreover, his nominations of cardinals were numerous and well thought out. Among them are worth noting his uncle C. Bandi, G. Archinto, L. Valenti Gonzaga, G. A. Archetti, G. Pallotta, S. Gerdil, A. Gioannetti, L. E. von Firmian, A. Mattei, G. Capece Zurlo, G. Doria Pamphili, G. Garampi, S. Borgia, I. Busca, F. Ruffo, and J. Maury.

Relations with the states quickly became difficult. At issue were problems of doctrine, jurisdictional disputes, and the Jesuit question. The excommunication of the bishops of the schismatic Church of Utrecht was confirmed, but the dispute with Emperor Joseph II's ecclesiastical reformism was especially violent. The emperor's initiatives concerned new dispositions relative to marriage dispensation, the suppression of monasteries and the reform of the confraternities, the reduction of feast days and pilgrimages, tolerance toward the Jews and non-Catholics, and the reorganization and valorization of parishes. His initiatives also aimed at the creation of a national Church within the framework of the Habsburg monarchy, in line with the episcopalian ideas spread in Austria by the writings of Febronius (Johann Nikolaus von Hontheim) and Valentin Eybel. In light of these developments, Pius VI resolved to undertake his famous journey to Vienna (1782), which brought no changes in imperial ecclesiastical policy but had great repercussions. It was chiefly popular acclaim of the pope that had important consequences. The enthusiasm and devotion aroused by the "apostolic pilgrim" as he traveled about confirmed the pope as leader of a growing opposition to reforms imposed from on high that were turning traditional life upside down. This was a significant stage in the process that would lead to the Sanfedist reaction.

However, the differences with Joseph II did not prevent the pope from playing a conciliatory role when violent uprisings broke out in 1790 in the Austrian Low Countries against ecclesiastical reform. Similar conflicts arose with the rulers of Prussia and Russia, who were refusing to put into effect Clement XIV's brief, promulgated in 1773, suppressing the Society of Jesus. With Catherine II, the dispute also concerned the nominations of bishops in White Russia, which the empress claimed as her own right. The skillful mediation of the pope's representatives counted for much in these conflicts. Noteworthy among them were the nuncios in Poland, Giovanni Andrea Archetti and Lorenzo Litta. On the other hand, relations were good with Spain and Portugal, where the anticlerical policy of the mid-century was gradually being dismantled. In Italy, the pope's severest problems were with Tuscany and the kingdom of Naples. There was serious disagreement with Grand Duke Leopold I, the brother of Joseph II. Inspired by the Jansenist bishop of Pistoia and Prato, Scipione de' Ricci, Leopold's ecclesiastical measures also favored the creation of a national Tuscan Church. The close connection between the ecclesiastical reform of the Jansenists (who placed their hopes for Church reform, hitherto unfulfilled by Rome, in political power) and the regalism of the monarchs (a situation that pertained also, though to a lesser extent, in Lombardy and the Austrian territories) produced a single, organized program. Together with measures similar to those of JOSEPHISM, de'Ricci's reformism introduced the novel idea of the creation of an ecclesiastical Patrimony (1783) that would reorganize the benefice system and use it to create *congruae portiones* for parishes. He also condemned popular, "facile" expressions of devotion typical of the Counter Reformation, which clashed with the rigorist ideal of a piety that was "enlightened" and sober. The synod of Pistoia, held in September 1786, which was the climax of the Tuscan effort toward episcopalian and parochial reform, would not be officially condemned by the pope until 1794, with the bull *Auctorem fidei*. At that time, in fact, the condemnation was aimed not only at Jansenist doctrine, JURISDICTIONALISM, and the regalism of sovereigns, but above all at the "parochialism" and "ecclesiastical democracy" that had led to revolutionary movements and France's Civil Constitution of the Clergy. Finally, in Naples, resumption of jurisdictionalist policy in the 1780s as well as impassioned regalist arguments, charged in this case with Febronian and Jansenist overtones, brought the kingdom to the brink of rupture with the Holy See. A concrete sign of these disputes was the refusal of the Neapolitan sovereign to pay the traditional feudal homage of a palfrey.

As temporal sovereign, Pius VI played an active and dynamic role. He gave a strong impetus to artistic and archaeological endeavors. During his pontificate, Rome swarmed with ARTISTS and gifted men of letters, both Italian and foreign. Archaeological finds, assembled in the Pio-Clementine MUSEUM, aroused great interest. But above all, the emphasis was on public works. The draining of the Pontine marshes, which lasted almost twenty years and placed a heavy burden on state finances, was a grandiose operation. The pope followed its progress personally. Nevertheless, it had no effect on production, nor did it increase landholdings. In fact, the restored lands were allotted to the great absentee owners, including Duke Braschi-Onesti, the pope's nephew. Despite these limitations, government interventions in the economics of the State were many and noteworthy. For the first time, they formed a body of measures organically linked to a precise plan for renewal. Behind them was not only a re-

forming intention designed especially to reduce the budget deficit and the huge public debt, but a definite will for the centralization and unification of the administration that was directed, not always successfully, against private systems and interests. This action would be continued and developed during the reforms of the Napoleonic period as well as the first and second papal restorations.

From the mid-1770s, there was a burgeoning of economic writings, agrarian journals, and academies, especially in the provinces, which sought to benefit from the experiences of other regions, in particular those of neighboring Tuscany. Propaganda encouraging the growth and modernization of agriculture and farming techniques intensified. Numerous publications were issued by theoreticians and reformers, most often Curia functionaries and local administrators, denouncing the structural weaknesses of the State and reflecting contemporary European economic thought, which was more advanced. Some authors wrote with originality and vigor, such as F. Milizia, F. Cacherano di Bricherasio, and N. Corona. Caught between opposed economic trends—some suggested a prudent liberalism and solutions of a physiocratic type, while many others favored a traditional mercantilist way of thinking—the pope's directives, during the 1780s, opted for a program of latter-day mercantilism as suggested by the treasurer Fabrizio Ruffo and his collaborators, Giovanni C. di Miller and Paolo Vergani. This program was designed to develop national manufacturing and trade rather than promote decisive agrarian reforms, which would inevitably have hurt the privileges and vested interests of the nobles, the ecclesiastics, and the capital. For this reason, legislative measures had to do with the customs system, with the abolition of domestic taxes that prevented the free circulation of products, and with the setting up of customs at frontiers, the encouragement of agriculture and new crops, the promotion of industry, especially textiles, measures taken to reduce monetary disorder and the spread of paper money, the organization of taxes, and the improvement of the judicial system. The introduction in the Papal States of the cadaster, later extended to the Roman Campagna, and the abolition in Rome of the levy on sheep and pigs as well as oil (1789) were of major importance. The second reform dealt the death blow to the ancient system of the annona, which favored the capital. Nevertheless, these initiatives frequently came up against strong resistance on the part of local interests and the privileged classes, often supported by the humbler strata of the population. Moreover, measures concerning taxes and customs, which exacerbated the old tension between Rome and the richest provinces of the States, ended up hastening disintegration rather than encouraging unification.

Other elements had a bearing on the pope's attempts at modernization. The attacks on Rome and the pontiff, inspired by the ideas of the Enlightenment, grew more numerous and violent. Especially in the 1780s, they denounced the anachronism, the poverty, and the absolute despotism of the Papal States. Meanwhile, as the dispute over administrative reform reached its peak under Pius VI, who had forcefully repelled the reforming trends at the heart of the Church and refused to talk with those who defended modern culture, a reaction was taking shape and coming to the defense of religion. Combative in nature, its aim was the mobilization and revival of Christianity. The papacy devised a shrewd strategy designed to reorganize society and recover influence on it. The strategy was based on the ever-growing consolidation of the relations of the Church with the lower, especially rural, classes. It was from these that the popular reaction, in defense of the faith, of the anti-French Sanfedist forces would arise. In another area, harsh criticism was directed against the pope's practice of nepotism. To prevent the family name from disappearing after his brothers died without heirs, the pope summoned to Rome his nephews *ex sorore*, Luigi and Romualdo Onesti, and then adopted them and gave them his name. Romualdo was named cardinal in 1786, and the elder nephew, Luigi, received the title Duke of Nemi, after the lands Pius VI had obtained for him. Following Luigi's marriage to Costanza Falconieri (1781), the pope decided to build the sumptuous Braschi Palace, based on plans by Cosimo Morelli. The notorious case of the Lepri inheritance and Luigi's rapid and shameless rise to riches also wealth tarnished the pope's image.

At the outbreak of the French Revolution, Pius VI, though hostile to it, initially adopted a prudent attitude. Faced with the first intrusions into religious affairs, he temporized. Then came the promulgation of the Civil Constitution of the Clergy (summer 1790) and the obligation placed on priests to swear fidelity to the new law. In his brief *Quod aliquantum* of 10 March 1791, the pope issued a block condemnation of the work of the constituent Assembly in ecclesiastical matters—since its aim, he said, was the destruction of the Catholic religion—as well as the principles of liberty and equality that had guided the constituents' actions in the political arena, which he defined as being contrary to the laws of God. His next brief (13 April) rejected the civic oath demanded of priest and annulled appointments of bishops made without papal assent. Diplomatic relations with France were officially broken off in May of that year, when Msgr. Antonio Dugnani left the Paris nunciature. Shortly afterward, France proclaimed the annexation of the two papal territories of Avignon and the Comtat Venaissin, ignoring the pope's protests. There began a huge exodus of clergy from France to the Papal States, where they were welcomed not without problems and with some anxiety. The assassination, in Rome, of the French representative Basseville (January 1793) followed, and the execution of

Louis XVI, which the pope learned of with great emotion. In a solemn address to the Sacred College, he described the deceased king as a "martyr." Finally, as the dechristianization of France got under way, the conflict between Rome and the Revolution became virulent. A violent and widespread press campaign accused the Revolution of being Satanic and the product of a vast anti-Catholic conspiracy, a definition that would long harm relations between the Catholic world and modern society. In 1796, when French troops bore down on Italy, threatening an invasion of the papal territories, the scurrilous accusations persisted, despite the official neutrality of the States. They relaunched the myth of the holy war and the crusades, calling on peoples and governments to defend the faith against the new barbarians. The campaign, accompanied by much prophesying, by the exaltation of new saints such as Benedict Joseph Labre, and by eschatological and miraculous ferment as expressed in the Marian "miracles" of 1796, was extremely effective, especially on the operational level. It also encouraged popular anti-French mobilization. After the Bologna armistice (23 June 1796), the breaking off of the negotiations, and military defeat, the peace treaty of Tolentino was signed with the French forces (19 February 1797), which would henceforth remain close to Rome. During the negotiations, the papal envoys, in particular Msgr. Lorenzo Caleppi, were ordered to yield on temporal questions but to remain steadfast in the spiritual domain. Papal policy came in for some harsh criticism from the most uncompromising members of the Curia, who were opposed to any agreement with the French. Yet when Avignon and Venaissin were definitively ceded and, above all, the legations of Bologna, Ferrara, and Ravenna were given up, even though these represented the first serious injury to the temporal sovereignty, the role and spiritual prestige of the pope in the end were reinforced, especially since the agreements in no way contradicted the religious policy measures he had adopted viv-à-vis the Revolution.

After the assassination in Rome of the French general Duphot (28 December 1797), the seizure by the French of the capital, and the proclamation of the Roman Republic (15 February 1798, the anniversary of Braschi's election), Pius VI was forced to go into exile, leaving his faithful collaborator Msgr. Michele Di Pietro as apostolic delegate. After a stop in Siena, he stayed confined in the charterhouse of Florence, where, despite the gradual deterioration of his health, he continued to busy himself with religious matters, maintain diplomatic contacts, and issue instructions to Catholics and to his subjects. In fact, he ordered functionaries to refuse to take the oath of fidelity to the Republic and of hatred for the monarchy that the new government was demanding. On 13 November 1798, he promulgated the bull *Quum nos*, in which, given the peculiar circumstances in which the Church found itself, he made arrangements against a possible vacancy of the papal see and set forth methods for the convening of a conclave should need arise. The grand duchy of Tuscany now being in the hands of the French, in March 1799 the pope was taken to Parma, and then set on the road to France. After a long and arduous journey, during which he crossed the Montegenèvre pass, he reached Briançon, where he remained about two months. Finally, amid fears of a rescue raid on the part of the Austrians and Russians in June, he was obliged to resume his travels in the direction of Valence, where he died on 29 August 1799.

Pius VI's remains were brought back to Rome in 1802. Yet already a myth and a hagiographic stereotype had begun to crystallize around the Church and the papacy, which had emerged from the Revolution wearing the halo of martyrdom. In the 19th century, these contributed, along with the revival of religious prestige and the reawakening of Catholicism, to the preservation of the temporal power and the return of the Church's role and of religion in society.

Marina Caffiero

Bibliography

Bourgin, G. *DTC*, XII, 1934, 1653–69.

Caffiero, M. *La nuova era. Miti e profezie dell' Italie in Rivoluzione*, Genoa, 1991.

Chadwick, O. *The Popes and the European Revolution*, Oxford, 1981.

Gendry, J. *Pie VI. Sa vie, son pontificat, 1771–99*, Paris, 1907.

Giuntella, V. E. *Roma nel Settecento*, Bologna, 1971.

Hales, E. E. Y. *Revolution and the Papacy 1769–1846*, London, 1960.

Menozzi, D. (ed.), *La chiesa italiana e la rivoluzione francese*, Bologna, 1990.

Pignatelli, G. *Aspetti della propaganda cattolica da Pio VI a Leone XII*, Rome, 1974.

Piscitelli, E. *La riforma di Pio VI e gli scrittori economici romani*, Milan, 1958.

Soranzo, G. *Peregrinus apostolicus. Lo spirito pubblico e il viaggio di Pio VI a Vienna*, Milan, 1937.

PIUS VII. *Barnaba (name in religion, Gregorio) Chiaramonti (b. Cesena, 14 August 1742, d. Rome, 20 August 1823). Elected pope in Venice on 14 March 1800, crowned in Venice on 21 March. Buried at St. Peter's in Rome.*

The memory of Pius VII is inextricably bound with that of the two men who had the strongest influence on the direction and guidance of his pontificate: on the one hand, Napoleon Bonaparte, an enemy, an ally, once again an implacable adversary, then pardoned; and on the other, Cardinal Ercole Consalvi, minister and diplomat without peer, for fifteen years his secretary of state. The pope's personality, his own perception of events, and his individual orientations are extremely hard to discern, but worth searching out in order to grasp the meaning of pontificate that marks the entry of the Church into the "new times" that emerged in the wake of the FRENCH REVOLUTION.

Barnaba Chiaramonti was born in the early years of BENEDICT XIV's pontificate in the little town of Cesena in Romagna, to Count Scipione Chiaramonti and Marchioness Giovanna Ghini. The family belonged to the old, impoverished urban nobility and was related to the Braschi, who produced the future Pius VI (born in Cesena twenty-five years earlier). Barnaba's father died when the boy was eight, and at the age of nine he became an oblate at the Benedictine monastery of Sta Maria del Monte in Cesena. There he received his primary education, and he entered the novitiate in 1756, when he was fourteen. Two years later, on 20 August 1758, he made his religious profession and took the Benedictine habit under the name Gregorio. His formation was continued at the monastery of Sta Giustina of Padua (1760–3), whose monks had scholarly ties with the French Maurists and were suspected of Jansenism by the Venetian INQUISITION, and then at the college of S. Anselmo in Rome (1763–6), where he was influenced by the reforming Jansenist trends current in the capital. On 21 September 1765, he was ordained priest, and the next year he became professor of theology.

When he was transferred to the abbey of S. Giovanni of Parma, where he taught theology and philosophy from 1766 to 1775, he participated in the heady climate of reform that characterized political and ecclesiastical life in the duchy. Ruled by the Bourbons and under French influence, the duchy had been governed by the minister Du Tillot, who came into open conflict with CLEMENT XIII in 1768. Here, too, Abbé de Condillac, the principal interpreter of sensualist philosophy, acted as tutor to the young duke. Don Gregorio was one of twenty-seven Parma subscribers to the *Encyclopédie* of Diderot and d'Alembert published in Leghorn. His library contained critical Maurist editions of the Fathers of the Church as well as erudite works by Mabillon, Montfaucon, le Nain de Tillemont, and Muratori. He also showed a lively but critical interest in the positivist ideas of Locke and de Condillac, whose *Essay on the Origin of Human Knowledge* (1754) he undertook to translate into Italian; it was published in Rome in 1784 with the endorsement of the papal censorship. After returning to Rome in 1775, thanks to the accession to the papal throne of his fellow countryman Gianangelo Braschi, he taught theology at the college of S. Anselmo, though he came under the suspicion of the other monks because of his openness to the new ideas. Having been appointed titular abbot of the

Benedictine monastery of Cesena so that he could escape his critics, he was soon elevated, thanks to Pius VI, to the diocese of Tivoli, on 11 December 1782. Two years later, on 14 February 1785, when he was only forty-two years old, the pope made him, as a relative and a client, CARDINAL and bishop of Imola in Romagna.

Gregorio Chiaramonti's fifteen-year episcopate at Imola was a period both of pastoral apprenticeship and of beginning awareness of the crisis of the Papal States in the last decades of the 18th century. The bishop proved painstaking in the fulfillment of his duties and attentive to the material and spiritual terms of his magisterium. In the spirit of reconciliation and firmness that is the distinctive feature of his personality, he strove especially to promote respect for the independence of the bishop vis-à-vis the legate and, to the minimal extent allowed by the theocratic constitution of the pope-king's temporal state, for the autonomy of the spiritual dimension as against the political interests of the supreme pontiff. Hence, the shock of the French invasion of 1796–7 (Bonaparte entered Bologna on 8 June 1796 and was at Imola again on 2 February 1797) caught him less off guard than it did many prelates. After the armistice of Bologna (23 June 1796), he even tried at Cesena and Imola to prevent the confrontation between the people and the French forces, which had led on 6 July to the sack of Lugo. After leaving for Rome on 2 February 1797 on the pope's orders, he recognized the impotence of General Colli's papal forces and maintained the negotiations that led to the signing of the treaty of Tolentino (19 February 1797) and the annexing of the Legations first by the Cispadane and then by the Cisalpine Republic. On 4 March, he sent his flock at Imola a pastoral letter from ST. PAUL's OUTSIDE THE WALLS calling on them to submit, "in the present circumstances of a change of temporal government," to the authority—all authority coming from God (Rom 13)—of the "victorious general at the head of the French army." He then immediately returned to his diocese. Faced with the increasingly violent fighting between the two sides in Romagna, and in order to respond to the pressure exerted by the republican delegates (including the poet Vincenzo Monti), on Christmas Day in 1797 he published a resounding homily, of which a rhetorical passage survives, unprecedented on papal territory at that time from the pen of a cardinal of the Roman Church: "The form of democratic government adopted among you, dearly beloved brethren, in no way contradicts the maxims I have previously stated, nor is it repugnant to the Gospel; on the contrary, it demands all the sublime virtues, which are learned only at the school of Jesus Christ and which, practiced religiously among you, will make for your happiness and contribute to the glory and renown of our Republic . . . Yes! my dear brothers, be good Christians, and you will be excellent democrats."

This republican homily of the future pope of the Empire and of the Restoration (which the *abbé* Henri Grégoire, rather maliciously, would translate and reedit in 1818, and which A. F. Artaud, Pius VII's first biographer, would attempt, erroneously, to attribute to other hands) is not an aberration dictated in urgency; it deserves to be appreciated in its whole structural context and carefully compared with the pastoral letter written by the bishop of Imola on 25 July 1799, when the Austrian forces succeeded to the French and put an end to the short-lived Republic (without in any way restoring the papal government). If both letters bear the weight of local circumstances and external pressures, and if neither is exempt from considerations of expediency, they still exhibit an undeniable continuity of thought. Twice, and in a contrary sense, Cardinal Chiaramonti refers to the same Pauline teaching on authority, and calls on the faithful to submit, with their hearts and minds, in the first instance "to the Republic and the constituted authorities," and in the second (it is true, with more conviction) to the authority "of the victorious Austro-Russian armies" and to that of the "unvanquished defender of the laws of the Church and of the Throne, the Most Pious Emperor Francis II." Twice, he utters words of civic peace; in 1797, he invites his flock not to imitate but to pity the "lost brethren" far removed from the Gospel, and in 1799, not without charity or courage amid the fury of anti-Jacobin reprisals, he urges them not to hate "the misguided brethren who have let themselves be seduced by new doctrines, but to separate the person from the fault committed," and not to take the law into their own hands. With the same firmness, he insists on the freedom of the Church, calls upon the authorities to protect the clergy and their flocks, and recalls each one to the demands of the Christian faith; in 1797, he calls to mind the religious guarantees written into the treaty of Tolentino, and in 1799, with sensitivity but in purely religious terms, the captivity of Pius VI.

Cardinal Chiaramonti thus sketches, in a dramatic context, an astonishingly modern line of thought, the fruit of long meditation on sacred texts and of a reading of secular ones. (The 1797 orator invokes not only "the Gospel of Jesus Christ, the whole body of revealed doctrine, the august traditions left to us by the Fathers and Doctors of Holy Church," but also "a philosophy founded on the maxims of natural and divine law," and quotes Sallust's *Conspiracy of Catiline* as well as Rousseau's *Émile*.) He presents his thoughts on the nature of the social bond, on the foundation of public authority and the common good, on the aim of civil society, and on the relation between temporal power and the demands placed upon the Christian; following others, he tries to arrive at a deep understanding in the light of the Gospel of the values born of the French Revolution and suddenly imposed on Italy. Finally, surrendering to the

PIUS VII

divine will, he confronts the meaning of history as it
thrust itself on him—and would continue to thrust itself
throughout his subsequent pontificate—in the form of a
violent upheaval of the old order, of bloody wars and civil
confrontations. "The Father of consolations," he wrote in
his 1799 homily, "loves to make known to man how great
he is in his compassion, even as he reveals how terrible he
is in his justice."

Pius VI died in Valence on 28 August 1799, as the Austrians and Russians were driving the French out of Italy
and the Counter-Revolution was winning the day in
Naples and Rome. On 1 December, Cardinal Chiaramonti
was among the thirty-five cardinals of the Church of
Rome who met in conclave in Venice, in the monastery
on the island of San Giorgio Maggiore, under the generous but onerous patronage of the emperor of Austria and
his minister Thugut. At once, the cardinal rallied to the
Braschi side, led by the weak cardinal nephew Romualdo
Braschi, Cardinal Giovan Francesco Albani, dean of the
Sacred College, and the cardinal of York, the last heir of
the Stuarts and the vice-dean. All these were behind the
candidature of Cardinal Bellisomi, a former protégé of
Pius VI and bishop of Cesena, who was supported also by
Spain, a *politicante* anxious for rapprochement with
France. But there loomed the threat of a minority bloc led
by the *zelante* Cardinal Leonardo Antonelli, supported by
Austria and its representative at the heart of the conclave,
Cardinal Herzan, and by Cardinal Maury, the personal
representative of the pretender to the French throne,
Louis XVIII. These men were totally opposed to reconciliation and obstructed the election by supporting the
candidature of Cardinal Alessandro Mattei, a signer of
the treaty of Tolentino (and thus the most likely, according to Austria's interested views, to give up the Legations
once again). The conclave would last 104 days; it was
marked by a state of impasse, by Austria's exclusive support of the Savoyard cardinal Hyacinthe Gerdil, first theologian of the Sacred College, and by the successive failure of the candidatures of Bellisomi, Mattei, Albani, and
Antonelli.

It was a young, forty-three-year-old prelate serving as
secretary to the conclave, Ercole Consalvi, who noticed
and put forward the compromise candidate, the cardinal
of Imola, member of the Braschi party, known for his
piety, moderation, and firmness, and a stranger to the dissensions of the Curia. In this, Consalvi had the support of
the auditor of the Rota for Spain, Antonio Despuig, as
well as of the highly political Cardinal Fabrizio Ruffo,
who had conquered the Revolution in Naples. Finally and
with great difficulty having been persuaded not to prolong further "the widowhood of the Church," Gregorio
Chiaramonti was unanimously elected on 14 March 1800
at the age of fifty-eight. He took the name Pius VII in
memory of his predecessor, and on 15 March chose as his
pro-secretary of state Ercole Consalvi, whom he would

make cardinal and secretary of state on 11 August.
Crowned on 21 March, not in the basilica of S. Marco,
which a bitter Austria had refused him, but at S. Giorgio
Maggiore, he issued in Venice his first ENCYCLICAL, *Diu
satis*, on 15 May 1800. It praised the sacrifice of Pius VI,
a martyr pope like MARTIN I (whom the Byzantine emperor deported to the Crimea), vigorously affirmed the
perenniality of the Church through times of tempest and
persecution, and placed his pontificate under the emblem
of a return to Church discipline and Catholic teaching
against the ravages of "philosophy"; one passage concerning France praises "the strength and constancy" of
the episcopate, the clergy, and the faithful in the face of a
"cruelty revisited from former times." Refusing to go to
Vienna at Francis II's invitation, Pius VII then once
again made for Rome, though without authorization to
cross the Legations. Traveling first by sea to Pesaro and
then by way of Ancona and Loreto, he made his solemn
entry into his capital city, still under Neapolitan occupation, on 3 July 1800.

The period from Pius VII's establishment in Rome up
to his enforced exile in 1809 represents, in terms of domestic politics, a first attempt to restore the pontifical
state, dismembered and destabilized after three years of
revolutionary wars. Under Consalvi's authority, and with
the help of reforming prelates (Alessandro Lante, Nicola
Nicolai, Paolo Vergani, all members of an economic
Congregation), a new way was revealed, one that saw the
beginnings of projects that Pius VI had for the most part
envisaged but had not been able or known how to complete. While a far-reaching amnesty had ended the Ja-
cobin period once and for all, four congregations of cardinals were instituted on 9 July to promote the
reorganization and reform of the State. The bull *Post di-
uturnas* (30 October 1800), with which their work concluded, reestablished Pius VI's former system of ecclesiastical government but at the same time introduced
substantial changes. These included the entry of lay
functionaries (chosen from the NOBILITY) into certain
sectors of the administration (the army, the ANNONA,
mortgages, the post, public spectacles), administrative
reform, the simplification of procedures, and the reorganization of tribunals. A BRIEF of 11 March 1801 established freedom of trade in the supplying of grain and
foodstuffs; another of 13 March extended the same liberal arrangements to industry. In the autumn of 1801, the
government put into effect a currency change so as to retire from circulation the defective coinage (*moneta
erosa*) that had piled up under Pius VI, the Republic, and
the Neapolitans, and to check inflation. A fiscal reform
(*motu proprio* of 19 March 1801) brought about the abolition of thirty-two duties or taxes, which were replaced
by a double property and personal tax, the *dativa*.

How to evaluate this ambitious body of reforms? Consalvi's policy proceeded from the conviction that the ec-

clesiastical state (whose existence was, in his view and that of Pius VII, the very condition of Church freedom) was viable, that its theocratic structure and ecclesiastical framework must be preserved, but that the Revolution had necessarily pointed the way to some indispensable changes. Pius VII's secretary of state here appears as a "conservative reformer" (Roger Aubert), in the tradition of the enlightened despotism of the monarchies of the second half of the 18th century. Yet he came up against obstacles. First of these was the incomprehension of the members of the staff of the ecclesiastical state: the most stubborn resistance to change appeared at the heart of the SACRED COLLEGE and among the PRELATURE. On the other hand, the nobility, in whose favor the Noble Guard had been created (11 May 1801), remained dissatisfied with its exclusion from most public posts. In part compromised with the Republic, this class in 1809 would rally massively to the cause of the Empire. Finally, the slenderness of the resources of the Papal State, now lacking the rich provinces of the Legations, and the almost complete absence of a commercial or industrial bourgeoisie, hamstrung any attempt at financial or economic reform of a liberal cast. As Consalvi wrote to the nuncio Della Genga (the future Leo XII) on 6 November 1800, "In vain I wear out my voice saying that the Revolution has achieved in the political and moral order what the Flood achieved in the physical order by changing the whole face of the earth; that Noah, when he left the ark, drank wine and ate meat and did everything in a quite different manner from before the Flood; that to say that this or that was not done in the old days, that our laws were excellent and must not be changed is to make a very serious mistake; and that, in short, such an opportunity to rebuild everything that was destroyed before will not come again." The 1801 reforms soon fell into abeyance under the weight of conservatism, dislike, and resistance. When Cardinal Consalvi was forced to leave the Secretariat of State in June 1806, his attempt at an enlightened transformation of the ecclesiastical state had already failed.

The new struggle between Church and Empire, of which Pius VII and Napoleon changed the particulars from 1800 to 1814 without fundamentally altering the content, has something to do with this failure. A *politicante* pope, Pius VII set as his first priority the reestablishment of the Church in Catholicism's leading nation, which for a decade had been revolutionizing Europe while waiting for the moment when it could, fleetingly, dominate it by force. The negotiations undertaken by the Holy See with the Republic to restore Catholicism in France seem today an extraordinary reversal of the course of history. Since 1792, the Revolution had been exiling and relentlessly persecuting the Church faithful to Rome; the Terror had crippled the constitutional Church which the Revolution had itself created; and since 1795, the Republic no longer either recognized or subsidized any reli-

gion, manifesting an attitude of alternating indifference and intolerance. Now the pope and the First Consul took a mere thirteen months (June 1800 to July 1801) to rebuild on new bases the concordatory edifice of the Ancien Régime. On 14 May 1800, Bonaparte was victorious over Austria at Marengo, reestablished French dominance in Italy, and consolidated his power. Before the battle, in Milan, and then after it, at Vercelli with the aged Cardinal Martiniana, he made the first overtures: "If the pope is reasonable," he told the cardinal, "if he understands the present situation, together we can reconcile France with the Church"; what had to be done was to "sweep away the Gallican Church." On 21 September, the papal negotiator Giuseppe Spina, who had closed Pius VI's eyes in Valence, left Rome. On 15 November, he was in Paris with the Servite theologian Caselli and met secretly with Abbé Bernier, the former negotiator of the peace of Vendée. The talks got bogged down. On 6 June, at the insistence of Ambassador Cacault, Cardinal Consalvi left Rome for Paris where he arrived on 20 June. After laborious compromises and ultimate rows, the CONCORDAT was signed on 15 July 1801.

It represented, at one and the same time, a considerable concession on the part of the Holy See to the principles of freedom of conscience and secularization of the state that came out of the French Revolution, a sort of coup d'état in the case of the Gallican Church, and a recognition of papal jurisdiction over the individual Churches. By the terms of a preamble, bitterly negotiated for months, the "Catholic, apostolic, and Roman" religion was no longer the religion of the state, the king, and the kingdom but of "the great majority of French citizens"—an utterly statistical formula that linked the privileged situation of Catholicism in France to the individual beliefs of faithful who henceforth were citizens. In exchange for this major concession (which was attenuated only by the reference to the "particular profession" of Catholicism made by consuls, a condition necessary to the exercise of their rights), the free public practice of Catholic worship was guaranteed (art. 1), the concordat of 1516 (granting to the sovereign the appointment of bishops and to the pope canonical investiture) was reestablished in principle (art. 4), places of worship were put at the disposal of the bishops (art. 12), and the state was responsible for clerical stipends (art. 14); for its part, the clergy was bound by oath, according to the formulas of the old concordat, to the new institutions (art. 6 to 8). The old Gallican Church was abolished by two articles that provided for a new division of the dioceses and a collective dismissal of the episcopate of 1787: the "tabula rasa" was accomplished. It made manifest the omnipotence of the pontifical jurisdiction: Pius VII, bishop of bishops, with the consent of the public powers, had overturned the thousand-year-old Gallican Church in order to build a new Church in France. The 1801 concordat, a compromise born of the Revolution and which was to last for a hundred years, thus constitutes a work of pastoral restoration, a plan for a lasting entente between Church and State, and an affirmation of the universality of the Roman Church. In this sense, it bore not so much the mark of Bonaparte as the stamp of the pope of "changes in temporal government."

The practical application of the concordat in the years following showed that Pius VII was determined, in his turn, to erase the doubts concerning and the downright opposition to the work of religious restoration and political reconciliation that he had undertaken. Already, while the negotiations were under way, he had turned down the hostile advice of Austria and Naples and imposed silence on Cardinal Maury, who represented the pretender-in-exile, Louis XVIII. When Consalvi returned to Rome on 9 August, the pope managed to obtain ratification of the agreement on 15 August, despite the hesitations of a large part of the Sacred College. On 24 August, the conciliating Cardinal Caprara was sent to Paris, at Bonaparte's request, as a legate *a latere* endowed with very extensive powers, to accelerate the reorganization of the Church. Meanwhile, in the brief *Pastoralis sollicitudo*, the pope firmly invited the bishops of the Ancien Régime to resign for the sake of religious peace: only fifty-two decided to do so, with forty-five refusing. On 8 September, the concordat was ratified by Bonaparte in his turn, and the exchange of ratifications took place two days later. On 29 November, the bull *Qui Christi Domini* abolished the 135 bishoprics of the old France, Belgium, and the left bank of the Rhine, taking away all jurisdiction from the old bishops. On 15 April, the reconciliation of the 12 old Constitutional bishops integrated into the concordatory episcopate (as against sixteen bishops of the Ancien Régime and thirty-two new arrivals) was assumed to be achieved: in 1805, Pius VII in person would hardly win more.

On 18 Germinal X (8 April 1802), the concordat was officially promulgated as a law of the French Republic. Immediately, however, the Organic Articles were appended to it, unilaterally decreed by the French state. These set strict legal and disciplinary limits, inspired by a narrow state Gallicanism, to the freedoms of the Church of France and its relations with Rome. The Holy See at once issued a solemn protest, but to no avail. On the other hand, the Organic Articles regarding Protestant worship, published on 4 April, had loudly proclaimed the equal protection that the Republic henceforth intended to offer each faith. On 17 January 1803, the pope promoted four French cardinals, among them Cardinal Fesch, Bonaparte's uncle, who was named ambassador to Rome on 8 April. He arrived accompanied by his secretary, the young Viscount de Chateaubriand, fresh with the success of his *Génie du christianisme*. On 16 September 1803, a concordat with the Italian Republic, on the French model,

was signed in Paris between Cardinal Caprara and Marescalchi. Far more favorable to the Roman Church (in Italy Catholicism was the state religion), the agreement was published by Melzi on 24 January 1804, albeit appended with executive decrees inspired by the Josephist tradition. A German concordat, aimed at reorganizing the Catholic Churches of the German lands following the suppression of the Holy Roman Empire and the secularization of the former ecclesiastical principalities, was finally negotiated from 1803, first in Vienna and then in Regensburg. But the efforts of the nuncio Annibale Della Genga were fruitless in face of the contradictory ambitions of France, Austria, and the German princes. Then, on 29 October 1804, Pius VII accepted the new emperor's invitation to crown him on 2 December at Notre-Dame: the pope's six-month stay in France (2 November 1804 to 16 May 1805) on this occasion was not only a transfer of sacral legitimacy (which Louis XVIII would never forgive him) but a dazzling official and popular witness to the restoration of Catholicism in the birthplace of the Revolution.

Yet a rupture between the pope and the emperor, whose victorious warring on the Continent was swelling a ravenous ambition, was close at hand. Having conquered Austria and Russia at Austerlitz in 1805 and Prussia at Jena in 1806, Napoleon set about redrawing the map of Europe to suit his convenience, erecting against England a European system under French domination and unifying under a dictatorship the civil, political, and ecclesiastical government of his lands. The conflict with the Holy See therefore became inextricably both a temporal and a spiritual one, waged through the suppression of the Papal States, a weak link in the apparatus of French domination in Italy, and the subjection of the Church to the interests of the Empire. On 8 June 1805, Napeolon introduced the Civil Code (including divorce) into the kingdom of Italy. The pope protested, in vain, on 11 July. On 18 October, General Gouvion-Saint-Cyr's troops occupied the port of Ancona, the chief stronghold of the Marches. In a personal letter to the emperor dated 13 November, Pius VII vigorously condemned this fresh and "cruel affront." On 15 February 1806, Gouvion-Saint-Cyr entered Naples, having crossed the Papal States without authorization. Napoleon drove out the Bourbons, who took refuge in Sicily, in order to set his brother Joseph and then his brother-in-law Murat on the throne. At the same time, he seized the port of Civitavecchia and demanded that the English, Russian, and Sardinian agents be expelled from Rome: "Your Holiness," he wrote, "is the sovereign of Rome, but I am its emperor. All my enemies must be yours."

On 19 February, the emperor named 15 August St. Napoleon's day. In vain, Cardinal Di Pietro protested at this uncrowning of the Virgin. On 10 April, Cardinal Fesch, deemed too conciliatory, was withdrawn from the

Roman embassy and replaced by Alquier, a former member of the National Convention (regicide). On 30 May, the weak Cardinal Caprara gave his approval in Paris to an imperial catechism which taught, "We owe in particular to Napoleon I, our Emperor, our love, respect, obedience, loyalty, military service, tributes ordered for the preservation and defense of the Empire, [and] fervent prayers for his safety and the spiritual and temporal prosperity of the State." Consalvi, who had been forced under French pressure to resign on 17 June, was replaced by the aged Cardinal Filippo Casoni; yet from this date Pius VII himself personally assumed direction of the Holy See's resistance to imperial policy. On 10 November, Napoleon summoned to Berlin Tommaso Arezzo, the nuncio in Saxony, to explain to him that the Papal States must support the Continental blockade of English commerce, begun on 21 November. Pius VII's adamant refusal was forwarded in December. During the whole of 1807, an embassy led in Paris by Cardinal de Bayane sought final accommodation. On 21 January 1808, Napoleon ordered the military occupation of Rome and the Papal States. On 2 February, General Miollis's troops entered the city and took possession of Castel Sant'Angelo. The pope was confined, a prisoner, in his Quirinal Palace.

From February 1808 to July 1809, the definitive rupture took effect while Napoleon attained the summit of his power. On 23 March 1808, General Miollis expelled fourteen cardinals born outside the Papal States, among them the short-lived pro-secretary of state Giuseppe Doria Pamphili, appointed in February to replace Cardinal Casoni; Pius VII replaced him on 26 March with Cardinal Giulio Gabrielli. On 27 March, the papal forces were incorporated into the imperial army. On 2 April, an imperial edict was proclaimed annexing the provinces of the Marches to the kingdom of Italy. Cardinal Gabrielli on 19 May issued a solemn protest and on 22 May sent the bishops the strictest instructions, ordering them to take a purely passive oath of loyalty to the new powers. He was arrested by the French occupation authorities on 16 June and dismissed to his diocese of Senigallia. On 19 June, Pius VII appointed in his place the *zelante* Cardinal Bartolomeo Pacca, a resolute champion of resistance; arrested in his turn on 6 September, he was freed by Pius VII himself and confined with the pope in the Quirinal. Finally, on 16 May 1809, an imperial decree signed by Napoleon in Schönbrunn annexed the Papal States to the Empire.

With the aid of Cardinals Pacca and Di Pietro, Pius VII thereupon drew up the bull *Quam memorandum*, dated 10 June, declaring the emperor excommunicated. It was posted on the walls and in the basilicas of Rome and then spread abroad clandestinely, so that it was hardly known in France and Europe. "By the authority of almighty God," wrote the pope, "by that of the holy apostles Peter and Paul and by our own, we declare that all those who, after the invasion of Rome and the ecclesiastical territory, after the sacrilegious violation of the Patrimony of St. Peter by the French forces, have committed, in Rome and in the Papal States, against ecclesiastical immunity, against even the temporal rights of the Church and the Holy See, those crimes, or some of the crimes which have aroused our just complaints [. . . . .] all their agents, supporters, counselors, or adherents; all those, in short, who have facilitated the execution of these violations or have themselves committed them, have incurred major excommunication."

"He's a raving lunatic, he should be locked up!" was the emperor's answer to Murat. During the night of 5 to 6 July 1809, General Radet attacked the Quirinal. The pope was forced to leave Rome in the morning of 6 July for an unknown destination, only Cardinal Pacca being allowed to accompany him. Taken to Grenoble (where Pacca was removed and imprisoned from August 1809 to January 1813 in the fortress of Fénestrelle), the pope was then brought to the small town of Savona, on the Ligurian coast, where he arrived on 17 August. He remained a prisoner there for close to three years, until June 1812, held first at the town hall and then at the bishop's palace. Kept in increasingly strict isolation, he was closely watched and spied on by the diligent prefect Chabrol. Meanwhile, in Paris, in his absence a system of radical reform of the relationship between the Church and the state was being worked out at the heart of the Empire. Napoleon, who in 1810 had summoned all the cardinals to Paris and had had the Vatican archives shipped there, in fact intended to create a Church subject to the interests of his Empire and opposed to the pope (who had refused, from then on, to confer investiture on bishops appointed by the emperor to vacant sees). On 17 February 1810, the metropolitan tribunal of Paris declared his childless marriage to Josephine de Beauharnais null and void. But on 2 April, thirteen cardinals out of twenty-seven (including Consalvi, Di Pietro, and Gabrielli) refused to witness the religious ceremony of his remarriage to Marie-Louise, the daughter of the Austrian emperor. The thirteen "black cardinals" were exiled and kept under close watch in eastern France. On 14 October 1810, the see of Paris was taken (after Cardinal Fesch had refused it) by the ambitious Cardinal Maury, who had moved from the service of Louis XVIII to that of Napoleon; he took possession of his see on 1 November. Pius VII issued a brief, dated 5 November, from Savona, formally prohibiting him from governing the diocese. A second brief, dated 18 December, declared all his administrative acts null and void. But Maury refused to take cognizance of either brief and on 1 January 1811 personally collaborated in the arrest of his grand vicar, d'Astros, who had been responsible for handing him the briefs. While the emperor was holding a national council of the bishops of the Empire, a deputation of bishops made its way to Savona. On 19 May 1811, they obtained from the weakened, isolated pope approval of a brief that allowed for a bishop's investiture by his metropolitan when a see had been six months vacant. However, the pope at once recovered himself and retracted his agreement. The national council that met in the cathedral of Notre-Dame of Paris from 17 June to 5 August 1811, while subscribing to Napoleon's imperial plans, nevertheless reaffirmed the unity of the Church around the pope, who, it demanded, should be set free. A deputation of the council, led by five cardinals who had rallied to the emperor, visited Savona from 3 to 20 September. With Pius VII anxious to avoid a schism, it obtained his approval of the principle of canonical institution by the metropolitan, but this approval was hedged about by so many reservations of principle concerning papal authority that Napoleon, in his turn, refused all concessions and, on the eve of his departure for the disastrous Russian campaign, ordered that the pope be moved close to the capital.

Wrested from Savona on 9 June 1812, ill and exhausted by a journey that resembled a police kidnapping, Pius VII reached Fontainebleau on 19 June, where he was installed in the palace. He remained there as a prisoner, and in isolation once again, until January 1814. When the vanquished emperor returned to France, in December 1812, negotiations were resumed through the mediation of Cardinal Doria and Bishop Duvoisin of Nantes. On 19 January 1813, Napoleon came in person to Fontainebleau. On 25 January, a broken Pius VII gave his approval to the major concession constituting the Fontainebleau agreement. He recognized the transfer of his temporal states, accepted the principle of investiture by the metropolitan as well as imperial endowment, and finally regained his freedom and that of his cardinals. But immediately racked by remorse for his weakness, and strengthened in his conviction by the return to his side of Cardinals Consalvi and Pacca, on 24 March the pope sent Napoleon a letter containing his retraction of the concordat, which the emperor had hastened to proclaim. The year 1813, marking the final collapse of the Empire at Leipzig, dragged along in pointless negotiations. Napoleon, threatened even in France by the irresistible advance of the allied armies, decided in January 1814 to move the pope far away, and once again sent the opposing cardinals into exile. On 23 January, Pius VII left Fontainebleau under heavy police escort. After a wide detour (designed to avoid the axis of the Rhône valley as well as the large cities) which took him through central, southwest, and southern France, where he was surrounded by excited and demoralized crowds, he reached his prison at Savona on 16 February. In March, he was finally permitted to return to Rome. The emperor, somewhat cynically, forced him to go by way of the Legations and the Marches in order to hamper King Murat's plans to annex Austria and the kingdom of Naples. The pope left Savona on 19 March crossed Austrian lines on the Taro on 25 March, and entered Bologna on the 31 March; he spent Holy Week in his former diocese of Imola and then stayed in his native Cesena from 20 April to 7 May. After giving thanks to the Virgin of Loreto, he made a triumphal entry into Rome on 24 May 1814, close to five years after his abduction. Meanwhile, the allies entered Paris, Louis XVIII was restored to the French throne, and the defeated emperor (whose mother and family the pope generously welcomed to Rome) made his way to the island of Elba.

"The triumph of divine compassion," Pius VII wrote from Cesena on 4 May, "has now been accomplished on our person, torn by an extraordinary act of violence from our peaceful seat and from the bosom of our well-beloved subjects, dragged from one province to another and condemned to suffer under constraint for close to five years. We have shed tears of grief in our prison, first for the Church committed to our care, because we knew her needs though we were powerless to help her, and then for the people subject to our authority, because the cry of their tribulations reached us without our being able to bring them comfort. The poignant affliction of our heart was tempered, however, by the ever lively confidence that the most clement God, once his just anger against our sins was appeased, would raise his invincible right hand, break the bow of the enemy, and shatter the chains binding his vicar on earth. Our confidence has not been disappointed. The pride of the madman who set himself up as equal of the Most High has been humbled, and our deliverance, toward which the august Alliance also gave its generous efforts, followed, prodigious and unhoped for. We acknowledge our debt to the all-powerful hand which holds the destiny of man, and we will never cease to bless it and to celebrate its glory. . . ." The pope, restored to his throne and his capital by an upheaval he ascribed to the order of Providence, would soon reach his seventy-second year. From then on—though it is not always possible to distinguish clearly between what grew out of his own inspiration and what grew out of the ideas of his advisers, Cardinal Consalvi in particular—he would dedicate the last nine years of his pontificate to the restoration of the temporal and spiritual foundation of the authority of the Holy See.

The first acts of the freed pope seem to have been inspired by the little group of *zelanti* prelates (Rivarola, Morozzo, Sala, Mauri, Della Genga) who made up his entourage in Imola and Cesena. The future Cardinal Rivarola, who restored the authority of papal government on 11 May 1814 in Rome, thus abolished with one stroke of the pen the mass of reforms introduced by the Napoleonic administration, suppressing the Civil Code, reinstating the ecclesiastical administration, and confining the Roman Jews in the ghetto. But the return of the first cardinals to Pius VII's side made for a provisional division of political tasks and orientations. Thus, on 17 May 1814, the pope once again entrusted the SECRETARIAT OF STATE to the *politicante* Cardinal Consalvi, whom he dispatched to the allied rulers to try to gain the complete restitution of the former Papal States. With him, as pro-secretary of state, he named the *zelante* Cardinal Pacca, to whom he entrusted the immediate restoration of the Church and the Papal States. Thus the 1814 restoration in the States would be characterized by a dual, contradictory movement, concordatory with regard to the restored princes, more and more intransigent on the ecclesiastical level, and voluntarily or involuntarily reactionary on the domestic level.

The extraordinary energy and matchless skill deployed by Cardinal Consalvi in the difficult year 1814–15 has captured the admiration of observers and historians from the beginning. After leaving Foligno on 20 May 1814, the cardinal reached Paris on 2 June: this was too late for him to take part in the negotiations concerning France that were concluded by the first treaty of Paris (confirming Louis XVIII's possession of Avignon and Venaissin), which had been signed by the allied powers three days before, but soon enough for the cardinal to take back from Della Genga the instructions calling into question the concordat of 1801. After being received by the king, he left Paris on 6 June and went to London, where he arrived on 10 June and was honorably received by the Prince Regent and Prime Minister Castlereagh. A first diplomatic note dated 23 June requested the restitution of the entire Papal States. Back in Paris on 9 July, he stayed there until 20 August in order to defend the concordatory work, and then journeyed to Vienna, where on 2 September 1814 he settled in for a stay of over nine months, taking part in the congress that was to fix the terms of peace in Europe. Thanks to Consalvi's efforts, the treaty of Vienna (9 June 1815) restored to the Holy See the Legations (south of the Po) and Romagna together with the enclaves of Pontecorvo and Benevento. A convention signed on 12 June with Metternich set the conditions for their evacuation. Finally, on 14 June, Consalvi made a solemn protest against the validity of the treaties of Tolentino (1797) and Paris.

Meanwhile, in Rome, Cardinal Pacca was not meeting with similar success. True, Pacca had achieved the spiritual and material recovery of the Roman Church and of the papal government; had (against Consalvi's recommendation) on 7 August 1814, by the constitution *Sollicitudo omnium ecclesiarum*, reestablished the Society of Jesus, which CLEMENT XIV had abolished in 1773; and had taken rigorous measures against those ecclesiastics who supported the Empire (two congregations were ordered to examine the conduct of bishops and priests in the former Papal States, and Cardinal Maury was imprisoned in Castel Sant'Angelo). However, he had not succeeded in mapping out an orientation of policy that did not imply

a simple return to the days of Pius VI. Moreover, his position was further weakened when Pius VII was forced to flee to Genoa from 22 March to 7 June 1815 during the Hundred Days, to evade Murat's military moves. On 2 July 1815, Cardinal Consalvi returned to Rome, amid the glory of his diplomatic triumph, and on 5 July he received from Cardinal Pacca's hands his former office as secretary of state.

Consalvi's diplomatic genius had saved the pontifical state for a half-century. Yet the secretary of state quickly showed that he was, despite all his political astuteness and organizational ability, unable to save the State from that process of "sacral rigidification" (to adopt Adolfo Omodeo's expression) that inevitably took over its structure and its future, until its subjects revolted and, a generation later, hastened the inexorable disintegration, to the benefit of Italian unity. True, the *motu proprio* of 6 July 1816 achieved, within the meaning of the 1800–2 reforms, a new administrative and judicial reorganization of the Papal States, taking up once again certain measures introduced by the imperial legislation. True, too, the feudal system was gradually abolished from 1818 on, and a policy of economic modernization consistently pursued. But the cardinal's isolation in the Sacred College and the Curia increased; he found no backing, any more than he had in 1800, from a political class or bourgeoisie, neither of which existed, while the carbonari and Freemasonry, once again solemnly condemned by a bull of 21 September 1821, found a growing response among the well-to-do youth of the cities, especially in the Legations and the Marches. It was on the diplomatic level that Consalvi, with the constant support of Metternich and a conservative Austria that henceforth would dominate the Italian peninsula, strengthened the pope's authority. He did so by managing to preserve in France the gains represented in the Napoleonic concordat of 1801—this despite the conclusion of the abortive concordats of 25 August 1816 and 11 June 1817, which sought to reestablish in its principle the old concordat of 1516. He also succeeded in drawing up the concordat of 24 October 1817 with the kingdom of Bavaria and that of 16 February 1818 with the kingdom of the Two Sicilies. In this way, concordatory policy, the advent of which was marked by the negotiations of 1801, anchored the Church in a new phase of transaction with the political and ecclesiastical modernity of post-Revolutionary Europe—without managing to disguise its growing political impotence or prevent the rise of an uncompromising current of opinion that was systematized in the publication in 1819 of Count de Maistre's *Du pape*, which Consalvi greeted with obvious suspicion.

Pius VII died at the age of eighty-one on 20 August 1823. Right up to the end, those around the pope kept from him the news of the fire at the abbey of St. Paul's Outside the Walls on 16 July, which completely destroyed the basilica that had been so dear to him since his young days as a monk and that would be completely restored by his successors LEO XII and GREGORY XVI. His death brought the immediate fall of Consalvi, who was overcome by a wave of bitterness. The Benedictine pope of Revolutionary times had died peacefully at the heart of a restoration which he perceived as a fresh moment in a history in the process of unfolding, through which he had lived in a spirit of loyalty to the heritage of his papal ministry and resignation to the divine will. Paradoxically, both in his hesitations and in his audacities, Pius VII had contributed not a little to opening up the Church of Rome to the "new times."

Philippe Boutry

Bibliography

Aquarone, A. "La Restaurazione nello Stato Pontificio ed i suoi indirizzi legislativi," *ASR*, LXX–VIII (1955), 119–88.

Aubert, R. "Pie VII," *Catholicisme*, XI, 261–8.

Bourgin, G. "Pie VII," *DTC*, XII/2 (1935), 1670–83.

Chappin, M. *Pie VII et les Pays-Bas. Tensions religieuses et tolérance civile, 1814–7*, Rome, 1984.

Chotard, H. *Le Pape Pie VII à Savone*, Paris, 1887.

Dal Pane, L. "Le riforme economiche di Pio VII," *Studi romagnoli* (Faenza), 16 (1965), 257–76.

de Mayol de Lupé, H. *La Captivité de Pie VII*, Paris, 1912.

Leflon, J. "Le pontificat de Pie VII (1800–23)," *La Crise révolutionnaire*, Paris, 1949, 159–376.

Leflon, J. *Pie VII. Des abbayes bénédictines à la papauté*, Paris, 1958.

Martinengo, D. and F. *Pio VII in Savona*, Turin, 1888.

Memorie del cardinale Ercole Consalvi, ed. M. Nasalli Rocca di Corneliano, Rome, 1950.

Moscarini, M. *La Restaurazione Pontificia nelle provincie di "primo recupero" (maggio 1814-marzo 1815)*, Rome, 1933.

O'Dwyer, M. M. *The Papacy in the Age of Napoleon and the Restoration: Pius VII, 1800–23*, Lanham, Md., 1985.

Pastor, L. "Ercole Consalvi prosegretario del conclave di Venezia," *ASR*, 83 (1960), 99–187; "Le Memorie sul conclave tenuto in Venezia di Ercole Consalvi," AHP, 3 (1965), 239–308.

Petrocchi, M. *La Restaurazione, il cardinale Consalvi e la riforma del 6 luglio 1816*, Florence, 1941; *La Restaurazione romana (1815–23)*, Florence, 1943.

Roveri, A. *La Missione Consalvi e il Congresso di Vienna*, Rome, 1970–3, 3 vols.; *La Santa Sede tra Rivoluzione e Restaurazione. Il cardinale Consalvi, 1813–5*, Florence, 1975.

Schmidlin, J. *Pius VII*, Munich, 1933.

Spada, I. *La Rivoluzione francese e il papa*, Bologna, 1989.

Vercesi, E. *Pio VII, Napoleone e la Restaurazione*, Rome, 1933.

von Ranke, L. *Kardinal Consalvi und seine Staatsverwaltung unter dem Pontifikat Pius VII.*, Leipzig, 1877.

Welschinger, H. *Le Pape et l'empereur*, Paris, 1905.

Zaghi, C. *Il generale Augereau, il cardinale Chiaramonti e il sacco di Lugo*, Ferrara, 1934.

PIUS VIII. *Francesco Saverio Castiglioni (b. Cingoli, 20 November 1761, d. Rome, 30 November 1830). Elected pope on 31 March 1829, crowned on 5 April. Buried at St. Peter's in Rome.*

The shortest pontificate of the 19th century (twenty months) was marked by three events of fundamental importance for the history of the Catholic Church: the definitive fall of the Bourbons in France, the birth of Belgium, and the abolition of the condemnation of lending at interest.

Like his three predecessors, Francesco Saverio Castiglioni was a product of the provincial NOBILITY, of the ecclesiastical state. His father was a patrician of the episcopal town of Cingoli in the Marches, and his mother, a Ghislieri, was related to PIUS V. Destined early on for a clerical career thanks to his legal training at the Montalto college in Bologna, he came to Rome in the autumn of 1785, and there he sat at the feet of Zaccaria and the canonist Devoti. The intellectual influence of the strict, anti-Jansenist circles of PIUS VI's Curia marked the formation and the career of the future pope: he was named vicar general of Anagni under Devoti in 1789, occupied the same position in Fano in 1790 under Severoli, was head of the *zelante* party at the CONCLAVE of 1823, and then served Cardinal Archetti at Ascoli Piceno in 1797. In the wake of the French Revolution, PIUS VII followed Severoli's advice and appointed Castiglioni, then thirty-eight, head of the diocese of Montalto, in the Marches.

For sixteen years (1800–16), the bishop of Montalto gave evidence of his pastoral zeal and his piety: he reformed the seminary, encouraged the veneration of the Sacred Heart, and intervened in Rome to advocate firmness toward Napoleon. When Napoleon invaded the Papal States, he refused to take the oath of allegiance to the imperial regime and was sentenced to exile, in Pavia, Mantua, and, finally, Milan. At the great promotion to the cardinalate of 8 March 1816, Pius VII raised him to the title of Sta Maria in Transpontina. After being appointed bishop of Cesena, the pope's native city, he was called to the Curia in 1821: he became Grand Penitentiary on 28 July; bishop of Frascati on 13 August, and prefect of the INDEX on 10 November. A moderate *zelante*, his attachment to Consalvi's conciliatory policy served him ill at the turbulent conclave of 1823 (where he was already marked as a *papabile*) but won him the votes of the "Party of the Crowns" on LEO XII's death.

Favored as a candidate by Metternich and de Chateaubriand, the French ambassador to Rome, Cardinal Castiglioni won election at a conclave (23 February to 31 March 1829) dominated by Albani, chief of the Austrian party, thanks to the division among the uncompromising candidates (Pacca, De Gregorio, Cappellari). Now seventy-six years old, fragile in health and sickly (a herpes in the neck obliged him to keep his head bent), the new pope took the name Pius in homage to Pius VII and appointed Albani as his secretary of state.

His first ENCYCLICAL, *Traditi humiliati nostrae* (24 May 1829), followed Leo XII's intransigent line in matters of ecclesiology and doctrine. He recalled his authority "not only over the lambs, that is, the Christian people, but also over the sheep, that is, the bishops" (which caused some indignation among the Gallicans), as well as condemning the Protestant Bible societies and religious indifference: "The sophists of this century, who claim that the gate of salvation is open to all religions, praise in equal measure truth and error, vice and virtue, honesty and turpitude." On 18 June, he announced the indulgence of the jubilee for Rome and the Christian world.

In Europe, Pius VIII, the last *politicante* pope of the aftermath of the 18th century, supported Metternich's and Albani's conservative and dynastic policy and kept a watchful eye on the balance of power. In July 1830, he considered granting the regency of Alger, conquered by France, to a Spanish prince. Faced with the affirmation of national rights, he oscillated between firmness of principle and practical concessions. Thus, in March 1830, Rome enjoined the Prussian clergy to tolerate "passively" laws governing mixed marriages that conferred the father's religion on the child. Prudence and a spirit of conciliation won the day in the two major crises of the summer of 1830. After the July Revolution in France, the pope, against the advice of the nuncio Lambruschini and a section of the legitimist episcopate, exhorted the clergy to remain at their posts: "When the flock is stricken by the storm, the shepherd must remain in the fold." He stipulated that they follow custom in the matter of oaths and prayers, and endowed Louis-Philippe with the title of Most Christian King. In the Low Countries, Cardinal Albani, together with the nuncio Capaccini, strove for a policy of appeasement toward King William I, in order to break the "monstrous" alliance of Catholics and liberals. But the Belgian revolution of 25 August 1830 brought about a definitive separation between the destinies of Holland and Belgium.

Pius VIII's reign also had an influence on the history of Christian morality. Hostile to Jansenism, which he fought as prefect of the Index, Pius VIII promoted the cause and work of Alphonsus Liguori. Under his influence, in the summer of 1830 both the HOLY OFFICE and the PENITENTIARY stipulated that the confessor who absolves a lender who has not exceeded the legal rate of interest (5 percent in France) "must not be harassed": the rejection of usury gave way to an attentive and benevolent approach to realities and individual conscience.

Pius VIII died on 30 November 1830: there were rumblings of revolt in Italy, and Lamennais's *L'Avenir* yoked together the Gospel and Liberty. Another century was dawning.

Philippe Boutry

Bibliography

Artaud de Montor, A. *Histoire du pape Pie VIII*, Paris, 1844.
Aubert, R. *Catholicisme*, XI (1988), 268–71.
Colapietra, R. "Il diario Brunelli del conclave del 1829," *Critica storica*, I (1962), 517–41, 636–61.
de Chateaubriand, F. R. *Mémoires d'outre tombe*, XXXI.
Fusi Pecci, O. *La Vita del Papa Pio VIII*, Rome, 1965.
Leflon, J. *La Crise révolutionnaire, 1789–1801* (*Histoire de l'Église*, XX), Paris, 1949, 409–25.
Schmidlin, J. *Histoire des papes à l'époque contemporaine*, Lyon, 1938, II, 138–84.

PIUS IX. *Giovanni Maria Mastai-Ferretti (b. Senigallia, near Ancona, 12 May 1792, d. Rome, 7 February 1878). Elected pope on 16 June 1846, crowned on 21 March. Buried at St. Peter's in Rome, then transferred in 1881 to S. Lorenzo fuori le Mura. Beatified, 2000.*

Neither a politician nor a diplomat, Pius IX was essentially a pastor. But because of the historical context of his papacy (the Risorgimento; that is, the territorial and political unification of Italy and the creation of a state based on the FRENCH REVOLUTION's principles of liberty and equality), he became embroiled despite himself in questions that were essentially, though not exclusively, political. Their immediate solution was beyond the pope's capabilities and those of his closest collaborator, Cardinal Antonelli, the secretary of state. The pope had chosen Antonelli because he had a political sense that Pius lacked. Nonetheless, Pius IX did succeed in giving a strong impetus to the spirituality and strictly religious renewal of the Church. On a political level, he failed because he lost Rome along with its temporal power and was unable to prevent the formation of the kingdom of Italy. But he succeeded in reviving anti-Jansenist piety, eliminating the last vestiges of Gallicanism, and reforming the clergy, both diocesan and religious.

The Mastai-Feretti family, which belonged to the petty provincial NOBILITY and was comfortably off without being wealthy, was rather strange. Obviously devout, pious in a lively and traditional way, it also showed a certain openness to new ideas (three of Giovanni Maria's brothers took part in the movements of 1831), and its members tended to push themselves forward beyond their capabilities. There were also several fraternal dis-

PIUS IX

putes—sometimes hushed up, sometimes in the open—
and failed marriages (among them, those of his sister Isabella and various nephews). His uncle Andrea had been
bishop of Pesaro, his uncle Paolino a high-ranking prelate
in Rome. From 1803 to 1809, Giovanni Maria studied at
the college of the Scolopi in Volterra, where he showed a
lively interest in the sciences. But toward the end of his
course of study he suffered severe attacks of epilepsy and
returned to Senigallia. His illness, on the nature of which
we have precise information, lasted through the period of
his ordination, making a dispensation necessary, but
stopped shortly afterward. Though genuinely cured,
throughout his life Gianmaria retained unmistakable
traces of the disease. Very emotional, he swung easily
from his customary joviality, a source of pleasure to those
who approached him in his "good" moments, to an abrupt
manner and harsh and unpredictable reproaches, both in
private and in public. With his precarious state of health
hampering the pursuit of his studies, he went to Rome, to
which PIUS VII had just returned. There he formed various friendships and was strongly attracted to certain
young women, as well as to Giacinta Milzetti-Machetti,
the wife of his great childhood friend, Giovanni. However, his feelings were always kept perfectly under control, and his profound piety, purity, and concern for the
poor remained intact.

In March 1816, when he was almost twenty-four, and
having talked over the matter with worthy ecclesiastics
and made several retreats, he decided to become a priest.
His idea was not to embark on a career but to be a shepherd of souls. After somewhat hasty studies at the Roman
COLLEGE, which had reopened insufficiently equipped (a
certain theological unpreparedness would prove a burden
to the pope), the young man was ordained priest in 1819.
Having given up the idea of becoming a JESUIT, for some
years he devoted his energies to the Tata Giovanni or-
phanage in Rome.

A combination of circumstances led young Mastai to
join the special mission sent by LEO XII to Chile at the request of the government. It was headed by Msgr. Muzi,
later bishop of Città di Castello. At first, he believed (at
least in part) that the venture was more missionary than
diplomatic, which was the reason he had put forward his
candidature. The mission did not achieve its aim because
of Muzi's lack of ability and the strong jurisdictional tendencies of the Chilean government. But the young man
returned to Rome with a good knowledge of Latin America and heightened apostolic zeal, of which he gave
proof, as well as of administrative and economic talents,
in his direction of the S. Michele Institute, one of the
most important relief agencies in Rome. As bishop of
Spoleto in 1827, when confronted with the 1831 revolution he followed his natural tendency toward moderation
and peace. After the surrender of the rebels, among them
Louis-Napoleon, the future emperor, whom he never met,

he arranged for their safe departure. On several occasions, he intervened with the new pope, GREGORY XVI,
on behalf of compromised diocesan clergy. Discouraged
by the predominance of a policy far removed from his
own moderation, he offered his resignation in late 1831.
But the pope remained as confident as ever in the pastor,
and one year later, in late November 1832, gave him a
larger and more difficult diocese: Imola, in Romagna,
where anticlericalism and opposition to temporal power
were more intense.

During this period, his thought was expressed in the
*Pensieri relativi all'Amministrazione pubblica dello
Stato Pontificio*, a program of reforms drawn up in 1845
and sent to Rome, and also in the letter he sent in 1833 to
his friend Cardinal Falconieri, archbishop of Ravenna: "I
hate and abominate to the marrow the thoughts and actions of the liberals; but I cannot sympathize with the fanaticism of the 'bigots.' The Christian middle way—and
not that diabolical one that is customary today—would
be the path I would wish to follow with the Savior's help:
but shall I succeed?"

He was named cardinal at the end of 1840. At the conclave of June 1846, after the death of Gregory XVI, his
candidature rapidly gained ground as the struggle proceeded between those defending the rigid and conservative Gregorian system, which favored the former secretary of state, Lambruschini, and the champions of a new,
more conciliatory orientation, who had long known the
archbishop of Imola and hoped to have found in him
"their man." Mastai-Ferretti was elected on the fourth
round of voting, on 16 April.

There soon followed a stream of religious initiatives
that were highly fruitful over the long term. The EN-
CYCLICAL-program *Qui pluribus* of 1 November 1846
followed the traditional line. It condemned religious indifference, rationalism, and a changing revelation, but it
also expressed the new pope's anguish, emphasizing the
need for strict selection and careful formation for candidates for the priesthood. Early October saw the institution of the Congregation *de statu regularium*, aimed at
overcoming the ultraconservatism of the existing dicasteries and encouraging the reform of the institutes of religion. Aided by the Capuchin Giusto da Camerino and
Msgr. Bizzarri, an expert in canon law and a tireless and
quick worker wholeheartedly committed to the new task,
the following June the pope published *Ubi primum*,
which recommended that the generals of the religious
orders exercise the utmost strictness in admission and
formation. Then followed an inquiry into the concrete
situation of religious in the Papal States. Simultaneously,
in August 1847, the CONCORDAT with Russia was signed.
If it had been faithfully applied, it might have ensured
freedom for the Catholics of the Latin and Byzantine
Churches, but it was never fully observed and was denounced by Russia in late 1866.

1192

Pius IX pursued the struggle begun by Gregory XVI against Portuguese interference in India. On several occasions, he rebuked the patriarch of Goa, the Benedictine Da Silva Torres, who, contrary to Gregory's precise instructions, did not recognize the authority of the apostolic vicars and claimed that he exercised jurisdiction over their territories. After long negotiations, Da Silva Torres, who was largely responsible for the "Goa schism" (between those who recognized the authority of the vicars and those who did not), was "promoted" to the Portuguese see of Braga. Nonetheless, Goa remained vacant for a long time. Important progress was also made in the Middle East, where the pope strove as far as possible to avoid French mediation by entering into direct relations with the Ottoman government and tried to set up, in Jerusalem, an authority that was directly dependent on Rome and capable of unifying the whole apostolate. In October 1847, the Latin patriarchate of Jerusalem was restored and entrusted to Msgr. Valerga, still controversial because of his latinizing tendencies. In January 1848, the Ferrieri mission led to the appointment of an apostolic delegate to Istanbul. On the other hand, the encyclical of 6 January of that year, *In suprema Petri sede*, inviting the heads of the Eastern Churches to meet in Rome, only gave rise to endless disputes. Characteristically, the Roman view considered Latin discipline and ritual the ideal. Thus there was no talk of dialogue, only of a return to unity, whence the failure of this premature and ill-prepared overture.

Yet at that juncture the fundamental problems were of a different nature. The 1848 revolution was close at hand, the result of an accumulation of disappointed hopes and the inevitable tensions that ensued. In 1843, the publication of Gioberti's *Primato morale e civile degli italiani* had aroused great enthusiasm among the minorities of the Italian liberal and intellectual bourgeoisie, who constituted one of the decisive factors in the revolution. Numerous contemporary accounts show how ardently these groups believed in a new era for Italy. Now emerged from the largely political decline of recent centuries, Italy had become one of the great powers. This meant that, as a reaction to the conservatism of Gregory XVI, people looked to the coming pope to provide encouragement in that direction. After the bloody trauma of the French Revolution, the Church and modern civilization could and should be reconciled, with the pope heading a confederation of the various Italian states.

At Imola, Pius IX had encountered these ideas and, although he did not quite share them, had not been insensitive to them. He envisaged a weakening of Austrian influence in Italy, a program of fairly limited political and administrative reforms, and a greater understanding among the Italian states. But his first measures, restrained in themselves, were soon deliberately interpreted by the Italian liberals as the confirmation of their dream. Thus

was born the myth of a liberal pope. Not only was Pius IX not immediately aware of the danger, but with a few sentences he helped aggravate the misunderstanding. Moreover, he himself had been touched by the widespread enthusiasm in Italy at the beginning of 1848 and, confusing the political and religious spheres, came to see in the Austrian crisis of that year the realization of the divine plan that would restore Italy to its former glory. The time soon came for the pope to make his position clear, but the delayed Vatican affirmations inevitably provoked a reaction of opposition. The myth of the liberal pope was replaced by the legend of the traitor pope.

From 1846 to the end of 1848, various secretaries of state appeared at the pope's side, modest men who were outstripped by events. All of them quickly resigned their posts. Gizzi (1846–7) withdrew because he was opposed to certain of the pope's concessions; Ferretti (second semester, 1847) because of his unstable character; Orioli and Soglia because of their lack of ability. Antonelli (March–April 1848) preferred to resign after contributing to a necessary clarification: shrewdly, he considered that his hour had not yet come and remained waiting in the wings. During this period, the most intelligent adviser was the open, disinterested, and loyal Msgr. Corboli Bussi of Urbino. Substitute secretary of state, then secretary for foreign affairs, he held the two most important posts after the SECRETARIAT OF STATE. He cooperated actively in the reformist policy and effectively accomplished important diplomatic missions in Italy. From mid-1848, he remained in a secondary position until his death in 1850 when he was still very young, which deprived the pope of an extremely valuable collaborator. Rosmini, sent to Rome by the kingdom of Sardinia in the second half of 1848, was about to be named to the cardinalate. He could have been named secretary of state, but the final crisis of 1848, and especially Antonelli's maneuvers, forced him to withdraw. From December 1848 to his death in 1876, Antonelli remained close to the pope, master of the situation. A deacon but not a priest, a believer who faithfully carried out his duties without ever being devout or pious (the accusations concerning his private life are groundless), cold, reserved, capable of playing a double game, attached to his family and bent on accumulating a fine inheritance, he was the perfect antithesis of Pius IX, who tended to be too expansive, sincere, incapable of dissimulation, extremely pious, and deeply devout. The cardinal's economic and political skill, in short the complementary relationship of the two men, explain this close collaboration, which was to last twenty-eight years.

Amid uncertainties and delays, pressures from the street, and obstruction from on high, a variety of reforms were enacted one after another beginning in July 1846. The amnesty of 16 July 1846, though limited, aroused a tumult of enthusiasm (in large measure intentional), causing the bishop of Gubbio, Giuseppe Pecci, and that of Iesi, Cardinal Corsi, to speak of a new era. Then, in 1847, came the granting of a consultative body, of the communal council of Rome, and of the ministerial council. This almost brought about the evolution, which Consalvi had begun, of the "chamber" system of government, with its various overlapping jurisdictions, into a "ministerial," centralized government. At the same time, from August to December, Corboli Bussi contacted various Italian heads of state in the hope of creating a customs alliance. The plan (which for Corboli represented a first step toward political alliance) failed because of the mistrust of certain rulers, in particular the king of Naples and the duke of Modena.

Still, 1848 was a decisive year. In France essentially socioeconomic, in Italy the revolution took on a clearly political coloration. The movement called for independence vis-à-vis Austria and for liberty. After the fall of Louis-Philippe in Paris and the promulgation of a constitution in Naples, Florence, and Turin, the same measure was taken in Rome, on 14 March. This highly complex constitution was an attempt to reconcile the independence of the pope as head of the Church with the ceding of legislative and executive power to other agencies. It was a difficult step that was powerless to prevent a crisis when Charles-Albert, king of Sardinia, declared war on Austria in the wake of the anti-Austrian uprisings in Milan and Venice. The pope allowed his army to advance to the frontiers in order to protect them. But the great independence shown by his generals and, especially, the protests and accusations rife in Vienna forced him to clear up ambiguities in his allocution of 29 April 1848. The autograph edition still shows traces of Pius IX's enthusiasm of 1848. But the official text, probably written by Antonelli, by then a master of the double game, reveals the anxiety not of the ruler of Italy but of the head of the universal Church, who cannot make war with his children no matter what their nationality. The pope tried to extricate himself from the trap he had fallen into, but the Italians were too inflamed with the delirium of those days to accept calmly the neutrality of the pope, an Italian sovereign, in the face of the national question. After various more or less feeble attempts at forms of government, Pius IX turned to an expert, the decisive Pellegrino Rossi. But Rossi, who had tried to restore order to the agitated capital, was assassinated on 15 November in the stairways of the Chancery Palace, where parliament was to reassemble. On 16 November, Pius IX, in order to avoid the worst, ended by accepting a cabinet imposed by the street, a crowd that shouted in front of the Quirinal. On 24 November, however, he fled Rome, according to a plan prepared by Antonelli, who had preceded him to Gaeta by sea. After attempts at agreement on the part of the Roman liberals, the breaking point was quickly reached. On 9 February 1849, the Roman parliament, elected 21–2 January, proclaimed the Republic. From Gaeta, the pope appealed to the Catholic powers. The most significant effective aid came from France, from the prince-president Louis-Napoleon, who sent an expeditionary force to Rome under the command of General Oudinot. In early July, despite strong resistance on the Janiculum, French troops entered the city, but it was not until 12 April 1850 that Pius IX could return to his capital. In September 1849, at Portici, near Naples, where the pope had moved, edicts had been promulgated establishing the new organization of the States of the Church. With the constitution abrogated, there took place what Corboli imaginatively called the "reactionary and ineffective restoration."

The relatively quiet years of 1850 to 1859 saw a number of initiatives. In 1850, the review CIVILTÀ CATTOLICA was founded. Taking advantage of the Jesuit Curci's astute proposal, Pius IX imposed this initiative on the indecisive superior General Roothaan, who feared lest his religious meddle in politics. The proclamation of the Immaculate Conception took place amid solemnity on 8 December 1854. It was the fruit of lengthy consultations with the episcopate since 1848, yet was still based exclusively on papal authority, a fact that announced the definition of the pontiff's personal infallibility. The method followed in the bull, which took as starting point existing agreement within the Church and interpreted past testimonies in light of it within a legitimate theological perspective, opened up new paths to theology which have been largely followed since then. The new dogma strengthened the devotion of the faithful and contributed to the triumph of the anti-Jansenist piety dear to Pius IX. In 1855, Rosmini's doctrine, the object of bitter polemics between Jesuits and Rosminians, was judged free of errors (*Dimittantur*, which continued to give rise to debate until LEO XIII issued his contrary judgment in 1888). At the same time, the Congregation *de statu regularium* introduced, through various measures, a perfect communal way of life at least into novitiates and seminaries, and instituted simple vows before solemn ones in order to make it easier for young religious to leave their orders.

Over the course of these years, numerous concordats were issued, two of which had particular resonance. The concordat with Austria, of 1855, should have marked the renunciation of JOSEPHISM and liberal principles and should have made Austria a Catholic state. In reality, the question of mixed marriages, the object of sterile decisions reiterated by Franz-Josef from 1860, was not resolved. In any case, Austria would become a liberal country, and the concordat was denounced in 1870. The concordat with Portugal, of 1857, meant, on the other hand, the abandonment of the policy of the early years and the recognition of Portuguese interference, even on English territories, in India. In fact, Lisbon never applied the treaty, Portugal having, paradoxically, bemoaned rather than rejoiced over what it considered an acceptance of Roman claims. Pius IX protested in vain to the king of Portugal and acknowledged the error. In the end, everything remained as it was in 1850, even if the Goa schism had ended and the excommunications hurled against rebellious ecclesiastics in Rome had been lifted. It was only in 1886, with Leo XIII, that a new agreement, this time signed with the active cooperation of the Indian bishops, made it possible to move toward a peaceful settlement of the anachronistic situation. Cardinal Barnabo, an energetic and effective worker, was prefect of the Propaganda in those years. He favored a policy of latinization of the Eastern Churches.

The years 1859–60 saw the new decisive phase of the Roman question, which concluded with the almost total loss of the Papal States, with the exception of Latium. This came about after a series of revolutions, the defeat of Castelfidardo, near Loreto, in September 1860, and a succession of excommunications that affected millions of Italians. On 18 March 1861, the kingdom of Italy was proclaimed. On 25 and 27 March, Camillo Cavour, president of the Council of the old kingdom of Sardinia since 1852, the true architect of Italian unification and arch-adversary of Pius IX, described in two speeches to parliament the objectives still outstanding: Rome should become the Italian capital, and an agreement should be reached with the pope, who could reap great benefits by giving up temporal power and accepting the liberty that the Italian government was promising him in exchange. On 6 June, Cavour died, at fifty-one, worn out by his efforts. Before his death, he received absolution from the Franciscan Giacomo da Poirino without in any way having recanted. In consequence, da Poirino was forbidden by Pius IX to hear confessions.

The polemics and thinking of those years stand out clearly in papal documents and pamphlets. Among them is one written anonymously by Viscount de La Gueronnière, *Le Pape et le Congrès* (1859), which was published in preparation for a congress that never took place, as well as a host of contemporary pastorals and books, partially collated by Saitta some thirty years ago. Bishop Dupanloup was the first to oppose de La Gueronnière, with Msgr. Pie and others following suit. Today, from a distance, it is easy to sum up the problems. Italian unification was an irreversible process, brought about by economic, political, and cultural factors and made possible by the astuteness of Cavour, who had found a way to assure himself of the support of Napoleon III. But unification could not be achieved without Rome. Pius IX, Antonelli, and the great majority of the episcopate, however, believed temporal power to be an effective, visible, and indispensable guarantee of the independence of the head of the Church. They did not have and perhaps could not have had the creative imagination necessary to find other

solutions. Furthermore, Pius IX was preoccupied by the Sardinian government's clearly secular orientation, which Cavour himself shared and defended. He therefore could not trust fine promises belied by the facts, and believed that a secular state would endanger the eternal salvation of his subjects. This last consideration, which was debatable, is today outdated, but it helped make the pope's stance more and more uncompromising.

In 1864, two documents came out at the same time: an encyclical, *Quanta cura*, a synthesis of the errors of the time, and a list of eighty erroneous and condemned propositions, the *SYLLABUS*. Both documents, which were long in preparation, were hastily drawn up from September to November 1864 by the Barnabite Bilio. Montalembert's two speeches, given at Mechelen in 1863, had been decisive. According to the viscount, it was useless to regret what was past. The liberty of the Church would be saved only by reference to the principle of general liberty. Freedom of religion was compatible with the Catholic religion. In a full refutation, Bilio evoked the long tradition to the contrary, the positive role of the state, the secular arm of the Church, and the evil posed by freedom of religion. Thus the final edition was arrived at.

Among the eighty propositions of the *Syllabus*, many had to do with idealism, lay morality, and the conception of the moral state, and passed by more or less unnoticed. But the last four theses aroused lively argument. The following were held to be errors: freedom of worship of non-Catholic minorities, the abandoning of the confessional state, full freedom of the press and of thought, and the claim that there could be reconciliation between the pope on the one hand and progress and modern civilization on the other. Bilio had extracted from previous papal documents some short phrases which, taken out of context, ended by having a quite other, and unacceptable, meaning. In any case, the condemnation of freedom of worship of non-Catholic minorities was clear. If Bilio wrote it, Pius IX remained the author juridically and historically responsible for the document, which was put together in a deplorable fashion, one capable of arousing arguments that might have been avoided. True, Pius IX accepted the distinction made immediately by Dupanloup between thesis (refusal of freedom of worship considered as an ideal) and hypothesis (its acceptance as a lesser, unavoidable evil), but in fact he continued intuitively to incline toward the thesis of an officially Christian society that would exclude religious tolerance. That is demonstrated in particular by his vain opposition to the Spanish constitution of 1876, which opened the door to moderate tolerance.

And yet it was precisely the publication of the *Syllabus* that gave the pope the idea of calling an ecumenical COUNCIL. The project quickly matured and was officially announced in 1867. It is more difficult to determine the moment when the pope turned his thoughts to a definition of infallibility and primacy. Certainly, these two definitions, which grew out of the 19th-century ultramontane movement as a whole, were present in the Curia at the time the council was officially announced, the definition of infallibility having been proposed by the semi-official *Civiltà cattolica* in February 1869. It provoked a wave of argument in France and Germany. Yet the council was not convened solely for that reason but especially to point the way toward a Christian renewal of society. The counterarguments of Hans Küng and August Bernhard Hasler, full of subjective a priori statements, are scientifically unacceptable.

On 8 December 1869, Pius IX solemnly opened the council. It was a move of great courage but one that showed he was far removed from political reality. True, the pope was the great organizer of the sessions. Antonelli, cold and somewhat distrustful, had no influence, whereas cardinal Bilio and the Jesuit theologians Franzelin, Kleutgen, Schrader, and Perrone played leading roles. It was the pope who decided upon and convened the council, determined its agenda, fixed its rules, and directed its progress from afar. Thus he moved from the initial freedom given to the fathers and the insistent presenters to modifying the rules, putting earlier in the agenda the discussion of primacy and infallibility, refusing the requests made *in extremis* by Bishop Dupanloup and other minority bishops opposed to INFALLIBILITY, and drily commanding Bilio to insert into the texts phrases that were weighty in their implication.

The end of April 1870 saw the unanimous approval of the constitution *Dei Filius*, which shed light on the relations between reason and faith. On 18 July, after the surprise vote of 13 July (25 percent of votes against), another constitution, *Pastor aeternus*, was promulgated, on the pope's universal primacy of jurisdiction and his personal infallibility. Fifty-five bishops of the opposition had left Rome the day before as a sign of protest. Nevertheless, the definitions of 18 July, according to the official council reports, stuck to a moderate line and reaffirmed the authority of the bishops and their effective collaboration in the pope's definitions. The minority critics had made a real and useful contribution. In a few months, the bishops who had been absent on 18 July gave their assent. The Old Catholics were now merely a restricted group, and the two constitutions reinforced the prestige and authority of the Holy See. At the end of October, the council was adjourned.

In fact, on 20 September, Italian troops had entered Rome. Up to the last moment, Pius IX had believed in some extraordinary aid, and even the realist Antonelli had failed to take the most elementary measures dictated by common sense. In the evening of 19 September, faced with the emphatic urgings of Kanzler, commander of the papal forces, the pope altered the letter ordering surren-

der at the first cannon shots and authorized resistance until a breach had been made in the city walls. Accordingly, on the morning of 20 September some fifty lay dead. The last piece of the Papal States had fallen, but the pope quickly decided, after consulting a few cardinals, to remain in Rome.

In late 1876, Antonelli died. He was replaced by Simeoni, a second-rank figure, chosen expressly to avoid emphasizing too strongly what the pope now regarded as a period of transition. The last years were marked by three long conflicts: with the Armenian Catholics, irritated by the provisions of *Reversurus* (1867), which restricted their freedom in the choice of bishops and the patriarch; with the Chaldeans, annoyed for the same reasons; and with Germany, where the stubborn resistance of the episcopate, especially the Prussian, and the pope in the face of Bismarck's measures prepared the way for the compromise favorable to the Church obtained under Leo XIII. On 9 January 1878, Victor Emmanuel II died at the QUIRINAL, where he had taken up residence, and on 7 February Pius IX died. Rome thus witnessed opposing demonstrations at the two solemn funerals. The Vatican and the Quirinal confronted each other, distrustful and hostile.

The pontificate ended with a complex balance sheet. There had been a broad victory over the vestiges of GALLICANISM and JANSENISM, a clear amelioration of the diocesan and religious clergy, an important affirmation of anti-Jansenist piety, an encouragement of Catholics in the struggle against secularization, and a reaffirmation of the independence of the Church and, in particular, of the Holy See. Over against these, however, were a stubborn incomprehension concerning the modern world and modern culture in all their aspects, a slowing down of ecclesiastical culture, and, in Italy, a noticeable tension between the two sides, one that would increase steadily under Leo XIII.

Giacomo Martina

Bibliography

Aubert, R. *Il pontificato di Pio IX*, Turin, 1971, Ital. ed. G. Martina.

Coppa, F. J. *Pope Pius IX, Crusader in a Secular Age*, Boston, 1979.

Croce, G. M. "Una fonte importante per la storia del pontificato di Pio IX e del Concilio Vaticano 1: i manoscritti inediti di Vincenzo Tizzani," *AHP*, 23 (1985), 217–345; 24 (1986), 273–363; 25 (1987), 263–363.

Crocella, C. *Augusta miseria, Aspetti delle finanze pontificie nell'età del capitalismo*, Milan, 1982.

Falconi, C. *Il giovane Mastai. Il futuro Pio IX dall'infanzia a Senigallia alla Roma della restaurazione, 1792–1827*, Milan, 1981.

Hales, E. E. Y. *Pio Nono: A Study in European Politics and Religion in the Nineteenth Century*, New York, 1954.

Hasler, A. B. *How the Pope Became Infallible: Pius IX and the Politics of Persuasion*, Garden City, N.Y., 1981.

Küng, H. *Infallible? An Unresolved Enquiry*, New York, 1994.

Martina, G. *Pio IX (1846–1850)*, Rome, 1974; *Pio IX (1851–1866)*, Rome, 1986; *Pio IX (1867–1878)*, Rome, 1990.

Mize, S. Y. "Defending Roman Loyalties and Republican Values: The 1848 Italian Revolution in American Catholic Apologetics," *Church History*, 60 (1991) pp. 480–92.

O'Malley, J. W. "On the Beatification of Pope Pius IX," *America* (Aug. 26–Sept. 2, 2000) pp. 6–11.

Wallace, L. P. *The Papacy and European Diplomacy, 1869–1878*, Chapel Hill, N.C., 1948.

PIUS X. *Giuseppe Melchiorre Sarto (b. Riese, 2 June 1835, d. Rome, 20 August 1914). Elected pope on 4 August 1903, crowned on 9 August. Buried in the Vatican Grottoes. Beatified on 3 June 1951, canonized on 29 May 1954.*

The second child of a large family of modest means, he was ordained priest on 18 September 1858 after studying at the seminary of Padua. He did pastoral work for seventeen years, first as vicar at Tombolo and then as parish priest in Salzano. In November 1875, he became a canon of the cathedral of Treviso, besides acting as CHANCELLOR of the CURIA and spiritual director of the seminary. In September 1884, he was appointed bishop of Mantua, where he took up his office in April 1885, after his episcopal ordination in Rome the previous November. In June 1893, he was named cardinal and patriarch of Venice, where he arrived in November 1894. On 4 August 1903, he was elected pope, which caused him much soul-searching. The CONCLAVE had been a tumultuous one on account of the Austrian emperor's VETO of Cardinal Rampolla, which the cardinals solemnly condemned and rejected.

This unusual pope offers one of those examples, rare in the last two hundred years, of a man whose ecclesiastical career brings him to the papacy after long years of pastoral activity and not a day's service in Vatican diplomacy. It is for this reason that Pius X would pick as his secretary of state a young prelate who had this very experience, Rafael Merry del Val.

Pius X had a rich pastoral background and a relatively meager cultural education, even if it was not as impoverished as some have liked to believe. These two elements are sufficient in themselves to account for the choices and programs of his pontificate. On the one hand, Pius X paid great attention to pastoral work, to catechesis, and to reforms of the liturgy and of sacred music that would help the faithful to a more intense life of prayer and a fuller participation in the sacraments. On the other hand, he harbored a constant mistrust of scientific research. Hence, a series of interventions and measures that, if justified by the need to react in the face of a serious crisis in the orientation of biblical and theological studies, also seems the fruit of a deficient education. He was incapable of understanding the problems of the researcher, whose difficult search for truth is not always or only a reckless desire for novelty at any price. Behind research can be a love of the Church, a love quite as profound as that of those who think, to the contrary, that the Church is best served by avoiding dangerous subjects that exclude predetermined solutions.

Over his years of pastoral service, first as parish priest and then as bishop, he had oriented his life according to a few simple and well thought-out guidelines: catechesis, above all of children, for whom he had put together a catechism in simple and vivid language; and the development of numerous social activities in a region in which the Catholic movement had a broad base and diverse expressions. Uncompromising politically, that is, totally opposed to choices that tended to favor politically liberal figures, he had nevertheless gradually abandoned his rigorist tendency, and had gone so far as to refrain from opposing an alliance between Catholics and liberals in the Venetian municipal administration. Still, he lost no opportunity to insist on the need for a complete subordination of the Catholic laity to the ecclesiastical hierarchy, even in specifically social and political matters. He had also clearly manifested his dislike of the political positions and programs of the group of young men, led by Romolo Murri, who were endeavoring to put themselves forward as a party in the name of CHRISTIAN DEMOCRACY. All these elements in a way represent the first fruits of the general principles guiding his pontificate, which are set forth in the earliest documents as a radical religious transformation summed up in the motto *Instaurare omnia in Christo*.

Pastoral Activity. The numerous activities undertaken by this pope account for the opinion of some historians that Pius X was the greatest reforming pope of the last few centuries. His interventions had to do with the whole range of ecclesiastical institutions. A few years into his papacy, he published decrees destined to effect a radical transformation of the Roman Curia. Similarly, with the *motu proprio Arduum sane munus* of March 1904 and the collaboration of the future Cardinal Gasparri, he undertook the codification of CANON LAW (an endeavor that would be completed only under BENEDICT XV).

Another significant initiative was the reorganization of the education and formation of the clergy. After lengthy work on the part of committees nominated by him, new programs of study and formation were published and implemented in the seminaries. In addition, regional seminaries, especially in southern Italy, were created to take in young men from dioceses unable to maintain effective establishments of their own. The decision, made after some hesitation, to reserve to Rome the responsibility for appointing the superiors and teachers at these seminaries ensured a satisfactory level in the quality of teaching, even though it stripped each diocese of its autonomy of decision.

The pope was also active in the area of liturgical prayer and of catechesis. The catechism he devised during his years as a parish priest would later be expanded and would become the *Catechism of Pius X*, disseminated throughout the world. His ENCYCLICAL *Acerbo nimis* (1905) concerned the teaching of Christian doctrine. That same year, he began a series of interventions regarding frequent communion, opposing the last vestiges of the Jansenist rigorism. Then he extended to children the invitation to the Eucharist, and in the end lowered the age at which first communion is received (decree *Quam singulari*, 8 August 1911).

Finally, he modified the existing practice whereby secular music was used in Church services, and restored Gregorian chant to its former place. In 1911, the constitution *Divino afflatu* reformed the breviary. Mention should also be made of his reorganization of the parishes of Rome in the interest of better pastoral service in the outskirts under development.

Sociopolitical Orientations. Described as the "religious pope" in contrast to his predecessor LEO XIII, Pius X had numerous opportunities to make social and political choices that aroused impassioned debate. The Italian political situation was still strongly conditioned by the breaking off of relations between the state and the Church, a consequence of the occupation of Rome in 1870. As a sign of protest, Italian Catholics took no part in political life, and Pius X did nothing in an official way to alter that state of affairs. However, he did permit bishops to decide "case by case" according to the needs of each region; thus, encouragement was given to candidates who could be called clerico-moderates. The Catholics supported moderate candidates from the liberal group, especially when these voices seemed useful for countering a possible victory by socialist candidates. Among other things, this choice made impracticable the creation of a Catholic party, or of a party of Catholics, such as was the hope of Romolo Murri and, in a certain sense, of Luigi Sturzo. To avoid any confusion and opposition, the pope affirmed on several occasions that it was the duty of the lay faithful to conform to the directives of the religious authorities, even in matters of politics.

Despite Leo XIII's policy of reconciliation, relations with France proved problematic, and in 1905, Pius X reacted by harshly condemning the Law of Separation approved by the French Senate. The pope refused to accept any form of compromise, because he believed there was great ambiguity in the possibility, then being offered to the dioceses, of holding on to some of their property on the condition that they form associations of worship, which might have given the state a real control over religious activities. This intransigence met with much criticism, including that of some French bishops, who, like Bishop Lacroix of Tarentaise, even tendered their resignations. Relations between state and Church deteriorated further in the wake of the "Montagnini affair," named after a Vatican diplomat who was accused of having exerted undue influence on French political personalities.

The subsequent condemnation of Le Sillon—the democratic movement of young French Catholics founded by Marc Sangnier—confirmed, if confirmation was needed, the problems posed by French Catholicism. The movement was accused of wanting to identify Catholicism with a form of democratic politics. (It should be recalled that the condemnation of the right-wing Action Française, decreed in 1926 by PIUS XI, was contemplated by Puis X himself.) On the other hand, his insistence on the matter of subordination to the ecclesiastical authorities led him to favor associations that were confessional in character. This attitude was confirmed in the encyclical *Singulari quadam* (1912), which nevertheless envisaged the acceptance of interconfessional trade unions, in certain local situations. German-speaking countries were especially interested in this problem, since they had both confessional and interconfessional social associations and trade union organisms. It was probably after this encyclical that Pius X adopted an even more rigid attitude, the result of a harsh campaign being waged by the integralist movements against interconfessionality. He did not intervene, however, even though certain signs made that seem likely, perhaps because certain persons, both ecclesiastical and lay, had persuaded the pope to renounce such an intervention.

The Struggle Against Modernism. The serious doctrinal crisis of the first years of the century, provoked by the consequences for Catholic culture of the progress made in biblical and theological sciences, impelled Pius X to take ever stricter measures to eradicate what the pope himself described as a synthesis of all the HERESIES—MODERNISM. Thus began a harsh and often exacerbated battle, which in the end drew in researchers of high repute, who were animated by an equal love for the Church. A climate of mistrust and vilification so convulsed great segments of the press that Pius X became convinced of the gravity of the situation and the need for a drastic solution. Because of this atmosphere and the war being led against modernism, certain historians in the end identified the pontificate of Pius X with the modernist crisis, with the result that all his action for reform was utterly neglected.

The condemnation of five works by the French exegete Alfred Loisy, promulgated a few months after Pius was elected pope, marked the beginning of a long series of similar gestures. Other scholars came in for disapproval over the following years—Laberthonnière and Le Roy, Tyrrell and Buoniauti, Fogazzaro, and Murri and Minocchi, to name only the best known. In July 1907, a decree from the Holy Office, *Lamentabili sane exitu*, and two months later the encyclical *Pascendi*, sanctioned the harsh and unequivocal condemnation of the modernist heresy, even attributing to it a thematic structure that none of the accused had so clearly expressed in his writings. Modernism was portrayed as a system of thought founded on agnosticism and immanentism, and therefore in total opposition to Catholic teaching. The condemnation grouped together not only philosophical, theological, and biblical trends but also specifically political ones, like those concerning the relations between Church and state and the believer's political autonomy with respect to the ecclesiastical hierarchy. A normative section followed, prescribing disciplinary measures and setting up surveillance structures that would prevent the repetition or diffusion of the incriminated doctrine.

The result was that persons of proven doctrinal integrity became suspect, owing to the formation of pressure groups that saw themselves as entrusted with a mission like that of Christ driving the moneylenders from the temple. All means were permitted them, including denunciation and slander, in the interest of destroying those they considered enemies. Some of them, under the direction of Umberto Benigni, formed a veritable espionage agency, the *Sodalicium pianum* (in memory of the great inquisitor pope, St. PIUS V), which was doubtless neither as vast nor as complex as some have wanted to believe, but was certainly far from admirable and without scruples of any kind. Historians continue to debate the question, much discussed in recent years, as to whether Pius X was informed of these maneuvers and the excesses they spawned. Certainly, in the end the climate also isolated and saddened a pope who had always agonized deeply over his mission. Those who knew him in the years before his pontificate remembered someone essentially jovial and serene.

The last months of his life were darkened by the deadly clouds of war that were gathering over Europe. Pius X experienced this eve of war as an unbearable tragedy, feeling his own impotence in the face of it. His appeal to Catholics the world over, issued on 2 August 1914 to express his horror and "bitter grief," in fact became the testament of a patriarch who saw his children confronting one another face to face. It could be said that it was really the awareness of his own impotence that killed him. The pope died on 20 August 1914.

Maurilio Guasco

Bibliography

Acta Apostolicae Sedis (1909–1914).

Acta Sanctae Sedis (1903–1908).

Agasso, D. *L'ultimo papa santo—Pio X*, Cinisello Balsamo, 1985.

Bentley, J. *God's Representatives: The Eight Twentieth-Century Popes*, London, 1997.

Canepa, A. M. "Pius X and the Jews: A Reappraisal" *Church History*, 61 (1992) pp. 362–72.

Dal Gal, G. *Il papa santo. Pio X*, Padua, 1954.

Disquisitio circa quasdam objectiones modum agendi servi Dei respicientes in modernismi debellatione, Vatican City, 1950.

Droulers, P. *Politique sociale et christianisme. Le père Desbuquois et l'Action populaire. Débuts, syndicalisme et intégristes (1903–1918)*, Paris, 1969.

Fernessole, P. *Pie X, essai historique*, 2 vols., Paris, 1952–3.

Lettere, ed. N. Vian, Rome, 1954, Padua, 1958.

Mayeur, J. M. *La Séparation des Églises et de l'État*, Paris, 1991.

Positio super introductione causae, Rome, 1942.

Positio super virtutibus, Vatican City, 1949.

Poulat, E. *Intégrisme et catholicisme intégral. Un réseau secret international antimoderniste: la "Sapinière" (1909–1921)*, Tournai, 1969.

Poulat, E. "La dernière bataille du pontificat de Pie X," *RSCI*, 1971.

Romanato, G. *Pio V. La vita di papa Sarto*, Milan, 1992.

Schmidlin, N. J. *Papstgeschichte der neusten Zeit*, III, Munich, 1934, 1–177.

Scoppola, P. *Crisi modernista e rinnovamento cattolico in Italia*, Bologna, 1969.

Sulle orme di Pio X. Giuseppe Sarto (1835–1914) dal microcosmo veneto alla dimensione universale, Salzano-Venice, 1986.

Tramontin, S., ed., *Le radici venete di San Pio X*, Brescia, 1987.

PIUS XI. *Achille Ratti (b. Desio, Lombardy, 31 May 1857, d. Rome, 10 February 1939). Elected pope on 6 February 1922, crowned on 12 February. Buried in the Vatican Grottoes.*

"He was a man who wanted and who knew what he wanted. He had set himself a goal and a program. . . . Because he had sought nothing but the reign of Christ, he dominated events and he dominated the men of his time." These lines of Saliège, written on the death of Pius XI, reflected the sentiment of a large body of opinion in 1939. Yet the question remains as to whether all the acts of this long and rich pontificate tally with such an appreciation. The historiography of Pius XI sees in him the pope of innovating impulses and the defense of the human person, yet certain aspects of his initiative have earned his pontificate the qualification *pontificato grigio*. What overall interpretation of this pontificate can be made?

Lombard, Librarian and Nuncio. Achille Ratti was a LOMBARD, by blood and by education. The family roots of his father, Francesco, and those of his mother, Teresa Galli, are to be found in the Brianza, and the Brianza roots are particularly important for understanding the psychology of the Ratti pope. His father settled in Desio only because of his work (Francesco Ratti managed a spinning factory there). Young Achille invariably spent his vacations at the home of his uncle Damiano, the provost of Asso, in the heart of the Brianza. But his education took place in the diocese of Milan, where the Ambrosian Church deeply influenced him. MILAN at that time was still marked by the memory and initiatives of Charles Borromeo. The era of the Catholic Reform was further exalted by the *Promessi sposi* of Manzoni, Achille Ratti's favorite author. Achille confided his precocious vocation to his uncle Damiano, and, in 1867, he entered the seminary of S. Pietro Martire in Seveso. He continued his studies at the seminary of Monza, learning German and becoming a Franciscan tertiary in 1874. A student at the major seminary of Milan from 1875 to 1879, he learned Hebrew, among other subjects, under the direction of Ceriani, the prefect of the Ambrosiana. His teachers had a marked influence on him, and he paid homage to the spiritual formation he received, in moving terms, twenty years after his ordination.

Achille Ratti taught in the minor seminary for a year and prepared for the priesthood before being sent to the Lombard College in Rome in 1879 to complete his formation. He enrolled in the faculty of law of the Gregorian University and on 20 December 1879 was ordained priest at St. John Lateran. He stayed in Rome until 1882, obtaining a triple doctorate in theology, canon law, and philosophy (this last doctorate was defended before F. Liberatore at the Academy of St. Thomas and won him a memorable AUDIENCE with LEO XIII). Back in Milan, Achille Ratti embarked on a long career, the course of which brings to light certain essential features. A vicar, then professor at the major seminary before being appointed to the Ambrosiana Library in November 1888, Fr. Achille belonged to the Oblates of St. Charles, of Borromean spirituality. Their charism was to serve the Church, to fill in for priests wherever they were sent, without any seeking after promotions. As chaplain of the Cenacle, Ratti left a lively impression. He increased the number of baptisms, inspired the months of Mary, and took an interest in the little street sweepers, the visible symbols of poverty. He was a leading figure in the diocese. Here he enjoyed loyal friendships and the support of Archbishop da Calabiana and his successor, Archbishop Ferrari. Fr. Achille was introduced into all the Milanese

circles, including the liberal ones, which entrée won him a reputation for openness of mind. But he was wary of making untimely declarations, and his sympathies for the Rosminians were revealed mainly in private.

In November 1888, thanks to his outstanding scientific reputation and his first research efforts, he was named "doctor" of the Ambrosiana under the direction of the prefect, Ceriani. Responsible for making known the library's treasures, Ratti led the austere life of a scholar, while pursuing his pastoral work and engaging in some intrepid mountaineering, which has since passed into legend. His publications were many and varied, as we shall see, but they centered particularly on St. Charles Borromeo and the Church of Milan. In 1907, he became prefect of the Ambrosiana, and prelate of His Holiness. He carried out the renovation of the celebrated library and the cataloguing of its holdings, and pursued research work that attracted notice in the scholarly world. Although soon appointed prefect of the Vatican Library under Fr. Ehrle, in 1912, Ratti continued to manage the Ambrosiana and to maintain close ties with Milan until his appointment as prefect at the Vatican Library became effective, in 1914. There, Ratti took on the considerable task of restoring codexes and publishing manuscripts. Very accessible, he exchanged a vast correspondence with the scholarly world. The Milanese priest was thenceforth at the center of the Church. He was on intimate terms with BENEDICT XV, with whom he frequently conferred during the difficult years of the world war. Meanwhile, he continued his scientific work and tried to maintain an attitude of sober reserve.

Nevertheless, it was this scholar whom Benedict XV appointed apostolic visitator to Poland on 25 April 1918. That country was undergoing a difficult time, and the pope was responding to a request from Archbishop Kakowski of Warsaw. Ratti's name was put forward by Cerretti, who stressed the Vatican prefect's knowledge of languages and his familiarity with the problems of the country. Ratti left for Warsaw in May, and traveled by way of Berlin. He received a triumphant welcome in Poland, and was deeply impressed by the devotion of the Polish people. He quickly familiarized himself with the Polish situation and became aware of the extreme complexity of the relations between politics and religion. Responsible for working toward a restoration of unity in Poland, the visitator was determined to keep aloof from party politics. His relations with the bishops were opposite in character. His objective was to gain a special place for the Catholic Church, while giving proof of moderation in other areas. Thus, when the Polish state was restored, he was able to be promoted to apostolic nuncio as well as archbishop of Lepanto, and he was ordained in Warsaw cathedral on 28 October 1919 by Archbishop Kakowski in the presence of twenty-two bishops and the president of the Republic,

Pilsudski. Msgr. Ratti, who thought of himself as a "Polish bishop," saw his stay in Warsaw extended until 1921. This nunciature phase, properly speaking, discloses a number of important features of Ratti's ideas and attitudes. While very attached to Poland, as nuncio he was suspicious of excessive nationalism and proved his talents as a negotiator, but he did not always move in the same direction as the Polish episcopate. Accredited to the Baltic states, he made only a brief though memorable stay there. In Poland, he acquired a reputation for courage, linked to his attitude at the time of the Bolshevik siege of Warsaw in August 1920. Nevertheless, his mission ended in ambiguity. Achille Ratti was named ecclesiastical high commissioner in Upper Silesia, a region that had a plebiscite system. Cardinal Bertram, archbishop of Breslau, asked those Polish priests who were not incardinated to abstain from all propaganda, a measure that favored the German clergy. The Warsaw nuncio was content to preach a spirit of peace, and was severely taken to task by the Polish press during the summer of 1920. This cast something of a shadow over the final period of his nunciature. But his unpopularity was only temporary. Ratti witnessed the rebirth of a nation, set a concordat in motion, and gave valuable advice to the Poles. On the personal level, he became aware of the excesses of nationalism and Bolshevism. In May 1921, Ratti was named archbishop of Milan, for which he left Warsaw on 4 June. On 13 June, Benedict XV officially assigned him the Ambrosian see and raised him to the cardinalate. In this way, the pope showed his confidence in and respect for the nuncio to Warsaw. In fact, he was appointing him to the first diocese of Italy, marked by the strong personality of Cardinal Ferrari, a dominant figure who had given his episcopate of Milan a Borromean tone. The close ties between Ratti and Ferrari, Ratti's firm yet conciliatory character, and his Milanese connections encouraged Benedict XV to entrust him with this great see, for which the Catholic University (which Ratti inaugurated) was requesting a bishop of intellectual ability. After making a brief pilgrimage to Lourdes, Ratti entered Milan on 8 September. His friendships there, his "Italian" personality, and his scientific talents were well received by Milanese opinion, enlightened by Angelo Novelli, the editor of *L'Italia*. Ratti's short-lived Milanese episcopate allowed him to assert himself as pastor and as a leading figure of the Italian Church. He attracted attention with his first homily by describing the pope as the *piu grande decoro e prestigio d'Italia*, an indication of his wish to see the Roman question resolved. His pastoral activity was intense: he visited within the diocese, presided at numerous ceremonies, imposed a uniform teaching of the catechism in all schools, and demanded that rooms be supplied in schools for the purpose (which he obtained on 22 December by municipal vote). Cardinal Ratti presided over the conference of Lombard bishops which ended, on 10 January 1922, with a collective letter on the subject of the education of youth and civil peace.

Benedict XV died on 22 January. On 24 January, Cardinal Ratti left for Rome. His brief episcopate in Milan had gained him a reputation throughout Italy as a bishop who tended to be conciliatory in political affairs and extremely active in the pastoral domain. Without putting him forward too much, the newspapers included him among the *papabili*.

Election and Personality. Achille Ratti was elected pope on 6 February 1922 on the fourteenth ballot. Both the pre-conclave and the conclave took place in an atmosphere seemingly dominated by Italian questions. The Italian press was full of rumors concerning the situation of the peninsula, which the foreign press saw chiefly as an obstacle to be surmounted by the government of the Church (thus concurring with the opinion of certain foreign cardinals). The "conservative" candidacy of Merry del Val (who gained no more than 17 votes) suffered the dual handicap of his being a foreigner and his having been labeled an Integralist. Gasparri led the "liberal" group, but very soon had to withdraw, probably acknowledging thereby that he could not win more than 24 votes. The French ambassador Jonnart believed that Achille Ratti was a third-party candidate. Whatever the case, the fact remains that, with 4 initial votes, he saw his name climb from the eighth round against Cardinal La Fontaine, more moderate than Merry del Val. Achille Ratti succeeded in securing the indispensable help of the liberal camp and won 42 votes. The election took place in a difficult Italian context, which resulted in obfuscating broader and more important issues, but the whole was highlighted by Galli, the SECRETARY OF BRIEFS TO PRINCES. The global implications of the election took precedence over church-state politics, and Cardinal O'Connell, who had arrived too late for the election, recalled with humor the importance of the United States! Pius XI was elected by virtue of the long-range thinking and experience he could offer. His prudence, his restraint, and his personal qualities failed to gain him the votes only of the Gasparri camp, and showed how generally attractive was a personality less flamboyant than Gasparri's but capable of moving in new directions.

What can be said, then, about the personality of this pope, whose "career" underwent such a transformation in four years? More than that of other popes, Achille Ratti's portrait has been subject to stereotypes long disseminated by the press and, moreover, having their origins in certain exceptional aspects of the man. Cardinal Confalonieri's affectionate testimony has clarified the portrait of this *Rex tremendae majestatis* (PAUL VI to Jean Guitton). Most notable is Pius XI's profound attachment to his Lombard roots. These were reflected in the circle closest to him (Carlo Confalonieri, Diego

Venini), both in its composition and in the relative intimacy the pope occasionally allowed himself to enjoy. In the spirituality of Achille Ratti, St. Ambrose and St. Charles Borromeo held pride of place, as did Cardinal Ferrari. The influence of the simple spirituality of the Brianza and Charles Borromeo's reign of reform account for Achille Ratti's deep attachment to Manzoni's work, which he so often quoted. Physically he was robust, and part of his legend—forged from the testimony of Angelo Novelli—is linked to his mountain-climbing days. His exploits were well recorded and remained in the collective memory. The image of an alpinist pope was a departure from the usual image and earned him wide popularity. Pius XI's coldness is also legendary, even if it was offset by outbursts of anger. What seems most characteristic of the Ratti pope is his deliberateness, his poise, and the firmness of his decisions. He spent a long time searching for the right word (Paul VI), could remain cool-headed when called on to analyze a situation, did not hesitate to gather documentary evidence "pen in hand," and early on was described by Archbishop de Calabiana as a "young old man." His firmness could sometimes turn into obstinacy. Pius XI had the soul of a leader (on many occasions, especially in Milan in 1898, he gave proof of personal courage) and a great aptitude for taking command (C. Confalonieri speaks of *virtù*). The energy of his gaze was hidden behind thick spectacles, but impressed all who met him.

This statue cast in bronze might leave an impression of coldness, of extreme reserve, were there no other facts to modify it. This "inaccessible" pope received thousands of young married couples, wept profusely at the consecration of Cardinal Verdier, and allowed glimpses of an extremely sensitive temperament. Pius XI's devotion to St. Thérèse of Lisieux disclosed a mystical side that he did not disguise.

His loyalty as a friend shows that he had a sensitive heart, expressed in the image he wanted to give of himself, that of the "father," even the "old father," presiding over the destinies of the universal Church. Formed in Ignatian spirituality, the faith of the pope was turned toward the Savior in all his rootedness in history. Pius XI drew the fundamental steadfastness of his faith from the Church "who has spoken with Christ," and would tolerate no shortcomings in her vicariate. Perhaps too obsessed with a certain image of the Church, he often defended her rights, ardently and wholeheartedly. At such times, his many-sided personality showed an assertive, even majestic side, but his vehemence could be intimidating. The spirituality of Pius XI was, it could be said, influenced by that of Charles Borromeo, whom he studied so deeply, and by the ideal of the Oblates of St. Charles: to be at the archbishop's disposal for any task that would serve the diocese. The pope's painstaking research had engrained in him a spirit of precision and encouraged him to exercise his lawyer's care for scrupulous definition and legislation.

When Benedict XV gave him the cardinal's hat, he in fact was honoring him as a man of diplomacy. Pius XI left behind him a considerable body of scientific work in the domain of scholarship and history. His major work is still the *Acta ecclesiae mediolanensis ab ejus initiis usque ad nostram aetatem*, three volumes of which were published between 1890 and 1897. He has to his credit an impressive list of meticulous articles not only concerning manuscripts and points of history, but also dealing with a whole range of subjects (such as his contribution to the *Geologia d'Italia* for the volume by G. Mercalli, *Vulcani e fenomeni vulcanici*, Milan, 1883). A painstaking scholar and an adventurous mountaineer, Pius XI was also a man of character. Yet it would be a mistake to think of him as a monolithic personality, for many aspects of his pontificate elude analysis. He was indeed a diplomat, one who to the fullest extent possible championed concord and conciliation. He demonstrated this as he blessed the crowd from the exterior loggia of St. Peter's on the day of his election, while at the same time giving out an explanation of the gesture. A partisan of agreement, the pope became uncompromising when he believed the rights of the Church or fundamental values were being called into question. In this way, he could give, at one and the same time, an impression of cold inflexibility and of openness, could be both the supreme pontiff and the "old father." The Church of Rome had to accustom itself to the first Milanese pope since the late 16th century.

The Chronology and Functioning of a Pontificate. The pontificate lasted seventeen years, and any analysis must take its duration into account. The activity of Pius XI has a fairly precise chronology, being articulated around a few nodal points, imposed on the pope but often resulting from his own actions. The 1920s, the period of Cardinal Gasparri's SECRETARIAT OF STATE, constitute a long phase in which the pontificate was getting under way. Continuing from the preceding pontificate and the First World War, this phase seems dominated by Italian affairs and by a policy aimed at giving the Church a place in the Europe of Versailles. Gasparri, a rigorous jurist and loyal executor, a man of dossiers, was placed in charge of these affairs, and his exceptional length of service at the Secretariat probably indicates his abilities. This period, with its far-reaching acts that shed light on the whole spirit of the pontificate, came to a definite caesura in 1929–30, with the solution of the Roman question in February 1929. The early 1930s, until 1936, were mainly pastoral in tone, starting from the creation of the Vatican City State, which gradually took shape. These years saw great documents on education, marriage, youth, social questions, statism, and the priesthood, which provide a substantial body of teaching, while the holy year of the Redemption (1933–4) indicates the extent to which the pontificate was rooted in Christology. The appointment of Cardinal Pacelli as secretary of state in January 1930 marked the caesura between the two periods. The pope was placing his trust in his secretary of state, an accomplished diplomat, and wanted him to be made known to public opinion as having had highly significant legations entrusted to him. The last part of the pontificate is clearly marked by the personal aura of Pius XI, magnified by his illness of 1936–7 determined to speak the essential in his resounding encyclicals of 1937. A patriarchal figure, the pope was now more than ever the "unquestionable pilot" of Catholics. This "white old man of the Vatican" was an important figure on the stage of the time, firm and authoritative, often prophetic. His relations with Cardinal Pacelli were more confidential than ever, Pius XI seeing in him his likely successor.

The great institutional innovations of the pontificate had to do with the creation of Vatican City. The Curia experienced no major upheaval. On the other hand, the promotions to the cardinalate, regarded by the pope as having an essential importance, underwent a change of rhythm at the end of the 1920s. The figures elevated to the cardinalate by the supreme pontiff were emblematic. Certain appointments were designed to provide him with veritable spokesmen in important countries (Schuster in Italy, Verdier in France, Villeneuve in Canada). Others rewarded the abilities or initiatives of prelates: Liénart was thanked for his social action, Mercati and Tisserant for their intellectual contributions, as was Baudrillart. The pope held major consistories, for example that of 16 December 1935, which profoundly changed the Sacred College. Although it was not truly international, by 1939 the college of cardinals included twenty-seven "foreigners" out of sixty-two members. At the Curia, Pius XI relied on tried-and-true personalities such as Montini and Ottaviani (Secretariat of State). In the case of Catholic Action, the trusted man was Pizzardo, whom he made a cardinal in 1937.

Outside Rome, too, in the late 1920s the pope put into practice his own episcopal policy. The appointments to the major dioceses are the best reflection of the pope's personal intention, but they often coincided with nominations to the cardinalate. The pontifical strategy varied according to the countries involved (in Italy, the pope is the natural head of an episcopate that is not constituted as a body, whereas elsewhere he maintains episcopal conferences or assemblies). Everywhere, under Pius XI, appointments were made that affected the Church's long-term future: this was the case for France and for the United States. A few episcopates showed a certain distrust of Rome (as apparently the Spanish episcopate did after 1936). At all events, Pius XI insisted often on the pastoral role proper to bishops and on the specific charac-

ter of their authority. His choices were frequently made in the interest of disseminating the fundamental message that was the supporting skeleton, the ossature, of his pontificate.

Preaching the Kingdom. In his inaugural encyclical, *Ubi arcano Dei* (23 December 1922), completed on 11 December 1925 by the encyclical *Quas primas* instituting the feast of Christ the King, Pius XI outlined a program he had long meditated. He wanted to establish "Christ's peace in Christ's kingdom" by setting up this kingdom in a contemporary world that was hostile to Christ in the political, economic, and social spheres. This, in a nutshell, was the constant preaching of the Ratti pope. It was of course elaborated and subjected to a variety of interpretations. Some commentators have seen in it the desire to rebuild a theocratic order, especially in the Iberian Peninsula. Some readers of our own day have tended to believe that hidden behind the program was a conscious desire to abolish a modernity that was dragging the human race down to barbarism. Pius XI's message, they believe, proceeded from an antiliberal theology that attempted to base the social on the religious, thereby challenging the fundamental objective of the French Revolution, the Rights of Man. The emotional messages of the last years of the pontificate, they say, can be seen as a veritable transformation of this pope as he faced the excesses of the totalitarian regimes. The dryness of the Thomistic and scholastic statements yielded, finally, to a certain biblical inspiration. And yet the early texts are in harmony with the rest, even as they provide a supporting framework for what unfolded later. The pope's programmatic documents offered a basic set of guidelines, which was supplemented by other documents and refined by specific teachings on ways of allowing the kingdom of Christ to enter the lives of individuals, families, and nations. The goal could seem old-fashioned, yet over the years the theoretical and practical refinements show an evolution in this conception of the Kingdom.

He defended the rights of the Church and the person without flagging. Having abandoned his plan for an ecumenical council, Pius XI presented less a universal and definitive statement than a general path to be followed, a method to be adapted to countries and circumstances. He had to advocate the return of Christ's kingdom to societies such as they were. Such is the key of a pontificate which, starting with a general orientation that was often complemented, chose to act by various methods. The encyclical *Miserentissimus Redemptor* (8 May 1928) shed light on this somewhat dry theological message. With the veneration of the Sacred Heart, Pius XI stressed the notion of atonement and the efficacy of prayer. In its context, the message was certainly a message of reconquest, but it was above all an urgent plea for conversion of heart to the Redeemer of the world. The pope's inaugural messages were indeed the ossature of a preaching that had to issue forth in an action illuminated by the encyclicals, the interior supporting structure of a teaching intended to "cast the light of doctrine on the most serious problems tormenting modern society" (Fr. Gemelli).

An Ecclesial Armature. The establishment of Christ's kingdom rested first of all on a solid Church, the base of all action, founded on the ministry of Peter, the "chair of truth." The pontificate may, in certain areas, have adopted a closed, even retrograde attitude, and the pope did not compromise in anything touching on ecclesial authority. Certain attitudes or statements seemed to freeze the Church. Accordingly, in the area of biblical scholarship, Pius XI seemed to disappoint the expectations. "The Holy Father has no desire to concern himself particularly with the biblical question" (Fr. Lagrange). The Ratti pope called a halt to the ecumenical movement, which he had encouraged until then, in the encyclical *Mortalium animos* (6 January 1928). In condemning the "pan-Christians," the pope was advocating the return to the Church of Rome of dissident Christians. True, he still took a lively interest in the Eastern Churches, but above all he favored the paths of unionism. The pope's doctrinal rigidity was affirmed also in the encyclical *Casti connubii* (31 December 1930), a virtual charter of Christian marriage, establishing a strict practice in conjugal relations. It is true that in both cases Pius XI felt the Church was being threatened by certain declarations made in Stockholm and by attitudes in the United States that he considered laxist. Catholic identity was reaffirmed by the celebration of the centenaries of leading saints, to whom he devoted some encyclicals: Thomas Aquinas and Francis de Sales in 1923, Francis of Assisi in 1926, Augustine in 1930. The pope produced a veritable treatise on holiness. The four new Doctors given by Pius XI to the Church—Peter Canisius, John of the Cross, Robert Bellarmine, and Albertus Magnus—each exemplified for him a teaching necessary to the Church of the 20th century. There were numerous canonizations during the pontificate.

Each of these deserves close study. All are interesting and instructive, from John Bosco to Joseph Benedict Cottolengo and Louise de Marillac in the field of education and charitable action, from Lucia Filippini to Madeleine Sophie Barat for the religious virtues, and from Jean de Brébeuf to Andrew Bobola for martyrdom (the blood shed for the Church was also celebrated by the beatification of the martyrs of various regions, notably those of September 1792 in Paris). Yet some names are highly symbolic of this teaching pontificate. The first canonization was that of Thérèse of Lisieux, the "star of the pontificate" of Pius XI, the "flower blooming in the enclosed garden of Carmel," the apostle of the way of spiritual childhood and courageous model of quotidian sanctity. The canonization of

Bernadette Soubirous affixed a seal to the mystery of Lourdes, and it also exalted humility and purity. One saint was presented as a model for the clergy: John Marie Vianney, the curé of Ars, the apostle of lowly hamlets. Pius XI designated Thérèse the patron saint of the missions and the curé of Ars the patron saint of parish priests. The chief apostle of the Church so taught was assuredly the priest. In the encyclical *Ad catholici sacerdotii* of 20 December 1935, Pius XI recalled the classic virtues of the priesthood. The priest, who holds the place of Christ, must mingle piety, chastity, knowledge, and action. The message of Pius XI in the ecclesial domain rested firmly on fidelity and on prayer as the basis of action. He frequently reminded all the faithful of the importance of the spiritual life. Two encyclicals were devoted to it: *Mens nostra*, of 20 December 1929, recommended the Exercises of St. Ignatius, and *Ingravescentibus malis*, of 29 September 1937, the rosary. It was out of a Church sure of herself and her traditions, rooted in Christological faith as was recalled in the encyclical *Lux veritatis* of 25 December 1931 on the council of Ephesus, that a Catholic action could be undertaken.

The Action of Catholics. Pius XI has often been called the "pope of Catholic Action." While he did not invent the movement, he did more than any other pope to popularize the term and to encourage all forms of apostolate that laid claim to it. Pius XI did not hesitate to define this organized apostolate of all Catholics: "the collaboration of the laity in the apostolate of the hierarchy."

The notion of apostolate was prominent in the thinking of the pope, who conceived of it in a profound and broad sense: "Whatever their age, whatever the social class to which they belong, all the faithful are called to collaborate in it, for all can work in the vineyard of the Lord" (exhortation to the Colombian episcopate, 14 February 1934). Still, no major encyclical was devoted to this grand design, so often invoked. Pius XI worked by small urgings and varied forms of encouragement, providing the necessary details at decisive moments: the letter to Cardinal Bertram (13 November 1928), the encyclical *Non abbiamo bisogno* (29 June 1931), and the encyclical *Firmissimam constantiamque* (28 March 1937) can be singled out from a host of declarations, speeches, and documents. Does the "apple of the eye" of this pontificate always take the same form? Certainly from 1928–29, if thought of in its overall conception. But it is clear that, in practice, Catholic Action underwent a translation in each country. The implementing of the general norms took on a different appearance according to attitudes and national necessities. In Italy, Catholic Action was animated by the clergy, the *assistente ecclesiastico* being an important figure in a movement that flooded the whole country: this "great family," organized and maintained by the pope, had to live with fascism, confronting it or indeed agreeing to cooperate with it, by emphasizing the spiritual. Its role, a highly variegated one, was appraised in a series of sectoral or regional studies. In Belgium, Cardjin's role, enhanced by the famous audience of March 1925, led to the development of homogeneous youth federations under the Association Catholique Jeunesse Belgique (ACJB). In France, "general" Catholic Action (long assimilated to the Fédération National Catholique [FNC]) coexisted with specialized groups. In the Iberian Peninsula, Pius XI expected much from Catholic Action in difficult national situations. Catholic Action was, then, a general framework for the action, privileged throughout the pontificate, of the Catholic laity. Through it, the pope became the reference point for a whole series of actions within national frameworks, all aiming, with their different sensibilities, at the rechristianizing of society.

Catholic apostolate was likewise undertaken outside Europe. The MISSIONS constituted another great theme of a pontificate devoted to evangelization. The apostolate concerned the clergy, but Pius XI did not exclude from it members of the laity eager to mobilize in support of missionary activity. Noting the worldwide character of the problems, in 1922 Pius launched a policy of centralization by transferring to Rome the work of the Propagation of the Faith (the operation was managed by Angelo Roncalli, later JOHN XXIII). Seeking to inform and motivate Catholics, he organized a highly educational Mission Exhibition in Rome in 1925. The great intention of the pontificate was to avoid national, and therefore nationalistic, monopolization of the missions. Pius XI indeed takes his place in line with the encyclical *Maximum illud* of Benedict XV, the orientations of which he intensified and drew out further in the encyclical *Rerum ecclesiae* (28 February 1926): he insists on the role of the bishops as apostles and calls for the formation of indigenous clergies and Churches. Missiology made great strides under Pius XI: the mobilization of the Christian West and the indigenization of the local Churches were the two main axes of his activity throughout the duration of his pontificate. The pope intended to highlight his missionary policy by means of the striking gesture made by the ordination of six Chinese bishops in Rome (28 October 1926), a gesture followed by a tour of these bishops through Europe. The impetus given by Pius XI is evident in both regions. China was a territory privileged by these initiatives (as demonstrated by Msgr. Costantini's initiative and the convening of a Chinese council in Shanghai in 1924). Many of the missionary works launched under Pius XI, as well as the impulses underlying them, would have important lasting effects after the Second World War.

Presence in the Contemporary World. Pius XI took the measure of what was unprecedented in the character of the contemporary world and attempted to establish a Christian presence in its midst. The influence of public opinion, his awareness of which grew keener over the course of his pontificate, led the pope to accord particular attention to this characteristic of the 20th century, the century of the masses. The pope tried to come to grips with this mysterious and multiform power by developing an interest in the "opinion-makers," beginning with the press. During the first part of his pontificate, the Ratti pope remained attached to a traditional type of teaching. The Catholic press must be "the school of civic virtues and of the faith." He was very attentive to the tone of newspapers that were, or were reputed to be, Catholic, as is demonstrated by the condemnation of *L'Action française*.

In the late 1920s (around 1927–8), and especially after the Lateran pacts of 1929, Pius XI encouraged a specifically Catholic press aimed at reaching broad strata of opinion. The organization of a World Exposition of the Press in Rome in 1935 revealed his preoccupation. At the center of the Church, *L'OSSERVATORE ROMANO*, edited by Count Dalla Torre, which had gradually become the only free newspaper in Italy, expressed the point of view of Pius XI but without being an official newspaper (the pope wanted to be linked to the paper only by means of his official acts; it should be noted, as Confalonieri reports, that his speeches were never reprinted and that the papal proposals were given in outline). In Italy, the pope encouraged the Catholic press to stay as free as possible despite the weight of fascist legislation: the support given to *L'Italia* and *L'Avvenire d'Italia* is highly significant. In France, after 1927, the newspaper *La Croix* was very close to the Holy See. Few newspapers, however, were labeled Catholic newspapers. A "press of Pius XI" expressing clearly the views of the pontificate (without perfect agreement with him, as is demonstrated by the withholding of certain issues) came into being in the late 1920s. During the 1930s, Pius XI became more and more interested in the vagaries of opinion properly so-called, and highly sensitive to the echoes of his own actions in the press, even the non-Catholic organs. The development of radio led him to contact Marconi in 1929 and to establish VATICAN RADIO, entrusted to Fr. Gianfranceschi. The pope delivered a memorable inaugural address in Latin on 12 February 1921, and was broadcast on Vatican Radio several other times, especially on the occasion of overseas eucharistic congresses. The cinema inspired the encyclical *Vigilanti cura* (29 June 1936), addressed to the bishops of the United States. The pope saw the cinema as having a triple status, as art, industry, and entertainment. He demonstrated that the cinema, by over-entertaining, could encourage evil: accordingly, films should be rated under the supervision of committees. The document has a tone that is above all defensive, and is not the great charter of the Catholic cinema that might have been expected. It signals a beginning awareness of modernity, but also the limitations of the pope's analyses in this specific area. Yet the pope did manifest his concern to have a presence in contemporary culture. This concern was clearest in the area of education. He recalled the great principles that ought to inform the Christian education of youth in the encyclical *Divini illius Magistri* (31 December 1929). The part that must be played by family and Church in education, the rights that must be claimed by these two actors against the role claimed by the state, are clearly defined. Pius XI, with his experience of Italian fascism, warned against an education that was totally controlled. His concern with education emerged also in the measures he took in the area of ecclesiastical studies. He established a precise framework for the course of studies in the seminaries and, in the apostolic constitution *Deus scientiarum Dominus* (24 May 1931), carefully determined the organization of higher ecclesiastical studies as well as of the conferring of degrees. The founding of the Pontifical Academy of Sciences, by the *motu proprio In multis solaciis* (28 October 1936), gives a clear picture of Pius XI's thinking with respect to a discipline so characteristic of the contemporary world. The pope, who had always shown a lively interest in the sciences, wanted to create a virtual scientific Senate, which would concern itself with pure, objective scientific knowledge. He spoke of the alliance of two magisteriums, that of the faith and that of science. He appointed non-Catholic and, particularly, Jewish scholars to that prestigious institution, the direction of which was entrusted to Fr. Gemelli.

One of the great problems of the period between the world wars was that of the economy and social relations. Here Pius XI took up a position directly in line with *Rerum novarum*, by actualizing certain of its teachings and presenting them in greater detail. In 1929, he intervened indirectly in favor of the Christian workers' unions in the north of France that were opposed to Catholic patronage. On 15 May 1931, the encyclical *Quadragesimo anno*, published on the anniversary of *Rerum novarum*, aimed to lay the foundations of a new social order. The document is uneven (it was drafted by several hands, Frs. Nell-Breuning, Muller, and Desbuquois) and often laborious, but rich in long-term thinking. The new Christian order must be based on an organization of a professional kind and reconcile order and freedom. Resolutely consecrated to a world in the midst of crisis, and justifying the engagement of Christians in economic and social affairs, the document, despite the vagueness of certain passages having to do with practical application, was designed to stimulate thinking about society and give rise to fundamental elements such as the principle of subsidiarity.

The Concert of Nations and Conciliation. Pius XI was acutely aware of the dysfunctionings of the contemporary world. He perceived them from the beginning of his pontificate and set them forth with sorrow, on 2 October 1931, in the encyclical *Nova impendet*, on the economic crisis and the arms race. He assigned the Holy See a place in the concert of nations: the sovereign papacy must contribute to the organization of peace (Yves de La Brière). The pope hoped for an international order guaranteeing that peace, a major axis of his pontificate. The Holy See, which did not take part in the League of Nations but was relieved of its ambiguous status in 1929, acted consistently in this direction. Pius XI was a pope of conciliation, in the international order first and foremost. The Holy See was an actor whose diplomatic activity increased from 1922 to 1939. True, the margin for maneuver was narrow. From a practical point of view, its intervention in the Genoa conference (1922) had little effect. In the Abyssinian affair, while Pius XI strove to support the Negus by diplomatic means, his speech to the Catholic nurses was interpreted in a variety of ways. The moderation of his speech *La vostra presenza* (14 September 1936) on the situation in Spain was soon contradicted by the attitudes of the Spanish episcopate in 1937. Despite these difficulties, Pius XI never stopped preaching peace and presenting himself as a defender of cooperation. The image of the pope was vastly changed from that of Benedict XV. People expected to hear him speak out on important happenings, and Edouard Herriot declared that he had been impressed by the consistorial allocution of 24 December 1930. Here, the pope spoke of the peace of Christ as different from "sentimental pacifism," contrasted patriotism and nationalism, and endorsed defensive precautions as indispensable to the maintenance of peace. The pontificate integrated into its reflection notions of the common good and international social justice, and constituted an important step in the elaboration of a doctrine on war. The application of these theories can be seen in Pius XI's policy regarding Germany: the pope voiced his reservations on the occupation of the Ruhr in 1923, welcomed the Lucarno accords in 1925, but later expressed his anxiety in the face of Hitler's maneuvers. His emotional appeal of 29 September 1938, on the eve of the Munich agreement, called for peace, but a peace founded on justice and charity.

The term "conciliation" was made official in order to define the LATERAN PACTS in 1929. It could be applied to the whole concordatory policy of Pius XI. A preferred expression for the relations among states, this policy was founded on grand principles and a certain pragmatism. The aim was above all to preserve the freedom of the Church and her apostolate, the rights of the family, and those of the human person. The best guarantee of the rights of the person being the Church, it seems clear that the ideal of Pius XI was the Catholic state (which he believed could be discerned in Dollfuss's Austria). Without any truly Catholic states, the pope had to rely on the virtues of the contract, and above all of the concordat. In this connection some have spoken of the Ratti pope's "concordatory mania." All the concordats insisted on the freedom of the Church, whatever the country concerned. This was the case with the "new" nations of central and eastern Europe (the Baltic states, Poland, Czechoslovakia, and Romania), which drew from the concordats a recognition of their identity, and formed a party in most of the agreements of the 1920s. The Holy See pursued this type of agreement, either general or partial, with Ecuador, Haiti, and Portugal. Pius XI may have thought that this concordatory policy guaranteed the rights of the Church and of the human person even if enacted with regimes of a totalitarian ideology, founded on the all-powerfulness of the state. The relations with fascist Italy were developed within the framework of this kind of thinking, and they have stirred up lively criticism from one segment of Italian historiography. Here, Pius XI, with the active help of Gasparri, wanted to resolve the gnawing Roman question and confer an international status on the sovereign papacy. But he also wanted to obtain guarantees for the Italian Church, and in particular for Catholic Action.

Negotiations with the government of Mussolini—who wanted to be the man who crowned the achievement of the Risorgimento—began in 1926. The way having been prepared by the elimination of the Italian Popular Party (PPI) and the exile of Luigi Sturzo; the pope failed to support to the Catholic party, which had become one of the fascists' favorite targets. The Lateran pacts were signed on 11 February 1929 and included a treaty instituting Vatican City and a concordat declaring Catholicism the state religion and granting the Church full guarantees for her freedom and apostolate. Pius even justified the treaty by the concordat. While the treaty worked fairly well, the concordat very soon showed its limitations. The status of Catholic youth and that of Catholic Action caused a violent crisis in 1931, pitting against each other two determined partners. This crisis of Catholic Action, well orchestrated by the fascist press, led to the encyclical *Non abbiamo bisogno* (29 June 1931), in which Pius XI strongly denounced idolatry of the state. After a compromise agreement (September 1931), the situation became even more delicate for the Holy See. How to preserve the Church from a multiform *consenso* and the risk of collusion with the regime? The pope was relying on Catholic Action, but the organization apparently failed to influence Catholic regional life, involving only one section of the clergy. Many facts point to an unmistakable collusion. Nevertheless, Pius XI was able to draw back on the brink of the unacceptable. The role of *L'Osservatore romano* can hardly be forgotten. Nor can the role of the FUCI, the Italian Catholic university federation, or of the *Movimento laureati*, whose clear-headed and courageous action took place under fascism, benefiting in a certain way from the the papal policy. It is true that, up to the end, the pope clung to this concordatory policy. Even when he de-

nounced the fascist legislation forbidding mixed marriages between Jews and "Aryans," he spoke of a "wound" (*vulnus*) to the concordat. Without altering his conception of the concordat and of the entente with fascism, Pius XI was able to stand up to the totalitarian state, and his voice was often the only one raised within a muzzled Italy.

In Germany, the concordatory policy reached its limits even more rapidly. Pius XI was familiar with German culture and the specific problems that the nation of the *Kulturkampf* posed for the Catholic minority. Also, because the constitution of the Weimar Republic allowed it, Pius XI entered into negotiations (led by the nuncio Pacelli) with a view to concordatory agreements with Catholic Bavaria. The Bavarian concordat (29 March 1924), followed later by a similar agreement with the Land of Baden (12 December 1932), was one of the concordats most favorable to the Church, particularly with regard to her freedom and teaching. Between these two agreements, an extremely important concordat was reached with Prussia, a state without a Catholic majority, on 24 June 1929. This accord, also negotiated by Msgr. Pacelli, was certainly less favorable to the Church, but it recognized the full right of worship as well as the Church's legal status. The concordat therefore seemed the right instrument for lessening the difficulties with Germany.

The rise to power of Hitler and national socialism, a movement the ideology of which had aroused anxiety and wariness among the German episcopate, gave Germany a chancellor armed with a totalitarian program. The terms of the question had been profoundly changed. Why, in the circumstances, the pope accepted the signing of a concordat, on 20 July 1933, with the whole German Reich, when he had so recently met with disillusionment in Italy, remains a puzzle. Perhaps influences on the German side (that of the Catholic von Papen) as well as Cardinal Pacelli's excellent knowledge of Germany—he who had been the principal negotiator—led the pope to accept an agreement that was both unexpected and unhoped for. Although the Centrist party disappeared, the Church won certain guarantees: recognition throughout the Reich and protection for youth associations and initiatives. Disturbed by the rise of Bolshevism in the Soviet Union, Pius XI probably believed he could tame the new German regime. Moreover, for the first time, an agreement had been signed with the whole of Germany. The temptation to agree to it had been strong, especially given Pius XI's confidence in contractual politics. Very soon, the pope and Cardinal Pacelli were able to measure the extent of their disappointment and their illusions. In October 1933, there began a lengthy deterioration that struck at the rights of the Church and, more seriously, at the principles of Christianity and the dignity of the human person. With France, no concordat was signed (with the exception of partial accords in 1926 and despite insistent rumors in 1929), and yet there was a growing harmony with the Republic, to the point that a "second Ralliement" was spoken of. The resumption of diplomatic relations was valuable (it was threatened only in 1924–5) and permitted the regime of the Separation of Church and state to function smoothly. As soon as he was elected, Pius XI applied the Briand-Ceretti agreements on episcopal appointments that had been concluded under Benedict XV, and on 28 January 1924, he authorized diocesan associations, in the encyclical *Maximam gravissimamque*, thus ending the delicate question regarding worship. The papal condemnation of Action Française in 1926 was motivated on important ideological ground: excessive nationalism, and paganism. Its effect was to redistribute the Catholic forces in France and consolidate the rapprochement with those leading the country. The pope certainly did not publish the great encyclical on nationalism that was expected, and some have preferred to interpret this development in a purely French context. In reality, the penetration of Catholic circles by Action Française counted for a great deal in an important action that had, certainly, mainly French consequences. Pius XI dealt a harsh blow to one of the principal adversaries of the democratic regime. A long period of entente followed, culminating in the visits of Cardinal Pacelli to France, in 1935 (Lourdes) and 1937 (Lisieux). Representatives of substance (Maglione and Charles-Roux) sustained courteous diplomatic relations. True, Pius XI was still distrustful of the governments of the Popular Front, and his Spanish policy was badly thought of by the French leaders. The pope did not approve of all the French Catholic attempts at openness (as is shown by the 1937 crisis of the newspaper *Sept*) and remained conservative (a subtle balance reigned among the various tendencies of French Catholicism). The fact remains that, without a concordat, a genuine policy of conciliation and entente could have ended there. The proof is to be found in the rousing homage given Pius XI on his death by the French Parliament. The condemnation of Action Française played a decisive role in consolidating the papal positions with respect to certain ideas; the Republic had no intention of imposing itself to the extent of keeping the Church under its thumb. The elements were in place for an agreement that was unique to the national circumstances.

Warnings and Condemnations. From being a pope of conciliation, Pius XI became a pope of rejection, even of anathema, when certain fundamental principles were called into question. The terms used in the denunciation of Action Française on 20 December 1926 showed the intensity of the pope's views. It was wrong to call into question the identity and independence of Catholicism. For Pius XI, warmongering, excessive nationalism, the all-powerfulness of the state, atheism or paganism, and, soon, racism were overstepping the limits. The pope was constantly preoccupied with the challenge in Mexico. That country was practicing a violently anticlerical policy, even one of persecution, and exhibiting strong communist influence. Some harsh-toned papal documents were issued on the subject. Three encyclicals concerned Mexico: *Iniquis afflictisque* (18 November 1926), *Acerba animi* (29 September 1932), and *Firmissimam constantiamque* (28 March 1937). The pontiff severely condemned the excesses of the Mexican government. While admitting the legitimacy of the Mexican resistance to oppression, he advocated above all social justice and the action of Catholics as a possible remedy for the excesses of the Mexican regime. Firmness was accompanied here by prudence, since Mexico had seen an armed Catholic resistance rise up and then be harshly repressed. Here Pius XI confronted, indirectly, the Marxist communism of which he had a genuine phobia, since for him the all-powerfulness of the state and militant atheism were mixed in together. Observers like Charles-Roux noted in the pope a veritable obsession with communism, to which his mission to Poland and Eastern Europe no doubt had contributed. Yet the pope was nonetheless fascinated by Russia, a country with which he wanted to remain in contact (his keen interest in the Eastern Churches, symbolized by the encyclical *Rerum orientalium* of 8 September 1925, is assuredly one of the signs of this fascination). In 1922, the pope set in motion a mission of aid to Russia and sought to open relations with the Russians at the Genoa conference. In 1924, he secured the liberation of Cieplak. When the regime hardened, the pope, in 1926, dispatched d'Herbigny to Russia to reconstitute a hierarchy. But in 1927, any likelihood of relations between Rome and Moscow collapsed when the Orthodox patriarch Sergius rallied to the side of the regime, and a new persecution was launched: the apostolic administrators who had been appointed were eliminated. Whatever Pius XI's intentions—the conversion of the Orthodox, a *modus vivendi* with Russia— even his mild policy of entente failed. His hopes for Russia underwent a major change in 1930: the pope launched a crusade of prayer and denounced the excesses of the regime in a chirograph of 2 February 1930 to Cardinal Pompilj. This solemn document, which prefigures *Divini Redemptoris*, brought the pontificate to an openly antibolshevik phase.

Bolshevism became Pius XI's "nightmare" and the Internationale his "bête noire" (Charles-Roux). Neveu, the successor to Msgr. d'Herbigny, at first stigmatized the term "crusade" but soon moved in the same direction. To many, the Vatican came to appear a rampart against Bolshevism. Whether this ideological rejection—which was based, moreover, on the precarious situation of the Church in Russia—impelled Pius XI to set out on unwelcome paths such as the signing of the German concordat remains a question. In any event, the encyclical *Divini Redemptoris* (19 March 1937) was the expression and the climax of a long reflection on communism. It is one of the three encyclicals published by the pope amid fanfare after his illness in March 1937. The document indeed condemns communist ideology. The pope reproaches atheistic communism as being "intrinsically perverse," for giving its followers an "idea of false redemption," for stripping "man of his liberty, the spiritual principle of moral conduct." Although the condemnation of doctrine takes up relatively little space in the encyclical, the terms used are strong. It is an ideology spreading throughout the whole world that the pope foresees here. The situation of Russia, in the thick of the Stalinist terror, certainly played a major role in the elaboration of the encyclical. After some attempts at coexistence, the pope took cognizance of a situation of total rupture. Nonetheless, for him, Russia remained above all "a terrain apt for experimenting with a theory that has been elaborated for dozens of years." The other terrains were Mexico (to which several documents were addressed) and Spain. The attitude of Pius XI during the Spanish civil war was conditioned by the "communist fury," in which he saw the source of the murders of bishops and priests. Personally, the pope adopted a somewhat reserved position vis-à-vis the Spanish war (his speech of 4 September 1936, *La vostra presenza*, condemned communism but did not call for a crusade). He had misgivings regarding the pastoral leadership of the Spanish bishops, who had preached such a crusade since July 1937. Pius XI had probably tried to negotiate with the Spanish Republic, even as he condemned the ideas inspiring it, for he mistrusted a Francoism linked to Germany. Franco's promises to defend Catholic principles tipped the balance in his favor in June 1938, and the pope—to the disadvantage of most of the Spanish bishops—removed the obstacles to the official recognition of the Burgos regime, obstacles that he had personally set in place. The solemn denunciation of communism marks one of the frustrations of the pontificate and well illustrates the disillusionment of Pius XI: all conciliation seemed to him out of the question.

With Hitler's Germany, all possibility of conciliation also seemed out of the question. Pius XI published, in German, the encyclical *Mit brennender Sorge*, dated 14 March 1937, which was read in all the churches of Germany on 21 March and published in Catholic newspapers the next day. The subtitle—"The Religious Situation in the German Empire"—did not, it is true, mention the national socialist ideology, but that party's principal ideas, over and above its practices, were certainly denounced: paganism and racism. The immediate reason for the publication of the document, the rough draft of which was prepared by Cardinal Faulhaber, the archbishop of Munich, was the collapse of the concordat. A large part of the text was in fact devoted to that concordat. But the pope firmly condemned racism, the abuse of religious terms by distortion of their meaning, and the belief in an impersonal God. He also reaffirmed the dignity of the human person: "Man, as a person, possesses rights which he holds from God and which must remain, vis-à-vis the community, safe from any assault that would tend to deny, abolish, or neglect them."

The almost simultaneous publication of these two encyclicals had great significance. Certain illusions could have been born out of discussions with these regimes or, worse, out of the hypothesis of a balancing of Bolshevism by Nazism. Having exhausted every possibility of amending the states, Pius XI firmly dismissed the two ideologies back to back, and denounced the unacceptable. It should be asked whether *Mit brennender Sorge*, devoted to Germany alone, contained a condemnation weaker than the condemnation of communism. The whole ending of the pontificate indicates that it did not. Whereas the declarations on communism became rare, the protests regarding Nazism and its offshoot, Italian racism, appeared in ever greater numbers. Furthermore, the efforts of Pius XI toward peace were intensified, and from 1936 the pope expressed his anxiety in the face of the Hitlerian expansion. Italy's alignment with Germany impelled him to leave Rome during Hitler's official visit on 8 May 1938. In Italy, the pope firmly denounced statism (while defending Catholic Action) and Italian racism in three speeches during the summer of 1938. On 6 September, before pilgrims representing Belgian radio, he spoke these definitive words: "Spiritually, we are all Semites." Four cardinals relayed this declaration against racism in explicit homilies. The pope, who was preparing to give a speech before the Italian bishops meeting in St. Peter's basilica, died on 10 February after a pontificate of seventeen years that was regarded as imposing by much of public opinion. Amid the universal emotion, people mourned the pope of peace, the pope of the human person. Despite the frequently criticized ambiguities, Pius XI had reaffirmed that religion could be a sustaining presence for the human race during the ominous years between the wars.

Marc Agostino

Bibliography

Acta apostolicae sedis, XIV–XXXI.

Actes de S.S. Pie XI, 17 vol., Paris, 1927–45.

Agostino, M. *Le Pape Pie XI et l'opinion (1922–1939)*, Rome, 1991.

Aubert, R. "Pie XI." *Catholicisme*, XI, Paris, 1988.

Bertetto, D. *Discorsi di Pio XI*, 3 vol., Turin, 1960–1.

Beyens B. *Quatre ans à Rome (1921–1926)*, Paris, 1934.

Chardavoine, E., ed. Le dépouillement de la presse, de certains annnuaires comme: *Annuaire pontifical catholique*, 15 vols., 1922–39.

Charles-Roux, F. *Huit ans au Vatican*, Paris, 1947.

Confalonieri, C. *Pio XI visto da vicino*, Turin, 1957.

Conzemius, V. "Le concordat du 20 juillet 1933 entre le Saint-Siège et l'Allemagne, esquisse d'un bilan de la recherche historique" *AHP*, 15, 1977.

Coutrot A. *Un courant de la pensée catholique, l'hebdomadaire Sept.* Paris, 1961.

Fontenelle, R. *Pie XI*, Paris, 1939.

Fouilloux, E. *Les Catholiques et l'unité chrétienne du XIXe au XXe siècle*, Paris, 1982.

Galbiati, G. *Papa Pio XI*, Milan, 1939. *Pio XI nel trentesimo della morte (1939–1969)*.

Gallarati-Scotti, T. *Interpretazioni e memorie*, Milan, 1961.

Giblin, M. "Quadragesimo Anno," *The New Dictionary of Catholic Social Thought*, J. A. Dwyer, ed., Collegeville, Minn., 1994, 802–13.

Hennesey, J. "Pius XI," *The New Dictionary of Catholic Social Thought*, J. A. Dwyer, ed., Collegeville, Minn., 1994, 739–41.

Jarlot, G. *Doctrine pontificale et Histoire*, II: *Pie XI. Doctrine et action (1922–1939)*, Rome, 1973.

Kent, P. C. "The Vatican and the Spanish Civil War," *European History Quarterly*, 16 (1986), pp. 441–64.

Kent, P. C. *The Pope and the Duce: The International Impact of the Lateran Agreements*, New York, 1981.

La Documentation catholique.

Maccarone, M. *Il nazionalo-socialismo e la Santa Sede*, Rome, 1947.

Margiotta-Brolio, F. *Italia e Santa Sede dalla Grande Guerra alla Conciliazione*, Bari, 1966.

Martini, A. *Studi sulla questione romana e la conciliazione*, Rome, 1963.

Novelli, A. *Pie XI*, Milan, 1922.

Passelecq, G., and Suchecky, B. *The Hidden Encyclical of Pius XI*, S. Randall, trans., New York, 1997.

Pecorari, L., ed. *Chiesa, Azione cattolica e fascismo nell'Italia settentrionale durante il pontificato di Pio XI (1922–1939)*, Milan, 1979.

Relations internationales, 27 (1961). "Les Églises Chrétiennes et la vie internationale au XXe siècle" (I).

Rémond, R. *Les Catholiques français dans les années trente*, Paris, 1979.

Rhodes, A. *The Vatican in the Age of the Dictators, 1992–1945*, London, 1973.

Rinoldi, A. "Pio XI," *Storia del movimento cattolico in Italia*, II, Casale Monferrato 1982.

Salvatorelli, L. *Pie XI e la sua eredita pontificale*, Turin, 1939.

Schmidlin, J. *Papstgeschichte der neuesten Zeit*, IV, Munich, 1939.

Scoppola, P. *La Chiesa e il fascismo. Documenti e interpretazione*, Bari, 1971.

Scritti alpinistici, Milan, 1932.

Scritti storici, Milan, 1932.

Wenger, A. *Rome et Moscou (1900–1950)*, Paris, 1987.

PIUS XII. *Eugenio Pacelli (b. Rome, 2 March 1876, d. Castel Gandolfo, 9 October 1958). Elected pope on 2 March 1939, crowned on 12 March. Buried in the Vatican Grottoes.*

A Roman Priest. With the election of Eugenio Pacelli, a Roman sat on the chair of St. Peter once again, after more than two hundred years. The fourteen popes since BENEDICT XIII, the last Roman pope, had all been Italians, over half of them originating in the PAPAL STATES. Born in Rome, Eugenio Pacelli belonged to a family closely linked to Vatican circles and the service of the Holy See. The youth grew up in Rome, which had become the capital of Italy. He studied in a public establishment, the Visconti high school. His family belonged to the Catholic world, the "other Rome." This community did not subscribe to the secular idea of a capital city destined to be the center of a new civilization, of science and secular thinking, in contrast to the obscurantism represented by the Catholic Church. This idea, which persisted among the dominant Italian clan, found support elsewhere. In 1881, in France, Renan was assigning to the new Rome the task of eliminating a system that ran counter to modern civilization: Catholicism.

The Pacelli thought very differently. The ending of temporal power had been a dramatic experience for them, as it had for most Catholics. The family had openly preserved its contacts with the Vatican. Filippo Pacelli, Eugenio's father, was a lawyer of the Roman ROTA and became a CONSISTORIAL ADVOCATE in 1896. Virginia Graziosi, his mother, came from a family known for its services to the Holy See, notably in the financial domain. One of Eugenio's cousins, Ernesto, played an important role in Vatican FINANCES, especially during the pontificate of LEO XIII: his work called for collaboration with both the Vatican and the civic government, when that liberal government was publicly opposed to the Rome of the popes. The Pacelli were a family of the lesser NOBILITY, distinguished in particular by their service to the Holy See. Francesco Pacelli, one of Filippo's four children and Eugenio's brother, became a consistorial advocate like his father. It was Francesco Pacelli, in fact, who played a leading role in the talks leading to the signing of the LATERAN PACTS in 1929. These solved the Roman question and, by recognizing the "sacred character" of the *urbs*, seemed destined to put an end to the opposition between the "two Romes." During this period, Eugenio Pacelli exercised great responsibility in the Vatican administration.

He had been ordained priest on 2 April 1899 by the vicar of Rome, Msgr. Cassetta, a friend of the family, in the presence of Cardinal Vincenzo Vannutelli and a few important members of the Catholic community of Rome such as Count Santucci. He prepared for his ordination by making a retreat with the Sulpicians, whom he had come to know through Msgr. Duchesne. He received his training at the Gregorian University (1894–99) as a student of the Capranica College in Rome. Then he completed his theological studies at the S. Apollinare Institute, where he obtained his license in theology and *in utroque jure* in 1902. He also took a year's courses, in 1895, at the faculty of letters and philosophy of the state university of Rome, La Sapienza. Here the young cleric showed a noticeable interest in cultural matters. He attended Msgr. Duchesne's Sunday conferences and the courses of the German historian Beloch. But his special study was the law, which resulted in his being appointed secretary of the Commission for the Codification of Canon Law by Cardinal Gasparri in 1904. He also published a study entitled "The Personality and Territoriality of Laws, Especially in Canon Law."

In the Service of the Holy See. In 1901, Cardinal Vannutelli recommended him to Msgr. Cavagnis, secretary of the Congregation for Extraordinary Ecclesiastical Affairs. This DICASTERY, which was responsible for the international relations of the Holy See, was headed by the then secretary of state, Cardinal Rampolla del Tindaro. Although he was still a student, Eugenio Pacelli had entered this congregation as an "apprentice," and there became MINUTANTE three years later. Under the pontificate of PIUS X, Cardinal Merry del Val had succeeded Cardinal Rampolla as secretary of state. Msgr. Gasparri, who was also involved in the codification of canon law, remained secretary of Extraordinary Ecclesiastical Affairs until 1907. From 1906, the undersecretary of this congregation was Msgr. Genigni, a figure at the center of the integrist and antimodernist organization.

During this period, young Pacelli, employed in Extraordinary Ecclesiastical Affairs, received a variety of offers to teach canon law, both at the Apollinare in Rome and at the Catholic University in Washington. But his superiors retained him at the Vatican. He taught public law at the Academy for Noble Ecclesiastics, the training center for Vatican diplomats. At twenty-eight, he was already secret CHAMBERLAIN, and at twenty-nine, domestic prelate. In 1911, he took Msgr. Benigni's place as undersecretary of Extraordinary Ecclesiastical Affairs, and thus became one of the leading figures of Vatican diplomacy. In 1912, Pius X appointed him secretary-adjunct and, in 1914, secretary of that congregation.

When BENEDICT XV was elected as pope (he had been substitute of the Secretariat of State until 1907, when he was named archbishop of Bologna), Msgr. Pacelli kept his post with the new secretary of state, Cardinal Gasparri. During the modernist crisis, his position had not been one of intransigence. He emerged from this period as the detached ecclesiastic, the servant of the Holy See, essentially aloof from the conflicts that were agitating Vatican milieus. His juridical background and diplomatic

gifts suited him admirably for service in the international relations of the Holy See.

Young Pacelli's experience was almost exclusively confined to Rome and the Vatican. His first trip abroad was to Paris, in 1896, with Lais, an Oratorian. In 1904, he returned to the French capital and also visited Belgium. In 1911, he went on his first official mission, as a member of the Vatican delegation to the coronation of George V, headed by Cardinal Granito Pignatelli di Belmonte. In Rome, Pacelli engaged in some pastoral activity, whatever was compatible with his employment at the Vatican. He attended the *Chiesa nuova* of the Oratorians, where he had celebrated his first mass, and served as chaplain of various women's religious institutions, among them the Sisters of the Assumption, who had been in Rome since 1888.

As secretary of Extraordinary Ecclesiastical Affairs, Msgr. Pacelli worked with Benedict XV on determining the position of the Holy See during the First WORLD WAR. His principal task was to concern himself with international relations. The Vatican's impartiality in the 1914–18 conflict prompted a series of interventions to reestablish relations between the belligerents and prevent any increase in the number of countries involved in the fighting. It was from this position that Msgr. Pacelli attempted to prevent Italy's entry into the war. In 1915, on the pope's behalf, he went to Vienna to recommend to the Austro-Hungarian authorities a greater understanding with respect to the Italian government. The NUNCIO Scapinelli was received by emperor Franz-Joseph, but it was Msgr. Pacelli who directed the Vienna operation.

Nuncio. Working closely with Cardinal Gasparri, Msgr. Pacelli was one of Benedict XV's principal collaborators in the peace and mediation initiatives undertaken by the Holy See during the war. In 1917, the pope appointed him to the important nunciature of Munich, still vacant, which was the sole papal representation to the German Empire. He was also ordained bishop, titular of the archbishopric of Sardis. A month after his appointment, he traveled to Berlin, where he was received by Chancellor Bethmann-Hollweg and left the interview with a positive impression concerning the possibilities for peace. But in July 1917 the formation of the Michaelis government, much closer to the military, marked a change of policy.

In the absence of a German reply, the Holy See sent all the belligerents the note of 1 August 1917. As nuncio, Pacelli got in touch with the German and Bavarian political milieus urging them to give a favorable reception to the pope's gesture, but the German attitude was on the whole disappointing. The nuncio experienced at first hand the turbulence of the Reich, the Munich revolution, and the birth of the Weimar Republic. He had formed close ties with the German episcopate and the Catholic community. During the twelve years of his nunciature, he visited German dioceses and attended the principal Catholic assemblages, among them the annual *Katholikentag*, at which he gave the closing address.

The nuncio's attitudes, in the certain respects different from that of the German episcopate, was, however, essentially favorable to the Catholic political experiment represented by the Center party. Msgr. Pacelli's concern was first and foremost the normalization of relations between the state and the Catholic Church in Germany. In 1920, the Holy See entered into diplomatic relations with Germany, impossible up to that time owing to Prussian hostility and the hostility of the imperial family. It was for that reason that Msgr. Pacelli, who had labored to achieve this outcome, was accredited as nuncio to Berlin. Nevertheless, he retained the Munich nunciature until the ratification of the concordat with Bavaria in 1925. In 1929, he concluded the concordat with Prussia, meanwhile continuing, after he had left Germany, to oversee the discussions with the Land of Baden and the German government. (The concordat with Baden was signed in 1932 and that with the Reich the following year.)

Berlin was a diplomatic observation post of the first rank both during the war and immediately after it. Here, Msgr. Pacelli had the opportunity to follow, in part, the contacts between the Holy See and the Soviet Union. In 1924, when Tchitcherine, who was responsible for Soviet international relations, visited Berlin, he was able to have several talks with him, which were later continued with Krestinsky. Certain Soviet proposals for the organization of Catholicism in the USSR, later judged unsatisfactory, were transmitted through the intermediary of the Berlin nunciature. At the end of his mission, Msgr. Pacelli was able to use his diplomatic post to note the crisis in the diplomatic dialogue between the Vatican and the USSR. During this period, in 1926, in the very offices of the Berlin nunciature and on PIUS XI's orders, he ordained as bishop the Jesuit d'Herbigny, whom the pope had made responsible for developing a clandestine Church in the Soviet Union. By the later 1920s, Msgr. Pacelli had become one of the most closely watched Vatican diplomats of his generation, like Marchetti Selvaggini, Cerretti, Maglione, Tedeschini, and others.

Secretary of State. His promotion to the cardinalate in 1929 came as no surprise. On the other hand, his nomination as secretary of state to succeed the mighty Cardinal Gasparri, with whom he had worked closely since the beginning of the century, caused a certain stupefaction. Pius XI, who was known to favor keeping a strong hand, probably wanted a collaborator less prone to compromise than old Cardinal Gasparri. Moreover, Cardinal Pacelli was one of the best prepared members of the college of cardinals: he was perfectly familiar with the administrative machinery of the Vatican and had wide international experience. He was a figure regarded as above the various parties, especially the group of cardinals who remained most closely linked to the legacy of the pontificate of Pius X.

His years of service as secretary of state were characterized by a profound identification with the directives of the pope, whose principal collaborator he was. Pius XI directed the Vatican administration in a personal, direct manner, and Cardinal Pacelli very soon became his scrupulous right-hand man, yet, chiefly because of the difference of generation, one who had more detachment from the pontiff than Cardinal Gasparri. It is difficult to reconstruct the role of this primary collaborator of the pope. The diplomats accredited to the Holy See, who were in continual contact with the secretary of state, retained the impression of a person extremely open to dialogue. The French ambassador, Charles-Roux, spoke of his "eagerness to give satisfaction."

Cardinal Pacelli played an important role (as we know today) in the concordatory policy of Pius XI. In particular, he followed closely the developments in Germany and, above all, the talks leading up to the signing of the 1933 concordat, after the Nazis seized power. After the Second WORLD WAR had come to an end, Pius XII felt the need to explain the motivations that had impelled the Holy See to take that action: "It was not that the Church, for her part, allowed herself to be deceived by exaggerated hopes, or that the concluding of the concordat in some way implied approval of the doctrine and tendencies of national socialism . . . Nevertheless, it should be recognized that the concordat, in the years following, did procure some advantages or, at least, prevent greater evils." It seemed difficult to reject Germany's willingness to come to an agreement with the Catholic Church on bases that were very close to what the Church was requesting. Cardinal Pacelli, however, had perceived the totalitarian aspect of Nazism.

In fact, the role of the secretary of state's with regard to Nazi Germany was, marked by firmness. This was evident most particularly in March 1937, with the appearance of the encyclical *Mit brennender Sorge*, the original text of which, prepared by Cardinal Faulhaber, the archbishop of Munich, was given added severity by Cardinal Pacelli. In 1938, the secretary of state criticized the attitude of the Austrian episcopate, which favored the Anschluss. He asked Cardinal Innitzer, the archbishop of Vienna, to come to Rome and demanded of him a declaration correcting this position. Nor was Cardinal Pacelli blind to the weaknesses of German Catholicism with regard to Nazism. This knowledge served him well when, during the Second World War, he had to adopt a policy with regard to Germany. His contacts with the German-speaking world were always numerous. The personal collaborators of the secretary of state and, above all, the pope, were German Jesuits such as Leiber, Hürth, and Gundlach.

German diplomacy, for its part, regarded Cardinal Pacelli as pro-French. His two trips to France (to Lourdes in 1935 and Paris and Lisieux in 1937) helped reinforce that impression. But during the course of his mandate the secretary of state visited a variety of countries. In 1934, Pius XI sent him as legate to Buenos Aires, and in 1938, to Budapest, where he took part in the Eucharistic congress. He was given an official reception by the president of Argentina and by the regent Horthy as heads of state. In 1936, he made an important private visit to the United States in order to learn about the American situation and establish contacts with the Catholic bishops of that country. Shortly before he left for Italy, Cardinal Pacelli met President Roosevelt, who had just been reelected. During his American stay, the secretary of state was accompanied in particular by the future cardinal archbishop of New York, Msgr. Spellman.

Pius XII and the War. It is undeniable that by the end of the 1930s Eugenio Pacelli was the most noted member of the college of cardinals at a time when relations among the future papal electors were relatively smooth. Pius XI had on certain occasions seemed to express the wish to have Pacelli succeed him. In fact, on his death, on 2 March 1939, Cardinal Pacelli was elected pope on the third ballot at a conclave that lasted less than twenty-four hours. The resident Italian cardinals were perplexed, as they would have preferred to see their votes go to the archbishop of Florence, Elia Dalla Costa. In any event, the brevity of the conclave confirmed the rumor, which spread over the next few days, that Cardinal Pacelli had been elected unanimously.

Pius XII chose as his secretary of state the former nuncio to Paris, Cardinal Maglione. The decision appeared to be influenced by the need for a collaborator who had close ties with France. Cardinal Maglione was Pius XII's only secretary of state. At the cardinal's death, in 1944, the pope resolved not to appoint a successor. Cardinal Tardini explained that "behind this decision there may have been the fear that his shyness might make him too vulnerable to another influence." Throughout his pontificate, the pope managed the affairs of the Holy See in a very direct fashion, employing the Secretariat of State, which he himself headed, as a filter. In a certain sense, as some American diplomats observed, he was his own secretary of state. In his governmental action, he relied particularly heavily on the collaboration of Msgr. Tardini, for international affairs, and of Msgr. Montini, who headed the second section of the Secretariat of State until the end of 1954. "I don't want collaborators, I want executors," the pope had said in communicating his decision not to appoint a successor to Cardinal Maglione.

The pontificate of Pius XII began with the difficult years of the Second World War. After his election, the new pope had in-depth talks with the four German cardinals then in Rome, who foresaw a hardening of the Nazi regime and the beginnings of a determined action against the Church. The invasion of Czechoslovakia, on 15 March, convinced Vatican diplomacy that war was imminent. Over the following months, the Holy See established a series of contacts with the European powers for the purpose of averting war and attempting a final mediation after the Munich agreements. The Molotov-Ribbentrop pact made it clear that there was no way war could be averted. The action of the Vatican then concentrated on trying to keep Italy out of the conflict, by exerting pressure on Mussolini and on the Italian groups that favored peace. In late 1939, Pius XII returned the Italian king's visit, by going to the Quirinal. It was the first time a pontiff had returned to the former residence of the popes. But neither his action nor his gesture bore fruit.

On 24 August, the pope had launched an appeal, in the drafting of which Msgr. Montini had collaborated, in which he made the notable declaration, "Nothing is lost with peace. All is lost with war." The pontiff maintained this position throughout the conflict, even though Vatican diplomacy was extremely limited at the time. The war years were a period of severe isolation for the Holy See, which was subject to a host of pressures from the opposed parties. After Germany invaded Russia, the Axis powers strove to give the war moral legitimacy as an "anti-Bolshevik crusade." Meanwhile, the Vatican was receiving information about Nazi atrocities, for example from the Polish government-in-exile, which asked the Holy See to intervene. Yet throughout the conflict, the attitude of the Vatican was essentially one of impartiality with regard to the warring sides.

During the war, the Catholic Church had to provide a mediating space between the belligerents, one offering asylum and communication. In a memorandum written in reply to a request for intervention from the Polish bishops on the subject of the German atrocities, Msgr. Tardini described the spirit in which the Holy See approached the situation: "In the first place, it would not be appropriate that a public act on the part of the Holy See should condemn and protest against so many injustices. Not for any lack of *substance* [. . .] but practical reasons for abstaining seem to assert themselves . . ." A condemnation would have been exploited "for political ends" by one of the parties; the German government "would intensify the persecutions" and prevent the Holy See's "work of charity" as well as the contacts with the Polish episcopate.

The Holy See did all in its power not to appear to side with one of the warring parties and to maintain its position as a potential mediator. Moreover, it recognized the need for a sorting out within the Catholic Church in view of the different national situations. Pius XII declared: "We leave to pastors on the spot the task of assessing whether, and to what extent, the danger of reprisals and pressure, and, perhaps, other circumstances due to the length and psychological climate of the war, counsel restraint—despite reasons that might exist for intervention—in order to avoid greater evils. This is one of the motives for the limitations we impose on ourselves in our declarations." The pope appreciated the bishops' unyielding stance. He had litttle respect for the French episcopate, but was close to the bishop of Berlin, von Preysing. In the city of Rome, which had been under German occupation following the Italian armistice, the pope allowed ecclesiastical institutions to be opened largely as places of asylum for Jews and other victims of persecution, even if he did not publicly intervene against the persecutions. This was a significant choice of attitude on the pope's part during the conflict.

It was probably impossible for the Vatican to act as mediator for the whole duration of the war. That is why it can be said that Vatican diplomacy to a certain extent failed during the Second World War: despite a constant desire to remain open and in touch, its plan for mediation rapidly collapsed. Relations with Nazi Germany were difficult, those with Italy uncomfortable, and there was no contact with the USSR. With France, relations were maintained with Pétain's government and proved problematic with de Gaulle. The United States was the only country with which the Holy See had fairly close ties throughout the war. At the end of 1939, in spite of the absence of diplomatic relations, President Roosevelt had appointed a personal representative, Myron Taylor, to the Holy See. This contact was extremely valuable for the pope himself during the isolation of the conflict, and afterwards it became an important channel of consultation on future international organization.

The "silence of Pius XII," that is, his not more forcefully condemning the Holocaust and other Nazi atrocities, has been, especially since 1962, the most widely controversial aspect of his pontificate. In that year Rolf Hochhuth's play *Der Stellvertreter* (English "The DEPUTY," but more properly "The Vicar [of Christ]") was published. The work was soon translated into other languages and aroused bitter controversy over the conduct of Pius XII during the Second World War. The outcry led Pope PAUL VI in 1963 to open the pertinent sections of the Vatican Secret Archives to a team of four Jesuit historians, which resulted in the publication of eleven volumes of documents (1966–81) that the editors believed would exculpate Pius XII. The publication of these documents did not, however, settle the controversy, which has continued to resurface. As late as 1999, for instance, two works were published that assess the Pope in almost diametrically opposed ways—*Hitler's Pope*, written by a Catholic layman, John Cornwell, is severely critical of the pope, whereas *Pius XII and the Second World War* by Pierre Blet, a French Jesuit and member of the original research team, offers a positive assessment. That same

year Pope JOHN PAUL II appointed a new commission of three Catholic and three Jewish historians to reexamine the issue. It disbanded inconclusively in 2001.

Even if new information is turned up by scholars in the future, it will almost certainly not resolve the issue. This is because what is at stake is not so much the facts as the criteria by which Pius is to be judged, which are not the same for the critics and the defenders of the pope. The former often demand of him a heroically prophetic stance that takes little account of consequences or of the historical reality of his situation, whereas the latter sometimes seem in principle unwilling to admit any serious missteps.

The basic policy guiding the Vatican was that public denunciation would do more harm than good. The pope and his advisers felt that empirical evidence such as the intensified persecution that occurred in certain Nazi-dominated territories after formal protests had been lodged confirmed the soundness of the policy. It is abundantly clear that through other means the Vatican under Pius XII helped save the lives of countless victims of Nazi fanaticism, including many Jews. Though the Vatican objected to some actions taken by the Allies, it much more strongly objected to those of the Axis. Whether its policy regarding public denunciation was the appropriate one, however, is what is at the center of the controversy concerning "the silence of Pius XII."

The Church, Educator of People and Nations. With his first encyclical, *Summi pontificatus* (20 October 1939), the pope began his denunciation of the causes of the international crisis that was leading to war. In a series of interventions issued over the course of the conflict, he tried to paint a general picture of the principles conducive to the establishment of peace and a new international order. Several radio messages—those for the fiftieth anniversary of *Rerum novarum* (1 June 1941), those of Christmas 1941 on the international order and of 1942 on the internal order of nations, and, finally, those of 1944, on Christian civilization (1 September) and on the problems of democracy (Christmas)—represented the most probing expressions of the pope's thinking on the organization of the postwar world. These texts expressed the need for a global order of international law and morality, founded on natural law, which the Catholic Church had the duty to propose and interpret. They constitute an inescapable point of reference for the action of Catholics in the years following the conflict.

The magisterium of Pius XII thus affirmed the primacy of the human person and the preeminence of the ethical in the organization of the life of society. It was only by returning to these "principles" of civilization, this "social metaphysic" (the inspirational role of the Jesuit G. Gundlach can be felt here) that it would be possible to establish a future of peace and justice for the whole world. And clearly in this context the Church had a vital role to play: "If the future belongs to democracy," Pius XII stated in his Christmas radio message of 1944, "an essential part of its achievement should concern the religion of Christ and the Church." In 1943, in the encyclical *Mystici corporis*, the pope had presented an ecclesiology in which the institutional elements were linked to the doctrine of the Church as a mystical body.

During the war, and especially in the postwar years, the pope became more and more convinced that the Church had to fulfill the function of "educator of people and of nations." Such were the thoughts the pope developed in his speech for the consistory of 1945, "Strength and Influence of the Church for the True Restoration of the World," in which he praised the supranationality of the Church, a model for the international order and one very different from the world's "empires." The pope claimed "the long experience of the Church as an educator of peoples": faced with the challenge of reconstruction, the pope and the Church did not intend to stand aside, "in the secrecy of temples," thus abandoning their mission, which was to form "the whole man."

Pius XII, who had witnessed the failure of Vatican diplomacy during the war years, discovered that public opinion and the masses were beginning to pay attention to his teaching. After the liberation of Rome, the Vatican was the setting for frequent meetings between the pope and visitors. Pius XII often made use of radio and, later, television, and his voice and image became familiar to Catholics. The communication between the pope and the people showed a new vitality. In 1949, the year the pontiff first appeared on American screens, he declared, "People have said that the papacy was dead or dying, and they will see the crowds overflowing on all sides of the vast St. Peter's Square to receive the pope's blessing and to hear his word."

The pontiff worked hard at his magisterium. He prepared his public interventions with care, conscious that a new attention was being paid to the Church and to his words. Moreover, the pope's teaching was a way of leading the Church directly by means of an active, militant presence in the contemporary world. The great mobilizations of Catholics, as for the HOLY YEAR of 1950 or the Marian year of 1954, were effective models of the pastoral conception of Pius XII. During the Second World War, in Western Europe, Catholic movements were organized in the political, economic, and trade-union spheres. It was in this way that European political life saw the rise of Christian political parties. In Italy, despite the opposition of some Vatican milieus wary of seeing the Church align itself with a political party, Pius XII endorsed the political unity of Catholics in a CHRISTIAN DEMOCRACY.

Pius XII and Communism. The great problem that dominated the pontificate from the war to its end was the confrontation with the communist regimes and parties. One of the consequences of the war was the penetration of communism into the heart of Europe, in traditionally Catholic countries such as Poland, Hungary, Czechoslovakia, Croatia, and Slovenia. This advance posed grave problems for the Catholic Churches of these nations. Relations between the Vatican and Moscow were marked by a total lack of understanding and a progressive estrangement, in spite of American diplomacy, which attempted to facilitate some sort of communication. However, Rome did not give up its representations in the Eastern countries, although the socialist governments did not welcome this Vatican presence. In 1950, the last representation of the Holy See in a country linked with Moscow was closed. In 1952, Marshal Tito broke off diplomatic relations with the Vatican following the nomination to the cardinalate of Archbishop Stepinac of Zagreb.

Opposition between the Catholic Church and the communist world was intense from the beginning of the postwar period, both in the Eastern countries and in Western Europe. The Vatican was convinced that the Soviets intended to limit drastically the Church's sphere and to loosen, if not break, the ties between the episcopates of the East and the Holy See. The arrest and trial of the primate of Hungary, Cardinal Mindszenty, in 1948 opened the public's eyes to the brutal attitude of the communist regimes with regard to the Church. The Hungarian cardinal had always been convinced of the inevitability of conflict and the need to adopt a firm stance.

During the late 1940s, the situation of Catholicism in the East was dramatic: Mindszenty and the Croatian Stepinac were in prison, the Czech Beran was prevented from exercising his ministry, and two whole Byzantine Churches, in Ukraine and in Romania, were forcibly incorporated into the Orthodox Church. At the Vatican, it was feared that Soviet and communist policy regarding Catholicism would result in the creation of national Churches, detached from Rome. The Holy Office's decree of July 1949 excommunicating the Communists set forth a solemn and definitive condemnation, which demonstrated the irreconcilability of communism and Catholicism. This measure, which aroused some perplexity within the Secretariat of State, conveyed Pius XII's determination to speak out loudly and forcefully against communism. In his speech for the beatification of INNOCENT XI, it was the "defense of the Christian world" that was exalted by the pontiff.

"Christian civilization," represented by the Church of Rome, was setting itself up in opposition to the other civilization, centered in Moscow. The pope descended into the arena for the confrontation: he denounced the antireligious persecution in the East and invited Catholics to come together to face the communist forces in the West. Henceforth, the Holy See's policy was one of total opposition. A few exceptions, which cannot be identified with ecclesiastical figures or movements favoring collaboration with the regimes, came in fact from the East, from the Church of Poland. In 1950, Wyszynski, the Polish primate, signed an agreement with the government granting the Church certain guarantees, and gave his support to the policy of defending national frontiers. This action, which was judged negatively in Rome, represented a significant moment in the strategy of the Polish primate, who was arrested shortly afterwards. In 1956, he renewed his support of the government in order to avoid the risk of a Soviet invasion.

Since the Second World War, Soviet policy with regard to the Holy See had been shaped by the desire to eliminate the social and political influence of Catholicism in countries over which Moscow intended to exercise total control. Rome's response had been to call attention to the danger and to prevent the infiltration of procommunist elements into the Churches, notably by means of solemn measures. In a particularly delicate situation, like that of Czechoslovakia, it was possible to set up a clandestine Church with bishops ordained in secret. But it was no longer an easily applied solution. Moreover, even toward the end of the pontificate, the Vatican saw no alternative to maintaining a firm policy, despite the grave crisis of the Eastern Churches. After Stalin's death, Moscow made a few tentative approaches, which Vatican diplomacy considered purely formal. For Pius XII, all that could be done was to wait until the situation evolved, something he did not believe was imminent, and meanwhile continue to pass on neighborly messages to the Eastern Churches and denounce the antireligious persecutions.

A Western Church. During Pius XII's pontificate, the Holy See was forcibly cut off from its Eastern Churches. On the other hand, it maintained active links with the Western world. Here were the principal centers of Catholicism, and from here came the greater part of the Holy See's concrete resources and its personnel—for example, the missionaries. And from a geopolitical point of view, in a world divided into blocks the Church appeared to side with the West, and communist propaganda often depicted the pope as the "chaplain of the West." Pius XII was aware of this and, despite his commitment against communism, did not want to confuse the Church's cause with Western politics. His perplexity with regard to Italy's membership in NATO, even though the Vatican favored the alliance in a general way, showed his fear that such a step on Italy's part could implicate the Holy See.

No doubt it was difficult for the Church to work out an impartial position in such a strong bipolar system. Nevertheless, the magisterium of Pius XII constantly stressed peace and equidistance from the two blocks, even if the pope did not cease to issue moral judgments, different ones, against the two sides. With regard to the East, obvi-

ously, his remarks were extremely severe. Yet the West, according to Pius XII, "likes to describe itself emphatically as 'the free world.' It is mistaken, and does not know itself [. . .] yet it does strive, still in large measure, consciously or not, to preserve natural law." The nuance is different, but the pope's reluctance to hide behind the Western world is plain.

In the West, the Catholic Church represented an important force in the life of society. In Italy, the pope expressed his preference for an outright representation of Catholics in a political party of Christian inspiration. In that country, the postwar period was characterized by the strong Catholic presence in political life and in the national leadership, such as had never before existed since the unification. In Germany, the situation was similar, and was followed closely by the pope, who endeavored to avert the excessive humiliation of the defeated country. The Catholics worked toward a political renaissance alongside the Protestants within a party of a Christian inspiration. The French situation was more complex. The Catholics were not united in the Republican People's Movement (MRP), nor did the Holy See openly intervene as it did for other Catholic parties.

After the war, the Vatican of Pius XII attempted to mitigate the estrangement of Franco's Spain from the democratic West. In 1953, the Holy See drew up a concordat with the Spanish government that recognized the Church's character as a "perfect society" and made Spain a country with an established Church. However, the civil authorities won the right to appoint bishops, which the Vatican negotiations had sought to eliminate in other concordats. In 1940, the Holy See had concluded a concordat with Portugal as well as a missionary agreement whereby the *padroado* was preserved in the colonies (it was partly modified in 1950). In spite of the differences, in the two Iberian states a privileged status for the Catholic Church survived, something that one section of the Roman Curia still considered a goal. For the pontiff, on the other hand, Iberia was no longer a model, but he wanted to maintain good relations with the two governments and counted on a gradual democratization of the regimes.

Pius XII kept a watchful eye on the process of European unification and intervened in order to ensure its historical and Christian foundations. *L'OSSERVATORE ROMANO* of 27 March 1957 hailed the treaties of Rome as "the most important and significant political event in the modern history of the Eternal City." For the Holy See, it was the culminating point of a process that, according to Cardinal Frings's words, had seen Pius XII committed to "achieving practical and realizable objectives in the unification of Europe." He was referring to a speech given during the second postwar period: in 1948, the pope took an explicit position in favor of European unity, knowing that he could also rely on the support of the Catholic ruling classes. Within the framework of the West, European unification represented for the pope one step toward the realization of an international order based on the Christian message, which he had proclaimed since the war. In 1957, Pius XII had declared, "We must build in Europe . . . a vast and solid majority of federalists, to sustain the principles of a healthy federalism."

Pastoral Role and Crisis. By his presence and his pronouncements, Pius XII represented the true leader of the Catholics. "You are finally militants," he told the young women of Catholic Action in 1955. "The Church must be engaged in society as a movement to affirm the values of Christian civilization." The 1950 holy year, in which Pius XII proclaimed the dogma of the Assumption of the Virgin Mary, represented a highly significant moment in the pope's pastoral mission. Catholics were urged to turn toward Rome and the pope's teaching. On that occasion, Pius XII called on his "children who are alienated, disillusioned, embittered" to return to the Church. The theme of Catholic mobilization was a constant one in the teaching of the pontiff. Such was the pastoral message that Rome transmitted to the dioceses. In 1952, the pope announced a movement of renewal for "a better world," which would radiate outward from Rome to embrace the whole Catholic world. The movement was inspired by a Jesuit close to the pope, Fr. Lombardi, who had been particularly influential in Italy and Latin America.

For things to change in the world, something had to change in the life of the Church. The religious themselves were summoned to make some transformations. The apostolic exhortation *Menti nostrae* of 1950 proposed that training for the priesthood should not take place "in a setting too isolated from the world." In 1951, in a speech to the World Congress for the Apostolate of the Laity, the pope, having outlined the commitment of laypersons and of the Catholic movement, expressed satisfaction that such a commitment was opposed to the "nefarious trend that also prevails among Catholics, which would confine the Church to what are called 'purely spiritual' questions." Concerning the internal life of the Church, the pontificate of Pius XII was marked by some changes the development of which the pope followed in order to make the pastoral mission more effective. The liturgy itself underwent a reform of the rites of Holy Week.

Pius XII, therefore, was convinced of the need to make changes in order to achieve a more active presence in contemporary society. Nevertheless, he did not conceal his anxiety when a process was set in motion that threatened a certain fundamental identity and developed independently from the Holy See. The encyclical *Humani generis* (1950) issued a warning to a new, mainly French, theological movement for overemphasizing the historical method and history and at the same time having ties to the very current and to highly unusual pastoral experiments. For the pontiff, as he told some of his interlocutors, these were "manifestations resembling those of modernism." The encyclical was the fruit of a compromise between those who wanted only a general rebuke and those who wanted a list of condemned positions. It was chiefly the "new theology" that it took issue with. This had developed in the French Church, which had enjoyed a burst of intellectual vitality after the Second World War and had inspired some novel pastoral experiments.

In France, where the Holy See was represented from 1944 to 1953 by Msgr. Roncalli, an experiment involving worker-priests had taken place, an important attempt to give the Church a new presence within the proletariat. The worker-priests enjoyed the support of an influential part of the French episcopate. The experiment lasted, amid much polemic, until 1954, the year Pius XII himself decided to discontinue it despite the contrary pressure of the French cardinals. Not that the pope was against new forms of commitment in the area of apostolate, but the life of the worker-priest seemed to him to call into question the identity of the Catholic priesthood. It was especially during the 1950s that the French Church was a cause of anxiety to the Vatican owing to what was seen as an excessive tendency to adapt pastoral methods to the modern world.

During the pontificate of Pius XII, Catholics had a presence in Western European governments and local administrations. Nonetheless, in spite of the "strength," of the Church, there were symptoms of problems. One interesting indication was a certain crisis in the recruitment of young priests, which began to manifest itself notably in France and Italy. In 1952, the pontiff spoke of a "fairly serious crisis" concerning vocations. Society did not seem to be accepting the models of behavior prescribed for it by the Church and Catholic tradition. The membership in Catholic organizations did not always live up to expectations or commitment. In the case of the city of Rome itself, the pope spoke of the existence of "little islands to evangelize, almost a missionary territory." The Church of Pius XII, despite its strong presence in society, surrounded by consensus, was beginning to come up against new kinds of resistance. It was a question not only of communist opposition to its influence but of a new and critical situation of having to do with the Church's role in a changed society.

The Third World. One circumstance characterizes the last years of the pontificate: the confrontation with the process of decolonization. The pope had only rarely tackled the problem (twice between 1948 and 1950, once between 1950 and 1954). After that, by contrast, the pope insistently affirmed the right of peoples to independence, for instance in the Christmas radio messages of 1954 and 1955. The discourse continued over the following period, in which certain responsibilities of the colonial powers were stressed. For a long time, the Roman CONGREGATION for the Propagation of the Faith, mainly under the guidance of Msgr. Costantini, whom Pius XII had named a cardinal in 1952, had been advocating the setting up of native hierarchies. The encyclical *Evangelii praecones* of 1951 represented the official sanction of the Church's new missionary teaching. The Holy See was preparing itself for the independence of nations.

For the Holy See, decolonization was inevitable and the missionary Churches should prepare for this new reality. On the other hand, the Secretariat of State and the pope himself did not disguise their fear that the confrontation between East and West would spread to the Third World countries, a possible area of development for communist ideology. In China, after Mao Tse-tung came to power, and in Vietnam, the Catholic Church found itself pitted against socialist regimes. The creation of the Chinese Patriotic Church appeared to the Vatican as the radical implementation of communist designs against the Church. After some hesitation between 1949 and 1951, Pius XII took a stand against the attempt to found a "Church separated from the Apostolic See" (1952). The Holy See maintained diplomatic relations with Taiwan by sending there the internuncio to Beijing, Msgr. Riberti, who had been expelled from China by the communist authorities.

The pope's apparent advocacy of making the colonies independent aroused negative reactions in the political circles of the colonial powers, especially in France. On the other hand, the United States, which the Vatican saw as a Western power with no colonial heritage, could, in its view, provide a brake upon the communist advance in the Third World. In the encyclical *Fidei donum* of 1957, Pius XII called for a new missionary commitment on the part of the whole Church, while at the same time confirming the value of the creation of indigenous hierarchies. He pointed out the dangers run by the fragile native Churches, coping with false nationalism, communism, Islam, and the influence of materialism and the consumer society of the West.

This new reflection on the Third World included concern for Latin America. The fragility of Catholicism on that continent impelled the pope to promote more careful coordination in a region of vital importance for the Church, as he stated in 1956 in a letter to Cardinal Piazza. The pope also had initiated a new coordination of effort on the part of the Latin American bishops, which led to the Rio de Janeiro meeting of 1955. It was from that meeting that an organic plan for the Latin American Church was born. Pius XII agreed to the bishops' request for the institution of a Latin American "Consejo Episcopal" with a permanent secretariat. In 1958, the pope established within the Roman Curia the Pontifical Commission for Latin America, responsible for coordinating and unifying Catholicism on the continent.

The Government of the Pope. The whole of Pius XII's government carried his strong personal stamp. He directly followed the majority of the questions submitted to the Holy See. In general, the process of decision was somewhat slow, not only because it was centralized in the person of the pope, but also because of the close attention devoted by Pius XII devoted to each question. The problem was particularly evident in the matter of appointments, where the pope's decision-making sometimes seemed laborious and hesitant. The college of cardinals was enlarged only in the consistories of 1945 and 1952. For that reason, especially in the last years of the pontificate, the number of cardinals declined sharply, while their age increased. During this period, the direction of several dicasteries was concentrated in the person of one and the same cardinal for lack of available cardinals. Over the course of the 1950s, a certain lassitude began to be felt in the ranks of the CURIA, which was smaller and older in its membership and accustomed to working under the direct control of a pope who was by now a sick man.

As far as the structure of the Curia is concerned, Pius XII carried out no reforms. No changes were made in the system of Vatican administration, even though ideas and plans for reform and internationalization had circulated in the first years of the pontificate. In fact, the pope did strengthen the role and responsibilities of the two sections of the Secretariat of State, an organ with a privileged position in his government of the Curia and the Church. Tardini and Montini (the latter until the end of 1954) were his chief collaborators, especially after the death of the secretary of state, Maglione.

Msgr. Tardini embodied the tradition and experience of papal diplomacy as applied throughout the 20th century. Msgr. Montini, in close touch with Catholic intellectual and political circles in Italy, was the contact for things French. He was generally thought more "open" than his colleague. His appointment to the archdiocese of Milan was interpreted as a victory for the most conservative elements of the Curia, among whom was Cardinal Ottaviani. In actual fact, the role of Cardinal Ottaviani, secretary of the HOLY OFFICE, was important in the Curia of Pius XII, but over these years no group of ecclesiastics had a dominant function. Cardinal Ottaviani represented a vision of the contemporary world marked by the confrontation between the Church and the "anti-Church," that is, international communism. Within the framework of this confrontation, he believed it necessary to assemble all the available forces, including Franco's Spain, the regime of which he thought closely resembled the model Catholic state. The dean of the SACRED COLLEGE, Cardinal Tisserant, saw things differently. He had doubts about the centralized authority of the pontificate and was particularly sensitive to relations with non-Catholic Christians. As the years passed, the number of cardinals declined in the absence of new consistories. The relations between the pope and his collaborators themselves grew weaker, partly owing to the illness of the pontiff; most questions were filtered through the Secretariat of State.

It could be said that even in the final period of the pontificate, in spite of the infrequent communication between the pope and the Curia or the bishops throughout the world, Pius XII still had a direct hand in governing the Church, although his control inevitably was exercised more slowly. He even strove to pursue his magisterium and keep in touch with the faithful. During his last years, the pope's teaching seemed to be tinged with a greater pessimism. At Easter 1957, he spoke of a "lost traveler," one "plunged in the darkness, an almost fatal darkness." His words ended, almost apocalyptically, with the invocation "Come, O Lord Jesus . . . make our night as bright as day." The pope died at Castel Gandolfo on 9 October 1958.

Andrea Riccardi

Bibliography

Actes et documents du Saint-Siège relatifs à la Seconde Guerre mondiale, ed. P. Blet, R. Graham, A. Martini, B. Schneider, Vatican City, 11 vols., 1965–81.

Alix, C. "Le Vatican et la décolonisation," *Les Églises chrétiennes et la décolonisation*, ed. M. Merle, Paris, 1967, 17–114.

Andreotti, G. *Pio XII*, Rome, 1965.

Aubert, R. "Le demi-siècle qui a préparé Vatican II," *Nouvelle Histoire de l'Église*, 5, L'Église dans le monde moderne, Paris, 1975, 556–689.

Bentley, J. *God's Representatives: The Eight Twentieth-Century Popes*, London, 1997.

Blet, P. *Pius XII and the Second World War: According to the Archives of the Vatican*, L. J. Johnson, trans., New York, 1999.

Breza, T. *La Porte de bronze. Chronique de la vie vaticane*, Paris, 1962.

Casula, C. F. *Domenico Tardini (1888–1961). L'azione della Santa Sede nella crisi fra le due guerre*, Rome, 1988.

Chelini, J., and d'Onorio, J.-B., ed., *Pie XII et la Cité. Actes du Colloque de la Faculté de droit d'Aix-en-Provence*, Paris, 1988.

Cheneaux, P. *Une Europe vaticane? Entre le plan Marshall et les traités de Rome*, Brussels, 1990.

Cornwell, J. *Hitler's Pope: The Secret History of Pius XII*, London, 1999.

Dalla Torre, G. *Memorie*, Milan, 1965.

Di Nolfo, E. *Vaticano e Stati Uniti (dalle carte di M.-C. Taylor)*, Milan, 1978.

Discorsi e Radiomessaggi di Sua Santità Pio XII, Vatican City, 1959–60, 20 vols.

Engel Janosi, F. *Il Vaticano fra fascismo e nazismo. Dal caos alla catastrofe*, Florence, 1976.

Falconi, C. *Il Pentagono vaticano*, Bari, 1958.

Falconi, C. *Pio XII*, Milan, 1966.

Fattorini, E. "Santa Sede e Germania alla vigilia della seconda guerra mondiale," *Dimensioni e problemi della ricerca storica*, 1990, 1, 99–117.

Galeazzi Lisi, R. *Dans l'ombre et dans la lumière de Pie XII*, Paris, 1960.

Giordani, I. *Pio XII, un grande papa*, Turin, 1961.

Graham, R. A. *The Vatican and Communism in World War II: What Really Happened?* San Francisco, 1996.

Gremigni, G. *Il Santo Padre Pio XII*, Vatican City, 1943.

Halecki, O. and Murray, J. F. *Pius XII*, New York, 1954.

Lehenert, P. *Pio XII. Il privilegio di servirlo*, Milan, 1984.

Leiber, R. *Pius XII., Stimmen der Zeit*, 1958. 81–100.

McInerny, R. *The Defamation of Pius XII*, South Bend, Ind., 2001.

Marchione, M. *Pope Pius XII: Architect for Peace*, New York, 2000.

Marchione, M. *Yours Is a Precious Witness: Memoirs of Jews and Catholics in Wartime Italy*, New York, 1997.

Mindszenty, J. *Erinnerungen*, Frankfurt/Berlin, 1974.

Pacelli, E. *Discorsi e panegirici, 1931–1938*, Vatican City, 1939.

Paxia, G. *The Artist and Moral Responsibility: Teachings of Pius XII and John XXIII*, San Francisco, 1999.

Phayer, M. *The Catholic Church and the Holocausts, 1930–1965*, Bloomington, Ind. 2000.

Poulat, E. *Une Église ébranlée. Changement, conflit, continuité de Pie XII à Jean Paul II*, Tournai, 1980.

Rhodes, A. *The Vatican in the Age of the Dictators, 1922–1945*, London, 1973.

Riccardi, A. *Il "partito romano" nel secondo dopoguerra (1945–1954)*, Brescia, 1983; *Pio XII*, Rome-Bari, 1984.

Riccardi, A. *Il potere del papa da Pio XII a Paolo VI*, Rome-Bari, 1988.

Riccardi, A., ed., *Le Chiese di Pio XII*, Rome-Bari, 1986.

Riccardi, A. Roma, "Città sacra"; *Dalla conciliazione all'operazione Sturzo*, Milan, 1979.

Roche, G., and Saint-Germain, P. *Pie XII devant l'histoire*, Paris, 1972.

Schambeck, H., ed., *Pius XII. Zum Gedächtnis*, Berlin, 1977.

Schneider, B. *Pio XII*, Rome, 1977.

Tardini, D. *Pio XII*, Vatican City, 1960.

Traniello, F. "Pio XII," *Dizionario storico del movimento cattolico in Italia*, ed. G. Campanini and F. Traniello, Casale Monferrato, 1982, II, 495–512.

Veneruso, D. *Pio XII e la seconda guerra mondiale*, Rome, 1969.

Weisbord, R. G., and Sillanpoa, W. P. *The Chief Rabbi,*

the Pope, and the Holocaust: An Era in Vatican-Jewish Relations, New Brunswick, N.J., 1992.

Zizolla, G. *Il microfono di Dio. Pio XII, Padre Lombardi e i cattolici italiani*, Milan, 1990.

Zuccotti, S. *Under His Very Windows: The Vatican and the Holocaust*, New Haven, Conn., 2000.

PLAGUE AND THE PAPACY. Humanity has suffered a variety of epidemics since the beginning of time, but the most lethal of all, the plague, raged during three quite limited periods: during the earliest Middle Ages, from 542 to 767; in the later Middle Ages up to modern times, from 1347 to 1722 (and until 1842 in the Middle East); finally, 1894 saw the beginning in southern China of a third pandemic outburst which was more or less contained only from around 1970 but hardly affected Europe.

Thus the papacy was not actually confronted with the plague except during the reigns of 36 popes in the earliest Middle Ages, from VIGILIUS to St. PAUL I, and of 48 from the later Middle Ages to modern times, from CLEMENT VI to INNOCENT XIII; among those, only a small number experienced an epidemic of the plague in their place of residence during their pontificates: 6 in the earliest Middle Ages and 19 during the second pandemic. Nevertheless, many popes obviously lived through the epidemic before they were elected, and several intervened at a time when epidemics were raging far from Rome.

When the plague first appeared in 542, the papacy was in tragic situation. And when the disease penetrated Italy in 543, the struggle between Pope Vigilius and the emperor was absorbing the general attention, and the plague, though exceptionally widespread, apparently elicited no particular action on the part of the pope, who in the end was arrested and exiled, on 22 November 545. The second eruption of the plague in Rome, in 570, also seems barely to have caught the notice of Pope JOHN III; in fact, it took place at the same time as the LOMBARD invasion and became merged with the overall misery and destruction of the period.

Far more important was the great plague of 590. It broke out at a time when Pope PELAGIUS II, an Ostrogoth by birth, had just succeeded in forcing the Lombards to withdraw, for a high price in gold, and in securing an alliance with the FRANKS to keep them at a distance. But Pelagius II was among the first victims of the epidemic (he is the only pope to have died of the plague), and Rome, in ruins, overcome by the calamities that had struck repeatedly since November 589 and having lost at least three-quarters of its inhabitants, elected a new pope, GREGORY I. He, a patrician, a former senator and prefect of Rome who had retired to a Benedictine monastery, initially regarded the task offered him as impossible. His first gesture was to refuse, but the emperor and the citizens forced him to accept.

Gregory's first action against the epidemic was to beg divine clemency by a novel means. A few years before, Pope PELAGIUS II had entrusted him with a mission to the emperor in Constantinople, where Gregory had seen the clergy lead the people in procession, singing psalms. He decided to introduce this custom to the Western Church, and organized the first procession. It crossed Rome from church to church, reciting *litaniae majores* composed for the occasion and singing canticles. Just when the faithful were intoning the *Regina Caeli*, they according to legend saw an exterminating angel appear in the sky over Hadrian's mausoleum, and sheathe his sword. The plague abated shortly thereafter, and Gregory, putting the Church to work in the place of the faltering civil authorities, had aid distributed to poor families suffering from the scourge. As Jacques Le Goff so well phrases it, in reference to the extraordinary calamities overwhelming the West at that time, "Gregory the Great, whose works were to have so great an influence throughout the Middle Ages, acted and wrote as though obsessed by the plague. For him, Job's pustules were buboes; in all respects he was the pope of the plague and of the coming of the Last Days." The plague returned to Rome yet again in 608 under Boniface IV, who no doubt followed the now established custom of distributing food to the needy. In 654, it made a final incursion into the city, but at that time Pope MARTIN I had already been in exile on Naxos for a year.

It was not until seven hundred years later, in 1348, that the disease reappeared in Rome at the time of the terrible Black Death, which, brought ashore at Marseille and Leghorn at the end of 1347, would unleash throughout the West one of the greatest hecatombs ever seen. In those days, Italy was in the grip of violent, inextricable political chaos. The pope, Clement VI, tried without much success to calm passions, but neither his safety nor his independence was assured in Rome, and, like his predecessors, he was forced to resign himself to staying on in Avignon. Queen Joan of Naples, accused of having had her husband, Andrew of Hungary, murdered, and ousted from her kingdom by her brother-in-law Louis of Hungary, disembarked at Marseille, where the epidemic was at its height, and on 15 March bravely made her way to Avignon, where, the day before, the pope had opened a new cemetery destined to receive eleven thousand bodies by the end of April. She begged audience with him, brought proof of her innocence, and, in order to obtain the funds necessary for regaining her kingdom, sold Avignon to him for eighty thousand gold florins; the deed would be approved the following 9 June.

From the time of his election to the papal throne in 1342, Clement VI threw himself into activity throughout the known world, striving to preserve or restore peace and helping all those, whether humble or powerful, who were in need.

In the face of the onslaught, he showed five major pre-occupations: to give the people the spiritual support they needed; to take medical measures, both preventive and curative, to combat the disease; to help those whom the epidemic had reduced to poverty; to protect the scape-goats whom slanderers accused of spreading the evil; and to condemn the manifestations of collective hysteria, which were reaching a level of dangerous excess.

In early January 1348, the Black Death made its appearance in Avignon. It began in the form of pneumonia in the convent of the Carmelites, killing all within two days—so quickly, says the chonicler Henry Kneighton, that the first people to enter the convent thought that the 66 brothers had all slaughtered one another. Confronted with an epidemic so horrifying Clement VI's first act was to keep himself informed by demanding a daily report of the number of deaths in Avignon. From this report, we know that the maximum number of fatalities took place in the three days after the Fourth Sunday of Lent, during which 1,412 deaths were counted, and that 94 out of some 450 curialists died, among them 7 cardinals including Giovanni Colonna, the pope's chief counsellor. (According to J. Enselme, "Gloses sur le passage dans la ville d'Avignon de la grande mortalité de 1348," contemporary registers show the percentages of mortality among the palace service staff: chaplaincy 42%, courier 32%, domestic officers 33%, penitentiary 30%, cardinals 30%, squires 30%, chancellery 14%.)

Despite the epidemic's massive invasion of his palace, Clement VI stayed his ground, and because he had little trust in the emerald he wore on his finger, which, according to Arab doctors, minimized the effect of poison or reduced infections depending on whether it was turned to the south or to the east respectively, he followed the counsels of his doctor Guy de Chauliac and was content to live attended by two domestics who carried lighted torches to purify the air he breathed.

Clement's principal concern was to help the faithful in this terrible time of testing. He therefore issued a decree reminding all priests, monks, and nuns that their duty was to visit, succor, and tend the sick as well as to administer the sacraments to the dying. Next, he appeased consciences by granting general absolution to all believers who died of the plague repenting of their sins, as well as a plenary indulgence to all those who, repenting with contrition, devoted themselves to tending the sick or burying the dead. Finally, he composed a special mass in time of plague, which he celebrated daily, and he blessed the Rhône so that all the bodies it carried in its waters might receive a minimum of religious ceremony from the Church.

On the advice of Guy de Chauliac, the pope took preventive and curative measures that were astonishingly advanced for his time. He purchased some land at the confluence of the Rhône and the Durance and there, sheltered in a ring of fortifications, had individual huts built in which all those sick of the plague could be housed, fed, cared for, and, above all, isolated. Made of wood, and simple to erect outside the city and in the fresh air, these lodgings would also be easy to disinfect by fire once the epidemic was over. An open-minded man, he authorized doctors to dissect the corpses of plague victims to help them penetrate the secret of the disease. (In 1281, Pope BONIFACE VIII had forbidden the University of Bologna to practice dissection.) Clement also paid for the recruitment of doctors to look after all poor victims in Avignon and the Comtat Venaissin. Accordingly, neither Clement VI nor Guy de Chauliac in this situation deserved the accusations heaped on them by Petrach.

The poor, moreover, were legion, their number increased by the unemployed, the widows, and the orphans, whose employer or breadwinner had died. La Pignotte, the office of papal charity founded in Avignon by JOHN XXII, was enlarged on two occasions, and every day distributed meals, clothing, and medicines; the number of loaves given out daily, which according to the account books totaled 9,500 before 1348, rose to 32,000 at the height of the epidemic.

From the onset of the plague, malevolent individuals believed that the disease had been spread willfully: the first to be accused were the lepers and beggars, and then, in April, the Jews. In many instances moneylenders, the Jews were seen by the common people as usurers; often doctors or apothecaries, as well, they were thought to have the ability to immunize themselves against poisons and infections. Twice, in a bull of 26 July and another of 26 September 1348, Clement VI took the Jews under his protection, condemned the massacres and extortions at their expense, and declared that they as much as the Christians were victims of the scourge. Finally, after carefully studying the activities of the flagellants, he refused to open the city of Avignon to a group that had come to ask for his approval. In a bull of 20 October 1349, he condemned them for secret association and various excesses, among them harassment of the Jews.

When the epidemic was almost at an end, he asked the religious orders to report on their losses and had a statement drawn up, area by area, which showed that the Black Death had killed 23,840,000 persons. To calm people's minds, he decreed a jubilee year for Rome in 1350. The influx of pilgrims was immense, but the English and Irish complained that they would not be able to make the journey because they had to cross a hostile France: on 17 August 1349, the pope granted them the graces of the jubilee even if they could not make the PILGRIMAGE. He also took advantage of the combatants' exhaustion as a result of the plague to renew the peace of Calais, which he had drawn up on 28 September 1347 between France and England. It was broken by Edward III, who, in July 1351, wanted to profit from the youth and inexperience of the new French king, John II the Good. Clement VI would succeed in having the truce renewed another three times; it was to last until 6 April 1354.

Finally, to erase the effects of the catastrophe on the Church as rapidly as possible, Clement VI authorized the ordination of young clerics and allowed youths who had not yet completed their formation to enter religious orders. He also approved the election of many bishops, abbots, and abbesses who were very young, and on 29 May 1348 he appointed as cardinal his nephew Pierre-Roger de Beaufort, only eighteen years of age, and then, on 17 December 1350, twelve other cardinals. But the loss of a good part of the clerical elites to the Black Death could not be undone.

Moreover, this was only the beginning of a new cycle of the plague. In early April 1361, the disease once again found its way into Avignon, where Pope INNOCENT VI found himself in a dramatic situation. Since December 1360, the town had been under siege by several bands of mercenaries. It may have been the spread of the plague, or some gold florins, that finally persuaded them to lift the siege on 22 April and leave for Aragon. Now famine joined forces with the plague, for the countryside had been laid waste for several months. Furthermore, the epidemic, which, according to Guy de Chauliac, was mainly attacking children, was no less virulent than that of 1348, causing around a hundred deaths, including those of nine cardinals in the pope's entourage. This second visitation of the plague and that of 1372–4 once again brought about a significant lowering of the intellectual and spiritual standard among the clergy, which indirectly would lead to the great crisis of the papacy in the late 14th century and possibly, over the long term, to that of the REFORMATION. During the schism, the Avignon pope CLEMENT VII was confronted with the plague of 1390, decided to flee, and took refuge in Beaucaire; as far as we know, this is the only instance of a pope fleeing from the plague.

Yet the plague may have forced several COUNCILS to move from one site to another. For example, the council of Constance, convened in 1414, was in danger of closing before it had even started. Tradition has it that a young monk suggested that prayers be offered to St. Roch. No sooner had the prayers and the procession in the saint's honor ended than the plague ceased and the council could begin. This incident established the reputation of St. Roch throughout Europe as the favored intercessor against the plague. Before they dispersed, the bishops also decided that another council should be held to provide for a general reform of the Church. Faithful to this promise, Pope MARTIN V convened a new council in Pavia in 1423. This time, however, the plague was raging before the bishops arrived, and he moved the council to Siena. Sixteen years later, in 1439, Pope EUGENE IV called a council in Ferrara to which, in an ecumenical

spirit, he invited JOHN VIII Palaeologus and the patriarch of Constantinople. But the plague threatened once again, and he was forced to transfer the council to Florence.

The details of every epidemic cannot be explored, but it is worth noting that in October 1637 URBAN VIII issued a bull authorizing the Capuchins of Franche-Comté, to push forward with ordinations in order to replace eighty brothers who had just been carried off by the plague; this action descended in a direct line from the measures taken by Clement VI, with the difference that, however terrible, the plague remained relatively restricted to central Europe.

Finally, it is worth noting that in 1720, Pope Clement XI, moved by the terrible plague overwhelming Marseille, assured the inhabitants of Marseille of his prayers and sent them a ship full of wheat.

Jean-Noël Biraben

Bibliography

Babord, I. "Quand les épidémies ravageaient Fécamp," *Paris-Normandie*, 4 June and 12–13 June 1965.

Bader, J. P., Oldra, A., and Naumicini, G. *Histoire illustrée de la médecine, de la magie préhistorique à la chirurgie moderne*, Paris, 1968.

Brossollet, J. "Quelques aspects religieux de la Grande Peste du XIVe siécle," *Revue d'histoire et de philosophie religieuses*, Faculté de théologie protestante, Strasbourg, 1984, 53–66.

Abbé Christophe, J. B. *Histoire de la papauté pendant le XIVe siècle*, 1 and 2, Paris, 1853.

Consideranda et observanda tempore pestis, Avignon, Bibliothèque du musée Calvet, manuscript 745, 403–5.

Mollaret, H. "Le dernier avatar de saint Roch," *Médecine et maladies infectieuses*, special issue, Nov. 1988, 663–6.

Morey, J. *Les Capucins en Franche-Comté*, Paris, 1881.

Pelissier, A. *Clément VI le Magnifique, premier pape limousin*, Brive, n.d.

PONTIAN. *(230–28 September 235).*

Peter's 17th successor replaced URBAN I as bishop of Rome. Very little is known about him, Eusebius of Caesarea merely stating that he reigned for six years. We do know that the end of Severus Alexander's reign was a time of peace and tolerance toward the Church. Thus, few salient events stand out, the only well-known one occurring within the Church. After two councils held in Alexandria under the presidency of the bishop, Demetrius condemned Origen and ousted him from his teaching post and from Alexandria. Pontian convoked a synod in Rome, which approved Demetrius's action (in 231). During his pontificate Hippolytus's schism persisted, although the pope's attitude toward it is unknown.

Maximinus Thrax, emperor since March 235, abandoned the policy of tolerance vis-à-vis the Christian community in Rome, and ordered those he considered its leaders, Pontian and Hippolytus, deported to the Sardinian mines. At that time Pontian chose to give up his papacy and abdicated on 28 September 235, the earliest date in the history of the popes that is known with certainty. He died, probably as a result of the harsh treatment he had received, on 29 or 30 October of that year. His second successor, the bishop Fabian, had the bodies of Pontian and Hippolytus brought back to Rome in 236 or 237. Pontian was placed in the crypt in Callistus's cemetery. A stele has been found there bearing his name and office in Greek: Pontian was the first bishop of Rome who was a martyr, with the evidence to prove it. His feastday is 19 November.

Bibliography

Amann, E. DTC, 1935, XII, 2, 2553–54.
Eusebius, B. HE, VI, 23, 3; 29, 1.
Jerome, Ep., 33, 4.
Weltin, E. G. NCE, 1967, VII, 548–49.

POOR RELIEF. Historians have generally studied the more opulent social groups, but in recent years, with some regret for past neglect, they have manifested a growing interest in subjects linked to poverty and, indirectly, to forms of social assistance intended to ameliorate poverty's most serious effects. This regret and the desire to shed light on historically neglected and disturbing problems is now granting some dignity and self-expression to those whom 19th century writers called the "dangerous classes." They were considered "dangerous" mainly because the unregulated life characteristic of people who have nothing to lose appeared to constitute a menace to society and its established order.

Contemporary research concentrates on various aspects of poverty and links them to the evolution of society, collective awareness, and the influence of ecclesiastical institutions and structures. In addition to general descriptions—for example, those by Bronislaw Geremek, who analyzes the process of formation of mental behaviors and modern social politics from the Middle Ages on—there are studies situating poverty within the urban context; J.-P. Gutton has thus studied assistance in Lyons during the modern era (16th–18th centuries), B. Pullan has concentrated on Venice during the Renaissance, and M. Mollat has undertaken extremely fruitful research on medieval pauperism. In general, there are fewer contributions specifically regarding the religious context, and there is a need to study the theme of pauperism as seen not only through well-known theological and canonical writings but also through pious texts, sermons, prayer books, and other documents. Nevertheless, some studies

have certainly contributed to drawing this subject from the recesses of memory and historical conscience. It is a history of suffering and penalizing exclusion but also of the will and immense effort of modern and preindustrial societies to assist and control larger and larger numbers of needy people. In the past, proposed solutions have come from many quarters, but even in the best cases, these remedies have proved largely insufficient. None has addressed class structures, social differences, and inequalities, or private and collective selfishness, within which pauperism reproduces and spreads. The battle against pauperism thus resembles the Sisyphus myth, a repetitive course of failures.

The poor were not conceived as a social entity until around the 15th century; late medieval culture had a more schematic and, at the same time, a more complex view of the poor. On the one hand, poverty was recognized as being caused and imposed by specific economic reversals or by unforeseen events, and so no reference to secular conditions of exploitation was made. On the other hand, it was seen as a voluntary condition, a chosen way of life and the application of rigorous and radical evangelical ideals. In the first case, poverty was obligatory and consequently passive; in the second, it was willingly accepted and engendered new energies. Public sentiment concentrated on poverty of the first type: raw, massive, and indiscreet. Efforts by the Church assumed particular importance when economic conditions were most difficult. Nonetheless, religious society truly accepted only the virtuous type of poverty that was chosen as a way of life. Thus, the model of ideal poverty that was still alive and motivational during the era of St. Francis and the great spiritual movements structured thought with respect to all other types of poverty. This model also influenced the kinds of remedies sought and the forms of assistance provided. The poor were accepted as long as they did not transgress the accepted ethical framework of social subordination and submission to the Church and the behaviors fixed by it. Indeed, medieval society perpetually vacillated between the poles of the model of the "Lord's poor" and concrete reality.

With the 15th century, however, new preoccupations came to be integrated into this view. Society was gradually emerging from one dominant religious mentality. Groups and classes were organizing, and nationalities were forming. Pauperism had become an embarrassment, though it still arose from social developments and economic inequalities. The Dominican St. Antoninus, archbishop of Florence (d. 1459), was an attentive observer of problems in the new urban setting. His reflection on pauperism was accompanied by knowledge of aspects of urban dynamism that relied on a very active middle class and a positive estimation of goods and exchanges. He did not see why the fact of possessing nothing must necessarily coincide with evangelical poverty, or, inversely, why the fact of possessing should be considered an unavoidable cause of losing one's soul. If necessary, the human heart should be changed.

Regarding the problem of pauperism, St. Antonino wrote that "many are mistaken" and rejected the kind of poverty advocated by heretics. It is obvious that preaching poverty was a precarious balance to maintain, and that interpretation was already tending to harden judgment of the lazy poor person, anticipating repercussions for the whole of society. On the other hand, it was necessary to determine which poor people deserved the charity and protection of the city. St. Antonino responded to this question by inviting the benefactor to consider certain factors permitting him to distinguish between true and false indigence as well as among degrees of poverty. This type of fiscal control, founded on the most visible aspects of poverty at the time, took into account the needy person's religiosity, degree of impoverishment, nature of infirmities or mutilations, and the social condition of the poor. Increasingly, social distinctions and classifications were made, a tendency that became excessive over the next centuries.

The reality of pauperism in the 15th century was most clearly perceived in the cities. This is where the Church developed a preoccupation with accepting the poor and with controlling, determining, and in some sense integrating poverty into the social framework. Charity became more operational. New forms of aid became widespread, such as the Monti di pietà of Franciscan inspiration. Hospitals were reorganized and became specialized; sometimes bishops allowed secular individuals and organizations to administer them. Modernity seems, therefore, to have already begun in the world of social assistance and in reflection on poverty. This intense activity in the areas of organized fiscal control and organized assistance was largely a product of the 16th century. The council of TRENT and the Counter Reformation motivated the bishops of the great dioceses to establish confraternities and other pious associations; for example, Carlo Borromeo founded numerous charitable institutions during this period. In the 16th century, penetrating new problems also arose: cities received massive immigration spurred not only by demographic growth but also by wars that ruined the countryside, sent prices plummeting, and caused shortages and epidemics. This general upheaval prompted an intellectual like the Spaniard Juan Luis Vives, author of a celebrated work (1526) on how to assist the poor, to press authorities to take serious measures and to warn them to be wary of dishonest individuals who would take advantage of this social malady. Thus, distinctions began to be made among the poor, and in response to an appeal made by Vives—a European who knew the phenomenon of pauperism well—a global and all-encompassing assistance plan needed to be conceived to address the various forms of existing misery. According to Vives, the problem could not be resolved simply within the uncontrollable and fluctuating framework of compassion. Instead, it was necessary to situate the approach within a rational perspective on urban structures, economy, and politics. Finally, he offered a subtle reminder of the specificity of problems whose solutions were better found within the scope of a larger enterprise than in the modest remedies offered by religion. This invitation to specificity and professionalism of services is apparent within the tight network of hospitals built during this period: not only were physical structures renovated, but new ways of considering the patient and illness were also introduced.

The Church in the 16th century was also questioning the ways it addressed these increasing needs. In the aftershock of the REFORMATION, clerics pondered how to address the problems posed by the new evangelization. In proposing solutions to these problems, the enormous effort made by the Church, especially in large cities, consisted mainly of presenting itself as the highest point of reference in social life. Consequently, a tight connection was gradually established between poverty and religion, not only because in religion all the events and conditions of human life can be understood in terms of ultimate significance, but also because only religion can alleviate the suffering of the weakest and most excluded elements of society. Thus, the apologetic sense of the Church's imposing structures becomes transparent, especially after the council of Trent.

The protagonists of this charity offensive were, even more than in the past, linked to ecclesiastical institutions. They were generally the founders of religious orders, mystics and intellectuals, bishops and priests, or laity. Numerous religious families were created to relieve specific types of suffering and poverty: the Camillians, the "Fate Bene Fratelli" in the 16th century, and the Lazarists in the 17th century. In addition, confraternities played a growing role. A new strategy for helping the poor was developed in the varied world of associations and volunteer groups. The kind piety required of members of brotherhoods—visiting the ill and moribund—was shaped, and large-scale urban economic assistance projects were launched. While the cities of the Counter Reformation are not all renowned for their churches and convents, they were well endowed with hospitals and asylums, centers for distributing bread and assigning pensions, and schools for the poor. Seats and tribunes were often improvised in town squares to harangue crowds of indigents. Missionaries traveled all over the countryside, even to the most remote regions, in search of souls to save and bodies to relieve of suffering. As a result, from the 16th to the 18th centuries pauperism gradually became the responsibility of people and structures linked to the Church. Only in recent centuries has the history of other forms of assistance, by civil and municipal institutions, begun to be recorded. These other institutions had their own characteristics, not necessarily in conflict with the Church, except in the case of great undertakings such as those realized under the absolute monarchy of Louis XIV of France.

In the 18th century, enlightened and reformist movements initiated another historic phase in views of the poor. In fact, indigence increased greatly over the course of this century. The war of the Spanish Succession caused new devastation in the countryside, followed by economic crises and shortages. In some cities, the proportion of the population living in poverty reached one-third. For L. Muratori and other representatives of social and economic reform, too many workers were idle and, moreover, too many indolent people populated the cities, encouraged by the charitable work of public institutions and private organizations. The remedy resided in abandoning fortuitous charity in favor of a renewable form of contingency assistance. Among the main objectives was to put the poor to work in new factories. The reformers believed that the poor should contribute to the city and stop being on the receiving end alone. This thought is not far from A. R. Turgot's conception, animated by a deep contempt for systems of traditional assistance. In his *Encyclopédie*, Turgot proposed to centralize assistance and to confiscate all Church property in favor of the State, since rather than reducing the number of poor, church charity only increased it. Applying Turgot's notions of assistance made the poor into socially useful individuals. Similar social experiments were carried out in Tuscany by Pietro Leopaldo.

The history of pauperism and assistance in the 19th and 20th centuries is very different from that in previous centuries, not only because the plans and solutions adopted in the past had been exhausted, but also because pauperism had become the heart of completely new and unsettling social and cultural processes. The Industrial Revolution radically modified the framework of traditional references and established, with the massive contribution of the lower classes, both structures and social organizations contributing to society's well-being and new forms of marginalization.

Rome, the Holy City, the seat of the papacy and the heart of Catholicism, offers an interesting case, nearly unique in the history of assistance. Pauperism was widespread, but numerous attempts were made to palliate its consequences through interventions dictated not by social or economic considerations but mainly by religious and spiritual ones. Limiting the field of observation to the 16th and 17th centuries, we can discover one origin of this policy in one of the most serious crises in the city—the imperial siege of 1527. Rome, which had 85,000 inhabitants under Leo X (1513–1521), retained only 32,000 in 1530. However, according to C.-B. Piazza, the most

significant devastation was inflicted on the religious organizations responsible for helping the poor. One of the most painful losses was that of the society of Divine Love, which administered the San Giacomo Hospital for the incurably ill. The resurgence of the city's interest in the poor was expressed in greater involvement of confraternities and secular groups dealing with old and new forms of poverty. One important event was the foundation of the Hospital of the Holy Trinity (Santissima Trinità) by the brotherhood of the same name and Philip Neri to care for foreign pilgrims. During the holy year 1550, some months after its founding, it succeeded in housing and nourishing 60,000 pilgrims. Also significant is the interest in the problem of Roman pauperism manifested by personages important in the history of the Church. For example, Ignacio de Loyola was particularly concerned about specific types of suffering, such as the condition of courtesans, Jews, and indigent prisoners; Philip Neri was especially interested in the ill abandoned in hospitals. Thus, awareness of and sensitivity to the ills of the city arose out of the convergent attitudes of the humble and devoted and of the great spiritual leaders—a synthesis of the simple and naive piety of an illiterate confraternity member and the reflected piety of the architects of great spiritual movements. This was one of the most original aspects of Roman assistance initiatives. Another characteristic element was the closer ideal and practical integration of the complex work carried out by confraternities and associations in the theological and cultural contexts typical of the Reformation and Counter Reformation. This was important because the Church saw in the social involvement of its faithful an implicit but effective response to the devaluation of works through the heretical affirmation of *sola fides*. Moreover, the Church saw charitable work as a providential instrument greatly aiding its plans to recover and expand its influence, especially in urban areas—one of the main objectives identified by the council of Trent. This relationship had also become very close and concrete, on the economical level, since financing was established and managed from the top down.

At the end of the 16th century, short works on the condition of the poor began to circulate. These concerned the problems of recognizing, assisting, and controlling the poor and indigent. Nothing compares to the celebrated work by Vives, which was sometimes banned from educational institutions because of Vives' suspect orthodoxy. Nevertheless, these small books at least enlightened readers about the intellectual infrastructure underpinning the Roman society addressing the problem. It is significant that most of the texts concern the practice of giving alms. Folco, De Angelis, Bellarmino, and later in the 17th century Sperelli, Bartoli, and Pinamonti speak only in traditional terms and relate only the superfluous giving of alms (*obole*), which constituted a right of the poor and could not be refused without committing a sin. This authorial preoccupation points to the fact that, in a society where there was significant accumulated wealth in the hands of a few (whether ecclesiastics, merchants, or aristocrats), the problem of knowing how and to what degree charity should be practiced was a crucial one. Roman theoreticians generally accepted the static and providential view of poverty. In one of his sermons in the Church of Santa Maria in Via, Bellarmino said that "poor men must live as poor men and, if they content themselves with their condition, God will help them more than He does in the present." This feeling that no possibility for deep structural change existed motivated all sorts of feverish attempts by the city to control rampant and increasingly visible pauperism. It is not surprising that dishonesty and dissimulation were widespread. In 1587, Sixtus V consolidated numerous small assistance initiatives to found a large hospice. The project was ambitious because the pope was responsible for ensuring a solid economic basis to found an enterprise aimed at resolving the problem of indigents incapable of working. However, the project was quickly changed and transformed into a mediocre hospital for the poor. The realization did not match the conception, it appears, because the difficulties encountered were more methodological than economic. Coercive methods condemned this project to mediocrity, as did the evident lack of interest of those most closely concerned with it.

This initiative presaged the 17th century, during which the number of poor greatly increased, as did attempts at assisting them. Some of these plans reiterated those originally adopted for Sixtus V's great hospice. Bishops' surveys in the cities show that Roman pauperism had become an increasingly aggressive imposition on churches and a disturbance for visiting pilgrims. Behind this phenomenon, however, lay a series of economic crises and crippling shortages in the years 1621, 1635, 1636, and 1647–1648 which exacerbated the already low level of existence of the masses. A priest at Santa Maria del Popolo wrote in a report of 1625 that numerous poor were dying in the streets of his parish, in slum housing, and in the quarries. Fifty years later, a census taken in several neighborhoods (Ponte, Regola, and Trevi in the center of the papal city) showed that there were 11,160 poor among the 27,092 inhabitants—40 percent of their population. Whatever the exact meaning given to the term "poor," it is clear that it denotes a person afflicted with weakness or need. A growing sense of frustration regarding the constant increase in impoverished masses may have made inevitable the creation of a single large hospice. During the last decades of the 17th century, Rome was just emerging from its mid-century crisis and had reached 150,000 inhabitants. It therefore needed a more efficient assistance structure on a larger scale. The great French hospices, conceived of as single centers for interning the poor, constituted a model to follow, albeit in a more ideal framework more closely linked to religious motivations. Innocent XII called on French designers, the Jesuit fathers Chaurand and Guevarre, to work on the Roman project. In 1693, he was able to inaugurate a grandiose hospice in the Lateran Palace, the last and best-organized effort to control what the popes saw as a disgrace to their city. With the apostolic hospice, the simple, improvised charity of the past was transformed into assistance organized and controlled by the state which underscored both piety and, even more strongly, the exigencies of rigorous discipline. The hospice had a brief and difficult existence; contemporary documents mention escapees, despite a rigorous surveillance system.

During the century that began with Sixtus V's (1585–1590) great initiative and concluded with the practical, similar experiment of Innocent XII (1691–1700), the city undertook many experiments and attempts to control pauperism, mendicancy, and indigence. Dominant ideas converged toward a unique solution. At first, the Church had attempted to give a response regarding the obligation of charity; the exact calculation of how much was to be given troubled such great 16th-century prelates as Alexander Farnese, Paul III's nephew, and noblewomen such as Eleonora Boncompagni. Yet opinions varied even regarding the duty of charity. The majority of moralists and directors of conscience thought it was just a matter of giving a superfluous sum; some however, believed that aid should be proportionate to the needs of the individual receiving it. As for the problem of hospices, the positions and solutions were varied. Those mentioned above were founded on constraint, and even another celebrated hospice, San Michele, kept poor people in seclusion. In contrast, the hospice of Santa Galla near the Theater of Marcellus, founded in 1657 and maintained by Cardinal Benedetto Odescalchi, offered the poor lodging and a hot meal without any obligation on their part. (There were a few religious gestures required, but no sacrifice of liberty for the poor benefiting from assistance.) The existence of the latter exempts Rome from the phrase applied to the hospices of France, *le grand renfermement* ("the great lock-up").

It is clear that the collective mind feared the poor and judged them severely. Once again, only the concrete lucidity of men such as Camillo de Lellis or the Spaniard José Calasanzio was able to go beyond appearances and discover, even in the most miserable of the poor, a brother or sister to assist, to respect. Calasanzio cared for the indigent in Trastevere and attempted to initiate educational programs to overcome misery and illiteracy in poor children and young people; he would say, with tranquil assurance, that the poor sustain this world with their pain and are the best part of it.

Luigi Fiorani

Bibliography

Fatica, M. "La reclusione dei poveri a Roma durante il pontificato di Innocenzo XII (1692–1700)," *Richerche per la storia religiosa di Roma*, 3 (1978), 133–179 (special issue on Roman pauperism).

Fiorani, L. "Religione e povertà: Il dibattito sul pauperismo a Roma tra Cinque e Seicento," *Ricerche per la storia religiosa di Roma*, 3 (1978), 43–131 (special issue on Roman pauperism).

Geremek, B. "Il pauperismo nell'età preindustriale (secoli XIV–XVIII), *Storia d'Italia*, 5, Turin, 1973, 669–98.

Geremek, B. *La Réforme de l'assistance publique au XVIe siècle et les controverses idéologiques*, Report on the Sixth Week of Studies of the Francesco Datini International Institute of Economic History, Prato, 1974.

Gutton, J. P. *La società e i poveri*, critical note by M. Rosa, Milan, 1977 (with bibliography on each European country).

Gutton, J. P. *La Société et les pauvres: L'exemple de la généralité de Lyon 1534–1789*, Paris, 1971.

Menozzi, D. *Chiesa, poveri, società nell'età moderna e contemporanea*, Brescia, 1979.

Mollat, M. "Assistance et assistés jusqu'à 1610," *Acts of the 97th meeting of the Congrès national des sociétés savantes, Nantes, 1972*, Paris 1979, 7–27.

Mollat, M. *Etudes sur l'histoire de la pauvreté (Moyen Âge–XVIe siècle)*, Paris, 1974.

Mollat, M. *Les Pauvres au Moyen Âge, étude sociale*, Paris, 1978.

Mollat, M. *Povertà e ricchezza nella spiritualità dei secoli XI e XII*, Todi, 1969.

Mollat, M., and Tillard, J. M. "Pauvreté chrétienne, III. Moyen Âge" and "IV. Vingtième siècle" *DS*, 12, 1, 647–689.

Monachino, V., da Alatri, M., and Villapadierna, I. D. *La carità cristiana in Roma*, Bologna, 1978 (Roma cristiana, X).

Morichini, C. L. *Degli istituti di carità per la sussistenza e l'educazione dei poveri e dei prigionieri in Roma*, Rome, 1870.

Paglia, V. *"La pietà dei carcerati": Confraternite e società a Roma nei secoli XVI–XVIII*, Rome, 1980.

Pullan, B. "Poveri, mendicanti e vagabondi (secoli XIV–XVII)," *Storia d'Italia, Annali*, 1, Turin, 1978, 981–1047.

Rosa, M. "Chiesa, idee sui poteri e assistenza in Italia dal Cinque al Settecento," *Società e storia*, 10 (1980), 775–806.

POPE. The most popular title used to designate the successor of St. Peter. From the Greek παππος, a term of affectionate respect that is found in Homer and that passed into usage in the Eastern Church to denote bishops and even priests. It did not appear in the West until the early 3rd century and over time came to be reserved for bishops: in Cyprian (*Epp.* 8, 8; 23, 30 [letter to the Roman clergy]; 31, 36), in Augustine, in Damasus, and by St. Jerome (Y. Congar). Its first use for the bishop of Rome is evidenced in an inscription from the DEACON Severus to St. CALLISTUS: "Jussu papae sui Marcellini." The title tends to become specific by the end of the 4th and during the course of the 5th centuries, but "Papa urbis Romae (aeternae)" shows that it was still being applied to all bishops. In the 6th century, the chancery of Constantinople addressed the bishop of Rome using the title *papa*. From the end of the 8th century, the bishops of Rome used it to designate themselves, without specification. Under GREGORY V (996–9), the COUNCIL of Pavia (998) demanded that the archbishop of Milan, Arnulf, cease using it. GREGORY VII (1073–85), in a DICTATUS PAPAE (XI), laid down that the title would be reserved for the successor of Peter: "Quod hoc unicum est in mundi" (Because he is unique in the world). The expression "Most Holy Father" that is used today goes back to the 12th century. It corresponds to the historical sense of "pope," παιπος, "Reverend Father," as does the expression *Pater patrum* (Father of Fathers), often employed by the bishops of Illyricum and AFRICA when addressing the successor of Peter in the first centuries of the Church (6th and 7th centuries).

The evolution of the term toward usage strictly reserved for the bishop of Rome belongs to the history of apostolic authority. The familiarity it gradually acquired has led to a philological controversy over the question of whether the Aramaic word *Abba* (Mk 14:36; Rom 8:15; Gal 4:6) used in the New Testament meant "papa" as in the usage by a child. James Barr has summed up the question in an article with the self-explanatory title "Abba Isn't Daddy." According to him, *abba*, a term employed in the Targums (translations of the Bible into Chaldean made when the Jews returned from exile), was the Semitic equivalent of *abi*, "my father," an expression used in prayer. And in the three New Testament passages (in particular Mk 14:36, on the verge of the Crucifixion), where the word *abba* is transliterated in Greek, the text expressly employs the explicative vocative: "Αββα ω πατερ" or "Father O [my] Father." The familiar Roman cry "Viva il Papa!" is not equivalent to "Viva Papa!" (Long live Daddy!).

Philippe Levillain

Bibliography

Barr, J. "Abba Isn't Daddy," *Journal of Theological Studies*, April 1988, 28–47.

Battifol, P. "Cathedra Petri," *Études d'histoire ancienne de l'Église*, Paris, 1938.

Bellarmine, R. *Tertia controversia generalis De Summo Pontifice*, II, Naples, 1836, 1, 420–3.

POPEMOBILE

Burn-Murdoch, H. *The Titles of the Papacy*, London, 1954, 72–73.

Congar, Y. "Titres donnés au Pape" in *Concilium*, 108 (1975), 55–64.

Margot, J. C. *Cahiers de traduction biblique*, 18 (1992), 15–16.

Marot, H. "La collégialité et le vocabulaire épiscopal du Ve au VIIe siécle," *Irénikon*, 36 (1963), 41–60 and 39 (1964), 198–221.

POPEMOBILE. See **Automobiles, Papal**.

PORTA PIA. See **Unity, Italian**.

PORTANTINA PAPALE. *Portantina* is the name given to the sedan chair used by the popes as they moved about Rome and in the apostolic palaces.

Introduced in the 12th century in INNOCENT IV's papal court, the *portantina* gradually came to be reserved for the pope's exclusive use for reasons of convenience and health. The first pontiff to use it in a ceremony was PAUL IV, who in 1555 went by sedan chair to take possession of his see as bishop of Rome in ST. JOHN LATERAN. PIUS V followed his example eleven years later, giving rise to a custom that lasted until the reign of PIUS VII in 1801. Even if the pope did not always sit in it himself, the chair, sometimes drawn by horses and sometimes by chamberlains, figured in his cortege (often in several richly decorated versions) and enhanced the splendor of the cavalcade of cardinals and prelates. From the 19th century, the *portantina* was employed only inside the apostolic palace. PIUS IX was content with a simple armchair, but LEO XIII brought back the sedan chair in his old age, using it up to the beginning of the 20th century. This pope had three at his disposal: the ordinary sedan chair lined in red damask, the "noble chair" made of gilded wood and decorated in red velvet, and the Naples chair offered by the faithful of that city for the pope's sacerdotal jubilee, but which was so richly ornamented in wood and silver that it was too heavy to carry! PIUS XII resorted to Leo XIII's ordinary sedan chair when, in his turn, he felt the fatigue of his advancing years.

Joël-Benoît d'Onorio

Bibliography

"La portantina papale," *Annuaire pontifical catholique*, Paris, 1902.

POSSESSO. The ceremony of the *possesso*, whereby the newly elected pope takes possession of the diocese of Rome, was originally held immediately after his CORONA-TION. But in the 16th century the two ceremonies were separated, on account of their length and the fatigue they imposed on the participants. The first mention of a *possesso* dates from 795, when LEO III became pope. It took its inspiration from Charlemagne's entry into Rome in 773, which itself was modeled on ancient Triumphs. The *possesso* thus took the form of a long procession across the city, symbolizing the taking hold of temporal power. The cavalcade began at the papal palace of the Vatican or, exceptionally, of the QUIRINAL, as with BENEDICT XIII, BENEDICT XIV, CLEMENT XIV, and PIUS VII. It followed the Via Papalis, passing by way of the Capitol, the Forum, and the Colosseum. The streets were festooned with window hangings and tapestries. Every church built a temporary altar close to the route and there displayed its finest gold and silver plate, often with exposition of the Blessed Sacrament. Two triumphal arches recalling ancient glories were erected along the route. The first, built by the "architect of the Roman people" at the entrance to the Capitol, afforded a view of the statue of Marcus Aurelius, believed at the time to be that of CONSTANTINE. CLEMENT XII, in a spirit of austerity, refused to have it constructed in 1730, but he went unheeded. Here the senator of Rome paid homage to the pope by handing him the keys of the city. The second arch, at the Forum near the entrance to the Farnese Gardens, represented the homage of the duke of Parma to his sovereign, and then that of his heir, the king of Naples.

The second part of the ceremony took place at ST. JOHN LATERAN. The pope, having been greeted in the atrium by the cardinal archpriest and by the chapter, sat on a throne, the *sedia stercoraria*, which took its name from the song of Hannah, intoned at this point: *Suscitat de pulvere egenum et de stercore elevat pauperem* (1 Sm 2: 8). After tossing coins to the people as a sign of scorn for the goods of this world, the pope entered the church and took his seat in the choir on another throne, for the ceremony of the kissing of the foot by the canons. He then made his way to the Lateran Palace, where he received the FERULA (*signum regiminis et correctionis*), the keys of the basilica and the palace, and twelve seals. Before blessing the people from the loggia, he presented a gift of silver to the chapter, with whom he proceeded to share a meal. Along the route, the procession halted at a special stopping place, situated first at CASTEL SANT' ANGELO, then at Monte Giordano, and finally near the Arch of Titus. Here the chief rabbi presented a Hebrew Bible to the pope, who in turn granted the Jewish people his protection. Until the end of the 18th century, the whole cortege was on horseback, including the pope. When Benedict XIV was thrown by his horse, he made the witty remark "But I am the successor of PETER, not of PAUL." The 19th century saw the introduction of coaches. After Italian UNITY no further ceremony took place until the *conciliazione*. PIUS XI took up the tradition in 1929 in a private form, and Pius XII felt compelled to tone down the splendor of the ceremony in a time of war. Thereafter, none of the popes has omitted this ritual ceremony, even JOHN PAUL I, who reigned only thirty-three days and was the last to enter the Lateran in the *SEDIA GESTATORIA*. As in the old days, the mayor of Rome pays homage to the supreme pontiff as the cortege, which today consists of nine AUTOMOBILES, passes by.

The ceremony has been memorialized iconographically in three ways. Taking its inspiration from the fresco in the Salone Sistino of the *possesso* of Sixtus V, a first series of engravings depicted the procession making its way from St. Peter's to St. John Lateran as a long sinuous line, and featured the most distinctive details and prominent points of reference along the route. Among the finest of these engravings are that executed by Giovanni Giacomo De Rossi in 1667 for the *possesso* of Clement XI, and that by Etienne Pleart in 1692 for INNOCENT XIII. The second group concentrates on the arches erected at the Capitol and the Forum. Executed from the architects' drawings so as to make their ephemeral works known and possibly inspire similar decorations, these have the sparseness of diagrams, save for those of Vasi, which show the arch in its natural setting. The last series, which contains fewer engravings, recalls the fireworks that closed the celebration and their allegorical "machines." In 1644, at the *possesso* of INNOCENT X, the Spanish ambassador erected in front of his palace a "Noah's Ark on Mt. Ararat" complete with exploding rockets. Rivaling it in magnificence was the contribution of the French ambassador, the marquess of Saint-Chamond, whose "Rome Triumphant Accompanied by the Four Corners of the World" blazed before the Borghese Palace.

Olivier Michel

See also FEASTS OF PAPAL ROME.

Bibliography

Cancellieri, F. *Storia de' solenni possessi de' sommi pontefici*, Rome, 1802.

Caraffa, F. "Possesso dei pontefici," *EC*, 9 (1952), 1834–5.

Moroni, G. "Coronazione," *Dizionario*, 17 (1842), 206–7; "Possesso de' papi," *Dizionario*, 54 (1852), 294–7.

von Erffa, H. M. "Die Ehrenpforten für den Possess der Päpste im 17. und 18. Jahrhundert," *Festschrift für Harald Keller*, Darmstadt, 1963, 335–70.

POSTAGE STAMPS. The Lateran agreement guaranteed the pope license to issue stamps valid in countries belonging to the Universal Postal Union, of which Vatican City has been a member since 1929. Production of the stamps is entrusted to a service of the Governorate,

the Ufficio Filatelico e Numismatico (Office of Philately and Coinage), which arranges for the printing to be done at the Istituto Poligrafico e Zecca dello Stato (State Polygraphic Institute and Mint), a public agency of the Italian state headquartered in Rome. However, certain series (one in 1981 and another in 1982) have been printed by the Oesterreichische Staatdruckeri (Austrian National Printing Press).

Five new series are issued each year, the print run varying considerably. After reaching a peak of 1.6 million copies during Paul VI's pontificate, the total print runs gradually dropped to 1 million copies, then, from 1989, stabilized at 450,000 copies. All the stamps issued since 16 October 1963 (the first issuance of Paul VI's pontificate) have an unlimited postage validity. Each year the Vatican also puts out an aerogram (around 300,000 copies) and various postcards (about 100,000 copies of each card). The choice of subject for the different series takes its inspiration from anniversaries or important events of the current year. For example, the choices for 1981 were Virgil's two-thousandth anniversary, the fourth International Eucharistic Congress, the sixth centenary of the death of the Flemish mystic Jan Van Ruysbroeck, the International Year of the Handicapped, and the pope's travels. The last series, which from then on was issued every year, has many different values, each of which corresponds to one segment of the pontifical trips. The inscriptions are usually in Italian, sometimes in Latin. The values are expressed in Italian lire.

François-Charles Uginet

Bibliography

The yearly publication *L'attività della Santa Sede* gives a color reproduction each year of all the new issues as well as an indication of their print run. In 1977, the Governorate published the official list of all issues since 1929. This list is published approximately every five years. For special printings (stamped sheets or envelopes, postcards, postal orders, etc.) cf. *I francobolli e gli interi postali dello Stato della Città del Vaticano*, Vatican City, 1988, which shows reproductions and complete lists, divided by pontificate, since 1929.

PREDICTIONS. See **Prophecies, Modern**.

PREFECT OF THE CITY. The Roman prefecture was an administrative position created by Augustus which became permanent in the year 13 A.D. The holder of the office, the urban prefect, was originally expected to take care of policing and maintaining order in the city of Rome, with the help of the soldiers belonging to the urban cohorts under his supervision. For this purpose, he was given powers of coercion and, not long afterward, criminal and civil jurisdiction—over troublemakers, cases concerning slaves, guardians, senators, and so on—which he exercised within a radius of a hundred *milia passuum* (90 miles/145 kilometers) of Rome. Appointed by the emperor from among the former consuls, he was the highest functionary of the order of senators. Wearing the toga, he remained above all else a civilian.

The prefect's powers were considerably extended under CONSTANTINE: he was given responsibility for maintaining supplies of wheat and oil, for overseeing the corporations that ensured the supply of food, for the nighttime police and for firefighting, for the departments of public works and the aqueducts, for construction at Ostia and the Port, and for the upkeep of the harbors. He thus became the superior of the functionaries who had previously handled these tasks: the prefect of the *annona*, the prefect of nightwatchmen, the superintendent of public works, the superintendent of water, and the *comes*, or count, of the port; from then on, a time when the emperor no longer resided in Rome, he was looked upon in the city as a kind of vice-emperor. He even presided over the SENATE. Moreover, he inherited from the consuls—who as a rule did not reside in Rome—certain functions belonging to the pagan priesthood: presiding at festivals and games and maintaining temples and tombs, at least until the reign of Gratian.

It was chiefly the policing and judicial aspects of the post that justified the prefect's direct participation in the great persecutions. The first evidence is to be found at the time of the persecution of Valerian in 258: St. Ambrose and Prudentius recount that the urban prefect ordered the deacon Lawrence to hand over the church treasure entrusted to his care; he then had him arrested, tried him, condemned him to death, and subsequently had him put to death on a gridiron. St. Cyprian, a contemporary witness, adds this general detail: "In Rome the prefects [of the city and of the praetorium], who devoted their days to this persecution, condemned to death those who were brought to them and seized their goods for the profit of the treasury." For the persecution of Diocletian, authentic texts are lacking; the only ones available are the Passions of the martyrs, written at the earliest in the 5th and 6th centuries. These are riddled with anachronisms and imaginary anecdotes; moreover, while they usually show martyrs being judged by the urban prefect, each Passion gives the prefect a totally fictitious name: Chromatius in the Acts of St. Sebastian, Symphronius in those of St. Agnes (that virgin martyr is even wooed by the son of the prefect, who then puts her on trial and drags her to the brothel). The actual name of the prefect in 304 was Aradius Rufinus. However, as far as the application of the first edict is concerned—it was pronounced in March 303—we know from St. Augustine that the Roman Church's places of worship and landholdings were confiscated, though not destroyed, by the urban prefect.

Later, the prefect continued to intervene in matters concerning the Roman Church by virtue of his policing authority. Athanasius relates that Emperor Constantius II wrote a letter to the prefect of the city ordering him to seize Pope LIBERIUS and send him, willing or not, to the court of Milan for having refused to subscribe to the decree condemning Athanasius himself; Ammienus Marcellinus notes that in 356 the bishop was arrested in the middle of the night by the offices of the prefect Leontius and immediately dispatched to Milan. Subsequently, the prefect was ordered to intervene with his police force when an episcopal election caused disturbances that quickly turned into riots. This happened twice: in 366–71 in connection with the rivalry of the two candidates, DAMASUS and URSINUS, and in 418–20 in connection with that of BONIFACE and EULALIUS. The first rivalry touched three successive prefectures, the second that of Anicius Symmachus. In theory, the prefect was not meant to take part in the dispute in person, his task being to restore order, inform the emperor, and enforce his decisions.

After the conversion of Constantine, the number of Christians within the Roman population, and even among the aristocracy, increased noticeably. Not surprisingly, some Christian members of the nobility acceded to the city prefecture. The first seems to have been Acilius Severus in 325, in the middle part of Constantine's reign. Another, as we know from his famous sarcophagus in the Vatican Grottoes, was Junius Bassus, who died during his prefecture in 359, at the age of forty-two, after having been baptized. Under Valentinian I (364–75), there was an equal alternation of pagan and Christian prefects, but this balance was broken off by his son Gratian (375–83), to the advantage of the Christians. Theodosius and Honorius returned to a certain balance between the two groups until 410; thereafter the Christians enjoyed a clear advantage, but pagans from time to time held the office throughout the remainder of the 5th century. Whatever the prefects' personal religion, it was not supposed to compromise in the least their detachment in carrying out their appointed tasks. Only one instance is known of provocative or sensational conduct in this regard: in 377, Furius Maecius Gracchus had himself solemnly baptized with his lictors and the insignia of his office, then proceeded to pull down statues of the pagan gods and close a Mithraic sanctuary, according to Prudentius and St. Jerome. The prefects did not participate directly in the Christian feasts, and they were still able to celebrate the pagan feasts as late as the 5th century: they took part, for example, in the games held each year on 27 January in honor of the Castor (*Ludi Castorum*), without, however, offering sacrifices or joining in any pagan rituals.

Following Gratian's decrees of 382, we have no further evidence of any involvement by the prefectural authorities in the repairing of a pagan temple. The one exception occurred during the usurpation of Eugenius, who reestablished the pagan regime for a short time in 394: the restoration of the temple of Hercules in Ostia by a prefect of the *annona*. On the other hand, from that time on the prefect did intervene alongside the pontifical authorities in connection with costly construction work at ST. PAUL'S OUTSIDE THE WALLS, when the basilica was enlarged from 383 to 387, as well as with some later restoration. A letter from Emperor Valentinia II to the prefect Sallustius is the first evidence we have of collaboration between the prefect and the pope. It also shows that from 382 the prefect had been given responsibility for important works, at least partly insured by the treasury, relative to buildings of Christian worship, in any event relative to the basilicas of St. Paul and St. Peter.

After 476, the prefect virtually disappears from the documentation, but he makes another appearance in 573, when Gregory held the office. Seventeen years later this prefect became Pope GREGORY the Great—the first and only time, as far as we know, that a former prefect became bishop of Rome. Under his pontificate, which began in 590, there was still a prefect of the city: Gregory announces the appointment of one such and indicates on that occasion that, under his control, the election was the prerogative not of the sovereign or the Senate, but of the bishops of the region together with the municipal leaders of Rome, notables who represented the people. The prefect was by now practically one of the pope's right-hand men. Gregory once again concerned himself with a prefect, one Johannes, the last one about whom there is evidence, in 599. In actual fact, the pope had gradually inherited the powers of the prefect, which had dwindled dramatically; from the beginning of the 7th century, he took over the whole body of Roman municipal services relative to buildings and the food supply, the last of them under the pontificate of HONORIUS I.

André Chastagnol

Bibliography

Arnaldi, G. "Rinascità, fine, reincarnazione e successive metamorphosi del Senato romano (secoli V–XII)," *ASR*, 105 (1982), 5–56.

Chastagnol, A. *La Préfecture urbaine à Rome sous le Bas-Empire*, Paris, 1960; *Les Fastes de la préfecture de Rome au Bas-Empire*, Paris, 1962.

Pietri, C. *Roma christiana. Recherches sur l'Église de Rome, son organisation, sa politique, son idólogie de Miltiade à Sixte III (311–440)*, 2 vols., Rome, 1976.

Stein, E. *Histoire du Bas-Empire*, I: *De l'État romain à l'État byzantin (284–476)* (Fr. trans.), 2 vols., Paris, 1959; II: *De la disparition de l'Empire d'Occident à la mort de Justinien (476–565)*, Paris, 1949.

Vigneaux, P. E. *Essai sur l'histoire de la Praefectura Urbis à Rome*, Paris, 1896.

Vitucci, G. *Ricerche sulla Praefectura Urbis in età imperiale* (sec. I–III), Rome, 1956.

von Haehling, R. *Die Religionszugehörigkeit der hohen Amstträger des Römischen Reiches seit Constantius I. Alleinherrschaft bis zum Ende der Theodosianischen Dynastie*, Bonn, 1978.

PREFECTURE FOR THE ECONOMIC AFFAIRS OF THE HOLY SEE. See **Administrative Offices, Roman**.

PREFECTURE OF THE PAPAL HOUSEHOLD.

This office, which is under the direction of a prefect of episcopal rank, came into being as a result of PAUL VI's efforts in 1967 and 1968 to simplify a group of tasks and agencies once characteristic of the papal court and its history—in this case, the offices of majordomo, master of the chamber of His Holiness, master of the Sacred Palace of the Ceremonial Congregation, and of the Heraldic Committee of the papal court.

The Prefecture of the Papal Household is a heavy responsibility. Assisting the prefect in his task is a prelate with the title of regent. The prefect's mission consists in aiding the pope "in the palace itself or wherever he goes." The prefecture thus has responsibility for scheduling papal audiences and ceremonies for the protocol section (the liturgical side being under the Office for Liturgical Celebrations and the Congregation for Divine Worship) and preparing and following the itinerary of the supreme pontiff, both in Rome and abroad. The Prefecture of the Papal Household, working with the SECRETARIAT OF STATE, determines the norms according to which individuals desirous of meeting the pope, or heads of state visiting Rome, will be received at the Vatican: personal audience in the Holy Father's library, private audience in a restricted group; *bacciamano* on leaving the Wednesday public audience; state visit, etc. Under the strict protocol of former days, visitors were selected on the basis of rigorously established hierarchies and Church interests. Today, a familiarity in the pope's contacts and unexpected decisions surrounding certain audiences, conversations, or visits all make the prefect's task of organization rather complex.

Philippe Levillain

Bibliography

Annuario pontificio per l'anno 2000, 1963–1972.

d'Onorio, J. B. *Le Pape et le gouvernement de l'Église*, Paris, 1992.

PREJUDICES. The complexity of the institutions of the Holy See and the spectacular character of the build-

ings inside the VATICAN CITY STATE have given rise to a number of stereotypes, some growing out of an old opposition to pontifical Rome and others out of erroneous interpretations based on factitious comparisons or over-hasty observations. The anti-Roman complex, to adopt Hans Urs von Balthasar's expression, which is widespread in countries of Protestant religion and culture, has developed certain themes that in the 19th century were amplified or simplified by secular Jacobinism and by anticlericalism: Rome is the modern Babylon, worshiping Mammon rather than God, and the headquarters of careerists hatching a neverending plot in order to maintain and extend their power, by claiming universality of teaching and by standing in the way of enlightenment by reason in the name of the defense of a faith that presides over obscurantism. The Vatican is thus depicted as a place of mystery, the beauty of whose monuments makes its fascination all the more perverse and cloaks an archaism of behavior and mentality that are peculiar to the Holy See and the Church. This stereotype, which VATICAN II largely did away with by reason of its promotion of ECUMENISM, persists in certain circles, especially anticlerical ones, for whom the Vatican has no meaning and the occupation of buildings belonging to the cultural heritage of all humanity constitutes a usurpation. Similarly, a political interpretation of the relations between the Holy See and Italy has it that the Vatican State in Rome is an enclave barely tolerated by the Italian capital, and that no real relations exist between the "two Romes." Conversely, the long tradition of an Italian pope and an almost exclusively Italian Curia until Vatican II has given rise to the stereotype of a Holy See in Italy's clutches, epitomizing, in its behavior, its way of life, and its language, the Italian temperament to the point of caricature. Anti-Italianism has long played a part in feeding the anti-Roman complex. By an irony of history, the changes in the Church since Vatican II having opened up the CURIA to non-Italians, this phenomenon itself is interpreted as an internationalization that has reduced the Italians' share to a bare minimum to the advantage of other countries. This is emphatically not so. The case is one in which a minimum dose of a novel remedy has masked the persistence of the underlying condition: the curial administration remains essentially Italian. But now there exist within the Curia, scattered among the CONGREGATIONS, various national groups, which, as in any administration, tend to form lobbies and whose influence depends solely on the authority of one or another of the compatriots heading such and such a DICASTERY, on the trust reposed in them by the supreme pontiff, and on the lack of organization of the other nationalities. Today the Poles and the Germans have influence. Yesterday the French were relatively influential. The Anglo-Saxons are without influence, yet are numerous. The Italians are a permanent fixture.

Today, the stereotype of Rome as the modern Babylon exists only to feed a polemical literature that has brought the old prejudices to bear on the question of the papal FINANCES, the existence and recent difficulties of which have been the object of scandal-provoking analyses having all the flavor of a detective novel. Careers, CONCLAVES, ties with certain persons or certain institutions like OPUS DEI, have—since 1978 and the unexpected death of JOHN PAUL I—been presented in terms of links with powerful networks hit by disasters that are the fruit of their own abuse of power, networks that are game for anything and have branches in the worlds of speculation, of the Mafia, of FREEMASONRY, etc., for which the Vatican, which should logically be their enemy, serves as a sanctuary or shield. The suggestion that the financial vexations of the Holy See are instead the result of the classic inexperience of clerics in money matters is considered a modern version of intransigentism. In other words, paradoxically, voicing skepticism as to a predilection for wrongdoing on the part of the Vatican functionaries is taken as a strenuous defense of the Holy See. Similarly, the universal interest in certain events that have been given media attention since 1962 (the year the opening of the council was shown on Eurovision)—such as the death of the pope, the conclave, and the papal TRAVELS—has restored to a position of honor certain misconceptions often presented as authoritative commentary.

A few examples should suffice. One is the use in public of the first person singular ("I") on the part first of John Paul I and then of JOHN PAUL II: the dropping of the majestic plural (the so-called royal "we"), with its sacred inflection, is presented as the formal manifestation of a freedom of expression sought by the pope in his dealings with the modern world. In actual fact, the popes of past centuries, especially the 19th, often used the singular. Again, during the conclaves (of 1958 and 1978) there have been expressions of astonishment at the results of the voting (JOHN XXIII, John Paul I, and John Paul II) accompanied by long dissertations on a Roman saying, the fruit of an ironical wisdom: "Whoever enters the conclave a pope leaves it a CARDINAL." Every deliberative assembly has it in its power to come up with surprises, and the Church of Rome is strict in its rule that no preliminary caucusing take place; nevertheless, it remains that the rapid election of John XXIII, of John Paul I, and of John Paul II was foreseen by some before the conclave began, that John XXIII knew it, and that John Paul I could have expected it. As for PIUS XII and Paul VI, the one the secretary of state and the other Pius XII's ill-used dauphin who was rehabilitated by John XXIII, both men entered the conclave as popes and left the conclave elected.

History itself feeds on stereotypical situations so as to give symbolic meaning to what is pure chance. After his election in 1878, LEO XIII failed to give the blessing *urbi et orbi* from the outer loggia of ST. PETER'S. The capture of Rome eight years before and the maintaining of a territory that was not a state made the incident significant of the type of relations that had been established between the Vatican and Italy. Quite simply, the rusty bolts on the loggia doors were what stood in the way: given the fussing that would be required, it was thought unwise to revive the custom of the pope's appearance outside. Contrary to what some might like to believe, whether one interprets everything coming out of the Vatican with favor or with antipathy, the part played by chance and circumstances is greater than the symbolic importance the history and patrimony of the Vatican allow it to manifest.

Philippe Levillain

PRELATURES. Until VATICAN II, the Church was divided into ecclesiastical jurisdictions based on a territorial criterion, either a certain geographical area or a group of faithful (for example, of the same rite) spread over several territories. The usual type of local division was the diocese, but depending on the nature of the area, the type of congregation or the Church's state of development, there were also other divisions known as apostolic VICARIATES, abbeys nullius (of which the Church held the abbatial dignity), and prelatures nullius (of which the Church held the prelatial dignity).

After Vatican II, however, the territorial criterion ceased to be the only one determining ecclesiastical jurisdictions. They could also be mapped out to people who qualified to belong to them. In addition, to meet the needs of global evangelization, new, specialized institutions were planned "for different groups in society, in any region or nation or in any part of the world." These institutions would be "international seminaries, or special dioceses or personal prelatures and similar institutions" (decree *Presbyterorum ordinis*, n. 10).

Territorial Prelature. This is the name given in the 1983 Code of Canon Law to the prelature called *nullius* or *nullius dioecesis*, that is, a prelate having his own territory separate from any diocese" (c. 319 1 of 1917 Code).

It was in the 9th or 10th century that prelates nullius appeared who exercised a fully episcopal jurisdiction over a territory separate from a diocese. The rapid increase in EXEMPTIONS that the rank carried with it (including exemptions for abbeys nullius) gave rise to numerous complaints on the part of the bishops. At the council of Constance (1418), MARTIN V revoked the exemptions granted during the GREAT SCHISM without the agreement of the ordinaries. LEO X determined the method of granting exemptions that was to be followed in the future (Fifth Lateran council, constitution *Regimini*, 4 May 1515). The council of Trent refused to abolish all exemp-

tions under the jurisdiction of ordinaries, instead limiting them and submitting them to the delegate of the Apostolic See (session XXIII, c. 1-0; XXIV, c. 9 *De reformatione*). New concessions were subsequently agreed on in favor of army chaplains. The First Vatican Council did not accept their full abrogation. In view of present conditions, the number of prelatures nullius has increased recently. This division is defined as a specific number of the people of God established within certain territorial boundaries and entrusted to a prelate who governs them as their pastor, like a diocesan bishop (Code of 1983, c 370). Unless otherwise evident (c 968), it is similar to a diocese. This is the reason the prelate is a local ordinary (c 134.2) and is equated with diocesan bishops unless it appears otherwise from the nature of the matter or from the prescription of the law (c.381.2). He usually receives episcopal consecration (Congregation for bishops, notification of 17 October 1977, in X. Ochoa, *Leges Ecclesiae posta Codicem Juris canonici, editae Rome*, 5, 7358–7359).

Present legislation no longer envisages the constitution of a territorial prelature that does not include at least three parishes and that, according to the 1917 Code (c. 319 2), is governed by its own peculiar law. They are therefore all governed by the general law of the 1983 Code.

Fifty-seven territorial prelatures were in existence in 2000, of which 45 are in the mission territories of Latin America (*Annuario pontificio*, 1992, 999–1013), six in the Philippines, five in Europe, and one in Africa: Aiquile (11 December 1961); Alto Parana (25 March 1968); Alto Sinú (25 April 1969); Ayaviri (30 July 1958); Batanes and Babuyan Islands (30 November 1950); Bocas del Toro (17 October 1962); Borba (13 July 1963); Cafayate (8 September 1969); Calama (21 July 1965); Camet (29 November 1952); Caravelí (21 November 1957); Chetumal (23 May 1970); Chota (7 April 1963); Chuquibamba (5 June 1962); Chuquibambilla (26 April 1968); Coari (13 July 1963); Corocoro (25 December 1949); Coxim (3 January 1978); Cristalândia (26 March 1956); De n Funes (25 January 1980); El Salto (10 June 1968); Escuintla (9 May 1969); Huamachuco (4 December 1961); Huari (15 May 1958); Huautla (8 October 1972); Humahuaca (8 September 1969); Illapel (30 April 1960); Infanta (25 April 1950); Ipil (24 December 1979); Isabela (12 October 1963); Itaituba (6 July 1988); Itocoatiara (13 July 1963); Jesús María (13 January 1962); Juli (3 August 1957); Labrea (1 May 1925); Libmanan (9 December 1989); Loretto (24 June 1965); Los Ríos (10 September 1951); Madera (25 April 1966); Marajó (14 April 1928); Marawi (20 November 1976); Mission de France ou de Pontigny (15 August 1954); Mixes (21 December 1964); Moyobamba (7 March 1948); Nuevo Casas Grandes (13 April 1977); Obidos (10 April 1957); Pompéi or the Blessed Virgin

Mary of the Most Holy Rosary (20 March 1926); Santo Domingo de los Colorados (5 January 1987); Sao Félix (13 May 1969); Sicuani (10 January 1959); Tef (11 August 1950); Tibú (16 November 1983); Tromsø (28 March 1979); Trondheim (28 March 1979); Tunis (9 July 1964); Xingú (16 August 1934); Yauyos (12 April 1957).

Personal Prelature. This juridical unit first appeared at the Second Vatican Council. It was designed to respond to pastoral challenges of the contemporary world that existing structures did not adequately meet. The criterion for the territorial distinction of ecclesiastical jurisdictions was corrected and modified *ratione apostolatus*, because of the demands of the apostolate. Concern for the communion of Churches, also evidenced at Vatican II, justified the historical development of the Church's hierarchical structures, always in accord with its unalterable constitutional core.

In the first stages of the council, the personal prelature was envisaged as being modeled on the Mission of France—a specialized pastoral structure designed to provide a missionary clergy to those French dioceses with a scarcity of priests. But the council fathers departed from that model and produced a new pattern that would make possible "not only a distribution adapted to the priests but also to the particular activities for the different groups in society, in any region or nation or any part of the world" (decree *Presbyterorum ordinis*). They believed that "it could be useful to create, to this end, international seminaries, special dioceses or personal prelatures, and other institutions of the same type." These entities would be able "to see some priests adapted or incardinated" for the common good of the whole Church (such is the reason for the erection by the Holy See of similar institutions) "according to modalities to be established in each case," and, in an important qualification, always respecting the rights of the local ordinaries (Decree *Presbyterorum ordinis*).

Within a broad framework for the application of the council (*motu proprio Ecclesiae Sanctae*), PAUL VI provided norms for the interpretation of this decree. After discussing the distribution of clergy (I, 1–3), he raised the question of the possibility that the Holy See might erect jurisdictional entities with a personal kind of common law, having both a prelate and a secular clergy, designed to carry out "individual, pastoral and missionary works, favoring different regions or groups in society needing special help" (I, 4). Besides consulting the conferences of bishops concerned with the apostolic work of these prelatures, Paul VI noted that the rights of the ordinaries must be respected. The council's thinking also implied that "there is nothing to prevent members of the laity, either single or married, who have met the standards for the prelature, from devoting themselves to serving the works and initiatives of that structure with their professional competence" (I, 4).

With the reorganization of the Roman Curia, prelatures were placed under the authority of the Congregation for Bishops. They alone are responsible for the configuration of the hierarchical structures of the Latin Church and the nomination of their prelate (apostolic constitution *Regimini Ecclesiae Universae*).

From the revisions of the Code—realized in conformity with what the council had set forth and with the council's norms of application—one can extract the following points: (a) throughout the successive schemas, personal prelatures were placed among the hierarchical structures governed by statutes established by the Church; (b) they were conceived to meet the ordinary pastoral needs of contemporary faithful; (c) but they were never conceived as particular Churches, since on many points they meet the norms relative to particular Churches (their own prelate, clergy and laity, incardination of clerics), and so the legislators applied the same norms where entities were similar and (d) they were never conceived as hierarchical structures, but are organized freely by the faithful.

These elements were included in the 1983 Code of Canon Law promulgated by JOHN PAUL II (25 January 1983), in which an autonomous place was given to the new configuration (c. 294–97) to emphasize that the personal prelature is not a local Church. Personal prelatures were instituted by the Apostolic See to promote an appropriate distribution of presbyters or to perform particular pastoral or missionary works for various regions or different social groups (c. 194). Harmonious relations with local Churches are guaranteed by the prior consultation of the conferences of the bishops involved, set up by the Holy See, as well as by the dispositions of the statutes peculiar to each prelature, which must determine its relations with the local ordinaries in whose particular Churches the prelature itself exercises or desires to exercise its pastoral or missionary works, with the prior consent of the diocesan bishop (c. 297).

These statutes were drawn up case by case by the Holy See (c. 295). In this way, highest authority determined the final form that would, in its view, meet the present needs of the pastoral leadership of the universal Church and the particular Churches. It also emphasized the personal prelature's characteristic jurisdictional structure.

The prelate, who is not necessarily of bishop's rank, is the proper ordinary of the personal prelature (c. 295, 1). He may erect a seminary, incardinate clerics, and promote them to orders under the title of service to the prelature (c. 295, 1). The expectation of the *motu proprio Ecclesiae Sanctae* can be seen here: layfolk may cooperate as members of the body in the tasks of the prelature, through bilateral agreements entered into with the prelature and according to the disposition of its statutes (c. 296, 2). The prelate exercises executive power according to both general law (c. 134) and the statutes of individual law, with regard to the clergy of the prelature—who are directly responsible to him—and to the layfolk incorporated in it. Concerning the latter, this power is limited to matters that are the object of the convention arranged between the prelature and the layperson. Depending on the nature of the personal prelature, the prelate's jurisdiction may extend to the same matters as concern the diocesan bishop, or to different matters. In the first case, the jurisdiction is described as cumulative; in the second, as juxtaposed, as in the prelature of the Holy Cross and Opus Dei, the first and today the only personal prelature erected by the Holy See. Personal prelatures are dependent on the Congregation for Bishops (apostolic constitution *Pastor bonus*).

Dominique Le Tourneau

Bibliography

Baucher, "Abbaye nullius," *DDC*, I (1935), 16–29.

Blanco, M. *El concepto de prelado en la lengua castellana siglos XIII–XVI*, Pamplona, 1989.

Caparros, E. "Une structure juridictionnelle issue de la préoccupation pastorale de Vatican II: les prélatures personnelles," *Studia Canonica*, 17 (1983), 487–531; "A New Hierarchical Structure for New Pastoral Needs: Personal Prelatures," *Philippiniana Sacra*, 24 (1989), 379–417.

Claeys Bouaert, F. "Prélat," *DDC*, VII (1965), 176–7.

Congregation for Bishops, declaration *Praelaturae personales*, 23 August 1982.

Dalla Torre, G. "Prelato e Prelatura," *Enciclopedia del diritto*, 34, 973–80.

de Fuenmayor, A. *Escritos sobre Prelaturas personales*, Pamplona, 1990.

Fornès, J. "El perfil jurídico de las prelaturas personales: Un comentario a la Constitución Apostólica *Ut sit* (28 Nov. 1982)," *Monitor Ecclesiasticus*, 108 (1983), 436–72.

Fox, J. *The Personal Prelature of the Second Vatican Council: An Historical Canonical Study*, 2 vols., Rome, 1987.

Fumagalli, O. "Las prelaturas personales en el Concilio Vaticano II," *Ius Canonicum*, 28 (1988), 753–64.

Garrido, M. "Un servicio del nuevo Código de Derecho Canónico. La identidad de personas e instituciones en la Iglesia," *Nova et Vetera*, 10 (1985), 103–13.

Ghirlanda, G. "Natura delle prelature personali e posizione dei laici," *Gregorianum*, 2 (1988), 299–314.

González del Valle, J.-M. "Zur Neue Rechtsfigur der Personalprälaturen," *Österreichsches Archiv für katholischen Kirchenrecht*, 34 (1983/1984), 131–40.

Green, T. J. "Personal Prelatures," *The Code of Canon Law: A Text and Commentary*, London, 1985, 240–2.

Gutiérrez, J. L. "De Praelatura personali iuxta leges eius constitutivas et Codicis iuris canonici normas," *Periodica de re morali, canonica, liturgica*, 72 (1983), 71–111.

Hervada, J. *Tempus otti: Fragmentos sobre los orígenes y el uso primitivo de los términos "Praelatus" y "Praelatura,"* Pamplona, 1991.

John Paul II, Code of Canon Law of 1983, c. 294–97, 368, 370; apostolic constitution *Pastor bonus*, 20 June 1988, art. 80.

Le Tourneau, D. "Les prélatures personnelles dans la pastorale de Vatican II," *L'Année canonique*, XXVIII (1984), 197–219; "Les prélatures personnelles vues par la doctrine," *Revue des sciences religieuses*, 60 (1986), 235–60.

Lo Castro, G. "Le prelature personali per lo svolgimento di specifiche funzioni pastorali," *Il Diritto ecclesiastico e Rassegna di diritto matrimoniale*, Jan.–June 1983, 85–146; *Le prelature personali. Profili giuridici*, Milan, 1988.

Lombardía, P., and Hervada, J. "Sobre prelaturas personales," *Ius Canonicum*, XXVII (1987), 11–76.

Madera López, L. "As Prelazias Pessoais no Novo Código di Direito Canonico," *Communio*, V (1986), 240–54.

Manzanares, J. "De Praelaturae personalis origine, natura et relatione cum Jurisdictione ordinaria," *Periodica de re morali, canonica, liturgica*, 69 (1980), 387–421.

Martinez-Torrón, J. *La configuración jurídica de las Prelaturas personales en el Concilio Vaticano II*, Pamplona, 1986.

Miras, J. *La noción canónica de "praelatus,"* Pamplona, 1987.

Navarro Valls, R. "Las Prelaturas personales en el derecho conciliar y docicial," *Estudios eclesiásticos*, 59 (1984), 431–58.

Ombres, R. "Opus Dei and Personal Prelatures," *Clergy Review*, 70 (1985) pp. 292–5.

O'Reilly, M. "Personal Prelatures and Ecclesial Communion," *Studia Canonica*, 18 (1984), 439–56.

Patruno, D. "Le prelature personali: enti istituzionali della Chiesa cattolica," *Monitor Ecclesiasticus*, 63 (1988), 259–63.

Paul VI, *motu proprio Ecclesiae Sanctae*, 6 August 1966, I, 4; apostolic constitution *Regimini Ecclesiae Universae*, 15 August 1967, no. 49, 1; Directory of Bishops *Ecclesiae imago*, 22 February 1973, no. 172.

Rodríguez, P. *Iglesias particulares y Prelaturas personales*, Pamplona, 2nd ed., 1986; "Prelaturas personales," *Palabra*, XII (1986), 621–24.

Rodríguez, P., and de Fuenmayor, A. "Sobre la naturaleza de las Prelaturas personales y su inserción dentro de la estructura de la Iglesia," *Ius Canonicum*, 24 (1984), 9–47.

Rodríguez Vidal, A. "Prelaturas personales: Una nueva figura jurídica," *Teología y Vida*, 24 (1983), 265–74.

Rodríguez Vidal, A., and Ibañez Langlois, J. M. "Nuevos frutos de la eclesiología conciliar: Las Prelaturas Personales," *Communio* (Latin America), III, 10, 1984, 74–81.

Roggendorf, J. "Die rechtliche Gestaltung der Personalprälaturen," *Theologische-praktische Quartalschrift*, 133 (1985), 247–48.

Schouppe, J. P. "Les prélatures personnelles: Réglementation canonique et contexte ecclésiologique," *Revue théologique de Louvain*, 17 (1986), 309–28.

Spinelli, L. "Riflessi canonistici di una nuova struttura pastorale (le prelature personale)," *Raccolta di scritti in onore di Pio Fedele*, Perugia, 1984, I, 591–612.

Stetson H., and Hervada, J. "Personal Prelatures from Vatican II to the New Code: An Hermeneutical Study of Canons 294–297," *The Jurist*, 45 (1985), 379–417.

Valdrini, P. "Prélature," *Catholicisme*, 11 (1988), 820–4.

Vatican II, decree *Presbyterorum ordinis*, 7 December 1965, no. 10.

PRESS OFFICE OF THE HOLY SEE. Long before it theorized about "social communications" and laid down rules for putting the theory into practice, the government of the Church, like all powerful institutions, used techniques for disseminating information in two opposite directions: from bottom to top for collating news and news analysis, and from top to bottom for the direct diffusion of news material elaborated by those in authority. These were two operations, and quite distinct. On the one hand was objective fact, bearing witness to an action performed; on the other, the completion of an interpretive process.

The Vatican's official gazette, the *Acta Apostolicae Sedis*, is the sole authorized source of public documentation. The various stages of its editing have always been a secret, any transgression of which was tantamount to violating the sacred and subject to ecclesiastical sanctions. Yet the external world—persons engaged in the enactment of history—needed to be informed of the activity of the Holy See, particularly as it affected the secular realm. From the beginning of the 20th century, such reports were channeled through chroniclers known as "Vaticanists," who had no official status and were tolerated for practical reasons and used in a calculated manner. They wormed their way around the Vatican relying on personal friendship and biased antechamber confidences, and interpreted the smallest hints of action in a seemingly static world. A Vatican that disdained the idea of "public relations" found them not just unacceptable but indecent.

Among the Vaticanists, who were highly jealous of their fief, the Italians and French were nationalist rivals, believing that, even in the 20th century, the Holy See should recognize that their two countries had historically privileged roles, no matter how tortuously enacted. The French retained traces of the arrogance of the kings of France, disguised behind a recent and exaggerated ultramontanism. The Italians mingled a critical allegiance to the pope-king with a new sense of pride in the house of Savoy. The writer who signed himself "Aventino" for *Action Française*, together with Jean Carrière for the *Journal des Dèbats*, Charles Pichon for the *Écho de Paris* and Silvio Negro for the *Corriere della Sera*, exemplify this type of "Vatican news." Fontenelle, the canon of St. Peter's, was the quasi-official correspondent for the French Catholic newspaper *La Croix*.

Before 1930, the future cardinals Pizzardo, secretary of the Congregation for Extraordinary Ecclesiastical Affairs, and Ottaviani, substitute of the Secretariat of State, attempted to counter the Vaticanists by using the Havas agency as a channel for information. The young writer Max Bergerre became the middleman for their delegate, Pucci, in the dissemination of straight news. The pope's speeches went through the same channel. Domenico Tardini used Havas as well, the process being entrusted to Antonio Samoré.

When Pius XI died, in February 1939, the Italian and foreign Vaticanists were locked up in a little room on the St. Damasus courtyard, with a few telephones. No news was to be had except what could be gleaned by observing the cardinals as they went back and forth. A prelate of the Secretariat of State, G.-B. Montini, on his own initiative set up a meeting in the editorial offices of the *Osservatore romano* to give out information on the CONCLAVE that elected Pius XII. That custom survived the war, and at the consistory of 1946, the press was admitted to a special gallery in St. Peter's, a privilege that Cardinal Cicognani would forbid at Vatican II. Around 1953, the first press service was established by the Secretariat of State in the offices of the *Osservatore romano*, under the supervision of the editor, Raimondo Manzini, who delegated the running of the office to the deputy editor-in-chief, Luciano Casimirri.

When Pius XII's reign ended, all prudence was tossed to the winds, all barriers torn down. Indeed, in October 1958 Pius XII died literally before the world's eyes, accompanied by bulletins that Vatican Radio broadcast several times an hour and dogged by the first television cameras. He was even betrayed by one of those nearest to him, his personal physician, who photographed the pope's agony in order to sell the negatives to international weeklies. This time it was not a question of blaming the world's journalists, but rather the ruthless nature of what the modern world called "news," abetted by the corruption of a disloyal servant.

With JOHN XXIII, who granted journalists one of his first public audiences, similarities to the practices of the secular political world increased. The cardinal secretary of state, Domenico Tardini, gave the first Vatican press conference on 16 March 1960 to make public John

XXIII's decision to enter into dialogue with the Eastern Church.

In the preparatory phase of VATICAN II, the question of the transmission of accurate news was posed, and Cardinal Tardini announced the creation of a press bureau on 30 September 1959. During the preliminary consultation, several bishops suggested a center for public relations. Instead of being entrusted to the Secretariat for Press and Public Ceremony, created in the spring of 1960 under the presidency of J. M. O'Connor, the "technical participation" of the press and radio in the workings of the council was placed under the supervision of the secretariat of the council and the Curia, and managed by a news-broadcasting press office.

Pericle Felici, secretary of the preparatory commission, did not mince words when he spoke to the general assembly of the Italian Catholic press on 3 December 1960. He recalled that the press had "created serious difficulties in the progress of the First Vatican Council." It was an accurate statement, except for the fact that the ones responsible had been a few council fathers and experts who, in the battle over papal infallibility, had exploited the only public medium of communication available at the time. Skirting this detail, Msgr. Felici threw out an unambiguous warning: "The press office will from time to time provide you with news that is usable and true and will answer your wishes as far as is possible. . . . Do not go anywhere where you cannot or may not remain. Only on this condition will we remain good friends."

Until the first session, the press service of the *Osservatore romano*, headed by Federico Alessandrini (1905-83) held its own. Alessandrini was the model of a journalist in the service of the Holy See, combining rigorous loyalty to the pope with an understanding of the pitfalls of the news business; he had joined the *Osservatore romano* in 1931. In 1946, he edited the *Quotidiano*, a Catholic paper based in Rome, then in 1950 returned to the *Osservatore romano*, becoming deputy director in 1961. In July 1970, he was appointed provisional director of the press office of the Holy See, retiring in June 1975.

This arrangement smoothed the transition between two methods of disseminating news. The long phase of grudging disclosure of matters that were secret by divine right had been handled by a layman, under the control of clerics behind the scenes. The press conferences were entrusted to a priest, Fausto Vallainc. Born in 1916, this amiable native of the Val d'Aosta, who agonized over his task, understood the needs of the press and was one of the very few Italian priests who were also professional journalists. First as the director of an information agency for diocesan periodicals, and then, in 1959, of the *Settimana del Clero*, he had also taken on the leadership of the National Bureau of the Catholic Press at the Italian bishops' conference. On 1 September 1966, Vallainc was ap-

pointed director of the press room of the Holy See. On 14 July 1970, he was made auxiliary bishop of Siena, at Colle Val d'Arno. He died in 1980 as bishop of Alba.

On 12 October 1961, Vallainc was called on to lead the press office in three capacities: editor of the *Osservatore romano*, which acted as press service to the public for the council; spokesman of the Secretariat; and spokesman of the central committee of the council. There were thus three degrees of subordination in the Vatican hierarchy. In the first degree, integration with *Osservatore romano*—which already acted as a press service—indicated continuity. Vatican control was next ensured by two functions that were peculiar to the council but emanated from the Roman Curia, the central committee acting as first court of appeal of the decisions issued by the all-powerful secretariat.

It is obvious that the channels of information were strictly supervised, all along the line. The press service never had any autonomy, even of management. Journalists appreciated the link with the *Osservatore romano* as a convenience and out of personal sympathy with Vallainc. But Cardinal Cicognani, secretary of state, would insist that Vallainc and his adjuncts be considered functionaries (*operatori*) of the secretariat, not journalists. Responsible for easing the tension between his superiors and accredited journalists, Vallainc, at the beginning of his mission, begged John XXIII to relieve him of it.

Under his leadership, several ecclesiastics distributed information for the seven language divisions. Father François Bernard, an Assumptionist and editor at *La Croix*, was the intermediary for the French-speaking sector. Inaugurated on 5 October 1962, the technical installations of the press room, at the entrance to St. Peter's square, perfectly met the needs of dissemination. Based on a daily bulletin, brochures were put out tracing the program of the council. Besides the official spokesmen, certain experts were called on to explain the documents. Some of the individuals on whom the pope had relied to prepare drafts of his great encyclicals presented these documents to the press room. The language was efficient and highly sensitive to the dangers of simplifying information. For instance, the future Cardinal Paul Poupard, who at that time worked in the French section of the Secretariat of State, provided an explanation with commentary of *Populorum progressio* that contributed greatly to the initial welcome that document received from the correspondents.

The flow of information was, from the outset, strictly controlled by the secretary general of the council, Felici. He approved the text of the communiqué that Vallainc wrote following each general congregation, in the form of a general summary. No names could be cited, nor could any of the speakers' remarks be quoted. As he transmitted the text to those responsible in the linguistic divisions, who were not allowed to attend sessions, Vallainc added oral commentaries. Thereafter, each responsible person held his own press conference. The official version thus went through a triple distillation.

Moreover, the journalists accredited to the council were selected according to the strictest criteria. The editor of a publication had "to guarantee that his representative would have a correct attitude toward the Holy See and the Catholic Church." The correspondent would have free access only to the press room and certain conciliar ceremonies. The old restriction remained in force: no access to Vatican City, no "approaching and consulting resident persons, employees and visitors" of that city. No photography was permitted without authorization. The card of accreditation would be taken away from those "whose presence in Vatican City is not judged opportune."

Only one comparison came to mind: "Most of the journalists were in the situation of the permanent or special envoy to Moscow, who only got his information by reading Pravda or Izvestia," wrote Philippe Levillain. Correspondents therefore set about removing the obstacles to obtaining ample and reliable information. The leading council Fathers set up networks of more or less direct leaks for the benefit of journalists—not in order to hand over or exploit some explosive secret, but to clarify the evolution and significance of the debates and to give journalists precise, in-depth knowledge of the issues at stake. The *Messaggero*, a Roman daily, was the first systematically to break through the censorship, by publishing the list of conciliar commissions prepared by the Curia. This made possible the first movement on the part of the council Fathers toward gaining their independence of the Curia.

From the preparatory period, in Rome and abroad, meetings mushroomed. Four international congresses of religious news reporters drew up alternative norms of communication, in order to avoid a situation where the press would come up against "a wall of silence, of dissimulation, or of defiance" and by accepting it, betray the truth. One of the documents submitted to these congresses stressed the paradoxical situation of Catholic journalists who, "not being able to take liberties with the information," had to allow the neutral press all the latitude of being "more and better informed."

During the few weeks of the first session, the system became untenable, first and foremost for the council Fathers themselves. Their intervention on the fringes of the Holy See was notorious. Cardinal Montini, archbishop of Milan, himself published his "Letters from the council" in the newspaper *Italia*. In Bologna, Cardinal Lercaro covered events for the daily *Avvenire d'Italia*, which published five pages a day on the council, deliberately breaking the secrecy.

Another example was that of the future cardinal secretary of state, Msgr. Jean Villot, archbishop coadjutor of Lyon and adjunct secretary of the council. His actions have to a large extent been revealed by his beneficiary, Father Wenger, editor-in-chief and correspondent of *La Croix*. "Wishing to ensure the good reputation of the council . . . , [Villot] decided to act as a journalist for *La Croix*," to which he gave articles—which were attributed to lay writers—and daily reports. *Le Figaro* also benefited from information gathered at the source by abbé René Laurentin, an expert at the council. Neither for him nor for Father Wenger, both journalists in the service of the Church, does the dual allegiance seem to have been a problem. "This privilege was envied," said abbé Laurentin, "and held to be discriminatory." Discriminatory it was indeed. As repositories of religious information, the clerics on principle got more credit than the laymen. However, unlike *La Croix, Le Figaro* was not an organ of the Church.

Seven centers of documentation and information, one for each language sector, were set up under the aegis of the national episcopates, without officially belonging to the conciliar agencies. At the time of the debate on the sources of Revelation, the issue of theological schools became tinged with nationalism. Opposition to the Roman Curia lent the debates a bitter tone. Frustrations and personal ambitions added to the confusion. Signs became reality; the rewording of comments became literal translation. The authorities of the Holy See were swamped, and the press no less. The press was divided between informed newspapers with good sources outside the press room, and others that used their own networks and improvised from chance encounters, with the result that the press often carried away versions of the council debates that were truncated, polemical, and had little to do with reality.

The situation quickly turned into a hotbed of misunderstanding that threatened collapse. This was averted by some improvised concessions, thanks to PAUL VI's decision to remove conciliar secrecy, at least in part. As a first step, Vaillainc's linguistic assistants were authorized to attend the debates they were meant to summarize. Direct links between council Fathers and journalists were in practice tolerated, and in an atmosphere of relative discretion. On the eve of the second session, reorganization centered on the two protagonists in the matter of information: the dispensing authority, and the journalists at the receiving end.

On his own, Paul VI discreetly put into action a radical reform, the significance of which extended beyond administration. The secretary general of the council was quietly relieved of his exclusive post. The press bureau, of which Vallainc remained director, was put under a Committee for the Council Press, presided over by Martin O'Connor, president of the Pontifical Commission for Motion Pictures, Radio and Television, and vice president of the Conciliar Commission for the Apostolate of the Laity. Members of this committee were chosen, on the one hand, from the council Fathers, according to the linguistic groups and geographical areas, and on the other from expert theologians already attached to the commission on the schema devoted to "The Church in the world of this time," a stipulation that made the new organization the most energetic of the council and gave it the dynamics of its most innovative pastoral intentions. Members were given complete freedom to have "direct and daily" contacts with the centers of documentation as well as accredited journalists, a signal proof that Paul VI had taken the question of information in hand. Moreover, with total discretion, he made plain his resolve to have done with the destructive methods of the Curia.

At the same time, under the aegis of Father Roberto Tucci, editor of *Civiltà Cattolica* (which most journalists respected), the representatives of 46 organizations of religious information set up a Center for Coordination of the Communications of the Council (CCCC), a blanket agency embracing national centers of documentation which drew up a large mass of files that shed light on the council debates. Without involving the Holy See, the center brought it the pledge of a cooperative office.

Both these reforms came into force with the second session, in the autumn of 1962. From then until the end of the council, the information system established equilibrium. The lateral news sources gave guarantees of seriousness, while the direct ones explained more precisely the basis of the debates, discouraging the journalists from trying to connect ideas to personalities. And yet, fed as it was with rumors and tendentious gossip, this kind of activity never completely disappeared. Certain texts—for instance, schema XIII on the Church in the world of our times, or the document on the Jews (finally incorporated into the constitution on non-Christian religions)—were launched into public discussion through the leaking of plans which aroused opinions and influenced the debates. The new mechanisms hit their stride, however, during the last two sessions of the council.

After the close of the council, the press bureau, which was reduced to a minimum by that time, nearly vanished. Paul VI caused it to be resurrected under the guise of a "press room (*sala stampa*) of the Holy See" within the Pontifical Commission for Social Communications, to take the place of the Conciliar Committee. On 1 September 1966, Vallainc was named as its head, thus ensuring continuity. From July 1970 to 1975, his "provisional" successor was Federico Alessandrini, deputy director of the *Osservatore romano*, a step that looked like a return to the pre-Council organization. In June 1976, Romeo Panciroli, a missionary and creator of many television programs on behalf of evangelization, took over. On 6 November 1984, JOHN PAUL II appointed as head of the press office a layman, Joachim Navarro Valls, a doctor who had become a Spanish press correspondent at the Vatican and was a member of Opus Dei. Under his aegis, the press office reached a high level of efficiency, sending out an abundant flow of documentation that was precise, open to the most modern methods of diffusion, and on a level equal to that of the best foreign information centers.

This evolution, dictated by the application of the instruction *Communio et progressio*, nevertheless did not happen without clashes between two ideas: evangelization, and what, for lack of a more appropriate term, might be called "pure information." When Paul VI inaugurated the pontiff's personal journeys around the world, which John Paul followed up, he was at first escorted by special envoys who sometimes paid more attention to picturesque incidents or differences of opinion vis-à-vis the authorities of the host countries than to the content of messages and their implications. Sometimes a correspondent saw his accreditation suspended for breaking the embargo on the publication of some text, or was excluded from the pontifical airplane because of commentaries that were judged inopportune. In 1983, the deputy director of the *Osservatore romano*, Don Vergilio Levi, was summarily dismissed for having commented too explicitly on the background of John Paul II's trip to Poland.

In October 1987, after a year of discussions, some internationally renowned Catholic newspapers—including the *National Catholic Reporter, Vida Nueva, Orientierung, Herder Korrespondenz, Il Regno*, and *Rocca*—published a manifesto inveighing against the return of ecclesiastical censorship of information, de facto if not de jure, particularly where priest-journalists were concerned. In 1985 in Palermo, Father Sorge, editor of *Civiltà Cattolica*, was replaced by Father Salvini, who lost the privilege of a bimonthly conversation with the pontiff because he had been censured by Curia functionaries. Vatican personnel were reminded not to have direct relations with journalists. Cardinal Jérôme Hammer, prefect of the Congregation for Religious, reminded the priests engaged with information of their duty to ensure "the transmission and correct, integral diffusion of the holy doctrine of the Church."

The modernization of the means of communication at the Church's disposal (plans for network television and press agencies) shows that complete mastery of this resource is now a fact, extended to global dimensions—an authentic instrument of power. Concern for open relations with those working in the news media is clear on the part of John Paul II. The pope has heeded them more than any of his predecessors—even, on 16 January 1988, going so far as to visit the offices of the Association of the Foreign Press in Italy, something inconceivable even in the papacy of Paul VI.

On 15 April 1983, in his message for the Seventeenth World Day of Social Communications, the pope expressed the wish to see the realization at an institutional level of "an order of communication that would guarantee an honest, just and constructive usage of information." This is an old internal debate familiar to the journalistic profession, but the pope's intervention does not necessarily mean it is about to end.

"Evangelization is communication, our paths converge," the pope told journalists, his companions as he traveled the world, on 27 January 1984. He also admonished them: "Nobody is a professional writer for his own eye. The social dimension is the raison d'être and perhaps the most delicate aspect of modern journalism. In an urgent, never-ending way it demands an effort of syntony over the wavelength of reality and a balanced discernment which safeguards, in clear fashion, the rights of truth and duties toward society."

These are metaphors on the technical level. The press is clearly welcome, but against the backdrop of a wider debate that is still going on over whether information should depend on an authority that exercises oversight over what can be published.

It took three years to find a compromise response in the daily workings of the press office. Some of the disagreements between the Holy See and journalists have to be relativized and compared with the clashes that arise whenever a secular government exerts pressure on those who chronicle its actions (a suspension of accreditation is nowhere exceptional). Yet there still exists a fundamental divergence, linked to the very nature of the transmission of Christ's message. Instructive documents on "the instruments of social communications" have eased the problem but have not abolished it. Sole custodian of the sacred trust of the faith, the Church will never permit uncontrolled interpretation of the faith without being given the final word, binding on individual consciences. The Church determines where information begins, and where interpretation begins. That is the privilege of any power, but it does not eliminate tension between the Holy See and the news media.

The notion of information as a corrective force is not completely academic. Could such a power exist within the Church? One can readily understand why plans for a "new world order of information," based on public control of the messages to be communicated, which UNESCO drew up at the inspiration of the Third World countries, were greeted by the Vatican with encouragement and favorable comments. The question of freedom of information will never be settled. This has not so much to do with the exercise of that freedom as with the contents of the information. One of the most reliable interpreters of Paul VI's thinking, Father Roberto Tucci, then editor in chief of *Civiltà Cattolica*, tackled the subject in 1966 in describing the relations between the freedom of the Catholic journalist and the authority of the Church. The first, he said, was very broad. Had not the constitution

Lumen gentium made it clear that layfolk have not merely the ability but the duty to "make their opinions known about things that concern the good of the Church"? Freedom of information, destined to form that public opinion praised by Pius XII and exalted by John XXIII in *Pacem in terris*, should recognize its own limits: dogmatic definitions and other doctrinal decisions.

Only very rarely are these considerations called into question in the actual diffusion of information. In 1964, Paul VI had, on the occasion of a speech to the staff of a Milan newspaper, formulated a point that revolutionized people's thinking: "A newspaper reports the news, states things as they are. . . . Information that wants to be truthful and complete is above all deeply independent of religion." Basically an objective reality, it "becomes a ferment of ideas" depending on the way in which it is presented.

As an acknowledgment of the ideological independence of truth, these words could have been a landmark as decisive as Pius XII's words about public opinion. By adopting an attitude of dialogue with the operators of the means of communication, the pope put an end to the confusion of domains that constantly muddled the diffusion of information about the Church by making the area of doctrine and dogma infringe on that of freedom of conscience. He liberated Catholic journalists from being torn between their secular duty to inform and the criticism allowed to those in authority over the expression of the truth. Reflection on this papal attitude has remained inconclusive, and the trend toward strict supervision, however "paternal" it calls itself, remains inherent in that authority.

Jacques Nobécourt

Bibliography

Bergerre, M. *Six papes, un journaliste*, Paris, 1979.

Caprile, G., S.J., *Il Concilio Vaticano, II*, Rome, 1965–8, 6 vols.

Civiltá Cattolica, 2780 (1966), II, 127–37.

Le IIe concile du Vatican (1959–1965): Colloque de l'École française de Rome, 28–30 May 1986, Rome, 1986 (CEFR, 113).

Levillain, P. *Le Mécanique politique de Vatican II*, Paris, 1975.

Paul VI et la modernité dans l'Église: Colloque de l'École française de Rome, 2–4 June 1983, Rome, 1984 (CEFR, 72).

Poupard, P. *Connaissance du Vatican*, Paris, 1987.

Vallainc, F. *Immagini del Concilio*, Vatican City, 1966.

Wenger, A. *Le Cardinal Villot (1905–1979)*, Paris, 1989.

Zizola, G. *Giovanni XXIII, la fede e la politica*, Bari, 1988.

PRIMACY, PAPAL. The Roman pontiff's function of primacy is defined as follows: "That which the Prince of Shepherds and great Shepherd of the sheep, Jesus Christ our Lord, established in the person of the blessed Apostle Peter to ensure the perpetual welfare and lasting good of the Church must, by the same institution, necessarily remain unceasingly in the Church" (Vatican Council I, dogmatic constitution *Pastor aeternus*, chapter 2). This function is designed to make the episcopate "one and undivided" and to keep the multitude of believers "in the oneness of faith and communion" (*ibid.*, introduction).

The aim of primacy is therefore a service that can be rendered only through the exercise of a function of divine origin that has been conferred on the pope for that purpose. It is also a service of unity, for which Jesus Christ "placed blessed Peter over the other apostles and instituted in him a permanent and visible source and foundation of unity of faith and fellowship" (Vatican Council II, dogmatic constitution *Lumen gentium*, n. 18).

Institution of the Primacy of Peter. VATICAN II reiterated and defined the principle that the apostle Peter was "established by the Lord Christ head of all the apostles and visible head of the Church militant," and that he received "directly and immediately from Christ our Lord" a primacy which is not merely honorary but "a primacy of jurisdiction, true and properly speaking" (chap. 2). This definition rests on the so-called promise texts: "Blessed art thou, Simon son of Jonah: for flesh and blood hath not revealed it [the divinity of Christ] unto thee, but my Father who is in heaven. And I say also unto thee, that thou art Peter, and upon this rock I will build my church: and the gates of hell shall not prevail against it. . . . and whatsoever thou shalt bind on earth shall be bound in heaven: and whatsoever thou shalt loose on earth shall be loosed in heaven" (Matt. 16, 17–19); and again, "Feed my lambs. . . . Feed my sheep" (John 21, 15, 16).

Perpetual Nature of the Apostolic Primacy in the Blessed Peter. Two principles are defined here by the Church's magisterium: (a) "the blessed Peter [has] a perpetual line of successors in the primacy over the universal Church"; and (b) "the Roman pontiff is the successor of blessed Peter in this primacy" (Vatican I, dogmatic constitution *Pastor aeternus*, chap. 2).

The principle of succession follows from the indefectibility and perpetuity of the Church tie: the impossibility that the Church should ever cease to exist or lose any of its essential character. Vatican II recalled that "the divine mission, entrusted by Christ to the apostles, will last until the end of the world (cf. Matt. 28: 20)" (dogmatic constitution *Lumen gentium*, n. 20). Succession in primacy is implied in the Gospel texts cited above. It is part of the permanent conviction of the Church: "No one doubts, and all centuries know, that the most blessed saint Peter, head of the apostles, column of the faith, foundation of the Catholic Church, received the keys of the kingdom from our Lord Jesus Christ, the Savior and Redeemer of the human race: now and for ever, he is the one who, in the person of his successors [the bishops of the see of Rome], lives and exercises the power to judge" (council of Ephesus, speech of the priest Philip, papal legate, 11 July 431).

Called on to pronounce on orthodox doctrine, St. Irenaeus refered to the apostolic succession, in particular "to the great Church, ancient and known to us all, founded and built in Rome by the glorious Peter and Paul . . . : all the Churches must be in accord with this Church, because of its most powerful authority (*propter potentiorem principalitatem*) . . . for it is in Her that is preserved the tradition that comes down from the apostles" (*Adversus haereses*, III, 3, 2).

Nature of Peter's Primacy. Vatican II described every episcopal ministry as "true service," called explicitly in the Bible *diakonia* or "ministry" (dogmatic constitution *Lumen gentium*, n. 24). The Roman pontiff, for his part, derives "full and supreme power in the Church by means of legitimate election accepted by him together with episcopal consecration" (Code of Canon Law of 1983, c. 332, 1). By virtue of his "function (charge) as vicar of Christ and Pastor of the universal Church on earth," the Roman pontiff holds "a full, supreme and universal power" which he "can always exercise . . . freely" (dogmatic constitution *Lumen gentium*, n. 22). This the Code of Canon Law defines even more closely as "a supreme, full, immediate and universal ordinary power which he can always freely exercise" (c. 331).

It is an ordinary power because it is comprised in the office of the pope of Rome. It is not, therefore, an extraordinary power, which the pope could only exercise in exceptional circumstances; nor is it a delegated power, which he would not receive with his office but through someone else's delegation. The pope exercises it in his own name.

It is a supreme power, in the sense that there exists no juridicial authority superior to the pope: "The First See is judged by no one" (c. 1404). The Roman pontiff is the head of the college of bishops (c. 336). His actions need no confirmation, given that he has the right to determine, "according to the needs of the Church," the "personal or collegial" way of exercising his function (c. 333, 2). His decisions cannot be the object of any appeal or recourse (c. 333, 3); recourse to the ecumenical council or the college of bishops against one of his actions is to be punished by censure (c. 1372).

It is plenary power, because it embraces all the questions that can arise in the life of the Church, no matter under what aspect they may appear. Thus, it is not a simple power "of inspection or direction," a theory that Vatican I condemned, explaining that this power is "full and supreme" over the whole Church, "not only in things which belong to faith and morals, but also in those which relate to discipline and government of the Church spread throughout the world"; it is not a question of "merely the principal part" but of "the fullness of the supreme power" (dogmatic constitution *Pastor aeternus*, chap. 3).

Primacy is an immediate power, because it comes directly from God, not from the will of the faithful or that of the college of bishops. The latter are merely "a group of equals who transfer their powers to their chairman" (dogmatic constitution *Lumen gentium*, preliminary explanatory note, n. 1).

It is a universal power over the whole Church, its pastors, and other faithful, and over all matters with which it concerns itself—a primacy of ordinary power that also extends "over all particular Churches and groupings of churches" (c. 333, 1). The Roman pontiff can exercise "his power at any time as he sees fit by reason of the demands of his office." In this, it differs from the power of the college of bishops, which "although it is always in existence, is not for that reason continually a strictly collegial activity" (dogmatic constitution *Lumen gentium*, preliminary explanatory note, n. 4).

Primacy is also a free power. It must be untouched by the interference of all other authorities, both ecclesiastic and civil.

The Roman pontiff thus is both bishop of Rome and of the Catholic Church. As bishop, he is responsible not only for sanctifying but also for teaching and governing the people of God (*ibid.*, n. 21). However, this primacy of the pope "is far . . . from being any prejudice to the ordinary and immediate power of episcopal jurisdiction [to] feed and govern, each his own flock as true pastors" (dogmatic constitution *Pastor aeternus*, chap. 3). The supreme pontiff is always "united in communion with the other bishops and with the universal Church" (c. 333, 2). This is because his power can never suppress or ignore the existence of the episcopate, which is also of divine right. Indeed, the exercise of episcopal power is "ultimately regulated by the supreme authority of the Church, and can be circumscribed by certain limits, for the advantage of the Church or of the faithful" (dogmatic constitution *Lumen gentium*, n. 27).

As for the *munus sanctificandi*, or function of sanctification, the pope can exercise it throughout the Church, without any need of the ministerial faculties of each bishop in his diocese nor of the dimissorial letters of the latter, to proceed to the ordination of his subjects, etc. The *munus docendi*, or task of teaching, is exercised by the pope in person, or collegially in the ordinary way (in communion with the bishops) or the extraordinary way (in council). The Roman pontiff is the supreme pastor and teacher of all the faithful of Christ (c. 749, 1) and his teaching, or *magisterium*, is infallible when "he proclaims by a definitive act that a doctrine of faith or morals is to be held" (*ibid.*).

The pope exercises his *munus regendi*, or function of government, first as supreme legislator, who issues laws for the universal Church and for the individual Churches or other ecclesial institutions. He can also change laws, depart from them, or dispense with them, the only limit being the divine right, natural or positive. This function has as its goal the "good of the Church" (dogmatic constitution *Lumen gentium*, preliminary explanatory note, no. 3).

As the "supreme judge for the entire Catholic world" (c. 1442), the Roman pontiff has the right to judge on his own, or through the ordinary tribunals of the Apostolic See—that is, the supreme tribunal of the Apostolic Signature (c. 1445) and the tribunal of the Roman Rota (c. 1443–1444), or through judges whom he has delegated. Certain matters are reserved for him alone without prejudice to those that he himself summons to his own tribunal (c. 1405, 1). Further, by virtue of primacy, any member of the faithful can freely refer to the Holy See or introduce to him "a case either contentious or penal in any grade of jurisdiction and at any stage of litigation" (c. 1417, 1).

The pope also holds the supreme executive power in the Church, as well as the direction of its central administration, for which he usually employs the Roman Curia (c. 360). By virtue of his primacy of government, the pope "is the supreme administrator and steward of all ecclesiastical goods" (c. 1273). But the juridical person who legitimately acquired these ecclesiastical goods holds the right of ownership "under the supreme authority of the Roman pontiff" (c. 1256).

Primacy and Collegiality. According to the most ancient discipline in force in the Church, "the bishops installed throughout the whole world lived in communion with one another and with the Roman Pontiff in a bond of unity, charity and peace; likewise the holding of councils in order to settle conjointly, in a decision rendered balanced and equitable by the advice of many, all questions of major importance." This indicates "the collegial character and structure of the episcopal order." Vatican II vigorously stressed the principle of collegiality: "As, by the Lord's will, St. Peter and the other apostles constituted one apostolic college, so in a similar way the Roman pontiff as the successor of Peter, and the bishops as the successors of the apostles, are joined together" (dogmatic constitution *Lumen gentium*, n. 22).

The essential elements of collegiality are therefore: (a) Our Lord's choice of the college of the 12 apostles, from which the college of bishops originates, of the apostolic succession, and of the continuity with which each of these colleges hands down the same faith and communicates to believers the same methods of salvation; (b) each bishop has responded to a personal, incommunicable vocation, which has placed him in a college and in an ontological bond with the other members of that college; (c) at the heart of the college, throughout the centuries, there has been transmitted "the office which the Lord confided to Peter alone, as first of the apostles, destined to be transmitted to his successors" (dogmatic constitution *Lumen gentium*, n. 20 and 21), together with the charism of the mission common to the 11 other apostles; and (d) this Petrine mission places Peter's successor in the college, as head and a permanent and visible source and foundation of unity of faith and fellowship (*ibid.*, n. 18). By this means, the episcopal college has no authority "unless it is simultaneously conceived of in terms of its head, the Roman pontiff, Peter's successor" (*ibid.*, n. 22). The college acts *cum Petro et sub Petro*. It agrees at all times and of necessity with its head, who retains wholly in the college his duty as vicar of Christ and pastor of the universal Church. In consequence, it is "not a distinction between the Roman pontiff and the bishops taken together but between the Roman pontiff by himself and the Roman pontiff along with the bishops" (*ibid.*, preliminary explanatory note, n. 3).

Collegiality is practiced in a special, complete way in the ecumenical councils. In order that the collegiality of the episcopal *ministerium* might be made manifest in the everyday life of the Church, Paul VI and Vatican II instituted the SYNOD of bishops (*motu proprio Apostolica sollicitudo*, 15 September 1965). The bishops' conferences, like the regional or provincial councils before them, are another contemporary way of practicing collegiality. A further sign of collegiality is the college of cardinals, especially in the consistories (c. 353 § 1). The visit *ad limina* which the bishop makes every five years is not strictly speaking an act of collegiality, but it takes its inspiration from this principle "and especially from the spirit of collegiality, thanks to which the members of the college always express their innate reference to their head" (Cardinal Lucas Moreira Neves, spiritual and pastoral note accompanying the Directory for the visit *ad limina*, 29 June 1988).

Dominique Le Tourneau

Bibliography

Antón, A. *Primado y colegialidad*, Madrid, 1970.

Baumann, R. *Des Petrus Bekenntnis und Schlüssel,* Stoccarda, 1950.

Betti, U. O. *La Costituzione dogmatica "Pastor aeternus" del Concilio Vaticano I*, Rome, 1961.

Buckley, M. J., et al. *Papal Primacy and the Episcopate: Towards a Relational Understanding*, New York, 1998.

Casamassa, A. *De primatu Romani Pontificis textus selecti*, Vatican City, 1943.

Collins, P. *Papal Power: A Proposal for Change in Catholicism's Third Millennium*, Blackburn, 1997.

Colombo, G. "Episcopato e Primato Pontificio nella vita della Chiesa," *La Scuola Cattolica*, 88, 1960, 401–34;

"Il Problema dell'episcopato nella Costituzione 'De Ecclesia catholica' del Concilio Vaticano I," *La Scuola Cattolica*, 89, 1961, 344–72.

Colson, J. *L'Épiscopat catholique: collégialité et primauté pendant les trois premiers siècles de l'Église*, Paris, 1963.

Congar, Y. M. J. *La Collégialité, épiscopale*, Paris, 1965; *Ministère et communion écclésiale*, Paris, 1971, 95–122, 187–227.

Cooke, B. *Papacy and the Church in the United States*, New York, 1989.

Cullmann, O. *L'Unité par la diversité*, Paris, 1987.

de Satgé, J. *Peter and the Single Church*, London, 1981.

Dejaifve, G. *Pape et evêques au premier concile du Vatican*, Bruges, 1961.

d'Onorio, J. B. *Le Pape et le gouvernement de l'Église*, Paris, 1992, 128–89.

El Colegio episcopal (ed. J. López Ortiz and J. Blazquez), Madrid, 1963.

Estrada, J. A. "La configuración monárquica del Primado Papal," *Estudios Eclesiásticos*, 62, 1988, 165–88.

Farmer, W. R., and Kereszty, R. *Peter and Paul in the Church of Rome: The Ecumenical Potential of a Forgotten Perspective*, New York, 1990.

Glez, G. "Primauté du pape," *DTC*, XIII, 1936, 247–344.

Graber, R. *Petrus der Fels, Fragen um den Primat*, Ettal, 1950.

Henn, W. *The Honor of My Brothers: A Short History of the Relation Between the Pope and the Bishops*, New York, 2000.

Il primato di Pietro nel pensiero contemporaneo, Bologna, 1965.

Journet, C. *Primaut, de Pierre dans la perspective protestante et dans la perspective catholique*, Paris, 1953.

Kasper, W. "Primat und Episkopat nach dem Vaticanum I.," *Tübinger theologische Quartalschrift*, 142, 1962, 47–83.

La Due, W. *The Chair of Peter: A History of the Papacy*, New York, 1999.

Le Guillou, M. J. "Chronique bibliographique: La primauté de Pierre," *Istina*, 10, 1964, 93–102.

Lecler, J. *Le Pape ou le concile*, Paris, 1973.

L'Épiscopat et l'église universelle (ed. Y. Congar and B. D. Dupuy), Paris, 1961.

Maccarrone, M. *Vicarius Christi*, Rome, 1952; "Apostolicit . . . , episcopato e primato di Pietro," *Lateranum*, 42/2, 1976, 1–355.

Meyendorff, J., ed. *The Primacy of Peter: Essays in Ecclesiology and the Early Church*, Crestwood, N.Y., 1992.

Minnerath, R. *Le Pape, évêque universel ou premier des évêques?*, Paris, 1978.

Papal Primacy and the Universal Church (ed. P. C. Empie and T. A. Murphy), Minneapolis, 1974.

Philips, G. *Primauté et collégialité: Le dossier de Gérard Philips sur la Nota explicativa praevia* (ed. J. Grootaers), Louvain, 1986.

Pottmeyer, H. J. *Towards a Papacy in Communion: Perspective from Vatican Councils I & II*, J. O'Connell, trans., New York, 1998.

Puglisi, J. F., ed. *Petrine Ministry and the Unity of the Church: Toward a Patient and Fraternal Dialogue*, Collegeville, 1999.

Quinn, J. R., et al. *The Exercise of the Primacy: Continuing the Dialogue*, P. Zagano and T. W. Tilley, eds., New York, 1998.

Rahner, K., and Ratzinger, J. *Episkopat und Primat*, Freibourg-in-Breisgau, 1962.

Ratzinger, J. "La collegialitá episcopale dal punto dei vista teologico," *La Chiesa del Vaticano II* (ed. G. Baraúna), Florence, 1965, 733–60.

Ray, S. K. *Upon this Rock: St. Peter and the Primacy of Rome in Scripture and the Early Church*, San Francisco, 1999.

Rincón, A. *Tu eres Pedro*, Pamplona, 1972.

Rouco, A. C. *Le Primat de l'évêque de Rome*, Freiburg, 1990.

Ryan, C., ed. *The Religious Roles of the Papacy: Ideals and Realities 1150–1300*, Toronto, 1989.

Saraiva Martins, J. M. "La collegialità episcopale nel pensiero di Giovanni Paolo II," *Apollinaris*, LV, 1982, 503–22.

Schatz, K. *Papal Primacy: From its Origins to the Present*, J. A. Otto and L. M. Maloney, trans., Collegeville, 1996.

Staffa, D. "De collegiali episcopatus ratione—La nature collégiale de l'épiscopat," *RTC*, XIV, 1964, 100–205.

Thils, G. *Primaute, pontificale: Les voies d'une révision*, Gembloux, 1972.

Tillard, J. M. *L'Évêque de Rome*, Paris, 1982.

Urresti, T. I. J. *El binomio "Primado-Episcopado,"* Bilbao, 1962.

The Historical Development of the Papal Office. In the first several generations after Christ, the diversity in church organization and structure was considerable. This diversity, however, did not seem to stand in the way of communion among the various churches and their members. From the Acts of the Apostles and the letters of the Pauline corpus, it is evident that a good number of Christians were traveling with some sort of regularity from one part of the Roman world to another. As they journeyed from town to town, they searched out fellow Christians who would offer them hospitality. They would join together in worship, but occasional and rather considerable differences in doctrinal emphasis and ecclesiastical organization did not seem to interrupt their communion with one another. With the death of the apostles in the second half of the 1st century, the apostolic office ceased, giving way to a multiplicity of organizational arrangements. For example, elders appeared very early in Antioch and Jerusalem. These leaders were appointed rather than ordained. In the Pauline communities there were prophets and teachers who were commissioned by the conferral of charisms by the Holy Spirit (I Thess 5:12). Luke's presbyters in Acts seem to have operated collegially. In Matthew's churches there were no elders, and decision-making apparently lay with the congregation, where honors and distinctions of any sort were frowned upon. In the Johannine communities discipleship was the controlling idea, and equality and fraternity were emphasized.

In the pastoral epistles, the churches possessed offices and, in some cases, held ordinations (I Tim 4:14), but the role of bishops and presbyters was not yet differentiated (Titus 1:5–7). The church organization revealed in the letters of Ignatius of Antioch (ca. 110) attests to the importance of the monarchical bishop in a good many churches, although Rome at that time was still governed by a college of presbyters or presbyter-bishops. As a matter of fact, it was not until the middle of the 2nd century that Rome had a monarchical bishop. A scholar from the East, Hegesippus, was probably the one who, around the period of the pontificate of Anicetus (ca. 155–66), set out a list of Roman clerics, from the time of St. Peter on, whom he labeled bishops of Rome. These individuals, including Linus, Clement, Evaristus, and Telesphorus, were in all probability historical figures who were prominent presbyters or presbyter-bishops in the Roman congregation. However, to place them in a continuous line of monarchical heads from Peter to Anicetus is not historically justifiable. The *First Letter of Clement*, written from Rome circa 95–96, reveals that at the turn of the century the Roman congregation felt some responsibility for guiding the development of one or another distant churches, such as Corinth. However, there were apparently only two Roman bishops from 189 to 257 who presumed to invoke jurisdictional authority over the dealings of church communities outside the environs of Rome, Victor (189–98) and Stephen (254–7). In both cases their intervention did not seem to have a lasting impression on the eastern congregations addressed. It is likely that Stephen was the first Roman bishop to ground his claim to jurisdictional authority over distant churches in Christ's promise to Peter (Mt. 16:18–19).

The period from 257 to the accession of Pope GREGORY I the Great (590–640) witnessed startling change in the role of the Roman pontiff. From DIONYSIUS (260–8) to DAMASUS I (366–84) and SIRICIUS (384–99) the position of the Roman bishop in the universal church evolved dramatically. These gains were consolidated under the reign of LEO I (440–61). In central and southern Italy, the pope was the sole metropolitan bishop, with his legislation and his synods exercising a controlling force in the area. After the fall of Carthage in 439, the Roman pontiff enjoyed what later came to be called a primacy of jurisdiction in the West, though he normally exercised his authority through the metropolitan of the several provinces. Only very rarely did the pope interfere directly in the affairs of individual dioceses. There is almost no evidence to indicate that he attempted as a matter of policy to control episcopal appointments in the western dioceses outside of central and southern Italy. He was the final arbiter of disputes in the West, and issued rulings on disputed issues of ecclesiastical procedure. In the East, however, the Roman pontiff had to deal with the ancient jurisdictional tradition of the patriarchs of Antioch (Syria), Alexandria, Jerusalem, and Constantinople. Although the East had always recognized a certain primacy of honor enjoyed by the popes, any sort of primacy of jurisdiction was quite another matter. There is no clear indication in the first four or five centuries, on the part of the Eastern churches, that Rome had the authority to govern or control the affairs of the Eastern patriarchates.

The letters of Gregory I reveal his understanding of the authority he possessed in both the East and the West. In the West outside of Italy he did have some influence on decision-making in the churches in Gaul. However, Spain, northern Africa, the Balkans, and Dalmatia were for the most part independent of his control. His many letters to the churches in the East indicate that he was acutely aware that the five patriarchs were the regional heads of their respective territories, with no one of them having anything approaching jurisdictional authority over the others.

During the 7th and 8th centuries the Roman, i.e., Byzantine, emperors became less concerned about the West due to pressing political problems of their own in the East. Thus the popes received little protection against their political rivals in Italy, especially the Lombards. Under Popes GREGORY II (715–31) and GREGORY III (731–41), Rome and the surrounding area in central Italy evolved as something of a distinct political entity that later came to be known as the Papal States. It was Charlemagne (768–814) who offered protection to the popes and their territories. As the descendents of Charlemagne became more and more ineffectual, popes like NICHOLAS I (858–67) and JOHN VIII (872–82) expanded their temporal and spiritual authority over all the churches, but these claims were never taken seriously in the East. By the end of the first millennium, the pope and the Eastern churches were drifting ineluctably apart.

The Carolingian Empire collapsed with the death of Charles the Fat in 882. The 10th century has been labeled the *saeculum obscurum*, the obscure century, because of the depths to which the papacy descended during that pe-

riod. After the protection of the Carolingians disappeared, the papacy was left to fight its own political battles. The papal office became the victim of the feuds of several Roman noble families. The ensuing anarchy was so profound that some of the popes were in office only a matter of days, and we hardly know their names. Besides, we cannot always be sure whether or not some of them were legitimately elected.

The Ottonine emperors of Germany eventually restored the prestige of the papal office in the 11th century by promoting the election of a number of German popes, especially LEO IX (1049–54) and VICTOR II (1054–7), who were animated by a reforming spirit. Leo IX initiated the development of the College of Cardinals as an organ of government of the universal church. But just after the death of Leo IX, Cardinal Humbert, the papal delegate, and Michael Cerularius, the patriarch of Constantinople, met in July of 1054 to improve relations between Rome and the Byzantine church that had been deteriorating for one hundred years or more. These two men were clearly the wrong players to effect a reconciliation, since both were strong-willed and hot-tempered. The result of their encounter was that Humbert excommunicated Cerularius, and Cerularius, with the consent of the Byzantine emperor, excommunicated Humbert. This marked the onset of the division between the Byzantine and the Roman churches that has remained to the present. The excommunications were withdrawn by Pope PAUL VI and the ecumenical patriarch, Athenagoras, in December 1965, but the split remains.

The reforms in the West initiated by Leo IX achieved significant results. His targets were the elimination of simony in the conferral of church offices, the eradication of concubinage among the clergy, and the curbing of lay investiture (the appointment of lay nobles to clerical posts). This movement of reform reached a high point in the pontificate of GREGORY VII (1073–85), who pursued his innovations largely through the agency of his traveling papal delegates. He also established the pattern of regular "AD LIMINA" VISITS to Rome for local bishops, and insisted that each resident bishop take a special oath of allegiance to the pope—thus binding the local ordinary more closely to papal authority. This period of ecclesiastical centralization, known as the Gregorian Reform, began in the mid-11th century and carried through until the First Lateran Council (1123), the first of the great western general councils. These western councils were very different from the first eight ecumenical councils that had been held in the East from 325 to 870. Those synods were conducted in the main by the Byzantine emperors and Eastern prelates, with the Eastern bishops and theologians as the principal contributors. However, the popes did send delegates to the councils and confirmed the conciliar enactments, usually after the fact.

Moreover it was during the 12th and 13th centuries that papal power became much more influential in the church in the West. Countless judicial disputes were brought to Rome for settlement, and ecclesiastical discipline became more uniform in the West through the enactments of the four Lateran Councils (1123, 1139, 1179, and 1215). These western general councils notably expanded the jurisdiction of the popes over such matters as the conferring of local ecclesiastical offices, the assessing of papal fees and taxes, and the granting of privileges and dispensations. The power and prestige of the popes reached a high point with INNOCENT III (1198–1216), who claimed for himself the fullness of spiritual power and occasionally utilized his authority to punish secular rulers when they acted against his wishes. By the time of INNOCENT IV (1243–54), the prestige of the popes among the European nations had declined considerably. Criticism of the papacy became widespread due to abuse of the papal reservation of benefices, the ever-increasing number of judicial appeals to Rome, and the dramatically expanded tax burdens inflicted by the pope on the local dioceses. The first general taxes on the local churches were assessed in 1199 and 1215 for the support of the fourth and fifth crusades.

By 1250 the papal power to tax the churches and the clergy had been firmly established, and this continuing insertion of curial interference was widely resented. The opposition to the expanding papal centralization took on a more national character among the emerging nations of Europe. With the accession of two French clerics to the papacy, URBAN IV (1261–4) and CLEMENT IV (1265–8), the depleted College of Cardinals was augmented by the addition of a number of French prelates, as the sympathy of the papal curia turned toward France. A series of rather weak popes during the 1270s and 1280s allowed the College of Cardinals to assume more and more authority and a greater share of the financial resources of the papal administration. The ecumenical synod at Vienne (1311–2) failed to come to grips with the pressing problems that were tearing the church apart—the centralization of decision-making in the papal curia that was emasculating local church government, and the growing burden of papal taxation that was alienating the national churches.

In 1309 Pope CLEMENT V (1305–14), a Frenchman who had spent most of his first four years as pontiff in France, settled down in Avignon, a papal territory, and there the popes remained for nearly seventy years. The eight pontiffs of the Avignon years, with their luxurious lifestyle and exploding bureaucracy, multiplied almost beyond the counting, the financial demands placed upon the various dioceses, parishes, and religious establishments all over western Christendom. (The revenues from the Papal States had of course been drastically reduced after the move to Avignon.) The pope's control over the conferring of benefices expanded to the point where almost every major office throughout the western church was granted by the papal curia. This situation gave the popes an almost unheard-of opportunity to levy taxes and fees on the new office holders, thus escalating the general unrest and increasing the level of frustration everywhere.

GREGORY XI ended the Avignon sojourn and returned to Rome in 1377. Six months after his death in 1378, however, there were two prelates who claimed the papacy—one in Rome and the other in Avignon. To solve this impossible situation, cardinals from both camps met at Pisa in 1409, creating a third papal line that only further exacerbated the turmoil. Through the efforts of a group of prelates, the moderate conciliarists, the Great Western Schism (1378–1417) was finally brought to a close at the Council of Constance (1414–8) after the deposition of two papal claimants, and the acceptance of the resignation of the third. The council then arranged for the valid election of a new pope, MARTIN V (1417–31). Martin V and his successor EUGENE IV (1431–47) managed to thwart the moderate conciliarists, and returned the papacy to its strictly monarchical moorings. The last half of the 15th century witnessed the rise of the Renaissance popes who proceeded to shrink the office down to the size and shape of a regional Italian duchy, whose lord and ruler manifested less and less interest in the wider concerns of the Christian world. The stage was now set for the cataclysmic Protestant-Reformation.

Pope HADRIAN VI of Utrecht (1522–3) had correctly diagnosed the seriousness of the situation in Rome after the corruption of Pope ALEXANDER VI (1492–1503) and the resistance to curial reform on the part of JULIUS II (1503–13) and LEO X (1513–21). But the Dutch pope notably underestimated the dimensions of the crisis brewing in Germany in the 1520s. It was Paul III (1534–49) who finally convoked the Council of Trent in 1545 to address the many critical problems of the time. Trent (1545–63) did go a long way to cope with the disciplinary abuses tearing the church apart. Also, its impressive series of doctrinal decrees refined for Catholics a number of beliefs that had previously been somewhat ambiguous. The Tridentine council confirmed, perhaps once and for all, the monarchical status of the pope, so that the modern papacy could be said to have taken shape at Trent.

The three reform pontiffs after the council—PIUS V (1566–72), GREGORY XIII (1572–85), and SIXTUS V (1585–90)—were responsible for initiating over time most of the needed disciplinary changes. In the 17th and 18th centuries, the papacy fell under the control of the kings of Spain, France, and the Habsburg Empire. CLEMENT XI's carelessly drafted bull, *Unigenitus* (1713), brought about a heated discussion on the irreformable character of the popes' teaching authority that was not fully resolved until Vatican I (1869–70). In the 19th century Popes GREGORY XVI (1831–46) and PIUS IX (1846–78) were determined to hold on to the Papal States, thus frustrating for decades the formation of a unified Italy. In addition, Pius IX's *Syllabus of Errors* (1864) left many inside and outside the church wondering whether the papacy would ever make peace with the modern world.

Pius IX opened the First Vatican Council in December 1869. His aim was to confront the errors of the age and clarify once and for all the issue of papal primacy. Perhaps as many as a quarter of the seven hundred or so delegates at the council were not in favor of dealing with papal prerogatives before a general treatment of the church's constitution and the role of the episcopal college. It was, however, the ultramontanists, those prelates bent on maximizing the prerogatives of the pope, who managed to control the agenda, so that papal jurisdictional supremacy and papal infallibility were discussed and defined first, before a general treatment of the church. The abrupt closure of the council in the summer of 1870—due to the political situation in Italy—foreclosed any possibility of situating those papal prerogatives within the context of the teaching and shepherding functions of the college of bishops.

Pius IX's negative views regarding the culture of the 19th century were reversed to a considerable degree by his successor, LEO XIII (1878–1903), who painted a more positive picture of the times in his many encyclicals. PIUS X (1903–14) narrowed the vision again, particularly in his bitter struggle with the modernists, many of whom were attempting to adapt Catholic theology and scriptural studies to the recent dramatic developments in biblical and historical scholarship. PIUS XI (1922–39) closed the case once and for all on the 'Roman question' in the Lateran Treaty of 1929, so that the church could settle in to the confines of Vatican City, and finally drop its claim to the Papal States. PIUS XII (1939–58) was a gracious and public figure whose pontificate was extremely monarchical, but his encyclicals opened the doors to a renaissance in biblical and liturgical studies, as well as new directions in ecclesiology.

These developments came to fruition in the Second Vatican Council, convoked by the visionary Pope JOHN XXIII (1958–63). Vatican II (1962–65) contextualized the papal office within the framework of the college of bishops (e.g., *The Constitution on the Church, The Decree on the Bishops*), and directed the Catholic Church into a more positive relationship with Protestant churches and the other religious bodies (e.g., *The Decree on Ecumenism, The Declaration on the Non-Christian Religions*), initiating a new era of inter-faith discussions. Moreover, it related the church to the world in a much more open and constructive way (e.g., *The Pastoral Constitution on the Church in the Modern World*). *Aggiornamento*, the task of bringing the Church into the modern age, remained the theme of PAUL

VI's pontificate (1963–78), except on the question of birth regulation (*Humanae vitae*, 1968), and on the absence of true dialogue in the various sessions of the World Synod of Bishops during his reign.

Pope JOHN PAUL II (1978–) brought a warm demeanor to the papacy, but a heart that was not deeply attuned to John XXIII's leitmotif of *aggiornamento*. In spite of his travels around the globe and his passion for meeting people, Christians and non-Christians alike, the pontiff's years can be evaluated, in the context of Vatican II, as a period of return to the highly monarchical popes operative since 1850. The organizational principles of collegiality, regionalism, and subsidiarity featured in the enactments of Vatican II have been replaced by an extremely centralized monarchical government that tends to shape the Catholic world into a uniformity uncharacteristic of its earliest and most sacred traditions. It is interesting to note that John Paul II himself, in his 1995 encyclical, *Ut unum sint*, has conceded that the current structure and operation of the papal role is an obstacle to Christian reunion, and he has acknowledged his responsibility to give the office a new shape and a new situation. In this encyclical he declares:

I insistently pray the Holy Spirit to shine his light upon us, enlightening all the pastors and theologians of our Churches, that all may seek—together of course—the forms in which this [papal] ministry may accomplish a service of love recognized by all concerned.

John Paul II, *That They May Be One*, Encyclical Letter, May 25, 1995 (Washington, DC: U. S. Catholic Conference, 1995): 106.

William J. La Due

Bibliography

Abbott, W. M., ed. *The Documents of Vatican II*, New York, 1966.

Alberigo, G., et al., *Decrees of the Ecumenical Councils*, vols. 1 and 2, Nicea I–Vatican II, english editor N. Tanner, Washington D.C. 1990.

Barraclough, G. *The Medieval Papacy*, New York, 1968.

Brown, R. E., and Meier, J. P., *Antioch and Rome*, New York, 1983.

Butler, D. C., *The Vatican Council 1869–70*, C. Butler, ed., Westminster, Md., 1962.

Chadwick, O. *The Popes and European Revolution*, Oxford, 1981.

Congar, Y. *L' Ecclésiologie du haut moyen age*, Paris, 1968.

Emerton, E., trans. *The Correspondence of Pope Gregory VII*, 1932; repr., New York, 1990.

Hales, E. E. Y. *Pio Nono*, New York, 1954.

Jedin, H., and Dolan, J., ed. *History of the Church*, vols. I–X, New York, 1980–9.

John Paul II. *That They May Be One*, encyclical letter, May 25, 1995, Washington, D.C., 1995.

La Due, W. J. *The Chair of Saint Peter*, Maryknoll, N.Y., 1999.

Lefebvre, C. M. P., and Chevailler, L. *L' Epoque Moderne*, tome XV, *Histoire du Droit et des Institutions de l' Eglise en Occident*, vol. I, G. LeBras and J. Gaudemet, ed., Paris, 1976.

Lortz, J. *How the Reformation Came*, O. M. Knab, trans., New York, 1964.

Mollat, G. *The Popes at Avignon 1305–78*, Love, trans., London, 1963.

Morris, C. *The Papal Monarchy. The Western Church from 1050 to 1250*, Oxford, 1989.

Oberman, H. A. *Luther*, New Haven, Conn., 1989.

Ostrogorsky, G. *History of the Byzantine State*, J. Hussey, trans., 1952, New Brunswick, N. J., 1969.

Tierney, B. *Foundations of the Conciliar Theory*, Cambridge, 1955.

Ullmann, W. *A Short History of the Papacy in the Middle Ages*, 1972, New York, 1982.

von Campenhausen, H. *Ecclesiastical Authority and Spiritual Power in the Church of the First Three Centuries*, J. A. Baker, trans., Stanford, Calif., 1969.

PRIVATE LIVES, POPES'. Interest in the daily life of the pope is a recent phenomenon. Strictly speaking, this was not a way in which the pope's image was represented. Until the abolition of the PAPAL STATES, the pope led a life governed by protocol at the heart of the pontifical court; its intimate side was visible only to his servants, who observed the strictest secrecy in this regard.

The description of the pontiff's bedroom, his eating habits, rhythm of work, and the objects arranged on his desk gradually came into the open in the 19th century, particularly under the pontificate of PIUS IX. Devotion to the martyr pope was inspired by a detailed portrayal of his simple, almost monastic way of life, presenting the pope's day-to-day existence as the very expression of a humble shepherd at the head of the universal Church.

Pius IX's successors restored a certain mystery to their daily lives by emphasizing the myth of the sovereign pontiff "captive" in the Vatican. PIUS XI embellished it; it was said that as the pope took his daily stroll in the Vatican gardens, he expressed nostalgia on hearing the trains going past his residence, because they reminded him of the freedom of his life before his election. The pope was known to be a good mountain-climber, liking exploration and travel.

His successor's daily life was more exposed to public view, even though PIUS XII distanced himself from this type of prying. Some chroniclers, and later his biographers, let it be known that during the war the pope had worn a hair-shirt, that he persisted in mortifications and lived extremely frugally. His last moments, which were photographed through the indelicacy of one of those close to him, were published in magazines. They showed the pope in pajamas, disfigured and in his final agony.

JOHN XXIII was the first pope of the 20th century to invite guests to his table, the council having encouraged him in this move. Information was given out about the pope's cuisine as well as his bons mots (*fioretti*). He was known to have had his bed brought from Venice and placed in Pius XII's former room, where the latter's bed still stood. People learned of John XXIII's sadness at the solitude that faced him the evening of his election. By contrast, his illness (cancer of the stomach) was not publicized until the pope's last days.

PAUL VI's daily life was protected from view, but at an Angelus, he replied indirectly to the accusations brought by a French writer about his morals on account of his positions regarding sexual morality. There was no public gawking at his death or the arthrosis of the knee which he endured for many years and which became evident from 1974.

The mysterious death of JOHN PAUL I brought about revelations of his impaired state of health even before his election. One example is an anecdote according to which he is said to have shown Cardinal Villot, his secretary of state, his swollen legs (a sign of cardiopathy) during a walk in the Vatican gardens.

But it was with JOHN PAUL II that the public view of the pope's daily life actually encompassed his private existence. Following the 1981 attempt on his life, when the operations he had to undergo were revealed in detail by the press, the pope occasionally allowed himself to be photographed at table; he let it be known who sat with him, as well as the names of the nuns who took care of his meals and his linen. The pope was surprised in a skiing outfit in the Abruzzi, or sitting at the foot of a tree. Only his love of swimming (in the pool at CASTEL GANDOLFO) was spared the curiosity of the media. Today the pope's private life is part of a minute observation of the mystery of his nature as sovereign pontiff. The public and especially media interest in the private life of the pontiff became acute throughout the 1990s as speculation increased concerning John Paul II's health.

Philippe Levillain

PRIVILEGES, PAULINE AND PETRINE.

Pauline Privilege. The term "Pauline privilege" refers to the possibility that marriage contracted between two unbaptized persons (implying that it is not sacramental) may be dissolved in consideration of the faith of one party who is converted and receives baptism. This Catholic doctrine takes its name from the First Epistle to the Corinthians (7, 12–15), in which St. Paul directs, "If any brother hath a wife that believeth not, and she be pleased to dwell with him, let him not put her away. For if a Christian woman has a non-Christian husband, who agrees to live with her, let her not repudiate her husband; for the non-Christian husband is sanctified by his wife; and the non-Christian wife is sanctified by her Christian husband. If the non-Christian party wants to be separated, let the separation take place under these conditions: neither the brother nor the sister is linked; for it is to live in peace that God has called you."

Tertullian (ca. 220) was the first theologian in the Roman Church to address this problem (*Ad uxorem*, 1, II, c. 2). The *Ambrosiaster*, attributed to St. Ambrose (397), developed Tertullian's opinion: "If the unbeliever [the unbaptized person] leaves out of a hatred of God, the believer will not be responsible for the dissolution of the marriage: God's cause is greater than that of marriage. No respect is owed to the marriage of one who has a hatred for the author of the marriage. . . . Contempt for the Creator in fact abolishes any right to marriage on the part of the one who is left behind, and if he is joined to another, he may not be the object of any accusation."

For St. Augustine (430), the Christian party was entitled to dismiss the unbelieving spouse, but he advised against this, because of the risk that the spouse would commit adultery. Innocent I (417) preached the same doctrine.

In contrast, Hincmar of Rheims (882), basing his argument on the *Ambrosiaster*, granted the converted spouse the right to leave the marriage, even if the non-Catholic party agreed to a peaceful life together (*De divortio Lotharii*, II, art. 866). Collections prior to Gratian's Decree adhere to the Augustinian doctrine.

Gratian (12th century) went back to the text of the *Ambrosiaster*, recognizing at the same time that marriage between two nonbelievers is a true marriage. But, not being sacramental, it is not *ratum* (valid marriage between baptized persons), and may therefore be dissolved. Further—and here Peter Lombard would agree—the converted spouse may repudiate his "unbelieving" spouse only if the latter refuses to continue to live together or makes their life together unbearable out of hatred of religion. In a dictum, Gratian explains that St. Paul's letter to the Corinthians does not apply if the marriage was contracted after one spouse had already been baptized, or if the spouse apostasized after the marriage ("caus." [?] XXVIII, q. II, c. 2).

INNOCENT III (1216) recognized the validity of the marriage of two unbelievers. The party who converted must return to his first wife after his conversion, unless she refuses, or accepts him only "while giving herself up to contempt of the Creator or seeking to draw her husband into sin" (decretal *Gaudemus in Domino*, l. [?] IV, tit. XIX, c. 7, 8).

Pauline privilege was governed by c. 1120–24 and 1126 of the 1917 Code of Canon Law. It is covered by c. 1143–47 of the Code of 1983.

The requisite conditions for the application of the Pauline privilege are as follows: (1) The marriage must be a legitimate one celebrated between two nonbaptized persons, one of whom is subsequently baptized (whether in the Catholic Church or in another faith that is not in full communion with the Catholic Church); and (2) the unbaptized party must refuse cohabitation (resulting in physical or material separation) or peaceful cohabitation (resulting in moral separation), that is, not insulting the Creator (*sine contumelia Creatoris*) or replying negatively to questioning about the intention to convert (formal separation). This distinction of the various situations of separation was elaborated by the Congregation of the Holy Office (replies of 4 July 1855, 8 July 1891). By "insulting the Creator" is meant anything that implies the danger of sin for the baptized party and for the children, as well as anything contrary to the integrity of the marriage—for example, preventing the baptized party from practicing the faith, putting obstacles in the way of the children's Christian education, injuring the sanctity of the marriage or practicing polygamy.

The Pauline privilege is said to work *in favorem fidei*, since it is designed to protect the faith and serenity of the baptized party by ensuring a peaceful life and forestalling a falling away from true faith. The use of the privilege enables the baptized party to remarry. The first marriage, even if consummated, is *ipso facto* dissolved when the new marriage is contracted (Congregation of the Holy Office, reply of 1 August 1759).

The baptized party has the right to contract a new marriage with a Catholic party not only when the other party replies negatively to questioning on intent to convert (effected according to c. 1144 and 1145), but also when the other party leaves the marriage without just cause after at first peacefully cohabiting without insult to the Creator (c. 1146).

In serious cases, the local ordinary may authorize the baptized party to contract marriage with a non-Catholic, whether baptized or not, following the norms established for mixed marriages (c. 1147).

Petrine Privilege. This term does not occur in the Code of Canon Law of 1983. It reflects the fact that, by virtue of his supreme power, the Roman pontiff may dissolve certain nonsacramental marriages.

The doctrine on Pauline privilege was sufficient to resolve cases that arose as a result of the conversion of monogamous Jews, Slavs, and Scandinavians. While the Council of Trent did not pronounce on Petrine privilege, the Roman Curia had to face it in the 16th century in connection with the evangelization of polygamous peoples in the Americas and East Indies. This presented new situations (notably regarding the questioning of the non-Catholic party on his intention of converting in his turn or, at the least, cohabiting without contempt for the Creator), to which the Pauline privilege could be applied only in an extended form.

The formal obligation to proceed with this questioning gave rise to an important development. PAUL III was responsible for setting it in motion (constitution *Altitudo*, 1 June 1537). He decreed that recently converted Indians who were polygamous and did not know which wife was their first could choose whichever wife they preferred. PIUS V confirmed this disposition (constitution *Romani Pontificis*, 2 August 1571). He authorized the convert to choose the wife he preferred, provided she agreed to convert and be baptized in turn, even if his first legitimate spouse—presuming he knew who she was—consented to live peaceably with her husband. The development was completed with GREGORY XIII (constitution *Populis ac nationibus*, 25 January 1585). He allowed converted slaves who had married according to the custom of their country of origin to remarry according to Christian custom, without the usual questioning of the first spouse, who (presumably) was still in Africa. There followed additional decrees and pontifical indults (dispensations or privileges regarding a law), from PAUL V (11 June 1611), URBAN VII (20 October 1626, 17 September 1627) and BENEDICT XIV (brief *In suprema*, 16 January 1745). This privilege was therefore exercised not only in favor of faith but also for the salvation of souls, this being the supreme law of the Church (c. 1752 of 1983 Code).

Under PIUS XI's papacy, the Holy See undertook to grant its blessings for the dissolution of nonsacramental marriages that were not covered by the Pauline privilege or by the three constitutions cited above. Concessions were granted on a case-by-case basis by the Roman pontiff; for example, a consummated marriage might be dissolved provided the nonbeliever agreed to be baptized into the Catholic Church (Holy Office, 5 November 1924), or provided the heretic—the baptized non-Catholic—converted to the true faith (Holy Office, 10 July 1924, 2 April 1929, 25 May 1933). The ever larger number of concessions led to the elaboration of "Norms to hasten the processing of cases of dissolution of the matrimonial bond in favor of the faith by the supreme authority of the sovereign pontiff" (Congregation of the Holy Office, reserved instruction of 1 May 1934). Pius XII confirmed that a marriage that is simply *ratum* but *non consummatum* may be dissolved "not only by virtue of the Pauline privilege but also by the Roman pontiff by virtue of his ministerial power" (discourse to audience of the Roman Rota, 3 October 1941).

Similarly, c. 1148 of the 1983 Code of Canon Law uses the Congregation's replies as sources for the authentic interpretation of the canons of the Code (25 January 1919 and 3 August 1919) and of the Congregation of the Holy Office (30 June 1937). In the case of polyandry, the law allows the wife to choose her husband, if it is difficult to remain with the first one, and to dismiss the others. The local ordinary would see to it that this dismissal is done with Christian charity and that the needs of the dismissed husbands are met (alimony is compulsory). The new marriage thus contracted must be according to the canonical form and, if need be, following the norms on mixed marriages.

Where imprisonment or persecution prevents conjugal cohabitation, the nonbaptized party who has received baptism into the Catholic Church may contract a marriage even if in the meantime the other party has been baptized—provided, however, that the first marriage, now sacramental, was not consummated (c. 1149).

Even though the writers of the Code did not cover the dissolution of a marriage contracted between a baptized and a nonbaptized party with the dispensation of the impediment of disparity of cult, the Petrine privilege may be applied here. In fact, waiving the instruction of 1 May 1934, the Congregation for the Doctrine of the Faith established that such a marriage may be dissolved if it is clear that, because of peculiar local circumstances—especially a small number of Catholics in the area concerned—the Catholic party cannot live in conformity with the Catholic faith within the marriage (instruction *Ut notum* on the dissolution of marriage in favor of faith, 6 December 1973). The Congregation must be informed of the publicity given to this marriage.

Dominique Le Tourneau

Bibliography

Arendt, G. "Quomodo in favorem fidei solvatur a S. Pontifice matrimonium in infidelitate contractum: Nota theologico-canonica circa canonem 1127," *Ephemerides theologicae lovanienses*, I, 1924, 174; "De clausula restrictiva canoni 1127 adiecta," *Ephemerides theologicae lovanienses*, III, 1926, 328– 37.

Boudon, J. *Mémento du privilège paulin*, Paris, 1949.

Bride, A. "Privilège paulin," *DTC*, XIII, 1932, 40000–14.

Chabagno, *Le Mariage des infidèles*, Yokohama, 1913.

Chaussegros de Léry, L. *Le Privilège de la foi*, Montreal, 1938.

Gréco, J. *Le Pouvoir du souverain pontife à l'égard des infidèles*, Rome, 1967.

Gregory, D. *The Pauline Privilege*, Washington, 1931.

Hopfenbeck, A. *Privilegium petrinum*, Saint Ottilien, 1976.

Huy, I. *Dissolutio matrimonii e privilegio fidei iuxta canonem 1127*, Rome, 1944.

Jombart, E. "Casus de dissolutione matrimonii paganorum," *Periodica de re morali, canonica, liturgica*, 14, 1925–26, 68 ff.

Kuntz, J. M. "The Petrine Privilege: A Study of Some Recent Cases," *The Jurist*, 28, 1968, 486–96.

Legrain, M. "Privilège paulin, privilège pétrinien," *Catholicisme*, Paris, 1051–55.

Navarrete, U. "De termino 'Privilegium petrinum' non adhibendum," *Periodica de re morali, canonica, liturgica*, 53, 1964, 323–73.

Oesterlé, G. "Privilegium paulinum in sua applicatione," *Apollinaris*, 29, 1956, 395–412; "Privilège paulin," *DDC*, VII, 1965, 229–80.

Reckers, *De favore quo matrimonium gaudet in iure canonico*, Rome, 1951.

Tobón Mejía, A. *Disolución de matrimonios no sacramentales por la potestad ministerial del Romano Pontifice*, Bogotá, 1963.

Tomko, J. "De dissolutione matrimonii in favorem fidei eiusque fundamento theologico," *Periodica de re morali, canonica, liturgica*, 64 (1975), 99 ff.

Vromant, "De dispensatione ab interpellationibus in ordine ad privilegium fidei: Applicationes practicae can. 1125," *Periodica de re morali, canonica, liturgica*, 20, 1031, 108 ff.

PROFESSION OF FAITH AND OATH OF FIDELITY. Both these formulas have their origin in the Tridentine profession of faith of 1564, completed in 1877 to include the definitions of the VATICAN I COUNCIL, and the antimodernist oath of 1910. The VATICAN II COUNCIL's preparatory theological commission failed to come up with a satisfactory formula. In December 1967, the Congregation for the Doctrine of Faith published a formula for the profession of faith to replace both the Tridentine formula and the antimodernist oath (*Enchiridion Vaticanum*, 2, 1146–48). Though concise, it did not make an adequate distinction between truths proposed as divine revelation and truths proposed in a definitive manner although not divinely revealed; nor did it mention the teachings of the supreme MAGISTERIUM that are neither divinely revealed nor definitively proposed. The antimodernist oath had been abolished, but there was no other mode of swearing fidelity to take its place.

Profession of Faith. To fill this lacuna, new formulas were devised that came into force on 1 March 1989. The new part of the profession of faith consists of three paragraphs covering the following: the truths of the faith, contained in tradition and Holy Scripture and proposed by the Church as divine revelation, either through a particular definition from the Roman pontiff or a common definition from the whole college of bishops, or by the ordinary and universal magisterium (all these truths call for a like assent of faith); and the truths on faith and morals proposed definitively by the Church but not divinely revealed (which must be firmly accepted and considered, without the need for the assent of faith); and the teachings of the authentic magisterium of the pope or the college of bishops, which are not intended to be put forward in a definitive manner (demanding the religious submission of will and intellect).

The text is as follows:

"I [name] with firm faith believe and profess all that is contained in the Symbol of the faith, both whole and separate, namely:

"I believe in one God the Father almighty, maker of heaven and earth, and of all things visible and invisible;

"And in one Lord Jesus Christ, the only-begotten Son of God, begotten of his Father before all worlds, God of God, Light of Light, Very God of Very God, begotten, not made, being of one substance with the Father, by whom all things were made: who for us men, and for our salvation came down from heaven, and was incarnate by the Holy Ghost of the Virgin Mary, and was made man, and was crucified also for us under Pontius Pilate. He suffered and was buried, and the third day he rose again according to the Scriptures, and ascended into heaven, and sitteth on the right hand of the Father. And he shall come again with glory to judge both the quick and the dead: whose kingdom shall have no end.

"And I believe in the Holy Ghost, the lord, the giver of life, who proceedeth from the Father and the Son, who with the Father and the Son together is worshipped and glorified, who spake by the prophets. And I believe one Holy Catholic and Apostolic Church. I acknowledge one baptism for the remission of sins. And I look for the resurrection of the dead, and the life of the world to come. Amen.

"With firm faith I believe also all that is contained in the word of God, written or handed down, and is proposed by the Church—either through solemn judgment or through the ordinary and universal magisterium—as divinely revealed and to be believed.

"I also firmly embrace and hold all and each truth that are definitively proposed by the Church concerning the doctrine of the faith and morals.

"Moreover, I adhere with religious respect and religious submission of will and intellect to the doctrines which either the Roman Pontiff or the college of bishops enunciate when they exercise the magisterium authenticum even if they intend to proclaim those doctrines by a non-definitive act."

The Latin text is as follows:

"Ego N. firma fide credo et profiteor omnia et singula quae continentur in Symbolo fide, videlicet:

"Credo in unum Deum Patrem omnipotentem, factorem coeli et terrae, visibilium et invisibilium et in unum Dominum Iesum Christum, Filium Dei unigenitum, et ex Patre natum ante omnia saecula, Deum de Deo, lumen de lumine, Deum verum de Deo vero, genitum non factum, consubstantialem Patri per quem omnia facta sunt, qui propter nos homines et propter nostram salutem descendit de coelis, et incarnatus est

de Spiritu Sancto, ex Maria Virgine, et homo factus est; crucifixus etiam pro nobis sub Pontio Pilato, passus et sepultus est; et resurrexit tertia die secundum Scripturas, et ascendit in coelum, sedet ad dexteram Patris, et iterum venturus est cum gloria iudicare vivos et mortuos, cuius regni non erit finis; et in Spiritum Sanctum Dominum et vivificantem, qui ex Patre Filioque procedit; qui cum Patre et Filio simul adoratur et conglorificator; qui locutus est per Prophetas; et unam sanctam catholicam et apostolicam Ecclesiam. Confiteor unum baptisma in remissionem peccatorum, et exspecto resurrectionem mortuorum, et vitam venturi saeculi. Amen.

"Firma fide quoque credo ea omnia quae in verbo Dei scripto vel tradito continentur et ab Ecclesia sive sollemni iudicio sive ordinario et universali Magisterio tamquam divinitus revelata credenda proponuntur.

"Insuper religioso voluntatis et intellectus obsequio doctrinis adhaereo quas sive Romanus Pontifex sive Collegium episcoporum enuntiunt cum Magisterium authenticum exercent etsi non definitivo actu easdem proclamare intendant."'

The last paragraph calls for a sincere adherence of intellect and will to the doctrines which the Church teaches by a non-definitive act, but in which the authentic magisterium of the Church in any case has the last word.

This obligation of conscience toward the authentic magisterium, which applies to all the faithful of the universal Church, independent of the particular profession of faith and oath of fidelity, is sworn by certain well-defined categories of the Faithful for several reasons: First, the magisterium represents a legitimate authority that acts in Christ's name. Second, there is an absolute guarantee of the general assistance of the Holy Spirit concerning universal fidelity for the transmission of the faith. Third, even if in a certain case the truth is not absolutely clear, there are sufficient moral guarantees of truth. Last, this teaching magisterium is combined with the power of jurisdiction which calls for obedience *hic et nunc* to its pronouncements.

The profession of faith also applies to those who work in the dicasteries of the Roman Curia, according to the provisions of the general rule of the Curia, 7 June 1992, annex I.

Oath of Fidelity. The Congregation for the Doctrine of the Faith published a formula for *Iusiurandum fidelitatis in suscipiendo officio nomine Ecclesiae exercendo*, or the "oath of fidelity," which complements the profession of faith. Whereas the profession of faith is the condition for assuming a function within the Church, the oath of fidelity is the public commitment to practice this function appropriately, taken before the Church and before the institutions and persons for whom the function has been assumed.

The oath came into force on 1 March 1989. Until then, only a bishop had to take the oath (Code of Canon Law of 1983, c. 380). Henceforth, the oath of fidelity must be sworn by the persons mentioned in c. 833, 5° to 8°, insofar as they assume a function that they must exercise in the name of the Church. These persons include vicars general, episcopal and judicial, who take the oath before the diocesan bishop or his delegate; curates, rectors of a seminary, professors of theology and philosophy in a seminary, who take the oath before the local ordinary or his delegate on assuming their function, as do those about to be promoted as deacons; the rector of an ecclesiastical or Catholic university on assuming his function, before the grand chancellor, or, if need be, the local ordinary or their delegates those teaching disciplines relating to faith or morals in the unversities, before the rector, if he is a priest, or before the local ordinary or their delegates, on assuming their function; and superiors in religious institutes and in clerical societies of apostolic life, according to the constitutions.

The text of this oath is as follows:

"I [name] on assuming the office of . . . promise that I shall always remain in communion with the Catholic Church, in my spoken words as well as in my manner of action.

"I shall fulfill with great diligence and fidelity the duties that I owe to the Church, universal and particular, in which I have been called to exercise my service according to the prescriptions of the law.

"In fulfilling my office, which has been granted to me in the name of the Church, I shall hand it over and explain it to others faithfully; I shall avoid all doctrines contrary to it.

"I shall follow the discipline common to the whole Church and I shall promote the observance of all ecclesiastical laws, especially those which are contained in the Code of Canon Law.

"I shall follow with Christian obedience what the sacred pastors, as authentic doctors and teachers of faith, declare, or as rulers of the Church prescribe. I shall also give assistance faithfully to the diocesan bishops, so that the apostolic action to be exercised in the name and by the mandate of the Church, should be accomplished in communion with the same Church.

"So help me God, and God's sacred Gospels, which I touch with my hands."

The Latin text is as follows:

"Ego N. in suscipiendo officio . . . promitto me cum catholica Ecclesia communionem semper servaturum, sive verbis a me prolatis, sive mea agendi ratione.

"Magna cum diligentia et fidelitate onera explebo quibus teneor erga Ecclesiam, tum universam, tum particularem, in qua ad meum servitium, secundum iuris praescripta, exercendum vocatus sum.

"In munere meo adimplendo, quod Ecclesiae nomine mihi commissum est, fidei depositum integrum servabo, fideliter tradam et illustrabo; quascumque igitur doctrinas iisdem contrarias devitabo.

"Disciplinam cunctae Ecclesiae communem sequar et fovebo observantiamque cunctarum legum ecclesiasticarum, earum imprimis quae in Codice Iuris Canonici continentur, servabo.

"Christiana oboedentia prosequar quae sacri Pastores, tamquam authentici fidei doctores et magistri declarant aut tamquam Ecclesiae rectores statuunt, atque Episcopis diocesanis fideliter auxilium dabo, ut actio apostolica, nomine et mandato Ecclesiae exercenda, in eiusdem Ecclesiae communione peragatur.

"Sic me Deus adiuvet et sancta Dei Evangelia, quae manibus mei tango."

Paragraphs 4 and 5 of the oath of fidelity are modified as follows for superiors in religious institutes and in clerical societies of apostolic life:

"I shall promote the discipline common to the whole Church, I shall urge the observance of all ecclesiastical laws, especially of those which are contained in the Code of Canon Law.

"I shall follow with Christian obedience what the sacred pastors, as authentic doctors and teachers of the faith, declare, or as rulers of the Church prescribe. I shall work willingly with the diocesan bishops, so that the apostolic action to be exercised in the name and by the mandate of the Church should be accomplished—with due regard for the character and purpose of my institute—in communion with the same Church."

The modified form in Latin is:

"Disciplinam cunctae Ecclesiae communem fovebo observantiamque cunctarum legum ecclesiasticarum urgebo, earum imprimis quae in Codice Iuris Canonici continentur.

"Christiana oboedentia prosequar quae sacri Pastores, tamquam authentici fidei doctores et magistri declarant, aut tamquam Ecclesiae rectores statuunt, atque cum Episcopis diocesanis libenter operam dabo, ut actio apostolica, nomine et mandato Ecclesiae exercenda, salvi indole et fine mei Instituti, in eiusdem Ecclesiae communione peragatur.'"

The oath is no longer a condition for the validity of the office, task, or function assigned, contrary to what the 1917 Code of Canon Law (c. 438) provided. Those who take the oath, besides the persons listed above, are as follows: all those who take part in the ecumenical or particular council, the synod of bishops of diocesan synod, whether they have a deliberative or consultative vote, take the oath before the president or his delegate, and the president swears it before the council or synod; those raised to the cardinalate, according to the statutes of the Sacred College; those who are promoted to the episcopate and those equivalent to them in law, before the pontifical

legate; and the diocesan administrator, before the college of consultors (c. 833, 1° to 4°).

The sole aim of the oath of fidelity is that each category of faithful bound to swear it should contribute "by words and actions, to the maintenance and increase of the communion in the bosom of the Church so that in the fact of considering, practicing and professing the faith that has been handed down, a complete agreement between pastors and faithful should be realized" (U. Betti, "Considerations," 12).

The general regulation of the Roman Curia stipulates the swearing of an oath of fidelity and of observance of professional secrecy. The terms of this oath are identical to those given above, with the addition of a penultimate paragraph concerning professional secrecy (annex II).

Dominique Le Tourneau

Bibliography

Betti, U. "Considérations doctrinales," *L'Osservatore Romano en langue française*, 7 March 1989, 11–12.

De Bhaldraithe, E. "The Oath of Fidelity and Ecumenism," *One in Christ*, 26, 1990, 358–61.

de Fleurquin, L. "The Profession of Faith and the Oath of Fidelity: A Manifestation of Seriousness and Loyalty in the Life of the Church (Can. 833)," *Studia Canonica*, 23, 1989, 485–99.

Fuentes, J. A. "Sujeción del fiel en las nuevas fórmulas de la profesión de fe y del juramento de fidelidad," *Ius Canonicum*, XXX, 1990, 517–45.

Galot, J. "La profession de foi et le serment de fidélité," *Esprit et Vie*, 51 (21 December 1989), 694–8.

Huels, J. M. "Focus on Canon Law: The Profession of Faith and Oath of Fidelity Revised," *New Theology Review*, 4, 1990, 79–84.

Pagé, R. "Le document sur la profession de foi et le serment de fidélité," *Studia Canonica*, 24, 1990, 51–68.

Schmitz, H. "'Professio fidei' und 'iusiurandum fidelitatis': Glaubensbekenntnis und Treueid. Wiederbelebung des Antimodernisteneides?," *Archiv für katholisches Kirchenrecht*, 157, 1988, 353–429.

Urrutia, F. J. "Iusiurandum fidelitatis," *Periodica de re morali, canonica, liturgica*, 80 (1991), 559–78.

PROPAGANDA FIDE, CONGREGATION OF. *(Sacred Congregation for the Propagation of the Faith). Since 1967: Congregation for the Evangelization of the Nations.*

On 6 January 1622, the Feast of the Epiphany, Pope GREGORY XV instituted within the Curia the Congregation *de propaganda fide*, to be the "head" (*caput*) of the propagation of the Catholic faith. On 14 January, the congregation, made up of 13 cardinals, 2 prelates, and a secretary, held its first plenary session. The next day, the sovereign pontiff solicited the collaboration of all the apostolic nuncios with the encyclical *Abbraccia il sommo officio*. Then, on 22 June, he promulgated the constitution *Inscrutabili*, which defined the congregation's task: to concern itself with "all and every one of the questions relating to the diffusion of the faith throughout the world." A second constitution (*Romanum*), issued the same day, provided for the DICASTERIES to receive regular income, in particular from a tax payable by newly selected cardinals, called a "cardinal's ring" tax. Financial management was entrusted to a special section directed by a cardinal "Prefect of the Economy" (the post was abolished in 1908). Finally, the constitution *Cum inter* gave Propaganda, the name by which the congregation is usually known, the privilege of EXEMPTION for its actions (14 December 1622).

The founding of a specialized agency for administering and encouraging missions is in line with the process of Roman centralization that took place in the 16th and 17th centuries. Propaganda's creation, which was preceded by a number of short-lived attempts, was strongly influenced by the Tridentine ecclesiology linking it closely to the pontifical ministry: "Called by the Holy Spirit to the government of the Church of Christ, we understand that our chief pastoral care consists in diligently and constantly striving, insofar as divine help allows, to bring the straying sheep to the fold of Christ in order to make known to them the master and shepherd of the flock, so that, drawn by divine grace, they will cease to wander in the unhappy pastures of faithlessness and heresy and to drink of mortal waters, but will enter the pastures of the true faith, the doctrine of salvation, and be led to the springs of living waters" (*Inscrutabili*, in *Collectanea*, 1907, no. 3).

The founding texts set no geographical or juridical limit on Propaganda's powers, since its prerogatives cover all missions, both domestic missions "to bring schismatics and heretics back to the fold" and overseas missions to the "heathen." One can conclude from this that Propaganda was the exclusive interlocutor in all these cases, and that it took the place of the other dicasteries, except for the internal forum, which continued to be dependent on the penitentiary. But such competition was hard for the Holy Office to accept; it was even in danger of being excluded from the non-Catholic world. It therefore arranged for the competences to be redefined. Contrary to the hopes of Propaganda's first secretary, Francesco Ingoli, the congregation found its independence gradually restricted. In 1632, it was placed under the authority of Cardinal Antonio Barberini, secretary of the Holy Office, which took over both duties.

After a period of hesitation, a decree of ALEXANDER VII settled the dispute on 11 September 1658, stating that "doubts" (*dubii*) on a theological question would have obligatorily to be submitted to the Holy Office. From then on, Propaganda was better integrated into the body of the Curia. However, being subordinate to the Holy Office, it lost the ability to acquire independent committees of theologians and canonists, which affected its ability to devise an innovative pastoral mission.

A palace on the Piazza di Spagna, given in 1622 by Msgr. Juan Batisto Vivés, a Spanish prelate who was a member of the new congregation, offered the dicastery a new setting worthy of its ambitions. Its organization, fixed in Gregory XV's papacy, had followed some tried-and-true models and was essentially preserved. At the top, the cardinal-prefect, sometimes aided by a pro-prefect, presided over the monthly meetings of the cardinal members; each cardinal originally was responsible for a particular area. Questions presenting special problems were dealt with by local congregations of cardinals (*congregazioni particolari*) appointed for the purpose. Some of these became permanent from 1638, the most important being the congregation for Chinese and Indian affairs (1664). Under the authority of a prefect, a prelate with the rank of secretary handled day-to-day administration. From 1649, he was often aided by a pro-secretary. He supervised a small number of clerics responsible for correspondence with the missions, the archiving of documents, and writing of reports (*ponenze*).

This spare structure was indispensable for carrying out the work of gathering information, which the secretary Ingoli had made a priority. The institution of a polyglot press on 3 June 1626 confirmed the central place given to written communication as a means of government and propagation of the Catholic faith.

After Ingoli's death (1649), the congregation's policy during the 17th and 18th centuries remained dominated by his dual aims: to remove overseas missions from the control of Catholic monarchies, and to put an end to the exemptions the religious congregations had accumulated. The congregation spared no effort to achieve these goals, under the guidance of a number of active prefects and secretaries—some of them exceptional, such as Stefano Borgia, who was successively secretary (1770–89), pro-prefect, and prefect (1802–4). It sought to train, at the heart of the College of Propaganda, or Collegio Urbaniano, priests from the mission countries who were imbued with "the spirit of Rome." It encouraged the creation of seminaries under its direct authority, gaining the Holy See's recognition of the seminary of the Society of Foreign Missions in Paris (1664). But it did not succeed in founding its own missionary institute of secular priests. Forced to give the religious wide autonomy, the congregation requested that proxies as procurators be appointed in Rome to represent their orders to Propaganda.

The congregation also drew up rules defining jurisdictions, as well as missionaries' obligations (they were forbidden to engage in commercial activity), relations with or between the religious congregations, and practices of pastoral leadership. It affirmed its determination to control orthodox teaching by forbidding the missions to print books without prior authorization. It also produced orientation texts that reflected deep thinking on the problems of external mission. For instance, the 1659 instruction to apostolic vicars leaving for China, Tonkin, and Cochin China includes a firm reminder of the missionary's subordination to the papacy. The instruction goes on to define the specifics of the missionary action vis-à-vis the political powers, warns against adopting an aggressive attitude toward local customs, and recommends that missionaries take account of "time and place." The primary goal, it stresses, is the training of a native clergy. Despite these initiatives, through the end of the 18th century large numbers of overseas missions continued to elude papal control. The realization of the objectives fixed in 1622 came up against political and ecclesiastical obstacles which Propaganda tried in vain to evade.

First among these was the inheritance of the system of *padroado*, or royal patronage, which had been instituted at the end of the 15th century and the beginning of the 16th to the advantage of the kings of Portugal and Spain. This delegation of power, which became unacceptable in the post-Tridentine climate, at first impelled Propaganda to combine temporal power with its missionary activities. When this very quickly met with resentment on the part of the states, the congregation had to find other ways. Its aim was either to neutralize or to circumvent the previously conceded rights. Examples of the first method were Rome's interventions aimed at confining royal patronage to the regions where the Spanish and Portuguese monarchies actually took charge of the people's religious interests. The result was endless conflicts over jurisdiction in Asia, since up to 1690 Rome refused to erect new episcopates depending on patronage. To avoid the danger of concurrent hierarchies named simultaneously by Rome and by the monarchy in the disputed territories, Propaganda dispatched apostolic vicars. The pope's personal representative, through the delegation of power, the apostolic vicar was given an episcopal see that no longer actually existed (*in partibus infidelium*) and did not come under the jurisdiction of the patronage bishops. The system was employed in India (1637), then in China and Indochina (1659). In spite of Portugal's protests, the network of apostolic vicariates, to which were added apostolic prefects (heads of missions, usually non-episcopal in nature), became the foundation of the whole Roman missionary strategy.

Another obstacle was that posed in the 17th century by French GALLICANISM in the colonies of New France (in North America), the Antilles, and the Indian Ocean. The rights of the papacy to appoint bishops (New France) and apostolic prefects was formally safeguarded by ambiguous compromises. In practice, the bishops and prefects were subject to royal power or to the administrators appointed by the Company of the East Indies.

To sum up, the congregation's missionary field of action was theoretically enormous but in practice very limited. Japan was closed to Europeans, and the interior regions of China and Africa (Ethiopia) were similarly inaccessible. The Spanish and Portuguese colonies in Latin America, the Philippines, part of India, and the Congo all depended on royal patronage. In the vast Ottoman Empire, Propaganda had to be content with ensuring a missionary presence. As for Protestant and Orthodox Europe, freedom of action was restricted. The congregation's main concern here was to maintain the ecclesiastical hierarchy, train an indigenous clergy, and provide religious books printed in the local languages.

Last, Rome's wish to impose its authority and rules on all the religious congregations was made singularly complicated by the constant barrage of missionary and political questions. Here, too, the results were apt to be disappointing. Superior generals' reports were far from regular. The abolition of exemptions to the advantage of a system of government with uniform powers was not carried out completely. And the required distinction between mission head and local religious superior was not satisfactorily applied.

Yet the meager results should not be attributed exclusively to the defense of political or congregationist interests. Faced with the challenge of acculturation in the affair of Chinese and Malabar (Indian) rites, Propaganda discovered how difficult it was to create a theology linking Catholicism and local cultures, and it showed it was incapable of working out an original solution, like that inspired by Jesuit experience. Widely informed and concerned for objectivity, as is attested by the abundant documentation compiled by the congregation for Asiatic affairs, Propaganda nevertheless had to refer the investigation of disputes to the Holy Office. Finally, the condemnation of rites by CLEMENT XI (1704) and BENEDICT XIV (1742–44) illustrated a trend toward basing decisions largely on Eurocentric considerations (the quarrel over JANSENISM). Initially concerned with extending its authority and spreading abroad uniform norms, by the late 18th century Propaganda was unable to impose a solution based on recognition of local realities, a measure which it nevertheless foreshadowed with its promotion of the study of languages and native customs.

In 1798, revolutionary ferment caused Propaganda to be suppressed as "a highly useless establishment," and first the prefect and then the secretary were forced to flee Rome. Thanks to improvised measures, it managed to survive precariously until PIUS VII returned to Rome in 1800. The Napoleonic Empire presented another period of uncertainty and displacement (the archives were moved to Paris), for which the reestablishment of the Paris Overseas Missions, and the Lazarists, was no compensation. From 1815, however, the horizon brightened and a new era dawned that was exceptionally fertile.

With the weakening of the Iberian powers in the 19th century, a new balance of forces was created that favored Rome in the matter of the *padroado*. GREGORY XVI took the initiative in China, where he appointed four apostolic vicars (1834–36). Pius IX followed the same path, but in India he was forced to retreat before the threat of a schism around the Lisbon-appointed archbishop of Goa. In 1857, he reached a concordat with Portugal, which was immediately regretted, and which papal diplomacy had the greatest difficulty abolishing and replacing with a second concordat in 1886. Essentially, since local disagreements continued up to 1950, the question of the *padroado* in India was settled. Meanwhile, owing to the exploration and colonization of Oceania and Africa, vast territories became available to missions over which Portugal could not seriously claim royal patronage.

In another important development, French Catholicism was the chief player in the missionary revival, making the greatest contribution of funds and manpower. It happened that, thanks to the Revolution, a majority of Catholics had been converted to an ULTRAMONTANISM that encouraged the agents of this missionary movement to turn toward Rome. The founders of religious congregations (Colin, Libermann, Lavigerie, and others) looked to the pope and to Propaganda for legitimacy, juridical recognition, and missionary territories. Thus, Propaganda had at its disposal more men and missionary institutions subject to its authority than it had been able to obtain since its founding.

At the same time, progress in transportation methods enabled the congregation to improve communication with distant missions and thus to widen its field of intervention and control. The importance of the function of prefect of Propaganda, who was nicknamed *papa rosso* "red pope," is illustrated by a number of remarkable and highly influential cardinals: Mauro Cappellari (the future pope GREGORY XVI), Fransoni, Barnabè, Franchi, Giovanni Simeoni, Ledochowski, and Gotti. All these factors led to a reinforcement of Propaganda in the 19th century, an extension of its authority, and the integration of missions into Church government.

In that century, the dicastery's organization and working became balanced. Rationalization of tasks was made possible by the geographic distribution of files among the *minutanti*. It was continued under Pius IX, who created a section specially responsible for the Churches of Eastern rites, called the Congregation of Propaganda for Oriental Affairs (1864). Although always under the authority of the prefect of Propaganda, this new section had its own staff and functioned independently of the Latin section. Important decisions were made in cardinals' plenary meetings (held monthly), while current business was settled in ordinary meetings of major and *minutanti* functionaries (held each Monday morning). Employees followed strict rules in their handling of the files. The archive system was streamlined by a reform begun in 1893. If need arose, specialized committees or consultors appointed by the pope to serve the congregation studied the files and made recommendations.

The benefits of centralization were reflected in the quantity and variety of matters treated. Instructions from Rome seemed to be more and more respected in the dispatch of reports every year and every five years, as well as extraordinary reports, all of which received attentive study. The institution of regional SYNODS in North America, Asia, and Australia was another efficient way of Romanizing and making uniform the formulation of doctrine as well as discipline, training of clergy, and liturgy; local decisions were subject to the recommendation of Rome, which did not hesitate to amend them. The congregation also began to send out apostolic delegates to all areas, who considered themselves—to quote Zaleski, the delegate for India (1892–1916)—the dicastery's "eyes and ears."

Omnipresent in the life of the missions, the Roman congregation was thus able to deploy a widespread normative activity in the most diverse areas. Still, it called increasingly on specialized dicasteries (such as those to do with rites and indulgences) to solve problems. The result was an impressive corpus of decisions emanating from the various congregations, which were collated under the title *Collectanea* in first one, then two large volumes of decrees, instructions, and rules for use by the missions. This systematic work of classification on the part of Propaganda paved the way for the Code of Canon Law of 1917.

Armed with a Roman legitimacy that was reinforced by VATICAN I as well as the personal action of the popes, by the 19th century's end Propaganda possessed instruments of government that bound missionary activity closely to the center, Rome. An undisputed master of the distribution of territories and of their assignment to a missionary society, the Piazza di Spagna in fact exercised the kind of power that was not defined officially until 1929, the *jus commissionis*. As a result, the granting of a mission, or "commission," was a Roman monopoly which Propaganda was entitled to end. The dicastery's expanding authority can also be seen in its many interventions to settle disputes, whether these had to do with conflicts of jurisdiction or a mission's internal problems.

Yet Propaganda's triumph was not yet complete in 1903. Direction of the chief works of aid to missions, founded in France—in particular, the Work of the Propagation of the Faith—did come directly under its authority. LEO XIII and the Curia tried unsuccessfully to have the seat of these associations moved to Rome.

Over and beyond direction, on its own or through papal interventions Propaganda also defined the objectives assigned to the missions. The most important documents were published between 1845 (instruction *Neminem perfecto* on indigenous clergy) and 1893 (instruction *Cum postremis* to the Indian bishops). Rather than providing a specifically missionary theology, the documents determined a pastoral strategy oriented toward the formation of Christianities that were homogeneous, manned over time by an indigenous staff of clergy and catechists, set in a network of parishes (or stations) and works (schools, workshops, dispensaries, etc.), and capable of meeting their own financial needs and attracting pagan converts. The implantation of the Church was a leading preoccupation, and the maturing of the seed thus sown was made concrete by the establishment of a hierarchy of residential bishops: Mauritius (1847), Australia (1848), Guadeloupe, Martinique, Réunion (1850), India (1886), New Zealand (1887), Japan (1891), and others.

On the other hand, the recognition of indigenous cultures hardly received equal treatment in the Roman texts. Timid proposals regarding adaptation came up against the traumatic memory of the question of rites that obliged missionaries bound for Asia to take a special oath. As in Europe, the plan to establish a Catholicism that was strongly Roman, complete, antiliberal, and social was paramount overseas.

The historical context of the 19th century gave missions particular political importance. Propaganda and the Secretariat of State harmonized their strategies in the Congregation for Extraordinary Ecclesiastical Affairs, created in 1814. The papacy made it a rule to refuse to sign agreements that would imply a ceding of part of its authority. That did not prevent it, however, from seeking the protection of missions by civil authorities. These two imperatives determined the variations in Rome's attitude toward the states and in the face of France's claim of a protectorate over the Eastern and Far Eastern missions.

PIUS X's papacy did not bring any major changes in Propaganda's doctrine or policy. However, he carried out a reform of the Curia (bull *Sapiento consilio* of 29 June 1908) that granted the dicastery those countries "in a mission state," that is, without an episcopal hierarchy or having "only an imperfect organization," even though a hierarchy had been set up. Northwest Europe (England, Scotland, Ireland, the Netherlands, Luxemburg) and English-speaking America (the United States, Canada, Newfoundland) were removed from Propaganda and included in the common law of specialized congregations. BENEDICT XV completed this task of specialization when he changed the Oriental section into a fully independent Congregation for the Oriental Church (*motu proprio Dei providentis* of 1 May 1917).

To match this, Propaganda's area of prerogatives was also limited. Everything having to do with faith, marriage, or rites was moved to the specialized congregations, thus ratifying practice. The Tribunal of the Rota was made responsible for legal claims. Religious were

dependent only on the congregation in their capacity as missionaries. The result was improved coherence but also a reduction of the importance of the Piazza da Spagna. World War I having demonstrated the dangers of the dependence of missions on Western nations, the training of native clergy now became a priority, along with a vigorous reminder of the supranationality of missionary action (*Maximum illud*, Benedict XV, 1919). Above all, the order for "indigenization" now applied to the local episcopate and brought about the consecration in Rome of the first six Chinese bishops (1926). On the other hand, the French protectorate over the Chinese missions was short-circuited in 1922 with the sending of an apostolic delegate dependent on Propaganda. At the same time, Pius XI took advantage of Propaganda's tricentenary, as well a reduction in France's financial contribution, to order that the seat of the Work of the Propagation of the Faith be moved to Rome (*motu proprio Romanorum pontificum*, 3 May 1922), and that associations be grouped within the Pontifical Missionary Works (OPM).

Between the two world wars, Propaganda took various measures to influence Catholic opinion. These included a Vatican missionary exhibition in 1925, the founding of the international agency Fides in 1927, monthly missionary intentions and missionary days. In 1926, the encyclical *Rerum Ecclesiae* called for a veritable mobilization behind Pius XI. There were other less spectacular but highly significant moves. Under the impulse of certain missionaries and the apostolic delegate to Peking, Costantini, later secretary (1935–53), Propaganda learned to adopt a positive approach toward cultures where theologians could seek out places where Christianity might be inserted. The Netherlands prefect van Rossum started university-level teaching of missiology at the Urbaniano. Courses in native art, as well as new regulations concerning the participation of Christians in public ceremonies in China and Japan and the authorization of Chinese rites in 1939, all were concrete examples of this marked development inspired by the idea of adaptation.

After 1945, the wave of decolonization led to increasing discussion in favor of indigenous Churches capable of being self-supporting. Despite the conflicts at that time, Rome's authority was not everywhere called into question, testifying to the strong bonds between the missionary periphery and the center of Catholicism. The VATICAN II council provided the best evidence of this unbroken evolution. The council texts (constitution *Lumen gentium* and the decree *Ad gentes*, 1965) and texts of application (*motu proprio Ecclesiae sanctae*, 1966) did not touch Propaganda's traditional functions, so that the congregation was still "the only competent dicastery" for missions. The call for internationalization of personnel led to the appointment of secretaries (Gantin, Lourdusamy) who were from the mission countries but had done part of their training in Rome.

The most innovative developments were in ecclesiology. Whereas missions had previously been entrusted to special institutes, now "the whole people of God" were told they had a missionary duty. "Commissions" were replaced by the recognition of fully responsible "local Churches," at least wherever the episcopal hierarchy had been set up, since vicariates, prefectures, and missions remained under a system of "mandate" granted to a religious institute (instruction *Relationes in territoriis*, 1969). The total area of territories that the congregation covered was considerable: over half the earth's surface and half the world's population.

Changes made after the council reflected the determination to preserve a system that had proved efficacious even as it responded to the young Churches' aspirations. Besides the choice of a less ambiguous name (Congregation for the Evangelization of Peoples), with PAUL VI's reform of the Curia in 1967 (apostolic constitution *Regimini Ecclesiae Universae*, completed by the instruction *Cum in Constitutione*), bishops, representatives of institutes, and missionary works were all associated with Propaganda's work. From 1971, various commissions (spirituality, catechesis, studies, theology, etc.) were set up to prepare plenary meetings and encourage communication with the national missionary episcopates, while pontifical councils created parallel collaborative structures: Council for interreligious dialogue with nonbelievers, of culture, and so on.

Yet the collegial dimension affirmed since Vatican II had to reckon with the Curia's tradition of centralization and independence. JOHN PAUL II's constitution *Pastor bonus* (1988) reaffirmed the difference between the agencies accustomed to a certain degree of self-government, like Propaganda, and the councils. In the end, the congregation's internal organization was not substantially affected by these reforms, which left matters of current business to the secretariat, remodeled along the lines of a more uniform hierarchy. It was still aided by a special administration for temporal matters and a council responsible for pontifical missionary Works (Propagation of the Faith, St. Peter the Apostle, Holy Childhood, Pontifical Missionary Union of the Clergy).

However, the constitution *Pastor bonus* retained the possibility of changes in the functioning of the congregation—for instance, in the call to the laity (as employees or consultants), or in the exercise of authority through the call for collaboration with the "local Churches." References in discourse to the theology of "inculturation"—that is, the expression of Christianity through new cultures—are another sign of these prudent but nevertheless real changes.

Prefects of Propaganda (1622–1990). Antonio Maria Sauli 1622. Ludovico Ludovisi 1622–32. Antonio Barberini Jr. 1632–71. Angelo Paluzzi degli Albertoni 1671–98. Carlo Barberini 1698–1704. Giuseppe Sacripanti 1704–27. Vincenzo Petra 1727–47. Silvio Valenti-Gonzaga 1747–56. Giuseppe Spinelli 1756–64. Giuseppe Maria Castelli 1763–80. Leonardo Antonelli 1780–95. Hyacinthe Sigismond Gerdil 1795–1802. Stefano Borgia 1802–4. Michele Di Pietro 1805–14. Lorenzo Litta 1814–18. Francesco Luigi Fontana 1818–22. Ercole Consalvi 1824. Bartolomeo Alberto (in religion, Mauro) Cappellari 1826–31. Carlo Maria Pedicini 1831–34. Giacomo Filippo Fransoni 1834–56. Alessandro Barnabè 1856–74. Alessandro Franchi 1874–78. Giovanni Simeoni 1878–92. Miczyslaw Halka Ledochowski (Poland) 1892–1902. Antonio Giovanni (in religion, Girolamo) Gotti 1902–16. Domenico Serafini 1916–18. Willem Marinus van Rossum (Netherlands) 1918–32. Pietro Fumasoni-Biondi 1933–60. Grigor Petros Agagianian (Armenia) 1960–70. Agnelo Rossi (Brazil) 1970–84. Dermot Ryan (pro-prefect) (Eire) 1984–85. Jozef Tomko (Slovakia) since 1985.

Claude Prud'homme

Bibliography

Arens, B. *Manuel des missions catholiques*, Louvain, 1925.

Collectanea S. Cong de Propaganda Fide seu Decreta, Instructiones, Rescripta pro Apostolicis Missionibus, Rome, 1907, 2 vols.

Grimaldi, F. *Les Congrégations romaines: Guide historique et pratique*, Rome, 1890.

Iuris Pontificii de Propaganda Fide Pars Prima complectens Bullas Brevia Acta S.S. a Congregationis institutione. . . cura ac studio Raphaelis De Martinis, 7 vols., Rome, 1888–1907; *Pars Secunda*, Rome, 1909.

Kowalski, N., and Metzler, J. *Inventory of the Historical Archives of the Sacred Congregation for the Evangelization of Peoples or "De Propaganda Fide,"* Rome, Pontificia Universitas Urbaniana, 1983.

Mioya, R. "S.C. per l'Evangelizzazione dei Popoli (1622)," *Dizionario degli Istituti di perfezione*, 8 (1988), 195–207.

Missiones catholicae ritus latini cura S.C.P.F. descriptae in annum . . . , Rome (yearly from 1886 to 1892; published irregularly from 1895).

Rommerskirchen, J., Dindinger, J., Kowalski, N., Metzler J., eds., *Bibliografia Missionaria*, Rome, from 1933.

Sacrae Congregationis De Propaganda Fide Memoria Rerum, 350 ans au service de la Mission, ed. J. Metzler, 3 vols. in 5 t., Rome, Freiburg, Vienna, Herder, 1971–76.

Song, R. H. *The Sacred Congregation for the Propagation of the Faith*, Washington, D. C. 1961.

Streit, R., Dindinger, J., and Rommerskirchen, J., Metzler, J., *Bibliotheca Missionum*, 30 vols., Münster, then Aix-la-Chapelle, then Freiburg-in-Breisgau, 1916–75.

Sylloge praecipuorum documentorum recentium Summorum Pontificum et S.C.P.F. . . . ad usum missionarumae, Vatican, 1939.

PROPAGATION OF THE FAITH. The most prestigious of the four pontifical missionary Works, had its small beginning in Lyon. Encouraged by her brother Philéas, then a seminarian at Largentière (Rhône), later at Saint-Sulpice (Paris), a young Lyons woman named Pauline-Marie Jaricot started collecting for Overseas Missions among female silk factory workers who at her initiative had been meeting in pious associations, both in Lyon and at the Saint-Vallier factory (Drôme) managed by her brother-in-law and one of her sisters. The money was sent to Philéas, who turned it over to the Overseas Missions seminary. Prayer groups benefiting establishments aimed at propagating the faith were started in the Overseas Missions seminary and approved by pontifical indult (30 November 1817).

Unsatisfied with these random collections, Pauline sought and, one autumn evening in 1819, found what she called "the plan," whose structure would be adopted throughout the world for over a century. The plan was a simple one: to form groups of ten people who would meet each week and bring the weekly sou they had collected. The person presiding over the meeting would give a reading concerning new sites of overseas missionary activity, and the group would spend a period in hopeful prayer. Pauline formed the leaders of ten groups of ten into "centenaries." They fanned out by the dozens, then by the hundreds, and soon the first "millenaries" came into being.

Meanwhile, there arrived in Lyon Angelo Ingelis, vicar general to Bishop Dubourg, of New Orleans. Twelve "Messieurs," including ten members of the (secret) Lyon Congregation, met on this occasion and discussed the question of expanding aid to the "Two Worlds" (Europe and America). One of Pauline's associates, Victor Girodon, presented the plan used to collect the weekly sou. The plan met with unanimous agreement.

No sooner was Pauline's plan adopted than it became the basis for the association which was created that day, 3 May 1822: the provisional council of the Society of the Propagation of the Faith was constituted. A century later, Pius XI made it a pontifical Work with an international center in Rome (*motu proprio Romanorum Pontificum,* 3 May 1922).

In recent years, the Work of the Propagation of the Faith has become increasingly concerned with missionary training. Nonetheless, appealing to the generosity of the faithful remains a central activity. Every year the pope issues a reminder of it on the occasion of World Missionary Week.

The aims of the Work are as follows: "(a) to arouse interest in universal evangelization in all sectors of the people of God: in families, basic communities, parishes, schools, movements, associations, so that the whole diocese may become aware of its universal missionary vocation . . . ; (b) to promote among the various local Churches, with the aim of world evangelization, spiritual and material cooperation and the exchange of apostolic personnel" (*Statutes of the Pontifical Missionary Works,* 26 June 1980, chap. II, art. II, I, n. 9). A central community fund has been set up to make possible a program of aid to the mission Churches.

"Education, information and missionary awareness are the Work's principal task" (*ibid.,* n. 10). This action reaches a climax on the penultimate Sunday in October, which in 1926 was proclaimed the day of universal mission in all dioceses throughout the world.

Dominique Le Tourneau

See also MISSIONS.

PROPHECIES, MODERN. Prophetism, in particular prophecies about the popes and the papacy, flourished from the end of the 18th century to the middle of the 19th. Even though prognostications of this kind had always been widespread, especially when the pontifical seat was vacant, over the years a new phenomenon appeared that had precise functions as well as political and ideological implications. Prophecy, in fact, underwent a renaissance during the crisis of the Catholic Church, when it was threatened by attacks from those imbued with the ideas of the Enlightenment and then by the French Revolution, and later by the resultant trend of growing secularization.

Prophecy usually was accompanied by visions and marvels. Along with less significant occurrences in the 18th century, the abolition of the Society of Jesus (1773) saw the beginning of a surge of prophetism. Shortly before the issuance of the decree dissolving the order, announcements threatening terrible chastisements began to circulate in the Papal States. These prophetic manifestations, accompanied by visions, came from a Dominican nun, Maria Teresa del Cuore di Gesú, and from a poor peasant woman, Bernardina Renzi; both women were from Valentano, in the diocese of Montefiascone. The prophetesses were encouraged and supported by a group of former JESUIT exiles from Bourbon Sicily, aided by some leading Roman personages. They soon became the center of a large network which broadcast—not only in Italy but also elsewhere, especially in France—"revelations" concerning the fate of the Jesuit order and the Church as a whole.

These revelations had a precise aim: to aid the cause of the Jesuits and those sectors of the Church favorable to the order. They acted as a powerful, efficient political tool, making full use of propaganda—a characteristic of every wave of prophetism, especially in periods of crisis and political and religious instability. It is no coincidence that Bernardina's prophecies about the imminent, unexpected death of CLEMENT XIV, as a punishment for his treatment of the Jesuits, and the ensuing "rebirth" of the order, were cited, during and after the Revolutionary turmoil, by intransigent Catholic publications, both Italian and French, which sought to show a causal link between the suppression of the Society of Jesus and the French Revolution. Many other instances of prophetism arose in the same period, while highly eschatological works, such as *La Venida del Mesias en gloria y magestad* by the Chilean Manuel Lacunza, were produced in former Jesuit circles.

The Jesuit cause was not the only one that relied on the influence of prophetism. A large sector of the Church employed it as a way of uniting the faithful and strengthening its own influence by appealing to popular emotion. Later, the Church found another source of support in the prophecies attributed to Benoît-Joseph Labre. He was a young French mendicant who died in Rome in 1783, whereupon his process of canonization was immediately begun. He became a symbol of the Church and the papacy, which were now under attack by philosophical movements as well as jurisdictional reforms on the part of the monarchies.

Prophecies about the Revolution attributed restrospectively to Labre, after the turmoil, fed the political current that arose from counter-revolutionary and pontifical propaganda. Moreover, with perfect timing, they coincided with the most celebrated of the "miraculous" and prophetic phenomena of the age, the "miracles" of the Marian images with moving eyes, which occurred in 1796, when French troops entered Italy. This phenomenon of mass enthusiasm, later linked to the anti-French rebellion—to which it gave its battle cry, "Viva Maria!"—was interpreted as a collection of signs of divine warning as well as protection, in the face of near and present danger. As a result, it was again put to use to help legitimize Catholic and pontifical causes.

Countering this effort was another form of prophetism. This was pro-revolutionary, or based on the expectation of a radical reform of the Church understood as regeneration; examples include the prophetess Suzette Labrousse, who was inspired to come to Rome in 1792, or the millenarist type of prophetism cultivated by pro-Jansenist groups. It confirmed *a contrario* the importance of the papacy at this time of expected renewal. Most typical were prophetic and apocalyptic interpretations of contemporary history. These were based, according to the schemas of uncompromising Catholicism, on the expression of divine wrath and punishment and the war of the last days between religion and the forces of Satan, unleashed by the modern world and conspiring

against the faith. Moreover, this interpretation extended to every social and cultural stratum, especially in anti-revolutionary literature (from the works of Joseph de Maistre to anonymous propaganda scribblings), and from the pulpit.

These prophetic expressions led to a hardening of thought critical of all forms of modernity, and to an active mobilization on the political and operational levels. Thus, prophetism and prophetic literature had a continuing, concrete influence on historical events. As people searched for a way to interpret terrible contemporary events, this encouraged the revival of old prophecies, which were adapted and applied to present happenings that could be explained in the light of renewal and the dawning of a new era.

These prophecies were often the same as those that had flourished in the 16th century, linked with the trauma of the Reformation. Not only did they observe the strict causal connection that Catholic polemics had established between the Reformation and the French Revolution; they were also made to serve a counter-revolutionary function, being centered on the specific question of the fate of the papacy and religion. Those years in Italy and France saw many reprintings, in the vernacular, of the prophecies contained in the famous *Mirabilis liber* and the *Vaticinia de summis pontificibus*. Based on the idea of the renewal of the Church and the world through the efforts of a saintly pope, these prophecies took on the functions of legitimist propaganda and political and religious restoration. First and foremost, they exalted the papacy—its absolute authority in the leadership of the Church and in society, as well as its eschatological role—presenting it as a guide to the faithful who were confused by the distractions of modernity.

It was because of the host of popular prophecies concerning the popes (the PROPHECIES OF MALACHY) that PIUS VI was called *peregrinus apostolicus*. Nor was it coincidental that the popular prophetic anthologies that proliferated throughout Italy in the second half of the 19th century—in the face of political, religious, and military threats to the papacy and the Church's temporal power—led intransigent Catholic culture to give new impetus to apocalyptic prophetism. In short, it was precisely because of this new link gradually established between the Church and prophecy, as well as prodigious happenings in general—a sort of "institutionalizing of the miraculous"—that the peculiar connection between the ecclesiastical institution and the popular (especially female) world was reinforced, making possible the renewal and redefinition of Catholicism in the 19th century.

Marina Caffiero

Bibliography

Caffiero, M. "Santità e controrivoluzione: Il caso di Benedetto Giuseppe Labre," *Dimensioni e problemi della ricerca storica*, 1989, 2, 83–103; *La nuova era: Miti e profezie dell'Italia in rivoluzione*, Genoa, 1991; "Le profetesse di Valentano," in G. Zarri (ed.), *Finzione e santità tra medioevo e età moderna*.

Garrett, C. *Respectable Folly: Millenarianism and the French Revolution in France and England*, Baltimore, 1974.

Kselman, T. A. *Miracles and Prophecies in Nineteenth-Century France*, New Brunswick, 1983.

Lecanu, A. F. *Dictionnaire des prophéties et des miracles*, 2 vols., Paris, 1852–4.

PROPHECIES OF MALACHY. Prophetic discourse—that is, discourse that claims to discern what will occur in the future—was an essential element of Old Testament thought. It was founded on revealed inspiration, which the Bible, up to the Book of Revelation, regarded as emanating from God's omniscience, wisdom, and goodness. The themes and varieties of prophetic speculation had to do almost exclusively with foreseeing and describing the last days, from the appearance of the Antichrist to the Last Judgment. This eschatological interpretation began to predominate during the imperial persecutions (2nd–3rd centuries), together with a millenarism that did not begin to decline until the middle of the 16th century.

Thereafter, the elaboration and diffusion of prophecies was encouraged by the progress of printing, although reports of prophecies still circulated orally, with all the attendant inaccuracies and distortions. One of the most striking prognoses that appeared at this time was the so-called Prophecies of Malachy (also known as the "Popes' Prophecies"); it is striking because, on the one hand, it is systematic and claims to be exhaustive, and on the other, because it concentrates on the history of the papacy traced through Peter's successors, and not on general history, as did Nostradamus's *Centuries*.

The name Malachy, the purported author of the prophecies, is probably a pseudonym and, despite the clear allusion, is not to be confused with the Old Testatement prophet Malachi ("my messenger"), the last of the 12 "Little Prophets" in the traditional order of the Hebrew canon. The problem of identifying the author of the Popes' Prophecies with St. Malachy, the 12th-century bishop of Armagh in Ireland, is trickier. Renowned beyond Ulster for his virtues and miraculous powers, and associated with many celestial marvels, Malachy had formed a friendship with Bernard de Clairvaux and most likely met Pope INNOCENT II (1130–43) when on pilgrimage to Rome, where, legend has it, the pope briefly crowned him with the pontifical tiara.

The list of popes evoked by the prophecy (118 in all) begins with CELESTINE II (1143–44), Innocent II's successor. The uncertainties that arose from the proliferation of antipopes at the time and the difficult situation the papal institution faced as a result, were most likely the psychological basis for the prophetic listing, which provided people with some sort of reassurance by concerning itself with the future. However, the first attested appearance of the text is no earlier than 1595, when a Benedictine of Flemish origin, Arnold (or Arnaud) of Wion, published his *Lignum Vitae ornamentum et decus Ecclesiae* (The Wood of Life, ornament and glory of the Church) in Venice. Some time later, certain scholars, led by the Jesuit Claude-François Ménestrier (*La Philosophie des images, énigmatiques*, Lyon, 1694), maintained that this prophecy had been concocted by a supporter of Cardinal Simoncelli, dean of the conclave of 1590 and bishop of Orvieto (Latin, *Urbs Vetus*), in whose favor the writer suggested the motto *ex antiquitate urbis* to speed the cardinals' decision. In the end, the motto was applied to GREGORY XIV, who was elected at the conclave. J.–P. Migne, at the end of the 19th century, accepted this hypothesis.

The coding of the list of prophecies is in fact based on a single principle, which makes its eventual interpretation dangerous. Every pope, from Celestine II to Peter II, the last sovereign pontiff (the name Peter supposedly signifying the end of the papal lineage), is given a motto meant to express a characteristic and essential trait of his person and pontificate. The many attempts at decoding that have been made up to the present have revealed a large number of references to the birthplaces of the popes in question, or to the episcopal residences they used before they became pope (e.g., for A. Roncalli, the patriarch of Venice and future John XXIII, *pastor et nauta*), as well as references to heraldry. The formulas all have several possible translations, varying considerably in coherence, and this pervasive polysemy diminishes the collection's force.

However, the historical method, for all its strictness, must pay attention upon encountering certain symbols or formulas that fit tolerably well with the reality under discussion. One example is the insistence on the lunar element marking the chief phases of the Ottoman conquest, which is symbolized by the crescent (first siege of Constantinople in 1422, motto 43; capture of the city in 1453, motto 54); or the use of the expression *religio depopulata* to refer to the papacy of BENEDICT XV (1914–22)—a double allusion, purportedly, to the slaughter of World War I and the process of de-Christianization then palpable at the heart of Western Christianity.

With other mottoes, though, these kinds of matches, even if far-fetched, hardly stand up. An obvious case is that of JOHN PAUL II (motto, *de labore solis*). The motto *axis in medietate signi*, given to pope SIXTUS V (1585–90), seems to make him the pivot of the prophetic list. From this motto, some audacious writers have deduced the date when the papacy will end: 442 years had elapsed between the accession of the first pope mentioned (Celestine, 1143) and that of Sixtus V (1585). By adding 442 more years to that date of 1585, one gets 2027 (or 2026, if one agrees to get rid of the inconvenient extra year), which would also be the date predicted by Michel Nostradamus (century X, quatrain 72). St. Malachy's prophecy states that at that time, "In the last persecution [or prosecution] of the Holy Roman Church, a Roman named Peter will be raised to the pontificate. He will feed the flock amidst a host of tribulations, which being at an end, the city of seven hills will be destroyed, and the dread judge will judge the world."

In spite of such meticulous readings, defined quite clearly, the systematic character of the text is obvious, and many problems remain, even though it is not necessary at this stage to prejudge the truth value of the prophecy. The singularity of the genre and the large number of times it has obviously failed would seem to counsel doubt. On the other hand, the prophecies also reveal a possible though bizarre way of regarding the unique institution of the papacy, which looks with faith toward the last days, a concept which it recognizes, accepts, and defends.

List of Popes' Mottoes (According to the so-called Prophecies of Malachy). Antipopes are given in brackets.

1. Celestine II (1143–4) — *Ex castro Tiberis*
2. Lucius II (1144–5) — *Inimicus expulsus*
3. Eugene III (1145–53) — *Ex magnitudine montis*
4. Anastasius IV (1153–4) — *Abbas Suburranus*
5. Hadrian IV (1154–59) — *De nire albo*
[6. Victor IV (1159–64) — *Ex tetro carcere*]
[7. Paschal III (1164–8) — *Via transtiberina*]
[8. Callistus III (1680–78) — *De Pannonica Tusciae*]
9. Alexander III (1159–81) — *Ex ansere custode*
10. Lucius III (1181–5) — *Lux in ostio*
11. Urban III (1185–7) — *Sus in cribro*
12. Gregory VIII (1187) — *Ensis Laurentii*
13. Clement III (1187–91) — *De schola exiet*
14. Celestine III (1191–8) — *De rure bovensi*
15. Innocent III (1198–1216) — *Comes signatus*
16. Honorius III (1216–27) — *Canonicus ex latere*
17. Gregory IX (1227–41) — *Avis ostiensis*
18. Celestine IV (1241) — *Leo Sabinus*
19. Innocent IV (1243–54) — *Comes Laurentius*
20. Alexander IV (1254–61) — *Signum ostiense*
21. Urban IV (1261–4) — *Jerusalem Campaniae*
22. Clement IV (1265–8) — *Draco depressus*
23. Gregory X (1271–6) — *Anguineus vir*
24. Innocent V (1276) — *Concionator Gallus*
25. Hadrian V (1276) — *Bonus comes*
26. John XXI (1276–7) — *Piscator Tuscus*
27. Nicholas III (1277–80) — *Rosa composita*
28. Martin IV (1281–5) — *Ex telonio liliacei Martini*
29. Honorius IV (1285–7) — *Ex rosa leonina*
30. Nicholas IV (1288–92) — *Picus inter escas*
31. Celestine V (1294) — *Ex eremo celsus*
32. Boniface VIII (1294–1303) — *Ex undarum benedictione*
33. Benedict XI (1303–4) — *Concionator Patareus*
34. Clement V (1305–14) — *De fasciis aquitanicis*
35. John XXII (1316–34) — *De sutore asseo*
[36. Nicholas V (1328–30) — *Corvus schismaticus*]
37. Benedict XII (1334–42) — *Frigidus abbas*
38. Clement VI (1342–52) — *De rosa atrebatensi*
39. Innocent VI (1352–62) — *De montibus Zammachii*
40. Urban V (1362–70) — *Gallus vicecomes*
41. Gregory XI (1370–8) — *Novus de virgine forti*
[42. Clement VII (1378–94) — *De cruce apostolica*]
[43. Benedict XIII (1394–1417) — *Luna cosmedina*]
[44. Clement VIII (1423–9) — *Schisma Barcinorum*]
45. Urban VI (1378–89) — *De inferno praegnanti*
46. Boniface IX (1389–1404) — *Cubus de mixtione*
47. Innocent VII (1404–6) — *De meliore sidere*
48. Gregory XII (1406–15) — *Nauta de Pontenegro*
[49. Alexander V (1409–10) — *Flagellum solis*]
[50. John XXIII (1410–15) — *Cervus siren*]
51. Martin V (1417–31) — *Corona veli aurei*
52. Eugene IV (1431–47) — *Lupa caelestina*
[53. Felix V (1439–49) — *Amator crucis*]
54. Nicholas V (1447–55) — *De modicitate lunae*
55. Callistus III (1455–8) — *Bos pascens*
56. Pius II (1458–64) — *De capra et albergo*
57. Paul II (1464–71) — *De cervo et leone*
58. Sixtus IV (1471–84) — *Piscator minorita*
59. Innocent VIII (1484–92) — *Praecursor Siciliae*
60. Alexander VI (1492–1503) — *Bos Albanus in portu*
61. Pius III (1503) — *De parvo homine*
62. Julius II (1503–13) — *Fructus Jovis juvabit*
63. Leo X (1513–21) — *De craticula Politiana*

64. Hadrian VI (1522–3)	*Leo Florentius*		108. Paul VI (1963–78)	*Flos florum*
65. Clement VII (1523–34)	*Flos pilae aegrae*		109. John Paul I (1978)	*De medietate lunae*
66. Paul III (1534–49)	*Hyacinthus medicorum*		110. John Paul II (1978–)	*De labore solis*
67. Julius III (1550–55)	*De corona montana*		111.	*De gloria divae*
68. Marcellus II (1555)	*Frumentum flaccidum*		112.	*Petrus Romanus*

Philippe Levillan

69. Paul IV (1555–9)	*De fide Petri*
70. Pius IV (1559–65)	*Aesculapii pharmacum*
71. Pius V (1566–72)	*Angelus nemorosus*
72. Gregory XIII (1572–85)	*Medium corpus pilarum*
73. Sixtus V (1585–90)	*Axis in medietate signi*
74. Urban VII (1590)	*De rore caeli*
75. Gregory XIV (1590–1)	*Ex antiquitate urbis*
76. Innocent IX (1591)	*Pia civitas in bello*
77. Clement VIII (1592–1605)	*Crux Romulea*
78. Leo XI (1605)	*Undosus vir*
79. Paul V (1605–21)	*Gens perversa*
80. Gregory XV (1621–3)	*In tribulatione pacis*
81. Urban VIII (1623–44)	*Lilium et rosa*
82. Innocent X (1644–55)	*Jucunditas crucis*
83. Alexander VII (1655–67)	*Montium custos*
84. Clement IX (1667–9)	*Sidus olorum*
85. Clement X (1670–6)	*De flumine magno*
86. Innocent XI (1676–89)	*Bellua insatiabilis*
87. Alexander VIII (1689–91)	*Poenitentia gloriosa*
88. Innocent XII (1691–1700)	*Rastrum in porta*
89. Clement XI (1700–21)	*Flores circumdati*
90. Innocent XIII (1721–4)	*De bona religione*
91. Benedict XIII (1724–30)	*Miles in bello*
92. Clement XII (1730–40)	*Columna excelsa*
93. Benedict XIV (1740–58)	*Animal rurale*
94. Clement XIII (1758–69)	*Rosa Umbriae*
95. Clement XIV (1769–74)	*Ursus velox*
96. Pius VI (1775–99)	*Peregrinus apostolicus*
97. Pius VII (1800–23)	*Aquilus rapax*
98. Leo XII (1823–9)	*Canis et coluber*
99. Pius VIII (1829–30)	*Vir religiosus*
100. Gregory XVI (1831–46)	*De balnis Etruriae*
101. Pius IX (1846–78)	*Crux de cruce*
102. Leo XIII (1878–1903)	*Lumen in caelo*
103. Pius X (1903–14)	*Ignis ardens*
104. Benedict XV (1914–22)	*Religio depopulata*
105. Pius XI (1922–39)	*Fides intrepida*
106. Pius XII (1939–58)	*Pastor angelicus*
107. John XXIII (1958–63)	*Pastor et nauta*

Bibliography

Binterim, A. J. *Die vorzüglichsten Denkwürdigkeiten der christ-katholischen Kirche aus den ersten, mittlern und letzten Zeiten*, Mainz, 1826.

de Fontbrune, J. C. *Prophéties des papes de saint Malachie*, Monaco, 1984.

Dollinger, *Der Weissagungsglaube und das Prophetentum in der christlichen Zeit, 1871.*

Forman, H. J. *Les Prophéties à travers les siècles*, Paris, 1969.

Honert, W. H. *Propheten-stimmen. Die Zukünftigen Schicksale der Kirche Christi, in Lichte der Weissagungen des Herrn und seiner Heiligen*, Regensburg, 1896.

Iguarta, J. M. *El enigma de la "Profecia de San Malaquias" sobre los papas*, Barcelona, 1976.

Ionescu, V. *Les Dernières victoires de Nostradamus*, Paris, 1992.

Lings, M. "Saint Malachy's Prophecy," *Parabola* 21 (February 1996), 83–9.

Maître, J. *Les Papes et la papauté, de 1143 à la fin du monde, d'aprés la prophétie attribuée à saint Malachie, étude historique*, Beaune, 1902.

Ménestrier, C. F., S. J., *La Philosophie des images énigmatiques*, Lyon, 1694.

PROTONOTARY. The term *protonotarius* has been in use at the pontifical CURIA since the 14th century. It was employed for the Chancery notaries (*notarii papae, notarii domini nostri*) to distinguish them from the notaries apostolic, also appointed by the pope or at least named *auctoritate apostolica*. In the 15th century, a distinction was made between the protonotaries *officio fungentes* or *participantes* and other protonotaries, who were honorary. The total number of protonotaries in the Chancery was seven. SIXTUS V increased this to twelve (1585), forming a COLLEGE, and at the same time made the office purchasable. In 1586, the college was granted vast privileges, in particular the rights to create notaries apostolic, to confer doctorates in law and theology after examination, to legitimize children born out of wedlock, and to wear pontifical robes and insignia at celebrations of the liturgy. In 1838, GREGORY XVI reduced the number of protonotaries *participantes* to seven. The protonotaries' function, powers, and privileges were the object of new measures undertaken by PIUS IX (1853), PIUS X (1905) and PIUS XI (1934). Henceforth, protonotaries were divided as follows: protonotaries *de numero participan-*

tium (who were employed at the apostolic Chancery and on various occasions took part in the life of the Curia); protonotaries *supranumerarii* (canon-prelates of the basilicas of ST. JOHN LATERAN, ST. PETER's, and ST. MARY MAJOR in Rome); protonotaries *ad instar participantium* (*ad vitam*, appointed by the pope by apostolic brief; or *durante munere*, canon-prelates of various Italian cities by explicit concession); and titular or honorary protonotaries (vicars general who are not bishops, *durante munere*). By the *motu proprio Pontificalis domus* (28 March 1968), PAUL VI reduced the grades to two: protonotaries *de numero participantium* and protonotaries *supranumerarii*.

Paulius Rabikauskas

Bibliography

Annuario pontificio 1992, Vatican City, 1992, 1245, 1735, 1933–2308 (passim).

Felici, G. "Protonotari apostolici," *EC*, 10 (1953), 200–2.

Hoffmann, L. "Protonotar, Apostolischer P.," *LTK*, 2nd ed., 7 (1963), 837.

Moroni, G. "Protonotari apostolici," *Dizionario di erudizione storico-ecclesiastica*, 56 (1852), 3–29.

Naz, R. "Protonotaires apostoliques," *DDC*, 7 (1958), 389–97.

Ortolani, T. "Cour romaine," *DTC*, 3 (1911), 1965–8.

Riganti, G. *De protonotariis apostolicis*, Rome, 1751.

PROVINCE, ECCLESIASTICAL. This term denotes a group of neighboring particular churches that are territorially defined (although there is nothing to prevent the Apostolic See from creating such groups based on other criteria). Ecclesiastical provinces become necessary where the expansion of the Church creates a greater number of particular churches. The aim of these groups is mainly a pastoral one, serving the particular churches that make them up. They are designed to promote the common pastoral activity of the various dioceses, and more effectively to encourage relationships among diocesan bishops (CODE OF CANON LAW of 1983, c. 431 § 1). Underlying the juridical approach to the region are the principle of subsidiarity (approved by the general assembly of the SYNOD OF BISHOPS of 1967, *Principia quae Codicis Iuris Canonice recognitionem dirigant*, no. 5) and the ecclesiological idea of the particular church worked out at VATICAN II (decree *Christus Dominus*, no. 11).

In the 2nd century, the bishops assembled to deal with disciplinary matters of interest to particular churches as well as to the Church as a whole: the date of Easter, the validity of baptism administered to heretics, or questions posed by the *lapsi* at the time of the persecutions. In the East, these meetings soon proliferated. The ecclesiastical province was an established fact by the time of the first council of Nicaea (325). In the West, it became institu-tionalized in the 4th century, with provinces like Milan, Aquilea, and Ravenna. Toward the end of that century, it appeared in Gaul. Generally, the grouping of provinces followed the model of the provinces of the Roman Empire, taking over the same metropolis and covering the same territory.

With the barbarian invasions, the institution suffered an eclipse, but it survived in places and rendered useful service to ecclesiastical discipline and the education of the population, as in Merovingian Gaul. The province reappeared with the Carolingian age and St. Boniface, persisting up to the time of the Gregorian reform, when power was centralized around the Apostolic See.

In the 1917 Code of Canon Law, the ecclesiastical province did not come in for special treatment. It was looked on as one division among many, but principally as regards the office of the metropolitan—that is, as a division over which the metropolitan had jurisdiction, providing an example of supervision and control over the suffragan dioceses, and more particularly their bishops.

At Vatican II, the territory was no longer a constituent element of the diocese. A similar view also affected the ecclesiastical province, which is a group of dioceses but does not necessarily constitute a new autonomous territory. These groups of particular churches in no way affect the autonomy of each diocese, which retains its own pastor, depending on the competence of the metropolitan.

Countries where the Church has sufficiently taken root have several provinces. Some countries make up a single province, such as the Netherlands. The province may also cover several nation states, like the province of Suva in the South Pacific. If a country has a large number of particular churches, neighboring ecclesiastical provinces may be combined into ecclesiastical regions (c. 433 § 1).

The organization of a province may respond to problems posed by a megalopolis. For example, the dioceses of Paris and Versailles were broken up in 1966 in order to make room for new dioceses and a new ecclesiastical province (apostolic constitution *Qui volente*, 9 October 1966).

In relation to the hierarchy, dioceses are either suffragan (that is, belonging to an ecclesiastical province presided over by the metropolitan) or exempt, otherwise known as *sui iuris*, or directly dependent on the Holy See. Exemption benefits neither the diocese nor the neighboring particular churches, so exempt dioceses are by now the exception and may soon cease to exist. They can be maintained solely for pastoral reasons (*Communicationes*, XII [1980], 253)—for instance, if the diocese is the only one a country has. However, for historic reasons, some Swiss and Swedish dioceses are directly dependent on the Holy See, these countries having no ecclesiastical province. In other cases, they are archepiscopal seats with no suffragans (Marseilles, Strasbourg, Metz, Luxemburg, etc.).

All the particular churches on a province's territory must belong to this province (c. 431§ 2). This arrangement corresponds to what was decreed at Vatican II "Dioceses which are now directly under the jurisdiction of the apostolic see and which are not united to any other diocese are either to be joined together into a new ecclesiastical province, if it is possible, or to be attached to whichever province is nearest or most suitable. They are then to come under the metropolitan jurisdiction of the archbishop according to the norm of common law" (*Christus Dominus*, III, 40, no. 2).

From this text, and from the use of *componantur* ("will be grouped") in c. 431 § 1, it is possible to deduce the obligatory nature of the province. The supreme authority of the Church, and it alone, may create, abolish, or alter ecclesiastical provinces (as in the case of the erection of particular churches). Prior to this, it will listen to the bishops involved (c. 431 § 3). Here it is no longer a question of consulting bishops' conferences, contrary to what PAUL VI provided for (*motu proprio Ecclesiae Sanctae*, I, no. 42), following the council, where we read: "It would be beneficial if competent episcopal conferences carefully examine the question of fixing the boundaries of ecclesiastical provinces . . . and should then submit their plans and proposals to the Apostolic See" (decree *Christus Dominus*, no. 41).

In the ecclesiastical province, authority is exercised by the provincial council, which is made up of all the bishops of the same ecclesiastical province meeting in a collegial assembly, together with the metropolitan (c. 432 § 1). The symbol of the metropolitan's authority over the ecclesiastical province is the *pallium*, which he must request of the pope (c. 437 § 1).

In the 1983 code, the metropolitan loses certain privileges he enjoyed under the previous legislation, his powers of supervision and control now having little importance. However, the *affectus collegialis* of the bishops of the province has increased because of more frequent joint actions. In practice, the ecclesiastical province may take on various configurations, for example as a result of the particular duties the metropolitan may be assigned by the Apostolic See (c. 436 § 2), as well as the convening of a provincial bishops' conference dependent or not on a national bishops' conference, etc.

Nothing is said about nonconciliar assemblies, the frequency with which they are held being left to the initiative of the bishops. But certain assemblies are covered by general law: to set up, at least every three years, a list of priests suitable for the episcopacy (c. 377 § 2); to determine what offering is to be made at Mass (c. 952 § 1); and to determine the taxes due for gracious acts, the execution of rescripts from the Apostolic See, and the administration of the sacraments and sacramentals (c. 1264).

The ecclesiastical province enjoys a juridical personality, based on its constitution (c. 114 § 1, c. 116 § 2). Thus, it has obligations and rights (c. 113 § 2) and is able to go to law and possess assets. The metropolitan represents it and acts in its name (c. 118).

Dominique Le Tourneau

Bibliography

Arrieta, J. I. "Instrumentos supradiocesanos para el gobierno de la Iglesia particular," *Ius Canonicum*, 24 (1984), 607–43; "Provincia y región eclesiástica," *Le Nouveau Code de droit canonique. Actes du Ve Congrès international de droit canonique; Ottawa 1984*, Ottawa, 1986, 607–25.

Cotalunga, M. "L'organizzazione in province e regioni ecclesiastiche," *Ius Canonicum*, 22 (1982), 749–62.

Mathorel, F. "Province et autonomie des Églises particulières en France," *L'Anneé canonique*, 30 (1987), 101–13; "Province ecclésiastique," *Catholicisme* (Paris), 1988, XII, 150–52.

Naz, R. "Province ecclésiastique," *DDC*, VII (1965), 397–8.

PROVISIONS, PAPAL. The collation of ecclesiastic benefices is independent of the tonsure of the cleric and the sacrament of orders granting him the right to certain benefices, which bear the responsibility of souls. However, it ensures for the cleric, and possibly the priest or the bishop, a benefice he must administer on both the spiritual and temporal levels. The revenue from this is his remuneration. From the early Middle Ages, the inevitable confusion between spiritual responsibility and temporal possession created constant conflicts of interest between the ecclesiastical and temporal authorities, whose rights have been conferred on it by history. The founder of a parish generally reserved the right to reap the benefits.

In theory, to become an ordinary collator for a diocese, the bishops, abbots, and cloistered priors were elected, while canons and priests were appointed by the bishop. In practice, the kings and leaders influenced elections beginning in the 8th century. The nobles and patrons, whose role was to submit proposals to the pastors were, in fact, the ones who had the real say in appointing candidates. The patron was the founder, or the virtually assured successor of the founder of a parish. His patronage entailed, in theory, a right to present a candidate to the ecclesiastical authority, but this soon became, in practice, a right to nominate. The collator—the bishop—had no real possibility of resisting a pressing request.

The intervention of laypersons, from the king to the simple nobleman and patron, brought about a situation that was denounced by the reformers in the 11th century. The Church was beset with all kinds of problems: trafficking in benefices, posts and responsibilities being handed down among family members, repayment by means of SIMONY. The Gregorian Reform in the second half of the 11th century changed this situation to a great extent. At the most, in certain cases, canons of cathedral chapters and monks from the abbies and priories were obliged to request authorization to elect some candidates. For bishoprics and monasteries, designated as royal because the king founded them, the authorization had to be accompanied by a royal recommendation for a person whose candidacy could hardly be overlooked.

From the 13th century onward, the popes intervened in many of the appointments made. They gave their judgment in disputes arising from elections where the results were called into question. They also intervened in disputes regarding benefices. In the 14th century, the pope increased the number of reservations, in other words, the number of cases where he could retain the collation of benefices for himself. The first reservations concerned benefices that had become vacant in the court of Rome, either due to the death or the resignation of the holder. The Avignon popes reserved the collation of all benefices for themselves, even those that were theoretically supposed to be conferred through election. This was because this practice afforded them precious remuneration for service and fidelity and also because it gave them the right to receive the annate. The immoderate recourse to the PETITION came to replace the ancient right of the patron. Princes, bishops, and even universities appealed to the pope to procure benefices for their protegés. They often requested dispensations from residence, and many a theologian condemned the harm caused to religious life as a result of this practice.

At the end of the 14th century, measures such as the removal of obediences were introduced and together with the COUNCILS of reformers in the first half of the 15th century, helped put an end to the usurpation of rights and benefits. The council of Basle, especially, put an end to all the general reservations, reintroduced free elections for major benefices, and made the ordinary collators once more responsible for the disposing of minor benefices (with the patrons having the right to present candidates). These measures were included in the decrees of 13 July 1433 and 24 March 1436. In fact, the compliance of a clergy preoccupied with its own interest continued to give free rein to the royal recommendations. In France there was the Pragmatic Sanction of Bourges (1438) that made executors within the kingdom of the canons of the council of Basle, previously approved by the clergy. The sanc-

tion placed the benefices in the possession of the king. A third of the benefices were reserved for university graduates. They had formed an important pressure group, having played a decisive role in the confrontations between the Western SCHISM and the councils.

Subsequent CONCORDATS only served to tighten the grip of the kings on the churches. The concordat of Bologna (1516) maintained an unequal division of prerogatives for the granting of major benefices. The king proposed a candidate to the pope, whom the latter could not refuse except in exceptionally serious cases. For minor benefices, the right of the bishop prevailed in his role as ordinary collator. However, the bishop also had to take account of the generally imperative presentations made by the king and other patrons. The system was improved during the 17th century by the intervention of the Royal Council, which expedited the process of inquiry into the candidates.

Jean Favier

Bibliography

Baix, F. "De la valeur des actes pontificaux de collation des bénéfices," *Hommage à Dom Ursmer Berlière*, Bruxelles, 1931, 57–66.

Barraclough, G. *Papal Provisions: Aspects of Church History, Constitutional, Legal and Administrative, in the Later Middle Ages*, Oxford, 1935; "The Executors of Papal Provisions in the Canonical Theory of the 13th and 14th Centuries," *Acta congressus iuridici internationalis Romae 1934*, 3, Rome, 1936, 109–150.

Deele, A. "Papal Provisions and Rights of Royal Patronage in the Early 14th Century," *English Historical Review*, 43 (1928), 497–527.

Edwards, R. D. "The King of England and Papal Provisions in Fifteenth-Century Ireland," *Medieval Studies Presented to Aubrey Gwynn*, Dublin, 1961, 265–80.

Lunt, W. E. *Papal Revenues in the Middle Ages*, 2 vols., New York, 1965.

Mollat, G. *La collation des bénéfices ecclésaistiques sous les papes d'Avignon, 1305–1378*, Paris, 1921.

Mollat, G. "Le roi de France et la collation plénière des bénéfices ecclésiastiques," *Mémoires présentés par divers savants a l'Académie des Inscriptions et Belles-Lettre*, 14-2 (1952), 107–252.

PROXIES. See Finances, Papal.

For Reference

Not to be taken from this room